This Missal belongs to

....

New *Saint Joseph*

WEEKDAY MISSAL

Complete Edition

Vol. I — Advent to Pentecost

This new Missal has been especially
designed to help you participate
at Mass . . . in the fullest and most
active way possible.

HOW EASY IT IS TO USE THIS MISSAL

- Refer to the Calendars (pp. [20]-[30] and
  and [32]-[37] or use the **St. Joseph Missal
  Guide** (No. 75).

- This arrow (**⍌**) means **continue to read.** This
  arrow (**➤**) indicates a **reference** back to the
  Order of Mass ("Ordinary") or to another part
  of the "Proper."

- **Boldface** type always indicates the **people's
  parts** that are to be recited aloud.

The People of God together with Christ worship the Father

New ... Saint Joseph

WEEKDAY MISSAL

COMPLETE EDITION

•

Vol. I — Advent to Pentecost

**With the Proper Mass Texts
for Every Weekday and Feast Day
in a Continuous and Easy-to-Use Arrangement**

**ALL READINGS FOR LITURGICAL YEARS I and II
IN THE "NEW AMERICAN BIBLE" TEXT**

**With the People's Parts
Printed in Boldface Type**

In accordance with the New Liturgy
as decreed by Vatican II

Dedicated to ST. JOSEPH
Patron of the Universal Church

CATHOLIC BOOK PUBLISHING CO.
New York, N.Y.

NIHIL OBSTAT: Daniel V. Flynn, J.C.D.
Censor Librorum

IMPRIMATUR: ✠ James P. Mahoney, D.D.
Vicar General, Archdiocese of New York

(T-920)

PREFACE

Content

This new **St. Joseph Weekday Missal** is a necessary companion to the **St. Joseph Sunday Missal**. It contains the Mass texts for all weekdays of the year. In doing so, it combines the Antiphons and Prayers found in the new **Sacramentary** together with the Readings and Intervenient Chants contained in the **Lectionary for Mass**. The faithful are thus given access to the biblical and liturgical riches that make up the treasury of the Church.

So great is the amount of this treasury that a complete Weekday Missal is not possible in one manageable volume. The present volume contains the texts for the weekday Masses from Advent to Pentecost. It also includes the most commonly used texts for Masses and Prayers for Various Needs and Occasions and Votive Masses (such as those for First Fridays and Saturdays).

Simplified Arrangement

All the texts in this Missal are clearly printed in large type, in an attractive and legible arrangement. All references are immediately visible and one always knows what comes next, and whose part it is. Succinct rubrics inform the reader of the options available and running heads identify the Masses on each page.

Participation Format

A simple, easy-to-understand method of instant identification of the parts of Mass ensures that everyone will do all of, but only, those parts of the Mass which pertain to his office. **Boldface** type is used for all people's parts; lightface type indicates the priest's or lector's parts. All the people's texts are arranged for congregational recitation.

Order (Ordinary) of the Mass

The complete text of the Order of Mass with all its options is printed in the center of the book and clearly marked for easy use. Each part is numbered to facilitate finding one's place quickly when turning from the Proper to the Ordinary. All the options are given and conveniently arranged. A valuable Introduction to the Order of Mass contains much useful information.

General Introduction

An extensive General Introduction provides a complete view of the liturgical year, the different liturgical days, the various classifications of celebrations and their make-up, the readings and chants, the color of vestments, and an important note on the type of participation to be attained.

Seasonal Introductions and Mass Themes

Every season of the liturgical year is prefixed by a useful Introduction providing necessary background for the better understanding of the liturgy and the easier use of the Missal. Each weekday Mass is prefaced by a short note focusing on one of the themes of the day's texts and inculcating some particular Christian attitude that may be found in them.

Concise Scriptural Commentaries

A completely original, especially written and very helpful series of commentaries gives the setting for the scripture readings and the lessons to be drawn from them, leading to a more fruitful hearing on the part of the people when they are proclaimed.

Calendars for Quick Reference

Two sets of Calendars are provided to help the reader find the Mass as quickly as possible. One is the General Calendar of feasts that may occur month by month. The second is the Calendar of Sundays and Feasts that gives the precise date for every Sunday and hence week of the year. There is also a more general Table of Principal Celebrations of the Liturgical Year which provides the dates for the two cycles of scripture readings until 1999.

Tables of Choices of Masses and Texts

Two handy tables give a bird's-eye view of the choices of Masses and texts available on any given day.

Aids to Prayer and Study

A popular selection of private prayers and devotions offers a fine starting point for a better prayer life. An invaluable Index section facilitates a deeper study of the Liturgy by listing all the Masses, Saints, Biblical Readings, Responsorial Psalms, and Prefaces.

In the Spirit of Vatican II

We trust that this Missal with its many outstanding features will enable all those who attend weekday Mass, in keeping with the desire of the Church, to "be led to that full, conscious, and active participation in liturgical celebrations which is demanded by the very nature of the liturgy" (Vatican II, **On the Sacred Liturgy,** no. 14).

CONTENTS

Proper of Saints

Common—Antiphons and Prayers

Common—Readings and Chants

Appendices

GENERAL INTRODUCTION

THE LITURGICAL YEAR

The Church celebrates the memory of Christ's saving work on appointed days in the course of the year. Every week the Church celebrates the memorial of the resurrection on Sunday, which is called the Lord's Day. This is also celebrated, together with the passion of Jesus, on the great feast of Easter once a year. Throughout the year the entire mystery of Christ is unfolded, and the birthdays (days of death) of the saints are commemorated.

By means of devotional exercises, instruction, prayer, and works of penance and mercy, the Church, according to traditional practices, completes the formation of the faithful during the various seasons of the liturgical year.

1. The Liturgical Day in General

Each day is made holy through liturgical celebrations of God's people, especially the eucharistic sacrifice and the divine office.

The liturgical day runs from midnight to midnight, but the observance of Sunday and of solemnities begins with the evening of the preceding day.

2. Sunday

The Church celebrates the paschal mystery on the first day of the week, known as the Lord's Day or Sunday. This follows a tradition handed down from the Apostles, which took its origin from the day of Christ's resurrection. Thus Sunday should be considered the original feast day.

Because of its special importance, the celebration of Sunday is replaced only by solemnities or by feasts of the Lord. The Sundays of Advent, Lent, and the Easter season, however, take precedence over all solemnities and feasts of the Lord. Solemnities that occur on these Sundays are observed on the preceding Saturday.

3. Solemnities, Feasts, and Memorials

In the course of the year, as the Church celebrates the mystery of Christ, Mary the Mother of God is especially honored, and the martyrs and other saints are proposed as examples for the faithful.

The celebration of the days of saints who have universal significance is required throughout the entire Church. The days of other saints are listed in the calendar as optional or are left to the veneration of particular churches, countries, or religious communities.

The different types of celebrations are distinguished from each other by their importance and are accordingly called solemnities, feasts, and memorials.

a) Solemnities are the days of greatest importance and begin with first vespers of the preceding day. Several solemnities have their own vigil Mass, to be used when Mass is celebrated in the evening of the preceding day.

The celebration of Easter and Christmas continues for eight days. Each octave is governed by its own rules.

b) Feasts are celebrated within the limits of a natural day. They do not have first vespers, with the exception of feasts of the Lord which fall on Sundays in ordinary time and Sundays of the Christmas season and which are substituted for the Sunday office.

c) Memorials are either obligatory or optional. Their observance is combined with the celebration of the occurring weekday according to norms given in the body of the Missal and seen at a glance in the Table of Choices of Masses and Texts, pp [18]-[19].

Obligatory memorials which occur on Lenten weekdays may be celebrated only as optional memorials.

Should more than one optional memorial fall on the same day, only one is celebrated; the others are omitted.

d) On Saturdays in ordinary time when there is no obligatory memorial, an optional memorial of the Blessed Virgin Mary may be observed.

4. Weekdays

The days following Sunday are called weekdays. They are celebrated in various ways according to the importance each one has:

a) Ash Wednesday and the days of Holy Week, from Monday to Thursday inclusive, are preferred to all other celebrations.

b) The weekdays of Advent from December 17 to December 24 inclusive and all the weekdays of Lent take precedence over obligatory memorials.

c) All other weekdays yield to solemnities and feasts and are combined with memorials.

d) Each weekday has its own special liturgical texts—at least, insofar as the Readings and Intervenient Chants are concerned (see p. [14]).

e) The weekdays of the major seasons have their own Antiphons and Prayers. The weekdays of Ordinary Time make use of the Antiphons and Prayers of the preceding Sunday or any of the thirty-four Sundays or those of Masses for Various Needs and Occasions as well as Votive Masses or even Masses for the Dead, as noted in the Tables of Choices of Masses and Texts, pp. [18]-[19].

5. Liturgical Seasons

a) The **Advent Season** begins with first vespers of the Sunday which falls on or closest to November 30 and ends before first vespers of Christmas. (See p. 1.)

b) The **Christmas season** runs from first vespers of Christmas until Sunday after Epiphany, or after January 6, inclusive. (See p. 90.)

c) **Lent** lasts from Ash Wednesday to the Mass of the Lord's Supper exclusive. (See p. 422.)

d) The **Easter Triduum** begins with the evening Mass of the Lord's Supper, reaches its high point in the Easter vigil, and closes with vespers on Easter Sunday. (See p. 583.)

e) The **Easter Season** comprises the fifty days from Easter Sunday to Pentecost which are celebrated as one feast day, sometimes called "the great Sunday." (See p. 720.)

f) **Ordinary Time** comprises the thirty-three or thirty-four weeks in the course of the year which celebrate no particular aspect of the mystery of Christ. Instead, especially on the last Sundays, the mystery of Christ in all its fullness is celebrated. This period is known as ordinary time.

Ordinary time begins on Monday after the Sunday following January 6 and continues until Tuesday before Ash Wednesday inclusive. (See p. 153.) It begins again on Monday after Pentecost and ends before first vespers of the First Sunday of Advent.

6. Readings and Intervenient Chants

a) On the weekdays of Advent, Christmas, Lent, and Easter there is a one-year cycle of Readings. These do not change from year to year.

b) On the weekdays of Ordinary Time, however, there is a two-year cycle for the First Readings and Responsorial Psalms. Those designated "Year I" are read on odd numbered years and those designated "Year II" are read on even numbered years.

c) This Missal has been arranged as follows: The Masses with invariable Readings (for example, those of Advent) are arranged in the traditional order of Antiphons, Prayers and Readings.

The Masses with variable Readings (for example, the weekdays in Ordinary Time or the Masses of the Commons) are arranged in two separate sections. One section contains the Antiphons and Prayers (Entrance Antiphon, Opening Prayer, Prayer over the Gifts,

Communion Antiphon, and Prayer after Communion) and the other the Readings and Intervenient Chants (Reading I, Responsorial Psalm, Reading II, Alleluia Verse, and Gospel).

COLOR OF VESTMENTS

Colors in vestments give an effective expression to the celebration of the mysteries of the faith and, in the course of the year, a sense of progress in the Christian life.

1. White is used in Masses of the Easter and Christmas Seasons; on feasts and commemorations of the Lord, other than of his passion; on feasts and memorials of Mary, the angels, saints who were not martyrs.

2. Red is used on Passion Sunday (Palm Sunday) and Good Friday, Pentecost, celebrations of the passion, birthday feasts of the apostles and evangelists, and feasts of martyrs.

3. Green is used in the offices and Masses of ordinary time.

4. Violet is used in Lent and Advent. It may also be used in offices and Masses for the dead.

5. Black may be used in Masses for the dead.

6. Rose may be used on Gaudete Sunday (Third Sunday of Advent) and Laetare Sunday (Fourth Sunday of Lent).

7. On more solemn days it is permitted to use more precious vestments even if not of the color of day.

8. Votive Masses of the Lord, the Blessed Virgin Mary, and the Saints may be said either with the color proper to the Mass, or with the color proper to the day or Season.

9. Masses for various needs may be said in the color proper either to the day or to the Season.

10. Ritual Masses are said in the color indicated in rubrics of the rite.

11. Adaptations to needs and culture of various regions may be proposed to the Holy See by Episcopal Conferences.

PARTICIPATION AT MASS

1. External and Internal Participation

a) The basic norm is that each one present at Mass has the right and duty to participate externally in the celebration—each one, however, doing wholly but solely what pertains to him by reason of the order to which he belongs or of the role assigned him.

b) In preparing liturgical celebrations, all concerned—whether of clergy or laity and whether directly interested in ritual or musical or pastoral aspects—should be consulted and should cooperate harmoniously under the leadership of the rector of the church.

c) In order that external participation may produce its full effects, something more is required than mere observance of laws governing valid and licit celebration. Participation should be **internal** also. This consists in right dispositions of faith and charity, cooperation with divine grace and effects.

d) Both internal and external participation is perfected by **spiritual,** and especially (when the law of Church permits) **sacramental**, Communion.

2. Participation of the Faithful

a) Every Mass is an action not only of Christ but of the Church. This is true even if none of the faithful is present; nor is the efficacy or value of the Mass as an action of the Church thereby nullified or essentially impaired. Yet by their presence and association with the celebrant and by the sacramental or at least spiritual Communion the faithful participate in the mystical communion of the Church with Christ in the Paschal Mystery. For it is the Church which is here and now acting in them.

b) Participation of the faithful is not a ministry but an office. This prerogative is theirs, not as individuals but insofar as they unite to form one assembly or congregation. For it is as a community that they are the sacramental sign of the Church. Hence, it is through incorporation into the community, just as it is through incorporation into the Church, that individuals are associated with Christ in the Easter Mystery of his dying and rising in glory.

c) It is of the highest importance, that, whether few or many, the faithful participate in the Mass as one body, united in faith and charity and avoiding every appearance of singularity or division. It is as a group that the Word of God is addressed to them and the body of the Lord is offered to them and that they are invited to pray, to sing, to perform certain actions and take certain positions. It is, therefore, as a group that they should respond. This common participation, lest it degenerate into more outward conformity for the sake of good order, should be motivated by a deep religious sense of their relation to one another and to God in Christ and of their office to be a sign of the mystery of the Church.

d) Special importance attaches to acclamations and responses of the faithful. These are not merely external signs of common celebration but effect and foster communion with the celebrant as a sacramental sign of Christ. This degree of active participation is the requisite minimum, in whatever form Mass is celebrated.

e) Next in importance are: the Penitential Rite; Profession of Faith; responses in the Prayer of the Faithful; the Lord's Prayer.

f) Other parts pertaining to the faithful—either alone, or together with celebrant or choir or chanter —are either rites in themselves or accompaniments of rites. To the **former** belong: the **Gloria;** Responsorial Psalm; **Sanctus;** anamnetic acclamation: hymn or silent prayer after Communion. To the **latter** belong: various processional chants (Entrance and Communion Antiphons); chant during preparations for a Gospel; **the Lamb of God** during the rite of the breaking of the bread.

HANDY TABLE OF CHOICES OF MASSES

MASS NOT OF DAY ON →	Funeral Requiem (4)	Requiem of Notification of a Death and on First Anniversary	"Daily" or Ordinary Requiem (1)	Nuptial Mass	For Grave Cause (2) with leave of Local Ordinary in Public Mass	For Just Cause (3) in judgment of Celebrant or Rector of church in Public Mass	Saint in Calendar or Martyrology of day	Votive, Public or Private
Easter Triduum — Sundays of Advent, Lent, Easter — Solemnities	No (4)	No	No	No (5)	No	No	No	No
Ash Wed. — Mon., Tues., Wed., of Holy Week	Yes	No	No	Yes	No	No	No	No
Mon. to Sat. of Octave of Easter	Yes	No	No	No (5)	No	No	No	No
Sundays in Seasons of Christmas and "of the year"	Yes	No	No	No (6)	Yes	No	No	No
Ferias of Advent from Dec.17 and of octave of Christmas	Yes	Yes	No	Yes	Yes	Yes	No (7)	No
Ferias of Lent (exc. Ash Wed. and Holy Week)	Yes	Yes	No	Yes	Yes	No	No (7)	No
Ferias of Seasons of Advent to Dec. 16, of Christmas from Jan. 2, and of Easter	Yes	Yes	No	Yes	Yes	Yes	Yes (8)	No
Feasts	Yes	No	No	Yes	Yes	No	No	No
Obligatory Memorial	Yes	Yes	No	Yes	Yes	Yes	No	No
Optional Memorial	Yes	Yes	No	Yes	Yes	Yes	Yes	No
Ferias in Season "of the year"	Yes	Yes	Yes	Yes	Yes	Yes	Yes	Yes

(1) Mass must be applied for deceased — (2) Reference is to Masses for special intentions, including votive Masses, if common good is involved in a serious way — (3) Reference is to same Masses as in (2), if common good is involved in a real, though not necessarily serious, way — (4) Funeral Requiem is permitted on a Solemnity, that is not a Holyday in place — (5) Mass of day is said instead, with marriage rite included. One of readings of nuptial Mass can be used in place of corresponding reading in Mass of Day, exc. in Easter Triduum, on Solemnity if a Holyday in place, and on Solemnities of Christmas, Epiphany, Ascension, Pentecost, and Corpus Christi — (6) Not forbidden, if Mass is not a parish Mass (7) If Saint is in general calendar, opening prayer in honor of the Saint may be said instead of opening prayer of Mass of the day — (8) Applies only to Saint in general or proper calendar.

Composed by: William T. Barry, C.SS.R.

[18]

HANDY TABLE OF CHOICES OF TEXTS

CHOICE OF TEXTS for → in ↓	ENTRANCE SONG	OPENING PRAYER	READING AND INTERVENIENT CHANTS	OFFERTORY SONG	PRAYER OVER GIFTS	COMMUNION SONG	PRAYER AFTER COMMUNION
Mass of Sunday	If sung: proper, as in Roman or Simple Gradual; or song approved by Bishops' Conference. — If not sung: antiphon in Missal (1)	Proper	Proper, as in Lectionary (2)	If sung: proper, as in Roman or Simple Gradual; or song approved by Bishops' Conference. — If not sung: it is omitted	Proper	If sung: proper, as in Roman or Simple Gradual; or song approved by Bishops' Conference. — If not sung: antiphon in Missal	Proper
Mass of Feria in Advent, Christmas, Lent, Easter Seasons	Same as above	Same as above (3)	Same as above (2)	Same as above	Same as above	Same as above	Same as above
Mass of Solemnity or Feast	Same as above. If no proper in Missal or Gradual: from Common	If no proper: from Common	If no proper: from Common (2)	If no proper in Gradual: from Common	Same as above. If no proper: from Common	Same as above. If no proper in Missal or Gradual: from Common	Same as above. If no proper: from Common
Mass of Memorial	Same as above	Same as above	Same as above (2)	Same as above	If no proper, from Common or current Feria	Same as above	If no proper: from Common or current Feria
Mass of Feria in Season "of year"	As for Mass of preceding Sunday or of any Sunday "of year"	As for Mass of preceding Sunday or of any Sunday "of year" or any Mass for Various Occasions or Various Prayers	Proper, as in Lectionary (2)	As for Mass of preceding Sunday or of any Sunday "of year"	Same as for Opening Prayer	As for Mass of preceding Sunday or of any Sunday "of year"	As for Mass of preceding Sunday or of any Sunday "of year" or any Mass for Various Occasions or Various Prayers
Mass of Dead	If sung: as in Roman or Simple Gradual; or an approved song. —If not sung: antiphon in Missal (1)	Any appropriate prayer for dead in Missal	Any appropriate readings for the dead in Lectionary (2)	If sung: as in Roman or Simple Gradual; or an approved song. If not sung: it is omitted	Any appropriate prayer for dead in Missal	If sung: as in Roman or Simple Gradual; or an approved song.—If not sung: antiphon in Missal	Any appropriate prayer for dead in Missal

(1) If current Missal is used, only antiphon is recited after 1st reading — (2) If responsorial psalm is recited, psalm assigned to reading in Lectionary is used. If it is sung, it is permitted to use say one of following: psalm assigned to reading in Lectionary; any psalm & response from common texts given in Lectionary for the season or class to which (in the case of a Solemnity, Feast, or Memorial) a Saint belongs; Gradual for the Mass given in Roman Gradual; the responsorial or alleluiatic psalm for the Mass given in Simple Gradual. If Alleluia or other chant before Gospel is not sung, it may be omitted — (3) If Memorial in General Calendar occurs on Feria from Dec. 17 to 24 or on Feria within octave of Christmas or (exc. Ash Wed. & Holy Week) on Feria of Lent, opening prayer of Memorial may be used in ferial Mass, instead of opening prayer proper to Mass.

Composed by: William T. Barry, C.SS.R.

GENERAL CALENDAR

JANUARY

1. Octave of Christmas
   SOLEMNITY OF MARY, MOTHER
   OF GOD   Solemnity
2. Basil the Great and Gregory Nazianzen,
   bishops and doctors   Memorial
3.
4. Elizabeth Ann Seton   Memorial
5. Blessed John Neumann, bishop   Memorial
6. EPIPHANY   Solemnity
7. *Raymond of Penyafort, priest**
8.
9.
10.
11.
12.
13. *Hilary, bishop and doctor*
14.
15.
16.
17. Anthony, abbot   Memorial
18.
19.
20. *Fabian, pope and martyr*
    Sebastian, martyr
21. Agnes, virgin and martyr   Memorial
22. *Vincent, deacon and martyr*
23.
24. Francis de Sales, bishop and doctor   Memorial
25. CONVERSION OF PAUL, APOSTLE   Feast
26. Timothy and Titus, bishops   Memorial
27. *Angela Merici, virgin*
28. Thomas Aquinas, priest and doctor   Memorial
29.
30.
31. John Bosco, priest   Memorial

Sunday after January 6: BAPTISM OF THE LORD   Feast

*When no rank is given, it is an optional memorial.

FEBRUARY

1.		
2.	PRESENTATION OF THE LORD	Feast
3.	*Blase, bishop and martyr*	
	Ansgar, bishop	
4.		
5.	Agatha, virgin and martyr	Memorial
6.	Paul Miki and companions, martyrs	Memorial
7.		
8.	*Jerome Emiliani*	
9.		
10.	Scholastica, virgin	Memorial
11.	*Our Lady of Lourdes*	
12.		
13.		
14.	Cyril, monk, and Methodius, bishop	Memorial
15.		
16.		
17.	*Seven Founders of the Order of Servites*	
18.		
19.		
20.		
21.	*Peter Damian, bishop and doctor*	
22.	CHAIR OF PETER, APOSTLE	Feast
23.	Polycarp, bishop and martyr	Memorial
24.		
25.		
26.		
27.		
28.		

MARCH

1.		
2.		
3.		
4.	*Casimir*	
5.		
6.		
7.	Perpetua and Felicity, martyrs	Memorial
8.	*John of God, religious*	
9.	*Frances of Rome, religious*	

10.
11.
12.
13.
14.
15.
16.
17. *Patrick, bishop*
18. *Cyril of Jerusalem, bishop and doctor*
19. JOSEPH, HUSBAND OF MARY   Solemnity
20.
21.
22.
23. *Turibius de Mongrovejo, bishop*
24.
25. ANNUNCIATION   Solemnity
26.
27.
28.
29.
30.
31.

APRIL

1.
2. *Francis of Paola, hermit*
3.
4. *Isidore, bishop and doctor*
5. *Vincent Ferrer, priest*
6.
7. John Baptist de la Salle, priest   Memorial
8.
9.
10.
11. *Stanislaus, bishop and martyr*
12.
13. *Martin I, pope and martyr*
14.
15.
16.
17.
18.
19.

25.
26.
27. *Cyril of Alexandria, bishop and doctor*
28. Irenaeus, bishop and martyr   Memorial
29. PETER AND PAUL, APOSTLES   Solemnity
30. *First Martyrs of the Church of Rome*

JULY

1.
2.
3. THOMAS, APOSTLE   Feast
4. *Elizabeth of Portugal*
    Independence Day
5. *Anthony Zaccaria, priest*
6. *Maria Goretti, virgin and martyr*
7.
8.
9.
10.
11. Benedict, abbot   Memorial
12.
13. *Henry*
14. *Camillus de Lellis, priest*
15. Bonaventure, bishop and doctor   Memorial
16. *Our Lady of Mount Carmel*
17.
18.
19.
20.
21. *Lawrence of Brindisi, priest and doctor*
22. Mary Magdalene   Memorial
23. *Bridget, religious*
24.
25. JAMES, APOSTLE   Feast
26. Joachim and Ann, parents of Mary   Memorial
27.
28.
29. Martha   Memorial
30. *Peter Chrysologus, bishop and doctor*
31. Ignatius of Loyola, priest   Memorial

AUGUST

1. Alphonsus Liguori, bishop and doctor   Memorial
2. *Eusebius of Vercelli, bishop*
3.
4. John Vianney, priest   Memorial
5. *Dedication of St. Mary Major*
6. TRANSFIGURATION   Feast
7. *Sixtus II, pope and martyr, and companions, martyrs*
   Cajetan, priest
8. Dominic, priest   Memorial
9.
10. LAWRENCE, DEACON AND MARTYR   Feast
11. Clare, virgin   Memorial
12.
13. *Pontian, pope and martyr, and Hippolytus, priest and martyr*
14.
15. ASSUMPTION   Solemnity
16. *Stephen of Hungary*
17.
18.
19. *John Eudes, priest*
20. Bernard, abbot and doctor   Memorial
21. Pius X, pope   Memorial
22. Queenship of Mary   Memorial
23. *Rose of Lima, virgin*
24. BARTHOLOMEW, APOSTLE   Feast
25. *Louis*
   Joseph Calasanz, priest
26.
27. Monica   Memorial
28. Augustine, bishop and doctor   Memorial
29. Beheading of John the Baptist, martyr   Memorial
30.
31.

SEPTEMBER

1.
2.
3. Gregory the Great, pope and doctor   Memorial
4.

5.
6.
7.
8. BIRTH OF MARY   Feast
9. Peter Claver, priest   Memorial
10.
11.
12.
13. John Chrysostom, bishop and doctor   Memorial
14. TRIUMPH OF THE CROSS   Feast
15. Our Lady of Sorrows   Memorial
16. Cornelius, pope and martyr, and
    Cyprian, bishop and martyr   Memorial
17. *Robert Bellarmine, bishop and doctor*
18.
19. *Januarius, bishop and martyr*
20.
21. MATTHEW, APOSTLE AND EVANGELIST   Feast
22.
23.
24.
25.
26. *Cosmas and Damian, martyrs*   Memorial
27. Vincent de Paul, priest   Memorial
28. *Wenceslaus, martyr*
29. MICHAEL, GABRIEL, AND RAPHAEL,
    ARCHANGELS   Feast
30. Jerome, priest and doctor   Memorial

OCTOBER

1. Theresa of the Child Jesus, virgin   Memorial
2. Guardian Angels   Memorial
3.
4. Francis of Assisi   Memorial
5.
6. *Bruno, priest*
7. Our Lady of the Rosary   Memorial
8.
9. *Denis, bishop and martyr, and companions,*
    martyrs
    John Leonardi, priest
10.

11.
12.
13.
14. *Callistus I, pope and martyr*
15. Teresa of Avila, virgin and doctor   Memorial
16. *Hedwig, religious*
    Margaret Mary Alacoque, virgin
17. Ignatius of Antioch, bishop and martyr   Memorial
18. LUKE, EVANGELIST   Feast
19. Isaac Jogues and John de Brébeuf, priests and
        martyrs, and companions, martyrs   Memorial
    Paul of the Cross, priest
20.
21.
22.
23. *John of Capistrano, priest*
24. *Anthony Claret, bishop*
25.
26.
27.
28. SIMON AND JUDE, APOSTLES   Feast
29.
30.
31.

NOVEMBER

1. ALL SAINTS   Solemnity
2. ALL SOULS
3. *Martin de Porres, religious*
4. Charles Borromeo, bishop   Memorial
5.
6.
7.
8.
9. DEDICATION OF ST. JOHN LATERAN   Feast
10. Leo the Great, pope and doctor   Memorial
11. Martin of Tours, bishop   Memorial
12. Josaphat, bishop and martyr   Memorial
13. Frances Xavier Cabrini, virgin   Memorial
14.
15. *Albert the Great, bishop and doctor*

16. *Margaret of Scotland*
    Gertrude, virgin
17. Elizabeth of Hungary, religious   Memorial
18. *Dedication of the churches of Peter and*
    Paul, apostles

19.
20.
21. Presentation of Mary   Memorial
22. Cecilia, virgin and martyr   Memorial
23. *Clement I, pope and martyr*
    Columban, abbot
24.
25.
26.
27.
28.
29.
30. ANDREW, APOSTLE   Feast
Fourth Thursday *Thanksgiving Day*
Last Sunday in Ordinary Time:
     CHRIST THE KING   Solemnity

DECEMBER

1.
2.
3. Francis Xavier, priest   Memorial
4. *John Damascene, priest and doctor*
5.
6. *Nicholas, bishop*
7. Ambrose, bishop and doctor   Memorial
8. IMMACULATE CONCEPTION   Solemnity
9.
10.
11. *Damasus I, pope*
12. Our Lady of Guadalupe   Memorial
    Jane Frances de Chantal, religious
13. Lucy, virgin and martyr   Memorial
14. John of the Cross, priest and doctor   Memorial
15.
16.
17.
18.

19.
20.
21. *Peter Canisius, priest and doctor*
22.
23. *John of Kanty, priest*
24.
25. CHRISTMAS   Solemnity
26. STEPHEN, FIRST MARTYR   Feast
27. JOHN, APOSTLE AND EVANGELIST   Feast
28. HOLY INNOCENTS, MARTYRS   Feast
29. *Thomas Becket, bishop and martyr*
30.
31. *Sylvester I, pope*

Sunday within the octave of Christmas or
if there is no Sunday within the octave,
December 30: HOLY FAMILY   Feast

PRINCIPAL CELEBRATIONS OF LITURGICAL YEAR

Year	Lectionary Weekday Cycle	Ash Wednes.	Easter	Ascension	Pentecost	Corpus Christi	First Sun. of Advent
1974	II	27 Feb.	14 Apr.	23 May	2 June	13 June	1 Dec.
1975	I	12 Feb.	30 Mar.	8 May	18 May	29 May	30 Nov.
1976	II	3 Mar.	18 Apr.	27 May	6 June	17 June	28 Nov.
1977	I	23 Feb.	10 Apr.	19 May	29 May	9 June	27 Nov.
1978	II	8 Feb.	26 Mar.	4 May	14 May	25 May	3 Dec.
1979	I	28 Feb.	15 Apr.	24 May	3 June	14 June	2 Dec.
1980	II	20 Feb.	6 Apr.	15 May	25 May	5 June	30 Nov.
1981	I	4 Mar.	19 Apr.	28 May	7 June	18 June	29 Nov.
1982	II	24 Feb.	11 Apr.	20 May	30 May	10 June	28 Nov.
1983	I	16 Feb.	3 Apr.	12 May	22 May	2 June	27 Nov.
1984	II	7 Mar.	22 Apr.	31 May	10 June	21 June	2 Dec.
1985	I	20 Feb.	7 Apr.	16 May	26 May	6 June	1 Dec.
1986	II	12 Feb.	30 Mar.	8 May	18 May	29 May	30 Nov.
1987	I	4 Mar.	19 Apr.	28 May	7 June	18 June	29 Nov.
1988	II	17 Feb.	3 Apr.	12 May	22 May	2 June	27 Nov.
1989	I	8 Feb.	26 Mar.	4 May	14 May	25 May	3 Dec.
1990	II	28 Feb.	15 Apr.	24 May	3 June	14 June	2 Dec.
1991	I	13 Feb.	31 Mar.	9 May	19 May	30 May	1 Dec.
1992	II	4 Mar.	19 Apr.	28 May	7 June	18 June	29 Nov.
1993	I	24 Feb.	11 Apr.	20 May	30 May	10 June	28 Nov.
1994	II	16 Feb.	3 Apr.	12 May	22 May	2 June	27 Nov.
1995	I	1 Mar.	16 Apr.	25 May	4 June	15 June	3 Dec.
1996	II	21 Feb.	7 Apr.	16 May	26 May	6 June	1 Dec.
1997	I	12 Feb.	30 Mar.	8 May	18 May	29 May	30 Nov.
1998	II	25 Feb.	12 Apr.	21 May	31 May	11 June	29 Nov.
1999	I	17 Feb.	4 Apr.	13 May	23 May	3 June	28 Nov.

YEAR A

Sunday or Feast	1986	1989	1992	1995	1998	2001
1st Sun. Advent	30 Nov.	3 Dec.	29 Nov.	3 Dec.	29 Nov.	2 Dec.
Immac. Concep.	8 Dec.	8 Dec.	8 Dec.	8 Dec.	8 Dec.	8 Dec.
2nd Sun. Advent	7 Dec.	10 Dec.	6 Dec.	10 Dec.	6 Dec.	9 Dec.
3rd Sun. Advent	14 Dec.	17 Dec.	13 Dec.	17 Dec.	13 Dec.	16 Dec.
4th Sun. Advent	21 Dec.	24 Dec.	20 Dec.	24 Dec.	20 Dec.	23 Dec.
Christmas	25 Dec.	25 Dec.	25 Dec.	25 Dec.	25 Dec.	25 Dec.
Holy Family	28 Dec.	31 Dec.	27 Dec.	31 Dec.	27 Dec.	30 Dec.

Sunday or Feast	1987	1990	1993	1996	1999	2002
Oct. of Christ.	1 Jan.	1 Jan.	1 Jan.	1 Jan.	1 Jan.	1 Jan.
Epiphany	4 Jan.	7 Jan.	3 Jan.	7 Jan.	3 Jan.	6 Jan.
Baptism of Lord	11 Jan.	—	10 Jan.	—	10 Jan.	13 Jan.
2nd Ord. Sun.	18 Jan.	14 Jan.	17 Jan.	14 Jan.	17 Jan.	20 Jan.
3rd Ord. Sun.	25 Jan.	21 Jan.	24 Jan.	21 Jan.	24 Jan.	27 Jan.
4th Ord. Sun.	1 Feb.	28 Jan.	31 Jan.	28 Jan.	31 Jan.	3 Feb.
5th Ord. Sun.	8 Feb.	4 Feb.	7 Feb.	4 Feb.	7 Feb.	10 Feb.
6th Ord. Sun.	15 Feb.	11 Feb.	14 Feb.	11 Feb.	14 Feb.	—
7th Ord. Sun.	22 Feb.	18 Feb.	21 Feb.	18 Feb.	—	—
8th Ord. Sun.	1 Mar.	25 Feb.	—	—	—	—
9th Ord. Sun.	—	—	—	—	—	—
1st Sun. of Lent	8 Mar.	4 Mar.	28 Feb.	25 Feb.	21 Feb.	17 Feb.
2nd Sun. of Lent	15 Mar.	11 Mar.	7 Mar.	3 Mar.	28 Feb.	24 Feb.
3rd Sun. of Lent	22 Mar.	18 Mar.	14 Mar.	10 Mar.	7 Mar.	3 Mar.
4th Sun. of Lent	29 Mar.	25 Mar.	21 Mar.	17 Mar.	14 Mar.	10 Mar.
5th Sun. of Lent	5 Apr.	1 Apr.	28 Mar.	24 Mar.	21 Mar.	17 Mar.
Palm Sun.	12 Apr.	8 Apr.	4 Apr.	31 Mar.	28 Mar.	24 Mar.
Holy Thurs.	16 Apr.	12 Apr.	8 Apr.	4 Apr.	1 Apr.	28 Mar.
Holy Thurs.	16 Apr.	12 Apr.	8 Apr.	4 Apr.	1 Apr.	28 Mar.
Good Friday	17 Apr.	13 Apr.	9 Apr.	5 Apr.	2 Apr.	29 Mar.
Easter Vigil	18 Apr.	14 Apr.	10 Apr.	6 Apr.	3 Apr.	30 Mar.
Easter Sunday	19 Apr.	15 Apr.	11 Apr.	7 Apr.	4 Apr.	31 Mar.
2nd Sun. Easter	26 Apr.	22 Apr.	18 Apr.	14 Apr.	11 Apr.	7 Apr.
3rd Sun. Easter	3 May	29 Apr.	25 Apr.	21 Apr.	18 Apr.	14 Apr.
4th Sun. Easter	10 May	6 May	2 May	28 Apr.	25 Apr.	21 Apr.
5th Sun. Easter	17 May	13 May	9 May	5 May	2 May	28 Apr.

YEAR A

Sunday or Feast	1987	1990	1993	1996	1999	2002
6th Sun. Easter	24 May	20 May	16 May	12 May	9 May	5 May
Ascension	28 May	24 May	20 May	16 May	13 May	9 May
7th Sun. Easter	31 May	27 May	23 May	19 May	16 May	12 May
Pentecost Sun.	7 June	3 June	30 May	26 May	23 May	19 May
Trinity Sun.	14 June	10 June	6 June	2 June	30 May	26 May
Body and Blood	21 June	17 June	13 June	9 June	6 June	2 June
9th Ord. Sun.	—	—	—	—	—	—
10th Ord. Sun.	—	—	—	—	—	9 June
11th Ord. Sun.	—	—	—	16 June	13 June	16 June
12th Ord. Sun.	—	24 June	20 June	23 June	20 June	23 June
13th Ord. Sun.	28 June	1 July	27 June	30 June	27 June	30 June
14th Ord. Sun.	5 July	8 July	4 July	7 July	4 July	7 July
15th Ord. Sun.	12 July	15 July	11 July	14 July	11 July	14 July
16th Ord. Sun.	19 July	22 July	18 July	21 July	18 July	21 July
17th Ord. Sun.	26 July	29 July	25 July	28 July	25 July	28 July
18th Ord. Sun.	2 Aug.	5 Aug.	1 Aug.	4 Aug.	1 Aug.	4 Aug.
19th Ord. Sun.	9 Aug.	12 Aug.	8 Aug.	11 Aug.	8 Aug.	11 Aug.
Assumption	15 Aug.	15 Aug.	15 Aug.	15 Aug.	15 Aug.	15 Aug.
20th Ord. Sun.	16 Aug.	19 Aug.	—	18 Aug.	—	18 Aug.
21st Ord. Sun.	23 Aug.	26 Aug.	22 Aug.	25 Aug.	22 Aug.	25 Aug.
22nd Ord. Sun.	30 Aug.	2 Sept.	29 Aug.	1 Sept.	29 Aug.	1 Sept.
23rd Ord. Sun.	6 Sept.	9 Sept.	5 Sept.	8 Sept.	5 Sept.	8 Sept.
24th Ord. Sun.	13 Sept.	16 Sept.	12 Sept.	15 Sept.	12 Sept.	15 Sept.
25th Ord. Sun.	20 Sept.	23 Sept.	19 Sept.	22 Sept.	19 Sept.	22 Sept.
26th Ord. Sun.	27 Sept.	30 Sept.	26 Sept.	29 Sept.	26 Sept.	29 Sept.
27th Ord. Sun.	4 Oct.	7 Oct.	3 Oct.	6 Oct.	3 Oct.	6 Oct.
28th Ord. Sun.	11 Oct.	14 Oct.	10 Oct.	13 Oct.	10 Oct.	13 Oct.
29th Ord. Sun.	18 Oct.	21 Oct.	17 Oct.	20 Oct.	17 Oct.	20 Oct.
30th Ord. Sun.	25 Oct.	28 Oct.	24 Oct.	27 Oct.	24 Oct.	27 Oct.
All Saints	1 Nov.	1 Nov.	1 Nov.	1 Nov.	1 Nov.	1 Nov.
31st Ord. Sun.	—	4 Nov.	31 Oct.	3 Nov.	31 Oct.	3 Nov.
32nd Ord. Sun.	8 Nov.	11 Nov.	7 Nov.	10 Nov.	7 Nov.	10 Nov.
33rd Ord. Sun.	15 Nov.	18 Nov.	14 Nov.	17 Nov.	14 Nov.	17 Nov.
34th Ord. Sun.	22 Nov.	25 Nov.	21 Nov.	24 Nov.	21 Nov.	24 Nov.

YEAR B

Sunday or Feast	1984	1987	1990	1993	1996	1999
1st Sun. Advent	2 Dec.	29 Nov.	2 Dec.	28 Nov.	1 Dec.	28 Nov.
Immac. Concep.	8 Dec.	8 Dec.	8 Dec.	8 Dec.	8 Dec.	8 Dec.
2nd Sun. Advent	9 Dec	6 Dec.	9 Dec.	5 Dec.	8 Dec.	5 Dec.
3rd Sun. Advent	16 Dec.	13 Dec.	16 Dec.	12 Dec.	15 Dec.	12 Dec.
4th Sun. Advent	23 Dec.	20 Dec.	23 Dec.	19 Dec.	22 Dec.	19 Dec.
Christmas	25 Dec.	25 Dec.	25 Dec.	25 Dec.	25 Dec.	25 Dec.
Holy Family	30 Dec.	27 Dec.	30 Dec	26 Dec.	29 Dec.	26 Dec.

Sunday or Feast	1985	1988	1991	1994	1997	2000
Oct. of Christ.	1 Jan.	1 Jan.	1 Jan.	1 Jan.	1 Jan.	1 Jan.
Epiphany	6 Jan.	3 Jan.	6 Jan.	2 Jan.	5 Jan.	2 Jan.
Baptism of Lord	13 Jan.	10 Jan.	13 Jan.	9 Jan.	12 Jan.	9 Jan.
2nd Ord. Sun.	20 Jan.	17 Jan.	20 Jan.	16 Jan.	19 Jan.	16 Jan.
3rd Ord. Sun.	27 Jan.	24 Jan.	27 Jan.	23 Jan.	26 Jan.	23 Jan.
4th Ord. Sun.	3 Feb.	31 Jan.	3 Feb.	30 Jan.	2 Feb.	30 Jan.
5th Ord. Sun.	10 Feb.	7 Feb.	10 Feb.	6 Feb.	9 Feb.	6 Feb.
6th Ord. Sun.	17 Feb.	14 Feb.	—	13 Feb.	—	13 Feb.
7th Ord. Sun.	—	—	—	—	—	20 Feb.
8th Ord. Sun.	—	—	—	—	—	27 Feb.
9th Ord. Sun.	—	—	—	—	—	5 Mar.
1st Sun. of Lent	24 Feb.	21 Feb.	17 Feb.	20 Feb.	16 Feb.	12 Mar.
2nd Sun. of Lent	3 Mar.	28 Feb.	24 Feb.	27 Feb.	23 Feb.	19 Mar.
3rd Sun. of Lent	10 Mar.	6 Mar	3 Mar.	6 Mar.	2 Mar.	26 Mar.
4th Sun. of Lent	17 Mar.	13 Mar	10 Mar	13 Mar.	9 Mar	2 Apr.
5th Sun. of Lent	24 Mar.	20 Mar	17 Mar	20 Mar.	16 Mar	9 Apr.
Palm Sun.	31 Mar.	27 Mar.	24 Mar.	27 Mar.	23 Mar.	16 Apr.
Holy Thurs.	4 Apr.	31 Mar.	28 Mar.	31 Mar.	27 Mar.	20 Apr.
Holy Thurs.	4 Apr.	31 Mar.	28 Mar.	31 Mar.	27 Mar.	20 Apr.
Good Friday	5 Apr.	1 Apr.	29 Mar.	1 Apr.	28 Mar.	21 Apr.
Easter Vigil	6 Apr.	2 Apr.	30 Mar.	2 Apr.	29 Mar.	22 Apr.
Easter Sunday	7 Apr.	3 Apr.	31 Mar.	3 Apr.	30 Mar.	23 Apr.
2nd Sun. Easter	14 Apr.	10 Apr.	7 Apr.	10 Apr.	6 Apr.	30 Apr.
3rd Sun. Easter	21 Apr.	17 Apr.	14 Apr.	17 Apr.	13 Apr.	7 May
4th Sun. Easter	28 Apr.	24 Apr.	21 Apr.	24 Apr.	20 Apr.	14 May
5th Sun. Easter	5 May	1 May	28 Apr.	1 May	27 Apr.	21 May

YEAR B

Sunday or Feast	1985	1988	1991	1994	1997	2000
6th Sun. Easter	12 May	8 May	5 May	8 May	4 May	28 May
Ascension	16 May	12 May	9 May	12 May	8 May	1 June
7th Sun. Easter	19 May	15 May	12 May	15 May	11 May	4 June
Pentecost Sun.	26 May	22 May	19 May	22 May	18 May	11 June
Trinity Sun.	2 June	29 May	26 May	29 May	25 May	18 June
Body and Blood	9 June	5 June	2 June	5 June	1 June	25 June
9th Ord. Sun.	—	—	—	—	—	—
10th Ord. Sun.	—	—	9 June	—	8 June	—
11th Ord. Sun.	16 June	12 June	16 June	12 June	15 June	—
12th Ord. Sun.	23 June	19 June	23 June	19 June	22 June	—
13th Ord. Sun.	30 June	26 June	30 June	26 June	29 June	2 July
14th Ord. Sun.	7 July	3 July	7 July	3 July	6 July	9 July
15th Ord. Sun.	14 July	10 July	14 July	10 July	13 July	16 July
16th Ord. Sun.	21 July	17 July	21 July	17 July	20 July	23 July
17th Ord. Sun.	28 July	24 July	28 July	24 July	27 July	30 July
18th Ord. Sun.	4 Aug.	31 July	4 Aug.	31 July	3 Aug.	6 Aug.
19th Ord. Sun.	11 Aug.	7 Aug.	11 Aug.	7 Aug.	10 Aug.	13 Aug.
Assumption	15 Aug.	15 Aug.	15 Aug.	15 Aug.	15 Aug.	15 Aug.
20th Ord. Sun.	18 Aug.	14 Aug.	18 Aug.	14 Aug.	17 Aug.	20 Aug.
21st Ord. Sun.	25 Aug.	21 Aug.	25 Aug.	21 Aug.	24 Aug.	27 Aug.
22nd Ord. Sun.	1 Sept.	28 Aug.	1 Sept.	28 Aug.	31 Aug.	3 Sept.
23rd Ord. Sun.	8 Sept.	4 Sept.	8 Sept.	4 Sept.	7 Sept.	10 Sept.
24th Ord. Sun.	15 Sept.	11 Sept.	15 Sept.	11 Sept.	14 Sept.	17 Sept.
25th Ord. Sun.	22 Sept.	18 Sept.	22 Sept.	18 Sept.	21 Sept.	24 Sept.
26th Ord. Sun.	29 Sept.	25 Sept.	29 Sept.	25 Sept.	28 Sept.	1 Oct.
27th Ord. Sun.	6 Oct.	2 Oct.	6 Oct.	2 Oct.	5 Oct.	8 Oct.
28th Ord. Sun.	13 Oct.	9 Oct.	13 Oct.	9 Oct.	12 Oct.	15 Oct.
29th Ord. Sun.	20 Oct.	16 Oct.	20 Oct.	16 Oct.	19 Oct.	22 Oct.
30th Ord. Sun.	27 Oct.	23 Oct.	27 Oct.	23 Oct.	26 Oct.	29 Oct.
All Saints	1 Nov.	1 Nov.	1 Nov.	1 Nov.	1 Nov.	1 Nov.
31st Ord. Sun.	3 Nov.	30 Oct.	3 Nov.	30 Oct.	2 Nov.	5 Nov.
32nd Ord. Sun.	10 Nov.	6 Nov.	10 Nov.	6 Nov.	9 Nov.	12 Nov.
33rd Ord. Sun.	17 Nov.	13 Nov.	17 Nov.	13 Nov.	16 Nov.	19 Nov.
34th Ord. Sun.	24 Nov.	20 Nov.	24 Nov.	20 Nov.	23 Nov.	26 Nov.

YEAR C

Sunday or Feast	1985	1988	1991	1994	1997	2000
1st. Sun. Advent	1 Dec.	27 Nov.	1 Dec.	27 Nov.	30 Nov.	3 Dec.
Immac. Concep.	8 Dec.	8 Dec.	8 Dec.	8 Dec.	8 Dec.	8 Dec.
2nd Sun. Advent	8 Dec.	4 Dec.	8 Dec.	4 Dec.	7 Dec.	10 Dec.
3rd Sun. Advent	15 Dec.	11 Dec.	15 Dec.	11 Dec.	14 Dec.	17 Dec.
4th Sun. Advent	22 Dec.	18 Dec.	22 Dec.	18 Dec.	21 Dec.	24 Dec.
Christmas	25 Dec.	25 Dec.	25 Dec.	25 Dec.	25 Dec.	25 Dec.
Holy Family	29 Dec.	—	29 Dec.	—	28 Dec.	31 Dec.

Sunday or Feast	1986	1989	1992	1995	1998	2001
Oct. of Christ.	1 Jan.	1 Jan.	1 Jan.	1 Jan.	1 Jan.	1 Jan.
Epiphany	5 Jan.	8 Jan.	5 Jan.	8 Jan.	4 Jan.	—
Baptism of Lord	12 Jan.	—	12 Jan.	—	11 Jan.	7 Jan.
2nd Ord. Sun.	19 Jan.	15 Jan.	19 Jan.	15 Jan.	18 Jan.	14 Jan.
3rd Ord. Sun.	26 Jan.	22 Jan.	26 Jan.	22 Jan.	25 Jan.	21 Jan.
4th Ord. Sun.	2 Feb.	29 Jan.	2 Feb.	29 Jan.	1 Feb.	28 Jan.
5th Ord. Sun.	9 Feb.	5 Feb.	9 Feb.	5 Feb.	8 Feb.	4 Feb.
6th Ord. Sun.	—	—	16 Feb.	12 Feb.	15 Feb.	11 Feb.
7th Ord. Sun.	—	—	23 Feb.	19 Feb.	22 Feb.	18 Feb.
8th Ord. Sun.	—	—	1 Mar.	26 Feb.	—	25 Feb.
9th Ord. Sun.	—	—	—	—	—	—
1st Sun. of Lent	16 Feb.	12 Feb.	8 Mar.	5 Mar.	1 Mar.	4 Mar.
2nd Sun. of Lent	23 Feb.	19 Feb.	15 Mar.	12 Mar.	8 Mar.	11 Mar.
3rd Sun. of Lent	2 Mar.	26 Feb.	22 Mar.	19 Mar.	15 Mar.	18 Mar.
4th Sun. of Lent	9 Mar.	5 Mar.	29 Mar.	26 Mar.	22 Mar.	25 Mar.
5th Sun. of Lent	16 Mar.	12 Mar.	5 Apr.	2 Apr.	29 Mar.	1 Apr.
Palm Sun.	23 Mar.	19 Mar.	12 Apr.	9 Apr.	5 Apr.	8 Apr.
Holy Thurs.	27 Mar.	23 Mar.	16 Apr.	13 Apr.	9 Apr.	12 Apr.
Holy Thurs.	27 Mar.	23 Mar.	16 Apr.	13 Apr.	9 Apr.	12 Apr.
Good Friday	28 Mar.	24 Mar.	17 Apr.	14 Apr.	10 Apr.	13 Apr.
Easter Vigil	29 Mar.	25 Mar.	18 Apr.	15 Apr.	11 Apr.	14 Apr.
Easter Sunday	30 Mar.	26 Mar.	19 Apr.	16 Apr.	12 Apr.	15 Apr.
2nd Sun. Easter	6 Apr.	2 Apr.	26 Apr.	23 Apr.	19 Apr.	22 Apr.
3rd Sun. Easter	13 Apr.	9 Apr.	3 May	30 Apr.	26 Apr.	29 Apr.
4th Sun. Easter	20 Apr.	16 Apr.	10 May	7 May	3 May	6 May
5th Sun. Easter	27 Apr.	23 Apr.	17 May	14 May	10 May	13 May

YEAR C

Sunday or Feast	1986	1989	1992	1995	1998	2001
6th Sun. Easter	4 May	30 Apr.	24 May	21 May	17 May	20 May
Ascension	8 May	4 May	28 May	25 May	21 May	24 May
7th Sun. Easter	11 May	7 May	31 May	28 May	24 May	27 May
Pentecost Sun.	18 May	14 May	7 June	4 June	31 May	3 June
Trinity Sun.	25 May	21 May	14 June	11 June	7 June	10 June
Body and Blood	1 June	28 May	21 June	18 June	14 June	17 June
9th Ord. Sun.	—	4 June	—	—	—	—
10th Ord. Sun.	8 June	11 June	—	—	—	—
11th Ord. Sun.	15 June	18 June	—	—	—	—
12th Ord. Sun.	22 June	25 June	—	25 June	21 June	24 June
13th Ord. Sun.	29 June	2 July	28 June	2 July	28 June	1 July
14th Ord. Sun.	6 July	9 July	5 July	9 July	5 July	8 July
15th Ord. Sun.	13 July	16 July	12 July	16 July	12 July	15 July
16th Ord. Sun	20 July	23 July	19 July	23 July	19 July	22 July
17th Ord. Sun.	27 July	30 July	26 July	30 July	26 July	29 July
18th Ord. Sun.	3 Aug.	6 Aug.	2 Aug.	6 Aug.	2 Aug.	5 Aug.
19th Ord. Sun.	10 Aug.	13 Aug.	9 Aug.	13 Aug.	9 Aug.	12 Aug.
Assumption	15 Aug.	15 Aug.	15 Aug.	15 Aug.	15 Aug.	15 Aug.
20th Ord. Sun.	17 Aug.	20 Aug.	16 Aug.	20 Aug.	16 Aug.	19 Aug.
21st Ord.Sun.	24 Aug.	27 Aug.	23 Aug.	27 Aug.	23 Aug.	26 Aug.
22nd Ord. Sun.	31 Aug.	3 Sept.	30 Aug.	3 Sept.	30 Aug.	2 Sept.
23rd Ord. Sun.	7 Sept.	10 Sept.	6 Sept.	10 Sept.	6 Sept.	9 Sept.
24th Ord. Sun.	14 Sept.	17 Sept.	13 Sept.	17 Sept.	13 Sept.	16 Sept.
25th Ord. Sun.	21 Sept.	24 Sept.	20 Sept.	24 Sept.	20 Sept.	23 Sept.
26th Ord. Sun.	28 Sept.	1 Oct.	27 Sept.	1 Oct.	27 Sept.	30 Sept.
27th Ord. Sun.	5 Oct.	8 Oct.	4 Oct.	8 Oct.	4 Oct.	7 Oct.
28th Ord. Sun.	12 Oct.	15 Oct.	11 Oct.	15 Oct.	11 Oct.	14 Oct.
29th Ord. Sun.	19 Oct.	22 Oct.	18 Oct.	22 Oct.	18 Oct.	21 Oct.
30th Ord. Sun.	26 Oct.	29 Oct.	25 Oct.	29 Oct.	25 Oct.	28 Oct.
All Saints	1 Nov.	1 Nov.	1 Nov.	1 Nov.	1 Nov.	1 Nov.
31st Ord. Sun.	2 Nov.	5 Nov.	—	5 Nov.	—	4 Nov.
32nd Ord. Sun.	9 Nov.	12 Nov.	8 Nov.	12 Nov.	8 Nov.	11 Nov.
33rd Ord. Sun.	16 Nov.	19 Nov.	15 Nov.	19 Nov.	15 Nov.	18 Nov.
34th Ord. Sun.	23 Nov.	26 Nov.	22 Nov.	26 Nov.	22 Nov.	25 Nov.

PROPER OF SEASONS

ADVENT SEASON

Creation, including ourselves, is submitted to a master-plan, which is in a process of being realized by the Creator. All creation groans and travails in pain till it will be delivered from its slavery to corruption into the freedom of the glory of the sons of God (see Rom. 8, 21-22).

But when, after millions of years, man, created in innocence, finally appeared on the scene—one of the highlights of this divinely-intended evolution—he chose not to cooperate with his process of mysterious growth into the image of the Creator (Gn 1, 27). Man's state of incompleteness became a sinful deficiency.

And since all have sinned (Rom 3, 23), this "sin of the world" brought about man's impotence to realize the divinely-intended freedom into which he is to grow. Hence, Redemption by Jesus, who took away the sin of the world (Jn 1, 29), became a necessity. Only in Christ has the earthy man the power to become the heavenly man, as intended by God (1 Cor 15, 45-49).

Advent is the time of more than usual eager longing, awaiting our revelation as sons of God (Rom 8, 19). It is the waiting for Christ's coming in grace on Christmas ever more to us (see Jn 14, 23) and for his final coming, when God's plan will be fully realized in all who have put on Christ by faith and baptism (Gal 3, 27).

God gives us this plan in the words of the prophets. And the Church gives us their words in Advent. To the great precursors of Isaiah and John the Baptizer, she now adds Baruch, Jeremiah, Zephaniah, and Micah. And then comes Jesus, whom St. Paul describes (2 Cor 1, 21) as the "Yes" or "Amen"—the fulfillment —of all the promises God has made.

1

From the day of the Annunciation onward, Mary, more than anyone else in the world, had the privilege of knowing that in all truth God is the One who comes into the world. It is by meditating on his mystery that we begin to understand that the One who is called 'the Son of the Most High" has linked our lot with his own by becoming man and that he will return to inaugurate his eternal kingdom by saving us.

The Book of Isaiah is one of those in which this Messianic hope is most strongly expressed. It contains the oracles of the great 8th-century-B.C. prophet himself as well as those of two disciples known as Second Isaiah and Third Isaiah. The readings from this book represent more than half of the first readings for Advent. The others are taken from various books and usually have a relation to the Gospel of the day, and some give important Messianic pronouncements. These texts provide a rich tableau of the hope that Christ has come to fulfill and transform.

The Infancy Gospels utilized during Advent and Christmas comprise a prologue to the Gospel which actually begins with the baptism of John (cf. Acts 1, 21ff). The evangelists of the infancy (Matthew and Luke) did not intend so much to give biographical detail as to show how he fulfilled God's promises and accomplished man's salvation. For Matthew, this meant underlining the signs of Jesus' fulfillment of Scripture: Jesus is the One expected by Israel, the One promised to Abraham and David, a new Moses. For Luke, this meant showing Jesus as the universal Savior, the One who reveals the Father's mercy to sinners and saves them by giving them the Spirit.

During Advent, our constant prayer should be: "Come, Lord Jesus!" (Rv 22, 20). We should "reject godless ways and worldly desires, and live temperately, justly, and devoutly in this age as we await our blessed hope, the appearing of the glory of the great God and our Savior Jesus Christ" (Ti 2, 12-13).

MONDAY OF THE FIRST WEEK OF ADVENT

Come, Lord Jesus. This welcome greeting reminds us that Jesus is to come again. His final coming will take place on the last day in the gathering together of the peoples from the east and the west. It will be the time of fulfillment when Jesus will bring peace. We await his glorious coming.

ENTRANCE ANT.   See Jer 31, 10; Is 35, 4

Nations, hear the message of the Lord, and make it known to the ends of the earth: Our Savior is coming. Have no more fear.   ➤ No. 2, p. 614

OPENING PRAYER

Lord our God,
help us to prepare
for the coming of Christ your Son.
May he find us waiting,
eager in joyful prayer.
We ask this through our Lord Jesus Christ, your Son,
who lives and reigns with you and the Holy Spirit,
one God, for ever and ever. ℟. **Amen.** ↓

READING I   Is 2, 1-5

In year A, when this reading is used on the First Sunday of Advent, the reading below (Is 4, 2-6) replaces it:

In his vision Isaiah sees that the Lord's house will be established over all. All peoples shall come and be instructed by God. They will then live in peace and brotherhood.

A reading from the book of the prophet Isaiah
This is what Isaiah, son of Amoz, saw concerning Judah and Jerusalem.
    In days to come,
The mountain of the Lord's house
    shall be established as the highest mountain
    and raised above the hills.

All nations shall stream toward it;
    many peoples shall come and say:
"Come, let us climb the Lord's mountain,
    to the house of the God of Jacob,
That he may instruct us in his ways,
    and we may walk in his paths."
For from Zion shall go forth instruction,
    and the word of the Lord from Jerusalem.
He shall judge between the nations,
    and impose terms on many peoples.
They shall beat their swords into plowshares
    and their spears into pruning hooks;
One nation shall not raise the sword against another,
    nor shall they train for war again.
O house of Jacob, come,
    let us walk in the light of the Lord!
This is the Word of the Lord. ℟. **Thanks to be God.** ℣

OR

READING I (for Year A)   Is 4, 2-6

The Messiah will come forth in Israel and bring salvation to those
who remained steadfast. Joy and happiness will be theirs for the Lord
will protect them.

A reading from the book of the prophet Isaiah
    On that day,
The branch of the Lord will be luster and glory,
    and the fruit of the earth will be honor and
        splendor
    for the survivors of Israel.
He who remains in Zion
    and he that is left in Jerusalem
Will be called holy:
    every one marked down for life in Jerusalem.
When the Lord washes away
    the filth of the daughters of Zion,
And purges Jerusalem's blood from her midst
    with a blast of searing judgment,

Then will the Lord create,
>over the whole site of Mount Zion
>and over her place of assembly,
A smoking cloud by day
>and a light of flaming fire by night.
For over all, his glory will be shelter and protection:
>shade from the parching heat of day,
>refuge and cover from storm and rain.
This is the Word of the Lord. ℟. **Thanks be to God.** ✓

Responsorial Psalm   Ps 122, 1-2. 3-4. (4-5. 6-7) 8-9

℟. (1) **I rejoiced when I heard them say:**
let us go to the house of the Lord.

I rejoiced because they said to me,
>"We will go up to the house of the Lord."
And now we have set foot
>within your gates, O Jerusalem. — ℟

Jerusalem, built as a city
>with compact unity.
To it the tribes go up,
>the tribes of the Lord. — ℟

According to the decree for Israel,
>to give thanks to the name of the Lord.
In it are set up judgment seats,
>seats for the house of David. — ℟

Pray for the peace of Jerusalem!
>May those who love you prosper!
May peace be within your walls,
>prosperity in your buildings. — ℟

Because of my relatives and friends
>I will say, "Peace be within you!"
Because of the house of the Lord, our God,
>I will pray for your good. — ℟ ✓

GOSPEL   Mt 8, 5-11

Alleluia (See Ps 79, 4)

℟. **Alleluia.** Come and save us, Lord our God;
let us see your face, and we shall be saved. ℟. **Alleluia.**

In place of the Alleluia given for each Weekday Mass, another may be selected from pp. 1267-1275.

Jesus heals the centurion's son. Jesus notes the faith of the centurion and at the same time shows that the kingdom of God is destined to extend to all men.

℣. The Lord be with you. ℟. **And also with you.**

✠ A reading from the holy gospel according to Matthew. ℟. **Glory to you, Lord.**

As Jesus entered Capernaum, a centurion approached him with this request: "Sir, my serving boy is at home in bed paralyzed, suffering painfully." He said to him, "I will come and cure him." "Sir," the centurion said in reply, "I am not worthy to have you under my roof. Just give an order and my boy will get better. I am a man under authority myself and I have troops assigned to me. If I give one man the order, 'Dismissed,' off he goes. If I say to another, 'Come here,' he comes. If I tell my slave 'Do this,' he does it." Jesus showed amazement on hearing this and remarked to his followers, "I assure you, I have never found this much faith in Israel. Mark what I say! Many will come from the east and the west and will find a place at the banquet in the kingdom of God with Abraham, Isaac, and Jacob."—This is the gospel of the Lord. ℟. **Praise to you, Lord Jesus Christ.**

PRAYER OVER THE GIFTS   ➤ No. 15, p. 623

Father,
from all you give us
we present this bread and wine.
As we serve you now,
accept our offering
and sustain us with your promise of eternal life.
Grant this through Christ our Lord.
℟. **Amen.**   ➤ No. 21, p. 626 (Pref. P 1)

COMMUNION ANT. See Ps 106, 4-5; Is 38, 3

Come to us, Lord, and bring us peace. We will rejoice in your presence and serve you with all our heart. ℣

PRAYER AFTER COMMUNION

Father,
may our communion
teach us to love heaven.
May its promise and hope
guide our way on earth.
We ask this through Christ our Lord.
℟. **Amen.** ─────────── ➔ No. 32, p. 650

TUESDAY OF THE FIRST WEEK OF ADVENT

Jesus is the promised Messiah who fills the needs that all men have.
We look to him that our faith will grow and that we may understand
the workings of God among his people.

ENTRANCE ANT. See Zec 14, 5. 7

See, the Lord is coming and with him all his saints. Then there will be endless day. ➔ No. 2, p. 614

OPENING PRAYER

God of mercy and consolation,
help us in our weakness and free us from sin.
Hear our prayers
that we may rejoice at the coming of your Son,
who lives and reigns with you and the Holy Spirit,
one God, for ever and ever. ℟. **Amen.** ℣

READING I Is 11, 1-10

Isaiah describes the power and virtue of the promised king in whom
God's covenant with David will be realized. The Spirit of the Lord
will make this king a man whose virtue, wisdom, and understanding
will go beyond all human dimensions. The Spirit of the Lord will rest
on him.

A reading from the book of the prophet Isaiah
On that day,
A shoot shall sprout from the stump of Jesse,
and from his roots a bud shall blossom.
The spirit of the Lord shall rest upon him:
a spirit of wisdom and of understanding,
A spirit of counsel and of strength,
a spirit of knowledge and of fear of the Lord,
and his delight shall be the fear of the Lord.
Not by appearance shall he judge,
nor by hearsay shall he decide,
But he shall judge the poor with justice,
and decide aright for the land's afflicted.
He shall strike the ruthless with the rod of his mouth,
and with the breath of his lips he shall slay the
wicked.
Justice shall be the band around his waist,
and faithfulness a belt upon his hips.
Then the wolf shall be a guest of the lamb,
and the leopard shall lie down with the kid;
The calf and the young lion shall browse together,
with a little child to guide them.
The cow and the bear shall be neighbors,
together their young shall rest;
the lion shall eat hay like the ox.
The baby shall play by the cobra's den,
and the child lay his hand on the adder's lair.
There shall be no harm or ruin on all my holy mountain;
for the earth shall be filled with knowledge of the
Lord,
as water covers the sea.

On that day,
The root of Jesse,
set up as a signal for the nations,
The Gentiles shall seek out,
for his dwelling shall be glorious.
This is the Word of the Lord. ℞. **Thanks be to God.** ℣

Responsorial Psalm Ps 72, 1. 7-8. 12-13. 17

℟. (7) **Justice shall flourish in his time,**
and fullness of peace for ever.

O God, with your judgment endow the king,
and with your justice, the king's son;
He shall govern your people with justice
and your afflicted ones with judgment. — ℟

Justice shall flower in his days,
and profound peace, till the moon be no more.
May he rule from sea to sea,
and from the River to the ends of the earth. — ℟

He shall rescue the poor man when he cries out,
and the afflicted when he has no one to help him.
He shall have pity for the lowly and the poor;
the lives of the poor he shall save. — ℟

May his name be blessed forever;
as long as the sun his name shall remain.
In him shall all the tribes of the earth be blessed;
all the nations shall proclaim his happiness. — ℟ ⍒

GOSPEL Lk 10, 21-24
Alleluia.
℟. **Alleluia.** Behold, our Lord shall come with power,
he will enlighten the eyes of his servants. ℟. **Alle-**
luia.

From Jesus' prayer of thanksgiving, it is clear that the Father reveals
the mystery of salvation to the little ones, the men of faith. It is only
by oneness of faith with Jesus, by looking at the Father through his
eyes, that men can come to know the unknown God.

℣. The Lord be with you. ℟. **And also with you.**
✠ A reading from the holy gospel according to Luke
℟. **Glory to you, Lord.**

Jesus rejoiced in the Holy Spirit and said: "I offer
you praise, O Father, Lord of heaven and earth, because what you have hidden from the learned and
the clever you have revealed to the merest children.

"Yes, Father, you have graciously willed it so.

"Everything has been given over to me by my Father. No one knows the Son except the Father and no one knows the Father except the Son—and anyone to whom the Son wishes to reveal him."

Turning to his disciples he said to them privately: "Blest are the eyes that see what you see. I tell you, many prophets and kings wished to see what you see but did not see it, and to hear what you hear but did not hear it."—This is the gospel of the Lord. ℞. **Praise to you, Lord Jesus Christ.**   ➤ No. 15, p. 623

PRAYER OVER THE GIFTS

Lord,
we are nothing without you.
As you sustain us with your mercy,
receive our prayers and offerings.
We ask this through Christ our Lord.
℞. **Amen.**   ➤ No. 21, p. 626 (Pref. P 1)

COMMUNION ANT.   2 Tm 4, 8

The Lord is just; he will award the crown of justice to all who have longed for his coming. ⱽ

PRAYER AFTER COMMUNION

Father,
you give us food from heaven.
By our sharing in this mystery,
teach us to judge wisely the things of earth
and to love the things of heaven.
Grant this through Christ our Lord.
℞. **Amen.** _____   ➤ No. 32, p. 650

WEDNESDAY OF THE FIRST WEEK OF ADVENT

Our thoughts today plunge us into the next life. We are reminded of the final judgment. As Jesus feeds the hungry in the desert, we come to hope in the banquet of the Lord where we shall be in God's kingdom. In every Eucharist we are already beginning to eat with the Lord and his heavenly court that feast of rich food and choice wine which in the time of Jesus Christ awaited us "on this mountain."

ENTRANCE ANT.   See Hb 2, 3; 1 Cor 4, 5

**The Lord is coming and will not delay; he will bring
every hidden thing to light and reveal himself to
every nation.**   → No. 2, p. 614

OPENING PRAYER

Lord our God,
grant that we may be ready
to receive Christ when he comes in glory
and to share in the banquet of heaven,
where he lives and reigns with you and the Holy
    Spirit,
one God, for ever and ever. ℞. **Amen.** ▼

READING I   Is 25, 6-10

Isaiah shows that on the great and final day toward which everything
is moving, the Lord and his heavenly court on Mount Zion will feast
unendingly with his people who are now seen to come from all over
the earth. The rich food and the choice wine which God provides for
all his people suggest perfect satisfaction. They show a loving God.

A reading from the book of the prophet Isaiah

On this mountain the Lord of hosts
    will provide for all peoples
A feast of rich food and choice wines,
    juicy, rich food and pure, choice wines.
On this mountain he will destroy
    the veil that veils all peoples,
The web that is woven over all nations;
    he will destroy death forever.
The Lord God will wipe away
    the tears from all faces;
The reproach of his people he will remove
    from the whole earth; for the Lord has spoken.
    On that day it will be said:
"Behold our God, to whom we looked to save us!
    This is the Lord for whom we looked;
    let us rejoice and be glad that he has saved us!"

For the hand of the Lord will rest on this mountain.
This is the Word of the Lord. ℟. **Thanks be to God.** ⍦

Responsorial Psalm   Ps 23, 1-3. 3-4. 5. 6
℟. (6) **I shall live in the house of the Lord
all the days of my life.**

The Lord is my shepherd; I shall not want.
    In verdant pastures he gives me repose;
Beside restful waters he leads me;
    he refreshes my soul. — ℟

He guides me in right paths
    for his name's sake.
Even though I walk in the dark valley
    I fear no evil; for you are at my side
With your rod and your staff
    that give me courage. — ℟

You spread the table before me
    in the sight of my foes;
You anoint my head with oil;
    my cup overflows. — ℟

Only goodness and kindness follow me
    all the days of my life;
And I shall dwell in the house of the Lord
    for years to come. — ℟ ⍦

GOSPEL   Mt 15, 29-37
Alleluia
℟. **Alleluia.** The Lord is coming to save his people;
happy are those prepared to meet him. ℟. **Alleluia.**

Jesus "wipes away the tears" by curing the sick, the blind, the
crippled. Here Jesus goes over the borders of Israel to indicate his
meal includes also the Gentiles. On a hilltop, he provides an abundant
heavenly banquet for them. Not only men of Israel, but pagans, see
wonders of God's salvation and the end of human miseries; they adore
a new God—"the God of Israel."

℣. The Lord be with you. ℟. **And also with you.**
✠ A reading from the holy gospel according to Matthew. ℟. **Glory to you, Lord.**

Jesus went along the Sea of Galilee. He went up onto the mountainside and sat down there. Large crowds of people came to him bringing with them cripples, the deformed, the blind, the mute, and many others besides. They laid them at his feet and he cured them. The result was great astonishment in the crowds as they beheld the mute speaking, the deformed made sound, cripples walking about, and the blind seeing. They glorified the God of Israel.

Jesus called his disciples to him and said: "My heart is moved with pity for the crowd. By now they have been with me three days, and have nothing to eat. I do not wish to send them away hungry, for fear they may collapse on the way." His disciples said to him, "How could we ever get enough bread in this deserted spot to satisfy such a crowd?" But Jesus asked them, "How many loaves of bread do you have?" "Seven," they replied, "and a few small fish." Then he directed the crowd to seat themselves on the ground. He took the seven loaves and the fish, and after giving thanks he broke them and gave them to the disciples, who in turn gave them to the crowds. All ate until they were full. When they gathered up the fragments left over, these filled seven hampers. —This is the gospel of the Lord. ℟. **Praise to you, Lord Jesus Christ.**   ➤ No. 15, p. 623

PRAYER OVER THE GIFTS

Lord,
may the gift we offer in faith and love
be a continual sacrifice in your honor
and truly become our eucharist and our salvation.
Grant this through Christ our Lord.
℟. **Amen.**   ➤ No. 21, p. 626 (Pref. P 1)

COMMUNION ANT.   Is 40, 10; see 34, 5

The Lord our God comes in strength and will fill his servants with joy. ℣

PRAYER AFTER COMMUNION

God of mercy,
may this eucharist bring us your divine help,
free us from our sins,
and prepare us for the birthday of our Savior,
who is Lord for ever and ever.
℟. **Amen.**

➤ No. 32, p. 650

THURSDAY OF THE FIRST WEEK OF ADVENT

In Advent we live in the hope of a reformed and re-established world.
All are called. The Lord gives hope to his people. Jesus shows his
care and concern for his fellowmen. He looks after both their bodily
and their spiritual needs. God takes care of those who come to him.

ENTRANCE ANT.   See Ps 119, 151-152

**Lord, you are near, and all your commandments are
just; long have I known that you decreed them for
ever.**

➤ No. 2, p. 614

OPENING PRAYER

Father,
we need your help.
Free us from sin and bring us to life.
Support us by your power.
Grant this through our Lord Jesus Christ, your Son,
who lives and reigns with you and the Holy Spirit,
one God, for ever and ever. ℟. **Amen.** ↓

READING I   Is 26, 1-6

Isaiah seems to be using a psalm that celebrates liturgically the entrance into the Holy City of God's remnant, a nation newly formed
out of the survivors of world devastation. They are God's poor. Isaiah
saw the root of Israel's sinfulness in its failure to trust the Lord. The
nation did not keep faith and did not live in the covenanted way that
God had given them. Isaiah sees the reborn Israel as a nation that
is just because it is one that trusts in the Lord forever and keeps faith
with him because he is their eternal Rock.

A reading from the book of the prophet Isaiah

On that day they will sing this song in the land of Judah:

"A strong city have we;
  he sets up walls and ramparts to protect us.
Open up the gates
  to let in a nation that is just,
  one that keeps faith.
A nation of firm purpose you keep in peace;
  in peace, for its trust in you."
Trust in the Lord forever!
  For the Lord is an eternal rock.
He humbles those in high places,
  and the lofty city he brings down;
He tumbles it to the ground,
  levels it with the dust.
It is trampled underfoot by the needy,
  by the footsteps of the poor.

This is the Word of the Lord. ℞. **Thanks be to God.** ℣

Responsorial Psalm   Ps 118, 1. 8-9. 19-21. 25-27

℞. (26) **Blessed is he who comes in the name of the Lord.**

Give thanks to the Lord, for he is good,
  for his mercy endures forever.
It is better to take refuge in the Lord
  than to trust in man.
It is better to take refuge in the Lord
  than to trust in princes. — ℞

Open to me the gates of justice;
  I will enter them and give thanks to the Lord.
This gate is the Lord's;
  the just shall enter it.
I will give thanks to you, for you have answered me
  and have been my savior. — ℞

O Lord, grant salvation!
  O Lord, grant prosperity!
Blessed is he who comes in the name of the Lord;
  we bless you from the house of the Lord.
The Lord is God, and he has given us light. — ℞ ℣

℞. Or: **Alleluia.** ℣

GOSPEL   Mt 7, 21. 24-27

Alleluia (Is 55, 6)

℞. **Alleluia.** Seek the Lord while he can be found.
Call on him while he is near. ℞. **Alleluia.**

All are called to this kingdom but not all will be admitted. Only the just
will be allowed inside the gates; i.e., those who keep faith, those who
are humble, those who accept the Messiah with their whole heart and
soul.

℣. The Lord be with you. ℞. **And also with you.**

✠ A reading from the holy gospel according to Matthew. ℞. **Glory to you, Lord.**

Jesus said to his disciples: "None of those who cry
out, 'Lord, Lord,' will enter the kingdom of God but
only the one who does the will of my Father in
heaven.

  "Anyone who hears my words and puts them into
practice is like the wise man who built his house on
rock. When the rainy season set in, the torrents came
and the winds blew and buffeted his house. It did not
collapse; it had been solidly set on rock. Anyone
who hears my words but does not put them into
practice is like the foolish man who built his house
on sandy ground. The rains fell, the torrents came,
the winds blew and lashed against his house. It col-
lapsed under all this and was completely ruined."—
This is the gospel of the Lord. ℞. **Praise to you, Lord
Jesus Christ.**   ➤ No. 15, p. 623

PRAYER OVER THE GIFTS

Father,
from all you give us
we present this bread and wine.
As we serve you now,
accept our offering
and sustain us with your promise of eternal life.
Grant this through Christ our Lord.
℟. **Amen.**   ➤ No. 21, p. 626 (Pref P 1)

COMMUNION ANT.   Ti 2, 12-13

Let our lives be honest and holy in this present age, as we wait for the happiness to come when our great God reveals himself in glory. ↓

PRAYER AFTER COMMUNION

Father,
may our communion
teach us to love heaven.
May its promise and hope
guide our way on earth.
We ask this through Christ our Lord.
℟. **Amen.** _____   ➤ No. 32, p. 650

FRIDAY OF THE FIRST WEEK OF ADVENT

Jesus is our light and our salvation. He came into the world to show us a way of life. It is through our faith and belief in him and our hope and trust in him that we come to know him and love him all the more.

ENTRANCE ANT.

The Lord is coming from heaven in splendor to visit his people, and bring them peace and eternal life.
➤ No. 2, p. 614

OPENING PRAYER

Jesus, our Lord,
save us from our sins.

Come, protect us from all dangers
and lead us to salvation,
for you live and reign with the Father and the
     Holy Spirit,
one God, for ever and ever. ℞. **Amen.** ℣

READING I   Is 29, 17-24

Isaiah sees the Messiah as a guiding light. From gloom and darkness,
the blind shall see. Evildoers will be cut off from him. The children
of Jacob shall give praise and honor to the Lord and reverence his
name.

A reading from the book of the prophet Isaiah
     Thus says the Lord God:
But a very little while,
     and Lebanon shall be changed into an orchard,
     and the orchard be regarded as a forest!
On that day the deaf shall hear
     the words of a book;
And out of gloom and darkness,
     the eyes of the blind shall see.
The lowly will ever find joy in the Lord,
 ˙ and the poor rejoice in the Holy One of Israel.
For the tyrant will be no more
     and the arrogant will have gone;
All who are alert to do evil will be cut off,
     those whose mere word condemns a man,
Who ensnare his defender at the gate,
     and leave the just man with an empty claim.
Therefore thus says the Lord,
     the God of the house of Jacob,
     who redeemed Abraham:
Now Jacob shall have nothing to be ashamed of,
     nor shall his face grow pale.
When his children see
     the work of my hands in his midst,
They shall keep my name holy;
     they shall reverence the Holy One of Jacob,
     and be in awe of the God of Israel.

Those who err in spirit shall acquire understanding,
    and those who find fault shall receive instruction.
This is the Word of the Lord. ℟. **Thanks be to God.** ↓

Responsorial Psalm   Ps 27, 1. 4. 13-14

℟. (1) **The Lord is my light and my salvation.**

The Lord is my light and my salvation;
    whom should I fear?
The Lord is my life's refuge;
    of whom should I be afraid? — ℟

One thing I ask of the Lord;
    this I seek:
To dwell in the house of the Lord
    all the days of my life,
That I may gaze on the loveliness of the Lord
    and contemplate his temple. — ℟

I believe that I shall see the bounty of the Lord
    in the land of the living.
Wait for the Lord with courage;
    be stouthearted, and wait for the Lord. — ℟ ↓

℟. Or: **Alleluia.** ↓

GOSPEL   Mt 9, 27-31

Alleluia

℟. **Alleluia.** Behold, our Lord shall come with power,
he will enlighten the eyes of his servants. ℟. **Alleluia.**

Jesus cures two blind men. To receive light, they had faith in Christ
and faith in God's infinite power and unlimited love for man. This is
a child's faith. It was a condition required by Christ before he would
work a miracle. Only this miracle-faith can receive the mystery of
light.

℣. The Lord be with you. ℟. **And also with you.**
✠ A reading from the holy gospel according to Matthew. ℟. **Glory to you, Lord.**

As Jesus moved on from Capernaum, two blind men
came after him crying out, "Son of David, have pity

on us!" When he got to the house, the blind men caught up with him. Jesus said to them, "Are you confident I can do this?" "Yes, Lord," they told him. At that he touched their eyes and said, "Because of your faith it shall be done to you"; and they recovered their sight. Then Jesus warned them sternly, "See to it that no one knows of this." But they went off and spread word of him through the whole area. —This is the gospel of the Lord. ℟. **Praise to you, Lord Jesus Christ.**   ➤ No. 15, p. 623

PRAYER OVER THE GIFTS

Lord,
we are nothing without you.
As you sustain us with your mercy,
receive our prayers and offerings.
We ask this through Christ our Lord.
℟. **Amen.**   ➤ No. 21, p. 626 (Pref. P 1)

COMMUNION ANT.   Phil 3, 20-21

We are waiting for our Savior, the Lord Jesus Christ; he will transfigure our lowly bodies into copies of his own glorious body. ℣

PRAYER AFTER COMMUNION

Father,
you give us food from heaven.
Teach us to live by your wisdom
and to love the things of heaven
by our sharing in this mystery.
Grant this through Christ our Lord.
℟. **Amen.**   ➤ No. 32, p. 650

_____

SATURDAY OF THE FIRST WEEK OF ADVENT

In the days of Isaiah the people did not want a shepherd. Their faith was weak and they were blinded. Today we are living in the time of Jesus. He tells us the harvest is good. Why is it that it rarely takes root in our lives?

ENTRANCE ANT. Ps 80, 4. 2

**Come, Lord, from your cherubim throne; let us see
your face, and we shall be saved.** → No. 2, p. 614

OPENING PRAYER

God our Father,
you loved the world so much
you gave your only Son to free us
from the ancient power of sin and death.
Help us who wait for his coming,
and lead us to true liberty.
We ask this through our Lord Jesus Christ, your Son,
who lives and reigns with you and the Holy Spirit,
one God, for ever and ever. ℟. **Amen.** ↓

READING I Is 30, 19-21. 23-26

Isaiah tells the people: "The Lord is waiting to show you favor and
he rises to pity you. . . . He will be gracious to you when you cry out;
as soon as he hears, he will answer you." Only their rejection of his
word, his shepherding, and their trust and reliance on what is crooked
and devious blocks the manifestation of his favor.

A reading from the book of the prophet Isaiah

Thus says the Lord God,
   the Holy One of Israel:
O people of Zion, who dwell in Jerusalem,
   no more will you weep;
He will be gracious to you when you cry out,
   as soon as he hears you he will answer you.
The Lord will give you the bread you need
   and the water for which you thirst.
No longer will your Teacher hide himself,
   but with your own eyes you shall see your Teacher,
While from behind, a voice shall sound in your ears:
   "This is the way; walk in it,"
   when you would turn to the right or to the left.
He will give rain for the seed
   that you sow in the ground,
And the wheat that the soil produces
   will be rich and abundant.

On that day your cattle will graze
   in spacious meadows;
The oxen and the asses that till the ground
   will eat silage tossed to them
   with shovel and pitchfork.
Upon every high mountain and lofty hill
   there will be streams of running water.
On the day of the great slaughter,
   when the towers fall,
The light of the moon will be like that of the sun
   and the light of the sun will be seven times
      greater
   [like the light of seven days].
On the day the Lord binds up the wounds of his
      people,
   he will heal the bruises left by his blows.
This is the Word of the Lord. ℟. **Thanks be to God.** ℣

Responsorial Psalm   Ps 147, 1-2. 3-4. 5-6

℟. (Is 30, 18) **Happy are all who long for the coming of the Lord.**

Praise the Lord, for he is good;
   sing praise to our God, for he is gracious;
   it is fitting to praise him.
The Lord rebuilds Jerusalem;
   the dispersed of Israel he gathers. — ℟

He heals the brokenhearted
   and binds up their wounds.
He tells the number of the stars;
   he calls each by name. — ℟

Great is our Lord and mighty in power:
   to his wisdom there is no limit.
The Lord sustains the lowly;
   the wicked he casts to the ground. — ℟ ℣

℟. Or: **Alleluia.** ℣

GOSPEL   Mt 9, 35—10, 1. 6-8

Alleluia (Is 33, 22)

℟. **Alleluia.** The Lord will judge us by his law;
he is our King and Savior. ℟. **Alleluia.**

The first half of our Gospel reading (9, 35-38) is a summary of the
situation which Jesus encountered during the early days of his mission
in Galilee. "He cured every sickness and disease." His heart is moved
to pity by much of what he sees, and he tells his disciples: "The
harvest is abundant, but more laborers are needed." Jesus communi-
cates his power to the apostles and sends them out to do the same
work that he is doing. They are to announce the Good News that the
kingdom is fast approaching.

℣. The Lord be with you. ℟. **And also with you.**
✠ A reading from the holy gospel according to Matthew. ℟. **Glory to you, Lord.**

Jesus toured all the towns and villages. He taught
in their synagogues, he proclaimed the good news of
God's reign, and he cured every sickness and disease.
At the sight of the crowds, his heart was moved with
pity. They were lying prostrate from exhaustion, like
sheep without a shepherd. He said to his disciples:
"The harvest is good but laborers are scarce. Beg the
harvest master to send out laborers to gather his
harvest."

Then he summoned his twelve disciples and gave
them authority to expel unclean spirits and to cure
sickness and disease of every kind. He gave them
these instructions: "Go instead after the lost sheep
of the house of Israel. As you go, make this announcement: 'The reign of God is at hand!' Cure the
sick, raise the dead, heal the leprous, expel demons.
The gift you have received, give as a gift."—This is
the gospel of the Lord. ℟. **Praise to you, Lord Jesus
Christ.** ➔ No. 15, p. 623

PRAYER OVER THE GIFTS

Lord,
may the gift we offer in faith and love
be a continual sacrifice in your honor

and truly become our eucharist and our salvation.
We ask this through Christ our Lord.
℞. **Amen.**   ➜ No. 21, p. 626 (Pref. P1)

COMMUNION ANT.   Rv 22, 12

**I am coming quickly, says the Lord, and will repay
each man according to his deeds.** ⌄

PRAYER AFTER COMMUNION

God of mercy,
may this eucharist bring us your divine help,
free us from our sins,
and prepare us for the birthday of our Savior,
who is Lord for ever and ever.
℞. **Amen.**   ➜ No. 32, p. 650

————————

MONDAY OF THE SECOND WEEK OF ADVENT

The Messiah will bring about peace and prosperity for which the
Israelites have prayed. Jesus responds to prayer, to faith, as he cures
the sick man. The sign of God's love is shown for his people. Our
response should be one of praise and thanks.

ENTRANCE ANT.   See Jer 31, 10; Is 35, 4

**Nations, hear the message of the Lord, and make it
known to the ends of the earth: Our Savior is coming.
Have no more fear.**   ➜ No. 2, p. 614

OPENING PRAYER

Lord,
free us from our sins and make us whole.
Hear our prayer,
and prepare us to celebrate the incarnation of your
   Son,
who lives and reigns with you and the Holy Spirit,
one God, for ever and ever.
℞. **Amen.** ⌄

READING I   Is 35, 1-10

Isaiah describes the extraordinary age of prosperity and peace. Yahweh will deliver the people from the bitterness of bondage as in the
great Exodus. The Exodus and the Exile restoration are types of the
New Exodus through the life, death, and resurrection of Jesus, the new
Moses. The blind will see; the ears of the deaf will be opened; the
lame will leap like a stag; the dumb will speak.

A reading from the book of the prophet Isaiah

The desert and the parched land will exult;
    the steppe will rejoice and bloom.
They will bloom with abundant flowers,
    and rejoice with joyful song.
The glory of Lebanon will be given to them,
    the splendor of Carmel and Sharon;
They will see the glory of the Lord,
    the splendor of our God.
Strengthen the hands that are feeble,
    make firm the knees that are weak,
Say to those whose hearts are frightened:
    Be strong, fear not!
Here is your God,
    he comes with vindication;
With divine recompense
    he comes to save you.
Then will the eyes of the blind be opened,
    the ears of the deaf be cleared;
Then will the lame leap like a stag,
    then the tongue of the dumb will sing.
Streams will burst forth in the desert,
    and rivers in the steppe.
The burning sands will become pools,
    and the thirsty ground, springs of water;
The abode where jackals lurk
    will be a marsh for the reed and papyrus.
A highway will be there,
    called the holy way;
No one unclean may pass over it,
    nor fools go astray on it.

No lion will be there,
    nor beast of prey go up to be met upon it.
It is for those with a journey to make,
    and on it the redeemed will walk.
Those whom the Lord has ransomed will return
    and enter Zion singing,
    crowned with everlasting joy;
They will meet with joy and gladness,
    sorrow and mourning will flee.
This is the Word of the Lord. ℟. **Thanks be to God.** ℣

Responsorial Psalm   Ps 85, 9-10. 11-12. 13-14
℟. (Is 35, 4) **Our God will come to save us!**
I will hear what the Lord God proclaims;
    the Lord—for he proclaims peace to his people.
Near indeed is his salvation to those who fear him,
    glory dwelling in our land. — ℟

Kindness and truth shall meet;
    justice and peace shall kiss.
Truth shall spring out of the earth,
    and justice shall look down from heaven. — ℟

The Lord himself will give his benefits;
    our land shall yield its increase.
Justice shall walk before him,
    and salvation, along the way of his steps. — ℟ ℣

GOSPEL   Lk 5, 17-26
Alleluia

℟. **Alleluia.** Behold, the king will come, the Lord of
    earth:
and he will set us free. ℟. **Alleluia.**

Jesus demonstrates the power of God over evil—moral and physical.
The lame man, now able to carry the mat, begins to glorify God. The
healing comes after faith; the response is one of praise and thanks
to God.

℣. The Lord be with you. ℟. **And also with you.**
✠ A reading from the holy gospel according to Luke
℟. **Glory to you, Lord.**

One day Jesus was teaching, and the power of the Lord made him heal. Sitting close by were Pharisees and teachers of the law who had come from every village of Galilee and from Judea and Jerusalem. Some men came along carrying a paralytic on a mat. They were trying to bring him in and lay him before Jesus; but they found no way of getting him through because of the crowd, so they went up on the roof. There they let him down with his mat through the tiles into the middle of the crowd before Jesus. Seeing their faith, Jesus said, "My friend, your sins are forgiven you."

The scribes and the Pharisees began a discussion, saying: "Who is this man who utters blasphemies? Who can forgive sins but God alone?" Jesus, however, knew their reasoning and answered them by saying: "Why do you harbor these thoughts? Which is easier: to say, 'Your sins are forgiven you,' or to say, 'Get up and walk'? In any case, to make it clear to you that the Son of Man has authority on earth to forgive sins"—he then addressed the paralyzed man: "I say to you, get up! Take your mat with you, and return to your house."

At once the man stood erect before them. He picked up the mat he had been lying on and went home praising God. At this they were all seized with astonishment. Full of awe, they gave praise to God, saying, "We have seen incredible things today!"— This is the gospel of the Lord. ℞. **Praise to you, Lord Jesus Christ.**   ➔ No.15, p. 623

PRAYER OVER THE GIFTS

Father,
from all you give us
we present this bread and wine
As we serve you now,
accept our offering
and sustain us with your promise of eternal life.

Grant this through Christ our Lord.
℟. **Amen.**   ➜ No. 21, p. 626 (Pref. P 1)

COMMUNION ANT.   See Ps 106, 4-5; Is 38, 3
**Come to us, Lord, and bring us peace. We will rejoice
in your presence and serve you with all our heart.** ⍦

PRAYER AFTER COMMUNION
Father,
may our communion
teach us to love heaven.
May its promise and hope
guide our way on earth.
We ask this through Christ our Lord.
℟. **Amen.**   _____   ➜ No. 32, p. 650

TUESDAY OF THE SECOND WEEK OF ADVENT

God cares for his people. He looks after them as a just, merciful,
and loving God. As he formerly looked after the people of Israel by
day and night, he will send his Son into the world to begin a new age
to look after his people now, even a single one who may stray.

ENTRANCE ANT.   See Zec 14, 5. 7

**See, the Lord is coming and with him all his saints.
Then there will be endless day.**   ➜ No. 2, p. 614

OPENING PRAYER
Almighty God,
help us to look forward
to the glory of the birth of Christ our savior:
his coming is proclaimed joyfully
to the ends of the earth,
for he lives and reigns with you and the Holy Spirit,
one God, for ever and ever.
℟. **Amen.** ⍦

READING I   Is 40, 1-11

Isaiah's central message is an announcement of the imminence of
salvation for exiled Israel. The punishment proceeds from Yahweh just
as he is also the source of comfort. The prophet reveals God as a
Shepherd-King, attracting and ever caring for his people.

A reading from the book of the prophet Isaiah

Comfort, give comfort to my people,
　　says your God.
Speak tenderly to Jerusalem, and proclaim to her
　　that her service is at an end,
　　her guilt is expiated;
Indeed, she has received from the hand of the Lord
　　double for all her sins.
　　A voice cries out:
In the desert prepare the way of the Lord!
　　Make straight in the wasteland a highway for our
　　　God!
Every valley shall be filled in,
　　every mountain and hill shall be made low;
The rugged land shall be made a plain,
　　the rough country, a broad valley.
Then the glory of the Lord shall be revealed,
　　and all mankind shall see it together;
　　for the mouth of the Lord has spoken.
A voice says, "Cry out!"
　　I answer, "What shall I cry out?"
"All mankind is grass,
　　and all their glory like the flower of the field.
The grass withers, the flower wilts,
　　when the breath of the Lord blows upon it.
　　[So then, the people is the grass.]
Though the grass withers and the flower wilts,
　　the word of our God stands forever."
Go up onto a high mountain,
　　Zion, herald of glad tidings;
Cry out at the top of your voice,
　　Jerusalem, herald of good news!
Fear not to cry out
　　and say to the cities of Judah:
　　Here is your God!
Here comes with power
　　the Lord God,
　　who rules by his strong arm;

Here is his reward with him,
     his recompense before him.
Like a shepherd he feeds his flock;
     in his arms he gathers the lambs,
Carrying them in his bosom,
     and leading the ewes with care.
This is the Word of the Lord. ℞. **Thanks be to God.** ℣

Responsorial Psalm   Ps 96, 1-2. 3. 10. 11-12. 13

℞. (Is 40, 9-10) **The Lord our God comes in strength.**
Sing to the Lord a new song;
     sing to the Lord, all you lands.
Sing to the Lord; bless his name;
     announce his salvation, day after day. — ℞

Tell his glory among the nations;
     among all peoples, his wondrous deeds.
Say among the nations: The Lord is king;
     he governs the peoples with equity. — ℞

Let the heavens be glad and the earth rejoice;
     let the sea and what fills it resound;
     let the plains be joyful and all that is in them!
Then shall all the trees of the forest exult. — ℞

They shall exult before the Lord, for he comes;
     for he comes to rule the earth.
He shall rule the world with justice
     and the peoples with his constancy. — ℞ ℣

GOSPEL   Mt 18, 12-14

Alleluia

℞. **Alleluia.** The day of the Lord is near:
he comes to save us. ℞. **Alleluia.**

The love of God for the individual is clear. Christ is not teaching that
one person equals ninety-nine, but that even one stray or lost one
must be sought out. The shepherds of the Church are called to live
the same loving, relentless pursuit of the lowly and sinful. Coaxing,
forgiving, looking after the sheep, today's shepherd guides the sheep
back to the Father.

℣. The Lord be with you. ℞. **And also with you.**

✠ A reading from the holy gospel according to Matthew. ℟. **Glory to you. Lord.**

Jesus said to his disciples: "What is your thought on this: A man owns a hundred sheep and one of them wanders away; will he not leave the ninety-nine out on the hills and go in search of the stray? If he succeeds in finding it, believe me he is happier about this one than about the ninety-nine that did not wander away. Just so, it is no part of your heavenly Father's plan that a single one of these little ones shall ever come to grief."—This is the gospel of the Lord. ℟. **Praise to you, Lord Jesus Christ.**

➨ No. 15, p. 623

PRAYER OVER THE GIFTS

Lord,
we are nothing without you.
As you sustain us with your mercy,
receive our prayers and offerings.
We ask this through Christ our Lord.
℟. **Amen.**   ➨ No. 21, p. 626 (Pref. P 1)

COMMUNION ANT.   2 Tm 4, 8

The Lord is just; he will award the crown of justice to all who have longed for his coming. ▼

PRAYER AFTER COMMUNION

Father,
you give us food from heaven.
By our sharing in this mystery,
teach us to judge wisely the things of earth
and to love the things of heaven.
Grant this through Christ our Lord.
℟. **Amen.**   ➨ No. 32, p. 650

WEDNESDAY OF THE
SECOND WEEK OF ADVENT

The secret of man's turning to God is twofold: to see creation in all its splendor and realize that these things are but toys in the hands of God, their Maker; and to experience the weakness and dependence of man. These two realities will leave man no other choice than to throw himself at the mercy of God and his providence. Come, Lord Jesus!

ENTRANCE ANT. See Hb 2, 3; 1 Cor 4, 5

The Lord is coming and will not delay; he will bring every hidden thing to light and reveal himself to every nation. → No. 2, p. 614

OPENING PRAYER

All-powerful Father,
we await the healing power of Christ your Son.
Let us not be discouraged by our weaknesses
as we prepare for his coming.
Keep us steadfast in your love.
We ask this through our Lord Jesus Christ, your Son,
who lives and reigns with you and the Holy Spirit,
one God, for ever and ever. ℟. **Amen.** ❧

READING I Is 40, 25-31

Isaiah has pleaded with the people to live in a way of holiness rather than in a life of wickedness. He calls the people to live a life worthy of the covenant that God has established with his people. Isaiah frequently calls God by the name "Holy One."

A reading from the book of the prophet Isaiah

To whom can you liken me as an equal?
    says the Holy One.
Lift up your eyes on high
    and see who has created these things:
He leads out their army and numbers them,
    calling them all by name.
By his great might and the strength of his power
    not one of them is missing!
Why, O Jacob, do you say,
    and declare, O Israel,

"My way is hidden from the Lord,
and my right is disregarded by my God"?
Do you not know
or have you not heard?
The Lord is the eternal God,
creator of the ends of the earth.
He does not faint nor grow weary,
and his knowledge is beyond scrutiny.
He gives strength to the fainting;
for the weak he makes vigor abound.
Though young men faint and grow weary,
and youths stagger and fall,
They that hope in the Lord will renew their strength,
they will soar as with eagles' wings;
They will run and not grow weary,
walk and not grow faint.
This is the Word of the Lord ℟. **Thanks be to God.** ℣

Responsorial Psalm   Ps 103, 1-2. 3-4. 8. 10

℟. (1) **O bless the Lord, my soul.**

Bless the Lord, O my soul;
and all my being, bless his holy name.
Bless the Lord, O my soul,
and forget not all his benefits. — ℟

He pardons all your iniquities,
he heals all your ills.
He redeems your life from destruction,
he crowns you with kindness and compassion.—℟

Merciful and gracious is the Lord,
slow to anger and abounding in kindness.
Not according to our sins does he deal with us,
nor does he requite us according to our crimes.—℟ ℣

GOSPEL   Mt 11, 28-30

Alleluia

℟. **Alleluia.** The Lord is coming to save his people;
happy are those prepared to meet him. ℟. **Alleluia.**

Matthew's gospel is very sensitive to the poor of spirit. He has preserved this tender invitation of the Good Shepherd to the weary and burdened sheep. Jesus can identify with the lowly and the poor to whom he has come to bring the Good News of Salvation.

℣. The Lord be with you. ℟. **And also with you.**
✠ A reading from the holy gospel according to Matthew. ℟. **Glory to you, Lord.**

Jesus said: "Come to me, all you who are weary and find life burdensome, and I will refresh you. Take my yoke upon your shoulders and learn from me, for I am gentle and humble of heart. Your souls will find rest, for my yoke is easy and my burden light."
—This is the gospel of the Lord. ℟. **Praise to you, Lord Jesus Christ.**   → No. 15, p. 623

PRAYER OVER THE GIFTS

Lord,
may the gift we offer in faith and love
be a continual sacrifice in your honor
and truly become our eucharist and our salvation.
Grant this through Christ our Lord.
℟. **Amen.**   → No. 21, p. 626 (Pref. P 1)

COMMUNION ANT.   Is 40, 10; see 34, 5

The Lord our God comes in strength and will fill his servants with joy. ℣

PRAYER AFTER COMMUNION

God of mercy,
may this eucharist bring us your divine help,
free us from our sins,
and prepare us for the birthday of our Savior,
who is Lord for ever and ever.
℟. **Amen.**   → No. 32, p. 650

THURSDAY OF THE SECOND WEEK OF ADVENT

God can become close to his people. The covenant (promise) is an intimate relationship between creature and creator. We are blessed to hear the Good News and respond to Christ's word that the reign of God may take root in us.

ENTRANCE ANT.   See Ps 119, 151-152

Lord, you are near, and all your commandments are just; long have I known that you decreed them for ever.   ➤ No. 2, p. 614

OPENING PRAYER

Almighty Father,
give us the joy of your love
to prepare the way for Christ our Lord.
Help us to serve you and one another.
We ask this through our Lord Jesus Christ, your Son,
who lives and reigns with you and the Holy Spirit,
one God, for ever and ever. ℟. **Amen.** ✟

READING I   Is 41, 13-20

In the Exodus, God offered his love as a saving God and to let the Hebrews be his people. Isaiah stresses the complete transcendence of God when he says: "I, the Lord, will answer them," and "The Holy One of Israel has created it." The blessings of the Messianic Kingdom are physical and material.

A reading from the book of the prophet Isaiah

I am the Lord, your God,
    who grasp your right hand;
It is I who say to you, "Fear not,
    I will help you."
Fear not, O worm Jacob,
    O maggot Israel;
I will help you, says the Lord;
    your redeemer is the Holy One of Israel.
I will make of you a threshing sledge,
    sharp, new, and double-edged,
To thresh the mountains and crush them.
    to make the hills like chaff.
When you winnow them, the wind shall carry them
        off
    and the storm shall scatter them.

But you shall rejoice in the Lord,
  and glory in the Holy One of Israel.
The afflicted and the needy seek water in vain,
  their tongues are parched with thirst.
I, the Lord, will answer them;
  I, the God of Israel, will not forsake them.
I will open up rivers on the bare heights,
  and fountains in the broad valleys;
I will turn the desert into a marshland,
  and the dry ground into springs of water.
I will plant in the desert the cedar,
  acacia, myrtle, and olive;
I will set in the wasteland the cypress,
  together with the plane tree and the pine,
That all may see and know,
  observe and understand,
That the hand of the Lord has done this,
  the Holy One of Israel has created it.
This is the Word of the Lord. ℟. **Thanks be to God.** ℣

Responsorial Psalm   Ps 145, 1. 9. 10-11. 12-13

℟. (8) **The Lord is kind and merciful;
  slow to anger, and rich in compassion.**

I will extol you, O my God and King,
  and I will bless your name forever and ever.
The Lord is good to all
  and compassionate toward all his works. — ℟

Let all your works give you thanks, O Lord,
  and let your faithful ones bless you.
Let them discourse of the glory of your kingdom
  and speak of your might. — ℟

Let them make known to men your might
  and the glorious splendor of your kingdom.
Your kingdom is a kingdom of all ages,
  and your dominion endures through all genera-
    tions. — ℟ ℣

GOSPEL   Mt 11, 11-15

Alleluia (Is 45, 8)

℟. **Alleluia.** Let the clouds rain down the Just One, and the earth bring forth a Savior. ℟. **Alleluia.**

The role of John the Baptizer in the history of man's salvation is stressed: "History has not known a man born of woman [who was] greater." He stands ahead of the great prophets like Moses, Elijah, Isaiah, and Amos, and points to the beginning of a new age.

℣. The Lord be with you. ℟. **And also with you.**
✠ A reading from the holy gospel according to Matthew. ℟. **Glory to you, Lord.**

Jesus said to the crowds: "I solemnly assure you, history has not known a man born of woman greater than John the Baptizer. Yet the least born into the kingdom of God is greater than he. From John the Baptizer's time until now the kingdom of God has suffered violence, and the violent take it by force. All the prophets as well as the law spoke prophetically until John. If you are prepared to accept it, he is Elijah, the one who was certain to come. Heed carefully what you hear!"—This is the gospel of the Lord. ℟. **Praise to you, Lord Jesus Christ.**

➤ No. 15, p. 623

PRAYER OVER THE GIFTS

Father,
from all you give us
we present this bread and wine.
As we serve you now,
accept our offering
and sustain us with your promise of eternal life.
Grant this through Christ our Lord.
℟. **Amen.**   ➤ No. 21, p. 626 (Pref. P 1)

COMMUNION ANT.   Ti 2, 12-13
Let our lives be honest and holy in this present age, as we wait for the happiness to come when our great God reveals himself in glory. ℣

PRAYER AFTER COMMUNION

Father,
may our communion
teach us to love heaven.
May its promise and hope
guide our way on earth.
We ask this through Christ our Lord.

℟. **Amen.** _____ ➔ No. 32, p. 650

FRIDAY OF THE SECOND WEEK OF ADVENT

In applying the imagery of the Messianic Kingdom that Isaiah uses, a poor, sickly, or lonely person without a family could well be close to God and abundantly wealthy ·in a spiritual sense; and someone wealthy, in good health, and with a large family might be very far from the Kingdom of God. Jesus taught by example, and how much we can learn from him! "Learn from me," he says on one occasion, "for I am gentle and humble of heart" (Mt 11, 29).

ENTRANCE ANT.

The Lord is coming from heaven in splendor to visit his people, and bring them peace and eternal life.

➔ No. 2, p. 614

OPENING PRAYER

All-powerful God,
help us to look forward in hope
to the coming of our Savior.
May we live as he has taught,
ready to welcome him with burning love and faith.
We ask this through our Lord Jesus Christ, your Son,
who lives and reigns with you and the Holy Spirit,
one God, for ever and ever. ℟. **Amen.** ✣

READING I   Is 48, 17-19

Isaiah offers a majestic summary of God's Messianic promises. He, the Holy One, will be our teacher, and to him who will listen, prosperity and descendants will come.

A reading from the book of the prophet Isaiah

Thus says the Lord, your redeemer,
    the Holy One of Israel:

I, the Lord, your God,
   teach you what is for your good,
   and lead you on the way you should go.
If you would hearken to my commandments,
   your prosperity would be like a river,
   and your vindication like the waves of the sea;
Your descendants would be like the sand,
   and those born of your stock like its grains,
Their name never cut off
   or blotted out from my presence.
This is the Word of the Lord. ℟. **Thanks be to God.** ℣

Responsorial Psalm   Ps 1, 1-2. 3. 4. 6

℟. (Jn 8, 12) **Those who follow you, Lord, will have
      the light of life.**

Happy the man who follows not
   the counsel of the wicked
Nor walks in the way of sinners,
   nor sits in the company of the insolent,
But delights in the law of the Lord
   and meditates on his law day and night. — ℟

He is like a tree
   planted near running water,
That yields its fruit in due season,
   and whose leaves never fade.
   [Whatever he does, prospers.] — ℟

Not so the wicked, not so;
   they are like chaff which the wind drives away.
For the Lord watches over the way of the just,
   but the way of the wicked vanishes. — ℟ ℣

GOSPEL   Mt 11, 16-19

Alleluia

℟. **Alleluia.** The Lord will come; go out to meet him!
He is the prince of peace. ℟. **Alleluia.**

Jesus' message is not accepted by everyone (neither was the message of John the Baptizer). Whatever message would involve change within the people's own hearts and religious beliefs is rejected immediately; so they reject John for his austerity, and they reject Jesus because he is not austere enough.

℣. The Lord be with you. ℟. **And also with you.**

✠ A reading from the holy gospel according to Matthew. ℟. **Glory to you, Lord.**

Jesus said to the crowds: "What comparison can I use to describe this breed? They are like children squatting in the town squares, calling to their playmates:

'We piped you a tune but you did not dance!

We sang you a dirge but you did not wail!'

In other words, John appeared neither eating nor drinking, and people say, 'He is mad!' The Son of Man appeared eating and drinking, and they say, 'This one is a glutton and drunkard, a lover of tax collectors and those outside the law!' Yet time will prove where wisdom lies."—This is the gospel of the Lord. ℟. **Praise to you, Lord Jesus Christ.**

➤ No. 15, p. 623

PRAYER OVER THE GIFTS

Lord,

we are nothing without you.

As you sustain us with your mercy,

receive our prayers and offerings.

We ask this through Christ our Lord.

℟. **Amen.** ➤ No. 21, p. 626 (Pref. P 1)

COMMUNION ANT.   Phil 3, 20-21

We are waiting for our Savior, the Lord Jesus Christ; he will transfigure our lowly bodies into copies of his own glorious body. ↓

PRAYER AFTER COMMUNION

Father,

you give us food from heaven.

Teach us to live by your wisdom
and to love the things of heaven
by our sharing in this mystery.
Grant this through Christ our Lord.
℟. **Amen.**

➤ No. 32, p. 650

SATURDAY OF THE SECOND WEEK OF ADVENT

We do not know the time or the day of the Parousia. It was thought, according to Malachi, that the "great and terrible day" would be inaugurated by the return of Elijah. This anticipates the second coming of Christ and "as to the exact day or hour, no one knows it" (Mk 13, 32). Let us be ready no matter what the hour.

ENTRANCE ANT.   Ps 80, 4. 2.

Come, Lord, from your cherubim throne; let us see your face, and we shall be saved.   ➤ No. 2, p. 614

OPENING PRAYER

Lord,
let your glory dawn to take away our darkness.
May we be revealed as the children of light
at the coming of your Son,
who lives and reigns with you and the Holy Spirit,
one God, for ever and ever.
℟. **Amen.** ℣

READING I   Sir 48, 1-4. 9-11

Sirach recounts the heroes of the Jewish faith; he recalls the fiery prophet Elijah who was taken up to heaven in a chariot. It is this prophet that the Jews were expecting to come to usher in the Messianic age, the Day of Yahweh.

A reading from the book of Sirach

Like a fire there appeared the prophet Elijah
    whose words were as a flaming furnace.
Their staff of bread he shattered,
    in his zeal he reduced them to straits;
By God's word he shut up the heavens
    and three times brought down fire.

How awesome are you, Elijah!
  Whose glory is equal to yours?
You were taken aloft in a whirlwind,
  in a chariot with fiery horses.
You are destined, it is written, in time to come
  to put an end to wrath before the day of the Lord,
To turn back the hearts of fathers toward their sons,
  and to re-establish the tribes of Jacob.
Blessed is he who shall have seen you before he dies.
This is the Word of the Lord. ℟. **Thanks be to God.** ℣

Responsorial Psalm   Ps 80, 2-3. 15-16. 18-19

℟. (4) **Lord, make us turn to you,**
  let us see your face and we shall be saved.

O shepherd of Israel, hearken,
  from your throne upon the cherubim, shine forth.
Rouse your power,
  and come to save us. — ℟

Once again, O Lord of hosts,
  look down from heaven, and see;
Take care of this vine,
  and protect what your right hand has planted
    [the son of man whom you yourself made
        strong]. — ℟

May your help be with the man of your right hand,
  with the son of man whom you yourself made
      strong.
Then we will no more withdraw from you;
  give us new life, and we will call upon your
      name. — ℟ ℣

GOSPEL   Mt 17, 10-13
Alleluia (Lk 3, 4. 6)

℟. **Alleluia.** Prepare the way for the Lord, make
    straight his paths:
all mankind shall see the salvation of God. ℟. **Alle-**
    luia.

The disciples of Jesus were aware of the tradition about Elijah. Jesus also mentioned that the time of decision will consume him just as it did John the Baptizer. The roles of Messiah and Suffering Servant are brought together.

℣. The Lord be with you. ℟. **And also with you.**

✠ A reading from the holy gospel according to Matthew. ℟. **Glory to you, Lord.**

As they were coming down the mountainside, the disciples put this question to Jesus: "Why do the scribes claim that Elijah must come first?" In reply he said: "Elijah is indeed coming, and he will restore everything. I assure you, though, that Elijah has already come, but they did not recognize him and they did as they pleased with him. The Son of Man will suffer at their hands in the same way." The disciples then realized that he had been speaking to them about John the Baptizer.—This is the gospel of the Lord. ℟. **Praise to you, Lord Jesus Christ.**

➤ No. 15, p. 623

PRAYER OVER THE GIFTS
Lord,
may the gift we offer in faith and love
be a continual sacrifice in your honor
and truly become our eucharist and our salvation.
Grant this through Christ our Lord.
℟. **Amen.** ➤ No. 21, p. 626 (Pref. P 1)

COMMUNION ANT. Rv 22, 12

I am coming quickly, says the Lord, and will repay each man according to his deeds. ℣

PRAYER AFTER COMMUNION
God of mercy,
may this eucharist bring us your divine help,
free us from our sins,
and prepare us for the birthday of our Savior,
who is Lord for ever and ever.
℟. **Amen.** ➤ No. 32, p. 650

MONDAY OF THE THIRD WEEK OF ADVENT

For the Masses from December 17 to 24, see pp. 61-89.

All authority in heaven and on earth comes from God. He shares it with us since we are his children, made to his image and likeness. Everyone who exercises this authority, however, must be accountable to God.

ENTRANCE ANT.   See Jer 31, 10; Is 35, 4

Nations, hear the message of the Lord, and make it known to the ends of the earth: Our Savior is coming. Have no more fear.   ➔ No. 2, p. 614

OPENING PRAYER

Lord,
hear our voices raised in prayer.
Let the light of the coming of your Son
free us from the darkness of sin.
We ask this through our Lord Jesus Christ, your Son,
who lives and reigns with you and the Holy Spirit,
one God, for ever and ever. ℟. **Amen.** ↓

READING I   Nm 24, 2-7. 15-17

Balaam foretells what Israel shall do to Moab in the days to come. The stars of Jacob shall prevail and the tribes of Israel shall rise up. Balaam's oracle is wholly and emphatically a blessing on Israel.

A reading from the book of Numbers

When Balaam raised his eyes and saw Israel en-
camped, tribe by tribe, the spirit of God came upon
him, and he gave voice to his oracle:
The utterance of Balaam, son of Beor,
    the utterance of the man whose eye is true,
The utterance of one who hears what God says,
    and knows what the Most High knows,
Of one who sees what the Almighty sees,
    enraptured, and with eyes unveiled:
How goodly are your tents, O Jacob;
    your encampments, O Israel!
They are like gardens beside a stream,
    like the cedars planted by the Lord.

His wells shall yield free-flowing waters,
  he shall have the sea within reach;
His king shall rise higher,
  and his royalty shall be exalted.
Balaam again gave voice to his oracle:
The utterance of Balaam, son of Beor,
  the utterance of the man whose eye is true,
The utterance of one who hears what God says,
  and knows what the Most High knows,
Of one who sees what the Almighty sees,
  enraptured and with eyes unveiled.
I see him, though not now;
  I behold him, though not near:
A star shall advance from Jacob,
  and a staff shall rise from Israel.
This is the Word of the Lord. ℟.**Thanks be to God.** ℣

Responsorial Psalm   Ps 25, 4-5. 6-7. 8-9

℟. (4) **Teach me your ways, O Lord.**

Your ways, O Lord, make known to me;
  teach me your paths,
Guide me in your truth and teach me,
  for you are God my savior. — ℟

Remember that your compassion, O Lord,
  and your kindness are from of old.
In your kindness remember me,
  because of your goodness, O Lord. — ℟

Good and upright is the Lord;
  thus he shows sinners the way.
He guides the humble to justice,
  he teaches the humble his way. ℟ ℣

GOSPEL   Mt 21, 23-27
Alleluia (Ps 85, 8)
℟. **Alleluia.** Lord, let us see your kindness,
and grant us your salvation. ℟. **Alleluia.**

The answer of Jesus to the chief priests is a counterquestion about the commission of John the Baptizer. Jesus' refusal to answer the question about his own commission is a tacit rejection of the authority of questioners.

℣. The Lord be with you. ℟. **And also with you.**
✠ A reading from the holy gospel according to Matthew. ℟. **Glory to you, Lord.**

After Jesus had entered the temple precincts and while he was teaching, the chief priests and elders of the people came up to him and said: "On what authority are you doing these things? Who has given you this power?" Jesus answered: "I too will ask a question. If you answer it for me, then I will tell you on what authority I do the things I do. What was the origin of John's baptism? Was it divine or merely human?" They thought to themselves, "If we say 'divine,' he will ask us, 'Then why did you not put faith in it?'; while if we say, 'merely human,' we shall have reason to fear the people, who all regard John as a prophet." So their answer to Jesus was, "We do not know." He said in turn, "Then neither will I tell you on what authority I do the things I do."—This is the gospel of the Lord. ℟. **Praise to you, Lord Jesus Christ.**

➤ No. 15, p. 623

PRAYER OVER THE GIFTS
Father,
from all you give us
we present this bread and wine.
As we serve you now,
accept our offering
and sustain us with your promise of eternal life.
Grant this through Christ our Lord.
℟. **Amen.**   ➤ No. 21, p. 626 (Pref. P 1)

COMMUNION ANT.   See Ps 106, 4-5; Is 38, 3

Come to us, Lord, and bring us peace. We will rejoice in your presence and serve you with all our heart. ℣

PRAYER AFTER COMMUNION

Father,
may our communion

teach us to love heaven.
May its promise and hope
guide our way on earth.
We ask this through Christ our Lord.
℞. **Amen.**   ➔ No. 32, p. 650

TUESDAY OF THE THIRD WEEK OF ADVENT

For the Masses from December 17 to 24, see pp. 61-89.
"The Lord is good to all and compassionate toward all his works"
(Ps 145, 9). His ways differ from ours since we are more like the
proud Pharisees. Jesus helps us become aware of our frailty and weakness. We must have sorrow for our sins.

ENTRANCE ANT.   See Zec 14, 5. 7

See, the Lord is coming and with him all his saints.
Then there will be endless day.   ➔ No. 2, p. 614

OPENING PRAYER

Father of love,
you made a new creation
through Jesus Christ your Son.
May his coming free us from sin
and renew his life within us,
for he lives and reigns with you and the Holy Spirit,
one God, for ever and ever. ℞. **Amen.** ℣

READING I   Zep 3, 1-2. 9-13

The time-honored formula for true piety was to hear the Lord (Jer 7,
28) and to trust in him (Hos 6, 5). Jerusalem has done neither. Zephaniah pictures an ideal future age in which the Lord triumphs and salvation is for all. There shall be no lying or deceit. The virtuous, truthful,
sincere remnant shall know peace and prosperity.

A reading from the book of the prophet Zephaniah

Woe to the city, rebellious and polluted,
    to the tyrannical city!
She hears no voice,
    accepts no correction;
In the Lord she has not trusted,
    to her God she has not drawn near.

I will change and purify
   the lips of the peoples,
That they all may call upon the name of the Lord,
   to serve him with one accord;
From beyond the rivers of Ethiopia
   and as far as the recesses of the North,
   they shall bring me offerings.
   On that day
You need not be ashamed
   of all your deeds,
   your rebellious actions against me;
For then will I remove from your midst
   the proud braggarts,
And you shall no longer exalt yourself
   on my holy mountain.
But I will leave as a remnant in your midst
   a people humble and lowly,
Who shall take refuge in the name of the Lord:
   the remnant of Israel.
They shall do no wrong
   and speak no lies;
Nor shall there be found in their mouths
   a deceitful tongue;
They shall pasture and couch their flocks
   with none to disturb them.
This is the Word of the Lord. ℟. **Thanks be to God.** ℣

Responsorial Psalm   Ps 34, 2-3. 6-7. 17-18. 19. 23

℟. (7) **The Lord hears the cry of the poor.**

I will bless the Lord at all times;
   his praise shall be ever in my mouth.
Let my soul glory in the Lord;
   the lowly will hear me and be glad. — ℟

Look to him that you may be radiant with joy,
   and your faces may not blush with shame.
When the afflicted man called out, the Lord heard,
   and from all his distress he saved him. — ℟

The Lord confronts the evildoers,
  to destroy remembrance of them from the earth.
When the just cry out, the Lord hears them,
  and from all their distress he rescues them. — ℟
The Lord is close to the brokenhearted;
  and those who are crushed in spirit he saves.
The Lord redeems the lives of his servants;
  no one incurs guilt who takes refuge in him.—℟ ✠

GOSPEL   Mt 21, 28-32
Alleluia

℟. **Alleluia.** Come, O Lord, do not delay:
forgive the sins of your people. ℟. **Alleluia.**

In this parable, the contrast is clear between verbal rebellion and ultimate obedience as opposed to verbal obedience and failure to act.
The adversaries themselves are compelled to admit that action is the
test of obedience. The parable no doubt reflects the faith of the
Gentiles as contrasted with the unbelief of the Jews.

℣. The Lord be with you. ℟. **And also with you.**
✠ A reading from the holy gospel according to Matthew. ℟. **Glory to you, Lord.**
Jesus said to the chief priests and elders of the
people: "What do you think of this case? There was
a man who had two sons. He approached the elder
and said, 'Son, go out and work in the vineyard
today.' The son replied, 'I am on my way, sir'; but he
never went. Then the man came to his second son
and said the same thing. This son said in reply, 'No,
I will not'; but afterward he regretted it and went.
Which of the two did what the father wanted?" They
said, "The second." Jesus said to them, "Let me make
it clear that tax collectors and prostitutes are entering the kingdom of God before you. When John came
preaching a way of holiness, you put no faith in him;
but the tax collectors and the prostitutes did believe
in him. Yet even when you saw that, you did not
repent and believe in him."—This is the gospel of the
Lord. ℟. **Praise to you, Lord Jesus Christ.**
➙ No. 15, p. 623

PRAYER OVER THE GIFTS

Lord,
we are nothing without you.
As you sustain us with your mercy,
receive our prayers and offerings.
We ask this through Christ our Lord.
℞. **Amen.**　　　　　　　➔ No. 21, p. 626 (Pref. P 1)

COMMUNION ANT.　　　　　　　　2 Tm 4, 8

The Lord is just; he will award the crown of justice to all who have longed for his coming. ↓

PRAYER AFTER COMMUNION

Father,
you give us food from heaven.
By our sharing in this mystery
teach us to judge wisely the things of earth
and to love the things of heaven.
We ask this through Christ our Lord.
℞. **Amen.**
　　　　　　　　　　　　　　　➔ No. 32, p. 650

WEDNESDAY OF THE THIRD WEEK OF ADVENT

For the Masses from December 17 to 24, see pp. 61-89.
In all our trials and temptations, divine Providence mercifully guides us and protects us. God endeavors to lead us and keep us to himself. As John sought to know the true identity of Christ through his own words, let us seek through the Gospels and Holy Scripture to find the words of our Savior as they expressly apply to us.

ENTRANCE ANT.　　　　　See Hb 2, 3; 1 Cor 4, 5

The Lord is coming and will not delay; he will bring every hidden thing to light and reveal himself to every nation.　　　　　　　➔ No. 2, p. 614

OPENING PRAYER

Father,
may the coming celebration of the birth of your Son
bring us your saving help
and prepare us for eternal life.

Grant this through our Lord Jesus Christ, your Son,
who lives and reigns with you and the Holy Spirit,
one God, for ever and ever. ℞. **Amen.** ℣

READING I   Is 45, 6-8. 18. 21-25

The year 587 marked an appalling catastrophe for Israel. Jerusalem
and the temple were destroyed by the Babylonians. Yet Israel, in spite
of its poor, desperate situation, did endure—a testimony to divine
mercy and the indestructibility of the divine plan. Isaiah preaches the
inevitable, glorious triumphs of Yahweh and the resurrection of Israel.

A reading from the book of the prophet Isaiah

I am the Lord, there is no other;
    I form the light, and create the darkness,
I make well-being and create woe;
    I, the Lord, do all these things.
Let justice descend, O heavens, like dew from above,
    like gentle rain let the skies drop it down.
Let the earth open and salvation bud forth;
    let justice also spring up!
    I, the Lord, have created this.
        For thus says the Lord,
The creator of the heavens,
    who is God,
The designer and maker of the earth
    who established it,
Not creating it to be a waste,
    but designing it to be lived in:
I am the Lord, and there is no other.
Who announced this from the beginning
    and foretold it from of old?
Was it not I, the Lord,
    besides whom there is no other God?
    There is no just and saving God but me.
Turn to me and be safe,
    all you ends of the earth,
    for I am God; there is no other!
By myself I swear,
    uttering my just decree
    and my unalterable word:

To me every knee shall bend;
  by me every tongue shall swear,
Saying, "Only in the Lord
  are just deeds and power.
Before him in shame shall come
  all who vent their anger against him.
In the Lord shall be the vindication and the glory
  of all the descendants of Israel."
This is the Word of the Lord. ℟. **Thanks be to God.** ℣

Responsorial Psalm   Ps 85, 9-10. 11-12. 13-14

℟. (Is 45, 8) **Let the clouds rain down the Just One,
  and the earth bring forth a savior.**

I will hear what God proclaims;
  the Lord—for he proclaims peace to his people.
Near indeed is his salvation to those who fear him,
  glory dwelling in our land. — ℟

Kindness and truth shall meet;
  justice and peace shall kiss.
Truth shall spring out of the earth,
  and justice shall look down from heaven. — ℟.

The Lord himself will give his benefits;
  our land shall yield its increase.
Justice shall walk before him,
  and salvation, along the way of his steps. — ℟ ℣

GOSPEL   Lk 7, 18-23

Alleluia (Is 40, 9. 10).

℟. **Alleluia.** Raise your voice and tell the Good News:
the Lord our God comes in strength. ℟. **Alleluia.**

John is told that Jesus is the great Prophet. The two disciples sent by
John to Jesus may represent the two witnesses prescribed by the law
for the establishment of the truth. That the poor have the Gospel
preached to them is the clearest sign that our Lord is the Messiah.

℣. The Lord be with you. ℟. **And also with you.**
✠ A reading from the holy gospel according to Luke
℟. **Glory to you, Lord.**

Summoning two of his disciples, John sent them to ask the Lord, "Are you 'He who is to come' or are we to expect someone else?" When the men came to him they said, "John the Baptizer sends us to you with this question: 'Are you "He who is to come" or do we look for someone else?'" (At that time he was curing many of their diseases, afflictions, and evil spirits; he also restored sight to many who were blind.) Jesus gave this response: "Go and report to John what you have seen and heard. The blind recover their sight, cripples walk, lepers are cured, the deaf hear, dead men are raised to life, and the poor have the good news preached to them. Blest is that man who finds no stumbling-block in me."— This is the gospel of the Lord. ℟. **Praise to you, Lord Jesus Christ.**   ➤ No. 15, p. 623

PRAYER OVER THE GIFTS

Lord,
may the gifts we offer in faith and love
be a continual sacrifice in your honor
and truly become our eucharist and our salvation.
Grant this through Christ our Lord.
℟. **Amen.**   ➤ No. 21, p. 626 (Pref. P 1)

COMMUNION ANT.   Is 40, 10; see 34, 5

The Lord our God comes in strength and will fill his servants with joy. ℣

PRAYER AFTER COMMUNION

God of mercy,
may this eucharist bring us your divine help,
free us from our sins,
and prepare us for the birthday of our Savior,
who is Lord for ever and ever.
℟. **Amen.**   ➤ No. 32, p. 650

THURSDAY OF THE THIRD WEEK OF ADVENT

For the Masses from December 17 to 24, see pp. 61-89.

In either the old law or the new law, who can doubt the love that God deserves from us? The answer is, only those who do not know him— only those who are either ignorant or forgetful of his divine perfection. Our Master frequently reminds us of the precept of charity and of our obligation to know God so that we will be led to love and serve him.

ENTRANCE ANT.   See Ps 119, 151-152

Lord, you are near, and all your commandments are just; long have I known that you decreed them for ever.   ➔ No. 2, p. 614

OPENING PRAYER

Lord,
our sins bring us unhappiness.
Hear our prayer for courage and strength.
May the coming of your Son
bring us the joy of salvation.
We ask this through our Lord Jesus Christ, your Son,
who lives and reigns with you and the Holy Spirit,
one God, for ever and ever. ℟. **Amen.** ↓

READING I   Is 54, 1-10

Isaiah places Israel's tragedy in proper perspective as he exhausts the resources of his language to emphasize the permanence of the new dispensation. The new covenant relationship will be unbreakable. The steadfast love is the inner bond of the covenant of peace which is also the everlasting covenant not to be removed.

A reading from the book of the prophet Isaiah

Raise a glad cry, you barren one who did not bear,
    break forth in jubilant song, you who were not in
    labor,
For more numerous are the children of the deserted
    wife
    than the children of her who has a husband, says
    the Lord.

Enlarge the space for your tent,
  spread out your tent cloths unsparingly;
  lengthen your ropes and make firm your stakes.
For you shall spread abroad to the right and to the
    left;
  your descendants shall dispossess the nations
  and shall people the desolate cities.
Fear not, you shall not be put to shame;
  you need not blush, for you shall not be disgraced.
The shame of your youth you shall forget,
  the reproach of your widowhood no longer remember.
For he who has become your husband is your Maker;
  his name is the Lord of hosts;
Your redeemer is the Holy One of Israel,
  called God of all the earth.
The Lord calls you back,
  like a wife forsaken and grieved in spirit,
A wife married in youth and then cast off,
  says your God.
For a brief moment I abandoned you,
  but with great tenderness I will take you back.
In an outburst of wrath, for a moment
  I hid my face from you;
But with enduring love I take pity on you,
  says the Lord, your Redeemer.
This is for me like the days of Noah,
  when I swore that the waters of Noah
  should never again deluge the earth;
So I have sworn not to be angry with you,
  or to rebuke you.
Though the mountains leave their place
  and the hills be shaken,
My love shall never leave you
  nor my covenant of peace be shaken,
  says the Lord, who has mercy on you.
This is the Word of the Lord. ℟. **Thanks be to God.** ∨

Responsorial Psalm   Ps 30, 2. 4. 5-6. 11-12. 13

℟. (2) **I will praise you, Lord,**
for you have rescued me.

I will extol you, O Lord, for you drew me clear
and did not let my enemies rejoice over me.

O Lord, you brought me up from the nether world;
you preserved me from among those going down
into the pit. — ℟

Sing praise to the Lord, you his faithful ones,
and give thanks to his holy name.

For his anger lasts but a moment;
a lifetime, his good will.

At nightfall, weeping enters in,
but with the dawn, rejoicing. — ℟

Hear, O Lord, and have pity on me;
O Lord, be my helper.

You changed my mourning into dancing;
O Lord, my God, forever will I give you
thanks. — ℟ ℣

GOSPEL   Lk 7, 24-30

Alleluia (Lk 3, 4. 6)

℟. **Alleluia.** Prepare the way for the Lord, make
straight his paths:

all mankind shall see the salvation of God. ℟. **Alle-**
luia.

John was a great prophet—and more than a prophet. But a new and
final epoch began with Jesus. Jesus proved he was the Messiah by his
miracles. In their baptism, sinners expressed their faith that God
would redeem them and, through the Messiah, reunite them to himself.

℣. The Lord be with you. ℟. **And also with you.**
✠ A reading from the holy gospel according to Luke
℟. **Glory to you, Lord.**

When the messengers of John had set off, Jesus
began to speak about him to the crowds. "What did
you go out to see in the desert—a reed swayed by
the wind? What, really, did you go out to see—someone dressed luxuriously? Remember, those who dress
in luxury and eat in splendor are to be found in royal

palaces. Then what did you go out to see—a prophet?
He is that, I assure you, and something more. This
is the man of whom Scripture says,

'I send my messenger ahead of you
to prepare your way before you.'

I assure you, there is no man born of woman greater
than John. Yet the least born into the kingdom of
God is greater than he."

The entire populace that had heard Jesus, even
the tax collectors, gave praise to God, for they had
received from John the baptismal bath he administered. The Pharisees and the lawyers, on the other
hand, by failing to receive his baptism defeated God's
plan in their regard.—This is the gospel of the Lord.
℟. **Praise to you, Lord Jesus Christ.**

➤ No. 15, p. 623

PRAYER OVER THE GIFTS

Father,
from all you give us
we present this bread and wine.
As we serve you now,
accept our offering
and sustain us with your promise of eternal life.
Grant this through Christ our Lord.
℟. **Amen.**   ➤No. 21, p. 626 (Pref. P 1)

COMMUNION ANT   Ti 2, 12-13
**Let our lives be honest and holy in this present age,
as we wait for the happiness to come when our great
God reveals himself in glory.** ↓

PRAYER AFTER COMMUNION

Father,
may our communion
teach us to love heaven.
May its promise and hope
guide our way on earth.
We ask this through Christ our Lord.
℟. **Amen.** _____ ➤ No. 32, p. 650

FRIDAY OF THE THIRD WEEK OF ADVENT

For the Masses from December 17 to 24, see pp. 61-89.

John the Baptizer was to prepare the way for Jesus. It is the work of every man to serve God. The Christ-bearer of today must be the lamp on the mountainside—directing, guiding, and leading to Jesus.

ENTRANCE ANT.

The Lord is coming from heaven in splendor to visit his people, and bring them peace and eternal life.

➔ No. 2, p. 614

OPENING PRAYER

All-powerful Father,
guide us with your love
as we await the coming of your Son.
Keep us faithful
that we may be helped through life
and brought to salvation.
We ask this through our Lord Jesus Christ, your Son,
who lives and reigns with you and the Holy Spirit,
one God, for ever and ever. ℞. **Amen.** ✟

READING I   Is 56, 1-3. 6-8

Isaiah proclaims that a man who does what is just will be happy. He is to love the Lord and the Lord will bring him into his house of prayer—a house for all people.

A reading from the book of the prophet Isaiah

Thus says the Lord:
Observe what is right, do what is just;
    for my salvation is about to come,
    my justice, about to be revealed.
Happy is the man who does this,
    the son of man who holds to it;
Who keeps the sabbath free from profanation,
    and his hand from any evildoing.
Let not the foreigner say,
    when he would join himself to the Lord,
    "The Lord will surely exclude me from his people."

The foreigners who join themselves to the Lord,
  ministering to him,
Loving the name of the Lord,
  and becoming his servants—
All who keep the sabbath free from profanation
  and hold to my covenant,
Them I will bring to my holy mountain
  and make joyful in my house of prayer;
Their holocausts and sacrifices
  will be acceptable on my altar,
For my house shall be called
  a house of prayer for all peoples.
Thus says the Lord God,
  who gathers the dispersed of Israel:
Others will I gather to him
  besides those already gathered.
This is the Word of the Lord. ℟. **Thanks be to God.** ✝

Responsorial Psalm   Ps 67, 2-3. 5. 7-8
℟. (4) **O God, let all the nations praise you!**

May God have pity on us and bless us;
  may he let his face shine upon us.
So may your way be known upon earth;
  among all nations, your salvation. — ℟

May the nations be glad and exult
  because you rule the peoples in equity;
  the nations on the earth you guide. — ℟

The earth has yielded its fruits;
  God, our God, has blessed us.
May God bless us,
  and may all the ends of the earth fear him! — ℟ ✝

GOSPEL   Jn 5, 33-36
Alleluia

℟. **Alleluia.** Come, Lord, bring to us your peace;
let us rejoice before you with a perfect heart. ℟.
    Alleluia.

Although John the Baptizer pointed out the way to Jesus by his prayer, fasting, and preaching, still the testimony of Jesus is far greater. The very works that Jesus performs speak for themselves. Only God can perform a miracle.

℣. The Lord be with you. ℞. **And also with you.**

✠ A reading from the holy gospel according to John

℞. **Glory to you, Lord.**

Jesus said to the Jews:

"You have sent to John,
who has testified to the truth.
(Not that I myself accept such human testimony—
I refer to these things only for your salvation.)
He was the lamp, set aflame and burning bright,
and for a while you exulted willingly in his light.
Yet I have testimony greater than John's
namely, the works the Father has given me to accomplish.
These very works which I perform
testify on my behalf
that the Father has sent me."

This is the gospel of the Lord. ℞. **Praise to you, Lord Jesus Christ.**   ➔ No. 15, p. 623

PRAYER OVER THE GIFTS
Lord,
we are nothing without you.
As you sustain us with your mercy,
receive our prayers and offerings.
We ask this through Christ our Lord.
℞. **Amen.**   ➔ No. 21, p. 626 (Pref. P 1)

COMMUNION ANT.   Phil 3, 20-21

We are waiting for our Savior, the Lord Jesus Christ; he will transfigure our lowly bodies into copies of his own glorious body. ↓

PRAYER AFTER COMMUNION

Father,
you give us food from heaven.
Teach us to live by your wisdom
and to love the things of heaven
by our sharing in this mystery.
Grant this through Christ our Lord.
℞. **Amen.**   ➤ No. 32, p. 650

WEEKDAYS OF ADVENT

from December 17 to December 24

The following Masses are used on the days assigned, with the exception of Sunday.

DECEMBER 17

Everyone is proud of his ancestry. God promised to send a Redeemer into the world. Today we profess our belief in Jesus that he is the Anointed One, the Son of God born of Mary, the Savior of the World.

ENTRANCE ANT.   See Is 49, 13

You heavens, sing for joy, and earth exult! Our Lord is coming; he will take pity on those in distress.

➤ No 2, p. 614

OPENING PRAYER

Father,
creator and redeemer of mankind,
you decreed, and your Word became man,
born of the Virgin Mary.
May we come to share the divinity of Christ,
who humbled himself to share our human nature,
for he lives and reigns with you and the Holy Spirit,
one God, for ever and ever. ℞. **Amen.** ☦

READING I   Gn 49, 2. 8-10

The sons of Jacob are assured that the strength and the scepter will not pass from Judah. They are to be the holders of authority and preserve the teaching until it can be presented to the one deserving of obedience.

A reading from the book of Genesis

Jacob called his sons and said to them:
"Assemble and listen, sons of Jacob,
   listen to Israel, your father.

"You, Judah, shall your brothers praise
   —your hand on the neck of your enemies;
   the sons of your father shall bow down to you.
Judah, like a lion's whelp,
   you have grown up on prey, my son.
He crouches like a lion recumbent,
   the king of beasts—who would dare rouse him?
The scepter shall never depart from Judah,
   or the mace from between his legs,
While tribute is brought to him,
   and he receives the people's homage."
This is the Word of the Lord. ℟. **Thanks to be God.** ⍯

Responsorial Psalm   Ps 72, 3-4. 7-8. 17

℟. (7) **Justice shall flourish in his time,
   and fullness of peace for ever.**

O God, with your judgment endow the king,
   and with your justice, the king's son;
He shall govern your people with justice
   and your afflicted ones with judgment. — ℟

The mountains shall yield peace for the people,
   and the hills justice.
He shall defend the afflicted among the people,
   save the children of the poor. — ℟

Justice shall flower in his days,
   and profound peace, till the moon be no more.
May he rule from sea to sea,
   and from the River to the ends of the earth. — ℟

May his name be blessed forever;
   as long as the sun his name shall remain.
In him shall all the tribes of the earth be blessed;
   all the nations shall proclaim his happiness. — ℟ ⍯

GOSPEL   Mt 1, 1-17
Alleluia

℟. **Alleluia.** Come
Wisdom of our God Most High,
guiding creation with power and love:
teach us to walk in the paths of knowledge. ℟. **Alleluia.**

The purpose of the genealogy is to show that Jesus is the Messiah,
the end of the history of salvation that was begun with the promise to
Abraham. The genealogy of Jesus is of particular significance in support of his claim to be the Messiah, the Son of David. The Savior's
Davidic descent was part of the primitive kerygma.

℣. The Lord be with you. ℟. **And also with you.**
✠ A reading from the holy gospel according to Matthew. ℟. **Glory to you, Lord.**
A family record of Jesus Christ, son of David, son of
Abraham. Abraham was the father of Isaac, Isaac
the father of Jacob, Jacob the father of Judah and his
brothers.

    Judah was the father of Perez and Zerah, whose
        mother was Tamar.
    Perez was the father of Hezron,
    Hezron the father of Ram.
    Ram was the father of Amminadab,
    Amminadab the father of Nahshon,
    Nahshon the father of Salmon.
    Salmon was the father of Boaz, whose mother
        was Rahab,
    Boaz was the father of Obed, whose mother was
        Ruth.
    Obed was the father of Jesse,
    Jesse the father of King David.
    David was the father of Solomon, whose mother
        had been the wife of Uriah.
    Solomon was the father of Rehoboam,
    Rehoboam the father of Abijah,
    Abijah the father of Asa.
    Asa was the father of Jehoshaphat,
    Jehoshaphat the father of Joram,

Joram the father of Uzziah.
Uzziah was the father of Jotham,
Jotham the father of Ahaz,
Ahaz the father of Hezekiah.
Hezekiah was the father of Manasseh,
Manasseh the father of Amos,
Amos the father of Josiah.
Josiah became the father of Jechoniah and his
     brothers at the time of the Babylonian
     exile.
After the Baylonian exile
Jechoniah was the father of Shealtiel,
Shealtiel the father of Zerubbabel.
Zerubbabel was the father of Abiud,
Abuid the father of Eliakim,
Eliakim the father of Azor.
Azor was the father of Zadok,
Zadok the father of Achim,
Achim the father of Eliud.
Eliud was the father of Eleazar,
Eleazar the father of Matthan,
Matthan the father of Jacob.
Jacob was the father of Joseph the husband of
     Mary.
It was of her that Jesus who is called the Mes-
     siah was born.
Thus the total number of generations is:
    from Abraham to David, fourteen genera-
      tions:
    from David to the Babylonian captivity, four-
      teen generations;
    from the Babylonian captivity to the Messiah,
      fourteen generations.
This is the gospel of the Lord. ℟. **Praise to you, Lord
Jesus Christ.**   ➤ No. 15, p. 623

PRAYER OVER THE GIFTS
Lord,
bless these gifts of your Church

and by this eucharist
renew us with the bread from heaven.
We ask this in the name of Jesus the Lord.
R̊. **Amen.** ➔ No. 21, p. 626 (Pref. P 2)

COMMUNION ANT. See Hg 2, 8

**The Desired of all nations is coming, and the house
of the Lord will be filled with his glory.** ⅴ

PRAYER AFTER COMMUNION
God our Father,
as you nourish us with the food of life,
give us also your Spirit,
so that we may be radiant with his light
at the coming of Christ your Son,
who is Lord for ever and ever.
R̊. **Amen.** ➔ No. 32, p. 650

DECEMBER 18

Isaiah gave a name to the future king—Immanuel, "God is with us."
Knowing the full course of revelation and history, we know that Jesus
alone has fulfilled the words and the hopes of the prophets. God has
come to live among his people.

ENTRANCE ANT.

**Christ our King is coming, the Lamb whom John pro-
claimed.** ➔ No. 2, p. 614

OPENING PRAYER
All-powerful God,
renew us by the coming feast of your Son
and free us from our slavery to sin.
Grant this through our Lord Jesus Christ, your Son,
who lives and reigns with you and the Holy Spirit,
one God, for ever and ever.
R̊. **Amen.** ⅴ

READING I Jer 23, 5-8

The Messianism here proposed is the fulfillment of sacred kingship as
the means chosen by God to realize the blessings of his covenant—
the peace and justice of his people in the promised land. Jeremiah
predicts the restoration of David's dynasty.

A reading from the book of the prophet Jeremiah
Behold, the days are coming, says the Lord,
    when I will raise up a righteous shoot to David;
As king he shall reign and govern wisely,
    he shall do what is just and right in the land.
In his days Judah shall be saved,
    Israel shall dwell in security,
This is the name they give him:
    "The Lord our justice."

Therefore, the days will come, says the Lord, when they shall no longer say, "As the Lord lives who brought the Israelites out of the land of Egypt"; but rather, "As the Lord lives, who brought the descendants of the house of Israel up from the land of the north"—and from all the lands to which I banished them; they shall again live on their own land.—This is the Word of the Lord. ℞. **Thanks be to God.** ⍄

Responsorial Psalm   Ps 72, 1-2. 12-13. 18-19

℞. **Justice shall flourish in his time,**
    and fullness of peace for ever.

O God, with your judgment endow the king,
    and with your justice, the king's son;
He shall govern your people with justice
    and your afflicted ones with judgment. — ℞

For he shall rescue the poor man when he cries out,
    and the afflicted when he has no one to help him.
He shall have pity for the lowly and the poor;
    the lives of the poor he shall save. — ℞

Blessed be the Lord, the God of Israel,
    who alone does wondrous deeds.
And blessed forever be his glorious name;
    may the whole earth be filled with his glory.
      Amen. Amen. — ℞ ⍄

GOSPEL   Mt 1, 18-24
Alleluia
℞. **Alleluia.** Come,

Leader of ancient Israel,
giver of the Law of Moses on Sinai:
rescue us with your mighty power. ℟. **Alleluia.**

Matthew's account of the birth of Christ makes Joseph the central
figure. He received the divine revelation through an angel in his
dream. Jesus' birth initiated the Messianic age of salvation which the
Old Testament anticipated, and Jesus realized the presence of God
among his people in an entirely new way.

℣. The Lord be with you. ℟. **And also with you.**
✠ A reading from the holy gospel according to Matthew. ℟. **Glory to you, Lord.**

Now this is how the birth of Jesus Christ came about.
When his mother Mary was engaged to Joseph, but
before they lived together, she was found with child
through the power of the Holy Spirit. Joseph her
husband, an upright man unwilling to expose her to
the law, decided to divorce her quietly. Such was his
intention when suddenly the angel of the Lord appeared in a dream and said to him: "Joseph, son of
David, have no fear about taking Mary as your wife.
It is by the Holy Spirit that she has conceived this
child. She is to have a son and you are to name him
Jesus because he will save his people from their
sins." All this happened to fulfill what the Lord had
said through the prophet:

"The virgin shall be with child
and give birth to a son,
and they shall call him Emmanuel,"

a name which means "God is with us." When Joseph
awoke he did as the angel of the Lord had directed
him and received her into his home as his wife. He
had no relations with her at any time before she
bore a son, whom he named Jesus.—This is the gospel of the Lord. ℟. **Praise to you, Lord Jesus Christ.**

➤ No. 15, p. 623

PRAYER OVER THE GIFTS
Lord,
may this sacrifice

bring us into the eternal life of your Son,
who died to save us from death,
for he is Lord for ever and ever.
℟. **Amen.**   ➤ No. 21, p. 626 (Pref. P 2)

COMMUNION ANT.   Mt 1, 23

**His name will be called Emmanuel, which means God
is with us.** ↓

PRAYER AFTER COMMUNION

Lord,
we receive mercy in your Church.
Prepare us to celebrate with fitting honor
the coming feast of our redemption.
We ask this in the name of Jesus the Lord.
℟. **Amen.**   ➤ No. 32, p. 650

_____

DECEMBER 19

John the Baptizer's mission was to prepare a people worthy to receive
the Lord. He went forth into the desert preaching repentance for sin
and a conversion of heart To concentrate only on the joy and celebration of the coming feast, and to ignore the spiritual preparation, is to
miss half of the message which the Church is setting before us
through the mouth of John during these weeks.

ENTRANCE ANT.   See Heb 10, 37

**He who is to come will not delay; and then there will
be no fear in our lands, because he is our Savior.**
                    ➤ No. 2, p. 614

OPENING PRAYER

Father,
you show the world the splendor of your glory
in the coming of Christ, born of the Virgin.
Give to us true faith and love
to celebrate the mystery of God made man.
We ask this through our Lord Jesus Christ, your Son,
who lives and reigns with you and the Holy Spirit,
one God, for ever and ever.
℟. **Amen.** ↓

READING I   Jgs 13, 2-7. 24-25

A nazirite was a person who was consecrated to God, at least for a specific time, in a very special way. The uncut hair, as the story of Samson later reveals, was a sign of strength resulting from this special consecration. The consecration with Samson, however, as with Samuel, was to be a perpetual consecration in order to accomplish a special service for God.

A reading from the book of Judges

There was a certain man from Zorah, of the clan of the Danites, whose name was Manoah. His wife was barren and had borne no children. An angel of the Lord appeared to the woman and said to her, "Though you are barren and have had no children, yet you will conceive and bear a son. Now, then, be careful to take no wine or strong drink and to eat nothing unclean. As for the son you will conceive and bear, no razor shall touch his head, for this boy is to be consecrated to God from the womb. It is he who will begin the deliverance of Israel from the power of the Philistines."

The woman went and told her husband, "A man of God came to me; he had the appearance of an angel of God, terrible indeed. I did not ask him where he came from, nor did he tell me his name. But he said to me, 'You will be with child and will bear a son. So take neither wine nor strong drink, and eat nothing unclean. For the boy shall be consecrated to God from the womb, until the day of his death.' "

The woman bore a son and named him Samson. The boy grew up and the Lord blessed him. The spirit of the Lord began to be with him.—This is the Word of the Lord. ℟. **Thanks be to God.** ℣

Responsorial Psalm   Ps 71, 3-4. 5-6. 16-17

℟. (8) **Fill me with your praise
and I will sing your glory!**

Be my rock of refuge,
    a stronghold to give me safety,
    for you are my rock and fortress.

O my God, rescue me from the hand of the wicked.
℞. **Fill me with your praise**
and I will sing your glory.
For you are my hope, O Lord;
   my trust, O God, from my youth.
On you I depend from birth;
   from my mother's womb you are my strength.—℞
I will treat of the mighty works of the Lord;
   O God, I will tell of your singular justice.
O God, you have taught me from my youth,
   and till the present I proclaim your wondrous
     deeds. — ℞ ↓

GOSPEL   Lk 1, 5-25
Alleluia
℞. **Alleluia.** Come,
Flower of Jesse's stem,
sign of God's love for all his people:
save us without delay! ℞. **Alleluia.**

The story of the conception of John the Baptizer is inseparably linked
with the narratives from the Old Testament, in particular the births of
Samuel and Samson. "He will be filled with the Holy Spirit from his
mother's womb."

℣. The Lord be with you. ℞. **And also with you.**
✠ A reading from the holy gospel according to Luke
℞. **Glory to you. Lord**.

In the days of Herod, king of Judea, there was a
priest named Zechariah of the priestly class of
Abijah; his wife was a descendant of Aaron named
Elizabeth. Both were just in the eyes of God, blamelessly following all the commandments and ordinances of the Lord. They were childless, for Elizabeth was sterile; moreover, both were advanced in
years.
    Once, when it was the turn of Zechariah's class
and he was fulfilling his functions as a priest before
God, it fell to him by lot according to priestly usage

to enter the sanctuary of the Lord and offer incense. While the full assembly of people was praying outside at the incense hour, an angel of the Lord appeared to him, standing at the right of the altar of incense. Zechariah was deeply disturbed upon seeing him, and overcome by fear.

The angel said to him: "Do not be frightened, Zechariah; your prayer has been heard. Your wife Elizabeth shall bear a son whom you shall name John. Joy and gladness will be yours, and many will rejoice at his birth; for he will be great in the eyes of the Lord. He will never drink wine or strong drink, and he will be filled with the Holy Spirit from his mother's womb. Many of the sons of Israel will he bring back to the Lord their God. God himself will go before him, in the spirit and power of Elijah, to turn the hearts of fathers to their children and the rebellious to the wisdom of the just, and to prepare for the Lord a people well-disposed."

Zechariah said to the angel: "How am I to know this? I am an old man; my wife too is advanced in age."

The angel replied: "I am Gabriel, who stand in attendance before God. I was sent to speak to you and bring you this good news. But now you will be mute—unable to speak—until the day when these things take place, because you have not trusted my words. They will all come true in due season." Meanwhile, the people were waiting for Zechariah, wondering at his delay in the temple. When he finally came out he was unable to speak to them, and they realized that he had seen a vision inside. He kept making signs to them, for he remained speechless.

Then, when his period of priestly service was over, he went home.

Afterward his wife Elizabeth conceived. She went into seclusion for five months, saying, "In these days the Lord is acting on my behalf; he has seen

fit to remove my reproach among men."—This is the
gospel of the Lord. ℟. **Praise to you, Lord Jesus
Christ.**   ➜ No. 15, p. 623

PRAYER OVER THE GIFTS

Lord of mercy,
receive the gifts we bring to your altar.
Let your power take away our weakness
and make our offerings holy.
We ask this in the name of Jesus the Lord.
℟. **Amen.**   ➜ No. 21, p. 626 (Pref. P 2)

COMMUNION ANT.   Lk 1, 78-79

**The dawn from on high shall break upon us, to guide
our feet on the road to peace.** ∀

PRAYER AFTER COMMUNION

Father,
we give you thanks for the bread of life.
Open our hearts in welcome
to prepare for the coming of our Savior,
who is Lord for ever and ever.
℟. **Amen.**   ➜ No. 32, p. 650

DECEMBER 20

Mary was the object of God's grace and favor. The words of Luke support
perfectly the doctrine of the Immaculate Conception—that from the first
moment of her existence, she was preserved free from all sin and filled
with grace, not because of any merit of her own, but to fit her for her role
to be the mother of the Incarnate Word.

ENTRANCE ANT.   See Is 11, 1; 40, 5; Lk 3, 6

**A shoot will spring from Jesse' stock, and all man-
kind will see the saving power of God.**
                                             ➜ No. 2, p. 614

OPENING PRAYER

God of love and mercy,
help us to follow the example of Mary,

always ready to do your will.
At the message of an angel
she welcomed your eternal Son
and, filled with the light of your Spirit,
she became the temple of your Word,
who lives and reigns with you and the Holy Spirit,
one God, for ever and ever.
℞. **Amen.** ⩔

READING I   Is 7, 10-14

The time, one of turmoil, is approximately 735 B.C. and Ahaz is reigning king of Judah in Jerusalem. Ahaz is weak and worldly, yet he is the legitimate heir to the throne. And so it is to him that God makes his offer. The solemnity of the sign and the use of the word "Immanuel" show that Isaiah is speaking of more than just a continuation of the royal line.

A reading from the book of the prophet Isaiah

The Lord spoke to Ahaz: Ask for a sign from the Lord, your God; let it be deep as the nether world, or high as the sky! But Ahaz answered, "I will not ask! I will not tempt the Lord!" Then he said: Listen, O house of David! Is it not enough for you to weary men, must you also weary my God? Therefore the Lord himself will give you this sign: the virgin shall be with child, and bear a son, and shall name him Immanuel [because "God is with us"].—This is the Word of the Lord. ℞. **Thanks be to God.** ⩔

Responsorial Psalm   Ps 24, 1-2. 3-4. 5-6

℞. (7. 10) **Let the Lord enter;**
    he is king of glory.

The Lord's are the earth and its fullness;
    the world and those who dwell in it.
For he founded it upon the seas
    and established it upon the rivers. — ℞

Who can ascend the mountain of the Lord?
    or who may stand in his holy place?
He whose hands are sinless, whose heart is clean,
    who desires not what is vain. — ℞

He shall receive a blessing from the Lord,
    a reward from God his savior.
Such is the race that seeks for him,
    that seeks the face of the God of Jacob.

℟. **Let the Lord enter;**
    he is king of glory. ℣

GOSPEL   Lk 1, 26-38
Alleluia

℟. **Alleuia.** Come,
Key of David,
opening the gates of God's eternal Kingdom:
free the prisoners of darkness! ℟. **Alleluia.**

Luke's Gospel now moves from the conception of the Baptizer to the
Incarnation of the Word of God. In response to the angel, Mary says:
"I am the maidservant of the Lord. Let it be done to me as you say."
Mary becomes the mother of Jesus.

℣. The Lord be with you. ℟. **And also with you.**
✠ A reading from the holy gospel according to Luke
℟. **Glory to you, Lord.**

In the sixth month, the angel Gabriel was sent from
God to a town of Galilee named Nazareth, to a virgin
betrothed to a man named Joseph, of the house of
David. The virgin's name was Mary. Upon arriving,
the messenger said to her: "Rejoice, O highly favored
daughter! The Lord is with you. Blessed are you
among women." She was deeply troubled by his
words, and wondered what his greeting meant. The
messenger went on to say to her: "Do not fear, Mary.
You have found favor with God. You shall conceive
and bear a son and give him the name Jesus. Great
will be his dignity and he will be called Son of the
Most High. The Lord God will give him the throne
of David his father. He will rule over the house of
Jacob forever and his reign will be without end."

    Mary said to the angel, "How can this be since I
do not know man?" The angel answered her: "The
Holy Spirit will come upon you and the power of the

Most High will overshadow you; hence, the holy offspring to be born will be called Son of God. Know
that Elizabeth your kinswoman has conceived a son
in her old age; she who was thought to be sterile
is now in her sixth month, for nothing is impossible
with God."

Mary said: "I am the maidservant of the Lord. Let
it be done to me as you say." With that the angel
left her.—This is the gospel of the Lord. ℟. **Praise
to you, Lord Jesus Christ.**   ➤ No. 15, p. 623

PRAYER OVER THE GIFTS

Lord,
accept this sacrificial gift.
May the eucharist we share
bring us to the eternal life
we seek in faith and hope.
Grant this through Christ our Lord.
℟. **Amen.**   ➤ No. 21, p. 626 (Pref. P 2)

COMMUNION ANT.   Lk 1, 31

**The angel said to Mary: you shall conceive and bear
a son, and you shall call him Jesus.** ℣

PRAYER AFTER COMMUNION

Lord,
watch over the people you nourish with this eucha-
    rist.
Lead them to rejoice in true peace.
We ask this in the name of Jesus the Lord.
℟. **Amen.**   ➤ No. 32, p. 650

DECEMBER 21

In the very first chapter of the Gospel we see New Testament spirituality
coming into play—that the Christian life is a life of service to others.
"Anyone among you who aspires to greatness must serve the rest"
(Mt 20, 26). Love of God and love of neighbor cannot be separated,
and, as the apostles warn us, love of neighbor without service is
empty and meaningless.

ENTRANCE ANT.   See Is 7, 14; 8, 10

Soon the Lord God will come, and you will call him Emmanuel, for God is with us.   ➤ No. 2, p. 614

OPENING PRAYER

Lord,
hear the prayers of your people.
May we who celebrate the birth of your Son as man
rejoice in the gift of eternal life when he comes in
    glory,
for he lives and reigns with you and the Holy Spirit,
one God, for ever and ever. ℞. **Amen.** ♦

One of the following readings may be chosen.

READING I   Sg 2, 8-14

The Song of Songs is interpreted in religious terms as a description of the love between God and his people and reflects the mood of lovers in particular situations, whether together or separated. In the beauty of the springtime, the bride awaits her lover as he swiftly speeds to her side.

A reading from the Song of Songs

Hark! my lover—here he comes
    springing across the mountains,
    leaping across the hills.
My lover is like a gazelle
    or a young stag.
Here he stands behind our wall,
    gazing through the windows,
    peering through the lattices.
My lover speaks; he says to me,
    "Arise, my beloved, my beautiful one,
    and come!
"For see, the winter is past,
    the rains are over and gone.
The flowers appear on the earth,
    the time of pruning the vines has come,
    and the song of the dove is heard in our land.

The fig tree puts forth its figs,
   and the vines, in bloom, give forth fragrance.
Arise, my beloved, my beautiful one,
   and come!
"O my dove in the clefts of the rock,
   in the secret recesses of the cliff,
Let me see you,
   let me hear your voice,
For your voice is sweet,
   and you are lovely."
This is the Word of the Lord. ℟. **Thanks be to God.** ℣

OR

READING I Zep 3, 14-18

The survivors of Israel, only a remnant without possessions, are invited to rejoice because their salvation is at hand. The Lord himself will stand at the head of Israel's army, and with such leadership the nation need fear no enemy.

A reading from the book of the prophet Zephaniah

Shout for joy, O daughter Zion!
   sing joyfully, O Israel!
Be glad and exult with all your heart,
   O daughter Jerusalem!
The Lord has removed the judgment against you,
   he has turned away your enemies;
The King of Israel, the Lord, is in your midst,
   you have no further misfortune to fear.
On that day, it shall be said to Jerusalem:
   Fear not, O Zion, be not discouraged!
The Lord, your God, is in your midst,
   a mighty savior;
He will rejoice over you with gladness,
   and renew you in his love.
He will sing joyfully because of you,
   as one sings at festivals.
This is the Word of the Lord. ℟. **Thanks be to God.** ℣

Responsorial Psalm   Ps 33, 2-3. 11-12. 20-21

℟. (1. 3) **Cry out with joy in the Lord, you holy ones;
sing a new song to him.**

Give thanks to the Lord on the harp;
   with the ten-stringed lyre chant his praises.
Sing to him a new song;
   pluck the strings skillfully, with shouts of glad-
      ness. — ℟

The plan of the Lord stands forever;
   the design of his heart, through all generations.
Happy the nation whose God is the Lord,
   the people he has chosen for his own inheri-
      tance. — ℟

Our soul waits for the Lord,
   who is our help and our shield,
For in him our hearts rejoice;
   in his holy name we trust. — ℟ ⍗

GOSPEL   Lk 1, 39-45

Alleluia

℟. **Alleluia.** Come, Emmanuel,
God's presence among us, our King, our Judge:
save us, Lord our God! ℟. **Alleluia.**

Mary visits her kinswoman to offer assistance and seek advice. The
theme of joy so connected with Messianic abundance and fulfillment is
continued in the words of Elizabeth. Mary proceeds with haste—the
greater to the lesser, Mary to Elizabeth, Christ to John.

℣. The Lord be with you. ℟. **And also with you.**

✠ A reading from the holy gospel according to Luke
℟. **Glory to you, Lord.**

Mary set out, proceeding in haste into the hill country to a town of Judah, where she entered Zechariah's
house and greeted Elizabeth. When Elizabeth heard
Mary's greeting, the baby stirred in her womb. Elizabeth was filled with the Holy Spirit, and cried out in

a loud voice: "Blessed are you among women and blessed is the fruit of your womb. But who am I that the mother of my Lord should come to me? The moment your greeting sounded in my ears, the baby stirred in my womb for joy. Blessed is she who trusted that the Lord's words to her would be fulfilled."—This is the gospel of the Lord. ℟. **Praise to you, Lord Jesus Christ.** ➤ No. 15, p. 623

PRAYER OVER THE GIFTS

Lord of love,
receive these gifts which you have given to your
    Church.
Let them become for us
the means of our salvation.
We ask this through Christ our Lord.
℟. **Amen.** ➤ No. 21, p. 626 (Pref. P 2)

COMMUNION ANT. Lk 1, 45

Blessed are you for your firm believing, that the promises of the Lord would be fulfilled. ↓

PRAYER AFTER COMMUNION

Lord,
help us to serve you
that we may be brought to salvation.
May this eucharist be our constant protection.
Grant this in the name of Jesus the Lord.
℟. **Amen.** ➤ No. 32, p. 650

DECEMBER 22

"God who is mighty has done great things for me" (Gospel). The words of our Blessed Lady speak for all men. God has selected her to be the mother of his Son and, in turn, he has given to us a Savior, a Redeemer—Christ, the Lord.

ENTRANCE ANT. Ps 24, 7

Gates, lift up your heads! Stand erect, ancient doors, and let in the King of glory. ➤ No. 2, p. 614

OPENING PRAYER

God our Father,
you sent your Son
to free mankind from the power of death.
May we who celebrate the coming of Christ as man
share more fully in his divine life,
for he lives and reigns with you and the Holy Spirit,
one God, for ever and ever.
℟. **Amen.** ↓

READING I

1 Sm 1, 24-28

Samuel is a symbol of a child dedicated from the womb to a special
service of God. Hannah fulfills her vow—that the child would be consecrated to God's service in the temple all the days of his life.

A reading from the first book of Samuel

Anna brought Samuel with her, along with a three-
year-old bull, an ephah of flour, and a skin of wine,
and presented him at the temple of the Lord in Shiloh. After the boy's father had sacrificed the young
bull, Hannah, his mother, approached Eli and said:
"Pardon, my lord! As you live, my lord, I am the
woman who stood near you here, praying to the
Lord. I prayed for this child, and the Lord granted
my request. Now I, in turn, give him to the Lord; as
long as he lives, he shall be dedicated to the Lord."
She left him there.—This is the Word of the Lord.
℟. **Thanks be to God.** ↓

Responsorial Psalm   1 Sm 2, 1. 4-5. 6-7. 8

℟. (1) **My heart rejoices in the Lord, my Savior.**

My heart exults in the Lord,
    my horn is exalted in my God.
I have swallowed up my enemies;
    I rejoice in my victory. — ℟

The bows of the mighty are broken,
    while the tottering gird on strength.
The well-fed hire themselves out for bread,

while the hungry batten on spoil.
The barren wife bears seven sons,
    while the mother of many languishes. — ℟

The Lord puts to death and gives life;
    he casts down to the nether world;
    he raises up again.
The Lord makes poor and makes rich,
    he humbles, he also exalts. — ℟

He raises the needy from the dust;
    from the ash heap he lifts up the poor,
To seat them with nobles
    and make a glorious throne their heritage. — ℟ ✟

GOSPEL   Lk 1, 46-56
Alleluia
℟. **Alleluia.** Come,
King of all nations,
source of your Church's unity and faith:
save all mankind, your own creation! ℟. **Alleluia.**

In the Magnificat, all of the Old Testament allusions to the Messiah are brought together in a hymn of thanksgiving with deep emotion and strong conviction. The fruits of faith and dependence on a merciful God are extolled. There is a prophetic or eschatological ring to Mary's words. God appears as the mighty one, caring for the needy.

℣. The Lord be with you. ℟. **And also with you.**

✠ A reading from the holy gospel according to Luke

℟. **Glory to you, Lord.**

Mary said:

"My being proclaims the greatness of the Lord,
    my spirit finds joy in God my savior,
For he has looked upon his servant in her lowliness;
    all ages to come shall call me blessed.
God who is mighty has done great things for me,
    holy is his name;
His mercy is from age to age
    on those who fear him.

"He has shown might with his arm;
   he has confused the proud in their inmost
      thoughts.
He has deposed the mighty from their thrones
   and raised the lowly to high places.
The hungry he has given every good thing,
   while the rich he has sent empty away.
He has upheld Israel his servant,
   ever mindful of his mercy;
Even as he promised our fathers,
   promised Abraham and his descendants forever."
Mary remained with Elizabeth about three months
and then returned home.—This is the gospel of the
Lord. ℟. **Praise to you, Lord Jesus Christ.**

➔ No. 15, p. 623

PRAYER OVER THE GIFTS

Lord God,
with confidence in your love
we come with gifts to worship at your altar.
By the mystery of this eucharist
purify us and renew your life within us.
We ask this through Christ our Lord.
℟. **Amen.**   ➔ No. 21, p. 626 (Pref. P 2)

COMMUNION ANT.   Lk 1, 46. 49

**My soul proclaims the greatness of the Lord, for
the Almighty has done great things for me.** ↓

PRAYER AFTER COMMUNION

Lord,
strengthen us by the sacrament we have received.
Help us to go out to meet our Savior
and to merit eternal life
with lives that witness to our faith.
We ask this in the name of Jesus the Lord.
℟. **Amen.**   ➔ No. 32, p. 650

DECEMBER 23

God wondrously intervenes among his people. The stage is now set
for that moment when God will bend down from heaven and offer us
his salvation in the person of his own Son, Jesus.

ENTRANCE ANT.   See Is 9, 6; Ps 71, 17

**A little child is born for us, and he shall be called the
mighty God; every race on earth shall be blessed in
him.**   ➜ No. 2, p. 614

OPENING PRAYER

Father,
we contemplate the birth of your Son.
He was born of the Virgin Mary
and came to live among us.
May we receive forgiveness and mercy
through our Lord Jesus Christ, your Son,
who lives and reigns with you and the Holy Spirit,
one God, for ever and ever. ℟. **Amen.** ↓

READING I   Mal 3, 1-4. 23-24

The fulfillment of the divine promise is announced in prophecy. Malachi
sees that one of the first tasks of the Messiah on the great day of the
Lord is to purify the sons of Levi and to restore once more to his
people a sacrifice worthy of the Lord.

A reading from the book of the prophet Malachi

Lo, I am sending my messenger
    to prepare the way before me;
And suddenly there will come to the temple
    the Lord whom you seek,
And the messenger of the covenant whom you desire.
    Yes, he is coming, says the Lord of hosts.
But who will endure the day of his coming?
    And who can stand when he appears?
For he is like the refiner's fire,
    or like the fuller's lye.
He will sit refining and purifying [silver],
    and he will purify the sons of Levi,

Refining them like gold or like silver
   that they may offer due sacrifice to the Lord.
Then the sacrifice of Judah and Jerusalem
   will please the Lord,
   as in the days of old, as in years gone by.
Lo, I will send you
   Elijah, the prophet,
Before the day of the Lord comes,
   the great and terrible day,
To turn the hearts of the fathers to their children,
   and the hearts of the children to their fathers,
Lest I come and strike
   the land with doom.
This is the Word of the Lord. ℟. **Thanks be to God.** ✟

Responsorial Psalm   Ps 25, 4-5. 8-9. 10. 14

℟. (Lk 21, 28) **Lift up your heads and see;
   your redemption is near at hand.**

Your ways, O Lord, make known to me;
   teach me your paths,
Guide me in your truth and teach me,
   for you are God my savior. — ℟

Good and upright is the Lord;
   thus he shows sinners the way.
He guides the humble to justice,
   he teaches the humble his way. — ℟

All the paths of the Lord are kindness and constancy
   toward those who keep his covenant and his decrees.
The friendship of the Lord is with those who fear
   him,
   and his covenant, for their instruction. — ℟ ✟

GOSPEL   Lk 1, 57-66
Alleluia

℟. **Alleluia.** Come, King of all nations,
source of your Church's unity and faith:
save all mankind, your own creation! ℟. **Alleluia.**

The birth of John the Baptizer is described. The name John, given him by the angel, signifies "Yahweh has shown favor," a name which symbolized the role of John in the redemptive plans of God.

℣. The Lord be with you. ℟. **And also with you.**

✠ A reading from the holy gospel according to Luke

℟. **Glory to you, Lord.**

When Elizabeth's time for delivery arrived, she gave birth to a son. Her neighbors and relatives, upon hearing that the Lord had extended his mercy to her, rejoiced with her. When they assembled for the circumcision of the child on the eighth day, they intended to name him after his father Zechariah. At this his mother intervened, saying, "No, he is to be called John."

They pointed out to her, "None of your relatives has this name." Then, using signs, they asked the father what he wished him to be called.

He signaled for a writing tablet and wrote the words, "His name is John." This astonished them all. At that moment his mouth was opened and his tongue loosed, and he began to speak in praise of God.

Fear descended on all in the neighborhood; throughout the hill country of Judea these happenings began to be recounted to the last detail. All who heard stored these things in their hearts, saying, "What will this child be?" and, "Was not the hand of the Lord upon him?"—This is the gospel of the Lord. ℟. **Praise to you, Lord Jesus Christ.**

➤ No. 15, p. 623

PRAYER OVER THE GIFTS

Lord,
you have given us this memorial
as the perfect form of worship.
Restore us to your peace
and prepare us to celebrate the coming of our Savior,
for he is Lord for ever and ever.

℟. **Amen.**   ➤ No. 21, p. 626 (Pref. P 2)

COMMUNION ANT.   Rv 3, 20

I stand at the door and knock, says the Lord. If any-
one hears my voice and opens the door, I will come
in and sit down to supper with him and he with me. ℣

PRAYER AFTER COMMUNION
Lord,
as you nourish us with the bread of life,
give peace to our spirits
and prepare us to welcome your Son with ardent
    faith.
We ask this through Christ our Lord.
℟. **Amen.** ──────────── ➤ No. 32, p. 650

DECEMBER 24

MASS IN THE MORNING

In preparing for the birth of Jesus, God asks of us the same openness
as Mary had. He is ready to come into our lives and fill us with himself if we put no obstacle in his way and if we are willing to adopt
Mary's attitude: "I am the maidservant of the Lord."

ENTRANCE ANT.   See Gal 4, 4
The appointed time has come; God has sent his Son
into the world.   ➤ No. 2, p. 614

OPENING PRAYER
Come Lord Jesus,
do not delay;
give new courage to your people who trust in your
    love.
By your coming, raise us to the joy of your kingdom,
where you live and reign with the Father and the
    Holy Spirit.
one God, for ever and ever. ℟. **Amen.** ℣

READING I   2 Sm 7, 1-5. 8-11. 16
David decides to build a temple. God reminds him that he has been
successful and has become rich and famous, not because of his own
power and strength, but through the fatherly care that God has shown
toward him. God promises to reward David by making him even
more successful and famous in the future. David's dynasty will last forever.

A reading from the second book of Samuel

When King David was settled in his palace, and the Lord had given him rest from his enemies on every side, he said to Nathan the prophet, "Here I am living in a house of cedar, while the ark of God dwells in a tent!" Nathan answered the king, "Go, do whatever you have in mind, for the Lord is with you." But that night the Lord spoke to Nathan and said: "Go, tell my servant David, 'Thus says the Lord: Should you build me a house to dwell in? The Lord of hosts has this to say: It was I who took you from the pasture and from the care of the flock to be commander of my people Israel. I have been with you wherever you went, and I have destroyed all your enemies before you. And I will make you famous like the great ones of the earth. I will fix a place for my people Israel; I will plant them so that they may dwell in their place without further disturbance. Neither shall the wicked continue to afflict them as they did of old, since the time I first appointed judges over my people Israel. I will give you rest from all your enemies. The Lord also reveals to you that he will establish a house for you. Your house and your kingdom shall endure forever before me; your throne shall stand firm forever.'"—This is the Word of the Lord. ℟. **Thanks be to God.** ℣

Responsorial Psalm   Ps 89, 2-3. 4-5. 27. 29

℟. (2) **For ever I will sing the goodness of the Lord.**

The favors of the Lord I will sing forever;
    through all generations my mouth shall proclaim
        your faithfulness.

For you have said, "My kindness is established forever";
    in heaven you have confirmed your faithfulness. — ℟

"I have made a covenant with my chosen one,
    I have sworn to David my servant:

Forever will I confirm your posterity
  and establish your throne for all generations."—℟

He shall say of me, "You are my father,
  my God, the Rock, my savior."

Forever I will maintain my kindness toward him,
  and my covenant with him stands firm. — ℟ ℣

GOSPEL   Lk 1, 67-79

Alleluia

℟. **Alleluia.** Come,
Radiant Dawn,
splendor of eternal light, sun of justice:
shine on those lost in the darkness of death! ℟.
Alleluia.

A solemn hymn of praise is attributed to Zechariah. This is the recognition of the Prophet of the Most High. The father praises his own son
and sees the son as a step closer to the fuller revelation of God.

℣. The Lord be with you. ℟. **And also with you.**

☩ A reading from the holy gospel according to Luke

℟. **Glory to you, Lord.**

Zechariah, the father of John, filled with the Holy
Spirit, uttered this prophecy:

  "Blessed be the Lord the God of Israel
    because he has visited and ransomed his people.
  He has raised a horn of saving strength for us
    in the house of David his servant,
  As he promised through the mouths of his holy
      ones,
    the prophets of ancient times:
  Salvation from our enemies
    and from the hands of all our foes.
  He has dealt mercifully with our fathers
    and remembered the holy covenant he made,
  The oath he swore to Abraham our father he
      would grant us:
    that, rid of fear and delivered from the enemy,

We should serve him devoutly, and through all
  our days,
  be holy in his sight.
And you, O child, shall be called
  prophet of the Most High;
For you shall go before the Lord
  to prepare straight paths for him,
Giving his people a knowledge of salvation
  in freedom from their sins.
All this is the work of the kindness of our God;
  he, the Dayspring, shall visit us in his mercy
To shine on those who sit in darkness and in the
  shadow of death,
  to guide our feet into the way of peace."
This is the gospel of the Lord. ℟. **Praise to you, Lord
Jesus Christ.** ➤ No. 15, p. 623

PRAYER OVER THE GIFTS

Father,
accept the gifts we offer.
By our sharing in this eucharist
free us from sin
and help us to look forward in faith
to the glorious coming of your Son,
who is Lord for ever and ever.
℟. **Amen.** ➤ No. 21, p. 626 (Pref. P 2)

COMMUNION ANT. Lk 1, 68

**Blessed be the Lord God of Israel, for he has visited
and redeemed his people.** ℣

PRAYER AFTER COMMUNION

Lord,
your gift of the eucharist has renewed our lives.
May we who look forward to the feast of Christ's
  birth
rejoice for ever in the wonder of his love,
for he is Lord for ever and ever.
℟. **Amen.** ➤ No. 32, p. 650

CHRISTMAS SEASON

The feasts of the liturgical year place before our minds the sign of some hidden sacred reality which must be applied to all of us. During the Christmas season this hidden sacred reality is the light, the life, and the joy beaming from Christ, the "Sun of Justice," upon mankind in the darkness of ignorance and sin (Mal 4, 2).

This mystery of our salvation is to be honored not as something that happened 2,000 years ago, but as something present, for while the act itself (Christ's birth and manifestation) is past, its effects are very present. The hidden reality in this mystery is ultimately Christ and his saving action. He is present in the mystery of Christmas-Epiphany, constantly interceding for us and communicating himself in holy symbols.

We should meditate on and celebrate the Christmas mystery as happening now to us and embrace its mystical effects with an open heart. After the time of waiting (Advent), we enjoy a fuller realization of Christ's presence in us. In the Word made flesh, we see that God is no stranger to the human condition; in the infant born in a stable to simple working people, we come to understand that God who is infinitely great is also one of us.

The readings of this season provide the salient features of this infant. He is the Servant of Yahweh and the Prince of Peace, whom Isaiah foretold. He is the Light and the Logos which is greater than human reason and perfects it (John). In him we encounter the Ultimate Transcendent Reality: he reveals the Father (Heb 1) who is gracious to men (Titus). This Father comforts and consoles us (Is 52) and promises to unite us his adopted sons in Jerusalem, symbols of the Church and brotherly love (Gal 4; Is 68).

Christmas celebrates the Father's gift to us: the revelation of his loving presence. This knowledge has been given to us through Israel and the prophets and supremely through Christ his Son. It must continue to be made manifest through Christ-in-us; "of his fullness we have all received" (John).

Dec. 25 — CHRISTMAS
See Vol. I (Sunday Missal), p. 110

Dec. 26 — ST. STEPHEN, First Martyr
2nd DAY WITHIN THE OCTAVE OF CHRISTMAS

St. Stephen received the commission from the apostles to gather food for the poor. The judges accused him before the Sanhedrin, being amazed at his wonderful miracles. St. Stephen, the Church tells us, was the first to give up his life for the Savior. He died praying for those who stoned him.

ENTRANCE ANT.

The gates of heaven opened for Stephen, the first of the martyrs; in heaven, he wears the crown of victory. ➤ No. 2, p. 614

OPENING PRAYER

Lord,
today we celebrate the entrance of St. Stephen
into eternal glory.
He died praying for those who killed him.
Help us to imitate his goodness
and to love our enemies.
We ask this through our Lord Jesus Christ, your Son,
who lives and reigns with you and the Holy Spirit,
one God, for ever and ever. ℟. **Amen.** ▼

READING I
Acts 6, 8-10; 7, 54-59

St. Stephen is "filled with grace and power" through his union with Christ and the presence of the Holy Spirit. The members of the "Synagogue of Roman Freedmen" are closed to God's action and rebel against the prophetic word spoken to them. They try to put Stephen's words out of their minds by stopping up their ears. They attack God's mouthpiece and put him to death.

A reading from the Acts of the Apostles

Stephen was a man filled with grace and power, who worked great wonders and signs among the people. Certain members of the so-called "Synagogue of Roman Freedmen" (that is, the Jews from Cyrene, Alexandria, Cicilia and Asia) would undertake to engage Stephen in debate, but they proved no match for the wisdom and spirit with which he spoke.

Those who listened to his words were stung to the heart; they ground their teeth in anger at him. Stephen meanwhile, filled with the Holy Spirit, looked to the sky above and saw the glory of God, and Jesus standing at God's right hand. "Look!" he exclaimed, "I see an opening in the sky, and the Son of Man standing at God's right hand." The onlookers were shouting aloud, holding their hands over their ears as they did so. Then they rushed at him as one man, dragged him out of the city, and began to stone him. The witnesses meanwhile were piling their cloaks at the feet of a young man named Saul. As Stephen was being stoned he could be heard praying, "Lord Jesus, receive my spirit."—This is the Word of the Lord. ℟. **Thanks be to God.** ⍗

Responsorial Psalm   Ps 31, 3-4. 6. 7. 8. 17. 21

℟. (6) **Into your hands, O Lord,**
  I entrust my spirit.
Be my rock of refuge,
  a stronghold to give me safety.
You are my rock and my fortress;
  for your name's sake you will lead and guide
    me. — ℟
Into your hands I commend my spirit;
  you will redeem me, O Lord, O faithful God.
But my trust is in the Lord.
  I will rejoice and be glad of your kindness. — ℟
Let your face shine upon your servant;
  save me in your kindness.
You hide them in the shelter of your presence
  from the plottings of men. — ℟ ⍗

GOSPEL Mt 10, 17-22

Alleluia (Ps 118, 26. 27)

℟. **Alleluia.** Blessed is he who comes in the name of
the Lord;
the Lord God shines upon us. ℟. **Alleluia.**

Christ tells his followers they will experience rejection because of him
as did Stephen. He tells them to be confident and courageous, to live
at peace with him so they can live at peace with themselves, and to
conform to his Gospel and live without fear.

℣. The Lord be with you ℟. **And also with you.**
✠ A reading from the holy gospel according to Matthew. ℟. **Glory to you, Lord.**

Jesus said to his apostles: "Be on your guard with
respect to others. They will hale you into court, they
will flog you in their synagogues. You will be brought
to trial before rulers and kings, to give witness before them and before the Gentiles on my account.
When they hand you over, do not worry about what
you will say or how you will say it. When the hour
comes, you will be given what you are to say. You
yourselves will not be the speakers; the Spirit of
your Father will be speaking in you.

"Brother will hand over brother to death, and the
father his child; children will turn against parents
and have them put to death. You will be hated by all
on account of me. But whoever holds out till the end
will escape death."—This is the gospel of the Lord.
℟. **Praise to you, Lord Jesus Christ.** ➤ No. 15, p. 623

PRAYER OVER THE GIFTS

Father,
be pleased with the gift we bring in your honor
as we celebrate the feast of St. Stephen.
Grant this through Christ our Lord.

➤ No. 21, p. 626 (Pref. P 3-5)

COMMUNION ANT. Acts 7, 58

**As they stoned him, Stephen prayed aloud: Lord
Jesus, receive my spirit.** ℣

PRAYER AFTER COMMUNION

Lord,
we thank you for the many signs of your love for us.
Save us by the birth of your Son
and give us joy in honoring St. Stephen the martyr.
We ask this through Christ our Lord.
℟. **Amen.**   ➤ No. 32, p. 650

Dec. 27 — ST. JOHN, Apostle and Evangelist

3rd DAY WITHIN THE OCTAVE OF CHRISTMAS

St. John is the apostle whom Jesus loved. It was he who reclined on
the bosom of the Savior at the Last Supper. He is the author of the
sublime Gospel which so emphatically proclaims the Divinity of Christ.
To him also our Lord, hanging on the cross, entrusted his beloved
Mother. He died about the year 100.

ENTRANCE ANT.   Sir 15, 5

**The Lord opened his mouth in the assembly, and fill-
ed him with the spirit of wisdom and understanding,
and clothed him in a robe of glory.
OR
At the last supper, John reclined close to the Lord.
Blessed apostle, to you were revealed the heavenly
secrets! Your life-giving words have spread over all
the earth!**   ➤ No. 2, p. 614

OPENING PRAYER

God our Father,
you have revealed the mysteries of your Word
through St. John the apostle.
By prayer and reflection
may we come to understand the wisdom he taught.
Grant this through our Lord Jesus Christ, your Son,
who lives and reigns with you and the Holy Spirit,
one God, for ever and ever. ℟. **Amen.** ✝

READING I   1 Jn 1, 1-4

John emphasizes that eternal life has been made known in the his-
torical Jesus and that the Church as an apostolic company actually
handled, saw, and heard the divine Logos who is the creative Mediator
of life.

The beginning of the first letter of John

This is what we proclaim to you:
what was from the beginning,
what we have heard,
what we have seen with our eyes,
what we have looked upon
and our hands have touched—
we speak of the word of life.
(This life became visible;
we have seen and bear witness to it,
and we proclaim to you the eternal life
that was present to the Father
and became visible to us.)
What we have seen and heard
we proclaim in turn to you
so that you may share life with us.
This fellowship of ours is with the Father
and with his Son, Jesus Christ.
Indeed, our purpose in writing you this
is that our joy may be complete.

This is the Word of the Lord. ℟. **Thanks be to God.** ℣

Responsorial Psalm   Ps 97, 1-2. 5-6. 11-12

℟. (12) **Let good men rejoice in the Lord.**

The Lord is king; let the earth rejoice;
    let the many isles be glad.
Clouds and darkness are round about him,
    justice and judgment are the foundation of his
        throne. — ℟

The mountains melt like wax before the Lord,
    before the Lord of all the earth.
The heavens proclaim his justice,
    and all peoples see his glory. — ℟

Light dawns for the just;
    and gladness, for the upright of heart.
Be glad in the Lord, you just,
    and give thanks to his holy name. — ℟ ℣

GOSPEL   Jn 20, 2-8
Alleluia

℞. **Alleluia.** We praise you, God; we acknowledge you as Lord;

your glorious band of apostles extols you. ℞. **Alleluia.**

John skillfully combines the tradition of the empty tomb with that of Resurrection appearances. Mary Magdalene reports to Peter and the "beloved disciples" that the stone has been removed, and the two disciples hurry to the tomb.

℣. The Lord be with you ℞. **And also with you.**

✠ A reading from the holy gospel according to John
℞. **Glory to you, Lord.**

On the first day of the week Mary Magdalene ran off to Simon Peter and the other disciple (the one Jesus loved) and told them, "The Lord has been taken from the tomb! We do not know where they have put him!"

At that, Peter and other disciple started out on their way toward the tomb. They were running side by side, but then the other disciple outran Peter and reached the tomb first. He did not enter but bent down to peer in, and saw the wrappings lying on the ground. Presently, Simon Peter came along behind him and entered the tomb. He observed the wrappings on the ground and saw the piece of cloth which had covered the head not lying with the wrappings, but rolled up in a place by itself. Then the disciple who had arrived first at the tomb went in. He saw and believed.—This is the gospel of the Lord. ℞. **Praise to you, Lord Jesus Christ.** ➤ No. 15, p. 623

PRAYER OVER THE GIFTS

Lord,
bless these gifts (we present to you).
With St. John may we share
in the hidden wisdom of your eternal Word
which you reveal at this eucharistic table.

We ask this in the name of Jesus the Lord.
℟. **Amen.**   ➤ No. 21, p. 626 (Pref. P 3-5)

COMMUNION ANT.   Jn 1, 14-16
**The Word of God became man, and lived among us.
Of his riches we have all received.** ⩔

PRAYER AFTER COMMUNION

Almighty Father,
St. John proclaimed that your Word became flesh
   for our salvation.
Through this eucharist may your Son always live in
   us,
for he is Lord for ever and ever.
℟. **Amen.**   ➤ No. 32, p. 650

Dec. 28 — HOLY INNOCENTS, Martyrs
4th DAY WITHIN THE OCTAVE OF CHRISTMAS

In the slaughter of the Innocents by Herod, the Infant Savior has
infant martyrs. Thus children are held up to our admiration from the
very first—in their death, as in their lives, a pattern to older Christians. All those who kill innocent children are like Herod and are to
be condemned. Even more corrupt are those who scandalize the
innocent and lead them into sin. Jesus pronounces a terrible punishment upon such people.

ENTRANCE ANT.

**These innocent children were slain for Christ. They
follow the spotless Lamb, and proclaim for ever:
Glory to you, Lord.**   ➤ No. 2, p. 614

OPENING PRAYER

Father,
the Holy Innocents offered you praise
by the death they suffered for Christ.
May our lives bear witness
to the faith we profess with our lips.
We ask this through our Lord Jesus Christ, your Son,
who lives and reigns with you and the Holy Spirit,
one God, for ever and ever. ℟. **Amen.** ⩔

READING I   1 Jn 1, 5—2, 2

John refutes the heretical claims to have fellowship with God and to
have no need for redemption from sin. "God is Light" means that God
is knowable, although invisible, for he reveals himself as Love; and
also that he is holy and morally perfect, for the darkness of sin does
not exist at all in his being. Every sin must be confessed in the
awareness that God knows all and that he is just. John writes to keep
"his little ones" from sin.

A reading from the first letter of John

Here, then, is the message
we have heard from Jesus Christ
and announce to you:
that God is light;
in him there is no darkness.
If we say, "We have fellowship with him,"
while continuing to walk in darkness,
we are liars and do not act in truth.
But if we walk in light,
as he is in the light,
we have fellowship with one another,
and the blood of his Son Jesus cleanses us from
    all sin.
If we say, "We are free of the guilt of sin,"
we deceive ourselves; the truth is not to be
    found in us.
But if we acknowledge our sins,
he who is just can be trusted
to forgive our sins
and cleanse us from every wrong.
If we say, "We have never sinned,"
we make him a liar
and his word finds no place in us.
My little ones,
I am writing this to keep you from sin.
But if anyone should sin,
we have in the presence of the Father,
Jesus Christ, an intercessor who is just.
He is an offering for our sins,

and not for our sins only,
but for those of the whole world.

This is the Word of the Lord. ℟. **Thanks be to God.** ℣

Responsorial Psalm   Ps 124, 2-3. 4-5. 7-8

℟. (7) **Our soul has escaped like a bird from the hunter's net.**

Had not the Lord been with us—
    when men rose up against us,
Then would they have swallowed us alive.
    When their fury was inflamed against us. — ℟
Then would the waters have overwhelmed us;
    the torrent would have swept us;
Over us then would have swept
    the raging waters. — ℟
Broken was the snare,
    and we were freed.
Our help is in the name of the Lord,
    who made heaven and earth. — ℟ ℣

GOSPEL   Mt 2, 13-18
Alleluia

℟. **Alleluia.** We praise you, God; we acknowledge you as Lord;

the radiant army of martyrs acclaims you. ℟. **Alleluia.**

The cruelty of Herod has become proverbial, even in Rome. He tries to destroy the child Jesus because he fails to see that the birth of this king was the dawning of hope for salvation. The quotation from Hosea, "Out of Egypt I have called my son," is based on the Hebrew text in which Jesus is presented as re-enacting in his own life the career of Israel, for he is the new Israel.

℣. The Lord be with you ℟. **And also with you.**

✠ A reading from the holy gospel according to Matthew. ℟. **Glory to you, Lord.**

After the Magi had left, the angel of the Lord suddenly appeared in a dream to Joseph with the command: "Get up, take the child and his mother, and flee to Egypt. Stay there until I tell you otherwise.

Herod is searching for the child to destroy him."
Joseph got up and took the child and his mother and
left that night for Egypt. He stayed there until the
death of Herod, to fulfill what the Lord had said
through the prophet:

"Out of Egypt I have called my son."

Once Herod realized that he had been deceived by
the astrologers, he became furious. He ordered the
massacre of all the boys two years old and under in
Bethlehem and its environs, making his calculations
on the basis of the date he had learned from the
astrologers. What was said through Jeremiah the
prophet was then fulfilled:

"A cry was heard at Ramah,
    sobbing and loud lamentation:
Rachel bewailing her children;
    no comfort for her, since they are no more."

This is the gospel of the Lord. ℟. **Praise to you, Lord
Jesus Christ.**   ➤ No. 15, p. 650

PRAYER OVER THE GIFTS

Lord,
you give us your life even before we understand.
Receive the offerings we bring in love,
and free us from sin.
We ask this in the name of Jesus the Lord.
℟. **Amen.**   ➤ No. 21, p. 626 (Pref. P 3-5)

COMMUNION ANT.   Rv 14, 4

**These have been ransomed for God and the Lamb as
the first-fruits of mankind; they follow the Lamb
wherever he goes.** ♥

PRAYER AFTER COMMUNION

Lord,
by a wordless profession of faith in your Son,
the innocents were crowned with life at his birth.

May all people who receive your holy gifts today
come to share in the fullness of salvation.
We ask this through Christ our Lord.
℟. **Amen.**   ➤ No. 32, p. 650

Dec. 29 — 5th DAY WITHIN THE OCTAVE OF CHRISTMAS

The Mass today stresses the necessity to observe the will of God in
obedience and humility. Christ's example of his respect for the law, in
the shedding of his precious blood in the rite of circumcision, had
nothing to do with sin. But to atone for that of men, he willingly
sacrificed himself. He obeyed the command of the old law to the
very letter.

ENTRANCE ANT.   Jn 3, 16

**God loved the world so much, he gave his only Son,
that all who believe in him might not perish, but
might have eternal life.**   ➤ No. 2, p. 614

OPENING PRAYER

All-powerful and unseen God,
the coming of your light into our world
has made the darkness vanish.
Teach us to proclaim the birth of your Son Jesus
    Christ,
who lives and reigns with you and the Holy Spirit,
one God, for ever and ever. ℟. **Amen.** ▼

READING I   1 Jn 2, 3-11

John urges his friends to realize that the one sure way to prove fellowship with God is to do the will of God. In keeping the Commandments,
the supreme example that comes to mind is the Lord's precept of love,
a commandment that is both old and yet of the new Christian revelation.

A reading from the first letter of John

The way we can be sure of our knowledge of Jesus
is to keep his commandments.
The man who claims, "I have known him,"
without keeping his commandments,
is a liar; in such a one there is no truth.

But whoever keeps his word
truly has the love of God made perfect in him.
The way we can be sure we are in union with him
is if one who claims to abide in him
conducts himself just as he did.
Dearly beloved,
it is no new commandment that I write to you,
but an old one which you had from the start.
The commandment, now old, is the word you have
    already heard.
On second thought, the commandment that I write
    you is new,
as it is realized in him and you,
for the darkness is over
and the real light begins to shine.
The man who claims to be in light,
hating his brother all the while,
is in darkness even now.
The man who continues in the light
is the one who loves his brother;
there is nothing in him to cause a fall.
But the man who hates his brother is in darkness.
He walks in shadows,
not knowing where he is going,
since the dark has blinded his eyes.
This is the Word of the Lord. ℟. **Thanks be to God.** ℣

Responsorial Psalm   Ps 96, 1-2. 2-3. 5-6

℟. (11) **Let heaven and earth exult in joy.**

Sing to the Lord a new song;
    sing to the Lord, all you lands.
Sing to the Lord; bless his name. — ℟
Announce his salvation, day after day.
    Tell his glory among the nations;
Among all peoples, his wondrous deeds. — ℟
The Lord made the heavens.
    Splendor and majesty go before him;
Praise and grandeur are in his sanctuary. — ℟ ℣

GOSPEL Lk 2, 22-35
Alleluia

℟. **Alleluia.** This is the light of revelation to the
nations,
and the glory of your people, Israel. ℟. **Alleluia.**

Mary is seen to be united with Jesus, and possibly with Joseph, in the
temple ceremony. Mary's uncleanness is not moral, but only ceremonial; but just as Jesus followed the full Mosaic law and completely
immersed himself in humanity, thereby to transform it, so Mary is
presented as one with all womankind in giving birth to her child. Her
purification, like Jesus' act of redemption, belongs to every one of
Israel.

℣. The Lord be with you ℟. **And also with you.**

✠ A reading from the holy gospel according to Luke
℟. **Glory to you, Lord.**

When the day came to purify them according to the
law of Moses, the couple brought Jesus up to Jerusalem so that he could be presented to the Lord, for
it is written in the law of the Lord, "Every first-born
male shall be consecrated to the Lord." They came
to offer in sacrifice "a pair of turtledoves or two
young pigeons," in accord with the dictate in the
law of the Lord.

There lived in Jerusalem a certain man named
Simeon. He was just and pious, and awaited the consolation of Israel, and the Holy Spirit was upon him.
It was revealed to him by the Holy Spirit that he
would not experience death until he had seen the
Anointed of the Lord. He came to the temple now,
inspired by the Spirit; and when the parents brought
in the child Jesus to perform for him the customary
ritual of the law, he took him in his arms and blessed
God in these words:

"Now, Master, you can dismiss your servant in
peace;
you have fulfilled your word.
For my eyes have witnessed your saving deed
displayed for all the peoples to see:

A revealing light to the Gentiles,
    the glory of your people Israel."

The child's father and mother were marveling at
what was being said about him. Simeon blessed them
and said to Mary his mother: "This child is destined
to be the downfall and the rise of many in Israel, a
sign that will be opposed—and you yourself shall be
pierced with a sword—so that the thoughts of many
hearts may be laid bare."—This is the gospel of the
Lord. ℟. **Praise to you, Lord Jesus Christ.**

➤ No. 15, p. 623

PRAYER OVER THE GIFTS

Lord,
receive our gifts in this wonderful exchange:
from all you have given us
we bring you these gifts,
and in return, you give us yourself.
We ask this through Christ our Lord.
℟. **Amen.**   ➤ No. 21, p. 626 (Pref. P 3-5)

*When Eucharistic Prayer I is used, the special Christ-
mas form of* In union with the whole Church *is said.*

COMMUNION ANT.   Lk 1, 78

**Through the tender compassion of our God, the dawn
from on high shall break upon us.** ↓

PRAYER AFTER COMMUNION

Father of love and mercy,
grant that our lives may always be founded
on the power of this holy mystery.
We ask this in the name of Jesus the Lord.
℟. **Amen.**   ➤ No. 32, p. 650

Dec. 30 — 6th DAY WITHIN THE OCTAVE OF CHRISTMAS

*When there is no Sunday within the octave of Christ-
mas, the feast of the Holy Family is celebrated today.
(See p. 1276.)*

We should turn our thoughts today, not to the hidden life of Jesus in general, but to that special period of it which formed his boyhood. Our Lord became truly man and went through the different stages of human life, from infancy to the fullness of manhood. He did not come into this world formed in that fullness all at once, as Adam came forth from his Creator's hand, but he came "made of a woman" (Gal 4, 4).

ENTRANCE ANT.   Wis 18, 14-15

When peaceful silence lay over all, and night had run half of her swift course, your all-powerful word, O Lord, leaped down from heaven, from the royal throne.   → No. 2, p. 614

OPENING PRAYER

All-powerful God,
may the human birth of your Son
free us from our former slavery to sin
and bring us new life.
We ask this through our Lord Jesus Christ, your Son,
who lives and reigns with you and the Holy Spirit,
one God, for ever and ever. ℟. **Amen.** ↓

READING I   1 Jn 2, 12-17

Observance of the law of Christ effectively removes the Christian from the influence of that world from which Christ prayed that his disciples might be free. John continues to address all his Christian readers as "little ones," whom, however, he now distinguishes as "fathers" and "young men" to emphasize that his appeal extends to the entire Christian community.

A reading from the first letter of John

Little ones, I address you,
   for through his Name your sins have been for-
      given.
Fathers, I address you,
   for you have known him who is from the begin-
      ning.
Young men, I address you,
   for you have conquered the evil one.
I address you, children,
   for you have known the Father.
I address you, fathers,

for you have known him who is from the beginning.
I address you, young men,
for you are strong,
and the word of God remains in you,
and you have conquered the evil one.
Have no love for the world,
nor the things that the world affords.
If anyone loves the world,
the Father's love has no place in him,
for nothing that the world affords
comes from the Father.
Carnal allurements,
enticements for the eye,
the life of empty show—
all these are from the world.
And the world with its seductions is passing away
but the man who does God's will
endures forever.
This is the Word of the Lord. ℟. **Thanks be to God.** ℣

Responsorial Psalm   Ps 96, 7-8. 8-9. 10

℟. (11) **Let heaven and earth exult in joy.**
Give to the Lord, you families of nations,
   give to the Lord glory and praise;
   give to the Lord the glory due his name! — ℟

Bring gifts, and enter his courts;
   worship the Lord in holy attire.
   Tremble before him, all the earth. — ℟

Say among the nations: The Lord is king.
   He has made the world firm, not to be moved;
   he governs the peoples with equity. — ℟ ℣

GOSPEL   Lk 2, 36-40
Alleluia

℟. **Alleluia.** A holy day has dawned upon us.
Today a great light has come upon the earth.
Come you nations and adore the Lord. ℟. **Alleluia.**

It is in the temple, the same place where Anna had for so many years poured out her heart to God, that God pours out his heart to her. Luke points out the necessity of our Lord's hidden life at Nazareth, that he might grow strong in the full experience of a human nature and thus be able to bring the spirit of God into immediate contact with every human area.

℣. The Lord be with you ℟. **And also with you.**

✠ A reading from the holy gospel according to Luke
℟. **Glory to you, Lord.**

There was a certain prophetess, Anna by name, daughter of Phanuel of the tribe of Asher. She had seen many days, having lived seven years with her husband after her marriage and then as a widow until she was eighty-four. She was constantly in the temple, worshiping day and night in fasting and prayer. Coming on the scene at this moment, she gave thanks to God and talked about the child to all who looked forward to the deliverance of Jerusalem.

When the pair had fulfilled all the prescriptions of the law of the Lord, they returned to Galilee and their own town of Nazareth. The child grew in size and strength, filled with wisdom, and the grace of God was upon him.—This is the gospel of the Lord.
℟. **Praise to you, Lord Jesus Christ.**

➜ No. 15, p. 623

PRAYER OVER THE GIFTS
Father,
in your mercy accept our gifts.
By sharing in this eucharist
may we come to live more fully the love we profess.
Grant this through Christ our Lord.
℟. **Amen.** ➜ No. 21, p. 626 (Pref. P 3-5)

COMMUNION ANT. Jn 1, 16
From his riches we have all received, grace for grace. ℣

PRAYER AFTER COMMUNION
God our Father,

in this eucharist you touch our lives.
Keep your love alive in our hearts
that we may become worthy of you.
We ask this through Christ our Lord.
℟. **Amen.**   ➔ No. 32, p. 650

_____

Dec. 31 — 7th DAY WITHIN THE OCTAVE OF CHRISTMAS

"False Christs and false prophets" come to seduce us in the guise of interesting literature and entertainment. These things have nothing in common with the teachings of Jesus. Jesus is the Way, the Truth, and the Life.

ENTRANCE ANT.   Is 9, 6

A child is born for us, a son is given to us; dominion is laid on his shoulders, and he shall be called Wonderful-Counselor.   ➔ No. 2, p. 614

OPENING PRAYER

Ever-living God,
in the birth of your Son
our religion has its origin and its perfect fulfillment.
Help us to share in the life of Christ
for he is the salvation of mankind,
who lives and reigns with you and the Holy Spirit,
one God, for ever and ever. ℟. **Amen.** ⍗

READING I   1 Jn 2, 18-21

By "antichrist," John alludes to any and all of the false teachers who afflict the Church in this "final hour." The false teachers who have separated themselves from the Church never truly shared in the Church's life of God. John speaks of this as a self-evident fact to which Christian experience must testify.

A reading from the first letter of John
Children, it is the final hour;
just as you heard that the Antichrist was coming,

so now many such antichrists have appeared.
It was from our ranks that they took their leave—
not that they really belonged to us;
for if they had belonged to us,
they would have stayed with us.
It only served to show that none of them was ours.
But you have the anointing that comes from the
   Holy One,
so that all knowledge is yours.
My reason for having written you
is not that you do not know the truth
but that you do,
and that no lie has anything in common with the
   truth.
This is the Word of the Lord. ℟. **Thanks be to God.** ℣

Responsorial Psalm   Ps 96, 1-2. 11-12. 13

℟. (11) **Let heaven and earth exult in joy.**

Sing to the Lord a new song;
   sing to the Lord, all you lands.
Sing to the Lord; bless his name;
   announce his salvation, day after day. — ℟

Let the heavens be glad and the earth rejoice;
   let the sea and what fills it resound;
Let the plains be joyful and all that is in them!
   Then shall all the trees of the forest exult before
      the Lord. — ℟

The Lord comes,
   he comes to rule the earth.
He shall rule the world with justice
   and the peoples with his constancy. — ℟ ℣

GOSPEL   Jn 1, 1-18

Alleluia (Jn 1, 14. 12)

℟. **Alleluia.** The Word of God became a man and
      lived among us.
He enabled those who accepted him
to become the children of God. ℟. **Alleluia.**

In the Old Testament, the Word of God is God's manifestation—the revelation of himself, whether in creation, in deeds of power and of grace, or in prophecy. All these trains of thought are taken up by John who shows that Christ, the Incarnate Word, is the ultimate and complete revelation of God.

℣. The Lord be with you ℟. **And also with you.**
✠ The beginning of the holy gospel according to John. ℟. **Glory to you, Lord.**

In the beginning was the Word;
the Word was in God's presence,
and the Word was God.
He was present to God in the beginning.
Through him all things came into being,
and apart from him nothing came to be.
Whatever came to be in him, found life,
life for the light of men.
The light shines on in darkness,
a darkness that did not overcome it.

There was a man named John sent by God, who came as a witness to testify to the light, so that through him all men might believe—but only to testify to the light, for he himself was not the light. The real light which gives light to every man was coming into the world.

He was in the world,
and through him the world was made,
yet the world did not know who he was.
To his own he came,
yet his own did not accept him.
Any who did accept him
he empowered to become children of God.

These are they who believe in his name—who were begotten not by blood, nor by carnal desire, nor by man's willing it, but by God.

The Word became flesh
and made his dwelling among us,
and we have seen his glory:
the glory of an only Son coming from the
Father,

filled with enduring love.
John testified to him by proclaiming: "This is he of
whom I said, 'The one who comes after me ranks
ahead of me, for he was before me.'"

> Of his fullness
> we have all had a share—
> love following upon love.

For while the law was a gift through Moses, this
enduring love came through Jesus Christ. No one
has ever seen God. It is God the only Son, ever at
the Father's side, who has revealed him.—This is the
gospel of the Lord. ℟. **Praise to you, Lord Jesus
Christ.** ➜ No. 15, p. 623

PRAYER OVER THE GIFTS

Father of peace,
accept our devotion and sincerity,
and by our sharing in this mystery
draw us closer to each other and to you.
We ask this in the name of Jesus the Lord.
℟. **Amen.** ➜ No. 21, p. 626 (Pref. P 3-5)

*When Eucharistic Prayer I is used, the special Christ-
mas form of* In union with the whole Church *is said.*

COMMUNION ANT. 1 Jn 4, 9

**God's love for us was revealed when he sent his only
Son into the world, so that we could have life through
him.** ⋎

PRAYER AFTER COMMUNION

Lord,
may this sacrament be our strength.
Teach us to value all the good you give us
and help us to strive for eternal life.
Grant this through Christ our Lord.
℟. **Amen.** ➜ No. 32, p. 650

ANTIPHONS AND PRAYERS FOR WEEKDAYS FROM JANUARY 2 TO EPIPHANY

MONDAY BEFORE EPIPHANY

After Epiphany, see p. 133.

The days between the Solemnity of Mary the Mother of God and the Epiphany are devoted to proclaiming the good news of the identity and work of the One who was born at Bethlehem. He is the Word made flesh, and we have known his glory. Christmas is a joyous time for us because the Son of Mary is the Son of God, the Messiah.

ENTRANCE ANT.

A holy day has dawned upon us. Come, you nations, and adore the Lord. Today a great light has come upon the earth.
➤ No. 2, p. 614

OPENING PRAYER

Lord,
keep us true in the faith,
proclaiming that Christ your Son,
who is one with you in eternal glory,
became man and was born of a virgin mother.
Free us from all evil
and lead us to the joy of eternal life.
We ask this through our Lord Jesus Christ, your Son,
who lives and reigns with you and the Holy Spirit,
one God, for ever and ever. ℟. **Amen.** ℣

READINGS AND INTERVENIENT CHANTS

The *weekday* readings and intervenient chants corresponding to the day of the month, pp. 119-132.

PRAYER OVER THE GIFTS

Lord,
receive our gifts in this wonderful exchange:
from all you have given us
we bring you these gifts,
and in return, you give you yourself.
We ask this through Christ our Lord.
℟. **Amen.**
➤ No. 21, p. 626 (P 3-5)

COMMUNION ANT. Jn 1, 14

We have seen his glory, the glory of the Father's only Son, full of grace and truth. ℣

PRAYER AFTER COMMUNION

Father of love and mercy,
grant that our gifts may always be founded
on the power of this holy mystery.
We ask this in the name of Jesus the Lord.
℟. **Amen.** ➔ No. 32, p. 650

TUESDAY BEFORE EPIPHANY

(After Epiphany, see p. 136)

The joy of Christmas must also provide room for penance for our sins. Jesus showed his love by coming to live among us and to offer himself for us, even while we were sinners. The spirit of holiness is given to those who welcome the One whom the Father has given.

ENTRANCE ANT. Ps 118, 26-27

Blessed is he who comes in the name of the Lord; the Lord God shines upon us. ➔ No. 2, p. 614

OPENING PRAYER

God our Father,
when your Son was born of the Virgin Mary
he became like us in all things but sin.
May we who have been reborn in him
be free from our sinful ways.
We ask this through our Lord Jesus Christ, your Son,
who lives and reigns with you and the Holy Spirit,
one God, for ever and ever. ℟ **Amen.** ℣

READINGS AND INTERVENIENT CHANTS

The *weekday* readings and intervenient chants corresponding to the day of the month, pp. 119-132.

PRAYER OVER THE GIFTS

Father,
in your mercy accept our gifts.

By sharing in this eucharist
may we come to live more fully the love we profess.
Grant this through Christ our Lord.

➔ No. 21, p. 626 (Pref. P 3-5)

COMMUNION ANT.   Eph 2, 4; Rom 8, 3

**God loved us so much that he sent his own Son in
the likeness of sinful flesh.** ∀

PRAYER AFTER COMMUNION

God our Father,
in this eucharist you touch our lives.
Keep your love alive in our hearts
that we may become worthy of you.
We ask this through Christ our Lord.
℞. **Amen.**
➔ No. 32, p. 650

_____

WEDNESDAY BEFORE EPIPHANY
(After Epiphany, see p. 139)

In the newly revised Missal, God's message in the readings becomes
our thought in the prayers. We renew our choice to be loyal to God,
rather than to follow evil. Jesus is our light and the source of all our
good. We ask the grace to follow him.

ENTRANCE ANT.   Is 9, 6

**The people who walked in darkness have seen a great
light; on those who lived in the shadow of death,
light has shone.**
➔ No. 2, p. 614

OPENING PRAYER

All-powerful Father,
you sent your Son Jesus Christ
to bring the new light of salvation to the world.
May he enlighten us with his radiance,
who lives and reigns with you and the Holy Spirit,
one God, for ever and ever. ℞. **Amen.** ∀

READINGS AND INTERVENIENT CHANTS

The *weekday* readings and intervenient chants corresponding to the day of the month, pp. 119-132.

PRAYER OVER THE GIFTS

Father of peace,
accept our devotion and sincerity,
and by our sharing in this mystery
draw us closer to each other and to you.
We ask this in the name of Jesus the Lord.
℟. **Amen.**   ➔ No. 21, p. 626 (Pref. P 3-5)

COMMUNION ANT.   1 Jn 1, 2

The eternal life which was with the Father has been revealed to us. ℣

PRAYER AFTER COMMUNION

Lord,
may this sacrament be our strength.
Teach us to value all the good you give us
and help us to strive for eternal life.
Grant this through Christ our Lord.
℟. **Amen.** _____ ➔ No. 32, p. 650

THURSDAY BEFORE EPIPHANY

(After Epiphany, see p. 143)

By the birth of Jesus, heaven came to earth, healing came to sin, and love broke through the darkness of loneliness and separation. Our Eucharist today is our gift of thanksgiving for God's gifts by which everything in life gains a new joy.

ENTRANCE ANT.   See Jn 1, 1

In the beginning, before all ages, the Word was God; that Word was born a man to save the world.
➔ No. 2, p. 614

OPENING PRAYER

Father,
you make known the salvation of mankind
at the birth of your Son.
Make us strong in faith
and bring us to the glory you promise.
We ask this through our Lord Jesus Christ, your Son,
who lives and reigns with you and the Holy Spirit,
one God, for ever and ever. ℟. **Amen.** ℣

READINGS AND INTERVENIENT CHANTS

The *weekday* readings and intervenient chants corresponding to the day of the month, pp. 119-132.

PRAYER OVER THE GIFTS

Lord,
receive our gifts in this wonderful exchange:
from all you have given us
we bring you these gifts,
and in return, you give us yourself.
We ask this through Christ our Lord.

➤ No. 21, p. 626 (Pref. P 3-5)

COMMUNION ANT.   Jn 3, 16

God loved the world so much, he gave his only Son, that all who believe in him might not perish, but might have eternal life. ℣

PRAYER AFTER COMMUNION

Father of love and mercy,
grant that our lives may always be founded
on the power of this holy mystery.
We ask this in the name of Jesus the Lord.
℞. **Amen.**
➤ No. 32, p. 650

FRIDAY BEFORE EPIPHANY
(After Epiphany, see p. 146)

Jesus, the child of Bethlehem, the Messiah, the Suffering Servant, the Risen Lord, pours out upon us the gifts of life, especially through the sacraments. Today's readings and prayers help us to be aware of how much the Son of God is with us and in us.

ENTRANCE ANT.   Ps 112, 4

The Lord is a light in darkness to the upright; he is gracious, merciful, and just.   ➤ No. 2, p. 614

OPENING PRAYER

Lord,
fill our hearts with your light.
May we always acknowledge Christ as our Savior

and be more faithful to his gospel,
for he lives and reigns with you and the Holy Spirit,
one God, for ever and ever.
℞. **Amen.** ℣

READINGS AND INTERVENIENT CHANTS

The *weekday* readings and intervenient chants corresponding to the day of the month, pp. 119-132.

PRAYER OVER THE GIFTS

Father,
in your mercy accept our gifts.
By sharing in this eucharist
may we come to live more fully the love we profess.
Grant this through Christ our Lord.
℞. **Amen.** ➤ No. 21, p. 626 (Pref. P 3-5)

COMMUNION ANT. 1 Jn 4, 9

**God's love for us was revealed when he sent his only
Son into the world, so that we could have life through
him.** ℣

PRAYER AFTER COMMUNION

God our Father,
in this eucharist you touch our lives.
Keep your love alive in our hearts
that we may become worthy of you.
We ask this through Christ our Lord.
℞. **Amen.** ➤ No. 32, p. 650

SATURDAY BEFORE EPIPHANY

(After Epiphany, see p. 149)

The Son of God came so that we might become the sons and daughters of God. The great danger to this present and future life is sin. As Jesus changed the water into wine at Cana, so he can change our minds and hearts by his grace. This is our prayer today.

ENTRANCE SONG Gal 4, 4-5

**God sent his own Son, born of a woman, so that we
could be adopted as his sons.** ➤ No. 2, p. 614

OPENING PRAYER

All-powerful and ever-living God,
you give us a new vision of your glory
in the coming of Christ your Son.
He was born of the Virgin Mary
and came to share our life.
May we come to share his eternal life
in the glory of your kingdom,
where he lives and reigns with you and the Holy
    Spirit,
one God, for ever and ever. ℟. **Amen.** ▾
℟. **Amen.** ▾

READINGS AND INTERVENIENT CHANTS

The *weekday* readings and intervenient chants corresponding to the day of the month, pp. 119-132.

PRAYER OVER THE GIFTS

Father of peace,
accept our devotion and sincerity,
and by our sharing in this mystery
draw us closer to each other and to you.
We ask this in the name of Jesus the Lord.
℟. **Amen.**   → No. 21, p. 626 (Pref. P 3-5)

COMMUNION ANT.   Jn 1, 16

From his riches we have all received, grace for grace.

PRAYER AFTER COMMUNION

Lord,
may this sacrament be our strength.
Teach us to value all the good you give us
and help us to strive for eternal life.
We ask this in the name of Jesus the Lord.
℟. **Amen.**   → No. 32, p. 650

READINGS AND INTERVENIENT CHANTS FOR WEEKDAYS FROM JANUARY 2 TO EPIPHANY

JANUARY 2

READING I   1 Jn 2, 22-28

"Christ" here has its full sense as the preferred New Testament designation of our Lord whose words and deeds have proclaimed him the divine Savior of mankind. It is only through the Son that the Father has completely revealed himself.

A reading from the first letter of John

Who is the liar?
He who denies that Jesus is the Christ.
He is the antichrist,
    denying the Father and the Son.
Anyone who denies the Son
has no claim on the Father,
but he who acknowledges the Son
can claim the Father as well.
As for you,
let what you heard from the beginning
remain in your hearts.
If what you heard from the beginning
does remain in your hearts,
then you in turn will remain in the Son and in
    the Father.
He himself made us a promise
and the promise is no less than this:
eternal life.
I have written you these things
about those who try to deceive you.
As for you,
the anointing you received from him
remains in your hearts.
This means you have no need
for anyone to teach you.
Rather, as his anointing teaches you about all
    things

and is true—free from any lie—
remain in him
as that anointing taught you.
Remain in him now, little ones,
so that when he reveals himself,
we may be fully confident
and not retreat in shame at his coming.
This is the Word of the Lord. ℟. **Thanks be to God.** ⱽ

Responsorial Psalm   Ps 98, 1. 2-3. 3-4
℟. (3) **All the ends of the earth have seen the saving power of God.**

Sing to the Lord a new song,
　for he has done wondrous deeds;
His right hand has won victory for him,
　his holy arm. — ℟

The Lord has made his salvation known:
　in the sight of the nations he has revealed his justice.
He has remembered his kindness and his faithfulness
　toward the house of Israel. — ℟

All the ends of the earth have seen
　the salvation by our God.
Sing joyfully to the Lord, all you lands;
　break into song; sing praise. ℟ ⱽ

GOSPEL   Jn 1, 19-28
Alleluia (Heb 1, 1-2)
℟. **Alleluia.** In the past God spoke to our fathers
　　through the prophets;
now he speaks to us through his Son. ℟. **Alleluia.**

The question, "Who are you?" is asked of John the Baptizer. As a prophet, he answers not by promoting himself but by announcing the presence of the Messiah whose servant and herald John is.

℣. The Lord be with you. ℟. **And also with you.**
✠ A reading from the holy gospel according to John
℟. **Glory to you, Lord.**

The testimony John gave when the Jews sent priests
and Levites from Jerusalem to ask "Who are you?"
was the absolute statement, "I am not the Messiah."
They questioned him further, "Who, then? Elijah?"
"I am not Elijah," he answered. "Are you the Prophet?" "No," he replied.

Finally they said to him: "Tell us who you are, so
that we can give some answer to those who sent us.
What do you have to say for yourself?" He said,
quoting the prophet Isaiah, "I am

'a voice in the desert, crying out:
Make straight the way of the Lord!' "

Those whom the Pharisees had sent proceeded to
question him further: "If you are not the Messiah,
nor Elijah, nor the Prophet, why do you baptize?"
John answered them: "I baptize with water. There
is one among you whom you do not recognize—the
one who is to come after me—the strap of whose
sandal I am not worthy to unfasten."

This happened in Bethany, across the Jordan,
where John was baptizing.—This is the gospel of the
Lord. ℟. **Praise to you, Lord Jesus Christ.**

——————————— ➤ No. 15, p. 623

JANUARY 3

READING I   1 Jn 2, 29—3, 6

In the truest and most absolute sense, God's gift of love is the gift
of his only Son as Savior of the world. It is this gift that makes it
possible for us to be called children of God. The apostle John describes
our likeness to God himself: holiness, love, adoption, purity, sin-
lessness.

A reading from the first letter of John

If you consider the holiness that is God's,
you can be sure that everyone who acts in holiness
has been begotten by him.
See what love the Father has bestowed on us
in letting us be called children of God!
Yet that is what we are.
The reason the world does not recognize us
is that it never recognized the Son.

Dearly beloved,
we are God's children now;
what we shall later be has not yet come to light.
We know that when it comes to light
we shall be like him,
for we shall see him as he is.
Everyone who has this hope based on him
keeps himself pure, as he is pure.
Everyone who sins acts lawlessly,
for sin is lawlessness.
You know well that the reason he revealed himself
was to take away sins;
in him there is nothing sinful.
The man who remains in him does not sin.
The man who sins has not seen him or known him.

This is the Word of the Lord. ℟. **Thanks be to God.** ℣

Responsorial Psalm   Ps 98, 1. 3-4. 5-6
℟. (3) **All the ends of the earth have seen the
saving power of God.**

Sing to the Lord a new song,
   for he has done wondrous deeds;
His right hand has won victory for him,
   his holy arm. — ℟

All the ends of the earth have seen
   the salvation by our God.
Sing joyfully to the Lord, all you lands;
   break into song; sing praise. — ℟

Sing praise to the Lord with the harp,
   with the harp and melodious song.
With trumpets and the sound of the horn
   sing joyfully before the King, the Lord. — ℟ ℣

GOSPEL   Jn 1, 29-34
Alleluia (Jn 1, 14. 12)

℟. **Alleluia.** The Word of God became a man and
   lived among us.

He enabled those who accepted him
  to become the children of God. ℟. **Alleluia.**

John the Baptizer brings together the prophecies of the Messiah.
Jesus is the lamb offered in sacrifice which accomplishes forgiveness.
God's Spirit is upon him, and he gives the Spirit to all who will
accept him.

℣. The Lord be with you. ℟. **And also with you.**
✠ A reading from the holy gospel according to John
℟. **Glory to you, Lord.**

When John caught sight of Jesus coming toward him,
he exclaimed:
  "Look there! The Lamb of God
  who takes away the sin of the world!
It is he of whom I said:
  'After me is to come a man
  who ranks ahead of me,
  because he was before me.'
I confess I did not recognize him, though the very
reason I came baptizing with water was that he
might be revealed to Israel."
  John gave this testimony also:
  "I saw the Spirit descend
  like a dove from the sky,
  and it came to rest on him.
  But I did not recognize him. The one who sent
me to baptize with water told me, 'When you see the
Spirit descend and rest on someone, it is he who is
to baptize with the Holy Spirit.' Now I have seen
for myself and have testified, 'This is God's chosen
One.' "—This is the gospel of the Lord. ℟. **Praise to
you, Lord Jesus Christ.**   → No. 15, p. 623

JANUARY 4

READING I   1 Jn 3, 7-10

God's word presents the choice between two allegiances, either to
God or to the devil whose kingdom is already being overcome by
Jesus. Virtue and sin are the two opposite characteristics for dis-
tinguishing children of God from the children of the devil.

A reading from the first letter of John

Little ones,
let no one deceive you;
the man who acts in holiness is holy indeed,
even as the Son is holy.
The man who sins belongs to the devil,
because the devil is a sinner from the beginning.
It was to destroy the devil's works
that the Son of God revealed himself.
No one begotten of God acts sinfully
because he remains of God's stock;
he cannot sin
because he is begotten of God.
That is the way to see who are God's children,
and who are the devil's.
No one whose actions are unholy belongs to God,
nor anyone who fails to love his brother.
This is the Word of the Lord. ℟. **Thanks be to God.** ❡

Responsorial Psalm   Ps 98, 1. 7-8. 9

℟. (3) **All the ends of the earth have seen the saving
    power of God.**

Sing to the Lord a new song,
    for he has done wondrous deeds;
His right hand has won victory for him,
    his holy arm. — ℟

Let the sea and what fills it resound,
    the world and those who dwell in it;
Let the rivers clap their hands,
    the mountains shout with them for joy before
    the Lord. — ℟

The Lord comes;
    he comes to rule the earth;
He will rule the world with justice
    and the peoples with equity. — ℟ ❡

GOSPEL   Jn 1, 35-42

Alleluia (Jn 1, 14. 12)

℟. **Alleluia.** The Word of God became a man and
   lived among us.
He enabled those who accepted him
to become the children of God. ℟. **Alleluia.**

Jesus receives his first disciples from John the Baptizer. Having
begun with curiosity, they quickly become convinced that **he is the
Anointed One of God.** The giving of a new name to Peter signifies the
taking on of a new way of life.

℣. The Lord be with you. ℟. **And also with you.**
✠ A reading from the holy gospel according to John
℟. **Glory to you, Lord.**

John was at Bethany across the Jordan with two of
his disciples. As he watched Jesus walk by he said:
"Look! There is the Lamb of God!" The two disciples
heard what he said, and followed Jesus. When Jesus
turned around and noticed them following him, he
asked them, "What are you looking for?" They said
to him, "Rabbi (which means Teacher), where do you
stay?" "Come and see," he answered. So they went
to see where he was lodged, and stayed with him
that day. (It was about four in the afternoon.)
    One of the two who had followed him after hear-
ing John was Simon Peter's brother Andrew. The
first thing he did was seek out his brother Simon
and tell him, "We have found the Messiah" (which
means the Anointed)! He brought him to Jesus, who
looked at him and said: "You are Simon, son of John;
your name shall be Cephas (which is rendered
Peter)."—This is the gospel of the Lord. ℟. **Praise to you,
Lord Jesus Christ.**   → No. 15, p. 623

JANUARY 5

READING I   1 Jn 3, 11-21

Charity is the way to life because hatred and selfishness mean
slavery to ourselves and to the goods of the world. God's own way is
love because he gives life and care to all. To love is to live in God.

A reading from the first letter of John

This, remember, is the message
you heard from the beginning:
we should love one another.
We should not follow the example of Cain
who belonged to the evil one
and killed his brother.
Why did he kill him?
Because his own deeds were wicked
while his brother's were just.
No need, then, brothers, to be surprised
if the world hates you.
That we have passed from death to life we know
because we love the brothers.
The man who does not love is among the living
    dead.
Anyone who hates his brother is a murderer,
and you know that eternal life
abides in no murderer's heart.
The way we came to understand love
was that he laid down his life for us;
we too must lay down our lives for our brothers.
I ask you, how can God's love survive in a man
who has enough of this world's goods
yet closes his heart to his brother
when he sees him in need?
Little children,
let us love in deed and in truth
and not merely talk about it.
This is our way of knowing we are committed to
    the truth
and are at peace before him
no matter what our consciences may charge us
    with;
for God is greater than our hearts
and all is known to him.
Beloved,
if our consciences have nothing to charge us with,

we can be sure that God is with us.
This is the Word of the Lord. ℟. **Thanks be to God.** ✙

Responsorial Psalm   Ps 100, 1-2. 3. 4. 5

℟. (1) **Let all the earth cry out to God with joy.**

Sing joyfully to the Lord, all you lands;
   serve the Lord with gladness;
   come before him with joyful song. — ℟

Know that the Lord is God;
   he made us, his we are;
   his people, the flock he tends. — ℟

Enter his gates with thanksgiving,
   his courts with praise;
Give thanks to him; bless his name. — ℟

The Lord is good:
   the Lord, whose kindness endures forever,
   and his faithfulness, to all generations. — ℟. ✙

GOSPEL   Jn 1, 43-51

Alleluia

℟. **Alleluia.** A holy day has dawned upon us.
Today a great light has come upon the earth.
Come you nations and adore the Lord. ℟. **Alleluia.**

Seemingly, Jesus knows of the thoughts and actions of Nathanael
without being present, and Nathanael responds to his call: "Follow
me." The opening of the sky is foretold in Jacob's vision in Genesis.
Jesus is the ladder, or link, between heaven and earth.

℣. The Lord be with you. ℟. **And also with you.**
✠ A reading from the holy gospel according to John
℟. **Glory to you, Lord.**

Jesus wanted to set out for Galilee, but first he came
upon Philip. "Follow me," Jesus said to him. Now
Philip was from Bethsaida, the same town as Andrew
and Peter. Philip sought out Nathanael and told him,
"We have found the one Moses spoke of in the law—
the prophets too— Jesus, son of Joseph, from Nazareth." Nathanael's response to that was, "Can any-

thing good come from Nazareth?" and Philip replied, "Come, see for yourself." When Jesus saw Nathanael coming toward him, he remarked: "This man is a real Israelite. There is no guile in him." "How do you know me?" Nathanael asked him. "Before Philip called you," Jesus answered, "I saw you under the fig tree." "Rabbi," said Nathanael, "you are the Son of God; you are the king of Israel." Jesus responded: "Do you believe just because I told you I saw you under the fig tree? You will see much greater things than that."

He went on to tell them, "I solemnly assure you, you shall see the sky opened and the angels of God ascending and descending on the Son of Man."— This is the gospel of the Lord. ℟. **Praise to you, Lord Jesus Christ.**

➤ No. 15, p. 623

JANUARY 6

READING I   1 Jn 5, 5-13

The risen Christ, who is not seen by us, is known to be present and active through the visible elements of the sacraments. The water of Baptism, the presence of the Spirit through Confirmation, and our sharing in the blood of Christ in the Eucharist are signs that God is giving us eternal life.

A reading from the first letter of John

Who, then, is conqueror of the world?
The one who believes that Jesus is the Son of God.
Jesus Christ it is who came through water and
    blood—
    not in water only,
    but in water and in blood.
It is the Spirit who testifies to this,
    and the Spirit is truth.
Thus there are three that testify,
    the Spirit and the water and the blood—
    and these three are of one accord.
Do we not accept human testimony?

The testimony of God is much greater:
   it is the testimony God has given
   on his own Son's behalf.
Whoever believes in the Son of God
   posseses that testimony with his heart.
Whoever does not believe God
   has made God a liar
   by refusing to believe in the testimony
   he has given on his own Son's behalf.
The testimony is this:
   God gave us eternal life,
   and this life is in his Son.
Whoever possesses the Son
   possesses life:
   whoever does not possess the Son of God
   does not possess life.

I have written this to you to make you realize
that you possess eternal life—you who believe in the
name of the Son of God.—This is the Word of the
Lord. ℟. **Thanks be to God.** ℣

Responsorial Psalm   Ps 147, 12-13. 14-15. 19-20
℟. (12) **Praise the Lord, Jerusalem.**

Glorify the Lord, O Jerusalem;
   praise your God, O Zion.
For he has strengthened the bars of your gates;
   he has blessed your children within you. — ℟

He has granted peace in your borders;
   with the best of wheat he fills you.
He sends forth his command to the earth;
   swiftly runs his word! — ℟

He has proclaimed his word to Jacob,
   his statutes and his ordinances to Israel.
He has not done thus for any other nation;
   his ordinances he has not made known to them.
      Alleluia. — ℟ ℣

℟. Or: **Alleluia.** ℣

GOSPEL   Mk 1, 7-11

Alleluia (See Mk 9, 6)

℟. **Alleluia.** The heavens were opened and the Father's voice was heard:
this is my beloved Son; hear him. ℟. **Alleluia.**

It is only when he baptizes Jesus that the Baptizer recognizes him as the Messiah. This recognition by John is the result of a divine intimation. The Spirit descends upon our Lord from heaven like a dove and rests upon him, and this promised heavenly sign reveals him. It is only then, and not before, that John is conscious of the wondrous truth.

℣. The Lord be with you. ℟. **And also with you.**
✠ A reading from the holy gospel according to Mark
℟. **Glory to you, Lord.**

The theme of John's preaching was: "One more powerful than I is to come after me. I am not fit to stoop and untie his sandal straps. I have baptized you in water; he will baptize you in the Holy Spirit."

During that time, Jesus came from Nazareth in Galilee and was baptized in the Jordan by John. Immediately on coming up out of the water he saw the sky rent in two and the Spirit descending on him like a dove. Then a voice came from the heavens: "You are my beloved Son. On you my favor rests."—This is the gospel of the Lord. ℟. **Praise to you, Lord Jesus Christ.**

➔ No. 15, p. 623

JANUARY 7

READING I   1 Jn 5, 14-21

God answers all proper prayers made in faith and with willingness for his will to be done. If our brothers commit sins, we pray for them in brotherly love. Fidelity to God's will is the necessary condition of the efficacy of prayer.

A reading from the first letter of John

We have this confidence in God: that he hears us whenever we ask for anything according to his will. And since we know that he hears us whenever we ask, we know that what we have asked him for is ours. Anyone who sees his brother sinning, if the sin is not deadly, should petition God and thus life will be given to the sinner. This is only for those whose sin is not deadly. There is such a thing as deadly sin; I do not say that one should pray about that. True, all wrongdoing is sin, but not all sin is deadly.

We know that no one begotten of God commits sin; rather, God protects the one begotten by him, and so the evil one cannot touch him. We know that we belong to God, while the whole world is under the evil one. We know, too, that the Son of God has come and has given us discernment to recognize the One who is true. And we are in the One who is true, for we are in his Son Jesus Christ. He is the true God and eternal life.

My little children, be on your guard against idols. —This is the Word of the Lord. ℟. **Thanks be to God.** ⍩

Responsorial Psalm   Ps 149, 1-2. 3-4. 5. 6. 9

℟. (4) **The Lord takes delight in his people.**

Sing to the Lord a new song
 of praise in the assembly of the faithful.
Let Israel be glad in their maker,
 let the children of Zion rejoice in their king. — ℟

Let them praise his name in the festive dance,
 let them sing praise to him with timbrel and harp.
For the Lord loves his people,
 and he adorns the lowly with victory. — ℟

Let the faithful exult in glory;
 let them sing for joy upon their couches;
 let the high praises of God be in their throats.
This is the glory of all his faithful. Alleluia. — ℟ ⍩

℟. Or: **Alleluia.** ⍩

GOSPEL   Jn 2, 1-12

Alleluia (Lk 7, 16)

℟. **Alleluia.** A great prophet has risen among us;
God has visited his people. ℟. **Alleluia.**

Jesus' first miracle, worked at the wedding party, shows his blessing upon married love and upon people having a good time together. It is a fitting occasion for his presence and for the act of almighty power which follows, for he is the bridegroom who has come into the world to take his spouse, the Church.

℣. The Lord be with you. ℟. **And also with you.**
✠ A reading from the holy gospel according to John
℟. **Glory to you, Lord.**

There was a wedding at Cana in Galilee, and the mother of Jesus was there. Jesus and his disciples had likewise been invited to the celebration. At a certain point the wine ran out, and Jesus' mother told him, "They have no more wine." Jesus replied, "Woman, how does this concern of yours involve me? My hour has not yet come." His mother instructed those waiting on table, "Do whatever he tells you." As prescribed for Jewish ceremonial washings, there were at hand six stone water jars, each one holding fifteen to twenty-five gallons. "Fill those jars with water," Jesus ordered, at which they filled them to the brim. "Now," he said, "draw some out and take it to the waiter in charge." They did as he instructed them. The waiter in charge tasted the water made wine, without knowing where it had come from; only the waiters knew, since they had drawn the water. Then the waiter in charge called the groom over and remarked to him: "People usually serve the choice wine first; then when the guests have been drinking awhile, a lesser vintage. What you have done is keep the choice wine until now." Jesus performed this first of his signs at Cana in Galilee. Thus did he reveal his glory, and his disciples believed in him.

After this he went down to Capernaum, along with his mother and brothers [and his disciples] but they stayed there only a few days. —This is the gospel of the Lord. ℟. **Praise to you, Lord Jesus Christ**

➤No. 15, p. 623

MONDAY AFTER EPIPHANY

God is willing and eager to give to us and to the world the gifts of the Spirit which are necessary for faith, unity, and holiness. As long as our minds and desires are in agreement with the Father's, he will hear us and keep us true to himself. Divine healing comes from such loyalty.

ENTRANCE ANT.

A holy day has dawned upon us. Come, you nations, and adore the Lord. Today a great light has come upon the earth.
➤ No. 2, p. 614

OPENING PRAYER

Lord,
let the light of your glory shine within us,
and lead us through the darkness of this world
to the radiant joy of our eternal home.
We ask this through our Lord Jesus Christ, your Son,
who lives and reigns with you and the Holy Spirit,
one God, for ever and ever. ℟. **Amen.** ⋎

READING I
1 Jn 3, 22-4, 6

A mysterious communion of life unites us with the Father and with one another. This is the work of the Spirit who enables us to hear, recognize, and accept the voice of Jesus and thus to remain in God.

A reading from the first letter of John

Whatever we ask we shall receive at God's hands.
Why? Because we are keeping his commandments
and doing what is pleasing in his sight.
His commandment is this:
we are to believe in the name of his Son, Jesus
    Christ,
and are to love one another as he commanded us.
Those who keep his commandments remain in him
and he in them.

And this is how we know that he remains in us:
from the Spirit that he gave us.
Beloved, do not trust every spirit,
but put the spirits to a test
to see if they belong to God,
because many false prophets have appeared in the
    world.
This is how you can recognize God's spirit:
every spirit that acknowledges Jesus Christ come
    in the flesh
belongs to God,
while every spirit that fails to acknowledge him
does not belong to God.
Such is the spirit of the antichrist
which, as you have heard, is to come;
in fact, it is in the world already.
You are of God, you little ones,
and thus you have conquered the false prophets.
For there is in you One greater
than there is in the world.
Those others belong to the world;
that is why theirs is the language of the world
and why the world listens to them.
We belong to God
and anyone who has knowledge of God gives us
    a hearing,
while anyone who is not of God refuses to hear us.
Thus do we distinguish the Spirit of truth
from the spirit of deception.
This is the Word of the Lord. ℟. **Thanks be to God.** ℣

Responsional Psalm   Ps 2, 7-8. 10-11

℟. (8) **I will give you all the nations for your heri-
tage.**
The Lord said to me, "You are my son;
    this day I have begotten you.
Ask of me and I will give you
    the nations for an inheritance
    and the ends of the earth for your possession." — ℟

And now, O kings, give heed;
    take warning, you rulers of the earth.
Serve the Lord with fear, and rejoice before him;
    with trembling, pay homage to him. — ℟ ✟

GOSPEL   Mt 4, 12-17. 23-25

Alleluia (Mt 4, 23)

℟. **Alleluia.** Jesus preached the Good News of the
        Kingdom
and healed all who were sick. ℟. **Alleluia.**

Jesus returns to Galilee, his own country, to proclaim the Reign.
His message is the Good News that the kingdom of heaven is at hand.
His proclamation is accompanied by healing which causes his fame
to spread, attracting followers from Jewish areas and from the lands
beyond.

℣. The Lord be with you. ℟. **And also with you.**
✠ A reading from the holy gospel according to Matthew. ℟. **Glory to you, Lord.**

When Jesus heard that John had been arrested, he
withdrew to Galilee. He left Nazareth and went
down to live in Capernaum by the sea near the territory of Zebulun and Naphtali, to fulfill what had
been said through Isaiah the prophet:

    "Land of Zebulun, land of Naphtali
    along the sea beyond the Jordan,
    heathen Galilee:
    a people living in darkness
    has seen a great light.
    On those who inhabit a land overshadowed by
        death,
    light has risen."

From that time on Jesus began to proclaim this
theme: "Reform your lives! The kingdom of heaven
it at hand."

    Jesus toured all of Galilee. He taught in their syna-
gogues, proclaimed the good news of the kingdom,
and cured the people of every disease and illness. As
a consequence of this, his reputation traveled the

length of Syria. They carried to him all those afflicted
with various diseases and racked with pain: the possessed, the lunatics, the paralyzed. He cured them
all. The great crowds that followed him came from
Galilee, the Ten Cities, Jerusalem and Judea, and
from across the Jordan.—This is the gospel of the
Lord. ℟. **Praise to you, Lord Jesus Christ.**

➜ No. 15, p. 623

PRAYER OVER THE GIFTS
Lord,
receive our gifts in this wonderful exchange:
from all you have given us
we bring you these gifts,
and in return, you give us yourself.
We ask this through Christ our Lord.
℟. **Amen.**   ➜ No. 21, p. 626 (Pref. P 6)

COMMUNION ANT.   Jn 1, 14
**We have seen his glory, the glory of the Father's
only Son, full of grace and truth.** ▼

PRAYER AFTER COMMUNION
Father of love and mercy,
grant that our lives may always be founded
on the power of this holy mystery.
We ask this in the name of Jesus the Lord.
℟. **Amen.**   ➜ No. 32, p. 650

TUESDAY AFTER EPIPHANY

Today we pray that we may become like God. This is a daring request,
but it is precisely the life to which we are invited. As we share in
this Eucharist, we receive Jesus who remains present within us in
order to mold us more and more into images of himself, with our
cooperation.

ENTRANCE ANT.   Ps 118, 26-27
**Blessed is he who comes in the name of the Lord;
the Lord God shines upon us.**   ➜ No. 2, p. 614

OPENING PRAYER

Father,
your Son became like us
when he revealed himself in our nature:
help us to become more like him,
who lives and reigns with you and the Holy Spirit,
one God, for ever and ever. ℟. **Amen.** ✟

READING I
1 Jn 4, 7-10

God's love expresses so clearly the personality and character of God that John can say, "God is love." The motive of love is the origin of love in God; whoever loves thereby proves that he has his own origin in the same God with whom he has fellowship. He is born of God.

A reading from the first letter of John

Beloved,
let us love one another
because love is of God;
everyone who loves is begotten of God
and has knowledge of God.
The man without love has known nothing of God,
for God is love.
God's love was revealed in our midst in this way:
he sent his only Son to the world
that we might have life through him.
Love, then, consists in this:
not that we have loved God,
but that he has loved us
and has sent his Son as an offering for our sins.
This is the Word of the Lord. ℟. **Thanks be to God.** ✟

Responsorial Psalm
Ps 72, 1-2. 3-4. 7-8

℟. (11) **Lord, every nation on earth will adore you.**

O God, with your judgment endow the king,
and with your justice, the king's son;
He shall govern your people with justice
and your afflicted ones with judgment. — ℟

The mountains shall yield peace for the people,
and the hills justice.

He shall defend the afflicted among the people,
    save the children of the poor. — ℟

Justice shall flower in his days,
    and profound peace, till the moon be no more.

May he rule from sea to sea,
    and from the River to the ends of the earth. — ℟ ℣

GOSPEL   Mk 6, 34-44

Alleluia (Lk 4, 18-19)

℟. **Alleluia.** The Lord sent me to bring Good News
        to the poor,
and freedom to prisoners. ℟. **Alleluia.**

Jesus' love leads him to provide for all of the needs of those who
come to him. The multiplication of the bread and fish foreshadows
the greater gift, the giving of himself in the sacred meal of the
Eucharist.

℣. The Lord be with you. ℟. **And also with you.**

✠ A reading from the holy gospel according to Mark
℟. **Glory to you, Lord.**

Jesus saw a vast crowd. He pitied them, for they
were like sheep without a shepherd; and he began
to teach them at great length. It was now getting
late and his disciples came to him with a suggestion:
"This is a deserted place and it is already late. Why
do you not dismiss them so that they can go to the
crossroads and villages around here and buy themselves something to eat?" "You give them something
to eat," Jesus replied. At that they said, "Are we to
go and spend two hundred days' wages for bread to
feed them?" "How many loaves have you?" Jesus
asked. "Go and see." When they learned the number
they answered, "Five, and two fish." He told them
to make the people sit down on the green grass in
groups or parties. The people took their places in
hundreds and fifties, neatly arranged like flower
beds. Then, taking the five loaves and two fish,
Jesus raised his eyes to heaven, pronounced a bless-

ing, broke the loaves, and gave them to the disciples to distribute. He divided the two fish among all of them and they ate until they had their fill. They gathered up enough leftovers to fill twelve baskets, besides what remained of the fish. Those who had eaten the loaves numbered five thousand men.— This is the gospel of the Lord. ℟. **Praise to you, Lord Jesus Christ.**   ➤ No. 15, p. 623

PRAYER OVER THE GIFTS

Father,
in your mercy accept our gifts.
By sharing in this eucharist
may we come to live more fully the love we profess.
Grant this through Christ our Lord.
℟. **Amen.**   ➤ No. 21, p. 626 (Pref. P 6)

COMMUNION ANT.   Eph 2, 4; Rom 8, 3

God loved us so much that he sent his own Son in the likeness of sinful flesh. ℣

PRAYER AFTER COMMUNION

God our Father,
in this eucharist you touch our lives.
Keep your love alive in our hearts
that we may become worthy of you.
We ask this through Christ our Lord.
℟. **Amen.**   _____   ➤ No. 32, p. 650

WEDNESDAY AFTER EPIPHANY

Today's liturgy provides motives for confidence in Jesus as true God and as the Savior. The authors of the Scriptures preserved the knowledge of the life, words, and miracles of Jesus so that we might be drawn to share in their faith. The zeal and apostolic love of the first Christians reaches down to us.

ENTRANCE ANT.   Is 9, 2

The people who walked in darkness have seen a great light; on those who lived in the shadow of death, light has shone.   ➤ No. 2, p. 614

OPENING PRAYER

God, light of all nations,
give us the joy of lasting peace,
and fill us with your radiance
as you filled the hearts of our fathers.
We ask this through our Lord Jesus Christ, your Son,
who lives and reigns with you and the Holy Spirit,
one God, for ever and ever. ℟. **Amen.** ✠

READING I   1 Jn 4, 11-18

John assumes the reality of God, the Invisible, and all that the prophetic faith of the Old Testament has taught about his nature and
will. John's primary desire is to urge Christians to treat one another
as God treats them—to love one another without self-interest, to have
faith in God's fatherly love, and to look forward to the "end of the
world" with eagerness rather than with fear.

A reading from the first letter of John

Beloved,
    if God has loved us so,
    we must have the same love for one another.
    No one has ever seen God.
    Yet if we love one another
    God dwells in us,
    and his love is brought to perfection in us.
    The way we know we remain in him
    and he in us
    is that he has given us of his Spirit.
    We have seen for ourselves, and can testify,
    that the Father has sent the Son as savior of the
        world.
    When anyone acknowledges that Jesus is the Son
        of God,
    God dwells in him
    and he in God.
    We have come to know and to believe
    in the love God has for us.
    God is love,
    and he who abides in love

abides in God,
and God in him.
Our love is brought to perfection in this,
that we should have confidence on the day of
judgment;
for our relation to this world is just like his.
Love has no room for fear;
rather, perfect love casts out all fear.
And since fear has to do with punishment,
love is not yet perfect in one who is afraid.
This is the Word of the Lord. ℟. **Thanks be to God.** ℣

Responsorial Psalm   Ps 72, 1-2. 10. 12-13
℟. (11) **Lord, every nation on earth will adore you.**
O God, with your judgment endow the king,
   and with your justice, the king's son;
He shall govern your people with justice
   and your afflicted ones with judgment. — ℟

The kings of Tarshish and the Isles shall offer gifts;
   the kings of Arabia and Seba shall bring tribute. — ℟

For he shall rescue the poor man when he cries out,
   and the afflicted when he has no one to help him.
He shall have pity for the lowly and the poor;
   the lives of the poor he shall save. — ℟ ℣

GOSPEL   Mk 6, 45-52
Alleluia (See 1 Tm 3, 16)
℟. **Alleluia.** Glory to Christ who is proclaimed to the
   world;
glory from all who believe in him! ℟. **Alleluia.**

By feeding the large crowd through a miracle, Jesus showed that the
great signs of God's presence in the world had resumed. In the events
on the lake, he shows that he has power and control over all of
creation, even over the physical characteristics of water. The apostles
are thus prepared for the growth of their faith and understanding.

℣. The Lord be with you. ℟. **And also with you.**
✠ A reading from the holy gospel according to Mark
℟. **Glory to you, Lord.**

[After the five thousand men were satiated] Jesus insisted that his disciples get into the boat and precede him to the other side toward Bethsaida, while he dismissed the crowd. When he had taken leave of them, he went off to the mountain to pray. As evening drew on, the boat was far out on the lake while he was alone on the land. Then, seeing them tossed about as they tried to row with the wind against them, he came walking toward them on the water; the time was between three and six in the morning. He meant to pass them by. When they saw him walking on the lake, they thought it was a ghost and they began to cry out. They had all seen him and were terrified. He hastened to reassure them: "Get hold of yourselves! It is I. Do not be afraid!" He got into the boat with them and the wind died down. They were taken aback by these happenings, for they had not understood about the loaves. On the contrary, their minds were completely closed to the meaning of the events.—This is the gospel of the Lord. ℟. **Praise to you, Lord Jesus Christ.**

➤ No. 15, p. 623

PRAYER OVER THE GIFTS

Father of peace,
accept our devotion and sincerity,
and by our sharing in this mystery
draw us closer to each other and to you.
We ask this in the name of Jesus the Lord.
℟. **Amen.**   ➤ No. 21, p. 626 (Pref. P 6)

COMMUNION ANT.   1 Jn 1, 2

The eternal life which was with the Father has been revealed to us. ℣

PRAYER AFTER COMMUNION

Lord,
may this sacrament be our strength.
Teach us to value all the good you give us

and help us to strive for eternal life.
Grant this through Christ our Lord.
℟. **Amen.**   ➤ No. 32, p. 650

THURSDAY AFTER EPIPHANY

Today our Epiphany proclamation of faith continues. We wish to show Jesus to one another and to everyone in the world. His teachings and his Spirit truly bring glad tidings to the poor, a new life of liberty, and a new spiritual vision.

ENTRANCE ANT.   See Jn 1, 1

In the beginning, before all ages, the Word was God: that Word was born a man to save the world.

➤ No. 2, p. 614

OPENING PRAYER

God our Father,
through Christ your Son
the hope of eternal life dawned on our world.
Give to us the light of faith
that we may always acknowledge him as our
    Redeemer
and come to the glory of his kingdom,
where he lives and reigns with you and the Holy
    Spirit,
one God, for ever and ever. ℟. **Amen.** ⍌

READING I   1 Jn 4, 19-5, 4

John warns against self-deception in love. No one can pretend to love God who does not love his brother. Christ's command is new in its extension to all men without distinction. Christ's love is not only the model but also the motive and cause of Christian charity.

A reading from the first letter of John

Beloved,
we, for our part, love God,
because he first loved us.
If anyone says, "My love is fixed on God,"
yet hates his brother,
he is a liar.
One who has no love for the brother he has seen

cannot love the God he has not seen.
The commandment we have from him is this:
Whoever loves God must also love his brother.
Everyone who believes that Jesus is the Christ
has been begotten of God.
Now, everyone who loves the father
loves the child he has begotten.
We can be sure that we love God's children
when we love God
and do what he has commanded.
The love of God consists in this:
that we keep his commandments—
and his commandments are not burdensome.
Everyone begotten of God conquers the world,
and the power that has conquered the world
is this faith of ours.

This is the Word of the Lord. ℟. **Thanks be to God.** ℣

Responsorial Psalm   Ps 72, 1-2. 14-15. 17

℟. (11) **Lord, every nation on earth will adore you.**

O God, with your judgment endow the king,
    and with your justice, the king's son;
He shall govern your people with justice
    and your afflicted ones with judgment. — ℟

From fraud and violence he shall redeem the poor,
    and precious shall their blood be in his sight.
May they be prayed for continually;
    day by day shall they bless him. — ℟.

May his name be blessed forever;
    as long as the sun his name shall remain.
In him shall all the tribes of the earth be blessed;
    all the nations shall proclaim his happiness.— ℟ ℣

GOSPEL   Lk 4, 14-22

Alleluia (Lk 4, 18-19)

℟. **Alleluia.** The Lord sent me to bring good news
        to the poor,
and freedom to prisoners. ℟. **Alleluia.**

Luke shows our Lord in Galilee as a great prophet, possessing the power of the Spirit. The inhabitants of the city in which the first twenty-nine years of his life had been spent listen to his message, and they can learn from it that the time of salvation has begun and that the Savior is present.

℣. The Lord be with you. ℞. **And also with you.**
✠ A reading from the holy gospel according to Luke
℞. **Glory to you, Lord.**

Jesus returned in the power of the Spirit to Galilee, and his reputation spread throughout the region. He was teaching in their synagogues, and all were loud in his praise.

He came to Nazareth where he had been reared, and entering the synagogue on the sabbath as he was in the habit of doing, he stood up to do the reading. When the book of the prophet Isaiah was handed him, he unrolled the scroll and found the passage where it was written:

> "The spirit of the Lord is upon me;
>   therefore he has anointed me.
> He has sent me to bring glad tidings to the poor,
>   to proclaim liberty to captives,
> Recovery of sight to the blind
>   and release to prisoners,
> To announce a year of favor from the Lord."

Rolling up the scroll he gave it back to the assistant and sat down. All in the synagogue had their eyes fixed on him. Then he began by saying to them, "Today this Scripture passage is fulfilled in your hearing." All who were present spoke favorably of him; they marveled at the appealing discourse which came from his lips.—This is the gospel of the Lord.
℞. **Praise to you. Lord Jesus Christ.** ➤ No. 15, p. 623

PRAYER OVER THE GIFTS

Lord,
receive our gifts in this wonderful exchange:
from all you have given us
we bring you these gifts,

and in return, you give us yourself.
We ask this through Christ our Lord.
℟. **Amen.**   → No. 21, p. 626 (Pref P 6)

COMMUNION ANT.   Jn 3, 16

God loved the world so much, he gave his only Son, that all who believe in him might not perish, but might have eternal life. ↓

PRAYER AFTER COMMUNION

Father of love and mercy,
grant that our lives may always be founded
on the power of this holy mystery.
We ask this in the name of Jesus the Lord.
℟. **Amen.**   → No. 32, p. 650

FRIDAY AFTER EPIPHANY

The Epiphany presented the journey of the wise men who were led by the star. Jesus himself is our star who draws us to himself as the light that shines out in the darkness. As he healed the leper, so he takes us to himself to heal us of leprosy of the spirit.

ENTRANCE ANT.   Ps 112, 4

The Lord is a light in darkness to the upright; he is gracious, merciful, and just   → No. 2, p. 614

OPENING PRAYER

All-powerful Father,
you have made known the birth of the Savior
by the light of a star.
May he continue to guide us with his light,
for he lives and reigns with you and the Holy Spirit,
one God, for ever and ever. ℟. **Amen.** ↓

READING I   1 Jn 5, 5-13

The light of faith is nourished by the water of baptism, the indwelling of the Spirit, the body and blood of the eucharist, and the testimony of the Father through signs and miracles. Eternal life is in the Son, to be enjoyed only by those who possess him.

A reading from the first letter of John

Who, then, is conqueror of the world?
The one who believes that Jesus is the Son of God.
Jesus Christ it is who came through water and
    blood—
not in water only,
but in water and in blood.
It is the Spirit who testifies to this,
and the Spirit is truth.
Thus there are three that testify,
the Spirit and the water and the blood—
and these three are of one accord.
Do we not accept human testimony?
The testimony of God is much greater:
it is the testimony God has given
on his own Son's behalf.
Whoever believes in the Son of God
possesses that testimony within his heart.
Whoever does not believe God
has made God a liar
by refusing to believe in the testimony
he has given on his own Son's behalf.
The testimony is this:
God gave us eternal life,
and this life is in his Son.
Whoever possesses the Son
possesses life;
whoever does not possess the Son of God
does not possess life.

I have written this to you to make you realize
that you possess eternal life—you who believe in the
name of the Son of God.—This is the Word of the
Lord. ℟. **Thanks be to God.** ℣

Responsorial Psalm   Ps 147, 12-13. 14-15. 19-20

℟. (12) **Praise the Lord, Jerusalem.**

Glorify the Lord, O Jerusalem;
    praise your God, O Zion.

For he has strengthened the bars of your gates;
    he has blessed your children within you. — ℟

He has granted peace in your borders;
    with the best of wheat he fills you.

He sends forth his command to the earth;
    swiftly runs his word! — ℟

He has proclaimed his word to Jacob,
    his statutes and his ordinances to Israel.

He has not done thus for any other nation;
    his ordinances he has not made known to
        them. — ℟ ℣

℟. Or: **Alleluia.** ℣

GOSPEL   Lk 5, 12-16

Alleluia (Mt 4, 23)

℟. **Alleluia.** Jesus preached the Good News of his
    kingdom
and healed all who were sick. ℟. **Alleluia.**

The misfortune of a leper was not only his disease but his enforced
isolation from family, friends, and the entire community. By reporting
to the priest after returning to health, the former leper could be re-
united with his family and re-enter the community. Similarly, Jesus
removes the leprosy of our sin and pride, and unites us with his
family, the Church.

℣. The Lord be with you. ℟. **And also with you.**
✠ A reading from the holy gospel according to Luke
℟. **Glory to you, Lord.**

On one occasion in a certain town, a man full of
leprosy came to Jesus. Seeing Jesus, he bowed down
to the ground and said to him, "Lord, if you will to
do so, you can cure me." Jesus stretched out his
hand to touch him and said, "I do will it. Be cured."
Immediately the leprosy left him. Jesus then instructed the man: "Tell no one, but go and show
yourself to the priest. Offer for your healing what
Moses prescribed; that should be a proof for them."
His reputation spread more and more, and great
crowds gathered to hear him and to be cured of their

maladies.—This is the gospel of the Lord. ℟. **Praise to you, Lord Jesus Christ.** ➔ No. 15, p. 623

PRAYER OVER THE GIFTS
Father,
in your mercy accept our gifts.
By sharing in this eucharist
may we come to live more fully the love we profess.
Grant this through Christ our Lord.
℟. **Amen.** ➔ No. 21, p. 626 (Pref. P 6)

COMMUNION ANT. 1 Jn 4, 9
God's love for us was revealed when he sent his only Son into the world, so that we could have life through him. ↓

PRAYER AFTER COMMUNION
God our Father,
in this eucharist you touch our lives.
Keep your love alive in our hearts
that we may become worthy of you.
We ask this through Christ our Lord.
℟. **Amen.** ➔ No. 32, p. 650

SATURDAY AFTER EPIPHANY

The word of God and the coming of Jesus make clear to us that this life and this world are not all that there is. There is a life which is so different that it is called a "new creation." The celebration of Christmas and Epiphany is genuine if it has the effect of changing us into new persons according to the pattern of Christ.

ENTRANCE ANT. Gal 4, 4-5
God sent his own Son, born of a woman, so that we could be adopted as his sons. ➔ No. 2, p. 614

OPENING PRAYER
God our Father,
through your Son you made us a new creation.
He shared our nature and became one of us;

with his help, may we become more like him,
who lives and reigns with you and the Holy Spirit,
one God, for ever and ever. ℟. **Amen.** ⍋

READING I   1 Jn 5, 14-21

The Scriptures do not divide body and soul, world and spirit as
sharply as we have learned to do from philosophy. The "world" is
human life that is ignorant of God and hostile to God's will and values.
Those who are in Christ are in the "spirit" and are delivered from
the "world" that is fading away.

A reading from the first letter of John

We have this confidence in God: that he hears us
whenever we ask for anything according to his will.
And since we know that he hears us whenever we
ask, we know that what we have asked him for is
ours. Anyone who sees his brother sinning, if the sin
is not deadly, should petition God, and thus life will
be given to the sinner. This is only for those whose
sin is not deadly. There is such a thing as a deadly
sin; I do not say that one should pray about that.
True, all wrongdoing is sin, but not all sin is deadly.

We know that no one begotten of God commits
sin; rather, God protects the one begotten by him,
and so the evil one cannot touch him. We know that
we belong to God, while the whole world is under
the evil one. We know, too, that the Son of God has
come and has given us discernment to recognize the
One who is true. And we are in the One who is true,
for we are in his Son Jesus Christ. He is the true God
and eternal life.

My little children, be on your guard against idols.
—This is the Word of the Lord. ℟. **Thanks be to
God.** ⍋

Responsorial Psalm   Ps 149, 1-2. 3-4. 5-6. 9
℟. (4) **The Lord takes delight in his people.**
Sing to the Lord a new song
    of praise in the assembly of the faithful.

Let Israel be glad in their maker,
  let the children of Zion rejoice in their king. — ℟

Let them praise his name in the festive dance,
  let them sing praise to him with timbrel and harp.

For the Lord loves his people,
  and he adorns the lowly with victory. — ℟

Let the faithful exult in glory;
  let them sing for joy upon their couches;

Let the high praises of God be in their throats.
  This is the glory of all his faithful. — ℟ ▼

℟. Or: **Alleluia.** ▼

GOSPEL   Jn 3, 22-30

Alleluia (Mt 4, 16)

℟. **Alleluia.** A people in darkness have seen a great
     light;

a radiant dawn shines on those lost in faith. ℟. **Alleluia.**

The law of Moses commanded many washings and sprinklings as ex-
pressions of life, purification, and renewal. John the Baptizer adopted
this meaningful custom, and Jesus perfected it in baptism—the
sacrament of forgiveness, holiness, life, and rebirth. Baptism is a gift
from on high by which Christ increases within us.

℣. The Lord be with you. ℟. **And also with you.**
✠ A reading from the holy gospel according to John
℟. **Glory to you, Lord.**

Jesus and his disciples came into Judean territory,
and he spent some time with them there baptizing.
John too was baptizing at Aenon near Salim where
water was plentiful, and people kept coming to be
baptized. (John, of course, had not yet been thrown
into prison.) A controversy about purification arose
between John's disciples and a certain Jew. So they
came to John, saying, "Rabbi, the man who was with
you across the Jordan—the one about whom you
have been testifying—is baptizing now, and everyone is flocking to him." John answered:

"No one can lay hold on anything
unless it is given him from on high.
You yourselves are witnesses to the fact that I
said: 'I am not the Messiah; I am sent before him.'
"It is the groom who has the bride.
The groom's best man
just waits there listening for him
and is overjoyed to hear his voice.
That is my joy, and it is complete.
He must increase,
while I must decrease."

This is the gospel of the Lord. ℟. **Praise to you, Lord Jesus Christ.**   ➤ No. 15, p. 623

PRAYER OVER THE GIFTS

Father of peace,
accept our devotion and sincerity,
and by our sharing in this mystery
draw us closer to each other and to you.
We ask this in the name of Jesus the Lord.
℟. **Amen.**   ➤ No. 21, p. 626 (Pref. P 6)

COMMUNION ANT.   Jn 1, 16

From his riches we have all received, grace for grace. ↓

PRAYER AFTER COMMUNION

Lord,
may this sacrament be our strength.
Teach us to value all the good you give us
and help us to strive for eternal life.
Grant this through Christ our Lord.
℟. **Amen.**   ➤ No. 32, p. 650

ORDINARY TIME

The Sundays and Weekdays of the major seasons of the year are distinguished by their relationship to the Solemnities of Christmas (Advent, Christmas) and Easter (Lent, Easter). On the other hand, Ordinary Time refers to all the other Sundays and Weekdays under the all-embracing heading of celebrations of the "Day of the Lord." These weeks number thirty-three or thirty-four according to the particular character of each year and are assigned to two parts of the liturgical year.

The first part begins with the Sunday after Epiphany (although this First Sunday is perpetually impeded by the Feast of the Baptism of the Lord) and continues until Ash Wednesday. Since the date of Easter varies each year, this part may include as few as four and as many as nine weeks.

The second part of Ordinary Time begins with the day after Pentecost and runs to the Saturday before the First Sunday of Advent. If the number of ordinary weeks is thirty-four, the week after Pentecost is the one which follows immediately the last week celebrated before Lent. The Masses of Pentecost, Trinity Sunday and (in countries where Corpus Christi is not observed as a holyday of obligation and is therefore celebrated on the following Sunday) Corpus Christi replace the Sunday Masses in these weeks. If the number of ordinary weeks is thirty-three, the first week which would otherwise follow Pentecost is omitted.

Some of the unique features of these weeks are:

The Gloria and the Profession of Faith are sung or said on Sundays; they are omitted on weekdays.

On Sundays one of the Prefaces for Sundays in Ordinary Time is sung or said; on Weekdays, a Weekday Preface.

Two Antiphons are given for Communion, the first from the Psalms, the second for the most part from the Gospel. Either one may be selected, but preference should be given to the Antiphon which may happen to come from the Gospel of the Mass.

The most important characteristic of this Ordinary Time is that, in accord with the pastoral needs of the people, any of the thirty-four Sunday Masses may be celebrated on any weekday, regardless of the particular week in which it falls. This does not refer to the readings and intervenient chants which form the "Lectionary texts" and should be taken from the weekday Lectionary for this period but to the processional chants (Entrance and Communion Antiphons) and presidential prayers (Opening Prayer, Prayer over the Gifts, and Prayer after Communion) which form the "Sacramentary texts."

Because of this fact, for this period of the year only, Lectionary texts will not be integrated into the Sacramentary texts in this Missal. The Sacramentary texts will be given first and the Lectionary texts will be given in another section. (Solely for the sake of convenience, cross-references according to weeks will be included.)

ANTIPHONS AND PRAYERS
FOR ORDINARY TIME

1st WEEK

Our heavenly Father knows all things. He has made us for himself. In him we live and move and are. Let us pray that all we do will be pleasing to him.

ENTRANCE ANT.

I saw a man sitting on a high throne, being worshiped by a great number of angels who were singing together: This is he whose kingdom will last for ever.

→ No. 2, p. 614

OPENING PRAYER

Father of love,
hear our prayers.
Help us to know your will
and to do it with courage and faith.
Grant this through our Lord Jesus Christ, your Son,
who lives and reigns with you and the Holy Spirit,
one God, for ever and ever. ℟. **Amen.** ⩔

READINGS AND INTERVENIENT CHANTS

The *weekday* readings and intervenient chants for each day of the 1st Week in Ordinary Time are found on pp. 209-231.

PRAYER OVER THE GIFTS

Lord,
accept our offering.
Make us grow in holiness
and grant what we ask you in faith.
We ask this in the name of Jesus the Lord.
℟. **Amen.** → No. 21, p. 626 (Pref. P 37-42)

COMMUNION ANT. Ps 36, 10

Lord, you are the source of life, and in the light of your glory we find happiness. ⩔

OR   Jn 10, 10

I came that men may have life, and have it to the full, says the Lord. ℣

PRAYER AFTER COMMUNION

All-powerful God,
you renew us with your sacraments.
Help us to thank you by lives of faithful service.
We ask this through Christ our Lord.
℞. **Amen.**   → No. 32, p. 650

_____

2nd WEEK

God has made heaven and earth. He made the stars in the heavens
and the seasons of the year. He has ordered them all well. Today we
pray that his peace and order may abound in the lives of all men.

ENTRANCE ANT.   Ps 66, 4

May all the earth give you worship and praise, and break into song to your name, O God, Most High.
                                → No. 2, p. 614

OPENING PRAYER

Father of heaven and earth,
hear our prayers,
and show us the way to peace in the world.
Grant this through our Lord Jesus Christ, your Son,
who lives and reigns with you and the Holy Spirit,
one God, for ever and ever. ℞. **Amen.** ℣

ALTERNATIVE OPENING PRAYER

Almighty and ever-present Father,
your watchful care reaches from end to end
and orders all things in such power
that even the tensions and the tragedies of sin
cannot frustrate your loving plans.
Help us to embrace your will,
give us the strength to follow your call,
so that your truth may live in our hearts
and reflect peace to those who believe in your love.
We ask this in the name of Jesus the Lord.
℞. **Amen.** ℣

READINGS AND INTERVENIENT CHANTS

The *weekday* readings and intervenient chants for each day of the 2nd Week in Ordinary Time are found on pp. 231-255.

PRAYER OVER THE GIFTS

Father,
may we celebrate the eucharist
with reverence and love,
for when we proclaim the death of the Lord
you continue the work of his redemption,
who is Lord for ever and ever.
℟. **Amen.**   → No. 21, p. 626 (Pref. P 37-42)

COMMUNION ANT.   Ps 23, 5

The Lord has prepared a feast for me: given wine in plenty for me to drink. ℣

OR   1 Jn 4, 16

We know and believe in God's love for us. ℣

PRAYER AFTER COMMUNION

Lord,
you have nourished us with bread from heaven.
Fill us with your Spirit,
and make us one in peace and love.
We ask this through Christ our Lord.
℟. **Amen**   → No. 32, p. 650

3rd WEEK

St. Paul reminds us that what we do, whether we eat, work or sleep, all must be done for God. Out of love Jesus came into the world. In return he asks our love.

ENTRANCE ANT.   Ps 96, 1. 6

Sing a new song to the Lord! Sing to the Lord, all the earth. Truth and beauty surround him, he lives in holiness and glory.   → No. 2, p. 614

OPENING PRAYER

All-powerful and ever-living God,
direct your love that is within us,
that our efforts in the name of your Son
may bring mankind to unity and peace.
We ask this through our Lord Jesus Christ, your Son,
who lives and reigns with you and the Holy Spirit,
one God, for ever and ever.
℟. **Amen.** ↓

ALTERNATIVE OPENING PRAYER

Almighty Father,
the love you offer
always exceeds the furthest expression of our human
    longing,
for you are greater than the human heart.
Direct each thought, each effort of our life,
so that the limits of our faults and weaknesses
may not obscure the vision of your glory
or keep us from the peace you have promised.
We ask this through Christ our Lord.
℟. **Amen.** ↓

READINGS AND INTERVENIENT CHANTS

The *weekday* readings and intervenient chants for each
day of the 3rd Week in Ordinary Time are found on pp.
255-278.

PRAYER OVER THE GIFTS

Lord,
receive our gifts.
Let our offerings make us holy
and bring us salvation.
Grant this through Christ our Lord.
℟. **Amen.**   → No. 21, p. 626 (Pref. P 37-42)

COMMUNION ANT.   Ps 34, 6

**Look up at the Lord with gladness and smile; your
face will never be ashamed.** ↓

OR   Jn 8, 12
I am the light of the world, says the Lord; the man who follows me will have the light of life. ⊻

PRAYER AFTER COMMUNION
God, all-powerful Father,
may the new life you give us increase our love
and keep us in the joy of your kingdom.
We ask this in the name of Jesus the Lord.
℟. **Amen.**   ➔ No. 32, p. 650

_____

4th WEEK

When Jesus came into the world, he left his place in heaven knowing that he was to suffer and die for all men. Greater love than this no man has: that he would lay down his life for his friend. Let us pray that we may love one another without reserve.

ENTRANCE ANT.   Ps 106, 47
Save us, Lord our God, and gather us together from the nations, that we may proclaim your holy name and glory in your praise.   ➔ No. 2, p. 614

OPENING PRAYER
Lord our God,
help us to love you with all our hearts
and to love all men as you love them.
Grant this through our Lord Jesus Christ, your Son,
who lives and reigns with you and the Holy Spirit,
one God, for ever and ever.
℟. **Amen.** ⊻

ALTERNATIVE OPENING PRAYER
Father in heaven,
from the days of Abraham and Moses
until this gathering of your Church in prayer,
you have formed a people in the image of your Son.
Bless this people with the gift of your kingdom.
May we serve you with our every desire

and show love for one another
even as you have loved us.
Grant this through Christ our Lord. ℟. **Amen.** ↯

READINGS AND INTERVENIENT CHANTS

The *weekday* readings and intervenient chants for each
day of the 4th Week in Ordinary Time are found on pp.
278-302.

PRAYER OVER THE GIFTS

Lord,
be pleased with the gifts we bring to your altar,
and make them the sacrament of our salvation.
We ask this through Christ our Lord.
℟. **Amen.**   ➔ No. 21, p. 626 (Pref. P 37-42)

COMMUNION ANT.   Ps 31, 17-18

**Let your face shine on your servant, and save me
by your love. Lord, keep me from shame, for I have
called to you.** ↯

OR   Mt 5, 3-4

**Happy are the poor in spirit; the kingdom of heaven
is theirs! Happy are the lowly; they shall inherit the
land.** ↯

PRAYER AFTER COMMUNION

Lord,
you invigorate us with this help to our salvation.
By this eucharist give the true faith continued growth
throughout the world.
We ask this in the name of Jesus the Lord.
℟. **Amen.**   ➔ No. 32, p. 650

5th WEEK

In Old Testament days God led his people out of bondage. He guided
them with a pillar of fire at night and a cloud during the day. He fed
them with manna in the desert. May God continue to watch over and
care for his people of today.

ENTRANCE ANT.   Ps 95, 6-7

**Come, let us worship the Lord. Let us bow down in
the presence of our maker, for he is the Lord our
God.**   ➤ No. 2, p. 614

OPENING PRAYER

Father,
watch over your family
and keep us safe in your care,
for all our hope is in you.
Grant this through our Lord Jesus Christ, your Son,
who lives and reigns with you and the Holy Spirit,
one God, for ever and ever. ℟. **Amen.** ℣

ALTERNATIVE OPENING PRAYER

In faith and love we ask you, Father,
to watch over your family gathered here.
In your mercy and loving kindness
no thought of ours is left unguarded,
no tear unheeded, no joy unnoticed.
Through the prayer of Jesus
may the blessings promised to the poor in spirit
lead us to the treasures of your heavenly kingdom.
We ask this in the name of Jesus the Lord.
℟. **Amen.** ℣

READINGS AND INTERVENIENT CHANTS

The *weekday* readings and intervenient chants for each
day of the 5th Week in Ordinary Time are found on pp.
306-330.

PRAYER OVER THE GIFTS

Lord our God,
may the bread and wine
you give us for our nourishment on earth
become the sacrament of our eternal life.
We ask this through Christ our Lord.
℟. **Amen.**   ➤ No. 21, p. 626 (Pref. P 37-42)

COMMUNION ANT.   Ps 107, 8-9

**Give praise to the Lord for his kindness, for his won-
derful deeds toward men. He has filled the hungry
with good things, he has satisfied the thirsty.** ℣

OR   Mt 5, 5-6

**Happy are the sorrowing; they shall be consoled.
Happy those who hunger and thirst for what is right;
they shall be satisfied.** ℣

PRAYER AFTER COMMUNION

God our Father,
you give us a share in the one bread and the one cup
and make us one in Christ.
Help us to bring your salvation and joy
to all the world.
We ask this through Christ our Lord.
℟. **Amen.**   ➤ No. 32, p. 650

6th WEEK

God made a covenant with the Israelites that he would be their God
and they would be his people. We pray today that he will look after
us and keep us safe from all harm.

ENTRANCE ANT   Ps 31, 3-4

**Lord, be my rock of safety, the stronghold that saves
me. For the honor of your name, lead me and guide
me.**   ➤ No. 2, p. 614

OPENING PRAYER

God our Father,
you have promised to remain for ever
with those who do what is just and right.
Help us to live in your presence.
We ask this through our Lord Jesus Christ, your Son,
who lives and reigns with you and the Holy Spirit,
one God, for ever and ever. ℟. **Amen.** ℣

ALTERNATIVE OPENING PRAYER

Father in heaven,
the loving plan of your wisdom took flesh in Jesus
    Christ,
and changed mankind's history
by his command of perfect love.
May our fulfillment of his command reflect your
    wisdom
and bring your salvation to the ends of the earth.
We ask this through Christ our Lord. ℟. **Amen.** ✛

READINGS AND INTERVENIENT CHANTS

The *weekday* readings and intervenient chants for each
day of the 6th Week in Ordinary Time are found on pp.
330-352.

PRAYER OVER THE GIFTS

Lord,
we make this offering in obedience to your word.
May it cleanse and renew us,
and lead us to our eternal reward.
We ask this in the name of Jesus the Lord
℟. **Amen.**   → No. 21, p. 626 (Pref. P 37-42)

COMMUNION ANT.   Ps 78, 29-30

**They ate and were filled; the Lord gave them what
they wanted: they were not deprived of their desire.** ✛

OR   Jn 3, 16

**God loved the world so much, he gave his only Son,
that all who believe in him might not perish, but
might have eternal life.** ✛

PRAYER AFTER COMMUNION

Lord,
you give us food from heaven.
May we always hunger
for the bread of life.

Grant this through Christ our Lord.
℞. **Amen.**   ⇥ No. 32, p. 650

7th WEEK

Solomon was renowned for his wisdom. Jesus confounded the scribes and Pharisees who tried to trick him. "Give to Caesar what is Caesar's and to God what is God's." May we abide by the revealed word of God and live always according to his commandments.

ENTRANCE ANT.   Ps 13, 6

Lord, your mercy is my hope, my heart rejoices in your saving power. I will sing to the Lord for his goodness to me.   ⇥ No. 2, p. 614

OPENING PRAYER

Father,
keep before us the wisdom and love
you have revealed in your Son.
Help us to be like him
in word and deed,
for he lives and reigns with you and the Holy Spirit,
one God, for ever and ever. ℞. **Amen.** ↓

ALTERNATIVE OPENING PRAYER

Almighty God,
Father of our Lord Jesus Christ,
faith in your word is the way to wisdom,
and to ponder your divine plan is to grow in the truth.
Open our eyes to your deeds,
our ears to the sound of your call,
so that our every act may increase our sharing
in the life you have offered us.
Grant this through Christ our Lord. ℞. **Amen.** ↓

READINGS AND INTERVENIENT CHANTS

The *weekday* readings and intervenient chants for each day of the 7th Week in Ordinary Time are found on pp. 353-373.

PRAYER OVER THE GIFTS

Lord,
as we make this offering,
may our worship in Spirit and truth
bring us salvation.
We ask this in the name of Jesus the Lord.
℟. **Amen.**   ➤ No. 21, p. 626 (Pref. P 37-42)

COMMUNION ANT.   Ps 9, 2-3

**I will tell all your marvelous works. I will rejoice and
be glad in you, and sing to your name, Most High.** ℣

OR   Jn 11, 27

**Lord, I believe that you are the Christ, the Son of
God, who was to come into this world.** ℣

PRAYER AFTER COMMUNION

Almighty God,
help us to live the example of love
we celebrate in this eucharist,
that we may come to its fulfillment in your presence.
We ask this through Christ our Lord.
℟. **Amen.**   ➤ No. 32, p. 650

8th WEEK

Everything lives in the ever-present "now" in the mind of God. We are
born only to live for a time wherein we are to serve God. We pray
that we may live lives pleasing to God, that we may live in joy and
peace.

ENTRANCE ANT.   Ps 18, 19-20

**The Lord has been my strength; he has led me into
freedom. He saved me because he loves me.**
                                        ➤ No. 2, p. 614

OPENING PRAYER

Lord,
guide the course of world events

and give your Church the joy and peace
of serving you in freedom.
We ask this through our Lord Jesus Christ, your Son,
who lives and reigns with you and the Holy Spirit,
one God, for ever and ever. ℟. **Amen.** ↓

ALTERNATIVE OPENING PRAYER

Father in heaven,
form in us the likeness of your Son
and deepen his life within us.
Send us as witnesses of gospel joy
into a world of fragile peace and broken promises.
Touch the hearts of all men with your love
that they in turn may love one another.
We ask this through Christ our Lord.
℟. **Amen.** ↓

READINGS AND INTERVENIENT CHANTS

The *weekday* readings and intervenient chants for each
day of the 8th Week in Ordinary Time are found on pp.
374-396.

PRAYER OVER THE GIFTS

God our Creator,
may this bread and wine we offer
as a sign of our love and worship
lead us to salvation.
Grant this through Christ our Lord.
℟. **Amen.**   ➔ No. 21, p. 626 (Pref. P 37-42)

COMMUNION ANT.   Ps 13, 6
**I will sing to the Lord for his goodness to me, I will
sing the name of the Lord, Most High.** ↓

OR   Mt 28, 20
**I, the Lord, am with you always, until the end of the
world.** ↓

PRAYER AFTER COMMUNION

God of salvation,
may this sacrament which strengthens us here on
   earth
bring us to eternal life.
We ask this in the name of Jesus the Lord.
℞. **Amen.**   ➤ No. 32, p. 650

9th WEEK

How much we take for granted as we live in a world of advanced progress. It is easy to become immersed in the affairs around us and they may easily ensnare us. May God who cares for us shield us from all dangers as he provides for our needs.

ENTRANCE ANT.   Ps 25, 16. 18

O look at me and be merciful, for I am wretched and alone. See my hardship and my poverty, and pardon all my sins.   ➤ No. 2, p. 614

OPENING PRAYER

Father,
your love never fails.
Hear our call.
Keep us from danger
and provide for all our needs.
Grant this through our Lord Jesus Christ, your Son,
who lives and reigns with you and the Holy Spirit,
one God, for ever and ever. ℞. **Amen.** ℣

ALTERNATIVE OPENING PRAYER

God our Father,
teach us to cherish the gifts that surround us.
Increase our faith in you
and bring our trust to its promised fulfillment
in the joy of your kingdom.
Grant this through Christ our Lord. ℞. **Amen.** ℣

READINGS AND INTERVENIENT CHANTS

The *weekday* readings and intervenient chants for each
day of the 9th Week in Ordinary Time are found on pp.
396-421.

PRAYER OVER THE GIFTS

Lord,
as we gather to offer our gifts
confident in your love,
make us holy by sharing your life with us
and by this eucharist forgive our sins.
We ask this through Christ our Lord.
℟. **Amen.**   ➤ No. 21, p. 626 (Pref. P 37-42)

COMMUNION ANT.   Ps 17, 6

**I call upon you, God, for you will answer me; bend
your ear and hear my prayer.** ✟

OR   Mk 11, 23-24

**I tell you solemnly, whatever you ask for in prayer,
believe that you have received it, and it will be yours,
says the Lord.** ✟

PRAYER AFTER COMMUNION

Lord,
as you give us the body and blood of your Son,
guide us with your Spirit
that we may honor you
not only with our lips,
but also with the lives we lead,
and so enter your kingdom.
We ask this in the name of Jesus the Lord.
℟. **Amen.**   ➤ No. 32, p. 650

———————————

10th WEEK

The life of the Holy Spirit dwells in those chosen by Jesus to carry on his work on earth. The openness of Christ to us through his Spirit is one of love and eternal presence. We are all called upon to be the means by which Christ may reach out to all mankind.

ENTRANCE ANT. Ps 26, 1-2

The Lord is my light and my salvation. Who shall frighten me? The Lord is the defender of my life. Who shall make me tremble? ➤ No. 2, p. 614

OPENING PRAYER

God of wisdom and love,
source of all good,
send your Spirit to teach us your truth
and guide our actions
in your way of peace.
We ask this through our Lord Jesus Christ, your Son,
who lives and reigns with you and the Holy Spirit,
one God, for ever and ever. ℟. **Amen.** ⅴ

ALTERNATIVE OPENING PRAYER

Father in heaven,
words cannot measure the boundaries of love
for those born to new life in Christ Jesus.
Raise us beyond the limits this world imposes,
so that we may be free to love as Christ teaches
and find our joy in your glory.
We ask this through Christ our Lord. ℟. **Amen.** ⅴ

READINGS AND INTERVENIENT CHANTS

The *weekday* readings and intervenient chants for the 1st to 9th Weeks in Ordinary Time on pp. 207-421.

PRAYER OVER THE GIFTS

Lord, look with love on our service.
Accept the gifts we bring
and help us grow in Christian love.
Grant this through Christ our Lord.
℟. **Amen.** ➤ No. 21, p. 626 (Pref. P 37-42)

COMMUNION ANT.   Ps 18, 3

**I can rely on the Lord; I can always turn to him for
shelter. It was he who gave me my freedom. My God,
you are always there to help me!** ℣

OR   1 Jn 4, 16

**God is love, and he who lives in love, lives in God,
and God in him.** ℣

PRAYER AFTER COMMUNION

Lord,
may your healing love
turn us from sin
and keep us on the way that leads to you.
We ask this in the name of Jesus the Lord.
℟. **Amen.**   ➜ No. 32, p. 650

11th WEEK

As Christians, we should remember that God's love as exemplified in
Christ's dying for all of mankind should bring us to a stronger and
more confident abandonment of ourselves in return to God and others.
May this Eucharistic liturgy strengthen our confidence in ourselves
as receivers and givers of God's love.

ENTRANCE ANT.   Ps 27, 7. 9.

**Lord, hear my voice when I call to you. You are my
help; do not cast me off, do not desert me, my Savior
God.**   ➜ No. 2, p. 614

OPENING PRAYER

Almighty God,
our hope and our strength,
without you we falter.
Help us to follow Christ
and to live according to your will.
We ask this through our Lord Jesus Christ, your Son,
who lives and reigns with you and the Holy Spirit,
one God, for ever and ever. ℟. **Amen.** ℣

ALTERNATIVE OPENING PRAYER

God our Father,
we rejoice in the faith that draws us together,
aware that selfishness can drive us apart.
Let your encouragement be our constant strength.
Keep us one in the love that has sealed our lives,
help us to live as one family
the gospel we profess.
We ask this through Christ our Lord. ℟. **Amen.** ✟

READINGS AND INTERVENIENT CHANTS

The *weekday* readings and intervenient chants for the
1st to 9th Weeks in Ordinary Time are found on pp.
207-421.

PRAYER OVER THE GIFTS

Lord God,
in this bread and wine
you give us food for body and spirit.
May the eucharist renew our strength
and bring us health of mind and body.
We ask this in the name of Jesus the Lord.
℟. **Amen.**   ➔ No. 21, p. 626 (Pref. P 37-42)

COMMUNION ANT.   Ps 27, 4

**One thing I seek: to dwell in the house of the Lord
all the days of my life.** ✟

OR   Jn 17, 11

**Father, keep in your name those you have given me,
that they may be one as we are one, says the Lord.** ✟

PRAYER AFTER COMMUNION

Lord,
may this eucharist
accomplish in your Church
the unity and peace it signifies.
Grant this through Christ our Lord.
℟. **Amen.**   ➔ No. 32, p. 650

12th WEEK

Jesus Christ is the Good Shepherd who protects us, his sheep. The sheep of his fold come first, and he will do all in his power to save them from harm. Christ our Shepherd laid down his life for us. How he has proved his love for us!

ENTRANCE ANT.   Ps 28, 8-9

God is the strength of his people. In him, we his chosen live in safety. Save us, Lord, who share in your life, and give us your blessings; be our shepherd for ever.

➤ No. 2, p. 614

OPENING PRAYER

Father,
guide and protector of your people,
grant us an unfailing respect for your name,
and keep us always in your love.
Grant this through our Lord Jesus Christ, your Son,
who lives and reigns with you and the Holy Spirit,
one God, for ever and ever. ℟. **Amen.** ⩔

ALTERNATIVE OPENING PRAYER

God of the universe,
we worship you as Lord.
God, ever close to us,
we rejoice to call you Father.
From this world's uncertainty we look to your covenant.
Keep us one in your peace, secure in your love.
We ask this through Christ our Lord. ℟. **Amen.** ⩔

READINGS AND INTERVENIENT CHANTS

The *weekday* readings and intervenient chants for the 1st to 9th Weeks in Ordinary Time are found on pp. 207-421.

PRAYER OVER THE GIFTS

Lord,
receive our offering,
and may this sacrifice of praise
purify us in mind and heart

and make us always eager to serve you.
We ask this in the name of Jesus the Lord.
℞. **Amen.**   ➤ No. 21, p. 626 (Pref. P 37-42)

COMMUNION ANT.   Ps 145, 15
The eyes of all look to you, O Lord, and you give them food in due season. ℣

OR   Jn 10, 11. 15
I am the Good Shepherd; I give my life for my sheep, says the Lord. ℣

PRAYER AFTER COMMUNION
Lord,
you give us the body and blood of your Son
to renew your life within us.
In your mercy, assure our redemption
and bring us to the eternal life
we celebrate in this eucharist.
We ask this through Christ our Lord. ℞. **Amen.**
                              ➤ No. 32, p. 650

13th WEEK

Jesus Christ, the Light of the World, gives us hope. He lights the way and guides us in the truth. Each day, his light comes to us to help us overcome the darkness. As children of light and followers of Christ, may we support each other and rely on the authority and power of Jesus to live a life of faith.

ENTRANCE ANT.   Ps 47, 2
All nations, clap your hands. Shout with a voice of joy to God.   ➤ No. 2, p. 614

OPENING PRAYER
Father,
you call your children
to walk in the light of Christ.
Free us from darkness
and keep us in the radiance of your truth.
We ask this through our Lord Jesus Christ, your Son,
who lives and reigns with you and the Holy Spirit,
one God, for ever and ever. ℞. **Amen. ℣**

ALTERNATIVE OPENING PRAYER

Father in heaven,
the light of Jesus
has scattered the darkness of hatred and sin.
Called to that light
we ask for your guidance.
Form our lives in your truth, our hearts in your
    love.
We ask this through Christ our Lord. ℟. **Amen.** ℣

READINGS AND INTERVENIENT CHANTS

The *weekday* readings and intervenient chants for the
1st to 9th Weeks in Ordinary Time are found on pp.
207-421.

PRAYER OVER THE GIFTS

Lord God,
through your sacraments
you give us the power of your grace.
May this eucharist
help us to serve you faithfully.
We ask this in the name of Jesus the Lord.
℟. **Amen.**   ➜ No. 21, p. 626 (Pref. P 37-42)

COMMUNION ANT.   Ps 103, 1

**O, bless the Lord, my soul, and all that is within me
bless his holy name.** ℣

OR   Jn 17, 20-21

**Father, I pray for them: may they be one in us, so
that the world may believe it was you who sent me.** ℣

PRAYER AFTER COMMUNION

Lord,
may this sacrifice and communion
give us a share in your life
and help us bring your love to the world.
Grant this through Christ our Lord.
℟. **Amen.**   ➜ No. 32, p. 650

14th WEEK

Each day we are witness to God's dominion over all things. He is the Master of the universe, the Ruler over life and death. All laws of nature are subject to him. We cannot merely recognize that God is all-powerful but must acknowledge that truth in a practical way by conducting our lives in obedience to his Divine Will.

ENTRANCE ANT.   Ps 48, 10-11

Within your temple, we ponder your loving kindness, O God. As your name, so also your praise reaches to the ends of the earth; your right hand is filled with justice.   ➤ No. 2, p. 614

OPENING PRAYER

Father,
through the obedience of Jesus,
your servant and your Son,
you raised a fallen world.
Free us from sin
and bring us the joy that lasts for ever.
We ask this through our Lord Jesus Christ, your Son,
who lives and reigns with you and the Holy Spirit,
one God, for ever and ever. ℟. **Amen.** ✟

ALTERNATIVE OPENING PRAYER

Father,
in the rising of your Son
death gives birth to new life.
The sufferings he endured restored hope to a fallen
    world.
Let sin never ensnare us
with empty promises of passing joy.
Make us one with you always,
so that our joy may be holy,
and our love may give life.
We ask this through Christ our Lord. ℟. **Amen.** ✟

READINGS AND INTERVENIENT CHANTS

The *weekday* readings and intervenient chants for the 1st to 9th Weeks in Ordinary Time are found on pp. 207-421.

PRAYER OVER THE GIFTS
Lord,
let this offering to the glory of your name
purify us and bring us closer to eternal life.
We ask this in the name of Jesus the Lord.
℞. **Amen.**   ➜ No. 21, p. 626 (Pref. P 37-42)

COMMUNION ANT.   Ps 34, 9
**Taste and see the goodness of the Lord; blessed is
he who hopes in God.** ℣

OR   Mt 11, 28
**Come to me, all you that labor and are burdened,
and I will give you rest, says the Lord.** ℣

PRAYER AFTER COMMUNION
Lord,
may we never fail to praise you
for the fullness of life and salvation
you give us in this eucharist.
We ask this through Christ our Lord.
℞. **Amen.**   ➜ No. 32, p. 650

─────────────────

15th WEEK

Jesus showed us that our God is a personal Father who knows the
sound of our voice and who always hears the prayers of those who
call on him. Jesus himself often prayed to his Father, remembering
all of God's goodness and giving him praise. Let us join Jesus in
praising the Father and thanking him for all that he has given us.

ENTRANCE ANT.   Ps 17, 15
**In my justice I shall see your face, O Lord; when
your glory appears, my joy will be full.**
                                        ➜ No. 2, p. 614
OPENING PRAYER
God our Father,
your light of truth
guides us to the way of Christ.
May all who follow him
reject what is contrary to the gospel.

We ask this through our Lord Jesus Christ, your Son,
who lives and reigns with you and the Holy Spirit,
one God, for ever and ever. ℟. **Amen.** ✠

ALTERNATIVE OPENING PRAYER

Father,
let the light of your truth
guide us to your kingdom
through a world filled with lights contrary to your
　own.
Christian is the name and the gospel we glory in.
May your love make us what you have called us to be.
We ask this through Christ our Lord. ℟. **Amen.** ✠

READINGS AND INTERVENIENT CHANTS

The *weekday* readings and intervenient chants for the
1st to 9th Weeks in Ordinary Time are found on pp.
207-421.

PRAYER OVER THE GIFTS

Lord,
accept the gifts of your Church.
May this eucharist
help us grow in holiness and faith.
We ask this in the name of Jesus the Lord.
℟. **Amen.**　　　　　　　➤ No. 21, p. 626 (Pref. P 37-42)

COMMUNION ANT.　　　　　　　　　Ps 84, 4-5

**The sparrow even finds a home, the swallow finds a
nest wherein to place her young, near to your altars,
Lord of hosts, my King, my God! How happy they
who dwell in your house! For ever they are praising
you.** ✠

OR　　　　　　　　　　　　　　　　Jn 6, 57

**Whoever eats my flesh and drinks my blood will live
in me and I in him, says the Lord.** ✠

PRAYER AFTER COMMUNION

Lord,
by our sharing in the mystery of this eucharist,

let your saving love grow within us.
Grant this through Christ our Lord.
℟. **Amen.** ———————— → No. 32, p. 650

16th WEEK

In his goodness and mercy, God has given to men the power to forgive
our sins and thereby restore us to friendship with him. He has given
to men the power to change bread and wine into his own Body and
Blood so that we may have the spiritual strength to meet the problems
and trials of life. May we thus serve God in faith, hope, and love!

ENTRANCE ANT.   Ps 54, 6. 8
**God himself is my help. The Lord upholds my life. I
will offer you a willing sacrifice; I will praise your
name, O Lord, for its goodness.**   → No. 2, p. 614

OPENING PRAYER
Lord,
be merciful to your people.
Fill us with your gifts
and make us always eager to serve you
in faith, hope, and love.
Grant this through our Lord Jesus Christ, your Son,
who lives and reigns with you and the Holy Spirit,
one God, for ever and ever. ℟. **Amen.** ⍗

ALTERNATIVE OPENING PRAYER
Father,
let the gift of your life
continue to grow in us,
drawing us from death to faith, hope, and love.
Keep us alive in Christ Jesus.
Keep us watchful in prayers,
and true to his teaching
till your glory is revealed in us.
Grant this through Christ our Lord. ℟. **Amen.** ⍗

READINGS AND INTERVENIENT CHANTS

The *weekday* readings and intervenient chants for the
1st to 9th Weeks in Ordinary Time are found on pp.
207-421.

PRAYER OVER THE GIFTS

Lord,
bring us closer to salvation
through these gifts which we bring in your honor.
Accept the perfect sacrifice you have given us,
bless it as you blessed the gifts of Abel.
We ask this through Christ our Lord.
R̸. **Amen.**   ➔ No. 21, p. 626 (Pref. P 37-42)

COMMUNION ANT.   Ps 111, 4-5

**The Lord keeps in our minds the wonderful things he
has done. He is compassion and love; he always provides for his faithful. ⱱ**

OR   Rv 3, 20

**I stand at the door and knock, says the Lord. If any-
one hears my voice and opens the door, I will come
in and sit down to supper with him, and he with
me. ⱱ**

PRAYER AFTER COMMUNION

Merciful Father,
may these mysteries
give us new purpose
and bring us to a new life in you.
We ask this in the name of Jesus the Lord.
R̸. **Amen.**   ➔ No. 32, p. 650

─────────────

17th WEEK

If we have faith in God, we can be assured that he will provide us with
all that we need. God's call is extended to all people, and we have
only to accept the invitation to share in his bountiful gifts.

ENTRANCE ANT.   Ps 68, 6-7. 36

**God is in his holy dwelling; he will give a home to
the lonely, he gives power and strength to his people.**
                                        ➔ No. 2, p. 614

OPENING PRAYER

God our Father and protector,
without you nothing is holy,
nothing has value.
Guide us to everlasting life
by helping us to use wisely
the blessings you have given to the world.
We ask this through our Lord Jesus Christ, your Son,
who lives and reigns with you and the Holy Spirit,
one God, for ever and ever. Ry. **Amen.** ℣

ALTERNATIVE OPENING PRAYER

God our Father,
open our eyes to see your hand at work
in the splendor of creation,
in the beauty of human life.
Touched by your hand our world is holy.
Help us to cherish the gifts that surround us,
to share your blessings with our brothers and sisters,
and to experience the joy of life in your presence.
We ask this through Christ our Lord. Ry. **Amen.** ℣

READINGS AND INTERVENIENT CHANTS

The *weekday* readings and intervenient chants for the
1st to 9th Weeks in Ordinary Time are found on pp.
207-421.

PRAYER OVER THE GIFTS

Lord,
receive these offerings
chosen from your many gifts.
May these mysteries make us holy
and lead us to eternal joy.
Grant this through Christ our Lord.
Ry. **Amen.**   ➔ No. 21, p. 626 (Pref. P 37-42)

COMMUNION ANT.   Ps 103, 2

O, bless the Lord, my soul, and remembers all his kindness. ℣

OR Mt 5, 7-8

Happy are those who show mercy; mercy shall be theirs. Happy are the poor of heart, for they shall see God. ℣

PRAYER AFTER COMMUNION

Lord,
we receive the sacrament
which celebrates the memory
of the death and resurrection of Christ your Son.
May this gift bring us closer to our eternal salvation.
We ask this through Christ our Lord.
℟. **Amen.** ➤ No. 32, p. 650

18th WEEK

The soul of man requires spiritual food. Jesus offers us himself as the Bread of Life which will fill our spiritual appetite so that we will never hunger again. All things of this world are as nothing to us in the presence of our Lord and Savior whom we receive in the Eucharist.

ENTRANCE ANT. Ps 70, 2. 6

God, come to my help. Lord, quickly give me assistance. You are the one who helps me and sets me free: Lord, do not be long in coming. ➤ No. 2, p. 614

OPENING PRAYER

Father of everlasting goodness,
our origin and guide,
be close to us
and hear the prayers of all who praise you.
Forgive our sins and restore us to life.
Keep us safe in your love.
Grant this through our Lord Jesus Christ, your Son,
who lives and reigns with you and the Holy Spirit,
one God, for ever and ever. ℟. **Amen.** ℣

ALTERNATIVE OPENING PRAYER

God our Father,
gifts without measure flow from your goodness

to bring us your peace.
Our life is your gift.
Guide our life's journey,
for only your love makes us whole.
Keep us strong in your love.
We ask this through Christ our Lord. ℟. **Amen.** ▼

READINGS AND INTERVENIENT CHANTS

The *weekday* readings and intervenient chants for the
1st to 9th Weeks in Ordinary Time are found on pp.
207-421.

PRAYER OVER THE GIFTS

Merciful Lord,
make holy these gifts,
and let our spiritual sacrifice
make us an everlasting gift to you.
We ask this in the name of Jesus the Lord.
℟. **Amen.**   ➜ No. 21, p. 626 (Pref. P 37-42)

COMMUNION ANT.   Wis 16, 20

**You gave us bread from heaven, Lord: a sweet-tasting
bread that was very good to eat.** ▼

OR   Jn 6, 35

**The Lord says: I am the bread of life. A man who
comes to me will not go away hungry, and no one
who believes in me will thirst.** ▼

PRAYER AFTER COMMUNION

Lord,
you give us the strength of new life
by the gift of the eucharist.
Protect us with your love
and prepare us for eternal redemption.
We ask this through Christ our Lord.
℟. **Amen.**   ➜ No. 32, p. 650

19th WEEK

We have been chosen to be the people of God and to hear the Good News of salvation. We have been reborn in the waters of baptism and we have received the gift of the Holy Spirit, our guide and our protector. We have nothing to fear.

ENTRANCE ANT.   Ps 74, 20. 19. 22. 23

Lord, be true to your covenant, forget not the life of your poor ones for ever. Rise up, O God, and defend your cause; do not ignore the shouts of your enemies.

➔ No. 2, p. 614

OPENING PRAYER

Almighty and ever-living God,
your Spirit made us your children,
confident to call you Father.
Increase your Spirit within us
and bring us to our promised inheritance.
Grant this through our Lord Jesus Christ, your Son,
who lives and reigns with you and the Holy Spirit,
one God, for ever and ever. ℟. **Amen.** ♥

ALTERNATIVE OPENING PRAYER

Father,
we come, reborn in the Spirit,
to celebrate our sonship in the Lord Jesus Christ.
Touch our hearts,
help them grow toward the life you have promised.
Touch our lives,
make them signs of your love for all men.
Grant this through Christ our Lord. ℟. **Amen.** ♥

READINGS AND INTERVENIENT CHANTS

The *weekday* readings and intervenient chants for the 1st to 9th Weeks in Ordinary Time are found on pp. 207-421.

PRAYER OVER THE GIFTS

God of power,
giver of the gifts we bring,

accept the offering of your Church
and make it the sacrament of our salvation.
We ask this through Christ our Lord.
℟. **Amen.**   ➔ No. 21, p. 626 (Pref. P 37-42)

COMMUNION ANT.   Ps 147, 12- 14
Praise the Lord, Jerusalem; he feeds you with the finest wheat. ↓

OR   Jn 6, 52
The bread I shall give is my flesh for the life of the world, says the Lord. ↓

PRAYER AFTER COMMUNION
Lord,
may the eucharist you give us
bring us to salvation
and keep us faithful to the light of your truth.
We ask this in the name of Jesus the Lord.
℟. **Amen.** _____   ➔ No. 32, p. 650

20th WEEK

The Lord's call is universal, meant for all mankind. We are all brothers and sisters in Christ. Each of us must support one another through our concern, and in this way we witness Jesus and his message.

ENTRANCE ANT.   Ps 84, 10-11
God, our protector, keep us in mind; always give strength to your people. For if we can be with you even one day, it is better than a thousand without you.   ➔ No. 2, p. 614

OPENING PRAYER
God our Father,
may we love you in all things and above all things
and reach the joy you have prepared for us
beyond all our imagining.
We ask this through our Lord, Jesus Christ, your Son,
who lives and reigns with you and the Holy Spirit,
one God, for ever and ever. ℟. **Amen.** ↓

ALTERNATIVE OPENING PRAYER

Almighty God, ever-loving Father,
your care extends beyond the boundaries of race and
    nation
to the hearts of all who live.
May the walls, which prejudice raises between us,
crumble beneath the shadow of your outstretched
    arm.
We ask this through Christ our Lord. ℟. **Amen.** ♦

READINGS AND INTERVENIENT CHANTS

The *weekday* readings and intervenient chants for the
1st to 9th Weeks in Ordinary Time are found on pp.
207-421.

PRAYER OVER THE GIFTS

Lord,
accept our sacrifice
as a holy exchange of gifts.
By offering what you have given us
may we receive the gift of yourself.
We ask this in the name of Jesus the Lord.
℟. **Amen.**   ➤ No. 21, p. 626 (Pref. P 37-42)

COMMUNION ANT.   Ps 130, 7

With the Lord there is mercy, and fullness of redemption. ♦

OR   Jn 6, 51-52

**I am the living bread from heaven, says the Lord; if
anyone eats this bread he will live for ever.** ♦

PRAYER AFTER COMMUNION

God of mercy,
by this sacrament you make us one with Christ.
By becoming more like him on earth,
may we come to share his glory in heaven,
where he lives and reigns for ever and ever.
℟. **Amen.**   ➤ No. 32, p. 650

21st WEEK

Jesus alone can lead us to his Father, but we owe him service in order for him to give us this life. We find this life in loving one another, the same way Christ loved his Church. He was willing to give up his life to save his Church.

ENTRANCE ANT.   Ps 86, 1-3

Listen, Lord, and answer me. Save your servant who trusts in you. I call to you all day long, have mercy on me, O Lord.   → No. 2, p. 614

OPENING PRAYER

Father,
help us to seek the values
that will bring us lasting joy in this changing world.
In our desire for what you promise
make us one in mind and heart.
Grant this through our Lord Jesus Christ, your Son,
who lives and reigns with you and the Holy Spirit,
one God, for ever and ever. ℟. **Amen.** ▼

ALTERNATIVE OPENING PRAYER

Lord our God,
all truth is from you,
and you alone bring oneness of heart.
Give your people the joy
of hearing your word in every sound
and of longing for your presence more than for life
    itself.
May all the attractions of a changing world
serve only to bring us
the peace of your kingdom which this world does
    not give.
Grant this through Christ our Lord. ℟. **Amen.** ▼

READINGS AND INTERVENIENT CHANTS

The *weekday* readings and intervenient chants for the 1st to 9th Weeks in Ordinary Time are found on pp. 207-421.

PRAYER OVER THE GIFTS
Merciful God,
the perfect sacrifice of Jesus Christ
made us your people.
In your love,
grant peace and unity to your Church.
We ask this through Christ our Lord.
℟. **Amen.** ➜ No. 21, p. 626 (Pref. P 37-42)

COMMUNION ANT. Ps 104, 13-15
Lord, the earth is filled with your gift from heaven; man grows bread from earth, and wine to cheer his heart. ☩

OR Jn 6, 55
The Lord says: The man who eats my flesh and drinks my blood will live for ever; I shall raise him to life on the last day. ☩

PRAYER AFTER COMMUNION
Lord,
may this eucharist increase within us
the healing power of your love.
May it guide and direct our efforts
to please you in all things.
We ask this in the name of Jesus the Lord.
℟. **Amen.** ➜ No. 32, p. 650

22nd WEEK

Christ calls all men to him, for all are sinners who need him. He calls us to come to him with repentance and he will not reject us. It is precisely because of our weakness that Christ holds out his hand of mercy and forgiveness to us.

ENTRANCE ANT. Ps 86, 3. 5
I call to you all day long, have mercy on me, O Lord. You are good and forgiving, full of love for all who call to you. ➜ No. 2, p. 614

OPENING PRAYER

Almighty God,
every good thing comes from you.
Fill our hearts with love for you,
increase our faith,
and by your constant care
protect the good you have given us.
We ask this through our Lord Jesus, your Son,
who lives and reigns with you and the Holy Spirit,
one God, for ever and ever. ℟. **Amen.** ℣

ALTERNATIVE OPENING PRAYER

Lord God of power and might,
nothing is good which is against your will,
and all is of value which comes from your hand.
Place in our hearts a desire to please you
and fill our minds with insight into love,
so that every thought may grow in wisdom
and all our efforts may be filled with your peace.
We ask this through Christ our Lord. ℟. **Amen.** ℣

READINGS AND INTERVENIENT CHANTS

The *weekday* readings and intervenient chants for the
1st to 9th Weeks in Ordinary Time are found on pp.
207-421.

PRAYER OVER THE GIFTS

Lord,
may this holy offering
bring us your blessing
and accomplish within us
its promise of salvation.
Grant this through Christ our Lord.
℟. **Amen.**   ➤ No. 21, p. 626 (Pref. P 37-42)

COMMUNION ANT.   Ps 31, 20

**Happy are the peacemakers; they shall be called sons
of God. Happy are they who suffer persecution for
justice' sake; the kingdom of heaven is theirs.** ℣

OR   Mt 5, 9-10

**O Lord, how great is the depth of the kindness which
you have shown to those who love you.** ℣

PRAYER AFTER COMMUNION
Lord,
you renew us at your table with the bread of life.
May this food strengthen us in love
and help us to serve you in each other.
We ask this in the name of Jesus the Lord.
℟. **Amen.**   ➤ No. 32, p. 650

23rd WEEK

In every age and in every place, God makes his presence known to
man. We have come to know God through his Son, Jesus. It is our task
to share our knowledge of Christ with others.

ENTRANCE ANT.   Ps 119, 137. 124

**Lord, you are just, and the judgments you make are
right. Show mercy when you judge me, your servant.**
➤ No. 2, p. 614

OPENING PRAYER
God our Father,
you redeem us
and make us your children in Christ.
Look upon us,
give us true freedom
and bring us to the inheritance you promised.
Grant this through our Lord Jesus Christ, your Son,
who lives and reigns with you and the Holy Spirit,
one God, for ever and ever. ℟. **Amen.** ℣

ALTERNATIVE OPENING PRAYER
Lord our God,
in you justice and mercy meet.
With unparalleled love you have saved us from death

and drawn us into the circle of your life.
Open our eyes to the wonders this life sets before us,
that we may serve you free from fear
and address you as God our Father.
We ask this in the name of Jesus the Lord.
℟. **Amen.** ⍍

READINGS AND INTERVENIENT CHANTS

The *weekday* readings and intervenient chants for the
1st to 9th Weeks in Ordinary Time are found on pp.
207-421.

PRAYER OVER THE GIFTS

God of peace and love,
may our offering bring you true worship
and make us one with you.
Grant this through Christ our Lord.
℟. **Amen.**   → No. 21, p. 626 (Pref. P 37-42)

COMMUNION ANT.   Ps 42, 2-3

**Like a deer that longs for running streams, my soul
longs for you, my God. My soul is thirsting for the
living God.** ⍍

OR   Jn 8, 12

**I am the light of the world, says the Lord; the man
who follows me will have the light of life.** ⍍

PRAYER AFTER COMMUNION

Lord,
your word and your sacrament
give us food and life.
May this gift of your Son
lead us to share his life for ever.
We ask this through Christ our Lord.
℟. **Amen.**   → No. 32, p. 650

24th WEEK

All of us are called to serve our heavenly Father in some unique way.
We must not bury or hide the talents he has given us; we must use
those talents by giving good example to others and living at peace.

ENTRANCE ANT.   See Sir 36, 18

**Give peace, Lord, to those who wait for you and
your prophets will proclaim you as you deserve. Hear
the prayers of your servant and of your people Israel.**

OPENING PRAYER

Almighty God,
our creator and guide,
may we serve you with all our heart
and know your forgiveness in our lives.
We ask this through our Lord Jesus Christ, your Son,
who lives and reigns with you and the Holy Spirit,
one God, for ever and ever. ℟. **Amen.** ✔

ALTERNATIVE OPENING PRAYER

Father in heaven, Creator of all,
look down upon your people in their moments of
    need,
for you alone are the source of our peace.
Bring us to the dignity which distinguishes the poor
    in spirit
and show us how great is the call to serve,
that we may share in the peace of Christ
who offered his life in the service of all.
We ask this through Christ our Lord. ℟. **Amen.** ✔

READINGS AND INTERVENIENT CHANTS

The *weekday* readings and intervenient chants for the
1st to 9th Weeks in Ordinary Time are found on pp.
207-421.

PRAYER OVER THE GIFTS

Lord,
hear the prayers of your people
and receive our gifts.
May the worship of each one here

bring salvation to all.
Grant this through Christ our Lord.
℟. **Amen.** ➔ No. 21, p. 626 (Pref. P 37-42)

COMMUNION ANT. Ps 36, 8

O God, how much we value your mercy! All mankind can gather under your protection. ❯

OR See 1 Cor 10, 16

The cup that we bless is a communion with the blood of Christ; and the bread that we break is a communion with the body of the Lord. ❯

PRAYER AFTER COMMUNION
Lord,
may the eucharist you have given us
influence our thoughts and actions.
May your Spirit guide and direct us in your way.
We ask this in the name of Jesus the Lord.
℟. **Amen.** ────────── ➔ No. 32, p. 650

25th WEEK

Love is a movement of the mind and heart. It is one of man's greatest and most powerful emotions. The world has many definitions for the word and places various interpretations upon it. The gospels tell us love is patient, kind, and never fails.

ENTRANCE ANT.

I am the Savior of all people, says the Lord. Whatever their troubles, I will answer their cry, and I will always be their Lord. ➔ No. 2, p. 614

OPENING PRAYER
Father, guide us, as you guide creation
according to your law of love.
May we love one another
and come to perfection
in the eternal life prepared for us.
Grant this through our Lord Jesus Christ, your Son,
who lives and reigns with you and the Holy Spirit,
one God, for ever and ever. ℟. **Amen.** ❯

ALTERNATIVE OPENING PRAYER

Father in heaven,
the perfection of justice is found in your love
and all mankind is in need of your law.
Help us to find this love in each other
that justice may be attained
through obedience to your law.
We ask this through Christ our Lord. ℞. **Amen.** ✟

READINGS AND INTERVENIENT CHANTS

The *weekday* readings and intervenient chants for the
1st to 9th Weeks in Ordinary Time on pp. 207-421.

PRAYER OVER THE GIFTS

Lord,
may these gifts which we now offer
to show our belief and our love
be pleasing to you.
May they become for us
the eucharist of Jesus Christ your Son,
who is Lord for ever and ever.
℞. **Amen.**   ➤ No. 21, p. 626 (Pref. P 37-42)

COMMUNION ANT.   Ps 119, 4-5

**You have laid down your precepts to be faithfully
kept. May my footsteps be firm in keeping your commands.** ✟

OR   Jn 10, 14

**I am the Good Shepherd, says the Lord; I know my
sheep, and mine know me.** ✟

PRAYER AFTER COMMUNION

Lord, help us with your kindness.
Make us strong through the eucharist.
May we put into action
the saving mystery we celebrate.
We ask this in the name of Jesus the Lord.
℞. **Amen.**   ➤ No. 32, p. 650

26th WEEK

When we are disobedient to the commandments given by God, we bring sorrow to others, to God, and, in the end, to ourselves. The people of God who shall live forever are those who do his will. Through obedience to God's word, men are enable to enter into a close personal relationship with our Divine Savior.

ENTRANCE ANT.   Dan 3, 31. 29. 30. 43. 42

O Lord, you had just cause to judge men as you did: because we sinned against you and disobeyed your will. But now show us your greatness of heart, and treat us with your unbounded kindness.

OPENING PRAYER   ➤ No. 2, p. 614

Father,
you show your almighty power
in your mercy and forgiveness.
Continue to fill us with your gifts of love.
Help us to hurry toward the eternal life you promise
and come to share in the joys of your kingdom.
Grant this through our Lord Jesus Christ, your Son,
who lives and reigns with you and the Holy Spirit,
one God, for ever and ever. ℟. **Amen.**

ALTERNATIVE OPENING PRAYER

Father of our Lord Jesus Christ,
in your unbounded mercy
you have revealed the beauty of your power
through your constant forgiveness of our sins.
May the power of this love be in our hearts
to bring your pardon and your kingdom to all we
    meet.
We ask this through Christ our Lord. ℟. **Amen.** ▼

READINGS AND INTERVENIENT CHANTS

The *weekday* readings and intervenient chants for the 1st to 9th Weeks in Ordinary Time on pp. 207-421.

PRAYER OVER THE GIFTS

God of mercy,
accept our offering

and make it a source of blessing for us.
We ask this in the name of Jesus the Lord.
℟. **Amen.**   ➜ No. 21, p. 626 (Pref. P 37-42)

COMMUNION ANT.   Ps 119, 49-50

**O Lord, remember the words you spoke to me, your
servant, which made me live in hope and consoled
me when I was downcast.** ✟

OR   1 Jn 3, 16

**This is how we know what love is: Christ gave up
his life for us; and we too must give up our lives for
our brothers.** ✟

PRAYER AFTER COMMUNION

Lord, may this eucharist
in which we proclaim the death of Christ
bring us salvation
and make us one with him in glory,
for he is Lord for ever and ever.
℟. **Amen.**   _____   ➜ No. 32, p. 650

27th WEEK

A just God is present. If we wish to find him, we must seek him. We
must not be misled by a world where just men suffer and unjust men
prosper. God has given us his Son to remain with us and to show
us the way to the Father.

ENTRANCE ANT.   Est 13, 9. 10-11

**O Lord, you have given everything its place in the
world, and no one can make it otherwise. For it is
your creation, the heavens and the earth and the
stars: you are the Lord of all.**

OPENING PRAYER

Father,
your love for us
surpasses all our hopes and desires.
Forgive our failings,
keep us in your peace
and lead us in the way of salvation.

We ask this through our Lord Jesus Christ, your Son,
who lives and reigns with you and the Holy Spirit,
one God, for ever and ever. ℞. **Amen.** ↓

ALTERNATIVE OPENING PRAYER

Almighty and eternal God,
Father of the world to come,
your goodness is beyond what our spirit can touch
and your strength is more than the mind can bear.
Lead us to seek beyond our reach
and give us the courage to stand before your truth.
We ask this through Christ our Lord. ℞. **Amen.** ↓

READINGS AND INTERVENIENT CHANTS

The *weekday* readings and intervenient chants for the
1st to 9th Weeks in Ordinary Time are found on pp.
207-421.

PRAYER OVER THE GIFTS

Father,
receive these gifts
which our Lord Jesus Christ
has asked us to offer in his memory.
May our obedient service
bring us to the fullness of your redemption.
We ask this in the name of Jesus the Lord.
℞. **Amen.**   ➔ No. 21, p. 626 (Pref. P 37-42)

COMMUNION ANT.   Lam 3, 25

**The Lord is good to those who hope in him, to those
who are searching for his love.** ↓

OR   See 1 Cor 10- 17

**Because there is one bread, we, though many, are
one body, for we all share in the one loaf and in the
one cup.** ↓

PRAYER AFTER COMMUNION

Almighty God,
let the eucharist we share
fill us with your life.

May the love of Christ
which we celebrate here
touch our lives and lead us to you.
We ask this in the name of Jesus the Lord.
℟. **Amen.** _____ ➤ No. 32, p. 650

28th WEEK

Jesus warns us against being overly concerned about the riches of
the world which can blind us to the spiritual wealth of the Father. In
our need to overcome spiritual ▌poverty, we must pray for a healthy
detachment from material riches and a realization of the true riches
of God.

ENTRANCE ANT.   Ps 130, 3-4

**If you, O Lord, laid bare our guilt, who could endure
it? But you are forgiving, God of Israel.**

➤ No. 2, p. 614

OPENING PRAYER

Lord, our help and guide,
make your love the foundation of our lives.
May our love for you express itself
in our eagerness to do good for others.
Grant this through our Lord Jesus Christ, your Son,
who lives and reigns with you and the Holy Spirit,
one God, for ever and ever. ℟. **Amen.** ⋁

ALTERNATIVE OPENING PRAYER

Father in heaven,
the hand of your loving kindness
powerfully yet gently guides all the moments of our
    day.
Go before us in our pilgrimage of life,
anticipate our needs and prevent our falling.
Send your Spirit to unite us in faith,
that sharing in your service,
we may rejoice in your presence.
We ask this through Christ our Lord. ℟. **Amen.** ⋁

READINGS AND INTERVENIENT CHANTS

The *weekday* readings and intervenient chants for the
1st to 9th Weeks in Ordinary Time are found on pp.
207-421.

PRAYER OVER THE GIFTS

Lord,
accept the prayers and gifts
we offer in faith and love.
May this eucharist bring us to your glory.
We ask this in the name of Jesus the Lord.
℟. **Amen.**　　　　→ No. 21, p. 626 (Pref. P 37-42)

COMMUNION ANT.　　　　Ps 34, 11

**The rich suffer want and go hungry, but nothing
shall be lacking to those who fear the Lord.** ⩔

OR　　　　1 Jn 3, 2

**When the Lord is revealed we shall be like him, for
we shall see him as he is.** ⩔

PRAYER AFTER COMMUNION

Almighty Father,
may the body and blood of your Son
give us a share in his life,
for he is Lord for ever and ever.
℟. **Amen.**　　　　→ No. 32, p. 650

29th WEEK

Carelessness and indifference may dim our vision; indeed, we may
be spiritually blind. Let us pray that we may see Jesus Christ as the
true spiritual guide of our lives and that we may see the light of
truth in what God has revealed.

ENTRANCE ANT.　　　　Ps 17, 6. 8

**I call upon you, God, for you will answer me; bend
your ear and hear my prayer. Guard me as the pupil
of your eye; hide me in the shade of your wings.**
　　　　→ No. 2, p. 614

OPENING PRAYER

Almighty and ever-living God,
our source of power and inspiration,
give us strength and joy
in serving you as followers of Christ,

who lives and reigns with you and the Holy Spirit,
one God, for ever and ever. R℣. **Amen.** ℣

ALTERNATIVE OPENING PRAYER

Lord our God, Father of all,
you guard us under the shadow of your wings
and search into the depths of our hearts.
Remove the blindness that cannot know you
and relieve the fear that would hide us from your
    sight.
We ask this through Christ our Lord. R℣. **Amen.** ℣

READINGS AND INTERVENIENT CHANTS

The *weekday* readings and intervenient chants for the
1st to 9th Weeks in Ordinary Time are found on pp.
207-421.

PRAYER OVER THE GIFTS

Lord God,
may the gifts we offer
bring us your love and forgiveness
and give us freedom to serve you with our lives.
We ask this in the name of Jesus the Lord.
R℣. **Amen.**   → No. 21, p. 626, (Pref. P 37-42)

COMMUNION ANT.   Ps 33, 18-19

**See how the eyes of the Lord are on those who fear
him, on those who hope in his love, that he may
rescue them from death and feed them in time of
famine.** ℣

OR   Mk 10, 45

**The Son of Man came to give his life as a ransom
for many.** ℣

PRAYER AFTER COMMUNION

Lord,
may this eucharist help us to remain faithful.
May it teach us the way to eternal life.
Grant this through Christ our Lord.
R℣. **Amen.**   → No. 32, p. 650

30th WEEK

The reign of God does not begin at the moment of our death. Rather, it begins in each of us at our baptism and continues to grow and flourish throughout our entire life. Let us celebrate and rejoice in the great riches we have as God's people through Christ.

ENTRANCE ANT.   Ps 105, 3-4

Let hearts rejoice who search for the Lord. Seek the Lord and his strength, seek always the face of the Lord.   ➔ No. 2, p. 614

OPENING PRAYER

Almighty and ever-living God,
strengthen our faith, hope, and love.
May we do with loving hearts
what you ask of us
and come to share the life you promise.
We ask this through our Lord Jesus Christ, your Son,
who lives and reigns with you and the Holy Spirit,
one God, for ever and ever. ℞. **Amen.** ⬇

ALTERNATIVE OPENING PRAYER

Praised be you, God and Father of our Lord Jesus
    Christ.
There is no power for good
    which does not come from your covenant,
and no promise to hope in,
that your love has not offered.
Strengthen our faith to accept your covenant
and give us the love to carry out your command.
We ask this through Christ our Lord. ℞. **Amen.** ⬇

READINGS AND INTERVENIENT CHANTS

The *weekday* readings and intervenient chants for the 1st to 9th Weeks in Ordinary Time on pp. 207-421.

PRAYER OVER THE GIFTS

Lord God of power and might,
receive the gifts we offer
and let our service give you glory.
Grant this through Christ our Lord.
℞. **Amen.**   ➔ No. 21, p. 626, (Pref. P 37-42)

COMMUNION ANT.   Ps 20, 6

We will rejoice at the victory of God and make our boast in his great name. ℣

OR   Eph 5, 2

Christ loved us and gave himself up for us as a fragrant offering to God. ℣

PRAYER AFTER COMMUNION

Lord,
bring to perfection within us
the communion we share in this sacrament.
May our celebration have an effect in our lives.
We ask this in the name of Jesus the Lord.
℟. **Amen.**   ➜ No. 32, p. 650

31st WEEK

The Church is the sacrament of Christ's presence in the world. The people of God constitute the Church, and to the extent that we follow Christ's teachings and have an effect on the world, Christ will be present in the world. Let us thank the Lord for his continued presence and love.

ENTRANCE ANT.   Ps 38, 22-23

Do not abandon me, Lord. My God, do not go away from me! Hurry to help me, Lord, my Savior.
➜ No. 2, p. 614

OPENING PRAYER

God of power and mercy,
only with your help
can we offer you fitting service and praise.
May we live the faith we profess
and trust your promise of eternal life.
Grant this through our Lord Jesus Christ, your Son,
who lives and reigns with you and the Holy Spirit,
one God, for ever and ever. ℟. **Amen.** ℣

ALTERNATIVE OPENING PRAYER

Father in heaven, God of power and Lord of mercy,
from whose fullness we have received,

direct our steps in our everyday efforts.
May the changing moods of the human heart
and the limits which our failings impose on hope
never blind us to you, source of every good.
Faith gives us the promise of peace
and makes known the demands of love.
Remove the selfishness that blurs the vision of faith.
Grant this through Christ our Lord. ℟. **Amen.** ↓

READINGS AND INTERVENIENT CHANTS

The *weekday* readings and intervenient chants for the
1st to 9th Weeks in Ordinary Time are found on pp.
207-421.

PRAYER OVER THE GIFTS

God of mercy,
may we offer a pure sacrifice
for the forgiveness of our sins.
We ask this through Christ our Lord.
℟. **Amen.**   ➔ No. 21, p. 626, (Pref. P 37-42)

COMMUNION ANT.   Ps 16, 11
**Lord, you will show me the path of life and fill me
with joy in your presence.** ↓

OR   Jn 6, 58
**As the living Father sent me, and I live because of
the Father, so he who eats my flesh and drinks my
blood will live because of me.** ↓

PRAYER AFTER COMMUNION

Lord,
you give us new hope in this eucharist.
May the power of your love
continue its saving work among us
and bring us to the joy you promise.
We ask this in the name of Jesus the Lord.
℟. **Amen.**   ➔ No. 32, p. 650

32nd WEEK

Jesus inspired the people of his day because his authority was from a source beyond this world, and the people were in awe as the Spirit worked in him. So, too, for us. We should be in awe as we look about us at all God's creation, at all that has been given to us.

ENTRANCE ANT. Ps 88, 3

Let my prayer come before you, Lord; listen, and answer me. ➤ No. 2, p. 614

OPENING PRAYER

God of power and mercy,
protect us from all harm.
Give us freedom of spirit
and health in mind and body
to do your work on earth.
We ask this through our Lord Jesus Christ, your Son,
who lives and reigns with you and the Holy Spirit,
one God, for ever and ever. ℟. **Amen.** ✟

ALTERNATIVE OPENING PRAYER

Almighty Father,
strong is your justice and great is your mercy.
Protect us in the burdens and challenges of life.
Shield our minds from the distortion of pride
and enfold our desire with the beauty of truth.
Help us to become more aware of your loving design
so that we may more willingly give our lives in service to all.
We ask this through Christ our Lord. ℟. **Amen.** ✟

READINGS AND INTERVENIENT CHANTS

The *weekday* readings and intervenient chants for the 1st to 9th Weeks in Ordinary Time, on pp. 207-421.

PRAYER OVER THE GIFTS

God of mercy,
in this eucharist we proclaim the death of the Lord.
Accept the gifts we present
and help us follow him with love,
for he is Lord for ever and ever.
℟. **Amen.** ➤ No. 21, p. 626, (Pref. P 37-42)

COMMUNION ANT. Ps 23, 1-2

The Lord is my shepherd; there is nothing I shall want. In green pastures he gives me rest, he leads me beside the waters of peace. ℣

OR Lk 24, 35

The disciples recognized the Lord Jesus in the breaking of bread. ℣

PRAYER AFTER COMMUNION

Lord,
we thank you for the nourishment you give us
through your holy gift.
Pour out your Spirit upon us
and in the strength of this food from heaven
keep us single-minded in your service.
We ask this in the name of Jesus the Lord.
℟. **Amen.** ———————— → No. 32, p. 650

33rd WEEK

Faith is our instrument of peace, and if it is sincere and good, we do not need miracles to keep it alive. We know that God is with us always, in times of trouble as well as in times of joy. Look about you and believe!

ENTRANCE ANT. Jer 29, 11. 12. 14

The Lord says: my plans for you are peace and not disaster; when you call to me, I will listen to you, and I will bring you back to the place from which I exiled you.

OPENING PRAYER

Father of all that is good,
keep us faithful in serving you,
for to serve you is our lasting joy.
We ask this through our Lord Jesus Christ, your Son,
who lives and reigns with you and the Holy Spirit,
one God, for ever and ever. ℟. **Amen.** ℣

ALTERNATIVE OPENING PRAYER

Father in heaven,
ever-living source of all that is good,

from the beginning of time you promised man salvation
through the future coming of your Son, our Lord
Jesus Christ.
Help us to drink of his truth
and expand our hearts with the joy of his promises,
so that we may serve you in faith and in love
and know for ever the joy of your presence.
We ask this through Christ our Lord. ℟. **Amen.** ↓

READINGS AND INTERVENIENT CHANTS

The *weekday* readings and intervenient chants for the
1st to 9th Weeks in Ordinary Time are found on pp.
207-421.

PRAYER OVER THE GIFTS

Lord God,
may the gifts we offer
increase our love for you
and bring us to eternal life.
We ask this in the name of Jesus the Lord.
℟. **Amen.**   ➜ No. 21, p. 626 (Pref. P 37-42)

COMMUNION ANT.   Ps 73, 28

It is good for me to be with the Lord and to put my
hope in him. ↓

OR   Mk 11, 23. 24

I tell you solemnly, whatever you ask for in prayer,
believe that you have received it, and it will be yours,
says the Lord. ↓

PRAYER AFTER COMMUNION

Father,
may we grow in love
by the eucharist we have celebrated
in memory of the Lord Jesus,
who is Lord for ever and ever.
℟. **Amen.**   ➜ No. 32, p. 650

34th WEEK

ENTRANCE ANT.   Ps 85, 9

**The Lord speaks of peace to his holy people, to those
who turn to him with all their heart.** → No. 2, p. 614

OPENING PRAYER

Lord, increase our eagerness to do your will
and help us to know the saving power of your love.
Grant this through our Lord Jesus Christ, your Son,
who lives and reigns with you and the Holy Spirit,
one God, for ever and ever. ℟. **Amen.** ↓

READINGS AND INTERVENIENT CHANTS

The *weekday* readings and intervenient chants for the
1st to 9th Weeks in Ordinary Time on pp. 207-421.

PRAYER OVER THE GIFTS

God of love,
may the sacrifice we offer
in obedience to your command
renew our resolution to be faithful to your word.
We ask this through Christ our Lord.
℟. **Amen.**   → No. 21, p. 626 (Pref. P 37-42)

COMMUNION ANT.   Ps 117, 1-2

**All you nations, praise the Lord, for steadfast is his
kindly mercy to us.** ↓

OR   Mt 28, 20

**I, the Lord, am with you always, until the end of the
world.**

PRAYER AFTER COMMUNION

Almighty God, in this eucharist
you give us the joy of sharing your life.
Keep us in your presence.
Let us never be separated from you.
We ask this in the name of Jesus the Lord.
℟. **Amen.**   → No. 32, p. 650

READINGS AND INTERVENIENT
CHANTS FOR ORDINARY TIME

INTRODUCTION FOR 1st to 4th WEEK

The Epistle to the Hebrews—*Written to a community of Christians afflicted with trials and in danger of lapsing into Judaizing practices, this Epistle describes most eloquently the eminent superiority of the new dispensation over the old. Inaugurated by the Son of God himself, this new dispensation was God's final revelation to man. It completed the message of the Prophets, and brought to perfection all that was of permanent value in the Mosaic covenant. The incarnate Son of God was its High Priest, and his glorious sacrifice was truly efficacious before God in the forgiveness of sin. As suffering and humiliation had an important place in his victory, his followers are exhorted to forego worldly advantage, to bear their trials patiently, and to persevere heroically in the faith.*

The Books of Samuel—*This single work comprises the history of about a century, describing the close of the age of the Judges and the beginnings of monarchy in Israel. By a series of episodes centered around the persons of Samuel, Saul, and David, the writer shows us the conditions and the problems of God's kingdom on earth. The most important spiritual values imparted are to be found in the work's relation to the messianic kingdom of Christ. Though David's earthly kingdom crumbled after his death, his greater achievement survived: the foundation of a spiritual kingdom that would never pass. The people of Israel, freed from their enemies, symbolize the Christian people delivered from spiritual foes.*

The Books of Kings — *In conjunction with the Books of Samuel, these two books, which are originally one work, extend the consecutive history of Israel* from the birth of Samuel to the destruction of Jerusalem in 587 B.C. The purpose of this latter work is to show that the happiness of the Chosen People was intimately associated with the observance of God's law. Hence, the author bitterly denounces the sins of the kings and people. The cardinal sin of the Kingdom of Israel was idolatry, while that of the Kingdom of Judah was the worship of either Yahweh on high places or false deities. The unified worship at the central sanctuary is stressed.

The Gospel of Mark — *Written at Rome about 70 A.D. by Mark, a companion of St. Paul and later a co-worker of St. Peter, this Gospel is short, vivid, concrete, and gives the impression of immediate contact with Jesus. It makes use of a familiar style that is occasionally awkward but always direct, and might almost be called photographic in its handling of details. Mark desires to establish a close bond between the Passion of Jesus and his Lordship, showing that the Son of Man had to endure the Cross before attaining his glory and that his destiny is that of the Suffering Servant prophesied by Isaiah (ch. 53). It is also his design to teach us that if we want to encounter the living Christ, we must follow his Way. We will deserve the name of his disciple only if we accept the same destiny as the Master.*

MONDAY OF THE FIRST WEEK
IN ORDINARY TIME

———— **YEAR I** ————

READING I   Heb 1, 1-6

Jesus is the Son of God. Jesus took upon himself our human nature so that as both God and man he could offer himself as a redemption. Paul stresses the uniqueness of Jesus' role, even far superior to the angels.

The beginning of the letter to the Hebrews

In times past, God spoke in fragmentary and varied ways to our fathers through the prophets; in this, the final age, he has spoken to us through his Son, whom he has made heir of all things and through whom he first created the universe. This Son is the reflection of the Father's being, and he sustains all things by his powerful word. When he had cleansed us from our sins, he took his seat at the right hand of the Majesty in heaven, as far superior to the angels as the name he has inherited is superior to theirs.

To which of the angels did God ever say,

"You are my son; today I have begotten you"?
Or again,

"I will be his father, and he shall be my son"?
And again when he leads his first-born into the world, he says,

"Let all the angels of God worship him."
This is the Word of the Lord. ℞. **Thanks be to God.** ℣

Responsorial Psalm   Ps 97, 1-2. 6-7. 9

℞. (7) **Let all his angels worship him.**

The Lord is king; let the earth rejoice;
  let the many isles be glad.
Justice and judgment are the foundation of his
      throne. — ℞

The heavens proclaim his justice,
  and all peoples see his glory.

All gods are prostrate before him. — ℟

Because you, O Lord, are the Most High over all the
   earth,
   exalted far above all gods. — ℟ ⩒

———— **YEAR II** ————

READING I   1 Sm 1, 1-8

Samuel's identity is established in terms of people and places. The
custom of an annual visit to the sanctuary may be taken as a favorable
comment on the piety of Elkanah and his family. The climax of the
pilgrimage comes with the sacrificial meal, the mood of which is one
of gaiety and joy in God.

   The beginning of the first book of Samuel

There was a certain man from Ramathaim, Elkanah
by name, a Zuphite from the hill country of Ephraim.
He was the son of Jeroham, son of Elihu, son of
Tohu, son of Zuph, an Ephraimite. He had two
wives, one named Hannah, the other Peninnah; Peninnah had children, but Hannah was childless. This
man regularly went on pilgrimage from his city to
worship the Lord of hosts and to sacrifice to him at
Shiloh, where the two sons of Eli, Hophni and Phinehas, were ministering as priests of the Lord. When
the day came for Elkanah to offer sacrifice, he used
to give a portion each to his wife Peninnah and to all
her sons and daughters, but a double portion to Hannah because he loved her, though the Lord had made
her barren. Her rival, to upset her, turned it into a
constant reproach to her that the Lord had left her
barren. This went on year after year; each time they
made their pilgrimage to the sanctuary of the Lord,
Peninnah would reproach her, and Hannah would
weep and refuse to eat. Her husband Elkanah used to
ask her: "Hannah, why do you weep, and why do you
refuse to eat? Why do you grieve? Am I not more to
you than ten sons?"—This is the Word of the Lord.
℟. **Thanks be to God.** ⩒

Responsorial Psalm Ps 116, 12-13. 14-17. 18-19

℟. (17) **To you, Lord, I will offer a sacrifice of praise.**

How shall I make a return to the Lord
  for all the good he has done for me?
The cup of salvation I will take up,
  and I will call upon the name of the Lord. — ℟

My vows to the Lord I will pay
  in the presence of all his people.
Precious in the eyes of the Lord
  is the death of his faithful ones.
O Lord, I am your servant;
  I am your servant, the son of your handmaid;
  you have loosed my bonds.
To you will I offer sacrifice of thanksgiving,
  and I will call upon the name of the Lord. — ℟

My vows to the Lord I will pay
  in the presence of all his people.
In the courts of the house of the Lord,
  in your midst, O Jerusalem. — ℟ ℣

℟. Or: **Alleluia.** ℣

——————— YEAR I AND II ———————

GOSPEL Mk 1, 14-20

Alleluia (Mk 1, 15)

℟. **Alleluia.** The kingdom of God is near, says the
    Lord;
repent and believe in the Good News! ℟. **Alleluia.**

Mark fixes the arrest of John as the decisive moment for the beginning of the ministry of our Lord. The way had been prepared by John.
Christ himself called his message the "good news" (Is 61, 1-2). Christ
bids his disciples to leave everything and follow him.

℣. The Lord be with you. ℟. **And also with you.**
✠ A reading from the holy gospel according to Mark
℟. **Glory to you, Lord.**

After John's arrest, Jesus appeared in Galilee, proclaiming the good news of God: "This is the time of

fulfillment. The reign of God is at hand! Reform your lives and believe in the good news!"

As he made his way along the Sea of Galilee, he observed Simon and his brother Andrew casting their nets into the sea; they were fishermen. Jesus said to them, "Come after me; I will make you fishers of men." They immediately abandoned their nets and became his followers. Proceeding a little farther along, he caught sight of James, Zebedee's son, and his brother John. They too were in their boat putting their nets in order. He summoned them on the spot. They abandoned their father Zebedee, who was in the boat with the hired men, and went off in his company.—This is the gospel of the Lord. ℟. **Praise to you, Lord Jesus Christ.**   ➔ No. 15, p. 623

TUESDAY OF THE FIRST WEEK IN ORDINARY TIME

—— YEAR I ——

READING I   Heb 2, 5-12

The world has been made subject to the glorified Son as the climax of an ascending movement that began in the humiliation of Christ's earthly life, suffering, and death. Here St. Paul regards all things as already subject to Christ in virtue of his exaltation. The designation of our Lord as leader announces the journey of the people of God to the place of rest, the heavenly sanctuary, in the footsteps of our Lord, their forerunner.

A reading from the letter to the Hebrews

For God did not make the world to come—that world of which we speak—subject to angels. Somewhere this is testified to, in the passage that says:

"What is man that you should be mindful of him,
      or the son of man that you should care for him?
You made him for a little while lower than the
      angels;

you crowned him with glory and honor,
and put all things under his feet."

In subjecting all things to him, God left nothing unsubjected. At present we do not see all things thus subject, but we do see Jesus crowned with glory and honor because he suffered death: Jesus, who was made for a little while lower than the angels, that through God's gracious will he might taste death for the sake of all men. Indeed, it was fitting that when bringing many sons to glory, God, for whom and through whom all things exist, should make their leader in the work of salvation perfect through suffering. He who consecrates and those who are consecrated have one and the same Father. Therefore he is not ashamed to call them brothers, saying,

"I will announce your name to my brothers,
I will sing your praise in the midst of the assembly."

This is the Word of the Lord. ℟. **Thanks be to God.** ℣

Responsorial Psalm Ps 8, 2. 5. 6-7. 8-9

℟. (7) **You gave your Son authority over all your creation.**

O Lord, our Lord,
how glorious is your name over all the earth!
What is man that you should be mindful of him,
or the son of man that you should care for him?—℟

You have made him little less than the angels,
and crowned him with glory and honor.
You have given him rule over the works of your hands,
putting all things under his feet: — ℟

All sheep and oxen,
yes, and the beasts of the field,
The birds of the air, the fishes of the sea,
and whatever swims the paths of the seas. — ℟ ℣

—— **YEAR II** ——

READING I   1 Sm 1, 9-20

Only the birth of a son will console Hannah. She has vowed that she
will dedicate her son, if she has one, to Yahweh. Her prayers are
answered. Hannah names her son Samuel. The name is entirely fitting
for one who bears a special mission from God.

A reading from the first book of Samuel

Hannah rose after a meal at Shiloh, and presented
herself before the Lord; at the time, Eli the priest
was sitting on a chair near the doorpost of the Lord's
temple. In her bitterness she prayed to the Lord,
weeping copiously, and she made a vow, promising:
"O Lord of hosts, if you look with pity on the misery
of your handmaid, if you remember me and do not
forget me, if you give your handmaid a male child, I
will give him to the Lord for as long as he lives;
neither wine nor liquor shall he drink, and no razor
shall ever touch his head." As she remained long at
prayer before the Lord, Eli watched her mouth, for
Hannah was praying silently; though her lips were
moving, her voice could not be heard. Eli, thinking
her drunk, said to her, "How long will you make a
drunken show of yourself? Sober up from your wine!"
"It isn't that, my lord," Hannah answered. "I am an
unhappy woman. I have had neither wine nor liquor;
I was only pouring out my troubles to the Lord. Do
not think your handmaid a ne'er-do-well; my prayer
has been prompted by my deep sorrow and misery."
Eli said, "Go in peace, and may the God of Israel
grant you what you have asked of him." She replied,
"Think kindly of your maidservant," and left. She
went to her quarters, ate and drank with her husband, and no longer appeared downcast. Early the
next morning they worshiped before the Lord, and
then returned to their home in Ramah.

When Elkanah had relations with his wife Hannah, the Lord remembered her. She conceived, and

at the end of her term bore a son whom she called Samuel, since she had asked the Lord for him.— This is the Word of the Lord. ℟. **Thanks be to God.** ↓

Responsorial Psalm 1 Sm 2, 1. 4-5. 6-7. 8

℟. (1) **My heart rejoices in the Lord, my Savior.**

My heart exults in the Lord,
    my horn is exalted in my God.
I have swallowed up my enemies;
    I rejoice in my victory. — ℟

The bows of the mighty are broken,
    while the tottering gird on strength.
The well-fed hire themselves out for bread,
    while the hungry batten on spoil.
The barren wife bears seven sons,
    while the mother of many languishes. — ℟

The Lord puts to death and gives life:
    he casts down to the nether world;
    he raises up again.
The Lord makes poor and makes rich,
    he humbles, he also exalts. — ℟

He raises the needy from the dust;
    from the ash heap he lifts up the poor,
To seat them with nobles
    and make a glorious throne their heritage. — ℟ ↓

———— **YEAR I AND II** ————

GOSPEL Mk 1, 21-28

Alleluia (1 Thes 2, 13)

℟. **Alleluia.** Receive this message not as the words
    of man,
but as truly the word of God. ℟. **Alleluia.**

The teaching and healing by our Lord in Capernaum illustrate his authority in word and act. Christ's teaching is connected with his miraculous power, and it causes amazement. His mighty words are immediately followed by a cluster of miracles, signs more wondrous even than the discourse to which they bore witness.

℣. The Lord be with you. ℟. **And also with you.**
✠ A reading from the holy gospel according to Mark
℟. **Glory to you, Lord.**

[In the city of Capernaum,] Jesus entered the synagague on the sabbath and began to teach. The people were spellbound by his teaching because he taught with authority and not like the scribes.

There appeared in their synagogue a man with an unclean spirit that shrieked: "What do you want of us, Jesus of Nazareth? Have you come to destroy us? I know who you are—the holy One of God!" Jesus rebuked him sharply: "Be quiet! Come out of the man!" At that the unclean spirit convulsed the man violently and with a loud shriek came out of him. All who looked on were amazed. They began to ask one another: "What does this mean? A completely new teaching in a spirit of authority! He gives orders to unclean spirits and they obey!" From that point on his reputation spread throughout the surrounding region of Galilee.—This is the gospel of the Lord.
℟. **Praise to you, Lord Jesus Christ.** ➔ No. 15, p. 623

WEDNESDAY OF THE FIRST WEEK
IN ORDINARY TIME

——— YEAR 1 ———

READING I Heb 2, 14-18

In the biblical sense, "flesh" means human nature considered in its weakness and frailty, and as such it is contrasted with "spirit" and God. Because of the connection between sin and death, the power of death was broken when Christ removed sin. Because of Jesus, the nature of death was changed.

A reading from the letter to the Hebrews

Since the children are men of blood and flesh, Jesus likewise had a full share in ours, that by his death he might rob the devil, the prince of death, of his power, and free those who through fear of death had

been slaves their whole life long. Surely he did not come to help angels, but rather the children of Abraham; therefore he had to become like his brothers in every way, that he might be a merciful and faithful high priest before God on their behalf, to expiate the sins of the people. Since he was himself tested through what he suffered, he is able to help those who are tempted.—This is the Word of the Lord.
℟. **Thanks be to God.** ♦

Responsorial Psalm   Ps 105, 1-2. 3-4. 6-7. 8-9

℟. (8) **The Lord remembers his covenant for ever.**

Give thanks to the Lord, invoke his name;
    make known among the nations his deeds.
Sing to him, sing his praise,
    proclaim all his wondrous deeds. — ℟

Glory in his holy name;
    rejoice, O hearts that seek the Lord!
Look to the Lord in his strength;
    seek to serve him constantly. — ℟

You descendants of Abraham, his servants,
    sons of Jacob, his chosen ones!
He, the Lord, is our God!
    throughout the earth his judgments prevail. — ℟

He remembers forever his covenant
    which he made binding for a thousand generations—
Which he entered into with Abraham
    and by his oath to Isaac. — ℟ ♦

℟. Or: **Alleluia.** ♦

——— **YEAR II** ———

READING I   1 Sm 3, 1-10. 19-20

In Israel the revelation of the Word of God was rare or precious, but the mention of it enhances the significance of the revelation to the young Samuel. He is recognized as a prophet throughout Israel and is represented here as the ruler of all Israel.

A reading from the first book of Samuel

During the time young Samuel was minister to the Lord under Eli, a revelation of the Lord was uncommon and vision infrequent. One day Eli was asleep in his usual place. His eyes had lately grown so weak that he could not see. The lamp of God was not yet extinguished, and Samuel was sleeping in the temple of the Lord where the ark of God was. The Lord called to Samuel, who answered, "Here I am." He ran to Eli and said, "Here I am. You called me." "I did not call you," Eli said. "Go back to sleep." So he went back to sleep. Again the Lord called Samuel, who rose and went to Eli. "Here I am," he said. "You called me." But he answered, "I did not call you, my son. Go back to sleep." At that time Samuel was not familiar with the Lord, because the Lord had not revealed anything to him as yet. The Lord called Samuel again, for the third time. Getting up and going to Eli, he said, "Here I am. You called me." Then Eli understood that the Lord was calling the youth. So he said to Samuel, "Go to sleep, and if you are called, reply, 'Speak, Lord, for your servant is listening.'" When Samuel went to sleep in his place, the Lord came and revealed his presence, calling out as before, "Samuel, Samuel!" Samuel answered, "Speak, for your servant is listening"

Samuel grew up, and the Lord was with him, not permitting any word of his to be without effect. Thus all Israel from Dan to Beer-sheba came to know that Samuel was an accredited prophet of the Lord.—This is the Word of the Lord. ℞. **Thanks be to God.** ℣

Responsorial Psalm   Ps 40, 2-5. 7-8. 8-9. 10

℞. (8. 9) **Here am I, Lord; I come to do your will.**

I have waited, waited for the Lord,
    and he stooped toward me.

Happy the man who makes the Lord his trust;
   who turns not to idolatry
   or to those who stray after falsehood. — ℟

Sacrifice or oblation you wished not,
   but ears open to obedience you gave me.

Holocausts or sin-offerings you sought not;
   then said I, "Behold I come." — ℟

"In the written scroll it is prescribed for me.
   To do your will, O my God, is my delight,
And your law is within my heart!" — ℟

I announced your justice in the vast assembly;
   I did not restrain my lips, as you, O Lord,
     know. — ℟ ℣

————— **YEAR I AND II** —————

GOSPEL   Mk 1, 29-39

Alleluia (Jn 10, 27)

℟. **Alleluia.** My sheep listen to my voice, says the
   Lord;
I know them, and they follow me. ℟. **Alleluia.**

Jesus cures Simon's mother-in-law. When the sun has set, the crowds
bring their sick to the Great Physician to be healed. Jesus enjoins
silence because he does not seek the reputation of a wonder-worker.
His own concept of Messiah is vastly different from that of his contemporaries.

℣. The Lord be with you. ℟. **And also with you.**
✠ A reading from the holy gospel according to Mark
℟. **Glory to you, Lord.**

Upon leaving the synagogue, Jesus entered the house
of Simon and Andrew with James and John. Simon's
mother-in-law lay ill with a fever, and the first thing
they did was to tell him about her. He went over to
her and grasped her hand and helped her up, and the
fever left her. She immediately began to wait on
them.

    After sunset, as evening drew on, they brought
him all who were ill and those possessed by demons.

Before long the whole town was gathered outside the door. Those whom he cured, who were variously afflicted, were many, and so were the demons he expelled. But he would not permit the demons to speak, because they knew him. Rising early the next morning, he went off to a lonely place in the desert; there he was absorbed in prayer. Simon and his companions managed to track him down, and when they found him, they told him, "Everybody is looking for you!" He said to them: "Let us move on to the neighboring villages so that I may proclaim the good news there also. That is what I have come to do." So he went into their synagogues preaching the good news and expelling demons throughout the whole of Galilee.—This is the gospel of the Lord. ℟. **Praise to you, Lord Jesus Christ.**

→ No. 15, p. 623

THURSDAY OF THE FIRST WEEK IN ORDINARY TIME

—— YEAR I ——

READING I   Heb 3, 7-14

God speaks to his people who should always be open to the voice of the Holy Spirit. The followers of Jesus are to support and encourage one another since all are partners in Christ.

A reading from the letter to the Hebrews

As the Holy Spirit says:

"Today, if you should hear his voice,
    harden not your hearts as at the revolt
        in the day of testing in the desert,
When your fathers tested and tried me,
    and saw my works for forty years.
Because of this I was angered with that generation
    and I said, 'They have always been of erring
        heart,
    and have never known my ways.'

Thus I swore in my anger,
'They shall never enter into my rest.' "
Take care, my brothers, lest any of you have an evil
and unfaithful spirit and fall away from the living
God. Encourage one another daily while it is still
"today," so that no one grows hardened by the deceit
of sin. We have become partners of Christ if only
we maintain to the end that confidence with which
we began.—This is the Word of the Lord. ℟. **Thanks
be to God.** ✟

Responsorial Psalm   Ps 95, 6-7. 8-9. 10-11

℟. (8) **If today you hear his voice,
harden not your hearts.**

Come, let us bow down in worship;
let us kneel before the Lord who made us.
For he is our God,
and we are the people he shepherds, the flock he
guides. — ℟

Oh, that today you would hear his voice:
"Harden not your hearts as at Meribah,
as in the day of Massah in the desert,
Where your fathers tempted me;
they tested me though they had seen my
works." — ℟

Forty years I loathed that generation,
and I said: They are a people of erring heart,
and they know not my ways.
Therefore I swore in my anger:
They shall not enter into my rest." — ℟ ✟

———   **YEAR II**   ———

READING I   1 Sm 4, 1-11

The Israelites are utterly defeated, the Ark is captured, and Eli's two
sons are killed. The Elders had felt that the presence of the Ark
among the troops would boost their morale. It was not commonly
carried to the front lines of battle.

A reading form the first book of Samuel

The Philistines gathered for an attack on Israel. Israel went out to engage them in battle and camped at Ebenezer, while the Philistines camped at Aphek. The Philistines then drew up in battle formation against Israel. After a fierce struggle Israel was defeated by the Philistines, who slew about four thousand men on the battlefield. When the troops retired to the camp, the elders of Israel said, "Why has the Lord permitted us to be defeated today by the Philistines? Let us fetch the ark of the Lord from Shiloh that it may go into battle among us and save us from the grasp of our enemies."

So the people sent to Shiloh and brought from there the ark of the Lord of hosts, who is enthroned upon the cherubim. The two sons of Eli, Hophni and Phinehas, were with the ark of God. When the ark of the Lord arrived in the camp, all Israel shouted so loudly that the earth resounded. The Philistines, hearing the noise of shouting, asked, "What can this loud shouting in the camp of the Hebrews mean?" On learning that the ark of the Lord had come into the camp, the Philistines were frightened. They said, "Gods have come to their camp." They said also, "Woe to us! This has never happened before. Woe to us! Who can deliver us from the power of these mighty gods? These are the gods that struck the Egyptians with various plagues and with pestilence. Take courage and be manly, Philistines; otherwise you will become slaves to the Hebrews, as they were your slaves. So fight manfully!" The Philistines fought and Israel was defeated; every man fled to his own tent. It was a disastrous defeat, in which Israel lost thirty thousand foot soldiers. The ark of God was captured, and Eli's two sons, Hophni and Phinehas, were among the dead.—This is the Word of the Lord. ℟. **Thanks be to God.** ℣

Responsorial Psalm   Ps 44, 10-11. 14-15. 25-26

℟. (27) **Save us, Lord, in your mercy.**

Yet now you have cast us off and put us in disgrace,
     and you go not forth with our armies.
You have let us be driven back by our foes;
     those who hated us plundered us at will. — ℟

You made us the reproach of our neighbors,
     the mockery and the scorn of those around us.
You make us a byword among the nations,
     a laughingstock among the peoples. — ℟

Why do you hide your face,
     forgetting our woe and our oppression?
For our souls are bowed down to the dust,
     our bodies are pressed to the earth. — ℟ ❖

————— **YEAR I AND II** —————

GOSPEL   Mk 1, 40-45

Alleluia (Mt 4, 23)

℟. **Alleluia.** Jesus preached the Good News of the
     Kingdom
and healed all who were sick. ℟. **Alleluia.**

The miracle of the leper's cure illustrates our Lord's power to save
those who had been excluded from Israel by the Mosaic law. Christ
puts forth his hand and touches the leper. The speech of the leper
implies a prayer. It is a touching profession of perfect faith and a
humble "Thy will be done."

℣. The Lord be with you. ℟. **And also with you.**
✠ A reading from the holy gospel according to Mark
℟. **Glory to you, Lord.**

A leper approached Jesus with a request, kneeling
down as he addressed him: "If you will to do so, you
can cure me." Moved with pity, Jesus stretched out
his hand, touched him, and said: "I do will it. Be
cured." The leprosy left him then and there, and he
was cured. Jesus gave him a stern warning and sent
him on his way. "Not a word to anyone, now," he

said. "Go off and present yourself to the priest and offer for your cure what Moses prescribed. That should be a proof for them." The man went off and began to proclaim the whole matter freely, making the story public. As a result of this, it was no longer possible for Jesus to enter a town openly. He stayed in desert places; yet people kept coming to him from all sides.—This is the gospel of the Lord. ℟. **Praise to you, Lord Jesus Christ.**

➜ No. 15, p. 623

FRIDAY OF THE FIRST WEEK
IN ORDINARY TIME
—— YEAR I ——

READING I   Heb 4, 1-5. 11

St. Paul uses New Testament terminology to describe entering heaven. Those who are faithful will enter God's abode, described as a place of rest, rather than as the heavenly sanctuary or the lasting city. There is no thought of hurrying into the rest, but rather of persevering in the effort needed to achieve it.

A reading from the letter to the Hebrews

While the promise of entrance into his rest still holds, we ought to be fearful of disobeying lest any one of you be judged to have lost his chance of entering. We have indeed heard the good news, as they did. But the word which they heard did not profit them, for they did not receive it in faith. It is we, who have believed, who enter into that rest, just as God said:

"Thus I swore in my anger,
'They shall never enter into my rest.' "

Yet God's work was finished when he created the world, for in reference to the seventh day Scripture somewhere says, "And God rested from all his work on the seventh day," and again, in the place we referred to, God says, "They shall never enter into my rest." Let us strive to enter into that rest, so that no one may fall in imitation of the example of Israel's unbelief.—This is the Word of the Lord. ℟. **Thanks be to God.** ⍒

Responsorial Psalm   Ps 78, 3. 4. 6-7. 8

℟. (7) **Do not forget the works of the Lord!**

What we have heard and know,
   and what our fathers have declared to us,
   we will declare to the generations to come
The glorious deeds of the Lord and his strength
   and the wonders that he wrought. — ℟

That they too may rise and declare to their sons
   that they should put their hope in God,
And not forget the deeds of God
   but keep his commands. — ℟

And not be like their fathers,
   a generation wayward and rebellious,
A generation that kept not its heart steadfast
   nor its spirit faithful toward God. — ℟ ⍒

———— **YEAR II** ————

READING I   1 Sm 8, 4-7. 10-22

Samuel's sons, not of the same caliber as their father, request a king (which amounts to rejecting Yahweh himself). Yahweh grants permission for the appointment of a king in response to the people's request. An unfavorable attitude to kingship is described.

A reading from the first book of Samuel

All the elders of Israel came in a body to Samuel at Ramah and said to him, "Now that you are old, and your sons do not follow your example, appoint a king over us, as other nations have, to judge us."

Samuel was displeased when they asked for a king to judge them. He prayed to the Lord, however, who said in answer: "Grant the people's every request. It is not you they reject, they are rejecting me as their king."

Samuel delivered the message of the Lord in full to those who were asking him for a king. He told them: "The rights of the king who will rule you will be as follows: He will take your sons and assign them to his chariots and horses, and they will run before his chariot. He will also appoint from among them his commanders of groups of a thousand and of a hundred soldiers. He will set them to do his plowing and his harvesting, and to make his implements of war and the equipment of his chariots. He will use your daughters as ointment-makers, as cooks, and as bakers. He will take the best of your fields, vineyards, and olive groves, and give them to his officials. He will tithe your crops and your vineyards, and give the revenue to his eunuchs and his slaves. He will take your male and female servants, as well as your best oxen and your asses, and use them to do his work. He will tithe your flocks and you yourselves will become his slaves. When this takes place, you will complain against the king whom you have chosen, but on that day the Lord will not answer you."

The people, however, refused to listen to Samuel's warning and said, "Not so! There must be a king over us. We too must be like other nations, with a king to rule us and to lead us in warfare and fight our battles." When Samuel had listened to all the people had to say, he repeated it to the Lord, who then said to him, "Grant their request and appoint a king to rule them."—This is the Word of the Lord. ℟. **Thanks be to God.** ℣

Responsorial Psalm   Ps 89, 16-17. 18-19

℟. (2) **For ever I will sing the goodness of the Lord.**

Happy the people who know the joyful shout;
  in the light of your countenance, O Lord, they
  walk.
At your name they rejoice all the day,
  and through your justice they are exalted. — ℟

For you are the splendor of their strength,
    and by your favor our horn is exalted.
For to the Lord belongs our shield,
    and to the Holy One of Israel, our king. — ℞ ✟

────── **YEAR I AND II** ──────

GOSPEL   Mk 2, 1-12
Alleluia (Lk 7, 16)

℞. **Alleluia.** A great prophet has risen among us;
God has visited his people. ℞. **Alleluia.**

Disease does, in a most convincing manner, set forth the nature of sin.
Disorders of the body aptly represent the disorders of the soul. An
almost insurmountable barrier is overcome because of the earnest
desire to bring the man sick with palsy to Jesus. Jesus says, "Your
sins are forgiven you."

℣. The Lord be with you. ℞. **And also with you.**
✠ A reading from the holy gospel according to Mark
℞. **Glory to you, Lord.**

Jesus came back to Capernaum after a lapse of several days and word got around that he was at home.
At that they began to gather in great numbers. There
was no longer any room for them, even around the
door. While he was delivering God's word to them,
some people arrived bringing a paralyzed man to
him. The four who carried him were unable to bring
him to Jesus because of the crowd, so they began to
open up the roof over the spot where Jesus was.
When they had made a hole, they let down the mat
on which the paralytic was lying. When Jesus saw
their faith, he said to the paralyzed man, "My son,
your sins are forgiven." Now some of the scribes
were sitting there asking themselves: "Why does the
man talk in that way? He commits blasphemy! Who
can forgive sins except God alone?" Jesus was immediately aware of their reasoning, though they kept
it to themselves, and he said to them: "Why do you
harbor these thoughts? Which is easier, to say to
the paralytic, 'Your sins are forgiven,' or to say,

'Stand up, pick up your mat, and walk again'? That you may know that the Son of Man has authority on earth to forgive sins" (he said to the paralyzed man), "I command you: Stand up! Pick up your mat and go home." The man stood and picked up his mat and went outside in the sight of everyone. They were awestruck; all gave praise to God, saying, "We have never seen anything like this!"—This is the gospel of the Lord. ℟. **Praise to you, Lord Jesus Christ.**

➤ No. 15, p. 623

SATURDAY OF THE FIRST WEEK
IN ORDINARY TIME
—— YEAR I ——

READING I   Heb 4, 12-16

St. Paul continues the warning to persevere, for the Word of God judges, and judges rightly. Nothing is unknown to the Word. In its light, those of the present generation will be judged worthy or unfit to enter God's rest. The saving Word of God speaks to men, inviting them to belief.

A reading from the letter to the Hebrews

God's word is living and effective, sharper than any two-edged sword. It penetrates and divides soul and spirit, joints and marrow; it judges the reflections and thoughts of the heart. Nothing is concealed from him; all lies bare and exposed to the eyes of him to whom we must render an account.

Since, then, we have a great high priest who has passed through the heavens, Jesus, the Son of God, let us hold fast to our profession of faith. For we do not have a high priest who is unable to sympathize with our weakness, but one who was tempted in every way that we are, yet never sinned. So let us confidently approach the throne of grace to receive mercy and favor and to find help in time of need.— This is the Word of the Lord. ℟. **Thanks be to God.** ⱽ

Responsorial Psalm   Ps 19, 8. 9. 10. 15

℟. (Jn 6, 64) **Your words, Lord, are spirit and life.**

The law of the Lord is perfect,
    refreshing the soul;
The decree of the Lord is trustworthy,
    giving wisdom to the simple. — ℟

The precepts of the Lord are right,
    rejoicing the heart;
The command of the Lord is clear,
    enlightening the eye. — ℟

The fear of the Lord is pure,
    enduring forever;
The ordinances of the Lord are true,
    all of them just. — ℟

Let the words of my mouth and the thought of my
    heart
    find favor before you,
    O Lord, my rock and my redeemer. — ℟ ↓

———— **YEAR II** ————

READING I   1 Sm 9, 1-4. 17-19; 10, 1

Saul, sent by his father to look for lost asses, is introduced by his
servant to Samuel. Samuel entertains Saul. Samuel anoints Saul with
oil as a token of consecration to the kingship. Saul is guaranteed signs
by which he will know the authority of what has transpired.

A reading from the first book of Samuel

There was a stalwart man from Benjamin named
Kish, who was the son of Abiel, son of Zeror, son of
Becorath, son of Aphiah, a Benjaminite. He had a son
named Saul, who was a handsome young man. There
was no other Israelite handsomer than Saul; he stood
head and shoulders above the people.

Now the asses of Saul's father, Kish, had wandered off. Kish said to his son Saul, "Take one of the
servants with you and go out and hunt for the asses."
Accordingly they went through the hill country of
Ephraim, and through the land of Shalishah. Not

finding them there they continued through the land of Shaalim without success. They also went through the land of Benjamin, but they failed to find the animals.

When Samuel caught sight of Saul, the Lord assured him, "This is the man of whom I told you; he is to govern my people."

Saul met Samuel in the gateway and said, "Please tell me where the seer lives." Samuel answered Saul: "I am the seer. Go up ahead of me to the high place and eat with me today. In the morning, before dismissing you, I will tell you whatever you wish."

From a flask Samuel had with him, he poured oil on Saul's head; he also kissed him, saying: "The Lord anoints you commander over his heritage. You are to govern the Lord's people Israel, and to save them from the grasp of their enemies round about."—This is the Word of the Lord. ℟. **Thanks be to God.** ↓

Responsorial Psalm Ps 21, 2-3. 4-5. 6-7

℟. (2) **Lord, your strength gives joy to the king.**

O Lord, in your strength the king is glad;
in your victory how greatly he rejoices!
You have granted him his heart's desire;
you refused not the wish of his lips. — ℟

For you welcomed him with goodly blessings,
you placed on his head a crown of pure gold.
He asked life of you: you gave him
length of days forever and ever. — ℟

Great is his glory in your victory;
majesty and splendor you conferred upon him.
For you made him a blessing forever;
you gladdened him with the joy of your presence. — ℟ ↓

——— YEAR I AND II ———

GOSPEL Mk 2, 13-17

Alleluia (Lk 4, 18-19)

℟. **Alleluia.** The Lord sent me to bring Good News
   to the poor,
and freedom to prisoners. ℟. **Alleluia.**

Jesus lived with his people. He associated with tax collectors and
sinners to the extent of eating with them. The scribes and Pharisees
were quick to criticize Christ. Our Lord gives them a triumphant
answer. The healthy man is in no need of a physician, whereas the
sick, or the sinners, are.

℣. The Lord be with you. ℟. **And also with you.**
✠ A reading from the holy gospel according to Mark
℟. **Glory to you, Lord.**

While Jesus went walking along the lakeshore, people kept coming to him in crowds and he taught
them. As he moved on he saw Levi the son of Alphaeus at his tax collector's post, and said to him,
"Follow me." Levi got up and became his follower.
While Jesus was reclining to eat in Levi's house,
many tax collectors and those known as sinners
joined him and his disciples at dinner. The number
of those who followed him was large. When the
scribes who belonged to the Pharisee party saw that
he was eating with tax collectors and offenders
against the law, they complained to his disciples,
"Why does he eat with such as these?" Overhearing
the remark, Jesus said to them, "People who are
healthy do not need a doctor; sick people do. I have
come to call sinners, not the self-righteous."—This
is the gospel of the Lord. ℟. **Praise to you, Lord
Jesus Christ.** ———— ➤ No. 15, p. 623

MONDAY OF THE SECOND WEEK
IN ORDINARY TIME
———— YEAR I ————

READING I   Heb 5, 1-10

Christ, "the anointed," was appointed to his heavenly office in the
way the priests of Israel were appointed. He "inherited" this office
from God who begot him as his Son. Priests are the dispensers of the
holy mysteries (1 Cor 4, 1). The priest is expected to exercise his office
faithfully and act according to the will of Christ whose steward he is.

A reading from the letter to the Hebrews

Every high priest is taken from among men and made their representative before God, to offer gifts and sacrifices for sins. He is able to deal patiently with erring sinners, for he is himself beset by weakness and so must make sin offerings for himself as well as for the people. One does not take this honor on his own initiative, but only when called by God as Aaron was. Even Christ did not glorify himself with the office of high priest; he received it from the One who said to him,

"You are my son;
    today I have begotten you";
just as he says in another place,
    "You are a priest forever,
    according to the order of Melchizedek."

In the days when he was in the flesh, he offered prayers and supplications with loud cries and tears to God, who was able to save him from death, and he was heard because of his reverence. Son though he was, he learned obedience from what he suffered; and when perfected, he became the source of eternal salvation for all who obey him, designated by God as high priest according to the order of Melchizedek.— This is the Word of the Lord. ℟. **Thanks be to God.** ℣

Responsorial Psalm   Ps 110, 1. 2. 3. 4

℟. (4) **You are a priest for ever, in the line of Melchizedek.**

The Lord said to my Lord: "Sit at my right hand
    till I make your enemies your footstool." — ℟

The scepter of your power the Lord will stretch forth
    from Zion:
    "Rule in the midst of your enemies." — ℟.

"Yours is princely power in the day of your birth,
    in holy splendor;
    before the daystar, like the dew, I have begotten
    you." — ℟

The Lord has sworn, and he will not repent:
  "You are a priest forever, according to the order
    of Melchizedek." — ℟ ℣

——— **YEAR II** ———

READING I   1 Sm 15, 16-23

Samuel declares that sacrifice without full obedience is of no value
and that Saul's disobedience is a rejection of God's Word. Saul explains his action in withholding the best cattle for sacrifice. What
was expected of Saul was his active obedience to God. The man who
works for God must be dependable—and Saul was not.

A reading from the first book of Samuel

Samuel said to Saul: "Stop! Let me tell you what the
Lord said to me last night." "Speak!" he replied.
Samuel then said: "Though little in your own esteem,
are you not leader of the tribes of Israel? The Lord
anointed you king of Israel and sent you on a mission, saying, 'Go and put the sinful Amalekites under a ban of destruction. Fight against them until
you have exterminated them.' Why, then, have you
disobeyed the Lord? You have pounced on the spoil,
thus displeasing the Lord." Saul answered Samuel:
"I did indeed obey the Lord and fulfill the mission
on which the Lord sent me. I have brought back
Agag, and I have destroyed Amalek under the ban.
But from the spoil the men took sheep and oxen,
the best of what had been banned, to sacrifice to
the Lord their God in Gilgal."

  But Samuel said:
"Does the Lord so delight in holocausts and sacri-
    fices
  as in obedience to the command of the Lord?
Obedience is better than sacrifice,
  and submission than the fat of rams.
For a sin like divination is rebellion,
  and presumption is the crime of idolatry.
Because you have rejected the command of the Lord,
  he, too, has rejected you as ruler."
This is the Word of the Lord. ℟. **Thanks be to God.** ℣

Responsorial Psalm   Ps 50, 8-9. 16-17. 21. 23

℟. (23) **To the upright I will show
    the saving power of God.**

Not for your sacrifices do I rebuke you,
    for your holocausts are before me always.
I take from your house no bullock,
    no goats out of your fold. — ℟

Why do you recite my statutes,
    and profess my covenant with your mouth,
Though you hate discipline
    and cast my words behind you? — ℟

When you do these things, shall I be deaf to it?
    Or do you think I am like yourself?
    I will correct you by drawing them up before your
        eyes.
He that offers praise as a sacrifice glorifies me;
    and to him that goes the right way I will show
        the salvation of God. — ℟ ⩕

——— **YEAR I AND II** ———

GOSPEL   Mk 2, 18-22

Alleluia (Heb 4, 12)

℟. **Alleluia.** The word of God is living and active;
it probes the thoughts and motives of our heart. ℟.
    Alleluia.

Because the "Bridegroom" is still with them, the significance of the
parable about fasting according to the old law indicates that Christ
realized his disciples were not yet ready for the new law—Christ's
law. Our Lord stresses the incompatibility of the new economy with
the old Mosaic law.

℣. The Lord be wth you. ℟. **And also with you.**
✠ A reading from the holy gospel according to Mark
℟. **Glory to you, Lord.**

John's disciples and the Pharisees were accustomed
to fast. People came to Jesus with the objection,
"Why do John's disciples and those of the Pharisees

fast while yours do not?" Jesus replied: "How can the guests at a wedding fast as long as the groom is still among them? So long as the groom stays with them, they cannot fast. The day will come, however, when the groom will be taken away from them; on that day they will fast. No one sews a patch of un- shrunken cloth on an old cloak. If he should do so, the very thing he has used to cover the hole would pull away—the new from the old—and the tear would get worse. Similarly, no man pours new wine into old wineskins. If he does so, the wine will burst the skins and both wine and skins will be lost. No, new wine is poured into new skins."—This is the gospel of the Lord. ℟. **Praise to you, Lord Jesus Christ.**

➤ No. 15, p. 623

_____

TUESDAY OF THE SECOND WEEK
IN ORDINARY TIME
—— YEAR I ——

READING I   Heb 6, 10-20

Zealous perseverance should mark all Christian work, founded in hope. Christian hope lies in what our Lord carried out in the eternal order of his sacrifice. He has not only entered the heavenly sanctuary, but entered as the "forerunner" of his brothers.

A reading from the letter to the Hebrews

God is not unjust; he will not forget your work and the love you have shown him by your service, past and present, to his holy people. Our desire is that each of you show the same zeal till the end, fully assured of that for which you hope. Do not grow lazy, but imitate those who, through faith and pa- tience, are inheriting the promises.

When God made his promise to Abraham, he swore by himself, having no one greater to swear by, and said, "I will indeed bless you, and multiply you." And so, after patient waiting, Abraham ob- tained what God had promised. Men swear by someone greater than themselves; an oath gives firmness to a promise and puts an end to all argument. God, wishing to give the heirs of his promise even clearer evidence that his purpose would not change, guaranteed it by oath, so that, by two things that are unchangeable, in which he could not lie, we who have taken refuge in him might be strongly encouraged to seize the hope which is placed before us. Like a sure and firm anchor, that hope extends beyond the veil through which Jesus, our forerunner, has entered on our behalf, being made high priest forever according to the order of Melchizedek.—This is the Word of the Lord. ℟. **Thanks be to God.** ℣

Responsorial Psalm   Ps 111, 1-2. 4-5. 9-10

℟. (5) **The Lord will remember his covenant for ever.**

I will give thanks to the Lord with all my heart
   in the company and assembly of the just.
Great are the works of the Lord,
   exquisite in all their delights. — ℟

He has won renown for his wondrous deeds;
   gracious and merciful is the Lord.
He has given food to those who fear him;
   he will forever be mindful of his covenant. — ℟

He has sent deliverance to his people;
   he has ratified his covenant forever;
   holy and awesome is his name.
His praise endures forever. — ℟ ℣

℟. Or: **Alleluia.** ℣

———— **YEAR II** ————

READING I   1 Sm 16, 1-13

The anointing of David is told with a certain suspense—the fear of Saul, the local color, the meeting with the Elders. Bethlehem came to occupy a special place in salvation history. The name "David" is unique in the Old Testament. Possession by the Spirit was not just a mark of God's favor but was virtually limited to leaders of the people—kings and prophets.

A reading from the first book of Samuel

The Lord said to Samuel: "How long will you grieve for Saul, whom I have rejected as king of Israel? Fill your horn with oil, and be on your way. I am sending you to Jesse of Bethlehem, for I have chosen my king from among his sons." But Samuel replied: "How can I go? Saul will hear of it and kill me." To this the Lord answered: "Take a heifer along and say, 'I have come to sacrifice to the Lord.' Invite Jesse to the sacrifice, and I myself will tell you what to do; you are to anoint for me the one I point out to you."

Samuel did as the Lord had commanded him. When he entered Bethlehem, the elders of the city came trembling to meet him and inquired, "Is your visit peaceful, O seer?" He replied: "Yes! I have come to sacrifice to the Lord. So cleanse yourselves and join me today for the banquet." He also had Jesse and his sons cleanse themselves and invited them to the sacrifice. As they came, he looked at Eliab and thought, "Surely the Lord's anointed is here before him." But the Lord said to Samuel: "Do not judge from his appearance or from his lofty stature, because I have rejected him. Not as man sees does God see, because man sees the appearance but the Lord looks into the heart." Then Jesse called Abinadab and presented him before Samuel, who said, "The Lord has not chosen him." Next Jesse presented Shammah but Samuel said, "The Lord has not chosen this one either." In the same way Jesse presented seven sons before Samuel but Samuel said to Jesse, "The Lord has not chosen any one of these." Then Samuel asked Jesse, "Are these all the sons you have?" Jesse replied, "There is still the youngest, who is tending the sheep." Samuel said to Jesse, "Send for him; we will not begin the sacrificial banquet until he arrives here." Jesse sent and had the young man brought to them. He was ruddy, a youth handsome to behold and making a splendid appearance. The Lord said, "There—anoint him, for this is he!" Then Samuel, with the horn of oil in hand, anointed him in the midst of his brothers; and from that day on, the spirit of the Lord rushed upon David. When Samuel took his leave, he went to Ramah. —This is the Word of the Lord. ℟. **Thanks be to God.** ⋁

Responsorial Psalm   Ps 89, 20. 21-22. 27-28
℟. (21) **I have found David, my servant.**

Once you spoke in a vision,
  and to your faithful ones you said:
"On a champion I have placed a crown;
  over the people I have set a youth." — ℟

I have found David, my servant;
  with my holy oil I have anointed him,
That my hand may be always with him,
  and that my arm may make him strong. — ℟

He shall say of me, "You are my father,
  my God the Rock, my savior."
And I will make him the first-born,
  highest of the kings of the earth. — ℟ ⋁

——— YEAR I AND II ———

GOSPEL   Mk 2, 23-28
Alleluia (See Eph 1, 17-18)
℟. **Alleluia.** May the Father of our Lord Jesus Christ
enlighten the eyes of our heart
that we might see how great is the hope
to which we are called. ℟. **Alleluia.**

Jesus answers the Pharisees' charge in rabbinic fashion with a counter-question. The Pharisees really do not accuse the disciples of theft, but of profaning the sabbath. However, the law, mercifully, allowed their present act. They were hungry.

℣. The Lord be with you. ℟. **And also with you.**

✠ A reading from the holy gospel according to Mark
℟. **Glory to you, Lord.**

It happened that the Lord was walking through
standing grain on the sabbath, and his disciples began
to pull off heads of grain as they went along. At this
the Pharisees protested: "Look! Why do they do a
thing not permitted on the sabbath?" He said to
them: "Have you never read what David did when
he was in need and he and his men were hungry?
How he entered God's house in the days of Abiathar
the high priest and ate the holy bread which only the
priests were permitted to eat? He even gave it to
his men." Then he said to them: "The sabbath was
made for man, not man for the sabbath. That is why
the Son of Man is lord even of the sabbath."—This
is the gospel of the Lord. ℟. **Praise to you, Lord
Jesus Christ.** _____ ➔ No. 15, p. 623

WEDNESDAY OF THE SECOND WEEK
IN ORDINARY TIME

—— **YEAR I** ——

READING I   Heb 7, 1-3. 15-17

It is strange that here Melchizedek is compared to Jesus, rather than
the reverse. Jesus received his exaltation after his death on the cross.
A priest is a channel of exchange between God and man. Christ is the
point of exchange through which pass man's submission to his Father
and his Father's life to man.

A reading from the letter to the Hebrews

Melchizedek, king of Salem and priest of the Most
High God, met Abraham returning from his defeat
of the kings and blessed him. And Abraham apportioned to him one tenth of all his booty. His name
means "king of justice"; he was also king of Salem,
that is, "king of peace." Without father, mother or
ancestry, without beginning of days or end of life,
like the Son of God he remains a priest forever.

The matter is clearer still if another priest is appointed according to the likeness of Melchizedek:

one who has become a priest, not in virtue of a law expressed in a commandment concerning physical descent but in virtue of the power of a life which cannot be destroyed. Scripture testifies: "You are a priest forever according to the order of Melchizedek." —This is the Word of the Lord. R̊. **Thanks be to God.** ↓

Responsorial Psalm   Ps 110, 1. 2. 3. 4

R̊. (4) **You are a priest for ever,
  in the line of Melchizedek.**

The Lord said to my Lord: "Sit at my right hand
  till I make your enemies your footstool." — R̊

The scepter of your power the Lord will stretch
  forth from Zion:
  "Rule in the midst of your enemies." — R̊

"Yours is princely power in the day of your birth,
  in holy splendor;
  before the daystar, like the dew, I have begotten
    you." — R̊

The Lord has sworn, and he will not repent:
  "You are a priest forever, according to the order
    of Melchizedek." — R̊ ↓

———— **YEAR II** ————

READING I   1 Sm 17, 32-33. 37. 40-51

Unable to wear Saul's armor, David goes out with only his sling. David affirms his loyalty to Yahweh, strikes Goliath down with his sling, and then dispatches him with the Philistine's own sword. The Philistines take this as a sign of the Israelites' superiority and flee.

A reading from the first book of Samuel

Then David spoke to Saul: "Let your majesty not lose courage. I am at your service to go and fight this Philistine." But Saul answered David, "You cannot go up against this Philistine and fight with him, for you are only a youth, while he has been a warrior from his youth."

David continued: "The Lord, who delivered me from the claws of the lion and the bear, will also keep me safe from the clutches of this Philistine." Saul answered David, "Go! the Lord will be with you."

Then, staff in hand, David selected five smooth stones from the wadi and put them in the pocket of his shepherd's bag. With his sling also ready to hand, he approached the Philistine.

With his shield-bearer marching before him, the Philistine also advanced closer and closer to David. When he had sized David up, and seen that he was youthful, and ruddy and handsome in appearance, he held him in contempt. The Philistine said to David, "Am I a dog that you come against me with a staff?" Then the Philistine cursed David by his gods and said to him, "Come here to me, and I will leave your flesh for the birds of the air and the beasts of the field." David answered him:

"You come against me with sword and spear and scimitar, but I come against you in the name of the Lord of hosts, the God of the armies of Israel that you have insulted. Today the Lord shall deliver you into my hand; I will strike you down and cut off your head. This very day I will leave your corpse and the corpses of the Philistine army for the birds of the air and the beasts of the field; thus the whole land shall learn that Israel has a God. All this multitude, too, shall learn that it is not by sword or spear that the Lord saves. For the battle is the Lord's, and he shall deliver you into our hands."

The Philistine then moved to meet David at close quarters, while David ran quickly toward the battle line in the direction of the Philistine. David put his hand into the bag and took out a stone, hurled it with the sling, and struck the Philistine on the forehead. The stone embedded itself in his brow, and he fell prostrate on the ground. [Thus David over-

came the Philistine with sling and stone; he struck
the Philistine mortally, and did it without a sword.]
Then David ran and stood over him; with the Philistine's own sword [which he drew from its sheath]
he dispatched him and cut off his head.—This is the
Word of the Lord. ℟. **Thanks be to God.** ⱱ

Responsorial Psalm   Ps 144, 1. 2. 9-10

℟. (1) **Blessed be the Lord, my Rock!**

Blessed be the Lord, my rock,
who trains my hands for battle, my fingers for
    war. — ℟

My refuge and my fortress,
  my stronghold, my deliverer,
My shield, in whom I trust,
  who subdues peoples under me. — ℟

O God, I will sing a new song to you;
  with a ten-stringed lyre I will chant your praise,
You who give victory to kings,
  and deliver David, your servant. — ℟ ⱱ

———— **YEAR I AND II** ————

GOSPEL   Mk 3, 1-6

Alleluia (Mt 4, 23)

℟. **Alleluia.** Jesus preached the Good News of the
    Kingdom
and healed all who were sick. ℟. **Alleluia.**

It is the sabbath and the scribes and Pharisees test Jesus. They
know now he always has compassion on those in need. Still they want
to find grounds for accusing him under the law. Christ knows their
murderous thoughts, but in his compassion, he heals the man. The
Pharisees hold their peace.

℣. The Lord be with you. ℟. **And also with you.**
✠ A reading from the holy gospel according to Mark
℟. **Glory to you, Lord.**

Jesus returned to the synagogue where there was a
man whose hand was shriveled up. The Pharisees

kept an eye on Jesus to see whether he would heal him on the sabbath, hoping to be able to bring an accusation against him. He addressed the man with the shriveled hand: "Stand up here in front!" Then he said to them: "Is it permitted to do a good deed on the sabbath—or an evil one? To preserve life—or to destroy it?" At this they remained silent. He looked around at them angrily, for he was deeply grieved that they had closed their minds against him. Then he said to the man, "Stretch out your hand." The man did so and his hand was perfectly restored. When the Pharisees went outside, they immediately began to plot with the Herodians on how they might destroy him.—This is the gospel of the Lord. ℟. **Praise to you, Lord Jesus Christ.** ➤ No 15, p. 623

THURSDAY OF THE SECOND WEEK IN ORDINARY TIME

———— YEAR I ————

READING I   Heb 7, 25-8, 6

The constant intercession that Jesus makes is a sequel of his completed sacrifice. Christ continues his mediating work on the basis of his unique work of atonement. In contrast to the earthly tabernacle set up by Moses, the heavenly tabernacle was set up by the Lord, and Christ is the ministering Priest.

A reading from the letter to the Hebrews

Jesus is always able to save those who approach God through him, since he forever lives to make intercession for them.

It was fitting that we should have such a high priest: holy, innocent, undefiled, separated from sinners, higher than the heavens. Unlike the other high priests, he has no need to offer sacrifice day after day, first for his own sins and then for those of the people; he did that once for all when he offered himself. For the law sets up as high priests men who are weak, but the word of the oath which came after the law appoints as priest the Son, made perfect forever.

The main point in what we are saying is this: we have such a high priest, who has taken his seat at the right hand of the throne of the Majesty in heaven, minister of the sanctuary and of that true tabernacle set up not by man but by the Lord. Now every high priest is appointed to offer gifts and sacrifices; hence the necessity for this one to have something to offer. If he were on earth he would not be a priest, for there are priests already offering the gifts which the law prescribes. They offer worship in a sanctuary which is only a copy and shadow of the heavenly one, for Moses, when about to erect the tabernacle, was warned, "See that you make everything according to the pattern shown you on the mountain." Jesus has obtained a more excellent ministry now, just as he is mediator of a better covenant, founded on better promises.—This is the Word of the Lord. ℟. **Thanks be to God.** ⍌

Responsorial Psalm   Ps 40, 7-8. 8-9. 10. 17
℟. (8) **Here am I, Lord;**
     I come to do your will.

Sacrifice or oblation you wished not,
     but ears open to obedience you gave me.
Holocausts or sin-offerings you sought not;
     then said I, "Behold I come." — ℟

"In the written scroll it is prescribed for me,
     to do your will, O my God, is my delight,
And your law is within my heart!" — ℟

I announced your justice in the vast assembly;
     I did not restrain my lips, as you, O Lord,
          know. — ℟

May all who seek you
     exult and be glad in you,
And may those who love your salvation
     say ever, "The Lord be glorified." — ℟ ⍌

____ YEAR II ____

READING I   1 Sm 18, 6-9; 19, 1-7

The women chant in David's honor. David becomes Saul's must successful general. Saul, in his envy, tries to persuade his men, Jonathan among them, to put David to death. Jonathan eloquently pleads David's case, and he is reinstated.

A reading from the first book of Samuel

At the approach of Saul and David (on David's return after slaying the Philistine), women came out from each of the cities of Israel to meet King Saul, singing and dancing, with tambourines, joyful songs, and sistrums. The women played and sang:

"Saul has slain his thousands,
    and David his ten thousands."

Saul was very angry and resentful of the song, for he thought: "They give David ten thousands, but only thousands to me. All that remains for him is the kingship." [And from that day on, Saul was jealous of David.]

Saul discussed his intention of killing David with his son Jonathan and with all his servants. But Saul's son Jonathan, who was very fond of David, told him: "My father Saul is trying to kill you. Therefore, please be on your guard tomorrow morning; get out of sight and remain in hiding. I, however, will go out and stand beside my father in the countryside where you are, and will speak to him about you. If I learn anything, I will let you know."

Jonathan then spoke well of David to his father Saul, saying to him: "Let not your majesty sin against his servant David, for he has committed no offense against you, but has helped you very much by his deeds. When he took his life in his hands and slew the Philistine, and the Lord brought about a great victory for all Israel through him, you were glad to see it. Why, then, should you become guilty of shedding innocent blood by killing David without cause?" Saul heeded Jonathan's plea and swore, "As the Lord lives, he shall not be killed." So Jonathan summoned David and repeated the whole conversation to him. Jonathan then brought David to Saul, and David served him as before.—This is the Word of the Lord. ℟. **Thanks be to God.** ⱽ

Responsorial Psalm   Ps 56, 2-3. 9-10. 10-12. 13-14

℟. (5) **In God I trust;**
   I shall not fear.

Have pity on me, O Lord, for men trample upon me;
   all the day they press their attack against me.
My adversaries trample upon me all the day;
   yes, many fight against me. — ℟

My wanderings you have counted;
   my tears are stored in your flask;
   are they not recorded in your book?
Then do my enemies turn back,
   when I call upon you. — ℟

Now I know that God is with me.
   In God, in whose promise I glory,
In God I trust without fear;
   what can flesh do against me? — ℟

I am bound, O God, by vows to you;
   your thank offerings I will fulfill.
For you have rescued me from death,
   my feet, too, from stumbling;
   that I may walk before God in the light of the
      living. — ℟ ⱽ

——— **YEAR I AND II** ———

GOSPEL   Mk 3, 7-12
Alleluia (2 Tm 1, 10)

℟. **Alleluia.** Our Savior Jesus Christ has done away
   with death,
and brought us life through his gospel. ℟. **Alleluia.**

This brief narrative shows the interest in the ministry of Jesus. People come from far and near as the rumors of his healings spread. Jesus enjoins silence upon the unclean spirits whose testimony might involve misconceptions about his mission.

℣. The Lord be with you. ℟. **And also with you.**

✠ A reading from the holy gospel according to Mark

℟. **Glory to you, Lord.**

Jesus withdrew toward the lake with his disciples. A great crowd followed him from Galilee, and an equally great multitude came to him from Judea, Jerusalem, Idumea, Transjordan, and the neighborhood of Tyre and Sidon, because they had heard what he had done. In view of their numbers, he told his disciples to have a fishing boat ready for him so that he could avoid the press of the crowd against him. Because he had cured many, all who had afflictions kept pushing toward him to touch him. Unclean spirits would catch sight of him, fling themselves down at his feet, and shout, "You are the Son of God!", while he kept ordering them sternly not to reveal who he was.—This is the gospel of the Lord.

℟. **Praise to you, Lord Jesus Christ.** ➤ No. 15, p. 623

FRIDAY OF THE SECOND WEEK
IN ORDINARY TIME
——— YEAR I ———

READING I   Heb 8, 6-13

Jesus' priesthood is an element of the new and better covenant of which he is mediator. The promise in the Old Covenant that God will be their God and they will be his people is also the promise in the New Covenant, but this relationship does not constitute the newness of the covenant.

A reading from the letter to the Hebrews

Jesus our high priest has obtained a more excellent ministry now, just as he is mediator of a better covenant, founded on better promises.

If that first covenant had been faultless, there would have been no place for a second one. But God, finding fault with them, says:

"Days are coming, says the Lord,
when I will make a new covenant with the house
of Israel
and with the house of Judah.
It will not be like the covenant I made with their
fathers
the day I took them by the hand
to lead them forth from the land of Egypt;
For they broke my covenant
and I grew weary of them, says the Lord.
But this is the covenant I will make with the house
of Israel
after those days, says the Lord:
I will place my laws in their minds
and I will write them upon their hearts;
I will be their God
and they shall be my people.
And they shall not teach their fellow citizens
or their brothers, saying, 'Know the Lord,'
for all shall know me, from least to greatest.
I will forgive their evildoing,
and their sins I will remember no more."
When he says, "a new covenant," he declares the
first one obsolete. And what has become obsolete
and has grown old is close to disappearing.—This is the
Word of the Lord. ℟. **Thanks be to God.** ↓

Responsorial Psalm   Ps 85, 8. 10. 11-12. 13-14
℟. (11) **Kindness and truth shall meet.**
Show us, O Lord, your kindness,
and grant us your salvation.
Near indeed is his salvation to those who fear him,
glory dwelling in our land. — ℟
Kindness and truth shall meet;
justice and peace shall kiss.
Truth shall spring out of the earth,
and justice shall look down from heaven. — ℟

The Lord himself will give his benefits;
    our land shall yield its increase.
Justice shall walk before him,
    and salvation, along the way of his steps. — ℟ ℣

_____ **YEAR II** _____

READING I   1 Sm 24, 3-21

Saul retires within a cave and unwittingly puts himself within David's
reach. David refuses to do any injury to the person of the Lord's
anointed. Saul acknowledges David's loyalty to his king and gives
David his blessing.

A reading from the first book of Samuel

Saul took three thousand picked men from all Israel
and went in search of David and his men in the
direction of the wild goat crags. When he came to
the sheepfolds along the way, he found a cave, which
he entered to ease nature. David and his men were
occupying the inmost recesses of the cave.

David's servants said to him, "This is the day of
which the Lord said to you, 'I will deliver your enemy into your grasp; do with him as you see fit.' "
So David moved up and stealthily cut off an end of
Saul's mantle. Afterward, however, David regretted
that he had cut off an end of Saul's mantle. He said
to his men, "The Lord forbid that I should do such
a thing to my master, the Lord's anointed, as to lay
a hand on him, for he is the Lord's anointed." With
these words David restrained his men and would
not permit them to attack Saul. Saul then left the
cave and went on his way. David also stepped out
of the cave, calling to Saul, "My lord the king!"
When Saul looked back, David bowed to the ground
in homage and asked Saul:

"Why do you listen to those who say, 'David is
trying to harm you'? You see for yourself today that
the Lord just now delivered you into my grasp in
the cave. I had some thought of killing you, but I
took pity on you instead. I decided, 'I will not raise
a hand against my lord, for he is the Lord's anointed

and a father to me.' Look here at this end of your mantle which I hold. Since I cut off an end of your mantle and did not kill you, see and be convinced that I plan no harm and no rebellion. I have done you no wrong, though you are hunting me down to take my life. The Lord will judge between me and you, and the Lord will exact justice from you in my case. I shall not touch you. The old proverb says, 'From the wicked comes forth wickedness.' So I will take no action against you. Against whom are you on campaign, O king of Israel? Whom are you pursuing? A dead dog, or a single flea! The Lord will be the judge; he will decide between me and you. May he see this, and take my part, and grant me justice beyond my reach!"

When David finished saying these things to Saul, Saul answered, "Is that your voice, my son David?" And he wept aloud. Saul then said to David: "You are in the right rather than I; you have treated me generously, while I have done you harm. Great is the generosity you showed me today, when the Lord delivered me into your grasp and you did not kill me. For if a man meets his enemy, does he send him away unharmed? May the Lord reward you generously for what you have done this day. And now, I know that you shall surely be king and that sovereignty over Israel shall come into your possession."
—This is the Word of the Lord. ℟. **Thanks be to God.** ▼

Responsial Psalm   Ps 57, 2. 3-4. 6. 11

℟. (2) **Have mercy on me, God, have mercy.**

Have pity on me, O God; have pity on me,
   for in you I take refuge.
In the shadow of your wings I take refuge,
   till harm pass by. — ℟

I call to God the Most High,
   to God, my benefactor.

May he send from heaven and save me;
>   may he make those a reproach who trample upon
>   me;
>   may God send his kindness and his faithful-
>   ness. — ℟

Be exalted above the heavens, O God;
>   above all the earth be your glory!
For your kindness towers to the heavens,
>   and your faithfulness to the skies. — ℟ ℣

____ YEAR I AND II ____

GOSPEL Mk 3, 13-19

Alleluia (2 Cor 5, 19)

℟. **Alleluia.** God was in Christ, to reconcile the
>   world to himself;
and the Good News of reconciliation he has en-
>   trusted to us. ℟. **Alleluia.**

Jesus withdraws to select the Twelve. (The number symbolizes the twelve tribes of Israel.) Jesus appoints them for the double purpose which is still the essential function of the Church—fellowship with himself and the proclamation of the Gospel. Simon is named first in the list.

℣. The Lord be with you. ℟. **And also with you.**
✠ A reading from the holy gospel according to Mark
℟. **Glory to you, Lord.**

Jesus went up the mountain and summoned the men he himself had decided on, who came and joined him. He named twelve as his companions whom he would send to preach the good news; they were likewise to have authority to expel demons. He appointed the Twelve as follows: Simon to whom he gave the name Peter; James, son of Zebedee; and John, the brother of James (he gave these two the name Boanerges, or "sons of thunder"); Andrew, Philip, Bartholomew, Matthew, Thomas, James son of Alphaeus; Thaddaeus, Simon of the Zealot party, and Judas Iscariot, who betrayed him.—This is the gospel of the Lord. ℟. **Praise to you, Lord Jesus Christ.** ➔ No. 15, p. 623

SATURDAY OF THE SECOND WEEK
IN ORDINARY TIME
——— YEAR I ———

READING I   Heb 9, 2-3. 11-14

St. Paul indicates that the perfect tabernacle is the heavenly region, the heavenly counterpart of the earthly outer tabernacle through which our Lord passed into the highest heaven, the abode of God, the counterpart of the inner tabernacle—the Holy of Holies.

A reading from the letter to the Hebrews

A tabernacle was constructed, the outer one, in which were the lampstand, and the table, and the showbread; this was called the holy place. Behind the second veil was the tabernacle called the holy of holies.

But when Christ came as high priest of the good things which came to be, he entered once for all into the sanctuary, passing through the greater and more perfect tabernacle not made by hands, that is, not belonging to this creation. He entered not with the blood of goats and calves but with his own blood, and achieved eternal redemption. For if the blood of goats and bulls and the sprinkling of a heifer's ashes can sanctify those who are defiled so that their flesh is cleansed, how much more will the blood of Christ, who through the eternal spirit offered himself up unblemished to God, cleanse our consciences from dead works to worship the living God!—This is the Word of the Lord. ℟. **Thanks be to God.** ℣

Responsorial Psalm   Ps 47, 2-3. 6-7. 8-9

℟. (6) **God mounts his throne to shouts of joy;
a blare of trumpets for the Lord.**

All you peoples, clap your hands,
　　shout to God with cries of gladness,
For the Lord, the Most High, the awesome,
　　is the great king over all the earth. — ℟

God mounts his throne amid shouts of joy;
  the Lord, amid trumpet blasts.
Sing praise to God, sing praise;
  sing praise to our king, sing praise. — ℟
For king of all the earth is God:
  sing hymns of praise.
God reigns over the nations,
  God sits upon his holy throne. — ℟ ℣

———— YEAR II ————

READING I   2 Sm 1, 1-4. 11-12. 19. 23-27

The news of the deaths of Saul and Jonathan reaches David at Ziklag.
David shows the usual signs of mourning. He composes an elegy in
honor of Saul and Jonathan. David extols the bravery and courage of
Saul and Jonathan and idealizes their union of spirit.

A reading from the second book of Samuel

David returned from his defeat of the Amalekites
and spent two days in Ziklag. On the third day a
man came from Saul's camp, with his clothes torn
and dirt on his head. Going to David, he fell to the
ground in homage. David asked him, "Where do you
come from?" He replied, "I have escaped from the
Israelite camp." "Tell me what happened," David
bade him. He answered that the soldiers had fled the
battle and that many of them had fallen and were
dead, among them Saul and his son Jonathan.

David seized his garments and rent them, and all
the men who were with him did likewise. They
mourned and wept and fasted until evening for Saul
and his son Jonathan, and for the soldiers of the
Lord of the clans of Israel, because they had fallen
by the sword.

David chanted this elegy for Saul and his son
Jonathan:

"Alas! the glory of Israel, Saul,
  slain upon your heights;
  how can the warriors have fallen!

"Saul and Jonathan, beloved and cherished,
  separated neither in life nor in death,
  swifter than eagles, stronger than lions!
Women of Israel, weep over Saul,
  who clothed you in scarlet and in finery,
  who decked your attire with ornaments of gold.
"How can the warriors have fallen—
  in the thick of the battle,
  slain upon your heights!
"I grieve for you, Jonathan my brother!
  most dear have you been to me;
More precious have I held love for you
  than love for women.
"How can the warriors have fallen,
  the weapons of war have perished!"
  This is the Word of the Lord. ℟. **Thanks be to God.** ⱴ

Responsorial Psalm   Ps 80, 2-3. 5-7

℟. (4) **Let us see your face, Lord,**
  and we shall be saved.

O shepherd of Israel, hearken,
  O guide of the flock of Joseph!
From your throne upon the cherubim, shine forth
  before Ephraim, Benjamin and Manasseh.
Rouse your power,
  and come to save us. — ℟

O Lord of hosts, how long will you burn with anger
  while your people pray?
You have fed them with the bread of tears
  and given them tears to drink in ample measure.
You have left us to be fought over by our neighbors,
  and our enemies mock us. — ℟ ⱴ

——— **YEAR I AND II** ———

GOSPEL   Mk 3, 20-21
Alleluia (See Acts 16, 14)

℟. **Alleluia.** Open our hearts, O Lord,
to listen to the words of your Son. ℟. **Alleluia.**

This statement seems to point out a course of conduct so unexpected and extraordinary that people failed to understand. Even those who knew Christ intimately did not realize his compassion and love for the crowd.

℣. The Lord be with you. ℟. **And also with you.**

✠ A reading from the holy gospel according to Mark

℟. **Glory to you, Lord.**

Jesus returned to the house with his disciples and again the crowd assembled, making it impossible for them to get any food whatever. When his family heard of this they came to take charge of him, saying, "He is out of his mind."—This is the gospel of the Lord. ℟. **Praise to you, Lord Jesus Christ.**

➤ No. 15, p. 623

——————

MONDAY OF THE THIRD WEEK
IN ORDINARY TIME

—— YEAR I ——

READING I   Heb 9, 15. 24-28

Christ as Mediator offered himself one time in the shedding of his blood. Man is to die but once and then is judged. Through his death, Jesus was offered to atone for sin. He will come a second time to judge mankind.

A reading from the letter to the Hebrews

Christ is mediator of a new covenant: since his death has taken place for deliverance from transgressions committed under the first covenant, those who are called may receive the promised eternal inheritance.

For Christ did not enter into a sanctuary made by hands, a mere copy of the true one; he entered heaven itself that he might appear before God now on our behalf. Not that he might offer himself there again and again, as the high priest enters year after year into the sanctuary with blood that is not his own; were that so, he would have had to suffer death over and over from the creation of the world. But now he has appeared at the end of the ages to take away sins once for all by his sacrifice. Just as it is appointed that men die once, and after death be judged, so Christ was offered up once to take away the sins of many; he will appear a second time not to take away sin but to bring salvation to those who eagerly await him.—This is the Word of the Lord. ℟. **Thanks be to God.** ℣

Responsorial Psalm   Ps 98, 1. 2-3. 3-4. 5-6
℟. (1) **Sing to the Lord a new song,**
    for he has done marvelous deeds.

Sing to the Lord a new song,
    for he has done wondrous deeds;
His right hand has won victory for him,
    his holy arm. — ℟

The Lord has made his salvation known:
    in the sight of the nations he has revealed his
        justice.
He has remembered his kindness and his faithfulness
    toward the house of Israel. — ℟

All the ends of the earth have seen
    the salvation by our God.
Sing joyfully to the Lord, all you lands;
    break into song; sing praise. — ℟

Sing praise to the Lord with the harp,
    with the harp and melodious song.
With trumpets and the sound of the horn
    sing joyfully before the King, the Lord. — ℟ ℣

————— **YEAR II** —————

READING I   2 Sm 5, 1-7. 10

David becomes king over all Israel, and his accession is ratified by a solemn covenant. He is anointed by the Elders of Israel. David and his men set out to capture Jerusalem. He grows in God's favor.

A reading from the second book of Samuel

All the tribes of Israel came to David in Hebron and said: "Here we are, your bone and your flesh. In days past, when Saul was our king, it was you who led the Israelites out and brought them back. And the Lord said to you, 'You shall shepherd my people Israel and shall be commander of Israel.'" When all the elders of Israel came to David in Hebron, King David made an agreement with them there before the Lord, and they anointed him king of Israel. David was thirty years old when he became king, and he reigned for forty years: seven years and six months in Hebron over Judah, and thirty-three years in Jerusalem over all Israel and Judah.

Then the king and his men set out for Jerusalem against the Jebusites who inhabited the region. David was told, "You cannot enter here: the blind and the lame will drive you away!" which was their way of saying, "David cannot enter here." But David did take the stronghold of Zion, which is the City of David.

David grew steadily more powerful, for the Lord of hosts was with him.—This is the Word of the Lord. ℟. **Thanks be to God.** ℣

Responsorial Psalm   Ps 89, 20. 21-22. 25-26

℟. (25) **My faithfulness and love shall be with him.**

Once you spoke in a vision,
 and to your faithful ones you said:
"On a champion I have placed a crown;
 over the people I have set a youth. — ℟

I have found David, my servant;
 with my holy oil I have anointed him,
That my hand may be always with him,
 and that my arm may make him strong. — ℟

My faithfulness and my kindness shall be with him,
 and through my name shall his horn be exalted.
I will set his hand upon the sea,
 his right hand upon the rivers." — ℟ ℣

─────── **YEAR I AND II** ───────

GOSPEL   Mk 3, 22-30

Alleluia (2 Tm 1, 10)

℟. **Alleluia.** Our Savior Jesus Christ has done away
     with death,
and brought us life through his gospel. ℟. **Alleluia.**

Jesus teaches that a house that is divided falls apart, and with his
almighty power he expels Satan by a firm command. Jesus promises
that every sin will be forgiven except that which blasphemes against
the Holy Spirit.

℣. The Lord be with you. ℟. **And also with you.**
✠ A reading from the holy gospel according to Mark
℟. **Glory to you, Lord.**

The scribes who arrived from Jerusalem said of
Jesus, "He is possessed by Beelzebul," and "He expels demons with the help of the prince of demons."
Summoning them, Jesus began to speak to them by
way of examples: "How can Satan expel Satan? If
a kingdom is torn by civil strife, that kingdom cannot last. If a household is divided according to loyal-
ties, that household will not survive. Similarly, if
Satan has suffered mutiny in his ranks and is torn
by dissension, he cannot endure; he is finished. No
one can enter a strong man's house and despoil his
property unless he has first put him under restraint.
Only then can he plunder his house.

   "I give you my word, every sin will be forgiven
mankind and all the blasphemies men utter, but whoever blasphemes against the Holy Spirit will never
be forgiven. He carries the guilt of his sin without
end." He spoke thus because they had said, "He is
possessed by an unclean spirit."—This is the gospel
of the Lord. ℟. **Praise to you, Lord Jesus Christ.**

➤ No. 15, p. 623

TUESDAY OF THE THIRD WEEK
IN ORDINARY TIME
—— YEAR I ——

READING I Heb 10, 1-10

The sacrifices of the Old Covenant only foreshadowed that of Christ. The one sacrifice of Christ Jesus is the source of remission of past sins (Heb 9, 15). Because of its perfection, no further sacrifice is necessary or possible. The offering of Christ's body means the same as the shedding of his blood.

A reading from the letter to the Hebrews

Since the law had only a shadow of the good things to come, and no real image of them, it was never able to perfect the worshipers by the same sacrifices offered continually year after year. Were matters otherwise, the priests would have stopped offering them, for the worshipers, once cleansed, would have had no sin on their conscience. But through those sacrifices there came only a yearly recalling of sins, because it is impossible for the blood of bulls and goats to take sins away. Wherefore, on coming into the world, Jesus said:

"Sacrifice and offering you did not desire,
but a body you have prepared for me;
Holocausts and sin offerings you took no delight in.
Then I said, 'As is written of me in the book,
I have come to do your will, O God.' "

First he says,

"Sacrifices and offerings, holocausts and sin offerings you neither desired nor delighted in."

(These are offered according to the prescriptions of the law.) Then he says,

"I have come to do your will."

In other words, he takes away the first covenant to establish the second.

By this "will," we have been sanctified through the offering of the body of Jesus Christ once for all.

—This is the Word of the Lord. ℞. **Thanks be to God.** ℣

Responsorial Psalm   Ps 40, 2. 4. 7-8. 10. 11

R. (8. 9) **Here am I, Lord;**
   I come to do your will.

I have waited, waited for the Lord,
   and he stooped toward me.
And he put a new song into my mouth,
   a hymn to our God. — R

Sacrifice or oblation you wished not,
   but ears open to obedience you gave me.
Holocausts or sin-offerings you sought not;
   then said I, "Behold I come." — R

I announced your justice in the vast assembly;
   I did not restrain my lips, as you, O Lord,
      know. — R

Your justice I kept not hid within my heart;
   your faithfulness and your salvation I have spoken
      of;
I have made no secret of your kindness and your
   truth in the vast assembly. — R ⱽ

——— **YEAR II** ———

READING I   2 Sm 6, 12-15. 17-19

The reception of the ark of the Lord into the City of David is the
occasion for exultant celebration. David offers sacrifice and blesses
the people. All the people of Israel join in the festivities and share
in the delightful repast.

   A reading from the second book of Samuel

David went to bring up the ark of God from the house
of Obed-edom into the City of David amid festivities.
As soon as the bearers of the ark of the Lord had
advanced six steps, he sacrificed an ox and a fat-
ling. Then David, girt with a linen apron, came dancing before the Lord with abandon, as he and all the
Israelites were bringing up the ark of the Lord with
shouts of joy and to the sound of the horn. The ark
of the Lord was brought in and set in its place
within the tent David had pitched for it. Then David

offered holocausts and peace offerings before the Lord. When he finished making these offerings, he blessed the people in the name of the Lord of hosts. He then distributed among all the people, to each man and each woman in the entire multitude of Israel, a loaf of bread, a cut of roast meat, and a raisin cake. With this, all the people left for their homes. —This is the Word of the Lord. R̷. **Thanks be to God.** ℣

Responsorial Psalm   Ps 24, 7. 8. 9. 10

R̷. (8) **Who is this king of glory?**
   It is the Lord!

Lift up, O gates, your lintels;
   reach up, you ancient portals,
   that the king of glory may come in! — R̷

Who is this king of glory?
   The Lord, strong and mighty,
   the Lord, mighty in battle. — R̷

Lift up, O gates, your lintels;
   reach up, you ancient portals,
   that the king of glory may come in! — R̷

Who is this king of glory?
   the Lord of hosts; he is the king of glory. — R̷ ℣

———   **YEAR I AND II**   ———

GOSPEL   Mk 3, 31-35

Alleluia (Mt 11, 25)

R̷. **Alleluia.** Blessed are you, Father, Lord of heaven and earth;
you have revealed to little ones the mysteries of the kingdom. R̷. **Alleluia.**

The reign of God makes demands on the personal commitment of a disciple which must transcend at times all natural family bonds. All are brothers in Christ who made this heavenly kinship possible by giving himself on the cross for our salvation.

℣. The Lord be with you. R̷. **And also with you.**

✠ A reading from the holy gospel according to Mark
℟. **Glory to you, Lord.**

The mother of Jesus and his brothers arrived, and as they stood outside they sent word to him to come out. The crowd seated around him told him, "Your mother and your brothers and sisters are outside asking for you." He said in reply, "Who are my mother and my brothers?" And gazing around him at those seated in the circle he continued, "These are my mother and my brothers. Whoever does the will of God is brother and sister and mother to me."—This is the gospel of the Lord. ℟.**Praise to you, Lord Jesus Christ.**

➤ No. 15, p. 623

WEDNESDAY OF THE THIRD WEEK
IN ORDINARY TIME
YEAR I

READING I   Heb 10, 11-18

There is an infinite contrast between the sacrifices of the Old Law for sin and the sublime sacrifice of Jesus. His sacrifice continues in heaven. Once God forgives sins, they are forgiven.

A reading from the letter to the Hebrews

Every other priest stands ministering day by day, and offering again and again those same sacrifices which can never take away sins. But Jesus offered one sacrifice for sins and took his seat forever at the right hand of God; now he waits until his enemies are placed beneath his feet. By one offering he has forever perfected those who are being sanctified. The Holy Spirit attests this to us, for after saying,

"This is the covenant I will make with them
    after those days, says the Lord:
I will put my laws in their hearts
    and I will write them on their minds,"

he also says,

"Their sins and their transgressions
    I will remember no more."

Once these have been forgiven, there is no further offering for sin.—This is the Word of the Lord. ℞. **Thanks be to God.** ℣

Responsorial Psalm   Ps 110, 1. 2. 3. 4

℞. (4) **You are a priest for ever,
in the line of Melchizedek.**

The Lord said to my Lord: "Sit at my right hand
    till I make your enemies your footstool." — ℞

The scepter of your power the Lord will stretch
    forth from Zion:
    "Rule in the midst of your enemies." — ℞

Yours is princely power in the day of your birth,
    in holy splendor;
    before the daystar, like the dew, I have begotten
    you." — ℞

The Lord has sworn, and he will not repent:
    "You are a priest forever, according to the order
    of Melchizedek." — ℞ ℣

——— **YEAR II** ———

READING I   2 Sm 7, 4-17

In a night vision, Nathan receives word that David should not build a temple but is to be given a promise that his house will continue and enjoy God's favor for all time. The promise to David is a personal one, but Israel, God's people, will enjoy peace and security.

A reading from the second book of Samuel

The Lord spoke to Nathan and said: "Go, tell my servant David, 'Thus says the Lord: Should you build me a house to dwell in? I have not dwelt in a house from the day on which I led the Israelites out of Egypt to the present, but I have been going about in a tent under cloth. In all my wanderings everywhere among the Israelites, did I ever utter a word to any one of the judges whom I charged to tend my people Israel, to ask: Why have you not built me a house of cedar?'

"Now then, speak thus to my servant David, 'The Lord of hosts has this to say: It was I who took you from the pasture and from the care of the flock to be commander of my people Israel. I have been with you wherever you went, and I have destroyed all your enemies before you. And I will make you famous like the great ones of the earth. I will fix a place for my people Israel; I will plant them so that they may dwell in their place without further disturbance. Neither shall the wicked continue to afflict them as they did of old, since the time I first appointed judges over my people Israel. I will give you rest from all your enemies. The Lord also reveals to you that he will establish a house for you. And when your time comes and you rest with your ancestors, I will raise up your heir after you, sprung from your loins, and I will make his kingdom firm. It is he who shall build a house for my name. And I will make his royal throne firm forever. I will be a father to him, and he shall be a son to me. And if he does wrong, I will correct him with the rod of men and with human chastisements; but I will not withdraw my favor from him as I withdrew it from your predecessor Saul, whom I removed from my presence. Your house and your kingdom shall endure forever before me; your throne shall stand firm forever.' "

Nathan reported all these words and this entire vision to David.—This is the Word of the Lord. ℟. **Thanks be to God.** ⱽ

Responsorial Psalm   Ps 89, 4-5. 27-28. 29-30

℟. (29) **For ever I will keep my love for him.**

I have made a covenant with my chosen one,
    I have sworn to David my servant:
For ever will I confirm your posterity
    and establish your throne for all generations.— ℟

He shall say of me, "You are my father,
    my God, the Rock, my savior."
And I will make him the first-born,
    highest of the kings of the earth. — ℟

Forever I will maintain my kindness toward him,
    and my covenant with him stands firm.
I will make his posterity endure forever
    and his throne as the days of heaveen. — ℟ ⊻

———— **YEAR I AND II** ————

GOSPEL   Mk 4, 1-20

Alleluia

℟. **Alleluia.** The seed is the word of God, Christ is
    the sower;
all who come to him will live for ever. ℟. **Alleluia.**

Jesus chooses images familiar to his hearers in order to enable them
to keep his teaching in daily remembrance. The seed is the Word
of God. The sower is Christ, who came forth from the Father.

℣. The Lord be with you. ℟. **And also with you.**
✠ A reading from the holy gospel according to Mark
℟. **Glory to you, Lord.**

On one occasion Jesus began to teach beside the
lake. Such a huge crowd gathered around him that
he went and sat in a boat on the water, while the
crowd remained on the shore nearby. He began to
instruct them at great length, by the use of parables,
and in the course of his teaching said: "Listen carefully to this. A farmer went out sowing. Some of
what he sowed landed on the footpath, where the
birds came along and ate it. Some of the seed landed
on rocky ground where it had little soil; it sprouted
immediately because the soil had no depth. Then,
when the sun rose and scorched it, it began to wither
for lack of roots. Again, some landed among thorns,
which grew up and choked it off, and there was no
yield of grain. Some seed, finally, landed on good
soil and yielded grain that sprang up to produce at a
rate of thirty- and sixty- and a hundredfold." Having
spoken this parable, he added: "Let him who has ears
to hear me, hear!"
    Now when he was away from the crowd, those
present with the Twelve questioned him about the

parables. He told them: "To you the mystery of the reign of God has been confided. To the others outside it is all presented in parables, so that they will look intently and not see, listen carefully and not understand, lest perhaps they repent and be forgiven."

He said to them: "You do not understand this parable? How then are you going to understand other figures like it? What the sower is sowing is the word. Those on the path are the ones to whom, as soon as they hear the word, Satan comes to carry off what was sown in them. Similarly, those sown on rocky ground are people who on listening to the word accept it joyfully at the outset. Being rootless, they last only a while. When some pressure or persecution overtakes them because of the word, they falter. Those sown among thorns are another class. They have listened to the word, but anxieties over life's demands, and the desire for wealth, and cravings of other sorts come to choke it off; it bears no yield. But those sown on good soil are the ones who listen to the word, take it to heart, and yield thirty- and sixty- and a hundredfold." This is the gospel of the Lord. ℟. **Praise to you, Lord Jesus Christ.**

➤ No. 15, p. 623

THURSDAY OF THE THIRD WEEK
IN ORDINARY TIME

—— YEAR I ——

READING I   Heb 10, 19-25

The sprinkling designates the purifying power of the sacrifice of Christ which gives salvation. Hope begins at baptism. The assembly is the gathering together of the community for the celebration of the Eucharist. Here Christians should encourage and support one another.

A reading from the letter to the Hebrews

Brothers, since the blood of Jesus assures our entrance into the sanctuary by the new and living path he has opened up for us through the veil (the "veil" means his flesh), and since we have a great priest who is over the house of God, let us draw near in utter sincerity and absolute confidence, our hearts sprinkled clean from the evil which lay on our conscience and our bodies washed in pure water. Let us hold unswervingly to our profession which gives us hope, for he who made the promise deserves our trust. We must consider how to rouse each other to love and good deeds. We should not absent ourselves from the assembly, as some do, but encourage one another; and this all the more because you see that the Day draws near.—This is the Word of the Lord. ℟. **Thanks be to God.** ℣

Responsorial Psalm   Ps 24, 1-2. 3-4. 5-6

℟. (6) **Lord, this is the people that longs to see your face.**

The Lord's are the earth and its fullness;
    the world and those who dwell in it.
For he founded it upon the seas
    and established it upon the rivers. — ℟

Who can ascend the mountain of the Lord?
    or who may stand in his holy place?
He whose hands are sinless, whose heart is clean,
    who desires not what is vain. — ℟

He shall receive a blessing from the Lord,
    a reward from God his savior.
Such is the race that seeks for him,
    that seeks the face of the God of Jacob. — ℟ ℣

—— **YEAR II** ——

READING I   2 Sm 7, 18-19. 24-29

David offers a prayer of gratitude to God for the promise and for the initial acts of favor shown to the nation in the Exodus and the settlement. David's conception of the Great Name achieved by Yahweh plays a vital part in subsequent thought.

A reading from the second book of Samuel

After Nathan had spoken to David, the king went in and sat before the Lord and said, "Who am I, Lord God, and who are the members of my house, that you have brought me to this point? Yet even this you see as too little, Lord God; you have also spoken of the house of your servant for a long time to come: this too you have shown to man, Lord God!

"You have established for yourself your people Israel as yours forever, and you, Lord, have become their God. And now Lord God, confirm for all time the prophecy you have made concerning your servant and his house, and do as you have promised. 'The Lord of hosts is God of Israel,' and the house of your servant David stands firm before you. It is you, Lord of hosts, God of Israel, who said in a revelation to your servant, 'I will build a house for you.' Therefore your servant now finds the courage to make this prayer to you. And now, Lord God, you are God and your words are truth; you have made this generous promise to your servant. Do, then, bless the house of your servant that it may be before you forever; for you, Lord God, have promised, and by your blessing the house of your servant shall be blessed forever."—This is the Word of the Lord. ℟. **Thanks be to God.** ℣

Responsorial Psalm   Ps 132, 1-2. 3-5. 11. 12. 13-14
℟. (Lk 1, 32) **God will give him the throne of David, his father.**

Remember, O Lord, for David
   all his anxious care:
How he swore to the Lord,
   vowed to the Mighty One of Jacob. — ℟

"I will not enter the house I live in,
   nor lie on the couch where I sleep;
I will give my eyes no sleep
   my eyelids no rest,

Till I find a place for the Lord,
a dwelling for the Mighty One of Jacob." — ℟

The Lord swore to David
a firm promise from which he will not withdraw:
"Your own offspring
I will set upon your throne. — ℟

If your sons keep my covenant
and the decrees which I shall teach them,
Their sons, too, forever
shall sit upon your throne." — ℟

For the Lord has chosen Zion;
he prefers her for his dwelling.
"Zion is my resting place forever;
in her will I dwell, for I prefer her." — ℟ ↓

———   **YEAR I AND II**   ———

GOSPEL   Mk 4, 21-25
Alleluia (Ps 119, 105)

℟. **Alleluia.** Your word is a lamp for my feet,
and a light on my path. ℟. **Alleluia.**

Jesus teaches that his doctrine should not be under a bushel. It is
for all men. To the apostles, Christ expounded all mysteries that
thereafter they might dispense Light to others also. Jesus warns the
apostles to listen: as you give so shall you receive.

℣. The Lord be with you. ℟. **And also with you.**
✠ A reading from the holy gospel according to Mark
℟. **Glory to you, Lord.**

Jesus said to the crowd: "Is a lamp acquired to be
put under a bushel basket or hidden under a bed?
Is it not meant to be put on a stand? Things are hidden only to be revealed at a later time; they are
covered so as to be brought out into the open. Let
him who has ears to hear me, hear!" He said to them
another time: "Listen carefully to what you hear. In
the measure you give you shall receive, and more
besides. To those who have, more will be given;
from those who have not, what little they have

will be taken away." — This is the gospel of the Lord.
℟. **Praise to you, Lord Jesus Christ.** → No. 15, p. 623

FRIDAY OF THE THIRD WEEK
IN ORDINARY TIME

—— YEAR I ——

READING I   Heb 10, 32-39

St. Paul recalls persecutions such as those of the Jerusalem church
which involved even the death of some (Acts 8, 1). The just man must
continue to live by faith, awaiting the return of Christ. If he loses
faith and falls away, he will displease God.

A reading from the letter to the Hebrews

Recall the days gone by when you endured a great
contest of suffering after you had been enlightened.
At times you were publicly exposed to insult and
trial; at other times you associated yourselves with
those who were being so dealt with. You even joined
in the sufferings of those who were in prison and
joyfully assented to the confiscation of your goods,
knowing that you had better and more permanent
possessions. Do not, then, surrender your confidence;
it will have a great reward. You need patience to do
God's will and receive what he has promised.

For, just "a brief moment,
    and he who is to come will come; he will not
        delay.
My just man will live by faith,"
    and "if he draws back
    I take no pleasure in him."

We are not among those who draw back and perish,
but among those who have faith and live—This is
the Word of the Lord. ℟. **Thanks be to God.** ↓

Responsorial Psalm   Ps 37, 3-4. 5-6. 23-24. 39-40
℟. (39) **The salvation of the just comes from the
    Lord.**

Trust in the Lord and do good,
    that you may dwell in the land and enjoy security.
Take delight in the Lord,
    and he will grant you your heart's requests. — ℟

Commit to the Lord your way;
    trust in him, and he will act.
He will make justice dawn for you like the light;
    bright as the noonday shall be your vindica-
        tion. — ℟

By the Lord are the steps of a man made firm,
    and he approves his way.
Though he fall, he does not lie prostrate,
    for the hand of the Lord sustains him. —℟

The salvation of the just is from the Lord;
    he is their refuge in time of distress.
And the Lord helps them and delivers them;
    he delivers them from the wicked and saves them,
    because they take refuge in him. — ℟ ↓

—— YEAR II ——

READING I   2 Sm 11, 1-4. 5-10. 13-17

The Ammonite campaign continues but David remains in Jerusalem. He
satisfies his lust for Bathsheba, Uriah's wife. To cover his own guilt,
David arranges for Uriah, who maintains his correct bearing throughout, to meet his death in battle.

A reading from the second book of Samuel

At the turn of the year, when kings go out on campaign, David sent out Joab along with his officers
and the army of Israel, and they ravaged the Ammonites and besieged Rabbah. David, however, remained in Jerusalem. One evening David rose from
his siesta and strolled about on the roof of the palace. From the roof he saw a woman bathing, who
was very beautiful. David had inquiries made about
the woman and was told, "She is Bathsheba, daughter of Eliam, and wife of [Joab's armorbearer] Uriah
the Hittite." Then David sent messengers and took

her. When she came to him, he had relations with her. The woman conceived, and sent the information to David, "I am with child."

David therefore sent a message to Joab, "Send me Uriah the Hittite." So Joab sent Uriah to David. When he came, David questioned him about Joab, the soldiers, and how the war was going, and Uriah answered that all was well. David then said to Uriah, "Go down to your house and bathe your feet." Uriah left the palace, and a portion was sent out after him from the king's table. But Uriah slept at the entrance of the royal palace with the other officers of his lord, and did not go down to his own house. David was told that Uriah had not gone home. On the day following, David summoned him, and he ate and drank with David, who made him drunk. But in the evening he went out to sleep on his bed among his lord's servants, and did not go down to his home. The next morning David wrote a letter to Joab which he sent by Uriah. In it he directed: "Place Uriah up front, where the fighting is fierce. Then pull back and leave him to be struck down dead." So while Joab was besieging the city, he assigned Uriah to a place where he knew the defenders were strong. When the men of the city made a sortie against Joab, some officers of David's army fell, and among them Uriah the Hittite died.—This is the Word of the Lord. ℟. **Thanks be to God.** ↓

Responsorial Psalm   Ps 51, 3-4. 5-6. 6-7. 10-11

℟. (3) **Be merciful, O Lord, for we have sinned.**

Have mercy on me, O God, in your goodness;
    in the greatness of your compassion wipe out my
        offense.
Thoroughly wash me from my guilt
    and of my sin cleanse me. — ℟

For I acknowledge my offense,
    and my sin is before me always:

"Against you only have I sinned,
   and done what is evil in your sight." — ℟

That you may be justified in your sentence,
   vindicated when you condemn.
Indeed, in guilt was I born,
   and in sin my mother conceived me. — ℟

Let me hear the sounds of joy and gladness;
   the bones you have crushed shall rejoice.
Turn away your face from my sins,
   and blot out all my guilt. — ℟ ⱽ

—— **YEAR I AND II** ——

GOSPEL   Mk 4, 26-34

Alleluia (Mt 11, 25)

℟. **Alleluia.** Blessed are you, Father, Lord of heaven
   and earth;
you have revealed to little ones the mysteries of the
      kingdom. ℟. **Alleluia.**

This is the parable of growing seed. Though the Gospel appears to
spread by human means, it is really God who nourishes it. As a seed
springs up and grows, mysteriously, so it is with the growth of Christ's
kingdom on earth.

℣. The Lord be with you. ℟. **And also with you.**
✠ A reading from the holy gospel according to Mark
℟. **Glory to you, Lord.**

Jesus said to the crowd: "This is how it is with the
reign of God. A man scatters seed on the ground. He
goes to bed and gets up day after day. Through it all
the seed sprouts and grows without his knowing
how it happens. The soil produces of itself first the
blade, then the ear, finally the ripe wheat in the ear.
When the crop is ready he 'wields the sickle, for the
time is ripe for harvest.'"

He went on to say: "What comparison shall we use
for the reign of God? What image will help to present
it? It is like mustard seed which, when planted in the
soil, is the smallest of all the earth's seeds, yet once

it is sown, springs up to become the largest of shrubs, with branches big enough for the birds of the sky to build nests in its shade." By means of many such parables he taught them the message in a way they could understand. To them he spoke only by way of parable, while he kept explaining things privately to his disciples.—This is the gospel of the Lord. ℟. **Praise to you, Lord Jesus Christ.**   ➔ No. 15, p. 623

SATURDAY OF THE THIRD WEEK IN ORDINARY TIME

——— YEAR I ———

READING I   Heb 11, 1-2. 8-19

Faith is the firm assurance of what is hoped for that is not seen. Christian living is marked by assurance that the good things promised by God will be fully possessed in the future. Jesus' saving death and his heavenly priesthood are indeed facts and not illusions.

A reading from the letter to the Hebrews

Faith is confident assurance concerning what we hope for, and conviction about things we do not see. Because of faith the men of old were approved by God. By faith Abraham obeyed when he was called and went forth to the place he was to receive as a heritage; he went forth, moreover, not knowing where he was going. By faith he sojourned in the promised land as in a foreign country, dwelling in tents with Isaac and Jacob, heirs of the same promise; for he was looking forward to the city with foundations, whose designer and maker is God. By faith Sarah received power to conceive though she was past the age, for she thought that the One who had made the promise was worthy of trust. As a result of this faith, there came forth from one man, who was himself as good as dead, descendants as numerous as the stars in the sky and the sands of the seashore.

All of these died in faith. They did not obtain what had been promised but saw and saluted it from afar.

By acknowledging themselves to be strangers and foreigners on the earth, they showed that they were seeking a homeland. If they had been thinking back to the place from which they had come, they would have had the opportunity of returning there. But they were searching for a better, a heavenly home. Wherefore God is not ashamed to be called their God, for he has prepared a city for them. By faith Abraham, when put to the test, offered up Isaac; he who had received the promises was ready to sacrifice his only son, of whom it was said, "Through Isaac shall your descendants be called." He reasoned that God was able to raise from the dead, and so he received Isaac back as a symbol.—This is the Word of the Lord. ℟. **Thanks be to God.** ℣

Responsorial Psalm   Lk 1, 69-70. 71-72. 73-75

℟. (68) **Blessed be the Lord God of Israel,**
   for he has visited his people.

He has raised a horn of saving strength for us
   in the house of David his servant,
As he promised through the mouths of his holy ones,
   the prophets of ancient times: — ℟

Salvation from our enemies
   and from the hands of all our foes.
He has dealt mercifully with our fathers
   and remembered the holy covenant. — ℟

The oath he swore to Abraham our father he would
      grant us:
   that, rid of fear and delivered from the enemy,
We should serve him devoutly, and through all our
      days,
   be holy in his sight. — ℟ ℣

———— **YEAR II** ————

READING I   2 Sm 12, 1-7. 10-17

This simple parable of the ewe lamb draws David into an untenable position. It elicits from David the expected judgment of himself.

Nathan points out to David that he stands self-condemned because of the wife of Uriah and that what he has done is unworthy of a prince who owes so much to Yahweh.

A reading from the second book of Samuel

The Lord sent Nathan to David, and when he came to him, he said: "Judge this case for me! In a certain town there were two men, one rich, the other poor. The rich man had flocks and herds in great numbers. But the poor man had nothing at all except one little ewe lamb that he had bought. He nourished her, and she grew up with him and his children. She shared the little food he had and drank from his cup and slept in his bosom. She was like a daughter to him. Now, the rich man received a visitor, but he would not take from his own flocks and herds to prepare a meal for the wayfarer who had come to him. Instead he took the poor man's ewe lamb and made a meal of it for his visitor." David grew very angry with that man and said to Nathan, "As the Lord lives, the man who has done this merits death! He shall restore the ewe lamb fourfold because he has done this and has had not pity."

Then Nathan said to David: "You are the man!

"Now, therefore, the sword shall never depart from your house, because you have despised me and have taken the wife of Uriah to be your wife. Thus says the Lord: 'I will bring evil upon you out of your own house. I will take your wives while you live to see it, and will give them to your neighbor. He shall lie with your wives in broad daylight. You have done this deed in secret, but I will bring it about in the presence of all Israel, and with the sun looking down.'"

Then David said to Nathan, "I have sinned against the Lord." Nathan answered David: "The Lord on his part has forgiven your sin: you shall not die. But since you have utterly spurned the Lord by this deed, the child born to you must surely die." Then Nathan returned to his house.

The Lord struck the child that the wife of Uriah had borne to David, and it became desperately ill. David besought God for the child. He kept a fast, retiring for the night to lie on the ground clothed in sackcloth. The elders of his house stood beside him urging him to rise from the ground; but he would not, nor would he take food with them.—This is the Word of the Lord. ℟. **Thanks be to God.** ⍗

Responsorial Psalm   Ps 51, 12-13. 14-15. 16-17

℟. (12) **Create a clean heart in me, O God.**

A clean heart create for me, O God,
  and a steadfast spirit renew within me.
Cast me not out from your presence,
  and your holy spirit take not from me. — ℟

Give me back the joy of your salvation,
  and a willing spirit sustain in me.
I will teach transgressors your ways,
  and sinners shall return to you. — ℟

Free me from blood guilt, O God, my saving God;
  then my tongue shall revel in your justice.
O Lord, open my lips,
  and my mouth shall proclaim your praise. — ℟ ⍗

———   **YEAR I AND II**   ———

GOSPEL   Mk 4, 35-41

Alleluia (Jn 3, 16)

℟. **Alleluia.** God loved the world so much, he gave
    us his only Son,
that all who believe in him might have eternal life.
    ℟. **Alleluia.**

The emphasis on the storm and the need of faith is a lesson in discipleship. Christ calms a violent storm. The doubt and fear of the apostles that he could save them shows that our Lord is trying their faith and awaiting their prayers.

℣. The Lord be with you. ℟. **And also with you.**
✠ A reading from the holy gospel according to Mark
℟. **Glory to you, Lord.**

One day as evening drew on Jesus said to his disciples, "Let us cross over to the farther shore." Leaving the crowd, they took him away in the boat in which he was sitting, while the other boats accompanied him. It happened that a bad squall blew up. The waves were breaking over the boat and it began to ship water badly. Jesus was in the stern through it all, sound asleep on a cushion. They finally woke him and said to him, "Teacher, doesn't it matter to you that we are going to drown?" He awoke and rebuked the wind and said to the sea: "Quiet! Be still!" The wind fell off and everything grew calm. Then he said to them, "Why are you so terrified? Why are you lacking in faith?" A great awe overcame them at this. They kept saying to one another, "Who can this be that the wind and the sea obey him?"—This is the gospel of the Lord. ℟ **Praise to you, Lord Jesus Christ.**

➙ No. 15, p. 623

MONDAY OF THE FOURTH WEEK IN ORDINARY TIME

—— YEAR I ——

READING I   Heb 11, 32-40

St. Paul passes summarily through some heroes of the Old Testament. The sufferings mentioned are principally those endured by the faithful Israelites during the persecution of the Maccabean revolt. The fulfillment the Old Testament saints awaited did not take place until the saving work of Christ was completed.

A reading from the letter to the Hebrews

What more shall I recount? I have no time to tell of Gideon, Barak, Samson, Jephthah, of David and Samuel and the prophets, who by faith conquered kingdoms, did what was just, obtained the promises;

they broke the jaws of lions, put out raging fires, escaped the devouring sword; though weak they were made powerful, became strong in battle, and turned back foreign invaders. Women received back their dead through resurrection. Others were tortured and did not receive deliverance, in order to obtain a better resurrection. Still others endured mockery, scourging, even chains and imprisonment. They were stoned, sawed in two, put to death at sword's point; they went about garbed in the skins of sheep or goats, needy, afflicted, tormented. The world was not worthy of them. They wandered about in deserts and on mountains, they dwelt in caves and in holes of the earth. Yet despite the fact that all of these were approved because of their faith, they did not obtain what had been promised. God had made a better plan, a plan which included us. Without us, they were not to be made perfect.— This is the Word of the Lord. ℟. **Thanks be to God.** ℣

Responsorial Psalm   Ps 31, 20. 21. 22. 23. 24

℟. (25) **Let your hearts take comfort,**
  all who hope in the Lord.

How great is the goodness, O Lord,
  which you have in store for those who fear you,
And which, toward those who take refuge in you,
  you show in the sight of men. — ℟

You hide them in the shelter of your presence
  from the plottings of men;
You screen them within your abode
  from the strife of tongues. — ℟

Blessed be the Lord whose wondrous kindness
  he has shown me in a fortified city. — ℟

Once I said in my anguish,
  "I am cut off from your sight";
Yet you heard the sound of my pleading
  when I cried out to you. — ℟

Love the Lord, all you his faithful ones!

The Lord keeps those who are constant,
but more than requites those who act
proudly. — ℟ ⊽

───────   **YEAR II**   ───────

READING I   2 Sm 15, 13-14. 30; 16, 5-13

David, alarmed at the news of the rebellion, leaves Jerusalem with
his troops. The ensuing events in David's flight are described suc-
cinctly; David is the hunted one. David is in dismay upon hearing
of Absalom's defection.

A reading from the second book of Samuel

An informant came to David with the report, "The
Israelites have transferred their loyalty to Absalom."
At this, David said to all his servants who were with
him in Jerusalem: "Up! Let us take flight, or none
of us will escape from Absalom. Leave quickly, lest
he hurry and overtake us, then visit disaster upon
us and put the city to the sword."

As David went up the Mount of Olives, he wept
without ceasing. His head was covered, and he was
walking barefoot. All those who were with him also
had their heads covered and were weeping as they
went.

As David was approaching Bahurim, a man named
Shimei, the son of Gera of the same clan as Saul's
family, was coming out of the place, cursing as he
came. He threw stones at David and at all the king's
officers, even though all the soldiers, including the
royal guard, were on David's right and on his left.
Shimei was saying as he cursed: "Away, away, you
murderous and wicked man! The Lord has requited
you for all the bloodshed in the family of Saul, in
whose stead you became king, and the Lord has
given over the kingdom to your son Absalom. And
now you suffer ruin because you are a murderer."
Abishai, son of Zeruiah, said to the king: "Why
should this dead dog curse my lord the king? Let

me go over, please, and lop off his head." But the
king replied: "What business is it of mine or of
yours, sons of Zeruiah, that he curses? Suppose the
Lord has told him to curse David; who then will dare
to say, 'Why are you doing this?'" Then the king
said to Abishai and to all his servants: "If my own
son, who came forth from my loins, is seeking my
life, how much more might this Benjaminite do so!
Let him alone and let him curse, for the Lord has
told him to. Perhaps the Lord will look upon my affliction and make it up to me with benefits for the
curses he is uttering this day." David and his men
continued on the road.—This is the Word of the Lord.
℟. **Thanks be to God.** ↓

Responsorial Psalm   Ps 3, 2-3. 4-5. 6-7
℟. (7) **Lord, rise up and save me.**

O Lord, how many are my adversaries!
    Many rise up against me!
Many are saying of me,
    "There is no salvation for him in God." — ℟

But you, O Lord, are my shield;
    my glory, you lift up my head!
When I call out to the Lord,
    he answers me from his holy mountain. — ℟

When I lie down in sleep,
    I wake again, for the Lord sustains me.
I fear not the myriads of people
    arrayed against me on every side.
Rise up, O Lord!
    Save me, my God! — ℟ ↓

————   **YEAR I AND II**   ————

GOSPEL   Mk 5, 1-20
Alleluia (Lk 7, 16)

℟. **Alleluia.** A great prophet has risen among us;
God has visited his people. ℟. **Alleluia.**

Mark dwells graphically on the impossibility of subduing the maniac. The miracle contains many hints as to the nature of demoniacal possession. At the direction of Christ, the healed demoniac returns to his family to tell them of the compassion and mercy of God.

℣. The Lord be with you. ℟. **And also with you.**
✠ A reading from the holy gospel according to Mark
℟. **Glory to you, Lord.**

Jesus and his disciples came to Gerasene territory on the other side of the lake. As he got out of the boat, he was immediately met by a man from the tombs who had an unclean spirit. The man had taken refuge among the tombs; he could no longer be restrained even with a chain. In fact, he had frequently been secured with handcuffs and chains, but had pulled the chains apart and smashed the fetters. No one had proved strong enough to tame him. Uninterruptedly night and day, amid the tombs and on the hillsides, he screamed and gashed himself with stones. Catching sight of Jesus at a distance, he ran up and did him homage, shrieking in a loud voice, "Why meddle with me, Jesus, Son of God Most High? I implore you in God's name, do not torture me!" (Jesus had been saying to him, "Unclean spirit, come out of the man!") "What is your name?" Jesus asked him. "Legion is my name," he answered. "There are hundreds of us." He pleaded hard with Jesus not to drive them away from that neighborhood.

It happened that a large herd of swine was feeding on the slope of the mountain. "Send us into the swine," they begged him. "Let us enter them." He gave the word, and with it the unclean spirits came out and entered the swine. The herd of about two thousand went rushing down the bluff into the lake, where they began to drown. The swineherds ran off and brought the news to field and village, and the people came to see what had happened. As they approached Jesus, they caught sight of the man who

had been possessed by Legion sitting fully clothed
and perfectly sane, and they were seized with fear.
The spectators explained what had happened to the
possessed man, and told them about the swine. Before long they were begging him to go away from
their district. As Jesus was getting into the boat,
the man who had been possessed was pressing to
accompany him. Jesus did not grant his request, but
told him instead: "Go home to your family and make
it clear to them how much the Lord in his mercy has
done for you." At that the man went off and began
to proclaim throughout the Ten Cities what Jesus
had done for him. They were all amazed at what
they heard.—This is the gospel of the Lord. ℟. **Praise
to you, Lord Jesus Christ.**   ➔ No. 15, p. 623

TUESDAY OF THE FOURTH WEEK
IN ORDINARY TIME
—— YEAR I ——

READING I   Heb 12, 1-4

All through life there are temptations, wants, and desires which
distract from Jesus. St. Paul reminds us to keep in the race with our
eyes focused on Jesus in whom we have faith. He did not give up the
fight even when faced with death.

A reading from the letter to the Hebrews

Since we for our part are surrounded by a cloud of
witnesses, let us lay aside every encumbrance of
sin which clings to us and persevere in running the
race which lies ahead; let us keep our eyes fixed on
Jesus, who inspires and perfects our faith. For the
sake of the joy which lay before him he endured
the cross, heedless of its shame. He has taken his
seat at the right of the throne of God. Remember
how he endured the opposition of sinners; hence do
not grow despondent or abandon the struggle. In
your fight against sin you have not yet resisted to

the point of shedding blood.—This is the Word of the Lord. ℟. **Thanks be to God. ✟**

Responsorial Psalm   Ps 22, 26-27. 28. 30. 31-32

℟. (27) **They will praise you, Lord, who long for you.**

I will fulfill my vows before those who fear him.
    The lowly shall eat their fill;
They who seek the Lord shall praise him:
    "May your hearts be ever merry!" — ℟

All the ends of the earth
    shall remember and turn to the Lord;
All the families of the nations
    shall bow down before him.
To him alone shall bow down
    all who sleep in the earth;
Before him shall bend
    all who go down into the dust. — ℟

And to him my soul shall live.
    My descendants shall serve him.
Let the coming generation be told of the Lord
    that they may proclaim to a people yet to be born
    the justice he has shown. — ℟ ✟

——— **YEAR II** ———

READING I   2 Sm 18, 9-10. 14. 24-25. 30-19, 3

Absalom is caught in a tree, and Joab thrusts three pikes in him. When the news of Absalom's death reaches David, he grieves together with the whole army.

    A reading from the second book of Samuel

Absalom unexpectedly came up against David's servants. He was mounted on a mule, and, as the mule passed under the branches of a large terebinth, his hair caught fast in the tree. He hung between heaven and earth while the mule he had been riding ran off. Someone saw this and reported to Joab that he had seen Absalom hanging from a terebinth. And taking three pikes in hand, Joab thrust for the heart of Absalom.

    Now David was sitting between the two gates,

and a lookout mounted to the roof of the gate above the city wall, where he looked about and saw a man running all alone. The lookout shouted to inform the king, who said, "If he is alone, he has good news to report." The king said, "Step aside and remain in attendance here." So he stepped aside and remained there. When the Cushite came in, he said, "Let my lord the king receive the good news that this day the Lord has taken your part, freeing you from the grasp of all who rebelled against you." But the king asked the Cushite, "Is young Absalom safe?" The Cushite replied, "May the enemies of my lord the king and all who rebel against you with evil intent be as that young man!"

The king was shaken, and went up to the room over the city gate to weep. He said as he wept, "My son Absalom! My son, my son Absalom! If only I had died instead of you, Absalom, my son, my son!"

Joab was told that the king was weeping and mourning for Absalom; and that day's victory was turned into mourning for the whole army when they heard that the king was grieving for his son.—This is the Word of the Lord. ℟. **Thanks be to God.** ℣

Responsorial Psalm   Ps 86, 1-2. 3-4. 5-6

℟. (1) **Listen, Lord, and answer me.**

Incline your ear, O Lord; answer me,
　　for I am afflicted and poor.
Keep my life, for I am devoted to you;
　　save your servant who trusts in you. — ℟

You are my God; have pity on me, O Lord,
　　for to you I call all the day.
Gladden the soul of your servant,
　　for to you, O Lord, I lift up my soul. — ℟

For you, O Lord, are good and forgiving,
　　abounding in kindness to all who call upon you.
Hearken, O Lord, to my prayer
　　and attend to the sound of my pleading. — ℟ ℣

—————— **YEAR I AND II** ——————

GOSPEL Mk 5, 21-43

Alleluia (Mt 8, 17)

℟. **Alleluia.** He took our sicknesses away,
and carried our diseases for us. ℟. **Alleluia.**

Jesus performs two miracles which are the result of deep faith—the
curing of the woman who was sick for years and the raising of Jairus'
daughter from death to life. Jesus shows how he responds to those
who come to him: "Ask and you shall receive."

℣. The Lord be with you. ℟. **And also with you.**
✠ A reading from the holy gospel according to Mark
℟. **Glory to you, Lord.**

When Jesus had crossed back to the other side of
the Sea of Galilee in the boat, a large crowd gathered around him and he stayed close to the lake.
One of the officials of the synagogue, a man named
Jairus, came near. Seeing Jesus, he fell at his feet
and made this earnest appeal: "My little daughter
is critically ill. Please come and lay your hands on
her so that she may get well and live." The two went
off together and a large crowd followed, pushing
against Jesus.

There was a woman in the area who had been afflicted with a hemorrhage for a dozen years. She had
received treatment at the hands of doctors of every
sort and exhausted her savings in the process, yet
she got no relief; on the contrary, she only grew
worse. She had heard about Jesus and came up behind him in the crowd and put her hand to his cloak.
"If I just touch his clothing," she thought, "I shall
get well." Immediately her flow of blood dried up
and the feeling that she was cured of her affliction
ran through her whole body. Jesus was immediately
conscious that healing power had gone out from him.
Wheeling about in the crowd, he began to ask, "Who
touched my clothing?" His disciples said to him,
"You can see how this crowd hems you in, yet you

ask, 'Who touched me?' Despite this, he kept looking around to see the woman who had done it. Fearful and beginning to tremble now as she realized what had happened, the woman came and fell in front of him and told him the whole truth. He said to her, "Daughter, it is your faith that has cured you. Go in peace and be free of this illness."

He had not finished speaking when people from the official's house arrived saying, "Your daughter is dead. Why bother the Teacher further?" Jesus disregarded the report that had been brought and said to the official: "Fear is useless. What is needed is trust." He would not permit anyone to follow him except Peter, James, and James' brother John. As they approached the house of the synagogue leader, Jesus was struck by the noise of people wailing and crying loudly on all sides. He entered and said to them: "Why do you make this din with your wailing? The child is not dead. She is asleep." At this they began to ridicule him. Then he put them all out.

Jesus took the child's father and mother and his own companions and entered the room where the child lay. Taking her hand he said to her, *"Talitha, koum,"* which means, "Little girl, get up." The girl, a child of twelve, stood up immediately and began to walk around. At this the family's astonishment was complete. He enjoined them strictly not to let anyone know about it, and told them to give her something to eat.—This is the gospel of the Lord.
℞. **Praise to you, Lord Jesus Christ.** ➔No. 15, p. 623

WEDNESDAY OF THE FOURTH WEEK IN ORDINARY TIME

—— YEAR I ——

READING I   Heb 12, 4-7. 11-15

It is evident that the local church addressed in the epistle shrinks from the thought of persecutions and suffering. However. the Christian should be aware that God trains his people in the hard school of suffering. Trials and suffering are proof of his Fatherly concern and certain'y not a sign of his anger.

A reading from the letter to the Hebrews

In your fight against sin you have not yet resisted to the point of shedding blood. Moreover, you have forgotten the encouraging words addressed to you as sons:

"My sons, do not disdain the discipline of the
     Lord nor lose heart when he reproves you;
For, whom the Lord loves, he disciplines;
     he scourges every son he receives."

Endure your trials as the discipline of God, who deals with you as sons. For what son is there whom his father does not discipline? At the time it is administered, all discipline seems a cause for grief and not for joy, but later it brings forth the fruit of peace and justice to those who are trained in its school. So strengthen your drooping hands and your weak knees. Make straight the paths you walk on, that your halting limbs may not be dislocated but healed.

Strive for peace with all men, and for that holiness without which no one can see the Lord. See to it that no one falls away from the grace of God; that no bitter root springs up through which many may become defiled.—This is the Word of the Lord. ℟. **Thanks be to God.** ℣

Responsorial Psalm   Ps 103, 1-2. 13-14. 17-18
℟. (17) **The Lord's kindness is everlasting to those who fear him.**

Bless the Lord, O my soul;
     and all my being, bless his holy name.
Bless the Lord, O my soul,
     and forget not all his benefits. — ℟

As a father has compassion on his children,

so the Lord has compassion on those who fear
 him,
For he knows how we are formed;
 he remembers that we are dust. — ℞

But the kindness of the Lord is from eternity
 to eternity toward those who fear him,
And his justice toward children's children
 among those who keep his covenant. — ℞ ℣

————— **YEAR II** —————

READING I   2 Sm 24, 2. 9-17

David orders a census of the Israelites, but he later repents for
testing the Lord. Three choices are given David, and he chooses pestilence for the punishment. God again spares his people.

A reading from the second book of Samuel

King David said to Joab and the leaders of the army
who were with him, "Tour all the tribes in Israel
from Dan to Beer-sheba and register the people, that
I may know their number."

Joab then reported to the king the number of
people registered: in Israel, eight hundred thousand
men fit for military service; in Judah, five hundred
thousand.

Afterward, however, David regretted having numbered the people, and said to the Lord: "I have sinned grievously in what I have done. But now, Lord,
forgive the guilt of your servant, for I have been
very foolish." When David rose in the morning, the
Lord had spoken to the prophet Gad, David's seer,
saying: "Go and say to David, 'This is what the
Lord says: I offer you three alternatives; choose
one of them and I will inflict it on you.'" Gad then
went to David to inform him. He asked: "Do you
want a three years' famine to come upon your land,
or to flee from your enemy three months while he
pursues you, or to have a three days' pestilence in
your land? Now consider and decide what I must

reply to him who sent me." David answered Gad: "I am in very serious difficulty. Let us fall by the hand of God, for he is most merciful; but let me not fall by the hand of man." Thus David chose the pestilence. Now it was the time of the wheat harvest when the plague broke out among the people. [The Lord then sent a pestilence over Israel from morning until the time appointed, and seventy thousand of the people from Dan to Beer-sheba died.] But when the angel stretched forth his hand toward Jerusalem to destroy it, the Lord regretted the calamity and said to the angel causing the destruction among the people, "Enough now! Stay your hand." The angel of the Lord was then standing at the threshing floor of Araunah the Jebusite. When David saw the angel who was striking the people, he said to the Lord: "It is I who have sinned; it is I, the shepherd, who have done wrong. But these are sheep; what have they done? Punish me and my kindred."
—This is the Word of the Lord. ℟. **Thanks be to God.** ℣

Responsorial Psalm   Ps 32, 1-2. 5. 6. 7
℟. (5) **Lord, forgive the wrong I have done.**

Happy is he whose fault is taken away,
    whose sin is covered.
Happy the man to whom the Lord imputes not guilt,
    in whose spirit there is no guile. — ℟

Then I acknowledged my sin to you,
    my guilt I covered not.
I said, "I confess my faults to the Lord,"
    and you took away the guilt of my sin. — ℟

For this shall every faithful man pray to you
    in time of stress.
Though deep waters overflow,
    they shall not reach him. — ℟

You are my shelter; from distress you will preserve
me;

with glad cries of freedom you will ring me
round. — ℟ ↓

——— **YEAR I AND II** ———

GOSPEL   Mk 6, 1-6

Alleluia (Jn 10, 27)

℟. **Alleluia.** My sheep listen to my voice, says the
Lord;

I know them, and they follow me. ℟. **Alleluia.**

Jesus is rejected by his fellow countrymen. It was a Jewish custom
to refer to a man as the son of his father. Thus, "son of Mary" may
be intended as an insult. Our Lord's miraculous power is rendered
ineffective by the disbelief in his countrymen.

℣. The Lord be with you. ℟. **And also with you.**
✠ A reading from the holy gospel according to Mark
℟. **Glory to you, Lord.**

Jesus went to his own part of the country followed
by his disciples. When the sabbath came he began
to teach in the synagogue in a way that kept his
large audience amazed. They said: "Where did he
get all this? What kind of wisdom is he endowed
with? How is it such miraculous deeds are accomplished by his hands? Isn't this the carpenter, the
son of Mary, a brother of James and Joses and Judas
and Simon? Aren't his sisters our neighbors here?"
They found him too much for them. Jesus' response
to all this was: "No prophet is without honor except
in his native place, among his own kindred, and in
his own house." He could work no miracle there,
apart from curing a few who were sick by laying
hands on them, so much did their lack of faith distress him. He made the rounds of the neighboring
villages instead, and spent his time teaching.—This
is the gospel of the Lord. ℟. **Praise to you, Lord
Jesus Christ.**

➤ No. 15, p. 623

THURSDAY OF THE FOURTH WEEK
IN ORDINARY TIME

——— YEAR I ———

READING I   Heb 12, 18-19. 21-24

St. Paul begins a contrast between the assembly of Israel gathered for the making of the Old Covenant and the giving of the law, and the assembly of those who have entered into the New Covenant.

A reading from the letter to the Hebrews

You have not drawn near to an untouchable mountain and a blazing fire, and gloomy darkness and storm and trumpet blast, and a voice speaking words such that those who heard begged that they be not addressed to them. Indeed, so fearful was the spectacle that Moses said, "I am terrified and trembling." No, you have drawn near to Mount Zion and the city of the living God, the heavenly Jerusalem, to myriads of angels in festal gathering, to the assembly of the first-born enrolled in heaven, to God the judge of all, to the spirits of just men made perfect, to Jesus, the mediator of a new covenant, and to the sprinkled blood which speaks more eloquently than that of Abel.—This is the Word of the Lord. ℟. **Thanks be to God.** ✟

Responsorial Psalm   Ps 48, 2-3. 3-4. 9. 10-11

℟. (10) **God, in your temple, we ponder your love.**

Great is the Lord and wholly to be praised
  in the city of our God.
His holy mountain, fairest of heights,
  is the joy of all the earth. — ℟

Mount Zion, "the recesses of the North,"
  is the city of the great King.
God is with her castles;
  renowned is he as a stronghold. — ℟

As we had heard, so have we seen
  in the city of the Lord of hosts,

In the city of our God;
  God makes it firm forever. — ℞
O God, we ponder your kindness
  within your temple.
As your name, O God, so also your praise
  reaches to the ends of the earth.
Of justice your right hand is full. — ℞ ℣

——— **YEAR II** ———

READING I   1 Kgs 2, 1-4. 10-12

Just before dying, David instructs Solomon to be courageous and
follow the decrees in the law of Moses. David dies and is buried in the
City of David. Thereupon, Solomon is seated on the throne of his
father.

A reading from the first book of Kings

When the time of David's death drew near, he gave
these instructions to his son Solomon: "I am going
the way of all mankind. Take courage and be a man.
Keep the mandate of the Lord, your God, following
his ways and observing his statutes, commands, ordinances, and decrees as they are written in the law
of Moses, that you may succeed in whatever you do,
wherever you turn, and the Lord may fulfill the
promise he made on my behalf when he said, 'If
your sons so conduct themselves that they remain
faithful to me with their whole heart and with their
whole soul, you shall always have someone of your
line on the throne of Israel.' "

David rested with his ancestors and was buried
in the City of David. The length of David's reign
over Israel was forty years: he reigned seven years
in Hebron and thirty-three years in Jerusalem.

Solomon was seated on the throne of his father
David, with his sovereignty firmly established.—This
is the Word of the Lord. ℞. **Thanks be to God.** ℣

Responsorial Psalm   1 Chr 29, 10. 11. 11-12, 12
℞. (12) **Lord, you are exalted over all.**

Blessed may you be, O Lord,
  God of Israel our father,
  from eternity to eternity.

℟. **Lord, you are exalted over all.**
Yours, O Lord, are grandeur and power,
  majesty, splendor, and glory. — ℟

Yours, O Lord, is the sovereignty;
  you are exalted as head over all.
  Riches and honor are from you. — ℟

And you have dominion over all.
  In your hand are power and might;
It is yours to give grandeur and strength to all.—℟ ⍎

——— **YEAR I AND II** ———

GOSPEL Mk 6, 7-13

Alleluia (Mk 1, 15)

℟. **Alleluia.** The kingdom of God is near:
believe the Good News! ℟. **Alleluia.**

St. Mark is the only evangelist who mentions that Christ began to send
his disciples forth in pairs. Two were considered better than one, for
if one fell, the companion could lift up his fellow. They work many
cures.

℣. The Lord be with you. ℟. **And also with you.**
✠ A reading from the holy gospel according to Mark
℟. **Glory to you, Lord.**

Jesus summoned the Twelve and began to send them
out two by two, giving them authority over unclean
spirits. He instructed them to take nothing on the
journey but a walking stick—no food, no traveling
bag, not a coin in the purses in their belts. They
were, however, to wear sandals. "Do not bring a
second tunic," he said, and added: "Whatever house
you find yourself in, stay there until you leave the
locality. If any place will not receive you or hear
you, shake its dust from your feet in testimony
against them as you leave." With that they went
off, preaching the need of repentance. They expelled
many demons, anointed the sick with oil, and worked

many cures.—This is the gospel of the Lord. ℞.
Praise to you, Lord Jesus Christ. ➤ No. 15, p. 623

FRIDAY OF THE FOURTH WEEK
IN ORDINARY TIME
——— YEAR I ———

READING I   Heb 13, 1-8

St. Paul speaks of brotherly love and appeals for hospitality. Ministry
to the basic needs of one's fellow man is mentioned to show that man
is judged on his behavior toward his fellow man. Much stress is laid
upon acts of mercy because they are within the reach of all.

A reading from the letter to the Hebrews

Love your fellow Christians always. Do not neglect
to show hospitality, for by that means some have
entertained angels without knowing it. Be as mindful of prisoners as if you were sharing their imprisonment, and of the ill-treated as yourselves, for you
may yet suffer as they do. Let marriage be honored
in every way and the marriage bed be kept undefiled, for God will judge fornicators and adulterers.
Do not love money but be content with what you
have, for God has said, "I will never desert you, nor
will I forsake you." Thus we may say with confidence:

"The Lord is my helper,
I will not be afraid;
What can man do to me?"

Remember your leaders who spoke the word of God
to you; consider how their lives ended, and imitate
their faith. Jesus Christ is the same yesterday, today, and forever.—This is the Word of the Lord.
℞. **Thanks be to God.** ⅴ

Responsorial Psalm   Ps 27, 1. 3. 5. 8-9

℞. (1) **The Lord is my light and my salvation.**

The Lord is my light and my salvation;
  whom should I fear?
The Lord is my life's refuge;
  of whom should I be afraid? — ℞

Though an army encamp against me,
 my heart will not fear;
Though war be waged upon me,
 even then will I trust. — ℟

For he will hide me in his abode
 in the day of trouble;
He will conceal me in the shelter of his tent,
 he will set me high upon a rock. — ℟

Your presence, O Lord, I seek.
 Hide not your face from me;
Do not in anger repel your servant.
 You are my helper: cast me not off. — ℟ ℣

--- **YEAR II** ---

READING I   Sir 47, 2-11

The Lord had given strength to David to slay the giant. The women
sang his praises. He destroyed the Philistines and ordered celebrations. The Lord also forgave him his sins.

  A reading from the book of Sirach

Like the choice fat of the sacred offerings,
 so was David in Israel.
He made sport of lions as though they were kids,
 and of bears, like lambs of the flock.
As a youth he slew the giant
 and wiped out the people's disgrace,
When his hand let fly the slingstone
 that crushed the pride of Goliath.
Since he called upon the Most High God,
 who gave strength to his right arm
To defeat the skilled warrior
 and raise up the might of his people,
Therefore the women sang his praises
 and ascribed to him tens of thousands.
When he assumed the royal crown, he battled
 and subdued the enemy on every side.
He destroyed the hostile Philistines
 and shattered their power till our own day.

With his every deed he offered thanks
   to God Most High, in words of praise.
With his whole being he loved his Maker
   and daily had his praises sung;
He added beauty to the feasts
   and solemnized the seasons of each year
With string music before the altar,
   providing sweet melody for the psalms
So that when the Holy Name was praised,
   before daybreak the sanctuary would resound.
The Lord forgave him his sins
   and exalted his strength forever;
He conferred on him the rights of royalty
   and established his throne in Israel.
This is the Word of the Lord. ℟. **Thanks be to God.** ⍦

Responsorial Psalm   Ps 18, 31. 47. 50. 51
℟. (47) **Blessed be God my salvation!**
God's way is unerring,
   the promise of the Lord is fire-tried;
     he is a shield to all who take refuge in him. — ℟
The Lord live! And blessed be my Rock!
   Extolled be God my savior.
Therefore will I proclaim you, O Lord, among the
     nations,
   and I will sing praise to your name. — ℟
You who gave great victories to your king
   and showed kindness to your anointed,
     to David and his posterity forever. — ℟ ⍦

————— **YEAR I AND II** —————

GOSPEL   Mk 6, 14-29
Alleluia (See Lk 8, 15)
℟. **Alleluia.** Happy are they who have kept the
     word with a generous heart,
and yield a harvest through perseverance. ℟. **Alle-
     luia.**

✠ The Gospel assigns John's rebuke of Herod's adultery as the reason for his death. When John denounces the adulterous connection of his royal hearer and demands that he put away the guilty woman as the only condition of salvation, John is shut up in prison and ultimately loses his life.

℣. The Lord be with you. ℟. **And also with you.**
✠ A reading from the holy gospel according to Mark
℟. **Glory to you, Lord.**

King Herod came to hear of Jesus whose reputation had become widespread and people were saying, "John the Baptizer has been raised from the dead; that is why such miraculous powers are at work in him." Others were saying, "He is Elijah"; still others, "He is a prophet equal to any of the prophets." On hearing of Jesus, Herod exclaimed, "John, whose head I had cut off, has been raised up!" Herod was the one who had ordered John arrested, chained, and imprisoned on acount of Herodias, the wife of his brother Philip, whom he had married. That was because John had told Herod, "It is not right for you to live with your brother's wife." Herodias harbored a grudge against him for this and wanted to kill him but was unable to do so. Herod feared John, knowing him to be an upright and holy man, and kept him in custody. When he heard him speak he was very much disturbed; yet he felt the attraction of his words. Herodias had her chance one day when Herod held a birthday dinner for his court circle, military officers, and the leading men of Galilee. Herodias' own daughter came in at one point and performed a dance which delighted Herod and his guests. The king told the girl, "Ask for anything you want and I will give it to you." He went so far as to swear to her: "I will grant you whatever you ask, even to half my kingdom!" She went out and said to her mother, "What shall I ask for?" The mother answered, "The head of John the Baptizer." At that the girl hurried back to the king's presence and made her request: "I want you to give me, at once, the head of John the Baptizer on a platter." The king bitterly regretted the request; yet because of his oath and the presence of the guests, he did not want to refuse her. He promptly dispatched an executioner, ordering him to bring back the Baptizer's head. The man went and beheaded John in the prison. He brought in the head on a platter and gave it to the girl, and the girl gave it to her mother. Later, when his disciples heard about this, they came and carried his body away and laid it in a tomb.—This is the gospel of the Lord. ℟. **Praise to you, Lord Jesus Christ.**   ➤ No. 15, p. 623

SATURDAY OF THE FOURTH WEEK IN ORDINARY TIME

—— YEAR I ——

READING I   Heb 13, 15-17. 20-21

St. Paul exhorts the Christians to praise God constantly through Jesus. They are bound to pray for their pastors, their missionaries, and their teachers. These required petitions and intercessions are as old as the Church itself. St. Paul prays that his people will receive from God all that is good.

A reading from the letter to the Hebrews

Through Jesus let us continually offer God a sacrifice of praise, that is, the fruit of lips which acknowledge his name.

Do not neglect good deeds and generosity; God is pleased by sacrifices of that kind. Obey your leaders and submit to them, for they keep watch over you as men who must render an account. So act that they may fulfill their task with joy, not with sorrow, for that would be harmful to you.

May the God of peace, who brought up from the dead the great Shepherd of the sheep in the blood of the eternal covenant, Jesus our Lord, furnish you with all that is good, that you may do his will. Through Jesus Christ may he carry out in you all that is pleasing to him. To Christ be glory forever! Amen.—This is the Word of the Lord. ℞. **Thanks be to God.**

Responsorial Psalm   Ps 23, 1-3. 3-4. 5-6

℞. (1) **The Lord is my shepherd;**
   there is nothing I shall want.

The Lord is my shepherd; I shall not want.
   In verdant pastures he gives me repose;
Beside restful waters he leads me;
   he refreshes my soul. — ℞

He guides me in right paths
   for his name's sake.
Even though I walk in the dark valley
   I fear no evil; for you are at my side
With your rod and your staff
   that give me courage. — ℞

You spread the table before me
   in the sight of my foes;
You anoint my head with oil;
   my cup overflows. — ℞

Only goodness and kindness follow me
   all the days of my life;
And I shall dwell in the house of the Lord
   for years to come. — ℞ ⍌

———— **YEAR II** ————

READING I   1 Kgs 3, 4-13

The Lord appears to Solomon in a dream telling him to ask any favor. Solomon prays for wisdom to know right from wrong. The Lord promises this and in addition great riches because Solomon has not asked for any selfish gain.

A reading from the first book of Kings

Solomon went to Gibeon to sacrifice there, because that was the most renowned high place. Upon its altar Solomon offered a thousand holocausts. In

Gibeon the Lord appeared to Solomon in a dream at night. God said, "Ask something of me and I will give it to you." Solomon answered: "You have shown great favor to your servant, my father David, because he behaved faithfully toward you, with justice and an upright heart; and you have continued this great favor toward him, even today, seating a son of his on his throne. O Lord, my God, you have made me, your servant, king to succeed my father David; but I am a mere youth, not knowing at all how to act. I serve you in the midst of the people whom you have chosen, a people so vast that it cannot be numbered or counted. Give your servant, therefore, an understanding heart to judge your people and to distinguish right from wrong. For who is able to govern this vast people of yours?"

The Lord was pleased that Solomon made this request. So God said to him: "Because you have asked for this—not for a long life for yourself, nor for riches, nor for the life of your enemies, but for understanding so that you may know what is right—I do as you requested. I give you a heart so wise and understanding that there has never been anyone like you up to now, and after you there will come no one to equal you. In addition, I give you what you have not asked for, such riches and glory that among kings there is not your like."—This is the Word of the Lord. ℟. **Thanks be to God.** ℣

Responsorial Psalm   Ps 119, 9. 10. 11. 12. 13. 14
℟. (12) **Lord, teach me your decrees.**

How shall a young man be faultless in his way?
  By keeping to your words. — ℟

With all my heart I seek you;
  let me not stray from your commands. — ℟

Within my heart I treasure your promise,
  that I may not sin against you. — ℟

Blessed are you, O Lord;
    teach me your statutes. — ℟

With my lips I declare
    all the ordinances of your mouth. — ℟

In the way of your decrees I rejoice,
    as much as in all riches. — ℟ ⩔

───── **YEAR I AND II** ─────

GOSPEL   Mk 6, 30-34
Alleluia (Jn 10, 27)

℟. **Alleluia.** My sheep listen to my voice, says the
    Lord;
I know them, and they follow me. ℟. **Alleluia.**

Jesus takes his apostles aside to converse with them and he teaches
them many things concerning the kingdom of God. His teaching is connected with his miraculous powers, and it causes amazement. Our
Lord's pity moves him to assuage the spiritual hunger of the shepherd-
less people by bringing God's revelation to them.

℣. The Lord be with you. ℟. **And also with you.**
✠ A reading from the holy gospel according to Mark
℟. **Glory to you, Lord.**

The apostles returned to Jesus and reported to him
all that they had done and what they had taught.
He said to them, "Come by yourselves to an out-of-
the-way place and rest a little." People were coming
and going in great numbers, making it impossible
for them to so much as eat. So Jesus and the apostles went off in the boat by themselves to a deserted
place. People saw them leaving, and many got to
know about it. People from all the towns hastened
on foot to the place, arriving ahead of them. Upon
disembarking Jesus saw a vast crowd. He pitied
them, for they were like sheep without a shepherd;
and he began to teach them at great length.—This
is the gospel of the Lord. ℟. **Praise to you, Lord
Jesus Christ.**   ➜ No. 15, p. 623

INTRODUCTION FOR 5th TO 9th WEEK

The Book of Genesis—*The first five books of the Bible (Genesis, Exodus, Leviticus, Numbers, and Deuteronomy) form what is called the Pentateuch. Though attributed en masse to Moses, they are really the result of a progressive fusion of traditions of diverse origins and times. Their principal theme is God's covenant with Israel, a contract of the living God with the people he had chosen and whose life he sustained through his fidelity.*

Genesis is the book of beginnings, the beginnings of the people of God and those of the world. The first eleven chapters paint in broad strokes the history of the world, from its beginning to Abraham, and form the setting for the history of salvation. They give two different pictures of creation, followed by the traditions about the life of the first men and the beginning of civilization, the flood, the repeopling of the earth and the dispersion of mankind, manifesting at the same time God's merciful love and man's sin.

Their basic purpose, however, is to interpret mankind's present condition and reveal every man's situation before God. Above all, they constitute a profession of faith in the absolute sovereignty of God, the origin and end of all reality, faith in the love and patience of God who has created man that he might become his partner and who constantly reestablishes relations with man in spite of the latter's repeated infidelities and incredulity.

The remaining chapters deal with the pre-history of the chosen people through the great patriarchs Abraham, Isaac, and Jacob and his twelve sons. They illustrate the fact that the God of the chosen people is not a far-off deity conceived by some philosopher. He is the God who has manifested himself to Abraham, Isaac, and Jacob, the God who made a covenant with them and made promises to them, among which is the promise of the Messiah.

The Epistle of James—*This epistle or letter is really a sermon set down about 62 A.D. by James, leader of the Jerusalem community and one of the relatives of Jesus. Its purpose was to counter the tendency toward an abstract, non-fruitful practice of Christianity threatening the particular churches known as "the twelve tribes of Israel." The author writes in the spirit of Old Testament wisdom literature and of the moral teaching of Tobit. He presupposes knowledge of the gospel on the part of his readers and concentrates on reminding them of how Christians ought to live. He also provides a beautiful reproduction of the moral teachings of our Lord's Sermon on the Mount.*

The Book of Sirach—*This book was written between 200 and 175 B.C. by a sage who lived in Jerusalem and was thoroughly imbued with love for the law, the priesthood, the temple, and divine worship. As a wise and experienced observer of life, he sets forth the true nature of wisdom and indicates the religious and social duties which must be performed in all the vicissitudes of life. It culminates in the personification of wisdom (ch. 24) which laid the groundwork for the revelation of the second person of the Trinity who is the personalized wisdom or word of God.*

The First Epistle of Peter—*This letter was most likely written by St. Peter about 64 A.D. and sets forth the nature of the Christian life begun in baptism as an experience of regeneration. By their acceptance of Christianity, the Christian communities of Asia Minor had become separated from their pagan countrymen, who were abusing and persecuting them. The apostle instructs his readers that Christianity is the true religion in spite of their trials and sufferings, and exhorts them to lead good Christian lives.*

The Book of Tobit—*Written in the second century B.C., this charming book uses the literary form* of religious novel (as do Jonah and Judith) for the purpose of instruction and edification. It contains numerous maxims like those found in the wisdom books as well as the customary sapiential themes: fidelity to the law, the intercessory function of angels, piety toward parents, the purity of marriage, reverence for the dead, and the value of almsgiving, prayer and fasting.

The Second Epistle of Peter—Probably written by an unknown author about 100-125 A.D., this epistle has a twofold purpose: to undergird faith in the second coming of Christ and to warn against false teachers. In addition to foretelling the imminent doom of the false teachers, the author recalls the apostolic witness as the basis of the Church's proclamation, points to the messianic prophecies of the Old Testament which have been confirmed by Christ's coming, and attributes the delay of the second coming to God's patience and forbearance.

The First Epistle to Timothy—The two Epistles to Timothy and the one to Titus are called the Pastoral Epistles because they are addressed directly, not to any church as a group, but to its head or pastor for his guidance in the rule of the church. This first Epistle was written between Paul's liberation from the first imprisonment (63 A.D.) and his death (67 A.D.) and has a twofold purpose: to provide guidance in the problems of church administration and to oppose false teaching of a speculative and moralistic type.

The Second Epistle to Timothy—This letter was written in 66 or 67 A.D. while St. Paul was a prisoner in Rome for the second and last time. It is a moving pastoral from a veteran missionary to a younger colleague urging endurance as the main quality of a preacher of the gospel.

MONDAY OF THE FIFTH WEEK
IN ORDINARY TIME

—— **YEAR I** ——

READING I   Gn 1, 1-19

Genesis presents a brief survey of the religious condition of mankind from the beginning to the time of Abraham. The one God is the sole author of all that exists (1, 1), and his created activity is unopposed (1, 2). His omnipotence is reflected in the total efficacy of his word which achieves its effects in the absolute correspondence of the created object to the creating will (1, 3 ff). Man surpasses all other created beings by reason of his special relationship to God. The whole visible world came into being as the result of God's divine activity.

The beginning of the book of Genesis

In the beginning, when God created the heavens and the earth, the earth was a formless wasteland, and darkness covered the abyss, while a mighty wind swept over the waters.

Then God said, "Let there be light," and there was light. God saw how good the light was. God then separated the light from the darkness. God called the light "day," and the darkness he called "night." Thus evening came, and morning followed—the first day.

Then God said, "Let there be a dome in the middle of the waters, to separate one body of water from the other." And so it happened: God made the dome, and it separated the water above the dome from the water below it. God called the dome "the sky." Evening came, and morning followed—the second day.

Then God said, "Let the water under the sky be gathered into a single basin, so that the dry land may appear." And so it happened: the water under the sky was gathered into its basin, and the dry land appeared. God called the dry land "the earth," and the basin of the water he called "the sea." God saw how good it was. Then God said, "Let the earth

bring forth vegetation: every kind of plant that bears
seed and every kind of fruit tree on earth that bears
fruit with its seed in it." And so it happened: the
earth brought forth every kind of plant that bears
seed and every kind of fruit tree on earth that bears
fruit with its seed in it. God saw how good it was.
Evening came, and morning followed—the third day.

Then God said: "Let there be lights in the dome
of the sky, to separate day from night. Let them
mark the fixed times, the days and the years, and
serve as luminaries in the dome of the sky, to shed
light upon the earth." And so it happened: God
made the two great lights, the greater one to govern
the day, and the lesser one to govern the night; and
he made the stars. God set them in the dome of the
sky, to shed light upon the earth, to govern the day
and the night, and to separate the light from the
darkness. God saw how good it was. Evening came,
and morning followed—the fourth day.—This is the
Word of the Lord. ℟. **Thanks be to God.** ℣

Responsorial Psalm   Ps 104, 1-2. 5-6. 10. 12. 24. 35
℟. (31) **May the Lord be glad in his works.**
Bless the Lord, O my soul!
   O Lord, my God, you are great indeed!
You are clothed with majesty and glory,
   robed in light as with a cloak. — ℟

You fixed the earth upon its foundation,
   not to be moved forever;
With the ocean, as with a garment, you covered it;
   above the mountains the waters stood. — ℟

You send forth springs into the watercourses
   that wind among the mountains.
Beside them the birds of heaven dwell;
   from among the branches they send forth their
      song. — ℟

How manifold are your works, O Lord!

In wisdom you have wrought them all—
the earth is full of your creatures;
Bless the Lord, O my soul! Alleluia. — ℟ ↓

———   **YEAR II**   ———

READING I   1 Kgs 8, 1-7. 9-13

The Elders and King Solomon go to Jerusalem to offer sacrifice. The priests take up the ark of the covenant. The Lord comes to dwell in a dark cloud and the Lord's glory fills the temple.

A reading from the first book of Kings

The elders of Israel and all the leaders of the tribes, the princes in the ancestral houses of the Israelites, came to King Solomon in Jerusalem, to bring up the ark of the Lord's covenant from the City of David [which is Zion]. All the men of Israel assembled before King Solomon during the festival in the month of Ethanim (the seventh month). When all the elders of Israel had arrived, the priests took up the ark; they carried the ark of the Lord and the meeting tent with all the sacred vessels that were in the tent. (The priests and Levites carried them.)

King Solomon and the entire community of Israel present for the occasion sacrificed before the ark sheep and oxen too many to number or count. The priests brought the ark of the covenant of the Lord to its place beneath the wings of the cherubim in the sanctuary, the holy of holies of the temple. The cherubim had their wings spread out over the place of the ark, sheltering the ark and its poles from above. There was nothing in the ark but the two stone tablets which Moses had put there at Horeb, when the Lord made a covenant with the Israelites at their departure from the land of Egypt.

When the priests left the holy place, the cloud filled the temple of the Lord so that the priests could no longer minister because of the cloud, since the Lord's glory had filled the temple of the Lord. Then Solomon said, "The Lord intends to dwell in

the dark cloud; I have truly built you a princely
house, a dwelling where you may abide forever."—
This is the Word of the Lord. ℟.**Thanks be to God.** ↓

Responsorial Psalm   Ps 132, 6-7. 8-10

℟. (8) **Lord, go up to the place of your rest!**

Behold, we heard of it in Ephratha;
  we found it in the fields of Jaar.
Let us enter into his dwelling,
  let us worship at his footstool. — ℟

Advance, O Lord, to your resting place
  you and the ark of your majesty.
May your priests be clothed with justice;
  let your faithful ones shout merrily for joy.
For the sake of David your servant,
  reject not the plea of your anointed. — ℟ ↓

———   **YEAR I AND II**   ———

GOSPEL   Mk 6, 53-56

Alleluia (Mt 4, 23)

℟. **Alleluia.** Jesus preached the Good News of the
    Kingdom
and healed all who were sick. ℟. **Alleuia.**

Many acts of mercy follow immediately after our Lord's going among
the people. Faith is an essential of salvation. Wherever Jesus goes,
those who are in need come to him.

℣. The Lord be with you. ℟. **And also with you.**
✠ A reading from the holy gospel according to Mark
℟. **Glory to you, Lord.**

Jesus and his disciples, after crossing the lake, came
ashore at Gennesaret, and tied up there. As they
were leaving the boat, people immediately recognized him. The crowds scurried about the adjacent
area and began to bring in the sick on bedrolls to
the place where they heard he was. Wherever he put
in an appearance, in villages, in towns, or at crossroads, they laid the sick in the marketplaces and
begged him to let them touch just the tassel of his

cloak. All who touched him got well.—This is the gospel of the Lord. ℟. **Praise to you, Lord Jesus Christ.**

→ No. 15, p. 623

TUESDAY OF THE FIFTH WEEK IN ORDINARY TIME

———— YEAR I ————

READING I   Gn 1, 20-2, 4

Animals are made superior to plants inasmuch as they are living beings and able to transmit life. Their procreative power is the result of a divine blessing. They are creatures of the one God and therefore good, but man alone is made in the image and likeness of God.

A reading from the book of Genesis

Then God said, "Let the water teem with an abundance of living creatures, and on the earth let birds fly beneath the dome of the sky." And so it happened: God created the great sea monsters and all kinds of swimming creatures with which the water teems, and all kinds of winged birds. God saw how good it was, and God blessed them, saying, "Be fertile, multiply, and fill the water of the seas; and let the birds multiply on the earth." Evening came, and morning followed—the fifth day.

Then God said, "Let the earth bring forth all kinds of living creatures: cattle, creeping things, and wild animals of all kinds." And so it happened: God made all kinds of wild animals, all kinds of cattle, and all kinds of creeping things of the earth. God saw how good it was. Then God said: "Let us make man in our image, after our likeness. Let them have dominion over the fish of the sea, the birds of the air, and the cattle, and over all the wild animals and all the creatures that crawl on the ground."

God created man in his image;
    in the divine image he created him;
    male and female he created them.

God blessed them, saying: "Be fertile and multiply;

fill the earth and subdue it. Have dominion over the fish of the sea, the birds of the air, and all the living things that move on the earth." God also said: "See, I give you every seed-bearing plant all over the earth and every tree that has seed-bearing fruit on it to be your food; and to all the animals of the land, all the birds of the air, and all the living creatures that crawl on the ground, I give all the green plants for food." And so it happened. God looked at everything he had made, and he found it very good. Evening came, and morning followed—the sixth day.

Thus the heavens and the earth and all their array were completed. Since on the seventh day God was finished with the work he had been doing, he rested on the seventh day from all the work he had undertaken. So God blessed the seventh day and made it holy, because on it he rested from all the work he had done in creation.

Such is the story of the heavens and the earth at their creation.—This is the Word of the Lord. ℞. **Thanks be to God.** ℣

Responsorial Psalm   Ps 8, 4-5. 6-7. 8-9

℞. (2) **O Lord, our God**
how beautiful your name in all the earth!

When I behold your heavens, the work of your fingers,
 the moon and the stars which you set in place—
What is man that you should be mindful of him,
 or the son of man that you should care for
  him? — ℞

You have made him little less than the angels,
 and crowned him with glory and honor.
You have given him rule over the works of your
  hands,
 putting all things under his feet. — ℞

All sheep and oxen,
 yes, and the beasts of the field,

The birds of the air, the fishes of the sea,
    and whatever swims the paths of the seas. — ℟ ▼

——— **YEAR II** ———

READING I   1 Kgs 8, 22-23. 27-30

Solomon prays for the people in the temple. He acknowledges the august power of the Lord who has chosen to dwell with his people on earth. Solomon asks that God listen to his people.

A reading from the first book of Kings

Solomon stood before the altar of the Lord in the presence of the whole community of Israel, and stretching forth his hands toward heaven, he said, "Lord, God of Israel, there is no God like you in heaven above or on earth below; you keep your covenant of kindness with your servants who are faithful to you with their whole heart.

"Can it indeed be that God dwells among men on earth? If the heavens and the highest heavens cannot contain you, how much less this temple which I have built! Look kindly on the prayer and petition of your servant, O Lord, my God, and listen to the cry of supplication which I, your servant, utter before you this day. May your eyes watch night and day over this temple, the place where you have decreed you shall be honored; may you heed the prayer which, I your servant, offer in this place. Listen to the petitions of your servant and of your people Israel which they offer in this place. Listen from your heavenly dwelling and grant pardon."—This is the Word of the Lord. ℟. **Thanks be to God.** ▼

Responsorial Psalm   Ps 84, 3. 4. 5. 10. 11

℟. (2) **How lovely is your dwelling-place,**
    Lord, mighty God!

My soul yearns and pines
    for the courts of the Lord.
My heart and my flesh
    cry out for the living God. — ℟

Even the sparrow finds a home,
  and the swallow a nest
  in which she puts her young—
Your altars, O Lord of hosts,
  my king and my God! — ℟

Happy they who dwell in your house!
  continually they praise you.
O God, behold our shield,
  and look upon the face of your anointed. — ℟

I had rather one day in your courts
  than a thousand elsewhere;
I had rather lie at the threshold of the house of my
      God
  than dwell in the tents of the wicked. — ℟ ℣

——— **YEAR I AND II** ———

GOSPEL   Mk 7, 1-13
Alleluia (Jn 17, 17)

℟. **Alleluia.** Your word, O Lord, is truth;
make us holy in the truth. ℟. **Alleluia.**

This Gospel contains two pronouncements which show our Lord's op-
position to the code of unwritten law so scrupulously observed by the
Pharisees. Christ is the Messiah whose mission extends beyond
Judaism and which contradicts the legalism and particularism of the
Pharisaic leaders.

℣. The Lord be with you. ℟. **And also with you.**
✠ A reading from the holy gospel according to Mark
℟. **Glory to you, Lord.**

The Pharisees and some of the experts in the law
who had come from Jerusalem gathered around
Jesus. They had observed a few of his disciples eating meals without having purified—that is to say,
washed—their hands. The Pharisees, and in fact all
Jews, cling to the custom of their ancestors and
never eat without scrupulously washing their hands.
Moreover, they never eat anything from the market
without first sprinkling it. There are many other
traditions they observe—for example, the washing

of cups and jugs and kettles. So the Pharisees and the scribes questioned him: "Why do your disciples not follow the tradition of our ancestors, but instead take food without purifying their hands?" He said to them: "How accurately Isaiah prophesied about you hypocrites when he wrote,

'This people pays me lip service
but their heart is far from me.
Empty is the reverence they do me
because they teach as dogmas mere human
precepts.'

You disregard God's commandment and cling to what is human tradition."

He went on to say: "You have made a fine art of setting aside God's commandment in the interests of keeping your traditions! For example, Moses said, 'Honor your father and your mother'; and in another place, 'Whoever curses father or mother shall be put to death.' Yet you declare, 'If a person says to his father or mother, Any support you might have had from me is *korban*' (that is, dedicated to God), you allow him to do nothing more for his father or mother. That is the way you nullify God's word in favor of the traditions you have handed on. And you have many other such practices besides."—This is the gospel of the Lord. ℟. **Praise to you, Lord Jesus Christ.**

➤ No. 15, p. 623

WEDNESDAY OF THE FIFTH WEEK IN ORDINARY TIME

—— YEAR I ——

READING I   Gn 2, 5-9. 15-17

The earth is destined for man's use. He has a special kind of life distinguishing him from all earthly beings, a life that comes from God. Man's enjoyment of the garden is a gift from God. God gives man a test; his happiness is consequent upon his remaining subject to God. In this concept lies the whole meaning of the garden.

A reading from the book of Genesis

At the time when the Lord God made the earth and the heavens—while as yet there was no field shrub on earth and no grass of the field had sprouted, for the Lord God had sent no rain upon the earth and there was no man to till the soil, but a stream was welling up out of the earth and was watering all the surface of the ground—the Lord God formed man out of the clay of the ground and blew into his nostrils the breath of life, and so man became a living being.

Then the Lord God planted a garden in Eden, in the east, and he placed there the man whom he had formed. Out of the ground the Lord God made various trees grow that were delightful to look at and good for food, with the tree of life in the middle of the garden and the tree of the knowledge of good and bad.

The Lord God then took the man and settled him in the garden of Eden, to cultivate and care for it. The Lord God gave man this order: "You are free to eat from any of the trees of the garden except the tree of the knowledge of good and bad. From that tree you shall not eat; the moment you eat from it you are surely doomed to die."—This is the Word of the Lord. ℟. **Thanks be to God.**

Responsorial Psalm   Ps 104, 1-2. 27-28. 29-30

℟. (1) **Oh, bless the Lord, my soul!**

Bless the Lord, O my soul!
    O Lord, my God, you are great indeed!
You are clothed with majesty and glory,
    robed in light as with a cloak. — ℟

All creatures look to you
    to give them food in due time.
When you give it to them, they gather it;
    when you open your hand, they are filled with
        good things. — ℟

If you take away their breath, they perish
    and return to their dust.
When you send forth your spirit, they are created,
    and you renew the face of the earth. — ℟ ↓

——— **YEAR II** ———

READING I   1 Kgs 10, 1-10

The Queen of Sheba comes to Jerusalem to see if all she has heard
about Solomon's wisdom, wealth, servants, and his rule is true. She is
amazed to find that all the reports were true far beyond her ex-
pectations.

A reading from the first book of Kings

The queen of Sheba, having heard of Solomon's
fame, came to test him with subtle questions. She
arrived in Jerusalem with a very numerous retinue,
and with camels bearing spices, a large amount of
gold, and precious stones. She came to Solomon and
questioned him on every subject in which she was
interested. King Solomon explained everything she
asked about, and there remained nothing hidden from
him that he could not explain to her.

When the queen of Sheba witnessed Solomon's
great wisdom, the palace he had built, the food at
his table, the seating of his ministers, the attendance and garb of his waiters, his banquet service,
and the holocausts he offered in the temple of the
Lord, she was breathless. "The report I heard in my
country about your deeds and your wisdom is true,"
she told the king. "Though I did not believe the report until I came and saw with my own eyes, I have
discovered that they were not telling me the half.
Your wisdom and prosperity surpass the report I
heard. Happy are your men, happy these servants of
yours, who stand before you always and listen to
your wisdom. Blessed be the Lord, your God, whom
it has pleased to place you on the throne of Israel.
In his enduring love for Israel, the Lord has made

you king to carry out judgment and justice." Then she gave the king one hundred and twenty gold talents, a very large quantity of spices, and precious stones. Never again did anyone bring such an abundance of spices as the queen of Sheba gave to King Solomon.—This is the Word of the Lord. ℟. **Thanks be to God.** ∨

Responsorial Psalm   Ps 37, 5-6. 30-31. 39-40

℟. (30) **The mouth of the just man murmurs wisdom.**

Commit to the Lord your way;
    trust in him, and he will act.
He will make justice dawn for you like the light;
    bright as the noonday shall be your vindica-
        tion. — ℟

The mouth of the just man tells of wisdom,
    and his tongue utters what is right.
The law of his God is in his heart,
    and his steps do not falter. — ℟

The salvation of the just is from the Lord;
    he is their refuge in time of distress.
And the Lord helps them and delivers them;
    he delivers them from the wicked and saves them,
        because they take refuge in him. — ℟ ∨

─────   **YEAR I AND II**   ─────

GOSPEL   Mk 7, 14-23

Alleluia (Jn 17, 17)

℟. **Alleluia.** Your word, O Lord, is truth;
make us holy in the truth. ℟. **Alleluia.**

Jesus teaches that thoughts and words which proceed from man's inmost self are those things which defile him. All sin proceeds out of the heart, but men are prone to blame external causes for temptation and so to excuse themselves. Wicked designs come from within.

℣. The Lord be with you. ℟. **And also with you.**
✠ A reading from the holy gospel according to Mark
℟. **Glory to you, Lord.**

Jesus summoned the crowd and said to them: "Hear me, all of you, and try to understand. Nothing that enters a man from the outside can make him impure; that which comes out of him, and only that, constitutes impurity. Let everyone heed what he hears!"

When he got home, away from the crowd, his disciples questioned him about the proverb. "Are you, too, incapable of understanding?" he asked them. "Do you not see that nothing that enters a man from outside can make him impure? It does not penetrate his being, but enters his stomach only and passes into the latrine." Thus did he render all foods clean. He went on: "What emerges from within a man, that and nothing else is what makes him impure. Wicked designs come from the deep recesses of the heart: acts of fornication, theft, murder, adulterous conduct, greed, maliciousness, deceit, sensuality, envy, blasphemy, arrogance, an obtuse spirit. All these evils come from within and render a man impure."—This is the gospel of the Lord. ℟. **Praise to you, Lord Jesus Christ.** → No. 15, p. 623

THURSDAY OF THE FIFTH WEEK IN ORDINARY TIME

—— **YEAR I** ——

READING I Gn 2, 18-25

Woman complements man. Man's deep sleep suggests the mystery of creation. The unity of marriage and its monogamous nature are God-ordered. Man and woman are creatures of God, redeemed by Christ; both are children of God and are called to the same supernatural destiny.

A reading from the book of Genesis

The Lord God said: "It is not good for the man to be alone. I will make a suitable partner for him." So the Lord God formed out of the ground various wild animals and various birds of the air, and he brought them to the man to see what he would call them; whatever the man called each of them would be its name. The man gave names to all the cattle, all the birds of the air, and all the wild animals; but none proved to be the suitable partner for the man.

So the Lord God cast a deep sleep on the man, and while he was asleep, he took out one of his ribs and closed up its place with flesh. The Lord God then built up into a woman the rib that he had taken from the man. When he brought her to the man, the man said:

"This one, at last, is bone of my bones
    and flesh of my flesh;
This one shall be called 'woman,'
    for out of 'her man' this one has been taken."

That is why a man leaves his father and mother and clings to his wife, and the two of them become one body.

The man and his wife were both naked, yet they felt no shame.—This is the Word of the Lord. ℟.
Thanks be to God. ℣

Responsorial Psalm   Ps 128, 1-2. 3. 4-5

℟. (1) **Happy are those who fear the Lord.**

Happy are you who fear the Lord,
    who walk in his ways!
For you shall eat the fruit of your handiwork;
    happy shall you be, and favored. — ℟

Your wife shall be like a fruitful vine
    in the recesses of your home;
Your children like olive plants
    around your table. — ℟

Behold, thus is the man blessed
    who fears the Lord.
The Lord bless you from Zion:
    may you see the prosperity of Jerusalem
    all the days of your life. — ℟ ℣

—— **YEAR II** ——

READING I   1 Kgs 11, 4-13

Solomon falls into worshiping false gods, unlike his father, David. The Lord is angry with him and vows to deprive Solomon's son of all but one tribe of the kingdom, which will be preserved only because of David.

A reading from the first book of Kings

When Solomon was old his wives had turned his heart to strange gods, and his heart was not entirely with the Lord, his God, as the heart of his father David had been. By adoring Astarte, the goddess of the Sidonians, and Milcom, the idol of the Ammonites, Solomon did evil in the sight of the Lord; he did not follow him unreservedly as his father David had done. Solomon then built a high place to Chemosh, the idol of Moab, and to Molech, the idol of the Ammonites, on the hill opposite Jerusalem. He did the same for all his foreign wives who burned incense and sacrificed to their gods. The Lord, therefore, became angry with Solomon, because his heart was turned away from the Lord, the God of Israel, who had appeared to him twice (for though the Lord had forbidden him this very act of following strange gods, Solomon had not obeyed him).

So the Lord said to Solomon: "Since this is what you want, and you have not kept my covenant and my statutes which I enjoined on you, I will deprive you of the kingdom and give it to your servant. I will not do this during your lifetime, however, for the sake of your father David; it is your son whom I will deprive. Nor will I take away the whole kingdom. I will leave your son one tribe for the sake of my servant David and of Jerusalem, which I have chosen."—This is the Word of the Lord. ℟. **Thanks be to God.** ℣

Responsorial Psalm   Ps 106, 3-4. 35-36. 37. 40

℟. (4) **Lord, remember us,**
   for the love you bear your people.

Happy are they who observe what is right,
who do always what is just.
Remember us, O Lord, as you favor your people;
visit us with your saving help. — ℞

But they mingled with the nations
and learned their works.
They served their idols,
which became a snare for them. — ℞

They sacrificed their sons
and their daughters to demons.
And the Lord grew angry with his people,
and abhorred his inheritance. — ℞ ↓

—— **YEAR I AND II** ——

GOSPEL Mk 7, 24-30

Alleluia. (Jas 1, 21)
℞. **Alleluia.** Receive and submit to the word planted
in you;
it can save your souls. ℞. **Alleluia.**

Jesus goes to the region of Tyre and Sidon into the coastal province of
Phoenicia, Gentile territory. This shows Jesus to be the savior of the
Gentiles as well as of the Jews. A woman asks that a demon be
expelled from her daughter.

℣. The Lord be with you. ℞. **And also with you.**
✠ A reading from the holy gospel according to Mark
℞. **Glory to you, Lord.**

Jesus went to the territory of Tyre and Sidon. He
retired to a certain house and wanted no one to recognize him; however, he could not escape notice.
Soon a woman, whose small daughter had an unclean spirit, heard about him. She approached him
and crouched at his feet. The woman who was Greek
—a Syro-Phoenician by birth—began to beg him to
expel the demon from her daughter. He told her:
"Let the sons of the household satisfy themselves at
table first. It is not right to take the food of the
children and throw it to the dogs." "Please, Lord,"

she replied, "even the dogs under the table eat the family's leavings." Then he said to her, "For such a reply, be off now! The demon has already left your daughter." When she got home, she found the child lying in bed and the demon gone.—This is the gospel of the Lord. R̸. **Praise to you, Lord Jesus Christ.**

➤ No. 15, p. 623

FRIDAY OF THE FIFTH WEEK IN ORDINARY TIME

—— YEAR I ——

READING I Gn 3, 1-8

Sin begins with some distortion of the truth. The serpent first denies the punishment, offering likeness to God as the result of eating of the tree. The whole of the human family was caught up in Adam's refusal to obey God's command, and by one man's sin, death came into the world for all.

A reading from the book of Genesis

Now the serpent was the most cunning of all the animals that the Lord God had made. The serpent asked the woman, "Did God really tell you not to eat from any of the trees in the garden?" The woman answered the serpent: "We may eat of the fruit of the trees in the garden; it is only about the fruit of the tree in the middle of the garden that God said, 'You shall not eat it or even touch it, lest you die.' " But the serpent said to the woman: "You certainly will not die! No, God knows well that the moment you eat of it you will be like gods who know what is good and what is bad." The woman saw that the tree was good for food, pleasing to the eyes, and desirable for gaining wisdom. So she took some of its fruit and ate it; and she also gave some to her husband, who was with her, and he ate it. Then the eyes of both of them were opened, and they realized that they were naked; so they sewed fig leaves together and made loincloths for themselves.

When they heard the sound of the Lord God moving about in the garden at the breezy time of the day, the man and his wife hid themselves from the' Lord God among the trees of the garden.—This is the Word of the Lord. ℟. **Thanks be to God.** ✟

Responsorial Psalm   Ps 32, 1-2. 5. 6-7

℟. (1) **Happy are those whose sins are forgiven.**

Happy is he whose fault is taken away,
    whose sin is covered.
Happy the man to whom the Lord imputes not guilt,
    in whose spirit there is no guile. — ℟

Then I acknowledged my sin to you,
    my guilt I covered not.
I said, "I confess my faults to the Lord,"
    and you took away the guilt of my sin. — ℟

For this shall every faithful man pray to you in time
        of stress.
Though deep waters overflow,
    they shall not reach him. — ℟

You are my shelter; from distress you will preserve
        me;
    with glad cries of freedom you will ring me
        round. — ℟ ✟

───── **YEAR II** ─────

READING I   1 Kgs 11, 29-32; 12, 19

Jeroboam leaves Jerusalem. By cutting up his cloak, Ahijah demonstrates how the kingdom will be divided and only one tribe will remain with the son of Solomon. The ten pieces represent the then northern tribes of Israel (cf. 2 Sm 19, 43).

A reading from the first book of Kings

At that time Jeroboam left Jerusalem, and the prophet Ahijah the Shilonite met him on the road. The two were alone in the area, and the prophet was wearing a new cloak. Ahijah took off his new cloak, tore it into twelve pieces, and said to Jeroboam:

"Take ten pieces for yourself; the Lord, the God of Israel, says: 'I will tear away the kingdom from Solomon's grasp and will give you ten of the tribes. One tribe shall remain to him for the sake of David my servant, and of Jerusalem, the city I have chosen out of the tribes of Israel.'"

Israel went into rebellion against David's house to this day.—This is the Word of the Lord. ℟. **Thanks be to God.** ✠

Responsorial Psalm   Ps 81, 10-11. 12-13. 14-15

℟. (11.9) **I am the Lord, your God:**
    hear my voice.

There shall be no strange god among you
    nor shall you worship any alien god.
I, the Lord, am your God
    who led you forth from the land of Egypt. — ℟

But my people heard not my voice,
    and Israel obeyed me not;
So I gave them up to the hardness of their hearts;
    they walked according to their own counsels. — ℟

If only my people would hear me,
    and Israel walk in my ways,
Quickly would I humble their enemies;
    against their foes I would turn my hand. — ℟ ✠

——— **YEAR I AND II** ———

GOSPEL   Mk 7, 31-37

Alleluia (See Acts 16, 14)

℟. **Alleluia.** Open our hearts, O Lord,
to listen to the words of your Son. ℟. **Alleluia.**

Friends bring a sick man to Christ for healing. Christ cures the man and charges the multitude to say nothing of the miracle, but so much the more do they publish it. The people are amazed at Jesus' powers.

℣. The Lord be with you. ℟. **And also with you.**
✠ A reading from the holy gospel according to Mark
℟. **Glory to you, Lord.**

Jesus left Tyrian territory and returned by way of Sidon to the Sea of Galilee, into the district of the Ten Cities. Some people brought him a deaf man who had a speech impediment and begged him to lay his hand on him. Jesus took him off by himself away from the crowd. He put his fingers into the man's ears and, spitting, touched his tongue; then he looked up to heaven and emitted a groan. He said to him, "Ephphatha!" (that is, "Be opened!") At once the man's ears were opened; he was freed from the impediment, and began to speak plainly. Then he enjoined them strictly not to tell anyone; but the more he ordered them not to, the more they proclaimed it. Their amazement went beyond all bounds: "He has done everything well! He makes the deaf hear and the mute speak!"—This is the gospel of the Lord. ℟. **Praise to you, Lord Jesus Christ.**

➤ No. 15, p. 623

SATURDAY OF THE FIFTH WEEK
IN ORDINARY TIME

—— YEAR I ——

READING I   Gn 3, 9-24

In the Garden, man enjoyed an intimacy with God which was disrupted by disobedience. As head of the family, man is questioned first. His response is the result of sin. The relationship between the power of evil and man is one of enmity that will continue throughout all generations.

A reading from the book of Genesis

The Lord God called to Adam and asked him, "Where are you?" He answered, "I heard you in the garden; but I was afraid, because I was naked, so I hid myself." Then he asked, "Who told you that you were naked? You have eaten, then, from the tree of which I had forbidden you to eat?" The man replied, "The woman whom you put here with me —she gave me fruit from the tree, and so I ate it."

The Lord God then asked the woman, "Why did you do such a thing?" The woman answered, "The serpent tricked me into it, so I ate it."

Then the Lord said to the serpent:

"Because you have done this, you shall be banned
    from all the animals
    and from all the wild creatures;
On your belly shall you crawl,
    and dirt shall you eat
    all the days of your life.
I will put enmity between you and the woman,
    and between your offspring and hers;
He will strike at your head,
    while you strike at his heel."

To the woman he said:

"I will intensify the pangs of your childbearing;
    in pain shall you bring forth children.
Yet your urge shall be for your husband,
    and he shall be your master."

To the man he said: "Because you listened to your wife and ate from the tree of which I had forbidden you to eat,

"Cursed be the ground because of you!
    In toil shall you eat its yield
    all the days of your life.
Thorns and thistles shall it bring forth to you,
    as you eat of the plants of the field.
By the sweat of your face
    shall you get bread to eat,
Until you return to the ground,
    from which you were taken;
For you are dirt,
    and to dirt you shall return."

The man called his wife Eve, because she became the mother of all the living.

For the man and his wife the Lord God made leather garments, with which he clothed them. Then the Lord God said: "See! The man has become like one of us, knowing what is good and what is bad! Therefore, he must not be allowed to put out his hand to take fruit from the tree of life also, and thus eat of it and live forever." The Lord God therefore banished him from the garden of Eden, to till the ground from which he had been taken. When he expelled the man, he settled him east of the garden of Eden; and he stationed the cherubim and the fiery revolving sword, to guard the way to the tree of life.—This is the Word of the Lord. ℟. **Thanks be to God.** ✠

Responsorial Psalm   Ps 90, 2. 3-4. 5-6. 12-13

℟. (1) **In every age, O Lord, you have been our refuge.**

Before the mountains were begotten
  and the earth and the world were brought forth,
  from everlasting to everlasting you are God. — ℟

You turn man back to dust,
  saying, "Return, O children of men."
For a thousand years in your sight
  are as yesterday, now that it is past,
  or as a watch of the night. — ℟

You make an end of them in their sleep;
  the next morning they are like the changing grass,
Which at dawn springs up anew,
  but by evening wilts and fades. — ℟

Teach us to number our days aright,
  that we may gain wisdom of heart.
Return, O Lord! How long?
  Have pity on your servants! — ℟ ✠

——— **YEAR II** ———

READING I   1 Kgs 12, 26-32; 13, 33-34

Jeroboam, in an effort to keep control over the people, builds altars to false gods and establishes feasts in their honor. He will be punished for this sin of leading the people into idolatry.

A reading from the first book of Kings

Jeroboam thought to himself: "The kingdom will return to David's house. If now this people go up to offer sacrifices in the temple of the Lord in Jerusalem, the hearts of this people will return to their master, Rehoboam, king of Judah, and they will kill me." After taking counsel, the king made two calves of gold and said to the people: "You have been going up to Jerusalem long enough. Here is your God, O Israel, who brought you up from the land of Egypt." And he put one in Bethel, the other in Dan. This led to sin, because the people frequented these calves in Bethel and in Dan. He also built temples on the high places and made priests from among the people who were not Levites. Jeroboam established a feast in the eighth month on the fifteenth day of the month to duplicate in Bethel the pilgrimage feast of Judah, with sacrifices to the calves he had made; and he stationed in Bethel priests of the high places he had built.

Jeroboam did not give up his evil ways after this event, but again made priests for the high places from among the common people. Whoever desired it was consecrated and became a priest of the high places. This was a sin on the part of the house of Jeroboam for which it was to be cut off and destroyed from the earth.—This is the Word of the Lord. ℟. **Thanks be to God.** ℣

Responsorial Psalm   Ps 106, 6-7. 19-20. 21-22

℟. (4) **Lord, remember us,**
   for the love you bear your people.

We have sinned, we and our fathers;
   we have committed crimes; we have done wrong.
Our fathers in Egypt
   considered not your wonders. — ℟

They made a calf in Horeb
   and adored a molten image;

They exchanged their glory
    for the image of a grass-eating bullock. — ℟
They forgot the God who had saved them,
    who had done great deeds in Egypt,
Wondrous deeds in the land of Ham,
    terrible things at the Red Sea. — ℟ ℣

─────── **YEAR I AND II** ───────

GOSPEL   Mk 8, 1-10

Alleluia (See Lk 8, 15)

℟. **Alleluia.** Happy are they who have kept the word
    with a generous heart,
and yield a harvest through perseverance. ℟. **Alleluia.**

Jesus continually cares for those who follow him. In this miracle of
the multiplying of the seven loaves and two fish, the disciples—not
our Lord—distribute the food to the multitude. All eat until they are
filled.

℣. The Lord be with you. ℟. **And also with you.**
✠ A reading from the holy gospel according to Mark
℟. **Glory to you, Lord.**

A large crowd assembled, and they were without
anything to eat. Jesus called the disciples over to
him and said: "My heart is moved with pity for the
crowd. By now they have been with me three days
and have nothing to eat. If I send them home hungry, they will collapse on the way. Some of them
have come a great distance." His disciples replied,
"How can anyone give these people sufficient bread
in this deserted spot?" Still he asked them, "How
many loaves do you have?" "Seven," they replied.
Then he directed the crowd to take their places on
the ground. Taking the seven loaves he gave thanks,
broke them, and gave them to his disciples to distribute, and they handed them out to the crowd.
They also had a few small fishes; asking a blessing
on the fish, he told them to distribute these also. The

people in the crowd ate until they had their fill; then they gathered up seven wicker baskets of leftovers. Those who had eaten numbered about four thousand.

He dismissed them and got into the boat with his disciples to go to the neighborhood of Dalmanutha. —This is the gospel of the Lord. ℞. **Praise to you, Lord Jesus Christ.**
➜ No. 15, p. 623

MONDAY OF THE SIXTH WEEK IN ORDINARY TIME

—— **YEAR I** ——

READING I Gn 4, 1-15. 25

The semi-nomadic life of Abel is contrasted to the sedentary life of Cain before the crime and the strictly nomadic life of Cain after killing his brother. The crime of murder confirms the fallen state of man. God, although merciful, shows how sin will be justly punished.

A reading from the book of Genesis

The man had relations with his wife Eve, and she conceived and bore Cain, saying, "I have produced a man with the help of the Lord." Next she bore his brother Abel. Abel became a keeper of flocks, and Cain a tiller of the soil. In the course of time Cain brought an offering to the Lord from the fruit of the soil, while Abel, for his part, brought one of the best firstlings of his flock. The Lord looked with favor on Abel and his offering, but on Cain and his offering he did not. Cain greatly resented this and was crestfallen. So the Lord said to Cain: "Why are you so resentful and crestfallen? If you do well, you can hold up your head; but if not, sin is a demon lurking at the door: his urge is toward you, yet you can be his master."

Cain said to his brother Abel, "Let us go out in the field." When they were in the field, Cain attacked his brother Abel and killed him. Then the

Lord asked Cain, "Where is your brother Abel?"
He answered, "I do not know. Am I my brother's
keeper?" The Lord then said: "What have you done!
Listen: your brother's blood cries out to me from
the soil! Therefore you shall be banned from the soil
that opened its mouth to receive your brother's blood
from your hand. If you till the soil, it shall no longer
give you its produce. You shall become a restless
wanderer on the earth." Cain said to the Lord: "My
punishment is too great to bear. Since you have now
banished me from the soil, and I must avoid your
presence and become a restless wanderer on the
earth, anyone may kill me at sight." "Not so!" the
Lord said to him. "If anyone kills Cain, Cain shall
be avenged sevenfold." So the Lord put a mark on
Cain, lest anyone should kill him at sight.

Adam again had relations with his wife, and she
gave birth to a son whom she called Seth. "God has
granted me more offspring in place of Abel," she
said, "because Cain slew him."—This is the Word
of the Lord. ℟. **Thanks be to God.** ✟

Responsorial Psalm   Ps 50, 1. 8. 16-17. 20-21

℟. (14) **Offer to God a sacrifice of praise.**

God the Lord has spoken and summoned the earth,
   from the rising of the sun to its setting.
Not for your sacrifice do I rebuke you,
   for your holocausts are before me always. — ℟

Why do you recite my statutes,
   and profess my covenant with your mouth
Though you hate discipline
   and cast my words behind you? — ℟

You sit speaking against your brother;
   against your mother's son you spread rumors.
When you do these things, shall I be deaf to it?
   Or think you that I am like yourself?
   I will correct you by drawing them up before your
   eyes. — ℟ ✟

—— **YEAR II** ——

READING I   Jas 1, 1-11

Trials are to be regarded as pure joy (cf. Mt 5, 10ff; Jn 10, 11). Spiritual maturity and full preparedness for the coming of Christ is achieved **by sustaining trials, cultivating endurance, and attaining perfection.** All this requires true wisdom which God readily grants to believing petitioners but withholds from those who doubt. From the religious point of view, the lot of the poor and the lowly is of greater value than that of the rich.

The beginning of the letter of James

To the twelve tribes in the dispersion, James, a servant of God and of the Lord Jesus Christ, sends greeting.

My brothers, count it pure joy when you are involved in every sort of trial. Realize that when your faith is tested this makes for endurance. Let endurance come to its perfection so that you may be fully mature and lacking in nothing.

If any of you is without wisdom, let him ask it from the God who gives generously and ungrudgingly to all, and it will be given him. Yet he must ask in faith, never doubting, for the doubter is like the surf tossed and driven by the wind. A person like this, devious and erratic in all that he does, must not expect to receive anything from the Lord.

Let the brother in humble circumstances take pride in his eminence and the rich man be proud of his lowliness, for he will disappear "like the flower of the field." When the sun comes up with its scorching heat it parches the meadow, the field flowers droop, and with that the meadow's loveliness is gone. Just so will the rich man wither away amid his many projects.—This is the Word of the Lord. ℟. **Thanks be to God.** ℣

Responsorial Psalm   Ps 119, 67. 68. 71. 72. 75. 86

℟. (77) **Be kind to me, Lord, and I shall live.**

Before I was afflicted I went astray,
    but now I hold to your promise. — ℞

You are good and bountiful;
    teach me your statutes. — ℞

It is good for me that I have been afflicted,
    that I may learn your statutes. — ℞

The law of your mouth is to me more precious
    than thousands of gold and silver pieces. — ℞

I know, O Lord, that your ordinances are just,
    and in your faithfulness you have afflicted me—℞

Let your kindness comfort me
    according to your promise to your servants. — ℞ ✠

————— **YEAR I AND II** —————

GOSPEL   Mk 8, 11-13

Alleluia (Jn 14, 5)

℞. **Alleluia.** I am the way, the truth, and the life,
    says the Lord;
no one comes to the Father, except through me.
    ℞. **Alleluia.**

Boldly, the Pharisees seek a sign from Christ that will substantiate
his claims. From their point of view, the request may have been
justified. Our Lord's answer is more than a refusal. God will give no
sign.

℣. The Lord be with you. ℞. **And also with you.**
✠ A reading from the holy gospel according to Mark
℞. **Glory to you, Lord.**

The Pharisees came forward and began to argue
with Jesus. They were looking for some heavenly
sign from him as a test. With a sigh from the depths
of his spirit he said, "Why does this age seek a sign?
I assure you, no such sign will be given it!" Then he
left them, got into the boat again, and went off to
the other shore.—This is the gospel of the Lord.
℞. **Praise to you, Lord Jesus Christ.** ➤ No. 15, p. 623

—————

TUESDAY OF THE SIXTH WEEK
IN ORDINARY TIME

────── YEAR I ──────

READING I Gn 6, 5-8; 7, 1-5. 10

This passage provides the theological connection between man's sin and the natural catastrophe of the flood. The account begins immediately with God's command to Noah to enter the ark. Noah is found "just" in God's sight. Noah's obedience is stressed; he does as directed.

A reading from the book of Genesis

When the Lord saw how great was man's wickedness on earth, and how no desire that his heart conceived was ever anything but evil, he regretted that he had made man on the earth, and his heart was grieved.

So the Lord said: "I will wipe out from the earth the men whom I have created, and not only the men, but also the beasts and the creeping things and the birds of the air, for I am sorry that I made them." But Noah found favor with the Lord.

Then the Lord said to Noah: "Go into the ark, you and all your household, for you alone in this age have I found to be truly just. Of every clean animal, take with you seven pairs, a male and its mate; and of the unclean animals, one pair, a male and its mate; likewise, of every clean bird of the air, seven pairs, a male and a female, and of all the unclean birds, one pair, a male and a female. Thus you will keep their issue alive over all the earth. Seven days from now I will bring rain down on the earth for forty days and forty nights, and so I will wipe out from the surface of the earth every moving creature that I have made." Noah did just as the Lord had commanded him.

As soon as the seven days were over, the waters of the flood came upon the earth.—This is the Word of the Lord. ℟. **Thanks be to God.** ⋎

Responsorial Psalm   Ps 29, 1-2. 3-4. 3. 9-10

℞. (11) **The Lord will bless his people with peace.**

Give to the Lord, you sons of God,
   give to the Lord glory and praise,
Give to the Lord the glory due his name;
   adore the Lord in holy attire. — ℞

The voice of the Lord is over the waters,
   the Lord, over vast waters.
The voice of the Lord is mighty;
   the voice of the Lord is majestic. — ℞

The God of glory thunders,
   and in his temple all say, "Glory!"
The Lord is enthroned above the flood;
   the Lord is enthroned as king forever. — ℞ ▼

—— **YEAR II** ——

READING I   Jas 1, 12-18

No man when he is tempted may try to evade responsibility by throwing the blame on God. God cannot be the source of temptation. Each man is led astray by his own desires. Sin, becoming mature, gives birth to death. By contrast, the things which come down from God are all good.

A reading from the letter of James

Happy the man who holds out to the end through trial! Once his worth has been proved, he will receive the crown of life the Lord has promised to those who love him. No one who is tempted is free to say, "I am being tempted by God." Surely God who is untouched by evil tempts no one. Rather the tug and lure of his own passion tempts every man. Once passion has conceived it gives birth to sin, and when sin reaches maturity it begets death.

Make no mistake about this, my dear brothers. Every worthwhile gift, every genuine benefit comes from above, descending from the Father of the heavenly luminaries, who cannot change and who is never shadowed over. He wills to bring us to birth

with a word spoken in truth so that we may be a
kind of firstfruits of his creatures.—This is the Word
of the Lord. ℟. **Thanks be to God.** ℣

Responsorial Psalm   Ps 94, 12-13. 14-15. 18-19

℟. (12) **Happy the man you teach, O Lord.**

Happy the man whom you instruct, O Lord,
  whom by your law you teach,
Giving him rest from evil days. — ℟

For the Lord will not cast off his people,
  nor abandon his inheritance;
But judgment shall again be with justice,
  and all the upright of heart shall follow it. — ℟

When I say, "My foot is slipping,"
  your kindness, O Lord, sustains me;
When cares abound within me,
  your comfort gladdens my soul. — ℟ ℣

———— **YEAR I AND II** ————

GOSPEL   Mk 8, 14-21

Alleluia (Jn 14, 23)

℟. **Alleluia.** If anyone loves me, he will hold to my
      words,
and my Father will love him, and we will come to
  him. ℟. **Alleluia.**

The disciples fail to make provision for their own personal needs.
Their usual food was bread. Our Lord warns his followers to beware of
the "yeast" of the Pharisees and the "yeast" of Herod-hypocrisy.
Christ's displeasure is for the disciples' distrust of his providence
and power which could have supplied bread.

℣. The Lord be with you. ℟. **And also with you.**
✠ A reading from the holy gospel according to Mark
℟. **Glory to you, Lord.**

The disciples had forgotten to bring any bread
along; except for one loaf they had none with them
in the boat. So when Jesus instructed them, "Keep
your eyes open! Be on your guard against the yeast of

the Pharisees and the yeast of Herod," they concluded among themselves that it was because they had no bread. Aware of this he said to them, "Why do you suppose that it is because you have no bread? Do you still not see or comprehend? Are your minds completely blinded? Have you eyes but no sight? Ears but no hearing? Do you remember when I broke the five loaves for the five thousand, how many baskets of fragments you gathered up." They answered, "Twelve." "When I broke the seven loaves for the four thousand, how many full hampers of fragments did you collect?" They answered, "Seven." He said to them again, "Do you still not understand?"—This is the gospel of the Lord. ℟. **Praise to you, Lord Jesus Christ.**   ➔ No. 15, p. 623

WEDNESDAY OF THE SIXTH WEEK IN ORDINARY TIME

YEAR I

READING I   Gn 8, 6. 13. 20-22

Note the suspense of the story. The earth is still covered with water when Noah sends the dove out. It comes back with an olive leaf. In another seven days, the dove is released again and it does not return. The flood story ends with an emphasis upon the restoration of man's life with God.

A reading from the book of Genesis

At the end of forty days Noah opened the hatch he had made in the ark, and he sent out a raven, to see if the waters had lessened on the earth. It flew back and forth until the waters dried off from the earth. Then he sent out a dove, to see if the waters had lessened on the earth. But the dove could find no place to alight and perch, and it returned to him in the ark, for there was water all over the earth. Putting out his hand, he caught the dove and drew it back to him inside the ark. He waited seven days more and again sent the dove out from the ark. In the evening the dove came back to him, and there in its bill was a plucked-off olive leaf! So Noah knew that the waters had lessened on the earth. He waited still another seven days and then released the dove once more; and this time it did not come back.

In the six hundred and first year of Noah's life, in the first month, on the first day of the month, the water began to dry up on the earth. Noah then removed the covering of the ark and saw that the surface of the ground was drying up.

Noah built an altar to the Lord, and choosing from every clean animal and every clean bird, he offered holocausts on the altar. When the Lord smelled the sweet odor, he said to himself: "Never again will I doom the earth because of man, since the desires of man's heart are evil from the start; nor will I ever again strike down all living beings, as I have done.

> As long as the earth lasts,
>> seedtime and harvest,
>> cold and heat,
> Summer and winter,
>> and day and night
>> shall not cease."

This is the Word of the Lord. ℟. **Thanks be to God.** ℣ .

Responsorial Psalm   Ps 116, 12-13. 14-15. 18-19

℟. (17) **To you, Lord, I will offer a sacrifice of praise.**
How shall I make a return to the Lord
    for all the good he has done for me?
The cup of salvation I will take up,
    and I will call upon the name of the Lord. — ℟
My vows to the Lord I will pay
    in the presence of all his people.
Precious in the eyes of the Lord
    is the death of his faithful ones. — ℟

My vows to the Lord I will pay
   in the presence of all his people,
In the courts of the house of the Lord,
   in your midst, O Jerusalem. — ℟ ✠

℟. Or: **Alleluia.** ✠

———— **YEAR II** ————

READING I   Jas 1, 19-27

The Christian must be prompt to hear the Word of God and put it into practice in his life. Happiness can result only from conformity of life to this ideal law of true freedom. A man cannot be devout without putting a rein on his tongue. Neither can he have true worship if he does not look after orphans and widows, that is, the defenseless and oppressed.

A reading from the letter of James

Keep this in mind, dear brothers.

Let every man be quick to hear, slow to speak, slow to anger; for a man's anger does not fulfill God's justice. Strip away all that is filthy, every vicious excess. Humbly welcome the word that has taken root in you, with its power to save you. Act on this word. If all you do is listen to it, you are deceiving yourselves.

A man who listens to God's word but does not put it into practice is like a man who looks into a mirror at the face he was born with; he looks at himself, then goes off and promptly forgets what he looked like. There is, on the other hand, the man who peers into freedom's ideal law and abides by it. He is no forgetful listener, but one who carries out the law in practice. Happy will this man be in whatever he does.

If a man who does not control his tongue imagines that he is devout, he is self-deceived; his worship is pointless. Looking after orphans and widows in their distress and keeping oneself unspotted by the world make for pure worship without stain before our God and Father.—This is the Word of the Lord. ℟.
Thanks be to God. ✠

Responsorial Psalm Ps 15, 2-3. 3-4. 5

℞. (1) **He who does justice shall live on the Lord's holy mountain.**

He who walks blamelessly and does justice;
  who thinks the truth in his heart
  and slanders not with his tongue. — ℞

Who harms not his fellow man,
  nor takes up a reproach against his neighbor;
By whom the reprobate is despised,
  while he honors those who fear the Lord. — ℞

Who lends not his money at usury
  and accepts no bribe against the innocent.
He who does these things
  shall never be disturbed. — ℞ ✠

———— **YEAR I AND II** ————

GOSPEL Mk 8, 22-26

Alleluia (See Eph 1, 17-18)

℞. **Alleluia.** May the Father of our Lord Jesus Christ
enlighten the eyes of our heart
that we might see how great is the hope
to which we are called. ℞. **Alleluia.**

Jesus cures the blind man, using signs and symbols. It is perhaps
implied here that he who came, as foretold, "to open the blind eyes"
will thus some time take by the hand those who sit in darkness and
guide them into his marvelous light. God spoke through his prophet
long before: "I will lead the blind . . . by paths unknown" (Is 42, 16).

℣. The Lord be with you. ℞. **And also with you.**
✠ A reading from the holy gospel according to Mark
℞. **Glory to you, Lord.**

When Jesus and his disciples arrived at Bethsaida,
some people brought him a blind man and begged
him to touch him. Jesus took the blind man's hand
and led him outside the village. Putting spittle on
his eyes he laid his hands on him and asked "Can
you see anything?" The man opened his eyes and

said, "I can see people but they look like walking trees!" Then a second time Jesus laid hands on his eyes, and he saw perfectly; his sight was restored and he could see everything clearly. Jesus sent him home with the admonition, "Do not even go into the village."—This is the gospel of the Lord. R̶.
Praise to you, Lord Jesus Christ. ➔ No. 15, p. 623

THURSDAY OF THE SIXTH WEEK
IN ORDINARY TIME

—— YEAR I ——

READING I   Gn 9, 1-13

The first epoch in the division of world's history ended with the flood. The second, marked by the covenant of Noah, supposes a theological disorder caused by sin and introduces as normal those adverse conditions of life that everyone encounters. Man's kingship is exercised, not in peace but through fear.

A reading from the book of Genesis

God blessed Noah and his sons and said to them: "Be fertile and multiply and fill the earth. Dread fear of you shall come upon all the animals of the earth and all the birds of the air, upon all the creatures that move about on the ground and all the fishes of the sea; into your power they are delivered. Every creature that is alive shall be yours to eat; I give them all to you as I did the green plants. Only flesh with its lifeblood still in it you shall not eat. For your own lifeblood, too, I will demand an accounting: from every animal I will demand it, and from man in regard to his fellow man I will demand an accounting for human life.

If anyone sheds the blood of man,
by man shall his blood be shed;
For in the image of God
has man been made.
Be fertile, then, and multiply; abound on the earth and subdue it."

God said to Noah and to his sons with him: "See, I am now establishing my covenant with you and your descendants after you and with every living creature that was with you: all the birds, and the various tame and wild animals that were with you and came out of the ark. I will establish my covenant with you, that never again shall all bodily creatures be destroyed by the waters of a flood; there shall not be another flood to devaste the earth." God added: "This is the sign that I am giving for all ages to come, of the covenant between me and you and every living creature with you: I set my bow in the clouds to serve as a sign of the covenant between me and the earth."—This is the Word of the Lord. ℟. **Thanks be to God.** ⅴ

Responsorial Psalm Ps 102, 16-18. 19-21. 29. 22-23
℟. (20) **From heaven the Lord looks down on the earth.**

The nations shall revere your name, O Lord,
    and all the kings of the earth your glory,
When the Lord has rebuilt Zion
    and appeared in his glory;
When he has regarded the prayer of the destitute,
    and not despised their prayer. — ℟

Let this be written for the generation to come,
    and let his future creatures praise the Lord:
"The Lord looked down from his holy height,
    from heaven he beheld the earth,
To hear the groaning of the prisoners,
    to release those doomed to die." — ℟

The children of your servants shall abide,
    and their posterity shall continue in your presence,
That the name of the Lord may be declared in Zion,
    and his praise, in Jerusalem,
When the peoples gather together,
    and the kingdoms, to serve the Lord. — ℟ ⅴ

———— **YEAR II** ————

READING I   Jas 2, 1-9

In the Christian community, there must be no discrimination against the poor or favoritism toward the rich based on a mistaken exaltation of status or wealth (cf Mt 23, 6). Rather, divine favor consists in God's promises, his election, and his rewards elicited by man's faith and response to his love. The impious rich who oppress the poor dishonor the name of Christ.

A reading from the letter of James

My brothers, your faith in our Lord Jesus Christ glorified must not allow of favoritism. Suppose there should come into your assembly a man fashionably dressed, with rings on his fingers, and at the same time a poor man dressed in shabby clothes. Suppose further you were to take notice of the well-dressed man and say, "Sit right here, please," whereas you were to say to the poor man, "You can stand!" or "Sit over there by my footrest." Have you not in a case like this discriminated in your hearts? Have you not set yourselves up as judges who hand down corrupt decisions?

Listen, dear brothers. Did not God choose those who are poor in the eyes of the world to be rich in faith and heirs of the kingdom he promised to those who love him? Yet you treated the poor man shamefully. Are not the rich exploiting you? They are the ones who hale you into the courts and who blaspheme that noble name which has made you God's own.

You are acting rightly, however, if you fulfill the law of the kingdom. Scripture has it, "You shall love your neighbor as yourself." But if you show favoritism you commit sin and are convicted by the law as transgressors.—This is the Word of the Lord.
℟. **Thanks be to God.** ⩔

Responsorial Psalm   Ps 34, 2-3. 4-5. 6-7
℟. (7) **The Lord hears the cry of the poor.**

I will bless the Lord at all times;
  his praise shall be ever in my mouth.
Let my soul glory in the Lord;
  the lowly will hear me and be glad. — ℟

Glorify the Lord with me,
  let us together extol his name.
I sought the Lord, and he answered me
  and delivered me from all my fears. — ℟

Look to him that you may be radiant with joy,
  and your faces may not blush with shame.
When the afflicted man called out, the Lord heard,
  and from all his distress he saved him. — ℟ ℣

——— **YEAR I AND II** ———

GOSPEL   Mk 8, 27-33
Alleluia (Jn 6, 64. 69)

℟. **Alleluia.** Your words, Lord, are spirit and life,
you have the words of everlasting life. ℟. **Alleluia.**

This passage climaxes our Lord's self-revelation to the disciples as
the Messiah. It also introduces the theme of the Suffering Messiah.
Peter is the first man to acknowledge openly that our Lord is the expected Deliverer. Christ then prepares the minds of the apostles for
his cross and passion.

℣. The Lord be with you. ℟. **And also with you.**
✠ A reading from the holy gospel according to Mark
℟. **Glory to you, Lord.**

Jesus and his disciples set out for the villages around
Caesarea Philippi. On the way he asked his disciples this question: "Who do people say that I am?"
They replied, "Some, John the Baptizer, other, Elijah,
still others, one of the prophets." "And you," he
went on to ask, "who do you say that I am?" Peter
answered him, "You are the Messiah!" Then he
strictly ordered them not to tell anyone about him.

    He then began to teach them that the Son of Man
had to suffer much, be rejected by the elders, the
chief priests, and the scribes, be put to death, and

rise three days later. He said this quite openly. Peter then took him aside and began to remonstrate with him. At this he turned around and, eyeing the disciples, reprimanded Peter in turn: "Get out of my sight, you satan! You are not judging by God's standards but by man's!"—This is the gospel of the Lord. ℞. **Praise to you, Lord Jesus Christ.**

FRIDAY OF THE SIXTH WEEK
IN ORDINARY TIME

——— **YEAR I** ———

READING I   Gn 11, 1-9

An ancient story, the building of the tower of Babel, is used to give the theological reason for the division of mankind. The sin of the first man resulted in the alienation of man from God (Gn 3, 22-24) and from his fellowman (Gn 5, 1-16). From sin now results the alienation of all human society from God, and men from one another.

A reading from the book of Genesis

The whole world spoke the same language, using the same words. While men were migrating in the east, they came upon a valley in the land of Shinar and settled there. They said to one another, "Come, let us mold bricks and harden them with fire." They used bricks for stone, and bitumen for mortar. Then they said, "Come, let us build ourselves a city and a tower with its top in the sky, and so make a name for ourselves; otherwise we shall be scattered all over the earth."

The Lord came down to see the city and the tower that the men had built. Then the Lord said: "If now, while they are one people, all speaking the same language, they have started to do this, nothing will later stop them from doing whatever they presume to do. Let us then go down and there confuse their language, so that one will not understand what another says." Thus the Lord scattered them from there all over the earth, and they stopped building the city. That is why it was called Babel, because there the Lord confused the speech of all the world. It was from that place that he scattered them all over the earth—This is the Word of the Lord. ℟. **Thanks be to God.** ℣

Responsorial Psalm   Ps 33, 10-11. 12-13. 14-15

℟. (12) **Happy the people the Lord has chosen to be his own.**

The Lord brings to nought the plans of nations;
  he foils the designs of peoples.
But the plan of the Lord stands forever;
  the design of his heart, through all genera-
    tions. — ℟

Happy the nation whose God is the Lord,
  the people he has chosen for his own inheritance.
From heaven the Lord looks down;
  he sees all mankind. — ℟

From his fixed throne he beholds
  all who dwell on the earth,
He who fashioned the heart of each,
  he who knows all their works. — ℟ ℣

——— **YEAR II** ———

READING I   Jas 2, 14-24. 26

Neither faith nor good works can merit salvation without the other. A living faith works through love, as opposed to a dead faith that lacks good works. James does not mean that genuine faith is insufficient for justification, but simply that faith without good works is not genuine. Thus there is no basic disagreement between James and Paul, for whom faith "works through love" (Gal 5, 6).

A reading from the letter of James

My brothers, what good is it to profess faith without practicing it? Such faith has no power to save one, has it? If a brother or sister has nothing to wear and no food for the day, and you say to them,

"Good-bye and good luck! Keep warm and be well fed," but do not meet their bodily needs, what good is that? So it is with the faith that does nothing in practice. It is thoroughly lifeless.

To such a person one might say, "You have faith and I have works—is that it?" Show me your faith without works, and I will show you the faith that underlies my works! Do you believe that God is one? You are quite right. The demons believe that and shudder. Do you want proof, you ignoramus, that without works faith is idle? Was not our father Abraham justified by his works when he offered his son Isaac on the altar? There you see proof that faith was both assisting his works and implemented by his works. You also see how the Scripture was fulfilled which says, "Abraham believed God, and it was credited to him as justice"; for this he received the title, "God's friend."

You must perceive that a person is justified by his works and not by faith alone. Be assured, then, that faith without works is as dead as a body without breath.—This is the Word of the Lord. ℟. **Thanks be to God.** ↓

Responsorial Psalm   Ps 112, 1-2. 3-4. 5-6

℟. (1) **Happy are those who do what the Lord commands.**

Happy the man who fears the Lord,
  who greatly delights in his commands.
His posterity shall be mighty upon the earth;
  the upright generation shall be blessed. — ℟

Wealth and riches shall be in his house;
  his generosity shall endure forever.
He dawns through the darkness, a light for the upright;
  he is gracious and merciful and just. — ℟

Well for the man who is gracious and lends,
  who conducts his affairs with justice;

He shall never be moved;
   the just man shall be in everlasting remem-
      brance. — ℟ ⍢

———— **YEAR I AND II** ————

GOSPEL   Mk 8, 34-9, 1
Alleluia (Jn 15, 15)

℟. **Alleluia.** I call you my friends, says the Lord,
for I have made known to you all that the Father
      has told me. ℟. **Alleluia.**

Christ's cross is a symbol of the redemptive suffering which all his
followers must bear: "Whoever does not take up [mark himself with]
his cross [that is, does not repent and dedicate himself wholly to
God], cannot be my disciple" (Lk 14, 27). The pleasures of the world
cannot be exchanged for heaven.

℣. The Lord be with you. ℟. **And also with you.**
✠ A reading from the holy gospel according to Mark
℟. **Glory to you, Lord.**

Jesus summoned the crowd with his disciples and
said to them: "If a man wishes to come after me, he
must deny his very self, take up his cross and follow
in my steps. Whoever would save his life will lose
it, but whoever loses his life for my sake and the
gospel's will save it. What profit does a man show
who gains the whole world and destroys himself in
the process? What can a man offer in exchange for
his life? If any one in this faithless and corrupt age
is ashamed of me and my doctrine, the Son of Man
will be ashamed of him when he comes with the holy
angels in his Father's glory."

   He also said to them: "I assure you, among those
standing here there are some who will not taste
death until they see the reign of God established in
power."—This is the gospel of the Lord. ℟. **Praise
to you, Lord Jesus Christ.**   ➔ No. 15, p. 623

SATURDAY OF THE SIXTH WEEK
IN ORDINARY TIME

——— **YEAR I** ———

READING I   Heb 11, 1-7

The Old Testament does not say why Abel's sacrifice was better than Cain's, but this Epistle takes for granted that it was his faith. Without faith, it is impossible to please God. Faith is God's spirit working within us, the "confident assurance concerning what we hope for, and conviction about things we do not see" (Heb 11, 1).

A reading from the letter to the Hebrews

Faith is confident assurance concerning what we hope for, and conviction about things we do not see. Because of faith the men of old were approved by God. Through faith we perceive that the worlds were created by the word of God, and that what is visible came into being through the invisible. By faith Abel offered God a sacrifice greater than Cain's. Because of this he was attested to be just, God himself having borne witness to him on account of his gifts; therefore, although Abel is dead, he still speaks. By faith Enoch was taken away without dying, and "he was seen no more because God took him." Scripture testifies that, before he was taken up, he was pleasing to God—but without faith, it is impossible to please him. Anyone who comes to God must believe that he exists, and that he rewards those who seek him. By faith Noah, warned about things not yet seen, revered God and built an ark that his household might be saved. He thereby condemned the world and inherited the justice which comes through faith.—This is the Word of the Lord. ℟. **Thanks be to God.** ↓

Responsorial Psalm   Ps 145, 2-3. 4-5. 10-11

℟. (1) **I will praise your name for ever, Lord**

Every day will I bless you,
    and I will praise your name forever and ever.

Great is the Lord and highly to be praised;
   his greatness is unsearchable. — ℞
Generation after generation praises your works
   and proclaims your might.
They speak of the splendor of your glorious majesty
   and tell of your wondrous works. — ℞
Let all your works give you thanks, O Lord,
   and let your faithful ones bless you.
Let them discourse of the glory of your kingdom
   and speak of your might. — ℞ ℣

———— **YEAR II** ————

READING I   Jas 3, 1-10

The use and abuse of the role of teaching are related to the good or
bad use of the tongue, the instrument through which teaching was
chiefly conveyed. The bit and the rudder are figures of the tongue's
control, just as the spark and destroying flames portray the evils of
unbridled speech. The tongue should be used to bless and praise God,
not curse one's fellowmen.

A reading from the letter of James

Not many of you should become teachers, my
brothers; you should realize that those of us who
do so will be called to the stricter account. All of
us fall short in many respects. If a person is without fault in speech he is a man in the fullest sense,
because he can control his entire body. When we
put bits into the mouths of horses to make them
obey us, we guide the rest of their bodies. It is the
same with ships: however large they are, and despite that fact that they are driven by fierce winds,
they are directed by very small rudders on whatever course the steerman's impulse may select. The
tongue is something like that. It is a small member,
yet it makes great pretensions.

See how tiny the spark is that sets a huge forest
ablaze! The tongue is such a flame. It exists among
our members as a whole universe of malice. The
tongue defiles the entire body. Its flames encircle our

course from birth, and its fire is kindled by hell. Every form of life, four-footed or winged, crawling or swimming, can be tamed, and has been tamed, by mankind; the tongue no man can tame. It is a restless evil, full of deadly poison. We use it to say, "Praised be the Lord and Father"; then we use it to curse men, though they are made in the likeness of God. Blessing and curse come out of the same mouth. This ought not to be, my brothers!—This is the Word of the Lord. ℟. **Thanks be to God.** ▼

Responsorial Psalm   Ps 12, 2-3. 4-5. 7-8

℟. (8) **You will protect us, Lord.**

Help, O Lord! for no one now is dutiful;
    faithfulness has vanished from among men.
Everyone speaks falsehood to his neighbor;
    with smooth lips they speak, and double heart.—℟

May the Lord destroy all smooth lips,
    every boastful tongue,
Those who say, "We are heroes with our tongues;
    our lips are our own; who is lord over us?" — ℟

The promises of the Lord are sure,
    like tried silver, freed from dross, sevenfold re-
        fined.
You, O Lord, will keep us
    and preserve us always from this genera-
        tion. — ℟ ▼

——— **YEAR I AND II** ———

GOSPEL   Mk 9, 2-13

Alleluia (See Mk 9, 6)

℟. **Alleluia.** The heavens were opened and the
    Father's voice was heard:
this is my beloved Son, hear him. ℟. **Alleluia.**

The original event of the transfiguration is obscure. Yet this story is based on some factual occurrence in which the disciples fleetingly recognize the truth of the revelation at Caesarea Philippi. Although Jesus' Messiahship involves suffering, he is truly the glorious Son of Man.

℣. The Lord be with you. ℟. **And also with you.**
✠ A reading from the holy gospel according to Mark
℟. **Glory to you, Lord.**

Jesus took Peter, James, and John off by themselves with him and led them up a high mountain. He was transfigured before their eyes and his clothes became dazzlingly white—whiter than the work of any bleacher could make them. Elijah appeared to them along with Moses; the two were in conversation with Jesus. Then Peter spoke to Jesus: "Rabbi, how good it is for us to be here. Let us erect three booths on this site, one for you, one for Moses, and one for Elijah." He hardly knew what to say, for they were all overcome with awe. A cloud came, overshadowing them, and out of the cloud a voice: "This is my Son, my beloved. Listen to him." Suddenly looking around they no longer saw anyone with them—only Jesus.

As they were coming down the mountain, he strictly enjoined them not to tell anyone what they had seen, before the Son of Man had risen from the dead. They kept this word of his to themselves, though they continued to discuss what "to rise from the dead" meant. Finally they put to him this question: "Why do the scribes claim that Elijah must come first?" He told them: "Elijah will indeed come first and restore everything. Yet why does Scripture say of the Son of Man that he must suffer much and be despised? Let me assure you, Elijah has already come. They did entirely as they pleased with him, as the Scriptures say of him."—This is the gospel of the Lord. ℟. **Praise to you, Lord Jesus Christ.**

— No. 15, p. 623

———————————

MONDAY OF THE SEVENTH WEEK
IN ORDINARY TIME

——— **YEAR I** ———

READING I   Sir 1, 1-10

All wisdom which comes from God always was and always will be.
Wisdom belongs to the Lord and he has placed his wisdom in the works
of creation, upon all his works and upon his friends.

The beginning of the book of Sirach

All wisdom comes from the Lord
   and with him it remains forever.
The sand of the seashore, the drops of rain,
   the days of eternity: who can number these?
Heaven's height, earth's breadth,
   the depth of the abyss: who can explore these?
Before all things else wisdom was created;
   and prudent understanding, from eternity.
To whom has wisdom's root been revealed?
   Who knows her subtleties?
There is but one, wise and truly awe-inspiring,
   seated upon his throne:
It is the Lord; he created her,
   has seen her and taken note of her.
He has poured her forth upon all his works,
   upon every living thing according to his bounty;
   he has lavished her upon his friends.
Fear of the Lord is glory and splendor,
   gladness and a festive crown.
Fear of the Lord warms the heart,
   giving gladness and joy and length of days.
This is the Word of the Lord. ℞. **Thanks be to God.** ℣

Responsorial Psalm   Ps 93, 1. 1-2. 5

℞. (1) **The Lord is king; he is robed in majesty.**

The Lord is king, in splendor robed;
   robed is the Lord and girt about with strength.— ℞

And he has made the world firm,
   not to be moved.

Your throne stands firm from of old;
  from everlasting you are, O Lord. — ℟

Your decrees are worthy of trust indeed:
  holiness befits your house,
    O Lord, for length of days. — ℟ ℣

———— **YEAR II** ————

READING I Jas 3, 13-18

Wisdom shines forth in humility. Jealousy and ambition are cunning. This leads to vile behavior. Wisdom from God, however, is innocent. It leads to a harvest of justice.

A reading from the letter of James

If one of you is wise and understanding, let him show this in practice through a humility filled with good sense. Should you instead nurse bitter jealousy and selfish ambition in your hearts, at least refrain from arrogant and false claims against the truth. Wisdom like this does not come from above. It is earthbound, a kind of animal, even devilish, cunning. Where there are jealousy and strife, there also are inconstancy and all kinds of vile behavior. Wisdom from above, by contrast, is first of all innocent. It is also peaceable, lenient, docile, rich in sympathy and the kindly deeds that are its fruits, impartial and sincere. The harvest of justice is sown in peace for those who cultivate peace.—This is the Word of the Lord. ℟. **Thanks be to God.** ℣

Responsorial Psalm Ps 19, 8. 9. 10. 15

℟. (9) **The precepts of the Lord give joy to the heart.**

The law of the Lord is perfect,
  refreshing the soul;
The decree of the Lord is trustworthy,
  giving wisdom to the simple. — ℟

The precepts of the Lord are right,
  rejoicing the heart;

The command of the Lord is clear,
  enlightening the eye. — ℟

The fear of the Lord is pure,
  enduring forever;

The ordinances of the Lord are true,
  all of them just. — ℟

Let the words of my mouth and the thought of my
    heart
  find favor before you,
  O Lord, my rock and my redeemer. — ℟ ℣

———— **YEAR I AND II** ————

GOSPEL   Mk 9, 14-29
Alleluia (2 Tm 1, 10)

℟. **Alleluia.** Our Savior Jesus Christ has done away
    with death,
and brought us life through his gospel. ℟. **Alleluia.**

A father asks Jesus to expel an evil spirit from his son. The begging
father prays for trust and faith in God. Because of faith Jesus orders
the demon out. Jesus teaches how important prayer is before acting.

℣. The Lord be with you. ℟. **And also with you.**
✠ A reading from the holy gospel according to Mark
℟. **Glory to you, Lord.**

[As Jesus came down the mountain with Peter,
James and John] and approached the disciples, they
saw a large crowd standing around, and scribes in
lively discussion with them. Immediately on catching sight of Jesus, the whole crowd was overcome
with awe. They ran up to greet him. He asked
them, "What are you discussing among yourselves?"
"Teacher," a man in the crowd replied, "I have
brought my son to you because he is possessed by
a mute spirit. Whenever it seizes him it throws him
down; he foams at the mouth and grinds his teeth
and becomes rigid. Just now I asked your disciples
to expel him, but they were unable to do so." He
replied by saying to the crowd, "What an unbeliev-

ing lot you are! How long must I remain with you? How long can I endure you? Bring him to me." When they did so the spirit caught sight of Jesus and immediately threw the boy into convulsions. As he fell to the ground he began to roll around and foam at the mouth. Then Jesus questioned the father: "How long has this been happening to him?" "From childhood," the father replied. "Often it throws him into the fire and into water. You would think it would kill him. If out of the kindness of your heart you can do anything to help us, please do!" Jesus said. " 'If you can?' Everything is possible to a man who trusts." The boy's father immediately exclaimed, "I do believe! Help my lack of trust!" Jesus, on seeing a crowd rapidly gathering, reprimanded the unclean spirit by saying to him, "Mute and deaf spirit, I command you: Get out of him and never enter him again!" Shouting, and throwing the boy into convulsions, it came out of him; the boy became like a corpse, which caused many to say, "He is dead." But Jesus took him by the hand and helped him to his feet. When Jesus arrived at the house his disciples began to ask him privately, "Why is it that we could not expel it?" He told them, "This kind you can drive out only by prayer."—This is the gospel of the Lord. ℟. **Praise to you, Lord Jesus Christ.** ➔No. 15, p. 623

TUESDAY OF THE SEVENTH WEEK IN ORDINARY TIME

—— **YEAR I** ——

READING I   Sir 2, 1-11
Sirach warns of trials that will come for one who accepts his teaching. Patience and trust in God are the means of emerging victoriously. Adversity is a test for the just man.

A reading from the book of Sirach

My son, when you come to serve the Lord,
  prepare yourself for trials.

Be sincere of heart and steadfast,
  undisturbed in time of adversity.
Cling to him, forsake him not;
  thus will your future be great.
Accept whatever befalls you,
  in crushing misfortune be patient;
For in fire gold is tested,
  and worthy men in the crucible of humiliation.
Trust God and he will help you;
  make straight your ways and hope in him.
You who fear the Lord, wait for his mercy,
  turn not away lest you fall.
You who fear the Lord, trust him,
  and your reward will not be lost.
You who fear the Lord, hope for good things,
  for lasting joy and mercy.
Study the generations long past and understand;
  has anyone hoped in the Lord and been disap-
    pointed?
Has anyone persevered in his fear and been forsaken?
  has anyone called upon him and been rebuffed?
Compassionate and merciful is the Lord;
  he forgives sins, he saves in time of trouble.
This is the Word of the Lord. ℟. **Thanks be to God.** ℣

Responsorial Psalm   Ps 37, 3-4. 18-19. 27-28. 39-40

℟. (5) **Commit your life to the Lord,**
  and he will help you.

Trust in the Lord and do good,
  that you may dwell in the land and enjoy security.
Take delight in the Lord,
  and he will grant you your heart's requests. — ℟

The Lord watches over the lives of the wholehearted;
  their inheritance lasts forever.
They are not put to shame in an evil time;
  in days of famine they have plenty. — ℟

Turn from evil and do good,
  that you may abide forever;

For the Lord loves what is right,
    and forsakes not his faithful ones. — ℟
The salvation of the just is from the Lord;
    he is their refuge in time of distress.
And the Lord helps them and delivers them;
    he delivers them from the wicked and saves them,
    because they take refuge in him. — ℟ ℣

———— **YEAR II** ————

READING I   Jas 4, 1-10

Ambition leads to conflicts and disputes, to envy, murder, squandering.
These are marks of the world which are contradictory to humility. The
Christian should submit to God and resist the devil. He should be
humble.

A reading from the letter of James

Where do the conflicts and disputes among you orig-
inate? Is it not your inner cravings that make war
within your members? What you desire you do not
obtain, and so you resort to murder. You envy and
you cannot acquire, so you quarrel and fight. You
do not obtain because you do not ask. You ask and
you do not receive because you ask wrongly, with a
view to squandering what you receive on your pleasures. O you unfaithful ones, are you not aware that
love of the world is enmity to God? A man is marked
out as God's enemy if he chooses to be the world's
friend. Do you suppose it is to no purpose that
Scripture says, "The spirit he has implanted in us
tends toward jealousy"? Yet he bestows a greater
gift, for the sake of which it is written,

    "God resists the proud
        but bestows his favor on the lowly."
Therefore submit to God; resist the devil and he will
take flight. Draw close to God, and he will draw
close to you. Cleanse your hands, you sinners; purify
your hearts, you backsliders. Begin to lament, to
mourn, and to weep; let your laughter be turned into

mourning and your joy into sorrow. Be humbled in the sight of the Lord and he will raise you on high. —This is the Word of the Lord. ℟. **Thanks be to God.** ℣

Responsorial Psalm   Ps 55, 7-8. 9-10. 10-11. 23

℟. (23) **Throw your cares on the Lord,
     and he will support you.**

And I say, "Had I but wings like a dove,
   I would fly away and be at rest.
Far away I would flee;
   I would lodge in the wilderness. — ℟

"I would hasten to find shelter
   from the violent storm and the tempest."
Engulf them, O Lord; divide their counsels. — ℟.

In the city I see violence and strife,
   day and night they prowl about upon its
      walls. — ℟

Cast your care upon the Lord,
   and he will support you;
   never will he permit the just man to be dis-
      turbed. — ℟ ℣

───── **YEAR I AND II** ─────

GOSPEL   Mk 9, 30-37

Alleluia (Gal 6, 14)

℟. **Alleluia.** My only glory is the cross of our Lord
      Jesus Christ,
which crucifies the world to me and me to the world.
      ℟. **Alleluia.**

Christ tries to give the disciples some preview of what lies before him. The disciples are to reverse the customary practice whereby those in authority rule by force. Their new norm of conduct—to be the servant of all—is made possible by Jesus' own example of his mission of service.

℣. The Lord be with you. ℟. **And also with you.**
✠ A reading from the holy gospel according to Mark
℟. **Glory to you, Lord.**

Jesus and his disciples came down the mountain and began a journey through Galilee, but he did not want anyone to know about it. He was teaching his disciples in this vein: "The Son of Man is going to be delivered into the hands of men who will put him to death; three days after his death he will rise." Though they failed to understand his words, they were afraid to question him.

They returned to Capernaum and Jesus, once inside the house, began to ask them, "What were you discussing on the way home?" At this they fell silent, for on the way they had been arguing about who was the most important. So he sat down and called the Twelve around him and said, "If anyone wishes to rank first, he must remain the last one of all and the servant of all." Then he took a little child, stood him in their midst, and putting his arms around him, said to them, "Whoever welcomes a child such as this for my sake welcomes me. And whoever welcomes me welcomes, not me, but him who sent me."—This is the gospel of the Lord. ℟.
Praise to you, Lord Jesus Christ. ➔ No. 15, p. 623

WEDNESDAY OF THE SEVENTH WEEK IN ORDINARY TIME

——— **YEAR I** ———

READING I   Sir 4, 11-19

True wisdom, which is found only in God and comes from him alone, brings God's blessings down on all who serve her. She puts man to the test until his heart is fully with her. Then she bestows glory and happiness on him.

A reading from the book of Sirach

Wisdom instructs her children
    and admonishes those who seek her.
He who loves her loves life;
    those who seek her out win her favor.

He who holds her fast inherits glory;
 wherever he dwells, the Lord bestows blessings.
Those who serve her serve the Holy One;
 those who love her the Lord loves.
He who obeys her judges nations;
 he who hearkens to her dwells in her inmost
  chambers.
If one trusts her, he will possess her;
 his descendants too will inherit her.
She walks with him as a stranger,
 and at first she puts him to the test;
Fear and dread she brings upon him
 and tries him with her discipline;
With her precepts she puts him to the proof,
 until his heart is fully with her.
Then she comes back to bring him happiness
 and reveal her secrets to him.
But if he fails her, she will abandon him
 and deliver him into the hands of despoilers.
This is the Word of the Lord. ℞. **Thanks be to God.** ⍦

Responsorial Psalm
    Ps 119, 165. 168. 171. 172. 174. 175

℞. (165) **O Lord, great peace have they who love
 your law.**

Those who love your law have great peace,
 and for them there is no stumbling block. — ℞

I keep your precepts and your decrees,
 for all my ways are before you. — ℞

My lips pour forth your praise,
 because you teach me your statutes. — ℞

May my tongue sing of your promise,
 for all your commands are just. — ℞

I long for your salvation, O Lord,
 and your law is my delight. — ℞

Let my soul live to praise you,
 and may your ordinance help me. — ℞ ⍦

—— **YEAR II** ——

READING I   Jas 4, 13-17

Tomorow is unknown. Life is like a vapor, appearing now and soon
vanishing. Only the will of God merits a reward. Not to do the right
thing means that a man sins.

A reading from the letter of James

Come now, you who say, "Today or tomorrow we
shall go to such and such a town, spend a year there,
trade, and come off with a profit!" You have no idea
what kind of life will be yours tomorrow. You are
a vapor that appears briefly and vanishes. Instead
of saying, "If the Lord wills it, we shall live to do
this or that," all you can do is make arrogant and
pretentious claims. All such boasting is reprehensi-
ble. When a man knows the right thing to do and
does not do it, he sins.—This is the Word of the
Lord. ℟. **Thanks be to God.** ⩣

Responsorial Psalm   Ps 49, 2-3. 6-7. 8-10. 11

℟. (Mt 5, 3) **Happy the poor in spirit;**
   the kingdom of heaven is theirs!

Hear this, all you peoples;
   hearken, all who dwell in the world,
Of lowly birth or high degree,
   rich and poor alike. — ℟

Why should I fear in evil days
   when my wicked ensnarers ring me round?
They trust in their wealth;
   the abundance of their riches is their boast. — ℟

Yet in no way can a man redeem himself,
   or pay his own ransom to God;
Too high is the price to redeem one's life; he would
      never have enough
   to remain alive always and not see destruc-
      tion. — ℟

For he can see that wise men die,

and likewise the senseless and the stupid pass
    away,
leaving to others their wealth. — ℟ ✝

——— **YEAR I AND II** ———

GOSPEL   Mk 9, 38-40
Alleluia (Jn 14, 5)
℟. **Alleluia.** I am the way, the truth, and the life,
    says the Lord;
no one comes to the Father, except through me.
    ℟. **Alleluia.**

Jesus warns against jealousy and intolerance toward good works,
such as exorcism, performed in his name by those whose faith is
imperfect. The saying in Mk 9, 40 is a broad principle of the divine
tolerance.

℣. The Lord be with you. ℟. **And also with you.**
✠ A reading from the holy gospel according to Mark.
℟. **Glory to you, Lord.**

John said to Jesus, "Teacher, we saw a man using
your name to expel demons and we tried to stop
him because he is not of our company." Jesus said
in reply: "Do not try to stop him. No one can perform
a miracle in my name and at the same time speak
ill of me. Anyone who is not against us is with us."
—This is the gospel of the Lord. ℟. **Praise to you,
Lord Jesus Christ.**   ➤ No. 15, p. 623

———————

THURSDAY OF THE SEVENTH WEEK
IN ORDINARY TIME

——— **YEAR I** ———

READING I   Sir 5, 1-8

Whoever has the misfortune to fall away from the Lord should never
delay returning to him. The Lord is, indeed, long-suffering and
forgiving, but he will not wait forever before sending his anger on
the unrepentant sinner.

A reading from the book of Sirach

Rely not on your wealth;
    say not: "I have the power."
Rely not on your strength
    in following the desires of your heart.
Say not: "Who can prevail against me?"
    for the Lord will exact the punishment.
Say not: "I have sinned, yet what has befallen me?"
    for the Lord bides his time.
Of forgiveness be not overconfident,
    adding sin upon sin.
Say not: "Great is his mercy;
    my many sins he will forgive."
For mercy and anger alike are with him;
    upon the wicked alights his wrath.
Delay not your conversion to the Lord,
    put it not off from day to day.
This is the Word of the Lord. ℟. **Thanks be to God.** ℣

Responsorial Psalm   Ps 1, 1-2. 3. 4. 6
℟. (Ps 40, 5) **Happy are they who hope in the Lord.**
Happy the man who follows not
    the counsel of the wicked
Nor walks in the way of sinners,
    nor sits in the company of the insolent,
But delights in the law of the Lord
    and meditates on his law day and night. — ℟
He is like a tree
    planted near running water,
That yields its fruit in due season,
    and whose leaves never fade.
      [Whatever he does, prospers.] — ℟
Not so the wicked, not so;
    they are like chaff which the wind drives away,
For the Lord watches over the way of the just,
    but the way of the wicked vanishes. — ℟ ℣

——— **YEAR II** ———

READING I   Jas 5, 1-6

Wealth and riches forebode miseries. Only what is stored up for the
last day counts. Those who sin in order to gain luxuries isolate themselves from the Lord.

A reading from the letter of James

You rich, weep and wail over your impending miseries. Your wealth has rotted, your fine wardrobe
has grown moth-eaten, your gold and silver have
corroded, and their corrosion shall be a testimony
against you; it will devour your flesh like a fire.
See what you have stored up for yourself against
the last days.

Here, crying aloud, are the wages you withheld
from the farmhands who harvested your fields. The
shouts of the harvesters have reached the ears of
the Lord of hosts. You lived in wanton luxury on
the earth: you fattened yourselves for the day of
slaughter. You condemned, even killed, the just man;
he does not resist you.—This is the Word of the
Lord. ℟. **Thanks be to God.** ℣

Responsorial Psalm Ps 49, 14-15. 15-16. 17-18. 19-20

℟. (Mt 5, 3) **Happy the poor in spirit;**
    the kingdom of heaven is theirs!

This is the way of those whose trust is folly,
    the end of those contented with their lot:
Like sheep they are herded into the nether world;
    death is their shepherd, and the upright rule over
        them. — ℟

Quickly their form is consumed;
    the nether world is their palace.
But God will redeem me
    from the power of the nether world by receiving
        me. — ℟

Fear not when a man grows rich,
    when the wealth of his house becomes great.

For when he dies, he shall take none of it;
   his wealth shall not follow him down. — ℞

Though in his lifetime he counted himself blessed,
   "They will praise you for doing well for yourself,"
He shall join the circle of his forebears
   who shall never more see light. — ℞ ↓

——— **YEAR I AND II** ———

GOSPEL   Mk 9, 41-50

Alleluia (1 Thes 2, 13)

℞. **Alleluia.** Receive this message not as the words
   of man,
but as truly the word of God. ℞. **Alleluia.**

A Christian must avoid giving scandal to others and be prepared to
sacrifice anything which is a scandal. He will then escape the torments
of hell, symbolized by the fire and worms that existed in the Valley
of Gehenna (a dumping ground near Jerusalem). To have the salt of
the Christian life means to be at peace with one another.

℣. The Lord be with you. ℞. **And also with you.**
✠ A reading from the holy gospel according to Mark.
℞. **Glory to you, Lord.**

Jesus said to his disciples: "Any man who gives you
a drink of water because you belong to Christ will
not, I assure you, go without his reward. But it
would be better if anyone who leads astray one of
these simple believers were to be plunged in the sea
with a great millstone fastened around his neck.

   "If your hand is your difficulty, cut it off! Better
for you to enter life maimed than to keep both hands
and enter Gehenna with its unquenchable fire. If
your foot is your undoing, cut it off! Better for you
to enter life crippled than to be thrown into Gehenna
with both feet. If your eye is your downfall, tear it
out! Better for you to enter the kingdom of God
with one eye than to be thrown with both eyes into
Gehenna, where 'the worm dies not and the fire is
never extinguished.' Everyone will be salted with
fire. Salt is excellent in its place; but if salt becomes

tasteless, how can you season it? Keep salt in your hearts and you will be at peace with one another."
—This is the gospel of the Lord. ℟. **Praise to you, Lord Jesus Christ.**   ➤ No. 15, p. 623

FRIDAY OF THE SEVENTH WEEK IN ORDINARY TIME

——— **YEAR I** ———

READING I   Sir 6, 5-17

A true friend is beyond comparison and should be diligently sought by all. He does not desert us in times of trial or turn against us as false friends do. He is a sturdy shelter, and he stands by us; he fears God just as we do.

A reading from the book of Sirach

A kind mouth multiplies friends,
    and gracious lips prompt friendly greetings.
Let your acquaintances be many,
    but one in a thousand your confidant.
When you gain a friend, first test him,
    and be not too ready to trust him.
For one sort of friend is a friend when it suits him,
    but he will not be with you in time of distress.
Another is a friend who becomes an enemy,
    and tells of the quarrel to your shame.
Another is a friend, a boon companion
    who will not be with you when sorrow comes.
When things go well, he is your other self,
    and lords it over your servants;
But if you are brought low, he turns against you
    and avoids meeting you.
Keep away from your enemies;
    be on your guard with your friends.
A faithful friend is a sturdy shelter;
    he who finds one finds a treasure.
A faithful friend is beyond price,
    no sum can balance his worth.

A faithful friend is a life-saving remedy,
  such as he who fears God finds;
For he who fears God behaves accordingly,
  and his friend will be like himself.
This is the Word of the Lord. ℟. **Thanks be to God.** ♦

Responsorial Psalm   Ps 119, 12. 16. 18. 27. 34. 35
℟. (35) **Guide me, Lord, in the way of your
    commands.**

Blessed are you, O Lord;
  teach me your statutes. — ℟

In your statutes I will delight;
  I will not forget your words. — ℟

Open my eyes, that I may consider
  the wonders of your law. — ℟

Make me understand the way of your precepts,
  and I will meditate on your wondrous deeds. — ℟

Give me discernment, that I may observe your law
  and keep it with all my heart. — ℟

Lead me in the path of your commands,
  for in it I delight. — ℟ ♦

——— **YEAR II** ———

READING I   Jas 5, 9-12

A Christian does not grumble. The judge stands and waits. The prophets
are past models of suffering; they have endured hardship patiently.
Speech should be open and honest.

A reading from the letter of James

Do not grumble against one another, my brothers,
lest you be condemned. See! The judge stands at
the gate. As your models in suffering hardships and
in patience, brothers, take the prophets who spoke
in the name of the Lord. Those who have endured
we call blessed. You have heard of the steadfast-
ness of Job, and have seen what the Lord, who is
compassionate and merciful, did in the end.

Above all else, my brothers, you must not swear

an oath, any oath at all, either "by heaven" or "by earth." Rather, let it be "yes" if you mean yes and "no" if you mean no. In this way you will not incur condemnation.—This is the Word of the Lord. ℟. **Thanks be to God.** ⩔

Responsorial Psalm   Ps 103, 1-2. 3-4. 8-9. 11-12

℟. (8) **The Lord is kind and merciful.**

Bless the Lord, O my soul;
    and all my being, bless his holy name.
Bless the Lord, O my soul,
    and forget not all his benefits. — ℟

He pardons all your iniquities,
    he heals all your ills.
He redeems your life from destruction,
    he crowns you with kindness and compassion.—℟

Merciful and gracious is the Lord,
    slow to anger and abounding in kindness.
He will not always chide,
    nor does he keep his wrath forever. — ℟

For as the heavens are high above the earth,
    so surpassing is his kindness toward those who
      fear him.
As far as the east is from the west,
    so far has he put our transgressions from us.—℟ ⩔

———— **YEAR I AND II** ————

GOSPEL   Mk 10, 1-12

Alleluia (Jn 17, 17)

℟. **Alleluia.** Your word, O Lord, is truth;
make us holy in the truth. ℟. **Alleluia.**

In answer to a test-question Jesus declares that divorce is not part of God's original plan for man and woman in marriage. They are no longer two but one flesh. Therefore, neither one can divorce the other.

℣. The Lord be with you. ℟. **And also with you.**
✠ A reading from the holy gospel according to Mark.
℟. **Glory to you, Lord.**

Jesus came to the district of Judea and across the Jordan. Once more crowds gathered around him and as usual he began to teach them. Then some Pharisees came up and as a test began to ask Jesus whether it was permissible for a husband to divorce his wife. In reply he said, "What command did Moses give you?" They answered, "Moses permitted divorce and the writing of a decree of divorce." But Jesus told them: "He wrote that commandment for you because of your stubbornness. At the beginning of creation God made them male and female; for this reason a man shall leave his father and mother and the two shall become as one. They are no longer two but one flesh. Therefore, let no man separate what God has joined." Back in the house again, the disciples began to question him about this. He told them, "Whoever divorces his wife and marries another commits adultery against her; and the woman who divorces her husband and marries another commits adultery."—This is the gospel of the Lord. ℟. **Praise to you, Lord Jesus Christ.** ➔ No. 15, p. 623

SATURDAY OF THE SEVENTH WEEK IN ORDINARY TIME

—— **YEAR I** ——

READING I Sir 17, 1-15

The Lord created man in his own image and likeness. He made him king of creation and bestowed marvelous blessings and gifts upon him. He made a covenant with him and exhorted him to do good and avoid evil. He continues to watch over him, and all man's actions are clear to him.

A reading from the book of Sirach

The Lord from the earth created man,
    and in his own image he made him.
Limited days of life he gives him
    and makes him return to earth again.

He endows man with a strength of his own,
  and with power over all things else on earth.
He puts the fear of him in all flesh,
  and gives him rule over beasts and birds.
He forms men's tongues and eyes and ears,
  and imparts to them an understanding heart.
With wisdom and knowledge he fills them;
  good and evil he shows them.
He looks with favor upon their hearts,
  and shows them his glorious works,
That they may describe the wonders of his deeds
  and praise his holy name.
He has set before them knowledge,
  a law of life as their inheritance;
An everlasting covenant he has made with them,
  his commandments he has revealed to them.
His majestic glory their eyes beheld,
  his glorious voice their ears heard.
He says to them, "Avoid all evil";
  each of them he gives precepts about his fellow
    men.
Their ways are ever known to him,
  they cannot be hidden from his eyes.
Over every nation he places a ruler,
  but the Lord's own portion is Israel.
All their actions are clear as the sun to him,
  his eyes are ever upon their ways.
This is the Word of the Lord. ℟. **Thanks be to God.** ℣

Responsorial Psalm   Ps 103, 13-14. 15-16. 17-18

℟. (17) **The Lord's kindness is everlasting
    to those who fear him.**

As a father has compassion on his children,
  so the Lord has compassion on those who fear
    him,
For he knows how we are formed;
  he remembers that we are dust. — ℟

Man's days are like those of grass;
  like a flower of the field he blooms;

The wind sweeps over him and he is gone,
  and his place knows him no more. — ℟

But the kindness of the Lord is from eternity
  to eternity toward those who fear him,

And his justice toward children's children
  among those who keep his covenant. — ℟ ✟

——— **YEAR II** ———

READING I Jas 5, 13-20

The Lord will answer the prayers of the just. Those who are sick should call in God's ministers to pray for them. If they are sincere, their sins will be forgiven. To help those in sin will merit a handsome reward.

A reading from the letter of James

If anyone among you is suffering hardship, he must pray. If a person is in good spirits, he should sing a hymn of praise. Is there anyone sick among you? He should ask for the elders of the church. They in turn are to pray over him, anointing him with oil in the Name [of the Lord]. This prayer uttered in faith will reclaim the one who is ill, and the Lord will restore him to health. If he has committed any sins, forgiveness will be his. Hence, declare your sins to one another, and pray for one another, that you may find healing.

The fervent petition of a holy man is powerful indeed. Elijah was only a man like us, yet he prayed earnestly that it would not rain and no rain fell on the land for three years and six months. When he prayed again, the sky burst forth with rain and the land produced its crop.

My brothers, the case may arise among you of someone straying from the truth, and of another bringing him back. Remember this: the person who brings a sinner back from his way will save his soul from death and cancel a multitude of sins.—This is the Word of the Lord. ℟. **Thanks be to God.** ✟

Responsorial Psalm   Ps 141, 1-2. 3. 8

℟. (2) **Let my prayer come like incense before you.**

O Lord, to you I call; hasten to me;
　hearken to my voice when I call upon you.
Let my prayer come like incense before you;
　the lifting up of my hands, like the evening sac-
　　rifice. — ℟

O Lord, set a watch before my mouth,
　a guard at the door of my lips.
For toward you, O God, my Lord, my eyes are turned;
　in you I take refuge; strip me not of life. — ℟ ℣

—————   **YEAR I AND II**   —————

GOSPEL   Mk 10, 13-16

Alleluia (Mt 11, 25)

℟. **Alleluia.** Blessed are you, Father, Lord of heaven
　　and earth;
you have revealed to little ones the mysteries of the
　　kingdom. ℟. **Alleluia.**

Children were the symbol Jesus used for the poor in spirit or the
lowly within the Christian community. Like the apostles, they have
surrendered personal possessions for total dedication to his ministry.
Jesus blesses the children.

℣. The Lord be with you. ℟. **And also with you.**
✠ A reading from the holy gospel according to Mark.
℟. **Glory to you, Lord.**

People were bringing their little children to Jesus to
have him touch them, but the disciples were scolding
them for this. Jesus became indignant when he noticed it and said to them: "Let the children come to
me and do not hinder them. It is to just such as these
that the kingdom of God belongs. I assure you that
whoever does not accept the kingdom of God like a
little child shall not enter into it." Then he embraced
them and blessed them, placing his hands on them.—
This is the gospel of the Lord. ℟. **Praise to you, Lord
Jesus Christ.** ➤ No. 15, p. 623

MONDAY OF THE EIGHTH WEEK
IN ORDINARY TIME

———— YEAR I ————

READING I   Sir 17, 19-27

The mercy of the Lord is great and God forgives all who return to him.
His mercy far surpasses that of man. Man must hate sin and offer
living praise to God while he has the opportunity to do so on earth.

A reading from the book of Sirach

But to the penitent he provides a way back,
  he encourages those who are losing hope!
Return to the Lord and give up sin,
  pray to him and make your offenses few.
Turn again to the Most High and away from sin,
  hate intensely what he loathes;
Who in the nether world can glorify the Most High
  in place of the living who offer their praise?
No more can the dead give praise than those who
    have never lived;
  they glorify the Lord who are alive and well.
How great the mercy of the Lord,
  his forgiveness of those who return to him!
The like cannot be found in men,
  for not immortal is any son of man.
Is anything brighter than the sun? Yet it can be
    eclipsed.
  How obscure then the thoughts of flesh and blood!
God watches over the hosts of highest heaven,
  while all men are dust and ashes.
This is the Word of the Lord. ℟. **Thanks be to God.** ℣

Responsorial Psalm   Ps 32, 1-2. 5. 6. 7

℟. (11) **Let the just exult and rejoice in the Lord.**

Happy is he whose fault is taken away,
  whose sin is covered.
Happy the man to whom the Lord imputes not guilt,
  in whose spirit there is no guile. — ℟

Then I acknowledged my sin to you,
   my guilt I covered not.
I said, "I confess my faults to the Lord."
   and you took away the guilt of my sin. — ℟
For this shall every faithful man pray to you
   in time of stress.
Though deep waters overflow,
   they shall not reach him. — ℟

You are my shelter; from distress you will preserve
   me;
   with glad cries of freedom you will ring me
     round. — ℟ ℣

———— **YEAR II** ————

READING I   1 Pt 1, 3-9

Through his resurrection Jesus has given to man a new hope, a new
birth. This is cause for rejoicing. It is by faith that men believe in
him to achieve salvation.

   A reading from the first letter of Peter
Praised be the God and Father of our Lord
   Jesus Christ,
   he who in his great mercy gave us new birth;
   a birth unto hope which draws its life
from the resurrection of Jesus Christ from the
   dead;
   a birth to an imperishable inheritance
incapable of fading or defilement,
   which is kept in heaven for you
who are guarded with God's power through faith;
   a birth to a salvation which stands ready
   to be revealed in the last days.
There is cause for rejoicing here. You may for a
time have to suffer the distress of many trials; but
this is so that your faith, which is more precious
than the passing splendor of fire-tried gold, may by
its genuineness lead to praise, glory and honor when
Jesus Christ appears. Although you have never seen

him, you love him, and without seeing him, you now
believe in him and rejoice with inexpressible joy
touched with glory because you are achieving faith's
goal, your salvation.—This is the Word of the Lord.
℟. **Thanks be to God.** ℣

Responsorial Psalm   Ps 111, 1-2. 5-6. 9. 10
℟. (5) **The Lord will remember his covenant for ever.**

I will give thanks to the Lord with all my heart
    in the company and assembly of the just.
Great are the works of the Lord,
    exquisite in all their delights. — ℟

He has given food to those who fear him;
    he will forever be mindful of his covenant.
He has made known to his people the power of his
      works,
    giving them the inheritance of the nations. — ℟

He has sent deliverance to his people;
    he has ratified his covenant forever;
    holy and awesome is his name.
His praise endures forever. — ℟ ℣

℟. Or: **Alleluia.** ℣

—— **YEAR I AND II** ——

GOSPEL   Mk 10, 17-27
Alleluia (2 Cor 8, 9)

℟. **Alleluia.** Jesus Christ was rich but he became
    poor,
to make you rich out of his poverty. ℟. **Alleluia.**

Jesus' contemporaries consider wealth a sign of divine favor. When
he denies this and shows that wealth can obstruct the spiritual percep-
tion of his message, the disciples conclude that virtually no one can
be saved. Jesus replies that the rich as well as the poor are dependent
on God for their salvation.

℣. The Lord be with you. ℟. **And also with you.**
✠ A reading from the holy gospel according to Mark.
℟. **Glory to you, Lord.**

As Jesus was setting out on a journey a man came running up, knelt down before him and asked, "Good Teacher, what must I do to share in everlasting life?" Jesus answered, "Why do you call me good? No one is good but God alone. You know the commandments:

'You shall not kill;
You shall not commit adultery;
You shall not steal;
You shall not bear false witness;
You shall not defraud;
Honor your father and your mother.' "

He replied, "Teacher, I have kept all these since my childhood." Then Jesus looked at him with love and told him, "There is one thing more you must do. Go and sell what you have and give to the poor; you will then have treasure in heaven. After that, come and follow me." At these words the man's face fell. He went away sad, for he had many possessions. Jesus looked around and said to his disciples, "How hard it is for the rich to enter the kingdom of God!" The disciples could only marvel at his words. So Jesus repeated what he had said: "My sons, how hard it is to enter the kingdom of God! It is easier for a camel to pass through a needle's eye than for a rich man to enter the kingdom of God."

They were completely overwhelmed at this, and exclaimed to one another, "Then who can be saved?" Jesus fixed his gaze on them and said, "For man it is impossible but not for God. With God all things are possible."—This is the gospel of the Lord. ℟. **Praise to you, Lord Jesus Christ.**   ➤ No. 15, p. 623

TUESDAY OF THE EIGHTH WEEK
IN ORDINARY TIME

—— YEAR I ——

READING I   Sir 35, 1-12

God is a God of justice, who knows no favorites. He always repays man for his good works, and he does so to the seventh degree, that is, to the perfect degree. Hence, man should observe God's commandments and present a perfect sacrifice to God.

A reading from the book of Sirach

To keep the law is a great oblation,
    and he who observes the commandments sacrifices
        a peace offering.
In works of charity one offers fine flour,
    and when he gives alms he presents his sacrifice
        of praise.
To refrain from evil pleases the Lord,
    and to avoid injustice is an atonement.
Appear not before the Lord empty-handed,
    for all that you offer is in fulfillment of the
        precepts.
The just man's offering enriches the altar
    and rises as a sweet odor before the Most High.
The just man's sacrifice is most pleasing,
    nor will it ever be forgotten.
In generous spirit pay homage to the Lord,
    be not sparing of freewill gifts.
With each contribution show a cheerful countenance,
    and pay your tithes in a spirit of joy.
Give to the Most High as he has given to you,
    generously, according to your means.
For the Lord is one who always repays,
    and he will give back to you sevenfold.
But offer no bribes, these he does not accept!
    Trust not in sacrifice of the fruits of extortion,
For he is a God of justice,
    who knows no favorites.
This is the Word of the Lord. ℟. **Thanks be to God.** ℣

Responsorial Psalm   Ps 50, 5. 6. 7-8. 14, 23

℟. (23) **To the upright I will show the saving power of God.**

"Gather my faithful ones before me,
  those who have made a covenant with me by
    sacrifice."
And the heavens proclaim his justice;
  for God himself is the judge. — ℟

"Hear, my people, and I will speak;
  Israel, I will testify against you;
  God, your God, am I.
Not for your sacrifices do I rebuke you,
  for your holocausts are before me always. — ℟

"Offer to God praise as your sacrifice
  and fulfill your vows to the Most High.
He that offers praise as a sacrifice glorifies me;
  and to him that goes the right way I will show
    the salvation of God." — ℟ ⋁

——— **YEAR II** ———

READING I   1 Pt 1, 10-16

The prophets were witnesses to the future coming of Christ. They
directed their lives to foreshadowing Jesus. Peter directs men to live
soberly, hoping in the fulfillment of the Gospel. Scripture says, "Be
holy, for I am holy."

A reading from the first letter of Peter

This is the salvation which the prophets carefully
searched out and examined. They prophesied the divine favor that was destined to be yours. They in-
vestigated the times and the circumstances which
the Spirit of Christ within them was pointing to, for
he predicted the sufferings destined for Christ and
the glories that would follow. They knew by revelation that they were providing, not for themselves but
for you, what has now been proclaimed to you by
those who preach the gospel to you, in the power of
the Holy Spirit sent from heaven. Into these matters
angels long to search.

So "gird the loins" of your understanding; live soberly; set all your hope on the gift to be conferred on you when Jesus Christ appears. As obedient sons, do not yield to the desires that once shaped you in your ignorance. Rather, become holy yourselves in every aspect of your conduct, after the likeness of the holy One who called you; remember, Scripture says, "Be holy, for I am holy."—This is the Word of the Lord. ℟. **Thanks be to God.** ℣

Responsorial Psalm   Ps 98, 1. 2-3. 3-4
℟. (2) **The Lord has made known his salvation.**

Sing to the Lord a new song,
    for he has done wondrous deeds;
His right hand has won victory for him,
    his holy arm. — ℟

The Lord has made his salvation known:
    in the sight of the nations he has revealed his
        justice.
He has remembered his kindness and his faithfulness
    toward the house of Israel. — ℟

All the ends of the earth have seen
    the salvation by our God.
Sing joyfully to the Lord, all you lands;
    break into song; sing praise. — ℟ ℣

——— **YEAR I AND II** ———

GOSPEL   Mk 10, 28-31
Alleluia (Mt 11, 25)
℟. **Alleluia.** Blessed are you, Father, Lord of heaven
    and earth;
you have revealed to little ones the mysteries of the
    kingdom. ℟. **Alleluia.**

Peter expresses the concern of all who follow Christ faithfully and closely in this life in spite of every difficulty. Jesus promises that voluntary renunciation of self, home, property, and relatives for his sake will be rewarded by God in this life and the next.

℣. The Lord be with you. ℟. **And also with you.**
✠ A reading from the holy gospel according to Mark.
℟. **Glory to you, Lord.**

Peter was moved to say to Jesus: "We have put aside everything to follow you!" Jesus answered: "I give you my word, there is no one who has given up home, brothers or sisters, mother or father, children or property, for me and for the gospel who will not receive in this present age a hundred times as many homes, brothers and sisters, mothers, children and property —and persecution besides—and in the age to come, everlasting life. Many who are first shall come last, and the last shall come first." —This is the gospel of the Lord. ℟. **Praise to you, Lord Jesus Christ.**

➤ No. 15, p. 623

WEDNESDAY OF THE EIGHTH WEEK IN ORDINARY TIME

YEAR I

READING I   Sir 36, 1. 5-6. 10-17

In the name of the people Sirach asks God to give new signs and work new wonders on their behalf. Thus the nations will know, as the people of God do, that there is no other God. They ask him to hear the prayers of his servants and so show that he is the eternal God.

A reading from the book of Sirach

Come to our aid, O God of the universe,
  and put all the nations in dread of you!
Thus they will know, as we know,
  that there is no God but you.
Give new signs and work new wonders.
Gather all the tribes of Jacob,
  that they may inherit the land as of old,
Show mercy to the people called by your name;
  Israel, whom you named your first-born.
Take pity on your holy city,
  Jerusalem, your dwelling place.

Fill Zion with your majesty,
　your temple with your glory.
Give evidence of your deeds of old;
　fulfill the prophecies spoken in your name,
Reward those who have hoped in you,
　and let your prophets be proved true.
Hear the prayer of your servants,
　for you are ever gracious to your people;
Thus it will be known to the very ends of the earth
　that you are the eternal God.
This is the Word of the Lord. ℟. **Thanks be to God.** ✟

Responsorial Psalm　　　　　　Ps 79, 8. 9. 11. 13

℟. (Sir 36, 16) **Show us, O Lord, the light of your
　kindness.**

Remember not against us the iniquities of the past;
　may your compassion quickly come to us,
　　for we are brought very low. — ℟

Help us, O God our savior,
　because of the glory of your name;
Deliver us and pardon our sins
　for your name's sake. — ℟

Let the prisoners' sighing come before you;
　with your great power free those doomed to death.
Then we, your people and the sheep of your pasture,
　will give thanks to you forever;
　　through all generations we will declare your
　　　praise. — ℟ ✟

——— **YEAR II** ———

READING I　　　　　　　　　　　1 Pt 1, 18-25

The faithful have been delivered not by gold or silver but by the
blood of Jesus Christ. Through him they are believers. By obedience
to him, they become purified. In this way men learn to love one
another.

　　　A reading from the first letter of Peter

Realize that you were delivered from the futile way
of life your fathers handed on to you, not by any

diminishable sum of silver or gold but by Christ's blood beyond all price: the blood of a spotless, unblemished lamb chosen before the world's foundation and revealed for your sake in these last days. It is through him that you are believers in God, the God who raised him from the dead and gave him glory. Your faith and hope, then, are centered in God.

By obedience to the truth you have purified yourselves for a genuine love of your brothers; therefore, love one another constantly from the heart. Your rebirth has come, not from a destructible but from an indestructible seed, through the living and enduring word of God. For,

"All mankind is grass,
and the glory of men is like the flower of the field.
The grass withers, the flower wilts,
but the word of the Lord endures forever."
Now this "word" is the gospel which was preached to you.—This is the Word of the Lord. ℟. **Thanks be to God.** ℣

Responsorial Psalm Ps 147, 12-13. 14-15. 19-20

℟. (12) **Praise the Lord, Jerusalem.**

Glorify the Lord, O Jerusalem;
praise your God, O Zion.
For he has strengthened the bars of your gates;
he has blessed your children within you. — ℟

He has granted peace in your borders;
with the best of wheat he fills you.
He sends forth his command to the earth;
swiftly runs his word! — ℟

He has proclaimed his word to Jacob,
his statutes and his ordinances to Israel.
He has not done thus for any other nation;
his ordinances he has not made known to them.
Alleluia. — ℟ ℣

℟. Or: **Alleluia.** ℣

───── **YEAR I AND II** ─────

GOSPEL Mk 10, 32-45

Alleluia (Jn 15, 15)

℟. **Alleluia.** I call you my friends, says the Lord, for I have made known to you all that the Father has told me. ℟. **Alleluia.**

Jesus predicts his passion once again and then emphasizes that whatever authority the disciples (and, of course, their successors) exercise is to be viewed, like the authority of Jesus, in terms of service to others rather than as a sign of personal eminence.

℣. The Lord be with you. ℟. **And also with you.**
✠ A reading from the holy gospel according to Mark.
℟. **Glory to you, Lord.**

The disciples were on the road going up to Jerusalem, with Jesus walking in the lead. Their mood was one of wonderment, while that of those who followed was fear. Taking the Twelve aside once more, he began to tell them what was going to happen to him. "We are on our way up to Jerusalem, where the Son of Man will be handed over to the chief priests and the scribes. They will condemn him to death and hand him over to the Gentiles, who will mock him and spit at him, flog him, and finally kill him. But three days later he will rise."

Zebedee's sons, James and John, approached him. "Teacher," they said, "we want you to grant our request." "What is it?" he asked. They replied, "See to it that we sit, one at your right and the other at your left, when you come into your glory." Jesus told them, "You do not know what you are asking. Can you drink the cup I shall drink or be baptized in the same bath of pain as I?" "We can," they told him. Jesus said in response, "From the cup I drink of you shall drink; the bath I am immersed in you shall share. But sitting at my right or my left is not mine to give; that is for those for whom it has been reserved." The other ten, on hearing this, became indignant at James and John. Jesus called them together and said to them: "You know how among the Gentiles those who seem to exercise authority lord it over them; their great ones make their importance felt. It cannot be like that with you. Anyone among you who aspires to greatness must serve the rest; whoever wants to rank first among you must serve the needs of all. The Son of Man has not come to be served but to serve—to give his life in ransom for the many."—This is the gospel of the Lord. ℟. **Praise to you, Lord Jesus Christ.**   ➤ No. 15, p. 623

THURSDAY OF THE EIGHTH WEEK
IN ORDINARY TIME

———   **YEAR I**   ———

READING I   Sir 42, 15-25

God is great and his glory fills all his works. His wisdom is almighty and he is from all eternity one and the same. His works are beautiful, and his creatures are all good, differing from one another, and filled with splendor.

A reading from the book of Sirach

Now will I recall God's works;
    what I have seen, I will describe.
At God's word were his works brought into being;
    they do his will as he has ordained for them.
As the rising sun is clear to all,
    so the glory of the Lord fills all his works;
Yet even God's holy ones must fail
    in recounting the wonders of the Lord,
Though God has given these, his hosts, the strength
    to stand firm before his glory.
He plumbs the depths and penetrates the heart;
    their innermost being he understands.
The Most High possesses all knowledge,
    and sees from of old the things that are to come:

He makes known the past and the future,
and reveals the deepest secrets.
No understanding does he lack;
no single thing escapes him.
Perennial is his almighty wisdom;
he is from all eternity one and the same,
With nothing added, nothing taken away;
no need of a counselor for him!
How beautiful are all his works!
even to the spark and the fleeting vision!
The universe lives and abides forever;
to meet each need, each creature is preserved.
All of them differ, one from another,
yet none of them has he made in vain,
For each in turn, as it comes, is good;
can one ever see enough of their splendor?
This is the Word of the Lord. ℟. **Thanks be to God.** ℣

Responsorial Psalm   Ps 33, 2-3. 4-5. 6-7. 8-9

℟. (6) **By the word of the Lord the heavens were made.**

Give thanks to the Lord on the harp;
with the ten-stringed lyre chant his praises.
Sing to him a new song;
pluck the strings skillfully, with shouts of
gladness. — ℟

For upright is the word of the Lord,
and all his works are trustworthy.
He loves justice and right;
of the kindness of the Lord the earth is full. — ℟

By the word of the Lord the heavens were made;
by the breath of his mouth all their host.
He gathers the waters of the sea as in a flask;
in cellars he confines the deep. — ℟

Let all the earth fear the Lord;
let all who dwell in the world revere him.
For he spoke, and it was made;
he commanded, and it stood forth. — ℟ ℣

———— **YEAR II** ————

READING I   1 Pt 2, 2-5. 9-12

Come to Jesus. He is the cornerstone and we are living stones. The faithful are a chosen people, a consecrated race. God delivers them to a marvelous light. They are not to be disturbed by slanderous criticism. By good works they give glory to God.

A reading from the first letter of Peter

Be as eager for milk as newborn babies—pure milk of the spirit to make you grow unto salvation, now that "you have tasted that the Lord is good."

Come to him, a living stone, rejected by men but approved, nonetheless, and precious in God's eyes. You too are living stones, built as an edifice of spirit, into a holy priesthood, offering spiritual sacrifices acceptable to God through Jesus Christ.

You, however, are "a chosen race, a royal priesthood, a consecrated nation, a people he claims for his own to proclaim the glorious works" of the One who called you from darkness into his marvelous light. Once you were "no people," but now you are God's people; once there was "no mercy for you," but now you have found mercy.

Beloved, you are strangers and in exile; hence I urge you not to indulge your carnal desires. By their nature they wage war on the soul. Though the pagans may slander you as troublemakers, conduct yourselves blamelessly among them. By observing your good works they may give glory to God on the day of visitation.—This is the Word of the Lord. ℟. **Thanks be to God.** ↓

Responsorial Psalm   Ps 100, 2. 3. 4. 5

℟. (2) **Come with joy into the presence of the Lord.**
Sing joyfully to the Lord, all you lands;
    serve the Lord with gladness;
    come before him with joyful song. — ℟
Know that the Lord is God;
    he made us, his we are;

his people, the flock he tends. — ℟

Enter his gates with thanksgiving,
  his courts with praise;
Give thanks to him;
  bless his name. — ℟

The Lord is good:
  his kindness endures forever,
  and his faithfulness, to all generations. — ℟ ℣

——— **YEAR I AND II** ———

GOSPEL Mk 10, 46-52

Alleluia (Jn 8, 12)

℟. **Alleluia.** I am the light of the world, says the
  Lord;
the man who follows me will have the light of life.
  ℟. **Alleluia.**

The blind man, unaffected by what he heard of Jesus' lowly condition,
addresses him with the messianic title, "Son of David." He asks to
be cured and his faith is rewarded.

℣. The Lord be wth you. ℟. **And also with you.**
✠ A reading from the holy gospel according to Mark.
℟. **Glory to you, Lord.**

As Jesus was leaving Jericho with his disciples and
a sizable crowd, there was a blind beggar Bartimaeus
("son of Timaeus") sitting by the roadside. On hearing that it was Jesus of Nazareth, he began to call
out, "Jesus, Son of David, have pity on me!" Many
people were scolding him to make him keep quiet,
but he shouted all the louder, "Son of David, have
pity on me!" Then Jesus stopped and said, "Call him
over." So they called the blind man over, telling him
as they did so, "You have nothing whatever to fear
from him! Get up! He is calling you!" He threw aside
his cloak, jumped up and came to Jesus. Jesus asked
him, "What do you want me to do for you?" "Rabboni," the blind man said, "I want to see." Jesus said

in reply, "Be on your way! Your faith has healed you." Immediately he received his sight and started to follow him up the road.—This is the gospel of the Lord. ℟. **Praise to you, Lord Jesus Christ.**

➤ No. 15, p. 623

FRIDAY OF THE EIGHTH WEEK
IN ORDINARY TIME

———   **YEAR I**   ———

READING I   Sir 44, 1. 9-13

The memory of good deeds and virtue is never blotted out, just as the merciful deeds of ancestors insured that their name would live on for generations. The glory of those who are faithful to God's covenant will endure forever.

A reading from the book of Sirach

Now will I praise those godly men,
    our ancestors, each in his own time.
But of others there is no memory,
    for when they ceased, they ceased.
And they are as though they had not lived,
    they and their children after them.
Yet these also were godly men
    whose virtues have not been forgotten;
Their wealth remains in their families,
    their heritage with their descendants;
Through God's covenant with them their family en-
        dures,
    their posterity, for their sake.
And for all time their progeny will endure,
    their glory will never be blotted out.
This is the Word of the Lord, ℟. **Thanks be to God.** ℣

Responsorial Psalm   Ps 149, 1-2. 3-4. 5-6. 9

℟. (4) **The Lord takes delight in his people.**

Sing to the Lord a new song
    of praise in the assembly of the faithful.
Let Israel be glad in their maker,
    let the children of Zion rejoice in their king. — ℟

Let them praise his name in the festive dance,
   let them sing praise to him with timbrel and harp.
For the Lord loves his people,
   and he adorns the lowly with victory. — ℟

Let the faithful exult in glory;
   let them sing for joy upon their couches;
   let the high praises of God be in their throats.
This is the glory of all his faithful. Alleluia. — ℟ ✣

————— **YEAR II** —————

READING I   1 Pt 4, 7-13

Love must be constant. It covers up for many sins. Followers of Christ
should not complain. They are to deliver the Gospel message and serve
one another. This gives glory to God.

A reading from the first letter of Peter

The consummation of all is close at hand. Therefore
do not be perturbed; remain calm so that you will
be able to pray. Above all, let your love for one
another be constant, for love covers a multitude of
sins. Be mutually hospitable without complaining.
As generous distributors of God's manifold grace,
put your gifts at the service of one another, each
in the measure he has received. The one who speaks
is to deliver God's message. The one who serves is
to do it with the strength provided by God. Thus,
in all of you God is to be glorified through Jesus
Christ: to him be glory and dominion throughout
the ages. Amen.
   Do not be surprised, beloved, that a trial by fire
is occurring in your midst. It is a test for you, but
it should not catch you off guard. Rejoice instead,
insofar as you share Christ's sufferings. When his
glory is revealed, you will rejoice exultantly.—This
is the Word of the Lord. ℟. **Thanks be to God.** ✣

Responsorial Psalm   Ps 96, 10. 11-12. 13
℟. (13) **The Lord comes to judge the earth.**

Say among the nations: The Lord is king.
He has made the world firm, not to be moved;
    he governs the peoples with equity. — ℟

Let the heavens be glad and the earth rejoice;
    let the sea and what fills it resound;
    let the plains be joyful and all that is in them! — ℟

They shall exult before the Lord, for he comes;
    for he comes to rule the earth.
He shall rule the world with justice
    and the people with his constancy. — ℟ ⱴ

——— **YEAR I AND II** ———

GOSPEL   Mk 11, 11-26

Alleluia (Jn 15, 16)

℟. **Alleluia.** I have chosen you from the world,
    says the Lord,
to go and bear fruit that will last. ℟. **Alleluia.**

Jesus curses a barren fig tree symbolizing his judgment on barren
Israel for failing to receive his teaching. Later he drives the money-
changers from the temple. Jesus insists that his house is a house of
prayer. Whoever is ready to believe will receive whatever he asks
for in prayer. Men must always forgive others and put their trust
completely in God.

℣. The Lord be with you. ℟. **And also with you.**
✠ A reading from the holy gospel according to Mark.
℟. **Glory to you, Lord.**

Jesus entered Jerusalem (amid acclamations from
the crowd) and went into the temple precincts. He
inspected everything there, but since it was already
late in the afternoon, he went out to Bethany accompanied by the Twelve.

    The next day when they were leaving Bethany
he felt hungry. Observing a fig tree some distance
off, covered with foliage, he went over to see if he
could find anything on it. When he reached it he
found nothing but leaves; it was not the time for figs.
Then addressing it he said, "Never again shall anyone
eat of your fruit!" His disciples heard all this.

When they reached Jerusalem he entered the temple precincts and began to drive out those who were engaged in buying and selling. He overturned the money-changers' tables and the stalls of the men selling doves; moreover, he would not permit anyone to carry things through the temple area.

Then he began to teach them: "Does not Scripture have it,

> 'My house shall be called a house of prayer for all peoples'?

but you have turned it into a den of thieves." The chief priests and the scribes heard of this and began to look for a way to destroy him. They were at the same time afraid of him because the whole crowd was under the spell of his teaching. When evening drew on, Jesus and his disciples went out of the city. Early next morning, as they were walking along, they saw the fig tree withered to its roots. Peter remembered and said to him, "Rabbi, look! The fig tree you cursed has withered up." In reply Jesus told them: "Put your trust in God. I solemnly assure you, whoever says to this mountain, 'Be lifted up and thrown into the sea,' and has no inner doubts but believes that what he says will happen, shall have it done for him. I give you my word, if you are ready to believe that you will receive whatever you ask for in prayer, it shall be done for you. When you stand to pray, forgive anyone against whom you have a grievance so that your heavenly Father may in turn forgive you your faults."—This is the gospel of the Lord. ℟. **Praise to you, Lord Jesus Christ.**

➤ No. 15, p. 623

SATURDAY OF THE EIGHTH WEEK IN ORDINARY TIME

—— YEAR I ——

READING I Sir 51, 12-20

True wisdom is a gift of God. Among other things she enables men to do good and avoid evil. They should ask God for her and thank him on receiving her, for she holds the key to eternal life.

A reading from the book of Sirach

I thank him and I praise him;
  I bless the name of the Lord.
When I was young and innocent,
  I sought wisdom.
She came to me in her beauty,
  and until the end I will cultivate her.
As the blossoms yielded to ripening grapes,
  the heart's joy,
My feet kept to the level path
  because from earliest youth I was familiar with
    her.
In the short time I paid heed,
  I met with great instruction.
Since in this way I have profited,
  I will give my teacher grateful praise.
I became resolutely devoted to her—
  the good I persistently strove for.
I burned with desire for her,
  never turning back.
I became preoccupied with her,
  never weary of extolling her.
My hand opened her gate
  and I came to know her secrets.
For her I purified even the soles of my feet;
  in cleanness I attained to her.
At first acquaintance with her, I gained under-
    standing
  such that I will never forsake her.
This is the Word of the Lord. ℟ **Thanks be to God.** ℣

Responsorial Psalm Ps 19, 8. 9. 10. 11

℟. (9) **The precepts of the Lord give joy to the heart.**

The law of the Lord is perfect,
  refreshing the soul;
The decree of the Lord is trustworthy,
  giving wisdom to the simple. — ℟

The precepts of the Lord are right,
  rejoicing the heart;
The command of the Lord is clear,
  enlightening the eye. — ℟

The fear of the Lord is pure,
  enduring forever;
The ordinances of the Lord are true,
  all of them just. — ℟

They are more precious than gold,
  than a heap of purest gold;
Sweeter also than syrup
  or honey from the comb. — ℟ ↓

———— **YEAR II** ————

READING I Jude 17. 20-25

Remember the teaching of the apostles. Persevere in the love of God.
Correct those who are confused. God can protect all of his people.
Glory to be to him forever.

A reading from the letter of Jude

Remember, beloved, the prophetic words of the apostles of our Lord Jesus Christ. Praying in the Holy Spirit, persevere in God's love, and welcome the mercy of our Lord Jesus Christ which leads to life eternal. Correct those who are confused; the others you must rescue, snatching them from the fire. Even with those you pity, be on your guard; abhor so much as their flesh-stained clothing.

There is One who can protect you from a fall and make you stand unblemished and exultant in the presence of his glory. Glory be to this only God our

Savior, through Jesus Christ our Lord. Majesty, too, be his, might and power from ages past, now and for ages to come. Amen.—This is the Word of the Lord. ℞. **Thanks be to God.** ⍒

Responsorial Psalm   Ps 63, 2. 3-4. 5-6

℞. (2) **My soul is thirsting for you, O Lord my God.**

O God, you are my God whom I seek;
　for you my flesh pines and my soul thirsts
　like the earth, parched, lifeless and without
　　water. — ℞

Thus have I gazed toward you in the sanctuary
　to see your power and your glory,
For your kindness is a greater good than life;
　my lips shall glorify you. — ℞

Thus will I bless you while I live;
　lifting up my hands, I will call upon your name.
As with the riches of a banquet shall my soul be
　satisfied,
　and with exultant lips my mouth shall praise
　　you. — ℞ ⍒

————— **YEAR I AND II** —————

GOSPEL   Mk 11, 27-33

Alleluia (Col 3, 16. 17)

℞. **Alleluia.** Give thanks to God our Father through
　　Jesus Christ our Lord,
and may the fullness of his message live within you.

Jesus shows by his verbal jousting with his opponents that he needs no "references." His authority imposes itself from within on all those whose heart is free of intrigue and self-service. But his message, like that of the Baptizer and the prophets, is opposed by the leaders who are jealous of their position.

℣. The Lord be with you. ℞. **And also with you.**
✠ A reading from the holy gospel according to Mark.
℞. **Glory to you, Lord.**

Jesus and his disciples returned once more to Jerusalem. As he was walking in the temple precincts the chief priests, the scribes, and the elders approached him and said to him, "On what authority are you doing these things? Who has given you the power to do them?" Jesus said to them, "I will ask you a question. If you give me an answer, I will tell you on what authority I do the things I do. Tell me, was John's baptism of divine origin or merely from men?" They thought to themselves, "If we say 'divine,' he will ask, 'Then why did you not put faith in it?' But can we say, 'merely human'?" (They had reason to fear the people, who all regarded John as a true prophet.) So their answer to Jesus was, "We do not know." In turn, Jesus said to them, "Then neither will I tell you on what authority I do the things I do."—This is the gospel of the Lord. ℟. **Praise to you, Lord Jesus Christ.** ➤ No. 15, p. 623

MONDAY OF THE NINTH WEEK IN ORDINARY TIME

——— **YEAR I** ———

READING I   Tb 1, 1. 2; 2, 1-9

The story of Tobit takes place during the exile in Babylon. Tobit and his family remain faithful to God in unfriendly surroundings and are outstanding for brotherly love. He shows his loyalty and trust regardless of criticism.

The beginning of the book of Tobit

This book tells the story of Tobit of the tribe of Naphtali, who during the reign of Shalmaneser, king of Assyria, was taken captive from Thisbe, which is south of Kedesh Naphtali in upper Galilee, above and to west of Asser, north of Phogor.

On our festival of Pentecost, the feast of Weeks, a fine dinner was prepared for me, and I reclined to eat. The table was set for me, and when many different dishes were placed before me, I said to my son Tobiah: "My son, go out and try to find a poor man from among our kinsmen exiled here in Nineveh. If he is a sincere worshiper of God, bring him back with you, so that he can share this meal with me. Indeed, son, I shall wait for you to come back."

Tobiah went out to look for some poor kinsman of ours. When he returned he exclaimed, "Father!" I said to him, "What is it, son?" He answered, Father, one of our people has been murdered! His body lies in the market place where he was just strangled!" I sprang to my feet, leaving the dinner untouched; and I carried the dead man from the street and put him in one of the rooms, so that I might bury him after sunset. Returning to my own quarters, I washed myself and ate my food in sorrow. I was reminded of the oracle pronounced by the prophet Amos against Bethel:
"Your festival shall be turned into mourning,
    and all your songs into lamentation."
And I wept. Then at sunset I went out, dug a grave, and buried him.

The neighbors mocked me, saying to one another: "Will this man never learn! Once before he was hunted down for execution because of this very thing; yet now that he has escaped, here he is again burying the dead!"

The same night I bathed, and went to sleep next to the wall of my courtyard. Because of the heat I left my face uncovered.—This is the Word of the Lord. ℟. **Thanks be to God.** ℣

Responsorial Psalm   Ps 112, 1-2. 3-4. 5-6
℟. (1) **Happy the man who fears the Lord**.
Happy the man who fears the Lord,
    who greatly delights in his commands.
His posterity shall be mighty upon the earth;
    the upright generation shall be blessed. — ℟
Wealth and riches shall be in his house;
    his generosity shall endure forever.

The Lord dawns through the darkness, a light for the
upright;
  he is gracious and merciful and just. — ℟

Well for the man who is gracious and lends,
  who conducts his affairs with justice;
He shall never be moved;
  the just man shall be in everlasting remem-
    brance. — ℟ ⅴ

℟. Or: **Alleluia.** ⅴ

────── **YEAR II** ──────

READING I   2 Pt 1, 2-7

God has given his people the means and grace for a holy life. In this
way they share in his divine nature. This is reason enough to live a
life of self-control leading to piety and care for one another.

      A reading from the second letter of Peter

May grace be yours and peace in abundance through
your knowledge of God and of Jesus, our Lord.

    That divine power of his has freely bestowed on
us everything necessary for a life of genuine piety
through knowledge of him who called us by his own
glory and power. By virtue of them he has bestowed
on us the great and precious things he promised,
so that through these you who have fled a world
corrupted by lust might become sharers of the divine nature. This is reason enough for you to make
every effort to undergird your virtue with faith,
your discernment with virtue, and your self-control
with discernment. This self-control, in turn, should
lead to perseverance, and perseverance to piety, and
piety to care for your brother, and care for your
brother, to love.—This is the Word of the Lord.
℟. **Thanks be to God.** ⅴ

Responsorial Psalm   Ps 91, 1-2. 14-15. 15-16

℟. (2) **In you, my God, I place my trust.**

You who dwell in the shelter of the Most High,

who abide in the shadow of the Almighty,
Say to the Lord, "My refuge and my fortress,
    my God, in whom I trust." — ℟
Because he clings to me, I will deliver him;
    I will set him on high because he acknowledges
        my name.
He shall call upon me, and I will answer him;
    I will be with him in distress. — ℟

I will deliver him and glorify him;
    with length of days I will gratify him
    and will show him my salvation. — ℟ ℣

——— YEAR I AND II ———

GOSPEL   Mk 12, 1-12

Alleluia (Rv 1, 5)
℟. **Alleluia.** Jesus Christ, you are the faithful wit-
    ness, firstborn from the dead;
you have loved us and washed away our sins in your
    blood. ℟. **Alleluia.**

In the parable, the servants who are killed represent the prophets,
and the son who is slain represents Jesus himself. However, his
death will become his victory. He will rise again as Lord, the keystone
of the Church, as foretold.

℣. The Lord be with you. ℟. **And also with you.**
✠ A reading from the holy gospel according to Mark.
℟. **Glory to you, Lord.**

Jesus began to address the chief priests, the scribes
and the elders once more in parables: "A man planted a vineyard, put a hedge around it, dug out a vat,
and erected a tower. Then he leased it to tenant
farmers and went on a journey. In due time he dispatched a man in his service to the tenants to obtain
from them his share of produce from the vineyard.
But they seized him, beat him, and sent him off
empty-handed. The second time he sent them another servant; him too they beat over the head and
treated shamefully. He sent yet another and they

killed him. So too with many others: some they
beat; some they killed. He still had one to send—
the son whom he loved. He sent him to them as a
last resort, thinking, 'They will have to respect my
son.' But those tenants said to one another, 'Here
is the one who will inherit everything. Come, let us
kill him, and the inheritance will be ours.' Then they
seized and killed him and dragged him outside the
vineyard. What do you suppose the owner of the
vineyard will do? He will come and destroy those
tenants and turn his vineyard over to others. Are
you not familiar with this passage of Scripture:

'The stone rejected by the builders
    has become the keystone of the structure.
It was the Lord who did it
    and we find it marvelous to behold'?''

They wanted to arrest him at this, yet they had
reason to fear the crowd. (They knew well enough
that he meant the parable for them.) Finally they
left him and went off.—This is the gospel of the
Lord. ℞. **Praise to you, Lord Jesus Christ.**

➤ No. 15, p. 623

TUESDAY OF THE NINTH WEEK
IN ORDINARY TIME

——— YEAR I ———

READING I   Tb 2, 9-14

In spite of exile, blindness, and his own misjudgments, Tobit still hopes
in God. God's watchful care will bring a solution to Tobit's problems.
He has trust in God.

A reading from the book of Tobit

One night I (Tobit) [fatigued from burying the dead]
went to sleep next to the wall of my courtyard.
Because of the heat I left my face uncovered. I did
not know there were birds perched on the wall above

me, till their warm droppings settled in my eyes, causing cataracts. I went to see some doctors for a cure, but the more they anointed my eyes with various salves, the worse the cataracts became, until I could see no more. For four years I was deprived of eyesight, and all my kinsmen were grieved at my condition. Ahiqar, however, took care of me for two years, until he left for Elymais.

At that time my wife Anna worked for hire at weaving cloth, the kind of work women do. When she sent back the goods to their owners, they would pay her. Late in winter she finished the cloth and sent it back to the owners. They paid her the full salary, and also gave her a young goat for the table. On entering my house the goat began to bleat. I called to my wife and said: "Where did this goat come from? Perhaps it was stolen! Give it back to its owners; we have no right to eat stolen food!" But she said to me, "It was given to me as a bonus over and above my wages." Yet I would not believe her, and told her to give it back to its owners. I became very angry with her over this. So she retorted: "Where are your charitable deeds now? Where are your virtuous acts? See! Your true character is finally showing itself!"—This is the Word of the Lord. ℟. **Thanks be to God.** ∀

Responsorial Psalm   Ps 112, 1-2. 7-8. 9

℟. (7) **The heart of the just man is secure, trusting in the Lord.**

Happy the man who fears the Lord,
    who greatly delights in his commands.
His posterity shall be mighty upon the earth;
    the upright generation shall be blessed. — ℟

An evil report he shall not fear;
    his heart is firm, trusting in the Lord.
His heart is steadfast; he shall not fear
    till he looks down upon his foes. — ℟

Lavishly he gives to the poor;
> his generosity shall endure forever;
> his horn shall be exalted in glory. — ℟ ♦

℟. Or: **Alleluia.** ♦

———— **YEAR II** ————

READING I   2 Pt 3, 12-15. 17-18

Anxiously the faithful await the coming of Jesus—a new heaven and a new earth. During this waiting the followers of Christ should be found without stain or sin. They should be on guard against false teaching.

A reading from the second letter of Peter

Look for the coming of the day of God and try to hasten it! Because of it, the heavens will be destroyed in flames and the elements will melt away in a blaze. What we await are new heavens and a new earth where, according to his promise, the justice of God will reside.

So, beloved, while waiting for this, make every effort to be found without stain or defilement, and at peace in his sight. Consider that our Lord's patience is directed toward salvation.

You are forewarned, beloved brothers. Be on your guard lest you be led astray by the error of the wicked, and forfeit the security you enjoy. Grow rather in grace, and in the knowledge of our Lord and Savior Jesus Christ. Glory be to him now and to the day of eternity! Amen.—This is the Word of the Lord. ℟. **Thanks be to God.** ♦

Responsorial Psalm   Ps 90, 2. 3-4. 10. 14. 16

℟. (1) **In every age, O Lord, you have been our refuge.**

Before the mountains were begotten
> and the earth and the world were brought forth,
> from everlasting to everlasting you are God. — ℟
You turn man back to dust,
> saying, "Return, O children of men."

For a thousand years in your sight
  are as yesterday, now that it is past,
  or as a watch of the night. — ℟

Seventy is the sum of our years,
  or eighty, if we are strong,
And most of them are fruitless toil,
  for they pass quickly and we drift away. — ℟

Fill us at daybreak with your kindness,
  that we may shout for joy and gladness all our
    days.
Let your work be seen by your servants
  and your glory by their children. — ℟ ℣

———— **YEAR I AND II** ————

GOSPEL   Mk 12, 13-17
Alleluia (See Eph 1, 17-18)
℟. **Alleluia.** May the Father of our Lord Jesus Christ
enlighten the eyes of our heart
that we might see how great is the hope
to which we are called. ℟. **Alleluia.**

Jesus answers a trick question with an important principle. Secularism
would exclude God from this world; some religionists would forget
the world in favor of God. Jesus uses the coin of tribute to teach
loyalty to God and country.

℣. The Lord be with you. ℟. **And also with you.**
✠ A reading from the holy gospel according to Mark
℟. **Glory to you, Lord.**
Some Pharisees and Herodians were sent after Jesus
to catch him in his speech. The two groups came and
said to him: "Teacher, we know you are a truthful
man, unconcerned about anyone's opinion. It is evident you do not act out of human respect but teach
God's way of life sincerely. Is it lawful to pay the
tax to the emperor or not? Are we to pay or not to
pay?" Knowing their hypocrisy he said to them,
"Why are you trying to trip me up? Bring me a
coin and let me see it." When they brought one, he

said to them, "Whose head is this and whose inscription is it?" "Caesar's," they told him. At that Jesus said to them, "Give to Caesar what is Caesar's but give to God what is God's." Their amazement at him knew no bounds.—This is the gospel of the Lord. ℟. **Praise to you, Lord Jesus Christ.**

➤ No. 15, p. 623

WEDNESDAY OF THE NINTH WEEK IN ORDINARY TIME

—— YEAR I ——

READING I   Tb 3, 1-11. 16

Tobit prays to God and summarizes God's blessings and the sins of his people. The author uses the trials and problems of Tobit and Sarah to show that God loves his people and will help them by his power, even when all seems lost.

A reading from the book of Tobit

Grief-striken in spirit, Tobit groaned and wept aloud.
Then with sobs he began to pray:
"You are righteous, O Lord,
    and all your deeds are just;
All your ways are mercy and truth;
    you are the judge of the world.
And now, O Lord, may you be mindful of me,
    and look with favor upon me.
Punish me not for my sins,
    nor for my inadvertent offenses,
    nor for those of my fathers.
"They sinned against you,
    and disobeyed your commandments.

So you handed us over to plundering, exile and death,
  till we were an object lesson, a byword, a reproach
  in all the nations among whom you scattered us.
"Yes, your judgments are many and true
  in dealing with me as my sins
  and those of my fathers deserve.
For we have not kept your commandments,
  nor have we trodden the paths of truth before you.
"So now, deal with me as you please,
  and command my life breath to be taken from me,
  that I may go from the face of the earth into dust.
It is better for me to die than to live,
  because I have heard insulting calumnies,
  and I am overwhelmed with grief.
"Lord, command me to be delivered from such anguish;
  let me go to the everlasting abode;
  Lord, refuse me not.
For it is better for me to die
  than to endure so much misery in life,
  and to hear these insults!"

On the same day, at Ecbatana in Media, it so happened that Raguel's daughter Sarah also had to listen to abuse, from one of her father's maids. For she had been married to seven husbands, but the wicked demon Asmodeus killed them off before they could have intercourse with her, as it is prescribed for wives. So the maid said to her: "You are the one who strangles your husbands! Look at you! You have already been married seven times, but you have had no joy with any one of your husbands. Why do you beat us? Because your husbands are dead? Then why not join them! May we never see a son or daughter of yours!"

That day she was deeply grieved in spirit. She went in tears to an upstairs room in her father's house with the intention of hanging herself. But she reconsidered, saying to herself: "No! People would level this insult against my father: 'You had only one beloved daughter, but she hanged herself because of ill fortune!' And thus would I cause my father in his old age to go down to the nether world laden with sorrow. It is far better for me not to hang myself, but to beg the Lord to have me die, so that I need no longer live to hear such insults."

At that time, then, she spread out her hands, and facing the window, poured out her prayer.

At that very time, the prayer of these two suppliants was heard in the glorious prescence of Almighty God. So Raphael was sent to heal them both.
—This is the Word of the Lord. ℞. **Thanks be to God.** ℣

Responsorial Psalm   Ps 25, 2-4. 4-5. 6-7. 8-9
℞. (1) **To you, O Lord, I lift my soul.**

O Lord, my God,
In you I trust; let me not be put to shame.
    let not my enemies exult over me.
No one who waits for you shall be put to shame;
    those shall be put to shame who heedlessly break
        faith. — ℞

Your ways, O Lord, make known to me;
    teach me your paths,
Guide me in your truth and teach me,
    for you are God my savior. — ℞

Remember that your compassion, O Lord,
    and your kindness are from of old.
In your kindness remember me,
    because of your goodness, O Lord. — ℞

Good and upright is the Lord;
    thus he shows sinners the way.
He guides the humble to justice,
    he teaches the humble his way. — ℞ ℣

—— **YEAR II** ——

READING I   2 Tm 1, 1-3. 6-12

Paul reminds Timothy to stir up the graces given him in Holy Orders. The spirit of God makes men strong. God has called his people to a holy life through the power of the Gospel.

The beginning of the second letter of Paul to Timothy

Paul, by the will of God an apostle of Christ Jesus sent to proclaim the promise of life in him, to Timothy, my dear child whom I love. May grace, mercy, and peace from God the Father and from Christ Jesus our Lord be with you.

I thank God, the God of my forefathers whom I worship with a clear conscience, whenever I remember you in my prayers—as indeed I do constantly, night and day.

For this reason, I remind you to stir into flame the gift of God bestowed when my hands were laid on you. The Spirit God has given us is no cowardly spirit but rather one that makes us strong, loving and wise. Therefore, never be ashamed of your testimony to our Lord, nor of me, a prisoner for his sake, but with the strength which comes from God bear your share of the hardship which the gospel entails.

God has saved us and has called us to a holy life, not because of any merit of ours but according to his own design—the grace held out to us in Christ Jesus before the world began but now made manifest through the appearance of our Savior. He has robbed death of its power and has brought life and immortality into clear light through the gospel. In the service of this gospel I have been appointed preacher and apostle and teacher, and for its sake I undergo present hardship. But I am not ashamed, for I know him in whom I have believed, and I am confident that he is able to guard what has been entrusted to me until that final Day.—This is the Word of the Lord. ℟. **Thanks be to God.** ℣

Responsorial Psalm Ps 123, 1-2. 2

℟. (1) **To you, O Lord, I lift up my eyes.**

To you I lift up my eyes
  who are enthroned in heaven.
Behold, as the eyes of servants
  are on the hands of their masters. — ℟

As the eyes of a maid
  are on the hands of her mistress,
So are our eyes on the Lord, our God,
  till he have pity on us. — ℟ ℣

–––––––– **YEAR I AND II** ––––––––

GOSPEL Mk 12, 18-27

Alleluia (Jn 11, 25. 26)

℟. **Alleluia.** I am the resurrection and the life,
  said the Lord:
he who believes in me will not die for ever. ℟. **Alleluia.**

St. Mark relates another trick question used to challenge Jesus. Jesus proclaims that the ancestors of the Jews are still alive and are with God. Marriage teaches love and prepares for the fullness of love in heaven. God is the God of the living, not the dead.

℣. The Lord be with you. ℟. **And also with you.**
✠ A reading from the holy gospel according to Mark
℟. **Glory to you, Lord.**

Then some Sadducees who hold there is no resurrection came to Jesus with a question: "Teacher, we were left this in writing by Moses: 'If anyone's brother dies leaving a wife but no child, his brother must take the wife and produce offspring for his brother.' There were these seven brothers. The eldest took a wife and died, leaving no children. The second took the woman, and he too died childless. The same thing happened to the third; in fact none of the seven left any children behind. Last of all, the woman also died. At the resurrection, when they all come back to life, whose wife will she be? All seven married her." Jesus said: "You are badly misled, because you fail to understand the Scriptures or the power of God. When people rise from the dead, they neither marry nor are given in marriage but live like angels in heaven. As to the raising of the dead, have you not read in the book of Moses, in the passage about the burning bush, how God told him,

'I am the God of Abraham, the God of Isaac,
    the God of Jacob'?

He is the God of the living, not of the dead. You are very much mistaken." —This is the gospel of the Lord. ℟. **Praise to you, Lord Jesus Christ.**

➤ No. 15, p. 623

THURSDAY OF THE NINTH WEEK
IN ORDINARY TIME

_____ **YEAR I** _____

READING I   Tb 6, 11; 7, 1. 9-14; 8, 4-7

The old saying holds that marriages are made in heaven. The young Tobiah and Sarah recognize that God is giving them to each other. They thank God and ask for his grace to live together to a happy old age.

A reading from the book of Tobit

The angel Raphael spoke thus to Tobiah, "Tonight we must stay with Raguel, who is a relative of yours. He has a daughter named Sarah." So he brought him to the house of Raguel, whom they found seated by his courtyard gate. They greeted him first. He said to them, "Greetings to you too, brothers! Good health to you and welcome!"

Afterward, Raguel slaughtered a ram from the flock and gave them a cordial reception. When they had bathed and reclined to eat, Tobiah said to Raphael, "Brother Azariah, ask Raguel to let me marry my kinswoman Sarah." Raguel overheard the words; so he said to the boy: "Eat and drink and be merry tonight, for no man is more entitled to marry my daughter Sarah than you, brother. Besides, not even I have the right to give her to anyone but you, because you are my closest relative. But I will explain the situation to you very frankly. I have given her in marriage to seven men, all of whom were kinsmen of ours, and all died on the very night they approached her. But now, son, eat and drink. I am sure the Lord will look after you both." Tobiah answered, "I will eat or drink nothing until you set aside what belongs to me."

Raguel said to him: "I will do it. She is yours according to the decree of the Book of Moses. Your marriage to her has been decided in heaven! Take your kinswoman; from now on you are her love, and she is your beloved. She is yours today and ever after. And tonight, son, may the Lord of heaven prosper you both. May he grant you mercy and peace." Then Raguel called his daughter Sarah, and she came to him. He took her by the hand and gave her to Tobiah with the words: "Take her according to the law. According to the decree written in the Book of Moses she is your wife. Take her and bring her back safely to your father. And may the God of heaven grant both of you peace and prosperity." He then called her mother and told her to bring a scroll, so that he might draw up a marriage contract stating that he gave Sarah to Tobiah as his wife according to the decree of the Mosaic law. Her mother brought the scroll, and he drew up the contract, to which they affixed their seals. Afterward they began to eat and drink.

Tobiah arose from bed and said to his wife, "My love, get up. Let us pray and beg our Lord to have mercy on us and to grant us deliverance." She got up, and they started to pray and beg that deliverance be theirs. He began with these words:

"Blessed are you, O God of our fathers;
    praised be your name for ever and ever.
Let the heavens and all your creation
    praise you forever.
You made Adam and you give him his wife Eve
    to be his help and support;
    and from these two the human race descended.
You said, 'It is not good for the man to be alone;
    let us make him a partner like himself.'
Now, Lord, you know that I take this wife of mine
    not because of lust,
    but for a noble purpose.
Call down your mercy on me and on her,
    and allow us to live together to a happy old
    age."

This is the Word of the Lord. ℟. **Thanks be to God.** ℣

Responsorial Psalm   Ps 128, 1-2. 3. 4-5

℟. (1) **Happy are those who fear the Lord.**

Happy are you who fear the Lord,
    who walk in his ways!
For you shall eat the fruit of your handiwork;
    happy shall you be, and favored. — ℟

Your wife shall be like a fruitful vine
    in the recesses of your home;
Your children like olive plants
    around your table. — ℟

Behold, thus is the man blessed
    who fears the Lord.
The Lord bless you from Zion:
    may you see the prosperity of Jerusalem
    all the days of your life. — ℟ ℣

—— **YEAR II** ——

READING I   2 Tm 2, 8-15

Paul preaches about Jesus Christ who is risen. In preaching Paul has
suffered much, but the word of God cannot be silenced. He directs

Timothy to keep reminding the people that if they deny Jesus, he will deny them. They must try to be worthy of God's approval.

A reading from the second letter of Paul to
Timothy

Remember that Jesus Christ, a descendant of David, was raised from the dead. This is the gospel I preach; in preaching it I suffer as a criminal, even to the point of being thrown into chains—but there is no chaining the word of God! Therefore I bear with all of this for the sake of those whom God has chosen, in order that they may obtain the salvation to be found in Christ Jesus and with it eternal glory.

You can depend on this:
> If we have died with him
>> we shall also live with him;
> If we hold out to the end
>> we shall reign with him.

But if we deny him he will deny us. If we are unfaithful he will still remain faithful, for he cannot deny himself.

Keep reminding people of these things and charge them before God to stop disputing about mere words. This does no good and can be the ruin of those who listen. Try hard to make yourself worthy of God's approval, following a straight course in preaching the truth.—This is the Word of the Lord. ℟. **Thanks be to God.** ℣

Responsorial Psalm   Ps 25, 4-5. 8-9. 10. 14

℟. (4) **Teach me your ways, O Lord.**

Your ways, O Lord, make known to me,
    teach me your paths,
Guide me in your truth and teach me,
    for you are God my savior. — ℟

Good and upright is the Lord.
    thus he shows sinners the way.
He guides the humble to justice,
    he teaches the humble his way. — ℟

All the paths of the Lord are kindness and constancy
toward those who keep his covenant and his decrees.
The friendship of the Lord is with those who fear
him,
and his covenant, for their instruction. — ℟ ℣

——— **YEAR I AND II** ———

GOSPEL   Mk 12, 28-34

Alleluia (Ps 119, 34)

℟. **Alleluia.** Teach me the meaning of your law, O
Lord,
and I will guard it with all my heart. ℟. **Alleluia.**

Jesus takes the two great commandments from the Old Testament,
and he makes them the spirit that must give life to every law. In this
way, the law teaches how men may truly love one another. This double
law brings life and the Kingdom.

℣. The Lord be with you. ℟. **And also with you.**
✠ A reading from the holy gospel according to Mark
℟. **Glory to you, Lord.**

One of the scribes came up to ask Jesus, "Which is
the first of all the commandments?" Jesus replied:
"This is the first:

'Hear, O Israel! The Lord our God is Lord
alone!
Therefore you shall love the Lord your God
with all your heart,
with all your soul,
with all your mind,
and with all your strength.'

This is the second,

'You shall love your neighbor as yourself.'

There is no other commandment greater than these."
The scribe said to him: "Excellent, Teacher! You
are right in saying, 'He is the One, there is no other
than he.' Yes, to love him with all our heart, with
all our thoughts and with all our strength, and to

love our neighbor as ourselves' is worth more than any burnt offering or sacrifice." Jesus approved the insight of this answer and told him, "You are not far from the reign of God." And no one had the courage to ask him any more questions.—This is the gospel of the Lord. ℟. **Praise to you, Lord Jesus Christ.**

➤ No. 15, p. 623

FRIDAY OF THE NINTH WEEK IN ORDINARY TIME

—— YEAR I ——

READING I Tb 11, 5-15

The trust of Anna is shown as she awaits her son's return. The story uses the medical ideas of its time, and the elder Tobit praises God in thanksgiving for his sight.

A reading from the book of Tobit

Anna sat watching the road by which her son was to come. When she saw him coming, she exclaimed to his father, "Tobit, your son is coming and the man who traveled with him!"

Raphael said to Tobiah before he reached his father: "I am certain that his eyes will be opened. Smear the fish gall on them. This medicine will make the cataracts shrink and peel off from his eyes; then your father will again be able to see the light of day."

Then Anna ran up to her son, threw her arms around him, and said to him, "Now that I have seen you again, son, I am ready to die!" And she sobbed aloud. Tobit got up and stumbled out through the courtyard gate. Tobiah went up to him with the fish gall in his hand, and holding him firmly, blew into his eyes. "Courage, father," he said. Next he smeared the medicine on his eyes, and made them smart. Then, beginning at the corners of Tobit's eyes, Tobiah used both hands to peel off the cataracts. When Tobit saw his son, he threw his arms around him and wept. He exclaimed, "I can see you, son, the light of my eyes!" Then he said:

"Blessed be God,
 and praised be his great name,
 and blessed be all his holy angels.
May his holy name be praised
 throughout all the ages,
Because it was he who scourged me,
 and it is he who has had mercy on me.
 Behold, I now see my son Tobiah!"

This is the Word of the Lord. ℟. **Thanks be to God.** ✟

Responsorial Psalm   Ps 146, 2. 7. 8-9. 9-10

℟. (2) **Praise the Lord, my soul!**

Praise the Lord, O my soul;
 I will praise the Lord all my life;
 I will sing praise to my God while I live. — ℟

The Lord keeps faith forever,
 secures justice for the oppressed,
 gives food to the hungry.
The Lord sets captives free. — ℟

The Lord gives sight to the blind.
 The Lord raises up those that were bowed down;
The Lord loves the just.
 The Lord protects strangers. — ℟

The fatherless and the widow he sustains,
 but the way of the wicked he thwarts.
The Lord shall reign forever;
 your God, O Zion, through all generations. Alleluia. — ℟ ✟

℟. Or: **Alleluia.** ✟

—————   **YEAR II**   —————

READING I   2 Tm 3, 10-17

Paul recalls for Timothy his persecutions because of teaching the Gospel message. Anyone who lives wholly for Jesus will be persecuted. The Scriptures are a source of wisdom. They are inspired by God, training us for holiness.

A reading from the second letter of Paul to
Timothy

You have followed closely my teaching and my
conduct. You have observed my resolution, fidelity,
patience, love, and endurance, through persecutions
and sufferings in Antioch, Iconium, and Lystra. You
know what persecutions I have had to bear, and you
know how the Lord saved me from them all. Anyone who wants to live a godly life in Christ Jesus
can expect to be persecuted. But all the while evil
men and charlatans will go from bad to worse, deceiving others, themselves deceived. You, for your
part, must remain faithful to what you have learned
and believed, because you know who your teachers
were. Likewise, from your infancy you have known
the sacred Scriptures, the source of the wisdom
which through faith in Jesus Christ leads to salvation. All Scripture is inspired of God and is useful
for teaching—for reproof, correction, and training
in holiness so that the man of God may be fully
competent and equipped for every good work.—This
is the Word of the Lord. ℟. **Thanks be to God.** ℣

Responsorial Psalm
                            Ps 119, 157. 160. 161. 165. 166. 168
℟. (165) **O Lord, great peace have they who love
    your law.**

Though my persecutors and my foes are many,
    I turn not away from your decrees. — ℟

Permanence is your word's chief trait;
    each of your just ordinances is everlasting. — ℟

Princes persecute me without cause
    but my heart stands in awe of your word. — ℟

Those who love your law have great peace,
    and for them there is no stumbling block. — ℟

I wait for your salvation, O Lord,
    and your commands I fulfill. — ℟

I keep your precepts and your decrees,
    for all my ways are before you. — ℟ ℣

——— **YEAR I AND II** ———

GOSPEL   Mk 12, 35-37

Alleluia (Jn 14, 23)

℟. **Alleluia.** If anyone loves me, he will hold to my
    words,
and my Father will love him, and we will come to
    him. ℟. **Alleluia.**

After being challenged by his enemies, Jesus poses a hard question
of his own. Jesus is both the Son of God and the Son of Man. He is
Lord and the Savior of his human brothers, in the one person.

℣. The Lord be with you. ℟. **And also with you.**
✠ A reading from the holy gospel according to Mark
℟. **Glory to you, Lord.**

As Jesus was teaching in the temple precincts he
went on to say: "How can the scribes claim, 'The
Messiah is David's son'? David himself, inspired by
the Holy Spirit, said,
    'The Lord said to my Lord: Sit at my right hand
        until I make your enemies your footstool.'
If David himself addresses him as 'Lord,' in what
sense can he be his son?" The majority of the crowd
heard this with delight.—This is the gospel of the
Lord. ℟. **Praise to you, Lord Jesus Christ.**

➤ No. 15, p. 623

———————

SATURDAY OF THE NINTH WEEK
IN ORDINARY TIME

——— **YEAR I** ———

READING I   Tb 12, 1. 5-15. 20

Tobit and his family discover that they have been aided by an angel
of God. Raphael recommends thanksgiving and almsgiving as pleasing
to God. God shows his care and concern for those who love him.

A reading from the book of Tobit

Tobit called his son Tobiah and said to him, "Son, see to it that you give what is due to the man who made the journey with you; give him a bonus too." So Tobiah called Raphael and said, "Take as your wages half of all that you have brought back, and go in peace."

Raphael called the two men aside privately and said to them: "Thank God! Give him the praise and the glory. Before all the living, acknowledge the many good things he has done for you, by blessing and extolling his name in song. Before all men, honor and proclaim God's deeds, and do not be slack in praising him. A king's secret it is prudent to keep, but the works of God are to be declared and made known. Praise them with due honor. Do good, and evil will not find its way to you. Prayer and fasting are good, but better than either is almsgiving accompanied by righteousness. A little with righteousness is better than abundance with wickedness. It is better to give alms than to store up gold; for almsgiving saves one from death and expiates every sin. Those who regularly give alms shall enjoy a full life; but those habitually guilty of sin are their own worst enemies.

"I will now tell you the whole truth; I will conceal nothing at all from you. I have already said to you, 'A king's secret it is prudent to keep, but the works of God are to be made known with due honor.' I can now tell you that when you, Tobit, and Sarah prayed, it was I who presented and read the record of your prayer before the Glory of the Lord; and I did the same thing when you used to bury the dead. When you did not hesitate to get up and leave your dinner in order to go and bury the dead, I was sent to put you to the test. At the same time, however, God commissioned me to heal you and your daughter-in-law Sarah. I am Raphael, one of the seven angels who enter and serve before the Glory of the Lord.

"So now get up from the ground and praise God. Behold, I am about to ascend to him who sent me; write down all these things that have happened to you."—This is the Word of the Lord. ℟. **Thanks be to God.** ✠

Responsorial Psalm   Tb 13, 2. 6

℟. (1) **Blessed be God, who lives for ever.**

God scourges and then has mercy;
   he casts down to the depths of the nether world,
   and he brings up from the great abyss.
No one can escape his hand. — ℟

So now consider what he has done for you,
   and praise him with full voice.
Bless the Lord of righteousness,
   and exalt the King of the ages. — ℟

In the land of my exile I praise him,
   and show his power and majesty to a sinful
      nation. — ℟

Turn back, you sinners! do the right before him:
   perhaps he may look with favor upon you
   and show you mercy. — ℟ ✠

—— **YEAR II** ——

READING I   2 Tm 4, 1-8

Paul exhorts Timothy to preach the good news at all times—correcting, reproving, appealing. But the time is coming when people will ignore sound doctrine. Paul admits he has fought a good fight and he awaits his crown in heaven.

A reading from the second letter of Paul to
Timothy

In the presence of God and of Christ Jesus, who is coming to judge the living and the dead, and by his appearing and his kingly power, I charge you to preach the word, to stay with this task whether convenient or inconvenient—correcting, reproving, appealing—constantly teaching and never losing patience. For the time will come when people will not tolerate sound doctrine, but, following their own desires, will surround themselves with teachers who tickle their ears. They will stop listening to the truth and will wander off to fables. As for you, be steady and self-possessed; put up with hardship, perform your work as an evangelist, fulfill your ministry.

For my part I am already being poured out like a libation. The time of my dissolution is near. I have fought the good fight, I have finished the race, I have kept the faith. From now on a merited crown awaits me; on that Day the Lord, just judge that he is, will award it to me—and not only to me but to all who have looked for his appearing with eager longing.—This is the Word of the Lord. ℟. **Thanks be to God.** ⩊

Responsorial Psalm   Ps 71, 8-9. 14-15. 16-17. 22

℟. (15) **I will sing of your salvation.**

My mouth shall be filled with your praise,
    with your glory day by day.
Cast me not off in my old age;
    as my strength fails, forsake me not. — ℟

But I will always hope
    and praise you ever more and more.
My mouth shall declare your justice,
    day by day your salvation. — ℟

I will treat of the mighty works of the Lord;
    O God, I will tell of your singular justice.
O God, you have taught me from my youth,
    and till the present I proclaim your wondrous
        deeds. — ℟

So will I give you thanks with music on the lyre,
    for your faithfulness, O my God!
I will sing your praises with the harp,
    O Holy One of Israel! — ℟ ⩊

——— YEAR I AND II ———

GOSPEL Mk 12, 38-44

Alleluia (Mt 5, 3)

℟. **Alleluia.** Happy the poor in spirit;
the kingdom of heaven is theirs! ℟. **Alleluia.**

Jesus teaches that outward show is vain. He uses the widow's mite by way of example. It is not the amount that is given that has value, but what matters in the sight of God is the spirit in which the gift is given. And so, the poor widow gave "more" than the rich gave.

℣. The Lord be with you. ℟. **And also with you.**
✠ A reading from the holy gospel according to Mark
℟. **Glory to you, Lord.**

In the course of his teaching Jesus said: "Be on guard against the scribes, who like to parade around in their robes and accept marks of respect in public, front seats in the synagogues, and places of honor at banquets. These men devour the savings of widows and recite long prayers for appearance' sake; it is they who will receive the severest sentence."

Taking a seat opposite the treasury, he observed the crowd putting money into the collection box. Many of the wealthy put in sizable amounts; but one poor widow came and put in two small copper coins worth about a cent. He called his disciples over and told them: "I want you to observe that this poor widow contributed more than all the others who donated to the treasury. They gave from their surplus wealth, but she gave from her want, all that she had to live on."—This is the gospel of the Lord.
℟. **Praise to you, Lord Jesus Christ.** ➤ No. 15, p. 623

LENTEN SEASON

The word "Lent" is an ancient word for spring. The season of Lent is a time in our personal lives for new life to appear, and for old frozen attitudes to disappear. It is a time to clear the ground, to clear away rubbish. A time for sowing, so that one day, the Day of the Lord, there will be a harvest.

Lent is six weeks. It is not too long to prepare for the Easter event, the Paschal mystery, that changed history and human life. Jesus went through this time of reflection that the forty days of Lent present to us. He made new choices. He thought about his direction in life, his awareness of the Father, his use of time, power, and personal gifts.

Jesus came into the world to share his life with us. We say we are "in him." We could examine the priorities in our lives with his mission in mind. His mission is to bring each man to human dignity, and all men to brotherhood, leading them to the Father. He sought to do the will of his Father. "My Father works . . . and I work, even to now," he said. What does that mean, for us?

Lent is a time of instruction. Faith comes by hearing, which certainly includes reading, and study, and good conversation. And today it would include the communication that comes from good film and art. Faith needs to grow, to ask questions, and to reflect on the answers. To grow in faith calls for an alert and attentive person, one who listens. The man of faith listens to others, and to himself, to one's speech and one's conscience. He also listens to the world.

In the early Christian centuries Lent was and (in parishes that prepare adults to enter the Church) still is a time of preparation for baptism on Easter Eve. If we are already baptized, then it is a time to think what that covenant should mean to us. Covenant is promise. Promise of what? Perhaps we promised nothing; it was all done for us. But should we look into that covenant and decide to renew it for ourselves? The Church provides a baptismal renewal at Easter. A serious spiritual effort in Lent will keep that renewal from becoming an empty gesture.

Lent is a time of listening. The Word of God is given to us in abundance. Look at the texts of the Lenten Sundays (and all the weekdays), the rich parables, the choice of Gospels, the great themes of faith, conversion, and turning back to a God who is already waiting and loving us. We are asked to do more than listen in this Lenten season. We are asked to make the Word of God a judgment upon our lives. Lent is a time for special penance and personal evaluation. We are reminded of the words of Christ that unless you do penance you shall all likewise perish. "Take up your cross and follow me" (Mt 16, 24).

The Gospel during Lent is chosen each day in accord with the major lenten themes and preparation for baptism: penance, prayer, effort to live a good Christian life, and acceptance of the mystery of salvation through the cross. Up until the end of the third week the texts are chosen from the Synoptic Gospels and follow one another without any real order. However, beginning with the fourth week, the Gospel of St. John is read in order. On the last day a text of Matthew's Gospel is read—the one concerning the betrayal by Judas.

The First Reading is taken every day from the Old Testament. It is chosen to accord with the theme of the Gospel or a lenten theme. On the last three days the songs of the Suffering Servant are read from the Book of Isaiah in order to prepare for the reading of the fourth Song on Good Friday, the Song which represents the spiritual summit of the Old Testament.

ASH WEDNESDAY

In today's Mass, ashes from olive branches or the branches of other trees, which were blessed in the preceding year, are blessed and imposed. In the Introductory Rites, the Penitential Rite is omitted since the giving of ashes takes its place. The ashes are blessed and given to the people after the Homily.

(The blessing and giving of ashes may also take place outside Mass. In this case, the Liturgy of the Word may be celebrated, using the Entrance Song, Opening Prayer, and the readings with their chants as at Mass. The Homily and the blessing and giving of ashes follow. The rite concludes with the General Intercessions.)

Ashes remind us of ancient forms of penance and also that the human glamor of this life will soon come to an end when God calls us to himself for judgment.

ENTRANCE ANT.   See Wis 11, 24. 25. 27

Lord, you are merciful to all, and hate nothing you have created. You overlook the sins of men to bring them to repentance. You are the Lord our God.

➤ No. 2, p. 614

OPENING PRAYER

Let us pray

[for the grace to keep Lent faithfully]

Lord,

protect us in our struggle against evil.
As we begin the discipline of Lent,
make this day holy by our self-denial.
Grant this through our Lord Jesus Christ, your Son,
who lives and reigns with you and the Holy Spirit,
one God, for ever and ever. ℟. **Amen.** ⱽ

ALTERNATIVE OPENING PRAYER

Let us pray

[in quiet remembrance of our need for redemption]

Father in heaven,
the light of your truth bestows sight
to the darkness of sinful eyes.
May this season of repentance
bring us the blessing of your forgiveness

and the gift of your light.
Grant this through Christ our Lord. ℟. **Amen.** ℣

READING I   Jl 2, 12-18

Joel warns that the Day of Yahweh is near. He recalls the actual
situation caused by the locust plague and pleads, in Yahweh's name,
for heartfelt repentance. The priests are invited to join in the general
penitence after they have proclaimed a national day of fasting and
prayer. The Lord's response implies he will send them food and
renew the gift of prophecy and wisdom.

A reading from the book of the prophet Joel

Even now, says the Lord,
    return to me with your whole heart,
    with fasting, and weeping, and mourning;
Rend your hearts, not your garments,
    and return to the Lord, your God.
For gracious and merciful is he,
    slow to anger, rich in kindness,
    and relenting in punishment.
Perhaps he will again relent
    and leave behind him a blessing,
Offerings and libations
    for the Lord, your God.
Blow the trumpet in Zion!
    proclaim a fast,
    call an assembly;
Gather the people,
    notify the congregation;
Assemble the elders,
    gather the children
    and the infants at the breast;
Let the bridegroom quit his room,
    and the bride her chamber.
Between the porch and the altar
    let the priests, the ministers of the Lord, weep,
And say, "Spare, O Lord, your people
    and make not your heritage a reproach,
    with the nations ruling over them!

Why should they say among the peoples,
'Where is their God?'"
Then the Lord was stirred to concern for his land
and took pity on his people.
This is the Word of the Lord. ℟.**Thanks be to God.** ↓

Responsorial Psalm   Ps 51, 3-4. 5-6. 12-13. 14. 17

℟. (3) **Be merciful, O Lord, for we have sinned.**

Have mercy on me, O God, in your goodness;
    in the greatness of your compassion wipe out my
        offense.
Thoroughly wash me from my guilt
    and of my sin cleanse me. — ℟

For I acknowledge my offense,
    and my sin is before me always:
"Against you only have I sinned,
    and done what is evil in your sight." — ℟

A clean heart create for me, O God,
    and a steadfast spirit renew within me.
Cast me not out from your presence,
    and your holy spirit take not from me. — ℟

Give me back the joy of your salvation,
    and a willing spirit sustain in me.
O Lord, open my lips,
    and my mouth shall proclaim your praise. — ℟ ↓

READING II   2 Cor 5, 20-6, 2

Paud describes an apostle's work. He is God's instrument. In one
sense, reconciliation is obtained with the acceptance of the first
justifying grace, but in another, it is not achieved until one enters
into definitive possession of the eternal reward.

A reading from the second letter of Paul to the
Corinthians

We are ambassadors for Christ, God as it were appealing through us. We implore you, in Christ's name:
be reconciled to God! For our sakes God made him
who did not know sin to be sin, so that in him we
might become the very holiness of God.

As your fellow workers we beg you not to receive the grace of God in vain. For he says, "In an acceptable time I have heard you; on a day of salvation I have helped you." Now is the acceptable time! Now is the day of salvation!—This is the Word of the Lord. ℟. **Thanks be to God.** ⍒

GOSPEL   Mt 6, 1-6. 16-18

Verse before the Gospel (Ps 95, 8)

℟. **Praise to you, Lord Jesus Christ, king of endless glory!**

If today you hear his voice,
harden not your hearts.

℟. **Praise to you, Lord Jesus Christ, king of endless glory!**

Righteousness is illustrated by three basic acts of Jewish piety: almsgiving, prayer, and fasting. Works of piety should not be done for vain display. The Pharisees were hypocrites. Prayer and fasting should be carried out joyfully without display. God will then give the reward.

℣. The Lord be with you. ℟. **And also with you.**
✠ A reading from the holy gospel according to Matthew. ℟. **Glory to you, Lord.**

Jesus said to his disciples: "Be on guard against performing religious acts for people to see. Otherwise expect no recompense from your heavenly Father. When you give alms, for example, do not blow a horn before you in synagogues and streets like hypocrites looking for applause. You can be sure of this much, they are already repaid. In giving alms you are not to let your left hand know what your right hand is doing. Keep your deeds of mercy secret, and your Father who sees in secret will repay you.

"When you are praying, do not behave like the hypocrites who love to stand and pray in synagogues or on street corners in order to be noticed. I give you my word, they are already repaid. Whenever you pray, go to your room, close your door, and pray to your Father in private. Then your Father, who sees what no man sees, will repay you.

"When you fast, you are not to look glum as the hypocrites do. They change the appearance of their faces so that others may see they are fasting. I assure you, they are already repaid. When you fast, see to it that you groom your hair and wash your face. In that way no one can see you are fasting but your Father who is hidden; and your Father who sees what is hidden will repay you."—This is the gospel of the Lord. ℟. **Praise to you, Lord Jesus Christ.** ✟

BLESSING AND GIVING OF ASHES

After the homily the priest joins his hands and says:

Dear friends in Christ, let us ask our Father to bless these ashes which we will use as the mark of our repentance. ✟

Pause for silent prayer

Lord,
bless the sinner who asks for your forgiveness
and bless ✛ all those who receive these ashes.
May they keep this lenten season
in preparation for the joy of Easter.
We ask this through Christ our Lord.
℟. **Amen.** ✟

OR:

Lord,
bless these ashes ✛
by which we show that we are dust.
Pardon our sins
and keep us faithful to the discipline of Lent,
for you do not want sinners to die
but to live with the risen Christ,
who reigns with you for ever and ever.
℟. **Amen.** ✟

He sprinkles the ashes with holy water in silence.

The priest then places ashes on those who come forward, saying to each:

Turn away from sin and be faithful to the gospel. (Mk 1, 15)

OR:

Remember, man, you are dust
and to dust you will return. (See Gn 3, 19)

Meanwhile some of the following antiphons or other appropriate songs are sung.

ANTIPHON 1   See Jl 2, 13
Come back to the Lord with all your heart; leave the past in ashes, and turn to God with tears and fasting, for he is slow to anger and ready to forgive.

ANTIPHON 2   See Jl 2, 17; Est 13, 17
Let the priests and ministers of the Lord lament before his altar, and say: Spare us, Lord; spare your people! Do not let us die for we are crying out to you.

ANTIPHON 3   Ps 51, 3
Lord, take away our wickedness.

These may be repeated after each verse of Psalm 51, Have mercy on me, O God.

RESPONSORY   See Bar 3, 5
Direct our hearts to better things, O Lord; heal our sin and ignorance. Lord, do not face us suddenly with death, but give us time to repent.

℟. **Turn to us with mercy, Lord; we have sinned against you.**

℣. **Help us, God our savior, rescue us for the honor of your name. (Ps 79, 9)**

℟. **Turn to us with mercy, Lord; we have sinned against you.**

*After the giving of ashes the priest washes his hands;
the rite concludes with the General Intercessions or
Prayer of the Faithful.*

The Profession of Faith is not said.

PRAYER OVER THE GIFTS

Lord,
help us to resist temptation
by our lenten works of charity and penance.
By this sacrifice
may we be prepared to celebrate
the death and resurrection of Christ our Savior
and be cleansed from sin and renewed in spirit.
We ask this through Christ our Lord.
℟. **Amen.**   ➤ No. 21, p. 626 (Pref. P 11)

COMMUNION ANT   Ps 1, 2-3

**The man who meditates day and night on the law of the
Lord will yield fruit in due season.** ↓

PRAYER AFTER COMMUNION

Lord,
through this communion
may our lenten penance give you glory
and bring us your protection.
We ask this in the name of Jesus the Lord.
℟. **Amen.**   _____ ➤ No. 32, p. 650

THURSDAY AFTER ASH WEDNESDAY

Just as the Israelites had to make a choice between good and evil
in the life they were to live, we must also make a choice between
what is good and pleasing to God, and what is evil and of the devil.
We should therefore gird ourselves with justice, truth, and good
works. The shield of faith, which teaches us how richly God rewards
virtue, gives us confidence in God and the hope of heaven.

ENTRANCE ANT.   See Ps 55, 17-20. 23

**When I cry to the Lord, he hears my voice and saves
me from the foes who threaten me. Unload your
burden onto the Lord, and he will support you.**
➤ No. 2, p. 614

OPENING PRAYER

Lord,
may everything we do
begin with your inspiration,
continue with your help,
and reach perfection under your guidance.
We ask this through our Lord Jesus Christ, your Son,
who lives and reigns with you and the Holy Spirit,
one God, for ever and ever. ℟. **Amen.** ⍌

READING I   Dt 30, 15-20

The liturgy of covenant renewal confronts the community with committing itself to a binding decision. The life in question is fullness
of life in the Promised Land. The calling of witnesses was an essential feature of ancient covenants. The Israelites were to choose
such a life.

A reading from the book of Deuteronomy

Moses said to the people: "Today I have set before
you life and prosperity, death and doom. If you obey
the commandments of the Lord, your God, which I
enjoin on you today, loving him, and walking in his
ways, and keeping his commandments, statutes and
decrees, you will live and grow numerous, and the
Lord, your God, will bless you in the land you are
entering to occupy. If, however, you turn away your
hearts and will not listen, but are led astray and
adore and serve other gods, I tell you now that you
will certainly perish; you will not have a long life
on the land which you are crossing the Jordan to
enter and occupy. I call heaven and earth today to
witness against you: I have set before you life and
death, the blessing and the curse. Choose life, then,
that you and your descendants may live, by loving
the Lord, your God, heeding his voice, and holding
fast to him. For that will mean life for you, a long
life for you to live on the land which the Lord swore
he would give to your fathers Abraham, Isaac and
Jacob."—This is the Word of the Lord. ℟. **Thanks
be to God.** ⍌

Responsorial Psalm   Ps 1, 1-2. 3. 4. 6

℟. (Ps 39, 5) **Happy are they who hope in the Lord.**

Happy the man who follows not
   the counsel of the wicked
Nor walks in the way of sinners,
   nor sits in the company of the insolent,
But delights in the law of the Lord
   and meditates on his law day and night. — ℟

He is like a tree
   planted near running water,
That yields its fruit in due season,
   and whose leaves never fade.
   [Whatever he does, prospers.] — ℟

Not so the wicked, not so;
   they are like chaff which the wind drives away.
For the Lord watches over the way of the just,
   but the way of the wicked vanishes. — ℟ ▼

GOSPEL   Lk 9, 22-25

Verse before the Gospel (Mt 4, 17)

℟. **Praise and honor to you, Lord Jesus Christ!**
Repent, says the Lord,
the kingdom of heaven is at hand.

℟. **Praise and honor to you, Lord Jesus Christ!**

Jesus foretells his passion and death. He warns that disciples too
must be prepared to suffer and die in true apostleship in imitation
of his suffering. The true disciple takes up his cross daily.

℣. The Lord be with you. ℟. **And also with you.**
✠ A reading from the holy gospel according to Luke
℟. **Glory to you, Lord.**

Jesus said to his disciples: "The Son of Man must
first endure many sufferings, be rejected by the elders, the high priests and the scribes, and be put to
death, and then be raised up on the third day."

   Jesus said to all: "Whoever wishes to be my follower must deny his very self, take up his cross each
day, and follow in my steps. Whoever would save

his life will lose it, and whoever loses his life for my sake will save it. What profit does he show who gains the whole world and destroys himself in the process?"—This is the gospel of the Lord. ℞. **Praise to you, Lord Jesus Christ.** ➔ No. 15, p. 623

PRAYER OVER THE GIFTS

Lord,
accept these gifts.
May they bring us your mercy
and give you honor and praise.
We ask this in the name of Jesus the Lord.
℞. **Amen.** ➔ No. 21, p. 626 (Pref. P 8-11)

COMMUNION ANT. Ps 51, 12

Create a clean heart in me, O God; give me a new and steadfast spirit. ℣

PRAYER AFTER COMMUNION

Merciful Father,
may the gifts and blessings we receive
bring us pardon and salvation.
Grant this through Christ our Lord.
℞. **Amen.** ➔ No. 32, p. 650

FRIDAY AFTER ASH WEDNESDAY

It is a good and holy practice to humble ourselves by abstaining from other than mere food for the body. The eye should abstain from all vain and curious sights, the ears from listening to idle talk, the tongue from detraction and frivolous words. True sorrow for past sins can best be expressed through acts of love and charity toward our brothers.

ENTRANCE ANT. Ps 30, 11

The Lord heard me and took pity on me. He came to my help. ➔ No. 2, p. 614

OPENING PRAYER

Lord,
with your loving care

guide the penance we have begun.
Help us to persevere with love and sincerity.
Grant this through our Lord Jesus Christ, your Son,
who lives and reigns with you and the Holy Spirit,
one God, for ever and ever. ℞. **Amen.** ℣

READING I   Is 58, 1-9

Fasting should unite rich and poor. Only the wealthy can fast; they
alone have something of which to deprive themselves. In fasting, they
share the lot of the poor who are always hungry. To fast and neglect
the poor is a form of conceit.

A reading from the book of the prophet Isaiah

Cry out full-throated and unsparingly,
    lift up your voice like a trumpet blast;
Tell my people their wickedness,
    and the house of Jacob their sins.
They seek me day after day,
    and desire to know my ways,
Like a nation that has done what is just
    and not abandoned the law of their God;
They ask me to declare what is due them,
    pleased to gain access to God.
"Why do we fast, and you do not see it?
    afflict ourselves, and you take no note of it?"
Lo, on your fast day you carry out your own pursuits,
    and drive all your laborers.
Yes, your fast ends in quarreling and fighting,
    striking with wicked claw.
Would that today you might fast
    so as to make your voice heard on high!
Is this the manner of fasting I wish,
    of keeping a day of penance:
That a man bow his head like a reed,
    and lie in sackcloth and ashes?
Do you call this a fast,
    a day acceptable to the Lord?
This, rather, is the fasting that I wish:
    releasing those bound unjustly,
    untying the thongs of the yoke;

Setting free the oppressed,
   breaking every yoke;
Sharing your bread with the hungry,
   sheltering the oppressed and the homeless;
Clothing the naked when you see them,
   and not turning your back on your own.
Then your light shall break forth like the dawn,
   and your wound shall quickly be healed.
Your vindication shall go before you,
   and the glory of the Lord shall be your rear guard.
Then you shall call, and the Lord will answer,
   you shall cry for help, and he will say: Here I am!
If you remove from your midst oppression
   false accusation and malicious speech.
This is the Word of the Lord. ℟. **Thanks be to God. ☩**

Responsorial Psalm   Ps 51, 3-4. 5-6. 18-19
℟. (19) **A broken, humbled heart, O God, you will
   not scorn.**
Have mercy on me, O God, in your goodness;
   in the greatness of your compassion wipe out my
      offense.
Thoroughly wash me from my guilt
   and of my sin cleanse me. — ℟
For I acknowledge my offense,
   and my sin is before me always:
"Against you only have I sinned,
   and done what is evil in your sight." — ℟
For you are not pleased with sacrifices;
   should I offer a holocaust, you would not accept it.
My sacrifice, O God, is a contrite spirit;
   a heart contrite and humbled, O God, you will not
      spurn. — ℟ ☩

GOSPEL   Mt 9, 14-15
Verse before the Gospel (Am 5, 14)
℟. **Glory and praise to you, Lord Jesus Christ!**

Seek good and not evil
so that you may live,
and the Lord will be with you.
℟. **Glory and praise to you, Lord Jesus Christ!**

In the Old Testament, fasting appears as a token of mourning or of
repentance. A fast meant abstinence from food for the entire day.
Jesus answers the question of not fasting by saying that his sojourn
with his disciples is considered a time of joy when fasting is out of
place.

℣. The Lord be with you. ℟. **And also with you.**
✠ A reading from the holy gospel according to Matthew. ℟. **Glory to you, Lord.**

When Jesus had crossed over into the territory of the Gerasenes, John's disciples came to him with the objection, "Why is it that while we and the Pharisees fast, your disciples do not?" Jesus said to them: "How can wedding guests go in mourning so long as the groom is with them? When the day comes that the groom is taken away, then they will fast."
—This is the gospel of the Lord. ℟. **Praise to you, Lord Jesus Christ.**   ➤ No. 15, p. 623

PRAYER OVER THE GIFTS
Lord,
through this lenten eucharist
may we grow in your love and service
and become an acceptable offering to you.
We ask this through Christ our Lord.
℟. **Amen.**   ➤ No. 21, p. 626 (Pref. P 8-11)

COMMUNION ANT.   Ps 25, 4
Teach us your ways, O Lord, and lead us in your paths. ℣

PRAYER AFTER COMMUNION
Lord,
may our sharing in this mystery
free us from our sins

and make us worthy of your healing.
We ask this in the name of Jesus the Lord.
℟. **Amen.**   _____   ➤ No. 32, p. 650

SATURDAY AFTER ASH WEDNESDAY

To serve God lovingly and to be content with few things always brings rich rewards, if not in this life, at least in the next. Christ promised the Kingdom of Heaven to the poor in spirit, that is, not only to the humble, but also to the poor who imitate Christ in all patience and resignation.

ENTRANCE ANT.   Ps 69, 17

Answer us, Lord, with your loving kindness, turn to us in your great mercy.   ➤ No. 2, p. 614

OPENING PRAYER

Father,
look upon our weakness
and reach out to help us with your loving power.
We ask this through our Lord Jesus Christ, your Son,
who lives and reigns with you and the Holy Spirit,
one God, for ever and ever. ℟. **Amen.** ⋎

READING I   Is 58, 9-14

The prophet's thoughts expand to include the eschatological day. When lowliness unites all men, then God will fill the need of the whole world with his glorious presence. Fasting makes the wealthy poor, and the poor will impart their spirit of humble waiting upon God to the wealthy.

A reading from the book of the prophet Isaiah

Thus says the Lord:
If you remove from your midst oppression,
    false accusation and malicious speech;
If you bestow your bread on the hungry
    and satisfy the afflicted;
Then light shall rise for you in the darkness,
    and the gloom shall become for you like midday;
Then the Lord will guide you always
    and give you plenty even on the parched land.

He will renew your strength,
and you shall be like a watered garden,
like a spring whose water never fails.
The ancient ruins shall be rebuilt for your sake,
and the foundations from ages past you shall
raise up;
"Repairer of the breach," they shall call you,
"Restorer of ruined homesteads."
If you hold back your foot on the sabbath
from following your own pursuits on my holy day;
If you call the sabbath a delight,
and the Lord's holy day honorable;
If you honor it by not following your ways,
seeking your own interests, or speaking with
malice—
Then you shall delight in the Lord,
and I will make you ride on the heights of the
earth;
I will nourish you with the heritage of Jacob, your
father,
for the mouth of the Lord has spoken.
This is the Word of the Lord. ℟. **Thanks be to God.** ℣

Responsorial Psalm   Ps 86, 1-2. 3-4. 5-6

℟. (11) **Teach me your way, O Lord, that I may be
faithful in your sight.**

Incline your ear, O Lord; answer me,
for I am afflicted and poor.
Keep my life, for I am devoted to you;
save your servant who trusts in you. — ℟

You are my God; have pity on me, O Lord,
for to you I call all the day.
Gladden the soul of your servant,
for to you, O Lord, I lift up my soul. — ℟

For you, O Lord, are good and forgiving,
abounding in kindness to all who call upon you.
Hearken, O Lord, to my prayer
and attend to the sound of my pleading. — ℟ ℣

GOSPEL   Lk 5, 27-32
Verse before the Gospel (Ez 33, 11)
℟. **Glory to you, Word of God, Lord Jesus Christ!**
I do not wish the sinner to die, says the Lord,
but to turn to me and live.
℟. **Glory to you, Word of God, Lord Jesus Christ!**

Jesus invites Levi (Matthew) to leave his tax post and follow him.
The Pharisees and scribes could not understand why Jesus would
eat with the unclean. Our Lord refers ironically to the self-righteous.
Jesus invites sinners who repent to become his guests at the heavenly
banquet.

℣. The Lord be with you. ℟. **And also with you.**
✠ A reading from the holy gospel according to Luke
℟. **Glory to you, Lord.**

Jesus saw a tax collector named Levi sitting at his
customs post. He said to him, "Follow me." Leaving
everything behind, Levi stood up and became his
follower. After that Levi gave a great reception for
Jesus in his house, in which he was joined by a large
crowd of tax collectors and others at dinner. The
Pharisees and the scribes of their party said to his
disciples, "Why do you eat and drink with tax collectors and non-observers of the law?" Jesus said to
them, "The healthy do not need a doctor; sick people
do. I have not come to invite the self-righteous to
a change of heart, but sinners."—This is the gospel
of the Lord. ℟. **Praise to you. Lord Jesus Christ.**

➔ No. 15, p. 623

PRAYER OVER THE GIFTS
Lord,
receive our sacrifice of praise and reconciliation.
Let it free us from sin
and enable us to give you loving service.
We ask this in the name of Jesus the Lord.
℟. **Amen.**   ➔ No. 21, p. 626 (Pref. P 8-11)

COMMUNION ANT.   Mt 9, 13

It is mercy that I want, and not sacrifice, says the Lord; I did not come to call the virtuous, but sinners. ℣

PRAYER AFTER COMMUNION

Lord,
we are nourished by the bread of life you give us.
May this mystery we now celebrate
help us to reach eternal life with you.
Grant this through Christ our Lord.
℟. **Amen.** _____ → No. 32, p. 650

MONDAY OF THE FIRST WEEK OF LENT

The same precept which binds us to love God also binds us to love our neighbor.We are bound to love our neighbor in thought, word, and deed from the motive of divine charity. This is a superior love and a higher order of charity, and it is grounded on faith and the love of God. Let us strive to purify ourselves of all our sins, and with the proper motive, perform good works with true charity and love toward God's "little ones."

ENTRANCE ANT.   Ps 123, 2-3

As the eyes of servants are on the hands of their master, so our eyes are fixed on the Lord our God, pleading for his mercy. Have mercy on us, Lord, have mercy.   → No. 2, p. 614

OPENING PRAYER

God our savior,
bring us back to you
and fill our minds with your wisdom.
May we be enriched by our observance of Lent.
Grant this through our Lord Jesus Christ, your Son,
who lives and reigns with you and the Holy Spirit,
one God, for ever and ever. ℟. **Amen.** ℣

READING I   Lv 19, 1-2. 11-18

The general theme of Leviticus is, "Be holy, because I, the Lord, your God, am holy." One directive comes out in a positive way in this passage: "You shall love your neighbor as yourself. . ." Men must not cheat or lie. There must be strict, impartial justice, no gossip, and no plotting against the life of a fellow-countryman.

A reading from the book of Leviticus

The Lord said to Moses, "Speak to the whole Israelite community and tell them: Be holy, for I, the Lord, your God, am holy.

"You shall not steal. You shall not lie or speak falsely to one another. You shall not swear falsely by my name, thus profaning the name of your God. I am the Lord.

"You shall not defraud or rob your neighbor. You shall not withhold overnight the wages of your day laborer. You shall not curse the deaf, or put a stumbling block in front of the blind, but you shall fear your God. I am the Lord.

"You shall not act dishonestly in rendering judgment. Show neither partiality to the weak nor deference to the mighty, but judge your fellow men justly. You shall not go about spreading slander among your kinsmen; nor shall you stand by idly when your neighbor's life is at stake. I am the Lord.

"You shall not bear hatred for your brother in your heart. Though you may have to reprove your fellow man, do not incur sin because of him. Take no revenge and cherish no grudge against your fellow countrymen. You shall love your neighbor as yourself. I am the Lord."—This is the Word of the Lord. ℟. **Thanks be to God.** ℣

Responsorial Psalm   Ps 19, 8. 9. 10. 15

℟. (Jn 6, 63) **Your words, Lord, are spirit and life.**

The law of the Lord is perfect,
    refreshing the soul;
The decree of the Lord is trustworthy,
    giving wisdom to the simple. — ℟

The precepts of the Lord are right,
    rejoicing the heart;

The command of the Lord is clear,
　　enlightening the eye. — ℟

The fear of the Lord is pure,
　　enduring forever;
The ordinances of the Lord are true,
　　all of them just. — ℟

Let the words of my mouth and the thought of my
　　　　heart
　　find favor before you,
　　O Lord, my rock and my redeemer. — ℟ ℣

GOSPEL　　　　　　　　　　　　　　　Mt 25, 31-46

Verse before the Gospel (2 Cor 6, 2)

℟. **Praise to you, Lord Jesus Christ, king of endless
　　glory!**

This is the favorable time,
this is the day of salvation.

℟. **Praise to you, Lord Jesus Christ, king of endless
　　glory!**

The final judgment by God will depend on how each man has lived.
The accent falls on Jesus' repeated phrase: Truly I say to you, as you
did it—or did it not—to one of the least of these my brothers, you did
it—or did it not—to me.

℣. The Lord be with you. ℟. **And also with you.**
✠ A reading from the holy gospel according to Matthew. ℟. **Glory to you, Lord.**

Jesus said to his disciples: "When the Son of Man
comes in his glory, escorted by all the angels of heav-
en, he will sit upon his royal throne and all the nations will be assembled before him. Then he will
separate them into two groups, as a shepherd separates sheep from goats. The sheep he will place on
his right hand, the goats on his left. The king will
say to those on his right: 'Come, you have my Father's blessing! Inherit the kingdom prepared for
you from the creation of the world. For I was hungry and you gave me food, I was thirsty and you
gave me drink. I was a stranger and you welcomed

me, naked and you clothed me. I was ill and you comforted me, in prison and you came to visit me.' Then the just will ask him: 'Lord, when did we see you hungry and feed you or see you thirsty and give you drink? When did we welcome you away from home or clothe you in your nakedness? When did we visit you when you were ill or in prison?' The king will answer them: 'I assure you, as often as you did it for one of my least brothers, you did it for me.'

"Then he will say to those on his left: 'Out of my sight, you condemned, into that everlasting fire prepared for the devil and his angels! I was hungry and you gave me no food, I was thirsty and you gave me no drink. I was away from home and you gave me no welcome, naked and you gave me no clothing. I was ill and in prison and you did not come to comfort me.' Then they in turn will ask: 'Lord, when did we see you hungry or thirsty or away from home or naked or ill or in prison and not attend you in your needs?' He will answer them: 'I assure you, as often as you neglected to do it to one of these least ones, you neglected to do it to me.' These will go off to eternal punishment and the just to eternal life."— This is the gospel of the Lord. R̸. **Praise to you, Lord Jesus Christ.**   ➜ No. 15, p. 623

PRAYER OVER THE GIFTS

Lord,
may this offering of our love
be acceptable to you.
Let it transform our lives
and bring us your mercy.
We ask this through Christ our Lord.
R̸. **Amen.**   ➜ No. 21, p. 626 (Pref. P 8-11)

COMMUNION ANT.   Mt 25, 40. 34

I tell you, anything you did for the least of my brothers, you did for me, says the Lord. Come, you whom

my Father has blessed; inherit the kingdom prepared
for you since the foundation of the world. ℣

PRAYER AFTER COMMUNION

Lord,
through this sacrament
may we rejoice in your healing power
and experience your saving love in mind and body.
We ask this in the name of Jesus the Lord.
℟. **Amen.**   _____   ➔ No. 32, p. 650

TUESDAY OF THE FIRST WEEK OF LENT

Lent is for special graces; marvelous things happen during this sacred
time. We overselves do not lay down the conditions for our salvation.
God does that. When we pray, we should mean what we say and keep
our mind on what we are doing. Glorify God, adore him, praise him—
then ask!

ENTRANCE ANT.   Ps 90, 1-2

**In every age, O Lord, you have been our refuge. From
all eternity, you are God.**   ➔ No. 2, p. 614

OPENING PRAYER

Father,
look on us, your children.
Through the discipline of Lent
help us to grow in our desire for you.
We ask this through our Lord Jesus Christ, your Son,
who lives and reigns with you and the Holy Spirit,
one God, for ever and ever. ℟. **Amen.** ℣

READING I   Is 55, 10-11

Isaiah directs his hearers to come to the Lord, especially when in
need. It is necessary to seek the Lord while he may be found. God
alone lays down the conditions for salvation.

A reading from the book of the prophet Isaiah

For just as from the heavens
    the rain and snow come down
And do not return there
    till they have watered the earth,
    making it fertile and fruitful,

Giving seed to him who sows
  and bread to him who eats,
So shall my word be
  that goes forth from my mouth;
It shall not return to me void,
  but shall do my will,
    achieving the end for which I sent it.
This is the Word of the Lord. ℞. **Thanks be to God.** ℣

Responsorial Psalm   Ps 34, 4-5. 6-7. 16-17 18-19

℞. (18) **From all their afflictions
God will deliver the just.**

Glorify the Lord with me,
  let us together extol his name.
I sought the Lord, and he answered me
  and delivered me from all my fears. — ℞

Look to him that you may be radiant with joy,
  and your faces may not blush with shame.
When the afflicted man called out, the Lord heard,
  and from all his distress he saved him. — ℞

The Lord has eyes for the just,
  and ears for their cry.
The Lord confronts the evildoers,
  to destroy remembrance of them from the
    earth. — ℞

When the just cry out, the Lord hears them,
  and from all their distress he rescues them.
The Lord is close to the brokenhearted;
  and those who are crushed in spirit he
    saves. — ℞ ℣

GOSPEL   Mt 6, 7-15
Verse before the Gospel (Mt 4, 4)

℞. **Praise and honor to you, Lord Jesus Christ!**
Man does not live by bread alone,
but on every word that comes from the mouth of God.
℞. **Praise and honor to you, Lord Jesus Christ!**

Jesus gives advice about prayer. He notes that sincerity and attention are required. Then he gives an example of how to pray. God forgives those who forgive others' faults.

℣. The Lord be with you. ℟. **And also with you.**
✠ A reading from the holy gospel according to Matthew. ℟. **Glory to you, Lord.**

Jesus said to his disciples: "In your prayer do not rattle on like the pagans. They think they will win a hearing by the sheer multiplication of words. Do not imitate them. Your Father knows what you need before you ask him. This is how you are to pray:

'Our Lord in heaven,
hallowed be your name,
your kingdom come,
your will be done
on earth as it is in heaven.
Give us today our daily bread,
and forgive us the wrong we have done
as we forgive those who wrong us.
Subject us not to the trial
but deliver us from the evil one.'

"If you forgive the faults of others, your heavenly Father will forgive you yours. If you do not forgive others, neither will your Father forgive you."—This is the gospel of the Lord. ℟. **Praise to you, Lord Jesus Christ.**   ➤ No. 15, p. 623

PRAYER OVER THE GIFTS

Father of creation,
from all you have given us
we bring you this bread and wine.
May it become for us the food of eternal life.
We ask this in the name of Jesus the Lord.
℟. **Amen.**   ➤ No. 21, 626 (Pref. P 8-11)

COMMUNION ANT.   Ps 4, 2

My God of justice, you answer my cry; you come to my help when I am in trouble. Take pity on me, Lord, and hear my prayer. ℣

PRAYER AFTER COMMUNION

Lord,
may we who receive this sacrament
restrain our earthly desires
and grow in love for the things of heaven.
Grant this through Christ our Lord.
℟. **Amen.** ──────────── ➤ No. 32, p. 650

WEDNESDAY OF THE FIRST WEEK OF LENT

Many of those now separated from God will again one day hear the voice of God as did the people of Nineveh. This should help us reflect on the tremendous love God has for his people. Let us consider Jesus' great love for us and we shall be led to offer him our love in return. Our Divine Master shows his love by his sufferings for us.

ENTRANCE ANT.   Ps 25, 6. 3. 22

Remember your mercies, Lord, your tenderness from ages past. Do not let our enemies triumph over us; O God, deliver Israel from all her distress.

➤ No. 2, p. 614

OPENING PRAYER

Lord,
look upon us and hear our prayer.
By the good works you inspire,
help us to discipline our bodies
and to be renewed in spirit.
Grant this through our Lord Jesus Christ, your Son,
who lives and reigns with you and the Holy Spirit,
one God for ever and ever. ℟. **Amen.** ▾

READING I   Jon 3, 1-10

Jonah was running away from his job of preaching penance to the people of Nineveh who were offending God by their wickedness. But God directs Jonah to encourage the people to repent. They listen and begin a fast. God is moved by their actions and spares them.

A reading from the book of the prophet Jonah

The word of the Lord came to Jonah: "Set out for the great city of Nineveh, and announce to it the message that I will tell you." So Jonah made ready and went to Nineveh, according to the Lord's bidding. Now Nineveh was an enormously large city; it took three days to go through it. Jonah began his journey through the city, and had gone but a single day's walk announcing, "Forty days more and Nineveh shall be destroyed," when the people of Nineveh believed God; they proclaimed a fast and all of them, great and small, put on sackcloth.

When the news reached the king of Nineveh, he rose from his throne, laid aside his robe, covered himself with sackcloth, and sat in the ashes. Then he had this proclaimed throughout Nineveh, by decree of the king and his nobles: "Neither man nor beast, neither cattle nor sheep, shall taste anything; they shall not eat, nor shall they drink water. Man and beast shall be covered with sackcloth and call loudly to God; every man shall turn from his evil way and from the violence he has in hand. Who knows, God may relent and forgive, and withhold his blazing wrath, so that we shall not perish." When God saw by their actions how they turned from their evil way, he repented of the evil that he had threatened to do to them; he did not carry it out.—This is the Word of the Lord. ℟. **Thanks be to God. ℣**

Responsorial Psalm   Ps 51, 3-4. 12-13. 18-19

℟. (19) **A broken, humbled heart,**
    O God, you will not scorn.

Have mercy on me, O God, in your goodness;
    in the greatness of your compassion wipe out my
        offense.
Thoroughly wash me from my guilt
    and of my sin cleanse me. — ℟

A clean heart create for me, O God,
    and a steadfast spirit renew within me.

Cast me not out from your presence,
  and your holy spirit take not from me. — ℞

For you are not pleased with sacrifices;
  should I offer a holocaust, you would not accept it.

My sacrifice, O God, is a contrite spirit;
  a heart contrite and humbled, O God, you will not
    spurn. — ℞ ℣

GOSPEL   Lk 11, 29-32

Verse before the Gospel (Jl 2, 12-13)

℞. **Glory and praise to you, Lord Jesus Christ!**
With all your heart turn to me
for I am tender and compassionate.
℞. **Glory and praise to you, Lord Jesus Christ!**

The Son of Man is a sign far greater than that of Jonah, but the scribes
and Pharisees are not converted. Jesus speaks as the one sent. He
is not only the prophet but also the Redeemer. Jesus praises the
people of Nineveh, but the present generation will be judged by their
response.

℣. The Lord be with you. ℞. **And also with you.**
✠ A reading from the holy gospel according to Luke
℞. **Glory to you, Lord.**

While the crowds pressed around Jesus, he began
to speak to them in these words: "This is an evil age.
It seeks a sign. But no sign will be given it except
the sign of Jonah. Just as Jonah was a sign to the
Ninevites, so will the Son of Man be a sign for the
present age. The queen of the south will rise at the
judgment along with the men of this generation, and
she will condemn them. She came from the farthest
corner of the world to listen to the wisdom of Solomon, but you have a greater than Solomon here. At
the judgment, the citizens of Nineveh will rise along
with the present generation, and they will condemn
it. For at the preaching of Jonah they reformed, but
you have a greater than Jonah here."—This is the
gospel of the Lord. ℞. **Praise to you, Lord Jesus
Christ.**
➤ No. 15, p. 623

PRAYER OVER THE GIFTS

Lord,
from all you have given us,
we bring you these gifts in your honor.
Make them the sacrament of our salvation.
We ask this through Christ our Lord.
℟. **Amen.**   ➔ No. 21, p. 626 (Pref. P 8-11)

COMMUNION ANT.   Ps 5, 12

Lord, give joy to all who trust in you; be their defender and make them happy for ever. ⍏

PRAYER AFTER COMMUNION

Father,
you have never fail to give us the food of life.
May this eucharist renew our strength
and bring us to salvation.
Grant this through Christ our Lord.
℟. **Amen.**   ➔ No. 32, p. 650

THURSDAY OF THE FIRST WEEK OF LENT

God promises the necessities of life and at the same time expects
us to perform our daily duties in order to obtain them. Let us avoid
all undue anxiety and inordinate care about the things of this life.
"Your heavenly Father knows all that you need. Seek first his kingship
over you, his way of holiness, and all these things will be given you
besides" (Mt 6, 32-33).

ENTRANCE ANT.   Ps 5, 2-3

**Let my words reach your ears, Lord; listen to my
groaning, and hear the cry of my prayer, O my King,
my God.**   ➔ No. 2, p. 614

OPENING PRAYER

Father,
without you we can do nothing.
By your Spirit help us to know what is right
and to be eager in doing your will.
We ask this through our Lord Jesus Christ, your Son,

who lives and reigns with you and the Holy Spirit,
one God, for ever and ever. ℟. **Amen.** ℣

READING I   Est C, 12. 14-16. 23-25

Esther, a Jewess, became queen of Persia, and King Assuerus fixed
a date for the extermination of all Jews. Esther intervenes, asking
help from the Lord, and the Jews are victorious. Esther's prayer and
penance earned God's care. This Book shows how God protected his
people.

A reading from the book of Esther

Queen Esther, seized with mortal anguish, had recourse to the Lord. She prayed to the Lord, the God
of Israel, saying: "My Lord, our King, you alone are
God. Help me, who am alone and have no help but
you, for I am taking my life in my hand. As a child
I was wont to hear from the people of the land of
my forefathers that you, O Lord, chose Israel from
among all peoples, and our fathers from among all
their ancestors, as a lasting heritage, and that you
fulfilled all your promises to them.

"Be mindful of us, O Lord. Manifest yourself in
the time of our distress and give me courage, King
of gods and Ruler of every power. Put in my mouth
persuasive words in the presence of the lion, and
turn his heart to hatred for our enemy, so that he
and those who are in league with him may perish.
Save us by your power, and help me, who am alone
and have no one but you, O Lord. You know all
things."—This is the Word of the Lord. ℟. **Thanks
be to God.** ℣

Responsorial Psalm   Ps 138, 1-2. 2-3. 7-8
℟. (3) **Lord, on the day I called for help,
    you answered me.**

I will give thanks to you, O Lord, with all my heart,
    [for you have heard the words of my mouth;]
        in the presence of the angels I will sing your
        praise;

I will worship at your holy temple
and give thanks to your name. — ℟

Because of your kindness and your truth;
for you have made great above all things
your name and your promise.

When I called, you answered me;
you built up strength within me. — ℟

Your right hand saves me.
The Lord will complete what he has done for me;
Your kindness, O Lord, endures forever;
forsake not the work of your hands. — ℟ ℣

GOSPEL   Mt 7, 7-12

Verse before the Gospel (Ps 51, 12. 14)

℟. **Glory to you, Word of God, Lord Jesus Christ!**
Create a clean heart in me, O God;
give back to me the joy of your salvation.
℟. **Glory to you, Word of God, Lord Jesus Christ!**

Jesus advised how important it is to keep clear the notion of God's
power and goodness, especially in prayer. The faith necessary for
prayer is really a firm hope that springs from belief in Jesus. God
will answer those who call upon him.

℣. The Lord be with you. ℟. **And also with you.**
✠ A reading from the holy gospel according to Matthew. ℟. **Glory to you, Lord.**

Jesus said to his disciples: "Ask, and you will receive.
Seek, and you will find. Knock, and it will be opened
to you. For the one who asks, receives. The one who
seeks, finds. The one who knocks, enters. Would
one of you hand his son a stone when he asks for a
loaf, or a poisonous snake when he asks for a fish?
If you, with all your sins, know how to give your
children what is good, how much more will your
heavenly Father give good things to anyone who
asks him!

"Treat others the way you would have them treat
you: this sums up the law and the prophets."—This

is the gospel of the Lord. ℟. **Praise to you, Lord Jesus Christ.**   ➤ No. 15, p. 623

PRAYER OVER THE GIFTS

Lord,
be close to your people,
accept our prayers and offerings,
and let us turn to you with all our hearts.
We ask this in the name of Jesus the Lord.
℟. **Amen.**   ➤ No. 21, p. 626 (Pref. P 8-11)

COMMUNION ANT.   Mt 7, 8

Everyone who asks will receive; whoever seeks shall find, and to him who knocks it shall be opened. ℣

PRAYER AFTER COMMUNION

Lord our God,
renew us by these mysteries.
May they heal us now
and bring us eternal salvation.
Grant this through Christ our Lord.
℟. **Amen.**   ➤ No. 32, p. 650

FRIDAY OF THE FIRST WEEK OF LENT

The second commandment is like the first in that it is concerned with love—the love of our neighbor as ourself. We must love our neighbor in thought, word, and deed—in thought, by never judging anything evil of him; in word, by carefully abstaining from any calumny or detraction; in deed, by being charitable in our actions. "Let us love in deed and in truth," says St. John, "and not merely talk about it" (1 John 3, 18).

ENTRANCE ANT.   Ps 25, 17-18

Lord, deliver me from my distress. See my hardship and my poverty, and pardon all my sins.

➤ No. 2, p. 614

OPENING PRAYER

Lord,
may our observance of Lent

help to renew us and prepare us
to celebrate the death and resurrection of Christ,
who lives and reigns with you and the Holy Spirit,
one God, for ever and ever. ℟. **Amen.** ⩣

READING I　　　Ez 18, 21-28

Ezekiel was the prophet during the Babylonian exile. Ezekiel preaches
the same message that Jeremiah did: Repent and all will be well. He
brings out personal accountability. A man lives only by keeping God's
law joyfully.

A reading from the book of the prophet Ezekiel

If the wicked man turns away from all the sins he
committed, if he keeps all my statutes and does
what is right and just, he shall surely live, he shall
not die. None of the crimes he committed shall be
remembered against him; he shall live because of
the virtue he has practiced. Do I indeed derive any
pleasure from the death of the wicked? says the
Lord God. Do I not rather rejoice when he turns from
his evil way that he may live?

And if the virtuous man turns from the path of
virtue to do evil, the same kind of abominable things
that the wicked man does, can he do this and still
live? None of his virtuous deeds shall be remembered,
because he has broken faith and committed sin; because of this, he shall die. You say, "The Lord's way
is not fair!" Hear now, house of Israel: Is it my way
that is unfair, or rather, are not your ways unfair?
When a virtuous man turns away from virtue to commit iniquity, and dies, it is because of the iniquity
he committed that he must die. But if a wicked man,
turning from the wickedness he has committed, does
what is right and just, he shall preserve his life; since
he has turned away from all the sins which he committed, he shall surely live, he shall not die.—This
is the Word of the Lord. ℟. **Thanks be to God.** ⩣

Responsorial Psalm　　　Ps 130, 1-2. 3-4. 4-6. 7-8
℟. (3) **If you, O Lord, laid bare our guilt
who could endure it?**

Out of the depths I cry to you, O Lord;
　　Lord, hear my voice!
Let your ears be attentive
　　to my voice in supplication. — ℞

If you, O Lord, mark iniquities,
　　Lord, who can stand?
But with you is forgiveness,
　　that you may be revered. — ℞

I trust in the Lord;
　　my soul trusts in his word.
My soul waits for the Lord
　　more than sentinels wait for the dawn.
Let Israel wait for the Lord. — ℞

For with the Lord is kindness
　　and with him is plenteous redemption;
And he will redeem Israel
　　from all their iniquities. — ℞ ⍒

GOSPEL Mt 5, 20-26

Verse before the Gospel (Ez 18, 31)

℞. **Praise to you, Lord Jesus Christ, king of endless
　　glory!**
Rid yourselves of all your sins;
and make a new heart and a new spirit.
℞. **Praise to you, Lord Jesus Christ, king of endless
　　glory!**

Christ talks about occasions of sin—do not get angry and you will
not be a murderer. It is not easy to understand the graduations of
guilt that our Lord mentions in this passage. A man is under God's
judgment when he cherishes hatred and anger. He should seek forgiveness of his brother if he wrongs him.

℣. The Lord be with you. ℞. **And also with you.**
✠ A reading from the holy gospel according to Matthew. ℞. **Glory to you, Lord.**
Jesus said to his disciples: "Unless your holiness
surpasses that of the scribes and Pharisees you shall
not enter the kingdom of God. You have heard the

commandment imposed on your forefathers, 'You shall not commit murder; every murderer shall be liable to judgment.' What I say to you is: everyone who grows angry with his brother shall be liable to judgment, any man who uses abusive language toward his brother shall be answerable to the Sanhedrin, and if he holds him in contempt he risks the fires of Gehenna. If you bring your gift to the altar and there recall that your brother has anything against you, leave your gift at the altar, go first to be reconciled with your brother, and then come and offer your gift. Lose no time; settle with your opponent while on your way to court with him. Otherwise your opponent may hand you over to the judge, who will hand you over to the guard, who will throw you into prison. I warn you, you will not be released until you have paid the last penny."—This is the gospel of the Lord. ℟. **Praise to you, Lord Jesus Christ.** ➜ No. 15, p. 623

PRAYER OVER THE GIFTS

Lord of mercy,
in your love accept these gifts.
May they bring us your saving power.
We ask this in the name of Jesus the Lord.
℟. **Amen.** ➜ No. 21, p. 626 (Pref. P 8-11)

COMMUNION ANT. Ez 33, 11

By my life, I do not wish the sinner to die, says the Lord, but to turn to me and live. ℣

PRAYER AFTER COMMUNION

Lord,
may the sacrament you give us
free us from our sinful ways and bring us new life.
May this eucharist lead us to salvation.
Grant this through Christ our Lord.
℟. **Amen.** ➜ No. 32, p. 650

SATURDAY OF THE FIRST WEEK OF LENT

St. Bernard tells us that perfection is a sincere purpose to go forward and increase in virtue, that is to say, in loving God and our neighbor. Prayer is a necessary means of perfection. The test of the repentant sinner is how courageously he can cut out the roots of evil habits and how wholeheartedly he is able to forgive his brother. The touch of the Divine Hand is never absent.

ENTRANCE ANT.   Ps 19, 8

The law of the Lord is perfect, reviving the soul; his commandments are the wisdom of the simple.

➤ No. 2, p. 614

OPENING PRAYER

Eternal Father,
turn our hearts to you.
By seeking your kingdom
and loving one another,
may we become a people who worship you
in spirit and truth.
Grant this through our Lord Jesus Christ, your Son,
who lives and reigns with you and the Holy Spirit,
one God, for ever and ever. ℟. **Amen.** ✠

READING I   Dt 26, 16-19

The Book of Deuteronomy literally means the Book of the Second Law which is concerned with the Ten Commandments. The Jewish people are told by God to observe these laws with all their heart and soul. It is in this pact that God makes the Jewish people a people chosen to be his own.

A reading from the book of Deuteronomy

Moses spoke to the people, saying: "This day the Lord, your God, commands you to observe these statutes and decrees. Be careful, then, to observe them with all your heart and with all your soul. Today you are making this agreement with the Lord: he is to be your God and you are to walk in his ways and observe his statutes, commandments and decrees, and to hearken to his voice. And today the Lord is making this agreement with you: you are to

be a people peculiarly his own, as he promised you;
and provided you keep all his commandments, he
will then raise you high in praise and renown and
glory above all other nations he has made, and you
will be a people sacred to the Lord, your God, as he
promised."—This is the Word of the Lord. ℟. **Thanks
be to God.** ✣

Responsorial Psalm   Ps 119, 1-2. 4-5. 7-8

℟. (1) **Happy are they who follow the law of the Lord.**

Happy are they whose way is blameless,
    who walk in the law of the Lord.
Happy are they who observe his decrees,
    who seek him with all their heart. — ℟

You have commanded that your precepts
    be diligently kept.
Oh, that I might be firm in the ways
    of keeping your statutes! — ℟

I will give you thanks with an upright heart,
    when I have learned your just ordinances.
I will keep your statutes;
    do not utterly forsake me. — ℟ ✣

GOSPEL   Mt 5, 43-48

Verse before the Gospel (2 Cor 6, 2)

℟. **Praise and honor to you, Lord Jesus Christ!**
This is the favorable time,
this is the day of salvation.
℟. **Praise and honor to you, Lord Jesus Christ!**

The law of Christian love is not hard to practice when no harm has
been done, but to love an enemy is difficult. Jesus' command is to
love our enemies and pray for our persecutors. In this way, man becomes perfect.

℣. The Lord be with you. ℟. **And also with you.**
✠ A reading from the holy gospel according to Matthew. ℟. **Glory to you, Lord.**

Jesus said to his disciples: "You have heard the commandment, 'You shall love your countryman but hate

your enemy.' My command to you is: love your enemies, pray for your persecutors. This will prove that you are sons of your heavenly Father, for his sun rises on the bad and the good, he rains on the just and the unjust. If you love those who love you, what merit is there in that? Do not tax collectors do as much? And if you greet your brothers only, what is so praiseworthy about that? Do not pagans do as much? In a word, you must be perfected as your heavenly Father is perfect."—This is the gospel of the Lord. ℟. **Praise to you, Lord Jesus Christ.**

➤ No. 15, p. 623

PRAYER OVER THE GIFTS

Lord,
may we be renewed by this eucharist.
May we become more like Christ your Son,
who is Lord for ever and ever.
℟. **Amen.**   ➤ No. 21, p. 626 (Pref. P 8-11)

COMMUNION ANT.   Mt 5, 48

Be perfect, as your heavenly Father is perfect, says the Lord. ℣

PRAYER AFTER COMMUNION

Lord,
may the word we share
be our guide to peace in your kingdom.
May the food we receive
assure us of your constant love.
We ask this in the name of Jesus the Lord.
℟. **Amen.**   ➤ No. 32, p. 650

MONDAY OF THE SECOND WEEK OF LENT

The Mass today teaches us not to look all around for someone to accuse and to blame. We should recognize our own personal sinfulness and not be too ready to give ourselves absolution. How often do we pray: "Forgive us our wrongdoings as we forgive those who do wrong to us"?

ENTRANCE ANT.   Ps 26, 11-12

Redeem me, Lord, and have mercy on me; my foot is set on the right path, I worship you in the great assembly.   ➤ No. 2, p. 614

OPENING PRAYER

God our Father,
teach us to find new life through penance.
Keep us from sin,
and help us live by your commandment of love.
We ask this through our Lord Jesus Christ, your Son,
who lives and reigns with you and the Holy Spirit,
one God, for ever and ever. ℟. **Amen.** ✟

READING I   Dn 9, 4-10

Daniel makes a sort of national act of contrition. Punishments on a people must be suffered right here when there is a question of corporate blame for defying God's law, or credit for keeping it.

A reading from the book of the prophet Daniel

"Lord, great and awesome God, you who keep your merciful covenant toward those who love you and observe your commandments! We have sinned, been wicked and done evil; we have rebelled and departed from your commandments and your laws. We have not obeyed your servants the prophets, who spoke in your name to our kings, our princes, our fathers, and all the people of the land. Justice, O Lord, is on your side; we are shamefaced even to this day: the men of Judah, the residents of Jerusalem, and all Israel, near and far, in all the countries to which you have scattered them because of their treachery toward you. O Lord, we are shamefaced, like our kings, our princes, and our fathers, for having sinned against you. But yours, O Lord, our God, are compassion and forgiveness! Yet we rebelled against you and paid no heed to your command, O Lord, our God, to live by the law you gave us through your

servants the prophets."—This is the Word of the
Lord. ℟. **Thanks be to God.** ℣

Responsorial Psalm   Ps 79, 8. 9. 11. 13

℟. (Ps 103, 10) **Lord, do not deal with us as our sins
    deserve.**

Remember not against us the iniquities of the past;
    may your compassion quickly come to us,
    for we are brought very low. — ℟

Help us, O God our savior,
    because of the glory of your name;
Deliver us and pardon our sins
    for your name's sake. — ℟

Let the prisoners' sighing come before you;
    with your great power free those doomed to death.
Then we, your people and the sheep of your pasture,
    will give thanks to you forever;
    through all generations we will declare your
        praise. — ℟ ℣

GOSPEL   Lk 6, 36-38

Verse before the Gospel (Jn 6, 64. 69)

℟. **Glory and praise to you, Lord Jesus Christ!**
Your words, Lord, are spirit and life;
you have the message of eternal life.
℟. **Glory and praise to you, Lord Jesus Christ!**

Jesus teaches that his disciples should be compassionate, should
not judge others, should not condemn. Pardon, forgiveness, generosity
are marks of a Christian. Measure for measure is the reward.

℣. The Lord be with you ℟. **And also with you.**
✠ A reading from the holy gospel according to Luke.
℟. **Glory to you, Lord.**

Jesus said to his disciples: "Be compassionate, as
your Father is compassionate. Do not judge, and
you will not be judged. Do not condemn, and you
will not be condemned. Pardon, and you shall be

pardoned. Give, and it shall be given to you. Good measure pressed down, shaken together, running over, will they pour into the fold of your garment. For the measure you measure with will be measured back to you."—This is the gospel of the Lord. ℟. **Praise to you, Lord Jesus Christ.**   ➤ No. 15, p. 623

PRAYER OVER THE GIFTS

Father of mercy,
hear our prayer.
May the grace of this mystery
prevent us from becoming absorbed in material
   things.
Grant this through Christ our Lord.
℟. **Amen.**   ➤ No. 21, p. 626 (Pref. P 8-11)

COMMUNION ANT.   Lk 6, 36

Be merciful as your Father is merciful, says the Lord. ⱽ

PRAYER AFTER COMMUNION

Lord,
may this communion bring us pardon
and lead us to the joy of heaven.
We ask this in the name of Jesus the Lord.
℟. **Amen.**   ➤ No. 32, p. 650

TUESDAY OF THE SECOND WEEK OF LENT

No advance in virtue is possible until one knows his faults, and knows them as God knows them. A full knowledge of past sinfulness ought to be reached by mere memory. But that faculty gives us only facts and figures. It takes no reckoning of guilt which enters the Christian's mind through a supernatural influence. One of our rudimentary graces is appreciation of sin.

ENTRANCE ANT.   Ps 13, 4-5

Give light to my eyes, Lord, lest I sleep in death, and my enemy say: I have overcome him.
➤ No. 2, p. 614

OPENING PRAYER

Lord,
watch over your Church,
and guide it with your unfailing love.
Protect us from what could harm us
and lead us to what will save us.
Help us always,
for without you we are bound to fail.
Grant this through our Lord Jesus Christ, your Son,
who lives and reigns with you and the Holy Spirit,
one God, for ever and ever. ℟. **Amen.** ℣

READING I   Is 1, 10. 16-20

The prophets talked out and most of them met a sudden death. "Your
hands are full of blood," Isaiah warns, and he tells the people to
wash themselves clean. In repentance sins are washed clean as snow.
The obstinate will suffer by the sword.

A reading from the book of the prophet Isaiah

Hear the word of the Lord,
    princes of Sodom!
Listen to the instruction of our God,
    people of Gomorrah!
    Wash yourselves clean!
Put away your misdeeds from before my eyes;
    cease doing evil; learn to do good.
Make justice your aim: redress the wronged,
    hear the orphan's plea, defend the widow.
Come now, let us set things right,
    says the Lord:
Though your sins be like scarlet,
    they may become white as snow;
Though they be crimson red,
    they may become white as wool.
If you are willing, and obey,
    you shall eat the good things of the land;
But if you refuse and resist,
    the sword shall consume you:
    for the mouth of the Lord has spoken!
This is the Word of the Lord. ℟. **Thanks be to God.** ℣

Responsorial Psalm   Ps 50, 8-9. 16-17. 21. 23

℟. (23) **To the upright**
  I will show the saving power of God.

Not for your sacrifices do I rebuke you,
  for your holocausts are before me always.
I take from your house no bullock,
  no goats out of your fold. — ℟

Why do you recite my statutes,
  and profess my covenant with your mouth,
Though you hate discipline
  and cast my words behind you? — ℟

When you do these things, shall I be deaf to it?
  Or think you that I am like yourself?
  I will correct you by drawing them up before your
    eyes.

He that offers praise as a sacrifice glorifies me;
  and to him that goes the right way I will show
    the salvation of God. — ℟ ✓

GOSPEL   Mt 23, 1-12

Verse before the Gospel (Ez 18, 31)

℟. **Glory to you, Word of God, Lord Jesus Christ!**
Rid yourselves of all your sins;
and make a new heart and a new spirit.
℟. **Glory to you, Word of God, Lord Jesus Christ!**

Christ complains about the rigor of scribal interpretation and the va-
nity and hypocrisy of the scribes and Pharisees. The Pharisees do
not practice what they preach. Jesus teaches by his humble example.

℣. The Lord be with you. ℟. **And also with you.**
✠ A reading from the holy gospel according to Matthew. ℟. **Glory to you, Lord.**

Jesus told the crowds and his disciples: "The scribes
and the Pharisees have succeeded Moses as teachers;
therefore, do everything and observe everything they
tell you. But do not follow their example. Their
words are bold but their deeds are few. They bind
up heavy loads, hard to carry, to lay on other men's

shoulders, while they themselves will not lift a finger to budge them. All their works are performed to be seen. They widen their phylacteries and wear huge tassels. They are fond of places of honor at banquets and the front seats in synagogues, of marks of respect in public and of being called 'Rabbi.' As to you, avoid the title 'Rabbi.' One among you is your teacher, the rest are learners. Do not call anyone on earth your father. Only one is your father, the One in heaven. Avoid being called teachers. Only one is your teacher, the Messiah. The greatest among you will be the one who serves the rest. Whoever exalts himself shall be humbled, but whoever humbles himself shall be exalted."—This is the gospel of the Lord. ℟. **Praise to you, Lord Jesus Christ.**

➤ No. 15, p. 623

PRAYER OVER THE GIFTS

Lord,
bring us closer to you by this celebration.
May it cleanse us from our faults
and lead us to the gifts of heaven.
We ask this through Christ our Lord.
℟. **Amen.**   ➤ No. 21, p. 626 (Pref. P 8-11)

COMMUNION ANT.   Ps 9, 2-3
I will tell all your marvelous works. I will rejoice and be glad in you, and sing to your name, Most High. ⱽ

PRAYER AFTER COMMUNION

Lord,
may the food we receive
bring us your constant assistance
that we may live better lives.
We ask this in the name of Jesus the Lord.
℟. **Amen.**   ➤ No. 32, p. 650

WEDNESDAY OF THE SECOND WEEK OF LENT

We should be honest enough to behave before men according to God's knowledge of men. How would our thoughts, words, and deeds stand examination before Christ? Let us follow the Master's maxim: "If any man desire to be first, he shall be the last of all and the minister of all" (Mark 9:35).

ENTRANCE ANT.   Ps 38, 22-23

Do not abandon me, Lord. My God, do not go away from me! Hurry to help me, Lord, my Savior.

➤ No. 2, p. 614

OPENING PRAYER

Father,
teach us to live good lives,
encourage us with your support
and bring us to eternal life.
We ask this through our Lord Jesus Christ, your Son,
who lives and reigns with you and the Holy Spirit,
one God, for ever and ever. ℟. **Amen.** ⍵

READING I   Jer 18, 18-20

"They are plotting against me," says Jeremiah, "but remember, I begged you, O Lord, to turn your wrath away from them." God's forgiveness has to be earned by a change of heart, by repentance. The prayer of vengeance is clear evidence of the fearful stress and strain imposed by Jeremiah's vocation.

A reading from the book of the prophet Jeremiah

The men of Judah and the citizens of Jerusalem said, "Let us contrive a plot against Jeremiah. It will not mean the loss of instruction from the priests, nor of counsel from the wise, nor of messages from the prophets. And so, let us destroy him by his own tongue; let us carefully note his every word."

Heed me, O Lord,
    and listen to what my adversaries say.
Must good be repaid with evil
    that they should dig a pit to take my life?
Remember that I stood before you
    to speak in their behalf,
    to turn away your wrath from them.
This is the Word of the Lord. ℟. **Thanks be to God.** ⍵

Responsorial Psalm   Ps 31, 5-6. 14. 15-16

℞. (17) **Save me, O Lord, in your steadfast love.**

You will free me from the snare they set for me,
  for you are my refuge.

Into your hands I commend my spirit;
  you will redeem me, O Lord, O faithful God. — ℞

I hear the whispers of the crowd, that frighten me
    from every side,
  as they consult together against me, plotting to
    take my life. — ℞

But my trust is in you, O Lord;
  I say, "You are my God."

In your hands is my destiny; rescue me
  from the clutches of my enemies and my perse-
    cutors. — ℞ ℣

GOSPEL   Mt 20, 17-28

Verse before the Gospel (Jn 8, 12)

℞. **Praise to you, Lord Jesus Christ, king of endless
    glory!**

I am the light of the world, says the Lord:
he who follows me will have the light of life.

℞. **Praise to you, Lord Jesus Christ, king of endless
    glory!**

The last journey to Jerusalem and the mentioning of the cross are
here used for the first time. The ransom of all men will be paid by
Christ by his own life. Jesus replies to the mother of Zebedee's sons
by promising they will drink his cup to the full but his Father alone
will award the places of honor in the next life. He who aspires to
greatness must be willing to serve.

℣. The Lord be with you. ℞. **And also with you.**

✠ A reading from the holy gospel according to Matthew. ℞. **Glory to you, Lord.**

As Jesus was starting to go up to Jerusalem, he
took the Twelve aside on the road and said to them:
"We are going up to Jerusalem now. There the Son
of Man will be handed over to the chief priests and
scribes, who will condemn him to death. They will

turn him over to the Gentiles, to be made sport of and flogged and crucified. But on the third day he will be raised up."

The mother of Zebedee's sons came up to him accompanied by her sons, to do him homage and ask of him a favor. "What is it you want?" he said. She answered, "Promise me that these sons of mine will sit, one at your right hand and the other at your left, in your kingdom." In reply Jesus said, "You do not know what you are asking. Can you drink of the cup I am to drink of?" "We can," they said. He told them, "From the cup I drink of you shall drink. Sitting at my right hand or my left is not mine to give. That is for those for whom it has been reserved by my Father." The other ten, on hearing this, became indignant at the two brothers. Jesus then called them together and said: "You know how those who exercise authority among the Gentiles lord it over them; their great ones make their importance felt. It cannot be like that with you. Anyone among you who aspires to greatness must serve the rest, and whoever wants to rank first among you, must serve the needs of all. Such is the case with the Son of Man who has come, not to be served by others but to serve, to give his own life as a ransom for the many."
—This is the gospel of the Lord. ℟. **Praise to you, Lord Jesus Christ.**   ➤ No. 15, p. 623

PRAYER OVER THE GIFTS
Lord,
accept this sacrifice,
and through this holy exchange of gifts
free us from the sins that enslave us.
We ask this in the name of Jesus the Lord.
℟. **Amen.**   ➤ No. 21, p. 626 (Pref. P 8-11)

COMMUNION ANT.   Mt 20, 28
The Son of Man did not come to be served, but to serve, and to give his life as a ransom for many. ↓

PRAYER AFTER COMMUNION

Lord our God,
may the eucharist you give us
as a pledge of unending life
help us to salvation.
Grant this through Christ our Lord.
℟. **Amen.**   ➜ No. 32, p. 650

THURSDAY OF THE SECOND WEEK OF LENT

To be detached from all material comforts for Jesus' sake is to be poor in spirit. We can be truly poor in spirit, not only by helping, but by deeply sympathizing with those who are poor. Poverty is closely related to holy wisdom. Jesus said of himself: "The foxes have lairs, the birds in the sky have nests, but the Son of Man has nowhere to lay his head" (Mt 8, 20).

ENTRANCE ANT.   Ps 139, 23-24

Test me, O God, and know my thoughts; see whether I step in the wrong path, and guide me along the everlasting way.   ➜ No. 2, p. 614

OPENING PRAYER

God of love,
bring us back to you.
Send your Spirit to make us strong in faith
and active in good works.
Grant this through our Lord Jesus Christ, your Son,
who lives and reigns with you and the Holy Spirit,
one God, for ever and ever. ℟. **Amen.** ⍐

READING I   Jer 17, 5-10

Jeremiah paints a beautiful pictures of fidelity in his prophecy. Just as a man cannot depend upon other human beings in some of the crises of life, so others cannot depend upon him either unless he has an authentic and direct relation to God.

A reading from the book of the prophet Jeremiah

Thus says the Lord:

Cursed is the man who trusts in human beings,
    who seeks his strength in flesh,
    whose heart turns away from the Lord.

He is like a barren bush in the desert
  that enjoys no change of season,
But stands in a lava waste,
  a salt and empty earth.
Blessed is the man who trusts in the Lord,
  whose hope is the Lord.
He is like a tree planted beside the waters
  that stretches out its roots to the stream:
It fears not the heat when it comes,
  its leaves stay green;
In the year of drought it shows no distress,
  but still bears fruit.
More tortuous than all else is the human heart,
  beyond remedy; who can understand it?
I, the Lord, alone probe the mind
  and test the heart,
To reward everyone according to his ways,
  according to the merit of his deeds.
This is the Word of the Lord. ℟. **Thanks be to God.** ℣

Responsorial Psalm   Ps 1, 1-2. 3. 4. 6
℟. (Ps 40, 5) **Happy are they who hope in the Lord.**
Happy the man who follows not
  the counsel of the wicked
Nor walks in the way of sinners
  nor sits in the company of the insolent,
But delights in the law of the Lord
  and meditates on his law day and night. — ℟
He is like a tree
  planted near running water,
That yields its fruit in due season,
  and whose leaves never fade.
  [Whatever he does, prospers.] — ℟
Not so, the wicked, not so;
  they are like chaff which the wind drives away.
For the Lord watches over the way of the just,
  but the way of the wicked vanishes. — ℟ ℣

GOSPEL Lk 16, 19-31

Verse before the Gospel (See Lk 8, 15)

℞. **Praise and honor to you, Lord Jesus Christ!**

Happy are they who have kept the word with a gene-
  ous heart,

and yield a harvest through perseverance.

℞. **Praise and honor to you, Lord Jesus Christ!**

In this story of the rich man and Lazarus, Our Lord addresses the
Pharisees who are fond of money. Those who make bad use of earthly riches will be punished with everlasting torments, while those who
follow Christ's example and lead poor but virtuous lives will be eternally rewarded.

℣. The Lord be with you. ℞. **And also with you.**

✠ A reading from the holy gospel according to Luke

℞. **Glory to you, Lord.**

Jesus said to the Pharisees: "Once there was a rich
man who dressed in purple and linen and feasted
splendidly every day. At his gate lay a beggar named
Lazarus, who was covered with sores. Lazarus longed
to eat the scraps that fell from the rich man's table.
The dogs even came and licked his sores. Eventually
the beggar died. He was carried by angels to the
bosom of Abraham. The rich man likewise died and
was buried. From the abode of the dead where he
was in torment, he raised his eyes and saw Abraham
afar off, and Lazarus resting in his bosom.

"He called out, 'Father Abraham, have pity on me.
Send Lazarus to dip the tip of his finger in water to
refresh my tongue, for I am tortured in these flames.'
'My child,' replied Abraham, 'remember that you
were well off in your lifetime, while Lazarus was in
misery. Now he has found consolation here, but you
have found torment. And that is not all. Between
you and us there is fixed a great abyss, so that those
who might wish to cross from here to you cannot
do so, nor can anyone cross from your side to us.'

" 'Father, I ask you, then,' the rich man said, 'send

him to my father's house where I have five brothers. Let him be a warning to them so that they may not end in this place of torment.' Abraham answered, 'They have Moses and the prophets. Let them hear them.' 'No, Father Abraham,' replied the rich man. 'But if someone would only go to them from the dead, then they would repent.' Abraham said to him, 'If they do not listen to Moses and the prophets, they will not be convinced even if one should rise from the dead.' "—This is the gospel of the Lord. ℟. **Praise to you, Lord Jesus Christ.**   ➜ No. 15, p. 623

PRAYER OVER THE GIFTS

Lord,
may this sacrifice bless our lenten observance.
May it lead us to sincere repentance.
We ask this through Christ our Lord.
℟. **Amen.**   ➜ No. 21, p. 626 (Pref. P 8-11)

COMMUNION ANT.   Ps 119, 1

Happy are those of blameless life, who follow the law of the Lord. ℣

PRAYER AFTER COMMUNION

Lord,
may the sacrifice we have offered strengthen our faith
and be seen in our love for one another.
We ask this in the name of Jesus the Lord.
℟. **Amen.**   ➜ No. 32, p. 650

FRIDAY OF THE SECOND WEEK OF LENT

Envy is either a kind of sadness because of another's prosperity or joy at his misfortunes. Such was the envy of Saul toward David, and of the Pharisees toward Christ. Envy is one of the most detestable of vices because it is so frequently found among us, and nothing else so destroys individual happiness as well as the welfare of whole nations.

ENTRANCE ANT. Ps 31, 2. 5

To you, Lord, I look for protection, never let me be disgraced. You are my refuge; save me from the trap they have laid for me. ➤ No. 2, p. 614

OPENING PRAYER

Merciful Father,
may our acts of penance bring us your forgiveness,
open our hearts to your love,
and prepare us for the coming feast of the resur-
    rection.
We ask this through our Lord Jesus Christ, your Son,
who lives and reigns with you and the Holy Spirit,
one God, for ever and ever. ℟. **Amen.** ℣

READING I Gn 37, 3-4. 12-13. 17-28

This reading reveals that God consistently brings good out of evil, success out of failure, triumph out of defeat. Joseph is a type of the redeeming Messiah. Jesus is loved by his Father, but rejected by his brothers, as Joseph was.

A reading from the book of Genesis

Israel loved Joseph best of all his sons, for he was the child of his old age; and he had made him a long tunic. When his brothers saw that their father loved him best of all his sons, they hated him so much that they would not even greet him.

One day, when his brothers had gone to pasture their father's flocks at Shechem, Israel said to Joseph, "Your brothers, you know, are tending our flocks at Shechem. Get ready; I will send you to them."

So Joseph went after his brothers and caught up with them in Dothan. They noticed him from a distance, and before he came up to them, they plotted to kill him. They said to one another: "Here comes that master dreamer! Come on, let us kill him and throw him into one of the cisterns here; we could say that a wild beast devoured him. We shall then see what comes of his dreams."

When Reuben heard this, he tried to save him from their hands, saying: "We must not take his life. Instead of shedding blood," he continued, "just throw him into that cistern there in the desert; but don't kill him outright." His purpose was to rescue him from their hands and restore him to his father. So when Joseph came up to them, they stripped him of the long tunic he had on; then they took him and threw him into the cistern, which was empty and dry.

They then sat down to their meal. Looking up, they saw a caravan of Ishmaelites coming from Gilead, their camels laden with gum, balm, and resin to be taken down to Egypt. Judah said to his brothers: "What is to be gained by killing our brother and concealing his blood? Rather, let us sell him to these Ishmaelites, instead of doing away with him ourselves. After all, he is our brother, our own flesh." His brothers agreed. They sold Joseph to the Ishmaelites for twenty pieces of silver.—This is the Word of the Lord. ℞. **Thanks be to God.** ✠

Responsorial Psalm   Ps 105, 16-17. 18-19. 20-21

℞. (5) **Remember the marvels the Lord has done.**

When the Lord called down a famine on the land
    and ruined the crop that sustained them,
He sent a man before them,
    Joseph, sold as a slave. — ℞

They had weighed him down with fetters,
    and he was bound with chains,
Till his prediction came to pass
    and the word of the Lord proved him true. — ℞

The king sent and released him,
    the ruler of the peoples set him free.
He made him lord of his house
    and ruler of all his possessions. — ℞ ✠

GOSPEL Mt 21, 33-43. 45-46

Verse before the Gospel (Jn 3, 16)

℟. **Glory and praise to you, Lord Jesus Christ!**

God loved the world so much, he gave us his only Son,

that all who believe in him might have eternal life.

℟. **Glory and praise to you, Lord Jesus Christ!**

The theme of Joseph is carried into the Gospel. It represents the same principle: what is rejected by men may become vital for salvation. The chosen people who reject Christ are really turning him over to the whole world.

℣. The Lord be with you. ℟. **And also with you.**

✠ A reading from the holy gospel according to Matthew. ℟. **Glory to you, Lord.**

Jesus said to the chief priests and elders of the people: "Listen to this parable. There was a property owner who planted a vineyard, put a hedge around it, dug out a vat, and erected a tower. Then he leased it out to tenant farmers and went on a journey. When vintage time arrived he dispatched his slaves to the tenants to obtain his share of the grapes. The tenants responded by seizing the slaves. They beat one, killed another, and stoned a third. A second time he dispatched even more slaves than before, but they treated them the same way. Finally he sent his son to them, thinking, 'They will respect my son.' When they saw the son, the tenants said to one another, 'Here is the one who will inherit everything. Let us kill him and then we shall have his inheritance!' With that they seized him, dragged him outside the vineyard, and killed him. What do you suppose the owner of the vineyard will do to those tenants when he comes?" They replied, "He will bring that wicked crowd to a bad end and lease his vineyard out to others, who will see to it that he has grapes at vintage time." Jesus said to them, "Did you never read in the Scriptures,

'The stone which the builders rejected
has become the keystone of the structure.
It was the Lord who did this
and we find it marvelous to behold'?
For this reason, I tell you, the kingdom of God will
be taken away from you and given to a nation that
will yield a rich harvest."

When the chief priests and the Pharisees heard
these parables, they realized he was speaking about
them. Although they sought to arrest him they had
reason to fear the crowds who regarded him as a
prophet.—This is the gospel of the Lord. R̲. **Praise
to you, Lord Jesus Christ.**   ➜ No. 15, p. 623

PRAYER OVER THE GIFTS

God of mercy,
prepare us to celebrate these mysteries.
Help us to live the love they proclaim.
We ask this in the name of Jesus the Lord.
R̲. **Amen.**   ➜ No. 21, p. 626 (Pref. P 8-11)

COMMUNION ANT.   1 Jn 4, 10

**God loved us and sent his Son to take away our
sins.** ℣

PRAYER AFTER COMMUNION

Lord,
may this communion so change our lives
that we may seek more faithfully
the salvation it promises.
Grant this through Christ our Lord.
R̲. **Amen.**   ➜ No. 32, p. 650

SATURDAY OF THE SECOND WEEK OF LENT

The two passages from the Bible for today's Mass are closely related. They are trustworthy testimony to the willingness of God the
Father to receive everyone at all times with the most compassionate

love. His love embraces even the greatest of sinners who truly repents. His mercy is unlimited for the contrite. How we must love God in his goodness!

ENTRANCE ANT. Ps 145, 8-9

The Lord is loving and merciful, to anger slow, and full of love; the Lord is kind to all, and compassionate to all his creatures. ➤ No. 2, p. 614

OPENING PRAYER

God our Father,
by your gifts to us on earth
we already share in your life.
In all we do,
guide us to the light of your kingdom.
Grant this through our Lord Jesus Christ, your Son,
who lives and reigns with you and the Holy Spirit,
one God, for ever and ever. ℟. **Amen.** ↓

READING I Mi 7, 14-15. 18-20

Micah denounced Israel's sins, particulary its social crimes, and he wrote about a new Israel. The latter idea may have a hidden reference to the future redemption of men by Christ and the founding of the kingdom of God. Micah is presenting God in his readiness to forgive the contrite.

A reading from the book of the prophet Micah

Shepherd your people with your staff,
    the flock of your inheritance,
That dwells apart in a woodland,
    in the midst of Carmel.
Let them feed in Bashan and Gilead,
    as in the days of old;
As in the days when you came from the land of
        Egypt,
    show us wonderful signs.
Who is there like you, the God who removes guilt
    and pardons sin for the remnant of his inheritance;
Who does not persist in anger forever,
    but delights rather in clemency,

And will again have compassion on us,
    treading underfoot our guilt?
You will cast into the depths of the sea
    all our sins;
You will show faithfulness to Jacob,
    and grace to Abraham,
As you have sworn to our fathers
    from days of old.
This is the Word of the Lord. ℟. **Thanks be to God.** ⋎

Responsorial Psalm   Ps 103, 1-2. 3-4. 9-10. 11-12

℟. (8) **The Lord is kind and merciful.**

Bless the Lord, O my soul!
    and all my being, bless his holy name.
Bless the Lord, O my soul,
    and forget not all his benefits. — ℟

He pardons all your iniquities,
    he heals all your ills.
He redeems your life from destruction,
    he crowns you with kindness and compassion. — ℟

He will not always chide,
    nor does he keep his wrath forever.
Not according to our sins does he deal with us,
    nor does he requite us according to our
        crimes — ℟

For as the heavens are high above the earth,
    so surpassing is his kindness toward those who
        fear him.
As far as the east is from the west,
    so far has he put our transgressions from us.— ℟ ⋎

GOSPEL   Lk 15, 1-3. 11-32
Verse before the Gospel (Lk 15, 18)

℟. **Glory to you, Word of God, Lord Jesus Christ!**
I will rise and go to my Father and tell him:
Father, I have sinned against heaven and against you.
℟. **Glory to you, Word of God, Lord Jesus Christ!**

The story of the Prodigal Son is the ideal story of contrition. He resents the boredom of family life and discipline and so asserts his rights, but he soon finds out that his total freedom is bringing him nothing but misery. The father receives his son back and forgives him.

℣. The Lord be with you. ℟. **And also with you.**
✠ A reading from the holy gospel according to Luke
℟. **Glory to you, Lord.**

The tax collectors and sinners were all gathering around Jesus to hear him, at which the Pharisees and the scribes murmured, "This man welcomes sinners and eats with them."

At this Jesus addressed this parable to them: "A man had two sons. The younger of them said to his father, 'Father, give me the share of the estate that is coming to me.' So the father divided up the property. Some days later this younger son collected all his belongings and went off to a distant land, where he squandered his money on dissolute living. After he had spent everything, a great famine broke out in that country and he was in dire need. So he attached himself to one of the propertied class of the place, who sent him to his farm to take care of the pigs. He longed to fill his belly with the husks that were fodder for pigs, but no one made a move to give him anything. Coming to his senses at last, he said: 'How many hired hands at my father's place have more than enough to eat, while here I am starving! I will break away and return to my father, and say to him, "Father, I have sinned against God and against you; I no longer deserve to be called your son. Treat me like one of your hired hands."' With that he set off for his father's house. While he was still a long way off, his father caught sight of him and was deeply moved. He ran out to meet him, threw his arms around his neck, and kissed him. The son said to him, 'Father, I have sinned against God and against you; I no longer deserve to be called your son.' The father said to his servants: 'Quick! bring out the finest robe and put it on him; put a ring on his finger and shoes on his feet. Take the fatted calf and kill it. Let us eat and celebrate because this son of mine was dead and has come back to life. He was lost and is found.' Then the celebration began.

"Meanwhile the elder son was out on the land. As he neared the house on his way home, he heard the sound of music and dancing. He called one of the servants and asked him the reason for the dancing and the music. The servant answered, 'Your brother is home, and your father has killed the fatted calf because he has him back in good health.' The son grew angry at this and would not go in; but his father came out and began to plead with him.

"He said to his father in reply: 'For years now I have slaved for you. I never disobeyed one of your orders, yet you never gave me so much as a kid goat to celebrate with my friends. Then, when this son of yours returns after having gone through your property with loose women, you kill the fatted calf for him.'

"'My son,' replied the father, 'you are with me always, and everything I have is yours. But we must celebrate and rejoice! This brother of yours was dead, and has come back to life. He was lost, and is found.'"—This is the gospel of the Lord. ℟. **Praise to you, Lord Jesus Christ.**   ➤ No. 15, p. 623

PRAYER OVER THE GIFTS

Lord,
may the grace of these sacraments
help us to reject all harmful things
and lead us to your spiritual gifts.
We ask this through Christ our Lord.
℟. **Amen.**   ➤ No. 21, p. 626 (Pref. P 8-11)

COMMUNION ANT.   Lk 15, 32

My son, you should rejoice, because your brother was
dead and has come back to life; he was lost and is
found. ℣

PRAYER AFTER COMMUNION

Lord,
give us the spirit of love
and lead us to share in your life.
We ask this in the name of Jesus the Lord.
℟. **Amen.** _____ ➤ No. 32, p. 650

OPTIONAL READINGS AND INTERVENIENT CHANTS
FOR THE THIRD WEEK OF LENT

*These readings and intervenient chants may be used on
any day of this week, especially when the Gospel of the
Samaritan woman is not read on the 3rd Sunday of
Lent.*

READING I   Ex 17, 1-7

The journey through the desert presents numerous difficulties for
the Israelites. They have been specially cared for by God, but now
they are without water. Impatient with Moses, they begin to complain.
When Moses asks God for help, water miraculously comes from out
of a rock.

A reading from the book of Exodus

From the desert of Sin the whole Israelite community journeyed by stages, as the Lord directed, and
encamped at Rephidim.

Here there was no water for the people to drink.
They quarreled, therefore, with Moses and said,
"Give us water to drink." Moses replied, "Why do
you quarrel with me? Why do you put the Lord to
a test?" Here, then, in their thirst for water, the
people grumbled against Moses, saying, "Why did
you ever make us leave Egypt? Was it just to have
us die here of thirst with our children and our livestock?" So Moses cried out to the Lord, "What shall

I do with this people? A little more and they will stone me!" The Lord answered Moses, "Go over there in front of the people, along with some of the elders of Israel, holding in your hand, as you go, the staff wtih which you struck the river. I will be standing there in front of you on the rock of Horeb. Strike the rock, and the water will flow from it for the people to drink." This Moses did, in the presence of the elders of Israel.—This is the Word of the Lord. ℟. **Thanks be to God.** ∀

Responsorial Psalm Ps 95, 1-2. 6-7. 8-9

℟. (7. 8) **If today you hear his voice, harden not your hearts.**

Come, let us sing joyfully to the Lord;
    let us acclaim the Rock of our salvation.
Let us greet him with thanksgiving;
    let us joyfully sing psalms to him. — ℟

Come, let us bow down in worship;
    let us kneel before the Lord who made us.
For he is our God,
    and we are the people he shepherds, the flock he
      guides. — ℟

Oh, that today you would hear his voice:
    "Harden not your hearts as at Meribah,
    as in the day of Massah in the desert,
Where your fathers tempted me;
    they tested me though they had seen my
      works." — ℟ ∀

GOSPEL Jn 4, 5-42

Verse before the Gospel (Jn 4, 42. 15)

℟. **Praise to you, Lord Jesus Christ, king of endless glory!**

Lord, you are truly the Savior of the world;
give me living water, that I may never thirst again.

℟. **Praise to you, Lord Jesus Christ, king of endless glory!**

Just as God gave water to the Israelites in the desert, Jesus offers
the Samaritan woman at the well life-giving water which will provide
eternal life. He also shows her that he knows her past. She recognizes
Jesus as prophet, and Jesus admits that he is the Messiash.

℣. The Lord be with you. ℟. **And also with you.**
✠ A reading from the holy gospel according to John
℟. **Glory to you, Lord.**

The journey of Jesus brought him to a Samaritan
town named Shechem near the plot of land which
Jacob had given to his son Joseph. This was the site
of Jacob's well. Jesus, tired from his journey, sat
down at the well.

   The hour was about noon. When a Samaritan
woman came to draw water, Jesus said to her, "Give
me a drink." (His disciples had gone off to the town
to buy provisions.) The Samaritan woman said to
him, "You are a Jew. How can you ask me, a Samaritan and a woman, for a drink?" (Recall that
Jews have nothing to do with Samaritans.) Jesus
replied:

   "If only you recognized God's gift,
   and who it is that is asking you for a drink,
   you would have asked him instead,
   and he would have given you living water."

"Sir," she challenged him, "you don't have a bucket
and this well is deep. Where do you expect to get
this flowing water? Surely you don't pretend to be
greater than our ancestor Jacob, who gave us this
well and drank from it with his sons and his flocks?"
Jesus replied:

   "Everyone who drinks this water
   will be thirsty again.
   But whoever drinks the water I give him
   will never be thirsty;
   no, the water I give
   shall become a fountain within him,
   leaping up to provide eternal life."

The woman said to him, "Give me this water, sir, so that I won't grow thirsty and have to keep coming here to draw water."

He told her, "Go, call your husband, and then come back here." "I have no husband," replied the woman. "You are right in saying you have no husband!" Jesus exclaimed. "The fact is, you have had five, and the man you are living with now is not your husband. What you said is true enough."

"Sir," answered the woman, "I can see you are a prophet. Our ancestors worshiped on this mountain, but you people claim that Jerusalem is the place where men ought to worship God." Jesus told her:

> "Believe me, woman,
> an hour is coming
> when you will worship the Father
> neither on this mountain
> nor in Jerusalem.
> You people worship what you do not understand,
> while we understand what we worship;
> after all, salvation is from the Jews.
> Yet an hour is coming, and is already here,
> when authentic worshipers
> will worship the Father in Spirit and truth.
> Indeed, it is just such worshipers
> the Father seeks.
> God is Spirit,
> and those who worship him
> must worship in Spirit and truth."

The woman said to him: "I know there is a Messiah coming. (This term means Anointed.) When he comes, he will tell us everything." Jesus replied, "I who speak to you am he."

His disciples, returning at this point, were surprised that Jesus was speaking with a woman. No one put a question, however, such as "What do you

want of him?" or "Why are you talking with her?"
The woman then left her water jar and went off into
the town. She said to the people, "Come and see
someone who told me everything I ever did! Could
this not be the Messiah?" With that they set out from
the town to meet him.

Meanwhile the disciples were urging him, "Rabbi,
eat something." But he told them:

"I have food to eat
of which you do not know."

At this the disciples said to one another, "You do
not suppose anyone has brought him something to
eat?" Jesus explained to them:

"Doing the will of him who sent me
and bringing his work to completion
is my food.
Do you not have a saying:
'Four months more
and it will be harvest!'?
Listen to what I say:
Open your eyes and see!
The fields are shining for harvest!
The reaper already collects his wages
and gathers a yield for eternal life,
that sower and reaper may rejoice together.
Here we have the saying verified:
'One man sows; another reaps.'
I sent you to reap
what you had not worked for.
Others have done the labor,
and you have come into their gain."

Many Samaritans from that town believed in him
on the strength of the woman's word of testimony:
"He told me everything I ever did." The result was
that, when these Samaritans came to him, they begged him to stay with them awhile. So he stayed there
two days, and through his own spoken word many
more came to faith. As they told the woman: "No

longer does our faith depend on your story. We have
heard for ourselves, and we know that this really
is the Savior of the Lord."—This is the gospel of
the Lord. ℟. **Praise to you, Lord Jesus Christ.**

———————————— ➤ No. 15, p. 623

MONDAY OF THE THIRD WEEK OF LENT

The Gentiles may not be as worthy as the Jews, but God in his mercy
has chosen us for his own. The Nazarenes despised Our Savior because of his humble birth, but when they learned of his miracles,
they asked that he would also heal their sick. But he refused their
request because they were without faith. If we desire not to be abandoned by God, as were the Nazarenes, we must have a lively faith.
This is a gift of God for which we should daily pray.

ENTRANCE ANT.   Ps 84, 3

**My soul is longing and pining for the courts of the
Lord; my heart and my flesh sing for joy to the living
God.**   ➤ No. 2, p. 614

OPENING PRAYER

God of mercy,
free your Church from sin
and protect it from evil.
Guide us, for we cannot be saved without you.
We ask this through our Lord Jesus Christ, your Son,
who lives and reigns with you and the Holy Spirit,
one God, for ever and ever. ℟. **Amen.** ☩

READING I   2 Kgs 5, 1-15

The story of the cure of Naaman represents an important point in the
process of the forgiveness of sin. The cure of leprosy is a good comparison. When Naaman is cured after doing what he is told, he cannot help exclaiming: "Now I know there is no God in all the earth
except in Israel!"

A reading from the second book of Kings

Naaman, the army commander of the king of Aram,
was highly esteemed and respected by his master,
for through him the Lord had brought victory to
Aram. But valiant as he was, the man was a leper.

Now the Arameans had captured from the land of Israel in a raid a little girl, who became the servant of Naaman's wife. "If only my master would present himself to the prophet in Samaria," she said to her mistress, "he would cure him of his leprosy." Naaman went and told his lord just what the slave girl from the land of Israel had said. "Go," said the king of Aram. "I will send along a letter to the king of Israel." So Naaman set out, taking along ten silver talents, six thousand gold pieces, and ten festal garments. To the king of Israel he brought the letter, which read: "With this letter I am sending my servant Naaman to you, that you may cure him of his leprosy."

When he read the letter, the king of Israel tore his garments and exclaimed: "Am I a god with power over life and death, that this man should send someone to me to be cured of leprosy? Take note! You can see he is only looking for a quarrel with me!" When Elisha, the man of God, heard that the king of Israel had torn his garments, he sent word to the king: "Why have you torn your garments? Let him come to me and find out that there is a prophet in Israel."

Naaman came with his horses and chariots and stopped at the door of Elisha's house. The prophet sent him the message: "Go and wash seven times in the Jordan, and your flesh will heal, and you will be clean." But Naaman went away angry, saying, "I thought that he would surely come out and stand there to invoke the Lord his God, and would move his hand over the spot, and thus cure the leprosy. Are not the rivers of Damascus, the Abana and the Pharpar, better than all the waters of Israel? Could I not wash in them and be cleansed?" With this, he turned about in anger and left.

But his servants came up and reasoned with him.

"My father," they said, "if the prophet had told you to do something extraordinary, would you not have done it? All the more now, since he said to you, 'Wash and be clean,' should you do as he said." So Naaman went down and plunged into the Jordan seven times at the word of the man of God. His flesh became again like the flesh of a little child, and he was clean.

He returned with his whole retinue to the man of God. On his arrival he stood before him and said, "Now I know that there is no God in all the earth, except in Israel."—This is the Word of the Lord. ℟. **Thanks be to God.** ℣

Responsorial Psalm   Pss 42, 2. 3; 43, 3. 4.

℟.(Ps 42, 3) **My soul is thirsting for the living God; when shall I see him face to face?**

As the hind longs for the running waters,
    so my soul longs for you, O God. — ℟

Athirst is my soul for God, the living God.
    When shall I go and behold the face of God? — ℟

Send forth your light and your fidelity;
    they shall lead me on
And bring me to your holy mountain,
    to your dwelling-place. — ℟

Then will I go in to the altar of God,
    the God of my gladness and joy;
Then will I give you thanks upon the harp,
    O God, my God! — ℟ ℣

GOSPEL   Lk 4, 24-30
Verse before the Gospel (Ps 130, 5. 7)
℟. **Praise and honor to you, Lord Jesus Christ!**
I hope in the Lord, I trust in his word;
with him there is mercy and fullness of redemption.
℟. **Praise and honor to you, Lord Jesus Christ!**

Our Lord reminds his hearers of the cure of the non-Jew Naaman. Part of his message was that he was not accepted by his own people and that, therefore, the wonders of his kingdom would be shared by so-called outsiders. A prophet is not without honor except in his native town.

℣ The Lord be with you. ℟. **And also with you.**

✠ A reading from the holy gospel according to Luke ℟. **Glory to you, Lord.**

When Jesus had come to Nazareth, he said to the people in the synagogue: "No prophet gains acceptance in his native place. Indeed, let me remind you, there were many widows in Israel in the days of Elijah when the heavens remained closed for three and a half years and a great famine spread over the land. It was to none of these that Elijah was sent, but to a widow of Zarephath near Sidon. Recall, too, the many lepers in Israel in the time of Elisha the prophet; yet not one was cured except Naaman the Syrian."

At these words the whole audience in the synagogue was filled with indignation. They rose up and expelled him from the town, leading him to the brow of the hill on which it was built and intending to hurl him over the edge. But he went straight through their midst and walked away.—This is the gospel of the Lord. ℟. **Praise to you, Lord Jesus Christ.**

➤ No. 15, p. 623

PRAYER OVER THE GIFTS

Father,
bless these gifts
that they may become the sacrament of our salvation.
We ask this in the name of Jesus the Lord.
℟. **Amen.** ➤ No. 21, p. 626 (Pref. P 8-11)

COMMUNION ANT. Ps 117, 1-2

All you nations, praise the Lord, for steadfast is his kindly mercy to us. ℣

PRAYER AFTER COMMUNION

Lord,
forgive the sins of those
who receive your sacrament,
and bring us together in unity and peace.
Grant this through Christ our Lord.
℞. **Amen.**　　　　　　　　　　　　→ No. 32, p. 650

TUESDAY OF THE THIRD WEEK OF LENT

We cannot expect forgiveness unless we forgive others. The first and most important disposition necessary for obtaining pardon in the sacrament of Penance is a sincere sorrow for having offended God, which includes a firm resolution of sinning no more and a willing intention of satisfying God's justice.

ENTRANCE ANT.　　　　　　　　　　　　Ps 17, 6. 8

I call upon you, God, for you will answer me; bend your ear and hear my prayer. Guard me as the pupil of your eye; hide me in the shade of your wings.

OPENING PRAYER　　　　　　　　　　→ No. 2, p. 614

Lord,
you call us to your service
and continue your saving work among us.
May your love never abandon us.
We ask this through our Lord Jesus Christ, your Son,
who lives and reigns with you and the Holy Spirit,
one God, for ever and ever. ℞. **Amen.** ⅴ

READING I　　　　　　　　　　　　Dn 3, 25. 34-43

Contrition for sin is a great act of worship. It takes deep faith, true humility, and complete obedience. The prayer of Azariah, whose Babylonian name was Abednego, is a national, public act of repentance. He prays to God with a contrite heart.

A reading from the book of the prophet Daniel

Azariah stood up in the fire and prayed aloud:
"For your name's sake, O Lord, do not deliver us up
　　forever,
　　or make void your covenant.

Do not take away your mercy from us,
   for the sake of Abraham, your beloved,
   Isaac your servant, and Israel your holy one,
To whom you promised to multiply their offspring
   like the stars of heaven,
   or the sand on the shore of the sea.
For we are reduced, O Lord, beyond any other nation,
   brought low everywhere in the world this day
   because of our sins.
We have in our day no prince, prophet, or leader,
   no holocaust, sacrifice, oblation, or incense,
   no place to offer first fruits, to find favor with you.
But with contrite heart and humble spirit
   let us be received;
As though it were holocausts of rams and bullocks,
   or thousands of fat lambs,
So let our sacrifice be in your presence today
   as we follow you unreservedly;
   for those who trust in you cannot be put to shame.
And now we follow you with our whole heart,
   we fear you and we pray to you.
Do not let us be put to shame,
   but deal with us in your kindness and great mercy.
Deliver us by your wonders,
   and bring glory to your name, O Lord."
This is the Word of the Lord. ℟. **Thanks be to God. ℣**

Responsorial Psalm   Ps 25, 4-5. 6-7. 8-9

℟. (6) **Remember your mercies, O Lord.**

Your ways, O Lord, make known to me;
   teach me your paths,
Guide me in your truth and teach me,
   for you are God my savior. — ℟

Remember that your compassion, O Lord,
   and your kindness are from of old.
In your kindness remember me,
   because of your goodness, O Lord. — ℟

Good and upright is the Lord;
   thus he shows sinners the way.
He guides the humble to justice,
   he teaches the humble his way. — ℞ ℣

GOSPEL   Mt 18, 21-35

Verse before the Gospel (Jl 2, 12-13)

℞. **Glory and praise to you, Lord Jesus Christ!**
With all your heart turn to me
for I am tender and compassionate.
℞. **Glory and praise to you, Lord Jesus Christ!**

Jesus teaches that forgiving others is a requirement for being forgiven. He presents an exaggerated difference of debt in the story. It is
not the statistic he is emphasizing, but the need of forgiving others.

℣. The Lord be with you. ℞. **And also with you.**
✠ A reading from the holy gospel according to Matthew. ℞. **Glory to you, Lord.**

Peter came up and asked Jesus, "Lord, when my
brother wrongs me, how often must I forgive him?
Seven times?" "No," Jesus replied, "not seven times;
I say, seventy times seven times. That is why the
reign of God may be said to be like a king who decided to settle accounts with his officials. When he
began his auditing, one was brought in who owed
him a huge amount. As he had no way of paying it,
his master ordered him to be sold, along with his
wife, his children, and all his property, in payment
of the debt. At that the official prostrated himself
in homage and said, 'My lord, be patient with me
and I will pay you back in full.' Moved with pity, the
master let the official go and wrote off the debt. But
when that same official went out he met a fellow
servant who owed him a mere fraction of what he
himself owed. He seized him and throttled him. 'Pay
back what you owe," he demanded. His fellow servant dropped to his knees and began to plead with
him, 'Just give me time and I will pay you back in
full.' But he would hear none of it. Instead, he had

him put in jail until he paid back what he owed. When his fellow servants saw what had happened they were badly shaken, and went to their master to report the whole incident. His master sent for him and said, 'You worthless wretch! I canceled your entire debt when you pleaded with me. Should you not have dealt mercifully with your fellow servant, as I dealt with you?' Then in anger the master handed him over to the torturers until he paid back all that he owed. My heavenly Father will treat you in exactly the same way unless each of you forgives his brother from his heart."—This is the gospel of the Lord. ℟. **Praise to you, Lord Jesus Christ.**

➤ No. 15, p. 623

PRAYER OVER THE GIFTS

Lord,
may the saving sacrifice we offer
bring us your forgiveness,
so that freed from sin, we may always please you.
Grant this through Christ our Lord.
℟. **Amen.**   ➤ No. 21, p. 626 (Pref. P 8-11)

COMMUNION ANT.   Ps 15, 1-2

Lord, who may stay in your dwelling place? Who shall live on your holy mountain? He who walks without blame and does what is right. ℣

PRAYER AFTER COMMUNION

Lord,
may our sharing in this holy mystery
bring us your protection, forgiveness and life.
We ask this in the name of Jesus the Lord.
℟. **Amen.**   ➤ No. 32, p. 650

WEDNESDAY OF THE THIRD WEEK OF LENT

The great obedience which shows our love of God is fidelity to conscience —to conscience enlightened by Christ's teaching in the Holy Church. To this is joined patient submission to God in our daily lives.

This is especially applicable in this time of renewal. Let us be aware that the Pope and all the Bishops involved in these changes are inspired by the Holy Spirit.

ENTRANCE ANT.   Ps 119, 133

Lord, direct my steps as you have promised, and let no evil hold me in its power.   ➔ No. 2, p. 614

OPENING PRAYER

Lord,
during this lenten season
nourish us with your word of life
and make us one in love and prayer.
Grant this through our Lord Jesus Christ, your Son,
who lives and reigns with you and the Holy Spirit,
one God, for ever and ever. ℟. **Amen.** ℣

READING I   Dt 4, 1. 5-9

This prayer of Moses is a beautiful prayer showing the relationship of man to God. It would serve as an ideal base for love of country and homeland. He admonishes that God's people should remember God's teachings and pass them on to their children.

A reading from the book of Deuteronomy

These are the words which Moses spoke to the people: "Now, Israel, hear the statutes and decrees which I am teaching you to observe, that you may live, and may enter in and take possession of the land which the Lord, the God of your fathers, is giving you. Therefore, I teach you the statutes and decrees as the Lord, my God, has commanded me, that you may observe them in the land you are entering to occupy. Observe them carefully, for thus will you give evidence of your wisdom and intelligence to the nations, who will hear of all these statutes and say, 'This great nation is truly a wise and intelligent people.' For what great nation is there that has gods so close to it as the Lord, our God, is to us whenever we call upon him? Or what great nation has statutes and decrees that are as just as this whole law which I am setting before you today?

"However, take care and be earnestly on your guard not to forget the things which your own eyes have seen, not let them slip from your memory as long as you live, but teach them to your children and to your children's children."—This is the Word of the Lord. ℟. **Thanks be to God.** ✣

Responsorial Psalm   Ps 147, 12-13. 15-16. 19-20

℟. (12) **Praise the Lord, Jerusalem.**

Glorify the Lord, O Jerusalem;
  praise your God, O Zion.
For he has strengthened the bars of your gates;
  he has blessed your children within you. — ℟

He sends forth his command to the earth;
  swiftly runs his word!
He spreads snow like wool;
  frost he strews like ashes. — ℟

He has proclaimed his word to Jacob,
  his statutes and his ordinances to Israel.
He has not done thus for any other nation;
  his ordinances he has not made known to
    them. — ℟ ✣

GOSPEL   Mt 5, 17-19

Verse before the Gospel (Jn 6, 64. 69)

℟. **Glory to you, Word of God, Lord Jesus Christ!**
Your words, Lord, are spirit and life;
you have the message of eternal life.
℟. **Glory to you, Word of God, Lord Jesus Christ!**

Jesus carries out the precept of obeying God's law. He did not come to change God's law but to carry it out to its fullest extent. Whoever keeps God's law will be great in his kingdom.

℣. The Lord be with you. ℟. **And also with you.**
✠ A reading from the holy gospel according to Matthew. ℟. **Glory to you, Lord.**

Jesus said to his disciples: "Do not think that I have come to abolish the law and the prophets. I have

come, not to abolish them, but to fulfill them. Of
this much I assure you: until heaven and earth pass
away, not the smallest letter of the law, not the
smallest part of a letter shall be done away with
until it all comes true. That is why whoever breaks
the least significant of these commands and teaches
others to do so shall be called least in the kingdom
of God. Whoever fulfills and teaches these commands shall be great in the kingdom of God."—This
is the gospel of the Lord. ℟. **Praise to you, Lord
Jesus Christ.** → No. 15, p. 623

PRAYER OVER THE GIFTS
Lord,
receive our prayers and offerings.
In time of danger,
protect all who celebrate this sacrament.
We ask this in the name of Jesus the Lord.
℟. **Amen.** → No. 21, p. 626 (Pref. P 8-11)

COMMUNION ANT.   Ps 16, 11
**Lord, you will show me the path of life and fill me
with joy in your presence.** ∨

PRAYER AFTER COMMUNION
Lord,
may this eucharist forgive our sins,
make us holy,
and prepare us for the eternal life you promise.
We ask this through Christ our Lord.
℟. **Amen.** → No. 32, p. 650

THURSDAY OF THE THIRD WEEK OF LENT

Whoever expects to reap a harvest of divine benefit other than through
faith in Christ will find his hopes and his labor in vain. It is only
by serving God alone that man is with and in God. He who is against
God can bring only destruction and damnation upon himself.

ENTRANCE ANT.

I am the Savior of all people, says the Lord. Whatever their troubles, I will answer their cry, and I will always be their Lord. ➜ No. 2, p. 614

OPENING PRAYER

Father,
help us to be ready to celebrate the great paschal mystery.
Make our love grow each day
as we approach the feast of our salvation.
We ask this through our Lord Jesus Christ, your Son,
who lives and reigns with you and the Holy Spirit,
one God, for ever and ever. ℟. **Amen.** ℣

READING I Jer 7, 23-28

Jeremiah speaks of what God commands his people. Nations are made up of individuals, but when the majority of individuals break away from God, the nation becomes godless even though a few righteous and holy people are scattered here and there. Because of deaf ears, the word of God is not among them.

A reading from the book of the prophet Jeremiah

Thus says the Lord: This is what I commanded my people: Listen to my voice; then I will be your God and you shall be my people. Walk in all the ways that I command you, so that you may prosper.

But they obeyed not, nor did they pay heed. They walked in the hardness of their evil hearts and turned their backs, not their faces, to me. From the day that your fathers left the land of Egypt even to this day, I have sent you untiringly all my servants the prophets. Yet they have not obeyed me nor paid heed; they have stiffened their necks and done worse than their fathers. When you speak all these words to them, they will not listen to you either; when you call to them, they will not answer you. Say to them: This is the nation which does not listen to the voice of the Lord, its God, or take correction. Faithfulness has disappeared; the word itself is banished from their speech.—This is the Word of the Lord. ℞. **Thanks be to God.** ℣

Responsorial Psalm   Ps 95, 1-2. 6-7. 8-9

℞. (7. 8) **If today you hear his voice, harden not your hearts.**

Come, let us sing joyfully to the Lord;
    let us acclaim the Rock of our salvation.
Let us greet him with thanksgiving;
    let us joyfully sing praise to him. — ℞

Come, let us bow down in worship;
    let us kneel before the Lord who made us.
For he is our God,
    and we are the people he shepherds, the flock he
       guides. — ℞

Oh, that today you would hear his voice:
    "Harden not your hearts as at Meribah,
    as in the day of Massah in the desert,
Where your fathers tempted me;
    they tested me though they had seen my
       works." — ℞ ℣

GOSPEL   Lk 11, 14-23

Verse before the Gospel (Jl 2, 12-13)

℞. **Praise to you, Lord Jesus Christ, king of endless glory!**
With all your heart turn to me
for I am tender and compassionate.
℞. **Praise to you, Lord Jesus Christ, king of endless glory!**

Jesus expels a devil. This text is an appropriate conclusion to the whole argument between our Lord and his enemies: "He that is not with me is against me, and he who does not gather with me scatters." There is no such thing as a neutral position in the kingdom of God.

℣. The Lord be with you. ℞. **And also with you.**
✠ A reading from the holy gospel according to Luke
℞. **Glory to you, Lord.**

Jesus was casting out a devil which was mute, and when the devil was cast out the dumb man spoke. The crowds were amazed at this. Some of them said, "It is by Beelzebul, the prince of devils, that he casts out devils." Others, to test him, were demanding of him a sign from heaven.

Because he knew their thoughts, he said to them: "Every kingdom divided against itself is laid waste. Any house torn by dissension falls. If Satan is divided against himself, how can his kingdom last?—since you say it is by Beelzebul that I cast out devils. If I cast out devils by Beelzebul, by whom do your people cast them out? In such case, let them act as your judges. But if it is by the finger of God that I cast out devils, then the reign of God is upon you.

"When a strong man fully armed guards his courtyard, his possessions go undisturbed. But when someone stronger than he comes and overpowers him, such a one carries off the arms on which he was relying and divides the spoils. The man who is not with me is against me. The man who does not gather with me scatters."—This is the gospel of the Lord. ℟. **Praise to you, Lord Jesus Christ.**

➤ No. 15, p. 623

PRAYER OVER THE GIFTS

Lord,
take away our sinfulness and be pleased with our
    offerings.
Help us to pursue the true gifts you promise
and not become lost in false joys.
Grant this through Christ our Lord.
℟. **Amen.** ➤ No. 21, p. 626 (Pref. P 8-11)

COMMUNION ANT. Ps 119, 4-5

You have laid down your precepts to be faithfully kept. May my footsteps be firm in keeping your commands. ∀

PRAYER AFTER COMMUNION

Lord,
may your sacrament of life
bring us the gift of salvation
and make our lives pleasing to you.
We ask this in the name of Jesus the Lord.
℟. **Amen.**   ➔ No. 32, p. 650

_____

FRIDAY OF THE THIRD WEEK OF LENT

The love of God is summed up in "the whole law and the prophets."
This love of God is the greatest and the First Commandment. The
Second is very like it and is next in importance in the eyes of the Lord.
Love for our brothers is true Christian charity. Christ says plainly,
"I say to you: Love your enemies; do good to them that hate you; and
pray for them that persecute you."

ENTRANCE ANT.   Ps 86, 8. 10

**Lord, there is no god to compare with you; you are
great and do wonderful things, you are the only God.**
                              ➔ No. 2, p. 614

OPENING PRAYER

Merciful Father,
fill our hearts with your love
and keep us faithful to the gospel of Christ.
Give us the grace to rise above our human weakness.
Grant this through our Lord Jesus Christ, your Son,
who lives and reigns with you and the Holy Spirit,
one God, forever and ever. ℟. **Amen.** ↓

READING I   Hos 14, 2-10

How many times the Jews turned from God. Through the prayer of the
prophet Hosea who lived about 750 B.C., God again shows his forgiveness and promises them a flourishing future. They shall bear
much fruit.

A reading from the book of the prophet Hosea

Return, O Israel, to the Lord, your God;
    you have collapsed through your guilt.
Take with you words,
    and return to the Lord;

Say to him, "Forgive all iniquity,
 and receive what is good, that we may render
 as offerings the bullocks from our stalls.
Assyria will not save us,
 nor shall we have horses to mount;
We shall say no more, 'Our god.'
 to the work of our hands;
 for in you the orphan finds compassion."
I will heal their defection,
 I will love them freely;
 for my wrath is turned away from them.
I will be like the dew for Israel:
 he shall blossom like the lily;
He shall strike root like the Lebanon cedar,
 and put forth his shoots.
His splendor shall be like the olive tree
 and his fragrance like the Lebanon cedar.
Again they shall dwell in his shade and raise grain;
They shall blossom like the vine,
 and his fame shall be like the wine of Lebanon.
Ephraim! What more has he to do with idols?
 I have humbled him, but I will prosper him.
"I am like a verdant cypress tree"—
 Because of me you bear fruit!
Let him who is wise understand these things;
 let him who is prudent know them.
Straight are the paths of the Lord,
 in them the just walk,
 but sinners stumble in them.
This is the Word of the Lord. ℞. **Thanks be to God.** ℣

Responsorial Psalm   Ps 81, 6-8. 8-9. 10-11. 14. 17

℞. (11. 9) **I am the Lord, your God:**
 hear my voice.

An unfamiliar speech I hear:
 "I relieved his shoulder of the burden;
 his hands were freed from the basket.
In distress you called, and I rescued you. — ℞

Unseen, I answered you in thunder;
  I tested you at the waters of Meribah.
Hear, my people, and I will admonish you;
  O Israel, will you not hear me? — ℟

There shall be no strange god among you
  nor shall you worship any alien god.
I, the Lord, am your God
  who led you forth from the land of Egypt. — ℟

If only my people would hear me,
  and Israel walk in my ways,
I would feed them with the best of wheat,
  and with honey from the rock I would fill
    them." — ℟ ⍭

GOSPEL   Mk 12, 28-34

Verse before the Gospel (Mt 4, 17)

℟. **Praise and honor to you, Lord Jesus Christ!**
Repent, says the Lord,
the kingdom of heaven is at hand.
℟. **Praise and honor to you, Lord Jesus Christ!**

In answering the question concerning the most important commandment, Jesus replies that the greatest commandment is to place the adoration of God above all else and the love of neighbor next.

℣. The Lord be with you. ℟. **And also with you.**
✠ A reading from the holy gospel according to Mark
℟. **Glory to you, Lord.**

One of the scribes came up to Jesus and asked him,
'Which is the first of all the commandments?" Jesus
replied: "This is the first:

    'Hear, O Israel! The Lord our God is Lord alone!
    Therefore you shall love the Lord your God
    with all your heart,
    with all your soul,
    with all your mind,
    and with all your strength.'
This is the second,
    'You shall love your neighbor as yourself.'
There is no other commandment greater than these."

The scribe said to him: "Excellent, Teacher! you are right in saying, 'He is the One, there is no other than he.' Yet, 'to love him with all our heart, with all our thought and with all our strength, and to love our neighbor as ourselves' is worth more than any burnt offering or sacrifice." Jesus approved the insight of this answer and told him, "You are not far from the reign of God." And no one had the courage to ask him any more questions.—This is the gospel of the Lord. ℟. **Praise to you, Lord Jesus Christ.**

➔ No. 15, p. 623

PRAYER OVER THE GIFTS

Lord,
bless the gifts we have prepared.
Make them acceptable to you
and a lasting source of salvation.
We ask this in the name of Jesus the Lord.
℟. **Amen.**   ➔ No. 21, p. 626 (Pref. P 8-11)

COMMUNION ANT.   See Mk 12, 33

To love God with all your heart, and your neighbor as yourself, is a greater thing than all the temple sacrifices. ℣

PRAYER AFTER COMMUNION

Lord,
fill us with the power of your love.
As we share in this eucharist,
may we come to know fully the redemption we have
   received.
We ask this through Christ our Lord.
℟. **Amen.**   _____   ➔ No. 32, p. 650

SATURDAY OF THE THIRD WEEK OF LENT

The Lord says, "What I want is love, not sacrifice; knowledge of God, not holocausts." This demand of our love by God applies even today when we celebrate the one and only Sacrifice of the New Covenant offered by Jesus Christ through the Mass. Even the Mass means nothing unless we turn to God with love!

ENTRANCE ANT.   Ps 103, 2-3

**Bless the Lord, my soul, and remember all his kind-
nesses, for he pardons all my faults.** ➜ No. 2, p. 614

OPENING PRAYER.

Lord,
make this lenten observance
of the suffering, death and resurrection of Christ
bring us to the full joy of Easter.
We ask this through our Lord Jesus Christ, your Son,
who lives and reigns with you and the Holy Spirit,
one God, for ever and ever. ℟. **Amen.** ℣

READING I   Hos 6, 1-6

Hosea was a prophet who sometimes is called the prophet of divine
love. He uses the imagery of a father's love for his son and the
husband's love for his wife in describing God's love for his people.
They are wayward people, but God pursues them, asking for their
love in return.

A reading from the book of the prophet Hosea

In their affliction, they shall look for me:
    "Come, let us return to the Lord,
For it is he who has rent, but he will heal us;
    he has struck us, but he will bind our wounds.
He will revive us after two days;
    on the third day he will raise us up,
    to live in his presence.
Let us know, let us strive to know the Lord;
    as certain as the dawn is his coming,
    and his judgment shines forth like the light of day!
He will come to us like the rain,
    like spring rain that waters the earth."
What can I do with you, Ephraim?
    What can I do with you, Judah?
Your piety is like a morning cloud,
    like the dew that early passes away.
For this reason I smote them through the prophets,
    I slew them by the words of my mouth;

For it is love that I desire, not sacrifice,
   and knowledge of God rather than holocausts.
This is the Word of the Lord. ℞. **Thanks be to God.** ℣

Responsorial Psalm   Ps 51, 3-4. 18-19. 20-21

℞. (Hos 6, 6) **It is steadfast love, not sacrifice,
   that God desires.**

Have mercy on me, O God, in your goodness;
   in the greatness of your compassion wipe out my
      offense.
Thoroughly wash me from my guilt
   and of my sin cleanse me. — ℞

For you are not pleased with sacrifices;
   should I offer a holocaust, you would not accept it.
My sacrifice, O God, is a contrite spirit;
   a heart contrite and humbled, O God, you will not
      spurn. — ℞

Be bountiful, O Lord, to Zion in your kindness
   by rebuilding the walls of Jerusalem;
Then shall you be pleased with due sacrifices,
   burnt offerings and holocausts. — ℞ ℣

GOSPEL   Lk 18, 9-14

Verse before the Gospel (Ps 95, 8)

℞. **Glory and praise to you, Lord Jesus Christ!**
If today you hear his voice,
harden not your hearts.
℞. **Glory and praise to you, Lord Jesus Christ!**

Jesus teaches by contrast. The Pharisee believes that his external
religious practices justify him before God. He assumes he is good,
while the other, a publican, begs for mercy and receives mercy. The
proud shall become humble.

℣. The Lord be with you. ℞. **And also with you.**
✠ A reading from the holy gospel according to Luke
℞. **Glory to you, Lord.**

Jesus spoke this parable addressed to those who believed in their own self-righteousness while holding

everyone else in contempt: "Two men went up to the temple to pray; one was a Pharisee, the other a tax collector. The Pharisee with head unbowed prayed in this fashion: "I give you thanks, O God, that I am not like the rest of men—grasping, crooked, adulterous—or even like this tax collector. I fast twice a week. I pay tithes on all I possess.' The other man, however, kept his distance, not even daring to raise his eyes to heaven. All he did was beat his breast and say, 'O God, be merciful to me, a sinner.' Believe me, this man went home from the temple justified but the other did not. For everyone who exalts himself shall be humbled while he who humbles himself shall be exalted.''—This is the gospel of the Lord. ℟. **Praise to you, Lord Jesus Christ.**

➔ No. 15, p. 623

PRAYER OVER THE GIFTS

Lord,
by your grace you enable us
to come to these mysteries with renewed lives.
May this eucharist give you worthy praise.
Grant this through Christ our Lord.

➔ No. 21, p. 626 (Pref. P 8-11)

COMMUNION ANT.   Lk 18, 13

He stood at a distance and beat his breast, saying: O God, be merciful to me, a sinner. ℣

PRAYER AFTER COMMUNION

God of mercy,
may the holy gifts we receive
help us to worship you in truth,
and to receive your sacraments with faith.
We ask this in the name of Jesus the Lord.
℟. **Amen.**

➔ No. 32, p. 650

OPTIONAL READINGS AND INTERVENIENT CHANTS
FOR THE FOURTH WEEK OF LENT

These reading and intervenient chants may be used on any day of this week, especially when the Gospel of the man born blind is not read on the Fourth Sunday of Lent.

READING I   Mi 7, 7-9

Micah says that God will be his Savior. Even though he is living in darkness, God will hear him when he prays to him. He has sinned and will be punished, but God will show him his justice.

A reading from the book of the prophet Micah

I will look to the Lord,
    I will put my trust in God my savior;
        my God will hear me!
Rejoice not over me, O my enemy!
    though I have fallen, I will arise;
        though I sit in darkness, the Lord is my light.
The wrath of the Lord I will endure
    because I have sinned against him,
Until he takes up my cause,
    and establishes my right.
He will bring me forth to the light;
    I will see his justice.
This is the Word of the Lord. ℟. **Thanks be to God.** ℣

Responsorial Psalm   Ps 27, 1. 7-8. 8-9. 13-14

℟. (1) **The Lord is my light and my salvation.**

The Lord is my light and my salvation;
    whom should I fear?
The Lord is my life's refuge;
    of whom should I be afraid? — ℟

Hear, O Lord, the sound of my call;
    have pity on me, and answer me.
Of you my heart speaks; you my glance seeks. — ℟
Your presence, O Lord, I seek.
    Hide not your face from me;

Do not in anger repel your servant.
   You are my helper: cast me not off. — ℟
I believe that I shall see the bounty of the Lord
   in the land of the living.
Wait for the Lord with courage;
   be stouthearted, and wait for the Lord. — ℟ ❣

GOSPEL   Jn 9, 1-41

Verse before the Gospel (Jn 8, 12)

℟. **Glory to you, Word of God, Lord Jesus Christ!**
I am the light of the world, says the Lord:
he who follows me will have the light of life.
℟. **Glory to you, Word of God, Lord Jesus Christ!**

The man who is cured from his blindness was chosen by God to show
forth the divine power of Jesus. The man believes in Jesus and obeys
him. There follows a full court investigation, but the man is faithful
in professing his anxious belief in the Son of Man regardless of
criticism or reprisal.

℣. The Lord be with you. ℟. **And also with you.**
✠ A reading from the holy gospel according to John
℟. **Glory to you, Lord.**

As Jesus walked along, he saw a man who had been
blind from birth. His disciples asked him, "Rabbi,
was it his sin or his parents' that caused him to be
born blind?" "Neither," answered Jesus:

      "It was no sin, either of this man
      or of his parents.
      Rather, it was to let God's works show forth
         in him.
      We must do the deeds of him who sent me
      while it is day.
      The night comes on
      when no one can work
      While I am in the world
      I am the light of the world."

With that Jesus spat on the ground, made mud with
his saliva, and smeared the man's eyes with the mud.
Then he told him, "Go, wash in the pool of Siloam."

(This name means "One who has been sent.") So the man went off and washed, and came back able to see.

His neighbors and the people who had been accustomed to see him begging began to ask, "Isn't this the fellow who used to sit and beg?" Some were claiming it was he; others maintained it was not but someone who looked like him. The man himself said, "I'm the one, all right." They said to him then, "How were your eyes opened?" He answered, "That man they call Jesus made mud and smeared it on my eyes, telling me to go to Siloam and wash. When I did go and wash, I was able to see." "Where is he?" they asked. He replied, "I have no idea."

Next, they took the man who had been born blind to the Pharisees. (Note that it was on a sabbath that Jesus had made the mud paste and opened his eyes.) The Pharisees, in turn, began to inquire how he had recovered his sight. He told them, "He put mud on my eyes. I washed it off, and now I can see." This prompted some of the Pharisees to assert, "This man cannot be from God because he does not keep the sabbath." Others objected, "If a man is a sinner, how can he perform signs like these?" They were sharply divided over him. Then they addressed the blind man again: "Since it was your eyes he opened, what do you have to say about him?" "He is a prophet," he replied.

The Jews refused to believe that he had really been born blind and had begun to see, until they summoned the parents of this man who now could see. "Is this your son?" they asked, "and if so, do you attest that he was blind at birth? How do you account for the fact that he now can see?" The parents answered, " We know this is our son, and we know he was blind at birth. But how he can see now, or who opened his eyes, we have no idea. Ask him. He is old enough to speak for himself." (His parents answered in this fashion because they were afraid of the Jews, who had already agreed among themselves that anyone who acknowledged Jesus as the Messiah would be put out of the synagogue. That was why his parents said, "He is of age—ask him.")

A second time they summoned the man who had been born blind and said to him, "Give glory to God! First of all, we know this man is a sinner." "I would not know whether he is a sinner or not," he answered. "I know this much: I was blind before; now I can see." They persisted: "Just what did he do to you? How did he open your eyes?" "I have told you once, but you would not listen to me," he answered them. "Why do you want to hear it all over again? Do not tell me you want to become his disciples too?" They retorted scornfully: "You are the one who is that man's disciple. We are disciples of Moses. We know that God spoke to Moses, but we have no idea where this man comes from." He came back at them, "Well, this is news! You do not know where he comes from, yet he opened my eyes. We know that God does not hear sinners, but that if someone is devout and obeys his will he listens to him. It is unheard of that anyone ever gave sight to a person blind from birth. If this man were not from God, he could never have done such a thing." "What!" they exclaimed. "You are steeped in sin from your birth, and you are giving us lectures?" With that they threw him out bodily.

When Jesus heard of his expulsion, he sought him out and asked him, "Do you believe in the Son of Man?" He answered, "Who is he, sir, that I may believe in him?" "You have seen him," Jesus replied. "He is speaking to you now." ["I do believe, Lord," he said, and bowed down to worship him. Then Jesus said:]

"I came into this world to divide it,
to make the sightless see
and the seeing blind."

Some of the Pharisees around him picked this up,

saying, "You are not counting us with the blind, are you?" To which Jesus replied:

"If you were blind
there would be no sin in that.
'But we see,' you say,
and your sin remains."

This is the gospel of the Lord. ℟. **Praise to you, Lord Jesus Christ.** ➤ No. 15, p. 623

MONDAY OF THE FOURTH WEEK OF LENT

Today we have placed before us the thoughts of our eternal happiness in heaven which we are to enjoy after the labors of this short life are ended. We may think of ourselves as mere pilgrims passing through for a time because it is the only way to our true home in heaven. Christ told his disciples that their journey through this vale of tears to his kingdom would last only a little while, and when they arrived, their sorrow would be turned to joy.

ENTRANCE ANT.   Ps 31, 7-8

Lord, I put my trust in you; I shall be glad and rejoice in your mercy, because you have seen my affliction. ➤ No. 2, p. 614

OPENING PRAYER

Father, creator,
you give the world new life by your sacraments.
May we, your Church, grow in your life
and continue to receive your help on earth.
Grant this through our Lord Jesus Christ, your Son,
who lives and reigns with you and the Holy Spirit,
one God, for ever and ever. ℟. **Amen.** ⩔

READING I   Is 65, 17-21

In an optimistic passage, Isaiah talks of renewal. This is God's response to man's interior renewal. Isaiah describes a Jerusalem of joy and happiness.

A reading from the book of the prophet Isaiah

Lo, I am about to create new heavens
and a new earth;

The things of the past shall not be remembered
  or come to mind.
Instead, there shall always be rejoicing and happiness
  in what I create;
For I create Jerusalem to be a joy
  and its people to be a delight;
I will rejoice in Jerusalem
  and exult in my people.
No longer shall the sound of weeping be heard there,
  or the sound of crying;
No longer shall there be in it
  an infant who lives but a few days,
  or an old man who does not round out his full lifetime;
He dies a mere youth who reaches but a hundred years,
  and he who fails of a hundred shall be thought accursed.
They shall live in the houses they build,
  and eat the fruit of the vineyards they plant.
This is the Word of the Lord. ℟. **Thanks be to God.** ℣

Responsorial Psalm   Ps 30, 2. 4. 5-6. 11-13

℟. (2) **I will praise you, Lord, for you have rescued me.**

I will extol you, O Lord, for you drew me clear
  and did not let my enemies rejoice over me.
O Lord, you brought me up from the nether world;
  you preserved me from among those going down
    into the pit. — ℟

Sing praise to the Lord, you his faithful ones,
  and give thanks to his holy name.
For his anger lasts but a moment;
  a lifetime, his good will.
At nightfall, weeping enters in,
  but with the dawn, rejoicing. — ℟

Hear, O Lord, and have pity on me;
  O Lord, be my helper.
You changed my mourning into dancing;
  O Lord, my God, forever will I give you
    thanks. — ℟ ✟

GOSPEL   Jn 4, 43-54

Verse before the Gospel (Am 5, 14)

℟. **Praise to you, Lord Jesus Christ, king of endless
    glory!**
Seek good and not evil
so that you may live,
and the Lord will be with you.

℟. **Praise to you, Lord Jesus Christ, king of endless
    glory!**

Jesus performed few miracles in his own Galilee. There was little
faith there and he was not accepted by his own. Presumably, the "royal
official" is not a native. He has only to believe the word of Jesus,
and he does so.

℣. The Lord be with you. ℟. **And also with you.**
✠ A reading from the holy gospel according to John
℟. **Glory to you, Lord.**

Jesus left [Samaria] for Galilee. (He himself had
testified that no one esteems a prophet in his own
country.) When he arrived in Galilee, the people
there welcomed him. They themselves had been at
the feast and had seen all that he had done in Jerusalem on that occasion.

He went to Cana in Galilee once more, where he
had made the water wine. At Capernaum there happened to be a royal official whose son was ill. When
he heard that Jesus had come back from Judea to
Galilee, he went to him and begged him to come
down and restore health to his son, who was near
death. Jesus replied, "Unless you people see signs
and wonders, you do not believe." "Sir," the royal
official pleaded with him, "come down before my
child dies." Jesus told him, "Return home. Your son

will live." The man put his trust in the word Jesus spoke to him, and started for home.

He was on his way there when his servant met him with the news that his boy was going to live. When he asked them at what time the boy had shown improvement, they told him, "The fever left him yesterday afternoon about one." It was at that very hour, the father realized, that Jesus had told him, "Your son is going to live." He and his whole household thereupon became believers. This was the second sign that Jesus performed on returning from Judea to Galilee.—This is the gospel of the Lord.
℟. **Praise to you, Lord Jesus Christ.** ➤ No. 15, p. 623

PRAYER OVER THE GIFTS

Lord,
through the gifts we present
may we receive the grace
to cast off the old ways of life
and to redirect our course toward the life of heaven.
We ask this in the name of Jesus the Lord.
℟. **Amen.**　　　　　　　➤ No. 21, p. 626 (Pref. P 8-11)

COMMUNION ANT.　　　　　　　　　　　　Ez 36, 27

I shall put my spirit within you, says the Lord; you will obey my laws and keep my decrees. ℣

PRAYER AFTER COMMUNION

Lord,
may your gifts bring us life and holiness
and lead us to the happiness of eternal life.
We ask this through Christ our Lord.
℟. **Amen.**　　　　　　　　　➤ No. 32, p. 650

_____

TUESDAY OF THE FOURTH WEEK OF LENT

Christ restores us to eternal life with God. This life comes through the Church and the sacraments. Baptism gives us supernatural life. The confessional brings the medicine to keep us alive. The Blessed Eucharist gives us strength. Left to ourselves, we have but a short cycle of life from birth to death. But through Christ and his Church, we have the promise of life forever.

ENTRANCE ANT.   See Is 55, 1

Come to the waters, all who thirst; though you have no money, come and drink with joy. ✝ No. 2, p. 614

OPENING PRAYER

Father,
may our lenten observance
prepare us to embrace the paschal mystery
and to proclaim your salvation with joyful praise.
We ask this through our Lord Jesus Christ, your Son,
who lives and reigns with you and the Holy Spirit,
one God, for ever and ever. ℟. **Amen.** ✝

READING I   Ez 47, 1-9. 12

Ezekiel uses the motif of the River of God with its life-giving waters, but in his own way he develops the concept of a temple-centered land. From beneath the threshold of the east gate of the Sanctuary, he sees a stream of water issue forth to the east, from the holy mount to the lifeless waters of the sea. Its waters become fresh and healthy.

A reading from the book of prophet Ezekiel

The angel brought me back to the entrance of the temple of the Lord, and I saw water flowing out from beneath the threshold of the temple toward the east, for the façade of the temple was toward the east; the water flowed down from the southern side of the temple, south of the altar. He led me outside by the north gate, and around to the outer gate facing the east, where I saw water trickling from the southern side. Then when he had walked off to the east with a measuring cord in his hand, he measured off a thousand cubits and had me wade through the water, which was ankle-deep. He measured off another thousand and once more had me wade through the water, which was now knee-deep. Again he measured off a thousand and had me wade; the water was up to my waist. Once more he measured off a thousand, but there was now a river through which

I could not wade; for the water had risen so high it had become a river that could not be crossed except by swimming. He asked me, "Have you seen this, son of man?" Then he brought me to the bank of the river, where he had me sit. Along the bank of the river I saw very many trees on both sides. He said to me, "This water flows into the eastern district down upon the Arabah, and empties into the sea, the salt waters, which it makes fresh. Wherever the river flows, every sort of living creature that can multiply shall live, and there shall be abundant fish, for wherever this water comes the sea shall be made fresh. Along both banks of the river, fruit trees of every kind shall grow; their leaves shall not fade, nor their fruit fail. Every month they shall bear fresh fruit, for they shall be watered by the flow from the sanctuary. Their fruit shall serve for food, and their leaves for medicine."—This is the Word of the Lord. ℟. **Thanks be to God.** ℣

Responsorial Psalm   Ps 46, 2-3. 5-6. 8-9

℟. (8) **The mighty Lord is with us;**
    the God of Jacob is our refuge.

God is our refuge and our strength,
    an ever-present help in distress.
Therefore we fear not, though the earth be shaken
    and mountains plunge into the depths of the
        sea. — ℟

There is a stream whose runlets gladden the city of
        God,
    the holy dwelling of the Most High.
God is in its midst; it shall not be disturbed;
    God will help it at the break of dawn. — ℟

The Lord of hosts is with us;
    our stronghold is the God of Jacob.
Come! behold the deeds of the Lord,
    the astounding things he has wrought on
        earth. — ℟ ℣

GOSPEL   Jn 5, 1-3. 5-16

Verse before the Gospel (Jn 11, 25. 26)

℞. **Praise and honor to you, Lord Jesus Christ!**

I am the resurrection and the life, said the Lord:
he who believes in me will not die for ever.

℞. **Praise and honor to you, Lord Jesus Christ!**

Water is featured again. The angel stirs the pool and all who enter
are made well and strong. The poor man who keeps trying to get in
has his faith rewarded when our Lord comes along. At last he is
cured.

℣. The Lord be with you. ℞. **And also with you.**

✠ A reading from the holy gospel according to John
℞. **Glory to you, Lord.**

On the occasion of a Jewish feast, Jesus went up to
Jerusalem. Now in Jerusalem by the Sheep Pool
there is a place with the Hebrew name Bethesda. Its
five porticoes were crowded with sick people lying
there blind, lame or disabled [waiting for the movement of the waters]. There was one man who had
been sick for thirty-eight years. Jesus, who knew
he had been sick a long time, said when he saw him
lying there, "Do you want to be healed?" "Sir," the
sick man answered, "I don't have anyone to plunge
me into the pool once the water has been stirred up.
By the time I get there, someone else has gone in
ahead of me." Jesus said to him, "Stand up! Pick up
your mat and walk!" The man was immediately
cured; he picked up his mat and began to walk.

The day was a sabbath. Consequently, some of the
Jews began telling the man who had been cured, "It
is the sabbath, and you are not allowed to carry that
mat around." He explained: "It was the man who
cured me who told me, 'Pick up your mat and walk.'"
"This person who told you to pick it up and walk,"
they asked, "who is he?" The man who had been
restored to health had no idea who it was. The crowd
in that place was so great that Jesus had been able
to slip away.

Later on, Jesus found him in the temple precincts and said to him: "Remember, now, you have been cured. Give up your sins so that something worse may not overtake you." The man went off and informed the Jews that Jesus was the one who had cured him.

It was because Jesus did things such as this on the sabbath that they began to persecute him.—This is the gospel of the Lord. ℟. **Praise to you, Lord Jesus Christ.**   ➔ No. 15, p. 623

PRAYER OVER THE GIFTS
Lord,
may your gifts of bread and wine
which nourish us here on earth
become the food of our eternal life.
Grant this through Christ our Lord.
℟. **Amen.**   ➔ No. 21, p. 626 (Pref. P 8-11)

COMMUNION ANT.   Ps 23, 1-2
The Lord is my shepherd; there is nothing I shall want. In green pastures he gives me rest, he leads me beside the waters of peace. ℣

PRAYER AFTER COMMUNION
Lord,
may your holy sacraments cleanse and renew us;
may they bring us your help
and lead us to salvation.
We ask this in the name of Jesus the Lord.
℟. **Amen.**   ➔ No. 32, p. 650

WEDNESDAY OF THE FOURTH WEEK OF LENT

Jesus is identified as the Suffering Servant of Isaiah. As Messiah and Prophet and Son of God, he fulfilled the role completely. In these days of Lent, we begin to discern more and more the significance of Christ's sufferings. Millions of people have suffered since time began, but the sufferings of the Son of God for us take on a special redemptive value. In those sufferings, Jesus was carrying out the special mission of uniting man with God.

ENTRANCE ANT.   Ps 69, 14

I pray to you, O God, for the time of your favor. Lord, in your great love, answer me.   → No. 2, p. 614

OPENING PRAYER

Lord,
you reward virtue
and forgive the repentant sinner.
Grant us your forgiveness
as we come before you confessing our guilt.
We ask this through our Lord Jesus Christ, your Son,
who lives and reigns with you and the Holy Spirit,
one God, for ever and ever. ℟. **Amen.** ⇓

READING I   Is 49, 8-15

Isaiah proclaims the wondrous reversal of Israel's fortunes. Salvation comes through God's pleasure. God is a shepherd leading his sheep along a new exodus. The Lord comforts his people but Zion exclaims, "The Lord has forsaken me..."

A reading from the book of the prophet Isaiah

Thus says the Lord:
In a time of favor I answer you,
    on the day of salvation I help you,
To restore the land
    and allot the desolate heritages,
Saying to the prisoners: Come out!
To those in darkness: Show yourselves!
Along the ways they shall find pasture,
    on every bare height shall their pastures be.
They shall not hunger or thirst,
    nor shall the scorching wind or the sun strike
        them;
For he who pities them leads them
    and guides them beside springs of water.
I will cut a road through all my mountains,
    and make my highways level.
See, some shall come from afar,
    others from the north and the west,
    and some from the land of Syene.

Sing out, O heavens, and rejoice, O earth,
    break forth into song, you mountains.
For the Lord comforts his people
    and shows mercy to his afflicted.
But Zion said, "The Lord has forsaken me;
    my Lord has forgotten me."
Can a mother forget her infant,
    be without tenderness for the child of her womb?
Even should she forget,
    I will never forget you.
This is the Word of the Lord. ℟. **Thanks be to God.** ℣

Resonsorial Psalm   Ps 145, 8-9. 13-14. 17-18

℟. (8) **The Lord is kind and merciful.**

The Lord is gracious and merciful,
    slow to anger and of great kindness.
The Lord is good to all
    and compassionate toward all his works. — ℟

The Lord is faithful in all his words
    and holy in all his works.
The Lord lifts up all who are falling
    and raises up all who are bowed down. — ℟

The Lord is just in all his ways
    and holy in all his works.
The Lord is near to all who call upon him,
    to all who call upon him in truth. ℟ ℣

GOSPEL   Jn 5, 17-30

Verse before the Gospel (Jn 3, 16)

℟. **Glory and praise to you, Lord Jesus Christ!**
God loved the world so much, he gave us his only
        Son,
that all who believe in him might have eternal life.
℟. **Glory and praise to you, Lord Jesus Christ!**

The Servant of Yahweh is Christ. God made his beloved Son the
source of life for all men. This is the specific meaning of "redeeming."
Jesus openly says that he has been appointed the supreme judge of
life and death.

℣. The Lord be with you. ℟. **And also with you.**
✠ A reading from the holy gospel according to John
℟. **Glory to you, Lord.**
Jesus said to the Jews:

"My Father is at work until now,
and I am at work as well."

The reason why the Jews were even more determined to kill him was that he not only was breaking the sabbath but, worse still, was speaking of God as his own Father, thereby making himself God's equal.

This was Jesus' answer:

"I solemnly assure you,
the Son cannot do anything by himself—
he can do only what he sees the Father doing.
For whatever the Father does,
the Son does likewise.
For the Father loves the Son
and everything the Father does he shows him.
Yes, to your great wonderment,
he will show him even greater works than these.
Indeed, just as the Father raises the dead and
grants life,
so the Son grants life to those to whom he
wishes.
The Father himself judges no one,
but has assigned all judgment to the Son,
so that all men may honor the Son
just as they honor the Father.
He who refuses to honor the Son
refuses to honor the Father who sent him.
I solemnly assure you,
the man who hears my word
and has faith in him who sent me
possesses eternal life.
He does not come under condemnation,
but has passed from death to life.
I solemnly assure you,

an hour is coming, has indeed come,
when the dead shall hear the voice of God's
Son,
and those who have heeded it shall live.
Indeed, just as the Father possesses life in himself,
so has he granted it to the Son to have life in
himself.
The Father has given over to him power to pass
judgment
because he is Son of Man;
no need for you to be surprised at this,
for an hour is coming
in which all those in the tombs
shall hear his voice and come forth.
Those who have done right shall rise to live;
the evildoers shall rise to be damned.
I cannot do anything of myself.
I judge as I hear,
and my judgment is honest
because I am not seeking my own will
but the will of him who sent me."

This is the gospel of the Lord. ℞. **Praise to you, Lord Jesus Christ.** ➤ No. 15, p. 623

PRAYER OVER THE GIFTS

Lord God,
may the power of this sacrifice wash away our sins,
renew our lives and bring us to salvation.
We ask this in the name of Jesus the Lord.
℞. **Amen.** ➤ No. 21, p. 626 (Pref. P 8-11)

COMMUNION ANT. Jn 3, 17

God sent his Son into the world, not to condemn it, but so that the world might be saved through him. ℣

PRAYER AFTER COMMUNION

Lord,
may we never misuse your healing gifts,

but always find in them a source of life and salvation.
Grant this through Christ our Lord.

℟. **Amen.**   ➜ No. 32, p. 650

————————————

THURSDAY OF THE FOURTH WEEK OF LENT

How often we refuse to bear witness to Christ and do not hear the
words of God. Sin darkens the understanding, blunts the spiritual
faculties, and deprives a man of true faith. Christ suffered and died
that we might be ransomed. We can help ourselves by learning more
and more of the depth of God's love for us by devout meditation on
Christ's sacred passion.

ENTRANCE ANT.   Ps 105, 3-4

**Let hearts rejoice who search for the Lord. Seek the
Lord and his strength, seek always the face of the
Lord.**   ➜ No. 2, p. 614

OPENING PRAYER

Merciful Father,
may the penance of our lenten observance
make us your obedient people.
May the love within us be seen in what we do
and lead us to the joy of Easter.
Grant this through our Lord Jesus Christ, your Son,
who lives and reigns with you and the Holy Spirit,
one God, for ever and ever. ℟. **Amen.** ℣

READING I   Ex 32, 7-14

While Moses is speaking to God, the Jewish people mold a golden
calf. God is angry but Moses implores God to forgive them. Moses
recalls the promise God had made to Abraham, Isaac and Jacob. So
God relents.

A reading from the book of Exodus

The Lord said to Moses, "Go down at once to your
people, whom you brought out of the land of Egypt,
for they have become depraved. They have soon
turned aside from the way I pointed out to them,
making for themselves a molten calf and worshiping it, sacrificing to it and crying out, 'This is your

God, O Israel, who brought you out of the land of
Egypt!' I see how stiff-necked this people is," continued the Lord to Moses. "Let me alone, then, that
my wrath may blaze up against them to consume
them. Then I will make of you a great nation."

But Moses implored the Lord, his God, saying,
"Why, O Lord, should your wrath blaze up against
your own people, whom you brought out of the land
of Egypt with such great power and with so strong
a hand? Why should the Egyptians say, 'With evil
intent he brought them out, that he might kill them
in the mountains and exterminate them from the face
of the earth'? Let your blazing wrath die down; relent in punishing your people. Remember your servants Abraham, Isaac and Israel, and how you swore
to them by your own self, saying, 'I will make your
descendants as numerous as the stars in the sky;
and all this land that I promised, I will give your
descendants as their perpetual heritage.'" So the
Lord relented in the punishment he had threatened
to inflict on his people.—This is the Word of the
Lord. ℟. **Thanks be to God.** ℣

Responsorial Psalm　　　　　Ps 106, 19-20. 21-22. 23

℟. (4) **Lord, remember us,**
　　for the love you bear your people.

Our fathers made a calf in Horeb
　　and adored a molten image;
They exchanged their glory
　　for the image of a grass-eating bullock. — ℟

They forgot the God who had saved them,
　　who had done great deeds in Egypt,
Wondrous deeds in the land of Ham,
　　terrible things at the Red Sea. — ℟

Then he spoke of exterminating them,
　　but Moses, his chosen one,
Withstood him in the breach
　　to turn back his destructive wrath. — ℟ ℣

GOSPEL   Jn 5, 31-47

Verse before the Gospel (Mt 4, 4)

℞. **Glory to you, Word of God, Lord Jesus Christ!**
Man does not live on bread alone,
but on every word that comes from the mouth of
   God.
℞. **Glory to you, Word of God, Lord Jesus Christ!**

Jesus says that John was his lamp. More than this, Jesus' divine works
must speak for themselves. Even the Scriptures foretold the works of
the Messiah. He has come in his Father's name.

℣. The Lord be with you. ℞. **And also with you.**
✠ A reading from the holy gospel according to John
℞. **Glory to you, Lord.**

Jesus said to the Jews:
      "If I witness on my own behalf,
      you cannot verify my testimony;
      but there is another who is testifying on my be-
         half,
      and the testimony he renders me
      I know can be verified.
      You have sent to John,
      who has testified to the truth.
      (Not that I myself accept such human testi-
         mony—
      I refer to these things only for your salvation.)
      He was the lamp, set aflame and burning bright,
      and for a while you exulted willingly in his light.
      Yet I have testimony greater than John's,
      namely, the works the Father has given me to
         accomplish.
      These very works which I perform
      testify on my behalf
      that the Father has sent me.
      Moreover, the Father who sent me
      has himself given testimony on my behalf.
      His voice you have never heard,
      his form you have never seen,

neither do you have his word abiding in your
    hearts
because you do not believe
the one he has sent.
Search the Scriptures
in which you think you have eternal life—
they also testify on my behalf.
Yet you are unwilling to come to me
to possess that life.
It is not that I accept human praise—
it is simply that I know you,
and you do not have the love of God in your
    hearts.
I have come in my Father's name,
yet you do not accept me.
But let someone come in his own name
and him you will accept.
How can people like you believe,
when you accept praise from one another
yet do not seek the glory that comes from the
    One [God]?
Do not imagine that I will be your accuser be-
    fore the Father;
the one to accuse you is Moses
on whom you have set your hopes.
If you believed Moses
you would then believe me,
for it was about me that he wrote.
But if you do not believe what he wrote,
how can you believe what I say?"

This is the gospel of the Lord. ℟. **Praise to you, Lord
Jesus Christ.**   ➔ No. 15, p. 623

PRAYER OVER THE GIFTS

All-powerful God,
look upon our weakness.
May the sacrifice we offer
bring us purity and strength.

We ask this in the name of Jesus the Lord.
℟. **Amen.**   ➤ No. 21, p. 626 (Pref. P 8-11)

COMMUNION ANT.   Jer 31, 33
I will put my law within them, I will write it on their hearts; then I shall be their God, and they will be my people. ⍗

PRAYER AFTER COMMUNION
Lord,
may the sacraments we receive
cleanse us of sin and free us from guilt,
for our sins bring us sorrow
but your promise of salvation brings us joy.
We ask this through Christ our Lord.
℟. **Amen.**   ➤ No. 32, p. 650

FRIDAY OF THE FOURTH WEEK OF LENT

The passion which we are approaching in the Sacred Liturgy will give us a supreme opportunity to concentrate our thoughts on that awful occasion which was brought about by the plots of wicked men. In the face of all that is human, remember the presence of that which is Divine. Let us be filled with cheerful certainty that in the Church, the time of sorrow will pass away and days of triumph and victory will return again.

ENTRANCE ANT.   Ps 54, 3-4
Save me, O God, by your power, and grant me justice! God, hear my prayer; listen to my plea.
                              ➤ No. 2, p. 614

OPENING PRAYER
Father, our source of life,
you know our weakness.
May we reach out with joy to grasp your hand
and walk more readily in your ways.
We ask this through our Lord Jesus Christ, your Son,
who lives and reigns with you and the Holy Spirit,
one God, for ever and ever. ℟. **Amen.** ⍗

READING I   Wis 2, 1. 12-22

The Book of Wisdom was written very close to the time of Christ—
perhaps only 50 years before him. It represents the whole history of
man's dealings with his fellows. Wickedness blinded those who were
mistaken and who doubted. They did not learn the counsels of God.
Let men uphold goodness and virtue and the observance of the Law.

A reading from the book of Wisdom

The wicked said among themselves, thinking not
aright:
"Let us beset the just one, because he is obnoxious
   to us;
   he sets himself against our doings,
Reproaches us for transgressions of the law
   and charges us with violations of our training.
He professes to have knowledge of God
   and styles himself a child of the Lord.
To us he is the censure of our thoughts;
   merely to see him is a hardship for us
Because his life is not like other men's,
   and different are his ways.
He judges us debased;
   he holds aloof from our paths as from things impure.
He calls blest the destiny of the just
   and boasts that God is his Father.
Let us see whether his words be true;
   let us find out what will happen to him.
For if the just one be the son of God, he will defend
   him
   and deliver him from the hand of his foes.
With revilement and torture let us put him to the
   test
   that we may have proof of his gentleness
   and try his patience.
Let us condemn him to a shameful death;
   for according to his own words, God will take
   care of him."

These were their thoughts, but they erred;
    for their wickedness blinded them,
And they knew not the hidden counsels of God;
    neither did they count on a recompense of holiness
    nor discern the innocent souls' reward.
This is the Word of the Lord. ℟. **Thanks be to God.** ℣

Responsorial Psalm   Ps 34, 17-18. 19-20. 21. 23

℟. (19) **The Lord is near to broken hearts.**

The Lord confronts the evildoers,
    to destroy remembrance of them from the earth.
When the just cry out, the Lord hears them,
    and from all their distress he rescues them. — ℟

The Lord is close to the brokenhearted;
    and those who are crushed in spirit he saves.
Many are the troubles of the just man,
    but out of them all the Lord delivers him. — ℟

He watches over all his bones;
    not one of them shall be broken.
The Lord redeems the lives of his servants;
    no one incurs guilt who takes refuge in
      him. — ℟ ℣

GOSPEL   Jn 7, 1-2. 10. 25-30

Verse before the Gospel (Mt 4, 4)

℟. **Praise to you, Lord Jesus Christ, king of endless
    glory!**
Man does not live on bread alone,
but on every word that comes from the mouth of
    God.
℟. **Praise to you, Lord Jesus Christ, king of endless
    glory!**

Those in Galilee begin to realize that Jesus is doomed. Voices are
heard in all directions asking, "Isn't this the man they want to kill?"
But Jesus faces them unafraid, and when he speaks in the temple, he
sets their malicious wills against him irrevocably.

℣. The Lord be with you. ℟. **And also with you.**
✠ A reading from the holy gospel accordidng to John
℟. **Glory to you, Lord.**

Jesus moved about within Galilee. He had decided not to travel in Judea because some of the Jews were looking for a chance to kill him. The Jewish feast of Booths drew near. Once his brothers had gone up to the festival he too went up, but as if in secret and not for all to see.

Some of the people of Jerusalem remarked, "Is this not the one they wan. 'o kill? Here he is speaking in public and they don't say a word to him! Perhaps even the authorities have decided that this is the Messiah. Still, we know where this man is from. When the Messiah comes, no one is supposed to know his origins."

At this, Jesus, who was teaching in the temple area, cried out:

"So you know me,
and you know my origins?
The truth is, I have not come of myself.
I was sent by One who has the right to send,
and him you do not know.
I know him because it is from him I come:
he sent me."

At this they tried to seize him, but no one laid a finger on him because his hour had not yet come.— This is the gospel of the Lord. ℟. **Praise to you, Lord Jesus Christ.** ➤ No. 15, p. 623

PRAYER OVER THE GIFTS

All-powerful God,
may the healing power of this sacrifice
free us from sin
and help us to approach you with pure hearts.
Grant this through Christ our Lord.
℟. **Amen.** ➤ No. 21, p. 626 (Pref. P 8-11)

COMMUNION ANT.
Eph 1, 7

In Christ, through the shedding of his blood, we have redemption and forgiveness of our sins by the abundance of his grace. ↓

PRAYER AFTER COMMUNION

Lord,
in this eucharist we pass from death to life.
Keep us from our old and sinful ways
and help us to continue in the new life.
We ask this in the name of Jesus the Lord.
℟. **Amen.**   ➔ No. 32, p. 650

SATURDAY OF THE FOURTH WEEK OF LENT

Jesus knows what we are thinking. He knows what we believe and
what we hesitate to believe and what we do not want to believe. But
once we accept him, we believe everything he tells us. A just God
probes our hearts.

ENTRANCE ANT.   Ps 18, 5-7

**The snares of death overtook me, the ropes of hell
tightened around me; in my distress I called upon the
Lord, and he heard my voice.**   ➔ No. 2, p. 614

OPENING PRAYER

Lord,
guide us in your gentle mercy,
for left to ourselves
we cannot do your will.
Grant this through our Lord Jesus Christ, your Son,
who lives and reigns with you and the Holy Spirit,
one God, for ever and ever. ℟. **Amen.** ℣

READING I   Jer 11, 18-20

This part of Jeremiah's prophecy gives a picture of his readiness to
suffer. As the prophet expresses his loving spirit, he would seem to
be unsuspecting. The vision is of patient resignation. His enemies
decide they must obliterate him.

A reading from the book of the prophet Jeremiah

I knew their plot because the Lord informed me; at
that time you, O Lord, showed me their doings. Yet
I, like a trusting lamb led to slaughter, had not realized that they were hatching plots against me: "Let

us destroy the tree in its vigor; let us cut him off
from the land of the living, so that his name will be
spoken no more.''

But, you, O Lord of hosts, O just Judge,
   searcher of mind and heart,
Let me witness the vengeance you take on
      them,
   for to you I have entrusted my cause!
This is the Word of the Lord. ℟. **Thanks be to God.** ℣

Responsorial Psalm   Ps 7, 2-3. 9-10. 11-12

℟. (2) **Lord, my God, I take shelter in you.**

O Lord, my God, in you I take refuge;
   save me from all my pursuers and rescue me,
Lest I become like the lion's prey,
   to be torn to pieces, with no one to rescue me.— ℟

Do me justice, O Lord, because I am just,
   and because of the innocence that is mine.
Let the malice of the wicked come to an end,
   but sustain the just,
   O searcher of heart and soul, O just God. — ℟

A shield before me is God,
   who saves the upright of heart;
A just judge is God,
   a God who punishes day by day. — ℟ ℣

GOSPEL   Jn 7, 40-53

Verse before the Gospel (Jn 3, 16)

℟. **Praise and honor to you, Lord Jesus Christ!**
God loved the world so much, he gave us his only
   Son,
that all who believe in him might have eternal life.
℟. **Praise and honor to you, Lord Jesus Christ!**

The scribes and Pharisees are discussing Christ. The last sentence in
this excerpt from St. John's gospel says everything: They all went
home! No consensus is reached. The major accusation against Jesus
is that he came from Galilee, and evidently Nazareth was the worst
place to come from in Galilee.

℣. The Lord be with you. ℟. **And also with you.**
✠ A reading from the holy gospel according to John
℟. **Glory to you, Lord.**

Some in the crowd who heard the words of Jesus
began to say, "This must be the Prophet." Others
were claiming, "He is the Messiah." But an objection was raised: "Surely the Messiah is not to come
from Galilee? Does not Scripture say that the Messiah, being of David's family, is to come from
Bethlehem, the village where David lived?" In this
fashion the crowd was sharply divided over him.
Some of them even wanted to apprehend him. However, no one laid hands on him.

When the temple guards came, the chief priests
and Pharisees asked them, "Why did you not bring
him in?" "No man ever spoke like that before," the
guards replied. "Do not tell us you too have been
taken in!" the Pharisees retorted. "You do not see
any of the Sanhedrin believing in him, do you? Or
the Pharisees? Only this lot, that knows nothing
about the law—and they are lost anyway!" One of
their own number, Nicodemus (the man who had
come to him), spoke up to say, "Since when does our
law condemn any man without first hearing him and
knowing the facts?" "Do not tell us you are a Galilean too," they taunted him. "Look it up. You will
not find the Prophet coming from Galilee."

Then each went off to his own house.—This is the
gospel of the Lord. ℟. **Praise to you, Lord Jesus
Christ.**   ➤ No. 15, p. 623

PRAYER OVER THE GIFTS

Father,
accept our gifts
and make our hearts obedient to your will.
We ask this in the name of Jesus the Lord.
℟. **Amen.**   ➤ No. 21, p. 626 (Pref. P 8-11)

COMMUNION ANT.   1 Pt 1, 19

We have been ransomed with the precious blood of Christ, as with the blood of a lamb without blemish or spot. ℣

PRAYER AFTER COMMUNION
Lord,
may the power of your holy gifts free us from sin
and help us to please you in our daily lives.
We ask this through Christ our Lord.
℟. **Amen.**   → No. 32, p. 650

The practice of covering crosses and images in the church may be observed, if the episcopal conference decides. The crosses are to be covered until the end of the celebration of the Lord's passion on Good Friday. Images are to remain covered until the beginning of the Easter vigil. _____

OPTIONAL READINGS AND INTERVENIENT CHANTS
FOR THE FIFTH WEEK OF LENT

These readings and intervenient chants may be used on any day of this week when the Gospel of Lazarus is not read on the Fifth Sunday of Lent.

READING I   2 Kgs 4, 18-21. 32-37

The son of the Shunammite woman becomes ill working in the field. He is carried home and dies in his mother's arms. Through the prayer of Elisha, the man of God, the boy's life is restored. How grateful is his mother.

A reading from the second book of Kings

The day came when the child of the Shunammite woman was old enough to go out to his father among the reapers. "My head hurts!" he complained to his father. "Carry him to his mother," the father said to a servant. The servant picked him up and carried him to his mother; he stayed with her until noon, when he died in her lap. The mother took him upstairs and laid him on the bed of the man of God. Closing the door on him, she went out.

When Elisha reached the house, he found the boy lying dead. He went in, closed the door on them both, and prayed to the Lord. Then he lay upon the child on the bed, placing his mouth upon the child's mouth, his eyes upon the eyes, and his hands upon the hands. As Elisha stretched himself over the child, the body became warm. He arose, paced up and down the room, and then once more lay down upon the boy, who now sneezed seven times and opened his eyes. Elisha summoned Gehazi and said, "Call the Shunammite." She came at his call, and Elisha said to her, "Take your son." She came in and fell at his feet in gratitude; then she took her son and left the room.—This is the Word of the Lord. R̂. **Thanks be to God.** ⱽ

Responsorial Psalm   Ps 17, 1. 6-7. 8. 15

R̂. (15) **Lord, when your glory appears,
    my joy will be full.**

Hear, O Lord, a just suit;
    attend to my outcry;
    hearken to my prayer from lips without deceit.—R̂

I call upon you, for you will answer me, O God;
    incline your ear to me; hear my word.
Show your wondrous kindness,
    O savior of those who flee
    from their foes to refuge at your right hand. — R̂

Hide me in the shadow of your wings.
    I in justice shall behold your face;
    on waking, I shall be content in your
        presence.— R̂ ⱽ

GOSPEL   Jn 11, 1-45

Verse before the Gospel Jn (11, 25. 26)

R̂. **Glory and praise to you, Lord Jesus Christ!**
I am the resurrection and the life, said the Lord:
he who believes in me will not die for ever.
R̂. **Glory and praise to you, Lord Jesus Christ!**

Jesus was a close friend of Mary, Martha, and Lazarus. When Lazarus becomes ill, his sisters send for Jesus. When Jesus arrives, he finds that Lazarus has been dead for four days. Jesus comforts Mary and Martha and brings Lazarus back to life.

℣. The Lord be with you. ℟. **And also with you.**

✠ A reading from the holy gospel according to John
℟. **Glory to you, Lord.**

There was a certain man named Lazarus who was sick. He was from Bethany, the village of Mary and her sister Martha. (This Mary whose brother Lazarus was sick was the one who anointed the Lord with perfume and dried his feet with her hair.) The sisters sent word to Jesus to inform him, "Lord, the one you love is sick." Upon hearing this, Jesus said:

"This sickness is not to end in death;
rather it is for God's glory,
that through it the Son of God may be glorified."

Jesus loved Martha and her sister and Lazarus very much. Yet, after hearing that Lazarus was sick, he stayed on where he was for two days more. Finally he said to his disciples, "Let us go back to Judea." "Rabbi," protested the disciples, "with the Jews only recently trying to stone you, you are going back up there again?" Jesus answered:

"Are there not twelve hours of daylight?
If a man goes walking by day he does not stumble,
because he sees the world bathed in light.
But if he goes walking at night he will stumble,
since there is no light in him."

After uttering these words, he added, "Our beloved Lazarus has fallen asleep, but I am going there to wake him." At this the disciples objected, "Lord, if he is asleep his life will be saved." Jesus had been speaking about his death, but they thought he meant sleep in the sense of slumber. Finally Jesus said plainly, "Lazarus is dead. For your sakes I am glad

I was not there, that you may come to believe. In any event, let us go to him." Then Thomas (the name means "Twin") said to his fellow disciples, "Let us go along, to die with him."

When Jesus arrived at Bethany, he found that Lazarus had already been in the tomb four days. The village was not far from Jerusalem—just under two miles—and many Jewish people had come out to console Martha and Mary over their brother. When Martha heard that Jesus was coming she went to meet him, while Mary sat at home. Martha said to Jesus, "Lord, if you had been here, my brother would never have died. Even now, I am sure that God will give you whatever you ask of him." "Your brother will rise again," Jesus assured her. "I know he will rise again," Martha replied, "in the resurrection on the last day." Jesus told her:

"I am the resurrection and the life:
whoever believes in me,
though he should die, will come to life;
and whoever is alive and believes in me
will never die."

Do you believe this?" "Yes, Lord, she replied. "I have come to believe that you are the Messiah, the Son of God: he who is to come into the world."

When she had said this she went back and called her sister Mary. "The Teacher is here, asking for you," she whispered. As soon as Mary heard this, she got up and started out in his direction. (Actually Jesus had not yet come into the village but was still at the spot where Martha had met him.) The Jews who were in the house with Mary consoling her saw her get up quickly and go out, so they followed her, thinking she was going to the tomb to weep there. When Mary came to the place where Jesus was, seeing him, she fell at his feet and said to him, "Lord, if you had been here my brother would never have died." When Jesus saw her weeping, and the Jewish folk who had accompanied her also weeping, he was troubled in spirit, moved by the deepest emotions. "Where have you laid him?" he asked. "Lord, come and see," they said. Jesus began to weep, which caused the Jews to remark, "See how much he loved him!" But some said, "He opened the eyes of that blind man. Why could he not have done something to stop this man from dying?" Once again troubled in spirit, Jesus approached the tomb.

It was a cave with a stone laid across it. "Take away the stone," Jesus directed. Martha, the dead man's sister, said to him, "Lord, it has been four days now; surely there will be a stench!" Jesus replied, "Did I not assure you that if you believed you would see the glory of God?" They then took away the stone and Jesus looked upward and said:

"Father, I thank you for having heard me.
I know that you always hear me
but I have said this for the sake of the crowd,
that they may believe that you sent me."

Having said this, he called loudly, "Lazarus, come out!" The dead man came out, bound hand and foot with linen strips, his face wrapped in a cloth. "Untie him," Jesus told them, "and let him go free."

This caused many of the Jews who had come to visit Mary, and had seen what Jesus did, to put their faith in him.—This is the gospel of the Lord.
℟. **Praise to you, Lord Jesus Christ.**   ➔ No. 15, p. 623

MONDAY OF THE FIFTH WEEK OF LENT

Jesus is the light of the world. In him we find perfect justice as he searches into the hearts of men. We live in an imperfect world and our human weakness often makes us prone to error. God alone is all just. He is triumphant in eternal vindication which is proven in the Resurrection. Jesus was judged by evil-minded men.

ENTRANCE ANT.   Ps 56, 2

God, take pity on me! My enemies are crushing me; all day long they wage war on me.   ➔ No. 2, p. 614

OPENING PRAYER

Father of love, source of all blessings,
help us to pass from our old life of sin
to the new life of grace.
Prepare us for the glory of your kingdom.
We ask this through our Lord Jesus Christ, your Son,
who lives and reigns with you and the Holy Spirit,
one God, for ever and ever. ℟. **Amen.** ✝

READING I

Dn 13, 1-9. 15-17. 19-30. 33-62 or 13, 41-62

[*If the "Short Form" is used, the indented text in brackets is omitted.*]

The last two chapters of the Book of Daniel develop stories about Daniel. In the shorter form of the story about Susanna, the author comes quickly to the point that in God there is perfect justice and vindication, whereas the judgment of men is always in danger of being erroneous.

A reading from the book of the prophet Daniel

[In Babylon there lived a man named Joakim, who married a very beautiful and God-fearing woman, Susanna, the daughter of Hilkiah; her pious parents had trained their daughter according to the law of Moses. Joakim was very rich; he had a garden near his house, and the Jews had recourse to him often because he was the most respected of them all.

That year, two elders of the people were appointed judges, of whom the Lord said, "Wickedness has come out of Babylon: from the elders who were to govern the people as judges." These men, to whom all brought their cases, frequented the house of Joakim. When the people left at noon, Susanna used to enter her husband's garden for a walk. When the old men saw her enter every day for her walk, they began to lust for her. They suppressed their consciences; they would not allow their eyes to look to heaven, and did not keep in mind just judgments.

One day, while they were waiting for the right moment, she entered the garden as usual, with two maids only. She decided to bathe, for the weather was warm. Nobody else was there except the two elders, who had hidden themselves and were watching her. "Bring me oil and soap," she said to the maids, "and shut the garden doors while I bathe."

As soon as the maids had left, the two old men got up and hurried to her. "Look," they said, "the garden doors are shut, and no one can see us; give in to our desire, and lie with us. If you refuse, we will testify against you that you dismissed your maids because a young man was here with you."

"I am completely trapped," Susanna groaned. "If I yield, it will be my death; if I refuse, I cannot escape your power. Yet it is better for me to fall into your power without guilt than to sin before the Lord." Then Susanna shrieked, and the old men also shouted at her, as one of them ran to open the garden doors. When the people in the house heard the cries from the garden, they rushed in by the side gate to see what had happened to her. At the accusations by the old men, the servants felt very much ashamed, for never had any such thing been said about Susanna.

When the people came to her husband Joakim the next day, the two wicked elders also came, fully determined to put Susanna to death. Before all the people they ordered: "Send for Susanna, the daughter of Hilkiah, the wife of Joakim." When she was sent for, she came with her parents, children and all her relatives. All her relatives and the onlookers were weeping.

In the midst of the people the two elders rose up and laid their hands on her head. Through her tears she looked up to heaven, for she trusted in the Lord wholeheartedly. The elders made this accusation: "As we were walking in the garden alone, this woman entered with two girls and shut the doors of the garden, dismissing the girls. A young man, who was hidden there, came and lay with her. When we, in a corner of the garden, saw this crime, we ran toward them. We saw them lying together, but the man we could not hold, because he was stronger than we; he opened the doors and ran off. Then we seized this one and asked who the young man was, but she refused to tell us. We testify to this."]

The assembly believed them, since they were elders and judges of the people, and they condemned her to death.

But Susanna cried aloud: "O eternal God, you know what is hidden and are aware of all things before they come to be: you know that they have testified falsely against me. Here I am about to die, though I have done none of the things with which these wicked men have charged me."

The Lord heard her prayer. As she was being led to execution, God stirred up the holy spirit of a young boy named Daniel, and he cried aloud: "I will have no part in the death of this woman." All the people turned and asked him, "What is this you are saying?" He stood in their midst and continued, "Are you such fools, O Israelites! To condemn a woman of Israel without examination and without clear evidence? Return to court, for they have testified falsely against her."

Then all the people returned in haste. To Daniel the elders said, "Come, sit with us and inform us, since God has given you the prestige of old age."

But he replied, "Separate these two far from one another that I may examine them."

After they were separated one from the other, he called one of them and said: "How you have grown evil with age! Now have your past sins come to term: passing unjust sentences, condemning the innocent, and freeing the guilty, although the Lord says, 'The, innocent and the just you shall not put to death.' Now, then, if you were a witness, tell me under what tree you saw them together." "Under a mastic tree," he answered. "Your fine lie has cost you your head," said Daniel; "for the angel of God shall receive the sentence from him and split you in two." Putting him to one side, he ordered the other one to be brought. "Offspring of Canaan, not of Judah," Daniel said to him, "beauty has seduced you, lust has subverted your conscience. This is how you acted with the daughters of Israel, and in their fear they yielded to you; but a daughter of Judah did not tolerate your wickedness. Now, then, tell me under what tree you surprised them together." "Under an oak," he said. "Your fine lie has cost you also your head," said Daniel; "for the angel of God waits with a sword to cut you in two so as to make an end of you both."

The whole assembly cried aloud, blessing God who saves those that hope in him. They rose up against the two elders, for by their own words Daniel had convicted them of perjury. According to the law of Moses, they inflicted on them the penalty they had plotted. Thus was innocent blood spared that day.
—This is the Word of the Lord. ℟. **Thanks be to God.** ℣

Responsorial Psalm   Ps 23, 1-3. 3-4. 5. 6
℟. (4) **Though I walk in the valley of darkness,**
   I fear no evil, for you are with me.
The Lord is my shepherd; I shall not want.
   In verdant pastures he gives me repose.

Beside restful waters he leads me;
  he refreshes my soul. — ℟

He guides me in right paths
  for his name's sake.

Even though I walk in the dark valley
  I fear no evil; for you are at my side

With your rod and your staff
  that give me courage. — ℟

You spread the table before me
  in the sight of my foes;

You anoint my head with oil;
  my cup overflows. — ℟

Only goodness and kindness follow me
  all the days of my life;

And I shall dwell in the house of the Lord
  for years to come. — ℟ ↓

GOSPEL   Jn 8, 1-11

Verse before the Gospel (Ez 33, 11)

℟. **Glory to you, Word of God, Lord Jesus Christ!**
I do not wish the sinner to die, says the Lord,
but to turn to me and live.

℟. **Glory to you, Word of God, Lord Jesus Christ!**

The Pharisees bring a woman accused of adultery to Jesus. They
ask him to judge the case in the light of their law. Without speaking,
Jesus writes in the sand. Let him who has no sin cast the first stone.
One by one, they leave and Jesus also forgives her.

℣. The Lord be with you. ℟. **And also with you.**
✠ A reading from the holy gospel according to John
℟. **Glory to you, Lord.**

Jesus went out to the Mount of Olives. At daybreak
he reappeared in the temple area; and when the people started coming to him, he sat down and began
to teach them. The scribes and the Pharisees led a
woman forward, who had been caught in adultery.
They made her stand there in front of everyone.
"Teacher," they said to him, "this woman has been

caught in the act of adultery. In the law, Moses ordered such women to be stoned. What do you have to say about the case?" (They were posing this question to trap him, so that they could have something to accuse him of.) Jesus simply bent down and started tracing on the ground with his finger. When they persisted in their questioning, he straightened up and said to them, "Let the man among you who has no sin be the first to cast a stone at her." A second time he bent down and wrote on the ground. Then the audience drifted away one by one, beginning with the elders. This left him alone with the woman, who continued to stand there before him. Jesus finally straightened up again and said to her, "Woman, where did they all disappear to? Has no one condemned you?" "No one, sir," she answered. Jesus said, "Nor do I condemn you. You may go. But from now on, avoid this sin."—This is the gospel of the Lord. ℟. **Praise to you, Lord Jesus Christ.**

➔ No. 15, p. 623

OR

When the above Gospel has been read on the preceding Sunday, the following text is used:

GOSPEL   Jn 8, 12-20

Verse before the Gospel (Ez 33, 11)

℟. **Glory to you, Word of God, Lord Jesus Christ!**
I do not wish the sinner to die, says the Lord,
but to turn to me and live.

℟. **Glory to you, Word of God, Lord Jesus Christ!**

This incident is connected with routing the accusers of the woman taken in adultery. Jesus says the worst thing he could have said to the Pharisees, the intellectuals of the Jewish people. "I," he says, "am the light of the world." This would mean "not you." And, of course, they react.

℣. The Lord be with you. ℟. **And also with you.**

✠ A reading from the holy gospel according to John
℟. **Glory to you, Lord.**

Jesus said to the Jews:

"I am the light of the world.
No follower of mine shall ever walk in darkness;
no, he shall possess the light of life."

This caused the Pharisees to break in with: "You
are your own witness. Such testimony cannot be
valid." Jesus answered:

"What if I am my own witness?
My testimony is valid nonetheless,
because I know where I came from
and where I am going;
you know neither the one nor the other.
You pass judgment according to appearances
but I pass judgment on no man.
Even if I do judge,
that judgment of mine is valid
because I am not alone:
I have at my side the One who sent me, the
    Father.
It is laid down in your law
that evidence given by two persons is valid.
I am one of those testifying in my behalf,
the Father who sent me is the other."

They pressed him: "And where is this 'Father' of
yours?" Jesus replied:

"You know neither me nor my Father.
If you knew me, you would know my Father
    too."

He spoke these words while teaching at the temple treasury. Still, he went unapprehended, because
his hour had not yet come.—This is the gospel of
the Lord. ℟. **Praise to you, Lord Jesus Christ.**

➤ No. 15, p. 623

PRAYER OVER THE GIFTS

Lord,
as we come with joy
to celebrate the mystery of the eucharist,
may we offer you hearts

purified by bodily penance.
Grant this through Christ our Lord.
℟. **Amen.**   ➜ No. 21, p. 626 (Pref. P 17)

COMMUNION ANT.   Ps 24, 10

When the gospel of the adultress is read (Year C):
                                      Jn 8, 10-11
**Has no one condemned you? The woman answered:
No one, Lord. Neither do I condemn you: go and do
not sin again.** ℣

When other gospels are read: Jn 8, 12
**I am the light of the world, says the Lord; the man
who follows me will have the light of life.** ℣

PRAYER AFTER COMMUNION
Father,
through the grace of your sacraments
may we follow Christ more faithfully
and come to the joy of your kingdom,
where he is Lord for ever and ever.
℟. **Amen.** _____   ➜ No. 32, p. 650

TUESDAY OF THE FIFTH WEEK OF LENT

In our humanity, the great obedience is fidelity to conscience—to
conscience enlightened by Christ's teachings in the Church. It must
be a prompt conformity to all lawful authority, beginning with our
parents in early days. This practice smoothes differences, blends
with kindness, and pleases God exceedingly.

ENTRANCE ANT.   Ps 27, 14

**Put your hope in the Lord. Take courage and be
strong.**   ➜ No. 2, p. 614

OPENING PRAYER
Lord,
help us to do your will
that your Church may grow
and become more faithful in your service.
Grant this through our Lord Jesus Christ, your Son,
who lives and reigns with you and the Holy Spirit,
one God, for ever and ever. ℟. **Amen.** ℣

READING I Nm 21, 4-9

Again the Israelites rebel against God and are punished. There is a deep symbolism in the mounting of the bronze serpent who saved those Israelites, victims of deadly stings in the desert. But first there is retribution for complaining against God.

A reading from the book of Numbers

From Mount Hor the Israelites set out on the Red Sea road, to by-pass the land of Edom. But with their patience worn out by the journey, the people complained against God and Moses, "Why have you brought us up from Egypt to die in this desert, where there is no food or water? We are disgusted with this wretched food!"

In punishment the Lord sent among the people saraph serpents, which bit the people so that many of them died. Then the people came to Moses and said, "We have sinned in complaining against the Lord and you. Pray the Lord to take the serpents from us." So Moses prayed for the people, and the Lord said to Moses, "Make a saraph and mount it on a pole, and if anyone who has been bitten looks at it, he will recover." Moses accordingly made a bronze serpent and mounted it on a pole, and whenever anyone who had been bitten by a serpent looked at the bronze serpent, he recovered.—This is the Word of the Lord. ℟. **Thanks be to God.** ℣

Responsorial Psalm Ps 102, 2-3. 16-18. 19-21

℟. (2) **O Lord, hear my prayer,**
and let my cry come to you.

O Lord, hear my prayer,
    and let my cry come to you.
Hide not your face from me
    in the day of my distress.
Incline your ear to me;
    in the day when I call, answer me speedily. — ℟

The nations shall revere your name, O Lord,
    and all the kings of the earth your glory,

When the Lord has rebuilt Zion
and appeared in his glory;
When he has regarded the prayer of the destitute,
and not despised their prayer. — ℟

Let this be written for the generation to come,
and let his future creatures praise the Lord:
"The Lord looked down from his holy height,
from heaven he beheld the earth,
To hear the groaning of the prisoners,
to release those doomed to die." — ℟ ℣

GOSPEL   Jn 8, 21-30

Verse before the Gospel

℟. **Praise to you, Lord Jesus Christ, king of endless
glory!**

The seed is the word of God, Christ is the sower;
all who come to him will live for ever.

℟. **Praise to you, Lord Jesus Christ, king of endless
glory!**

Jesus' words are clear only for those who are disposed to believe. His
words may be wasted on the Pharisees to whom he is speaking, but
there are others listening who may be saved. In this passage Jesus
speaks as one who is sent with authority.

℣. The Lord be with you. ℟. **And also with you.**

✠ A reading from the holy gospel according to John

℟. **Glory to you, Lord.**

Jesus said to the Pharisees:
"I am going away. You will look for me
but you will die in your sins.
Where I am going you cannot come."
At this some of the Jews began to ask, "Does he
mean he will kill himself when he claims, 'Where I
am going you cannot come'?" He went on:
"You belong to what is below;
I belong to what is above.
You belong to this world—
a world which cannot hold me.
That is why I said you would die in your sins.

You will surely die in your sins
unless you come to believe that I AM."

"Who are you, then?" they asked him. Jesus answered:

"What I have been telling you from the beginning.
I could say much about you in condemnation,
but no, I only tell the world
what I have heard from him,
the truthful One, who sent me."

They did not grasp that he was speaking to them of the Father. Jesus continued:

"When you lift up the Son of Man,
you will come to realize that I AM
and that I do nothing by myself.
I say only what the Father has taught me.
The One who sent me is with me.
He has not deserted me
since I always do what pleases him."

Because he spoke this way, many came to believe in him.—This is the gospel of the Lord. ℞. **Praise to you, Lord Jesus Christ.**   ➤ No. 15, p. 623

PRAYER OVER THE GIFTS

Merciful Lord,
we offer this gift of reconciliation
so that you will forgive our sins
and guide our wayward hearts.
We ask this through Christ our Lord.
℞. **Amen.**   ➤ No. 21, p. 626 (Pref. P 17)

COMMUNION ANT.   Jn 12, 32

When I am lifted up from the earth, I will draw all men to myself, says the Lord. ℣

PRAYER AFTER COMMUNION

All-powerful God,
may the holy mysteries we share in this eucharist

make us worthy to attain the gift of heaven.
We ask this in the name of Jesus the Lord.
℟. **Amen.** ➤ No. 32, p. 650

_____

WEDNESDAY OF THE FIFTH WEEK OF LENT

We are slaves to sin, slaves to envy and hatred of our brothers, bound
to human weakness from which, without true repentance and faith in
the grace of God, we can never know spiritual freedom. We must
realize that we have been called to live in freedom, but not to give
free rein to freedom of the flesh. Love for our brother assures for us
this freedom.

ENTRANCE ANT.   Ps 18, 48-49

**Lord, you rescue me from raging enemies, you lift
me up above my attackers, you deliver me from
violent men.** ➤ No. 2, p. 614

OPENING PRAYER

Father of mercy,
hear the prayers of your repentant children
who call on you in love.
Enlighten our minds and sanctify our hearts.
We ask this through our Lord Jesus Christ, your Son,
who lives and reigns with you and the Holy Spirit,
one God, for ever and ever. ℟. **Amen.** ⅴ

READING I   Dn 3, 14-20. 91-92. 95

Nebuchadnezzar builds a golden statue and commands all men to
worship it. The three youths do not obey, and being denounced to the
king by certain Chaldeans, they are thrown into a furnace of extreme
heat. Nevertheless, they are not consumed, but walk unharmed in the
midst of the fire. With them is a fourth, whose aspect is like a "Son
of God."

A reading from the book of the prophet Daniel

King Nebuchadnezzar said: "Is it true, Shadrack,
Meshach, and Abednego, that you will not serve my
god, or worship the golden statue that I set up? Be
ready now to fall down and worship the statue I had
made, whenever you hear the sound of the trumpet,
flute, lyre, harp, psaltery, bagpipe, and all the other

musical instruments; otherwise, you shall be instantly cast into the white-hot furnace; and who is the God that can deliver you out of my hands?" Shadrach, Meshach, and Abednego answered King Nebuchadnezzar, "There is no need for us to defend ourselves before you in this matter. If our God, whom we serve, can save us from the white-hot furnace and from your hands, O king, may he save us! But even if he will not, know, O king, that we will not serve your god or worship the golden statue which you set up."

Nebuchadnezzar's face became livid with utter rage against Shadrach, Meshach, and Abednego. He ordered the furnace to be heated seven times more than usual and had some of the strongest men in his army bind Shadrach, Meshach, and Abednego and cast them into the white-hot furnace.

Nebuchadnezzar rose in haste and asked his nobles, "Did we not cast three men bound into the fire?" "Assuredly, O king," they answered. "But," he replied, "I see four men unfettered and unhurt, walking in the fire, and the fourth looks like a son of God." Nebuchadnezzar exclaimed, "Blessed be the God of Shadrach, Meshach, and Abednego, who sent his angel to deliver the servants that trusted in him; they disobeyed the royal command and yielded their bodies rather than serve or worship any god except their own God."—This is the Word of the Lord.
℟. **Thanks be to God.** ↯

Responsorial Psalm   Dn 3, 52. 53. 54. 55. 56

℟. (52) **Glory and praise for ever!**

Blessed are you, O Lord, the God of our fathers,
   praiseworthy and exalted above all forever;
And blessed is your holy and glorious name,
   praiseworthy and exalted above all for all ages.—℟

Blessed are you in the temple of your holy glory,
   praiseworthy and glorious above all forever. — ℟

Blessed are you on the throne of your kingdom,
   praiseworthy and exalted above all forever. — ℞

Blessed are you who look into the depths
   from your throne upon the cherubim,
   praiseworthy and exalted above all forever. — ℞

Blessed are you in the firmanent of heaven,
   praiseworthy and glorious forever. — ℞ ♥

GOSPEL   Jn 8, 31-42

Verse before the Gospel (See Lk 8, 15)

℞. **Praise and honor to you, Lord Jesus Christ!**
Happy are they who have kept the word with a
   generous heart,
and yield a harvest through perseverance.
℞. **Praise and honor to you, Lord Jesus Christ!**

The Jews who were listening to Jesus' words were definitely hoping
to become a world power through some indomitable leader. Christ
was dispelling such notions by insisting that his mission was to redeem men from themselves, that is, from sin—a slavery to self.

℣. The Lord be with you. ℞. **And also with you.**
✠ A reading from the holy gospel according to John
℞. **Glory to you, Lord.**

Jesus said to those Jews who believed in him:
   "If you live according to my teaching,
   you are truly my disciples;
   then you will know the truth,
   and the truth will set you free."
"We are descendants of Abraham," was their answer. "Never have we been slaves to anyone. What
do you mean by saying, 'You will be free'?" Jesus
answered them:
   "I give you my assurance,
   everyone who lives in sin
   is the slave of sin.
   (No slave has a permanent place in the family,
   but the son has a place there forever.)
   That is why, if the son frees you,

you will really be free.
I realize you are of Abraham's stock.
Nonetheless, you are trying to kill me
because my word finds no hearing among you.
I tell what I have seen in the Father's presence;
    you do what you have heard from your father."
They retorted, "Our father is Abraham." Jesus told
them:

"If you were Abraham's children,
you would be following Abraham's example.
The fact is, you are trying to kill me,
a man who has told you the truth
which I have heard from God.
Abraham did nothing like that.
Indeed you are doing your father's works!"
They cried, "We are no illegitimate breed! We have
but one father and that is God himself." Jesus answered:

"Were God your father
you would love me,
for I came forth from God, and am here.
I did not come of my own will;
    it was he who sent me."
This is the gospel of the Lord. ℟. **Praise to you, Lord
Jesus Christ.**
➤ No. 15, p. 623

PRAYER OVER THE GIFTS
Lord,
you have given us these gifts to honor your name.
Bless them,
and let them become a source of health and strength.
We ask this through Christ our Lord.
℟. **Amen.**
➤ No. 21, p. 626 (Pref. P 17)

COMMUNION ANT.
Col. 1, 13-15
**God has transferred us into the kingdom of the Son
he loves; in him we are redeemed, and find forgiveness of our sins.** ⋎

PRAYER AFTER COMMUNION

Lord,
may the mysteries we receive heal us,
remove sin from our hearts,
and make us grow strong
under your constant protection.
Grant this through Christ our Lord.
℟. **Amen.** _____ ➔ No. 32, p. 650

THURSDAY OF THE FIFTH WEEK OF LENT

Almighty God is eager to forgive us. With his gift of his only Son to be our salvation, he waits for us to come to him, and it will be the same until the Second Coming. We should waste no time in putting our house in order and be ready for that great summons!

ENTRANCE ANT. Heb 9, 15

Christ is the mediator of a new covenant so that, since he has died, those who are called may receive the eternal inheritance promised to them.

➔ No. 2, p. 614

OPENING PRAYER

Lord,
come to us:
free us from the stain of our sins.
Help us to remain faithful to a holy way of life,
and guide us to the inheritance you have promised.
Grant this through our Lord Jesus Christ, your Son,
who lives and reigns with you and the Holy Spirit,
one God, for ever and ever. ℟. **Amen.** ⅴ

READING I Gn 17, 3-9

Abram, "the father," becomes Abraham, indicating "father of a multitude." The new item here is the extension of the covenant to succeeding generations, and the promise of the land is here stated solemnly. Abraham and his descendants are to keep the covenant.

A reading from the book of Genesis

When Abram prostrated himself, God spoke to him:
"My covenant with you is this: you are to become

the father of a host of nations. No longer shall you be called Abram; your name shall be Abraham, for I am making you the father of a host of nations. I will render you exceedingly fertile; I will make nations of you; kings shall stem from you. I will maintain my covenant with you and your descendants after you throughout the ages as an everlasting pact, to be your God and the God of your descendants after you. I will give to you and to your descendants after you the land in which you are now staying, the whole land of Canaan, as a permanent possession; and I will be their God."

God also said to Abraham: "On your part, you and your descendants after you must keep my covenant throughout the ages."—This is the Word of the Lord. R̄. **Thanks be to God.** ♦

Responsorial Psalm　　　　　Ps 105, 4-5. 6-7. 8-9

R̄. (8) **The Lord remembers his covenant for ever.**

Look to the Lord in his strength;
　　seek to serve him constantly.
Recall the wondrous deeds that he has wrought,
　　his portents, and the judgments he has
　　　　uttered. — R̄

You descendants of Abraham, his servants,
　　sons of Jacob, his chosen ones!
He, the Lord, is our God;
　　throughout the earth his judgments prevail. — R̄

He remembers forever his covenant
　　which he made binding for a thousand generations—
Which he entered into with Abraham
　　and by his oath to Isaac. — R̄ ♦

GOSPEL　　　　　　　　　　　　Jn 8, 51-59

Verse before the Gospel (Ps 95, 8)

R̄. **Glory and praise to you, Lord Jesus Christ!**

If today you hear his voice,
harden not your hearts.

℟. **Glory and praise to you, Lord Jesus Christ!**

Still superficial in their judgment, the Jews protest the possibility
of Christ giving eternal life. Jesus answers that it is the testimony of
the Father that is involved—the testimony which they refuse to receive. Abraham himself knew that the promises made to him pointed
to a blessedness to come.

℣. The Lord be with you. ℟. **And also with you.**

✠ A reading from the holy gospel according to John

℟. **Glory to you, Lord.**

Jesus said to the Jews:
    "I solemnly assure you,
        if a man is true to my word
        he shall never see death."

"Now we are sure you are possessed," the Jews retorted. "Abraham is dead. The prophets are dead.
Yet you claim, 'A man shall never know death if he
keeps my word.' Surely you do not pretend to be
greater than our father Abraham, who died! Or the
prophets, who died! Whom do you make yourself
out to be?"

Jesus answered:
    "If I glorify myself,
        that glory comes to nothing.
    He who gives me glory is the Father,
        the very one you claim for your God,
        even though you do not know him.
    But I know him.
    Were I to say I do not know him,
        I would be no better than you—a liar!
    Yes, I know him well,
        and I keep his word.
    Your father Abraham rejoiced
        that he might see my day.
    He saw it and was glad."

At this the Jews objected: "You are not yet fifty!
How can you have seen Abraham?" Jesus answered
them:

"I solemnly declare it:
before Abraham came to be, I AM."
At that they picked up rocks to throw at Jesus, but
he hid himself and slipped out of the temple precincts.—This is the gospel of the Lord. ℟. **Praise to
you, Lord Jesus Christ.** ➔ No. 15, p. 623

PRAYER OVER THE GIFTS
Merciful Lord,
accept the sacrifice we offer you
that it may help us grow in holiness
and advance the salvation of the world.
We ask this in the name of Jesus the Lord.
℟. **Amen.** ➔ No. 21, p. 626 (Pref. P 17)

COMMUNION ANT. Rom 8, 32
**God did not spare his own Son, but gave him up for
us all: with Christ he will surely give us all things. ⱽ**

PRAYER AFTER COMMUNION
Lord of mercy,
let the sacrament which renews us
bring us to eternal life.
We ask this through Christ our Lord.
℟. **Amen.** ➔ No. 32, p. 650

FRIDAY OF THE FIFTH WEEK OF LENT

Faith alone is not sufficient for salvation. "Be assured, then, that
faith without works is as dead as a body without breath," says St.
James (2, 26); and, again, "Do you believe that God is one? You are
quite right. The demons believe that, and shudder" (2, 19). We
should believe as if our salvation depended on God alone and work as
if it depended only on us. God will listen to those who come to him.

ENTRANCE ANT. Ps 31, 10. 16. 18
**Have mercy on me, Lord, for I am in distress; rescue
me from the hands of my enemies. Lord, keep me
from shame, for I have called to you.** ➔ No. 2, p. 614

OPENING PRAYER

Lord,
grant us your forgiveness,
and set us free from our enslavement to sin.
We ask this through our Lord Jesus Christ, your Son,
who lives and reigns with you and the Holy Spirit,
one God, for ever and ever. ℟. **Amen.** ✝

READING I　　　　　　　　　　　　　Jer 20, 10-13

Jeremiah knows that God is with him. This confidence has its foundation in Yahweh's promise which the prophet often recalls. In the
midst of strong contradictions, he keeps his faith in God's loyalty.

A reading from the book of the prophet Jeremiah

I hear the whispering of many:
　　"Terror on every side!
　　Denounce! let us denounce him!"
All those who were my friends
　　are on the watch for any misstep of mine.
"Perhaps he will be trapped; then we can prevail,
　　and take our vengeance on him."
But the Lord is with me, like a mighty champion;
　　my persecutors will stumble, they will not
　　　　triumph.
In their failure they will be put to utter shame,
　　to lasting, unforgettable confusion.
O Lord of hosts, you who test the just,
　　who probe mind and heart,
Let me witness the vengeance you take on them,
　　for to you I have entrusted my cause.
Sing to the Lord,
　　praise the Lord,
For he has rescued the life of the poor
　　from the power of the wicked!
This is the Word of the Lord. ℟. **Thanks be to God.** ✝

Responsorial Psalm　　　　　　Ps 18, 2-3. 3-4. 5-6. 7

℟. (7) **In my distress I called upon the Lord,
　　and he heard my voice.**

I love you, O Lord, my strength,
  O Lord, my rock, my fortress, my deliverer. — ℟

My God, my rock of refuge,
  my shield, the horn of my salvation, my strong-
    hold!

Praised be the Lord, I exclaim,
  and I am safe from my enemies. — ℟

The breakers of death surged round about me,
  the destroying floods overwhelmed me;

The cords of the nether world enmeshed me,
  the snares of death overtook me. — ℟

In my distress I called upon the Lord,
  and cried out to my God;

From his temple he heard my voice,
  and my cry to him reached his ears. — ℟ ⍖

GOSPEL   Jn 10, 31-42

Verse before the Gospel (Jn 6, 64-69)

℟. **Glory to you, Word of God, Lord Jesus Christ!**
Your words, Lord, are spirit and life;
you have the message of eternal life.
℟. **Glory to you, Word of God, Lord Jesus Christ!**

The sinful men who wanted to stone our Lord when they had accused
him of blasphemy heard what Jesus spoke when he said he was of
one substance with the Father. He is known for who he is because he
does the work of the Father. The people recall what John taught about
Jesus.

℣. The Lord be with you. ℟. **And also with you.**
✠ A reading from the holy gospel according to John
℟. **Glory to you, Lord.**

When the Jews reached for rocks to stone him, Jesus
protested to them, "Many good deeds have I shown
you from the Father. For which of these do you stone
me?" "It is not for any 'good deed' that we are ston-
ing you," the Jews retorted, "but for blaspheming.
You who are only a man are making yourself God."
Jesus answered:

"Is it not written in your law,
 'I have said, You are gods'?
 If it calls those men gods
 to whom God's word was addressed—
 and Scripture cannot lose its force—
 do you claim that I blasphemed
 when, as he whom the Father consecrated
 and sent into the world,
 I said, 'I am God's Son'?
 If I do not perform my Father's works,
 put no faith in me.
 But if I do perform them,
 even though you put no faith in me,
 put faith in these works,
 so as to realize what it means
 that the Father is in me
 and I in him."

At these words they again tried to arrest him, but he eluded their grasp.

Then he went back across the Jordan to the place where John had been baptizing earlier, and while he stayed there many people came to him. "John may never have performed a sign," they commented, "but whatever John said about this man was true." In that place, many came to believe in him.—This is the gospel of the Lord. ℞. **Praise to you, Lord Jesus Christ.**   ➤ No. 15, p. 623

PRAYER OVER THE GIFTS

God of mercy,
may the gifts we present at your altar
help us to achieve eternal salvation.
Grant this through Christ our Lord.
℞. **Amen.**   ➤ No. 21, p. 626 (Pref. P 17)

COMMUNION ANT.   1 Pt 2, 24

Jesus carried our sins in his own body on the cross so that we could die to sin and live in holiness; by his wounds we have been healed. ⱽ

PRAYER AFTER COMMUNION

Lord,

may we always receive the protection of this
    sacrifice.

May it keep us safe from all harm.

We ask this in the name of Jesus the Lord.

℟. **Amen.** ———————— ➤ No. 32, p. 650

SATURDAY OF THE FIFTH WEEK OF LENT

Jesus offered his life for all of us. This is the example of ultimate
love. By thinking of this we can gradually transform and motivate
ourselves to become more understanding of one another. We too, like
Christ, can give of ourselves in prayer, thought, word, and action.

ENTRANCE ANT. Ps 22, 20. 7

**Lord, do not stay away; come quickly to help me!
I am a worm and no man: men scorn me, people
despise me.** ➤ No. 2, p. 614

OPENING PRAYER

God our Father,

you always work to save us,

and now we rejoice in the great love

you give to your chosen people.

Protect all who are about to become your children,

and continue to bless those who are already baptized.

Grant this through our Lord Jesus Christ, your Son,

who lives and reigns with you and the Holy Spirit,

one God, for ever and ever. ℟. **Amen.** ⱱ

READING I Ez 37, 21-28

The union of all tribes is a frequent element in messianic prophecy.
God is to unite the nation in a new covenant in which there are five
essential elements: Yahweh, its God; Israel, his people; life, "on the
land where their fathers lived"; "my sanctuary among them," as a
sign of the presence of the Lord and law; David, as the one shepherd
over them.

A reading from the book of the prophet Ezekiel

Thus speaks the Lord God: I will take the Israelites
from among the nations to which they have come,

and gather them from all sides to bring them back to their land. I will make them one nation upon the land, in the mountains of Israel, and there shall be one prince for them all. Never again shall they be two nations, and never again shall they be divided into two kingdoms.

No longer shall they defile themselves with their idols, their abominations, and all their transgressions. I will deliver them from all their sins of apostasy, and cleanse them so that they may be my people and I may be their God. My servant David shall be prince over them, and there shall be one shepherd for them all; they shall live by my statutes and carefully observe my decrees. They shall live on the land which I gave to my servant Jacob, the land where their fathers lived; they shall live on it forever, they, and their children, and their children's children, with my servant David their prince forever. I will make with them a covenant of peace; it shall be an everlasting covenant with them, and I will multiply them, and put my sanctuary among them forever. My dwelling shall be with them; I will be their God, and they shall be my people. Thus the nations shall know that it is I, the Lord, who make Israel holy, when my sanctuary shall be set up among them forever.—This is the Word of the Lord. ℟. **Thanks be to God.** ℣

Responsorial Psalm   Jer 31, 10. 11-12. 13

℟. (10) **The Lord will guard us,**
   like a shepherd guarding his flock.

Hear the word of the Lord, O nations,
   proclaim it on distant coasts, and say:
He who scattered Israel, now gathers them together,
   he guards them as a shepherd his flock. — ℟

The Lord shall ransom Jacob,
   he shall redeem him from the hand of his conqueror.
Shouting, they shall mount the heights of Zion,
   they shall come streaming to the Lord's blessings:

The grain, the wine, and the oil,
> the sheep and the oxen. — ℟

Then the virgins shall make merry and dance,
> and young men and old as well.

I will turn their mourning into joy,
> I will console and gladden them after their sorrows. — ℟ ℣

GOSPEL   Jn 11, 45-57

Verse before the Gospel (Ez 18, 31)

℟. **Praise to you, Lord Jesus Christ, king of endless
>   glory!**

Rid yourselves of all your sins;
and make a new heart and a new spirit.

℟. **Praise to you, Lord Jesus Christ, king of endless
>   glory!**

With each day the hatred of the Jews increases, and the more astounding the deeds Jesus performs, the more determined they are to put him to death. Caiaphas prophesies: "It is better for you to have one man die for the people than to have the whole nation destroyed."

℣. The Lord be with you. ℟. **And also with you.**

✠ A reading from the holy gospel according to John
℟. **Glory to you, Lord.**

Many of the Jews who had come to visit Mary, and had seen what Jesus did, put their faith in him. Some others, however, went to the Pharisees and reported what Jesus had done. The result was that the chief priests and the Pharisees called a meeting of the Sanhedrin. "What are we to do," they said, "with this man performing all sorts of signs? If we let him go on like this, the whole world will believe in him. Then the Romans will come in and sweep away our sanctuary and our nation." One of their number named Caiaphas, who was high priest that year, addressed them at this point: "You have no understanding whatever! Can you not see that it is better for you to have one man die [for the people] than to have the whole nation destroyed?" (He did not say this on his own. It was rather as high priest for that year that he prophesied that Jesus would die for the nation—and not for this nation only, but to gather into one all the dispersed children of God.)

From that day onward there was a plan afoot to kill him. In consequence, Jesus no longer moved about freely in Jewish circles. He withdrew instead to a town called Ephraim in the region near the desert, where he stayed with his disciples

The Jewish Passover was near, which meant that people from the country went up to Jerusalem for Passover purification. They were on the lookout for Jesus, various people in the temple vicinity saying to each other, "What do you think? Is he likely to come for the feast?" (The chief priests and the Pharisees had given orders that anyone who knew where he was should report it, so that they could apprehend him.)—This is the gospel of the Lord. ℞. **Praise to you, Lord Jesus Christ.**   ➤ No. 15, p. 623

PRAYER OVER THE GIFTS

Ever-living God,
in baptism, the sacrament of our faith,
you restore us to life.
Accept the prayers and gifts of your people:
forgive our sins and fulfill our hopes and desires.
We ask this in the name of Jesus the Lord.
℞. **Amen.**   ➤ No. 21, p. 626 (Pref. P 17)

COMMUNION ANT.   Jn 11, 52

Christ was sacrificed so that he could gather together the scattered children of God. ℣

PRAYER AFTER COMMUNION

Father of mercy and power,
we thank you for nourishing us
with the body and blood of Christ

and for calling us to share in his divine life,
for he is Lord for ever and ever.
℟. **Amen.** ➤ No. 32, p. 650

MONDAY OF HOLY WEEK

We are in the final week of the New Creation. Jesus makes it clear that all of us have varied tasks and responsibilities in the kingdom of God. In working out our salvation we must be careful to attend to them and uproot our failings and sins that turn us away from God.

ENTRANCE ANT.   Ps 35, 1-2; 140, 8

Defend me, Lord, from all my foes: take up your arms and come swiftly to my aid for you have the power to save me. ➤ No. 2, p. 614

OPENING PRAYER

All-powerful God,
by the suffering and death of your Son,
strengthen and protect us in our weakness.
We ask this through our Lord Jesus Christ, your Son,
who lives and reigns with you and the Holy Spirit,
one God, for ever and ever. ℟. **Amen.** ✔

READING I   Is 42, 1-7

The Suffering Servant represents the finest qualities of Israel and her great leaders. In this song he is a "chosen one" like Moses, David, and all Israel. As the Servant, he fulfills the role of Davidic king and prophet.

A reading from the book of the prophet Isaiah
Here is my servant whom I uphold,
    my chosen one with whom I am pleased,
Upon whom I have put my spirit;
    he shall bring forth justice to the nations,
Not crying out, not shouting,
    not making his voice heard in the street.
A bruised reed he shall not break,
    and a smoldering wick he shall not quench,
Until he establishes justice on the earth;
    the coastlands will wait for his teaching.

Thus says God, the Lord,
   who created the heavens and stretched them out,
   who spreads out the earth with its crops,
Who gives breath to its people
   and spirit to those who walk on it:
I, the Lord, have called you for the victory of justice,
   I have grasped you by the hand;
I formed you, and set you
   as a covenant of the people,
   a light for the nations,
To open the eyes of the blind,
   to bring out prisoners from confinement,
   and from the dungeon, those who live in darkness.
This is the Word of the Lord. ℟. **Thanks be to God.** ✟

Responsorial Psalm   Ps 27, 1. 2. 3. 13-14

℟. (1) **The Lord is my light and my salvation.**

The Lord is my light and my salvation;
   whom should I fear?
The Lord is my life's refuge;
   of whom should I be afraid? — ℟

When evildoers come at me
   to devour my flesh,
My foes and my enemies
   themselves stumble and fall. — ℟

Though an army encamp against me,
   my heart will not fear;
Though war be waged upon me,
   even then will I trust. — ℟

I believe that I shall see the bounty of the Lord
   in the land of the living.
Wait for the Lord with courage;
   be stouthearted, and wait for the Lord. — ℟ ✟

GOSPEL   Jn 12, 1-11
Verse before the Gospel
℟. **Praise and honor to you, Lord Jesus Christ!**

Let us greet our king;
he alone showed mercy for our sins.
℟. **Praise and honor to you, Lord Jesus Christ!**

John describes the supper at Bethany on the sabbath before the Passover. Martha waits upon Jesus as he reclines at the table. Mary anoints the feet of Jesus with ointment and wipes his feet with her hair. Judas objects to the use of the expensive ointment, making religion a cloak for his covetousness.

℣. The Lord be with you. ℟. **And also with you.**
✠ A reading from the holy gospel according to John
℟. **Glory to you, Lord.**

Six days before Passover Jesus came to Bethany, the village of Lazarus whom Jesus had raised from the dead. There they gave him a banquet, at which Martha served. Lazarus was one of those at table with him. Mary brought a pound of costly perfume made from genuine aromatic nard, with which she anointed Jesus' feet. Then she dried his feet with her hair, and the house was filled with the ointment's fragrance. Judas Iscariot, one of his disciples (the one about to hand him over), protested: "Why was this perfume not sold? It could have brought three hundred silver pieces, and the money have been given to the poor." (He did not say this out of concern for the poor, but because he was a thief. He held the purse, and used to help himself to what was deposited there.) To this Jesus replied, "Leave her alone. Let her keep it against the day they prepare me for burial. The poor you always have with you, but me you will not always have."

The great crowd of Jews discovered he was there and came out, not only because of Jesus but also to see Lazarus, whom he had raised from the dead. The fact was, the chief priests planned to kill Lazarus too, because many Jews were going over to Jesus and believing in him on account of Lazarus.—This is the gospel of the Lord. ℟. **Praise to you, Lord Jesus Christ.** ➤ No. 15, p. 623

PRAYER OVER THE GIFTS

Lord,
look with mercy on our offerings.
May the sacrifice of Christ, your Son,
bring us to eternal life,
for he is Lord for ever and ever.
℟. **Amen.**   ➤ No. 21, p. 626 (Pref. P 18)

COMMUNION ANT.   Ps 102, 3

**When I am in trouble, Lord, do not hide your face
from me; hear me when I call, and answer me
quickly. ℣**

PRAYER AFTER COMMUNION

God of mercy,
be close to your people.
Watch over us who receive this sacrament of salvation,
and keep us in your love.
We ask this in the name of Jesus the Lord.
℟. **Amen.**   ➤ No. 32, p. 650

TUESDAY OF HOLY WEEK

In times of trial and discouragement, we might conceivably lose sight
of the fact that God has in store for us things never dreamed of in
the mind of men. In spite of our weakness and errors, he has extended
his mission to the "ends of the earth." We should seek our reward
with God because we trust him to reveal the fruit of our efforts.

ENTRANCE ANT.   Ps 27, 12

**False witnesses have stood up against me, and my
enemies threaten violence; Lord, do not surrender
me into their power!**   ➤No. 2, p. 614

OPENING PRAYER

Father,
may we receive your forgiveness and mercy
as we celebrate the passion and death of the Lord,

who lives and reigns with you and the Holy Spirit,
one God, for ever and ever. ℟. **Amen.** ✔

READING I   Is 49, 1-6

The second Servant Song presents the Servant as another Jeremiah:
He is called from his mother's womb (Jer 1, 5); he has a vocation to
the Gentiles (Jer 1, 10); he brings a message of both doom and happiness (Jer 16, 19-21).

A reading from the book of the prophet Isaiah

Hear me, O coastlands,
   listen, O distant peoples.
The Lord called me from birth,
   from my mother's womb he gave me my name.
He made of me a sharp-edged sword
   and concealed me in the shadow of his arm.
He made me a polished arrow,
   in his quiver he hid me.
You are my servant, he said to me,
   Israel, through whom I show my glory.
Though I thought I had toiled in vain,
   and for nothing, uselessly, spent my strength,
Yet my reward is with the Lord,
   my recompense is with my God.
For now the Lord has spoken
   who formed me as his servant from the womb,
That Jacob may be brought back to him
   and Israel gathered to him;
And I am made glorious in the sight of the Lord,
   and my God is now my strength!
It is too little, he says, for you to be my servant,
   to raise up the tribes of Jacob,
      and restore the survivors of Israel;
I will make you a light to the nations,
   that my salvation may reach to the ends of the
      earth.
This is the Word of the Lord. ℟. **Thanks be to God.** ✔

Responsorial Psalm   Ps 71, 1-2. 3-4. 5-6. 17
℟. (15) **I will sing of your salvation.**

In you, O Lord, I take refuge;
  let me never be put to shame.
    In your justice rescue me, and deliver me;
    incline your ear to me, and save me. — ℟

Be my rock of refuge,
  a stronghold to give me safety,
  for you are my rock and my fortress.

O my God, rescue me from the hand of the
    wicked. — ℟

For you are my hope, O Lord;
  my trust, O God, from my youth.

On you I depend from birth;
  from my mother's womb you are my strength.— ℟

My mouth shall declare your justice,
  day by day your salvation,
  though I know not their extent.

O God, you have taught me from my youth,
  and till the present I proclaim your wondrous
    deeds. — ℟ ↓

GOSPEL   Jn 13, 21-33. 36-38

Verse before the Gospel

℟. **Glory and praise to you, Lord Jesus Christ!**
Hail to our king, obedient to his Father,
he went to his crucifixion like a gentle lamb.
℟. **Glory and praise to you, Lord Jesus Christ!**

Our Lord's statement that one of the Twelve will betray him strikes
fear in the hearts of each of them. Peter understands nothing of the
mystery of the cross and suspects that Christ doubts his courage or
his zeal. Jesus tells Peter that Peter will deny even knowing him
"three times before the cock crows."

℣. The Lord be with you. ℟. **And also with you.**

✠ A reading from the holy gospel according to John
℟. **Glory to you, Lord.**

Jesus, reclining with his disciples, grew deeply troubled. He went on to give this testimony:
    "I tell you solemnly,
    one of you will betray me."

The disciples looked at one another, puzzled as to whom he could mean. One of them, the disciple whom Jesus loved, reclined close to him as they ate. Simon Peter signaled him to ask Jesus whom he meant. He leaned back against Jesus' chest and said to him, "Lord, who is he?" Jesus answered, "The one to whom I give the bit of food I dip in the dish." He dipped the morsel, then took it and gave it to Judas, son of Simon Iscariot. Immediately after, Satan entered his heart. Jesus addressed himself to him, "Be quick about what you are to do." (Naturally, none of those reclining at table understood why Jesus said this to him. A few had the idea that, since Judas held the common purse, Jesus was telling him to buy what was needed for the feast, or to give something to the poor.) No sooner had Judas eaten the morsel than he went out. It was night.

Once Judas had left, Jesus said:

"Now is the Son of Man glorified
and God is glorified in him.
[If God has been glorified in him,]
God will, in turn, glorify him in himself,
and will glorify him soon.
My children, I am not to be with you much
    longer.
You will look for me,
but I say to you now
what I once said to the Jews:
'Where I am going, you cannot come.'"

"Lord," Simon Peter said to him, "where do you mean to go?" Jesus answered:

"I am going where you cannot follow me now;
    later on you shall come after me."

"Lord," Peter said to him, "why can I not follow you now? I will lay down my life for you!" "You will lay down your life for me, will you?" Jesus answered. "I tell you truly, the cock will not crow be-

fore you have three times disowned me!"—This is
the gospel of the Lord. ℞. **Praise to you, Lord Jesus
Christ.**   ➤ No. 15, p. 623

PRAYER OVER THE GIFTS

Lord,
look with mercy on our offerings.
May we who share the holy gifts
receive the life they promise.
We ask this in the name of Jesus the Lord.
℞. **Amen.**   ➤ No. 21, p. 626 (Pref. P 18)

COMMUNION ANT.   Rom 8, 32

**God did not spare his own Son, but gave him up for
us all.** ⋎

PRAYER AFTER COMMUNION

God of mercy,
may the sacrament of salvation
which now renews our strength
bring us a share in your life for ever.
Grant this through Christ our Lord. ➤ No. 32, p. 650

WEDNESDAY OF HOLY WEEK

It should always be remembered that those who suffer persecution
in the defense of the truth, the faith, and Christian virtues and who
cling firmly to God and permit nothing to turn them from their duties
as Christians will, like the saints, receive the heavenly crown. God
will be our Redeemer and our helper. All who live in Christ, our Lord,
shall suffer persecution (2 Tm 3, 12).

ENTRANCE ANT.   Phil 2, 10. 8. 11

**At the name of Jesus every knee must bend, in heav-
en, on earth, and under the earth: Christ became obedient for us even to death, dying on the cross. Therefore, to the glory of God the Father, Jesus is Lord.**
                                        ➤ No. 2, p. 614

OPENING PRAYER

Father,
in your plan of salvation
your Son Jesus Christ accepted the cross
and freed us from the power of the enemy.
May we come to share the glory of his resurrection,
for he lives and reigns with you and the Holy Spirit,
one God, for ever and ever. ℟. **Amen.** ✟

READING I   Is 50, 4-9

Isaiah speaks with a spirit of resignation. The Suffering Servant
opens with the statement that God's Word is the source of salvation.
The servant must first be a disciple, prayerfully receiving God's words,
before he can presume to teach others.

A reading from the book of the prophet Isaiah

The Lord God has given me
   a well-trained tongue,
That I might know how to speak to the weary
   a word that will rouse them.
Morning after morning
   he opens my ear that I may hear;
And I have not rebelled,
   have not turned back.
I gave my back to those who beat me,
   my cheeks to those who plucked my beard;
My face I did not shield
   from buffets and spitting.
The Lord God is my help,
   therefore I am not disgraced;
I have set my face like flint,
   knowing that I shall not be put to shame.
He is near who upholds my right;
   if anyone wishes to oppose me,
   let us appear together.
Who disputes my right?
   Let him confront me.
See, the Lord God is my help.
This is the Word of the Lord. ℟. **Thanks be to God.** ✟

Responsorial Psalm   Ps 69, 8-10. 21-22. 31. 33-34

℟. (14) **Lord, in your great love, answer me.**

For your sake I bear insult,
  and shame covers my face.
I have become an outcast to my brothers,
  a stranger to my mother's sons.
Because zeal for your house consumes me,
  and the insults of those who blaspheme you fall
    upon me. — ℟

Insult has broken my heart, and I am weak,
  I looked for sympathy, but there was none;
  for comforters, and I found none.
Rather they put gall in my food,
  and in my thirst they gave me vinegar to drink.—℟

I will praise the name of God in song,
  and I will glorify him with thanksgiving:
"See, you lowly ones, and be glad;
  you who seek God, may your hearts be merry!
For the Lord hears the poor,
  and his own who are in bonds he spurns
    not." — ℟ ✟

GOSPEL

Verse before the Gospel   Mt 26, 14-25
As above, pp. 566, 570.

"One of the Twelve" is to betray Jesus. The enormity of the deed
is underlined by the fact that it was done for money, for thirty pieces
of silver. Jesus predicts that Judas is the betrayer.

℣. The Lord be with you. ℟. **And also with you.**
✠ A reading from the holy gospel according to Matthew. ℟. **Glory to you, Lord.**

One of the Twelve whose name was Judas Iscariot
went off to the chief priests and said, "What are you
willing to give me if I hand him over to you?" They
paid him thirty pieces of silver, and from that time
on he kept looking for an opportunity to hand him
over.

On the first day of the feast of Unleavened Bread, the disciples came up to Jesus and said, "Where do you wish us to prepare the Passover supper for you?" He said, "Go to this man in the city and tell him, 'The Teacher says, My appointed time draws near. I am to celebrate the Passover with my disciples in your house.' "

The disciples then did as Jesus had ordered, and prepared the Passover supper.

When it grew dark he reclined at table with the Twelve. In the course of the meal he said, "I give you my word, one of you is about to betray me." Distressed at this, they began to say to him one after another, "Surely it is not I, Lord?" He replied: "The man who has dipped his hand into the dish with me is the one who will hand me over. The Son of Man is departing, as Scripture says of him, but woe to that man by whom the Son of Man is betrayed. Better for him if he had never been born."

Then Judas, his betrayer, spoke: "Surely it is not I, Rabbi?" Jesus answered, "It is you who have said it."—This is the gospel of the Lord. ℟. **Praise to you, Lord Jesus Christ.**   ➤ No. 15, p. 623

PRAYER OVER THE GIFTS

Lord,
accept the gifts we present
as we celebrate this mystery
of the suffering and death of your Son.
May we share in the eternal life he won for us,
for he is Lord for ever and ever.
℟. **Amen.**   ➤ No. 21, p. 626 (Pref. P 18)

COMMUNION ANT.   Mt 20, 28

The Son of Man did not come to be served, but to serve, and to give his life as a ransom for many. ❧

PRAYER AFTER COMMUNION

All-powerful God,
the eucharist proclaims the death of your Son.
Increase our faith in its saving power
and strengthen our hope in the life it promises.
We ask this in the name of Jesus the Lord.
℟. **Amen.**   ➔ No. 32, p. 650

HOLY THURSDAY

CHRISM MASS

This Mass, which the bishop concelebrates with his presbyterium and at which the oils are blessed, shows the communion of the priests with their bishops. It is thus desirable that, if possible, all the priests take part in it, together with parish representatives, and receive communion under both kinds. To show the unity of the presbyterium, the priests who concelebrate with the bishop should come from different parts of the diocese. This day also is dedicated to the renewal of priestly ministry.

ENTRANCE ANT.   Rv 1, 6

Jesus Christ has made us a kingdom of priests to serve his God and Father: glory and kingship be his for ever and ever. Amen.   ➔ No. 2, p. 614

The Gloria *is sung or said.*

OPENING PRAYER

Father,
by the power of the Holy Spirit
you anointed your only Son Messiah and Lord of
      creation;
you have given us a share in his consecration
to priestly service in your Church.
Help us to be faithful witnesses in the world
to the salvation Christ won for all mankind.
We ask this through our Lord Jesus Christ, your Son,
who lives and reigns with you and the Holy Spirit,
one God, for ever and ever. ℟. **Amen.** ↓

READING I   Is 61, 1-3. 6. 8-9

Isaiah the prophet, anointed by God to bring the Good News to the poor, proclaims a message filled with hope. It is one that replaces mourning with gladness. Their descendants wlil be renowned among all nations. God has blessed them.

A reading from the book of the prophet Isaiah

The spirit of the Lord God is upon me,
    because the Lord has anointed me;
He has sent me to bring glad tidings to the lowly,
    to heal the brokenhearted,
To proclaim liberty to the captives
    and release to the prisoners,
To announce a year of favor from the Lord
    and a day of vindication by our God,
        to comfort all who mourn;
To place on those who mourn in Zion
    a diadem instead of ashes,
To give them oil of gladness in place of mourning,
    a glorious mantle instead of a listless spirit.
You yourselves shall be named priests of the Lord,
    ministers of our God you shall be called.
I will give them their recompense faithfully,
    a lasting covenant I will make with them.
Their descendants shall be renowned among the
        nations,
    and their offspring among the peoples;
All who see them shall acknowledge them as a race
        the Lord has blessed.
This is the Word of the Lord. ℟. **Thanks be to God.** ☩

Responsorial Psalm   Ps 89, 21-22. 25. 27
℟. (2) **For ever I will sing the goodness of the Lord.**
I have found David, my servant;
    with my holy oil I have anointed him,
That my hand may be always with him,
    and that my arm may make him strong. — ℟
My faithfulness and my kindness shall be with him,
    and through my name shall his horn be exalted.

"He shall say of me, 'You are my father,
    my God, the rock, my savior.' " — ℟ ⩛

READING II
Rv 1, 5-8

God says, "I am the beginning and the end, the One who is and who
was and who is to come, the Almighty!" All shall see God as he comes
amid the clouds.

A reading from the book of Revelation

[Grace and peace to you] from Jesus Christ the faithful witness, the first-born from the dead and ruler
of the kings of earth. To him who loves us and freed
us from our sins by his own blood, who has made
us a royal nation of priests in the service of his God
and Father—to him be glory and power forever and
ever! Amen.
See, he comes amid the clouds!
    Every eye shall see him,
    even of those who pierced him.
All the peoples of the earth
    shall lament him bitterly.
    So it is to be! Amen!
    The Lord God says, "I am the Alpha and the
Omega, the One who is and who was and who is to
come, the Almighty!"—This is the Word of the Lord.
℟. Thanks be to God. ⩛

GOSPEL
Lk 4, 16-21

Verse before the Gospel (Is 61, 1: cited in Lk 4, 18)
℟. **Glory to you, Word of God, Lord Jesus Christ!**
The spirit of the Lord is upon me;
he sent me to bring Good News to the poor.
℟. **Glory to you, Word of God, Lord Jesus Christ!**

Jesus reads in the synagogue at Nazareth the words of Isaiah quoted
in the first reading. Jesus is the Anointed One. He tells the people
that today Isaiah's prophecy is fulfilled in their hearing.

℣. The Lord be with you. ℟. **And also with you.**
✠ A reading from the holy gospel according to Luke
℟. **Glory to you, Lord.**

Jesus came to Nazareth where he had been reared, and entering the synagogue on the sabbath as he was in the habit of doing, he stood up to do the reading. When the book of the prophet Isaiah was handed him, he unrolled the scroll and found the passage where it was written:

"The spirit of the Lord is upon me;
    therefore he has anointed me.
He has sent me to bring glad tidings to the
    poor,
    to proclaim liberty to captives,
Recovery of sight to the blind
    and release to prisoners,
To announce a year of favor from the Lord."

Rolling up the scroll, he gave it back to the assistant and sat down. All in the synagogue had their eyes fixed on him. Then he began by saying to them, "Today this Scripture passage is fulfilled in your hearing."—This is the gospel of the Lord. ℟. **Praise to you, Lord Jesus Christ.**

In his Homily the bishop should urge the priests to be faithful in fulfilling their office in the Church and should invite them to renew publicly their priestly promises.

Renewal of Commitment to Priestly Service

After the Homily the bishop speaks to the priests in these or similar words:

My brothers,
today we celebrate the memory of the first eucharist,
at which our Lord Jesus Christ
shared with his apostles and with us
his call to the priestly service of his Church.
Now, in the presence of your bishop and God's only
    people,
are you ready to renew your own dedication to Christ
as priests of his new covenant?

Priests: I am.

Bishop: At your ordination
you accepted the responsibilities of the priesthood
out of love for the Lord Jesus and his Church.
Are you resolved to unite yourselves more closely
    to Christ
and to try to become more like him
by joyfully sacrificing your own pleasure and ambi-
    tion
to bring his peace and love to your brothers and
    sisters?

Priests: I am

Bishop: Are you resolved
to be faithful ministers of of the mysteries of God,
to celebrate the eucharist and the other liturgical
    services
with sincere devotion?
Are you resolved to imitate Jesus Christ,
the head and shepherd of the Church,
by teaching the Christian faith
without thinking of your own profit,
solely for the well-being of the people
you were sent to serve?

Priests: I am.

Then the bishop addresses the people:

My brothers and sisters,
pray for your priests.
Ask the Lord to bless them with the fullness of his
    love,
to help them be faithful ministers of Christ the High
    Priest,
so that they will be able to lead you to him,
the fountain of your salvation.

**People: Lord Jesus Christ, hear us and answer our
    prayer.**

Bishop: Pray also for me
that despite my own unworthiness
I may faithfully fulfill the office of apostle
which Jesus Christ has entrusted to me.
Pray that I may become more like
our High Priest and Good Shepherd,
the teacher and servant of all,
and so be a genuine sign
of Christ's loving presence among you.

People: Lord Jesus Christ, hear us and answer our prayer.

Bishop: May the Lord in his love
keep you close to him always,
and may he bring all of us,
his priests and people,
to eternal life.
All: Amen.

The Profession of Faith and General Intercessions are omitted.   ➔ No. 17, p. 624

PRAYER OVER THE GIFTS
Lord God,
may the power of this sacrifice
cleanse the old weakness of our human nature.
Give us a newness of life
and bring us to salvation.
Grant this through Christ our Lord. ℟. **Amen.** ♥

PREFACE (P 20)

℣. The Lord be with you. ℟. **And also with you.**
℣. Lift up your hearts. ℟. **We lift them up to the Lord.** ℣. Let us give thanks to the Lord our God.
℟. **It is right to give him thanks and praise.** ♥

Father, all-powerful and ever-living God,
we do well always and everywhere to give you thanks.
By your Holy Spirit

you anointed your only Son
High Priest of the new and eternal covenant.
With wisdom and love you have planned
that this one priesthood should continue in the
    Church.
Christ gives the dignity of a royal priesthood
to the people he has made his own.
From these, with a brother's love,
he chooses men to share his sacred ministry
by the laying on of hands.
He appoints them to renew in his name
the sacrifice of our redemption
as they set before your family his paschal meal.
He calls them to lead your holy people in love,
nourish them by your word,
and strengthen them through the sacraments.
Father, they are to give their lives in your service
and for the salvation of your people
as they strive to grow in the likeness of Christ
and honor you by their courageous witness of faith
    and love.
We praise you Lord, with all the angels and saints
in their song of joy: → No. 23, p. 627

COMMUNION ANT.   Ps 89, 2
**For ever I will sing the goodness of the Lord: I will
proclaim your faithfulness to all generations.** ℣

PRAYER AFTER COMMUNION
Lord God almighty,
you have given us fresh strength
in these sacramental gifts.
Renew in us the image of Christ's goodness.
We ask this in the name of Jesus the Lord.
℟. **Amen.**   → No. 32, p. 650

Optional Solemn Blessings, p. 682, and Prayers over the People, p. 689

EASTER TRIDUUM

The Evening Mass of the Lord's Supper commemorates the institution of the Holy Eucharist and the sacrament of Holy Orders. It was at this Mass that Jesus changed bread and wine into his Body and Blood. He then directed his disciples to carry out this same ritual: "As often as you do this, do it in my memory."

EVENING MASS OF THE LORD'S SUPPER

According to the Church's ancient tradition, all Masses without a congregation are prohibited on this day.

The Mass of the Lord's Supper is celebrated in the evening, at a convenient hour, with the full participation of the whole local community and with all the priests and clergy exercising their ministry.

Priest who have already celebrated the chrism Mass or a Mass for the convenience of the faithful may concelebrate again at the evening Mass.

For pastoral reasons the local Ordinary may permit another Mass to be celebrated in churches and public or semipublic oratories in the evening or, in the case of genuine necessity, even in the morning, but exclusively for those who are in no way able to take part in the evening Mass. Such Masses must not be celebrated for the advantage of private persons or prejudice the principal evening Mass.

Holy communion may be given to the faithful only during Mass, but may be brought to the sick at any hour of the day.

In the United States, communion may be given under both kinds, in accordance with the judgment of the Ordinary, at Masses on Holy Thursday.

If the local Ordinary permits one or more additional Masses of the Lord's Supper, in accord with the rubrics, the washing of feet may take place at such Masses.

Introductory Rites and Liturgy of the Word

The tabernacle should be entirely empty; a sufficient amount of bread should be consecrated at this Mass for the communion of clergy and laity today and tomorrow.

ENTRANCE ANT.   See Gal 6, 14

We should glory in the cross of our Lord Jesus Christ, for he is our salvation, our life and our resurrection; through him we are saved and made free. ➤ p. 614

During the singing of the Gloria, *the church bells are rung and then remain silent until the Easter Vigil, unless the conference of bishops or the Ordinary decrees otherwise.*

OPENING PRAYER

God our Father,
we are gathered here to share in the supper
which your only Son left to his Church to reveal his
    love.
He gave it to us when he was about to die
and commanded us to celebrate it as the new and
    eternal sacrifice.
We pray that in this eucharist
we may find the fullness of love and life.
Grant this through our Lord Jesus Christ, your Son,
who lives and reigns with you and the Holy Spirit,
one God, for ever and ever. ℟. **Amen.** ▼

READING I   Ex 12, 1-8. 11-14

For the protection of the Jewish people, strict religious and dietary instructions are given to Moses by God. The law of the Passover meal requires that the doorposts and lintels of each house be marked with the blood of the sacrificial animal so that the Lord can "go through Egypt striking down every first-born of the land, both man and beast."

A reading from the book of Exodus

The Lord said to Moses and Aaron in the land of Egypt, "This month shall stand at the head of your calendar; you shall reckon it the first month of the year. Tell the whole community of Israel: On the tenth of this month every one of your families must procure for itself a lamb, one apiece for each household. If a family is too small for a whole lamb, it shall join the nearest household in procuring one and shall share in the lamb in proportion to the number of persons who partake of it. The lamb must be a year-old male and without blemish. You may take it from either the sheep or the goats. You shall keep it until the fourteenth day of this month, and then, with the whole assembly of Israel present, it shall be slaughtered during the evening twilight. They shall take some of its blood and apply it to the two doorposts and the lintel of every house in which they partake of the lamb. That same night they shall eat its roasted flesh with unleavened bread and bitter herbs.

"This is how you are to eat it: with your loins girt, sandals on your feet and your staff in hand, you shall eat like those who are in flight. It is the Passover of the Lord. For on this same night I will go through Egypt, striking down every first-born of the land, both man and beast, and executing judgment on all the gods of Egypt—I, the Lord! But the blood will mark the houses where you are. Seeing the blood, I will pass over you; thus, when I strike the land of Egypt, no destructive blow will come upon you.

"This day shall be a memorial feast for you, which all your generations shall celebrate with pilgrimage to the Lord, as a perpetual institution."—This is the Word of the Lord. ℞. **Thanks be to God.** ℣

Responsorial Psalm   Ps 116, 12-13. 15-16. 17-18

℞. (See 1 Cor 10, 16) **Our blessing-cup is a communion with the blood of Christ.**

How shall I make a return to the Lord
    for all the good he has done for me?
The cup of salvation I will take up,
    and I will call upon the name of the Lord. — ℞

Precious in the eyes of the Lord
    is the death of his faithful ones.
I am your servant, the son of your handmaid;
    you have loosed my bonds. — ℞

To you will I offer sacrifice of thanksgiving,
    and I will call upon the name of the Lord.
My vows to the Lord I will pay
    in the presence of all his people. — ℞ ℣

READING II   1 Cor 11, 23-26

Paul recounts the events of the Last Supper which were handed down
to him. The changing of bread and wine into the Body and Blood of the
Lord proclaimed again his death. It was to be a sacrificial meal.

A reading from the first letter of Paul to the
Corinthians

I received from the Lord what I handed on to you,
namely, that the Lord Jesus on the night in which
he was betrayed took bread, and after he had given
thanks, broke it and said, "This is my body, which
is for you. Do this in remembrance of me." In the
same way, after the supper, he took the cup, saying,
"This cup is the new covenant in my blood. Do this,
whenever you drink it, in remembrance of me."
Every time, then, you eat this bread and drink this
cup, you proclaim the death of the Lord until he
comes!—This is the Word of the Lord. ℟. **Thanks be
to God.** ♥

GOSPEL   Jn 13, 1-15
Verse before the Gospel (Jn 13, 34)
℟. **Praise to you, Lord Jesus Christ, king of endless
glory!**
I give you a new commandment:
love one another as I have loved you.
℟. **Praise to you, Lord Jesus Christ, king of endless
glory!**

Jesus washes the feet of his disciples to prove to them his sincere
love and great humility which they should imitate. He teaches them
that, although free from sin and not unworthy to receive his most
holy body and blood, they should be purified of all evil inclinations.

℣. The Lord be with you. ℟. **And also with you.**
✠ A reading from the holy gospel according to John
℟. **Glory to you, Lord.**

Before the feast of Passover, Jesus realized that the
hour had come for him to pass from this world to
the Father. He had loved his own in this world, and

would show his love for them to the end. The devil had already induced Judas, son of Simon Iscariot, to hand Jesus over; and so, during the supper, Jesus —fully aware that he had come from God and was going to God, the Father who had handed everything over to him—rose from the meal and took off his cloak. He picked up a towel and tied it around himself. Then he poured water into a basin and began to wash his disciples' feet and dry them with the towel he had around him. Thus he came to Simon Peter, who said to him, "Lord, are you going to wash my feet?" Jesus answered, "You may not realize now what I am doing, but later you will understand." Peter replied, "You shall never wash my feet!" "If I do not wash you," Jesus answered, "you will have no share in my heritage." "Lord," Simon Peter said to him, "then not only my feet, but my hands and head as well." Jesus told him, "The man who has bathed has no need to wash [except for his feet]; he is entirely cleansed, just as you are; though not all." (The reason he said, "Not all are washed clean," was that he knew his betrayer.)

After he had washed their feet, he put his cloak back on and reclined at table once more. He said to them:

"Do you understand what I just did for you?
You address me as 'Teacher' and 'Lord,'
and fittingly enough,
for that is what I am.
But if I washed your feet—
I who am Teacher and Lord—
then you must wash each other's feet.
What I just did was to give you an example:
as I have done, so you must do."

This is the gospel of the Lord. ℟. **Praise to you, Lord Jesus Christ.** ℣

The Homily should explain the principal mysteries which are commemorated in this Mass: the institution of the eucharisti, the institution of the priesthood, and Christ's commandment of brotherly love.

Washing of Feet

Depending on pastoral circumstances, the washing of feet follows the Homily.

The men who have been chosen are led by the ministers to chairs prepared in a suitable place. Then the priest (removing his chasuble if necessary) goes to each man. With the help of the ministers, he pours water over each one's feet and dries them.

Meanwhile some of the following antiphons or other appropriate songs are sung.

ANTIPHON 1　　　　　　　　　See Jn 13, 4. 5. 15

The Lord Jesus,
when he had eaten with his disciples,
poured water into a basin
and began to wash their feet, saying:
This example I leave you.

ANTIPHON 2　　　　　　　　　Jn 13, 6. 7. 8

Lord, do you wash my feet?
Jesus said to him:
If I do not wash your feet,
you can have no part with me.

℣. So he came to Simon Peter,
who said to him:
Lord, do you wash my feet?

℣. Now you do not know what I am doing,
but later you will understand.
Lord, do you wash my feet?

ANTIPHON 3　　　　　　　　　See Jn 13, 14

If I, your Lord and Teacher, have washed your feet,
then surely you must wash one another's feet.

ANTIPHON 4　　　　　　　　　Jn 13, 35

If there is this love among you,
all will know that you are my disciples.

℣. **Jesus said to his disciples:**
If there is this love among you,
all will know that you are my disciples.

ANTIPHON 5   Jn 13, 34

I give you a new commandment:
love one another as I have loved you, says the Lord.

ANTIPHON 6   1 Cor 13, 13

Faith, hope, and love,
let these endure among you;
and the greatest of these is love.

The General Intercessions follow the washing of feet,
or, if this does not take place, they follow the Homily.
The Profession of Faith is not said in this Mass.

The Liturgy of the Eucharist

At the beginning of the liturgy of the eucharist, there
may be a procession of the faithful with gifts for the
poor. During the procession the following may be sung,
or another appropriate song.

Ant. **Where charity and love are found, there is God.**
℣. **The love of Christ has gathered us together into**
     one.
℣. **Let us rejoice and be glad in him.**
℣. **Let us fear and love the living God,**
℣. **and love each other from the depths of our heart.**
Ant. **Where charity and love are found, there is God.**
℣. **Therefore when we are together,**
℣. **let us take heed not to be divided in mind.**
℣. **Let there be an end to bitterness and quarrels,**
     an end to strife,
℣. **and in our midst be Christ our God.**
Ant. **Where charity and love are found, there is God.**
℣. **And, in company with the blessed, may we see**
℣. **your face in glory, Christ our God,**
℣. **pure and unbounded joy**
℣. **for ever and for ever.**
Ant. **Where charity and love are found, there is God.**

➤ No. 17, p. 624

PRAYER OVER THE GIFTS

Lord,
make us worthy to celebrate these mysteries.
Each time we offer this memorial sacrifice,
the work of our redemption is accomplished.
We ask this in the name of Jesus the Lord.

℟. **Amen**   → No. 21, p. 626 (Pref. P 47)

*When Eucharistic Prayer I is used, the special Holy
Thursday forms of* In union with the whole Church,
Father, accept this offering,*and* The day before he suf-
fered *are said:*

In union with the whole Church
we celebrate that day
when Jesus Christ, our Lord,
was betrayed for us.
We honor Mary,
the ever-virgin mother of Jesus Christ our Lord and
    God.
We honor Joseph, her husband,
the apostles and martyrs
Peter and Paul, Andrew,
(James, John, Thomas,
James, Philip,
Bartholomew, Matthew, Simon and Jude;
we honor Linus, Cletus, Clement, Sixtus,
Cornelius, Cyprian, Lawrence, Chrysogonus,
John and Paul, Cosmas and Damian)
and all the saints.
May their merits and prayers
gain us your constant help and protection.
(Through Christ our Lord. Amen.)

Father, accept this offering
from your whole family
in memory of the day when Jesus Christ, our Lord,
gave the mysteries of his body and blood
for his disciples to celebrate.

Grant us your peace in this life,
save us from final damnation,
and count us among those you have chosen.
(Through Christ our Lord. Amen.)

Bless and approve our offering;
make it acceptable to you,
an offering in spirit and in truth.
Let it become for us
the body and blood of Jesus Christ,
your only Son, our Lord.

The day before he suffered
to save us and all men,
that is today,
he took bread in his sacred hands
and looking up to heaven,
to you, his almighty Father,
he gave you thanks and praise.
He broke the bread,
gave it to his disciples, and said:

Take this, all of you, and eat it:
this is my body which will be given up for you.

The rest follows the Roman canon, pp. 630-632.

COMMUNION ANT.   1 Cor 11, 24-25
**This body will be given for you. This is the cup of
the new covenant in my blood; whenever you receive
them, do so in remembrance of me.** ℣

*After the distribution of communion, the ciborium with
hosts for Good Friday is left on the altar.*

*A period of silence may be observed after communion,
or a psalm or song of praise may be sung.*

PRAYER AFTER COMMUNION

Almighty God,
we receive new life
from the supper your Son gave us in this world.
May we find full contentment
in the meal we hope to share
in your eternal kingdom.
We ask this through Christ our Lord. ℞. **Amen.**

The Mass concludes with this prayer.

Transfer of the Holy Eucharist

*After the prayer the priest stands before the altar and
puts incense in the thurible. Kneeling, he incenses the
Blessed Sacrament three times. Then he receives the
humeral veil, takes the ciborium, and covers it with the
ends of the veil.*

*The Blessed Sacrament is carried through the church
in procession, led by a cross-bearer and accompanied by
candles and incense, to the place of reposition prepared
in a chapel suitably decorated for the occasion. During
the procession the hymn* Pange, lingua *(exclusive of the
last two stanzas) or some other eucharistic song is sung.*

PANGE LINGUA

Sing my tongue, the Savior's glory,
Of his flesh the mystery sing;
Of his blood all price exceeding,
Shed by our immortal king,
Destined for the world's redemption,
From a noble womb to spring.

Of a pure and spotless Virgin
Born for us on earth below,
He, as man with man conversing,
Stayed the seeds of truth to sow;
Then he closed in solemn order
Wondrously his life of woe.

On the night of that Last Supper,
Seated with his chosen band,
He, the paschal victim eating,

First fulfills the law's command;
Then as food to all his brethren
Gives himself with his own hand.

Word made Flesh, the bread of nature,
By his word to flesh he turns;
Wine into his blood he changes:
What though sense no change discerns,
Only be the heart in earnest,
Faith her lesson quickly learns.

When the procession reaches the place of reposition, the priest sets the ciborium down. Then he puts incense in the thurible and, kneeling, incenses the Blessed Sacrament, while Tantum ergo Sacramentum *is sung. The tabernacle of reposition is then closed.*

Down in adoration falling,
Lo! the sacred host we hail,
Lo! o'er ancient forms departing
Newer rites of grace prevail;
Faith for all defects supplying,
Where the feeble senses fail.

To the everlasting Father,
And the Son who reigns on high
With the Holy Spirit proceeding
Forth from each eternally,
Be salvation, honor, blessing,
Might and endless majesty. Amen.

After a period of silent adoration, the priest and ministers genuflect and return to the sacristy.

Then the altar is stripped and, if possible, the crosses are removed from the church. It is desirable to cover any crosses which remain in the church.

Evening Prayer is not said by those who participate in the evening Mass.

The faithful should be encouraged to continue adoration before the Blessed Sacrament for a suitable period of time during the night, according to local circumstances, but there should be no solemn adoration after midnight.

INTRODUCTION TO THE
ORDER OF MASS

by REV. JOHN C. KERSTEN, S.V.D.

1. CELEBRATIONS

A bicentennial of freedom and self-determination is a reason for celebration. A nation does not want to forget this great event of the past. Likewise, we annually celebrate Thanksgiving Day, Independence Day, Washington's and Lincoln's birthdays. These memorials foster our gratitude and our awareness as a nation under God.

The Jews celebrate their Exodus from bondage in Egypt, which is their birthday as a free nation, with the annual Passover. The remarkable thing is that they attribute their redemption expressly to the intervention of almighty God and celebrate it annually with a detailed ritual. Until the destruction of the Jewish temple in Jerusalem (70 A.D.) this ritual consisted of the Passover sacrifice (offering God a lamb as a symbol of appreciation) and a sacrificial repast (symbolizing both communion with God, to whom the victim was offered, and communion with fellow worshipers). Afterward the Jewish Passover became, what it still is, only a memorial meal.

Nevertheless, this celebration is not just a grateful remembrance of the past; rather past and present coincide. At the Passover, Jews identify themselves with those who actually did leave Egypt. As Jewish

595

tradition has it: "From generation to generation everyone must consider himself as having personally gone out of Egypt. Therefore we must thank him [God] and praise him who led our fathers and us through these wonderful things out of slavery to freedom" (Mishna Pes. 10, 5).

2.   THE CHRISTIAN PASSOVER

As a faithful Jew, Jesus celebrated the annual Passover. In the Gospels, we have detailed information about the last time he celebrated it with his disciples on the night before his death. This event is known as "The Last Supper." After the Passover lamb had been sacrificed to God in the temple, it was brought to the upper room where Jesus and his friends ate it as a sacrificial repast according to Jewish ritual.

At this Last Supper, Jesus did a remarkable thing. He gave this ancient sacrifice and sacred meal (the Jewish Passover) a new meaning. Referring to his cruel death on the cross, he said in other words: "From now on I am that Passover lamb, sacrificed to deliver you figuratively from the slavery in Egypt and actually from all evil. Do this as a memorial of me." In meditating on our Lord's death on the cross, the early Church saw Jesus as a Jewish high priest offering sacrifice to God. This sacrifice, however, was not a lamb; it was his own body and blood, shed to set us free from the bondage of evil (Heb 9, 10).

Following this trend of thought, we understand Paul when he says: "Christ, our Passover, has been sacrificed" (1 Cor 5, 7). Our Eucharistic celebration is a Jewish Passover with a new meaning. The Jews celebrate Passover as a memorial of their redemption from bondage in Egypt, brought about by God's mighty hand. We Christians celebrate the Eucharist as a memorial of our redemption from the slavery of evil, brought about by Christ's death on the cross.

3. HOW TO CELEBRATE

In celebrating the memorial of our redemption, the Eucharist [Mass], we do what our Lord has told us to do: "Do this as a remembrance of me" (Lk 22, 19). Moreover, we look to the early Church of Jerusalem, closest to the source of Christianity. In Acts we read: "The community of believers were of one heart and one mind" (Acts 4, 32). "They devoted themselves to the apostles' instruction and the communal life, to the breaking of the bread and the prayers" (Acts 2, 42). These early Christians were very much aware of our Lord's promise: "Where two or three are gathered in my name, there am I in their midst" (Mt 18, 20).

"In the celebration of Mass, which perpetuates the sacrifice of the cross, Christ is really present in the assembly itself, which is gathered in his name" (General Instruction of the Roman Missal, ch. II, no. 7). All Christians share in Christ's royal priesthood, which is a function of intercession for all fellowmen. Hence, the celebration of the Eucharist is the action of the whole Church. All should participate. However, through the sacrament of orders, some Christians are singled out to exercise a special ministry in this priestly people, whose "spiritual sacrifice to God is accomplished through the ministry of presbyters [priests], in union with the sacrifice of Christ, our one and only Mediator" (Ibid., no. 5).

In summary, "the celebration of Mass is the action of Christ and the people of God hierarchically [in graded order] assembled" (Ibid., ch. I, no. 1), of one heart and mind, each playing his role in the great memorial drama of our redemption, the Eucharist.

4. STRUCTURE

Mass is made up of the Liturgy of the Word (Bible readings and Homily) and the Liturgy of the Eucharist. There are also introductory rites, which prepare us for both the table of God's word and the table of Christ's body and blood, and a concluding rite which consists of a final blessing and dismissal. Assembled "in graded order," we listen to the prayers assigned to the priest, actively take part in the dialogues, sing wholeheartedly, meditatively apply God's word to our own life situation, make Christ's sacrifice, present in the signs of bread and wine, a token of our own self-surrender to God, and make Communion an intimate encounter with our Lord.

There is no time for idle dreaming. If properly understood, participating in the Eucharist is exciting —even without the usual trappings we associate with excitement, such as a swinging band! Music at Mass is meaningful only if it underlines and fosters activities of heart and mind.

5. THE LANGUAGE OF SYMBOLS

Religious symbolism points to beautiful realities often more effectively than mere words can do. Entering the church, I make the sign of the cross with holy water. It reminds me of my baptism. Likewise, the sprinkling with holy water, which may replace the penitential rite, points to cleansing from sin. Genuflecting is a sign of respect for the Blessed Sacrament, kneeling is a symbol of humility, and standing in prayer expresses respect for Almighty God. (Do we not stand up to shake hands?)

Incense clouds may symbolize my prayers going up to God, and striking one's breast is a confession of sinfulness. The handshake of peace should be a genuine symbol of love and concern for all fellow members. As religious people, we should develop a feeling for symbolism and make it meaningful. Void symbolism is boring.

6. INTRODUCTORY RITES OF THE MASS

The introductory rites consist of songs and prayers which precede the Liturgy of the Word and the Liturgy of the Eucharist.

a) The **Entrance Antiphon** deepens the unity of the people and introduces us to the mystery of the season or feast.

b) Within the sanctuary there stands that which is the very heart of the church—the altar. Since we in the Catholic tradition give high preference to the Liturgy of the Eucharist, the altar is central, not the pulpit. Entering the sanctuary **the priest venerates the altar with a kiss.** The altar bears the gift which Christ will offer to the heavenly Father.

c) The **Penitential Rite** speaks for itself. We should worship with a clean heart. Notice that the "I confess" of the new rite mentions the much overlooked "in what I have failed to do." ("During this past week where have I failed to be the kind of person I should be in the eyes of my Maker?")

d) **Praise to Christ.** The "Lord, Have Mercy" (Kyrie) is an acclamation which praises the Lord and implores his mercy. The "Glory to God" (Gloria) is an ancient hymn in which the Church assembled in the Spirit praises and prays to the Father and the Lamb.

e) **Opening Prayer.** The Introductory Rites conclude with a prayer which expresses the theme of the celebration and addresses a petition in the people's name to God the Father through the mediation of Christ in the Holy Spirit. The people make the prayer their own and give their assent by the acclamation: Amen.

7. LITURGY OF THE WORD

a) First we listen to a reading from the Hebrew Bible, which we call the Old Testament. Since the

Church sees all the aspirations of the ancient Hebrews fulfilled in Christ, we must read the Old Testament in order to understand its Christian interpretation, which is the New Testament. The Hebrew Bible contains a wealth of God-inspired wisdom. We must especially bear in mind that the Bible never tells stories for a story's sake. In telling a story, the sacred writer wants to teach religious values. Hence, the reader should always try to find the point of the story, which is **God's word to us.**

As for the **Responsorial Psalm,** we should become acquainted with the way the Church re-interprets the Psalms and gives them a Christian meaning. Often the refrain indicates how we should adapt a particular psalm in its liturgical setting on Sunday.

b) The second reading is usually taken from **letters composed by the apostles.** As the early Jerusalem Church has done, we devote ourselves to the apostles' instruction. (See no. 3 above.) The Church is apostolic! Both the first and the second reading are usually done by lay members of the congregation.

c) The Liturgy of the Word culminates in **the reading of the Gospel,** which deals directly with God's manifestation in Jesus Christ. Candlelight (Christ is the light of the world!) and incense (sign of respect) can be used to help emphasize the importance of the Gospel reading. Christ is present and speaks to us.

d) As a rule, the **Homily** develops some point of the Bible readings. Indeed, the congregation may rightfully expect that the priest will be well acquainted with Biblical theology and prepare his sermons carefully. On the other hand, the congregation must be realistic. One cannot expect a spectacular performance every Sunday. Neither may we expect that the preacher will say only "nice things." Paul told the young bishop Timothy: "I charge you to preach the word [of God], to stay with this task whether convenient or inconvenient—teaching, reproving, appealing—constantly teaching and never losing patience" (2 Tm 4, 2). The priest has to do his duty and apply the Bible message to the life situation of the congregation.

e) The **Profession of Faith** is our assent to the word of God, which we have heard in the readings and Homily. And exercising our priestly function (see no. 3 above) **we make intercession** for all mankind by saying the petitions and/or underlining them by our response.

8. THE LITURGY OF THE EUCHARIST

At the Last Supper, Christ took bread, gave thanks and praise to the Father, broke it, and gave it to his disciples, saying: "Take this and eat it: this is my body." Then he took the cup, again gave thanks, and gave it to his disciples, saying: "Take this and drink from it: this is the cup of my blood. Do this in memory of me." (See no. 2, above.) Corresponding to these words and actions of our Lord, the Church has ararnged the celebration of the Eucharist as follows.

Preparation of the gifts. Bread, wine and water are brought to the sanctuary.

The Eucharistic prayer (which means "prayer of thanksgiving and sanctification"). It has a preface (introduction), followed by the preface acclamation, the "Holy, holy, . . ." by the congregation. In this framework of thanksgiving, the offerings of bread and wine become the body and blood of Christ and are offered to God in sacrifice.

Communion rite (a sign of the unity of the faithful). In communion all receive the body and blood of Christ as a sacrificial repast. (See nos. 1 and 2, above.)

PREPARATION OF THE GIFTS

Members of the congregation bring the gifts of bread and wine to the altar. We should pay attention to its symbolism. Bread and wine (in Oriental setting, daily food) stand for all of us, who want to offer ourselves as "an everlasting gift to God" (Euch. Pr. III). Other gifts (collection) are added. This money is used for the poor and the support of the church. All of this should be seen as a symbolical giving of self.

The presentation song, prayers, lifting up of the gifts, and incense, if used, underline the idea of self-giving. "Lord God, we ask you to receive us and be pleased with the sacrifice we offer you with humble and contrite hearts" (Prayer by priest). All of this symbolism has only so much meaning as **you** give to it by giving **yourself** to God. You can show this by a heartfelt Amen to the Prayer over the Gifts, which asks the Father's blessing.

EUCHARISTIC PRAYER

At a farewell party for a retiring employee most of the time is taken up by speaking words of thanks and appreciation for services rendered, and only at the end is a token of appreciation offered, a gift which signifies whatever has been said.

The Eucharistic Prayer should be considered in a similar setting. Most of it consists of words of praise and thanksgiving, and in that framework time and again we offer Almighty God a token of our gratitude, namely, the body and blood of Christ (Christ himself in the signs of bread and wine), offered in sacrifice on the altar of the cross "once for all" (Heb 10, 10).

The Roman Missal offers a choice of many Prefaces and four versions of the Eucharistic Prayer proper. All contain the following elements.

a) **Preface.** We should wholeheartedly join in the dialogue, in which we are invited to give thanks to God, and the acclamation, the "Holy, holy . . . ," said/sung in union with all the angels of heaven.

b) **Epiclesis** (Invocation). These are the prayers before the Consecration in which the priest and we with him invoke God's power and ask him that the gifts offered by men may be consecrated, that is, become the body and blood of Christ and source of salvation for those who partake. "[God] let your Spirit come upon these gifts to make them holy, so that they may become for us the body and blood of our Lord, Jesus Christ" (Euch. Pr. II).

c) **Narrative of the Institution and Consecration.** We celebrate the sacrifice which Jesus Christ instituted at the Last Supper when in the signs of bread and wine he offered his body and blood (himself), gave them to the apostles, and told them to do the same "in memory" of him.

d) **Anamnesis** (a calling to mind). Calling to mind our Lord's death, resurrection, and ascension, we offer God in thanksgiving "this holy and living sacrifice," the body and blood of Christ, and in and with him ourselves "as an everlasting gift" to the Almighty (Euch. Pr. III). (See also nos. 2 and 3, above.)

e) **Intercessions,** which we should make our own.

f) **Final Doxology** (hymn of praise), which we should confirm with our acclamation "Amen" (So be it!).

COMMUNION RITE

At a banquet we celebrate togetherness (communion) not only with the host and hostess but also with the fellow guests. Intending not to meet certain people could be a reason to decline an invitation.

The night before his death, our Lord ate the Passover lamb with his disciples as a sacrificial repast.

(See nos. 1 and 2, above.) Traditionally, eating from the lamb which had been offered to God symbolized communion with God and fellow worshipers. We should see "Holy Communion" in a similar vein. We eat "our Passover, which has been sacrificed" (1 Cor 5, 7, see no. 2, above), and should realize that by doing so we signify our oneness not only with God in Jesus Christ, but also with all who partake. This is clearly indicated by the preparatory rites which lead directly to it.

a) **The Lord's Prayer.** This is a petition both for daily food, which for Christians means also the Eucharistic bread, and for forgiveness from sin, "forgive us . . . as we forgive those who trespass against us." Without taking this prayer seriously, signifying communion with Christ and fellowmen would be a void symbolism.

b) **Rite of Peace.** Before we share the table of the Lord, we shake hands as a sign of love for one another. With the priest we ask for peace and unity in Christ's kingdom.

c) **Breaking of Bread.** In early Christianity the Eucharist (Mass) was known as "The Breaking of Bread" (See no. 3, above). Using a loaf of bread, its breaking was a necessity for distributing it, but simultaneously it was seen as a beautiful symbolism: All are one in partaking of the one loaf of bread, Jesus Christ (1 Cor 10, 17). For practical reasons we now use small altar breads and one large one, which is broken when the congregation prays/sings "The Lamb of God." Symbolism is still there. The priest shows the broken bread. Christ was "broken," sacrificed, as a spotless lamb to take away the sin of the world.

d) The **Communion Antiphon** expresses the spiritual union of all who partake in the Eucharistic banquet. Note that in Biblical language the words "flesh, body, blood" do not indicate the things as such but the whole person and the event which they signify, namely, Jesus Christ giving himself in his meritorious death, in which we share when we partake in the Eucharist.

e) **Silent Prayer.** If spontaneous silent prayer does not work too well, meditatively you could pray again the Responsorial Psalm to the first Bible reading or the Communion Psalm in your Missal, and take a thought that strikes you as a starting point for private prayer. Our personal prayer is summed up in a final prayer by the priest (Prayer after Communion). We make it our prayer by our acclamation, Amen—So be it!

9. CONCLUDING RITE

The presiding priest greets us, gives his blessing, and dismisses the congregation with the mission to love and serve the Lord. Partaking in the Eucharist means a renewed commitment to God and fellowmen. We have prayed: "[God] we offer you in thanksgiving this holy and living sacrifice. Look with favor on your Church's offering, and see the Victim [Christ] whose death has reconciled us to yourself. . . . May he [Christ] make us an everlasting gift to you" (Euch. Pr. III). We hope to make this commitment real during the week "strengthened by the bread of heaven." Not even caring enough to try to do so would make our partaking in the Eucharist a void and meaningless symbolism. Symbolize only reality!

COMMUNION PRAYERS

PRAYERS BEFORE HOLY COMMUNION

Act of Faith

Lord Jesus Christ, I firmly believe that you are present in this Blessed Sacrament as true God and true Man, with your Body and Blood, Soul and Divinity. My Redeemer and my Judge, I adore your Divine Majesty together with the angels and saints. I believe, O Lord; increase my faith.

Act of Hope

Good Jesus, in you alone I place all my hope. You are my salvation and my strength, the Source of all good. Through your mercy, through your Passion and Death, I hope to obtain the pardon of my sins, the grace of final perseverance and a happy eternity.

Act of Love

Jesus, my God, I love you with my whole heart and above all things, because you are the one supreme Good and an infinitely perfect Being. You have given your life for me, a poor sinner, and in your mercy you have even offered yourself as food for my soul.

My God, I love you. Inflame my heart so that I may love you more.

Act of Contrition

O my Savior, I am truly sorry for having offended you because you are infinitely good and sin displeases you. I detest all the sins of my life and I desire to atone for them. Through the merits of your Precious Blood, wash from my soul all stain of sin, so that, cleansed in body and soul, I may worthily approach the Most Holy Sacrament of the Altar.

Act of Desire

Jesus, my God and my all, my soul longs for you. My heart yearns to receive you in Holy Communion.

Come, Bread of heaven and Food of angels, to nourish my soul and to rejoice my heart. Come, most lovable Friend of my soul, to inflame me with such love that I may never again be separated from you.

Prayer of St. Thomas Aquinas

Almighty and ever-living God,
I approach the sacrament of your only-begotten Son,
    our Lord Jesus Christ.
I come sick to the doctor of life,
unclean to the fountain of mercy,
blind to the radiance of eternal light,
and poor and needy to the Lord of heaven and earth.
Lord, in your great generosity,
heal my sickness, wash away my defilement,
enlighten my blindness, enrich my poverty,
and clothe my nakedness.
May I receive the bread of angels,
the King of kings and Lord of lords,
with humble reverence,
with the purity and faith,
the repentance and love, and the determined purpose
that will help to bring me to salvation.
May I receive the sacrament of the Lord's body
    and blood,
and its reality and power.
Kind God,
may I receive the body of your only-begotten Son,
    our Lord Jesus Christ,
born from the womb of the Virgin Mary,
and so be received into his mystical body
and numbered among his members.
Loving Father,
as on my earthly pilgrimage
I now receive your beloved Son
under the veil of a sacrament,
may I one day see him face to face in glory,
who lives and reigns with you for ever Amen.

PRAYERS AFTER HOLY COMMUNION

Act of Faith

Jesus, I firmly believe that you are present within me as God and Man, to enrich my soul with graces and to fill my heart with the happiness of the blessed. I believe that you are Christ, the Son of the living God!

Act of Adoration

With deepest humility, I adore you, my Lord and God; you have made my soul your dwelling place. I adore you as my Creator from whose hands I came and with whom I am to be happy forever.

Act of Love

Dear Jesus, I love you with my whole heart, my whole soul, and with all my strength. May the love of your own Sacred Heart fill my soul and purify it so that I may die to the world for love of you, as you died on the Cross for love of me. My God, you are all mine; grant that I may be all yours in time and in eternity.

Act of Thanksgiving

From the depths of my heart I thank you, dear Lord, for your infinite kindness in coming to me. How good you are to me! With your most holy Mother and all the angels, I praise your mercy and generosity toward me, a poor sinner. I thank you for nourishing my soul with your Sacred Body and Precious Blood. I will try to show my gratitude to you in the Sacrament of your love, by obedience to your holy commandments, by fidelity to my duties, by kindness to my neighbor and by an earnest endeavor to become more like you in my daily conduct.

Prayer to Christ the King

O Christ Jesus, I acknowledge you King of the universe. All that has been created has been made for

you. Exercise upon me all your rights. I renew my
baptismal promises, renouncing Satan and all his
works and pomps. I promise to live a good Christian
life and to do all in my power to procure the triumph
of the rights of God and your Church.

Divine Heart of Jesus, I offer you my poor actions in order to obtain that all hearts may ackowl-
edge your sacred Royalty, and that thus the reign
of your peace may be established throughout the
universe. Amen.

Prayer of St. Thomas Aquinas

Lord, Father all-powerful and ever-living God,
I thank you,
for even though I am a sinner, your unprofitable
    servant,
not because of my worth but in the kindness of your
    mercy,
you have fed me
with the precious body and blood of your Son, our
    Lord Jesus Christ.
I pray that this holy communion
may not bring me condemnation and punishment
but forgiveness and salvation.
May it be a helmet of faith
and a shield of good will.
May it purify me from evil ways
and put an end to my evil passions.
May it bring me charity and patience,
humility and obedience,
and growth in the power to do good.
May it be my strong defense
against all my enemies, visible and invisible,
and the perfect calming of all my evil impulses,
bodily and spiritual.
May it unite me more closely to you,
the one true God,
and lead me safely through death

and everlasting happiness with you.
And I pray that you will lead me, a sinner,
to the banquet where you,
with your Son and Holy Spirit,
are true and perfect light,
total fulfillment, everlasting joy,
gladness without end,
and perfect happiness to your saints.
Grant this through Christ our Lord. Amen.

Prayer to Our Redeemer

Soul of Christ, make me holy.
Body of Christ, be my salvation.
Blood of Christ, let me drink your wine.
Water flowing from the side of Christ, wash me
   clean.
Passion of Christ, strengthen me.
Kind Jesus, hear my prayer;
hide me within your wounds
and keep me close to you.

Defend me from the evil enemy.
Call me at my death
to the fellowship of your saints,
that I may sing your praise with them
through all eternity. Amen.

Prayer to Jesus Christ Crucified

My good and dear Jesus,
I kneel before you,
asking you most earnestly
to engrave upon my heart
a deep and lively faith, hope, and charity,
with true repentance for my sins,
and a firm resolve to make amends.
As I reflect upon your five wounds,
and dwell upon them with deep compassion and
   grief.

I recall, good Jesus, the words the prophet David spoke
long ago concerning yourself:
they have pierced my hands and my feet,
they have counted all my bones!

A *plenary indulgence* is granted on each Friday of Lent and Passiontide to the faithful, who after Communion piously recite the above prayer before an image of Christ crucified; on other days of the year the indulgence is *partial. (No. 22)*

Prayer to Mary

O Jesus living in Mary, come and live in your servants, in the spirit of your holiness, in the fulness of your power, in the perfection of your ways, in the truth of your mysteries. Reign in us over all adverse power by your Holy Spirit, and for the glory of the Father. Amen.

Mary, I come to you with childlike confidence and earnestly beg you to take me under your powerful protection. Grant me a place in your loving motherly Heart. I place my immortal soul into your hands and give you my own poor heart.

Prayer to St. Joseph

Guardian of virgins, and holy father Joseph, to whose faithful custody Christ Jesus, innocence itself, and Mary, Virgin of virgins, were committed; I beg you, by these dear pledges, Jesus and Mary, that, being preserved from all uncleanness, I may with spotless mind, pure heart and chaste body, ever serve Jesus and Mary most chastely all the days of my life. Amen.

PLAN OF THE MASS

INTRODUCTORY RITES
1. Entrance Antiphon **(Proper)**
2. Greeting
3. Rite of Blessing and Sprinkling Holy Water
4. Penitential Rite
5. Kyrie
6. Gloria
7. Opening Prayer **(Proper)**

LITURGY OF THE WORD
8. First Reading **(Proper)**
9. Responsorial Psalm **(Proper)**
10. Second Reading **(Proper)**
11. Alleluia **(Proper)**
12. Gospel **(Proper)**
13. Homily
14. Profession of Faith
15. General Intercessions

(Eucharistic Prayer)
16. Offertory Song
17. Preparation of the Bread
18. Preparation of the Wine
19. Invitation to Prayer
20. Prayer over the Gifts **(Proper)**

LITURGY OF THE EUCHARIST
21. Introductory Dialogue
22. Preface
23. Sanctus
Eucharistic Prayer 1 — p. 628
Eucharistic Prayer 2 — p. 633
Eucharistic Prayer 3 — p. 637
Eucharistic Prayer 4 — p. 641

(Communion Rite)
24. Lord's Prayer
25. Sign of Peace
26. Breaking of the Bread
27. Prayers before Communion
28. Reception of Communion
29. Communion Ant. **(Proper)**
30. Silence after Communion
31. Prayer after Communion **(Proper)**

CONCLUDING RITE
32. Greeting
33. Blessing
34. Dismissal

613

THE ORDER OF MASS

Options are indicated by A, B, C, D in the margin.

INTRODUCTORY RITES

Acts of prayer and penitence prepare us to meet Christ as he comes in Word and Sacrament. We gather as a worshiping community to celebrate our unity with him and with one another in faith.

1 ENTRANCE ANTIPHON

STAND

If it is not sung, it is recited by all or some of the people.

Joined together as Christ's people, we open the celebration by raising our voices in praise of God who is present among us. This song should deepen our unity as it introduces the Mass we celebrate today.

> **> Turn to Today's Mass**

2 GREETING (3 forms)

When the priest comes to the altar, he makes the customary reverence with the ministers and kisses the altar. Then, with the ministers, he goes to his seat. After the entrance song, all make the sign of the cross:

Priest: In the name of the Father, and of the Son, and of the Holy Spirit.

PEOPLE: Amen.

614

The priest welcomes us in the name of the Lord. We show our union with God, our neighbor, and the priest by a united response to his greeting.

A

Priest: The grace of our Lord Jesus Christ and the love of God and the fellowship of the Holy Spirit be with you all.

PEOPLE: **And also with you.**

—————————— OR ——————————

B

Priest: The grace and peace of God our Father and the Lord Jesus Christ be with you.

PEOPLE: **Blessed be God, the Father of our Lord Jesus Christ.**

    or:

    And also with you.

—————————— OR ——————————

C

Priest: The Lord be with you.

PEOPLE: **And also with you.**

    [Bishop: Peace be with you.

    People: **And also with you.**

3 RITE OF BLESSING and SPRINKLING HOLY WATER

The rite of blessing and sprinkling holy water may be celebrated in all churches and chapels at all Sunday Masses celebrated on Sunday or Saturday evening, see p. 652-654.

4 PENITENTIAL RITE (3 forms)

(Omitted when the rite of blessing and sprinkling holy water has taken place or some part of the liturgy of the hours has preceded)

Before we hear God's word, we acknowledge our sins humbly, ask for mercy, and accept his pardon.

Invitation to repent:

After the introduction to the day's Mass, the priest invites the people to recall their sins and to repent of them in silence:

A As we prepare to celebrate the mystery of Christ's love,
let us acknowledge our failures
and ask the Lord for pardon and strength.

B Coming together as God's family,
with confidence let us ask the Father's forgiveness,
for he is full of gentleness and compassion.

C My brothers and sisters,
to prepare ourselves to celebrate the sacred mysteries,
let us call to mind our sins.

Then, after a brief silence, one of the following forms is used.

A

Priest and **PEOPLE:**

> I confess to almighty God,
> and to you, my brothers and sisters,
> that I have sinned through my own fault

They strike their breast:

> in my thoughts and in my words,
> in what I have done,

and in what I have failed to do;
and I ask blessed Mary, ever virgin,
all the angels and saints,
and you, my brothers and sisters,
to pray for me to the Lord our God.

——— OR ———

B

Priest: Lord, we have sinned against you:
Lord, have mercy.
PEOPLE: Lord, have mercy.
Priest: Lord, show us your mercy and love.
PEOPLE:: And grant us your salvation.

——— OR ———

C

Priest or other minister:

You were sent to heal the contrite:
Lord, have mercy.
PEOPLE: Lord, have mercy.
Priest or other minister:

You came to call sinners:
Christ, have mercy.
PEOPLE: Christ, have mercy.
Priest or other minister:

You plead for us at the right hand of the
Father:
Lord, have mercy.
PEOPLE: Lord, have mercy.

(Other invocations may be used as on pp. 655-657.)

Absolution:

At the end of any of the forms of the penitential rite:

Priest: May almighty God have mercy on us,
           forgive us our sins,
           and bring us to everlasting life.

PEOPLE: Amen.

5 KYRIE

Unless included in the penitential rite, the Kyrie is sung or said by all, with alternating parts for the choir or cantor and for the people:

℣. Lord, have mercy.

℟. **Lord, have mercy.**

℣. Christ, have mercy.

℟. **Christ, have mercy.**

℣. Lord, have mercy.

℟. **Lord, have mercy.**

6 GLORIA

As the Church assembled in the Spirit, we praise and pray to the Father and the Lamb.

When the Gloria is sung or said, the priest or the cantors or everyone together may begin it:

**Glory to God in the highest,
    and peace to his people on earth.
Lord God, heavenly King,
almighty God and Father,
    we worship you, we give you thanks,
    we praise you for your glory.**

Lord Jesus Christ, only Son of the Father,
Lord God, Lamb of God,
you take away the sin of the world:
   have mercy on us;
you are seated at the right hand of the Father:
   receive our prayer.
For you alone are the Holy One,
you alone are the Lord,
you alone are the Most High,
   Jesus Christ,
   with the Holy Spirit,
   in the glory of God the Father. Amen.

7 OPENING PRAYER

The priest invites us to pray silently for a moment and then, in our name, expresses the theme of the day's celebration and petitions God the Father through the mediation of Christ in the Holy Spirit.

Priest: Let us pray.

> **→ Turn to Today's Mass**

Priest and people pray silently for a while. Then the priest says the opening prayer and concludes:

Priest: For ever and ever.

PEOPLE: Amen.

LITURGY OF THE WORD

The proclamation of God's Word is always centered on Christ, present through his Word. Old Testament writings prepare for him; New Testament books speak of him directly. All of scripture calls us to believe once more and to follow. After the reading we reflect upon God's words and respond to them.

As in Today's Mass

SIT

8 FIRST READING

At end of reading: Reader: This is the Word of the Lord.
PEOPLE: Thanks be to God.

9 RESPONSORIAL PSALM

The people repeat the response sung by the cantor the first time and then after each verse.

10 SECOND READING

At end of reading: Reader: This is the Word of the Lord.
PEOPLE: Thanks be to God.

11 ALLELUIA (Gospel Acclamation) STAND

Jesus will speak to us in the gospel. We rise now out of respect and prepare for his message with the alleluia.

The people repeat the alleluia after cantor's alleluia and then after the verse.
During Lent one of the following invocations is used as a response instead of the alleluia:

(A) Praise to you, Lord Jesus Christ, king of endless glory!
(B) Praise and honor to you, Lord Jesus Christ!
(C) Glory and praise to you, Lord Jesus Christ!
(D) Glory to you, Word of God, Lord Jesus Christ!

12 GOSPEL

Before proclaiming the gospel, the deacon asks the priest: Father, give me your blessing. *The priest says*:

The Lord be in your heart and on your lips
that you may worthily proclaim his gospel.
In the name of the Father, and of the Son, ✠ and
of the Holy Spirit. *The deacon answers*: **Amen.**

If there is no deacon, the priest says quietly:

Almighty God, cleanse my heart and my lips
that I may worthily proclaim your gospel.

Deacon (or priest):

The Lord be with you.

PEOPLE: And also with you.

Deacon (or priest):

✠ A reading from the holy gospel according
to N.

PEOPLE: Glory to you, Lord.

At the end:

Deacon (or priest):

This is the gospel of the Lord.

PEOPLE: Praise to you, Lord Jesus Christ.

Then the deacon (or priest) kisses the book, saying quietly: May the words of the gospel wipe away our sins.

13 HOMILY   `SIT`

God's word is spoken again in the homily. The Holy Spirit speaking through the lips of the preacher explains and applies today's biblical readings to the needs of this particular congregation. He calls us to respond to Christ through the life we lead.

`STAND`

14 PROFESSION OF FAITH (CREED)

As a people we express our acceptance of God's message in the scriptures and homily. We summarize our faith by proclaiming a creed handed down from the early Church.

All say the profession of faith on Sundays.

We believe in one God,
the Father, the Almighty,
maker of heaven and earth,
of all that is seen and unseen.
We believe in one Lord, Jesus Christ,
the only Son of God,
eternally begotten of the Father,
God from God, Light from Light,
true God from true God,
begotten, not made, one in Being with the
Father.
Through him all things were made.
For us men and for our salvation
he came down from heaven:

All bow at the following words up to: and became man.

by the power of the Holy Spirit
he was born of the Virgin Mary, and
became man.

For our sake he was crucified under Pontius
Pilate;
he suffered, died, and was buried.
On the third day he rose again
in fulfillment of the Scriptures;
he ascended into heaven
and is seated at the right hand of the
Father.
He will come again in glory to judge the
living and the dead,
and his kingdom will have no end.

We believe in the Holy Spirit, the Lord,
the giver of life,
who proceeds from the Father and the Son.
With the Father and the Son he is worshiped
and glorified.
He has spoken through the Prophets.
We believe in one holy catholic and apostolic Church.
We acknowledge one baptism for the forgiveness of sins.
We look for the resurrection of the dead,
and the life of the world to come. Amen.

15 GENERAL INTERCESSIONS

(Prayer of the Faithful)

As a priestly people we unite with one another to pray for
today's needs in the Church and the world.

*After the priest gives the introduction the deacon or
other minister sings or says the invocations.*

PEOPLE: Lord, hear our prayer.

(or other response, according to local custom)
At the end the priest says the concluding prayer:

PEOPLE: Amen.

LITURGY OF THE EUCHARIST

Made ready by reflection on God's Word, we enter now into the eucharistic sacrifice itself, the Supper of the Lord. We celebrate the memorial which the Lord instituted at his Last Supper. We are God's new people, the redeemed brothers of Christ, gathered by him around his table. We are here to bless God and to receive the gift of Jesus' body and blood so that our faith and life may be transformed.

SIT

16 OFFERTORY SONG

The bread and wine for the Eucharist, with our gifts for the Church and the poor, are gathered and brought to the altar. We prepare our hearts by song or in silence as the Lord's table is being set.

While the gifts of the people are brought forward to the priest and are placed on the altar, the offertory song is sung.

17 PREPARATION OF THE BREAD

Before placing the bread on the altar, the priest says quietly:

Blessed are you, Lord, God of all creation.
Through your goodness we have this bread to offer,
which earth has given and human hands have made.
It will become for us the bread of life.

If there is no singing, the priest may say this prayer aloud, and the people may respond:

People: **Blessed be God for ever.**

18 PREPARATION OF THE WINE

When he pours wine and a little water into the chalice, the deacon (or the priest) says quietly:

By the mystery of this water and wine
may we come to share in the divinity of Christ,
who humbled himself to share in our humanity.

Before placing the chalice on the altar, he says:

Blessed are you, Lord, God of all creation.
Through your goodness we have this wine to offer,
fruit of the vine and work of human hands.
It will become our spiritual drink.

If there is no singing, the priest may say this prayer aloud, and the people may respond:

People: **Blessed be God for ever.**

The priest says quietly:

Lord God, we ask you to receive us
and be pleased with the sacrifice we offer you
with humble and contrite hearts.

Then he washes his hands, saying:

Lord, wash away my iniquity;
cleanse me from my sin.

19 INVITATION TO PRAYER

Priest: Pray, brethren, that our sacrifice may be
acceptable to God, the almighty Father.

PEOPLE:

**May the Lord accept the sacrifice at your hands,
for the praise and glory of his name,
for our good, and the good of all his Church.**

20 PRAYER OVER THE GIFTS   `STAND`

The priest, speaking in our name, asks the Father to bless
and accept these gifts.

> **➤ Turn to Today's Mass**

At the end,   **PEOPLE:** **Amen.**

EUCHARISTIC PRAYER

We begin the eucharistic service of praise and thanksgiving, the center of the entire celebration, the central prayer of worship. At the priest's invitation we lift our hearts to God and unite with him in the words he addresses to the Father through Jesus Christ. Together we join Christ in his sacrifice, celebrating his memorial in the holy meal and acknowledging with him the wonderful works of God in our lives.

21 INTRODUCTORY DIALOGUE

Priest: The Lord be with you.

PEOPLE: And also with you.

Priest: Lift up your hearts.

PEOPLE: We lift them up to the Lord.

Priest: Let us give thanks to the Lord our God.

PEOPLE: It is right to give him thanks and praise.

22 PREFACE

As indicated in the individual Masses throughout this Missal, the priest may say one of the following Prefaces (listed in numerical order).

626

23 ACCLAMATION

Priest and **PEOPLE:**

Holy, holy, holy Lord, God of power and might, heaven and earth are full of your glory.

> **Hosanna in the highest.**

Blessed is he who comes in the name of the Lord.

> **Hosanna in the highest.**

KNEEL

Then the priest continues with one of the following Eucharistic Prayers.

The Roman Canon

(This Eucharistic Prayer is especially suitable for Sundays and Masses with proper "Communicantes" and "Hanc igitur.")

[The words within brackets may be omitted.]

[*Praise to the Father*]

We come to you, Father,
with praise and thanksgiving,
through Jesus Christ your Son.
Through him we ask you to accept and bless
these gifts we offer you in sacrifice.

[*Intercessions: For the Church*]

We offer them for your holy Catholic Church,
watch over it, Lord, and guide it;
grant it peace and unity throughout the world.
We offer them for N. our Pope,
for N. our bishop,
and for all who hold and teach the catholic faith
that comes to us from the apostles.

Remember, Lord, your people,
especially those for whom we now pray, N. and N.

Remember all of us gathered here before you.
You know how firmly we believe in you
and dedicate ourselves to you.
We offer you this sacrifice of praise

for ourselves and those who are dear to us.
We pray to you, our living and true God,
for our well-being and redemption.

[*In Communion with the Saints*]
In union with the whole Church *
we honor Mary,
the ever-virgin mother of Jesus Christ our Lord and
    God.
We honor Joseph, her husband,
the apostles and martyrs
Peter and Paul, Andrew,
[James, John, Thomas,
James, Philip,
Bartholomew, Matthew, Simon and Jude;
we honor Linus, Cletus, Clement, Sixtus,
Cornelius, Cyprian, Lawrence, Chrysogonus,
John and Paul, Cosmas and Damian]
and all the saints.
May their merits and prayers
gain us your constant help and protection.
[Through Christ our Lord. Amen.]
Father, accept this offering *
from your whole family.
Grant us your peace in this life,
save us from final damnation,
and count us among those you have chosen.
[Through Christ our Lord. Amen.]
Bless and approve our offering;
make it acceptable to you,
an offering in spirit and in truth.
Let it become for us
the body and blood of Jesus Christ,
your only Son, our Lord.

* *See page* **684** *for Special Communicantes and Hanc Igitur.*

1

The day before he suffered
he took bread in his sacred hands
and looking up to heaven,
to you, his almighty Father,
he gave you thanks and praise.
He broke the bread,
gave it to his disciples, and said:

Take this, all of you, and eat it:
this is my body which will be given up for you.

When supper was ended,
he took the cup.
Again he gave you thanks and praise,
gave the cup to his disciples, and said:

Take this, all of you, and drink from it:
this is the cup of my blood,
the blood of the new and everlasting covenant.
It will be shed for you and for all men
so that sins may be forgiven.
Do this in memory of me.

[*Memorial Acclamation*]

Priest: Let us proclaim the mystery of faith.

PEOPLE:

A   Christ has died,
      Christ is risen,
      Christ will come again.

B   Dying you destroyed our death,
      rising you restored our life.
      Lord Jesus, come in glory.

C   When we eat this bread and drink this cup,
we proclaim your death, Lord Jesus,
until you come in glory.

D   Lord, by your cross and resurrection
you have set us free.
You are the Savior of the world.

[*The Memorial Prayer*]

Father, we celebrate the memory of Christ, your Son.
We, your people and your ministers,
recall his passion,
his resurrection from the dead,
and his ascension into glory;
and from the many gifts you have given us
we offer to you, God of glory and majesty,
this holy and perfect sacrifice:
the bread of life
and the cup of eternal salvation.
Look with favor on these offerings
and accept them as once you accepted
the gifts of your servant Abel,
the sacrifice of Abraham, our father in faith,
and the bread and wine offered by your priest
   Melchisedech.
Almighty God,
we pray that your angel may take this sacrifice
to your altar in heaven.
Then, as we receive from this altar
the sacred body and blood of your Son,
let us be filled with every grace and blessing.
[Through Christ our Lord. Amen.]

1

[*For the Dead*]

Remember, Lord, those who have died
and have gone before us marked with the sign of
  faith,
especially those for whom we now pray, *N.* and *N.*
May these, and all who sleep in Christ,
find in your presence
light, happiness, and peace.
[Through Christ our Lord. Amen.]
For ourselves, too, we ask
some share in the fellowship of your apostles and
  martyrs,
with John the Baptist, Stephen, Matthias, Barnabas,
[Ignatius, Alexander, Marcellinus, Peter,
Felicity, Perpetua, Agatha, Lucy,
Agnes, Cecilia, Anastasia]
and all the saints.
Though we are sinners,
we trust in your mercy and love.
Do not consider what we truly deserve,
but grant us your forgiveness.
Through Christ our Lord
you give us all these gifts.
You fill them with life and goodness,
you bless them and make them holy.

Through him,   [*Concluding Doxology*]
with him,
in him,
in the unity of the Holy Spirit,
all glory and honor is yours,
almighty Father,
for ever and ever.
All reply: **Amen.**

Continue with the Mass, as on p. **646.**

2

(This Eucharistic Prayer is particularly suitable on Weekdays or for special circumstances)

℣. The Lord be with you.
℟. **And also with you.**
℣. Lift up your hearts.
℟. **We lift them up to the Lord.**
℣. Let us give thanks to the Lord our God.
℟. **It is right to give him thanks and praise.**

STAND

PREFACE   [*Praise to the Father*]

Father, it is our duty and our salvation,
always and everywhere
to give you thanks
through your beloved Son, Jesus Christ.

He is the Word through whom you made the
   universe,
the Savior you sent to redeem us.

By the power of the Holy Spirit
he took flesh and was born of the Virgin Mary.

For our sake he opened his arms on the cross;
he put an end to death
and revealed the resurrection.

In this he fulfilled your will
and won for you a holy people.

And so we join the angels and the saints
in proclaiming your glory
as we sing (say):

2 SANCTUS

[*First Acclamation of the People*]

**Holy, holy, holy Lord, God of power and might,
heaven and earth are full of your glory.**
  Hosanna in the highest.
Blessed is he who comes in the name of the Lord.
  Hosanna in the highest.   `KNEEL`

[*Invocation of the Holy Spirit*]

Lord, you are holy indeed,
the fountain of all holiness.

Let your Spirit come upon these gifts to make them
  holy,
so that they may become for us
the body and blood of our Lord, Jesus Christ.

[*The Lord's Supper*]

Before he was given up to death,
a death he freely accepted,
he took bread and gave you thanks.
He broke the bread,
gave it to his disciples, and said:
Take this, all of you, and eat it:
this is my body which will be given up for you.
When supper was ended, he took the cup.
Again he gave you thanks and praise,
gave the cup to his disciples, and said:
Take this, all of you, and drink from it:
this is the cup of my blood,
the blood of the new and everlasting covenant.
It will be shed for you and for all men
so that sins may be forgiven.
Do this in memory of me.

[*Memorial Acclamation*]

Priest: Let us proclaim the mystery of faith.

PEOPLE:

A   Christ has died,
   Christ is risen,
   Christ will come again.

B   Dying you destroyed our death,
   rising you restored our life.
   Lord Jesus, come in glory.

C   When we eat this bread and drink this cup,
   we proclaim your death, Lord Jesus,
   until you come in glory.

D   Lord, by your cross and resurrection
   you have set us free.
   You are the Savior of the world.

[*The Memorial Prayer*]

In memory of his death and resurrection,
we offer you, Father, this life-giving bread,
this saving cup.

We thank you for counting us worthy
to stand in your presence and serve you.

[*Invocation of the Holy Spirit*]

May all of us who share in the body and blood of
   Christ
be brought together in unity by the Holy Spirit.

2

[*Intercessions: For the Church*]

Lord, remember your Church throughout the world;
make us grow in love,
together with N. our Pope,
N. our bishop, and all the clergy.*

Remember our brothers and sisters   [*For the Dead*]
who have gone to their rest
in the hope of rising again;
bring them and all the departed
into the light of your presence.

[*In Communion with the Saints*]

Have mercy on us all;
make us worthy to share eternal life
with Mary, the virgin mother of God,
with the apostles,
and with all the saints who have done your will
    throughout the ages.

May we praise you in union with them,
and give you glory
through your Son, Jesus Christ.

Through him,   [*Concluding Doxology*]
with him,
in him,
in the unity of the Holy Spirit,
all glory and honor is yours,
almighty Father,
for ever and ever.

All reply: **Amen.**
    Continue with the Mass, as on p. **646.**

---

* In Masses for the Dead the following may be added:
Remember N., whom you have called from this life.
In baptism he (she) died with Christ:
may he (she) also share his resurrection.

(This Eucharistic Prayer may be used with any Preface and preferably on Sundays and feast days)

KNEEL

[Praise to the Father]

Father, you are holy indeed,
and all creation rightly gives you praise.
All life, all holiness comes from you
through your Son, Jesus Christ our Lord,
by the working of the Holy Spirit.
From age to age you gather a people to yourself,
so that from east to west
a perfect offering may be made
to the glory of your name.

[Invocation of the Holy Spirit]

And so, Father, we bring you these gifts.
We ask you to make them holy by the power of your
   Spirit,
that they may become the body and blood
of your Son, our Lord Jesus Christ,
at whose command we celebrate this eucharist.

[The Lord's Supper]

On the night he was betrayed,
he took bread and gave you thanks and praise.
He broke the bread, gave it to his disciples, and said:

Take this, all of you, and eat it:
this is my body which will be given up for you.

637

3 When supper was ended, he took the cup.
Again he gave you thanks and praise,
gave the cup to his disciples, and said:

Take this, all of you, and drink from it:
this is the cup of my blood,
the blood of the new and everlasting covenant.
It will be shed for you and for all men
so that sins may be forgiven.
Do this in memory of me.

[*Memorial Acclamation*]

Priest: Let us proclaim the mystery of faith.

PEOPLE:

A   Christ has died,
      Christ is risen,
      Christ will come again.

B   Dying you destroyed our death,
      rising you restored our life.
      Lord Jesus, come in glory.

C   When we eat this bread and drink this cup,
      we proclaim your death, Lord Jesus,
      until you come in glory.

D   Lord, by your cross and resurrection
      you have set us free.
      You are the Savior of the world.

[*The Memorial Prayer*]

Father, calling to mind the death your Son endured
for our salvation,

his glorious resurrection and ascension into heaven, **3**
and ready to greet him when he comes again,
we offer you in thanksgiving this holy and living
   sacrifice.
Look with favor on your Church's offering,
and see the Victim whose death has reconciled us to
   yourself.

[*Invocation of the Holy Spirit*]

Grant that we, who are nourished by his body and
   blood,
may be filled with his Holy Spirit,
and become one body, one spirit in Christ.

[*Intercessions: In Communion with the Saints*]

May he make us an everlasting gift to you
and enable us to share in the inheritance of your
   saints,
with Mary, the virgin mother of God;
with the apostles, the martyrs,
(Saint *N.*) and all your saints,
on whose constant intercession we rely for help.

[*For the Church*]

Lord, may this sacrifice, which has made our peace
   with you,
advance the peace and salvation of all the world.
Strengthen in faith and love your pilgrim Church on
   earth:
your servant, Pope *N.*, our bishop *N.*,
and all the bishops,
with the clergy and the entire people your Son has
   gained for you.
Father, hear the prayers of the family you have
   gathered here before you.

3 In mercy and love unite all your children
wherever they may be.*

[*For the Dead*]

Welcome into your kingdom our departed brothers
and sisters,
and all who have left this world in your friendship.
We hope to enjoy for ever the vision of your glory,
through Christ our Lord, from whom all good things
come.

[*Concluding Doxology*]

Through him,
with him,
in him,
in the unity of the Holy Spirit,
all glory and honor is yours,
almighty Father,
for ever and ever.

All reply: **Amen.**

Continue with the Mass, as on p. 646.

___

* In Masses for the Dead the following is said:
Remember *N*.
In baptism he (she) died with Christ:
may he (she) also share his resurrection,
when Christ will raise our mortal bodies
and make them like his own in glory.
Welcome into your kingdom our departed brothers and
sisters,
and all who have left this world in your friendship.
There we hope to share in your glory
when every tear will be wiped away.
On that day we shall see you, our God, as you are.
We shall become like you
and praise you for ever through Christ our Lord,
from whom all good things come.
Through him, etc., *as above.*

EUCHARISTIC PRAYER No. 4

℣. The Lord be with you. **STAND**

℟. **And also with you.**

℣. Lift up your hearts.

℟. **We lift them up to the Lord.**

℣. Let us give thanks to the Lord our God.

℟. **It is right to give him thanks and praise.**

PREFACE

Father in heaven, it is right that we should give you thanks and glory:

you alone are God, living and true.

Through all eternity you live in unapproachable light.

Source of life and goodness, you have created all things, to fill your creatures with every blessing and lead all men to the joyful vision of your light.

Countless hosts of angels stand before you to do your will;

they look upon your splendor

and praise you, night and day.

United with them, and in the name of every creature under heaven,

we too praise your glory as we sing (say):

SANCTUS   [*First Acclamation of the People*]

Holy, holy, holy Lord, God of power and might, heaven and earth are full of your glory.

    Hosanna in the highest.

Blessed is he who comes in the name of the Lord.

    Hosanna in the highest.   **KNEEL**

[*Praise to the Father*]

Father, we acknowledge your greatness:

all your actions show your wisdom and love.

641

4 You formed man in your own likeness
and set him over the whole world
to serve you, his creator,
and to rule over all creatures.
Even when he disobeyed you and lost your friendship
you did not abandon him to the power of death,
but helped all men to seek and find you.
Again and again you offered a covenant to man,
and through the prophets taught him to hope for
    salvation.
Father, you so loved the world
that in the fullness of time you sent your only Son
    to be our Savior.
He was conceived through the power of the Holy
    Spirit, and born of the Virgin Mary,
a man like us in all things but sin.
To the poor he proclaimed the good news of salva-
    tion,
to prisoners, freedom,
and to those in sorrow, joy.
In fulfillment of your will
he gave himself up to death;
but by rising from the dead,
he destroyed death and restored life.
And that we might live no longer for ourselves but
    for him,
he sent the Holy Spirit from you, Father,
as his first gift to those who believe,
to complete his work on earth
and bring us the fullness of grace.

[*Invocation of the Holy Spirit*]

Father, may this Holy Spirit sanctify these offerings.
Let them become the body and blood of Jesus Christ
    our Lord

4

as we celebrate the great mystery
which he left us as an everlasting covenant.

[*The Lord's Supper*]

He always loved those who were his own in the
 world.
When the time came for him to be glorified by you,
 his heavenly Father,
he showed the depth of his love.
While they were at supper,
he took bread, said the blessing, broke the bread
and gave it to his disciples, saying:

Take this, all of you, and eat it:
this is my body which will be given up for you.

In the same way, he took the cup, filled with wine.
He gave you thanks, and giving the cup to his disciples, said:

Take this, all of you, and drink from it:
this is the cup of my blood,
the blood of the new and everlasting covenant.
It will be shed for you and for all men
so that sins may be forgiven.
Do this in memory of me.

[*Memorial Acclamation*]

Priest: Let us proclaim the mystery of faith.

PEOPLE:

A **Christ has died,**
 Christ is risen,
 Christ will come again.

B   Dying you destroyed our death,
rising you restored our life.
Lord Jesus, come in glory.

C   When we eat this bread and drink this cup,
we proclaim your death, Lord Jesus,
until you come in glory.

D   Lord, by your cross and resurrection
you have set us free.
You are the Savior of the world.

[*The Memorial Prayer*]

Father, we now celebrate this memorial of our redemption.

We recall Christ's death, his descent among the dead,
his resurrection, and his ascension to your right
hand;

and, looking forward to his coming in glory, we
offer you his body and blood,

the acceptable sacrifice which brings salvation to
the whole world.

Lord, look upon this sacrifice which you have given
to your Church;

and by your Holy Spirit, gather all who share this
bread and wine

into the one body of Christ, a living sacrifice of
praise.

[*Intercessions: For the Church*]

Lord, remember those for whom we offer this sacrifice.

especially N., our Pope,
N., our bishop, and bishops and clergy everywhere.

Remember those who take part in this offering,
those here present and all your people,
and all who seek you with a sincere heart.

[*For the Dead*]

Remember those who have died in the peace of
    Christ
and all the dead whose faith is known to you alone.

[*In Communion with the Saints*]

Father, in your mercy grant also to us, your chil-
    dren,
to enter into our heavenly inheritance
in the company of the Virgin Mary, the mother of
    God,
and your apostles and saints.

Then, in your kingdom, freed from the corruption of
    sin and death,
we shall sing your glory with every creature through
    Christ our Lord,
through whom you give us everything that is good.

Through him,   [*Concluding Doxology*]
with him,
in him,
in the unity of the Holy Spirit,
all glory and honor is yours,
almighty Father,
for ever and ever.

All reply: **Amen.**

COMMUNION RITE

To prepare for the paschal meal, to welcome the Lord, we pray for forgiveness and exchange a sign of peace. Before eating Christ's body and drinking his blood, we must be one with him and with all our brothers in the Church.

24 LORD'S PRAYER

STAND

Priest:

A Let us pray with confidence to the Father
in the words our Savior gave us:

B Jesus taught us to call God our Father,
and so we have the courage to say:

C Let us ask our Father to forgive our sins
and to bring us to forgive those who sin against us.

D Let us pray for the coming of the kingdom
as Jesus taught us.

Priest and **PEOPLE:**

**Our Father, who art in heaven,
hallowed be thy name;
thy kingdom come;
thy will be done on earth as it is in heaven.
Give us this day our daily bread;
and forgive us our trespasses
as we forgive those who trespass against us;
and lead us not into temptation,
but deliver us from evil.**

Priest: Deliver us, Lord, from every evil,
and grant us peace in our day.
In your mercy keep us free from sin

646

and protect us from all anxiety
as we wait in joyful hope
for the coming of our Savior, Jesus Christ.

**PEOPLE: For the kingdom, the power, and the
glory are yours, now and for ever.**

25 SIGN OF PEACE

The Church is a community of Christians joined by the
Spirit in love. It needs to express, deepen, and restore its
peaceful unity before eating the one Body of the Lord and
drinking from the one cup of salvation. We do this by a sign
of peace.

The priest says the prayer for peace:

Lord Jesus Christ, you said to your apostles:
I leave you peace, my peace I give you.
Look not on our sins, but on the faith of your
    Church,
and grant us the peace and unity of your kingdom
where you live for ever and ever.

PEOPLE: Amen.

Priest: The peace of the Lord be with you al-
    ways.

PEOPLE: And also with you.

Deacon (or priest):

    Let us offer each other the sign of peace.

*The people exchange a sign of peace and love, ac-
cording to local custom.*

26 BREAKING OF THE BREAD

Christians are gathered for the "breaking of the bread,"
another name for the Mass. In communion, though many
we are made one body in the one bread, which is Christ.

Then the following is sung or said:

PEOPLE:

**Lamb of God, you take away the sins of the
    world:**

   have mercy on us.

**Lamb of God, you take away the sins of the
    world:**

   have mercy on us.

**Lamb of God, you take away the sins of the
    world:**

   grant us peace.

> *The hymn may be repeated until the breaking of
> the bread is finished, but the last phrase is al-
> ways: "Grant us peace."*

> *Meanwhile the priest breaks the host over the
> paten and places a small piece in the chalice,
> saying quietly:*

May this mingling of the body and blood of our Lord
    Jesus Christ

bring eternal life to us who receive it.

27 PRAYERS BEFORE COMMUNION

We pray in silence and then voice words of humility and
hope as our final preparation before meeting Christ in the
Eucharist.

> *Before communion, the priest says quietly one of
> the following prayers:*

Lord Jesus Christ, Son of the living God, by the will
of the Father and the work of the Holy Spirit your
death brought life to the world. By your holy body
and blood free me from all my sins and from every
evil. Keep me faithful to your teaching, and never
let me be parted from you.

OR: Lord Jesus Christ, with faith in your love and mercy, I eat your body and drink your blood. Let it not bring me condemnation, but health in mind and body.

28 RECEPTION OF COMMUNION

The priest genuflects. Holding the host elevated slightly over the paten, the priest says:

Priest: This is the Lamb of God
who takes away the sins of the world.
Happy are those who are called to his supper.

Priest and **PEOPLE** (once only):

Lord, I am not worthy to receive you,
but only say the word and I shall be healed.

Before receiving communion, the priest says quietly: May the body of Christ bring me to everlasting life. May the blood of Christ bring me to everlasting life. *He then gives communion to the people.*

Priest: The body of Christ: Communicant. **Amen.**

29 COMMUNION SONG or ANTIPHON

The Communion Psalm or other appropriate Song or Hymn is sung while Communion is given to the faithful. If there is no singing, the Communion Antiphon is said:

> **➤ Turn to Today's Mass**

The vessels are cleansed by the priest or deacon. Meanwhile he says quietly:

Lord, may I receive these gifts in purity of heart. May they bring me healing and strength, now and for ever.

30 PERIOD OF SILENCE or Song of Praise

After communion there may be a period of silence, or a song of praise may be sung.

31 PRAYER AFTER COMMUNION   STAND

The priest prays in our name that we may live the life of faith since we have been strengthened by Christ himself. Our Amen makes his prayer our own.

Priest: Let us pray.

Priest and people may pray silently for a while. Then the priest says the prayer after communion.

> **→ Turn to Today's Mass**

At the end,   **PEOPLE:** **Amen.**

CONCLUDING RITE

We have heard God's Word and eaten the body of Christ. Now it is time for us to leave, to do good works, to praise and bless the Lord in our daily lives.

32 GREETING   STAND

After any brief announcements (sit), the blessing and dismissal follow:

Priest: The Lord be with you.

PEOPLE: **And also with you.**

33 BLESSING

A Simple form

Priest: May almighty God bless you, the **Father,** and the Son, ✠ and the Holy Spirit.

PEOPLE: Amen.

On certain days or occasions another more solemn form of blessing or prayer over the people may be used as the rubrics direct.

B Solemn blessing

Texts of all the solemn blessings are given on pp. 682-689.

Deacon: Bow your heads and pray for God's blessing.

The priest always concludes the solemn blessing by adding:

May almighty God bless you,
the Father, and the Son, ✠ and the Holy Spirit.

PEOPLE: Amen.

C Prayer over the people

Texts of all prayers over the people are given on pp. 689-693.

After the prayer over the people, the priest always adds:

And may the blessing of almighty God,
the Father, and the Son, ✠ and the Holy Spirit,
come upon you and remain with you for ever.

PEOPLE: Amen.

34 DISMISSAL

Deacon (or priest):

A Go in the peace of Christ.

B The Mass is ended, go in peace.

C Go in peace to love and serve the Lord.

PEOPLE: Thanks be to God.

If any liturgical service follows immediately, the rite of dismissal is omitted.

RITE OF BLESSING AND
SPRINKLING HOLY WATER

When this rite is celebrated it takes the place of the penitential rite at the beginning of Mass. The Kyrie is also omitted.

After greeting the people the priest remains standing at his chair. A vessel containing the water to be blessed is placed before him. Facing the people, he invites them to pray, using these or similar words:

Dear friends,
this water will be used
to remind us of our baptism.
Let us ask God to bless it,
and to keep us faithful
to the Spirit he has given us.

After a brief silence, he joins his hands and continues:

A.

God our Father,
your gift of water
brings life and freshness to the earth;
it washes away our sins
and brings us eternal life.

We ask you now
to bless ✠ this water,
and to give us your protection on this day
which you have made your own.
Renew the living spring of your life within us
and protect us in spirit and body,
that we may be free from sin
and come into your presence
to receve your gift of salvation.
We ask this through Christ our Lord. ℟. **Amen.**

B. Or:

Lord God almighty,
creator of all life,
of body and soul,

652

we ask you to bless ✚ this water:
as we use it in faith
forgive our sins
and save us from all illness
and the power of evil.

Lord,
in your mercy
give us living water,
always springing up as a fountain of salvation:
free us, body and soul, from every danger,
and admit us to your presence
in purity of heart.
Grant this through Christ our Lord.

C.   Or (during the Easter season):

Lord God almighty,
hear the prayers of your people:
we celebrate our creation and redemption.
Hear our prayers and bless ✚ this water
which gives fruitfulness to the fields,
and refreshment and cleansing to man.
You chose water to show your goodness
when you led your people to freedom
through the Red Sea
and satisfied their thirst in the desert
with water from the rock.
Water was the symbol used by the prophets
to foretell your new covenant with man.
You made the water of baptism holy
by Christ's baptism in the Jordan:
by it you give us a new birth
and renew us in holiness.
May this water remind us of our baptism,
and let us share the joy
of all who have been baptized at Easter.
We ask this through Christ our Lord.

*Where it is customary, salt may be mixed with the holy
water. The priest blesses the salt, saying:*

Almighty God,
we ask you to bless ✝ this salt
as once you blessed the salt scattered over the water
by the prophet Elisha.
Wherever this salt and water are sprinkled,
drive away the power of evil,
and protect us always
by the presence of your Holy Spirit.
Grant this through Christ our Lord.

Then he pours the salt into the water in silence.

*Taking the sprinkler, the priest sprinkles himself and
his ministers, then the rest of the clergy and people.
He may move through the church for the sprinkling of
the people. Meanwhile, an antiphon or another appropriate song is sung.*

*When he returns to his place and the song is finished,
the priest faces the people and, with joined hands, says:*

May almighty God cleanse us of our sins,
and through the eucharist we celebrate
make us worthy to sit at his table
in his heavenly kingdom.

The people answer: Amen.

When it is prescribed, the Gloria *is then sung or said.*

PENITENTIAL RITE

ALTERNATIVE FORMS FOR C p. 617

ii

Priest or other minister:
Lord Jesus, you came to gather the nations
into the peace of God's kingdom:
Lord, have mercy.

People: **Lord, have mercy.**

Priest or other minister:
You come in word and sacrament to strengthen us in
   holiness:
Christ, have mercy.

People: **Christ, have mercy.**

Priest or other minister:
You will come in glory with salvation for your people:
Lord, have mercy.

People: **Lord, have mercy.**   (➤ p. 617)

iii

Priest or other minister:
Lord Jesus, you are mighty God and Prince of peace:
Lord, have mercy.

People: **Lord, have mercy.**

Priest or other minister:
Lord Jesus, you are Son of God and Son of Mary:
Christ, have mercy.

People: **Christ, have mercy.**

Priest or other minister:
Lord Jesus, you are Word made flesh and splendor of
   the Father:
Lord, have mercy.

People: **Lord, have mercy.**   (➤ p. 617)

655

iv

Priest or other minister:
Lord Jesus, you came to reconcile us
to one another and to the Father:
Lord, have mercy.

People: **Lord, have mercy.**

Priest or other minister:
Lord Jesus, you heal the wounds of sin and division:
Christ, have mercy.

People: **Christ, have mercy.**

Priest or other minister:
Lord Jesus, you intercede for us with your Father:
Lord, have mercy.

People: **Lord, have mercy.**   (➤ p. 617)

v

Priest or other minister:
You raise the dead to life in the Spirit:
Lord, have mercy.

People: **Lord, have mercy.**

Priest or other minister:
You bring pardon and peace to the sinner:
Christ, have mercy.

People: **Christ, have mercy.**

Priest or other minister:
You bring light to those in darkness:
Lord, have mercy.

People: **Lord, have mercy.**   (➤ p. 617)

vi

Priest or other minister:
Lord Jesus, you raise us to new life:
Lord, have mercy.

People: **Lord, have mercy.**

Priest or other minister:
Lord Jesus, you forgive us our sins:
Christ, have mercy.

People: **Christ, have mercy.**

Priest or other minister:
Lord Jesus, you feed us with your body and blood:
Lord, have mercy.

People: **Lord, have mercy.**   (➤ p. 617)

vii

Priest or other minister:
Lord Jesus, you have shown us the way to the Father:
Lord, have mercy.

People: **Lord, have mercy.**

Priest or other minister:
Lord Jesus, you have given us the consolation of the
   truth:
Christ, have mercy.

People: **Christ, have mercy.**

Priest or other minister:
Lord Jesus, you are the Good Shepherd,
leading us into everlasting life:
Lord, have mercy.

People: **Lord, have mercy.**   (➤ p. 617)

viii

Priest or other minister:
Lord Jesus, you healed the sick:
Lord, have mercy.

People: **Lord, have mercy.**

Priest or other minister:
Lord Jesus, you forgave sinners:
Christ, have mercy.

People: **Christ, have mercy.**

Priest or other minister:
Lord Jesus, you give us yourself to heal us and bring us
   strength:
Lord, have mercy.

People: **Lord, have mercy.**   (➤ p. 617)

PREFACES
ADVENT I (P 1)

The Two Comings of Christ
(From the First Sunday of Advent to December 16)

Father, all-powerful and ever-living God,
we do well always and everywhere to give you thanks
through Jesus Christ our Lord.

When he humbled himself to come among us as a man,
he fulfilled the plan you formed long ago
and opened for us the way to salvation.

Now we watch for the day
hoping that the salvation promised us will be ours
when Christ our Lord will come again in his glory.

And so, with all the choirs of angels in heaven
we proclaim your glory
and join in their unending hymn of praise: ➤ No. 23, p. 627

ADVENT II (P 2)

Waiting for the Two Comings of Christ
(From December 17 to December 24)

Father, all-powerful and ever-living God,
we do well always and everywhere to give you thanks
through Jesus Christ our Lord.

His future coming was proclaimed by all the prophets.
The virgin mother bore him in her womb
   with love beyond all telling.
John the Baptist was his herald
and made him known when at last he came.

In his love he has filled us with joy
as we prepare to celebrate his birth,
so that when he comes he may find us watching in prayer,
our hearts filled with wonder and praise.

And so, with all the choirs of angels in heaven
we proclaim your glory
and join in their unending hymn of praise: ➤ No. 23, p. 627

CHRISTMAS I (P 3)

Christ the Light
(From Christmas to Saturday before Epiphany)

Father, all-powerful and ever-living God,
we do well always and everywhere to give you thanks
through Jesus Christ our Lord.

In the wonder of the incarnation
your eternal Word has brought to the eyes of faith
a new and radiant vision of your glory.
In him we see our God made visible
and so are caught up in love of the God we cannot see.

And so, with all the choirs of angels in heaven
we proclaim you glory
and join in the unending hymn of praise:➤ No. 23, p. 627

CHRISTMAS II (P 4)

Christ Restores Unity to All Creation
(From Christmas to Saturday before Epiphany)

Father, all-powerful and ever-living God,
we do well always and everywhere to give you thanks
through Jesus Christ our Lord.

Today you fill our hearts with joy
as we recognize in Christ the revelation of your love.
No eye can see his glory as our God,
yet now he is seen as one like us.

Christ is your Son before all ages,
yet now he is born in time.
He has come to lift up all things to himself,
to restore unity to creation,
and to lead mankind from exile into your heavenly
    kingdom.

With all the angels of heaven
we sing our joyful hymn of praise: ➤ No. 23, p. 627

CHRISTMAS III (P 5)

Divine and Human Exchange in the Incarnation of the Word
(From Christmas to Saturday before Epiphany)

Father, all-powerful and ever-living God,
we do well always and everywhere to give you thanks

through Jesus Christ our Lord.
Today in him a new light has dawned upon the world:
God has become one with man,
and man has become one again with God.

Your eternal Word has taken upon himself our human
   weakness,
giving our mortal nature immortal value.
So marvelous is this oneness between God and man
that in Christ man restores to man the gift of everlasting
   life.

In our joy we sing to your glory
with all the choirs of angels: ➤ No. 23, p. 627

EPIPHANY (P 6)

Christ the Light of the Nations

Father, all-powerful and ever-living God,
we do well always and everywhere to give you thanks.

Today you revealed in Christ your eternal plan of salvation
and showed him as the light of all peoples.
Now that his glory has shone among us
you have renewed humanity in his immortal image.

Now, with angels and archangels,
and the whole company of heaven,
we sing the unending hymn of your praise:
➤ No. 23, p. 627

LENT I (P 8)

The Spiritual Meaning of Lent

Father, all-powerful and ever-living God,
we do well always and everywhere to give you thanks
through Jesus Christ our Lord.

Each year you give us this joyful season
when we prepare to celebrate the paschal mystery
with mind and heart renewed.
You give us a spirit of loving reverence for you,
   our Father,
and of willing service to our neighbor.

As we recall the great events that gave us new life in
   Christ,
you bring the image of your Son to perfection within us.

Now, with angels and archangels,
and the whole company of heaven,
we sing the unending hymn of your praise: → No. 23, p. 627

LENT II (P 9)

The Spirit of Penance

Father, all-powerful and ever-living God,
we do well always and everywhere to give you thanks.

This great season of grace is your gift to your family
to renew us in spirit.
You give us strength to purify our hearts,
to control our desires,
and so to serve you in freedom.

You teach us how to live in this passing world
with our heart set on the world that will never end.

Now, with all the saints and angels,
we praise you for ever: → No. 23, p. 627

LENT III (P 10)

The Fruits of Self-denial

Father, all-powerful and ever-living God,
we do well always and everywhere to give you thanks.

You ask us to express our thanks by self-denial.
We are to master our sinfulness and conquer our pride.
We are to show to those in need your goodness to ourselves.

Now, with all the saints and angels,
we praise you for ever: → No. 23, p. 627

LENT IV (P 11)

The Reward of Fasting

Father, all-powerful and ever-living God,
we do well always and everywhere to give you thanks.

Through our observance of Lent
you correct our faults and raise our minds to you,
you help us grow in holiness,
and offer us the reward of everlasting life
through Jesus Christ our Lord.

Through him the angels and all the choirs of heaven
worship in awe before your presence.
May our voices be one with theirs
as they sing with joy the hymn of your glory:

➤ No. 23, p. 627

PASSION OF THE LORD I (P 17)

The Power of the Cross

Father, all-powerful and ever-living God,
we do well always and everywhere to give you thanks.

The suffering and death of your Son
brought life to the whole world,
moving our hearts to praise your glory.

The power of the cross reveals your judgment on this
    world
and the kingship of Christ crucified.

We praise you, Lord,
with all the angels and saints in their song of joy:

➤ No. 23, p. 627

PASSION OF THE LORD II (P 18)

The Victory of the Passion

Father, all-powerful and ever-living God,
we do well always and everywhere to give you thanks
through Jesus Christ our Lord.

The days of his life-giving death and glorious resurrection
    are approaching.
This is the hour when he triumphed over Satan's pride.
tl.e time when we celebrate the great event of our redemption.

Through Christ
the angels of heaven offer their prayer of adoration
as they rejoice in your presence for ever.
May our voices be one with theirs
in their triumphant hymn of praise: ➤ No. 23, p. 627

EASTER I (P 21)
The Paschal Mystery
(Easter Vigil, Easter Sunday and during the octave)

Father, all-powerful and ever-living God,
we do well always and everywhere to give you thanks
through Jesus Christ our Lord.

We praise you with greater joy than ever
on this Easter night (day),
when Christ became our paschal sacrifice.

He is the true Lamb who took away the sins of the world.
By dying he destroyed our death;
by rising he restored our life.

And so, with all the choirs of angels in heaven
we proclaim your glory
and join in their unending hymn of praise: ➤ No. 23, p. 627

EASTER II (P 22)
New Life in Christ

Father, all-powerful and ever-living God,
we do well always and everywhere to give you thanks
through Jesus Christ our Lord.

We praise you with greater joy than ever in this
    Easter season,
when Christ became our paschal sacrifice.

He has made us children of the light,
rising to new and everlasting life.
He has opened the gates of heaven
to receive his faithful people.
His death is our ransom from death;
his resurrection is our rising to life.

The joy of the resurrection renews the whole world,
while the choirs of heaven sing for ever to your glory:

➤ No. 23, p. 627

EASTER III (P 23)
Christ Lives and Intercedes for Us For Ever

Father, all-powerful and ever-living God,
we do well always and everywhere to give you thanks
through Jesus Christ our Lord.

We praise you with greater joy than ever in this
   Easter season,
when Christ became our paschal sacrifice.

He is still our priest,
our advocate who always pleads our cause.
Christ is the victim who dies no more,
the Lamb, once slain, who lives for ever.

The joy of the resurrection renews the whole world,
while the choirs of heaven sing for ever to your glory:

➤ No. 23, p. 627

EASTER IV (P 24)

*The Restoration of the Universe through the
Paschal Mystery*

Father, all-powerful and ever-living God,
we do well always and everywhere to give you thanks
through Jesus Christ our Lord.

We praise you with greater joy than ever in this
   Easter season,
when Christ became our paschal sacrifice.

In him a new age has dawned,
the long reign of sin is ended,
a broken world has been renewed,
and man is once again made whole.

The joy of the resurrection renews the whole world,
while the choirs of heaven sing for ever to your glory:

➤ No. 23, p. 627

EASTER V (P 25)

Christ Is Priest and Victim

Father, all-powerful and ever-living God,
we do well always and everywhere to give you thanks
through Jesus Christ our Lord.

We praise you with greater joy than ever in this
   Easter season,
when Christ became our paschal sacrifice.

As he offered his body on the cross,
his perfect sacrifice fulfilled all others.

As he gave himself into your hands for our salvation,
he showed himself to be the priest, the altar, and the lamb
   of sacrifice.

The joy of the resurrection renews the whole world,
while the choirs of heaven sing for ever to your glory:

> ➤ No. 23, p. 627

ASCENSION I (P 26)
The Mystery of the Ascension
(Ascension to the Saturday before Pentecost inclusive)

Father, all-powerful and ever-living God,
we do well always and everywhere to give you thanks.

[Today] the Lord Jesus, the king of glory,
the conqueror of sin and death,
ascended to heaven while the angels sang his praises.

Christ, the mediator between God and man,
judge of the world and Lord of all,
has passed beyond our sight,
not to abandon us but to be our hope.
Christ is the beginning, the head of the Church;
where he has gone, we hope to follow.

The joy of the resurrection and ascension renews the
   whole world,
while the choirs of heaven sing for ever to your glory:

> ➤ No. 23, p. 627

ASCENSION II (P 27)
The Mystery of the Ascension
(Ascension to the Saturday before Pentecost inclusive)

Father, all-powerful and ever-living God,
we do well always and everywhere to give you thanks
through Jesus Christ our Lord.

In his risen body he plainly showed himself to his disciples
and was taken up to heaven in their sight
to claim for us a share in his divine life.

And so, with all the choirs of angels in heaven
we proclaim your glory
and join in their unending hymn of praise:➤ No. 23, p. 627

WEEKDAYS I (P 37)

All Things Made One in Christ
(For Masses without Proper or Seasonal Preface)

Father, all-powerful and ever-living God,
we do well always and everywhere to give you thanks
through Jesus Christ our Lord.

In him you have renewed all things
and you have given us all a share in his riches.

Though his nature was divine,
he stripped himself of glory
and by shedding his blood on the cross
he brought his peace to the world.

Therefore he was exalted above all creation
and became the source of eternal life
to all who serve him.

And so, with all the choirs of angels in heaven
we proclaim your glory
and join in their unending hymn of praise:

➜ No. 23, p. 627

WEEKDAYS II (P 38)

Salvation Through Christ
(For Masses without Proper or Seasonal Preface)

Father, all-powerful and ever-living God,
we do well always and everywhere to give you thanks.

In love you created man,
in justice you condemned him,
but in mercy you redeemed him,
through Jesus Christ our Lord.

Through him the angels and all the choirs of heaven
worship in awe before your presence.
May our voices be one with theirs
as they sing with joy
the hymn of your glory:

➜ No. 23, p. 627

WEEKDAYS III (P 38)

Praise of God in Creation and through the Conversion of Man
(For Masses without Proper or Seasonal Preface)

Father, all-powerful and ever-living God,
we do well always and everywhere to give you thanks.

Through your beloved Son
you created our human family.
Through him you restored us to your likeness.

Therefore it is your right
to receive the obedience of all creation,
the praise of the Church on earth,
the thanksgiving of your saints in heaven.

We too rejoice with the angels
as we proclaim your glory for ever: ➤ No. 23, p. 627

WEEKDAYS IV (P 40)

Praise of God Is His Gift
(For Masses without Proper or Seasonal Preface)

Father, all-powerful and ever-living God,
we do well always and everywhere to give you thanks.

You have no need of our praise,
yet our desire to thank you is itself your gift.
Our prayer of thanksgiving adds nothing to your greatness,
but makes us grow in your grace,
through Jesus Christ our Lord.

In our joy we sing to your glory
with all the choirs of angels:

WEEKDAYS V (P 41)

The Mystery of Christ Is Proclaimed
(For Masses without Proper or Seasonal Preface)

Father, all-powerful and ever-living God,
we do well always and everywhere to give you thanks
through Jesus Christ our Lord.

With love we celebrate his death.
With living faith we proclaim his resurrection.
With unwavering hope we await his return in glory.

Now, with the saints and all the angels
we praise you for ever: ➤ No. 23, p. 627

WEEKDAYS VI (P 42)

Salvation in Christ

(For Masses without Proper or Seasonal Preface)

Father, it is our duty and our salvation,
always and everywhere
to give you thanks
through your beloved Son, Jesus Christ.

He is the Word through whom you made the universe,
the Savior you sent to redeem us.
By the power of the Holy Spirit
he took flesh and was born of the Virgin Mary.

For our sake he opened his arms on the cross;
he put an end to death
and revealed the resurrection.
In this he fulfilled your will
and won for you a holy people.

And so we join the angels and the saints
in proclaiming your glory: ➤ No. 23, p. 627

HOLY EUCHARIST I (P 47)

Father, all-powerful and ever-living God,
we do well always and everywhere to give you thanks
through Jesus Christ our Lord.

He is the true and eternal priest
who established this unending sacrifice.
He offered himself as a victim for our deliverance
and taught us to make this offering in his memory.
As we eat his body which he gave for us.
we grow in strength.
As we drink his blood which he poured out for us,
we are washed clean.

Now, with angels and archangels,
and the whole company of heaven,
we sing the unending hymn of your praise: ➤ No. 23, p. 627

HOLY EUCHARIST II (P 48)

Father, all-powerful and ever-living God,
we do well always and everywhere to give you thanks
through Jesus Christ our Lord.

At the last supper,
as he sat at table with his apostles,
he offered himself to you as the spotless lamb,
the acceptable gift that gives you perfect praise.
Christ has given us this memorial of his passion
to bring us its saving power until the end of time.

In this great sacrament you feed your people
and strengthen them in holiness,
so that the family of mankind
may come to walk in the light of one faith,
in one communion of love.
We come then to this wonderful sacrament
to be fed at your table
and grow into the likeness of the risen Christ.

Earth unites with heaven
to sing the new song of creation
as we adore and praise you for ever: ➤ No. 23, p. 627

DEDICATION OF A CHURCH I (P 52)

In the Dedicated Church

Father, all-powerful and ever-living God,
we do well always and everywhere to give you thanks.

We thank you now for this house of prayer
in which you bless your family
as we come to you on pilgrimage.

Here you reveal your presence
by sacramental signs,
and make us one with you
through the unseen bond of grace.
Here you build your temple of living stones,
and bring the Church to its full stature
as the body of Christ throughout the world,
to reach its perfection at last
in the heavenly city of Jerusalem,

which is the vision of your peace.

In communion with all the angels and saints
we bless and praise your greatness
in the temple of your glory: → No. 23, p. 627

DEDICATION OF A CHURCH II (P 53)

Outside the Dedicated Church

Father, all-powerful and ever-living God,
we do well always and everywhere to give you thanks.

Your house is a house of prayer,
and your presence makes it a place of blessing.
You give us grace upon grace
to build the temple of your Spirit,
creating its beauty from the holiness of our lives.

Your house of prayer
is also the promise of the Church in heaven.
Here your love is always at work.
preparing the Church on earth
for its heavenly glory
as the sinless bride of Christ,
the joyful mother of a great company of saints.

Now, with the saints and all the angels
we praise you for ever: → No. 23, p. 627

HOLY SPIRIT I (P 54)

(For Votive Masses of the Holy Spirit)

Father, all-powerful and ever-living God,
we do well always and everywhere to give you thanks
through Jesus Christ our Lord.

He ascended above all the heavens,
and from his throne at your right hand
poured into the hearts of your adopted children
the Holy Spirit of your promise.

With steadfast love
we sing your unending praise;
we join with the hosts of heaven
in their triumphant song: → No. 23, p. 627

HOLY SPIRIT II (P 55)

(For Votive Masses of the Holy Spirit)

Father, all-powerful and ever-living God,
we do well always and everywhere to give you thanks.
You give your gifts of grace
for every time and season
as you guide the Church
in the marvelous ways of your providence.

You give us your Holy Spirit
to help us always by his power,
so that with loving trust
we may turn to you in all our troubles,
and give you thanks in all our joys,
through Jesus Christ our Lord.

In our joy we sing to your glory
with all the choirs of angels: ➤ No. 23, p. 627

BLESSED VIRGIN MARY I (P 56)

Motherhood of Mary

Father, all-powerful and ever-living God,
we do well always and everywhere to give you thanks
(as we celebrate . . . of the Blessed Virgin Mary).
(as we honor the Blessed Virgin Mary).

Through the power of the Holy Spirit,
she became the virgin mother of your only Son,
our Lord Jesus Christ,
who is for ever the light of the world.

Through him the choirs of angels
and all the powers of heaven
praise and worship your glory.
May our voices blend with theirs
as we join in their unending hymn: ➤ No. 23, p. 627

BLESSED VIRGIN MARY II (P 57)

The Church Echoes Mary's Song of Praise

Father, all-powerful and ever-living God,
we do well always and everywhere to give you thanks,
and to praise you for your gifts
as we contemplate your saints in glory.

In celebrating the memory of the Blessed Virgin Mary,
it is our special joy to echo her song of thanksgiving.
What wonders you have worked throughout the world.
All generations have shared the greatness of your love.
When you looked on Mary your lowly servant,
you raised her to be the mother of Jesus Christ, your
  Son, our Lord,
the savior of all mankind.

Through him the angels of heaven
offer their prayer of adoration
as they rejoice in your presence for ever.
May our voices be one with theirs
in their triumphant hymn of praise: ➤ No. 23, p. 627

ANGELS (P 60)

The Glory of God in the Angels

Father, all-powerful and ever-living God,
we do well always and everywhere to give you thanks.

In praising your faithful angels and archangels,
we also praise your glory,
for in honoring them, we honor you, their creator.
Their splendor shows us your greatness,
which surpasses in goodness the whole of creation.

Through Christ our Lord
the great army of angels rejoices in your glory.
In adoration and joy
we make their hymn of praise our own: ➤ No. 23, p. 627

APOSTLES I (P 64)

The Apostles Are Shepherds of God's People
(For Masses of the apostles)

Father, all-powerful and ever-living God,
we do well always and everywhere to give you thanks.

You are the eternal Shepherd
who never leaves his flock untended.
Through the apostles
you watch over us and protect us always.
You made them shepherds of the flock
to share in the work of your Son,
and from their place in heaven they guide us still.

And so, with all the choirs of angels in heaven
we proclaim your glory
and join in their unending hymn of praise: ➤ No. 23, p. 627

APOSTLES II (P 65)

Apostolic Foundation and Witness
(For Masses of the apostles and evangelists)

Father, all-powerful and ever-living God,
we do well always and everywhere to give you thanks.
You founded your Church on the apostles
to stand firm for ever
as the sign on earth of your infinite holiness
and as the living gospel for all men to hear.
With steadfast love
we sing your unending praise:
we join with the hosts of heaven
in their triumphant song: ➤ No. 23, p. 627

MARTYRS (P 66)

The Sign and Example of Martyrdom
(For solemnities and feasts of martyrs)

Father, all-powerful and ever-living God,
we do well always and everywhere to give you thanks.
Your holy martyr N. followed the example of Christ,
and gave his (her) life for the glory of your name.
His (her) death reveals your power
shining through our human weakness.
You choose the weak and make them strong
in bearing witness to you,
through Jesus Christ our Lord.
In our unending joy we echo on earth
the song of the angels in heaven
as they praise your glory for ever: ➤ No. 23, p. 627

PASTORS (P 67)

The Presence of Shepherds in the Church
(For solemnities and feasts of pastors)

Father, all-powerful and ever-living God,
we do well always and everywhere to give you thanks.

You give the Church this feast in honor of Saint N.;
you inspire us by his holy life,
instruct us by his preaching,
and give us your protection in answer to his prayers.

We join the angels and the saints
as they sing their unending hymn of praise:

→ No. 23, p. 627

VIRGINS AND RELIGIOUS (P 68)

The Sign of a Life Consecrated to God

(For solemnities and feasts of virgins and religious)

Father, all-powerful and ever-living God,
we do well always and everywhere to give you thanks.

Today we honor your saints
who consecrated their lives to Christ
for the sake of the kingdom of heaven.
What love you show us
as you recall mankind to its innocence,
and invite us to taste on earth
the gifts of the world to come!

Now, with the saints and all the angels
we praise you for ever: → No. 23, p. 627

HOLY MEN AND WOMEN I (P 69)

The Glory of the Saints

(For Masses of all saints, patrons, and titulars of churches, and
on the solemnities and feasts of saints which have no Proper Preface)

Father, all-powerful and ever-living God,
we do well always and everywhere to give you thanks.

You are glorified in your saints,
for their glory is the crowning of your gifts.
In their lives on earth
you give us an example.
In our communion with them,
you give us their friendship.
In their prayer for the Church
you give us strength and protection.
This great company of witnesses spurs us on to victory,
to share their prize of everlasting glory,
through Jesus Christ our Lord.

With angels and archangels
and the whole company of saints
we sing our unending hymn of praise: ➤ No. 23, p. 627

HOLY MEN AND WOMEN II (P 70)

The Activity of the Saints

(For Masses of all saints, patrons, and titulars of churches, and on the solemnities and feasts of saints which have no Proper Preface)

Father, all-powerful and ever-living God,
we do well always and everywhere to give you thanks.

You renew the Church in every age
by raising up men and women outstanding in holiness,
living witnesses of your unchanging love.
They inspire us by their heroic lives,
and help us by their constant prayers
to be the living sign of your saving power.

We praise you, Lord, with all the angels and saints
in their song of joy: ➤ No. 23, p. 627

RELIGIOUS PROFESSION (P 75)

Father, all-powerful and ever-living God,
we do well always and everywhere to give you thanks
through Jesus Christ our Lord.

He came, the son of a virgin mother,
named those blessed who were pure of heart,
and taught by his whole life the perfection of chastity.

He chose always to fulfill your holy will,
and became obedient even to dying for us,
offering himself to you as a perfect oblation.

He consecrated more closely to your service
those who leave all things for your sake,
and promised that they would find a heavenly treasure.

And so, with all the angels and saints
we proclaim your glory
and join in their unending hymn of praise: ➤ No. 23, p. 627

CHRISTIAN UNITY (P 76)

Father, all-powerful and ever-living God,
we do well always and everywhere to give you thanks
through Jesus Christ our Lord.

Through Christ you bring us to the knowledge of your
     truth,
that we may be united by one faith and one baptism
to become his body.
Through Christ you have given the Holy Spirit to all peo-
     ples.
How wonderful are the works of the Spirit,
revealed in so many gifts!
Yet how marvelous is the unity
the Spirit creates from their diversity,
as he dwells in the hearts of your children,
filling the whole Church with his presence
and guiding it with his wisdom!

In our joy we sing to your glory
with all the choirs of angels: ➤ No. 23, p. 627

CHRISTIAN DEATH I (P 77)

Father, all-powerful and ever-living God,
we do all always and everywhere to give you thanks
through Jesus Christ our Lord.

In him, who rose from the dead,
our hope of resurrection dawned.
The sadness of death gives way
to the bright promise of immortality.

Lord, for your faithful people life is changed, not ended.
When the body of our earthly dwelling lies in death
we gain an everlasting dwelling place in heaven.

And so, with all the choirs of angels in heaven
we proclaim your glory
and join in their unending hymn of praise:

     ➤ No. 23, p. 627

CHRISTIAN DEATH II (P 78)

Father, all-powerful and ever-living God,
we do well always and everywhere to give you thanks
through Jesus Christ our Lord.

He chose to die
that he might free all men from dying.
He gave his life
that we might live to you alone for ever.

In our joy we sing to your glory
with all the choirs of angels: ➤ No. 23, p. 627

CHRISTIAN DEATH III (P 79)

Father, all-powerful and ever-living God,
we do all always and everywhere to give you thanks
through Jesus Christ our Lord.

In him the world is saved,
man is reborn,
and the dead rise again to life.

Through Christ the angels of heaven
offer their prayer of adoration
as they rejoice in your presence for ever.
May our voices be one with theirs
in their triumphant hymn of praise: ➤ No. 23, p. 627

CHRISTIAN DEATH IV (P 80)

Father, all-powerful and ever-living God,
we do well always and everywhere to give you thanks.

By your power you bring us to birth.
By your providence you rule our lives.
By your command you free us at last from sin
as we return to the dust from which we came.
Through the saving death of your Son
we rise at your word to the glory of the resurrection.

Now we join the angels and the saints
as they sing their unending hymn of praise:

➤ No. 23, p. 627

CHRISTIAN DEATH V (P 81)

Father, all-powerful and ever-living God,
we do well always and everywhere to give you thanks
through Jesus Christ our Lord.

Death is the just reward for our sins,
yet, when at last we die,
your loving kindness calls us back to life
in company with Christ
whose victory is our redemption.

Our hearts are joyful,
for we have seen your salvation,
and now with the angels and saints
we praise you for ever:

➤ No. 23, p. 627

INDEPENDENCE DAY AND OTHER CIVIC OBSERVANCES I (P 82)

Father, all-powerful and ever-living God,
we do well to sing your praise for ever,
and to give you thanks in all we do
through Jesus Christ our Lord.

He spoke to men a message of peace
and taught us to live as brothers.
His message took form in the vision of our fathers
as they fashioned a nation
where men might live as one.
This message lives on in our midst
as a task for men today
and a promise for tomorrow.

We thank you, Father, for your blessings in the past
and for all that, with your help, we must yet achieve.
And so, with hearts full of love,
we join the angels today and every day of our lives,
to sing your glory in a hymn of endless praise:

➤ No. 23, p. 627

INDEPENDENCE DAY AND OTHER CIVIC OBSERVANCES II (P 83)

Father, all-powerful and ever-living God,
we praise your oneness and truth.

We praise you as the God of creation,
and the Father of Jesus, the Savior of mankind,
in whose image we seek to live.
He loved the children of the lands he walked
and enriched them with his witness of justice and truth.
He lived and died that we might be reborn in the Spirit
and filled with love of all men.

And so, with hearts full of love,
we join the angels, today and every day of our lives,
to sing your glory in a hymn of endless praise:

➤ No. 23, p. 627

THANKSGIVING DAY (P 84)

Father,
we do well to join all creation,
in heaven and on earth,
in praising you, our mighty God
through Jesus Christ our Lord.

You made man to your own image
and set him over all creation.
Once you chose a people
and gave them a destiny
and, when you brought them out of bondage to freedom,
they carried with them the promise
that all men would be blessed
and all men could be free.

What the prophets pledged
was fulfilled in Jesus Christ,
your Son and our saving Lord.
It has come to pass in every generation
for all men who have believed that Jesus
by his death and resurrection
gave them a new freedom in his Spirit.

It happened to our fathers,
who came to this land as if out of the desert
into a place of promise and hope.
It happens to us still, in our time,
as you lead all men through your Church
to the blessed vision of peace.

And so, with hearts full of love,
we join the angels, today and every day of our lives,
to sing your glory in a hymn of endless praise:

➤ No. 23, p. 627

PROPER COMMUNICANTES
AND HANC IGITUR
FOR EUCHARISTIC PRAYER I

Communicantes for Christmas

In union with the whole Church
we celebrate that day (night)
when Mary without loss of her virginity
gave this world its savior.
We honor her,
the ever-virgin mother of Jesus Christ, our Lord and
   God, etc., p. 629.

Communicantes for the Epiphany

In union with the whole Church
we celebrate that day
when your only Son,
sharing your eternal glory,
showed himself in a human body.
We honor Mary, etc., p. 629.

Communicantes for Easter

In union with the whole Church
we celebrate that day (night)
when Jesus Christ, our Lord,
rose from the dead in his human body.
We honor Mary, etc., p. 629.

Hanc Igitur for Easter

Father, accept this offering
from your whole family
and from those born into the new life
of water and the Holy Spirit,
with all their sins forgiven.
Grant us your peace in this life,
save us from final damnation,
and count us among those you have chosen.
[Through Christ our Lord. Amen.]

➤ *Canon, p. 629: Bless, etc.*

Communicantes for the Ascension

In union with the whole Church
we celebrate that day
when your only Son, our Lord,
took his place with you
and raised our frail human nature to glorv.
We honor Mary, etc., p. 629.

Communicantes for Pentecost

In union with the whole Church
we celebrate the day of Pentecost
when the Holy Spirit appeared to the apostles
in the form of countless tongues.
We honor Mary, etc., p. 629.

Hanc Igitur for Pentecost

Father, accept this offering
from your whole family
and from those born into the new life
of water and the Holy Spirit,
with all their sins forgiven.
Grant us your peace in this life,
save us from final damnation,
and count us among those you have chosen.
[Through Christ our Lord. Amen.]

➤ *Canon,* **p. 629:** *Bless, etc.*

SOLEMN BLESSINGS

The following blessings may be used, at the discretion of the priest, at the end of Mass, or after the liturgy of the word, the office, and the celebration of the sacraments.

The deacon, or in his absence the priest himself, gives the invitation: Bow your heads and pray for God's blessing. *Another form of invitation may be used. Then the priest extends his hands over the people while he says or sings the blessings. All respond:* Amen.

I. Celebrations during the Proper of Seasons

1. ADVENT

You believe that the Son of God once came to us;
you look for him to come again.
May his coming bring you the light of his holiness
and free you with his blessing. ℟. **Amen.**

May God make you steadfast in faith,
joyful in hope, and untiring in love
all the days of your life. ℟. **Amen.**

You rejoice that our Redeemer came to live with us as
 man.
When he comes again in glory,
may he reward you with endless life. ℟. **Amen.**

May almighty God bless you,
the Father, and the Son, ✢ and the Holy Spirit. ℟. **Amen.**

2. CHRISTMAS

When he came to us as man,
the Son of God scattered the darkness of this world,
and filled this holy night (day) with his glory.
May the God of infinite goodness
scatter the darkness of sin
and brighten your hearts with holiness. ℟. **Amen.**

God sent his angels to shepherds
to herald the great joy of our Savior's birth.
May he fill you with joy
and make you heralds of his gospel. ℟. **Amen.**

When the Word became man,
earth was joined to heaven.
May he give you his peace and good will,
and fellowship with all the heavenly host. ℟. **Amen.**

May almighty God bless you,
the Father, and the Son, ✠ and the Holy Spirit. ℟. **Amen.**

3. BEGINNING OF THE NEW YEAR

Every good gift comes from the Father of light.
May he grant you his grace and every blessing,
and keep you safe throughout the coming year. ℟. **Amen.**

May he grant you unwavering faith,
constant hope, and love that endures to the end. ℟. **Amen.**

May he order your days and work in his peace,
hear your every prayer,
and lead you to everlasting life and joy. ℟. **Amen.**

May almighty God bless you,
the Father, and the Son, ✠ and the Holy Spirit, ℟. **Amen.**

4. EPIPHANY

God has called you out of darkness
into his wonderful light.
May you experience his kindness and blessings,
and be strong in faith, in hope, and in love. ℟. **Amen.**

Because you are followers of Christ,
who appeared on this day as a light shining in darkness,
may he make you a light to all your sisters and brothers.
℟. **Amen.**

The wise men followed the star,
and found Christ who is light from light.
May you too find the Lord
when your pilgrimage is ended. ℟. **Amen.**

May almighty God bless you,
the Father, and the Son, ✠ and the Holy Spirit. ℟. **Amen.**

5. PASSION OF THE LORD

The Father of mercies has given us an example of unselfish love
in the sufferings of his only Son.
Through your service of God and neighbor
may you receive his countless blessings. ℟. **Amen.**

You believe that by his dying
Christ destroyed death for ever.
May he give you everlasting life. ℟. **Amen.**

He humbled himself for our sakes.
May you follow his example
and share in his resurrection. ℟. **Amen.**

May almighty God bless you,
the Father, and the Son, ✝ and the Holy Spirit. ℟. **Amen.**

6. EASTER VIGIL AND EASTER SUNDAY

May almighty God bless you on this solemn feast of
  Easter,
and may he protect you against all sin. ℟. **Amen.**

Through the resurrection of his Son
God has granted us healing.
May he fulfill his promises,
and bless you with eternal life. ℟. **Amen.**

You have mourned for Christ's sufferings;
now you celebrate the joy of his resurrection.
May you come with joy to the feast which lasts for ever.
  ℟. **Amen.**

May almighty God bless you,
the Father, and the Son, ✝ and the Holy Spirit. ℟. **Amen.**

7. EASTER SEASON

Through the resurrection of his Son
God has redeemed you and made you his children.
May he bless you with joy. ℟. **Amen.**

The Redeemer has given you lasting freedom.
May you inherit his everlasting life. ℟. **Amen.**

By faith you rose with him in baptism.
May your lives be holy,
so that you will be united with him for ever. ℟. **Amen.**

May almighty God bless you,
the Father, and the Son, ✝ and the Holy Spirit. ℟. **Amen.**

8. ASCENSION

May almighty God bless you on this day
when his only Son ascended into heaven

to prepare a place for you. ℟. **Amen.**

After his resurrection, Christ was seen by his disciples.
When he appears as judge
may you be pleasing for ever in his sight. ℟. **Amen.**

You believe that Jesus has taken his seat in majesty
at the right hand of the Father.
May you have the joy of experiencing
that he is also with you to the end of time,
according to his promise. ℟. **Amen.**

May almighty God bless you,
the Father, and the Son, ✚ and the Holy Spirit. ℟. **Amen.**

9. HOLY SPIRIT

(This day) the Father of light
has enlightened the minds of the disciples
by the outpouring of the Holy Spirit.
May he bless you
and give you the gifts of the Spirit for ever. ℟. **Amen.**

May that fire which hovered over the disciples
as tongues of flame
burn out all evil from your hearts
and made them glow with pure light. ℟. **Amen.**

God inspired speech in different tongues
to proclaim one faith.
May he strengthen your faith
and fulfill your hope of seeing him face to face. ℟. **Amen.**

May almighty God bless you,
the Father, and the Son, ✚ and the Holy Spirit. ℟. **Amen.**

10. ORDINARY TIME I

Blessing of Aaron (Num 6:24-26)

May the Lord bless you and keep you. ℟. **Amen.**
May his face shine upon you,
and be gracious to you. ℟. **Amen.**

May he look upon you with kindness,
and give you his peace. ℟. **Amen.**

May almighty God bless you,
the Father, and the Son, ✚ and the Holy Spirit. ℟. **Amen.**

11. ORDINARY TIME II   (Phil 4:7)

May the peace of God
which is beyond all understanding
keep your hearts and minds
in the knowledge and love of God
and of his Son, our Lord Jesus Christ. ℟. **Amen.**

May almighty God bless you,
the Father, and the Son, ✛ and the Holy Spirit. ℟. **Amen.**

12. ORDINARY TIME III

May almighty God bless you in his mercy,
and make you always aware of his saving wisdom.
    ℟. **Amen.**

May he strengthen your faith with proofs of his love,
so that you will persevere in good works. ℟. **Amen.**

May he direct your steps to himself,
and show you how to walk in charity and peace. ℟. **Amen.**

May almighty God bless you,
the Father, and the Son, ✛ and the Holy Spirit. ℟. **Amen.**

13. ORDINARY TIME IV

May the God of all consolation
bless you in every way
and grant you peace all the days of your life. ℟. **Amen.**

May he free you from all anxiety
and strengthen your hearts in his love. ℟. **Amen.**

May he enrich you with his gifts of faith, hope, and love,
so that what you do in this life
will bring you to the happiness of everlasting life.
    ℟. **Amen.**

May almighty God bless you,
the Father, and the Son, ✛ and the Holy Spirit. ℟. **Amen.**

14. ORDINARY TIME V

May almighty God keep you from all harm
and bless you with every good gift. ℟. **Amen.**

May he set his Word in your heart
and fill you with lasting joy. ℟. **Amen.**

May you walk in his ways,

always knowing what is right and good,
until you enter your heavenly inheritance. ℟. **Amen.**

May almighty God bless you,
the Father, and the Son, ✠ and the Holy Spirit. ℟. **Amen.**

II. Celebrations of Saints

15. BLESSED VIRGIN MARY

Born of the Blessed Virgin Mary,
the Son of God redeemed mankind.
May he enrich you with his blessings. ℟. **Amen.**

You received the author of life through Mary.
May you always rejoice in her loving care. ℟. **Amen.**
You have come to rejoice at Mary's feast.
May you be filled with the joys of the Spirit
and the gifts of your eternal home. ℟. **Amen.**

May almighty God bless you,
the Father, and the Son, ✠ and the Holy Spirit. ℟. **Amen.**

16. PETER AND PAUL

The Lord has set you firm within his Church,
which he built upon the rock of Peter's faith.
May he bless you with a faith that never falters. ℟. **Amen.**

The Lord has given you knowledge of the faith
through the labors and preaching of St. Paul.
May his example inspire you to lead others to Christ
by the manner of your life. ℟. **Amen.**

May the keys of Peter, and the words of Paul,
their undying witness and their prayers,
lead you to the joy of that eternal home
which Peter gained by his cross, and Paul by the sword.
℟. **Amen.**

May almighty God bless you,
the Father, and the Son, ✠ and the Holy Spirit. ℟. **Amen.**

17. APOSTLES

May God who founded his Church upon the apostles
bless you through the prayers of St. N. (and St. N.).
℟. **Amen.**

May God inspire you to follow the example of the apostles,
and give you witness to the truth before all men.
R̲. **Amen.**

The teaching of the apostles has strengthened your faith.
May their prayers lead you
to your true and eternal home. R̲. **Amen.**
May almighty God bless you,
the Father, and the Son, ✛ and the Holy Spirit.   **Amen.**

18. ALL SAINTS

God is the glory and joy of all his saints,
whose memory we celebrate today.
May his blessing be with you always. R̲. **Amen.**

May the prayers of the saints deliver you from the present
evil.
May their example of holy living
turn your thoughts to service of God and neighbor.
R̲. **Amen.**

God's holy Church rejoices that her saints
have reached their heavenly goal,
and are in lasting peace.
May you come to share all the joys of our Father's house.
R̲. **Amen.**

May almighty God bless you,
the Father, and the Son, ✛ and the Holy Spirit. R̲. **Amen.**

III. Other Blessings

19. DEDICATION OF A CHURCH

The Lord of earth and heaven
has assembled you before him this day
to dedicate this house of prayer
(to recall the dedication of this church).
May he fill you with the blessings of heaven. R̲. **Amen.**

God the Father wills that all his children
scattered throughout the world
become one family in his Son.
May he make you his temple,
the dwelling-place of his Holy Spirit. R̲. **Amen.**

May God free you from every bond of sin,
dwell within you and give you joy.
May you live with him for ever
in the company of all his saints.
May almighty God bless you,
the Father, and the Son, ✠ and the Holy Spirit. ℟. **Amen.**

20. THE DEAD

In his great love,
the God of all consolation gave man the gift of life.
May he bless you with faith
in the resurrection of his Son,
and with the hope of rising to new life. ℟. **Amen.**

To us who are alive
may he grant forgiveness,
and to all who have died
a place of light and peace. ℟. **Amen.**

As you believe that Jesus rose from the dead,
so may you live with him for ever in joy. ℟. **Amen.**

May almighty God bless you,
the Father, and the Son, ✠ and the Holy Spirit. ℟. **Amen.**

PRAYERS OVER THE PEOPLE

*The following prayers may be used, at the discretion of
the priest, at the end of the Mass, or after the liturgy of
the word, the office, and the celebration of the sacraments.*

*The deacon, or in his absence the priest himself, gives
the invitation:* Bow your heads and pray for God's
blessing. *Another form of invitation may be used. Then
the priest extends his hands over the people while he
says or sings the prayer. All respond:* Amen.

After the prayer, the priest always adds:

And may the blessing of almighty God,
the Father, and the Son, ✠ and the Holy Spirit,
come upon you and remain with you for ever. ℟. **Amen.**

1. Lord,
have mercy on your people.
Grant us in this life the good things
that lead to the everlasting life you prepare for us.
We ask this through Christ our Lord.

2. Lord,
   grant your people your protection and grace.
   Give them health of mind and body,
   perfect love for one another,
   and make them always faithful to you.
   Grant this through Christ our Lord.

3. Lord,
   may all Christian people both know and cherish
   the heavenly gifts they have received.
   We ask this in the name of Jesus the Lord.

4. Lord,
   bless your people and make them holy
   so that, avoiding evil,
   they may find in you the fulfillment of their longing.
   We ask this through Christ our Lord.

5. Lord,
   bless and strengthen your people.
   May they remain faithful to you
   and always rejoice in your mercy.
   We ask this in the name of Jesus the Lord.

6. Lord,
   you care for your people even when they stray.
   Grant us a complete change of heart,
   so that we may follow you with greater fidelity.
   Grant this through Christ our Lord.

7. Lord,
   send your light upon your family.
   May they continue to enjoy your favor
   and devote themselves to doing good.
   We ask this through Christ our Lord.

8. Lord,
   we rejoice that you are our creator and ruler.
   As we call upon your generosity,
   renew and keep us in your love.
   Grant this through Christ our Lord.

9. Lord,
   we pray for your people who believe in you.
   May they enjoy the gift of your love,

share it with others,
and spread it everywhere.
We ask this in the name of Jesus the Lord.

10. Lord,
bless your people who hope for your mercy.
Grant that they may receive
the things they ask for at your prompting.
Grant this through Christ our Lord.

11. Lord,
bless us with your heavenly gifts,
and in your mercy make us ready to do your will.
We ask this through Christ our Lord.

12. Lord,
protect your people always,
that they may be free from every evil
and serve you with all their hearts.
We ask this through Christ our Lord.

13. Lord,
help your people to seek you with all their hearts
and to deserve what you promise.
Grant this through Christ our Lord.

14. Father,
help your people to rejoice in the mystery of redemption
and to win its reward.
We ask this in the name of Jesus the Lord.

15. Lord,
have pity on your people;
help them each day to avoid what displeases you
and grant that they may serve you with joy.
We ask this through Christ our Lord.

16. Lord,
care for your people and purify them.
Console them in this life
and bring them to the life to come.
We ask this in the name of Jesus the Lord.

17. Father,
look with love upon your people,

the love which our Lord Jesus Christ showed us
when he delivered himself to evil men
and suffered the agony of the cross,
for he is Lord for ever.

18. Lord,
grant that your faithful people
may continually desire to relive the mystery of the
eucharist
and so be reborn to lead a new life.
We ask this through Christ our Lord.

19. Lord God,
in your great mercy,
enrich your people with your grace
and strengthen them by your blessing
so that they may praise you always.
Grant this through Christ our Lord.

20. May God bless you with every good gift from on high.
May he keep you pure and holy in his sight at all times.
May he bestow the riches of his grace upon you,
bring you the good news of salvation,
and always fill you with love for all men.
We ask this through Christ our Lord.

21. Lord,
make us pure in mind and body,
that we will avoid all evil pleasures
and always delight in you.
We ask this in the name of Jesus the Lord.

22. Lord,
bless your people and fill them with zeal.
Strengthen them by your love to do your will.
We ask this through Christ our Lord.

23. Lord,
come, live in your people
and strengthen them by your grace.
Help them to remain close to you in prayer
and give them a true love for one another.
Grant this through Christ our Lord.

24. Father,
   look kindly on your children who put their trust in you;
   bless them and keep them from all harm,
   strengthen them against the attacks of the devil.
   May they never offend you
   but seek to love you in all they do.
   We ask this through Christ our Lord.

FEASTS OF SAINTS

25. God our Father,
   may all Christian people rejoice in the glory of your
      saints.
   Give us fellowship with them
   and unending joy in your kingdom.
   We ask this in the name of Jesus the Lord.

26. Lord,
   you have given us many friends in heaven.
   Through their prayers we are confident
   that you will watch over us always
   and fill our hearts with your love.
   Grant this through Christ our Lord.

GOOD FRIDAY

CELEBRATION OF THE LORD'S PASSION

The liturgy of Good Friday recalls graphically the passion and death of Jesus. The reading of the passion describes the suffering and death of Jesus. Today we show great reverence for the crucifix, the sign of our redemption.

1. *According to the Church's ancient tradition, the sacraments are not celebrated today or tomorrow.*

2. *The altar should be completely bare, without cloths, candles, or cross.*

3. *The celebration of the Lord's passion takes place in the afternoon, about three o'clock, unless pastoral reasons suggest a later hour. The celebration consists of three parts: liturgy of the word, veneration of the cross, and holy communion.*

In the United States, if the size or nature of a parish or other community indicates the pastoral need for an additional liurgical service, the local Ordinary may permit the service to be repeated later.

Holy communion may be given to the faithful only at the celebration of the Lord's passion, but may be brought at any hour of the day to the sick who cannot take part in this service.

4. *The priest and deacon, wearing red Mass vestments, go to the altar. There they make a reverence and prostrate themselves, or they may kneel. All pray silently for a while.*

5. *Then the priest goes to the chair with the ministers. He faces the people and, with hands joined, says one of the following prayers.*

PRAYER

(Let us pray is not said.)

Lord, by shedding his blood for us
your Son, Jesus Christ,
established the paschal mystery.
In your goodness, make us holy
and watch over us always.
We ask this through Christ our Lord. ℟. **Amen.**

OR

Lord, by the suffering of Christ, your Son,
you have saved us all from the death
we inherited from sinful Adam.
By the law of nature
we have borne the likeness of his manhood;
may the sanctifying power of grace
help us to put on the likeness of our Lord in heaven,
who lives and reigns for ever and ever. ℟. **Amen.**

PART ONE: LITURGY OF THE WORD

6. *All sit.*

READING I   Is 52, 13-53, 12

The Suffering Servant shall be raised up and exalted. The Servant
remains one with all people in sorrow and yet distinct from each of
them in innocence of life and total service to God. The doctrine of
expiatory suffering finds supreme expression in these words.

A reading from the book of the prophet Isaiah

See, my servant shall prosper,
    he shall be raised high and greatly exalted.
Even as many were amazed at him—
    so marred was his look beyond that of man,
    and his appearance beyond that of mortals—
So shall he startle many nations,
    because of him kings shall stand speechless;
For those who have not been told shall see,
    those who have not heard shall ponder it.
Who would believe what we have heard?
    To whom has the arm of the Lord been revealed?
He grew up like a sapling before him,
    like a shoot from the parched earth;
There was in him no stately bearing to make us look
        at him,
    nor appearance that would attract us to him.
He was spurned and avoided by men,
    a man of suffering, accustomed to infirmity,

One of those from whom men hide their faces,
  spurned, and we held him in no esteem.
Yet it was our infirmities that he bore,
  our sufferings that he endured,
While we thought of him as stricken,
  as one smitten by God and afflicted.
But he was pierced for our offenses,
  crushed for our sins;
Upon him was the chastisement that makes us whole,
  by his stripes we were healed.
We had all gone astray like sheep,
  each following his own way;
But the Lord laid upon him
  the guilt of us all.
Though he was harshly treated, he submitted
  and opened not his mouth;
Like a lamb led to the slaughter
  or a sheep before the shearers,
  he was silent and opened not his mouth.
Oppressed and condemned, he was taken away,
  and who would have thought any more of his
    destiny?
When he was cut off from the land of the living,
  and smitten for the sin of his people,
A grave was assigned him among the wicked
  and a burial place with evildoers,
Though he had done no wrong
  nor spoken any falsehood.
[But the Lord was pleased
  to crush him in infirmity.]
If he gives his life as an offering for sin,
  he shall see his descendants in a long life,
    and the will of the Lord shall be accomplished
      through him.
Because of his affliction
  he shall see the light in fullness of days;
Through his suffering, my servant shall justify many,
  and their guilt he shall bear.

Therefore I will give him his portion among the
    great,
    and he shall divide the spoils with the mighty,
Because he surrendered himself to death
    and was counted among the wicked;
And he shall take away the sins of many,
    and win pardon for their offenses.
This is the Word of the Lord. ℟. **Thanks be to God.** ✔

Responsorial Psalm   Ps 31, 2. 6. 12-13. 15-16. 17. 25

℟. (Lk 23, 46) **Father, I put my life in your hands.**
In you, O Lord, I take refuge;
    let me never be put to shame.
    In your justice rescue me.
Into your hands I commend my spirit;
    you will redeem me, O Lord, O faithful God. — ℟

For all my foes I am an object of reproach,
    a laughingstock to my neighbors, and a dread to
        my friends;
    they who see me abroad flee from me.
I am forgotten like the unremembered dead;
    I am like a dish that is broken. — ℟

But my trust is in you, O Lord;
    I say, "You are my God."
In your hands is my destiny; rescue me
    from the clutches of my enemies and my perse-
        cutors. — ℟

Let your face shine upon your servant;
    save me in your kindness.
Take courage and be stouthearted,
    all you who hope in the Lord. — ℟ ✔

7. READING II   Heb 4, 14-16; 5, 7-9

The theme of the compassionate high priest appears again in this
passage. In him the Christian can approach God confidently and without fear. Christ learned obedience from his sufferings whereby he
became the source of eternal life for all.

A reading from the letter of Paul to the Hebrews

We have a great high priest who has passed through the heavens, Jesus, the Son of God; let us hold fast to our profession of faith. For we do not have a high priest who is unable to sympathize with our weakness, but one who was tempted in every way that we are, yet never sinned. So let us confidently approach the throne of grace to receive mercy and favor and to find help in time of need.

In the days when he was in the flesh, Christ offered prayers and supplications with loud cries and tears to God, who was able to save him from death, and he was heard because of his reverence. Son though he was, he learned obedience from what he suffered; and when perfected, he became the source of eternal salvation for all who obey him.—This is the Word of the Lord. ℟. **Thanks be to God.** ☩

GOSPEL   Jn 18, 1—19, 42

Verse before the Gospel (Phil 2, 8-9)

℟. **Praise and honor to you, Lord Jesus Christ!**
Christ became obedient for us even to death,
dying on the cross.
Therefore God raised him on high
and gave him the name above all other names.
℟. **Praise and honor to you, Lord Jesus Christ!**

8. *Finally the passion is read in the same way as on the preceding Sunday. The narrator is noted by C (Chronista), the words of Jesus by a ☩ and the words of others by S (Synagoga), groups in the account by SS. The words of the narrator enclosed in brackets may be omitted. The parts of the Synagoga marked with SS and printed in boldface type may be recited by the people.*

The Passion of our Lord Jesus Christ
according to John

The beginning scene is Christ's agony in the garden. The soldiers are from the Roman garrison, whose help Christ's enemies sought when they were planning to denounce him to the Romans as a seditionist. Our Lord knows what is to happen. The Scriptures recount the betrayal, the trial, the condemnation, and the crucifixion of Jesus.

1. JESUS ARRESTED

C. Jesus went out with his disciples across the Kidron Valley. There was a garden there, and he and his disciples entered it. The place was familiar to Judas as well (the one who was to hand him over) because Jesus had often met there with his disciples. Judas took the cohort as well as guards supplied by the chief priest and the Pharisees, and came there with lanterns, torches, and weapons. Jesus, aware of all that would happen to him, stepped forward and said to them, ✠ "Who is it you want?" **C.** [They replied,] **SS. "Jesus the Nazorean."** **C.** He answered, ✠ "I am he." **C.** (Now, Judas, the one who was to hand him over, was there with them.) As Jesus said to them, "I am he," they retreated slightly and fell to the ground. Jesus put the question to them again, ✠ "Who is it you want?" **C.** They repeated, **SS. "Jesus the Nazorean."** **C.** [Jesus said,] ✠ "I have told you, I am he. If I am the one you want, let these men go." **C.** (This was to fulfill what he had said, "I have not lost one of those you gave me.") Then Simon Peter, who had a sword, drew it and struck the slave of the high priest, severing his right ear. (The slave's name was Malchus.) At that Jesus said to Peter, ✠ "Put your sword back in its sheath. Am I not to drink the cup the Father has given me?" **C.** Then the soldiers of the cohort, their tribune, and the Jewish guards arrested Jesus and bound him. They led him first to Annas, the father-in-law of Caiaphas who was high priest that year. (It was Caiaphas who had proposed to the Jews the advantage of having one man die for the people.)

2. PETER'S FIRST DENIAL

Simon Peter, in company with another disciple, kept following Jesus closely. This disciple, who was known to the high priest, stayed with Jesus as far as the high priest's courtyard, while Peter was left standing at the gate. The disciple known to the high priest came out and spoke to the woman at the gate and then brought Peter in. This servant girl who kept the gate said to Peter, **S.** "Are you not one of this man's followers?" **C.** [He replied,] "Not I." **C.** Now the night was cold, and the servants and the guards who were standing around had made a charcoal fire to warm themselves by. Peter joined them and stood there warming himself.

3. THE INQUIRY BEFORE ANNAS

The high priest questioned Jesus, first about his disciples then about his teaching. Jesus answered by saying, ✠ "I have spoken publicly to any who would listen. I always taught in a synagogue or in the temple area where all the Jews come together. There was nothing secret about anything I said. Why do you question me? Question those who heard me when I spoke. It should be obvious they will know what I said." **C.** At this reply, one of the guards who was standing nearby gave Jesus a sharp blow on the face. He said, **S.** "Is that the way to answer the high priest?" **C.** Jesus replied, ✠ "If I said anything wrong produce the evidence, but if I spoke the truth why hit me?" **C.** Annas next sent him, bound, to the high priest Caiaphas.

4. THE FURTHER DENIALS

All through this, Simon Peter had been standing there warming himself. They said to him, **SS.** "Are you not a disciple of his?" **C.** [He denied:] **S.** "I am not!" **C.** One of the high priests' slaves—as it happened, a relative of the man whose ear Peter had severed—insisted, **S.** "But did I not see you with him in the garden?" **C.** Peter denied it again. At that moment a cock began to crow.

5. JESUS BROUGHT BEFORE PILATE

At daybreak they brought Jesus from Caiaphas to the praetorium. They did not enter the praetorium themselves, for they had to avoid ritual impurity if they were to eat the Passover supper. Pilate came out to them and demanded, **S.** "What accusation do you bring against this man?" **C.** They retorted, **SS. "If he were not a criminal we would certainly not have handed him over to you." C.** At this Pilate said, **S.** "Why do you not take him and pass judgment on him according to your law?" **C.** The Jews answered, **SS. "We may not put anyone to death." C.** (This was to fulfill what Jesus had said, indicating the sort of death he had to die.)

6. JESUS QUESTIONED BY PILATE

Pilate went back into the praetorium and summoned Jesus. He asked him, **S.** "Are you the King of the Jews?" **C.** Jesus answered, ✠ "Are you saying this on your own, or have others been telling you about me?" **C.** Pilate retorted, **S.** "I am no Jew! It is your own people and the chief priests who have handed you over to me. What have you done?" **C.** Jesus answered, ✠ "My kingdom does not belong to this world. If my kingdom were of this world, my subjects would be fighting to save me from being handed over to the Jews. As it is, my kingdom is not here." **C.** At this Pilate said to him, **S.** "So, then, you are a king?" **C.** [Jesus replied,] ✠ "Is it you who say I am a king? The reason I was born, the reason why I came into the world, is to testify to the truth. Anyone committed to the truth hears my voice." **C.** Pilate said, **S.** "Truth! What does that mean?"

7. BARABBAS CHOSEN OVER JESUS

C. After this remark, Pilate went out again to the Jews and said to them: **S.** "Speaking for myself, I find no case against this man. Recall your custom whereby I release to you someone at Passover time. Do you want me to release to you the king of the Jews?" **C.** They shouted back, **SS. "We want Barabbas, not this one!" C.** (Barabbas was an insurrectionist.)

8. JESUS IS SCOURGED

Pilate's next move was to take Jesus and have him scourged. The soldiers then wove a crown of thorns and fixed it on his head, throwing around his shoulders a cloak of royal purple. Repeatedly they came up to him and while slapping his face said, **SS. "All hail, King of the Jews!"**

9. JESUS IS PRESENTED TO THE CROWD

C. Pilate went out a second time and said to the crowd: **S.** "Observe what I do. I am going to bring him out to you to make you realize that I find no case against him." **C.** When Jesus came out wearing the crown of thorns and the purple cloak, Pilate said to them, **S.** "Look at the man!" **C.** As soon as the chief priests and the temple guards saw him they shouted, **SS. "Crucify him! Crucify him!" C.** Pilate said, **S.** "Take him and crucify him yourselves; I find no case against him." **C.** The Jews responded, **SS. "We have our law and according to that law he must die because he made himself God's Son." C.** When Pilate heard this kind of talk, he was more afraid than ever.

10. JESUS AGAIN QUESTIONED BY PILATE

Going back into the praetorium, he said to Jesus, **S.** "Where do you come from?" **C.** Jesus would not give him any answer. Pilate asked him, **S.** "Do you refuse to speak to me? Do you not know that I have the power to release you and the power to crucify you?" **C.** [Jesus answered,] ✠ "You would have no power over me whatever unless it were given you from above. That is why he who handed me over to you is guilty of the greater sin."

11. JESUS SENTENCED TO BE CRUCIFIED

C. After this, Pilate was eager to release him, but the Jews shouted, **SS. "If you free this man you are no 'Friend of Caesar.' Anyone who makes himself a king becomes Caesar's rival." C.** Pilate heard what they were saying, then brought Jesus outside and took a seat on a judge's bench at the place called the Stone Pavement—Gabbatha in Hebrew. (It was the Preparation Day for Passover, and the hour was about noon.) He said to the Jews, **S.** "Look at your king!" **C.** At this they shouted, **SS. "Away with him! Away with him! Crucify him!" C.** Pilate exclaimed, **S.** "What! Shall I crucify your king?" **C.** The chief priests replied, **SS. "We have no king but Caesar." C.** In the end, Pilate handed Jesus over to be crucified.

12. CRUCIFIXION AND DEATH

Jesus was led away, and carrying the cross by himself, went out to what is called the Place of the Skull (in Hebrew, Golgotha). There they crucified him, and two others with him: one on either side, Jesus in the middle. Pilate had an inscription placed on the cross which read, JESUS THE NAZOREAN, THE KING OF THE JEWS. This inscription, in Hebrew, Latin, and Greek, was read by many of the Jews, since the place where Jesus was crucified was near the city. The chief priests of the Jews tried to tell Pilate, **SS. "You should not have written, 'The King of the Jews.' Write instead, 'This man claimed to be King of the Jews.'" C.** Pilate replied, **S.** "What I have written, I have written." **C.** After the soldiers had crucified Jesus they took his garments and divided them four ways, one for each soldier. There was also his tunic, but this tunic was woven in one piece from top to bottom and had no seam. They said to each other, **SS. "We should not tear it. Let us throw dice to see who gets it." C.** (The purpose of this was to have the Scripture fulfilled: "They divided my garments among them; for my clothing they cast lots.") And this was what the soldiers did. Near the cross of Jesus there stood his mother, his mother's sister, Mary the wife of Clopas, and Mary Magdalene. Seeing his mother there with the disciple whom he loved, Jesus said to his mother. ☩ "Woman, there is your son." **C.** In turn he said to the disciple, ☩ "There is your mother." **C.** From that hour onward, the disciple took her into his care. After that, Jesus, realizing that everything was now finished, said to fulfill the Scripture, ☩ "I am thirsty." **C.** There was a jar there full of common wine. They stuck a sponge soaked in this wine on some hyssop and raised it to his lips. When Jesus took the wine, he said, ☩ "Now it is finished." **C.** Then he bowed his head, and delivered over his spirit. (HERE KNEEL AND PAUSE MOMENTARILY)

13. THE BLOOD AND WATER

Since it was the Preparation Day the Jews did not want to have the bodies left on the cross during the sabbath, for that sabbath was a solemn feast day. They asked Pilate that the legs be broken and the bodies be taken away. Accordingly, the soldiers came and broke the legs of the men crucified with Jesus, first of one, then of the other. When they came to Jesus and saw that he was already dead, they did not break his legs. One of the soldiers ran a lance into his side, and immediately blood and water flowed out. (This testimony has been given by an eyewitness, and his testimony is true. He tells what he knows is true, so that you may believe.) These events took place for the fulfillment of Scripture: "Break none of his bones." There is still another Scripture passage which says: "They shall look on him whom they have pierced."

14. BURIAL OF JESUS

Afterward, Joseph of Arimathea, a disciple of Jesus (although a secret one for fear of the Jews), asked Pilate's permission to remove Jesus' body. Pilate granted it, so they came and took the body away. Nicodemus (the man who had first come to Jesus at night) likewise came, bringing a mixture of myrrh and aloes which weighed about a hundred pounds. They took Jesus' body, and in accordance with Jewish burial custom, bound it up in wrappings of cloth with perfumed oils. In the place where he had been crucified there was a garden, and in the garden a new tomb in which no one had ever been buried. Because of the Jewish Preparation Day they buried Jesus there, for the tomb was close at hand. —This is the gospel of the Lord. ℟. **Praise to you, Lord Jesus Christ.** ➤ No. 15, p. 623

9. *After the reading of the passion there may be a brief Homily.*

GENERAL INTERCESSIONS

10. *The general intercessions conclude the liturgy of the word. The priest stands at the chair, or he may be at the lectern or altar. With his hands joined, he sings or says the introduction in which each intention is stated. All kneel and pray silently for some period of time, and then the priest, with hands extended, sings or says the prayer. The people may either kneel or stand throughout the entire period of the general intercessions.*

11. *The conference of bishops may provide an acclamation for the people to sing before the priest's prayer or decree that the deacon's traditional invitation to kneel and pray be continued: Let us kneel—let us stand. In the United States, if desired, an appropriate accla-*

*mation by the people may be introduced before each of
the solemn prayers of intercession, or the traditional
period of kneeling at each of the prayers (at the invitation of the deacon) may be continued.*

12. *In case of serious public need, the local Ordinary
may permit or decree the addition of a special intention.*

13. *The priest may choose from the prayers in the missal those which are more appropriate to local circumstances, provided the series follows the rule for the
General Intercessions (see General Instruction of the
Roman Missal, no. 46).*

I. For the Church

Let us pray, dear friends,
for the holy Church of God throughout the world,
that God the almighty Father
guide it and gather it together
so that we may worship him
in peace and tranquility.

Silent prayer. Then the priest sings or says:

Almighty and eternal God,
you have shown your glory to all nations
in Christ, your Son.
Guide the work of your Church.
Help it to persevere in faith,
proclaim your name
and bring your salvation to people everywhere.
We ask this through Christ our Lord. ℟. **Amen.**

II. For the pope

Let us pray
for our Holy Father, Pope N.,
that God who chose him to be bishop
may give him health and strength
to guide and govern God's holy people.

Silent prayer. Then the priest sings or says:

Almighty and eternal God,
you guide all things by your word,

you govern all Christian people.
In your love protect the pope you have chosen for us.
Under his leadership deepen our faith
and make us better Christians.
We ask this through Christ our Lord. ℞. **Amen.**

III. For the clergy and laity of the Church

Let us pray
for N., our bishop;
for all bishops, priests and deacons;
for all who have a special ministry in the Church
and for all God's people.

Silent prayer. Then the priest sings or says:

Almighty and eternal God,
your Spirit guides the Church
and makes it holy.
Listen to our prayers
and help each of us
in his own vocation
to do your work more faithfully.
We ask this through Christ our Lord. ℞. **Amen.**

IV. For those preparing for baptism

Let us pray
for those [among us] preparing for baptism,
that God in his mercy
make them responsive to his love,
forgive their sins through the waters of new birth,
and give them life in Jesus Christ our Lord.

Silent prayer. Then the priest sings or says:

Almighty and eternal God,
you continually bless your Church with new members.
Increase the faith and understanding
of those [among us] preparing for baptism.
Give them a new birth in these living waters
and make them members of your chosen family.
We ask this through Christ our Lord. ℞. **Amen.**

V. For the unity of Christians

Let us pray
for all our brothers and sisters
who share our faith in Jesus Christ,
that God may gather and keep together in one
    Church
all those who seek the truth with sincerity.

Silent prayer. Then the priest sings or says:

Almighty and eternal God,
you keep together those you have united.
Look kindly on all who follow Jesus your Son.
We are all consecrated to you by our common bap-
    tism.
Make us one in the fullness of faith,
and keep us one in the fellowship of love.
We ask this through Christ our Lord. ℟. **Amen.**

VI. For the Jewish people

Let us pray
for the Jewish people,
the first to hear the word of God,
that they may continue to grow in the love of his
    name
and in faithfulness to his covenant.

Silent prayer. Then the priest sings or says:

Almighty and eternal God,
long ago you gave your promise to Abraham and his
    posterity.
Listen to your Church as we pray
that the people you first made your own
may arrive at the fullness of redemption.
We ask this through Christ our Lord. ℟. **Amen.**

VII. For those who do not believe in Christ

Let us pray
for those who do not believe in Christ,
that the light of the Holy Spirit
may show them the way to salvation.

Silent prayer. Then the priest sings or says:
Almighty and eternal God,
enable those who do not acknowledge Christ
to find the truth
as they walk before you in sincerity of heart.
Help us to grow in love for one another,
to grasp more fully the mystery of your godhead,
and to become more perfect witnesses of your love
in the sight of men.
We ask this through Christ our Lord. ℟. **Amen.**

VIII. For those who do not believe in God

Let us pray
for those who do not believe in God,
that they may find him
by sincerely following all that is right.

Silent prayer. Then the priest sings or says:
Almighty and eternal God,
you created mankind
so that all might long to find you
and have peace when you are found.
Grant that, in spite of the hurtful things
that stand in their way,
they may all recognize in the lives of Christians
the tokens of your love and mercy,
and gladly acknowledge you
as the one true God and Father of us all.
We ask this through Christ our Lord. ℟. **Amen.**

IX. For all in public office

Let us pray
for those who serve us in public office,
that God may guide their minds and hearts,
so that all men may live in true peace and freedom.

Silent prayer. Then the priest sings or says:
Almighty and eternal God,
you know the longings of men's hearts

and you protect their rights.
In your goodness,
watch over those in authority,
so that people everywhere may enjoy
religious freedom, security, and peace.
We ask this through Christ our Lord. ℟. **Amen.**

X. For those in special need

Let us pray, dear friends,
that God the almighty Father
may heal the sick,
comfort the dying,
give safety to travelers,
free those unjustly deprived of liberty,
and rid the world of falsehood,
hunger, and disease.

Silent prayer. Then the priest sings or says:
Almighty, ever-living God,
you give strength to the weary
and new courage to those who have lost heart.
Hear the prayers of all who call on you in any
    trouble
that they may have the joy of receiving your help
    in their need.
We ask this through Christ our Lord. ℟. **Amen.**

PART TWO: VENERATION OF THE CROSS

14.   *After the General Intercessions, the veneration of
the cross takes place. Pastoral demands will determine
which of the two forms is more effective and should be
chosen.*

First Form of Showing the Cross

15.   *The veiled cross is carried to the altar, accompanied
by two ministers with lighted candles, Standing at the
altar, the priest takes the cross, uncovers the upper part
of it, then elevates it and begins the invitation* This is
the wood of the cross. *He is assisted in the singing by
the deacon or, if convenient, by the choir. All respond:*

Come, let us worship. *At the end of the singing all kneel. and venerate the cross briefly in silence; the priest remains standing and holds the cross high.*

Then the priest uncovers the right arm of the cross, lifts it up, and again begins the invitation This is the wood of the cross, *and the rite is repeated as before.*

Finally he uncovers the entire cross, lifts it up, and begins the invitation This is the wood of the cross *a third time, and the rite is repeated as before.*

16. *Accompanied by two ministers with lighted candles, the priest then carries the cross to the entrance of the sanctuary or to another suitable place. There he lays the cross down or hands it to the ministers to hold. Candles are placed on either side of the cross, and the veneration follows as below, no. 18.*

Second Form of Showing the Cross

17. *The priest or deacon, accompanied by the ministers or by another suitable minister, goes to the church door. There he takes the (uncovered) cross, and the ministers take lighted candles. They go in procession through the church to the sanctuary. Near the entrance of the church, in the middle of the church, and at the entrance to the sanctuary, the one carrying the cross stops, lifts it up and sings the invitation* This is the wood of the cross. *All respond:* Come, let us worship. *After each response all kneel and venerate the cross briefly in silence as above.*

Then the cross and candles are placed at the entrance to the sanctuary.

INVITATION

℣. This is the wood of the cross, on which hung the Savior of the world.

℟. **Come, let us worship.**

Veneration of the Cross

18. *The priest, clergy, and faithful approach to venerate the cross in a kind of procession. They make a simple genuflection or perform some other appropriate sign of reverence according to local custom, for example, kissing the cross.*

During the veneration the antiphon We worship you. Lord, *the reproaches or other suitable songs are sung.*

All who have venerated the cross return to their places and sit.

19.   *Only one cross should be used for the veneration. If the number of people makes it impossible for everyone to venerate the cross individually, the priest may take the cross, after some of the faithful have venerated it, and stand in the center in front of the altar. In a few words he invites the people to venerate the cross and then holds it up briefly for them to worship in silence.*

In the United States, if pastoral reasons suggest that there be individual veneration even though the number of people is very large, a second or third cross may be used.

20.   *After the veneration, the cross is carried to its place at the altar, and the lighted candles are placed around the altar or near the cross.*

Songs at the Veneration of the Cross

Individual parts are indicated by no. 1 (first choir) and no. 2 (second choir); parts sung by both choirs together are indicated by nos. 1 and 2.

ANTIPHON

1 and 2: Antiphon
**We worship you, Lord,
we venerate your cross,
we praise your resurrection.
Through the cross you brought joy to the world.**

1: Psalm 67, 2
**May God be gracious and bless us;
and let his face shed its light upon us.**

1 and 2: Antiphon
**We worship you, Lord,
we venerate your cross,
we praise your resurrection.
Through the cross you brought joy to the world.**

I
REPROACHES

1 and 2: **My people, what have I done to you?
How have I offended you? Answer me!**

1:    I led you out of Egypt, from slavery to freedom,
      but you led your Savior to the cross.

2.   My people, what have I done to you?
      How have I offended you? Answer me!

1:    Holy is God!

2:    Holy and strong!

1:    Holy immortal One,
      have mercy on us!

1 and 2: For forty years I led you safely through the
         desert.
      I fed you with manna from heaven,
      and brought you to a land of plenty;
      but you led your Savior to the cross.

1:    Holy is God!

2:    Holy and strong!

1:    Holy immortal One,
      have mercy on us!

1 and 2:   What more could I have done for you?
      I planted you as my fairest vine,
      but you yielded only bitterness:
      when I was thirsty you gave me vinegar to drink,
      and you pierced your Savior with a lance.

1:    Holy is God!

2:    Holy and strong!

1:    Holy immortal One,
      have mercy on us!

II

1:    For your sake I scourged your captors and their
         firstborn sons,
      but you brought your scourges down on me.

2:    My people, what have I done to you?
      How have I offended you? Answer me!

1:    I led you from slavery to freedom
      and drowned your captors in the sea,
      but you handed me over to your high priests.

2:   My people, what have I done to you?
How have I offended you? Answer me!

1:   I opened the sea before you,
but you opened my side with a spear.

2:   My people, what have I done to you?
How have I offended you? Answer me!

1:   I led you on your way in a pillar of cloud,
but you led me to Pilate's court.

2:   My people, what have I done to you?
How have I offended you? Answer me!

1:   I bore you up with manna in the desert,
but you struck me down and scourged me.

2:   My people, what have I done to you?
How have I offended you? Answer me!

1:   I gave you saving water from the rock,
but you gave me gall and vinegar to drink.

2:   My people, what have I done to you?
How have I offended you? Answer me!

1:   For you I struck down the kings of Canaan,
but you struck my head with a reed.

2:   My people, what have I done to you?
How have I offended you? Answer me!

1:   I gave you a royal scepter,
but you gave me a crown of thorns.

2:   My people, what have I done to you?
How have I offended you? Answer me!

1:   I raised you to the height of majesty,
but you have raised me high on a cross.

2:   My people, what have I done to you?
How have I offended you? Answer me!

HYMN: PANGE LINGUA

Sing, my tongue, the Savior's glory;
   tell his triumph far and wide;
Tell aloud the famous story

of his body crucified;
How upon the cross a victim,
  vanquishing in death, he died.

Eating of the tree forbidden,
  man had sunk in Satan's snare,
When our pitying Creator did
  this second tree prepare;
Destined, many ages later,
  that first evil to repair.

Such the order God appointed
  when for sin he would atone;
To the serpent thus opposing
  schemes yet deeper than his own;
Thence the remedy procuring,
  when the fatal wound had come.

So when now at length the fullness
  of the sacred time drew nigh,
Then the Son, the world's Creator,
  left his Father's throne on high;
From a virgin's womb appearing,
  clothed in our mortality.

All within a lowly manger,
  lo, a tender babe he lies!
See his gentle Virgin Mother
  lull to sleep his infant cries!
While the limbs of God incarnate
  round with swathing bands she ties.

Thus did Christ to perfect manhood
  in our mortal flesh attain:
Then of his free choice he goeth
  to a death of bitter pain;
And as a lamb, upon the altar of the cross,
  for us is slain.

Lo, with gall his thirst he quenches!
  See the thorns upon his brow!
Nails his tender flesh are rending!

See, his side is opened now!
Whence, to cleanse the whole creation,
  streams of blood and water flow.

Lofty tree, bend down thy branches,
  to embrace thy sacred load;
Oh, relax the native tension
  of that all too rigid wood;
Gently, gently bear the members
  of thy dying King and God.

Tree, which solely wast found worthy
  the world's great Victim to sustain.
Harbor from the raging tempest!
  Ark, that saved the world again!
Tree, with sacred blood anointed
  of the Lamb for sinners slain.

Blessing, honor everlasting,
  to the immortal Deity;
To the Father, Son, and Spirit,
  equal praises ever be;
Glory through the earth and heaven
  to Trinity in Unity. Amen.

PART THREE: HOLY COMMUNION

21. *The altar is covered with a cloth and the corporal and book are placed on it. Then the deacon or, if there is no deacon, the priest brings the ciborium with the Blessed Sacrament from the place of reposition to the altar without any procession, while all stand in silence. Two ministers with lighted candles accompany him and they place their candles near the altar or on it.*

22. *The deacon places the ciborium on the altar and uncovers it. Meanwhile the priest comes from his chair, genuflects, and goes up to the altar. With hands joined, he says aloud:*

Let us pray with confidence to the Father
in the words our Savior gave us:

He extends his hands and continues, with all present:
Our Father . . .

With hands extended, the priest continues alone:

Deliver us, Lord, from every evil,
and grant us peace in our day.
In your mercy keep us free from sin
and protect us from all anxiety
as we wait in joyful hope
for the coming of our Savior, Jesus Christ.

He joins his hands. The people end the prayer with the acclamation:

**For the kingdom, the power, and the glory are yours,
   now and for ever.**

23.   *Then the priest joins his hands and says quietly:*

Lord Jesus Christ, with faith in your love and mercy
   I eat your body and drink your blood.
Let it not bring me condemnation, but health in mind
   and body.

24.   *The priest genuflects. Taking the host, he raises it slightly over the ciborium and, facing the people, says aloud:*

This is the Lamb of God
who takes away the sins of the world.
Happy are those who are called to his supper.

He adds, once only, with the people:

**Lord, I am not worthy to receive you,
but only say the word and I shall be healed.**

Facing the altar, he reverently consumes the body of Christ.

25.   *Then communion is distributed to the faithful. Any appropriate song may be sung during communion.*

26.   *When the communion has been completed, a suitable minister may take the ciborium to a place prepared outside the church or, if circumstances require, may place it in the tabernacle.*

27.   *A period of silence may now be observed. The priest then says the following prayer:*

Let us pray.
Almighty and eternal God,

you have restored us to life
by the triumphant death and resurrection of Christ.
Continue this healing work within us.
May we who participate in this mystery
never cease to serve you.
We ask this in the name of Jesus the Lord. ℞. **Amen.**

28. *For the dismissal the priest faces the people, extends his hands towards them, and says the following prayer:*

PRAYER OVER THE PEOPLE

Lord,
send down your abundant blessing
upon your people who have devoutly recalled the
   death of your Son
in the sure hope of the resurrection.
Grant them pardon; bring them comfort.
May their faith grow stronger
and their eternal salvation be assured.
We ask this through Christ our Lord. ℞.**Amen.**

All depart in silence. The altar is stripped at a convenient time.

29. *Evening Prayer is not said by those who participate in this afternoon liturgical service.*

HOLY SATURDAY

On Holy Saturday the Church waits at the Lord's tomb, meditating on his suffering and death. The altar is left bare, and the sacrifice of the Mass is not celebrated. Only after the solemn vigil during the night, held in anticipation of the resurrection, does the Easter celebration begin, with a spirit of joy that overflows into the following period of fifty days.

On this day holy communion may be given only as viaticum.

EASTER SEASON

In our analysis of Advent, we mentioned that creation and ourselves in it, as unfinished beings, are in a process of evolution. The Creator evolves his plan and the first creature in whom this master-plan was fully realized is our risen Lord Jesus Christ. Creation, where it became self-conscious man, did not cooperate. Man sinned; hence God re-established all things in Christ Jesus (Eph 1, 10).

According to the purpose of God's will, we are predestined to grow into the full realization of that divine plan (Eph 1, 5), presupposing the cooperation we have given during Lent. In Christ all will be made to live. But each in his own turn, Christ as first fruits, then they who are Christ's, who have believed, at his coming (1 Cor 15, 22-23).

It is through faith and baptism that we now share in Christ's glorious resurrection, till we fully share in it by partaking in his ascension into heaven. Therefore both mysteries: Christ's resurrection and our partaking in it through baptism, are celebrated in the Easter Liturgy.

And after we had heard the good news of our salvation and believed in it, we were sealed with the Holy Spirit (Eph 1, 13). Our full initiation into God's people is by Confirmation. The feast of Pentecost celebrates the outpouring of this pledge of our inheritance (Eph 1, 14).

Again, both Easter, Ascension and Pentecost are not past but present to us. (Note "this day" in the Propers of these feasts.)

We should read about God's plan of salvation in Eph 1, 3-14 and consider prayerfully how it is celebrated at Easter, the Ascension and Pentecost.

There is no Easter victory unless there is a personal victory in which love becomes stronger than hate, moving us to forgive each other and to live together in mutual respect and brotherhood. If we are "Easter men," as St. Augustine called us, we should also be a joyous people. There is no reason for prolonged sadness at life's defeats or the end that death brings to our visible existence. Easter is a reminder that death has lost its victory and its sting. Sin will always be with us, but the knowledge that this man Jesus seeks out sinners and eats with them, as the Gospel often relates, will lead us to show our gratitude in a good life and a glad heart.

The Gospels for the first week of Easter reproduce the accounts of the Resurrection as found in the four Gospels. In the ensuing weeks the Gospel of John is read omitting the parts already used for Lent. We can thus meditate on the message of Jesus as seen in the light of Easter.

The First Readings for the entire season are taken from the Acts of the Apostles. In this way the Church sets before us the history of the primitive community with its accent on the joy and fervor of Christians flowing from the knowledge of Christ's Resurrection.

EASTER SUNDAY

During the Night

THE EASTER VIGIL

1. *In accord with ancient tradition, this night is one of vigil for the Lord (Ex 12, 42). The Gospel of Luke (12, 35ff) is a reminder to the faithful to have their lamps burning ready, to be like men awaiting their master's return so that when he arrives he will find them wide awake and will seat them at his table.*

2. *The night vigil is arranged in four parts: (a) a brief service of light; (b) the liturgy of the word, when the Church meditates on all the wonderful things God has done for his people from the beginning; (c) the liturgy of baptism, when new members of the Church are reborn as the day of resurrection approaches; and (d) the liturgy of the eucharist, when the whole Church is called to the table which the Lord has prepared for his people through his death and resurrection.*

3. *The entire celebration of the Easter Vigil takes place at night. It should not begin before nightfall; it should end before daybreak on Sunday.*

In the United States, although it is never permitted to celebrate the entire Easter Vigil more than once in a given church or to anticipate the Mass of Easter before the vigil, in those places where the local Ordinary permits the anticipation of Sunday Masses on Sunday evening, for pastoral reasons an additional Mass may be celebrated after the Mass of the Easter Vigil. Such a Mass may follow the liturgy of the word of the Mass of the Easter Vigil (nos. 23-26) and other texts of that Mass and should include the renewal of baptismal promises (nos. 46-47).

4. *Even if the vigil Mass takes place before midnight, the Easter Mass of the resurrection is celebrated.*

Those who participate in the Mass at night may receive communion again at the second Mass of Easter Sunday.

In the United States, communion may be given under both kinds in accordance with the judgment of the Ordinary, at the Mass of the Easter Vigil.

5. *Those who celebrate or concelebrate the Mass at night may celebrate or concelebrate the second Mass of Easter Sunday.*

6. *The priest and deacon wear white Mass vestments. Candles should be prepared for all who take part in the vigil.*

PART ONE

SOLEMN BEGINNING OF THE VIGIL: THE SERVICE OF LIGHT

7. *All the lights in the church are put out.*

A large fire is prepared in a suitable place outside the church. When the people have assembled, the priest goes there with the ministers, one of whom carries the Easter candle.

If it is not possible to light the fire outside the church, the rite is carried out as in no. 13 below, p. 725.

8. *The priest greets the congregation in the usual manner and briefly instructs them about the vigil in these or similar words:*

Dear friends in Christ,
on this most holy night,
when our Lord Jesus Christ passed from death to life,
the Church invites her children throughout the world
to come together in vigil and prayer.
This is the passover of the Lord:
if we honor the memory of his death and resurrection
by hearing his word and celebrating his mysteries,
then we may be confident
that we shall share his victory over death
and live with him for ever in God.

9. *Then the fire is blessed.*

Let us pray.
Father,
we share in the light of your glory
through your Son, the light of the world.
Make this new fire ✠ holy, and inflame us with new
    hope.

Purify our minds by this Easter celebration,
and bring us one day to the feast of eternal light.
We ask this through Christ our Lord. ℟. **Amen.**

The Easter candle is lighted from the new fire.

Preparation of the Candle

10. *Depending on the nature of the congregation, it may seem appropriate to stress the dignity and significance of the Easter candle with other symbolic rites. This may be done as follows:*

After the blessing of the new fire, an acolyte or one of the ministers brings the Easter candle to the celebrant, who cuts a cross in the wax with a stylus. Then he traces the Greek letter alpha above the cross, the letter omega below, and the numerals of the current year between the arms of the cross. Meanwhile he says:

1. Christ yesterday and today *(as he traces the vertical arm of the cross),*
2. the beginning and the end *(the horizontal arm),*
3. Alpha *(alpha, above the cross),*
4. and Omega *(omega, below the cross);*
5. all time belongs to him *(the first numeral, in the upper left corner of the cross),*
6. and all the ages *(the second numeral in the upper right corner);*
7. to him be glory and power *(the third numeral in the lower left corner),*
8. through every age and for ever. Amen. *(the last numeral in the lower right corner).*

```
       A
    1  |  9
       |
    7  |
       Ω
```

11. *When the cross and other marks have been made, the priest may insert five grains of incense in the candle. He does this in the form of a cross, saying:*

1. By his holy
2. and glorious wounds   1
3. may Christ our Lord   4 2 5
4. guard us   3
5. and keep us. Amen.

12. The priest lights the candle from the new fire, saying:

May the light of Christ, rising in glory,
dispel the darkness of our hearts and minds.

Any or all of the preceding rites may be used, depending on local pastoral circumstances. The conferences of bishops may also determine other rites better adapted to the culture of the people.

---

13. Where it may be difficult to have a large fire, the blessing of the fire is adapted to the circumstances. When the people have assembled in the church as on other occasions, the priest goes with the ministers (carrying the Easter candle) to the church door. If possible, the people turn to face the priest.

The greeting and brief instruction take place as in above in no. 8. Then the fire is blessed (no. 9) and, if desired, the candle is prepared and lighted as above in nos. 10-12.

Procession

14. Then the deacon or, if there is no deacon, the priest takes the Easter candle, lifts it high, and sings alone:

Christ our light.

All answer:

Thanks be to God.

The conferences of bishops may determine a richer acclamation.

15. Then all enter the church, led by the deacon with the Easter candle. If incense is used, the thurifer goes before the deacon.

At the church door the deacon lifts the candle high and sings a second time:

Christ our light.

All answer:

Thanks be to God.

All light their candles from the Easter candle and continue in the procession.

When the deacon arrives before the altar, he faces the people and sings a third time:

Christ our light.

All answer:

Thanks be to God.

Then the lights in the church are put on.

Easter Proclamation (Exsultet)

16.   *When he comes to the altar, the priest goes to his chair. The deacon places the Easter candle on a stand in the middle of the sanctuary or near the lectern. If incense is used, the priest puts some in the censer, as at the gospel of Mass. Then the deacon asks the blessing of the priest, who says in a low voice:*

The Lord be in your heart and on your lips,
that you may worthily proclaim his Easter praise.
In the name of the Father, and of the Son, ✠ and of
the Holy Spirit. ℟. **Amen.**

This blessing is omitted if the Easter proclamation is sung by one who is not a deacon.

17.   *The book and candle may be incensed. Then the deacon or, if there is no deacon, the priest sings the Easter proclamation at the lectern or pulpit. All stand and hold lighted candles.*

If necessary, the Easter proclamation may be sung by one who is not a deacon. In this case the words My dearest friends *up to the end of the introduction are omitted, as is the greeting* The Lord be with you.

The Easter proclamation may be sung either in the long or short form. The conferences of bishops may also adapt the text by inserting acclamations for the people.

Long Form of the Easter Proclamation (Exsultet)

18.   Rejoice, heavenly powers! Sing, choirs of angels!
         Exult, all creation around God's throne!
         Jesus Christ, our King, is risen!
         Sound the trumpet of salvation!

      Rejoice, O earth, in shining splendor,
         radiant in the brightness of your King!

Christ has conquered! Glory fills you!
Darkness vanishes for ever!

Rejoice, O Mother Church! Exult in glory!
The risen Savior shines upon you!
Let this place resound with joy,
echoing the mighty song of all God's people!

[My dearest friends, standing with me in this
holy light,
join me in asking God for mercy,
that he may give his unworthy minister
grace to sing his Easter praises.]

[℣. The Lord be with you.
℟. **And also with you.**]
℣. Lift up your hearts.
℟. **We lift them up to the Lord.**
℣. Let us give thanks to the Lord our God.
℟. **It is right to give him thanks and praise. ▼**

It is truly right
that with full hearts and minds and voices
we should praise the unseen God, the all-powerful
Father,
and his only Son, our Lord Jesus Christ.
For Christ has ransomed us with his blood,
and paid for us the price of Adam's sin
to our eternal Father!

This is our passover feast,
when Christ, the true Lamb, is slain,
whose blood consecrates the homes of all believers.

This is the night when first you saved our fathers:
you freed the people of Israel from their slavery
and led them dry-shod through the sea.

This is the night when the pillar of fire
destroyed the darkness of sin!

This is the night when Christians everywhere,
washed clean of sin
and freed from all defilement,

are restored to grace and grow together in holiness.

This is the night when Jesus Christ
broke the chains of death
and rose triumphant from the grave.

What good would life have been to us,
had Christ not come as our Redeemer?

Father, how wonderful your care for us!
How boundless your merciful love!
To ransom a slave
you gave away your Son.

O happy fault, O necessary sin of Adam,
which gained for us so great a Redeemer!

Most blessed of all nights, chosen by God
to see Christ rising from the dead!

Of this night scripture says:
"The night will be as clear as day:
it will become my light, my joy."

The power of this holy night
dispels all evil, washes guilt away,
restores lost innocence, brings mourners joy;
it casts out hatred, brings us peace, and humbles
earthly pride.

Night truly blessed when heaven is wedded to earth
and man is reconciled with God!

Therefore, heavenly Father, in the joy of this night,
receive our evening sacrifice of praise,
your Church's solemn offering.

Accept this Easter candle,
a flame divided but undimmed,
a pillar of fire that glows to the honor of God.

Let it mingle with the lights of heaven
and continue bravely burning
to dispel the darkness of this night!

May the Morning Star which never sets find this
flame still burning:

Christ, that Morning Star, who came back from
　　the dead,
and shed his peaceful light on all mankind,
　　your Son who lives and reigns for ever and ever.
℟. **Amen.**

Short Form of the Easter Proclamation (Exsultet)
19.

Rejoice, heavenly powers! Sing, choirs of angels!
　　Exult, all creation around God's throne!
　　Jesus Christ, our King, is risen!
　　Sound the trumpet of salvation!

Rejoice, O earth, in shining splendor,
　　radiant in the brightness of your King!
　　Christ has conquered! Glory fills you!
　　Darkness vanishes for ever!

Rejoice, O Mother Church! Exult in glory!
　　The risen Savior shines upon you!
　　Let this place resound with joy,
　　echoing the mighty song of all God's people!

[℣. The Lord be with you.
℟. **And also with you.**]
℣. Lift up your hearts.
℟. **We lift them up to the Lord.**
℣. Let us give thanks to the Lord our God.
℟. **It is right to give him thanks and praise. ✟**

It is truly right
that with full hearts and minds and voices
we should praise the unseen God, the all-powerful
　　Father,
and his only Son, our Lord Jesus Christ.

For Christ has ransomed us with his blood,
　　and paid for us the price of Adam's sin
　　to our eternal Father!

This is our passover feast,
　　when Christ, the true Lamb, is slain,

whose blood consecrates the homes of all believers.

This is the night when first you saved our fathers:
you freed the people of Israel from their slavery
and led them dry-shod through the sea.

This is the night when Christians everywhere,
washed clean of sin
and freed from all defilement,
are restored to grace and grow together in holiness.

This is the night when Jesus Christ
broke the chains of death
and rose triumphant from the grave.

Father, how wonderful your care for us!
How boundless your merciful love!
To ransom a slave
you gave away your Son.

O happy fault, O necessary sin of Adam,
which gained for us so great a Redeemer!

The power of this holy night
dispels all evil, washes guilt away,
restores lost innocence, brings mourners joy.

Night truly blessed when heaven is wedded to earth
and man is reconciled with God!

Therefore, heavenly Father, in the joy of this night,
receive our evening sacrifice of praise,
your Church's solemn offering.

Accept this Easter candle.
May it always dispel the darkness of this night!

May the Morning Star which never sets find this
flame still burning:
Christ, that Morning Star, who came back from
the dead,
and shed his peaceful light on all mankind,
your Son who lives and reigns for ever and ever.

℞. **Amen.**

PART TWO

LITURGY OF THE WORD

20. *In this vigil, the mother of all vigils, nine readings are provided, seven from the Old Testament and two from the New Testament (the epistle and gospel).*

21. *The number of readings from the Old Testament may be reduced for pastoral reasons, but it must always be borne in mind that the reading of the word of God is the fundamental element of the Easter Vigil. At least three readings from the Old Testament should be read, although for more serious reasons the number may be reduced to two. The reading of Exodus 14, however, is never to be omitted.*

22. *After the Easter proclamation, the candles are put aside and all sit down. Before the readings begin, the priest speaks to the people in these or similar words:*

Dear friends in Christ,
we have begun our solemn vigil.
Let us now listen attentively to the word of God,
recalling how he saved his people throughout history
and, in the fullness of time,
sent his own Son to be our Redeemer.
Through this Easter celebration,
may God bring to perfection
the saving work he has begun in us.

23. *The readings follow. A reader goes to the lectern and proclaims the first reading. Then the cantor leads the psalm and the people respond. All rise and the priest sings or says* Let us pray. *When all have prayed silently for a while, he sings or says the prayer.*

Instead of the responsorial psalm a period of silence may be observed. In this case the pause after Let us pray *is omitted.*

24. READING I Gn 1, 1—2, 2 or 1, 1. 26-31

God created the world and all that is in it. He saw that it was good. This reading from the first book of the Bible shows that God loved all that he made.

[If the "Short Form" is used, the indented text in brackets is omitted.]

920-13

The beginning of the book of Genesis

In the beginning, when God created the heavens and the earth,

[the earth was a formless wasteland, and darkness covered the abyss, while a mighty wind swept over the waters.

Then God said, "Let there be light," and there was light. God saw how good the light was. God then separated the light from the darkness. God called the light "day," and the darkness he called "night." Thus evening came, and morning followed—the first day.

Then God said, "Let there be a dome in the middle of the waters, to separate one body of water from the other." And so it happened: God made the dome, and it separated the water above the dome from the water below it. God called the dome "the sky." Evening came, and morning followed—the second day.

Then God said, "Let the water under the sky be gathered into a single basin, so that the dry land may appear." And so it happened: the water under the sky was gathered into its basin, and the dry land appeared. God called the dry land "the earth," and the basin of the water he called "the sea." God saw how good it was. Then God said, "Let the earth bring forth vegetation: every kind of plant that bears seed and every kind of friut tree on earth that bears fruit with its seed in it." And so it happened: the earth brought forth every kind of plant that bears seed and every kind of fruit tree on earth that bears fruit with its seed in it. God saw how good it was. Evening came, and morning followed—the third day.

Then God said: "Let there be lights in the dome of the sky, to separate day from night. Let them mark the fixed times, the days and the years, and serve as luminaries in the dome of the sky, to shed light upon the earth." And so it happened: God made the two great lights, the greater one to govern the day, and the lesser one to govern the night; and he made the stars. God set them in the dome of the sky, to shed light upon the earth, to govern the day and the night, and to separate the light from the darkness. God saw how good it was. Evening came, and morning followed—the fourth day.

Then God said, "Let the water teem with an abundance of living creatures, and on the earth let birds fly beneath the dome of the sky." And so it happened: God created the great sea monsters and all kinds of swimming creatures with which the water teems, and all kinds of winged birds. God saw how good it was, and God blessed them, saying, "Be fertile, multiply, and fill the water of the seas; and let the birds multiply on the earth." Evening came, and morning followed—the fifth day.

Then God said, "Let the earth bring forth all kinds of living creatures: cattle, creeping things, and wild animals of all kinds." And so it happened: God made all kinds of wild animals, all kinds of cattle, and all kinds of creeping things of the earth. God saw how good it was. Then] God said: "Let us make man in our image, after our likeness. Let them have dominion over the fish of the sea, the birds of the air, and the cattle, and over all the wild animals and all the creatures that crawl on the ground."

God created man in his image;
in the divine image he created him;
male and female he created them.

God blessed them, saying: "Be fertile and multiply;

fill the earth and subdue it. Have dominion over the fish of the sea, the birds of the air, and all the living things that move on the earth." God also said: "See, I give you every seed-bearing plant all over the earth and every tree that has seed-bearing fruit on it to be your food; and to all the animals of the land, all the birds of the air, and all the living creatures that crawl on the ground, I give all the green plants for food." And so it happened. God looked at everything he had made, and he found it very good.

[Evening came, and morning followed—the sixth day.

Thus the heavens and the earth and all their array were completed. Since on the seventh day God was finished with the work he had been doing, he rested on the seventh day from all the work he had undertaken.]

This is the Word of the Lord. ℟. **Thanks be to God.** ℣

Responsorial Psalm
Ps 104, 1-2. 5-6. 10. 12. 13-14. 24. 35

℟. (30) **Lord, send out your Spirit,
and renew the face of the earth.**

Bless the Lord, O my soul!
   O Lord, my God, you are great indeed!
You are clothed with majesty and glory,
   robed in light as with a cloak. — ℟

You fixed the earth upon its foundation,
   not to be moved forever;
With the ocean, as with a garment, you covered it;
   above the mountains the waters stood. — ℟

You send forth springs into the watercourses
   that wind among the mountains.
Beside them the birds of heaven dwell;
   from among the branches they send forth their
   song. — ℟

You water the mountains from your palace;
   the earth is replete with the fruit of your works.

You raise grass for the cattle,
   and vegetation for men's use,
Producing bread from the earth. — ℟

How manifold are your works, O Lord!
   In wisdom you have wrought them all—
   the earth is full of your creatures.
Bless the Lord, O my soul! Alleluia. — ℟ ✟

OR

Responsorial Psalm   Ps 33, 4-5. 6-7. 12-13. 20-22

℟. (5) **The earth is full of the goodness of the Lord.**

Upright is the word of the Lord,
   and all his works are trustworthy.
He loves justice and right;
   of the kindness of the Lord the earth is full. — ℟

By the word of the Lord the heavens were made;
   by the breath of his mouth all their host.
He gathers the waters of the sea as in a flask;
   in cellars he confines the deep. — ℟

Happy the nation whose God is the Lord,
   the people he has chosen for his own inheritance.
From heaven the Lord looks down;
   he sees all mankind. — ℟

Our soul waits for the Lord,
   who is our help and our shield.
May your kindness, O Lord, be upon us
   who have put our hope in you. — ℟ ✟

PRAYER

Let us pray.
Almighty and eternal God,
you created all things in wonderful beauty and order.
Help us now to perceive
how still more wonderful is the new creation
by which in the fullness of time
you redeemed your people
through the sacrifice of our passover, Jesus Christ,
who lives and reigns for ever and ever. ℟. **Amen.** ✟

OR

PRAYER (on the creation of man)

Let us pray.
Lord God,
the creation of man was a wonderful work,
his redemption still more wonderful.
May we persevere in right reason
against all that entices to sin
and so attain to everlasting joy.
We ask this through Christ our Lord. ℟. **Amen.** ✟

25. READING II
Gn 22, 1-18 or 22, 1-2. 9. 10-13. 15-18

Abraham is obedient to the will of God. Because God asks him, without
hesitation he prepares to sacrifice his son Isaac. In the new order,
God sends his Son to redeem man by his death on the cross.

[*If the "Short Form" is used, the indented text in
brackets is omitted.*]

A reading from the book of Genesis

God put Abraham to the test. He called to him,
"Abraham!" "Ready!" he replied. Then God said:
"Take your son Isaac, your only one, whom you love,
and go to the land of Moriah. There you shall offer
him up as a holocaust on a height that I will point
out to you."

[Early the next morning Abraham saddled
his donkey, took with him his son Isaac, and
two of his servants as well, and with the wood
that he had cut for the holocaust, set out for
the place of which God had told him.

On the third day Abraham got sight of the
place from afar. Then he said to his servants:
"Both of you stay here with the donkey, while
the boy and I go on over yonder. We will worship and then come back to you." Thereupon
Abraham took the wood for the holocaust and

laid it on his son Isaac's shoulders, while he himself carried the fire and the knife. As the two walked on together, Isaac spoke to his father Abraham. "Father!" he said. "Yes, son," he replied. Isaac continued, "Here are the fire and the wood, but where is the sheep for the holocaust?" "Son," Abraham answered, "God himself will provide the sheep for the holocaust." Then the two continued going forward.]

When they came to the place of which God had told him, Abraham built an altar there and arranged the wood on it.

[Next he tied up his son Isaac, and put him on top of the wood on the altar.]

Then he reached out and took the knife to slaughter his son. But the Lord's messenger called to him from heaven, "Abraham, Abraham!" "Yes, Lord," he answered. "Do not lay your hand on the boy," said the messenger. "Do not do the least thing to him. I know now how devoted you are to God, since you did not withhold from me your own beloved son." As Abraham looked about, he spied a ram caught by its horns in the thicket. So he went and took the ram and offered it up as a holocaust in place of his son.

[Abraham named the site Yahweh-yireh; hence people now say, "On the mountain the Lord will see."]

Again the Lord's messenger called to Abraham from heaven and said: "I swear by myself, declares the Lord, that because you acted as you did in not withholding from me your beloved son, I will bless you abundantly and make your descendants as countless as the stars of the sky and the sand of the seashore; your descendants shall take possession of the gates of their enemies, and in your descendants all the nations of the earth shall find blessing—all this because you obeyed my command."—This is the Word of the Lord. ℟. **Thanks be to God.** ℣

Responsorial Psalm   Ps 16, 5. 8. 9-10. 11

℟. (1) **Keep me safe, O God;**
       you are my hope.

O Lord, my allotted portion and my cup,
    you it is who hold fast my lot.
I set the Lord ever before me;
    with him at my right hand I shall not be dis-
    turbed. — ℟

Therefore my heart is glad and my soul rejoices,
    my body, too, abides in confidence;
Because you will not abandon my soul to the nether
    world,
    nor will you suffer your faithful one to undergo
    corruption. — ℟

You will show me the path to life,
    fullness of joys in your presence,
    the delights at your right hand forever. — ℟ ♦

PRAYER

Let us pray.
God and Father of all who believe in you,
you promised Abraham that he would become the
    father of all nations,
and through the death and resurrection of Christ
you fulfill that promise:
everywhere throughout the world you increase your
    chosen people.
May we respond to your call
by joyfully accepting your invitation to the new life
    of grace.
We ask this through Christ our Lord. ℟. **Amen.** ♦

26.   READING III   Ex 14, 15—15, 1

Moses leads the Israelites out of Egypt. He opens a path of escape
through the Red Sea. God protects his people. Through the waters of
baptism, men are freed from sin.

A reading from the book of Exodus

The Lord said to Moses, "Why are you crying out
to me? Tell the Israelites to go forward. And you,

lift up your staff and, with hand outstretched over the sea, split the sea in two, that the Israelites may pass through it on dry land. But I will make the Egyptians so obstinate that they will go in after them. Then I will receive glory through Pharaoh and all his army, his chariots and charioteers. The Egyptians shall know that I am the Lord, when I receive glory through Pharaoh and his chariots and charioteers."

The angel of God, who had been leading Israel's camp, now moved and went around behind them. The column of cloud also, leaving the front, took up its place behind them, so that it came between the camp of the Egyptians and that of Israel. But the cloud now became dark, and thus the night passed without the rival camps coming any closer together all night long. Then Moses stretched out his hand over the sea, and the Lord swept the sea with a strong east wind throughout the night and so turned it into dry land. When the water was thus divided, the Israelites marched into the midst of the sea on dry land, with the water like a wall to their right and to their left.

The Egyptians followed in pursuit; all Pharaoh's horses and chariots and charioteers went after them right into the midst of the sea. In the night watch just before dawn the Lord cast through the column of the fiery cloud upon the Egyptian force a glance that threw it into a panic; and he so clogged their chariot wheels that they could hardly drive. With that the Egyptians sounded the retreat before Israel, because the Lord was fighting for them against the Egyptians.

Then the Lord told Moses, "Stretch out your hand over the sea, that the water may flow back upon the Egyptians, upon their chariots and their charioteers." So Moses stretched out his hand over the sea, and at dawn the sea flowed back to its normal depth. The Egyptians were fleeing head on toward the sea, when the Lord hurled them into its midst. As the water flowed back, it covered the chariots and the charioteers of Pharaoh's whole army which had followed the Israelites into the sea. Not a single one of them escaped. But the Israelites had marched on dry land through the midst of the sea, with the water like a wall to their right and to their left. Thus the Lord saved Israel on that day from the power of the Egyptians. When Israel saw the Egyptians lying dead on the seashore and beheld the great power that the Lord had shown against the Egyptians, they feared the Lord and believed in him and in his servant Moses.

Then Moses and the Israelites sang this song to the Lord:

I will sing to the Lord, for he is gloriously triumphant;
> horse and chariot he has cast into the sea.

This is the Word of the Lord. ℟. **Thanks be to God.** ↓

Responsorial Psalm   Ex 15, 1-2. 3-4. 5-6. 17-18

℟. (1) **Let us sing to the Lord;
he has covered himself in glory.**

I will sing to the Lord, for he is gloriously triumphant;
> horse and chariot he has cast into the sea.
My strength and my courage is the Lord,
> and he has been my savior.
He is my God, I praise him;
> the God of my father, I extol him. — ℟

The Lord is a warrior,
> Lord is his name!
Pharaoh's chariots and army he hurled into the sea;
> the elite of his officers were submerged into the Red Sea. — ℟

The flood waters covered them,
> they sank into the depths like a stone.
Your right hand, O Lord, magnificent in power,
> your right hand, O Lord, has shattered the enemy. — ℟

You brought in the people you redeemed
and planted them on the mountain of your inheritance.
The place where you made your seat, O Lord,
the sanctuary, O Lord, which your hands established.
The Lord shall reign forever and ever. — ℟ ♥

PRAYER

Let us pray.
Father, even today we see the wonders
of the miracles you worked long ago.
You once saved a single nation from slavery,
and now you offer that salvation to all through bap-
tism.
May the peoples of the world become true sons of
Abraham
and prove worthy of the heritage of Israel.
We ask this through Christ our Lord. ℟. **Amen.** ♥

OR

PRAYER

Let us pray.
Lord God, in the new covenant
you shed light on the miracles you worked in ancient
times:
the Red Sea is a symbol of our baptism,
and the nation you freed from slavery
is a sign of your Christian people.
May every nation
share the faith and privilege of Israel,
and come to new birth in the Holy Spirit.
We ask this through Christ our Lord. ℟. **Amen.** ♥

27.   READING IV   Is 54, 5-14

For a time, God hid from his people, but his love for them is everlasting. He takes pity on them and promises them prosperity.

A reading from the book of the prophet Isaiah

He who has become your husband is your Maker;
his name is the Lord of hosts;

Your redeemer is the Holy One of Israel,
  called God of all the earth.
The Lord calls you back,
  like a wife forsaken and grieved in spirit,
A wife married in youth and then cast off,
  says your God.
For a brief moment I abandoned you,
  but with great tenderness I will take you back.
In an outburst of wrath, for a moment
  I hid my face from you;
But with enduring love I take pity on you,
  says the Lord, your redeemer.
This is for me like the days of Noah,
  when I swore that the waters of Noah
  should never again deluge the earth;
So I have sworn not to be angry with you,
  or to rebuke you.
Though the mountains leave their place
  and the hills be shaken,

My love shall never leave you
  nor my covenant of peace be shaken,
  says the Lord, who has mercy on you.
O afflicted one, storm-battered and unconsoled,
  I lay your pavements in carnelians,
  and your foundations in sapphires;
I will make your battlements of rubies,
  your gates of carbuncles,
  and all your walls of precious stones.
All your sons shall be taught by the Lord,
  and great shall be the peace of your children.
In justice shall you be established,
  far from the fear of oppression,
  where destruction cannot come near you.
This is the Word of the Lord. ℟. **Thanks be to God.** ℣

Responsorial Psalm   Ps 30, 2. 4. 5-6. 11-12. 13
℟. (2) **I will praise you, Lord,**
  for you have rescued me.

I will extol you, O Lord, for you drew me clear
and did not let my enemies rejoice over me.
O Lord, you brought me up from the nether world;
you preserved me from among those going down
into the pit. — ℟

Sing praise to the Lord, you his faithful ones,
and give thanks to his holy name.
For his anger lasts but a moment;
a lifetime, his good will.
At nightfall, weeping enters in,
but with the dawn, rejoicing. — ℟

Hear, O Lord, and have pity on me;
O Lord, be my helper.
You changed my mourning into dancing;
O Lord, my God, forever will I give you
thanks. — ℟ ✟

PRAYER

Let us pray.
Almighty and eternal God,
glorify your name by increasing your chosen people
as you promised long ago.
In reward for their trust,
may we see in the Church the fulfillment of your
promise.
We ask this through Christ our Lord. ℟. **Amen.** ✟

*Prayers may also be chosen from those given after the
following readings, if the readings are omitted.*

28.   READING V   Is 55, 1-11

God is a loving Father and he calls his people back. He promises an
everlasting covenant with them. God is merciful, generous, and forgiving.

A reading from the book of the prophet Isaiah

Thus says the Lord:
All you who are thirsty,
come to the water!
You who have no money,

come, receive grain and eat;
Come, without paying and without cost,
    drink wine and milk!
Why spend your money for what is not bread;
    your wages for what fails to satisfy?
Heed me, and you shall eat well,
    you shall delight in rich fare.
Come to me heedfully,
    listen, that you may have life.
I will renew with you the everlasting covenant,
    the benefits assured to David.
As I made him a witness to the peoples,
    a leader and commander of nations,
So shall you summon a nation you knew not,
    and nations that knew you not shall run to you,
Because of the Lord, your God,
    the Holy One of Israel, who has glorified you.
Seek the Lord while he may be found,
    call him while he is near.
Let the scoundrel forsake his way,
    and the wicked man his thoughts;
Let him turn to the Lord for mercy;
    to our God, who is generous in forgiving.
For my thoughts are not your thoughts,
    nor are your ways my ways, says the Lord.
As high as the heavens are above the earth,
    so high are my ways above your ways
    and my thoughts above your thoughts.
For just as from the heavens
    the rain and snow come down
And do not return there
    till they have watered the earth,
    making it fertile and fruitful,
Giving seed to him who sows
    and bread to him who eats,
So shall my word be
    that goes forth from my mouth;
It shall not return to me void,
    but shall do my will,

achieving the end for which I sent it.
This is the Word of the Lord. ℟. **Thanks be to God.** ℣

Responsorial Psalm   Is 12, 2-3. 4. 5-6
℟. (3) **You will draw water joyfully from the springs
    of salvation.**

God indeed is my savior;
    I am confident and unafraid.
My strength and my courage is the Lord,
    and he has been my savior.
With joy you will draw water
    at the fountain of salvation. — ℟

Give thanks to the Lord, acclaim his name;
    among the nations make known his deeds,
    proclaim how exalted is his name. — ℟

Sing praise to the Lord for his glorious achievement;
    let this be known throughout all the earth.
Shout with exultation, O city of Zion,
    for great in your midst
    is the Holy One of Israel! — ℟ ℣

PRAYER
Let us pray.
Almighty, ever-living God,
only hope of the world,
by the preaching of the prophets
you proclaimed the mysteries we are celebrating
    tonight.
Help us to be your faithful people,
for it is by your inspiration alone
that we can grow in goodness.
We ask this through Christ our Lord. ℟. **Amen.** ℣

29.   READING VI   Bar 3, 9-15. 32—4, 4

Baruch tells the people of Israel to walk in the ways of God. They have
to learn prudence, wisdom, understanding. Then they will have peace
forever.

A reading from the book of the prophet Baruch

Hear, O Israel, the commandments of life:
   listen, and know prudence!
How is it, Israel,
   that you are in the land of your foes,
   grown old in a foreign land,
Defiled with the dead,
   accounted with those destined for the nether
     world?
You have forsaken the fountain of wisdom!
   Had you walked in the way of God,
   you would have dwelt in enduring peace.
Learn where prudence is,
   where strength, where understanding;
That you may know also
   where are length of days, and life,
   where light of the eyes, and peace.
Who has found the place of wisdom,
   who has entered into her treasuries?

He who knows all things knows her;
   he has probed her by his knowledge—
He who established the earth for all time,
   and filled it with four-footed beasts;
He who dismisses the light, and it departs,
   calls it, and it obeys him trembling;
Before whom the stars at their posts
   shine and rejoice;
When he calls them, they answer, "Here we are!"
   shining with joy for their Maker.
Such is our God;
   no other is to be compared to him:
He has traced out all the way of understanding,
   and has given her to Jacob, his servant,
   to Israel, his beloved son.
Since then she has appeared on earth,
   and moved among men.
She is the book of the precepts of God,
   the law that endures forever;
All who cling to her will live,

but those will die who forsake her.
Turn, O Jacob, and receive her:
  walk by her light toward splendor.
Give not your glory to another,
  your privileges to an alien race.
Blessed are we, O Israel;
  for what pleases God is known to us!
This is the Word of the Lord. ℟. **Thanks be to God.** ⍆

Responsorial Psalm   Ps 19, 8. 9. 10. 11

℟. (Jn 6, 69) **Lord, you have the words of everlasting life.**

The law of the Lord is perfect,
  refreshing the soul;
The decree of the Lord is trustworthy,
  giving wisdom to the simple. — ℟

The precepts of the Lord are right,
  rejoicing the heart;
The command of the Lord is clear,
  enlightening the eye. — ℟

The fear of the Lord is pure,
  enduring forever;
The ordinances of the Lord are true,
  all of them just. — ℟

They are more precious than gold,
  than a heap of purest gold;
Sweeter also than syrup
  or honey from the comb. — ℟ ⍆

PRAYER

Let us pray.
Father, you increase your Church
by continuing to call all people to salvation.
Listen to our prayers
and always watch over those you cleanse in baptism.
We ask this through Christ our Lord. ℟. **Amen.** ⍆

30.   READING VII   Ez 36, 16-28

Ezekiel, as God's prophet, speaks for God who is to keep his name
holy among his people. All shall know the holiness of God. He will

cleanse his people from idol worship and make them his own again. This promise is again fulfilled in baptism in the restored order of redemption.

A reading from the book of the prophet Ezekiel

Thus the word of the Lord came to me: Son of man, when the house of Israel lived in their land, they defiled it by their conduct and deeds. In my sight their conduct was like the defilement of a menstruous woman. Therefore I poured out my fury upon them [because of the blood which they poured out on the ground, and because they defiled it with idols]. I scattered them among the nations, dispersing them over foreign lands; according to their conduct and deeds I judged them. But when they came among the nations [wherever they came], they served to profane my holy name, because it was said to them: "These are the people of the Lord, yet they had to leave their land." So I have relented because of my holy name which the house of Israel profaned among the nations where they came. Therefore say to the house of Israel: Thus says the Lord God: Not for your sakes do I act, house of Israel, but for the sake of my holy name, which you profaned among the nations to which you came. I will prove the holiness of my great name, profaned among the nations, in whose midst you have profaned it. Thus the nations shall know that I am the Lord, says the Lord God, when in their sight I prove my holiness through you. For I will take you away from among the nations, gather you from all the foreign lands, and bring you back to your own land. I will sprinkle clean water upon you to cleanse you from all your impurities, and from all your idols I will cleanse you. I will give you a new heart and place a new spirit within you, taking from your bodies your stony hearts and giving you natural hearts. I will put my spirit within you and make you live by my statutes, careful to observe my decrees. You shall live in the land I gave your fathers; you shall be my people, and I will be your God.—This is the Word of the Lord. ℟. **Thanks be to God.** ✟

Responsorial Psalm   Ps 42, 3. 5; 43, 3. 4

℟. (Ps 42, 2) **Like a deer that longs for running streams,**
my soul longs for you, my God.

Athirst is my soul for God, the living God.
When shall I go and behold the face of God? — ℟

I went with the throng
and led them in procession to the house of God,
Amid loud cries of joy and thanksgiving,
with the multitude keeping festival. — ℟

Send forth your light and your fidelity;
they shall lead me on
And bring me to your holy mountain,
to your dwelling-place. — ℟

Then will I go into the altar of God,
the God of my gladness and joy;
Then will I give you thanks upon the harp,
O God, my God! — ℟ ✟

OR

When baptism is celebrated, the responsorial psalm after Reading V (Is 12, 2-3. 4. 5-6) as above, p. 745, may be used; or the following:

Responsorial Psalm   Ps 51, 12-13. 14-15. 18-19

℟. (12) **Create a clean heart in me, O God.**

A clean heart create for me, O God,
and a steadfast spirit renew within me.
Cast me not out from your presence,
and your holy spirit take not from me. — ℟

Give me back the joy of your salvation,
and a willing spirit sustain in me.
I will teach transgressors your ways,
and sinners shall return to you. — ℟

For you are not pleased with sacrifices;

should I offer a holocaust, you would not accept it.
My sacrifice, O God, is a contrite spirit;
a heart contrite and humbled, O God, you will not
spurn. — ℟ ✝

PRAYER

Let us pray.
God of unchanging power and light,
look with mercy and favor on your entire Church.
Bring lasting salvation to mankind,
so that the world may see
the fallen lifted up,
the old made new,
and all things brought to perfection,
through him who is their origin,
our Lord Jesus Christ,
who lives and reigns for ever and ever. ℟. **Amen.** ✝

OR

PRAYER

Let us pray.
Father, you teach us in both the Old and the New Testament
to celebrate this passover mystery.
Help us to understand your great love for us.
May the goodness you now show us
confirm our hope in your future mercy.
We ask this through Christ our Lord. ℟. **Amen.** ↓

OR

(if there are candidates to be baptized)

PRAYER

Let us pray.
Almighty and eternal God,
be present in this sacrament of your love.
Send your Spirit of adoption
on those to be born again in baptism.
And may the work of our humble ministry
be brought to perfection by your mighty power.
We ask this through Christ our Lord. ℟. **Amen.** ✝

31. *After the last reading from the Old Testament with its responsory and prayer, the altar candles are lighted, and the priest intones the* Gloria, *which is taken up by all present. The church bells are rung, according to local custom.*

32. *At the end of the hymn, the priest sings or says the opening prayer in the usual way.*

OPENING PRAYER

Let us pray.
Lord God, you have brightened this night
with the radiance of the risen Christ.
Quicken the spirit of sonship in your Church;
renew us in mind and body
to give you whole-hearted service.
Grant this through our Lord Jesus Christ, your Son,
who lives and reigns with you and the Holy Spirit,
one God, for ever and ever. ℟. **Amen.** ⱽ

33. *Then a reader proclaims the reading from the Apostle Paul.*

EPISTLE   Rom 6, 3-11

Baptism introduces man into union with Christ, suffering and dying. In the same way the Christian will be with Jesus in the rewards of his resurrection. Death no longer has power over him. The Christian is alive for God in Jesus.

A reading from the letter of Paul to the Romans

Are you not aware that we who were baptized into Christ Jesus were baptized into his death? Through baptism into his death we were buried with him, so that, just as Christ was raised from the dead by the glory of the Father, we too might live a new life. If we have been united with him through likeness to his death, so shall we be through a like resurrection. This we know: our old self was crucified with him so that the sinful body might be destroyed and we might be slaves to sin no longer. A man who is dead has been freed from sin. If we have died with Christ, we believe that we are also to live with him. We know that Christ, once raised from the dead, will never die again; death has no more power over him. His death was death to sin, once for all; his life is life for God. In the same way, you must consider yourselves dead to sin but alive for God in Christ Jesus.—This is the Word of the Lord. Ṙ. **Thanks be to God.** ✠

34. *After the Epistle all rise, and the priest solemnly intones the* alleluia, *which is repeated by all present.*

The cantor sings the psalm and the people answer Alleluia. *If necessary, the cantor of the psalm may himself intone the* alleluia.

Responsorial Psalm   Ps 118, 1-2. 16. 17. 22-23

Ṙ. **Alleluia. Alleluia. Alleluia.**

Give thanks to the Lord, for he is good,
    for his mercy endures forever.
Let the house of Israel say,
    "His mercy endures forever." — Ṙ

The right hand of the Lord has struck with power;
    the right hand of the Lord is exalted.
I shall not die, but live,
    and declare the works of the Lord. — Ṙ

The stone which the builders rejected
    has become the cornerstone.
By the Lord has this been done;
    it is wonderful in our eyes. — Ṙ ✠

35. *Incense may be used at the Gospel, but candles are not carried.*

(Year A)

GOSPEL   Mt 28, 1-10

Jesus has risen; he is not here. The cross has yielded to the empty tomb. Although Peter is singled out, the Easter message is first announced to the faithful, devoted women who followed Jesus. They hurry to share the Good News with the disciples.

Ṿ. The Lord be with you. Ṙ. **And also with you.**
✠ A reading from the holy gospel according to Matthew. Ṙ. **Glory to you, Lord.**

After the sabbath, as the first day of the week was

dawning, Mary Magdalene came with the other Mary
to inspect the tomb. Suddenly there was a mighty
earthquake, as the angel of the Lord descended from
heaven. He came to the stone, rolled it back, and sat
on it. In appearance he resembled a flash of light-
ning while his garments were as dazzling as snow.
The guards grew paralyzed with fear of him and fell
down like dead men. Then the angel spoke, addressing the women: "Do not be frightened. I know you
are looking for Jesus the crucified, but he is not here.
He has been raised, exactly as he promised. Come
and see the spot where he was laid. Then go quickly
and tell his disciples: 'He has been raised from the
dead and now goes ahead of you to Galilee, where
you will see him.' That is the message I have for
you."

They hurried away from the tomb half-overjoyed,
half-fearful, and ran to carry the good news to his
disciples. Suddenly, without warning, Jesus stood
before them and said, "Peace!" The women came up,
embraced his feet and did him homage. At this Jesus
said to them, "Do not be afraid! Go and carry the
news to my brothers that they are to go to Galilee,
where they will see me."—This is the gospel of the
Lord. R̷. **Praise to you, Lord Jesus Christ.**

(Year B)

GOSPEL   Mk 16, 1-8

Crucified and entombed on Good Friday, Jesus is living anew. On
Sunday morning his tomb is found empty. But those of his disciples
who believe in the testimony of the women who went to the tomb
will be able in their turn to see the risen Lord.

V̷. The Lord be with you. R̷. **And also with you.**
✠ A reading from the holy gospel according to Mark
R̷. **Glory to you, Lord.**

When the sabbath was over, Mary Magdalene, Mary
the mother of James, and Salome bought perfumed
oils with which they intended to go and anoint Jesus.

Very early, just after sunrise, on the first day of the week they came to the tomb. They were saying to one another, "Who will roll back the stone for us from the entrance to the tomb?" When they looked, they found that the stone had been rolled back. (It was a huge one.) On entering the tomb they saw a young man sitting at the right, dressed in a white robe. This frightened them thoroughly, but he reassured them: "You need not be amazed! You are looking for Jesus of Nazareth, the one who was crucified. He has been raised up; he is not here. See the place where they laid him. Go now and tell his disciples and Peter, 'He is going ahead of you to Galilee, where you will see him just as he told you.'" They made their way out and fled from the tomb bewildered and trembling; and because of their great fear, they said nothing to anyone.—This is the gospel of the Lord.
R̲. **Praise to you, Lord Jesus Christ.**

(Year C)

GOSPEL   Lk 24, 1-12

Mary of Magdala, Joanna, and Mary, the mother of James, are the three women named by Luke as the ones who bring spices and oils to anoint the body of Jesus on the first day of the week. Upon reaching the tomb, they find the stone rolled back, and when they enter the tomb, they find it empty. Peter also sees only the wrappings of the burial in the tomb.

V̲. The Lord be with you. R̲. **And also with you.**
✠ A reading from the holy gospel according to Luke
R̲. **Glory to you, Lord.**

On the first day of the week, at dawn, the women came to the tomb bringing the spices they had prepared. They found the stone rolled back from the tomb; but when they entered the tomb, they did not find the body of the Lord Jesus. While they were still at a loss what to think of this, two men in dazzling garments appeared beside them. Terrified, the women bowed to the ground. The men said to them:

"Why do you search for the living One among the dead? He is not here; he has been raised up. Remember what he said to you while he was still in Galilee —that the Son of Man must be delivered into the hands of sinful men, and be crucified, and on the third day rise again." With this reminder, his words came back to them.

On their return from the tomb, they told all these things to the Eleven and the others. The women were Mary of Magdala, Joanna, and Mary the mother of James. The other women with them also told the apostles, but the story seemed like nonsense and they refused to believe them. Peter, however, got up and ran to the tomb. He stooped down but could see nothing but the wrappings. So he went away full of amazement at what had occurred.—This is the gospel of the Lord. ℟. **Praise to you, Lord Jesus Christ.**

36. *The Homily follows the Gospel, and then the liturgy of baptism begins.*

PART THREE

LITURGY OF BAPTISM

37. *The priest goes with the ministers to the baptismal font, if this can be seen by the congregation. Otherwise a vessel of water is placed in the sanctuary.*

If there are candidates to be baptized, they are called forward and presented by their godparents. If they are children, the parents and godparents bring them forward in front of the congregation.

38. *Then the priest speaks to the people in these or similar words:*

If there are candidates to be baptized

Dear friends in Christ,
as our brothers and sisters approach the waters of
    rebirth,
let us help them by our prayers,
and ask God, our almighty Father,
to support them with his mercy and love.

If the font is to be blessed, but there is no one to be baptized

Dear friends in Christ,
let us ask God, the almighty Father,
to bless this font,
that those reborn in it
may be made one with his adopted children in Christ.

39. *The litany is sung by two cantors. All present stand (as is customary during the Easter season) and answer.*

If there is to be a procession of some length to the baptistery, the litany is sung during the procession. In this case those who are to be baptized are first called forward. Then the procession begins: the Easter candle is carried first, followed by the candidates with their godparents, and the priest with the ministers. The above instruction is given before the blessing of the water.

40. *If there is no one to be baptized and the font is not to be blessed the litany is omitted, and the blessing of water (no. 45) takes place at once.*

41. *In the litany some names of saints may be added, especially the titular of the church, the local patrons, or the saints of those to be baptized.*

Lord, have mercy.
Lord, have mercy.
Christ, have mercy.
Christ, have mercy.
Lord, have mercy.
Lord, have mercy.
Holy Mary, Mother of God, **pray for us.**
St. Michael, **pray for us.**
Holy angels of God, **pray for us.**
St. John the Baptist, **pray for us.**
St. Joseph, **pray for us.**
St. Peter and St. Paul, **pray for us.**
St. Andrew, **pray for us.**
St. John, **pray for us.**

St. Mary Magdalene, **pray for us.**
St. Stephen, **pray for us.**
St. Ignatius, **pray for us.**
St. Lawrence, **pray for us.**
St. Perpetua and St. Felicity, **pray for us.**
St. Agnes, **pray for us.**
St. Gregory, **pray for us.**
St. Augustine, **pray for us.**
St. Athanasius, **pray for us.**
St. Basil, **pray for us.**
St. Martin, **pray for us.**
St. Benedict, **pray for us.**
St. Francis and St. Dominic, **pray for us.**
St. Francis Xavier, **pray for us.**

St. John Vianney, **pray for us.**

St. Catherine, **pray for us.**

St. Teresa, **pray for us.**

All holy men and women, **pray for us.**

Lord, be merciful, **Lord, save your people**

From all evil, **Lord, save your people.**

From every sin, **Lord, save your people.**

From everlasting death, **Lord, save your people.**

By your coming as man, **Lord, save your people.**

By your death and rising to new life, **Lord, save your people.**

By your gift of the Holy Spirit, **Lord, save your people.**

Be merciful to us sinners, **Lord, hear our prayer.**

If there are candidates to be baptized

Give new life to these chosen ones by the grace of baptism, **Lord, hear our prayer.**

If there is no one to be baptized

By your grace bless this font where your children will be reborn, **Lord, hear our prayer.**

Jesus, Son of the living God, **Lord, hear our prayer.**

Christ, hear us, **Christ, hear us.**

Lord Jesus, hear our prayer, **Lord Jesus, hear our prayer.**

Blessing of Water

42. *The priest then blesses the baptismal water. With hands joined, he sings or says the following prayer:*

Father, you give us grace through sacramental signs,
which tell us of the wonders of your unseen power.

In baptism we use your gift of water,
which you have made a rich symbol
of the grace you give us in this sacrament.

At the very dawn of creation
your Spirit breathed on the waters,
making them the wellspring of all holiness.

The waters of the great flood
you made a sign of the waters of baptism,
that make an end of sin and a new beginning of goodness.

Through the waters of the Red Sea
    you led Israel out of slavery,
        to be an image of God's holy people,
        set free from sin by baptism.

In the waters of the Jordan
    your Son was baptized by John
    and anointed with the Spirit.

Your Son willed that water and blood
    should flow from his side
    as he hung upon the cross.

After his resurrection he told his disciples:
    "Go out and teach all nations,
    baptizing them in the name of the Father,
    and of the Son, and of the Holy Spirit."

Father, look now with love upon your Church,
    and unseal for her the fountain of baptism.

By the power of the Spirit
    give to the water of this font
    the grace of your Son.

You created man in your own likeness:
    cleanse him from sin in a new birth of innocence
    by water and the Spirit.

The priest may lower the Easter candle into the water either once or three times, as he continues:

We ask you, Father, with your Son
    to send the Holy Spirit upon the waters of this
        font.

He holds the candle in the water:

May all who are buried with Christ
    in the death of baptism
    rise also with him to newness of life.

We ask this through Christ our Lord. ℟. **Amen.**

43. *Then the candle is taken out of the water as the people sing the acclamation:*

**Springs of water, bless the Lord.
Give him glory and praise for ever.**

Any other appropriate acclamation may be sung.

44. *Those who are to be baptized renounce the devil individually. Then they are questioned about their faith and are baptized.*

Adults are confirmed immediately after baptism if a bishop or a priest with the faculty to confirm is present.

Celebration of Baptism *

[*The parts of the rite preceding the celebration of the sacrament are celebrated at a convenient time and place before the Easter Vigil. The celebration of the sacrament takes place after the blessing of the water.*]

RENUNCIATION OF SIN AND PROFESSION OF FAITH

The celebrant speaks to the parents and godparents in these words [in the case of the baptism of adults, he addresses his words to the candidates directly and refers to their own faith and responsibility]:

Dear parents and godparents:

You have come here to present these children for baptism. By water and the Holy Spirit they are to receive the gift of new life from God, who is love.

On your part, you must make it your constant care to bring them up in the practice of the faith. See that the divine life which God gives them is kept safe from the poison of sin, to grow always stronger in their hearts.

If your faith makes you ready to accept this responsibility, renew now the vows of your own baptism. Reject sin; profess your faith in Christ Jesus. This is the faith of the Church. This is the faith in which these children are about to be baptized.

The celebrant questions the candidates and the parents and godparents:

---

* The text is from the Rite of Baptism for Children, with the appropriate adaptations to adult candidates made, since the rite for the baptism of adults has not yet been published in revised form. See Rite of Baptism for Children, Introduction, no. 28.

A

Celebrant: Do you reject Satan?

Candidates, parents and godparents: I do.

Celebrant: And all his works?

Candidates, parents and godparents: I do.

Celebrant: And all his empty promises?

Candidates, parents and godparents: I do.

OR

B

Celebrant: Do you reject sin, so as to live in the freedom of God's children?

Candidates, parents and godparents: I do.

Celebrant: Do you reject the glamor of evil, and refuse to be mastered by sin?

Candidates, parents and godparents: I do.

Celebrant: Do you reject Satan, father of sin and prince of darkness?

Candidates, parents and godparents: I do.

Next the celebrant asks for the threefold profession of faith from the candidates, parents and godparents:

Celebrant: Do you believe in God, the Father almighty, creator of heaven and earth?

Candidates, parents and godparents: I do.

Celebrant: Do you believe in Jesus Christ, his only Son, our Lord, who was born of the Virgin Mary, was crucified, died and was buried, rose from the dead and is now seated at the right hand of the Father?

Candidates, parents and godparents: I do.

Celebrant: Do you believe in the Holy Spirit, the holy Catholic Church, the communion of saints, the forgiveness of sins, the resurrection of the body, and life everlasting?

Candidates, parents and godparents: I do.

BAPTISM OF ADULTS

The celebrant invites the first of the candidates to the font with his Godparents. Using the name of the candidate, he questions him.

Celebrant: Is it your will to be baptized in the faith of the Church, which we have all professed with you?

Candidate: It is.

He baptizes the candidate, saying:

N., I baptize you in the name of the Father,

He immerses the candidate or pours water upon him.

and of the Son,

He immerses the candidate or pours water upon him a second time.

and of the Holy Spirit.

He immerses the candidate or pours water upon him a third time. He asks the same question and performs the same action for each candidate.

After each baptism it is appropriate for the people to sing a short acclamation (from the Rite of Baptism for Children, nos. 225-245) such as:

Blessed be God who chose you in Christ.

If baptism is done by immersion, the godparent holds or touches the candidate. If baptism is done by the pouring of water, the godparent places his right hand upon the right shoulder of the candidate.

BAPTISM OF CHILDREN

The celebrant invites the first of the families to the font. Using the name of the individual child, he questions the parents and godparents.

Celebrant: Is it your will that N. should be baptized in the faith of the Church, which we have all professed with you?

Candidate: It is.

He baptizes the child in the same way as the adult, above.

If the baptism is performed by the pouring of water, it is preferable that the child be held by the mother (or father). Where, however, it is felt that the existing custom should be retained, the godmother (or godfather) may hold the child. If baptism is by immersion, the mother or father (godmother or godfather) lifts the child out of the font.

If the number of children to be baptized is large, and other priests or deacons are present, these may baptize some of the children in the way described above, and with the same form.

ANOINTING WITH CHRISM

Then the celebrant says:

God the Father of our Lord Jesus Christ has freed you from sin, given you a new birth by water and the Holy Spirit, and welcomed you into his holy people. He now anoints you with the chrism of salvation. As Christ was anointed Priest, Prophet, and King, so may you live always as members of this body, sharing everlasting life.

All: **Amen.**

Next, the celebrant anoints each of the newly baptized on the crown of the head with chrism, in silence.

If the number is large and other priests or deacons are present, these may anoint some of the newly baptized with chrism.

CLOTHING WITH WHITE GARMENT

The celebrant says:

(N., N.,) you have become a new creation, and have clothed yourselves in Christ.

See in this white garment the outward sign of your Christian dignity. With your family and friends to help you by word and example, bring that dignity unstained into the everlasting life of heaven.

All: **Amen.**

The white garments are placed on the newly baptized. A different color is not permitted unless demanded by local custom. It is desirable that the families provide the garments.

———

45. *If no one is to be baptized and the font is not to be blessed, the priest blesses the water with the following prayer:*

My brothers and sisters,
let us ask the Lord our God
to bless this water he has created,
which we shall use to recall our baptism.
May he renew us
and keep us faithful to the Spirit
we have all received.

*All pray silently for a short while. With hands joined,
the priest continues:*

Lord our God,
this night your people keep prayerful vigil.
Be with us as we recall the wonder of our creation
and the greater wonder of our redemption.
Bless this water: it makes the seed to grow,
it refreshes us and makes us clean.
You have made of it a servant of your loving kind-
    ness:
through water you set your people free,
and quenched their thirst in the desert.
With water the prophets announced a new covenant
that you would make with man.
By water, made holy by Christ in the Jordan,
you make our sinful nature new
in the bath that gives rebirth.
Let this water remind us of our baptism;
let us share the joys of our brothers
who are baptized this Easter.
We ask this through Christ our Lord. ℞. **Amen.**

Renewal of Baptismal Promises

46. *When the rite of baptism (and confirmation) has
been completed or, if there is no baptism, immediately
after the blessing of the water, all present stand with
lighted candles and renew their baptismal profession of
faith.*

*The priest speaks to the people in these or similar
words:*

Dear friends,
through the paschal mystery

we have been buried with Christ in baptism,
so that we may rise with him to a new life.
Now that we have completed our lenten observance,
let us renew the promises we made in baptism
when we rejected Satan and his works,
and promised to serve God faithfully
in his holy catholic Church.

And so:

Priest: Do you reject Satan?

All: **I do.**

Priest: And all his works?

All: **I do.**

Priest: And all his empty promises?

All: **I do.**

OR

Priest: Do you reject sin, so as to live in the freedom
of God's children?

All: **I do.**

Priest: Do you reject the glamor of evil, and refuse
to be mastered by sin?

All: **I do.**

Priest: Do you reject Satan, father of sin and prince
of darkness?

All: **I do.**

*According to circumstances, this second form may be
adapted to local needs by the conferences of bishops.
Then the priest continues:*

Priest: Do you believe in God, the Father almighty,
creator of heaven and earth?

All: **I do.**

Priest: Do you believe in Jesus Christ, his only Son,
our Lord,
who was born of the Virgin Mary,
was crucified, died, and was buried,
rose from the dead,
and is now seated at the right hand of the
Father?

All: **I do.**

Priest: Do you believe in the Holy Spirit,
the holy Catholic Church, the communion of
saints,
the forgiveness of sins, the resurrection of
the body,
and life everlasting?

All: **I do.**

The priest concludes:

God, the all-powerful Father of our Lord Jesus
Christ,
has given us a new birth by water and the Holy
Spirit,
and forgiven all our sins.
May he also keep us faithful to our Lord Jesus Christ
for ever and ever.

All: **Amen.**

47. *The priest sprinkles the people with the blessed water, while all sing:* I saw water; *or any other song which is baptismal in character may be sung.*

ANTIPHON   See Ez 47, 1-2. 9

I saw water flowing
from the right side of the temple, alleluia.
It brought God's life and his salvation,
and the people sang in joyful praise:
alleluia, alleluia.

48. *Meanwhile the newly baptized are led to their place among the faithful.*
If the blessing of the baptismal water does not take place in the baptistery, the ministers reverently carry the vessel of water to the font.
If the blessing of the font does not take place, the blessed water is put in a convenient place.

49. *After the people have been sprinkled, the priest returns to the chair. The Profession of Faith is omitted, and the priest directs the General Intercessions, in which the newly baptized take part for the first time.*

PART FOUR

LITURGY OF THE EUCHARIST

50. *The priest goes to the altar and begins the liturgy of the eucharist in the usual way.*

51. *It is fitting that the bread and wine be brought forward by the newly baptized.*

52.   PRAYER OVER THE GIFTS

Lord, accept the prayers and offerings of your people.
With your help
may this Easter mystery of our redemption
bring to perfection the saving work you have begun
    in us.
We ask this through Christ our Lord. ℟. **Amen.**

53.   *Preface of Easter I (P 21: on this Easter day), p.* 663.

When Eucharistic Prayer I is used, the special Easter forms of In union with the whole Church, *and* Father, accept this offering *are said.*

54.   COMMUNION ANT.   1 Cor 5, 7-8

Christ has become our paschal sacrifice; let us feast with the unleavened bread of sincerity and truth, alleluia. ℣

55.   PRAYER AFTER COMMUNION

Lord, you have nourished us with your Easter sacraments.
Fill us with your Spirit
and make us one in peace and love.
We ask this through Christ our Lord. ℟. **Amen.**

56.   *The deacon (or the priest) sings or says the dismissal as follows:*

Go in the peace of Christ, alleluia, alleluia.

OR

The Mass is ended, go in peace, alleluia, alleluia.

OR

Go in peace to love and serve the Lord, alleluia, alleluia.

℟. **Thanks be to God, alleluia, alleluia.**

MONDAY OF THE OCTAVE OF EASTER

Jesus Christ has risen from the dead. He allowed himself to undergo the sufferings of the cross, but then he was raised to life. In Jesus we live and move and have our being. Let us rejoice and be glad for the Lord is risen. Alleluia.

ENTRANCE ANT. Ex 13, 5. 9

The Lord brought you to a land flowing with milk and honey, so that his law would always be given honor among you, alleluia.

OR:

The Lord has risen from the dead, as he foretold. Let there be happiness and rejoicing for he is our King for ever, alleluia. → No. 2, p. 614

OPENING PRAYER

Father,
you give your Church constant growth
by adding new members to your family.
Help us put into action in our lives
the baptism we have received with faith.
We ask this through our Lord Jesus Christ, your Son,
who lives and reigns with you and the Holy Spirit,
one God, for ever and ever. ℟. **Amen.** ↓

READING I Acts 2, 14. 22-32

In short summary, St. Peter proposes the name, works, death and resurrection of Jesus. He speaks to the Jews and all in Jerusalem, and he includes the facts about the resurrection.

A reading from the Acts of the Apostles
[On the day of Pentecost] Peter stood up with the Eleven, raised his voice, and addressed them: "You who are Jews, indeed all of you staying in Jerusalem! Listen to what I have to say.

"Jesus the Nazorean was a man whom God sent to you with miracles, wonders and signs as his credentials. These God worked through him in your midst, as you well know. He was delivered up by the set purpose and plan of God; you even made use of pagans to crucify and kill him. God freed him from death's bitter pangs, however, and raised him up again, for it was impossible that death should keep its hold on him. David says of him:

'I have set the Lord ever before me,
    with him at my right hand I shall not be disturbed.
My heart has been glad and my tongue has rejoiced,
    my body will live on in hope,
for you will not abandon my soul to the nether world,
    nor will you suffer your faithful one to undergo corruption.
You have shown me the paths of life;
    you will fill me with joy in your presence.'

"Brothers, I can speak confidently to you about our father David. He died and was buried, and his grave is in our midst to this day. He was a prophet and knew that God had sworn to him that one of 'his descendants would sit upon his throne.' He said that he was 'not abandoned to the nether world,' nor did his body 'undergo corruption,' thus proclaiming beforehand the resurrection of the Messiah. This is the Jesus God has raised up, and we are his witnesses." —This is the Word of the Lord. ℞. **Thanks be to God.** ℣

Responsorial Psalm   Ps 16, 1-2. 5. 7-8. 9-10. 11

℞. (1) **Keep me safe, O God;**
    you are my hope.

Keep me, O God, for in you I take refuge;
    I say to the Lord, "My Lord are you."
O Lord, my allotted portion and my cup,
    you it is who hold fast my lot. — ℞

I bless the Lord who counsels me;
    even in the night my heart exhorts me.
I set the Lord ever before me;
    with him at my right hand I shall not be disturbed. — ℞

Therefore my heart is glad and my soul rejoices,
   my body, too, abides in confidence;
Because you will not abandon my soul to the nether
    world,
   nor will you suffer your faithful one to undergo
     corruption. — ℟
You will show me the path to life,
   fullness of joys in your presence,
   the delights at your right hand forever. — ℟ ♦

℟. Or: **Alleluia.** ♦

Sequence (Optional)

One of the following texts may be chosen for the Sequence.

(Prose text)

**To the Paschal Victim let Christians offer a sacrifice
of praise.**

    The Lamb redeemed the sheep. Christ, sinless, reconciled sinners to the Father.

    **Death and life were locked together in a unique
struggle. Life's captain died; now he reigns, never
more to die.**

Tell us, Mary, "What did you see on the way?"

    **"I saw the tomb of the now living Christ. I saw
the glory of Christ, now risen.**

    **"I saw angels who gave witness; the cloths too
which once had covered head and limbs.**

    **"Christ my hope has arisen. He will go before his
own into Galilee."**

    **We know that Christ has indeed risen from the
dead. Do you, conqueror and king, have mercy on
us. Amen, Alleluia.** ♦

OR

(Poetic text)

**Christians, to the Paschal Victim * offer your thankful praises! * A Lamb the sheep redeems: Christ, *
who only is sinless, * reconciles sinners to the Fa-**

ther. * Death and life have contended in that combat
stupendous: * The Prince of life, who died, reigns
immortal.

Speak, Mary, declaring * what you saw, wayfar-
ing. * "The tomb of Christ, who is living, * the glory
of Jesus' resurrection; * bright angels attesting, * the
shroud and napkin resting. * Yes, Christ my hope
is arisen: * to Galilee he goes before you."

Christ indeed from death is risen, our new life
obtaining. * Have mercy, victor King, ever reigning! *
Amen. Alleluia. ℣

GOSPEL　　　　　　　　　　　　　　　　　　Mt 28, 8-15
Alleluia (Ps 118, 24)
℟. **Alleluia.** This is the day the Lord has made;
　　let us rejoice and be glad. ℟. **Alleluia.**

The apparition of Christ himself completes the Resurrection narrative. The empty tomb has ceased to be a place of mourning and
has become a place of exultant joy. Jesus repeats to the women the
message the angel has already given for the disciples. Even now the
elders and chief priests continue their scheme of plotting against
the Jews.

℣. The Lord be with you. ℟. **And also with you.**
✠ A reading from the holy gospel according to Matthew. ℟. **Glory to you, Lord.**

The women hurried away from the tomb half-overjoyed, half-fearful, and ran to carry the good news
to his disciples. Suddenly, without warning, Jesus
stood before them and said, "Peace!" The women
came up and embraced his feet and did him homage.
At this Jesus said to them, "Do not be afraid! Go
and carry the news to my brothers that they are to
go to Galilee, where they will see me."

As the women were returning, some of the guard
went into the city and reported to the chief priests
all that had happened. They, in turn, convened with
the elders and worked out their strategy, giving the
soldiers a large bribe with the instructions: "You
are to say, 'His disciples came during the night and

stole him while we were asleep.' If any word of this gets to the procurator, we will straighten it out with him and keep you out of trouble." The soldiers pocketed the money and did as they had been instructed. This is the story that circulates among the Jews to this very day.—This is the gospel of the Lord. ℟. **Praise to you, Lord Jesus Christ.** ➤ No. 15, p. 623

PRAYER OVER THE GIFTS

Father,
you have given us new light by baptism
and the profession of your name.
Accept the gifts of your children
and bring us to eternal joy in your presence.
We ask this in the name of Jesus the Lord.
℟. **Amen.** ➤ No. 21, p. 626 (Pref. P 21)

When Eucharistic Prayer I is used, the special Easter forms of In union with the whole Church *and* Father, accept this offering *are said.*

COMMUNION ANT. Rom 6, 9

Christ now raised from the dead will never die again; death no longer has power over him, alleluia. ℣

PRAYER AFTER COMMUNION

Lord,
may the life we receive in these Easter sacraments continue to grow in our hearts.
As you lead us along the way of eternal salvation, make us worthy of your many gifts.
Grant this through Christ our Lord.
℟. **Amen.** ➤ No. 32, p. 650

TUESDAY OF THE OCTAVE OF EASTER

If our love of God is perfect and unselfish as was Mary's, shown in her grief and tenderness as she stood at the empty tomb, we can express this kind of love and loyalty by our sincere desire to keep God's commands. Our love will be from the heart which binds us to God and also binds us to our neighbor. For his sake, may we love our neighbor in thought, word, and deed.

ENTRANCE ANT.   Sir 15, 3-4

If men desire wisdom, she will give them the water of knowledge to drink. They will never waver from the truth; they will stand firm for ever, alleluia.

➤ No. 2, p. 614

OPENING PRAYER

Father,
by this Easter mystery you touch our lives
with the healing power of your love.
You have given us the freedom of the sons of God.
May we who now celebrate your gift
find joy in it for ever in heaven.
Grant this through our Lord Jesus Christ, your Son,
who lives and reigns with you and the Holy Spirit,
one God, for ever and ever. ℟. **Amen.** ▼

READING I   Acts 2, 36-41

St. Peter reminds the Jews that Christ has been crucified and they are summoned to penance and to conversion which will be accomplished by the mystery of baptism in the name of Jesus Christ. Three thousand are baptized that very day.

A reading from the Acts of the Apostles

[On the day of Pentecost] Peter said to the Jews: "Let the whole house of Israel know beyond any doubt that God has made both Lord and Messiah this Jesus whom you crucified."

When they heard this, they were deeply shaken. They asked Peter and the other apostles, "What are we to do, brothers?" Peter answered: "You must reform and be baptized, each one of you, in the name of Jesus Christ, that your sins may be forgiven; then you will receive the gift of the Holy Spirit. It was to you and your children that the promise was made, and to all those still far off whom the Lord our God calls."

In support of his testimony he used many other arguments, and kept urging, "Save yourselves from this generation which has gone astray." Those who accepted his message were baptized; some three thousand were added that day.—This is the Word of the Lord. ℟. **Thanks be to God.** ✛

Responsorial Psalm   Ps 33, 4-5. 18-19. 20. 22

℟. (5) **The earth is full of the goodness of the Lord.**

Upright is the word of the Lord,
   and all his works are trustworthy.
He loves justice and right;
   of the kindness of the Lord the earth is full. — ℟

See, the eyes of the Lord are upon those who fear
      him,
   upon those who hope for his kindness,
To deliver them from death
   and preserve them in spite of famine. — ℟

Our soul waits for the Lord,
   who is our help and our shield.
May your kindness, O Lord, be upon us
   who have put our hope in you. — ℟

℟. Or: **Alleluia.**

➜ Sequence (Optional), p. 769

GOSPEL   Jn 20, 11-18

Alleluia (Ps 118, 24)

℟. **Alleluia.** This is the day the Lord has made;
   let us rejoice and be glad. ℟. **Alleluia.**

As Mary Magdalene stands weeping at Jesus' tomb, she believes the Lord has been taken away. But he appears, and at first Mary fails to recognize him. It is sufficient for Jesus to call Mary by name for her to recognize him.

℣. The Lord be with you. ℟. **And also with you.**
✠ A reading from the holy gospel according to John
℟. **Glory to you, Lord.**

Mary stood weeping beside the tomb. Even as she wept, she stooped to peer inside, and there she saw two angels in dazzling robes. One was seated at the head and the other at the foot of the place where Jesus' body had lain. "Woman," they asked her, "why are you weeping?" She answered them, "Because the Lord has been taken away, and I do not know where they have put him." She had no sooner said this than she turned around and caught sight of Jesus standing there. But she did not know him. "Woman," he asked her, "why are you weeping? Who is it you are looking for?" She supposed he was the gardener, so she said, "Sir, if you are the one who carried him off, tell me where you have laid him and I will take him away." Jesus said to her, "Mary!" She turned to him and said [in Hebrew], "Rabboni!" (meaning "Teacher"). Jesus then said: "Do not cling to me, for I have not yet ascended to the Father. Rather, go to my brothers and tell them, 'I am ascending to my Father and your Father, to my God and your God!'" Mary Magdalene went to the disciples. "I have seen the Lord!" she announced. Then she reported what he had said to her.—This is the gospel of the Lord. ℟. **Praise to you, Lord Jesus Christ.**   ➔ No. 15, p. 623

PRAYER OVER THE GIFTS

Lord,
accept these gifts from your family.
May we hold fast to the life you have given us
and come to the eternal gifts you promise.
We ask this in the name of Jesus the Lord.
℟. **Amen.**   ➔ No. 21, p. 626 (Pref. P 21)

When Eucharistic Prayer I is used, the special Easter forms of In union with the whole Church *and* Father, accept this offering *are said.*

COMMUNION ANT.   Col. 3, 1-2

If you have been raised with Christ, seek the things that are above, where Christ is seated at the right hand of God, alleluia. ⍐

PRAYER AFTER COMMUNION

All-powerful Father,
hear our prayers.

Prepare for eternal joy
the people who have renewed in baptism.
We ask this through Christ our Lord. ℟. **Amen.** ✠

➤ No. 32, p. 650

WEDNESDAY OF THE OCTAVE OF EASTER

The glorious mystery of the Holy Eucharist is in itself a continuing miracle of the love of God for his children. Christ our Lord expects us to prepare for the worthy reception of it. Through our work and in the company of our brothers, we shall help to bring to completion the creative and redemptive work of God. Each day through the Eucharist we will then move one step closer to attaining the fullness of Christ.

ENTRANCE ANT. Mt 25, 34

Come, you whom my Father has blessed; inherit the kingdom prepared for you since the foundation of the world, alleluia.

➤ No. 2, p. 614

OPENING PRAYER

God our Father,
on this solemn feast you give us the joy of recalling
the rising of Christ to new life.
May the joy of our annual celebration
bring us to the joy of eternal life.
We ask this through our Lord Jesus Christ, your Son,
who lives and reigns with you and the Holy Spirit,
one God, for ever and ever. ℟. **Amen.** ✠

READING I Acts 3, 1-10

Our Lord's healing ministry is continued by his chosen apostles. It is Peter who speaks and acts for the Twelve. Peter's admission that he had neither silver nor gold shows the depth of his faith and prepares for the name of Jesus as a powerful source of salvation.

A reading from the Acts of the Apostles

Once, when Peter and John were going up to the temple for prayer at the three o'clock hour, a man crippled from birth was being carried in. They would bring him every day and put him at the temple gate called "the Beautiful" to beg from the people as they entered. When he saw Peter and John on their way in, he begged them for an alms. Peter fixed his gaze on the man; so did John. "Look at us!" Peter said. The cripple gave them his whole attention, hoping to get something. Then Peter said: "I have neither silver nor gold, but what I have I give you! In the name of Jesus Christ the Nazorean, walk!" Then Peter took him by the right hand and pulled him up. Immediately the beggar's feet and ankles became strong; he jumped up, stood for a moment, then began to walk around. He went into the temple with them—walking, jumping about, and praising God. When the people saw him moving and giving praise to God, they recognized him as that beggar who used to sit at the Beautiful Gate of the temple. They were struck with astonishment—utterly stupefied at what had happened to him.—This is the Word of the Lord. ℟. **Thanks be to God.** ⩒

Responsorial Psalm   Ps 105, 1-2. 3-4. 6-7. 8-9

℟. (5) **The earth is full of the goodness of the Lord.**

Give thanks to the Lord, invoke his name;
  make known among the nations his deeds.
Sing to him, sing his praise,
  proclaim all his wondrous deeds. — ℟

Glory in his holy name;
  rejoice, O hearts that seek the Lord!
Look to the Lord in his strength;
  seek to serve him constantly. — ℟

You descendants of Abraham, his servants,
  sons of Jacob, his chosen ones!
He, the Lord, is our God;
  throughout the earth his judgments prevail. — ℟

He remembers forever his covenant
  which he made binding for a thousand generations—
Which he entered into with Abraham
  and by his oath to Isaac. — ℟

℟. Or: **Alleluia.**   ➔ Sequence (Optional) p. 769

GOSPEL   Lk 24, 13-35

Alleluia (Ps 118, 24)

℟. **Alleluia.** This is the day the Lord has made;
let us rejoice and be glad. ℟. **Alleluia.**

While walking on the road to Emmaus, the two disciples are troubled
and do not understand why Jesus is absent. They seem to recognize
Jesus in the stranger but do not believe their senses. After recognition, these men do not hesitate to believe. Once recognized, Jesus
disappears.

℣. The Lord be with you. ℟. **And also with you.**
✠ A reading from the holy gospel according to Luke
℟. **Glory to you, Lord.**

Two of the disciples of Jesus that same day [the first
day of the week] were making their way to a village
named Emmaus seven miles distant from Jerusalem,
discussing as they went all that had happened. In
the course of their lively exchange, Jesus approached
and began to walk along with them. However, they
were restrained from recognizing him. He said to
them, "What are you discussing as you go your
way?" They halted in distress, and one of them,
Cleopas by name, asked him, "Are you the only resi-
dent of Jerusalem who does not know the things that
went on there these past few days?" He said to them,
"What things?" They said: "All those that had to do
with Jesus of Nazareth, a prophet powerful in word
and deed in the eyes of God and all the people; how
our chief priests and leaders delivered him up to be
condemned to death, and crucified him. We were
hoping that he was the one who would set Israel
free. Besides all this, today, the third day since these
things happened, some women of our group have
just brought us some astonishing news. They were
at the tomb before dawn and failed to find his body,
but returned with the tale that they had seen a vision
of angels who declared he was alive. Some of our
number went to the tomb and found it to be just as
the women said; but him they did not see."

Then he said to them, "What little sense you have! How slow you are to believe all that the prophets have announced! Did not the Messiah have to undergo all this so as to enter into his glory?" Beginning, then, with Moses and all the prophets, he interpreted for them every passage of Scripture which referred to him. By now they were near the village to which they were going, and he acted as if he were going farther. But they pressed him: "Stay with us. It is nearly evening—the day is practically over." So he went to stay with them.

When he had seated himself with them to eat, he took bread, pronounced the blessing, then broke the bread and began to distribute it to them. With that their eyes were opened and they recognized him; whereupon he vanished from their sight. They said to one another, "Were not our hearts burning inside us as he talked to us on the road and explained the Scriptures to us? They got up immediately and returned to Jerusalem, where they found the Eleven and the rest of the company assembled. They were greeted with, "The Lord has been raised! It is true! He has appeared to Simon." Then they recounted what had happened on the road and how they had come to know him in the breaking of bread.—This is the gospel of the Lord. ℟. **Praise to you, Lord Jesus Christ.**   → No. 15, p. 623

PRAYER OVER THE GIFTS
Lord,
accept this sacrifice of our redemption
and accomplish in us salvation of mind and body.
Grant this through Christ our Lord.
℟. **Amen.**   → No. 21, p. 626 (Pref. P 21)

When Eucharistic Prayer I is used, the special Easter forms of In union with the whole Church *and* Father, accept this offering *are said.*

COMMUNION ANT.
Lk 24, 35

The disciples recognized the Lord Jesus in the breaking of bread, alleluia. ℣

PRAYER AFTER COMMUNION

Lord,
may this sharing in the sacrament of your Son
free us from our old life of sin
and make us your new creation.
We ask this in the name of Jesus the Lord.
℟. **Amen.** _____ ➔ No. 32, p. 650

THURSDAY OF THE OCTAVE OF EASTER

May our faith have the strength to make us pleasing to God. We should ever guard and preserve the gift of true faith. We cannot expose it to danger. In a manner of speaking, we are engraved on Jesus' hands and feet and in his heart. We are strengthened by these sacred wounds. Let us strive, therefore, to live so that these wounds may be our consolation.

ENTRANCE ANT.
Wis 10, 20-21

Your people praised your great victory, O Lord. Wisdom opened the mouth that was dumb, and made the tongues of babies speak, alleluia. ➔ No. 2, p. 614

OPENING PRAYER

Father,
you gather the nations to praise your name.
May all who are reborn in baptism
be one in faith and love.
Grant this through our Lord Jesus Christ, your Son,
who lives and reigns with you and the Holy Spirit,
one God, for ever and ever. ℟. **Amen.** ℣

READING I
Acts 3, 11-26

Peter refuses as false any claim that the miracle was wrought because of either John's or his piety. He stresses the power of prayer. Peter tells the people how they killed Jesus but God raised him from the dead.

A reading from the Acts of the Apostles

As the lame man who had been cured stood clinging to Peter and John, the whole crowd rushed over to them excitedly in Solomon's Portico. When Peter saw this, he addressed the people as follows: "Fellow Israelites, why does this surprise you? Why do you stare at us as if we had made this man walk by some power or holiness of our own? The 'God of Abraham, of Isaac, and of Jacob, the God of our fathers,' has glorified his Servant Jesus, whom you handed over and disowned in Pilate's presence when Pilate was ready to release him. You disowned the Holy and Just One and preferred instead to be granted the release of a murderer. You put to death the Author of life. But God raised him from the dead, and we are his witnesses. It is his name, and trust in this name, that has strengthened the limbs of this man whom you see and know well. Such faith has given him perfect health, as all of you can observe.

"Yet I know, my brothers, that you acted out of ignorance, just as your leaders did. God has brought to fulfillment by this means what he announced long ago through the prophets: that his Messiah would suffer. Therefore, reform your lives! Turn to God, that your sins may be wiped away! Thus may a season of refreshment be granted you by the Lord when he sends you Jesus, already designated as your Messiah. Jesus must remain in heaven until the time of universal restoration which God spoke of long ago through his holy prophets. For Moses said:

"The Lord God will raise up for you a prophet like me from among your own kinsmen: you shall listen to him in everything he says to you. Anyone who does not listen to that prophet shall be ruthlessly cut off from the people.'

"Moreover, all the prophets who have spoken, from Samuel onward, have announced the events of these days. You are the children of those prophets, you are the heirs of the covenant God made with your fathers when he said to Abraham, 'In your offspring, all the families of the earth shall be blessed.'

When God raised up his servant, he sent him to you first to bless you by turning you from your evil ways." —This is the Word of the Lord. ℞. **Thanks be to God.** ℣

Responsorial Psalm   Ps 8, 2. 5. 6-7. 8-9

℞. (2) **O Lord, our God,**
  how wonderful your name in all the earth!

O Lord, our Lord,
  how glorious is your name over all the earth!
What is man that you should be mindful of him,
  or the son of man that you should care for him?—℞

You have made him little less than the angels,
  and crowned him with glory and honor.
You have given him rule over the works of your hands,
  putting all things under his feet: — ℞

All sheep and oxen,
  yes, and the beasts of the field,
The birds of the air, the fishes of the sea,
  and whatever swims the paths of the seas.— ℞

℞. Or: **Alleluia.**   → Sequence (Optional), p. 436

GOSPEL Alleluia (Ps 118, 24)   Lk 24, 35-48

℞. **Alleluia.** This is the day the Lord has made;
  let us rejoice and be glad. ℞. **Alleluia.**

Without a sound or a step being heard, "Jesus stood in their midst." Peace, the last word of the prophecy of Zechariah, is the first word which is heard from Jesus' lips when he is risen from the dead. He shows them his hands and his feet, and the apostles are convinced.

℣. The Lord be with you. ℞. **And also with you.**
✠ A reading from the holy gospel according to Luke
℞. **Glory to you, Lord.**

The disciples recounted what had happened on the road to Emmaus and how they had come to know Jesus in the breaking of bread.

  While they were still speaking about all this, Jesus himself stood in their midst [and said to them, "Peace to you."] In their panic and fright they thought they were seeing a ghost. He said to them, "Why are you disturbed? Why do such ideas cross your mind? Look at my hands and my feet; it is really I. Touch me, and see that a ghost does not have flesh and bones as I do." [As he said this he showed them his hands and feet.] They were still incredulous for sheer joy and wonder, so he said to them, "Have you anything here to eat?" They gave him a piece of cooked fish, which he took and ate in their presence. Then he said to them, "Recall those words I spoke to you when I was still with you: everything written about me in the law of Moses and the prophets and psalms had to be fulfilled." Then he opened their minds to the understanding of the Scriptures.

He said to them: "Thus it is written that the Messiah must suffer and rise from the dead on the third day. In his name, penance for the remission of sins is to be preached to all the nations, beginning at Jerusalem. You are witnesses of all this."—This is the gospel of the Lord. ℟. **Praise to you, Lord Jesus Christ.**   → No. 15, p. 623

PRAYER OVER THE GIFTS

Lord,
accept our gifts
and grant your continuing protection
to all who have received new life in baptism.
We ask this in the name of Jesus the Lord.
℟. **Amen.**   → No. 21, p. 626 (Pref. P 21)

When Eucharistic Prayer I is used, the special Easter forms of In union with the whole Church *and* Father, accept this offering *are said.*

COMMUNION ANT.   1 Pt 2, 9

You are a people God claims as his own, to praise him who called you out of darkness into his marvelous light, alleluia. ▾

PRAYER AFTER COMMUNION

Lord,
may this celebration of our redemption
help us in this life
and lead us to eternal happiness.
We ask this through Christ our Lord.
℟. **Amen.** ────────────── ➤ No. 32, p. 650

FRIDAY OF THE OCTAVE OF EASTER

True faith in the name of Jesus and its power to save us is one
that firmly believes all that God has revealed, whether written or unwritten. It imposes upon us a life in accordance with that faith. This
we do for the love of God who is eternal Truth and cannot be deceived.
In a small way, we must suffer "martyrdom" by crucifying the flesh,
in the words of St. John Chrysostom, "that you may obtain the
martyr's crown."

ENTRANCE ANT.   Ps 78, 53

**The Lord led his people out of slavery. He drowned
their enemies in the sea, alleluia.** ➤ No. 2, p. 614

OPENING PRAYER

Eternal Father,
you gave us the Easter mystery
as our covenant of reconciliation.
May the new birth we celebrate
show its effects in the way we live.
We ask this through our Lord Jesus Christ, your Son,
who lives and reigns with you and the Holy Spirit,
one God, for ever and ever. ℟. **Amen.** ✠

READING I   Acts 4, 1-12

The arrest of Peter and John at the moment when salvation is being
announced to Israel begins the tide of opposition. Peter explains that
the miracle of curing the lame man was done in the name of Jesus.
He reminds the Jews how they rejected Jesus, the cornerstone.
Only in the name of Jesus is salvation possible.

A reading from the Acts of the Apostles

While Peter and John were still addressing the
crowd [after the lame man was healed] the priests,

the captain of the temple guard, and the Sadducees came up to them, angry because they were teaching the people and proclaiming the resurrection of the dead in the person of Jesus. It was evening by now, so they arrested them and put them in jail for the night. Despite this, many of those who had heard the speech believed; the number of the men came to about five thousand.

When the leaders, the elders, and the scribes assembled the next day in Jerusalem, Annas the high priest, Caiaphas, John, Alexander, and all who were of the high-priestly class were there. They brought Peter and John before them and began the interrogation in this fashion: "By what power or in whose name have men of your stripe done this?"

Then Peter, filled with the Holy Spirit, spoke up: "Leaders of the people! Elders! If we must answer today for a good deed done to a cripple and explain how he was restored to health, then you and all the people of Israel must realize that it was done in the name of Jesus Christ the Nazorean whom you crucified and whom God raised from the dead. In the power of that name this man stands before you perfectly sound. This Jesus is 'the stone rejected by you the builders which has become the cornerstone.' There is no salvation in anyone else, for there is no other name in the whole world given to men by which we are to be saved."—This is the Word of the Lord. ℟. **Thanks be to God.** ✠

Responsorial Psalm   Ps 118, 1-2. 4. 22-24. 25-27

℟. (22) **The stone rejected by the buliders has become the cornerstone.**

Give thanks to the Lord, for he is good,
    for his mercy endures forever.
Let the house of Israel say,
    "His mercy endures forever."
Let those who fear the Lord say,
    "His mercy endures forever." — ℟

The stone which the builders rejected
  has become the cornerstone.
By the Lord has this been done;
  it is wonderful in our eyes.
This is the day the Lord has made;
  let us be glad and rejoice in it. — ℟

O Lord, grant salvation!
  O Lord, grant prosperity!
Blessed is he who comes in the name of the Lord;
  we bless you from the house of the Lord.
  The Lord is God, and he has given us light. — ℟
℟. Or: **Alleluia.**   ➤ Sequence (Optional), p. 769

GOSPEL   Jn 21, 1-14

Alleluia (Ps 118, 24)
℟. **Alleluia.** This is the day the Lord has made;
  let us rejoice and be glad. ℟. **Alleluia.**

Jesus shows himself to his disciples again collectively while they
are fishing unsuccessfuly. At his word they cast all their nets, and
the miracle of fish proves that Jesus is with them. Peter swims to
shore to be with Jesus.

℣. The Lord be with you. ℟. **And also with you.**
✠ A reading from the holy gospel according to John
℟. **Glory to you, Lord.**

Jesus showed himself to the disciples [once again]
at the Sea of Tiberias. This is how the appearance
took place. Assembled were Simon Peter, Thomas
("the Twin"), Nathanael (from Cana in Galilee),
Zebedee's sons, and two other disciples. Simon Peter
said to them, "I am going out to fish." "We will join
you," they replied, and went off to get into their
boat. All through the night they caught nothing.
Just after daybreak Jesus was standing on the shore,
though none of the disciples knew it was Jesus. He
said to them, "Children, have you caught anything
to eat?" "Not a thing," they answered. "Cast your
net off to the starboard side," he suggested, "and
you will find something." So they made a cast, and

took so many fish that they could not haul the net in. Then the disciple Jesus loved cried out to Peter, "It is the Lord!" On hearing it was the Lord, Simon Peter threw on some clothes—he was stripped— and jumped into the water.

Meanwhile the other disciples came in the boat, towing the net full of fish. Actually they were not far from land—no more than a hundred yards.

When they landed, they saw a charcoal fire there with a fish laid on it and some bread. "Bring some of the fish you just caught," Jesus told them. Simon Peter went aboard and hauled ashore the net loaded with sizable fish—one hundred fifty-three of them! In spite of the great number, the net was not torn.

"Come and eat your meal," Jesus told them. Not one of the disciples presumed to inquire "Who are you?" for they knew it was the Lord. Jesus came over, took the bread and gave it to them, and did the same with the fish. This marked the third time that Jesus appeared to the disciples after being raised from the dead.—This is the gospel of the Lord. ℟. **Praise to you, Lord Jesus Christ.**

➤ No. 15, p. 623

PRAYER OVER THE GIFTS

Lord,
bring to perfection the spirit of life
we receive from these Easter gifts.
Free us from seeking after the passing things in life
and help us set our hearts on the kingdom of heaven.
Grant this through Christ our Lord.
℟. **Amen.**   ➤ No. 21, p. 626 (Pref. P 21)

When Eucharistic Prayer I is used, the special Easter forms of In union with the whole Church *and* Father, accept this offering *are said.*

COMMUNION ANT.   See Jn 21, 12-13

Jesus said to his disciples: Come and eat. And he took the bread and gave it to them, alleluia. ▼

PRAYER AFTER COMMUNION

Lord,
watch over those you have saved in Christ.
May we who are redeemed by his suffering and death
always rejoice in his resurrection,
for he is Lord for ever and ever.
℟. **Amen.** ━━━━━━━ ➤ No. 32, p. 650

SATURDAY OF THE OCTAVE OF EASTER

In applying the doubts of the apostles to our own frequent doubts, we should have in mind that though the assent of faith is in a sense obscure, it is still most reasonable. When God reveals his truths to us, he provides us with abundant motives for believing and gives us his own authority for them. If we are blessed with the gift of true faith, we can never forget that it is bestowed through the mercy and goodness of God and the merits of Jesus Christ and not because of any merit of ourselves.

ENTRANCE ANT. Ps 105, 43

The Lord led his people to freedom and they shouted with joy and gladness, alleluia. ➤ No. 2, p. 614

OPENING PRAYER

Father of love,
by the outpouring of your grace
you increase the number of those who believe in you.
Watch over your chosen family.
Give undying life to all
who have been born again in baptism.
Grant this through our Lord Jesus Christ, your Son,
who lives and reigns with you and the Holy Spirit,
one God, for ever and ever. ℟. **Amen.** ⅴ

READING I Acts 4, 13-21

The fearlessness of the apostles astonishes the elders and priests. It was known that they were uneducated men, but their self-assurance is a traditional attribute of the preaching of God's word. No legal fault can be found with the preaching of the Gospel.

A reading from the Acts of the Apostles

The priests and elders were amazed as they observed the self-assurance of Peter and John and realized

that the speakers were uneducated men of no standing. Then they recognized these men as having been with Jesus. When they saw the man who had been cured standing there with them, they could think of nothing to say, so they ordered them out of the court while they held a consultation. "What shall we do with these men? Everyone who lives in Jerusalem knows what a remarkable show of power took place through them. We cannot deny it. To stop this from spreading further among the people we must give them a stern warning never to mention that man's name to anyone again." So they called them back and made it clear that under no circumstances were they to speak the name of Jesus or teach about him. Peter and John answered, "Judge for yourselves whether it is right in God's sight for us to obey you rather than God. Surely we cannot help speaking of what we have heard and seen." At that point they were dismissed with further warnings. The court could find no way to punish them because of the people, all of whom were praising God for what had happened.—This is the Word of the Lord.
℟. **Thanks be to God.** ℣

Responsorial Psalm   Ps 118, 1. 14-15. 16-18. 19-21
℟. (21) I praise you, Lord,
    for you have answered me.
Give thanks to the Lord, for he is good,
    for his mercy endures forever.
My strength and my courage is the Lord,
    and he has been my savior.
The joyful shout of victory
    in the tents of the just. — ℟
The right hand of the Lord is exalted;
    "The right hand of the Lord has struck with
       power."
I shall not die, but live,
    and declare the works of the Lord.

Though the Lord has indeed chastised me,
yet he has not delivered me to death. — ℟

Open to me the gates of justice;
I will enter them and give thanks to the Lord.

This gate is the Lord's;
the just shall enter it.

I will give thanks to you, for you have answered me
and have been my savior. — ℟

℟. Or: **Alleluia.**   ➤ Sequence (Optional), p. 769

GOSPEL   Mk 16, 9-15

Alleluia (Ps 118, 24)

℟. **Alleluia.** This is the day the Lord has made;
let us rejoice and be glad. ℟. **Alleluia.**

Jesus rose from the dead and appeared to Mary Magdalene, but the
faithful followers refuse to believe. Jesus rebukes the apostles for
disbelieving the evidence of Mary Magdalene and the others. He
then tells the apostles to proclaim the Good News to all creation.

℣. The Lord be with you. ℟. **And also with you.**
✠ A reading from the holy gospel according to Mark
℟. **Glory to you, Lord.**

Jesus rose from the dead early on the first day of
the week. He first appeared to Mary Magdalene, out
of whom he had cast seven demons. She went to announce the good news to his followers, who were
now grieving and weeping. But when they heard
that he was alive and had been seen by her, they
refused to believe it. Later on, as two of them were
walking along on their way to the country, he was
revealed to them completely changed in appearance.
These men retraced their steps and announced the
good news to the others; but the others put no more
faith in them than in Mary Magdalene. Finally, as
they were at table, Jesus was revealed to the Eleven.
He took them to task for their disbelief and their
stubbornness, since they had put no faith in those
who had seen him after he had been raised.

Then he told them: "Go into the whole world and proclaim the good news to all creation."—This is the gospel of the Lord. ℟. **Praise to you, Lord Jesus Christ.**

➤ No. 15, p. 623

PRAYER OVER THE GIFTS

Lord,
give us joy by these Easter mysteries.
Let the continuous offering of this sacrifice
by which we are renewed
bring us to eternal happiness.
We ask this in the name of Jesus the Lord.
℟. **Amen.**   ➤ No. 21, p. 626 (Pref. P 21)

When Eucharistic Prayer I is used, the special Easter forms of In union with the whole Church *and* Father, accept this offering *are said.*

COMMUNION ANT.   Gal 3, 27

All you who have been baptized have been clothed in Christ, alleluia. ℣

PRAYER AFTER COMMUNION

Lord,
look on your people with kindness
and by these Easter mysteries
bring us to the glory of the resurrection.
We ask this in the name of Jesus the Lord.
℟. **Amen.** _____   ➤ No. 32, p. 650

MONDAY OF THE SECOND WEEK OF EASTER

"Be renewed in the spirit of your mind, and put on the new man." To accomplish this we must make a radical and complete change in all our ways. We may have lived what is called a virtuous life, but if we have not had the proper spirit and motive, our actions will not have rendered us pleasing and holy in the sight of God.

ENTRANCE ANT.   Rom 6, 9

Christ now raised from the dead will never die again; death no longer has power over him, alleluia.

➤ No. 2, p. 614

OPENING PRAYER

Almighty and ever-living God,
your Spirit made us your children,
confident to call you Father.
Increase your Spirit of love within us
and bring us to our promised inheritance.
Grant this through our Lord Jesus Christ, your Son,
who lives and reigns with you and the Holy Spirit,
one God, for ever and ever. ℟. **Amen.** ℣

READING I　　　　　　　　　　　　　　　Acts 4, 23-31

When the believers prayed, they were supported by their faith in the omnipotence of God who made heaven and earth. This is one of the original and fundamental truths of revelation from which faith continually derives. They were filled with the Holy Spirit.

A reading from the Acts of the Apostles

Peter and John, after being released, went back to their own people and told them what the priests and elders had said. All raised their voices in prayer to God on hearing the story: "Sovereign Lord, 'who made heaven and earth and sea and all that is in them,' you have said by the Holy Spirit through the lips of our father David your servant:

'Why did the Gentiles rage,
　　the peoples conspire in folly?
The kings of the earth were aligned,
　　the princes gathered together
　　　　against the Lord and against his anointed.'

Indeed, they gathered in this very city against your holy Servant, Jesus, 'whom you anointed'—Herod and Pontius Pilate in league with 'the Gentiles' and 'the peoples' of Israel. They have brought about the very things which in your powerful providence you planned long ago. But now, O Lord, look at the threats they are leveling against us. Grant to your servants, even as they speak your words, complete assurance by stretching forth your hand in cures and signs and wonders to be worked in the name of Jesus, your holy Servant."

The place where they were gathered shook as they prayed. They were filled with the Holy Spirit and continued to speak God's word with confidence.— This is the Word of the Lord. ℞. **Thanks be to God.** ✔

Responsorial Psalm   Ps 2, 1-3. 4-6. 7-9

℞. (12) **Happy are all who put their trust in the Lord.**

Why do the nations rage
   and the peoples utter folly?
The kings of the earth rise up,
   and the princes conspire together
   against the Lord and against his anointed:
"Let us break their fetters
   and cast their bonds from us!" — ℞

He who is throned in heaven laughs;
   the Lord derides them.
Then in anger he speaks to them;
   he terrifies them in his wrath:
"I myself have set up my king
   on Zion, my holy mountain."
I will proclaim the decree of the Lord. — ℞

The Lord said to me, "You are my son;
   this day I have begotten you.
Ask of me and I will give you
   the nations for an inheritance
   and the ends of the earth for your possession.
You shall rule them with an iron rod;
   you shall shatter them like an earthen dish."—℞ ✔
℞. Or: **Alleluia.** ✔

GOSPEL   Jn 3, 1-8
Alleluia (Col 3, 1)

℞. **Alleluia.** If then you have been raised with Christ,
   seek the things that are above,
where Christ is seated at the right hand of God.
   ℞. **Alleluia.**

In view of the official opposition to Jesus, Nicodemus could only have come to see him secretly. Nicodemus' profession of faith would be of no value unless it fixed itself upon our Lord as he really is. The kingdom of God can only be experienced through a spiritual rebirth.

℣. The Lord be with you. ℟. **And also with you.**

✠ A reading from the holy gospel according to John ℟. **Glory to you, Lord.**

A certain Pharisee named Nicodemus, a member of the Jewish Sanhedrin, came to Jesus at night. "Rabbi," he said, "we know you are a teacher come from God, for no man can perform signs and wonders such as you perform unless God is with him." Jesus gave him this answer:

"I solemnly assure you,
no one can see the rule of God
unless he is begotten from above."

"How can a man be born again once he is old?" retorted Nicodemus. "Can he return to his mother's womb and be born all over again!" Jesus replied:

"I solemnly assure you,
no one can enter into God's kingdom
without being begotten of water and Spirit.
Flesh begets flesh,
Spirit begets spirit.
Do not be surprised that I tell you
you must all be begotten from above.
The wind blows where it will.
You hear the sound it makes
but you do not know where it comes from,
or where it goes.
So it is with everyone begotten of the Spirit."

This is the gospel of the Lord. ℟. **Praise to you, Lord Jesus Christ.**   → No. 15, p. 623

PRAYER OVER THE GIFTS

Lord,
receive these gifts from your Church.
May the great joy you give us
come to perfection in heaven.

Grant this through Christ our Lord.
℟. **Amen.**   ➤ No. 21, p. 626 (Pref. P 22-25)

COMMUNION ANT.   Jn 20, 19
**Jesus came and stood among his disciples and said to
them: Peace be with you, alleluia.** ℣

PRAYER AFTER COMMUNION
Lord,
look on your people with kindness
and by these Easter mysteries
bring us to the glory of the resurrection.
We ask this in the name of Jesus the Lord.
℟. **Amen.**   ➤ No. 32, p. 650

TUESDAY OF THE SECOND WEEK OF EASTER

The real proof of our love of God is our hatred of sin and our sincere
desire to keep his commandments. If this love strives for perfection,
we will love our neighbor, whom we are bound to love in thought,
word and deed, from the motive of divine charity. This is a superior
love and a higher order of charity which is grounded on faith and
the love of God.

ENTRANCE ANT.   Rv 19, 7. 6
**Let us shout out our joy and happiness, and give
glory to God, the Lord of all, because he is our King,
alleluia.**   ➤ No. 2, p. 614

OPENING PRAYER
All-powerful God,
help us to proclaim the power of the Lord's resur-
    rection.
May we who accept this sign of the love of Christ
come to share the eternal life he reveals,
for he lives and reigns with you and the Holy Spirit,
one God, for ever and ever. ℟. **Amen.** ℣

READING I   Acts 4, 32-37
The union in spirit among the disciples was not only a union in faith,
but also one in brotherly love, and demonstrates that the Christians
were truly regenerated and in a state of grace. Barnabas gives his
wealth to the Church.

A reading from the Acts of the Apostles

The community of believers were of one heart and one mind. None of them ever claimed anything as his own; rather, everything was held in common. With power the apostles bore witness to the resurrection of the Lord Jesus, and great respect was paid to them all; nor was there anyone needy among them, for all who owned property or houses sold them and donated the proceeds. They used to lay them at the feet of the apostles to be distributed to everyone according to his need.

There was a certain Levite from Cyprus named Joseph, to whom the apostles gave the name Barnabas (meaning "son of encouragement"). He sold a farm that he owned and made a donation of the money, laying it at the apostles' feet.—This is the Word of the Lord. ℟. **Thanks be to God.** ℣

Responsorial Psalm   Ps 93, 1. 1-2. 5

℟. **The Lord is king;**
   he is robed in majesty.

The Lord is king, in splendor robed;
    robed is the Lord and girt about with strength.—℟

And he has made the world firm,
    not to be moved.
Your throne stands firm from of old;
    from everlasting you are, O Lord. — ℟

Your decrees are worthy of trust indeed:
    holiness befits your house,
    O Lord, for length of days. — ℟ ℣

℟. Or: **Alleluia.** ℣

GOSPEL   Jn 3, 7-15

Alleluia (Col 3, 1)

℟. **Alleluia.** If then you have been raised with Christ,
    seek the things that are above,
where Christ is seated at the right hand of God.
    ℟. **Alleluia.**

The "heavenly things" of which Christ has spoken cannot be grasped by any man at will. Nicodemus asks how and Jesus alone can answer with authority since he is the only person who has come down from heaven. Those who believe in him will have eternal life.

℣. The Lord be with you. ℟. **And also with you.**
✠ A reading from the holy gospel according to John
℟. **Glory to you, Lord.**

Jesus said to Nicodemus:

"I solemnly assure you,
do not be surprised that I tell you
you must all be begotten from above.
The wind blows where it will.
You hear the sound it makes
but you do not know where it comes from,
or where it goes.
So it is with everyone begotten of the Spirit."

"How can such a thing happen?" asked Nicodemus.
Jesus responded: "You hold the office of teacher of Israel and still you do not understand these matters?

"I solemnly assure you,
we are talking about what we know,
we are testifying to what we have seen.
You are the ones who do not accept our testimony.
If you do not believe
when I tell you about earthly things,
how are you to believe
when I tell you about those of heaven?
No one has gone up to heaven
except the One who came down from there—
the Son of Man [who is in heaven].
Just as Moses lifted up the serpent in the desert,
so must the Son of Man be lifted up,
that all who believe
may have eternal life in him."

This is the gospel of the Lord. ℟. **Praise to you, Lord Jesus Christ.**

➤ No. 15, p. 623

PRAYER OVER THE GIFTS
Lord,
give us joy by these Easter mysteries.
Let the continuous offering of this sacrifice
by which we are renewed
bring us to eternal happiness.
We ask this in the name of Jesus the Lord.
℞. **Amen.**   ➔ No. 21, p. 626 (Pref. P 22-25)

COMMUNION ANT.   See Lk 24, 46. 26
**Christ had to suffer and to rise from the dead, and
so enter into his glory, alleluia. ℣**

PRAYER AFTER COMMUNION
Lord,
may this celebration of our redemption
help us in this life
and lead us to eternal happiness.
We ask this through Christ our Lord.
℞. **Amen.**   ➔ No. 32, p. 650

WEDNESDAY OF THE SECOND WEEK OF EASTER

Even the just suffer tribulations and are surrounded by dangers of
every kind. Friends prove false; sickness strikes; death and misfortunes may follow. But if God is with us, the winds of adversity blow
in vain. God in his mercy will not permit us to be tried beyond our
strength.

ENTRANCE ANT.   Ps 18, 50; 21, 23
**I will be a witness to you in the world, O Lord. I
will spread the knowledge of your name among my
brothers, alleluia.**   ➔ No. 2, p. 614

OPENING PRAYER
God of mercy,
you have filled us with the hope of resurrection
by restoring man to his original dignity.
May we who relive this mystery each year
come to share it in perpetual love.

Grant this through our Lord Jesus Christ, your Son, who lives and reigns with you and the Holy Spirit, one God, for ever and ever. ℟. **Amen.** ℣

READING I   Acts 5, 17-26
The apostles are arrested but they are delivered by the angel who opens the prison doors and brings them forth. The guard and high priests cannot understand the release of the prisoners who are free and teaching the people.

A reading from the Acts of the Apostles

The high priest and all his supporters (that is, the party of the Sadducees), filled with jealousy, arrested the apostles and threw them into the public jail. During the night, however, an angel of the Lord opened the gates of the jail, led them forth, and said, "Go out now and take your place in the temple precincts and preach to the people all about this new life." Accordingly they went into the temple at dawn and resumed their teaching.

When the high priest and his supporters arrived they convoked the Sanhedrin, the full council of the elders of Israel. They sent word to the jail that the prisoners were to be brought in. But when the temple guard got to the jail they could not find them, and they hurried back with the report, "We found the jail securely locked and the guards at their posts outside the gates, but when we opened it we found no one inside."

On hearing this report, the captain of the temple guard and the high priests did not know what to make of the affair. Someone then came up to them, pointing out, "Look, there! Those men you put in jail are standing over there in the temple, teaching the people." At that, the captain went off with the guard and brought them in, but without any show of force, for fear of being stoned by the crowd.— This is the Word of the Lord. ℟. **Thanks be to God.** ℣

Responsorial Psalm   Ps 34, 2-3. 4-5. 6-7. 8-9
℟. (7) **The Lord hears the cry of the poor.**

I will bless the Lord at all times;
  his praise shall be ever in my mouth.
Let my soul glory in the Lord;
  the lowly will hear me and be glad. — ℟

Glorify the Lord with me,
  let us together extol his name.
I sought the Lord, and he answered me
  and delivered me from all my fears. — ℟

Look to him that you may be radiant with joy,
  and your faces may not blush with shame.
When the afflicted man called out, the Lord heard,
  and from all his distress he saved him. — ℟

The angel of the Lord encamps
  around those who fear him, and delivers them.
Taste and see how good the Lord is;
  happy the man who takes refuge in him. — ℟ ↯

℟. Or: **Alleluia.** ↯

GOSPEL   Jn 3, 16-21

Alleluia (Jn 3, 16)

℟. **Alleluia.** God loved the world so much, he gave
    us his only Son,
that all who believe in him might have eternal life.
    ℟. **Alleluia.**

The gift of eternal life made possible in the Redemption is the result
of God's incredible love for the world. Christ has been sent into the
world to bring eternal life. The evildoer is the child of darkness.
Christ, the Light, "acts in truth."

℣. The Lord be with you. ℟. **And also with you.**
✠ A reading from the holy gospel according to John
℟. **Glory to you, Lord.**

Jesus said to Nicodemus:
    "Yes, God so loved the world
    that he gave his only Son,
    that whoever believes in him may not die
    but may have eternal life.
    God did not send the Son into the world
    to condemn the world,

but that the world might be saved through him.
Whoever believes in him avoids condemnation,
but whoever does not believe is already condemned
for not believing in the name of God's only Son.
The judgment in question is this:
the light came into the world,
but men loved darkness rather than light
because their deeds were wicked.
Everyone who practices evil
hates the light;
he does not come near it
for fear his deeds will be exposed.
But he who acts in truth
comes into the light,
to make clear
that his deeds are done in God."

This is the gospel of the Lord. ℟. **Praise to you, Lord
Jesus Christ.**   ➜ No. 15, p. 623

PRAYER OVER THE GIFTS

Lord God,
by this holy exchange of gifts
you share with us your divine life.
Grant that everything we do
may be directed by the knowledge of your truth.
We ask this in the name of Jesus the Lord.
℟. **Amen.**   ➜ No. 21, p. 626 (Pref. P 22-25)

COMMUNION ANT.   See Jn 15, 16. 19

**The Lord says, I have chosen you from the world
to go and bear fruit that will last, alleluia.** ↓

PRAYER AFTER COMMUNION

Merciful Father,
may these mysteries give us new purpose
and bring us to a new life in you.
Grant this through Christ our Lord.
℟. **Amen.**   _____   ➜ No. 32, p. 650

THURSDAY OF THE SECOND WEEK OF EASTER

One of the greatest miracles of all time was the marvelous establishment of the Christian religion itself—rapid, universal, and lasting in character. It has been victorious over innumerable persecutions. We are blessed in having been given the faith that guides our eternal salvation. The Divine Word given to us by the successors of Christ and the apostles still has the same power it had when Christ and the apostles first preached it, for "our faith stands not on the wisdom of men, but on the power of God."

ENTRANCE ANT.   See Ps 68, 8-9. 20

When you walked at the head of your people, O God, and lived with them on their journey, the earth shook at your presence, and the skies poured forth their rain, alleluia.   ➔ No. 2, p. 614

OPENING PRAYER

God of mercy,
may the Easter mystery we celebrate
be effective throughout our lives.
Grant this through our Lord Jesus Christ, your Son,
who lives and reigns with you and the Holy Spirit,
one God, for ever and ever. ℞. **Amen.** ↓

READING I   Acts 5, 27-33

The Jewish leaders clearly feel powerless in preventing the teaching of Christ by the apostles. The people are enthusiastic and listen with great attention. The disciples continue to preach the "Good News." It is better to obey God than men.

A reading from the Acts of the Apostles

When the attendants had led the apostles in and made them stand before the Sanhedrin, the high priest began the interrogation in this way: "We gave you strict orders not to teach about that name, yet you have filled Jerusalem with your teaching and are determined to make us responsible for that man's blood." To this, Peter and the apostles replied: "Better for us to obey God than men! The God of our fathers has raised up Jesus whom you put to death, 'hanging him on a tree.' He whom God has exalted at his right hand as ruler and savior is to bring repentance to Israel and forgiveness of sins. We testify to this. So too does the Holy Spirit, whom God has given to those that obey him."

When the Sanhedrin heard this, they were stung to fury and wanted to kill them.—This is the Word of the Lord. ℟. **Thanks be to God.** ✣

Responsorial Psalm   Ps 34, 2. 9. 17-18. 19-20

℟. (7) **The Lord hears the cry of the poor.**

I will bless the Lord at all times;
  his praise shall be ever in my mouth.
Taste and see how good the Lord is;
  happy the man who takes refuge in him. — ℟

The Lord confronts the evildoers,
  to destroy remembrance of them from the earth.
When the just cry out, the Lord hears them,
  and from all their distress he rescues them. — ℟

The Lord is close to the brokenhearted;
  and those who are crushed in spirit he saves.
Many are the troubles of the just man,
  but out of them all the Lord delivers him. — ℟ ✣

℟. Or: **Alleluia.** ✣

GOSPEL   Jn 3, 31-36

Alleluia (Jn 20, 29)

℟. **Alleluia.** You believe in me, Thomas, because you
  have seen me;
happy those who have not seen me, but still believe!
  ℟. **Alleluia.**

Jesus brings eternal life. Whoever receives the testimony of Christ testifies to God's truthfulness, even as God certifies to the truthfulness of Christ. Since Christ is the Messenger of God, the fullness of God's revelation has come only in Christ.

℣. The Lord be with you. ℟. **And also with you.**
✠ A reading from the holy gospel according to John
℟. **Glory to you, Lord.**

Jesus said to Nicodemus:
  "The One who comes from above is above all;

the one who is of the earth is earthly,
and he speaks on an earthly plane.
The One who comes from heaven [who is above
    all]
testifies to what he has seen and heard,
but no one accepts his testimony.
Whoever does accept this testimony
certifies that God is truthful.
For the One whom God has sent
speaks the words of God;
he does not ration his gift of the Spirit.
The Father loves the Son
and has given everything over to him.
Whoever believes in the Son
has life eternal.
Whoever disobeys the Son
will not see life,
but must endure the wrath of God."

This is the gospel of the Lord. ℟. **Praise to you, Lord Jesus Christ.**
➤ No. 15, p. 623

PRAYER OVER THE GIFTS

Lord,
accept our prayers and offerings.
Make us worthy of your sacraments of love
by granting us your forgiveness.
We ask this in the name of Jesus the Lord.
℟. **Amen.**   ➤ No. 21, p. 626 (Pref. P 22-25)

COMMUNION ANT.   Mt 28, 20
I, the Lord, am with you always, until the end of the world, alleluia. ↓

PRAYER AFTER COMMUNION

Almighty and ever-living Lord,
you restored us to life
by raising Christ from death.
Strengthen us by this Easter sacrament;
may we feel its saving power in our daily life.

We ask this through Christ our Lord.
℟. **Amen.**   ➔ No. 32, p. 650

FRIDAY OF THE SECOND WEEK OF EASTER

Jesus fed about five thousand by the miraculous multiplication of the loaves and fishes. This was the foreshadowing of the supreme Banquet of the Most Holy Sacrament—the spiritual food he has given to us for all time for the attainment of our eternal life. Our Savior delights to be with the children of men. He invites us to the Divine Banquet to comfort and console us. "Come to me, all you that labor, and are burdened, and I will refresh you" (Mt 11, 28).

ENTRANCE ANT.   Rv 5, 9-10

By your blood, O Lord, you have redeemed us from every tribe and tongue, from every nation and people: you have made us into the kingdom of God, alleluia.

➔ No. 2, p. 614

OPENING PRAYER

Father,
in your plan of salvation
your Son Jesus Christ accepted the cross
and freed us from the power of the enemy.
May we come to share the glory of his resurrection,
for he lives and reigns with you and the Holy Spirit,
one God, for ever and ever. ℟. **Amen.** ↓

READING I   Acts 5, 34-42

Gamaliel cautions the Sanhedrin because he is well aware of their motives in the trial of Jesus. Gamaliel is expedient and prudent, but he also has knowledge of God. The Sanhedrin are eager to "save face" and are willing to punish the apostles by having them flogged and then released.

A reading from the Acts of the Apostles

A certain member of the Sanhedrin stood up and had the apostles ordered out of court for a few minutes, and then said to the assembly, "Fellow Israelites, think twice about what you are going to do with these men. Not long ago a certain Theudas came on the scene and tried to pass himself off as someone of importance. About four hundred men joined him. However he was killed, and all those who had been so easily convinced by him were disbanded. In the end it came to nothing. Next came Judas the Galilean at the time of the census. He too built up quite a following, but likewise died, and all his followers were dispersed. The present case is similar. My advice is that you have nothing to do with these men. Let them alone. If their purpose or activity is human in its origins it will destroy itself. If, on the other hand, it comes from God, you will not be able to destroy them without fighting God himself.''

This speech persuaded them. In spite of it, however, the Sanhedrin called in the apostles and had them whipped. They ordered them not to speak again about the name of Jesus, and afterward dismissed them. The apostles for their part left the Sanhedrin full of joy that they had been judged worthy of ill-treatment for the sake of the Name. Day after day, both in the temple and at home, they never stopped teaching and proclaiming the good news of Jesus the Messiah.—This is the Word of the Lord. ℟. **Thanks be to God.** ℣

Responsorial Psalm   Ps 27, 1. 4. 13-14

℟. (4) **One thing I seek:**
  to dwell in the house of the Lord.

The Lord is my light and my salvation;
  whom should I fear?
The Lord is my life's refuge;
  of whom should I be afraid? — ℟

One thing I ask of the Lord;
  this I seek:
To dwell in the house of the Lord
  all the days of my life,
That I may gaze on the loveliness of the Lord
  and contemplate his temple. — ℟

I believe that I shall see the bounty of the Lord
  in the land of the living.
Wait for the Lord with courage;
  be stouthearted, and wait for the Lord. — ℟ ✔

℟. Or: **Alleluia.** ✔

GOSPEL   Jn 6, 1-15
Alleluia (Mt 4, 4)
  ℟. **Alleluia.** Man does not live on bread alone,
but on every word that comes from the mouth of God.
    ℟. **Alleluia.**

John recounts the multiplication of the loaves. The miracle is a
Eucharistic symbol. The people correctly see in this miracle an
indication that Jesus is the Prophet, like Moses, come to found the
New Israel. Jesus promises his flesh to eat and his blood to drink.

℣. The Lord be with you. ℟. **And also with you.**
✠ A reading from the holy gospel according to John
℟. **Glory to you, Lord.**

Jesus crossed the Sea of Galilee [to the shore] of
Tiberias; a vast crowd kept following him because
they saw the signs he was performing for the sick.
Jesus then went up the mountain and sat down there
with his disciples. The Jewish feast of Passover was
near; when Jesus looked up and caught sight of a
vast crowd coming toward him, he said to Philip,
"Where shall we buy bread for these people to eat?"
(He knew well what he intended to do but he asked
this to test Philip's response.) Philip replied, "Not
even with two hundred days' wages could we buy
loaves enough to give each of them a mouthful."

One of Jesus' disciples, Andrew, Simon Peter's
brother, remarked to him, "There is a lad here who
has five barley loaves and a couple of dried fish, but
what good is that for so many?" Jesus said, "Get
the people to recline." Even though the men numbered about five thousand, there was plenty of grass
for them to find a place on the ground. Jesus then
took the loaves of bread, gave thanks, and passed

them around to those reclining there; he did the same with the dried fish, as much as they wanted. When they had had enough, he told his disciples, "Gather up the crusts that are left over so that nothing will go to waste." At this, they gathered twelve baskets full of pieces left over by those who had been fed with the five barley loaves.

When the people saw the sign he had performed they began to say, "This is undoubtedly the Prophet who is to come into the world." At that, Jesus realized that they would come and carry him off to make him king, so he fled back to the mountain alone.— This is the gospel of the Lord. ℟. **Praise to you, Lord Jesus Christ.** ➤ No. 15, p. 623

PRAYER OVER THE GIFTS

Lord,
accept these gifts from your family.
May we hold fast to the life you have given us
and come to the eternal gifts you promise.
We ask this in the name of Jesus the Lord.
℟. **Amen.** ➤ No. 21, p. 626 (Pref. P 22-25)

COMMUNION ANT. Rom 4, 25

Christ our Lord was put to death for our sins; and he rose again to make us worthy of life, alleluia. ∨

PRAYER AFTER COMMUNION

Lord,
watch over those you have saved in Christ.
May we who are redeemed by his suffering and death
always rejoice in his resurrection,
for he is Lord for ever and ever.
℟. **Amen.** ─────────── ➤ No. 32, p. 650

SATURDAY OF THE SECOND WEEK OF EASTER

The Church is a community of persons created in God's image. The human family is a unity—a family of sons with but one Father. Like the early Christians, we should strive for complete brotherhood of man so that we become true sons of a disciple's loving Father. Growth in the love of the Father is accomplished only by the sacrifice of self-love.

ENTRANCE ANT. 1 Pt 2, 9

You are a people God claims as his own, to praise him who called you out of darkness into his marvelous light, alleluia. ➥ No. 2, p. 614

OPENING PRAYER

God our Father,
look upon us with love.
You redeem us and make us your children in Christ.
Give us true freedom
and bring us to the inheritance you promised.
We ask this through our Lord Jesus Christ, your Son,
who lives and reigns with you and the Holy Spirit,
one God, for ever and ever. ℟. **Amen.** ↓

READING I Acts 6, 1-7

The followers of Jesus are now an international group. The apostles select deacons to carry out the works of religion among the poor and to help instruct the people about the new life.

A reading from the Acts of the Apostles

In those days as the number of disciples grew, the ones who spoke Greek complained that their widows were being neglected in the daily distribution of food, as compared with the widows of those who spoke Hebrew. The Twelve assembled the community of the disciples and said, "It is not right for us to neglect the word of God in order to wait on the tables. Look around among your own number, brothers, for seven men acknowledged to be deeply spiritual and prudent, and we shall appoint them to this task. This will permit us to concentrate on prayer and the ministry of the word." The proposal was unanimously accepted by the community. Following this they selected Stephen, a man filled with faith and the Holy Spirit; Philip, Prochorus, Nicanor, Timon, Parmenas and Nicolaus of Antioch, who had been a convert to Judaism. They presented these men to the apostles, who first prayed over them and then imposed hands on them.

The word of God continued to spread, while at the same time the number of the disciples in Jerusalem enormously increased. There were many priests among those who embraced the faith.—This is the Word of the Lord. ℟. **Thanks be to God.** ℣

Responsorial Psalm   Ps 33, 1-2. 4-5. 18-19

℟. (22) **Lord, let your mercy be on us,**
     as we place our trust in you.

Exult, you just, in the Lord;
     praise from the upright is fitting.
Give thanks to the Lord on the harp;
     with the ten-stringed lyre chant his praises. — ℟

Upright is the word of the Lord,
     and all his works are trustworthy.
He loves justice and right;
     of the kindness of the Lord the earth is full. — ℟

See, the eyes of the Lord are upon those who fear
       him,
     upon those who hope for his kindness,
To deliver them from death
     and preserve them in spite of famine. — ℟ ℣

℟. Or: **Alleluia.** ℣

GOSPEL   Jn 6, 16-21
Alleluia

℟. **Alleluia.** Christ is risen, and makes all things new;
he has shown pity to all mankind. ℟. **Alleluia.**

When Jesus walks upon the water and comes to the disciples, they become frightened. But he assures them there is no need to be afraid.

℣. The Lord be with you. ℟. **And also with you.**
✠ A reading from the holy gospel according to John
℟. **Glory to you, Lord.**

As evening drew on, the disciples of Jesus came down to the lake. They embarked, intending to cross the lake toward Capernaum. By this time it was dark, and Jesus had still not joined them; moreover, with a strong wind blowing, the sea was becoming rough. Finally, when they had rowed three or four miles, they sighted Jesus approaching the boat, walking on the water. They were frightened, but he told them, "It is I; do not be afraid." They wanted to take him into the boat, but suddenly it came aground on the shore they had been approaching.— This is the gospel of the Lord. ℟. **Praise to you, Lord Jesus Christ.**   → No. 15, p. 623

PRAYER OVER THE GIFTS

Merciful Lord,
make holy these gifts
and let our spiritual sacrifice
make us an everlasting gift to you.
We ask this in the name of Jesus the Lord.
℟. **Amen.**   → No. 21, p. 626 (Pref. P 22-25)

COMMUNION ANT.   Jn 17, 24

Father, I want the men you have given me to be with me where I am, so that they may see the glory you have given me, alleluia.

PRAYER AFTER COMMUNION

Lord,
may this eucharist,
which we have celebrated in memory of your Son,
help us to grow in love.
We ask this in the name of Jesus the Lord.
℟. **Amen.**   → No. 32, p. 650

MONDAY OF THE THIRD WEEK OF EASTER

The persecution of the early Christians served to spread the rapid growth of the Church into the far reaches of the then-civilized world.

In our day, we may not expect to suffer martyrdom; still, this is a continual reminder of the suffering offered by Christ to the Father. Our frustrations and disappointments must be taken up daily by those who would serve with Christ our Lord.

ENTRANCE ANT.

The Good Shepherd is risen! He who laid down his life for his sheep, who died for his flock, he is risen, alleluia.   ➤ No. 2, p. 614

OPENING PRAYER

God our Father,
your light of truth
guides us to the way of Christ.
May all who follow him
reject what is contrary to the gospel.
We ask this through our Lord Jesus Christ, your Son,
who lives and reigns with you and the Holy Spirit,
one God, for ever and ever. ℞. **Amen.** ↓

READING I   Acts 6, 8-15

The deacon, St. Stephen, is filled with the Holy Spirit through the grace of the risen Christ. He courageously gives witness that Jesus fulfills the promises of the Scriptures. In the Spirit, he faces his trial without fear.

A reading from the Acts of the Apostles

Stephen, filled with grace and power, worked great wonders and signs among the people. Certain members of the so-called "Synagogue of Roman Freedmen" (that is, the Jews from Cyrene, Alexandria, Cilicia and Asia) would undertake to engage Stephen in debate, but they proved no match for the wisdom and spirit with which he spoke. They persuaded some men to make the charge that they had heard him speaking blasphemies against Moses and God, and in this way they incited the people, the elders, and the scribes. All together they confronted him, seized him, and led him off to the Sanhedrin. There they brought in false witnesses, who said: "This man never stops making statements against the holy

place and the law. We have heard him claim that
Jesus the Nazorean will destroy this place and change
the customs which Moses handed down to us." The
members of the Sanhedrin who sat there stared at
him intently. Throughout, Stephen's face seemed like
that of an angel. This is the Word of the Lord. R.
Thanks be to God. ℣

Responsorial Psalm   Ps 119, 23-24. 26-27. 29-30

℟. (1) **Happy are those of blameless life.**

Though princes meet and talk against me,
   your servant meditates on your statutes.
Yes, your decrees are my delight;
   they are my counselors. — ℟

I declared my ways, and you answered me;
   teach me your statutes.
Make me understand the way of your precepts,
   and I will meditate on your wondrous deeds. — ℟

Remove from me the way of falsehood,
   and favor me with your law.
The way of truth I have chosen;
   I have set your ordinances before me. — ℟ ℣

℟. Or: **Alleluia.** ℣

GOSPEL   Jn 6, 22-29

Alleluia (Mt 4, 4)

℟. **Alleluia.** Man does not live on bread alone,
but on every word that comes from the mouth of God.
   ℟. **Alleluia.**

The crowd wants to proclaim Jesus their Messiah, but he leaves
from among them, alone. The people search for him. When found,
Jesus tells them of their concern—that they are looking for signs,
wonders, perishable food.

℣. The Lord be with you. ℟. **And also with you.**
✠ A reading from the holy gospel according to John
℟. **Glory to you, Lord.**

The crowd remained on the other side of the lake.
The next day they realized that there had been only

one boat there and that Jesus had not left in it with
his disciples; rather, they had set out by themselves.
Then some boats came out from Tiberias near the
place where they had eaten the bread after the Lord
had given thanks. Once the crowd saw that neither
Jesus nor his disciples were there, they too embarked in the boats and went to Capernaum looking
for Jesus.

When they found him on the other side of the
lake, they said to him, "Rabbi, when did you come
here?" Jesus answered them:

"I assure you,
you are not looking for me because you have
    seen signs
but because you have eaten your fill of the
    loaves.
You should not be working for perishable food
but for food that remains unto life eternal,
food which the Son of Man will give you;
it is on him that God the Father has set his
    seal."

At this they said to him, "What must we do to perform the works of God?" Jesus replied:

"This is the work of God:
have faith in the One whom he sent."

This is the gospel of the Lord. ℞. **Praise to you, Lord
Jesus Christ.**   ➤ No. 15, p. 623

PRAYER OVER THE GIFTS

Lord,
accept our prayers and offerings.
Make us worthy of your sacraments of love
by granting us your forgiveness.
We ask this in the name of Jesus the Lord.
℞. **Amen.**   ➤ No. 21, p. 626 (Pref. P 22-25)

COMMUNION ANT.   Jn 14, 27

**The Lord says, peace I leave with you, my own peace
I give you; not as the world gives, do I give, alleluia.** ℣

PRAYER AFTER COMMUNION

Almighty and ever-living Lord,
you restored us to life
by raising Christ from death.
Strengthen us by this Easter sacrament.
We ask this through Christ our Lord.
℟. **Amen.** _____ ➔ No. 32, p. 650

TUESDAY OF THE THIRD WEEK OF EASTER

Severe as the accusations were, they did not disturb Stephen because
his conscience acquitted him. There is no greater tormentor than a
bad conscience and no better defender than a good one, for a
good conscience is a continual feast (Prv 15, 15). It is the best com-
forter in all adversity; it goes with us into prison, is with us in
distress, in death, and even before the judgment seat of God.

ENTRANCE ANT.   Rv 19, 5; 12, 10

**All you who fear God, both the great and the small,
give praise to him! For his salvation and strength
have come, the power of Christ, alleluia.**

                                    ➔ No. 2, p. 614

OPENING PRAYER

Father,
you open the kingdom of heaven
to those born again by water and the Spirit.
Increase your gift of love in us.
May all who have been freed from sins in baptism
receive all that you have promised.
We ask this through our Lord Jesus Christ, your Son,
who lives and reigns with you and the Holy Spirit,
one God, for ever and ever. ℟. **Amen.** ℣

READING I   Acts 7, 51-8, 1

Stephen boldly reminds the Sanhedrin of how Jesus suffered and died. Those
who listen become angered and begin to stone him. Stephen prays for his persecutors. Saul agrees to the execution, but later is to become the great St. Paul.

A reading from the Acts of the Apostles
Stephen said to the people and elders and scribes:

"You stiff-necked people, uncircumcised in heart and ears, you are always opposing the Holy Spirit just as your fathers did before you. Was there ever any prophet whom your fathers did not persecute? In their day, they put to death those who foretold the coming of the Just One; now you in your turn have become his betrayers and murderers. You who received the law through the ministry of angels have not observed it."

Those who listened to his words were stung to the heart; they ground their teeth in anger at him. Stephen meanwhile, filled with the Holy Spirit, looked to the sky above and saw the glory of God, and Jesus standing at God's right hand. "Look!" he exclaimed, "I see an opening in the sky, and the Son of Man standing at God's right hand." The onlookers were shouting aloud, holding their hands over their ears as they did so. Then they rushed at him as one man, dragged him out of the city, and began to stone him. The witnesses meanwhile were piling their cloaks at the feet of a young man named Saul. As Stephen was being stoned he could be heard praying, "Lord Jesus, receive my spirit." He fell to his knees and cried out in a loud voice, "Lord, do not hold this sin against them." And with that he died.

Saul, for his part, concurred in the act of killing. —This is the Word of the Lord. ℟. **Thanks be to God.** ✠

Responsorial Psalm   Ps 31, 3-4. 6. 7. 8. 17. 21

℟. (6) **Into your hands, O Lord,**
   I entrust my spirit.

Be my rock of refuge,
   a stronghold to give me safety.
You are my rock and my fortress;
   for your name's sake you will lead and guide
      me. — ℟

Into your hands I commend my spirit;
   you will redeem me, O Lord, O faithful God.

My trust is in the Lord;
  I will rejoice and be glad of your kindness. — ℟
Let your face shine upon your servant;
  save me in your kindness.
You hide them in the shelter of your presence
  from the plotting of men. — ℟ ✟

℟. Or: **Alleluia.** ✟

GOSPEL   Jn 6, 30-35
Alleluia

℟. **Alleluia.** Christ has risen and shines upon us,
whom he has redeemed by his blood. ℟. **Alleluia.**

Jesus teaches that the manna provided to the Hebrews in the desert
during the Exodus was a symbol of the true bread from heaven that
he would give. Jesus explains that he is the bread of life. Those who
come to him will never hunger or thirst again.

℣. The Lord be with you. ℟. **And also with you.**
✟ A reading from the holy gospel according to John
℟. **Glory to you, Lord.**

The crowd said to Jesus: "What sign are you going
to perform for us to see so that we can put faith in
you? What is the 'work' you do? Our ancestors had
manna to eat in the desert; according to Scripture,
'He gave them bread from the heavens to eat.' "
Jesus said to them:
      "I solemnly assure you,
      it was not Moses who gave you bread from the
          heavens;
      it is my Father who gives you the real heav-
          enly bread.
      God's bread
      comes down from heaven
      and gives life to the world."
"Sir, give us this bread always," they besought him.
  Jesus explained to them:
      "I myself am the bread of life.
      No one who comes to me shall ever be hungry,
      no one who believes in me shall thirst again."

This is the gospel of the Lord. ℟. **Praise to you, Lord Jesus Christ.**   ➔ No. 15, p. 623

PRAYER OVER THE GIFTS

Lord,
receive these gifts from your Church.
May the great joy you give us
come to perfection in heaven.
Grant this through Christ our Lord.
℟. **Amen.**   ➔ No. 21, p. 626 (Pref. P 22-25)

COMMUNION ANT.   Rom 6, 8

Because we have died with Christ, we believe that we shall also come to life with him, alleluia. ℣

PRAYER AFTER COMMUNION

Lord,
look on your people with kindness
and by these Easter mysteries
bring us to the glory of the resurrection.
We ask this in the name of Jesus the Lord.
℟. **Amen.**   _____   ➔ No. 32, p. 650

WEDNESDAY OF THE THIRD WEEK OF EASTER

Regardless of what sins we have committed, nothing is too vicious to be forgiven if we have true repentance. If we can no longer hear the voice of God calling us to repentance and can no longer ask for mercy and forgiveness, our condition is indeed serious. But we must never despair of God's mercy, for "the Lord is good to all and compassionate toward all his works" (Ps 145, 9). When the grace of God touches the sinner's heart, tears of repentance will follow.

ENTRANCE ANT.   Ps 71, 8. 23

Fill me with your praise and I will sing your glory; songs of joy will be on my lips, alleluia.
                              ➔ No. 2, p. 614

OPENING PRAYER

Merciful Lord,
hear the prayers of your people.
May we who have received your gift of faith

share for ever in the new life of Christ.
Grant this through our Lord Jesus Christ, your Son,
who lives and reigns with you and the Holy Spirit,
one God, for ever and ever. ℟. **Amen.** ⩔

READING I   Acts 8, 1-8

The violent death of the deacon Stephen begins a general persecution. The Christian faithful disperse to safer areas and bring the
word of God to many more people. God certifies the truth of their
words by miracles and signs.

A reading from the Acts of the Apostles

A certain day saw the beginning of a great persecution of the church in Jerusalem. All except the apostles scattered throughout the countryside of Judea
and Samaria. Devout men buried Stephen, bewailing
him loudly as they did so. After that, Saul began to
harass the church. He entered house after house,
dragged men and women out, and threw them into
jail.

The members of the church who had been dispersed went about preaching the word. Philip, for
example, went down to the town of Samaria and
there proclaimed the Messiah. Without exception,
the crowds that heard Philip and saw the miracles
he performed attended closely to what he had to say.
There were many who had unclean spirits, which
came out shrieking loudly. Many others were para-
lytics or cripples, and these were cured. The rejoicing in that town rose to fever pitch—This is the
Word of the Lord. ℟. **Thanks be to God.** ⩔

Responsorial Psalm   Ps 66, 1-3. 4-5. 6-7
℟. (1) **Let all the earth cry out to God with joy.**
Shout joyfully to God, all you on earth,
    sing praise to the glory of his name;
    proclaim his glorious praise.
Say to God, "How tremendous are your deeds! — ℟
Let all on earth worship and sing praise to you,
    sing praise to your name!"

Come and see the works of God,
　　his tremendous deeds among men. — ℞

He has changed the sea into dry land;
　　through the river they passed on foot;
　　therefore let us rejoice in him.

He rules by his might forever. — ℞ ℣

℞. Or: **Alleluia.** ℣

GOSPEL　　　　　　　　　　　　　　Jn 6, 35-40

Alleluia (Jn 6, 40)

℞. **Alleluia.** This is the will of my Father, says the
　　Lord,
all who believe in the Son will have eternal life
and I will raise them to life again on the last day.
　　℞. **Alleluia.**

St. John continues his presentation of the words of Jesus about the
Bread of Life, the Holy Eucharist. Those who eat his Body and drink
his Blood will share in the risen life of Christ and will have their
spiritual hunger satisfied.

℣. The Lord be with you. ℞. **And also with you.**
✠ A reading from the holy gospel according to John
℞. **Glory to you, Lord.**

Jesus explained to the crowd:
　　"I myself am the bread of life.
　　No one who comes to me shall ever be hungry,
　　no one who believes in me shall thirst again.
　　But as I told you—
　　though you have seen me, you still do not be-
　　　　lieve.
　　All that the Father gives me shall come to me;
　　no one who comes will I ever reject,
　　because it is not to do my will
　　that I have come down from heaven,
　　but to do the will of him who sent me.
　　It is the will of him who sent me
　　that I should lose nothing of what he has given
　　　　me;

rather, that I should raise it up on the last day.
Indeed, this is the will of my Father,
that everyone who looks upon the Son
and believes in him
shall have eternal life.
Him I will raise up on the last day."
This is the gospel of the Lord. ℟. **Praise to you, Lord Jesus Christ.**
➤ No. 15, p. 623

PRAYER OVER THE GIFTS
Lord,
restore us by these Easter mysteries.
May the continuing work of our Redeemer
bring us eternal joy.
We ask this through Christ our Lord.
℟. **Amen.**   ➤ No. 21, p. 626 (Pref. P 22-25)

COMMUNION ANT.
Christ has risen and shines upon us, whom he has redeemed by his blood, alleluia. ℣

PRAYER AFTER COMMUNION
Lord,
may this celebration of our redemption
help us in this life
and lead us to eternal happiness.
We ask this through Christ our Lord.
℟. **Amen.**   ——————   ➤ No. 32, p. 650

THURSDAY OF THE THIRD WEEK OF EASTER

We who have the precious treasure of faith have a grave responsibility. It is not enough to be satisfied with mere profit from the message we have received. We must also communicate it to others. Thus we shall assist in the good work of spreading the Gospel of Christ and share in the reward promised by God to those who lead others to grace and virtue.

ENTRANCE ANT.   Ex 15, 1-2
Let us sing to the Lord, he has covered himself in glory! The Lord is my strength, and I praise him: he is the Savior of my life, alleluia. ➤ No. 2, p. 614

OPENING PRAYER

Father,
in this holy season
we come to know the full depth of your love.
You have freed us from the darkness of error and sin.
Help us to cling to your truths with fidelity.
We ask this through our Lord Jesus Christ, your Son,
who lives and reigns with you and the Holy Spirit,
one God, for ever and ever. ℟. **Amen.** ↓

READING I   Acts 8, 26-40

In a mysterious way Philip meets a man anxious to hear the Gospel.
The prophecy of the sufferings of the Messiah is applied to Christ.
Philip brings the man into the life of the risen Christ by baptizing
him, and the man rejoices in God's gift.

A reading from the Acts of the Apostles

An angel of the Lord addressed himself to Philip:
"Head south toward the road which goes from Jerusalem to Gaza, the desert route." Philip began the
journey. It happened that an Ethiopian eunuch, a
court official in charge of the entire treasury of Can-
dace (a name meaning queen) of the Ethiopians, had
come on a pilgrimage to Jerusalem and was returning home. He was sitting in his carriage reading
the prophet Isaiah. The Spirit said to Philip, "Go and
catch up with that carriage." Philip ran ahead and
heard the man reading the prophet Isaiah. He said
to him, "Do you really grasp what you are reading?"
"How can I," the man replied, "unless someone explains it to me?" With that, he invited Philip to get
in and sit down beside him. This was the passage of
Scripture he was reading:

"Like a sheep he was led to the slaughter,
   like a lamb before its shearer he was silent
   and opened not his mouth.
In his humiliation he was deprived of justice.
Who will ever speak of his posterity,
   for he is deprived of his life on earth?"
The eunuch said to Philip, "Tell me, if you will, of

whom the prophet says this—himself or someone else?" Philip launched out with this Scripture passage as his starting point, telling him the good news of Jesus. As they moved along the road they came to some water, and the eunuch said, "Look, there is some water right there. What is to keep me from being baptized?" He ordered the carriage stopped, and Philip went down into the water with the eunuch and baptized him. When they came out of the water, the Spirit of the Lord snatched Philip away and the eunuch saw him no more. Nevertheless the man went on his way rejoicing. Philip found himself at Azotus next, and he went about announcing the good news in all the towns until he reached Caesarea.—This is the Word of the Lord. ℟. **Thanks be to God.** ℣

Responsorial Psalm   Ps 66, 8-9. 16-17. 20

℟. (1) **Let all the earth cry out to God with joy.**

Bless our God, you peoples,
  loudly sound his praise;
He has given life to our souls,
  and has not let our feet slip. — ℟

Hear now, all you who fear God, while I declare
  what he has done for me.
When I appealed to him in words,
  praise was on the tip of my tongue. — ℟

Blessed be God who refused me not
  my prayer or his kindness! — ℟ ℣

℟. Or: **Alleluia.** ℣

GOSPEL   Jn 6, 44-51

Alleluia (Jn 6, 51-52)

℟. **Alleluia.** I am the living bread from heaven, says
  the Lord;
if anyone eats this bread he will live for ever. ℟. **Al-
luia.**

Jesus teaches that the only way to life is through himself. He reveals the Father and his will. Through faith and the Eucharist, we will not die, but we will share in the life of the Father forever.

℣. The Lord be with you. ℟. **And also with you.**
✠ A reading from the holy gospel according to John
℟. **Glory to you, Lord.**

Jesus said to the crowds:

"No one can come to me
unless the Father who sent me draws him;
I will raise him up on the last day.
It is written in the prophets:
'They shall all be taught by God.'
Everyone who has heard the Father
and learned from him
comes to me.
Not that anyone has seen the Father—
only the one who is from God
has seen the Father.
Let me firmly assure you,
he who believes has eternal life.
I am the bread of life.
Your ancestors ate manna in the desert, but
they died.
This is the bread that comes down from heaven,
for a man to eat and never die.
I myself am the living bread
come down from heaven.
If anyone eats this bread
he shall live forever;
the bread I will give
is my flesh, for the life of the world."

This is the gospel of the Lord. ℟. **Praise to you, Lord,
Lord Jesus Christ.**   → No. 15, p. 623

PRAYER OVER THE GIFTS

Lord God,
by this holy exchange of gifts
you share with us your divine life.
Grant that everything we do
may be directed by the knowledge of your truth.
We ask this in the name of Jesus the Lord.
℟. **Amen.**   → No. 21, p. 626 (Pref. P 22-25)

COMMUNION ANT.   2 Cor 5, 15

Christ died for all, so that living men should not live for themselves, but for Christ who died and was raised to life for them, alleluia. ℣

PRAYER AFTER COMMUNION
Merciful Father,
may these mysteries give us new purpose
and bring us to a new life in you.
Grant this through Christ our Lord.
℟. **Amen.**   ➔ No. 32, p. 650

_____

FRIDAY OF THE THIRD WEEK OF EASTER

St. Paul in his life, as after his death by martyrdom, worked numberless miracles. He had so deeply impressed the name of Jesus in his heart that it was almost continually on his lips, "for out of the fullness of the heart, the mouth speaks." Would that we loved Jesus as St. Paul loved him, to be ready to do his will and suffer for him.

ENTRANCE ANT.   Rv 5, 12

The Lamb who was slain is worthy to receive strength and divinity, wisdom and power and honor, alleluia.
                    ➔ No. 2, p. 614

OPENING PRAYER
Father,
by the love of your Spirit,
may we who have experienced
the grace of the Lord's resurrection
rise to the newness of life in joy.
Grant this through our Lord Jesus Christ, your Son,
who lives and reigns with you and the Holy Spirit,
one God, for ever and ever. ℟. **Amen.** ℣

READING I   Acts 9. 1-20

Saul is stricken from his horse on the road to Damascus and has a vision of Jesus as the Lord. Christ himself has been persecuted by Saul's attacks upon the faithful. Saul receives the gift of faith.

A reading from the Acts of the Apostles
Saul, breathing murderous threats against the Lord's

disciples, went to the high priest and asked him for letters to the synagogues in Damascus which would empower him to arrest and bring to Jerusalem anyone he might find, man or woman, living according to the new way. As he traveled along and was approaching Damascus, a light from the sky suddenly flashed about him. He fell to the ground and at the same time heard a voice saying, "Saul, Saul, why do you persecute me?" "Who are you, sir?" he asked. The voice answered, "I am Jesus, the one you are persecuting. Get up and go into the city, where you will be told what to do." The men who were traveling with him stood there speechless. They had heard the voice but could see no one. Saul got up from the ground unable to see, even though his eyes were open. They had to take him by the hand and lead him into Damascus. For three days he continued blind, during which time he neither ate nor drank.

There was a disciple in Damascus named Ananias to whom the Lord had appeared in a vision. "Ananias!" he said. "Here I am, Lord," came the answer. The Lord said to him, "Go at once to Straight Street, and at the house of Judas ask for a certain Saul of Tarsus. He is there praying." (Saul saw in a vision a man named Ananias coming to him and placing his hands on him so that he might recover his sight.) But Ananias protested: "Lord, I have heard from many sources about this man and all the harm he has done to your holy people in Jerusalem. He is here now with authorization from the chief priests to arrest any who invoke your name." The Lord said to him: "You must go! This man is the instrument I have chosen to bring my name to the Gentiles and their kings and to the people of Israel. I myself shall indicate to him how much he will have to suffer for my name." With that Ananias left. When he entered the house he laid his hands on Saul and said, "Saul, my brother, I have been sent by the Lord Jesus who appeared to you on the way here, to help you recover your sight and be filled with the Holy Spirit." Immediately something like scales fell from his eyes and he regained his sight. He got up and was baptized, and his strength returned to him after he had taken food.

Saul stayed some time with the disciples in Damascus, and soon began to proclaim in the synagogues that Jesus was the Son of God.—This is the Word of the Lord. ℟. **Thanks be to God.** ℣

Responsorial Psalm   Ps 117, 1. 2.

℟. (Mk 16, 15) **Go out to all the world, and tell the Good News.**

Praise the Lord, all you nations;
    glorify him, all you peoples! — ℟

For steadfast is his kindness toward us,
    and the fidelity of the Lord endures forever.— ℟ ℣

℟. Or: **Alleluia.** ℣

GOSPEL   Jn 6, 52-59

Alleluia (Jn 6, 57)

℟. **Alleluia.** Whoever eats my flesh and drinks my blood

will live in me and I in him, says the Lord. ℟. **Alleluia.**

The announcement of his flesh and blood as food and drink produces wonderment and objection, but Jesus stresses the real meaning of his words. Whoever eats the flesh of the Son of Man and drinks his blood remains in Jesus and will live forever.

℣. The Lord be with you. ℟. **And also with you.**
✠ A reading from the holy gospel according to John
℟. **Glory to you, Lord.**

The Jews quarreled among themselves, saying, "How can this man give us his flesh to eat?" Thereupon Jesus said to them:

"Let me solemnly assure you,
    if you do not eat the flesh of the Son of Man

and drink his blood,
you have no life in you.
He who feeds on my flesh
and drinks my blood
has life eternal,
and I will raise him up on the last day.
For my flesh is real food
and my blood real drink.
The man who feeds on my flesh
and drinks my blood
remains in me, and I in him.
Just as the Father who has life sent me
and I have life because of the Father,
so the man who feeds on me
will have life because of me.
This is the bread that came down from heaven.
Unlike your ancestors who ate and died nonetheless,
the man who feeds on this bread shall live forever."

He said this in a synagogue instruction at Capernaum.—This is the gospel of the Lord. ℟. **Praise to
you, Lord Jesus Christ.**   ➔ No. 15, p. 623

PRAYER OVER THE GIFTS

Merciful Lord,
make holy these gifts
and let our spiritual sacrifice
make us an everlasting gift to you.
We ask this in the name of Jesus the Lord.
℟. **Amen.**   ➔ No. 21, p. 626 (Pref. P 22-25)

COMMUNION ANT.

**The man who died on the cross has risen from the
dead, and has won back our lives from death, alleluia.** ⍒

PRAYER AFTER COMMUNION

Lord,
may this eucharist,

which we have celebrated in memory of your Son,
help us to grow in love.
We ask this in the name of Jesus the Lord.
℟. **Amen.**   ➜ No. 32, p. 650

_____

SATURDAY OF THE THIRD WEEK OF EASTER

Jesus said: "Without me you can do nothing" (Jn 16, 5). Our grace
must come from God, and it enables us to practice good works. By
prayer and a lively faith, we can do anything! We have but to ask
with every confidence in God's will and power to help us. This is the
reason why all the saints and the spiritual writers insist upon the
practice of prayer as an essential means of salvation.

ENTRANCE ANT.   Col 2, 12

**In baptism we have died with Christ, and we have
risen to new life in him, because we believed in the
power of God who raised him from the dead, alleluia.**
➜ No. 2, p. 614

OPENING PRAYER
God our Father,
by the waters of baptism
you give new life to the faithful.
May we not succumb to the influence of evil
but remain true to your gift of life.
We ask this through our Lord Jesus Christ, your Son,
who lives and reigns with you and the Holy Spirit,
one God, for ever and ever. ℟. **Amen.** ▼

READING I   Acts 9, 31-42

During his missionary journeys, St. Peter cures the sick and raises
the dead. The signs that Jesus performed are now done by the
apostles, but by prayer to Christ rather than by their own personal
power.

A reading from the Acts of the Apostles

Throughout all Judea, Galilee and Samaria the
church was at peace. It was being built up and was
making steady progress in the fear of the Lord; at
the same time it enjoyed the increased consolation
of the Holy Spirit.

Once when Peter was making numerous journeys, he went—among other places—to God's holy people living in Lydda. There he found a man named Aeneas, a paralytic who had been bedridden for eight years. Peter said to him, "Aeneas, Jesus Christ cures you! Get up and make your bed." The man got up at once. All the inhabitants of Lydda and Sharon, upon seeing him, were converted to the Lord.

Now in Joppa there was a certain woman convert named Tabitha (in Greek Dorcas, meaning a gazelle). Her life was marked by constant good deeds and acts of charity. At about that time she fell ill and died. They washed her body and laid it out in an upstairs room. Since Lydda was near Joppa, the disciples who had heard that Peter was there sent two men to him with the urgent request, "Please come over to us without delay." Peter set out with them as they asked. Upon his arrival they took him upstairs to the room. All the widows came to him in tears and showed him the various garments Dorcas had made when she was still with them. Peter first made everyone go outside; then he knelt down and prayed. Turning to the dead body, he said, "Tabitha, stand up." She opened her eyes, then looked at Peter and sat up. He gave her his hand and helped her to her feet. The next thing he did was to call in those who were believers and the widows to show them that she was alive. This became known all over Joppa, and because of it, many came to believe in the Lord.—This is the Word of the Lord. ℟. **Thanks be to God.** ✟

Responsorial Psalm   Ps 116, 12-13. 14-15. 16-17

℟. (12) **What return can I make to the Lord**
    for all that he gives to me?

How shall I make a return to the Lord
    for all the good he has done for me?

The cup of salvation I will take up,
    and I will call upon the name of the Lord. — R̅⁊
My vows to the Lord I will pay
    in the presence of all his people.
Precious in the eyes of the Lord
    is the death of his faithful ones. — R̅⁊

O Lord, I am your servant;
    I am your servant, the son of your handmaid;
    you have loosed my bonds.
To you will I offer sacrifice of thanksgiving,
    and I will call upon the name of the Lord. — R̅⁊ ⅴ

R̅⁊. Or: **Alleluia.** ⅴ

GOSPEL Jn 6, 60-69

Alleluia (Jn 6, 64. 69)
R̅⁊. **Alleluia.** Your words, Lord, are spirit and life;
you have the message of eternal life. R̅⁊. **Alleluia.**

The Bread of Life discourse leads many of Jesus' followers to abandon him. Jesus explains that his promise is possible because of his
coming passage into the risen life of heaven. Jesus challenges his
apostles to accept his words because of their faith in him.

Ⅴ. The Lord be with you. R̅⁊. **And also with you.**
✠ A reading from the holy gospel according to John
R̅⁊. **Glory to you, Lord.**

Many of the disciples of Jesus remarked, "This sort
of talk is hard to endure! How can anyone take it
seriously?" Jesus was fully aware that his disciples
were murmuring in protest at what he had said.
"Does it shake your faith?" he asked them.

    "What, then, if you were to see the Son of Man
       ascend to where he was before . . . ?
    It is the spirit that gives life;
       the flesh is useless.
    The words I spoke to you
       are spirit and life.
    Yet among you there are some who do not be-
       lieve."

(Jesus knew from the start, of course, the ones who refused to believe, and the one who would hand him over.) He went on to say:

"This is why I have told you
that no one can come to me
unless it is granted him by the Father."

From this time on, many of his disciples broke away and would not remain in his company any longer. Jesus then said to the Twelve, "Do you want to leave me too?" Simon Peter answered him, "Lord, to whom shall we go? You have the words of eternal life. We have come to believe; we are convinced that you are God's holy one."—This is the gospel of the Lord.
R. **Praise to you, Lord Jesus Christ.** ➔ No. 15, p. 623

PRAYER OVER THE GIFTS

Lord,
accept these gifts from your family.
May we hold fast to the life you have given us
and come to the eternal gifts you promise.
We ask this in the name of Jesus the Lord.
R̃. **Amen.**   ➔ No. 21, p. 626 (Pref. P 22-25)

COMMUNION ANT.   Jn 17, 20-21

Father, I pray for them: may they be one in us, so that the world may believe it was you who sent me, alleluia. ⱽ

PRAYER AFTER COMMUNION

Lord,
watch over those you have saved in Christ.
May we who are redeemed by his suffering and death
always rejoice in his resurrection,
for he is Lord for ever and ever.
R̃. **Amen.**   ➔ No. 32, p. 650

MONDAY OF THE FOURTH WEEK OF EASTER

More than nineteen centuries have passed since Christ founded the Church upon the blessed apostle Peter, and although thousands of heresies have risen from the pool of hell, the foundation yet stands unshaken, serene and unharmed in apostolic dignity. We, like Peter, should assist in spreading the Gospel of Christ, remembering that "the person who brings a sinner back from his way will save his soul from death and cancel a multitude of sins" (Jas 5, 20).

ENTRANCE ANT.   Rom 6, 9

Christ now raised from the dead will never die again; death no longer has power over him, alleluia.

➤ No. 2, p. 614

OPENING PRAYER

Father,
through the obedience of Jesus,
your servant and your Son,
you raised a fallen world.
Free us from sin
and bring us the joy that lasts for ever.
We ask this through our Lord Jesus Christ, your Son,
who lives and reigns with you and the Holy Spirit,
one God, for ever and ever. ℟. **Amen.** ⍦

READING I   Acts 11, 1-18

By receiving a Roman family into the Church, Peter sets off a major controversy about the obligation of the law of Moses after the coming of Christ. Peter explains the will of Christ, thus opening the Church to the Gentiles, that is, to non-Jews, without imposing the Mosaic law.

A reading from the Acts of the Apostles

The apostles and the brothers heard that Gentiles, too, had accepted the word of God. As a result, when Peter went up to Jerusalem some among the circumcised took issue with him, saying, "You entered the house of uncircumcised men and ate with them." Peter then explained the whole affair to them step by step from the beginning: "I was at prayer in the city of Joppa when, in a trance, I saw a vision. An object like a big canvas came down; it was lowered down to me from the sky by its four corners. As I stared at it I could make out four-legged creatures of the earth, wild beasts and reptiles, and birds of the sky. I listened as a voice said to me, 'Get up, Peter! Slaughter, then eat.' I replied: "Not for a moment, sir! Nothing unclean or impure has ever entered my mouth!' A second time the voice from the heavens spoke out: 'What God has purified you are not to call unclean.' This happened three times; then the canvas with everything in it was drawn up again into the sky.

"Immediately after that, the three men who had been sent to me from Caesarea came to the house where we were staying. The Spirit instructed me to accompany them without hesitation. These six brothers came along with me, and we entered the man's house. He informed us that he had seen an angel standing in his house and that the angel had said: 'Send someone to Joppa and fetch Simon, known also as Peter. In the light of what he will tell you, you shall be saved, and all your household.' As I began to address them the Holy Spirit came upon them, just as it had upon us at the beginning. Then I remembered what the Lord had said: 'John baptized with water but you will be baptized with the Holy Spirit.' If God was giving them the same gift he gave us when we first believed in the Lord Jesus Christ, who was I to interfere with him?" When they heard this they stopped objecting, and instead began to glorify God in these words: "If this be so, then God has granted life-giving repentance even to the Gentiles."—This is the Word of the Lord. ℟. **Thanks be to God.** ℣

Responsorial Psalm   Pss 42, 2-3; 43, 3. 4.
℟. (Ps 41, 3) **My soul is thirsting for the living God.**
As the hind longs for the running waters,
    so my soul longs for you, O God.
Athirst is my soul for God, the living God.

When shall I go and behold the face of God? — ℞

Send forth your light and your fidelity;
   they shall lead me on
And bring me to your holy mountain,
   to your dwelling-place. — ℞

Then will I go in to the altar of God,
   the God of my gladness and joy;
Then will I give you thanks upon the harp,
   O God, my God! — ℞ ℣

℞. Or: **Alleluia.** ℣

GOSPEL   Jn 10, 1-10

Alleluia (Jn 10, 14)

℞. **Alleluia.** I am the good shepherd, says the Lord;
I know my sheep and mine know me. ℞. **Alleluia.**

By using two related comparisons, that of a shepherd leading his
flock and that of a sheepfold protecting the sheep, Jesus promises
that whoever enters the fold through him will be safe.

℣. The Lord be with you. ℞. **And also with you.**
✠ A reading from the holy gospel according to John
℞. **Glory to you, Lord.**

Jesus said:
      "Truly I assure you:
      Whoever does not enter the sheepfold through
         the gate
      but climbs in some other way
      is a thief and a marauder.
      The one who enters through the gate
      is shepherd of the sheep;
      the keeper opens the gate for him.
      The sheep hear his voice
      as he calls his own by name
      and leads them out.
      When he has brought out [all] those that are his,
      he walks in front of them,
      and the sheep follow him
      because they recognize his voice.

> They will not follow a stranger;
> such a one they will flee,
> because they do not recognize a stranger's
>   voice."

Even though Jesus used this figure with them, they did not grasp what he was trying to tell them. He therefore said [to them again]:

> "My solemn word is this:
> I am the sheepgate.
> All who came before me
> were thieves and marauders
> whom the sheep did not heed.
> "I am the gate.
> Whoever enters through me
> will be safe.
> He will go in and out,
> and find pasture.
> The thief comes
> only to steal and slaughter and destroy.
> I came that they might have life
> and have it to the full."

This is the gospel of the Lord. ℞. **Praise to you, Lord Jesus Christ.**   ➔ No. 15, p. 623

OR

In year A, when the above Gospel is read on the preceding Sunday, the following text is used.

GOSPEL   Jn 10, 11-18

Alleluia (Jn 10, 14)

℞. **Alleluia.** I am the good shepherd, says the Lord; I know my sheep and mine know me. ℞. **Alleluia.**

Christ is the good shepherd. He loves his sheep and lays down his life for them. The Father loves him because he lays down his life freely. Jesus announces that he has other sheep who will one day be part of the one fold.

℣. The Lord be with you. ℞. **And also with you.**
✠ A reading from the holy gospel accoridng to John
℞. **Glory to you, Lord.**

Jesus said:
"I am the good shepherd;
the good shepherd lays down his life for the sheep.
The hired hand, who is no shepherd
nor owner of the sheep,
catches sight of the wolf coming
and runs away, leaving the sheep
to be snatched and scattered by the wolf.
That is because he works for pay;
he has no concern for the sheep.
"I am the good shepherd.
I know my sheep
and my sheep know me
in the same way that the Father knows me
and I know the Father;
for these sheep I will give my life.
I have other sheep
that do not belong to this fold.
I must lead them, too,
and they shall hear my voice.
There shall be one flock then, one shepherd.
The Father loves me for this:
that I lay down my life
to take it up again.
No one takes it from me;
I lay it down freely.
I have power to lay it down,
and I have power to take it up again.
This command I received from my Father."

This is the gospel of the Lord. ℟. **Praise to you, Lord Jesus Christ.** ➤ No. 15, p. 623

PRAYER OVER THE GIFTS

Lord,
receive these gifts from your Church.
May the great joy you give us
come to perfection in heaven.
Grant this through Christ our Lord.
℟. **Amen.** ➤ No. 21, p. 626 (Pref. P 22-25)

COMMUNION ANT.   Jn 20, 19

**Jesus came and stood among his disciples and said
to them: Peace be with you, alleluia.** ℣

PRAYER AFTER COMMUNION

Lord,
look on your people with kindness
and by these Easter mysteries
bring us to the glory of the resurrection.
We ask this in the name of Jesus the Lord.
℟. **Amen.**   ➔ No. 32, p. 650

TUESDAY OF THE FOURTH WEEK OF EASTER

In all places they reached, the disciples established Christian communities. Jesus cast aside Paganism and Judaism and promulgated
a new religion and founded this true Church. There is but one flock
and one shepherd. The apostolic Church thus founded and continued
was watered with the blood of thousands of holy martyrs. We must
be ever ready to show our gratitude and to suffer, if required, to
foster the faith that is our gift from God.

ENTRANCE ANT.   Rv 19, 7. 6

**Let us shout out our joy and happiness, and give glory
to God, the Lord of all, because he is our King, alleluia.**   ➔ No. 2, p. 614

OPENING PRAYER

Almighty God,
as we celebrate the resurrection,
may we share with each other
the joy the risen Christ has won for us.
We ask this through our Lord Jesus Christ, your Son,
who lives and reigns with you and the Holy Spirit,
one God, for ever and ever. ℟. **Amen.** ℣

READING I   Acts 11, 19-26

The message of Christ reaches Greek areas, especially Cyprus. Barnabas has been commissioned to oversee the development of the
Church in Antioch. Barnabas in turn selects Paul to work with him.

A reading from the Acts of the Apostles

Those in the community who had been dispersed by the persecution that arose because of Stephen went as far as Phoenicia, Cyprus and Antioch, making the message known to none but Jews. However, some men of Cyprus and Cyrene among them who had come to Antioch began to talk even to the Greeks, announcing the good news of the Lord Jesus to them. The hand of the Lord was with them and a great number of them believed and were converted to the Lord. News of this eventually reached the ears of the church in Jerusalem, resulting in Barnabas' being sent to Antioch. On his arrival he rejoiced to see the evidence of God's favor. He encouraged them all to remain firm in their commitment to the Lord, since he himself was a good man filled with the Holy Spirit and faith. Thereby large numbers were added to the Lord. Then Barnabas went off to Tarsus to look for Saul; once he had found him, he brought him back to Antioch. For a whole year they met with the church and instructed great numbers. It was in Antioch that the disciples were called Christians for the first time.—This is the Word of the Lord. ℟. **Thanks be to God. ⅴ**

Responsorial Psalm   Ps 87, 1-3. 4-5. 6-7

℟. (Ps 117, 1) **All you nations, praise the Lord.**

His foundation upon the holy mountains
    the Lord loves:
The gates of Zion,
    more than any dwelling of Jacob.
Glorious things are said of you,
    O city of God! — ℟

I tell of Egypt and Babylon
    among those that know the Lord;
Of Philistia, Tyre, Ethiopia:
    "This man was born there."
And of Zion they shall say:

"One and all were born in her;
And he who has established her
   is the Most High Lord." — ℟
They shall note, when the peoples are enrolled:
   "This man was born there."
And all shall sing, in their festive dance:
   "My home is within you." — ℟ ℣

℟. Or: **Alleluia.** ℣

GOSPEL   Jn 10, 22-30
Alleluia (Jn 10, 27)

℟. **Alleluia.** My sheep listen to my voice, says the
   Lord;
I know them and they follow me. ℟. **Alleluia.**

John recorded many statements by Jesus concerning his identity as
the Son of God. In this Gospel passage, Jesus says he and the
Father are one, and he directs our attention to the works that he has
done. These works prove his claim.

℣. The Lord be with you. ℟. **And also with you.**
✠ A reading from the holy gospel according to John
℟. **Glory to you, Lord.**

It was winter, and the time came for the feast of the
Dedication in Jerusalem. Jesus was walking in the
temple area, in Solomon's Portico, when the Jews
gathered around him and said, "How long are you
going to keep us in suspense? If you really are the
Messiah, tell us so in plain words." Jesus answered:

   "I did tell you, but you do not believe.
   The works I do in my Father's name
   give witness in my favor,
   but you refuse to believe
   because you are not my sheep.
   My sheep hear my voice.
   I know them,
   and they follow me.
   I give them eternal life,
   and they shall never perish.

No one shall snatch them out of my hand.
My Father is greater than all, in what he has
     given me,
and there is no snatching out of his hand.
The Father and I are one."

This is the gospel of the Lord. ℟. **Praise to you, Lord Jesus Christ.**   ➤ No. 15, p. 623

PRAYER OVER THE GIFTS

Lord,
give us joy by these Easter mysteries;
let the continuous offering of this sacrifice
by which we are renewed
bring us to eternal happiness.
We ask this in the name of Jesus the Lord.
℟. **Amen.**   ➤ No. 21, p. 626 (Pref. P 22-25)

COMMUNION ANT.   See Lk 24, 46. 26
Christ had to suffer and to rise from the dead, and so enter into his glory, alleluia. ✣

PRAYER AFTER COMMUNION

Lord,
may this celebration of our redemption
help us in this life
and lead us to eternal happiness.
We ask this through Christ our Lord.
℟. **Amen.**   ➤ No. 32, p. 650

WEDNESDAY OF THE FOURTH WEEK OF EASTER

Jesus is the Way by his holy doctrine and example. He is the Truth by the fulfillment of all prophecies, by his mysteries, his promises and warnings. He is the Life because by his death he has obtained for us the life of grace and glory. We have but to listen and obey.

ENTRANCE ANT.   Ps 18, 50; 21, 23
I will be a witness to you in the world, O Lord. I will spread the knowledge of your name among my brothers, alleluia.   ➤ No. 2, p. 614

OPENING PRAYER

God our Father,
life of the faithful,
glory of the humble,
happiness of the just,
hear our prayer.
Fill our emptiness
with the blessing of this eucharist,
the foretaste of eternal joy.
We ask this through our Lord Jesus Christ, your Son,
who lives and reigns with you and the Holy Spirit,
one God, for ever and ever. ℟. **Amen.** ℣

READING I   Acts 12, 24-13, 5

As the community of believers spreads in numbers and in area,
preachers and ministers are added to the original twelve apostles.
Barnabas and Paul are ordained by the will of the Spirit and accepted
into the college of the apostles.

A reading from the Acts of the Apostles

The word of the Lord continued to spread and increase.

Barnabas and Saul returned to Jerusalem upon
completing the relief mission, taking with them John
Mark.

There were in the church at Antioch certain prophets and teachers: Barnabas, Symeon known as Niger,
Lucius of Cyrene, Manaen (who had been brought
up with Herod the tetrarch), and Saul. On one occasion, while they were engaged in the liturgy of the
Lord and were fasting, the Holy Spirit spoke to
them: "Set apart Barnabas and Saul for me to do
the work for which I have called them." Then, after
they had fasted and prayed, they imposed hands on
them and sent them off.

These two, sent forth by the Holy Spirit, went
down to the port of Seleucia and set sail from there
for Cyprus. On their arrival in Salamis they proclaimed the word of God in the Jewish synagogues.

—This is the Word of the Lord. ℟. **Thanks to be God.** ✔

Responsorial Psalm   Ps 67, 2-3. 5. 6. 8

℟. (4) **O God, let all the nations praise you!**

May God have pity on us and bless us;
    may he let his face shine upon us.
So may your way be known upon earth;
    among all nations, your salvation. — ℟

May the nations be glad and exult
    because you rule the peoples in equity;
    the nations on the earth you guide. — ℟

May the peoples praise you, O God;
    may all the peoples praise you!
May God bless us,
    and may all the ends of the earth fear him! — ℟ ✔

℟. Or: **Alleluia.** ✔

GOSPEL   Jn 12, 44-50

Alleluia (Jn 8, 12)

℟. **Alleluia.** I am the light of the world, says the Lord: he who follows me will have the light of life. ℟. **Alleluia.**

Jesus teaches that he is the light of the world. The Jews followed a pillar of light out of slavery into the promised land. Jesus is the light leading all men to eternal life. Whoever rejects Jesus and does not believe already has his judge.

℣. The Lord be with you. ℟. **And also with you.**

✠ A reading from the holy gospel according to John
℟. **Glory to you, Lord.**

Jesus proclaimed aloud:
    "Whoever puts faith in me
    believes not so much in me
    as in him who sent me;
    and whoever looks on me
    is seeing him who sent me.
    I have come to the world as its light,
    to keep anyone who believes in me

from remaining in the dark.
If anyone hears my words and does not keep
    them,
I am not the one to condemn him,
for I did not come to condemn the world
but to save it.
Whoever rejects me and does not accept my
    words
already has his judge,
namely, the word I have spoken—
it is that which will condemn him on the last
    day.
For I have not spoken on my own;
no, the Father who sent me
has commanded me
what to say and how to speak.
Since I know that his commandment means
    eternal life,
whatever I say
is spoken just as he instructed me."
This is the gospel of the Lord. ℟. **Praise to you, Lord
Jesus Christ.**
                            ➤ No. 15, p. 623

PRAYER OVER THE GIFTS
Lord God,
by this holy exchange of gifts
you share with us your divine life.
Grant that everything we do
may be directed by the knowledge of your truth.
We ask this in the name of Jesus the Lord.
℟. **Amen.**   ➤ No. 21, p. 626 (Pref. P 22-25)

COMMUNION ANT.   See Jn 15, 16. 19
**The Lord says, I have chosen you from the world to
go and bear fruit that will last, alleluia.** ↓

PRAYER AFTER COMMUNION
Merciful Father,
may these mysteries give us new purpose

and bring us to a new life in you.
Grant this through Christ our Lord.
℟. **Amen.**   ➤ No. 32, p. 650

_____

THURSDAY OF THE FOURTH WEEK OF EASTER

Even in the most difficult of circumstances, nothing is impossible to God. We should ever be aware that God abandons no one, no matter what his sin and weakness, if he is truly repentant. How anxious God is to care for all of us. We need but come to him as we do at Mass today.

ENTRANCE ANT.   See Ps 68, 8-9. 20

When you walked at the head of your people, O God, and lived with them on their journey, the earth shook at your presence and the skies poured forth their rain, alleluia.   ➤ No. 2, p. 614

OPENING PRAYER

Father,
in restoring human nature
you have given us a greater dignity
than we had in the beginning.
Keep us in your love
and continue to sustain those
who have received new life in baptism.
We ask this through our Lord Jesus Christ, your Son,
who lives and reigns with you and the Holy Spirit,
one God, for ever and ever. ℟. **Amen.** ▼

READING I   Acts 13, 13-25

Paul gives a summary of the case for Jesus Christ as the promised Messiah to groups of Jews he meets during his travels. Jesus fulfills the Old Testament. Jewish history has been the preparation for the coming of Christ.

A reading from the Acts of the Apostles

From Paphos, Paul and his companions put out to sea and sailed to Perga in Pamphylia. There John left them and returned to Jerusalem. They continued to travel on from Perga and came to Antioch in

Pisidia. On the sabbath day they entered the synagogue and sat down. After the reading of the law and of the prophets, the leading men of the synagogue sent this message to them: "Brothers, if you have any exhortation to address to the people please speak up."

So Paul arose, motioned to them for silence, and began: "Fellow Israelites and you others who reverence our God, listen to what I have to say! The God of the people Israel once chose our fathers. He made this people great during their sojourn in the land of Egypt, and 'with an outstretched arm' he led them out of it. For forty years 'he put up with them in the desert'; then he destroyed 'seven nations' in the land of Canaan to give them that country as their heritage at the end of some four hundred and fifty years. Later on he set up judges to rule them until the time of the prophet Samuel. When they asked for a king, God gave them Saul son of Kish, of the tribe of Benjamin, who ruled for forty years. Then God removed him and raised up David as their king; on his behalf God testified, 'I have found David son of Jesse to be a man after my own heart who will fulfill my every wish.'

"According to his promise, God has brought forth from this man's descendants Jesus, a savior for Israel. John heralded the coming of Jesus by proclaiming a baptism of repentance to all the people of Israel. As John's career was coming to an end, he would say, 'What you suppose me to be I am not. Rather, look for the one who comes after me. I am not worthy to unfasten the sandals on his feet.' "— This is the Word of the Lord. ℟. **Thanks be to God.** ℣

Responsorial Psalm   Ps 89, 2-3. 21-22. 25. 27

℟. (2) **For ever I will sing the goodness of the Lord.**

The favors of the Lord I will sing forever;
    through all generations my mouth shall proclaim
        your faithfulness.

For you have said, "My kindness is established for-
    ever";
  in heaven you have confirmed your faithful-
    ness. — ℞

I have found David, my servant;
  with my holy oil I have anointed him,
That my hand may be always with him,
  and that my arm may make him strong. — ℞

My faithfulness and my kindness shall be with him,
  and through my name shall his horn be exalted.
"He shall say of me, 'You are my father,
  my God, my Rock, my savior.' " — ℞ ℣

℞. Or: **Alleluia.** ℣

GOSPEL   **Alleluia** (Rv 1, 5)   Jn 13, 16-20

℞. **Alleluia.** Jesus Christ, you are the faithful witness,
  first-born from the dead;
you have loved us and washed away our sins in your
  blood. ℞. **Alleluia.**

The scene is that of the Last Supper. Jesus washed the feet of his
apostles, thus showing his love and self-sacrifice for them. He expects
his followers to love one another as he has loved all men and to
help those who preach his coming.

℣. The Lord be with you. ℞. **And also with you.**
✠ A reading from the holy gospel according to John
℞. **Glory to you, Lord.**

[After Jesus has washed the feet of the disciples he
said:]
     "I solemnly assure you,
      no slave is greater than his master;
      no messenger outranks the one who sent him.
      Once you know all these things,
      blest will you be if you put them into practice.
      What I say is not said of all,
      for I know the kind of men I chose.
      My purpose here is the fulfillment of Scripture:
      'He who partook of bread with me

has raised his heel against me.'
I tell you this now, before it takes place,
so that when it takes place you may believe
    that I AM.
I solemnly assure you,
he who accepts anyone I send
accepts me,
and in accepting me
accepts him who sent me."

This is the gospel of the Lord. ℟. **Praise to you, Lord Jesus Christ.**   ➤ No. 15, p. 623

PRAYER OVER THE GIFTS

Lord,
accept our prayers and offerings.
Make us worthy of your sacraments of love
by granting us your forgiveness.
We ask this in the name of Jesus the Lord.
℟. **Amen.**   ➤ No. 21, p. 626 (Pref. P 22-25)

COMMUNION ANT.   Mt 28, 20

I, the Lord, am with you always, until the end of the world, alleluia. ℣

PRAYER AFTER COMMUNION

Almighty and ever-living Lord,
you restored us to life
by raising Christ from death.
Strengthen us by this Easter sacrament;
may we feel its saving power in our daily life.
We ask this through Christ our Lord.
℟. **Amen.**   ➤ No. 32, p. 650

FRIDAY OF THE FOURTH WEEK OF EASTER

By his death and resurrection, Jesus has rendered perfect satisfaction and effected man's redemption. But we must not imagine there is no further need for doing penance or for working out our salvation. As the children of Israel, though freed from Pharaoh's bondage, had to fight long and constantly against many enemies in order to gain the

Promised Land, so also we, though freed by Christ, must battle against our enemies to the end of our lives to obtain the promised heavenly land.

ENTRANCE ANT.   Rv 5, 9-10

By your blood, O Lord, you have redeemed us from every tribe and tongue, from every nation and people: you have made us into the kingdom of God, alleluia.

➔ No. 2, p. 614

OPENING PRAYER

Father of our freedom and salvation,
hear the prayers of those redeemed by your Son's
    suffering.
Through you may we have life;
with you may we have eternal joy.
We ask this through our Lord Jesus Christ, your Son,
who lives and reigns with you and the Holy Spirit,
one God, for ever and ever. ℟. **Amen.** ↓

READING I   Acts 13, 26-33

Paul tries to convert to Christ the Jews who are settled in the cities of the Roman empire. He goes to their synagogues, and he proclaims that God's plan was fulfilled by the death and the resurrection of Jesus Christ, the Savior and the Son of God.

A reading from the Acts of the Apostles

[When Paul came to Antioch in Pisidia, he said in the synagogue:] "My brothers, children of the family of Abraham and you others who reverence our God, it was to us that this message of salvation was sent forth. The inhabitants of Jerusalem and their rulers failed to recognize him, and in condemning him they fulfilled the words of the prophets which we read sabbath after sabbath. Even though they found no charge against him which deserved death, they begged Pilate to have him executed. Once they had thus brought about all that had been written of him, they took him down from the tree and laid him in a tomb. Yet God raised him from the dead, and for many days thereafter Jesus appeared to those who had come up with him from Galilee to Jerusalem. These are his witnesses now before the people.

"We ourselves announce to you the good news that what God promised our fathers he has fulfilled for us, their children, in raising up Jesus, according to what is written in the second psalm, 'You are my son; this day I have begotten you.' "—This is the Word of the Lord. ℟. **Thanks be to God.** ℣

Responsorial Psalm   Ps 2, 6-7. 8-9. 10-11

℟. (7) **You are my Son;**
    this day have I begotten you.

"I myself have set up my king
    on Zion, my holy mountain."
I will proclaim the decree of the Lord:
    The Lord said to me, "You are my son;
    this day I have begotten you." — ℟

"Ask of me and I will give you
    the nations for an inheritance
    and the ends of the earth for your possession.
You shall rule them with an iron rod;
    you shall shatter them like an earthen dish." — ℟

And now, O kings, give heed;
    take warning, you rulers of the earth.
Serve the Lord with fear, and rejoice before him;
    with trembling pay homage to him. — ℟ ℣

℟. Or: **Alleluia.** ℣

GOSPEL   Jn 14, 1-6

Alleluia (Jn 14, 5)

℟. **Alleluia.** I am the way, the truth, and the life,
    says the Lord;
no one comes to the Father, except through me.
    ℟. **Alleluia.**

Before Easter Sunday, Jesus foretold his death and resurrection. He passed over into heaven to prepare a place for his followers, his brothers and sisters. Thus, Jesus is the way, the truth, and the life.

℣. The Lord be with you. ℟. **And also with you.**
✠ A reading from the holy gospel according to John
℟. **Glory to you, Lord.**

Jesus said to his disciples,

"Do not let your hearts be troubled.
Have faith in God
and faith in me.
In my Father's house there are many dwelling
    places;
otherwise, how could I have told you
that I was going to prepare a place for you?
I am indeed going to prepare a place for you,
and then I shall come back to take you with me,
that where I am you also may be.
You know the way that leads where I go."

"Lord," said Thomas, "we do not know where you are going. How can we know the way?" Jesus told him:

"I am the way, and the truth, and the life;
    no one comes to the Father but through me."

This is the gospel of the Lord. ℟. **Praise to you, Lord Jesus Christ.**   ➔ No. 15, p. 623

PRAYER OVER THE GIFTS

Lord,
accept these gifts from your family.
May we hold fast to the life you have given us
and come to the eternal gifts you promise.
We ask this in the name of Jesus the Lord.
℟. **Amen.**   ➔ No. 21, p. 626 (Pref. P 22-25)

COMMUNION ANT.   Rom 4, 25

Christ our Lord was put to death for our sins; and he rose again to make us worthy of life, alleluia. ℣

PRAYER AFTER COMMUNION

Lord,
watch over those you have saved in Christ.
May we who are redeemed by his suffering and death
always rejoice in his resurrection,
for he is Lord for ever and ever.
℟. **Amen.**   _____   ➔ No. 32, p. 650

SATURDAY OF THE FOURTH WEEK OF EASTER

May God grant us a lively and firm faith, one secure in the knowledge that through our Lord Jesus Christ we have all the knowledge that is necessary to make us pleasing to God. Let us often pray with the apostles, "Lord, increase our faith."

ENTRANCE ANT.   1 Pt 2, 9

You are a people God claims as his own, to praise him who called you out of darkness into his marvelous light, alleluia.   ➔ No. 2, p. 614

OPENING PRAYER

Father,
may we whom you renew in baptism
bear witness to our faith by the way we live.
By the suffering, death, and resurrection of your Son
may we come to eternal joy.
We ask this through our Lord Jesus Christ, your Son,
who lives and reigns with you and the Holy Spirit,
one God, for ever and ever. ℟. **Amen.** ↓

READING I   Acts 13, 44-52

Since the teaching of the apostles is not always well received and Paul is rejected by some of the Jews of Antioch, he turns his work to the Gentiles who welcome the new faith. Rejected by his own people, Paul then continues his journeys.

A reading from the Acts of the Apostles

On another sabbath, almost the entire city gathered to hear the word of God. When the Jews saw the crowds, they became very jealous and countered with violent abuse whatever Paul said. Paul and Barnabas spoke out fearlessly, nonetheless: "The word of God has to be declared to you first of all; but since you reject it and thus convict yourselves as unworthy of everlasting life, we now turn to the Gentiles. For thus were we instructed by the Lord: 'I have made you a light to the nations, a means of salvation to the ends of the earth.' " The Gentiles were delighted when they heard this and responded to the word of the Lord with praise. All who were destined for life everlasting believed in it. Thus the word of God was carried throughout that area.

But some of the Jews stirred up their influential women sympathizers and the leading men of the town, and in that way got a persecution started against Paul and Barnabas. The Jews finally expelled them from their territory. So the two shook the dust from their feet in protest and went on to Iconium. The disciples could not but be filled with joy and the Holy Spirit.—This is the Word of the Lord. ℟. **Thanks be to God.** ℣

Responsorial Psalm   Ps 98, 1. 2-3. 3-4

℟. (3) **All the ends of the earth have seen the saving power of God.**

Sing to the Lord a new song,
    for he has done wondrous deeds;
His right hand has won victory for him,
    his holy arm. — ℟

The Lord has made his salvation known:
    in the sight of the nations he has revealed his
        justice.
He has remembered his kindness and his faithfulness
    toward the house of Israel. — ℟

All the ends of the earth have seen
    the salvation by our God.
Sing joyfully to the Lord, all you lands;
    break into song; sing praise. — ℟ ℣

℟. Or: **Alleluia.** ℣

GOSPEL   Jn 14, 7-14

Alleluia (Jn 8, 31-32)

℟. **Alleluia.** If you stay in my word, you will indeed be my disciples,
and you will know the truth, says the Lord. ℟. **Alleluia.**

Jesus teaches the disciples that he and the Father are fully and equally the one God, and yet that Father and Son are distinct from one another. Philip asks to see the Father. Jesus promises that anything asked from the Father in his name will be granted.

℣. The Lord be with you. ℟. **And also with you.**
✠ A reading from the holy gospel according to John
℟. **Glory to you, Lord.**

Jesus said to his disciples,

"If you really knew me, you would know my
   Father also.
From this point on you know him; you have
   seen him."

"Lord," Philip said to him, "show us the Father
and that will be enough for us." "Philip," Jesus replied, "after I have been with you all this time, you
still do not know me?

"Whoever has seen me has seen the Father.
How can you say, 'Show us the Father'?
Do you not believe that I am in the Father
   and the Father is in me?
The words I speak are not spoken of myself;
it is the Father who lives in me accomplishing
   his works.
Believe me that I am in the Father
   and the Father is in me,
or else, believe because of the works I do.
I solemnly assure you,
the man who has faith in me
will do the works I do,
and greater far than these.
Why? Because I go to the Father,
and whatever you ask in my name
I will do,
so as to glorify the Father in the Son.
Anything you ask me in my name
I will do."

This is the gospel of the Lord. ℟. **Praise to you, Lord
Jesus Christ.**   ➤ No. 15, p. 623

PRAYER OVER THE GIFTS

Merciful Lord,
make holy these gifts

and let our spiritual sacrifice
make us an everlasting gift to you.
We ask this in the name of Jesus the Lord.
℟. **Amen.** ➤ No. 21, p. 626 (Pref. P 22-25)

COMMUNION ANT. Jn 17, 24

**Father, I want the men you have given me to be
with me where I am, so that they may see the glory
you have given me, alleluia.** ℣

PRAYER AFTER COMMUNION
Lord,
may this eucharist,
which we have celebrated in memory of your Son,
help us to grow in love.
We ask this in the name of Jesus the Lord.
℟. **Amen.** ➤ No. 32, p. 650

MONDAY OF THE FIFTH WEEK OF EASTER

All Christians should learn to be obedient to the commandments of
God and of the Church. God has united life or death, blessing or rejection, with obedience or disobedience to his commandments, and
the Bible shows that obedience pleases God more than sacrifices. If
our obedience is meant with all our heart, we show the Father our
greatest love and gratitude and eagerness always to be pleasing to him.

ENTRANCE ANT.

**The Good Shepherd is risen! He who laid down his
life for his sheep, who died for his flock, he is risen,
alleluia.** ➤ No. 2, p. 614

OPENING PRAYER
Father,
help us to seek the values
that will bring us eternal joy in this changing world.
In our desire for what you promise
make us one in mind and heart.
Grant this through our Lord Jesus Christ, your Son,
who lives and reigns with you and the Holy Spirit,
one God, for ever and ever. ℟. **Amen.** ℣

READING I Acts 14, 5-18

Paul cures a crippled man in Lystra, a stronghold of pagan belief. The darkness of paganism shows itself in the reaction. Paul patiently tries to explain the truth.

A reading from the Acts of the Apostles

A move was made [in Iconium] by Gentiles and Jews, together with their leaders, to abuse and stone Paul and Barnabas. When they learned of this, they fled to the Lycaonian towns of Lystra and Derbe and to the surrounding country, where they continued to proclaim the good news.

At Lystra there was a man who was lame from birth; he used to sit crippled, never having walked in his life. On one occasion he was listening to Paul preaching, and Paul looked directly at him and saw that he had the faith to be saved. He called out to him in a loud voice, "Stand up! On your feet!" The man jumped up and began to walk around. When the crowds saw what Paul had done, they cried out in Lycaonian, "Gods have come to us in the form of men!" They named Barnabas Zeus; Paul they called Hermes, since he was the spokesman. Even the priest of the temple of Zeus, which stood outside the town, brought oxen and garlands to the gates because he wished to offer sacrifice to them with the crowds.

When the apostles Barnabas and Paul heard of this, they tore their garments and rushed out into the crowd. "Friends, why do you do this?" they shouted frantically. "We are only men, human like you. We are bringing you the good news that will convert you from just such follies as these to the living God, 'the one who made heaven and earth and the sea and all that is in them.' In past ages he let the Gentiles go their way. Yet in bestowing his benefits, he has not hidden himself completely without a clue. From the heavens he sends down rain and rich harvests; your spirits he fills with food and delight." Yet even with a speech such as this, they

could scarcely stop the crowds from offering sacrifice
to them.—This is the Word of the Lord. ℟. **Thanks
be to God.** ℣

Responsorial Psalm   Ps 115, 1-2. 3-4. 15-16

℟. (1) **Not to us, O Lord,**
  but to your name give the glory.

Not to us, O Lord, not to us
  but to your name give glory
    because of your kindness, because of your truth.
Why should the pagans say,
  "Where is their God?" — ℟

Our God is in heaven;
  whatever he wills, he does.
Their idols are silver and gold,
  the handiwork of men. — ℟

May you be blessed by the Lord,
  who made heaven and earth.
Heaven is the heaven of the Lord,
  but the earth he has given to the children of
    men. — ℟ ℣

℟. Or: **Alleluia.** ℣

GOSPEL   Jn 14, 21-26

Alleluia (Jn 14, 26)

℟. **Alleluia.** The Holy Spirit will teach you all things,
and remind you of all I have said to you. ℟. **Alleluia.**

Jesus teaches that an understanding of God depends upon good will
and the gift of faith. He sent the Holy Spirit into the world that man
may understand and follow God's word. The Holy Spirit will emphasize
the message Jesus preached.

℣. The Lord be with you. ℟. **And also with you.**
✠ A reading from the holy gospel according to John
℟. **Glory to you, Lord.**

Jesus said to his disciples:
    "He who obeys the commandments he has from
      me
    is the man who loves me;

and he who loves me will be loved by my Father.

I too will love him
and reveal myself to him."

Judas (not Judas Iscariot) said to him, "Lord, why is it that you will reveal yourself to us and not to the world?" Jesus answered:

"Anyone who loves me
will be true to my word,
and my Father will love him;
we will come to him
and make our dwelling place with him.
He who does not love me does not keep my words.
Yet the word you hear is not mine;
it comes from the Father who sent me.
This much have I told you while I was still with you;
the Paraclete, the Holy Spirit
whom the Father will send in my name,
will instruct you in everything,
and remind you of all that I told you."

This is the gospel of the Lord. ℟. **Praise to you, Lord Jesus Christ.**   ➤ No. 15, p. 623

PRAYER OVER THE GIFTS

Lord,
accept our prayers and offerings.
Make us worthy of your sacraments of love
by granting us your forgiveness.
We ask this in the name of Jesus the Lord.
℟. **Amen.**   ➤ No. 21, p. 626 (Pref. P 22-25)

COMMUNION ANT.   Jn 14, 27

The Lord says, peace I leave with you, my own peace I give you; not as the world gives, do I give, alleluia. ℣

PRAYER AFTER COMMUNION

Almighty and ever-living Lord,

858 TUESDAY OF 5th WEEK OF EASTER

you restored us to life
by raising Christ from death.
Strengthen us by this Easter sacrament.
We ask this through Christ our Lord.
℟. **Amen.** ➤ No. 32, p. 650

TUESDAY OF THE FIFTH WEEK OF EASTER

By faith, true Christian faith, we are imbued with love and gratitude
to God. As believers of his word, we are his witnesses. The further
we advance in the ways of faith, the deeper becomes that faith. If
we but approach the Gospels as the Word of God inspired by the Holy
Spirit, we will find in them eternal life.

ENTRANCE ANT. Rv 19, 5; 12, 10

**All you who fear God, both the great and the small,
give praise to him! For his salvation and strength
have come, the power of Christ, alleluia.**

➤ No. 2, p. 614

OPENING PRAYER
Father,
you restored your people to eternal life
by raising Christ your Son from death.
Make our faith strong and our hope sure.
May we never doubt that you will fulfill
the promises you have made.
Grant this through our Lord Jesus Christ, your Son,
who lives and reigns with you and the Holy Spirit,
one God, for ever and ever. ℟. **Amen.** ✠

READING I Acts 14, 19-28

Paul and his companion Barnabas complete their first great missionary journey, bringing the faith to many far-distant towns, but also
encountering much opposition. They willingly accept the trials, as
Christ did, to build the kingdom.

A reading from the Acts of the Apostles

In those days some Jews from Antioch and Iconium
arrived and won the people over. They stoned Paul

and dragged him out of the town, leaving him there for dead. His disciples quickly formed a circle about him, and before long he got up and went back into the town. The next day he left with Barnabas for Derbe. After they had proclaimed the good news in that town and made numerous disciples, they retraced their steps to Lystra and Iconium first, then to Antioch. They gave their disciples reassurances, and encouraged them to persevere in the faith with this instruction: "We must undergo many trials if we are to enter into the reign of God." In each church they installed elders and, with prayer and fasting, commended them to the Lord in whom they had put their faith.

Then they passed through Pisidia and came to Pamphylia. After preaching the message in Perga, they went down to Attalia. From there they sailed back to Antioch, where they had first been commended to the favor of God for the task they had now completed. On their arrival, they called the congregation together and related all that God had helped them accomplish, and how he had opened the door of faith to the Gentiles. Then they spent some time there with the disciples.—This is the Word of the Lord. ℟. **Thanks be to God.** ℣

Responsorial Psalm   Ps 145, 10-11. 12-13. 21

℟. (12) **Your friends tell the glory of your kingship, Lord.**

Let all your works give you thanks, O Lord,
  and let your faithful ones bless you.
Let them discourse of the glory of your kingdom
  and speak of your might. — ℟

Making known to men your might
  and the glorious splendor of your kingdom.
Your kingdom is a kingdom for all ages,
  and your dominion endures through all generations. — ℟

May my mouth speak the praise of the Lord,
and may all flesh bless his holy name forever and
ever. — ℟ ✟

℟. Or: **Alleluia.** ✟

GOSPEL   Jn 14, 27-31

Alleluia (Lk 24, 26)

℟. **Alleluia.** Christ had to suffer and to rise from the
dead,
and so enter into his glory. ℟. **Alleluia.**

Jesus speaks of peace only a few hours before his sufferings and
death. His victory over death meant that peace is possible, but only
if his followers take up the cross of self-sacrifice as Jesus himself
did.

℣. The Lord be with you. ℟. **And also with you.**

✠ A reading from the Holy gospel according to John
℟. **Glory to you, Lord.**

Jesus said to his disciples:
  " 'Peace' is my farewell to you,
  my peace is my gift to you;
  I do not give it to you as the world gives peace.
  Do not be distressed or fearful.
  You have heard me say,
  'I go away for a while and I come back to you.'
  If you truly loved me
  you would rejoice to have me go to the Father,
  for the Father is greater than I.
  I tell you this now, before it takes place,
  so that when it takes place you may believe.
  I shall not go on speaking to you longer;
  the Prince of this world is at hand.
  He has no hold on me,
  but the world must know that I love the Father
  and do as the Father has commanded."

This is the gospel of the Lord. ℟. **Praise to you, Lord
Jesus Christ.**   ➤ No. 15, p. 623

PRAYER OVER THE GIFTS

Lord,

receive these gifts from your Church.
May the great joy you give us
come to perfection in heaven.
Grant this through Christ our Lord.
℟. **Amen.**   ➤ No. 21, p. 626 (Pref. P 22-25)

COMMUNION ANT.   Rom 6, 8

**Because we have died with Christ, we believe that
we shall also come to life with him, alleluia.** ℣

PRAYER AFTER COMMUNION

Lord,
look on your people with kindness
and by these Easter mysteries
bring us to the glory of the resurrection.
We ask this in the name of Jesus the Lord.
℟. **Amen.**   ➤ No. 32, p. 650

————————

WEDNESDAY OF THE FIFTH WEEK OF EASTER

We are incapable of judging the degree of success or failure in which
the work of anyone results in the sight of God. Often the most ap-
parently successful results are the saddest failures, just as the most
shining piety, which obtains for a man the respect of his neighbors,
is not always the most solid or the most perfect in the sight of God.
"Unless the Lord build the house, they labor in vain that build it"
(Ps 127,1).

ENTRANCE ANT.   Ps 71, 8. 23

**Fill me with your praise and I will sing your glory;
songs of joy will be on my lips, alleluia.**

➤ No. 2, p. 614

OPENING PRAYER

Father of all holiness,
guide our hearts to you.
Keep in the light of your truth
all those you have freed from the darkness of un-
    belief.
We ask this through our Lord Jesus Christ, your Son,

who lives and reigns with you and the Holy Spirit,
one God, for ever and ever. ℟. **Amen.** ℣

READING I   Acts 15, 1-6

Agitation to impose the Mosaic law upon Christians was a repeated
difficulty faced by the apostles. Paul holds that the gift of faith
upon so many pagans is a sign that the law of Moses cannot be made
an obligation under the New Covenant in Christ.

A reading from the Acts of the Apostles

Some men came down to Antioch from Judea and
began to teach the brothers: "Unless you are circumcised according to Mosaic practice, you cannot be
saved." This created dissension and much controversy between them and Paul and Barnabas. Finally
it was decided that Paul, Barnabas, and some others
should go up to see the apostles and elders in Jerusalem about this question.

The church saw them off and they made their way
through Phoenicia and Samaria, telling everyone
about their conversion of the Gentiles as they went.
Their story caused great joy among the brothers.
When they arrived in Jerusalem they were welcomed
by that church, as well as by the apostles and the
elders, to whom they reported all that God had helped them accomplish. Some of the converted Pharisees
then got up and demanded that such Gentiles be
circumcised and told to keep the Mosaic law.

The apostles and the elders accordingly convened
to look into the matter.—This is the Word of the
Lord. ℟. **Thanks be to God.** ℣

Responsorial Psalm   Ps 122, 1-2. 3-4. 4-5

℟. (1) **I rejoiced when I heard them say:**
    let us go to the house of the Lord.

I rejoiced because they said to me,
    "We will go up to the house of the Lord."
And now we have set foot
    within your gates, O Jerusalem. — ℟

Jerusalem, built as a city
　　with compact unity.
To it the tribes go up,
　　the tribes of the Lord. — ℟

According to the decree for Israel,
　　to give thanks to the name of the Lord.
In it are set up judgment seats,
　　seats for the house of David. — ℟ ℣

℟. Or: **Alleluia.** ℣

GOSPEL　　　　　　　　　　　　　　Jn 15, 1-8

Alleluia (Jn 15, 4-5)

℟. **Alleluia.** Live in me and let me live in you, says
the Lord;
my branches bear much fruit. ℟. **Alleluia.**

The symbol of the vine and the branches is similar to Paul's image
of the Mystical Body. True life and adoptive relationship to the Father
depend on union with Christ. Jesus teaches that only the branch that
is connected to the vine will bear fruit.

℣. The Lord be with you. ℟. **And also with you.**

✠ A reading from the holy gospel according to John
℟. **Glory to you, Lord.**

Jesus said to his disciples:
　　　　"I am the true vine
　　　　and my Father is the vinegrower.
　　　　He prunes away
　　　　every barren branch,
　　　　but the fruitful ones
　　　　he trims clean
　　　　to increase their yield.
　　　　You are clean already,
　　　　thanks to the word I have spoken to you.
　　　　Live on in me, as I do in you.
　　　　No more than a branch can bear fruit of itself
　　　　apart from the vine,
　　　　can you bear fruit
　　　　apart from me.

I am the vine, you are the branches.
He who lives in me and I in him,
will produce abundantly,
for apart from me you can do nothing.
A man who does not live in me
is like a withered, rejected branch,
picked up to be thrown in the fire and burnt.
If you live in me,
and my words stay part of you,
you may ask what you will—
it will be done for you.
My Father has been glorified
in your bearing much fruit
and becoming my disciples."

This is the gospel of the Lord. ℞. **Praise to you, Lord Jesus Christ.**
➤ No. 15, p. 623

PRAYER OVER THE GIFTS

Lord,
restore us by these Easter mysteries.
May the continuing work of our Redeemer
bring us eternal joy.
We ask this through Christ our Lord.
℞. **Amen.**
➤ No. 21, p. 626 (Pref. P 22-25)

COMMUNION ANT.

Christ has risen and shines upon us, whom he has redeemed by his blood, alleluia. ⍒

PRAYER AFTER COMMUNION

Lord,
may this celebration of our redemption
help us in this life
and lead us to eternal happiness.
We ask this through Christ our Lord.
℞. **Amen.**
➤ No. 32, p. 650

THURSDAY OF THE FIFTH WEEK OF EASTER

We should always remember that we are all one under the Good Shepherd. We cannot bar anyone from our circle of friends. All men are our brothers and friends, and our belief in the Father is proof that we are brothers of every human being. Faith imposes upon us this underlying unity and is the foundation of lasting peace. Christ our Lord showed charity and love in the salvation of all men.

ENTRANCE ANT. Ex 15, 1-2

Let us sing to the Lord, he has covered himself in glory! The Lord is my strength, and I praise him: he is the Savior of my life, alleluia. ➤ No. 2, p. 614

OPENING PRAYER

Father,
in your love you have brought us
from evil to good and from misery to happiness.
Through your blessings
give the courage of perseverance
to those you have called and justified by faith.
Grant this through our Lord Jesus Christ, your Son,
who lives and reigns with you and the Holy Spirit,
one God, for ever and ever. ℟. **Amen.** ↓

READING I

Acts 15, 7-21

The apostles, as the divinely appointed guides and teachers of the Church, decide that the Old Testament regulations were a preparation for Christ and had passed away. James urges the faithful to be considerate of the feelings of their Jewish brethren.

A reading from the Acts of the Apostles

After much discussion, Peter took the floor and said to the apostles and the elders: "Brothers, you know well enough that from the early days God selected me from your number to be the one from whose lips the Gentiles would hear the message of the gospel and believe. God, who reads the hearts of men, showed his approval by granting the Holy Spirit to them just as he did to us. He made no distinction between them and us, but purified their hearts by means of faith also. Why, then, do you put God to the test by trying to place on the shoulders of these converts a yoke which neither we nor our fathers were able to bear? Our belief is rather that we are saved by the favor of the Lord Jesus and so are they." At that the whole assembly fell silent. They listened to Barnabas and Paul as the two described all the signs and wonders God had worked among the Gentiles through them.

When they concluded their presentation, James spoke up: "Brothers, listen to me. Symeon has told you how God first concerned himself with taking from among the Gentiles a people to bear his name. The words of the prophets agree with this, where it says in Scripture, 'Hereafter I will return and rebuild the fallen hut of David: from its ruins I will rebuild it and set it up again, so that all the rest of mankind and all the nations that bear my name may seek out the Lord. Thus says the Lord who accomplishes these things known to him from of old.' It is my judgment, therefore, that we ought not to cause God's Gentile converts any difficulties. We should merely write to them to abstain from anything contaminated by idols, from illicit sexual union, from the meat of strangled animals, and from eating blood. After all, for generations now Moses has been proclaimed in every town and has been read aloud in the synagogues on every sabbath."—This is the Word of the Lord. ℟. **Thanks be to God.** ℣

Responsorial Psalm   Ps 96, 1-2. 2-3. 10

℟. (3) **Proclaim his marvelous deeds to all the nations.**

Sing to the Lord a new song;
    sing to the Lord, all you lands.
    Sing to the Lord; bless his name. — ℟

Announce his salvation, day after day.
    Tell his glory among the nations;
    among all peoples, his wondrous deeds. — ℟

Say among the nations: The Lord is king.
He has made the world firm, not to be moved;
he governs the peoples with equity. — ℟ ℣
℟. Or: **Alleluia.** ℣

GOSPEL Jn 15, 9-11

Alleluia (Jn 10, 27)

℟. **Alleluia.** My sheep listen to my voice, says the
Lord;
I know them and they follow me, ℟. **Alleluia.**

Jesus gives the spirit of obedience to the law. The letter kills, but
the spirit gives life. The Christian obeys because of his love, and so
he shares in the love and in the life of God.

℣. The Lord be with you. ℟. **And also with you.**
✠ A reading from the holy gospel according to Luke
℟. **Glory to you, Lord.**

Jesus said to his disciples:
"As the Father has loved me,
so I have loved you.
Live on in my love.
You will live in my love
if you keep my commandments,
even as I have kept my Father's commandments,
and live in his love.
All this I tell you
that my joy may be yours
and your joy may be complete."
This is the gospel of the Lord. ℟. **Praise to you, Lord
Jesus Christ.** ➔ No. 15, p. 623

PRAYER OVER THE GIFTS
Lord God,
by this holy exchange of gifts
you share with us your divine life.
Grant that everything we do
may be directed by the knowledge of your truth.
We ask this in the name of Jesus the Lord.
℟. **Amen.** ➔ No. 21, p. 626 (Pref. P 22-25)

COMMUNION ANT.   2 Cor 5, 15

Christ died for all, so that living men should not live for themselves, but for Christ who died and was raised to life for them, alleluia. ℣

PRAYER AFTER COMMUNION

Merciful Father,
may these mysteries give us new purpose
and bring us to a new life in you.
Grant this through Christ our Lord.
℟. **Amen.**   ➤ No. 32, p. 650

———————————

FRIDAY OF THE FIFTH WEEK OF EASTER

It is our duty to bear witness to the divinity of Christ and his teaching by the example of our own Christ-like virtues by which all men should recognize us as faithful followers of our Divine Master. The virtue of charity, or love, is then the true test of the Christian. It is a most essential characteristic. If we are without it, we are not of Christ.

ENTRANCE ANT.   Rv 5, 12

The Lamb who was slain is worthy to receive strength and divinity, wisdom and power and honor, alleluia.

➤ No. 2, p. 614

OPENING PRAYER

Lord,
by this Easter mystery
prepare us for eternal life.
May our celebration of Christ's death and resurrection
guide us to salvation.
We ask this through our Lord Jesus Christ, your Son,
who lives and reigns with you and the Holy Spirit,
one God, for ever and ever. ℟. **Amen. ℣**

READING I   Acts 15, 22-31

The decision by the apostles about the Mosaic law clearly shows the authoritative position that they held in the young Church. They state that their decisions are guaranteed by the Holy Spirit. Their letter is read by the faithful teachers of the Gospel to those embracing the faith.

A reading from the Acts of the Apostles

It was resolved by the apostles and elders, in agreement with the whole Jerusalem church, that representatives be chosen from among their number and sent to Antioch along with Paul and Barnabas. Those chosen were leading men of the community, Judas, known as Barsabbas, and Silas. They were to deliver this letter:

"The apostles and the elders, your brothers, send greetings to the brothers of Gentile origin in Antioch, Syria and Cilicia. We have heard that some of our number without any instructions from us have upset you with their discussions and disturbed your peace of mind. Therefore we have unanimously resolved to choose representatives and send them to you, along with our beloved Barnabas and Paul, who have dedicated themselves to the cause of our Lord Jesus Christ. Those whom we are sending you are Judas and Silas, who will convey this message by word of mouth: 'It is the decision of the Holy Spirit, and ours too, not to lay on you any burden beyond that which is strictly necessary, namely, to abstain from meat sacrificed to idols, from blood, from the meat of strangled animals, and from illicit sexual union. You will be well advised to avoid these things. Farewell.' "

Thus were the representatives sent on their way to Antioch; and upon their arrival there they called the assembly together to deliver the letter. When it was read there was a great delight at the encouragement it gave.—This is the Word of the Lord. ℟. **Thanks be to God.** ℣

Responsorial Psalm   Ps 57, 8-9. 10-12

℟. (10) **I will praise you among the nations, O Lord.**

My heart is steadfast, O God; my heart is steadfast;
    I will sing and chant praise.
Awake, O my soul; awake, lyre and harp!
I will wake the dawn — ℟

I will give thanks to you among the peoples, O Lord,
  I will chant your praise among the nations.
Be exalted above the heavens, O God;
  above all the earth be your glory! — ℟ ℣

℟. Or: **Alleluia.** ℣

GOSPEL   Jn 15, 12-17

Alleluia (Jn 15, 15)

℟. **Alleluia.** I call you my friends, says the Lord,
for I have made known to you all that the Father
  has told me. ℟. **Alleluia.**

The theme of the law is continued with the announcement of the
supreme law of Christ, the law of love. Jesus gives the perfect
example of how men are to love one another, that is, with complete
unselfishness and without expecting thanks from others.

℣. The Lord be with you. ℟. **And also with you.**
✠ A reading from the holy gospel according to John
℟. **Glory to you, Lord.**

Jesus said to his disciples,
      "This is my commandment:
      love one another
      as I have loved you.
      There is no greater love than this:
      to lay down one's life for one's friends.
      You are my friends
      if you do what I command you.
      I no longer speak of you as slaves,
      for a slave does not know what his master is
          about.
      Instead I call you friends,
      since I have made known to you all that I heard
          from my Father.
      It was not you who chose me,
      it was I who chose you
      to go forth and bear fruit.
      Your fruit must endure,
      so that all you ask the Father in my name he
          will give you.

The command I give you is this,
that you love one another."
This is the gospel of the Lord. ℟. **Praise to you, Lord
Jesus Christ.**   ➤ No. 15, p. 623

PRAYER OVER THE GIFTS

Merciful Lord,
make holy these gifts
and let our spiritual sacrifice
make us an everlasting gift to you.
We ask this in the name of Jesus the Lord.
℟. **Amen.**   ➤ No. 21, p. 626 (Pref. P 22-25)

COMMUNION ANT.

**The man who died on the cross has risen from the
dead, and has won back our lives from death, alleluia.** ℣

PRAYER AFTER COMMUNION

Lord,
may this eucharist,
which we have celebrated in memory of your Son,
help us to grow in love.
We ask this in the name of Jesus the Lord.
℟. **Amen.**   ➤ No. 32, p. 650

SATURDAY OF THE FIFTH WEEK OF EASTER

The true Christian has no easy task to live and be pleasing to God. The
unjust persecute him on all sides, but if he is abused, he must pray
for those who abuse him. As Christians we must not be ashamed
because the world despises us and opposes our virtuous life. This
was the lot of the apostles, and even of Christ himself. They entered
heaven only through suffering trials and many persecutions.

ENTRANCE ANT.   Col 2, 12

**In baptism we have died with Christ, and we have
risen to new life in him, because we believed in the
power of God who raised him from the dead, alleluia.**
                                        ➤ No. 2, p. 614

OPENING PRAYER

Loving Father,
through our rebirth in baptism
you give us your life and promise immortality.
By your unceasing care,
guide our steps toward the life of glory.
Grant this through our Lord Jesus Christ, your Son,
who lives and reigns with you and the Holy Spirit,
one God, for ever and ever. ℟. **Amen.** ℣

READING I   Acts 16, 1-10

After his first journey, Paul goes forth again on a longer and more difficult missionary tour. As he teaches, many plead for the faith. God directs the work of his chosen missionary.

A reading from the Acts of the Apostles

Paul arrived at Derbe; then he came to Lystra, where there was a disciple named Timothy, whose mother was a Jew and a believer, and whose father was a Greek. Since the brothers in Lystra and Iconium spoke highly of him, Paul was anxious to have him come along on the journey. Paul had him circumcised because of the Jews of that region, for they all knew that it was only his father who was Greek. As they made their way from town to town, they transmitted to the people for observance the decisions which the apostles and elders had made in Jerusalem.

Through all this, the congregations grew stronger in faith and daily increased in numbers.

They next traveled through Phrygia and Galatian territory because they had been prevented by the Holy Spirit from preaching the message in the province of Asia. When they came to Mysia they tried to go on into Bithynia, but again the Spirit of Jesus would not allow them. Crossing through Mysia instead, they came down to Troas. There one night Paul had a vision. A man of Macedonia stood before him and invited him, "Come over to Macedonia and help us."

After this vision, we immediately made efforts to get across to Macedonia, concluding that God had summoned us to proclaim the good news there.— This is the Word of the Lord. ℞. **Thanks be to God.** ℣

Responsorial Psalm   Ps 100, 1-2. 3. 5

℞. **Let all the earth cry out to God with joy.**

Sing joyfully to the Lord, all you lands;
    serve the Lord with gladness;
    come before him with joyful song. — ℞

Know that the Lord is God;
    he made us, his we are;
    his people, the flock he tends. — ℞

The Lord is good:
    his kindness endures forever,
    and his faithfulness, to all generations. — ℞ ℣

℞. Or: **Alleluia.** ℣

GOSPEL   Jn 15, 18-21

Alleluia (Col 3, 1)

℞. **Alleluia.** If then you have been raised with Christ,
    seek the things that are above,
where Christ is seated at the right hand of God.
    ℞. **Alleluia.**

Jesus warns that the Christian cannot be fully at home in the world. The "world" means society insofar as it is contrary to the plan of God and ignores God. The follower of Christ is to have different values in life, based on his hope in the coming of Christ.

℣. The Lord be with you. ℞. **And also with you.**
✠ A reading from the holy gospel according to John
℞. **Glory to you, Lord.**

Jesus said to his disciples:
        "If you find that the world hates you,
        know it has hated me before you.
        If you belonged to the world,
        it would love you as its own;
        the reason it hates you

is that you do not belong to the world.
But I chose you out of the world.
Remember what I told you:
no slave is greater than his master.
They will harry you
as they harried me.
They will respect your words
as much as they respected mine.
All this they will do to you because of my name,
for they know nothing of him who sent me."

This is the gospel of the Lord. ℟. **Praise to you, Lord Jesus Christ.**　　　　　　　➔ No. 15, p. 623

PRAYER OVER THE GIFTS

Lord,
accept these gifts from your family.
May we hold fast to the life you have given us
and come to the eternal gifts you promise.
We ask this in the name of Jesus the Lord.
℟. **Amen.**　　　　➔ No. 21, p. 626 (Pref. P 22-25)

COMMUNION ANT.　　　　　　　　　Jn 17, 20-21

Father, I pray for them: may they be one in us, so that the world may believe it was you who sent me, alleluia. ℣

PRAYER AFTER COMMUNION

Lord,
watch over those you have saved in Christ.
May we who are redeemed by his suffering and death
always rejoice in his resurrection,
for he is Lord for ever and ever.
℟. **Amen.**　　　　　　　　➔ No. 32, p. 650

MONDAY OF THE SIXTH WEEK OF EASTER

We are born of God by the saving waters of baptism by which the merits of Christ are applied to our souls. Our faith overcomes the world. By this faith we truly believe that Jesus is the Son of God who saved us not merely by the waters of baptism, but by his own blood. What a deep debt of gratitude man owes to his Creator.

ENTRANCE ANT.   Rom 6, 9

Christ now raised from the dead will never die again; death no longer has power over him, alleluia.

➤ No. 2, p. 614

OPENING PRAYER

God of mercy,
may our celebration of your Son's resurrection
help us to experience its effect in our lives.
We ask this through our Lord Jesus Christ, your Son,
who lives and reigns with you and the Holy Spirit,
one God, for ever and ever. ℟. **Amen.** ♥

READING I   Acts 16, 11-15

The writer of Acts, St. Luke, now says "we," indicating that he accompanied St. Paul. The kingdom of God is spread not by the Spirit alone, but by men and women who cooperate with the Spirit and who work with one another.

A reading from the Acts of the Apostles

We put out to sea from Troas and set a course straight for Samothrace, and the next day on to Neapolis; from there we went to Philippi, a leading city in the district of Macedonia and a Roman colony. We spent some time in that city. Once, on the sabbath, we went outside the city gate to the bank of the river, where we thought there would be a place of prayer. We sat down and spoke to the women who were gathered there. One who listened was a woman named Lydia, a dealer in purple goods from the town of Thyatira. She already reverenced God, and the Lord opened her heart to accept what Paul was saying. After she and her household had been baptized, she extended us an invitation: "If you are convinced that I believe in the Lord, come and stay at my house." She managed to prevail on us.—This is the Word of the Lord. ℟. **Thanks be to God.** ♥

Responsorial Psalm   Ps 149, 1-2. 3-4. 5-6. 9

℟. (4) **The Lord takes delight in his people.**

Sing to the Lord a new song
  of praise in the assembly of the faithful.
Let Israel be glad in their maker,
  let the children of Zion rejoice in their king. —℟

Let them praise his name in the festive dance,
  let them sing praise to him with timbrel and harp.
For the Lord loves his people,
  and he adorns the lowly with victory. — ℟

Let the faithful exult in glory;
  let them sing for joy upon their couches.
Let the high praises of God be in their throats.
  This is the glory of all his faithful. Alleluia. — ℟ ·℣

℟. Or: **Alleluia.** ℣

GOSPEL   Jn 15, 26-16, 4

Alleluia (Jn 15, 26. 27)

℟. **Alleluia.** The Spirit of truth will bear witness to
  me, says the Lord,
and you also will be my witnesses. ℟. **Alleluia.**

The message of Christ is the means to eternal salvation. Nevertheless,
he entrusts the future of his work to chosen men. Therefore, Christ
promises to give the Spirit, who will preserve his words accurately
throughout the centuries. The Holy Spirit will bear witness to the
Good News.

℣. The Lord be with you. ℟. **And also with you.**
✠ A reading from the holy gospel according to John
℟. **Glory to you, Lord.**

Jesus said to his disciples:
    "When the Paraclete comes,
    the Spirit of truth who comes from the Father—
    and whom I myself will send from the Father—
    he will bear witness on my behalf.
    You must bear witness as well,
    for you have been with me from the beginning.
    I have told you all this
    to keep your faith from being shaken.

Not only will they expel you from synagogues;
a time will come
when anyone who puts you to death
will claim to be serving God!
All this they will do [to you]
because they know neither the Father nor me.
But I have told you these things
that when their hour comes
you may remember my telling you of them."
This is the gospel of the Lord. ℟. **Praise to you, Lord
Jesus Christ.**   ➤ No. 15, p. 623

PRAYER OVER THE GIFTS
Lord,
receive these gifts from your Church.
May the great joy you give us
come to perfection in heaven.
Grant this through Christ our Lord.
℟. **Amen.**   ➤ No. 21, p. 626 (Pref. P 22-25)

COMMUNION ANT.   Jn 20, 19
**Jesus came and stood among his disciples and said
to them: Peace be with you, alleluia.** ℣

PRAYER AFTER COMMUNION
Lord,
look on your people with kindness
and by these Easter mysteries
bring us to the glory of the resurrection.
We ask this in the name of Jesus the Lord.
℟. **Amen.**   ➤ No. 32, p. 650

TUESDAY OF THE SIXTH WEEK OF EASTER

Though the assent of faith is in a sense obscure, it is still most
reasonable, for when God reveals his truths to us, he provides us
with abundant motives for believing and gives us his own authority
for them. Nothing increases the rich flow of his grace and love to us
so much as our humble thankfulness for and acknowledgment of
his mercy and kindness.

ENTRANCE ANT.   Rv 19, 7. 6

Let us shout out our joy and happiness, and give glory to God, the Lord of all, because he is our King, alleluia.   ➤ No. 2, p. 614

OPENING PRAYER

God our Father,
may we look forward with hope to our resurrection,
for you have made us your sons and daughters,
and restored the joy of our youth.
We ask this through our Lord Jesus Christ, your Son,
who lives and reigns with you and the Holy Spirit,
one God, for ever and ever. ℟. **Amen.** ⅴ

READING I   Acts 16, 22-34

Sᵵ. Paul is arrested, flogged, and jailed. Freed by the Lord, his faith and his firm commitment stimulate faith in his jailer. Today, strong faith and patient forgiveness will be a sign that we have indeed found God, and will draw others to him.

A reading from the Acts of the Apostles

The crowd [of Philippians] joined in the attack on Paul and Silas, and the magistrates stripped them and ordered them to be flogged. After receiving many lashes they were thrown into prison, and the jailer was given instructions to guard them well. Upon receipt of these instructions he put them in maximum security, going so far as to chain their feet to a stake.

About midnight, while Paul and Silas were praying and singing hymns to God as their fellow prisoners listened, a severe earthquake suddenly shook the place, rocking the prison to its foundations. Immediately all the doors flew open and everyone's chains were pulled loose. The jailer woke up to see the prison gates wide open. Thinking that the prisoners had escaped, he drew his sword to kill himself; but Paul shouted to him, "Do not harm yourself! We are all still here." The jailer called for a light, then rushed in and fell trembling at the feet of Paul and

Silas. After a brief interval he led them out and said, "Men, what must I do to be saved?" Their answer was, "Believe in the Lord Jesus and you will be saved, and all your household." They proceeded to announce the word of God to him and to everyone in his house. At that late hour of the night he took them in and bathed their wounds; then he and his whole household were baptized. He led them up into his house, spread a table before them, and joyfully celebrated with his whole family his newfound faith in God.—This is the Word of the Lord. ℟. **Thanks be to God.** ✟

Responsorial Psalm   Ps 138, 1-2. 2-3. 7-8

℟. (7) **Your right hand has saved me, O Lord.**

I will give thanks to you, O Lord, with all my heart,
  [for you have heard the words of my mouth;]
In the presence of the angels I will sing your praise;
  I will worship at your holy temple,
  and give thanks to your name. — ℟

Because of your kindness and your truth,
  you have made great above all things
  your name and your promise.
When I called, you answered me;
  you built up strength within me. — ℟

Your right hand saves me.
  The Lord will complete what he has done for me;
Your kindness, O Lord, endures forever;
  forsake not the work of your hands. — ℟ ✟

℟. Or: **Alleluia.** ✟

GOSPEL   Jn 16, 5-11

Alleluia (Jn 16, 7. 13)

℟. **Alleluia.** I will send you the Spirit of truth, says the Lord;

he will lead you to the whole truth. ℟. **Alleluia.**

Jesus says that he has to go in order for the Holy Spirit to come. Jesus promises the coming of the Spirit by passing over into the presence of the Father as the perfect gift.

℣. The Lord be with you. ℟. **And also with you.**
✠ A reading from the holy gospel according to John
℟. **Glory to you, Lord.**

Jesus said to his disciples,

"Now that I go back to him who sent me,
not one of you asks me, 'Where are you going?'
Because I have had all this to say to you,
you are overcome with grief.
Yet I tell you the sober truth:
It is much better for you that I go.
If I fail to go,
the Paraclete will never come to you,
whereas if I go,
I will send him to you.
When he comes,
he will prove the world wrong
about sin,
about justice,
about condemnation.
About sin—
in that they refuse to believe in me;
about justice—
from the fact that I go to the Father
and you can see me no more;
about condemnation—
for the prince of this world has been condemned."

This is the gospel of the Lord. ℟. **Praise to you, Lord
Jesus Christ.**   ➤ No. 15, p. 623

PRAYER OVER THE GIFTS

Lord,
give us joy by these Easter mysteries;
let the continuous offering of this sacrifice
by which we are renewed
bring us to eternal happiness.
We ask this in the name of Jesus the Lord.
℟. **Amen.**   ➤ No. 21, p. 626 (Pref. P 22-25)

COMMUNION ANT.   See Lk 24, 46. 26

**Christ had to suffer and to rise from the dead, and
so enter into his glory, alleluia.** ℣

PRAYER AFTER COMMUNION

Lord,
may this celebration of our redemption
help us in this life
and lead us to eternal happiness.
We ask this through Christ our Lord.
℟. **Amen.** _____ ➤ No. 32, p. 650

WEDNESDAY OF THE SIXTH WEEK OF EASTER

Our greatest source of encouragement, strength and consolation, as
we labor in the Lord's vineyard, is absolute certainty that we are
guided in our efforts by the Holy Spirit. He is our divine and infal-
lible guide to God in the teachings and precepts of the Church. This
is the sublime promise of our Savior. The Holy Spirit will always
guide us in the right direction.

ENTRANCE ANT.   Ps 18, 50; 22, 23

**I will be a witness to you in the world, O Lord. I will
spread the knowledge of your name among my brothers, alleluia.** ➤ No. 2, p. 614

OPENING PRAYER

Lord,
as we celebrate your Son's resurrection,
so may we rejoice with all the saints
when he returns in glory,
who lives and reigns with you and the Holy Spirit,
one God, for ever and ever. ℟. **Amen.** ℣

READING I   Acts 17, 15. 22—18, 1

When he reaches Athens, the center of Greek culture, Paul presents
the message of Christ in a way adapted to his hearers' habits of
thought. In God all live and move and are. Some are baptized and
others ask to hear Paul again.

A reading from the Acts of the Apostles

Paul was taken as far as Athens by an escort, who

then returned with instructions for Silas and Timothy to join him as soon as possible.

Then Paul stood up in the Areopagus and delivered this address: "Men of Athens, I note that in every respect you are scrupulously religious. As I walked around looking at your shrines, I even discovered an altar inscribed, 'To a God Unknown.' Now, what you are thus worshiping in ignorance I intend to make known to you. For the God who made the world and 'all that is in it,' the Lord of heaven and earth, does not dwell in sanctuaries made by human hands; no more does he receive man's service as if he were in need of it. Rather, it is he 'who gives' to all life and 'breath' and everything else. From one stock he made every nation of mankind to dwell on the face of the earth. It is he who set limits to their epochs and 'fixed the boundaries' of their regions. They were to seek God, yes, to grope for him and perhaps eventually to find him—though he is not really far from any one of us. 'In him we live and move and have our being,' as some of your own poets have put it, 'for we too are his offspring.' If we are in fact God's offspring, we ought not to think of divinity as something like a statue of gold or silver or stone, a product of man's genius and his art. God may well have overlooked bygone periods when men did not know him; but now he calls on all men everywhere to reform their lives. He has set the day on which he is going to 'judge the world with justice' through a man he has appointed—one whom he has endorsed in the sight of all by raising him from the dead."

When they heard about the raising of the dead, some sneered, while others said, "We must hear you on this topic some other time." At that point, Paul left them. A few did join him, however, to become believers. Among these were Dionysius, a member of the court of the Areopagus, a woman named

Damaris, and a few others.

After that, Paul left Athens and went to Corinth.
This is the Word of the Lord. ℟. **Thanks be to God.** ✠

Responsorial Psalm   Ps 148, 1-2. 11-12. 12-14. 14
℟. **Heaven and earth are filled with your glory.**

Praise the Lord from the heavens,
  praise him in the heights;
Praise him, all you his angels,
  praise him, all you his hosts. — ℟

Let the kings of the earth and all peoples,
  the princes and all the judges of the earth,
Young men too, and maidens,
  old men and boys. — ℟

Praise the name of the Lord,
  for his name alone is exalted;
His majesty is above earth and heaven. — ℟

He has lifted up the horn of his people;
  be this his praise from all his faithful ones,
From the children of Israel, the people close to him.
    Alleluia. — ℟ ✠
℟. Or: **Alleluia.** ✠

GOSPEL   Jn 16, 12-15
Alleluia (Jn 14, 16)

℟. **Alleluia.** The Father will send you the Holy Spirit,
  says the Lord,
to be with you for ever. ℟. **Alleluia.**

Jesus promises that when the Spirit comes, he will guide men to
all truth. He will teach of things to come.

℣. The Lord be with you. ℟. **And also with you.**
✠ A reading from the holy gospel according to John
℟. **Glory to you, Lord.**

Jesus said to his disciples,
    "I have much more to tell you,
    but you cannot bear it now.
    When he comes, however,
    being the Spirit of truth

he will guide you to all truth.
He will not speak on his own,
but will speak only what he hears,
and will announce to you the things to come.
In doing this he will give glory to me,
because he will have received from me
what he will announce to you.
All that the Father has belongs to me.
That is why I said that what he will announce
     to you
he will have from me."

This is the gospel of the Lord. ℟. **Praise to you, Lord Jesus Christ.**   ➤ No. 15, p. 623

PRAYER OVER THE GIFTS

Lord God,
by this holy exchange of gifts
you share with us your divine life.
Grant that everything we do
may be directed by the knowledge of your truth.
We ask this in the name of Jesus the Lord.
℟. **Amen.**   ➤ No. 21, p. 626 (Pref. P 22-25)

COMMUNION ANT.   See Jn 15, 16. 19

The Lord says, I have chosen you from the world to go and bear fruit that will last, alleluia. ⅴ

PRAYER AFTER COMMUNION

Merciful Father,
may these mysteries give us new purpose
and bring us to a new life in you.
Grant this through Christ our Lord.
℟. **Amen.**   ➤ No. 32, p. 650

THURSDAY OF THE SIXTH WEEK OF EASTER

This Mass is celebrated in countries where the celebration of the Ascension is transferred to the Seventh Sunday of Easter. (See Sunday Missal, pp. 327, 701, 1062.)

Jesus came into the world to give us an example of how we are to live. In him we live and move and are. Just as the apostles of the early Church taught about Jesus in both word and act, we, as the apostles of today born into the faith, should share our belief with others. Let us be conscious today of our every thought, word, and deed that they may reflect the life of Jesus.

ENTRANCE ANT.   See Ps 68, 8-9. 20

When you walked at the head of your people, O God, and lived with them on their journey, the earth shook at your presence, and the skies poured forth their rain, alleluia.   ➔ No. 2, p. 614

OPENING PRAYER

Father,
may we always give you thanks
for raising Christ our Lord to glory,
because we are his people
and share the salvation he won,
for he lives and reigns with you and the Holy Spirit,
one God, for ever and ever. ℟. **Amen.** ↓

READING I   Acts 18, 1-8

Paul relies upon the help of zealous lay people in making Christ known. He preaches that Jesus was the Messiah. When he is persecuted by his fellow countrymen, he turns to the Gentiles.

A reading from the Acts of the Apostles

Paul left Athens and went to Corinth. There he found a Jew named Aquila, a native of Pontus recently arrived from Italy with his wife Priscilla. An edict of Claudius had ordered all Jews to leave Rome. Paul went to visit the pair, whose trade he had in common with them. He took up lodgings with them and they worked together as tentmakers. Every sabbath, in the synagogue, Paul led discussions in which he persuaded certain Jews and Greeks.

When Silas and Timothy came down from Macedonia, Paul was absorbed in preaching and giving evidence to the Jews that Jesus was the Messiah. When they opposed him and insulted him, he would shake out his garments in protest and say to them: "Your blood be on your own heads. I am not to blame! From now on, I will turn to the Gentiles."

Later, Paul withdrew and went to the house of a Gentile named Titus Justus, who reverenced God; his house was next door to the synagogue. A leading man of the synagogue, Crispus, along with his whole household, put his faith in the Lord. Many of the Corinthians, too, who heard Paul believed and were baptized.—This is the Word of the Lord. ℟. **Thanks be to God.** ℣

Responsorial Psalm Ps 98, 1. 2-3. 3-4

℟. (2) **The Lord has revealed to the nations his saving power.**

Sing to the Lord a new song,
    for he has done wondrous deeds;
His right hand has won victory for him,
    his holy arm. — ℟

The Lord has made his salvation known:
    in the sight of the nations he has revealed his
        justice.
He has remembered his kindness and his faithfulness
    toward the house of Israel. — ℟

All the ends of the earth have seen
    the salvation by our God.
Sing joyfully to the Lord, all you lands;
    break into song; sing praise. — ℟ ℣

℟. Or: **Alleluia.** ℣

GOSPEL Jn 16, 16-20

Alleluia. (Jn 14, 18)

℟. **Alleluia.** The Holy Spirit will teach you all things, and remind you of all I have said to you. ℟. **Alleluia.**

As the Hebrews passed over from Egypt to the Promised Land, so Jesus will pass over from this alienated world to the right hand of the Father. Jesus predicts his leaving this world. The disciples fail to understand and they question him. In the end Jesus promises their sorrow will be turned to joy.

℣. The Lord be with you. ℟. **And also with you.**
✠ A reading from the holy gospel according to John
℟. **Glory to you, Lord.**

Jesus said to his disciples:

"Within a short time you will lose sight of me,
but soon after that you shall see me again."

At this some of his disciples asked one another,
"What can he mean, 'Within a short time you will
lose sight of me, but soon after that you will see
me'? And did he not say that he is going back to the
Father?" They kept asking, "What does he mean by
this 'short time'? We do not know what he is talking
about." Since Jesus was aware that they wanted to
question him, he said: "You are asking one another
about my saying, 'Within a short time you will lose
sight of me, but soon after that you will see me.

"I tell you truly:
you will weep and mourn
while the world rejoices;
you will grieve for a time,
but your grief will be turned into joy."

This is the gospel of the Lord. ℟. **Praise to you, Lord
Jesus Christ.** ➔ No. 15, p. 623

PRAYER OVER THE GIFTS

Lord,
accept our prayers and offerings.
Make us worthy of your sacraments of love
by granting us your forgiveness.
We ask this in the name of Jesus the Lord.
℟. **Amen.** ➔ No. 21, p. 626 (Pref. P 22-25)

COMMUNION ANT. Mt 28, 20

**I, the Lord, am with you always, until the end of
the world, alleluia.** ℣

PRAYER AFTER COMMUNION

Almighty and ever-living Lord,
you restored us to life

by raising Christ from death.
Strentghen us by this Easter sacrament;
may we feel its saving power in our daily life.
We ask this through Christ our Lord.
℞. **Amen.**   ➤ No. 32, p. 650

———————

FRIDAY OF THE SIXTH WEEK OF EASTER

Jesus is our mediator, and although we may be depressed with the
memory of our many weaknesses and transgressions, we should have
confidence that he is always helping us. We must first let him take
us under his protecting arm, and then we shall be certain to receive
every good gift for which we ask.

ENTRANCE ANT.   See Rv 5, 9-10
**By your blood, O Lord, you have redeemed us from
every tribe and tongue, from every nation and people:
you have made us into the kingdom of God, alleluia.**
                            ➤ No. 2, p. 614

OPENING PRAYER
Father,
you have given us eternal life
through Christ your Son who rose from the dead
and now sits at your right hand.
When he comes again in glory,
may he clothe with immortality
all who have been born again in baptism.
We ask this through our Lord Jesus Christ, your Son,
who lives and reigns with you and the Holy Spirit,
one God, for ever and ever. ℞. **Amen.** ↓

*In countries where the Ascension is celebrated on the
Seventh Sunday of Easter, the following opening prayer
is said:*
Lord,
hear our prayer
that your gospel may reach all men
and that we who receive salvation through your Word
may be your children in deed as well as in name.
We ask this through our Lord Jesus Christ, your Son,

who lives and reigns with you and the Holy Spirit,
one God, for ever and ever. ℟. **Amen.** ℣

READING I   Acts 18, 9-18

Luke recounts more of the difficulties encountered by Paul. In a vision
the Lord encourages Paul. Paul is brought to trial, but the judge
sees it is a political trial and discontinues the hearing.

A reading from the Acts of the Apostles

[When Paul was in Corinth] one night in a vision the
Lord said to him: "Do not be afraid. Go on speaking
and do not be silenced, for I am with you. No one
will attack you or harm you. There are many of my
people in this city." Paul ended by settling there for
a year and a half, teaching them the word of God.
    During Gallio's proconsulship in Achaia, the Jews
rose in a body against Paul and brought him before
the bench. "This fellow," they charged, "is influenc-
ing people to worship God in ways that are against
the law." Paul was about to speak in self-defense
when Gallio said to the Jews: "If it were a crime or
a serious fraud, I would give you Jews a patient and
reasonable hearing. But since this is a dispute about
terminology and titles and your own law, you must
see to it yourselves. I refuse to judge such matters."
With that, he dismissed them from the court. Then
they all pounced on Sosthenes, a leading man of the
synagogue, and beat him in full view of the bench;
but Gallio paid no attention to it.
    Paul stayed on in Corinth for quite a while; but
eventually he took leave of the brothers and sailed
for Syria, in the company of Priscilla and Aquila.
At the port of Cenchreae he shaved his head because
of a vow he had taken.—This is the Word of the
Lord. ℟. **Thanks be to God.** ℣

Responsorial Psalm   Ps 47, 2-3. 4-5. 6-7
℟. (8) **God is king of all the earth.**

All you peoples, clap your hands,
    shout to God with cries of gladness,
For the Lord, the Most High, the awesome,
    is the great king over all the earth. — ℞

He brings peoples under us;
    nations under our feet.
He chooses for us our inheritance,
    the glory of Jacob, whom he loves. — ℞

God mounts his throne amid shouts of joy;
    the Lord, amid trumpet blasts.
Sing praise to God, sing praise;
    sing praise to our king, sing praise. — ℞ ✟

℞. Or: **Alleluia.** ✟

GOSPEL   Jn 16, 20-23

Alleluia (Lk 24, 26)

℞. **Alleluia.** Christ had to suffer and to rise from
    the dead,
and so enter into his glory. ℞. **Alleluia.**

The coming of the kingdom is described in terms of childbirth. The
process requires time and patient endurance, but the result will be a
joy that will never be taken away.

℣. The Lord be with you. ℞. **And also with you.**
✠ A reading from the holy gospel according to John
℞. **Glory to you, Lord.**

Jesus said to his disciples:
        "I tell you truly:
        you will weep and mourn
        while the world rejoices;
        you will grieve for a time,
        but your grief will' be turned into joy.
        When a woman is in labor
        she is sad that her time has come.
        When she has borne her child,
        she no longer remembers her pain,
        for joy that a man has been born into the world.
        In the same way, you are sad for a time,

but I shall see you again;
then your hearts will rejoice
with a joy no one can take from you.
On that day you will have no questions to ask
me."

This is the gospel of the Lord. ℟. **Praise to you, Lord
Jesus Christ.**   ➔ No. 15, p. 623

PRAYER OVER THE GIFTS

Lord,
accept these gifts from your family.
May we hold fast to the life you have given us
and come to the eternal gifts you promise.
We ask this in the name of Jesus the Lord.
℟. **Amen.**   ➔ No. 21, p. 626

*If the Ascension has been celebrated on Thursday of
this week: Preface of Ascension I or II (P 26-27). If
the Ascension is celebrated on the Seventh Sunday of
Easter: Preface of Easter II-V (P 22-25).*

COMMUNION ANT.   Rom 4, 25

**Christ our Lord was put to death for our sins; and
he rose again to make us worthy of life, alleluia.** ℣

PRAYER AFTER COMMUNION

Lord,
watch over those you have saved in Christ.
May we who are redeemed by his suffering and death
always rejoice in his resurrection,
for he is Lord for ever and ever.
℟. **Amen.** _____   ➔ No. 32, p. 650

SATURDAY OF THE SIXTH WEEK OF EASTER

Jesus himself has expressly promised that our prayers shall be heard
if only we ask them in his name through the Father. It is a mistake
to imagine that consideration or meditation on the eternal truths is
a spiritual exercise reserved for those who have specially consecrated
their lives to the service of God in the religious state. It is necessary
for all the faithful. Let us recall our Lord's promise: "If you ask the
Father anything in my name, he will give it to you."

ENTRANCE ANT.   1 Pt 2, 9

You are a people God claims as his own, to praise
him who called you out of darkness into his mar-
velous light, alleluia.   ➤ No. 2, p. 614

OPENING PRAYER

Father,
at your Son's ascension into heaven
you promised to send the Holy Spirit on your apos-
    tles.
You filled them with heavenly wisdom:
fill us also with the gift of your Spirit.
Grant this through our Lord Jesus Christ, your Son,
who lives and reigns with you and the Holy Spirit,
one God, for ever and ever. ℟. **Amen.** ⋎

In countries where the Ascension is celebrated on the
Seventh Sunday of Easter, the following opening prayer
is said:

Lord,
teach us to know you better
by doing good to others.
Help us to grow in your love
and come to understand the eternal mystery
of Christ's death and resurrection.
We ask this through our Lord Jesus Christ, your Son,
who lives and reigns with you and the Holy Spirit,
one God, for ever and ever. ℟. **Amen.** ⋎

READING I   Acts 18, 23-28

The Christian preacher Apollos shows from the Scriptures that Jesus
was the Messiah. He preaches fearlessly. Since he had only heard of
John's baptism, Priscilla and Aquila instruct him in greater depth
about Jesus.

A reading from the Acts of the Apostles

After spending some time in Antioch, Paul set out
again, traveling systematically through the Galatian
country and Phrygia to reassure all his disciples.

A Jew named Apollos, a native of Alexandria and
a man of eloquence, arrived by ship at Ephesus. He

was both an authority on Scripture and instructed in the new way of the Lord. Apollos was a man full of spiritual fervor. He spoke and taught accurately about Jesus, although he knew only of John's baptism. He too began to express himself fearlessly in the synagogue. When Priscilla and Aquila heard him, they took him home and explained to him God's new way in greater detail. He wanted to go on to Achaia, and so the brothers encouraged him by writing the disciples there to welcome him. When he arrived, he greatly strengthened those who through God's favor had become believers. He was vigorous in his public refutation of the Jewish party as he went about establishing from the Scriptures that Jesus is the Messiah.—This is the Word of the Lord. ℞. **Thanks be to God.** ℣

Responsorial Psalm　　　　　　Ps 47, 2-3. 8-9. 10

℞. (8) **God is king of all the earth.**

All you peoples, clap your hands,
　　shout to God with cries of gladness,
For the Lord, the Most High, the awesome,
　　is the great king over all the earth. — ℞

For king of all the earth is God;
　　sing hymns of praise.
God reigns over the nations,
　　God sits upon his holy throne. — ℞

The princes of the people are gathered together
　　with the people of the God of Abraham.
For God's are the guardians of the earth;
　　he is supreme. — ℞ ℣

℞. Or: **Alleluia.** ℣

GOSPEL　　　　　　　　　　　　Jn 16, 23-28

Alleluia (Jn 16, 28)

℞. **Alleluia.** I went from the Father and came into the world;

and now I leave the world to return to the Father.
℟. **Alleluia.**

Jesus is not only willing to present prayers to the Father; he strongly urges his followers to ask "in his name," that is, according to what is truly good according to the wisdom of God.

℣. The Lord be with you. ℟. **And also with you.**
✠ A reading from the holy gospel according to John
℟. **Glory to you, Lord.**

Jesus said to his disciples,

"I give you my assurance,
whatever you ask the Father,
he will give you in my name.
Until now you have not asked for anything in
    my name.
Ask and you shall receive,
that your joy may be full.
I have spoken these things to you in veiled lan-
    guage.
A time will come when I shall no longer do so,
but shall tell you about the Father in plain
    speech.
On that day you will ask in my name
and I do not say that I will petition the Father
    for you.
The Father already loves you,
because you have loved me
and have believed that I came from God.
[I did indeed come from the Father;]
I came into the world.
Now I am leaving the world
  to go to the Father."

This is the gospel of the Lord. ℟. **Praise to you, Lord
Jesus Christ.**   ➤ No. 15, p. 623

PRAYER OVER THE GIFTS
Merciful Lord,
make holy these gifts,
and let our spiritual sacrifice
make us an everlasting gift to you.

We ask this in the name of Jesus the Lord.
℞. **Amen.**   ➤ No. 21, p. 626

*If the Ascension has been celebrated on Thursday of
this week: Preface of Ascension I or II (P 26-27). If
the Ascension is celebrated on the Seventh Sunday of
Easter: Preface of Easter II-V (P 22-25).*

COMMUNION ANT.   Jn 17, 24

**Father, I want the men you have given me to be with
me where I am, so that they may see the glory you
have given me, alleluia. ℣**

PRAYER AFTER COMMUNION

Lord,
may this eucharist,
which we have celebrated in memory of your Son,
help us to grow in love.
We ask this in the name of Jesus the Lord.
℞. **Amen.**   ➤ No. 32, p. 650

MONDAY OF THE SEVENTH WEEK OF EASTER

When the Holy Spirit descended upon the apostles and made the
power of God's grace manifest, he came to dwell for all time in the
hearts of the faithful. The gift of divine charity was thus infused
into their souls. We should examine ourselves and see what results
have been produced in us by the many visits of the Holy Spirit which
we have been privileged to receive. The gift of the Holy Spirit is the
secret of the complete change of heart, true conversion.

ENTRANCE ANT.   Acts 1, 8

**You will receive power when the Holy Spirit comes
upon you. You will be my witnesses to all the world,
alleluia.**   ➤ No. 2, p. 614

OPENING PRAYER

Lord,
send the power of your Holy Spirit upon us
that we may remain faithful
and do your will in our daily lives.
We ask this through our Lord Jesus Christ, your Son,

who lives and reigns with you and the Holy Spirit, one God, for ever and ever. ℟. **Amen.** ⱽ

READING I   Acts 19, 1-8

The giving of the Holy Spirit to the twelve men by Paul is called "Little Pentecost." The event is a Scriptural indication of the sacraments of baptism and confirmation. Through Christ, the Spirit is available to all. Paul continues to preach Jesus as the Lord, the Risen Savior.

A reading from the Acts of the Apostles

While Apollos was in Corinth, Paul passed through the interior of the country and came to Ephesus. There he found some disciples to whom he put the question, "Did you receive the Holy Spirit when you became believers?" They answered, "We have not so much as heard that there is a Holy Spirit." "Well, how were you baptized?" he persisted. They replied, "With the baptism of John." Paul then explained, "John's baptism was a baptism of repentance. He used to tell the people about the one who would come after him in whom they were to believe—that is, Jesus." When they heard this, they were baptized in the name of the Lord Jesus. As Paul laid his hands on them, the Holy Spirit came down on them and they began to speak in tongues and to utter prophecies. There were in the company about twelve men in all.

Paul entered the synagogue, and over a period of three months debated fearlessly, with persuasive arguments, about the kingdom of God.—This is the Word of the Lord. ℟. **Thanks be to God.** ⱽ

Responsorial Psalm   Ps 68, 2-3. 4-5. 6-7
℟. (33) **Sing to God, O kingdoms of the earth.**

God arises; his enemies are scattered,
    and those who hate him flee before him.
As smoke is driven away, so are they driven;
    as wax melts before the fire. — ℟

But the just rejoice and exult before God;
   they are glad and rejoice.
Sing to God, chant praise to his name;
   his name is the Lord; exult before him. — ℞

The father of orphans and the defender of widows
   is God in his holy dwelling.
God gives a home to the forsaken;
   he leads forth prisoners to prosperity. — ℞ ♦

℞. Or: **Alleluia.** ♦

GOSPEL   Jn 16, 29-33

Alleluia. (Col 3, 1)

℞. **Alleluia.** If then you have been raised with Christ,
   seek the things that are above,
where Christ is seated at the right hand of God. ℞.
   Alleluia.

The disciples finally make a profession of their belief in Jesus. They
admit that he is from God. Jesus then warns them of their future,
their sufferings, but he promises that he will overcome the world.

℣. The Lord be with you. ℞. **And also with you.**
✠ A reading from the holy gospel according to John
℞. **Glory to you, Lord.**

The disciples said to Jesus:

   "At last you are speaking plainly without talking
in veiled language! We are convinced that you know
everything. There is no need for anyone to ask you
questions. We do indeed believe you came from God."

   Jesus answered them:

      "Do you really believe?
      An hour is coming—has indeed already come—
   when you will be scattered and each will go his
      way,
   leaving me quite alone.
   (Yet I can never be alone;
   the Father is with me.)
   I tell you all this
   that in me you may find peace.

You will suffer in the world.
But take courage!
I have overcome the world."
This is the gospel of the Lord. ℟. **Praise to you, Lord Jesus Christ.**   ➜ No. 15, p. 623

PRAYER OVER THE GIFTS
Lord,
may these gifts cleanse us from sin
and make our hearts live with your gift of grace.
Grant this through Christ our Lord.
℟. **Amen.**   ➜ No. 21, p. 626 (Pref. P 26-27)

COMMUNION ANT.   Jn 14, 18; 16, 22
The Lord said: I will not leave you orphans. I will come back to you, and your hearts will rejoice, alleluia. ℣

PRAYER AFTER COMMUNION
Merciful Father,
may these mysteries give us new purpose
and bring us to a new life in you.
Grant this through Christ our Lord.
℟. **Amen.**   ➜ No. 32, p. 650

TUESDAY OF THE SEVENTH WEEK OF EASTER

The final proof of our redemption which was given through the Incarnation and Passion was completed when our Savior took his place as true God and as true man at the right hand of his Eternal Father in the kingdom of heaven. Our faith is that which the apostles and their successors received with their commission to preach and teach and to bear witness to the truths of the Gospel. Our faith, too, must be ever steadfast, and it will become strong as we imitate our Divine Master.

ENTRANCE ANT.   Rv 1, 17-18
I am the beginning and the end of all things. I have met death, but I am alive, and I shall live for eternity, alleluia.   ➜ No. 2, p. 614

OPENING PRAYER

God of power and mercy,
send your Holy Spirit
to live in our hearts
and make us temples of his glory.
We ask this through our Lord Jesus Christ, your Son,
who lives and reigns with you and the Holy Spirit,
one God, for ever and ever. ℟. **Amen.** ▼

READING I   Acts 20, 17-27

Luke exposes the inner spirit of the great apostle Paul. He has abandoned any thought of a life for himself and has become the servant
of the plan of God. He finds his joy in serving others. He wants to
finish the race of life and attain the crown of victory.

A reading from the Acts of the Apostles

Paul sent word from Miletus to Ephesus, summoning the elders of that church. When they came to
him he delivered this address: "You know how I
lived among you from the first day I set foot in the
province of Asia—how I served the Lord in humility
through the sorrows and trials that came my way
from the plottings of certain Jews. Never did I shrink
from telling you what was for your own good, or
from teaching you in public or in private. With Jews
and Greeks alike I insisted solemnly on repentance
before God and on faith in our Lord Jesus. But now,
as you see, I am on my way to Jerusalem, compelled
by the Spirit and not knowing what will happen to
me there—except that the Holy Spirit has been warning me from city to city that chains and hardships
await me. I put no value on my life if only I can finish
my race and complete the service to which I have
been assigned by the Lord Jesus, bearing witness to
the gospel of God's grace. I know as I speak these
words that none of you among whom I went about
preaching the kingdom will ever see my face again.
Therefore I solemnly declare this day that I take the
blame for no man's conscience, for I have never

shrunk from announcing to you God's design in its entirety."—This is the Word of the Lord. ℞. **Thanks be to God.** ✝

Responsorial Psalm   Ps 68, 10-11. 20-21

℞. (33) **Sing to God, O kingdoms of the earth.**

A bountiful rain you showered down, O God, upon
    your inheritance;
  you restored the land when it languished;
Your flock settled in it;
  in your goodness, O God, you provided it for the
    needy. — ℞

Blessed day by day be the Lord,
  who bears our burdens; God, who is our salvation.
God is a saving God for us;
  the Lord, my Lord, controls the passageways of
    death. — ℞ ✝

℞. Or: **Alleluia.** ✝

GOSPEL   Jn 17, 1-11

Alleluia (Jn 14, 16)

℞. **Alleluia.** The Father will send you the Holy Spirit,
  says the Lord,
to be with you for ever. ℞. **Alleluia.**

Jesus speaks of his coming death. The Son of Man will suffer and enter into his glory at the right hand of the Father. He prays about how the chosen disciples have heard the message of the Father. Jesus prays especially for them since they, too, belong to the Father.

℣. The Lord be with you. ℞. **And also with you.**

✠ A reading from the holy gospel according to John
℞. **Glory to you, Lord.**

Jesus looked up to heaven and said:
  "Father, the hour has come!
  Give glory to your Son
  that your Son may give glory to you,
  inasmuch as you have given him authority over
    all mankind,
  that he may bestow eternal life on those you
    gave him.

(Eternal life is this:
to know you, the only true God,
and him whom you have sent, Jesus Christ.)
I have given you glory on earth
by finishing the work you gave me to do.
Do you now, Father, give me glory at your side,
a glory I had with you before the world began.
I have made your name known
to those you gave me out of the world.
These men you gave me were yours;
they have kept your word.
Now they realize
that all that you gave me comes from you.
I entrusted to them
the message you entrusted to me,
and they received it.
They have known that in truth I came from you,
they have believed it was you who sent me.
"For these I pray—
not for the world
but for these you have given me,
for they are really yours.
(Just as all that belongs to me is yours,
so all that belongs to you is mine.)
It is in them that I have been glorified.
I am in the world no more,
but these are in the world
as I come to you."

This is the gospel of the Lord. ℟. **Praise to you, Lord
Jesus Christ.**   ➔ No. 15, p. 623

PRAYER OVER THE GIFTS

Father,
accept the prayers and offerings of your people
and bring us to the glory of heaven,
where Jesus is Lord for ever and ever.
℟. **Amen.**   ➔ No. 21, p. 626 (Pref. P 26-27)

COMMUNION ANT.   Jn 14, 26

The Lord says, the Holy Spirit whom the Father will send in my name will teach you all things, and remind you of all I have said to you, alleluia. ℣

PRAYER AFTER COMMUNION

Lord,
may this eucharist,
which we have celebrated in memory of your Son,
help us to grow in love.
We ask this in the name of Jesus the Lord.
℟. **Amen.**   ➔ No. 32, p. 650

WEDNESDAY OF THE SEVENTH WEEK OF EASTER

The apostolic mission of the Church is the same as Christ's mission from the Father. The Church shows us the love of Almighty God for man and reminds us how noble, generous, and truly divine is the charity of our Heavenly Father. When God created us, he did so because he was goodness and love itself, and our Lord Jesus Christ was one with him. In humility, let us try to be one with the Father and the Son, to be holy and pleasing to the Creator through our Blessed Savior.

ENTRANCE ANT.   Ps 47, 2

All nations, clap your hands. Shout with a voice of joy to God, alleluia.   ➔ No. 2, p. 614

OPENING PRAYER

God of mercy,
unite your Church in the Holy Spirit
that we may serve you with all our hearts
and work together with unselfish love.
Grant this through our Lord Jesus Christ, your Son,
who lives and reigns with you and the Holy Spirit,
one God, for ever and ever. ℟. **Amen.** ℣

READING I   Acts 20, 28-38

Paul entrusts the protection of the true faith and the guidance of the faithful to the appointed ministers of each community. He warns of false teachers. Paul refers to his own example, and before leaving Ephesus he prays with the community.

A reading from the Acts of the Apostles

Paul spoke to the elders of the church of Ephesus: "Keep watch over yourselves, and over the whole flock the Holy Spirit has given you to guard. Shepherd the church of God, which he has acquired at the price of his own blood. I know that when I am gone, savage wolves will come among you who will not spare the flock. From your own number, men will present themselves distorting the truth and leading astray any who follow them. Be on guard, therefore. Do not forget that for three years, night and day, I never ceased warning you individually even to the point of tears. I commend you now to the Lord, and to that gracious word of his which can enlarge you, and give you a share among all who are consecrated to him. Never did I set my heart on anyone's silver or gold or envy the way he dressed. You yourselves know that these hands of mine have served both my needs and those of my companions. I have always pointed out to you that it is by such hard work that you must help the weak. You need to recall the words of the Lord Jesus himself, who said, 'There is more happiness in giving than receiving.'"

After this discourse, Paul knelt down with them all and prayed. They began to weep without restraint, throwing their arms around him and kissing him, for they were deeply distressed to hear that they would never see his face again. Then they escorted him to the ship.—This is the Word of the Lord. ℟. **Thanks be to God.** ⩔

Responsorial Psalm   Ps 68, 29-30. 33-35. 35-36
℟. (33) **Sing to God, O kingdoms of the earth.**
Show forth, O God your power,
    the power, O God, with which you took our part;
For your temple in Jerusalem
    let the kings bring you gifts. — ℟

You kingdoms of the earth, sing to God,
    chant praise to the Lord
    who rides on the heights of the ancient heavens.
Behold, his voice resounds, the voice of power:
    "Confess the power of God!" — ℟

Over Israel is his majesty;
    his power is in the skies.
Awesome in his sanctuary is God, the God of Israel;
    he gives power and strength to his people. — ℟ ℣

℟. Or: **Alleluia.** ℣

GOSPEL   Jn 17, 11-19

Alleluia. (Jn 17, 17)

℟. **Alleluia.** Your word, O Lord, is truth;
make us holy in the truth. ℟. **Alleluia.**

Jesus prays at the Last Supper that all may be one. The mutual bond
of the followers of Jesus is that all are the adopted sons of the
Father, gathered to hear him and to worship him. Jesus ask that these
followers be guarded from the evil one.

℣. The Lord be with you. ℟. **And also with you.**
✠ A reading from the holy gospel according to John
℟. **Glory to you, Lord.**

Jesus looked up to heaven and prayed:
    "O Father most holy,
    protect them with your name which you have
        given me,
    [that they may be one, even as we are one.]
    As long as I was with them,
    I guarded them with your name which you gave
        me.
    I kept careful watch,
    and not one of them was lost,
    none but him who was destined to be lost—
    in the fulfillment of Scripture.
    Now, however, I come to you;
    I say all this while I am still in the world
    that they may share my joy completely.
    I gave them your word,

and the world has hated them for it;
they do not belong to the world,
[any more than I belong to the world].
I do not ask you to take them out of the world,
but to guard them from the evil one.
They are not of the world,
any more than I am of the world.
Consecrate them by means of truth—
'Your word is truth.'
As you have sent me into the world,
so I have sent them into the world;
I consecrate myself for their sakes now,
that they may be consecrated in truth."

This is the gospel of the Lord. ℟. **Praise to you, Lord Jesus Christ.**   ➤ No. 15, p. 623

PRAYER OVER THE GIFTS

Lord,
accept this offering we make at your command.
May these sacred mysteries by which we worship you
bring your salvation to perfection within us.
We ask this in the name of Jesus the Lord.
℟. **Amen.**   ➤ No. 21, p. 626 (Pref. P 26-27)

COMMUNION ANT.   Jn 15, 26-27

The Lord says: When the Holy Spirit comes to you, the Spirit whom I shall send, the Spirit of truth who proceeds from the Father, he will bear witness to me, and you also will be my witnesses, alleluia. ⱱ

PRAYER AFTER COMMUNION

Lord,
may our participation in the eucharist
increase your life in us,
cleanse us from sin,
and make us increasingly worthy of this holy sacrament.
We ask this through Christ our Lord.
℟. **Amen.**   _____   ➤ No. 32, p. 650

THURSDAY OF THE SEVENTH WEEK OF EASTER

As courage was infused into Paul by God before what was to be the end of his missionary work, the Church endeavors to renew our courage and strength and a trust and confidence in his mercy and power. No matter what our condition may be, we must never despair of God's mercy, for "the Lord is good to all and compassionate toward all his works" (Ps 145, 9).

ENTRANCE ANT. Heb 4, 16

Let us come to God's presence with confidence, because we will find mercy, and strength when we need it, alleluia. ➜ No. 2, p. 614

OPENING PRAYER
Father,
let your Spirit come upon us with power
to fill us with his gifts.
May he make our hearts pleasing to you,
and ready to do your will.
We ask this through our Lord Jesus Christ, your Son,
who lives and reigns with you and the Holy Spirit,
one God, for ever and ever. ℟. **Amen.** ⩔

READING I Acts 22, 30; 23, 6-11

After reaching Jerusalem at the end of his third journey, Paul is arrested. Even then, he witnesses to the resurrection of Jesus and influences many. At night God appears to Paul to give him courage to persevere.

A reading from the Acts of the Apostles

The commander released Paul from prison, intending to look carefully into the charge which the Jews were bringing against him. He summoned the chief priests and the whole Sanhedrin to a meeting; then he brought Paul down and made him stand before them.

Paul, it should be noted, was aware that some of them were Sadducees and some Pharisees. Consequently he spoke out before the Sanhedrin: "Brothers, I am a Pharisee and was born a Pharisee. I find myself on trial now because of my hope in the resurrection of the dead." At these words, a dispute arose between Pharisees and Sadducees which divided the whole assembly. (The Sadducees, of course, maintain that there is no resurrection and that there are neither angels nor spirits, while the Pharisees believe in all these things.) A loud uproar ensued. Finally, some scribes of the Pharisee party arose and declared emphatically: "We do not find this man guilty of any crime. If a spirit or an angel has spoken to him. . . ." At this, the dispute grew worse and the commander feared they would tear Paul to pieces. He therefore ordered his troops to go down and rescue Paul from their midst and take him back to headquarters. That night the Lord appeared at Paul's side and said: "Keep up your courage! Just as you have given testimony to me here in Jerusalem, so must you do in Rome."—This is the Word of the Lord. ℞. **Thanks be to God.** ℣

Responsorial Psalm   Ps 16, 1-2. 5. 7-8. 9-10. 11

℞. (1) **Keep me safe, O God;
    you are my hope.**

Keep me, O God, for in you I take refuge;
    I say to the Lord, "My Lord are you."
O Lord, my allotted portion and my cup,
    you it is who hold fast my lot. — ℞

I bless the Lord who counsels me;
    even in the night my heart exhorts me.
I set the Lord ever before me;
    with him at my right hand I shall not be disturbed. — ℞

Therefore my heart is glad and my soul rejoices,
    my body, too, abides in confidence;
Because you will not abandon my soul to the nether world,
    nor will you suffer your faithful one to undergo corruption. — ℞

You will show me the path to life,
> fullness of joys in your presence,
> the delights at your right hand forever. — ℟

℟. Or: **Alleluia.** ℣

GOSPEL   Jn 17, 20-26

Alleluia (Jn 17, 21)

℟. **Alleluia.** May all be one as you are, Father, and
> I in you;

let the world believe that you sent me, says the Lord.
> ℟. **Alleluia.**

Jesus prays for unity so that men will believe in him and in his gospel.
He prays that all may be one in the Father and him. Jesus reveals the
Father and will continue to carry out his mission.

℣. The Lord be with you. ℟. **And also with you.**

✠ A reading from the holy gospel according to John

℟. **Glory to you, Lord.**

Jesus looked up to heaven and said:
> "I do not pray for my disciples alone.
> I pray also for those who will believe in me
> > through their word,
> that all may be one
> as you, Father, are in me, and I in you;
> I pray that they may be [one] in us,
> that the world may believe that you sent me.
> I have given them the glory you gave me
> that they may be one, as we are one—
> I living in them, you living in me—
> that their unity may be complete.
> So shall the world know that you sent me,
> and that you loved them as you loved me.
> Father,
> all those you gave me
> I would have in my company
> where I am,
> to see this glory of mine
> which is your gift to me,
> because of the love you bore me before the
> > world began.

Just Father,
the world has not known you,
but I have known you;
and these men have known that you sent me.
To them I have revealed your name,
and I will continue to reveal it
so that your love for me may live in them,
and I may live in them."

This is the gospel of the Lord. ℟. **Praise to you, Lord Jesus Christ.**　　　➤ No. 15, p. 623

PRAYER OVER THE GIFTS

Merciful Lord,
make holy these gifts,
and let our spiritual sacrifice
make us an everlasting gift to you.
We ask this in the name of Jesus the Lord.
℟. **Amen.**　　　➤ No. 21, p. 626 (Pref. P 26-27)

COMMUNION ANT.　　　Jn 16, 7

This is the word of Jesus: It is best for me to leave you; because if I do not go, the Spirit will not come to you, alleluia. ℣

PRAYER AFTER COMMUNION

Lord,
renew us by the mysteries we have shared.
Help us to know you
and prepare us for the gifts of the Spirit.
We ask this through Christ our Lord.
℟. **Amen.**　　　➤ No. 32, p. 650

FRIDAY OF THE SEVENTH WEEK OF EASTER

We should refrain from judging others and even examining their motives. Let us leave all judgment in the hands of God. Thus, we shall have prepared the way of the Lord according to his own directions, and by his grace we shall be prepared to meet him by receiving Holy Communion. Jesus Christ is the Lamb of God who takes away the sins of the world.

ENTRANCE ANT.   Rv 1, 5-6
Christ loved us and has washed away our sins with his blood, and has made us a kingdom of priests to serve his God and Father, alleluia.   ➤ No. 2, p. 614

OPENING PRAYER
Father,
in glorifying Christ and sending us your Spirit,
you open the way to eternal life.
May our sharing in this gift increase our love
and make our faith grow stronger.
Grant this through our Lord Jesus Christ, your Son,
who lives and reigns with you and the Holy Spirit,
one God, for ever and ever. ℞. **Amen.** ↓

READING I   Acts 25, 13-21

The imprisonment of Paul brings much good. Several high Roman officials hear of Jesus Christ and of Paul's firm conviction that Jesus is the risen Lord. Paul will soon announce the Good News in Rome itself.

A reading from the Acts of the Apostles

King Agrippa and Bernice arrived in Caesarea and paid Festus a courtesy call. Since they were to spend several days there, Festus referred Paul's case to the king. "There is a prisoner here," he said, "whom Felix left behind in custody. While I was in Jerusalem the chief priests and the elders of the Jews presented their case against this man and demanded his condemnation. I replied that it was not the Roman practice to hand an accused man over before he had been confronted with his accusers and given a chance to defend himself against their charges. When they came here with me, I did not delay the matter. The very next day I took my seat on the bench and ordered the man brought in. His accusers surrounded him but they did not charge him with any of the crimes I expected. Instead they differed with him over issues in their own religion, and about a certain Jesus who had died but who Paul claimed is alive. Not knowing how to decide the case, I asked whether the prisoner was willing to go to Jerusalem and stand trial there on these charges. Paul appealed to be kept here until there would be an imperial investigation of his case, so I issued orders that he be kept in custody until I could send him to the emperor."—This is the Word of the Lord. ℟. **Thanks be to God.** ✟

Responsorial Psalm Ps 103, 1-2. 11-12. 19-20

℟. (19) **The Lord has set his throne in heaven.**

Bless the Lord, O my soul;
    and all my being, bless his holy name.
Bless the Lord, O my soul,
    and forget not all his benefits; — ℟

For as the heavens are high above the earth,
    so surpassing is his kindness toward those who
        fear him.
As far as the east is from the west,
    so far has he put our transgressions from us. — ℟

The Lord has established his throne in heaven,
    and his kingdom rules over all.
Bless the Lord, all you his angels,
    you mighty in strength, who do his bidding. — ℟ ✟

℟. Or: **Alleluia.** ✟

GOSPEL Jn 21, 15-19

Alleluia (Jn 14, 26)

℟. **Alleluia.** The Holy Spirit will teach you all things, and remind you of all I have said to you. ℟. **Alleluia.**

Jesus makes the apostle Peter the shepherd of his flock on earth after Peter answers the threefold question of Jesus. Then Jesus foretells how Peter will die.

℣. The Lord be with you. ℟. **And also with you.**
✠ A reading from the holy gospel according to John
℟. **Glory to you, Lord.**

When [Jesus manifested himself to his disciples and] they had eaten their meal, he said to Simon Peter, "Simon, son of John, do you love me more than these?" "Yes, Lord," Peter said, "you know that I love you." At which Jesus said, "Feed my lambs."

A second time he put his question, "Simon, son of John, do you love me?" "Yes, Lord," Peter said, "you know that I love you." Jesus replied, "Tend my sheep."

A third time Jesus asked him, "Simon, son of John, do you love me?" Peter was hurt because he had asked a third time, "Do you love me?" So he said to him: "Lord, you know everything. You know well that I love you." Jesus told him, "Feed my sheep."

"I tell you solemnly:
as a young man
you fastened your belt
and went about as you pleased;
but when you are older
you will stretch out your hands,
and another will tie you fast
and carry you off against your will."

(What he said indicated the sort of death by which Peter was to glorify God.) When Jesus had finished speaking he said to him, "Follow me."—This is the gospel of the Lord. ℟. **Praise to you, Lord Jesus Christ.**   → No. 15, p. 623

PRAYER OVER THE GIFTS

Father of love and mercy,
we place our offering before you.
Send your Holy Spirit to cleanse our lives
so that our gifts may be acceptable.
We ask this through Christ our Lord.
℟. **Amen.**   → No. 21, p. 626 (Pref. P 26-27)

COMMUNION ANT.   Jn 16, 13

When the Spirit of truth comes, says the Lord, he will lead you to the whole truth, alleluia. ℣

PRAYER AFTER COMMUNION

God our Father,
the eucharist is our bread of life
and the sacrament of our forgiveness.
May our sharing in this mystery
bring us to eternal life,
where Jesus is Lord for ever and ever.
℟. **Amen.** ➔ No. 32, p. 650

SATURDAY OF THE SEVENTH WEEK OF EASTER
MASS IN THE MORNING

We should be aware that the chosen people of Israel, favored though they were by God's most special care, are but a figure of us, enriched as we have been by God's choicest favors. We should try to realize that we are often called to repentance, but we have been careless in accepting such tender invitations. Let us purify the "holy temple" by casting out all affection for sin and its occasions.

ENTRANCE ANT. Acts 1, 14

The disciples were constantly at prayer together, with Mary the mother of Jesus, the other women, and the brothers of Jesus, alleluia. ➔ No. 2, p. 614

OPENING PRAYER

Almighty Father,
let the love we have celebrated in this Easter season
be put into practice in our daily lives.
We ask this through our Lord Jesus Christ, your Son,
who lives and reigns with you and the Holy Spirit,
one God, for ever and ever. ℟. **Amen.** ↓

READING I Acts 28, 16-20. 30-31

This passage concludes the Acts of the Apostles. The faith has been planted according to the directions of Jesus to teach all men. Paul is held in custody but welcomes any visitors. He preaches the reign of God and teaches about Jesus.

A reading from the Acts of the Apostles

Upon entry into Rome, Paul was allowed to take a lodging of his own, although a soldier was assigned to keep guard over him.

Three days later Paul invited the prominent men of the Jewish community to visit him. When they had gathered he said: "My brothers, I have done nothing against our people or our ancestral customs; yet in Jerusalem I was handed over to the Romans as a prisoner. The Romans tried my case and wanted to release me because they found nothing against me deserving of death. When the Jews objected, I was forced to appeal to the emperor, though I had no cause to make accusations against my own people. This is the reason, then, why I have asked to see you and speak with you. I wear these chains solely because I share the hope of Israel."

For two full years Paul stayed on in his rented lodgings, welcoming all who came to him. With full assurance, and without any hindrance whatever, he preached the reign of God and taught about the Lord Jesus Christ—This is the Word of the Lord. ℞. **Thanks to be God.** ✟

Responsorial Psalm   Ps 11, 4. 5. 7

℞. (7) **The just will gaze on your face, O Lord.**

The Lord is in his holy temple;
    the Lord's throne is in heaven.
His eyes behold,
    his searching glance is on mankind. — ℞

The Lord searches the just and the wicked;
    the lover of violence he hates.
For the Lord is just, he loves just deeds;
    the upright shall see his face. — ℞ ✟

℞. Or: **Alleluia.** ✟

GOSPEL   Jn 21, 20-25

Alleluia (Jn 16, 7. 13)

℞. **Alleluia.** I will send you the Spirit of truth, says
    the Lord;
he will lead you to the whole truth. ℞. **Alleluia.**

John speaks of himself as the disciple whom Jesus loved and as the witness to the events of Christ's life. Peter asks about John but Jesus reminds him of his mission. John ends his account by admitting much more could have been written about Jesus.

℣. The Lord be with you. ℟. **And also with you.**
✠ A reading from the holy gospel according to John
℟. **Glory to you, Lord.**

As Peter followed Jesus, he turned around and noticed that the disciple whom Jesus loved was following (the one who had leaned against Jesus' chest during the supper and said, "Lord, which one will hand you over?"). Seeing him, Peter was prompted to ask Jesus, "But Lord, what about him?" "Suppose I want him to stay until I come," Jesus replied, "how does that concern you? Your business is to follow me." This is how the report spread among the brothers that this disciple was not going to die. Jesus never told him, as a matter of fact, that the disciple was not going to die; all he said was, "Suppose I want him to stay until I come. [How does that concern you]?"

It is this same disciple who is the witness to these things; it is he who wrote them down and his testimony, we know, is true. There are still many other things that Jesus did, yet if they were written about in detail, I doubt there would be room enough in the entire world to hold the books to record them.—This is the gospel of the Lord. ℟. **Praise to you, Lord Jesus Christ.**   ➜ No. 15, p. 623

PRAYER OVER THE GIFTS
Lord,
may the coming of the Holy Spirit
prepare us to receive these holy sacraments,
for he is our forgiveness.
We ask this in the name of Jesus the Lord.
℟. **Amen.**   ➜ No. 21, p. 626 (Pref. P 26-27)

COMMUNION ANT.   Jn 16, 14
**The Lord says: The Holy Spirit will give glory to me,
because he takes my words from me and will hand
them to you, alleluia.** ℣

PRAYER AFTER COMMUNION
Father of mercy,
hear our prayers
that we may leave our former selves behind
and serve you with holy and renewed hearts.
Grant this through Christ our Lord.
℟. **Amen.**   ➤ No. 32, p. 650

PROPER OF SAINTS

"In celebrating the annual cycle of Christ's mysteries, holy Church honors with special love the Blessed Mary, Mother of God, who is joined by an inseparable bond to the saving work of her Son. In her the Church holds up and admires the most excellent fruit of the redemption, and joyfully contemplates, as in a faultless model, that which she herself wholly desires and hopes to be.

"The Church has also included in the annual cycle days devoted to the memory of the martyrs and the other saints. Raised up to perfection by the manifold grace of God, and already in possession of eternal salvation, they sing God's perfect praise in heaven and offer prayers for us. By celebrating the passage of these saints from earth to heaven the Church proclaims the paschal mystery as achieved in the saints who have suffered and been glorified with Christ; she proposes them to the faithful as examples who draw all to the Father through Christ, and through their merits she pleads for God's favors" (Vatican II Constitution on the Sacred Liturgy, nos. 103-104).

Solemnities and Feasts

A proper Mass is provided in its entirety for each solemnity and feast. There is no substitute for the processional chants, presidential prayers, and special readings and intervenient chants given for these days.

Obligatory Memorials

1) Processional Chants and Presidential Prayers

a) Proper texts, given on some days, should always be used.

b) When there is a reference to a particular common, appropriate texts should be chosen according to the principles at the beginning of the Commons. The page reference in each case indicates only the beginning of the common to which reference is made.

c) *If the reference is to more than one common, one or the other may be used, according to pastoral need. It is always permissible to interchange texts from several Masses within the same common.*

For example, if a saint is both a martyr and a bishop, either the Common of Martyrs or the Common of Pastors (for bishops) may be used.

d) *In addition to the commons which express a special characteristic holiness, (e.g., of martyrs, virgins, or pastors), the texts from the Common of Holy Men and Women, referring to holiness in general, may always be used.*

For example, in the case of a saint who is both a virgin and a martyr, texts from the Common of Holy Men and Women in general may be used, in addition to texts from the Common of Martyrs or the Common of Virgins.

e) *The Prayers over the Gifts and after Communion, unless there are proper prayers, may be taken either from the common or from the current liturgical season.*

2) *Readings and Intervenient Chants*

a) *The weekday readings and intervenient chants are to be preferred.*

b) *However, sometimes special readings are assigned, that is, readings which mention the saint or mystery being celebrated; these are to be said in place of the weekday readings. (Whenever this is the case, a clear indication is given in this Missal.)*

c) *In all other cases the readings found in the Proper of Saints are used only if special reasons (particularly of a pastoral nature) exist. Sometimes, these readings will be appropriate, that is, they will shed light on some outstanding trait of the saint's spiritual life. Others will be simply references to the general readings in the Commons so as to facilitate a selection. However, they are only suggestions; in place of these appropriate readings or suggested gen-*

eral *readings, any other reading from the common indicated may be said.*

d) *Whenever there are compelling reasons for doing so, readings can always be chosen from the Common of Holy Men and Women.*

Optional Memorials

The category of Optional Memorials is like that of Obligatory Memorials as far as choice of texts is concerned but it allows many more options of Masses to be chosen. In place of the Mass of the Optional Memorial, the priest has the option to choose the Mass of the Weekday, or of one of the saints commemorated or mentioned in the martyrology on that day, or a Mass for Various Needs and Occasions or a Votive Mass. Masses of the saints from the martyrology can be taken from the Mass of a saint in the Missal who is in a similar category, e.g., a martyr, priest, etc.

— NOVEMBER —

Nov. 30 — ST. ANDREW, Apostle

Feast

St. Andrew, the brother of St. Peter, was a native of the town of Bethsaida in Galilee. A fisherman by profession and a disciple of St. John the Baptist, he and his brother, St. Peter, joined Jesus as members of the Apostolic College. After the dispersion of the Apostles, St. Andrew preached in Greece and several other countries. He suffered martyrdom in Patras, Greece, and according to common opinion, by crucifixion on a cross made in the form of the letter X.

ENTRANCE ANT.   See Mt 4, 18-19

By the Sea of Galilee the Lord saw two brothers, Peter and Andrew. He called them: come and follow me, and I will make you fishers of men.

➤ No. 2, p. 614

OPENING PRAYER

Lord,
in your kindness hear our petitions.
You called Andrew the apostle
to preach the gospel and guide your Church in faith.
May he always be our friend in your presence
to help us with his prayers.
We ask this through our Lord Jesus Christ, your Son,
who lives and reigns with you and the Holy Spirit,
one God, for ever and ever. ℟. **Amen.** ✣

READING I   Rom 10, 9-18

An inward faith is demanded that will guide the whole man, but it is also an assent to an expression of that faith. The man seeking justification and salvation is called on to acknowledge Christ as the risen Lord.

A reading from the letter of Paul to the Romans

If you confess with your lips that Jesus is Lord, and believe in your heart that God raised him from the dead, you will be saved. Faith in the heart leads to justification, confession on the lips to salvation.

Scripture says, "No one who believes in him will be put to shame." Here there is no difference between Jew and Greek; all have the same Lord, rich in mercy toward all who call upon him. "Everyone who calls on the name of the Lord will be saved."

But how shall they call on him in whom they have not believed? And how can they believe unless they have heard of him? And how can they hear unless there is someone to preach? And how can men preach unless they are sent? Scripture says, "How beautiful are the feet of those who announce good news!" But not all have believed the gospel. Isaiah asks, "Lord, who has believed what he has heard from us?" Faith, then, comes through hearing, and what is heard is the word of Christ. I ask you, have they not heard? Certainly they have, for " their voice has sounded over the whole earth, and their words to the limits of the world."—This is the Word of the Lord. ℟. **Thanks be to God. ⩔**

Responsorial Psalm   Ps 19, 2-3. 4-5

℟. (5) **Their message goes out through all the earth.**
The heavens declare the glory of God,
    and the firmament proclaims his handiwork.
Day pours out the word to day,
    and night to night imparts knowledge. — ℟
Not a word nor a discourse
    whose voice is not heard;
Through all the earth their voice resounds,
    and to the end of the world, their message. — ℟ ⩔

GOSPEL   Mt 4, 18-22

Alleluia (Mt 4, 19)
℟. **Alleluia.** Come, follow me, says the Lord,
and I will make you fishers of men. ℟. **Alleluia.**

Peter, Andrew, James and John follow our Lord immediately. They drop their fishing net, leave their families and become disciples. The promise of Christ to make them "fishers of men" is an intimation of the apostolic office.

℣. The Lord be with you. ℟. **And also with you.**
✠ A reading from the holy gospel according to Matthew. ℟. **Glory to you, Lord.**

As Jesus was walking along the Sea of Galilee he watched two brothers, Simon now known as Peter, and his brother Andrew, casting a net into the sea. They were fishermen. He said to them, "Come after me and I will make you fishers of men." They immediately abandoned their nets and became his followers. He walked along farther and caught sight of two other brothers, James, Zebedee's son, and his brother John. They too were in their boat, getting their nets in order with their father Zebedee. He called them, and immediately they abandoned boat and father to follow him.—This is the gospel of the Lord. ℟. **Praise to you, Lord Jesus Christ.**

➤ No. 15, p. 623

PRAYER OVER THE GIFTS

All-powerful God,
may these gifts we bring on the feast of St. Andrew
be pleasing to you
and give life to all who receive them.
We ask this in the name of Jesus the Lord
℟. **Amen.**   ➤ No. 21, p. 626 (Pref. P 64-65)

COMMUNION ANT.   Jn 1, 41-42

Andrew told his brother Simon: We have found the Messiah, the Christ; and he brought him to Jesus. ℣

PRAYER AFTER COMMUNION

Lord,
may the sacrament we have received give us courage
to follow the example of Andrew the apostle.
By sharing in Christ's suffering
may we live with him for ever in glory,
for he is Lord for ever and ever.
℟. **Amen.**   ➤ No. 32, p. 650

— DECEMBER —

Dec. 3 — ST. FRANCIS XAVIER, Priest

Memorial

St. Francis Xavier was born in Navarre, Spain, 1506. From St. Ignatius Loyola, he heard the words: "What does it profit a man, if he gain the whole world, but suffer the loss of his own soul?" He renounced his worldly life, and became one of the most zealous apostles who have ever preached.

Common of Pastors: for Missionaries, p. 1077.

OPENING PRAYER

God our Father,
by the preaching of Francis Xavier
you brought many nations to yourself.
Give his zeal for the faith to all who believe in you,
that your Church may rejoice in continued growth
throughout the world.
Grant this through our Lord Jesus Christ, your Son,
who lives and reigns with you and the Holy Spirit,
one God, for ever and ever. ℟. **Amen.** ↓

Reading I (1 Cor 9, 16-19. 22-23), p. 1165, no. 4.
Responsorial Psalm (Ps 96), p. 1162, no. 4.
Gospel (Mk 16, 15-20), p. 1172, no. 5.

PRAYER OVER THE GIFTS

Lord,
receive the gifts we bring on the feast of Francis
   Xavier.
As his zeal for the salvation of mankind
led him to the ends of the earth,
may we be effective witnesses to the gospel
and come with our brothers and sisters
to be with you in the joy of your kingdom.
We ask this through Christ our Lord.
℟. **Amen.**   ➤ No. 21, p. 626 (Pref. P 1)

PRAYER AFTER COMMUNION

Lord God,
may this eucharist fill us with the same love
that inspired Francis Xavier
to work for the salvation of all.
Help us to live in a manner more worthy of our
    Christian calling
and so inherit the promise of eternal life.   ____
We ask this in the name of Jesus the Lord.
℞. **Amen.**   ➔ No. 32, p. 650

_____

Dec. 4 — ST. JOHN DAMASCENE, Priest and Doctor

Optional Memorial

St. John distinguished himself against the Emperor of
Constantinople for his defense of the veneration of
sacred images. He was famous for his great knowledge
and for his theological method. He died in the 8th century.

Common of Pastors, p. 1071; *or Common of Doctors of
the Church, p.* 1082.

OPENING PRAYER

Lord,
may the prayers of St. John Damascene help us,
and may the true faith he taught so well
always be our light and our strength.
We ask this through our Lord Jesus Christ, your Son,
who lives and reigns with you and the Holy Spirit,
one God, for ever and ever. ℞. **Amen.**

Reading I (2 Tm 1, 13-14; 2, 1-3), p. 1168, no. 11.
Responsorial Psalm (Ps 19), p. 1180, no. 1.
Gospel (Mt 25, 14-30), p. 1224, no. 9.

_____

Dec. 6 — ST. NICHOLAS, Bishop

Optional Memorial

St. Nicholas is distinguished in the Church for his holy
austerity and childlike innocence. Chosen as Bishop of
Myra in Licia, Asia Minor, he distinguished himself for
his charity and liberality. He was particularly solicitous

for the care of the young, and thus is venerated as the patron of children.

Common of Pastors: for Bishops, p. 1069.

OPENING PRAYER

Father,
hear our prayers for mercy,
and by the help of St. Nicholas
keep us safe from all danger,
and guide us on the way of salvation.
Grant this through our Lord Jesus Christ, your Son,
who lives and reigns with you and the Holy Spirit,
one God, for ever and ever. ℟. **Amen.**

Reading I (Is 6, 1-8), p. 1156, no. 4.
Responsorial Psalm (Ps 40), p. 218.
Gospel (Lk 10, 1-9), p. 1174, no. 7.

Dec. 7 — ST. AMBROSE, Bishop and Doctor

Memorial

St. Ambrose was one of the four great Latin Fathers and Doctors of the Western Church. As Bishop of Milan, he witnessed the conversation of St. Augustine, whom he baptized in 387. He enriched Latin literature with many works on Scripture, the priesthood, doctrinal subjects and hymnology. The liturgy of Milan is known as the "Ambrosian Rite." He died in 397.

Common of Pastors: for Bishops, p. 1069; or Common of Doctors of the Church, p. 1082.

OPENING PRAYER

Lord,
you made St. Ambrose
an outstanding teacher of the Catholic faith
and gave him the courage of an apostle.
Raise up in your Church more leaders after your
    own heart,
to guide us with courage and wisdom.
We ask this through our Lord Jesus Christ, your Son,
who lives and reigns with you and the Holy Spirit,
one God, for ever and ever. ℟. **Amen.**

Reading I (Eph 3, 8-12), p. 1183, no. 4.
Responsorial Psalm (Ps 89), p. 1161, no. 3.
Gospel (Jn 10, 11-16), p. 1175, no. 9.

PRAYER OVER THE GIFTS

Lord,
as we celebrate these holy rites,
send your Spirit to give us the light of faith
which guided St. Ambrose to make your glory
     known.
We ask this in the name of Jesus the Lord.
℟. **Amen.** → No. 21, p. 626 (Pref. P 1)

PRAYER AFTER COMMUNION

Father,
you have renewed us by the power of this sacrament.
Through the teachings of St. Ambrose,
may we follow your way with courage
and prepare ourselves for the feast of eternal life.
Grant this through Christ our Lord.
℟. **Amen.** → No. 32, p. 650

Dec. 8 — Immaculate Conception

See Vol. I, Sunday Missal, p. 1331.

Dec. 11 — ST. DAMASUS I, Pope

Optional Memorial

Born in Spain, St. Damasus governed the Church from
366 to 384. He commanded St. Jerome to translate the
New Testament into Latin, combatted the Apollinarist
and Macedonian heresies and confirmed the second
ecumenical council of Constantinople which had condemned the Arian heresy. He died in 384.

Common of Pastors: for Popes, p. 1066.

OPENING PRAYER

Father,
as St. Damasus loved and honored your martyrs,
so may we continue to celebrate their witness for
     Christ,

who lives and reigns with you and the Holy Spirit,
one God, for ever and ever. ℟. **Amen.**

Reading I (Acts 20, 17-18. 28-32. 36), p. 1159, no. 2.
Responsorial Psalm (Ps 110), p. 1163, no. 5.
Gospel (Jn 15, 9-17), p. 1232, no. 21.

———————

[In the dioceses of the United States]

Dec. 12 — OUR LADY OF GUADALUPE

Memorial

The Shrine of Our Lady of Guadalupe, near Mexico
City, is one of the most celebrated places of pilgrimages
in North America. On Dec. 9, 1531, the Blessed Virgin
Mary appeared to an Indian convert, Juan Diego, and
left with him a picture of herself impressed upon his
cloak. Devotion to Mary under this title has continually
increased and today she is Patroness of the Americas.

Common of the Blessed Virgin Mary, p. 1040.

OPENING PRAYER

God of power and mercy,
you blessed the Americas at Tepeyac
with the presence of the Virgin Mary of Guadalupe.
May her prayers help all men and women
to accept each other as brothers and sisters.
Through your justice present in our hearts
may your peace reign in the world.
We ask this through our Lord Jesus Christ, your Son,
who lives and reigns with you and the Holy Spirit,
one God, for ever and ever. ℟. **Amen.**

Reading I (Zec 2, 14-17), p. 1124, no. 11.
Responsorial Psalm (Lk 1), p. 1128, no. 5.
Gospel (Lk 11, 27-28), p. 1136, no. 9.

———————

The Same Day, Dec. 12

ST. JANE FRANCES DE CHANTAL, Religious

Optional Memorial

Under the direction of St. Francis de Sales, St. Jane
Frances de Chantal founded the "Order of the Visitation." She died at Moulins, in 1641.

Common of Holy Men and Women: for Religious, p.
1097.

OPENING PRAYER
Lord,
you chose St. Jane Frances to serve you
both in marriage and in religious life.
By her prayers
help us to be faithful in our vocation
and always to be the light of the world.
We ask this through our Lord Jesus Christ, your Son,
who lives and reigns with you and the Holy Spirit,
one God, for ever and ever. ℟. **Amen.**

Reading I (Prv 31, 10-31. 19-20. 30-31), p. 1200, no. 11.
Responsorial Psalm (Ps 131), p. 1210, no. 8.
Gospel (Mk 3, 31-35), p. 1226, no. 11.

Dec. 13 — ST. LUCY, Virgin and Martyr

Memorial

St. Lucy is the name of an early martyr of Syracuse
(Sicily) honored in the Roman Church from the 6th
century onward. She is invoked for protection against
eye ailments.

Common of Martyrs, p. 1056; or Common of Virgins, p.
1085.

OPENING PRAYER
Lord,
give us courage through the prayers of St. Lucy.
As we celebrate her entrance into eternal glory,
we ask to share her happiness in the life to come.
Grant this through our Lord Jesus Christ, your Son,
who lives and reigns with you and the Holy Spirit,
one God, for ever and ever. ℟. **Amen.**

Reading I (2 Cor 10, 17—11, 2), p. 1212, no. 4.
Responsorial Psalm (Ps 31), p. 1144, no. 1.
Gospel (Mt 25, 1-13), p. 1223, no. 8.

Dec. 14 — ST. JOHN OF THE CROSS,
Priest and Doctor

Memorial

John Yepez was born at Fontiberas in Old Castile, Spain, in 1524. He took the Carmelite habit in 1563 and gave himself up to the practice of the greatest austerities. Later he collaborated with St. Teresa of Avila in reforming the Carmelite Order. He is known in the Church as one of the greatest contemplatives and teachers of mystical theology. After much physical and mental suffering, he died in peace in 1591.

ENTRANCE ANT.   Gal 6, 14

I should boast of nothing but the cross of our Lord Jesus Christ; through him the world is crucified to me, and I to the world.   → No. 2, p. 614

OPENING PRAYER

Father,
you endowed John of the Cross with a spirit of self-denial
and a love of the cross.
By following his example,
may we come to the eternal vision of your glory.
We ask this through our Lord Jesus Christ, your Son,
who lives and reigns with you and the Holy Spirit,
one God, for ever and ever. ℟. **Amen.**

Readings and Intervenient Chants are taken from the Common of Doctors of the Church, p. 1177, or the Common of Holy Men and Women: for Religious, p. 1195.

Reading I (1 Cor 2, 1-10), p. 1182, no. 2.
Responsorial Psalm (Ps 37), p. 1181, no. 2.
Gospel (Lk 14, 25-33), p. 1230, no. 19.

PRAYER OVER THE GIFTS

Almighty God,
look upon the gifts we offer
in memory of St. John of the Cross.
May we imitate the love we proclaim
as we celebrate the mystery

of the suffering and death of Christ,
who is Lord for ever and ever.
℟. **Amen.**   ➔ No. 21, p. 626 (Pref. P.1)

COMMUNION ANT.   Mt 16, 24
**If anyone wishes to come after me, he must re-
nounce himself, take up his cross, and follow me,
says the Lord.** ✟

PRAYER AFTER COMMUNION
God our Father,
you have shown us the mystery of the cross
in the life of St. John.
May this sacrifice make us strong,
keep us faithful to Christ
and help us to work in the Church
for the salvation of all mankind.
We ask this in the name of Jesus the Lord.
℟. **Amen.**   ➔ No. 32, p. 650

Dec. 21 — ST. PETER CANISIUS, Priest and Doctor

Optional Memorial

This eminent Jesuit, who was born in Holland, became
the second great Apostle of Germany. He enriched the
Church with his standard Catechism and won the title
of Doctor of the Church. He died in 1598.

*Common of Pastors, p. 1071; or Common of Doctors of
the Church, p. 1082.*

OPENING PRAYER
Lord,
you gave St. Peter Canisius
wisdom and courage to defend the Catholic faith.
By the help of his prayers
may all who seek the truth rejoice in finding you,
and may all who believe in you
be loyal in professing their faith.
Grant this through our Lord Jesus Christ, your Son,
who lives and reigns with you and the Holy Spirit,
one God, for ever and ever. ℟. **Amen.**

Reading I (2 Tm 4, 1-5), p. 1169, no. 12.
Responsorial Psalm (Ps 40), p. 218.
Gospel (Mt 5, 13-16), p. 1220, no. 2.

Dec. 23 — ST. JOHN OF KANTY, Priest

Optional Memorial

Born at Kanty, Poland, St. John attended the University of Cracow, where he later became a professor. He was famous for his charity and love for the poor. He died in 1473.

Common of Pastors, p. 1071; or Common of Holy Men and Women: for Those Who Work for the Underprivileged, p. 1099.

OPENING PRAYER

Almighty Father,
through the example of John of Kanty
may we grow in the wisdom of the saints.
As we show understanding and kindness to others,
may we receive your forgiveness.
We ask this through our Lord Jesus Christ, your Son,
who lives and reigns with you and the Holy Spirit,
one God, for ever and ever. ℟. **Amen.**

Reading I (Jas 2, 14-17), p. 1215, no. 12.
Responsorial Psalm (Ps 112), p. 1209, no. 6.
Gospel (Mt 25, 31-46), p. 1225, no. 10.

Dec. 26, 27, 28

See pp. 91-101.

Dec. 29 — ST. THOMAS BECKET, Bishop and Martyr

Optional Memorial

Thomas Becket, after having served as chancellor of Henry II, was made Archbishop of Canterbury. He fought against the King for the liberty of the Church. He was slain, December 29, 1171.

Common of Martyrs, p. 1056; or Common of Pastors: for Bishops, p. 1069.

OPENING PRAYER

Almighty God,
you granted the martyr Thomas
the grace to give his life for the cause of justice.
By his prayers
make us willing to renounce for Christ
our life in this world
so that we may find it in heaven.
We ask this through our Lord Jesus Christ, your Son,
who lives and reigns with you and the Holy Spirit,
one God, for ever and ever. ℟. **Amen.**

Reading I (2 Tm 2, 8-13; 3, 10-12), p. 1148, no. 5.
Responsorial Psalm (Ps 34), p. 1144, no. 2.
Gospel (Mt 16, 24-27), p. 1222, no. 5.

Dec. 31 — ST. SYLVESTER I, Pope

Optional Memorial

Little is known of the reign of Pope Sylvester I. He took
an active part in the negotiations in regard to the
heresy of Arius and the first Ecumenical Council of
Nicea in 325. He died in 335.

Common of Pastors: for Popes, p. 1066.

OPENING PRAYER

Lord,
help and sustain your people
by the prayers of Pope Sylvester.
Guide us always in this present life
and bring us to the joy that never ends.
We ask this through our Lord Jesus Christ, your Son,
who lives and reigns with you and the Holy Spirit,
one God, for ever and ever. ℟. **Amen.**

Reading I (Ez 34, 11-16), p. 1158, no. 9.
Responsorial Psalm (Ps 23), p. 1161, no. 2.
Gospel (Mt 28, 16-20), p. 1171, no. 3.

— JANUARY —

Jan. 2 — STS. BASIL THE GREAT AND GREGORY NAZIANZEN, Bishops and Doctors

Memorial

St. Basil, one of the four great Doctors of the East, was born at Cappadocia in Asia Minor. He became a monk and combatted the Arian heresy with great zeal. He wrote the famous Basilian rule of monasticism and framed the Basilian Liturgy. He died in 379.

St. Gregory, called "The Theologian," because of his profound knowledge of Sacred Scripture, was born at Nazianzen of Cappadocia, Asia Minor. He became successively the Bishop of Sosina, Nazianzen, and Patriach of Constantinople. He died in the latter part of the 4th century after having written many pious works of Scriptural eloquence.

Common of Pastors: for Bishops, p. 1069; or Common of Doctors of the Church, p. 1082.

OPENING PRAYER

God our Father,
you inspired the Church
with the example and teaching of your saints Basil
    and Gregory.
In humility may we come to know your truth
and put it into action with faith and love.
Grant this through our Lord Jesus Christ, your Son,
who lives and reigns with you and the Holy Spirit,
one God, for ever and ever. ℟. **Amen.**

Reading I (Eph 4, 1-7. 11-13), p. 1167, no. 8.
Responsorial Psalm (Ps 23), p. 1161, no. 2.
Gospel (Mt 23, 8-12), p. 1171, no. 2.

[In the dioceses of the United States]

Jan. 4 — ST. ELIZABETH ANN SETON, Widow

Memorial

Upon the death of her husband, by whom she had five children, Elizabeth Seton became a convert and in 1809 established a religious community of teaching sisters. She died in 1821 at the age of 46 and was beatified in 1963. She was canonized in September 1975.

Common of Holy Men and Women, p. 1090.

OPENING PRAYER

Lord God,
you blessed Elizabeth Seton with gifts of grace
as wife and mother, educator and foundress,
so that she might spend her life in service to your
   people.
Through her example and prayers
may we learn to express our love for you
in love for our fellow men and women . . .
We ask this . . . ℟. **Amen.**

Reading I (Phil 3, 8-14), p. 1214, no. 9.
Responsorial Psalm (Ps 16), p. 1207, no. 3.
Gospel (Mk 9, 34-37), p. 1226, no. 12.

[In the dioceses of the United States]

Jan. 5 — BL. JOHN NEUMANN, Bishop
Memorial

Born in Bohemia in 1811, John Neumann came to the United States, became a priest, and joined the Redemptorists. In 1852 he was consecrated bishop of Philadelphia and labored zealously to establish parish schools and erect many parishes. He died in 1860 and was beatified in 1963.

Common of Pastors: for Bishops, p. 1069,

OPENING PRAYER

Father,
you called blessed John Neumann to labor for the
   gospel
among the people of the new world.
His ministry strengthened many others in the Christian faith:
through his prayers may faith grow strong in this
   land.

Grant this ... ℟. **Amen.**

Reading I (2 Cor 4, 1-2. 5-7), p. 1166, no. 6.
Responsorial Psalm (Ps 16), p. 1160, no. 1.
Gospel (Lk 22, 24-30), p. 1174, no. 8.

Jan. 7 — ST. RAYMOND OF PENYAFORT, Priest

Optional Memorial

Born at Barcelona, Spain, in 1175, St. Raymond labored
zealously for the redemption of slaves. By order of Gregory IX he wrote five books of Decretals which are now
a valuable part of the Canon Law of the Church. He
died in 1275.

Common of Pastors, p. 1071.

OPENING PRAYER

Lord,
you gave St. Raymond the gift of compassion
in his ministry to sinners.
May his prayers free us from the slavery of sin
and help us to love and serve you in liberty.
We ask this through our Lord Jesus Christ, your Son,
who lives and reigns with you and the Holy Spirit,
one God, for ever and ever. ℟. **Amen.**

Reading I (2 Cor 5, 14-20), p. 1166, no. 7.
Responsorial Psalm (Ps 103), p. 1208, no. 5.
Gospel (Lk 12, 35-40), p. 1230, no. 18.

Jan. 13 — ST. HILARY, Bishop and Doctor

Optional Memorial

St. Hilary, Bishop of Poitiers, one of the greatest religious luminaries of France in the 4th century, strenuously defended the Church against the Arian heresy.
He wrote 12 books about the Holy Trinity. He died in
368.

*Common of Pastors: for Bishops, p. 1069; or Common
of Doctors of the Church, p. 1082.*

OPENING PRAYER

All-powerful God,
as St. Hilary defended the divinity of Christ your
    Son,

give us a deeper understanding of this mystery
and help us to profess it in all truth.
Grant this through our Lord Jesus Christ, your Son,
who lives and reigns with you and the Holy Spirit,
one God, for ever and ever. ℞. **Amen.** ▼

READING I   1 Jn 2, 18-25

John warns that many antichrists have appeared. They show that they
are imposters because of what they say and do. They are not of the
truth, and they deny that Jesus is the Christ, the Son of God. Jesus
alone is the promise of eternal life.

A reading from the first letter of John

Children, it is the final hour;
just as you heard that the Antichrist was coming,
so now many such antichrists have appeared.
This makes us certain that it is the final hour.
It was from our ranks that they took their leave—
not that they really belonged to us;
for if they had really belonged to us,
they would have stayed with us.
It only served to show that none of them was ours.
But you have the anointing that comes from the
    Holy One,
so that all knowledge is yours.
My reason for having written you
is not that you do not know the truth
but that you do,
and that no lie has anything in common with the
    truth.
Who is the liar?
He who denies that Jesus is the Christ.
He is the antichrist,
denying the Father and the Son.
Anyone who denies the Son
has no claim on the Father,
but he who acknowledges the Son
can claim the Father as well.
As for you,
let what you heard from the beginning
remain in your hearts.

If what you heard from the beginning
does remain in your hearts,
then you in turn will remain in the Son and in the
Father.
He himself made us a promise
and the promise is no less than this:
eternal life.
This is the Word of the Lord. ℟. **Thanks be to God.** ✠

Responsorial Psalm Ps 110, 1. 2. 3. 4

℟. (4) **You are a priest for ever,
in the line of Melchizedek.**

The Lord said to my Lord: "Sit at my right hand
till I make your enemies your footstool." — ℟

The scepter of your power the Lord will stretch
forth from Zion:
"Rule in the midst of your enemies. — ℟

Yours is princely power in the day of your birth,
in holy spendor;
before the daystar, like the dew, I have begotten
you." — ℟

The Lord has sworn, and he will not repent:
"You are a priest forever, according to the order
of Melchizedek." — ℟ ✠

Gospel (Mt 5, 13-16), p. 1186, no. 1.

Jan. 17 — ST. ANTHONY, Abbot

Memorial

At eighteen years of age, St. Anthony retired to the desert. He is called the Patriarch of Monks, not that before his advent the monastical life was non-existent, but precisely because he was the first Abbot to form a stable rule for his family of monks dedicated to Divine Service. He died in 356, at 105 years of age.

ENTRANCE ANT. Ps 92, 13-14

The just man will flourish like the palm tree. Planted in the courts of God's house, he will grow like the cedars of Lebanon.

➤ No. 2, p. 614

OPENING PRAYER

Father,
you called St. Anthony
to renounce the world
and serve you in the solitude of the desert.
By his prayers and example,
may we learn to deny ourselves
and to love you above all things.
We ask this through our Lord Jesus Christ, your Son,
who lives and reigns with you and the Holy Spirit,
one God, for ever and ever. ℞. **Amen.**

*Readings and Intervenient Chants from the Common of
Holy Men and Women: for Religious, p. 1195.*

Reading I (Eph 6, 10-13. 18), p. 1213, no. 8.
Responsorial Psalm (Ps 16), p. 1160, no. 1.

GOSPEL   Mt 19, 16-26

Alleluia (Jn 8, 31-32)

℞. **Alleluia.** If you stay in my word, you will indeed
   be my disciples,
and you will know the truth, says the Lord. ℞. **Alleluia.**

Jesus teaches that to attain everlasting life, it is necessary to keep
the commandments. To seek absolute perfection, however, Jesus
counsels his disciples to sell all their possessions, give to the poor,
and then follow him.

℣. The Lord be with you. ℞. **And also with you.**
✠ A reading from the holy gospel according to Matthew. ℞. **Glory to you, Lord.**

A man came up to Jesus and said, "Teacher, what
good must I do to possess everlasting life?" He answered, "Why do you question me about what is
good? There is One who is good. If you wish to enter
into life, keep the commandments." "Which ones?"
he asked. Jesus replied, " 'You shall not kill'; 'You
shall not commit adultery'; 'You shall not steal'; 'You
shall not bear false witness'; 'Honor your father and
your mother'; and 'Love your neighbor as yourself.' "
The young man said to him, "I have kept all these;

what do I need to do further?" Jesus told him, "If you seek perfection, go, sell your possessions, and give to the poor. You will then have treasure in heaven. Afterward, come back and follow me." Hearing these words, the young man went away sad, for his possessions were many.

Jesus said to his disciples: "I assure you, only with difficulty will a rich man enter into the kingdom of God. I repeat what I said: it is easier for a camel to pass through a needle's eye than for a rich man to enter the kingdom of God." When the disciples heard this they were completely overwhelmed, and exclaimed, "Then who can be saved?" Jesus looked at them and said, "For man it is impossible; but for God all things are possible."—This is the gospel of the Lord. ℟. **Praise to you, Lord Jesus Christ.**

➤ No. 15, p. 623

PRAYER OVER THE GIFTS

Lord,
accept the sacrifice we offer at your altar
in commemoration of St. Anthony.
May no earthly attractions keep us from loving you.
Grant this through Christ our Lord.
℟. **Amen.**   ➤ No. 21, p. 626, (Pref. P 37-42)

COMMUNION ANT.   Mt 19, 21

If you wish to be perfect, go, sell what you own, give it all to the poor, then come, follow me. ⱽ

PRAYER AFTER COMMUNION

Lord,
you helped St. Anthony conquer the powers of darkness.
May your sacrament strengthen us
in our struggle with evil.
We ask this in the name of Jesus the Lord.
℟. **Amen.**   ➤ No. 32, p. 650

Jan. 20 — ST. FABIAN, Pope and Martyr

Optional Memorial

St. Fabian, Supreme Pontiff, suffered martyrdom in 250 during the persecution of Decius.

Common of Martyrs, p. 1056; or Common of Pastors: for Popes, p. 1066.

OPENING PRAYER

God our Father, glory of your priests,
may the prayers of your martyr Fabian
help us to share his faith
and offer you loving service.
Grant this through our Lord Jesus Christ, your Son,
who lives and reigns with you and the Holy Spirit,
one God, for ever and ever. ℟. **Amen.**

Reading I (1 Pt 5, 1-4), p. 1169, no. 13.
Responsorial Psalm (Ps 40), p. 218.
Gospel (Jn 21, 15-17), p. 1176, no. 11.

The Same Day, Jan. 20
ST. SEBASTIAN, Martyr

St. Sebastian, finding life too easy in his native city of Milan, went to Rome where Christians were valiantly suffering for their faith. He became their companion and "he too suffered and was crowned" (St. Ambrose).

Common of Martyrs, p. 1056.

OPENING PRAYER

Lord,
fill us with that spirit of courage
which gave your martyr Sebastian
strength to offer his life in faithful witness.
Help us to learn from him to cherish your law
and to obey you rather than men.
We ask this through our Lord Jesus Christ, your Son,
who lives and reigns with you and t he Holy Spirit,
one God, for ever and ever. ℟. **Amen.**

Reading I (1 Pt 3, 14-17), p. 1149, no. 8.
Responsorial Psalm (Ps 34), p. 1144, no. 2.
Gospel (Mt 10, 28-33), p. 1151, no. 2.

Jan. 21 — ST. AGNES, Virgin and Martyr

Memorial

According to St. Augustine and St. Ambrose, St. Agnes, a noble Roman virgin, was about thirteen years of age when she won the martyr's crown. She was tortured by fire or decapitated in 304. Her name is inscribed in Eucharistic Prayer No. 1, and she is universally venerated as the Patroness of the Children of Mary Sodality.

Common of Martyrs, p. 1056; or Common of Virgins, p. 1085.

OPENING PRAYER

Almighty, eternal God,
you choose what the world considers weak
to put the worldly power to shame.
May we who celebrate the birth of St. Agnes into
    eternal joy
be loyal to the faith she professed.
Grant this through our Lord Jesus Christ, your Son,
who lives and reigns with you and the Holy Spirit,
one God, for ever and ever. ℞. **Amen.**

Reading I (1 Cor 1, 26-31), p. 1211, no. 2.
Responsorial Psalm (Ps 23), p. 1161, no. 2.
Gospel (Mt 13, 44-46), p. 1221, no. 4.

Jan. 22 — ST. VINCENT, Deacon and Martyr

Optional Memorial

St. Vincent, born at Huesca in Spain, is one of the great Deacons of the Church. For his defense of Christianity he suffered martyrdom about 300.

Common of Martyrs, p. 1056.

OPENING PRAYER

Eternal Father,
you gave St. Vincent
the courage to endure torture and death for the
    gospel:
fill us with your Spirit

and strengthen us in your love.
We ask this through our Lord Jesus Christ, your Son,
who lives and reigns with you and the Holy Spirit,
one God, for ever and ever. ℞. **Amen.**

Reading I (2 Cor 4, 7-15), p. 1147, no. 3.
Responsorial Psalm (Ps 34), p. 1144, no. 2.
Gospel (Mt 10, 17-22), p. 1151, no. 1.

Jan. 24 — ST. FRANCIS DE SALES,
Bishop and Doctor

Memorial

St. Francis was born near Annecy in Savoy in 1567.
After many victories and conversions which were the
fruits of his apostolic zeal in combatting Calvinism, St.
Francis succeeded to the bishopric of Geneva. With St.
Frances de Chantal he founded the *Visitation Order*.
After writing several devout treatises for the edification
of the faithful, he died at Lyons, France in 1622. He
was canonized in 1655, and in 1877, Pius IX placed him
among the Doctors of the Church.

*Common of Pastors: for Bishops, p. 1069; or Common
of Doctors of the Church, p. 1082.*

OPENING PRAYER

Father,
you gave Francis de Sales the spirit of compassion
to befriend all men on the way to salvation.
By his example, lead us to show your gentle love
in the service of our fellow men.
Grant this through our Lord Jesus Christ, your Son,
who lives and reigns with you and the Holy Spirit,
one God, for ever and ever. ℞. **Amen.**

Reading I (Eph 3, 8-12), p. 1183, no. 4.
Responsorial Psalm (Ps 37), p. 1181, no. 2.
Gospel (Jn 15, 9-17), p. 1232, no. 21.

PRAYER OVER THE GIFTS

Lord,
by this offering
may the divine fire of your Holy Spirit.

which burned in the gentle heart of Francis de Sales,
inspire us with compassion and love.
We ask this through Christ our Lord.
℞. **Amen.** ➤ No. 21, p. 626

PRAYER AFTER COMMUNION

Merciful Father,
may the sacrament we have received
help us to imitate Francis de Sales in love and
    service;
bring us to share with him the glory of heaven.
We ask this in the name of Jesus the Lord.
℞. **Amen.** ➤ No. 32, p. 650

Jan. 25 — CONVERSION OF ST. PAUL, Apostle

Feast

The conversion of Saul while journeying to Damascus
is perhaps the greatest miracle in the history of the
Primitive Church. The doctrine of the Mystical Body of
Christ which teaches us that all the faithful are members of the same Body, whose Head Christ is, receives a
very clear meaning in the words of Christ addressed to
Saul, the persecutor of Christians: "Saul, Saul, why do
you persecute me?"

ENTRANCE ANT. 2 Tm 1, 12; 4, 8

**I know whom I have believed. I am sure that he, the
just judge, will guard my pledge until the day of
judgment.** ➤ No. 2, p. 614

OPENING PRAYER

God our Father,
you taught the gospel to all the world
through the preaching of Paul your apostle.
May we who celebrate his conversion to the faith
follow him in bearing witness to your truth.
We ask this through our Lord Jesus Christ, your Son,
who lives and reigns with you and the Holy Spirit,
one God, for ever and ever. ℞. **Amen.** ⩔

READING I   Acts 22, 3-16

Before the mission to the Gentiles is officially begun, Luke must
incorporate Saul into the early Church. The narrative of Saul's
conversion is introduced. It is not merely a conversion story; it is
rather the story of his call "to the Gentiles."

A reading from the Acts of the Apostles

Paul told the people: "I am a Jew, born in Tarsus
in Cilicia, but I was brought up in this city. Here I
sat at the feet of Gamaliel and was educated strictly
in the law of our fathers. I was a staunch defender
of God, just as all of you are today. Furthermore I
persecuted this new way to the point of death. I arrested and imprisoned both men and women.

"On this point the high priest and the whole council of elders can bear me witness, for it was from
them that I received letters to our brother Jews in
Damascus. I set out with the intention of bringing
the prisoners I would arrest back to Jerusalem for
punishment. As I was traveling along, approaching
Damascus around noon, a great light from the sky
suddenly flashed all about me. I fell to the ground
and heard a voice say to me, 'Saul, Saul, why do you
persecute me?' I answered, 'Who are you, sir?' He
said to me, 'I am Jesus the Nazorean whom you are
persecuting.' My companions saw the light but did
not hear the voice speaking to me. 'What is it I must
do, sir?' I asked, and the Lord replied, 'Get up and go
into Damascus. There you will be told about everything you are destined to do.' But since I could not
see because of the brilliance of the light, I had to be
taken by the hand and led into Damascus by my
companions.

"A certain Ananias, a devout observer of the law
and well spoken of by all the Jews who lived there,
came and stood by me. 'Saul, my brother,' he said,
'recover your sight.' In that instant I regained my
sight and looked at him. The next thing he said was,
'The God of our fathers long ago designated you to
know his will, to look upon the Just One, and to hear

the sound of his voice; before all men you are to be his witness to what you have seen and heard. Why delay, then? Be baptized at once and wash away your sins as you call upon his name.' "—This is the Word of the Lord. ℟. **Thanks be to God.** ℣

OR

READING I   Acts 9, 1-22

Saul in his former life persecuted the Church founded by Jesus Christ. The reality of Saul's vision on the road to Damascus is recognized as the operation of grace bestowed upon him by the Lord. Henceforth, Jesus will make of him a servant and take possession of him.

A reading from the Acts of the Apostles

Saul, still breathing murderous threats against the Lord's disciples, went to the high priest and asked him for letters to the synagogues in Damascus which would empower him to arrest and bring to Jerusalem anyone he might find, man or woman, living according to the new way. As he traveled along and was approaching Damascus, a light from the sky suddenly flashed about him. He fell to the ground and at the same time heard a voice saying, "Saul, Saul, why do you persecute me?" "Who are you, sir?" he asked. The voice answered, "I am Jesus, the one you are persecuting. Get up and go into the city, where you will be told what to do." The men who were traveling with him stood there speechless. They had heard the voice but could see no one. Saul got up from the ground unable to see, even though his eyes were open. They had to take him by the hand and lead him into Damascus. For three days he continued blind, during which time he neither ate nor drank.

There was a disciple in Damascus named Ananias to whom the Lord had appeared in a vision. "Ananias!" he said. "Here I am, Lord," came the answer. The Lord said to him, "Go at once to Straight Street, and at the house of Judas ask for a certain Saul of Tarsus. He is there praying." (Saul saw in a vision a man named Ananias coming to him and placing his

hands on him so that he might recover his sight.) But
Ananias protested: "Lord, I have heard from many
sources about this man and all the harm he has done
to your holy people in Jerusalem. He is here now
with authorization from the chief priests to arrest
any who invoke your name." The Lord said to him:
"You must go! This man is the instrument I have
chosen to bring my name to the Gentiles and their
kings and to the people of Israel. I myself shall indicate to him how much he will have to suffer for my
name." With that Ananias left. When he entered the
house he laid his hands on Saul and said, "Saul, my
brother, I have been sent by the Lord Jesus who appeared to you on the way here, to help you recover
your sight and be filled with the Holy Spirit." Immediately something like scales fell from his eyes
and he regained his sight. He got up and was baptized, and his strength returned to him after he had
taken food.

Saul stayed some time with the disciples in Damascus, and soon began to proclaim in the synagogues that Jesus was the Son of God. Any who
heard it were greatly taken aback. They kept saying:
"Isn't this the man who worked such havoc in Jerusalem among those who invoke this name? Did he
not come here purposely to apprehend such people
and bring them before the chief priests?"

Saul for his part grew steadily more powerful, and
reduced the Jewish community of Damascus to silence with his proofs that this Jesus was the Messiah.
—This is the Word of the Lord. ℟. **Thanks be to
God.** ℣

Responsorial Psalm   Ps 117, 1. 2

℟. (Mk 16, 15) **Go out to all the world,
    and tell the Good News.**

Praise the Lord, all you nations;
    glorify him, all you peoples! — ℟

For steadfast is his kindness toward us,
    and the fidelity of the Lord endures forever.— ℟ ⍖

℟. Or: **Alleluia.** ⍖

GOSPEL Mk 16, 15-18

Alleluia (Jn 15, 16)

℟. **Alleluia.** I have chosen you from the world,
    says the Lord,
to go and bear fruit that will last. ℟. **Alleluia.**

Christ's commission to his disciples is emphatic. Repentance and remission of sins is to be preached among all nations. In spreading this gospel, they are to be saved from danger.

℣. The Lord be with you. ℟. **And also with you.**
✠ A reading from the holy gospel according to Mark
℟. **Glory to you, Lord.**

Jesus appeared to the Eleven and said to them: "Go into the whole world and proclaim the good news to all creation. The man who believes in it and accepts baptism will be saved; the man who refuses to believe in it will be condemned. Signs like these will accompany those who have professed their faith: they will use my name to expel demons, they will speak entirely new languages, they will be able to handle serpents, they will be able to drink deadly poison without harm, and the sick upon whom they lay their hands will recover."—This is the gospel of the Lord. ℟. **Praise to you, Lord Jesus Christ.**

➤ No. 15, p. 623

PRAYER OVER THE GIFTS
Lord,
may your Spirit who helped Paul the apostle
to preach your power and glory
fill us with the light of faith
as we celebrate this holy eucharist.
We ask this in the name of Jesus the Lord.
℟. **Amen.**
➤ No. 21, p. 626 (Pref. P 64-65)

COMMUNION ANT. Gal 2, 20
I live by faith in the Son of God, who loved me and sacrificed himself for me. ⍖

PRAYER AFTER COMMUNION

Lord God,
you filled Paul the apostle
with love for all the churches:
may the sacrament we have received
foster in us this love for your people.
Grant this through Christ our Lord.
R̸. **Amen.** → No. 32, p. 650

Jan. 26 — STS. TIMOTHY AND TITUS, Bishops

Memorial

When St. Paul preached at Ephesus, Timothy admired his virtues, renounced all his worldly possessions in order to be his disciple, and accompanied him in the evangelization of many cities. He was consecrated Bishop of Ephesus by St. Paul. He died in the year 97.

St. Titus was the friend and disciple of St. Paul. He was also ordained Bishop of Crete by St. Paul. One of the canonical epistles addressed by St. Paul to Titus forms part of the New Testament. He died at the age of 105. St. John Chrysostom and St. Jerome eulogized him.

Common of Pastors: for Bishops, p. 1069.

OPENING PRAYER

God our Father,
you gave your saints Timothy and Titus
the courage and wisdom of the apostles:
may their prayers help us to live holy lives
and lead us to heaven, our true home.
Grant this through our Lord Jesus Christ, your Son,
who lives and reigns with you and the Holy Spirit,
one God, for ever and ever. R̸. **Amen.** ♥

Reading I is special in this Memorial and one of the following is always to be read.

READING I   2 Tm 1, 1-8

Paul sees God's power at work in the souls of all Christians and in his fellow worker, Timothy. Paul reminds Timothy of God's gift of grace which dwells in him as a result of the imposition of hands. As an office-bearer, Timothy has received, together with this gift of grace, the Spirit of strength and love.

The beginning of the second letter of Paul to
Timothy

Paul, by the will of God an apostle of Christ Jesus
sent to proclaim the promise of life in him, to Timothy, my child whom I love. May grace, mercy, and
peace from God the Father and from Christ Jesus
our Lord be with you.

I thank God, the God of my forefathers whom I
worship with a clear conscience, whenever I remember you in my prayers—as indeed I do constantly,
night and day. Recalling your tears when we parted,
I yearn to see you again. That would make my happiness complete. I find myself thinking of your sincere faith—faith which first belonged to your grand-
mother Lois and to your mother Eunice, and which
(I am confident) you also have.

For this reason, I remind you to stir into flame
the gift of God bestowed when my hands were laid
on you. The Spirit God has given us is no cowardly
spirit, but rather one that makes us strong, loving,
and wise. Therefore, never be ashamed of your testimony to our Lord, nor of me, a prisoner for his
sake, but with the strength which comes from God
bear your share of the hardship which the gospel
entails.—This is the Word of the Lord. ℟. **Thanks
be to God.** ⅴ

OR

READING I   Ti 1, 1-5

In the beginning of his letter to Titus, Paul calls himself an apostle.
Without reservation, he acknowledges his mission to spread the work
of God. Paul tells Titus to carry on the work he started, especially to
appoint more leaders in the Church.

The beginning of the letter of Paul to Titus

Paul, a servant of God, sent as an apostle of Jesus
Christ for the sake of the faith of those whom God
has chosen, and to promote their knowledge of the
truth as our religion embodies it, in the hope of that
eternal life which God, who cannot lie, promised in

endless ages past. This he has now manifested in
his own good time as his word, in the preaching entrusted to me by the command of God our Savior.
Paul to Titus, my own true child in our common
faith: May grace and peace from God our Father,
and Christ Jesus our Savior, be with you.

My purpose in leaving you in Crete was that you
might accomplish what had been left undone, especially the appointment of presbyters in every town,
as I instructed you.—This is the Word of the Lord.
℟. **Thanks be to God.** ♥

Responsorial Psalm   Ps 37, 3-4. 5-6. 23-24. 39-40
℟. (39) **The salvation of the just comes from the
    Lord.**

Trust in the Lord and do good,
    that you may dwell in the land and enjoy security.
Take delight in the Lord,
    and he will grant you your heart's requests. —℟

Commit to the Lord your way;
    trust in him, and he will act.
He will make justice dawn for you like the light;
    bright as the noonday shall be your vindica-
        tion. — ℟

By the Lord are the steps of a man made firm,
    and he approves his way.
Though he fall, he does not lie prostrate,
    for the hand of the Lord sustains him. — ℟

The salvation of the just is from the Lord;
    he is their refuge in time of distress.
And the Lord helps them and delivers them;
    he delivers them from the wicked and saves them,
        because they take refuge in him. — ℟ ♥

Gospel (Lk 10, 1-9), p. 1174, no. 7.

Jan. 27 — ST. ANGELA MERICI, Virgin

Optional Memorial

St. Angela was born on the shores of Lake Giarda. She founded the Order of the *Ursulines,* the first teaching Order for women approved by the Church. She died in 1540.

Common of Virgins, p. 1085; or Common of Holy Men and Women: for Teachers, p. 1101.

OPENING PRAYER

Lord,
may St. Angela commend us to your mercy;
may her charity and wisdom help us
to be faithful to your teaching
and to follow it in our lives.
We ask this through our Lord Jesus Christ, your Son,
who lives and reigns with you and the Holy Spirit,
one God, for ever and ever. ℟. **Amen.**

Reading I (1 Pt 4, 7-11), p. 1216, no. 14.
Responsorial Psalm (Ps 148), p. 1191, no. 2.
Gospel (Mk 9, 34-37), p. 1226, no. 12.

Jan. 28 — ST. THOMAS AQUINAS, Priest and Doctor

Memorial

His undisputed mastery in scholastic theology gained for him the title of *Angelic Doctor.* He is one of the greatest glories of the Dominican Order. Pope Leo XIII declared him patron of all Catholic Schools. He left the great monument of his learning, the *Summa Theologica,* unfinished, for, on his way to the Council of Lyons, in 1274, he fell sick and died in the Cistercian monastery of Fossa Nuova, Italy.

Common of Doctors of the Church, p. 1082; or Common of Pastors, p. 1071.

OPENING PRAYER

God our Father,
you made Thomas Aquinas known for his holiness
   and learning.
Help us to grow in wisdom by his teaching,

and in holiness by imitating his faith.
Grant this through our Lord Jesus Christ, your Son,
who lives and reigns with you and the Holy Spirit,
one God, for ever and ever. ℟.

*Readings and Intervenient Chants may also be taken
from the Common of Holy Men and Women: for Religious, p. 1195.*

Reading I (Wis 7, 7-10. 15-16), p. 1177, no. 2.
Responsorial Psalm (Ps 19), p. 1180, no. 1.
Gospel (Mt 23, 8-12), p. 1186, no. 2.

Jan. 31 — ST. JOHN BOSCO, Priest

Memorial

This admirable "Apostle of Youth" is almost our con-
temporary. He founded the Salesian Society of St.
Francis de Sales, and the Daughters of Mary, Help of
Christians. His lifework was consecrated to the care of
young boys and girls. He died in 1888 and was canonized
by Pope Pius XI in 1934. The motto on the Salesian
coat of arms: "Give me only souls and keep the rest,"
bears witness to Don Bosco's Christian ideal.

*Common of Pastors, p. 1071; or Common of Holy Men
and Women: for Teachers, p. 1101.*

OPENING PRAYER

Lord,
you called John Bosco
to be a teacher and father to the young.
Fill us with love like his:
may we give ourselves completely to your service
and to the salvation of mankind.
We ask this through our Lord Jesus Christ, your Son,
who lives and reigns with you and the Holy Spirit,
one God, for ever and ever. ℟. **Amen.**

Reading I (Phil 4, 4-9), p. 1214, no. 10.
Responsorial Psalm (Ps 112), p. 1209, no. 6.
Gospel (Mt 18, 1-4), p. 1222, no. 6.

— FEBRUARY —

Feb. 2 — PRESENTATION OF THE LORD

Feast

We have evidence going back to the 5th century of the celebration at Jerusalem of the feast of the Presentation of the Lord in the temple. The feast was accepted at Rome in the 7th century under the name Hypapante. Beginning with the 10th century Western liturgical books emphasized the purification of Mary, which henceforth gave its name to the feast. In full accord with the traditions of the Eastern Church, the Code of Rubrics in 1960 established that this must be regarded as a feast of the Lord.

Candles are blessed on this day, a symbolic representation of the words of holy Simeon concerning Christ: "A light of revelation to the Gentiles." A procession of the faithful with lighted candles is held to commemorate the entry of Christ, the Light of the World, into the temple of Jerusalem.

Blessing of Candles and Procession
FIRST FORM: PROCESSION

The people gather in a chapel or other suitable place outside the church where the Mass will be celebrated. They carry unlighted candles. The priest and his ministers wear white vestments. The priest may wear the cope instead of the chasuble during the procession.

While the candles are being lighted, this canticle or another hymn is sung:

The Lord will come with mighty power,
and give light to the eyes of all who serve him, alleluia.

The priest greets the people as usual, and briefly invites the people to take an active part in this celebration. He may use these or similar words:

Forty days ago we celebrated the joyful feast of the birth of our Lord Jesus Christ. Today we recall the holy day on which he was presented in the temple, fulfilling the law of Moses and at the same time going to meet his faithful people. Led by the Spirit, Simeon and Anna came to the temple, recognized

Christ as their Lord, and proclaimed him with joy.
United by the Spirit, may we now go to the house
of God to welcome Christ the Lord. There we shall
recognize him in the breaking of bread until he
comes again in glory.

Then the priest joins his hands and blesses the candles:

Let us pray.
God our Father, source of all light,
today you revealed to Simeon
your Light of revelation to the nations.
Bless ✣ these candles and make them holy.
May we who carry them to praise your glory
walk in the path of goodness
and come to the light that shines for ever.
Grant this through Christ our Lord. ℟. **Amen.** ▼

OR

Let us pray.
God our Father, source of eternal light,
fill the hearts of all believers
with the light of faith.
May we who carry these candles in your church
come with joy to the light of glory.
We ask this through Christ our Lord. ℟. **Amen.** ▼

He sprinkles the candles in silence
*The priest then takes the candle prepared for him, and
the procession begins with the acclamation:*

Let us go in peace to meet the Lord.

*During the procession, the following canticle or another
hymn is sung:*

ANTIPHON

**Christ is the light of the nations
and the glory of Israel his people.**

CANTICLE

**Now, Lord, you have kept your word:
let your servant go in peace.**

The Antiphon is repeated: "Christ is the light, etc."

With my own eyes I have seen the salvation which you have prepared in the sight of every people.

The Antiphon is repeated: "Christ is the light, etc."

A light to reveal you to the nations and the glory of your people Israel.

The Antiphon is repeated: "Christ is the light, etc."

As the procession enters the church, the Entrance Antiphon of the Mass is sung. When the priest reaches the altar, he venerates it, and may incense it. Then he goes to the chair (and replaces the cope with the chasuble). After the Gloria, *he sings or says the Opening Prayer. The Mass continues as usual.*

SECOND FORM: SOLEMN ENTRANCE

The people, carrying unlighted candles, assemble in the church. The priest, vested in white, is accompanied by his ministers and by a representative group of the faithful. They go to a suitable place (either in front of the door or in the church itself) where most of the congregation can easily take part.

Then the candles are lighted while the antiphon, Christ is the light, *or another hymn is sung.*

After the greeting and introduction, he blesses the candles, as above, and goes in procession to the altar, while all are singing. The Mass is as described above.

The Mass

ENTRANCE ANT.   Ps 48, 10-11

Within your temple, we ponder your loving kindness, O God. As your name, so also your praise reaches to the ends of the earth; your right hand is filled with justice.

→ No. 2, p. 614

OPENING PRAYER

All-powerful Father,
Christ your Son became man for us
and was presented in the temple.
May he free our hearts from sin
and bring us into your presence.
We ask this through our Lord Jesus Christ, your Son,

who lives and reigns with you and the Holy Spirit,
one God, for ever and ever. ℞. **Amen.** ▼

*When this feast occurs apart from Sunday, only one of
the first two readings is read before the Gospel.*

READING I   Mal 3, 1-4
Malachi presents the eschatological moment in the language of God's
great interventions in sacred history. Malachi does not reject the
Jerusalem sacrifice altogether, but he awaits its transformation just
as he expects the priestly messenger of the covenant to be perfected
and transcended by the Lord.

A reading from the book of the prophet Malachi

The Lord God said:
   Lo, I am sending my messenger
   to prepare the way before me;
   and suddenly there will come to the temple
   the Lord whom you seek,
      and the messenger of the covenant whom you
         desire.
   Yes, he is coming, says the Lord of hosts.
   But who will endure the day of his coming?
   And who can stand when he appears?
   For he is like the refiner's fire,
   or like the fuller's lye.
   He will sit refining and purifying [silver],
   and he will purify the sons of Levi,
   refining them like gold or like silver
   that they may offer due sacrifice to the Lord.
   Then the sacrifice of Judah and Jerusalem
   will please the Lord,
   as in the days of old, as in years gone by.
This is the Word of the Lord. ℞. **Thanks be to God.** ▼

Responsorial Psalm   Ps 24, 7. 8. 9. 10

℞. (8) **Who is this king of glory?**
   It is the Lord!

Lift up, O gates, your lintels;
   reach up, you ancient portals,
   that the king of glory may come in! — ℞

Who is this king of glory?

The Lord, strong and mighty,
  the Lord, mighty in battle. — ℟

Lift up, O gates, your lintels;
  reach up, you ancient portals,
    that the king of glory may come in! — ℟

Who is this king of glory?
  The Lord of hosts; he is the king of glory. — ℟ ℣

READING II   Heb 2, 14-18

In the biblical sense, "flesh" means human nature considered in its weakness and frailty. It is contrasted with "spirit" and God. Because of the connection between sin and death, Christ overcomes the power of death through his priestly work. In Christ's death and resurrection, the nature of death is changed.

A reading from the letter to the Hebrews

Now, since the children are men of blood and flesh, Jesus likewise had a full share in these, that by his death he might rob the devil, the prince of death, of his power, and free those who through fear of death had been slaves their whole life long. Surely he did not come to help angels, but rather the children of Abraham; therefore he had to become like his brothers in every way, that he might be a merciful and faithful high priest before God on their behalf, to expiate the sins of the people. Since he was himself tested through what he suffered, he is able to help those who are tempted.—This is the Word of the Lord. ℟. **Thanks be to God.** ℣

GOSPEL   Lk 2, 22-40 or 1, 22-32
Alleluia

℟. **Alleluia.** This is the light of revelation to the nations,
and the glory of your people, Israel. ℟. **Alleluia.**

Mary and Joseph come with the Christ Child to the temple ceremony to present Jesus according to the prescriptions of the Jewish law. Jesus is formally stamped as a member of God's chosen people through whom world salvation is to be achieved.

[If the "Short Form" is used, the indented text in brackets is omitted.]

℣. The Lord be with you. ℟. **And also with you.**
✠ A reading from the holy gospel according to Luke
℟. **Glory to you, Lord.**

When the day came to purify them according to the law of Moses, the couple brought Jesus up to Jerusalem so that he could be presented to the Lord, for it is written in the law of the Lord, "Every first-born male shall be consecrated to the Lord." They came to offer in sacrifice "a pair of turtledoves or two young pigeons," in accord with the dictate in the law of the Lord.

There lived in Jerusalem at the time a certain man named Simeon. He was just and pious, and awaited the consolation of Israel, and the Holy Spirit was upon him. It was revealed to him by the Holy Spirit that he would not experience death until he had seen the Anointed of the Lord. He came to the temple now, inspired by the Spirit; and when the parents brought in the child Jesus to perform for him the customary ritual of the law, he took him in his arms and blessed God in these words:

"Now, Master, you can dismiss your servant
    in peace;
  you have fulfilled your word.
For my eyes have witnessed your saving deed
    displayed for all the peoples to see:
A revealing light to the Gentiles,
    the glory of your people Israel."

[The child's father and mother were marveling at what was being said about him. Simeon blessed them and said to Mary his mother: "This child is destined to be the downfall and the rise of many in Israel, a sign that will be opposed—and you yourself shall be pierced with a sword—so that the thoughts of many hearts may be laid bare."

There was also a certain prophetess, Anna by name, daughter of Phanuel of the tribe of Asher. She had seen many days, having lived seven years with her husband after her marriage and then as a widow until she was eighty-four. She was constantly in the temple, worshiping day and night in fasting and prayer. Coming on the scene at this moment, she gave thanks to God and talked about the child to all who looked forward to the deliverance of Jerusalem.

When the pair had fulfilled all the prescriptions of the law of the Lord, they returned to Galilee and their own town of Nazareth. The child grew in size and strength, filled with wisdom, and the grace of God was upon him.]

This is the gospel of the Lord. ℟. **Praise to you, Lord Jesus Christ**
➔ No. 15, p. 623

PRAYER OVER THE GIFTS

Lord,
accept the gifts your Church offers you with joy,
since in fulfillment of your will
your Son offered himself as a lamb without blemish
for the life of the world.
We ask this through Christ our Lord. ℟. **Amen.** ♥

PREFACE (P 49)

℣. The Lord be with you. ℟. **And also with you.**
℣. Lift up your hearts. ℟. **We lift them up to the Lord.** ℣. Let us give thanks to the Lord our God.
℟. **It is right to give him thanks and praise.**

Father, all-powerful and ever-living God,
we do well always and everywhere to give you thanks
through Jesus Christ our Lord.

Today your Son,
who shares your eternal splendor,
was presented in the temple,

and revealed by the Spirit
as the glory of Israel
and the light of all peoples.

Our hearts are joyful,
for we have seen your salvation,
and now with the angels and saints
we praise you for ever:　　　　　　➜ No. 23, p. 627

COMMUNION ANT.　　　　　　　　　　Lk 2, 30-31

**With my own eyes I have seen the salvation which
you have prepared in the sight of all the nations.** ℣

PRAYER AFTER COMMUNION

Lord,
you fulfilled the hope of Simeon,
who did not die
until he had been privileged to welcome the Messiah.
May this communion perfect your grace in us
and prepare us to meet Christ
when he comes to bring us into everlasting life,
for he is Lord for ever and ever.
℟. **Amen.**　　　　　　　　　　　➜ No. 32, p. 650

*Optional Solemn Blessings, p. 682, and Prayers over
the People, p. 689.*

Feb. 3 — ST. BLASE, Bishop and Martyr

Optional Memorial

St. Blase, Bishop of Sebaste, was beheaded after terrible
torments, under Licinius in 317. Among his many miracles, there is cited one in which he cured a boy who was
choking from a fishbone. Thus, he is venerated as the
patron saint against diseases of the throat.

*Common of Martyrs, p. 1056; or Common of Pastors:
for Bishops, p. 1069.*

OPENING PRAYER

Lord,
hear the prayers of your martyr Blase.
Give us the joy of your peace in this life

and help us to gain the happiness that will never end.
Grant this through our Lord Jesus Christ, your Son,
who lives and reigns with you and the Holy Spirit,
one God, for ever and ever. ℟. **Amen.**

Reading I (Rom 5, 1-5), p. 1146, no. 1.
Responsorial Psalm (Ps 117), p. 1163, no. 6.
Gospel (Mk 16, 15-20), p. 1172, no. 5.

The Same Day, Feb. 3

ST. ANSGAR, Bishop

Optional Memorial

St. Ansgar died in Bremen, Germany, on February 3,
865. Since the holy apostles of Germany, England and
the Slavic countries were added to the liturgical calendar in the 19th century, it was only right to include the
apostle of Denmark and Switzerland in the latest calendar reform.

*Common of Pastors: for Missionaries, p. 1077, or for
Bishops, p. 1069.*

OPENING PRAYER

Father,
you sent St. Ansgar
to bring the light of Christ to many nations.
May his prayers help us
to walk in the light of your truth.
We ask this through our Lord Jesus Christ, your Son,
who lives and reigns with you and the Holy Spirit,
one God, for ever and ever. ℟. **Amen.**

Reading I (Is 52, 7-10), p. 1156, no. 5.
Responsorial Psalm (Ps 96), p. 1162, no. 4.
Gospel (Mk 1, 14-20), p. 1172, no. 4.

Feb. 5 — ST. AGATHA, Virgin and Martyr

Memorial

St. Agatha, an illustrious Sicilian virgin, was martyred
at Catania in 251, for refusing the solicitations of a
Roman Senator. Her name appears in the First Eucharistic Prayer.

Common of Martyrs, p. 1056; *or Common of Virgins,*
p. 1085.

OPENING PRAYER

Lord,
let your forgiveness be won for us
by the pleading of St. Agatha,
who found favor with you by her chastity
and by her courage in suffering death for the gospel.
Grant this through our Lord Jesus Christ, your Son,
who lives and reigns with you and the Holy Spirit,
one God, for ever and ever. ℟. **Amen.**

Reading I (1 Cor 1, 26-31), p. 1211, no. 2.
Responsorial Psalm (Ps 31), p. 1144, no. 2.
Gospel (Lk 9, 23-26), p. 1152, no. 4.

Feb. 6 — STS. PAUL MIKI and COMPANIONS, Martyrs

Memorial

St. Paul Miki and his twenty-five companions were crucified at Nagasaki, Japan, on February 5, 1597. They
were the first martyrs of the Far East to be canonized
(1862) and included priests and laymen, European
missionaries and Japanese Christians.

Common of Martyrs, p. 1049.

OPENING PRAYER

God our Father,
source of strength for all your saints,
you led Paul Miki and his companions
through the suffering of the cross
to the joy of eternal life.
May their prayers give us the courage
to be loyal until death in professing our faith.
We ask this through our Lord Jesus Christ, your Son,
who lives and reigns with you and the Holy Spirit,
one God, for ever and ever. ℟. **Amen.**

Reading I (Gal 2, 19-20), p. 1212, no. 5.
Responsorial Psalm (Ps 126), p. 1145, no. 4.
Gospel (Mt 28, 16-20), p. 1171, no. 3.

Feb. 8 — ST. JEROME EMILIANI

Optional Memorial

St. Jerome was born in Venice and left everything for the sake of the Lord. He founded a Congregation which was dedicated to the education of children, orphanages, and schools. He died of the plague in 1537.

Common of Holy Men and Women: for Teachers, p. 1101.

OPENING PRAYER

God of mercy,
you chose Jerome Emiliani
to be a father and friend of orphans:
May his prayers keep us faithful
to the Spirit we have received,
who makes us your children.
Grant this through our Lord Jesus Christ, your Son,
who lives and reigns with you and the Holy Spirit,
one God, for ever and ever. ℟. **Amen.**

Reading I (Tb 12, 6-13), p. 1198, no. 8.
Responsorial Psalm (Ps 103), p. 1208, no. 5.
Gospel (Mk 10, 17-30 or 17-27), p. 1227, no. 14.

Feb. 10 — ST. SCHOLASTICA, Virgin

Memorial

St. Scholastica was the twin sister of St. Benedict. Embracing the rule of her brother, she founded the Order of Benedictine nuns. She died in 542.

Common of Virgins, p. 1085; or Common of Holy Men and Women: for Religious, p. 1097.

OPENING PRAYER

Lord,
as we recall the memory of St. Scholastica,
we ask that by her example
we may serve you with love and obtain perfect joy.
Grant this through our Lord Jesus Christ, your Son,
who lives and reigns with you and the Holy Spirit,
one God, for ever and ever. ℟. **Amen.**

Reading I (Sg 8, 6-7), p. 1188, no. 1.
Responsorial Psalm (Ps 148), p. 1191, no. 2.
Gospel (Lk 10, 38-42), p. 1194, no. 3.

Feb. 11 — OUR LADY OF LOURDES

Optional Memorial

The first of the eighteen apparitions of the Blessed
Virgin Mary to the humble Bernadette took place at
Lourdes on February 11, 1858. On March 25, when Bernadette asked the Beautiful Lady her name, she replied:
"I am the Immaculate Conception." The devotion of
people in all parts of the world to our Lady of Lourdes,
together with the countless miracles that have been
wrought through her intercession, has caused one of the
most marvelous spiritual regenerations in the history
of the Church.

Common of the Blessed Virgin Mary, p. 1040.

OPENING PRAYER

God of mercy,
we celebrate the feast of Mary,
the sinless mother of God.
May her prayers help us
to rise above our human weakness.
We ask this through our Lord Jesus Christ, your Son,
who lives and reigns with you and the Holy Spirit,
one God, for ever and ever. R̶. **Amen.**

READING I   Is 66, 10-14

The power of the Lord is manifest to his servants. They are to rejoice and
exult in the fulfillment that he gives them. He will give them wealth and
comfort.

A reading from the book of the prophet Isaiah

Rejoice with Jerusalem and be glad because of her,
  all you who love her;
Exult, exult with her,
  all you who were mourning over her!
Oh, that you may suck fully
  of the milk of her comfort,
That you may nurse with delight
  at her abundant breasts!

For thus says the Lord:
Lo, I will spread prosperity over her like a river,
    and the wealth of the nations like an overflowing
      torrent.
As nurslings, you shall be carried in her arms,
    and fondled in her lap;
As a mother comforts her son,
    so will I comfort you;
    in Jerusalem you shall find your comfort.
When you see this, your heart shall rejoice,
    and your bodies flourish like the grass;
The Lord's power shall be known to his servants.
This is the Word of the Lord. ℟. **Thanks be to God.**

Responsorial Psalm (Jdt 13), p. 1126, no. 2.
Gospel (Jn 2, 1-11), p. 1136, no. 10.

Feb. 14 — STS. CYRIL, Monk, and METHODIUS, Bishop   *Memorial*

Born in Thessalonica, these two brothers evangelized Moravia, Bohemia and Bulgaria. Consecrated Bishops by Pope Adrian II, St. Cyril died at Rome in the year 869 and St. Methodius in the year 885.

Common of Pastors: for Founders of Churches, p. 1075, or for Missionaries, p. 1077.

OPENING PRAYER
Father,
you brought the light of the gospel to the Slavic
    nations
through St. Cyril and his brother St. Methodius.
Open our hearts to understand your teaching
and help us to become one in faith and praise.
Grant this through our Lord Jesus Christ, your Son,
who lives and reigns with you and the Holy Spirit,
one God, for ever and ever. ℟. **Amen.**

Reading I (Acts 13, 46-49), p. 1159, no. 1.
Responsorial Psalm (Ps 117), p. 1163, no. 6.
Gospel (Lk 10, 1-9), p. 1174, no. 7.

Feb. 17 — SEVEN FOUNDERS OF THE ORDER OF SERVITES

Optional Memorial

In 1233 seven members of a Florentine Confraternity founded the Order of Servites of the Blessed Virgin Mary. The Servites led an austere life, meditating constantly on the Passion of our Lord and venerating the Blessed Virgin as Our Lady of Sorrows.

Common of Holy Men and Women: for Religious, p. 1097.

OPENING PRAYER

Lord,
fill us with the love
which inspired the seven holy brothers
to honor the mother of God with special devotion
and to lead your people to you.
We ask this through our Lord Jesus Christ, your Son,
who lives and reigns with you and the Holy Spirit,
one God, for ever and ever. ℟. **Amen.**

Reading I (Rom 8, 26-30), p. 1210, no. 1.
Responsorial Psalm (Ps 34), p. 1207, no. 4.
Gospel (Mk 10, 17-30 or 10, 17-27), p. 1227, no. 14.

Feb. 21 — ST. PETER DAMIAN, Bishop and Doctor

Optional Memorial

Peter Damian a Benedictine monk, rendered immense services to Gregory VII in his struggle for the rights of the Church. He died in 1072.

Common of Doctors of the Church, p. 1082; or Common of Pastors: for Bishops, p. 1069.

OPENING PRAYER

All-powerful God,
help us to follow the teachings and example of Peter Damian.
By making Christ and the service of his Church
the first love of our lives,
may we come to the joys of eternal light,

where he lives and reigns with you and the Holy
   Spirit,
one God, for ever and ever. ℞. **Amen.**

Reading I (2 Tm 4, 1-5), p. 1185, no. 7.
Responsorial Psalm (Ps 16), p. 1207, no. 3.
Gospel (Jn 15, 1-8), p. 1231, no. 20.

Feb. 22 — CHAIR OF ST. PETER, Apostle

Feast

The feast of the Chair of St. Peter was originally celebrated on February 22. However in Gaul it came to be
celebrated on January 18. Pope Paul IV believed that
there were two different feasts; therefore in 1558 he
doubled the original feast: on January 18 he placed St.
Peter's Pontificate at Rome and on February 22 his
Pontificate at Antioch. As of 1961, the duplicate feast
of January 18 was abolished and the original feast remains in honor of St. Peter's Pontifical Authority.

ENTRANCE ANT.   Lk 22, 32
**The Lord said to Simon Peter: I have prayed that
your faith may not fail; and you in your turn must
strengthen your brothers.**   ➤ No. 2, p. 614

OPENING PRAYER
All-powerful Father,
you have built your Church
on the rock of St. Peter's confession of faith.
May nothing divide or weaken
our unity in faith and love.
Grant this through our Lord Jesus Christ, your Son,
who lives and reigns with you and the Holy Spirit,
one God, for ever and ever. ℞. **Amen.** ✟

READING I   1 Pt 5, 1-4
The presbyters are entrusted with an administrative function in the
Christian community. The pastoral care of the Church is entrusted to
the elders. Christ in his parousia is depicted in the role of shepherd,
bringing out the pastoral aspects of his activity and his relationship
to others in the Church.

    A reading from the first letter of Peter

To the elders among you I, a fellow elder, a witness
of Christ's sufferings and sharer in the glory that

is to be revealed, make this appeal. God's flock is
in your midst; give it a shepherd's care. Watch over
it willingly as God would have you do, not under
coercion; and not for shameful profit either, but
generously. Be examples to the flock, not lording
it over those assigned to you, so that when the chief
shepherd appears you will win for yourselves the
unfading crown of glory.—This is the Word of the
Lord. ℟. **Thanks be to God.** ℣

Responsorial Psalm   Ps 23, 1-3. 3-4. 5. 6

℟. (1) **The Lord is my shepherd;
     there is nothing I shall want.**

The Lord is my shepherd; I shall not want.
    In verdant pastures he gives me repose;
Beside restful waters he leads me;
    he refreshes my soul. — ℟

He guides me in right paths
    for his name's sake.
Even though I walk in the dark valley
    I fear no evil; for you are at my side
With your rod and your staff
    that give me courage. — ℟

You spread the table before me
    in the sight of my foes;
You anoint my head with oil;
    my cup overflows. — ℟

Only goodness and kindness follow me
    all the days of my life;
And I shall dwell in the house of the Lord
    for years to come. — ℟ ℣

GOSPEL   Mt 16, 13-19

Alleluia (Mt 16, 18)

℟. **Alleluia.** You are Peter, the rock on which I will
        build my Church;
the gates of hell will not hold out against it. ℟. **Al-
        leluia.**

The question of Jesus concerns his messianic title, the Son of Man. He directly puts the question to the disciples. It is a challenge. Peter answers for all with a profession that Christ is the Messiah. Simon is given the name by which he is usually known in the New Testament.

℣. The Lord be with you. ℟. **And also with you.**

✠ A reading from the holy gospel according to Matthew. ℟. **Glory to you, Lord.**

When Jesus came to the neighborhood of Caesarea Philippi, he asked his disciples this question: "Who do people say that the Son of Man is?" They replied, "Some say John the Baptizer, others Elijah, still others Jeremiah or one of the prophets." "And you," he said to them, "who do you say that I am?" "You are the Messiah," Simon Peter answered, "the Son of the living God!" Jesus replied, "Blest are you, Simon son of John! No mere man has revealed this to you, but my heavenly Father. I for my part declare to you, you are 'Rock,' and on this rock I will build my Church, and the jaws of death shall not prevail against it. I will entrust to you the keys of the kingdom of heaven. Whatever you declare bound on earth shall be bound in heaven; whatever you declare loosed on earth shall be loosed in heaven."— This is the gospel of the Lord. ℟. **Praise to you, Lord Jesus Christ.**   ➔ No. 15, p. 623

PRAYER OVER THE GIFTS

Lord,
accept the prayers and gifts of your Church.
With St. Peter as our shepherd,
keep us true to the faith he taught
and bring us to your eternal kingdom.
We ask this through Christ our Lord.
℟. **Amen.**   ➔ No. 21, p. 626 (Pref. P 64-65)

COMMUNION ANT.   Mt 16, 16. 18

Peter said: You are the Christ, the Son of the living God. Jesus answered: You are Peter, the rock on which I will build my Church. ℣

PRAYER AFTER COMMUNION

God our Father,
you have given us the body and blood of Christ
as the food of life.
On this feast of Peter the apostle,
may this communion bring us redemption
and be the sign and source of our unity and peace.
We ask this in the name of Jesus the Lord.
℟. **Amen.**   ➔ No. 32, p. 650

Feb. 23 — ST. POLYCARP, Bishop and Martyr
Memorial

St. Polycarp was a disciple of St. John the Evangelist,
who converted him to Christianity. Late in life he was
elevated to the Bishopric of Smyrna. When he was
carried to the amphitheatre, the pro-consul exhorted
him to renounce Jesus Christ, and he responded: "For
eighty-six years I have served him and he has never
wronged me; how can I renounce the king who has
saved me?" He suffered martyrdom about the year 155.

*Common of Martyrs, p. 1056; or Common of Pastors:
for Bishops, p. 1069.*

OPENING PRAYER

God of all creation
you gave your bishop Polycarp
the privilege of being counted among the saints
who gave their lives in faithful witness to the gospel.
May his prayers give us the courage
to share with him the cup of suffering
and to rise to eternal glory.
We ask this through our Lord Jesus Christ, your Son,
who lives and reigns with you and the Holy Spirit,
one God, for ever and ever. ℟. **Amen.**

READING I   Rv 2, 8-11

To the church in Smyrna, John is directed to write that there will be
suffering and poverty in spite of riches. The devil will bring about
imprisonment and persecution, but for those who are faithful, the
crown of life will be received. The victor will not suffer a second
death.

A reading from the book of Revelation

To the presiding spirit of the church in Smyrna, write this:

"The First and the Last who once died but now lives has this to say: I know of your tribulation and your poverty, even though you are rich. I know the slander you endure from self-styled Jews who are nothing other than members of Satan's assembly. Have no fear of the sufferings to come. The devil will indeed cast some of you into prison to put you to the test; you will be tried over a period of ten days. Remain faithful until death and I will give you the crown of life.

"Let him who has ears to hear heed the Spirit's word to the churches! The victor shall never be harmed by the second death."—This is the Word of the Lord. ℟. **Thanks be to God.**

Responsorial Psalm (Ps 31), p. 1144, no. 1.
Gospel (Jn 15, 18-21), p. 1153, no. 6.

MARCH

Mar. 4 — ST. CASIMIR

Optional Memorial

St. Casimir was the son of King Casimir IV of Poland and Elizabeth of Austria. Amidst the moral dangers of the court, he was an example of piety and above all preserved his chastity. While on a journey to Lithuania, he died at the court of Grodno, March 4, 1484.

Common of Holy Men and Women, p. 1090.

OPENING PRAYER

All-powerful God,
to serve you is to reign:
by the prayers of St. Casimir,
help us to serve you in holiness and justice.
Grant this through our Lord Jesus Christ, your Son,
who lives and reigns with you and the Holy Spirit,
one God, for ever and ever. ℟. **Amen.**

Reading I (Phil 3, 8-14), p. 1214, no. 9.
Responsorial Psalm (Ps 15), p. 1206, no. 2.
Gospel (Jn 15, 9-17), p. 1232, no. 21.

Mar. 7 — PERPETUA and FELICITY, Martyrs
Memorial

Perpetua, a noble lady of Carthage with a nursing child, and Felicity, an expectant mother, were exposed to the ferocity of wild beasts. They were finally beheaded in the year 202 during the persecution of Severus.

Common of Martyrs, p. 1049; or Common of Holy Men and Women, p. 1102.

OPENING PRAYER

Father,
your love gave the saints Perpetua and Felicity
courage to suffer a cruel martyrdom.
By their prayers, help us to grow in love of you.
We ask this through our Lord Jesus Christ, your Son,
who lives and reigns with you and the Holy Spirit,
one God, for ever and ever. ℟. **Amen.**

Reading I (Rom 8, 31-39), p. 1146, no. 2.
Responsorial Psalm (Ps 124), p. 1145, no. 3.
Gospel (Mt 10, 34-39), p. 1152, no. 3.

Mar. 8 — ST. JOHN OF GOD, Religious
Optional Memorial

After a stormy youth, St. John listened to the word of God when he was forty years old, and lived thereafter a penitent life. He founded the Order of "Brothers Hospitallers of St. John of God," who devote themselves to the healing of sick bodies and souls. He died in 1550.

Common of Holy Men and Women: for Religious, p. 1097, or for Those Who Work for the Underprivileged, p. 1099.

OPENING PRAYER

Father,
you gave John of God
love and compassion for others.

Grant that by doing good for others
we may be counted among the saints in your kingdom.
We ask this through our Lord Jesus Christ, your Son,
who lives and reigns with you and the Holy Spirit,
one God, for ever and ever. R̷. **Amen.**

Reading I (1 Jn 3, 14-18), p. 1217, no. 15.
Responsorial Psalm (Ps 112), p. 1209, no. 6.
Gospel (Mt 25, 31-46 or 31-40), p. 1225, no. 10.

Mar. 9 — ST. FRANCES OF ROME, Religious
Optional Memorial

At eleven years of age, St. Frances married Lorenzo de
Ponziani, with whom she had six children. She was the
perfect Christian spouse. She founded the Benedictine
Oblate Congregation of Tor di Specchi, and died in
1440.

*Common for Holy Men and Women: for Religious, p.
1097.*

OPENING PRAYER
Merciful Father,
in Frances of Rome
you have given us a unique example of love in marriage
as well as in religious life.
Keep us faithful in your service,
and help us to see and follow you
in all the aspects of life
We ask this through our Lord Jesus Christ, your Son,
who lives and reigns with you and the Holy Spirit,
one God, for ever and ever. R̷. **Amen.**

Reading I (Prv 31, 10-31. 19-20. 30-31), p. 1200, no. 11.
Responsorial Psalm (Ps 34), p. 1207, no. 4.
Gospel (Mt 16, 24-27), p. 1222, no. 5.

Mar. 17 — ST. PATRICK, Bishop

Optional Memorial

St. Patrick, Apostle and Patron of Ireland, was born in
Scotland in 387. Pope St. Celestine commissioned him to
evangelize Ireland, and in the thirty-three years of his
apostolate, he succeeded in converting the whole country, which, in the Middle Ages, was known as "Island of
Saints," resplendent with churches and monasteries.
St. Patrick died in the year 464.

*Common of Pastors: for Missionaries, p. 1077, or for
Bishops, p. 1069.*

OPENING PRAYER

Let us pray
  [that like St. Patrick the missionary
  we will be fearless witnesses
  to the gospel of Jesus Christ]

God our Father,
you sent St. Patrick
to preach your glory to the people of Ireland.
By the help of his prayers,
may all Christians proclaim your love to all men.
Grant this through our Lord Jesus Christ, your Son,
who lives and reigns with you and the Holy Spirit,
one God, for ever and ever. ℟. **Amen.** ℣

ALTERNATIVE OPENING PRAYER

Let us pray
  [that, like St. Patrick,
  we may be loyal to our faith in Christ]

Father in heaven,
you sent the great bishop Patrick
to the people of Ireland to share his faith
and to spend his life in loving service.
May our lives bear witness
to the faith we profess,
and our love bring others
to the peace and joy of your gospel.
We ask this through Christ our Lord. ℟. **Amen.**

Reading I (1 Pt 4, 7-11), p. 1216, no. 14.
Responsorial Psalm (Ps 96), p 1162, no. 4.
Gospel (Lk 5, 1-11), p. 1173, no. 6.

Mar. 18 — CYRIL OF JERUSALEM, Bishop and Doctor
Optional Memorial

When he was a simple priest, St. Cyril instructed the Catechumens during Lent. His instructions which are extant show conclusively that Catholic doctrine was the same then as now. The Arians exiled him three times. He died in 386.

Common of Pastors: for Bishops, p. 1069; or Common of Doctors of the Church, p. 1082.

OPENING PRAYER
Father,
through Cyril of Jerusalem
you led your Church to a deeper understanding
of the mysteries of salvation.
Let his prayers help us to know your Son better
and to have eternal life in all its fullness.
We ask this through our Lord Jesus Christ, your Son,
who lives and reigns with you and the Holy Spirit,
one God, for ever and ever. ℞. **Amen.**

Reading I (1 Jn 5, 1-5), p. 1218, no. 17.
Responsorial Psalm (Ps 19), p. 1180, no. 1.
Gospel (Jn 15, 1-8), p. 1231, no. 20.

Mar. 19 — JOSEPH, HUSBAND OF MARY
Solemnity

From the end of the 10th century St. Joseph has been honored on March 19 in many Western calendars. His feast was accepted at Rome in 1479 and established on the same date; and in 1621 it was inserted into the universal calendar. Since the Solemnity of St. Joseph always falls in Lent, the episcopal conferences have the faculty to transfer it to another day, outside Lent.

ENTRANCE ANT.   Lk 12, 42
The Lord has put his faithful servant in charge of his household.   ➡ No. 2, p. 614

OPENING PRAYER

Let us pray

[that the Church will continue
the saving work of Christ]

Father,

you entrusted our Savior to the care of St. Joseph.
By the help of his prayers
may your Church continue to serve its Lord, Jesus
Christ,

who lives and reigns with you and the Holy Spirit,
one God, for ever and ever. ℟. **Amen.** ✠

READING I   2 Sm 7, 4-5. 12-14. 16

This text probes deeply into the stupendous mystery of the Incarnation.
God is the Father of his eternal Son, Jesus Christ, and Mary is his
mother by the power of the Holy Spirit. But Jesus is also the Son of
David. Joseph was of the Davidic line, and so was Mary.

A reading from the second book of Samuel

The Lord spoke to Nathan and said: "Go, tell my
servant David, 'When your time comes and you rest
with your ancestors, I will raise up your heir after
you, sprung from your loins, and I will make his
kingdom firm. It is he who shall build a house for
my name. And I will make his royal throne firm forever. I will be a father to him, and he shall be a son
to me. Your house and your kingdom shall endure
forever before me; your throne shall stand firm forever.' "—This is the Word of the Lord. ℟. **Thanks be
to God.** ✠

Responsorial Psalm   Ps 89, 2-3. 4-5. 27. 29

℟. (37) **The son of David will live for ever.**

The favors of the Lord I will sing forever;
through all generations my mouth shall proclaim
your faithfulness.

For you have said, "My kindness is established forever";
in heaven you have confirmed your faithfulness. — ℟

"I have made a covenant with my chosen one,
  I have sworn to David my servant:
Forever will I confirm your posterity
  and establish your throne for all generations."—℞
"He shall say of me, 'You are my father,
  my God, the Rock, my savior.'
Forever I will maintain my kindness toward him,
  and my covenant with him stands firm." — ℞ ❡

READING II   Rom 4, 13. 16-18. 22

St. Paul brings full pressure to bear on faith as we think over the
mystery of God's coming to earth under the protection of Joseph.
Abraham's faith is held up to us as the ideal. Joseph's faith was like
Abraham's, and by that faith he became the spiritual father of millions.

A reading from the letter of Paul to the Romans

Certainly the promise made to Abraham and his descendants that they would inherit the world did not
depend on the law; it was made in view of the justice that comes from faith. Hence, all depends on
faith, everything is a grace. Thus the promise holds
true for all Abraham's descendants, not only for
those who have the law but for all who have his
faith. He is father of us all, which is why Scripture
says, "I have made you father of many nations."
Yes, he is our father in the sight of God in whom
he believed, the God who restores the dead to life
and calls into being those things which had not been.
Hoping against hope, Abraham believed and so became the father of many nations, just as it was once
told him, "Numerous as this shall your descendants
be." Thus his faith was credited to him as justice.—
This is the Word of the Lord. ℞. **Thanks be to God.** ❡

GOSPEL   Mt 1, 16. 18-21. 24
Alleluia (Ps 84, 1)
(℞. **Alleluia.**) How happy they who dwell in your
  house, O Lord;
continually they sing your praise! (℞. **Alleluia.**)

Joseph's faith was tested from the start. First there was a crisis of integrity, and a great tension arose in his just heart. Mary was with child. Then an angel of the Lord revealed the whole majestic and unspeakable truth. Mary had conceived by the Holy Spirit. She was the all-holy tabernacle of our redemption.

℣. The Lord be with you. ℟. **And also with you.**

✠ A reading from the holy gospel according to Matthew. ℟. **Glory to you, Lord.**

Jacob was the father of Joseph the husband of Mary. It was of her that Jesus who is called the Messiah was born. Now this is how the birth of Jesus Christ came about. When his mother Mary was engaged to Joseph, but before they lived together, she was found with child through the power of the Holy Spirit. Joseph her husband, an upright man unwilling to expose her to the law, decided to divorce her quietly. Such was his intention when suddenly the angel of the Lord appeared in a dream and said to him: "Joseph, son of David, have no fear about taking Mary as your wife. It is by the Holy Spirit that she has conceived this child. She is to have a son and you are to name him Jesus because he will save his people from their sins." When Joseph awoke he did as the angel of the Lord had directed him.—This is the gospel of the Lord. ℟. **Praise to you, Lord Jesus Christ.**   ➤ No. 14, p. 622

OR

GOSPEL   Lk 2, 41-51

Alleluia. (Ps 84, 1)

(℟. **Alleluia.**) How happy they who dwell in your house, O Lord;

continually they sing your praise! (℟. **Alleluia.**)

Mary and Joseph were religious people and they observed the Passover. During the return journey from Jerusalem, Jesus was lost. His parents found him in the temple. Jesus returned with them to Nazareth and was obedient to them.

℣. The Lord be with you. ℟. **And also with you.**

✠ A reading from the holy gospel according to Luke ℟. **Glory to you, Lord.**

The parents of Jesus used to go every year to Jerusalem for the feast of the Passover, and when he was twelve they went up for the celebration as was their custom. As they were returning at the end of the feast, the child Jesus remained behind unknown to his parents. Thinking he was in the party, they continued their journey for a day, looking for him among their relatives and acquaintances.

Not finding him, they returned to Jerusalem in search of him. On the third day they came upon him in the temple sitting in the midst of the teachers, listening to them and asking them questions. All who heard him were amazed at his intelligence and his answers.

When his parents saw him they were astonished, and his mother said to him: "Son, why have you done this to us? You see that your father and I have been searching for you in sorrow." He said to them: "Why did you search for me? Did you not know I had to be in my Father's house?" But they did not grasp what he said to them.

He went down with them then and came to Nazareth, and was obedient to them.—This is the gospel of the Lord. ℟. **Praise to you, Lord Jesus Christ.**

➤ No. 14, p. 623

PRAYER OVER THE GIFTS

Father,
with unselfish love St. Joseph cared for your Son, born of the Virgin Mary.
May we also serve you at your altar with pure hearts.
We ask this in the name of Jesus the Lord.
℟. **Amen.** ↓

PREFACE (P 62)

℣. The Lord be with you. ℟. **And also with you.**
℣. Lift up your hearts. ℟. **We lift them up to the Lord.** ℣. Let us give thanks to the Lord our God.
℟. **It is right to give him thanks and praise.**

Father, all-powerful and ever-living God,
we do well always and everywhere to give you thanks

as we honor St. Joseph.

He is that just man,
that wise and loyal servant,
whom you placed at the head of your family.
With a husband's love he cherished Mary,
the virgin Mother of God.
With fatherly care he watched over Jesus Christ
   your Son,
conceived by the power of the Holy Spirit.

Through Christ the choirs of angels
and all the powers of heaven
praise and worship your glory.
May our voices blend with theirs
as we join in their unending hymn: ➜ No. 23, p. 627

COMMUNION ANT.   Mt 25, 21

**Come, good and faithful servant! Share the joy of
your Lord! ⱽ**

PRAYER AFTER COMMUNION

Lord,
today you nourish us at this altar
as we celebrate the feast of St. Joseph.
Protect your Church always,
and in your love watch over the gifts you have given
   us.
Grant this through Christ our Lord.
℟. **Amen.**   ➜ No. 32, p. 650

———————————

Mar. 23 — ST. TURIBIUS DE MONGROVEJO, Bishop

Optional Memorial

St. Turibius Alphonsus de Mongrovejo died at Lima,
Peru, on March 23, 1606. He was canonized in 1726. He
has been inscribed in the general calendar because of
his important contribution toward the establishment of
ecclesiastical discipline in the Church of Latin America.

Common of Pastors: for Bishops, p. 1069.

OPENING PRAYER

Lord,
through the apostolic work of St. Turibius
and his unwavering love of truth,
you helped your Church to grow.
May your chosen people continue to grow
in faith and holiness.
Grant this through our Lord Jesus Christ, your Son,
who lives and reigns with you and the Holy Spirit,
one God, for ever and ever. ℟. **Amen.**

Reading I (2 Tm 1, 13-14; 2, 1-3), p. 1168, no. 11.
Responsorial Psalm (Ps 96), p. 1162, no. 4.
Gospel (Mk 1, 14-20), p. 1172, no. 4.

Mar. 25 — ANNUNCIATION

Solemnity

The Solemnity of the Annunciation, of Eastern origin,
was accepted at Rome in the 7th century under the title
"Annunciation of the Lord" as attested by the "Liber
Pontificalis." The Eastern Rites as well as the Ambrosian Rite have always regarded it as a feast of the Lord.
Hence the name of this Solemnity has now been changed. It is called the "Annunciation of the Lord" to make
it more evident that it is above all a feast of the Lord.

ENTRANCE ANT.   Heb 10, 5. 7

**As Christ came into the world, he said: Behold! I
have come to do your will, O God.** ➔ No. 2, p. 614

OPENING PRAYER

Let us pray
   [that Christ, the Word made flesh,
   will make us more like him]
God our Father,
your Word became man and was born of the Virgin
   Mary.
May we become more like Jesus Christ,
whom we acknowledge as our redeemer, God and
   man.

We ask this . . .   ℞. **Amen.** ℣

ALTERNATIVE OPENING PRAYER

Let us pray
  [that we may become more like Christ
    who chose to become one of us]

Almighty Father of our Lord Jesus Christ,
you have revealed the beauty of your power
by exalting the lowly virgin of Nazareth
and making her the mother of our Savior.
May the prayers of this woman
bring Jesus to the waiting world
and fill the void of incompletion
with the presence of her child,
who lives and reigns with you and the Holy Spirit,
one God, for ever and ever. ℞. **Amen.** ℣

READING I   Is 7, 10-14

On this feast of the Incarnation of our Lord, we celebrate the moment
of his taking on of our flesh in the womb of his mother by the power
of the Holy Spirit.

    A reading from the book of the prophet Isaiah
The Lord spoke to Ahaz: Ask for a sign from the
Lord, your God; let it be deep as the nether world,
or high as the sky! But Ahaz answered, "I will not
ask! I will not tempt the Lord!" Then he said: Listen,
O house of David! Is it not enough for you to weary
men, must you also weary my God? Therefore the
Lord himself will give you this sign: the virgin shall
be with child, and bear a son, and shall name him
Immanuel.—This is the Word of the Lord. ℞. **Thanks
be to God.** ℣

Responsorial Psalm   Ps 40, 7-8. 8-9. 10. 11
℞. (8. 9) **Here am I, Lord;**
  I come to do your will.
Sacrifice or oblation you wished not,
  but ears open to obedience you gave me.

Holocausts or sin-offerings you sought not;
   then said I, "Behold I come; — ℟

In the written scroll it is prescribed for me,
To do your will, O my God, is my delight,
   and your law is within my heart!" — ℟

I announced your justice in the vast assembly;
   I did not restrain my lips, as you, O Lord, know.—℟

Your justice I kept not hid within my heart;
   your faithfulness and your salvation I have spoken
   of;
I have made no secret of your kindness and your
   truth
   in the vast assembly. — ℟ ℣

READING II   Heb 10, 4-10

Christ is shown making a free offering of himself for us. It was an
act of his all-holy will to be the Son of Mary and Brother of us all.
Mary is God's mother; Jesus is God's Son. We will be made holy by
the offering of his body!

   A reading from the letter to the Hebrews

It is impossible for the blood of bulls and goats to
take sins away. Wherefore, on coming into the world,
Jesus said:
   "Sacrifice and offering you did not desire,
      but a body you have prepared for me;
   Holocausts and sin offerings you took no de-
      light in.
   Then I said, 'As is written of me in the book,
      I have come to do your will, O God.' "
First he says,
   "Sacrifices and offerings, holocausts and sin
      offerings
      you neither desired nor delighted in."
(These are offered according to the prescriptions of
the law.) Then he says,
   "I have come to do your will."
In other words, he takes away the first covenant to
establish the second.
   By this "will," we have been sanctified through

the offering of the body of Jesus Christ once for all.
—This is the Word of the Lord. ℟. **Thanks be to God.** ⍊

GOSPEL   Lk 1, 26-38

Alleluia. (Jn 1, 14)

(℟. **Alleluia.**) The Word of God became man and
    lived among us;
and we saw his glory. (℟. **Alleluia.**)

St. Luke tells the story. The most we know about the doctrine of the
Incarnation is contained in these few paragraphs. This is an event
that puts Christ in the middle of all history. And the exquisite lady
who received the message gave herself with her newly conceived Son.

℣. The Lord be with you. ℟. **And also with you.**
✠ A reading from the holy gospel according to Luke
℟. **Glory to you, Lord.**

The angel Gabriel was sent from God to a town of
Galilee named Nazareth, to a virgin betrothed to a
man named Joseph, of the house of David. The virgin's name was Mary. Upon arriving, the angel said
to her: "Rejoice, O highly favored daughter! The
Lord is with you. Blessed are you among women."
She was deeply troubled by his words, and wondered what his greeting meant. The angel went on
to say to her: "Do not fear, Mary. You have found
favor with God. You shall conceive and bear a son
and give him the name Jesus. Great will be his dignity and he will be called Son of the Most High. The
Lord God will give him the throne of David his father. He will rule over the house of Jacob and his
reign will be without end."

Mary said to the angel, "How can this be since
I do not know man?" The angel answered her: "The
Holy Spirit will come upon you and the power of the
Most High will overshadow you; hence, the holy offspring to be born will be called Son of God. Know
that Elizabeth your kinswoman has conceived a son
in her old age; she who was thought to be sterile is
now in her sixth month, for nothing is impossible
with God."

Mary said: "I am the maidservant of the Lord. Let it be done to me as you say." With that the angel left her.—This is the gospel of the Lord. ℞. **Praise to you, Lord Jesus Christ.**   ➤ No. 14, p. 623

In the Profession of Faith, all genuflect at the words, and became man.

PRAYER OVER THE GIFTS

Almighty Father,
as we recall the beginning of the Church
when your Son became man,
may we celebrate with joy today
this sacrament of your love.
We ask this through Christ our Lord. ℞. **Amen.** ⱽ

PREFACE (P 44)

℣. The Lord be with you. ℞. **And also with you.**
℣. Lift up your hearts. ℞. **We lift them up to the Lord.** ℣. Let us give thanks to the Lord our God.
℞. **It is right to give him thanks and praise.**
Father, all-powerful and ever-living God,
we do well always and everywhere to give you thanks
through Jesus Christ our Lord.

He came to save mankind by becoming a man himself.
The Virgin Mary, receiving the angel's message in faith,
conceived by the power of the Spirit
and bore your Son in purest love.

In Christ, the eternal truth,
your promise to Israel came true.
In Christ, the hope of all peoples,
man's hope was realized beyond all expectation.

Through Christ the angels of heaven
offer their prayer of adoration
as they rejoice in your presence for ever.
May our voices be one with theirs
in their triumphant hymn of praise. ➤ No. 23, p. 627

COMMUNION ANT.   Is 7, 14

The Virgin is with child and shall bear a son, and she will call him Emmanuel. ℣

PRAYER AFTER COMMUNION

Lord,
may the sacrament we share
strengthen our faith and hope in Jesus, born of a
    virgin
and truly God and man.
By the power of his resurrection
may we come to eternal joy.
We ask this in the name of Jesus the Lord.
℟. **Amen.**   → No. 32, p. 650

— APRIL —

Apr. 2 — ST. FRANCIS OF PAOLA, Hermit

Optional Memorial

St. Francis founded the Order of Minims, whose name shows that they wished to be regarded as the least in the household of God. He died in 1507.

Common of Holy Men and Women: for Religious, p. 1097.

OPENING PRAYER

Father of the lowly,
you raised St. Francis of Paola
to the glory of your saints.
By his example and prayers,
may we come to the rewards
you have promised the humble.
We ask this through our Lord Jesus Christ, your Son,
who lives and reigns with you and the Holy Spirit,
one God, for ever and ever. ℟. **Amen.**

Reading I (Phil 3, 8-14), p. 1214, no. 9.
Responsorial Psalm (Ps 16), p. 1160, no. 1.
Gospel (Lk 12, 32-34), p. 1229, no. 17.

Apr. 4 — ST. ISIDORE, Bishop and Doctor

Optional Memorial

St. Isidore, who restored Catholicism in Spain, was admired for his preaching, his miracles, his work for the liturgy and ecclesiastical discipline. He presided at the Council of Toledo (633) and died in 636.

Common of Pastors: for Bishops, p. 1069; or Common of Doctors of the Church, p. 1082.

OPENING PRAYER

Lord,
hear the prayers we offer in commemoration of St.
    Isidore.
May your Church learn from his teaching
and benefit from his intercession.
Grant this through our Lord Jesus Christ, your Son,
who lives and reigns with you and the Holy Spirit,
one God, for ever and ever. ℟. **Amen.**

Reading I (2 Cor 4, 1-2. 5-7), p. 1166, no. 6.
Responsorial Psalm (Ps 37), p. 1181, no. 2.
Gospel (Mt 23, 8-12), p. 1186, no. 2.

Apr. 5 — ST. VINCENT FERRER, Priest

Optional Memorial

St. Vincent Ferrer was born in Valencia, Spain, January 23, 1350. He was educated at the Dominican school in Barcelona, and later entered the Order. He is said to have had the gift of tongues, so amazing was the speed with which he mastered the many varied dialects of Western Europe. He converted thousands of sinners, Jews and infidels by his preaching. He died in France in 1419.

Common of Pastors: for Missionaries, p. 1077.

OPENING PRAYER

Father,
you called St. Vincent Ferrer
to preach the gospel of the last judgment.
Through his prayers may we come with joy

to meet your Son in the kingdom of heaven,
where he lives and reigns with you and the Holy
  Spirit,
one God, for ever and ever. ℟. **Amen.**

*Readings and Intervenient Chants may also be taken
from the Common of Holy Men and Women: for Religious, p. 1195.*

Reading I (2 Tm 4, 1-5), p. 1169, no. 12.
Responsorial Psalm (Ps 40), p. 218.
Gospel (Lk 12, 35-40), p. 1230, no. 18.

Apr. 7 — ST. JOHN BAPTIST DE LA SALLE, Priest

Memorial

Founder of the Institute of the *Brothers of the Christian
Schools,* St. John Baptist de la Salle is called the father
of modern pedagogy. In 1678 he was ordained to the
priesthood and received his doctorate in theology in
1680. In 1691 he founded his first novitiate of *Brothers*
at Vangirard, France. He died in Rouen, in 1719, and
was canonized on May 24, 1900.

*Common of Pastors, p. 1071; or Common of Holy Men
and Women: for Teachers, p. 1101.*

OPENING PRAYER

Father,
you chose St. John Baptist de la Salle
to give young people a Christian education.
Give your Church teachers who will devote themselves
to helping your children grow
as Christian men and women.
We ask this through our Lord Jesus Christ, your Son,
who lives and reigns with you and the Holy Spirit,
one God, for ever and ever. ℟. **Amen.**

Reading I (2 Tm 1, 13-14; 2, 1-3), p. 1168, no. 11.
Responsorial Psalm (Ps 1), p. 1206, no. 1.
Gospel (Mt 18, 1-4), p. 1222, no. 6.

Apr. 11 — STANISLAUS, Bishop and Martyr

Optional Memorial

St. Stanislaus was born in Poland. As Bishop of Cracow he reproached King Boleslaw II for his dissolute life. Boleslaw slew him during the Holy Sacrifice of the Mass, in 1079.

Common of Martyrs, p. 1061; or Common of Pastors: for Bishops p. 1069.

OPENING PRAYER

Father,
to honor you, St. Stanislaus faced martyrdom with
   courage.
Keep us strong and loyal in our fath until death.
Grant this through our Lord Jesus Christ, your Son,
who lives and reigns with you and the Holy Spirit,
one God, for ever and ever. ℟. **Amen.**

Reading I (Rv 12, 10-12), p. 1143, no. 3.
Responsorial Psalm (Ps 34), p. 1144, no. 2.
Gospel (Jn 17, 11-19), p. 1153, no. 7.

Apr. 13 — ST. MARTIN I, Pope and Martyr

Optional Memorial

St. Martin was continually persecuted by the heretics of his time. The horrible treatment to which he was subjected hastened his death in 655.

Common of Martyrs, p. 1061; or Common of Pastors: for Popes, p. 1066.

OPENING PRAYER

Merciful God, our Father,
neither hardship, pain, nor the threat of death
could weaken the faith of St. Martin.
Through our faith, give us courage
to endure whatever sufferings the world may inflict
   upon us.
We ask this through our Lord Jesus Christ, your Son,
who lives and reigns with you and the Holy Spirit,
one God, for ever and ever. ℟. **Amen.**

Reading I (2 Tm 2, 8-13; 3, 10-12), p. 1148, no. 5.
Responsorial Psalm (Ps 126), p. 1145, no. 4.
Gospel (Jn 15, 18-21), p. 1153, no. 6.

Apr. 21 — ST. ANSELM, Bishop and Doctor

Optional Memorial

A Benedictine Monk, St. Anselm governed the Monastery of Bec and was elevated to the Archbishopric of Canterbury. He died in 1109 and is called the Father of Scholastic Theology.

Common of Pastors: for Bishops, p. 1069; or Common of Doctors of the Church, p. 1082.

OPENING PRAYER

Father,
you called St. Anselm
to study and teach the sublime truths you have revealed.
Let your gift of faith come to the aid of our understanding
and open our hearts to your truth.
Grant this through our Lord Jesus Christ, your Son,
who lives and reigns with you and the Holy Spirit,
one God, for ever and ever. ℟. **Amen.**

Readings and Intervenient Chants may also be taken from the Common of Holy Men and Women: for Religious, p. 1195.

Reading I (Eph 3, 14-19), p. 1213, no. 7.
Responsorial Psalm (Ps 34), p. 1207, no. 4.
Gospel (Mt 18, 1-4), p. 1222, no. 6.

Apr. 23 — ST. GEORGE, Martyr

Optional Memorial

Son of an illustrious family of Cappadocia, St. George was elevated at a young age by Diocletian to one of the highest offices of the Imperial ministry. When the Emperor promulgated an edict against the Christians, St. George professed his faith publicly. He died in 303. He is the Patron Saint of England.

Common of Martyrs, p. 1061.

OPENING PRAYER

Lord,
hear the prayers of those who praise your mighty
 power.
As St. George was ready to follow Christ in suffering
 and death,
so may he be ready to help us in our weakness.
We ask this through our Lord Jesus Christ, your Son,
who lives and reigns with you and the Holy Spirit,
one God, for ever and ever. ℟. **Amen.**

Reading I (Rv 21, 5-7), p. 1143, no. 4.
Responsorial Psalm (Ps 126), p. 1145, no. 4.
Gospel (Lk 9, 23-26), p. 1152, no. 4.

_____

Apr. 24 — ST. FIDELIS OF SIGMARINGEN,
Priest and Martyr

Optional Memorial

St. Fidelis was born at Sigmaringen, Germany, in 1577.
He was at first "the Advocate of the poor." He then
entered the Order of Friars Minor, preached the Word
of God. He was martyred in the Capuchin reform in
1622 and is the Protomartyr of the *Propaganda Fidei*.

Common of Martyrs, p. 1061; or Common of Pastors, p.
1071.

OPENING PRAYER

Father,
you filled St. Fidelis with the fire of your love
and gave him the privilege of dying
that the faith might live.
Let his prayers keep us firmly grounded in your love,
and help us to come to know the power of Christ's
 resurrection.
We ask this through our Lord Jesus Christ, your Son,
who lives and reigns with you and the Holy Spirit,
one God, for ever and ever. ℟. **Amen.**

Reading I (Col 1, 24-29), p. 1167, no. 9.
Responsorial Psalm (Ps 34), p. 1144, no. 2.
Gospel (Jn 15, 9-17), p. 1232, no. 21.

_____

Apr. 25 — ST. MARK, Evangelist

Feast

St. Mark was a disciple of St. Paul and the author of the second Gospel under the inspiration of the Holy Spirit. He begins his account with the Mission of John the Baptizer, "crying in the desert"; thus he is represented with a lion at his feet, since the lion, one of the symbolic living creatures of Ezekiel's vision, shakes the desert with his roars. He founded the Church at Alexandria in Egypt and was martyred there in the latter part of the 1st century.

ENTRANCE ANT.   Mk 16, 15

Go out to the whole world, and preach the gospel to all creation, alleluia.   → No. 2, p. 14

OPENING PRAYER

Father,
you gave St. Mark
the privilege of proclaiming your gospel.
May we profit by his wisdom
and follow Christ more faithfully.
Grant this through our Lord Jesus Christ, your Son,
who lives and reigns with you and the Holy Spirit,
one God, for ever and ever. ℟. **Amen.** ⍱

READING I   1 Pt 5, 5-14

St. Peter tells us that we are to be obedient toward those in authority and humble toward one another, with complete trust in God's loving care. As a reward for our faith and trust in God, we will be strengthened and attain glory in Christ.

A reading from the first letter of Peter

In your relations with one another, clothe yourselves with humility, because God "is stern with the arrogant but to the humble he shows kindness." Bow humbly under God's mighty hand, so that in due time he may lift you high. Cast all your cares on him because he cares for you. Stay sober and alert. Your opponent the devil is prowling like a roaring lion looking for someone to devour. Resist him, solid in your faith, realizing that the brotherhood of believers is undergoing the same sufferings throughout the world. The God of all grace, who called you to his everlasting glory in Christ, will himself restore, confirm, strengthen and establish those who have suffered a little while. Dominion be his throughout the ages! Amen.

I am writing briefly through Silvanus, whom I take to be a faithful brother to you. Herewith are expressed my encouragement and my testimony that this is the true grace of God. Be steadfast in it. The church in Babylon sends you greeting, as does Mark my son. Greet one another with the embrace of true love. To all of you who are in Christ, peace—This is the Word of the Lord. ℞. **Thanks be to God.** ℣

➤ No. 15, p. 623

Responsorial Psalm　　　　Ps 89, 2-3. 6-7. 16-17

℞. (2) **For ever I will sing the goodness of the Lord.**

The favors of the Lord I will sing forever;
　　through all generations my mouth shall proclaim
　　　　your faithfulness.

For you have said, "My kindness is established forever";
　　in heaven you have confirmed your faithfulness. — ℞

The heavens proclaim your wonders, O Lord,
　　and your faithfulness, in the assembly of the holy
　　　　ones.

For who in the skies can rank with the Lord?
　　Who is like the Lord among the sons of God?—℞

Happy the people who know the joyful shout;
　　in the light of your countenance, O Lord, they
　　　　walk.

At your name they rejoice all the day,
　　and through your justice they are exalted. — ℞ ℣

℞. Or: **Alleluia.** ℣

GOSPEL Mk 16, 15-20

Alleluia (1 Cor 1, 23-24)

℞. **Alleluia.** We preach a Christ who was crucified; he is the power and the wisdom of God. ℞. **Alleluia.**

Together with Christ, our human nature has been glorified at God's right hand. To those who have this certitude Jesus entrusts the mission to continue his work of salvation; and he promises them his help.

℣. The Lord be with you. ℞. **And also with you.**

✠ A reading from the holy gospel according to Mark ℞. **Glory to you, Lord.**

Jesus appeared to the Eleven and told them: "Go into the world and proclaim the good news to all creation. The man who believes in it and accepts baptism will be saved; the man who refuses to believe in it will be condemned. Signs like these will accompany those who have professed their faith: they will use my name to expel demons, they will speak entirely new languages, they will be able to handle serpents, they will be able to drink deadly poison without harm, and the sick upon whom they lay their hands will recover." Then, after speaking to them, the Lord Jesus was taken up into heaven and took his seat at God's right hand. The Eleven went forth and preached everywhere. The Lord continued to work with them throughout and confirm the message through the signs which accompanied them.—This is the gospel of the Lord. ℞. **Praise to you, Lord Jesus Christ.** ➤ No. 15, p. 623

PRAYER OVER THE GIFTS

Lord,
as we offer the sacrifice of praise
on the feast of St. Mark,
we pray that your Church may always be faithful
to the preaching of the gospel.
We ask this through Christ our Lord.
℞. **Amen.** ➤ No. 21, p. 626 (Pref. P 65)

COMMUNION ANT.   Mt 28, 20

I, the Lord, am with you always, until the end of the world, alleluia. ℣

PRAYER AFTER COMMUNION
All-powerful God,
may the gifts we have received at this altar
make us holy, and strengthen us
in the faith of the gospel preached by St. Mark.
We ask this in the name of Jesus the Lord.
℞. **Amen.**   ➜ No. 32, p. 650

Apr. 28 — ST. PETER CHANEL, Priest and Martyr

Optional Memorial

St. Peter Chanel died a martyr's death on the island of Futuna in Polynesia, April 28, 1841. He was canonized in 1954. It seems quite fitting that the first martyr of Oceania should be inscribed in the general calendar of the Church.

Common of Martyrs, p. 1061; or Common of Pastors: for Missionaries, p. 1077.

OPENING PRAYER
Father,
you called St. Peter Chanel to work for your Church
and gave him the crown of martyrdom.
May our celebration of Christ's death and resurrection
make us faithful witnesses to the new life he brings,
for he lives and reigns with you and the Holy Spirit,
one God, for ever and ever. ℞. **Amen.**

Reading I (1 Cor 1, 18-25), p. 1164, no. 2.
Responsorial Psalm (Ps 117), p. 1163, no. 6.
Gospel (Mk 1, 14-20), p. 1172, no. 4.

Apr. 29 — ST. CATHERINE OF SIENA,
Virgin and Doctor

Memorial

A Dominican tertiary, St. Catherine pacified the civil discords of her country and was largely responsible for the return of Pope Gregory XI from Avignon to Rome. She was imprinted with the sacred Stigmata and died at Rome in 1380 at thirty-three years of age. In 1970 Pope Paul VI proclaimed her a Doctor of the Church.

ENTRANCE ANT.

Here is a wise and faithful virgin who went with lighted lamp to meet her Lord, alleluia.

➤ No. 2, p. 12

OPENING PRAYER

Father,
in meditating on the sufferings of your Son
and in serving your Church,
St. Catherine was filled with the fervor of your love.
By her prayers,
may we share in the mystery of Christ's death
and rejoice in the revelation of his glory,
for he lives and reigns with you and the Holy Spirit,
one God, for ever and ever. ℟. **Amen.** ℣

Readings and Intervenient Chants from the Common of Virgins, p. 1188, or the Common of Doctors of the Church, p. 1177.

READING I   1 Jn 1, 5—2, 2

The blood of Jesus Christ cleanses us of all sin. We are saved through the blood of Christ who is the perfect offering for our sins.

A reading from the first letter of John

Here, then, is the message
we have heard from him
and announce to you:
that God is light;
in him there is no darkness.
If we say, "We have fellowship with him,"
while continuing to walk in darkness,

we are liars and do not act in truth.
But if we walk in light,
as he is in the light,
we have fellowship with one another,
and the blood of his Son Jesus cleanses us from all
    sin.
If we say, "We are free of the guilt of sin,"
we deceive ourselves; the truth is not to be found
    in us.
But if we acknowledge our sins,
he who is just can be trusted
to forgive our sins
and cleanse us from every wrong.
If we say, "We have never sinned,"
we make him a liar
and his word finds no place in us.
My little ones,
I am writing this to keep you from sin.
But if anyone should sin,
we have, in the presence of the Father,
Jesus Christ, an intercessor who is just.
He is an offering for our sins,
and not for our sins only,
but for those of the whole world.
This is the Word of the Lord. ℟. **Thanks be to God.**

Responsorial Psalm (Ps 103), p. 1208, no. 5.
Gospel (Mt 11, 25-30), p. 1221, no. 3.

PRAYER OVER THE GIFTS

Lord,
accept this saving sacrifice
we offer on the feast of St. Catherine.
By following her teaching and example,
may we offer more perfect praise to you.
Grant this through Christ our Lord.
℟. **Amen.**   ➤ No. 21, p. 626, (Pref. P 22-25)

COMMUNION ANT.   1 Jn 1, 7

If we walk in the light, as God is in light, there is fellowship among us, and the blood of his Son, Jesus Christ, will cleanse us from all sin, alleluia. ℣

PRAYER AFTER COMMUNION

Lord,
may the eucharist,
which nourished St. Catherine in this life,
bring us eternal life.
We ask this in the name of Jesus the Lord.
℟. **Amen.**   → No. 32, p. 650

Apr. 30 — ST. PIUS V, Pope

Optional Memorial

St. Pius V, of the Dominican Order, was a Pope of great sanctity. His pontificate was one of most glorious of the 16th century. He enforced obedience to the decrees of the Council of Trent, and revised the Missal and the Breviary. He died in 1572.

Common of Pastors: for Popes, p. **1066.**

OPENING PRAYER

Father,
you chose St. Pius V as pope of your Church
to protect the faith and give you more fitting wor-
    ship.
By his prayers,
help us to celebrate your holy mysteries
with a living faith and an effective love.
We ask this through our Lord Jesus Christ, your Son,
who lives and reigns with you and the Holy Spirit,
one God, for ever and ever. ℟. **Amen.**

Reading I (1 Cor 4, 1-5), p. 1165, no. 3.
Responsorial Psalm (Ps 110), p. 1163, no. 5.
Gospel (Jn 21, 15-17), p. 1176, no. 11.

— MAY —

May 1 — ST. JOSEPH THE WORKER

Optional Memorial

The feast of St. Joseph the Worker was instituted in 1955 by Pope Pius XII, and its celebration fixed on May 1, which is the day on which man's labor is honored in many countries.

ENTRANCE ANT.   Ps 128, 1-2

Happy are all who fear the Lord and walk in his ways. You shall enjoy the fruits of your labor, you will prosper and be happy, alleluia. ➤No. 2, p. 614

OPENING PRAYER

God our Father,
creator and ruler of the universe,
in every age you call man
to develop and use his gifts for the good of others.
With St. Joseph as our example and guide,
help us to do the work you have asked
and come to the rewards you have promised.
We ask this through our Lord Jesus Christ, your Son,
who lives and reigns with you and the Holy Spirit,
one God, for ever and ever. ℟. **Amen.** ⬧

READING I   Gn 1, 26—2, 3

God has given the world he created into the care of men. We are to work with it, subdue it and rule over it. It is our responsibility to develop the essential goodness that God has given to all creation.

A reading from the book of Genesis

God said: "Let us make man in our image, after our likeness. Let them have dominion over the fish of the sea, the birds of the air, and the cattle, and over all the wild animals and all the creatures that crawl on the ground."

God created man in his image;
in the divine image he created him;
male and female he created them.

God blessed them, saying: "Be fertile and multiply; fill the earth and subdue it. Have dominion over the fish of the sea, the birds of the air, and all the living things that move on the earth." God also said: "See, I give you every seed-bearing plant all over the earth and every tree that has seed-bearing fruit on it to be your food; and to all the animals of the land, all the birds of the air, and all the living creatures that crawl on the ground, I give all the green plants for food." And so it happened. God looked at everything he had made, and he found it very good. Evening came, and morning followed— the sixth day.

Thus the heavens and the earth and all their array were completed. Since on the seventh day God was finished with the work he had been doing, he rested on the seventh day from all the work he had undertaken. So God blessed the seventh day and made it holy, because on it he rested from all the work he had done in creation.—This is the Word of the Lord. ℟. **Thanks be to God.** ⅴ

OR

READING I   Col 3, 14-15. 17. 23-24

Everything we do must be done in the name of the Lord Jesus, for all we have and do comes to us through him from the Father. We must give our all in the service of the Lord.

A reading from the letter of Paul to the Colossians

Over all the virtues put on love, which binds the rest together and makes them perfect. Christ's peace must reign in your hearts, since as members of the one body you have been called to that peace. Dedicate yourselves to thankfulness. Whatever you do, whether in speech or in action, do it in the name of the Lord Jesus. Give thanks to God the Father through him.

Whatever you do, work at it with your whole being. Do it for the Lord rather than for men, since you know full well you will receive an inheritance from him as your reward. Be slaves of Christ the Lord.—This is the Word of the Lord. ℟. **Thanks be to God.** ↓

Responsorial Psalm   Ps 90, 2. 3-4. 12-13. 14. 16

℟. (17) **Lord, give success to the work of our hands.**

Before the mountains were begotten
   and the earth and the world were brought forth,
     from everlasting to everlasting you are God. — ℟
You turn man back to dust,
   saying, "Return, O children of men."
For a thousand years in your sight
   are as yesterday, now that it is past,
   or as a watch of the night. — ℟
Teach us to number our days aright,
   that we may gain wisdom of heart.
Return, O Lord! How long?
   Have pity on your servants! — ℟
Fill us at daybreak with your kindness,
   that we may shout for joy and gladness all our
     days.
Let your work be seen by your servants
   and your glory by their children. — ℟ ↓

The Gospel is special in this Optional Memorial.

GOSPEL   Mt 13, 54-58

Alleluia (Ps 67, 20)

℟. **Alleluia.** Blessed be the Lord day after day, the God who saves us and bears our burdens. ℟. **Alleluia.**

The people of Nazareth spurned Jesus because they knew he was the son of a simple carpenter. If only they had had the vision to see how noble was the work of Joseph and Jesus, they might not have rejected Jesus out of hand.

℣. The Lord be with you. ℟. **And also with you.**
✠ A reading from the holy gospel according to Matthew. ℟. **Glory to you, Lord.**

Jesus went to his native place and spent his time teaching the people in their synagogue. They were filled with amazement, and said to one another, "Where did this man get such wisdom and miraculous powers? Isn't this the carpenter's son? Isn't Mary known to be his mother and James, Joseph, Simon, and Judas his brothers? Aren't his sisters our neighbors? Where did he get all this?" They found him altogether too much for them. Jesus said to them, "No prophet is without honor except in his native place, indeed in his own house." And he did not work many miracles there because of their lack of faith.—This is the gospel of the Lord. ℟. **Praise to you, Lord Jesus Christ.**   ➔ No. 15, p. 623

PRAYER OVER THE GIFTS

Lord God,
fountain of all mercy,
look upon our gifts on this feast of St. Joseph.
Let our sacrifice
become the protection of all who call on you.
We ask this in the name of Jesus the Lord.
℟. **Amen.**   ➔ Pref. P 62, p. 979

COMMUNION ANT.   Col. 3, 17

Let everything you do or say be in the name of the Lord with thanksgiving to God, alleluia. ℣

PRAYER AFTER COMMUNION

Lord,
hear the prayers of those you nourish in this eucharist.
Inspired by the example of St. Joseph,
may our lives manifest your love;
may we rejoice for ever in your peace.
Grant this through Christ our Lord.
℟. **Amen.** ——————————— ➔ No. 32, p. 650

May 2 — ST. ATHANASIUS, Bishop and Doctor

Memorial

St. Athanasius was born at Alexandria toward the end of the 3rd century. Elevated to the Bishopric of Alexandria, he became the champion of the Faith against Arianism. He died in 373, leaving many religious and apologetic writings.

Common of Pastors: for Bishops, p. 1069; or Common of Doctors of the Church, p. 1082.

OPENING PRAYER

Father,
you raised up St. Athanasius
to be an outstanding defender
of the truth of Christ's divinity.
By his teaching and protection
may we grow in your knowledge and love.
Grant this through our Lord Jesus Christ, your Son,
who lives and reigns with you and the Holy Spirit,
one God, for ever and ever. ℟. **Amen.**

Reading I (1 Jn 5, 1-5), p. 1150.
Responsorial Psalm (Ps 37), p. 1181, no. 2.

GOSPEL   Alleluia (Mt 5, 10)   Mt 10, 22-25

℟. **Alleluia.** Happy are they who suffer persecution
   for justice' sake;
the kingdom of heaven is theirs. ℟. **Alleluia.**

The missionaries are told not to risk their lives unnecessarily. Jesus implies, not that he expects the Second Coming and God's final judgment before the termination of his disciples' mission, but rather that the divine plan of Israel's salvation will not be completed before the Second Coming because of hostility.

℣. The Lord be with you. ℟. **And also with you.**
✠ A reading from the holy gospel according to Matthew. ℟. **Glory to you, Lord.**

Jesus said to his disciples: "You will be hated by all on account of me. But whoever holds out till the end will escape death. When they persecute you in one town, flee to the next. I solemnly assure you, you will not have covered the towns of Israel before the Son of Man comes.

  "No pupil outranks his teacher, no slave his master. The pupil should be glad to become like his

teacher, the slave like his master."—This is the
gospel of the Lord. ℞. **Praise to you, Lord Jesus
Christ.**   ➤ No. 15, p. 623

PRAYER OVER THE GIFTS

Lord,
look upon the gifts we offer
on the feast of St. Athanasius.
Keep us true to the faith he professed
and let our own witness to your truth
bring us closer to salvation.
We ask this through Christ our Lord.
℞. **Amen.**   ➤ No. 21, p. 626 (Pref. **P 22-25**)

PRAYER AFTER COMMUNION

All-powerful God,
we join St. Athanasius in professing our belief
in the true divinity of Christ your Son.
Through this sacrament
may our faith always give us life and protection.
We ask this through Christ our Lord.
℞. **Amen.**   ➤ No. 32, p. 650

May 3 — STS. PHILIP AND JAMES, Apostles

Feast

St. Philip, like Peter and Andrew, was of Bethsaida. He
was crucified at Hierapolis in Phrygia where he preached the gospel. St. James the Less was a cousin of our
Lord and a brother of the apostle Jude. He wrote one
of the Epistles of the New Testament. He was hurled
down from the terrace of the temple and clubbed to
death.

ENTRANCE ANT.

**The Lord chose these holy men for their unfeigned
love, and gave them eternal glory, alleluia.**
                                   ➤ No. 2, p. 614

OPENING PRAYER

God our Father,
every year you give us joy

on the festival of the apostles Philip and James.
By the help of their prayers
may we share in the suffering, death, and resurrection
of your only Son
and come to the eternal vision of your glory.
We ask this through our Lord Jesus Christ, your Son,
who lives and reigns with you and the Holy Spirit,
one God, for ever and ever. ℟. **Amen.** ⱽ

READING I   1 Cor 15, 1-8

In this reading, St. Paul summarizes the most basic facts of the Good
News of Christ. Our faith rests upon the eyewitness testimony of the
apostles, who saw Jesus after his death and resurrection. Our faith
rests also upon the successors of the apostles today, our bishops.

A reading from the first letter of Paul to the
Corinthians

Brothers, I want to remind you of the gospel I
preached to you, which you received and in which
you stand firm. You are being saved by it at this
very moment if you retain it as I preached it to you.
Otherwise you have believed in vain. I handed on to
you first of all what I myself received, that Christ
died for our sins in accord with the Scriptures; that
he was buried and, in accord with the Scriptures,
rose on the third day; that he was seen by Cephas,
then by the Twelve. After that he was seen by five
hundred brothers at once, most of whom are still
alive, although some have fallen asleep. Next he
was seen by James; then by all the apostles. Last of
all he was seen by me, as one born out of the normal
course.—This is the Word of the Lord. ℟. **Thanks
be to God.** ⱽ

Responsorial Psalm   Ps 19, 2-3. 4-5
℟. (5) **Their message goes out through all the earth.**
The heavens declare the glory of God,
    and the firmament proclaims his handiwork.
Day pours out the word to day,
    and night to night imparts knowledge. — ℟

Not a word nor a discourse
  whose voice is not heard;
Through all the earth their voice resounds,
  and to the ends of the world, their message. — ℟ ℣

℟. Or: **Alleluia.** ℣

GOSPEL   Jn 14, 6-14

Alleluia (Jn 14, 6. 9)

℟. **Alleluia.** I am the way, the truth, and the life,
  says the Lord;
Philip, whoever sees me sees the Father. ℟. **Alleluia.**

The question of Philip, who is honored today, was answered by Christ
with a clear statement of his divinity. The apostles are to share in
the saving mission of the Son of God, who will watch over them and
will answer their needs.

℣. The Lord be with you. ℟. **And also with you.**
✠ A reading from the holy gospel according to John
℟. **Glory to you, Lord.**

Jesus told Thomas:
  "I am the way, and the truth, and the life;
  no one comes to the Father but through me.
  If you really knew me, you would know my Father
    also.
  From this point on you know him; you have seen
    him."

  "Lord," Philip said to him, "show us the Father
and that will be enough for us." "Philip," Jesus replied, "after I have been with you all this time, you
still do not know me?

  "Whoever has seen me has seen the Father.
  How can you say, 'Show us the Father'?
  Do you not believe that I am in the Father and
    the Father is in me?
  The words I speak are not spoken of myself;
  it is the Father who lives in me accomplishing
    his works.
  Believe me that I am in the Father
  and the Father is in me,
  or else, believe because of the works I do.

I solemnly assure you,
the man who has faith in me
will do the works I do,
and greater far than these.
Why? Because I go to the Father,
and whatever you ask in my name
I will do,
so as to glorify the Father in the Son.
Anything you ask me in my name
I will do."

This is the gospel of the Lord. ℟. **Praise to you, Lord Jesus Christ.** ➤ No. 15, p. 623

PRAYER OVER THE GIFTS

Lord,
accept our gifts
at this celebration in honor of the apostles Philip
and James.
Make our religion pure and undefiled.
We ask this through Christ our Lord.
℟. **Amen.** ➤ No. 21, p. 626 (Pref. P 64-65)

COMMUNION ANT. Jn 14, 8-9

Lord, let us see the Father, and we shall be content. And Jesus said: Philip, he who sees me, sees the Father, alleluia. ℣

PRAYER AFTER COMMUNION

Father,
by the holy gifts we have received
free our minds and hearts from sin.
With the apostles Philip and James
may we see you in your Son
and be found worthy to have eternal life.
We ask this through Christ our Lord.
℟. **Amen.** ➤ No. 32, p. 650

May 12 — STS. NEREUS and ACHILLEUS, Martyrs

Optional Memorial

Nereus and Achilleus were Roman soldiers who embraced the true faith and refused to serve any longer. As a result, they were martyred, probably during the reign of Diocletian. Their tomb is located in the cemetery on the Via Ardeatina, where a basilica was erected in their honor.

Common of Martyrs, p. 1049 or 1059.

OPENING PRAYER

Father,
we honor Saints Nereus and Achilleus for their courage
in dying to profess their faith in Christ.
May we experience the help of their prayers
at the throne of your mercy.
Grant this through our Lord Jesus Christ, your Son,
who lives and reigns with you and the Holy Spirit,
one God, for ever and ever. ℟. **Amen.**

Reading I (Rv 7, 9-17), p. 1142, no. 2.
Responsorial Psalm (Ps 124), p. 1145, no. 3.
Gospel (Mt 11, 25-30), p. 1221, no. 3.

The Same Day, May 12
ST. PANCRAS, Martyr

Optional Memorial

St. Pancras was martyred at the age of fourteen, during the reign of Diocletian about 304. He was buried on the Via Aurelia and Pope Symmachus built a church over his tomb.

Common of Martyrs, p. 1056 or 1061.

OPENING PRAYER

God of mercy,
give your Church joy and confidence
through the prayers of St. Pancras.
Keep us faithful to you
and steadfast in your service.

We ask this through our Lord Jesus Christ, your Son,
who lives and reigns wtih you and the Holy Spirit,
one God, for ever and ever. ℟. **Amen.**

Reading I (Rv 19, 1. 5-9), p. 1205, no. 3.
Responsorial Psalm (Ps 103), p. 1208, no. 5.
Gospel (Mt 11, 25-30), p. 1221, no. 3.

May 14 — ST. MATTHIAS, Apostle

Feast

After the Ascension of our Lord, St. Peter proposed that
the disciples draw lots to select an Apostle to take the
place of Judas. "The choice fell to Matthias; and he was
added to the eleven Apostles." He propagated the Faith
in Palestine, and was stoned to death in the year 64.

ENTRANCE ANT.   Jn 15, 16

**You have not chosen me; I have chosen you. Go
and bear fruit that will last, alleluia.** ➤ No. 2, p. 614

OPENING PRAYER

Father,
you called St. Matthias to share in the mission of
    the apostles.
By the help of his prayers
may we receive with joy the love you share with us
and be counted among those you have chosen.
We ask this through our Lord Jesus Christ, your Son,
who lives and reigns with you and the Holy Spirit,
one God, for ever and ever. ℟. **Amen.** ⋎

READING I   Acts 1, 15-17. 20-26

Peter discusses the question of Judas and his replacement. Two men of
irreproachable life are nominated; Joseph Barsabbas and Matthias. Then
lots are drawn by the disciples and the choice falls on Matthias, who is
added to the apostles.

A reading from the Acts of the Apostles

In those days, Peter stood up in the center of the
brothers; there must have been a hundred and
twenty gathered together. "Brothers," he said, "the

saying in Scripture uttered long ago by the Holy
Spirit through the mouth of David was destined to
be fulfilled in Judas, the one that guided those who
arrested Jesus. He was one of our number and he
had been given a share in this ministry of ours.

"It is written in the Book of Psalms,
     'Let his encampment be desolate.
          May no one dwell on it.'
And again,
     'May another take his office.'
It is entirely fitting, therefore, that one of those
who was of our company while the Lord Jesus
moved among us, from the baptism of John until
the day he was taken up from us, should be named
as witness with us to his resurrection." At that
they nominated two, Joseph (called Barsabbas, also
known as Justus) and Matthias. Then they prayed:
"O Lord, you read the hearts of men. Make known
to us which of these two you choose for this apostolic ministry, replacing Judas, who deserted the
cause and went the way he was destined to go."
They then drew lots between the two men. The
choice fell to Matthias, who was added to the eleven apostles.—This is the Word of the Lord. ℟.
Thanks be to God. ℣

Responsorial Psalm   Ps 113, 1-2. 3-4. 5-6. 7-8
℟. (8) **The Lord will give him a seat with the leaders
     of his people.**
Praise, you servants of the Lord,
     praise the name of the Lord.
Blessed be the name of the Lord
     both now and forever. — ℟
From the rising to the setting of the sun
     is the name of the Lord to be praised.
High above all nations is the Lord;
     above the heavens is his glory. — ℟

Who is like the Lord, our God, who is enthroned
    on high
    and looks upon the heavens and the earth be-
      low? — ℟

He raises up the lowly from the dust;
    from the dunghill he lifts up the poor
To seat them with princes,
    with the princes of his own people. — ℟ ↓

℟. Or: **Alleluia.** ↓

GOSPEL   Jn 15, 9-17

Alleluia (Jn 15, 16)

℟. **Alleluia.** I have chosen you from the world,
    says the Lord,
to go out and bear fruit that will last. ℟. **Alleluia.**

Jesus admonishes the disciples to continue the love he has shown to
them. Their keeping of the commandments will be a proof of this.
"You are to love one another... It was I who chose you."

V. The Lord be with you. ℟. **And also with you.**

✠ A reading from the holy gospel according to John
℟. **Glory to you, Lord.**

Jesus said to his disciples:
    "As the Father has loved me,
    so I have loved you.
    Live on in my love.
    You will live in my love
    if you keep my commandments,
    even as I have kept my Father's commandments
    and live in his love.
    All this I tell you
    that my joy may be yours
    and your joy may be complete.
    This is my commandment:
    love one another
    as I have loved you.
    There is no greater love than this:
    to lay down one's life for one's friends.
    You are my friends
    if you do what I command you.

I no longer speak of you as slaves,
for a slave does not know what his master is
    about.
Instead, I call you friends,
since I have made known to you all that I heard
    from my Father.
It was not you who chose me,
it was I who chose you
to go forth and bear fruit.
Your fruit must endure,
so that all you ask the Father in my name
he will give you.
The command I give you is this,
that you love one another."

This is the gospel of the Lord. ℟. **Praise to you,
Lord Jesus Christ.**   ➤ No. 15, p. 623

PRAYER OVER THE GIFTS
Lord,
accept the gifts your Church offers
on the feast of the apostle, Matthias,
and by this eucharist
strengthen your grace within us.
We ask this through Christ our Lord.
℟. **Amen.**   ➤ No. 21, p. 626 (Pref. P 64-65)

COMMUNION ANT.   Jn 15, 12
**This is my commandment: love one another as I
have loved you.** ℣

PRAYER AFTER COMMUNION
Lord,
you constantly give life to your people
in this holy eucharist.
By the prayers of the apostle Matthias
prepare us to take our place
among your saints in eternal life.
We ask this through Christ our Lord.
℟. **Amen.**   ➤ No. 32, p. 650

[In the dioceses of the United States]

May 15 — ST. ISIDORE

Optional Memorial

St. Isidore was born at Madrid, Spain, in the latter half of the 12th century. For the greater part of his life he was employed as a laborer on a farm outside the city. Many marvelous happenings accompanied his lifelong work in the fields and continued long after his death. St. Isidore was canonized in 1622. In 1947, he was proclaimed the patron of the National Rural Life Conference in the United States.

Common of Holy Men and Women, p. 1090.

OPENING PRAYER

Lord God,
all creation is yours, and you call us to serve you
by caring for the gifts that surround us.
May the example of St. Isidore urge us
to share our food with the hungry
and to work for the salvation of mankind.
We ask this through our Lord Jesus Christ, your Son,
who lives and reigns with you and the Holy Spirit,
one God, for ever and ever. ℟. **Amen.**

Reading I (Rv 3, 14. 20-22), p. 1204, no. 2.
Responsorial Psalm (Ps 23), p. 1161, no. 2.
Gospel (Mt 25, 14-30), p. 1224, no. 9.

May 18 — ST JOHN I, Pope and Martyr

Optional Memorial

St. John I was Pope under the Arian King Theodoric. Captured and brought to Ravenna, he died in prison shortly after in 526.

Common of Martyrs, p. 1056 or 1061; or Common of Pastors: for Popes, p. 1066.

OPENING PRAYER

God our Father,
rewarder of all who believe,

hear our prayers
as we celebrate the martyrdom of Pope John.
Help us to follow him in loyalty to the faith.
Grant this through our Lord Jesus Christ, your Son,
who lives and reigns with you and the Holy Spirit,
one God, for ever and ever. ℟. **Amen.**

Reading I (Rv 3, 14. 20-22), p. 1204, no. 2.
Responsorial Psalm (Ps 23), p. 1161, no. 2.
Gospel (Lk 22, 24-30), p. 1174, no. 8.

May 20 — ST. BERNARDINE OF SIENA, Priest

Optional Memorial

St. Bernardine, born of noble parentage, left all and entered the Franciscan Order and became one of its chief
glories. He preached everywhere devotion to the Name
of Jesus, and died in 1444.

Common of Pastors: for Missionaries, p. 1077.

OPENING PRAYER

Father,
you gave St. Bernardine a special love
for the holy name of Jesus.
By the help of his prayers,
may we always be alive with the spirit of your love.
We ask this through our Lord Jesus Christ, your Son,
who lives and reigns with you and the Holy Spirit,
one God, for ever and ever. ℟. **Amen.**

*Readings and Intervenient Chants may be taken from
the Common of Pastors: for Missionaries, p. 1154, or
Common of Holy Men and Women: for Religious, p.
1195.*

READING I   Acts 4, 8-12

Peter explains the cure of the cripple. It was a miracle performed in
the name of Jesus, whom the people had rejected and crucified. There
is no salvation except in Jesus.

A reading from the Acts of the Apostles

Peter, filled with the Holy Spirit, spoke up: "Leaders
of the people! Elders! If we must answer today for

a good deed done to a cripple and explain how he was restored to health, then you and all the people of Israel must realize that it was done in the name of Jesus Christ the Nazorean whom you crucified and whom God rased from the dead. In the power of that name this man stands before you perfectly sound. This Jesus is 'the stone rejected by you the builders which has become the cornerstone.' There is no salvation in anyone else, for there is no other name in the whole world given to men by which we are to be saved."—This is the Word of the Lord. ℞. **Thanks be to God.**

Responsorial Psalm (Ps 40), p. 218.
Gospel (Lk 9, 57-62), p. 1228, no. 15.

May 25 — ST. BEDE THE VENERABLE, Priest and Doctor

Optional Memorial

St. Bede, who lived in the 8th century, was a member of the Order of St. Benedict. Because of the enormous amount of his writings, full of sound doctrine, he was called "Venerable" while still living. He is rightly called "The Father of English History," He died in 735.

Common of Doctors of the Church, p. 1082; or Common of Holy Men and Women: for Religious, p. 1097.

OPENING PRAYER

Lord,
you have enlightened your Church
with the learning of St. Bede.
In your love
may your people learn from his wisdom
and benefit from his prayers.
Grant this through our Lord Jesus Christ, your Son,
who lives and reigns with you and the Holy Spirit,
one God, for ever and ever. ℞. **Amen.**

Reading I (1 Cor 2, 10-16), p. 1183, no. 3.
Responsorial Psalm (Ps 119), p. 1181, no. 3.
Gospel (Mt 5, 13-16), p. 1186, no. 1.

The Same Day, May 25
ST. GREGORY VII, Pope

Optional Memorial

Before ascending the Papacy, St. Gregory was known as Hildebrand, a monk of the Benedictine Order. As a monk and Pope (1073) he fought against the abuses within the Church. He died in 1085.

Common of Pastors: for Popes, p. 1066.

OPENING PRAYER

Lord,
give your Church
the spirit of courage and love for justice
which distinguished Pope Gregory.
Make us courageous in condemning evil
and free us to pursue justice with love.
We ask this through our Lord Jesus Christ, your Son,
who lives and reigns with you and the Holy Spirit,
one God, for ever and ever. ℟. **Amen.**

Reading I (Acts 20, 17-18. 28-32. 36), p. 1159, no. 2.
Responsorial Psalm (Ps 110), p. 1163, no. 5.
Gospel (Mt 16, 13-19), p. 1171, no. 1.

The Same Day, May 25
ST. MARY MAGDALENE DE PAZZI, Virgin

Optional Memorial

At ten years of age, St. Mary Magdalene consecrated her virginity to God. When she was nineteen, she received the Carmelite habit. Her constant exclamation was: "To suffer and not to die." She died in 1607.

Common of Virgins, p. 1085; or Common of Holy Men and Women: for Religious, p. 1097.

OPENING PRAYER

Father,
you love those who give themselves completely to
  your service,
and you filled St. Mary Magdalene de Pazzi
with heavenly gifts and the fire of your love.
As we honor her today

may we follow her example of purity and charity.
Grant this through our Lord Jesus Christ, your Son,
who lives and reigns with you and the Holy Spirit,
one God, for ever and ever. ℟. **Amen.**

Reading I (1 Cor 7, 25-35), p. 1191, no. 1.
Responsorial Psalm (Ps 148), p. 1191, no. 2.
Gospel (Mk 3, 31-35), p. 1226, no. 11.

May 26 — ST. PHILIP NERI, Priest

Memorial

St. Philip Neri was born at Florence. Ordained a priest,
he founded the Congregation of the Priests of the
Oratory. He is noted for his zeal in converting sinners
by means of the confessional. He died at 80 years of
age, in 1595, after having demonstrated many miraculous gifts.

*Common of Pastors, p. 1071; or Common of Holy Men
and Women: for Religious, p. 1097.*

OPENING PRAYER

Father,
you continually raise up your faithful
to the glory of holiness.
In your love
kindle in us the fire of the Holy Spirit
who so filled the heart of Philip Neri.
We ask this through our Lord Jesus Christ, your Son,
who lives and reigns with you and the Holy Spirit,
one God, for ever and ever. ℟. **Amen.**

Reading I (Phil 4, 4-9), p. 1214, no. 10.
Responsorial Psalm (Ps 34), p. 1207, no. 4.
Gospel (Jn 17, 20-26), p. 1233, no. 22.

PRAYER OVER THE GIFTS

Lord,
help us who offer you this sacrifice of praise
to follow the example of St. Philip.
Keep us always cheerful in our work
for the glory of your name and the good of our
    neighbor.

Grant this through Christ our Lord.
℟. **Amen.**   ➜ No. 21, p. 626

PRAYER AFTER COMMUNION
Lord,
strengthen us with the bread of life.
May we always imitate St. Philip
by hungering after this sacrament
in which we find true life.
We ask this in the name of Jesus the Lord.
℟. **Amen.**   ➜ No. 32, p. 650

May 27 — ST. AUGUSTINE OF CANTERBURY, Bishop

Optional Memorial

St. Augustine was sent by St. Gregory the Great to
England to convert the people to Christianity. At Canterbury he erected a monastery, and there established
his Episcopal See. He is said to have baptized thousands
of Englishmen in one day. He died in the year 604.

*Common of Pastors: for Missionaries, p. 1077; or for
Bishops, p. 1069.*

OPENING PRAYER
Father,
by the preaching of St. Augustine of Canterbury,
you led the people of England to the gospel.
May the fruits of his work continue in your Church.
Grant this through our Lord Jesus Christ, your Son,
who lives and reigns with you and the Holy Spirit,
one God, for ever and ever. ℟. **Amen.**

Reading I (1 Thes 2, 2-8), p. 1168, no. 10.
Responsorial Psalm (Ps 96), p. 1162, no. 4.
Gospel (Mt 16, 15-20), p. 1172, no. 5.

May 31 — VISITATION

Feast

The feast of the Visitation was instituted in 1389 by
Urban VI to obtain the end of the Western schism, and
it was inserted in the Roman Calendar on July 2, the
date on which it had already been celebrated by the
Franciscans since 1263. Its new date (May 31) places
this feast between the Solemnity of the Annunciation
of the Lord and the Birth of St. John the Baptist, to
conform more closely to the gospel account.

ENTRANCE ANT.   Ps 66, 16

**Come, all you who fear God, and hear the great things
the Lord has done for me.**   ➤ No. 2, p. 614

OPENING PRAYER

Eternal Father,
you inspired the Virgin Mary, mother of your Son,
to visit Elizabeth and assist her in her need.
Keep us open to the working of your Spirit,
and with Mary may we praise you for ever.
We ask this through our Lord Jesus Christ, your Son,
who lives and reigns with you and the Holy Spirit,
one God, for ever and ever. ℞. **Amen.** ⇓

READING I   Zep 3, 14-18

"Shout for joy ... the Lord is in your midst." The chosen people are
told they are understood and forgiven; therefore, they have nothing
to fear. Their hearts are to be filled with joy and gladness as he is
renewing them in his love.

A reading from the book of the prophet
Zephaniah

Shout for joy, O daughter Zion!
  sing joyfully, O Israel!
Be glad and exult with all your heart,
  O daughter Jerusalem!
The Lord has removed the judgment against you,
  he has turned away your enemies;
The King of Israel, the Lord, is in your midst,
  you have no further misfortune to fear.

On that day, it shall be said to Jerusalem:
    Fear not, O Zion, be not discouraged!
The Lord, your God, is in your midst,
    a mighty savior;
He will rejoice over you with gladness,
    and renew you in his love.
He will sing joyfully because of you,
    as one sings at festivals.
This is the Word of the Lord. ℞. **Thanks be to God.** ℣

OR

READING I   Rom 12, 9-16

"Your love must be sincere." Be patient, hospitable, concerned,
sympathetic, brotherly to the lowly. By these ways, you serve the
Lord, and you can rejoice in hope.

A reading from the letter of Paul to the Romans

Your love must be sincere. Detest what is evil, cling
to what is good. Love one another with the affection of brothers. Anticipate each other in showing
respect. Do not grow slack but be fervent in spirit;
he whom you serve is the Lord. Rejoice in hope, be
patient under trial, persevere in prayer. Look on the
needs of the saints as your own; be generous in offering hospitality. Bless your persecutors; bless and
do not curse them. Rejoice with those who rejoice,
weep with those who weep. Have the same attitude
toward all. Put away ambitious thoughts and associate with those who are lowly.—This is the Word
of the Lord. ℞. **Thanks be to God.** ℣

Responsorial Psalm   Is 12, 2-3. 4. 5-6
℞. (6) **Among you is the great and Holy One of Israel.**
God indeed is my savior;
    I am confident and unafraid.
My strength and my courage is the Lord,
    and he has been my savior.
With joy you will draw water
    at the fountain of salvation. — ℞

Give thanks to the Lord, acclaim his name;
   among the nations make known his deeds,
   proclaim how exalted is his name. — ℟

Sing praise to the Lord for his glorious achievement;
   let this be known throughout all the earth.

Shout with exultation, O city of Zion,
   for great in your midst
   is the Holy One of Israel! — ℟ ▼

GOSPEL   Lk 1, 39-56

Alleluia (Lk 1, 45)

℟. **Alleluia.** Blessed are you, O Virgin Mary, for
   your firm believing,
that the promises of the Lord would be fulfilled.
   ℟. **Alleluia.**

Filled with unutterable joy, Mary had to share her feelings with
Elizabeth, who was mentioned by the angel. Joyfully, they revealed
their secrets and found themselves exultantly praising God in all his
ways.

℣. The Lord be with you. ℟. **And also with you.**

✠ A reading from the holy gospel according to Luke

℟. **Glory to you, Lord.**

Mary set out, proceeding in haste into the hill country to a town of Judah, where she entered Zechariah's house and greeted Elizabeth. When Elizabeth
heard Mary's greeting, the baby stirred in her womb.
Elizabeth was filled with the Holy Spirit and cried
out in a loud voice: "Blessed are you among women
and blessed is the fruit of your womb. But who am
I that the mother of my Lord should come to me?
The moment your greeting sounded in my ears, the
baby stirred in my womb for joy. Blessed is she who
trusted that the Lord's words to her would be fulfilled."

Then Mary said:

   "My being proclaims the greatness of the Lord,
      my spirit finds joy in God my savior,
   For he has looked upon his servant in her low-
      liness;

all ages to come shall call me blessed.
God who is mighty has done great things for
    me,
    holy is his name;
His mercy is from age to age
    on those who fear him.
"He has shown might with his arm;
    he has confused the proud in their inmost
       thoughts.
He has deposed the mighty from their thrones
    and raised the lowly to high places.
The hungry he has given every good thing,
    while the rich he has sent empty away.
He has upheld Israel his servant,
    ever mindful of his mercy;
Even as he promised our fathers,
    promised Abraham and his descendants for
       ever."

Mary remained with Elizabeth about three months
and then returned home.—This is the gospel of the
Lord. ℟. **Praise to you, Lord Jesus Christ.**

➤ No. 15, p. 623

PRAYER OVER THE GIFTS

Father,
make our sacrifice acceptable and holy
as you accepted the love of Mary,
the mother of your Son, Jesus Christ,
who is Lord for ever and ever.
℟. **Amen.**
➤ No. 21, p. 626 (Pref. P 56-57)

COMMUNION ANT.   Lk 1, 48-49

**All generations will call me blessed, for the Almighty
has done great things for me. Holy is his name.** ▼

PRAYER AFTER COMMUNION

Lord,
let the Church praise you
for the great things you have done for your people.

May we always recognize with joy
the presence of Christ in the eucharist we celebrate,
as John the Baptist hailed the presence
of our Savior in the womb of Mary.
We ask this through Christ our Lord.
℟. **Amen.** ➔ No. 32, p. 650

Saturday following the Second Sunday after Pentecost

IMMACULATE HEART OF MARY

Optional Memorial

Our Lady of Fatima is said to have asked for the Consecration of the world to her Immaculate Heart in order to obtain world peace and the conversion of Russia. To it must be added devout prayers, true repentance and penance for the sins of men. In 1942, Pope Pius XII consecrated the world to the Immaculate Heart of Mary. In 1945, the sovereign Pontiff established this new Feast to promote devotion to the Immaculate Heart of Mary and extended it to the Universal Church.

ENTRANCE ANT. Ps 13, 6

My heart rejoices in your saving power. I will sing to the Lord for his goodness to me. ➔ No. 2, p. 614

OPENING PRAYER

Father,
you prepared the heart of the Virgin Mary
to be a fitting home for your Holy Spirit.
By her prayers
may we become a more worthy temple of your glory.
Grant this through our Lord Jesus Christ, your Son,
who lives and reigns with you and the Holy Spirit,
one God, for ever and ever. ℟. **Amen.**

Readings and Intervenient Chants from the Common of the Blessed Virgin Mary, p. 1118.

Reading I (Is 61, 9-11), p. 1123, no. 9.
Responsorial Psalm (1 Sm 2), p. 1125, no. 1.

The Gospel is special in this Optional Memorial:

GOSPEL   Lk 2, 41-51

Alleluia (See Lk 2, 19)

℞. **Alleluia.** Blessed is the Virgin Mary who kept
the word of God,
and pondered it in her heart. ℞. **Alleluia.**

Jesus and his parents go to Jerusalem for the Passover. Upon returning,
Jesus is separated from them. Mary and Joseph find him in the temple
teaching. When Mary asked why, Jesus replies that he must be doing
his Father's work. Jesus returns with Mary and Joseph to Nazareth.

℣. The Lord be with you. ℞. **And also with you.**

✠ A reading from the holy gospel according to Luke

℞. **Glory to you, Lord.**

The parents of Jesus used to go every year to Jerusalem for the feast of the Passover, and when he was
twelve they went up for the celebration as was their
custom. As they were returning at the end of the
feast, the child Jesus remained behind unknown to
his parents. Thinking he was in the party, they continued their journey for a day, looking for him among
their relatives and acquaintances.

Not finding him, they returned to Jerusalem in
search of him. On the third day they came upon him
in the temple sitting in the midst of the teachers,
listening to them and asking them questions. All who
heard him were amazed at his intelligence and his
answers.

When his parents saw him they were astonished,
and his mother said to him: "Son, why have you done
this to us? You see that your father and I have been
searching for you in sorrow." He said to them: "Why
did you search for me? Did you not know I had to be
in my Father's house?" But they did not grasp what
he said to them.

He went down with them then, and came to
Nazareth, and was obedient to them. His mother
meanwhile kept all these things in memory.—This
is the gospel of the Lord. ℞. **Praise to you, Lord
Jesus Christ.**   ➜ No. 15, p. 623

PRAYER OVER THE GIFTS

Lord,
accept the prayers and gifts we offer
in honor of Mary, the Mother of God.
May they please you
and bring us your help and forgiveness.
We ask this in the name of Jesus the Lord.
℟. **Amen.**   ➜ No. 21, p. 626 (P 56-57)

COMMUNION ANT.   Lk 2, 19

Mary treasured all these words and pondered them in her heart. ℣

PRAYER AFTER COMMUNION

Lord,
you have given us the sacrament of eternal redemption.
May we who honor the mother of your Son
rejoice in the abundance of your blessings
and experience the deepening of your life within us.
We ask this through Christ our Lord.
℟. **Amen.**   No. 32, p. 650

———————————

— JUNE —

June 1 — ST. JUSTIN, Martyr

Memorial

St. Justin was converted from a pagan philosopher to Christianity. He then became the most illustrious opponent of pagan philosophers. He addressed two Apologies to the Emperor Antoninus and the Roman Senate. He died in 165.

ENTRANCE ANT.   See Ps 119, 85. 46

The wicked tempted me with their fables against your law, but I proclaimed your decrees before kings without fear or shame.   ➜ No. 2, p. 614

OPENING PRAYER

Father,
through the folly of the cross
you taught St. Justin the sublime wisdom of Jesus
   Christ.
May we too reject falsehood
and remain loyal to the faith.
We ask this through our Lord Jesus Christ, your Son,
who lives and reigns with you and the Holy Spirit,
one God, for ever and ever. ℟. **Amen.**

*Readings and Intervenient Chants from the Common of
Martyrs, p. 1138.*

READING I   1 Cor 1, 18-25

Paul says our wisdom is foolishness to the world. What does the world
know about the cross, or eternal life? "God's folly is wiser than men,
and his weakness more powerful."

A reading from the first letter of Paul to the
Corinthians

The message of the cross is complete absurdity to
those who are headed for ruin, but to us who are experiencing salvation it is the power of God. Scripture says,

   "I will destroy the wisdom of the wise,
      and thwart the cleverness of the clever."

Where is the wise man to be found? Where is the
scribe? Where is the master of worldly argument?
Has not God turned the wisdom of this world into
folly? Since in God's wisdom the world did not come
to know him through wisdom, it pleased God to
save those who believe through the absurdity of the
preaching of the gospel. Yes, Jews demand "signs"
and Greeks look for "wisdom," but we preach Christ
crucified, a stumbling block to Jews and an absurdity
to Gentiles, but to those who are called, Jews and
Greeks alike, Christ the power of God and the wisdom of God. For God's folly is wiser than men, and
his weakness more powerful than men.—This is
the Word of the Lord. ℟. **Thanks be to God.**

Responsorial Psalm (Ps 34), p. 1144, no. 2.
Gospel (Mt 5, 13-16), p. 1186, no. 1.

PRAYER OVER THE GIFTS

Lord,
help us to worship you as we should
when we celebrate these mysteries
which St. Justin vigorously defended.
We ask this in the name of Jesus the Lord.
℞. **Amen.**   ➤ No. 21, p. 626

COMMUNION ANT.   1 Cor 2, 2

**I resolved that while I was with you I would think
of nothing but Jesus Christ and him crucified.** ℣

PRAYER AFTER COMMUNION

Lord,
hear the prayer of those you renew with spiritual
    food.
By following the teaching of St. Justin
may we offer constant thanks for the gifts we receive.
Grant this through Christ our Lord.
℞. **Amen.** _____ ➤ No. 32, p. 650

June 2 — STS. MARCELLINUS and PETER, Martyrs

Optional Memorial

The exorcist Peter succeeded in converting his jailer and
his family. All were baptized by St. Marcellinus. Both
were beheaded in 304.

Common of Martyrs, p. 1049 or 1059.

OPENING PRAYER

Father,
may we benefit from the example
of your martyrs Marcellinus and Peter,
and be supported by their prayers.
Grant this through our Lord Jesus Christ, your Son,
who lives and reigns with youand the Holy Spirit,
one God, for ever and ever. ℞. **Amen.**

Reading I (2 Cor 6, 4-10), p. 1147, no. 4.
Responsorial Psalm (Ps 124), p. 1145, no. 3.
Gospel (Jn 17, 11-19), p. 1153, no. 7.

June 3 — STS. CHARLES LWANGA and COMPANIONS, Martyrs

Memorial

St. Charles Lwanga and his Companions, martyrs of Uganda, are the first martyrs of black Africa. St. Charles was martyred with twelve companions near Rubaga on June 3, 1886; the others were killed between May 26, 1886 and January 27, 1887. They were canonized in 1964.

Common of Martyrs, p. 1049 or 1059.

OPENING PRAYER

Father,
you have made the blood of the martyrs
the seed of Christians.
May the witness of St. Charles and his companions
and their loyalty to Christ in the face of torture
inspire countless men and women
to live the Christian faith.
We ask this through our Lord Jesus Christ, your Son,
who lives and reigns with you and the Holy Spirit,
one God, for ever and ever. R̶. **Amen.**

Reading I (2 Mc 7, 1-2. 9-14), p. 1139, no. 3.
Responsorial Psalm (Ps 124), p. 1145, no. 3.
Gospel (Mt 5, 1-12), p. 1220, no. 1.

PRAYER OVER THE GIFTS

Lord,
accept the gifts we present at your altar.
As you gave your holy martyrs courage to die rather
    than sin,
help us to give ourselves completely to you.
We ask this in the name of Jesus the Lord.
R̶. **Amen.**   ➔ No. 21, p. 626.

PRAYER AFTER COMMUNION

Lord,
at this celebration of the triumph of your martyrs,
we have received the sacraments
which helped them endure their sufferings.
In the midst of our own hardships
may this eucharist keep us steadfast in faith and love.
Grant this through Christ our Lord.
℟. **Amen.**   ➤ No. 32, p. 650

June 5 — ST. BONIFACE, Bishop and Martyr

Memorial

Born in England about 680, St. Boniface became a Benedictine monk. He preached in Germany and later was
consecrated first Bishop of Germany by Pope Gregory
II. He died a martyr together with thirty companions,
in 754.

*Common of Martyrs, p. 1056 or 1061; or Common of
Pastors: for Missionaries, p. 1077.*

OPENING PRAYER

Lord,
your martyr Boniface
spread the faith by his teaching
and witnessed to it with his blood.
By the help of his prayers
keep us loyal to our faith
and give us the courage to profess it in our lives.
Grant this through our Lord Jesus Christ, your Son,
who lives and reigns with you and the Holy Spirit,
one God, for ever and ever. ℟. **Amen.**

Reading I (Acts 26, 19-23), p. 1160, no. 3.
Responsorial Psalm (Ps 117), p. 1163, no. 6.
Gospel (Jn 10, 11-16), p. 1175, no. 9.

June 6 — ST. NORBERT, Bishop

Optional Memorial

St. Norbert was born at Xanten, Germany, in 1080. After a somewhat worldly and licentious life, he retired to Prémontre and there founded the Premonstratensians under the rule of St. Augustine. He died in 1134 while holding the exalted office of Archbishop of Magdeburg.

Common of Pastors: for Bishops, p, 1069; or Common of Holy Men and Women: for Religious, p. 1097.

OPENING PRAYER

Father,
you made the bishop Norbert
an outstanding minister of your Church,
renowned for his preaching and pastoral zeal.
Always grant to your Church faithful shepherds
to lead your people to eternal salvation.
We ask this through our Lord Jesus Christ, your Son,
who lives and reigns with you and the Holy Spirit,
one God, for ever and ever. ℞. **Amen.**

Reading I (Ez 34, 11-16), p. 1158, no. 9.
Responsorial Psalm (Ps 23), p. 1161, no. 2.
Gospel (Lk 14, 25-33), p. 1230, no. 19.

June 9 — ST. EPHREM, Deacon and Doctor

Optional Memorial

St. Ephrem, of Nisibis in Mesopotamia, was cast forth from his home by his father, a pagan priest. He lived as a hermit but was later ordained a Deacon of Edessa and became renowned as a poet, orator, and holy monk. He died in 373.

Common of Doctors of the Church, p. 1082.

OPENING PRAYER

Lord,
in your love fill our hearts with the Holy Spirit,
who inspired the deacon Ephrem to sing the praise
    of your mysteries

and gave him strength to serve you alone.
Grant this through our Lord Jesus Christ, your Son,
who lives and reigns with you and the Holy Spirit,
one God, for ever and ever. ℟. **Amen.**

Reading I (1 Pt 4, 7-11), p. 1216, no. 14.
Responsorial Psalm (Ps 37), p 1181, no. 2.
Gospel (Mk 3, 31-35), p. 1226, no. 11.

June 11 — ST. BARNABAS, Apostle

Memorial

St. Barnabas was the companion of St. Paul in the evangelization of the pagans in Cyprus. After having conquered many souls for Christ, Barnabas died a martyr
at Cyprus during Nero's reign with the Gospel of St.
Matthew, written by his own hand, on his chest.

ENTRANCE ANT.   See Acts 11, 24
**Blessed are you, St. Barnabas: you were a man of
faith filled with the Holy Spirit and counted among
the apostles.**   ➜ No. 2, p. 614

OPENING PRAYER

God our Father,
you filled St. Barnabas with faith and the Holy Spirit,
and sent him to convert the nations.
Help us to proclaim the gospel by word and deed.
We ask this through our Lord Jesus Christ, your Son,
who lives and reigns with you and the Holy Spirit,
one God, for ever and ever. ℟. **Amen.** ↓

Reading I is special in this Memorial.

READING I   Acts 11, 21-26; 13, 1-3
Today's saint, Barnabas, is commended as a man full of the Holy Spirit
and faith. St. Barnabas introduced St. Paul to the Christian community. Together, they were added to the number of the apostles and were sent to the
Gentiles.

A reading from the Acts of the Apostles

A great number believed and were converted to the
Lord. News of this eventually reached the ears of

the church in Jerusalem, resulting in Barnabas' being sent to Antioch. On his arrival he rejoiced to
see the evidence of God's favor. He encouraged them
all to remain firm in their commitment to the Lord,
since he himself was a good man filled with the Holy
Spirit and faith. Thereby large numbers were added
to the Lord. Then Barnabas went off to Tarsus to look
for Saul; once he had found him, he brought him
back to Antioch. For a whole year they met with
the church and instructed great numbers. It was in
Antioch that the disciples were called Christians for
the first time.

There were in the church at Antioch certain prophets and teachers: Barnabas, Symeon known as Niger,
Lucius of Cyrene, Manaen (who had been brought
up with Herod the tetrarch), and Saul. On one occasion, while they were engaged in the liturgy of the
Lord and were fasting, the Holy Spirit spoke to
them: "Set apart Barnabas and Saul for me to do
the work for which I have called them." Then, after
they had fasted and prayed, they imposed hands on
them and sent them off.—This is the Word of the
Lord. ℟. **Thanks be to God.** ℣

Responsorial Psalm   Ps 98, 1. 2-3. 3-4. 5-6

℟. (2) **The Lord has revealed to the nations his
saving power.**

Sing to the Lord a new song,
    for he has done wondrous deeds;
His right hand has won victory for him,
    his holy arm. — ℟

The Lord has made his salvation known:
    in the sight of the nations he has revealed his
    justice.
He has remembered his kindness and his faithfulness
    toward the house of Israel. — ℟

All the ends of the earth have seen
    the salvation by our God.

Sing joyfully to the Lord, all you lands;
　　break into song; sing praise. — ℟

Sing praise to the Lord with the harp,
　　with the harp and melodious song.

With trumpets and the sound of the horn
　　sing joyfully before the King, the Lord. — ℟ ❣

GOSPEL Mt 10, 7-13

Alleluia.

℟. **Alleluia.** We praise you, God; we acknowledge
　　you as Lord;
your glorious band of apostles extols you. ℟. **Alle-
　　luia.**

Jesus empowered his apostles to work wonders and miracles, to
prove their teaching about Christ. The greater miracles are men who
still leave everything today, in order to preach the Good News.
Miracles of grace accompany such dedication.

℣. The Lord be with you. ℟. **And also with you.**
✠ A reading from the holy gospel according to Matthew. ℟. **Glory to you, Lord.**

Jesus said to his disciples: "As you go, make this
announcement: 'The reign of God is at hand!' Cure
the sick, raise the dead, heal the leprous, expel demons. The gift you have received, give as a gift.
Provide yourselves with neither gold nor silver nor
copper in your belts; no traveling bag, no change of
shirt, no sandals, no walking staff. The workman,
after all, is worth his keep.

　　"Look for a worthy citizen in every town or village you come to and stay with him until you leave.
As you enter his home bless it. If the home is deserving, your blessing will descend on it. If it is not,
your blessing will return to you."—This is the gospel of the Lord. ℟. **Praise to you, Lord Jesus Christ.**

➜ No. 15, p. 623

PRAYER OVER THE GIFTS

Lord,
bless these gifts we present to you.
May they kindle in us the flame of love
by which St. Barnabas brought the light of the gospel
to the nations.
Grant this through Christ our Lord.
℟. **Amen.**   ➤ No. 21, p. 626 (Pref. P 64-65)

COMMUNION ANT.   Jn 15, 15

**No longer shall I call you servants, for a servant
knows not what his master does. Now I shall call
you friends, for I have revealed to you all that I have
heard from my Father.** ✣

PRAYER AFTER COMMUNION

Lord,
hear the prayers of those who receive the pledge of
    eternal life.
on the feast of St. Barnabas.
May we come to share the salvation
we celebrate in this sacrament.
We ask this in the name of Jesus the Lord.
℟. **Amen.**   ➤ No. 32, p. 650

_____

COMMON OF SAINTS
ANTIPHONS AND PRAYERS

1) *The following Mass formularies are used for all Masses of Saints who have no complete formulary in the Proper of Saints. In each case, an appropriate rubric gives the page number of the specific Common or Commons that may be used.*

2) *In the individual Commons, several Mass formularies, with antiphons and prayers, are arranged for convenience.*

The priest, however, may interchange antiphons and prayers of the same Common choosing according to the circumstances those texts which seem pastorally appropriate.

In addition, for Masses of Memorial, the Prayer over the Gifts and the Prayer after Communion may be taken from the weekdays of the current liturgical season as well as from the Commons.

3) *In the Common of Martyrs and in the Common of Holy Men and Women, all the prayers may be used of men or women with the necessary change of gender.*

4) *In the individual Commons, texts in the singular may be changed to the plural and vice versa.*

5) *Certain Masses which are given for specific seasons and circumstances should be used for those seasons and circumstances.*

6) *During the Easter Season an alleluia should be added at the end of the Entrance and Communion Antiphons.*

7) *In accord with the rules given in the Introduction to the Proper of Saints, the Readings and Intervenient Chants in the Common of Saints may always be used in any individual celebration in honor of the Saints when there are pastoral reasons for doing so.*

COMMON OF THE DEDICATION OF A CHURCH

The Common of the Dedication of a Church comprises three formularies. The first is said on the day of the dedication. The others are used on the anniversary of the dedication: the second in the dedicated church itself, for example, the parish church; and the third outside the dedicated church, for example on the feast of St. John Lateran (Nov. 9) or of the Cathedral of the local diocese.

1. ON THE DAY OF DEDICATION

ENTRANCE ANT. See Gn 28, 17

This is a place of awe; this is God's house, the gate of heaven, and it shall be called the royal court of God. ➤ No. 2, p. 614

OPENING PRAYER

All powerful and ever-living God,
fill this church with your love
and give your help to all who call on you in faith.
May the power of your word and sacraments in this place
bring strength to the people gathered here.
We . . . for ever and ever. ℟. **Amen.** ⅴ

READINGS AND INTERVENIENT CHANTS

See pp. 1106-1118.

PRAYER OVER THE GIFTS

Lord,
accept the gifts of your Church
which we offer with joy.
May all your people gathered in this holy place
come to eternal salvation by these mysteries.
Grant this in the name of Jesus the Lord.
℟. **Amen.** ➤ No. 21, p. 626 (Pref. P 52)

COMMUNION ANT.

Mt 21, 13; Lk 11, 19

My house shall be called a house of prayer, says the Lord; ask here and you shall receive, seek and you shall find, knock and the door will open. ⅴ

PRAYER AFTER COMMUNION

Lord,
may your truth grow in our hearts
by the holy gifts we receive.
May we worship you always in your holy temple
and come to rejoice with all the saints in your presence.
We ask this through Christ our Lord.
℞. **Amen.** → No. 32, p. 650

---

2. ANNIVERSARY OF DEDICATION

A. IN THE DEDICATED CHURCH

ENTRANCE ANT Ps 68, 36

Greatly to be feared is God in his sanctuary; he, the God of Israel, gives power and strength to his people. Blessed be God! → No. 2, p. 614

OPENING PRAYER

Father,
each year we recall the dedication of this church
  to your service.
Let our worship always be sincere
and help us to find your saving love in this church.
Grant this through our Lord Jesus Christ, your Son,
who lives and reigns with you and the Holy Spirit,
one God, for ever and ever. ℞. **Amen.** ↓

READINGS AND INTERVENIENT CHANTS

See pp. 1106-1118.

PRAYER OVER THE GIFTS

Lord,
as we recall the day you filled this church
with your glory and holiness,
may our lives also become an acceptable offering
  to you.
Grant this in the name of Jesus the Lord.
℞. **Amen.** → No. 21, p. 626 (Pref. P 52)

COMMUNION ANT.   1 Cor 3, 16-17

You are the temple of God, and God's Spirit dwells in you. The temple of God is holy; you are that temple. ⍩

PRAYER AFTER COMMUNION

Lord,
we know the joy and power of your blessing in our
   lives.
As we celebrate the dedication of this church,
may we give ourselves once more to your service.
Grant this through Christ our Lord.
℟. **Amen.**   ➤ No. 32, p. 650

_____

B. OUTSIDE THE DEDICATED CHURCH

ENTRANCE ANT.   Rv 21, 2

I saw the holy city, new Jerusalem, coming down from God out of heaven, like a bride adorned in readiness for her husband.   ➤ No. 2, p. 614

OPENING PRAYER

God our Father,
from living stones, your chosen people,
you built an eternal temple to your glory.
Increase the spiritual gifts you have given to your
   Church,
so that your faithful people may continue to grow
into the new and eternal Jerusalem.
We ask this through our Lord Jesus Christ, your Son,
who lives and reigns with you and the Holy Spirit,
one God, for ever and ever. ℟. **Amen.** ⍩

OR

Father,
you called your people to be your Church.
As we gather together in your name,
may we love, honor, and follow you
to eternal life in the kingdom you promise.

Grant this through our Lord Jesus Christ, your Son,
who lives and reigns with you and the Holy Spirit,
one God, for ever and ever. ℟. **Amen.** ↓

READINGS AND INTERVENIENT CHANTS
See pp. 1106-1118.

PRAYER OVER THE GIFTS
Lord,
receive our gifts.
May we who share this sacrament
experience the life and power it promises,
and hear the answer to our prayers.
We ask this in the name of Jesus the Lord.
℟. **Amen.**   ➤ No. 21, p. 626 (Pref. P 53)

COMMUNION ANT.   1 Pt 2, 5
**Like living stones let yourselves be built on Christ
as a spiritual house, a holy priesthood.** ↓

PRAYER AFTER COMMUNION
Father,
you make your Church on earth
a sign of the new and eternal Jerusalem.
By sharing in this sacrament
may we become the temple of your presence
and the home of your glory.
Grant this in the name of Jesus the Lord.
℟. **Amen.**   ➤ No. 32, p. 650

COMMON OF THE BLESSED
VIRGIN MARY

The Common of the Blessed Virgin Mary comprises six Mass formularies and one Prayer formulary. These are used on feasts of the Virgin Mary during the year as indicated in the Missal. They are also utilized for the Mass of the Blessed Virgin Mary on Saturday in Ordinary Time when there is no feast higher than an optional Memorial.

These Masses are also used for the Saturday celebrations of the Blessed Virgin Mary and for votive Masses of the Blessed Virgin Mary.

1

ENTRANCE ANT. Sedulius
**Hail, holy Mother! The child to whom you gave birth
is the King of heaven and earth for ever.**

➤ No. 2, p. 614

OPENING PRAYER

Lord, God,
give to your people the joy
of continual health in mind and body.
With the prayers of the Virgin Mary to help us,
guide us through the sorrows of this life
to eternal happiness in the life to come.
Grant this through our Lord Jesus Christ, your Son,
who lives and reigns with you and the Holy Spirit,
one God, for ever and ever. ℞. **Amen.** ⱽ

OR

Lord,
take away the sins of your people.
May the prayers of Mary the mother of your Son
    help us,
for alone and unaided we cannot hope to please you.
We ask this through our Lord Jesus Christ, your Son,
who lives and reigns with you and the Holy Spirit,
one God, for ever and ever. ℞. **Amen.** ⱽ

READINGS AND INTERVENIENT CHANTS

See pp. 1118-1137.

PRAYER OVER THE GIFTS

Father,
the birth of Christ your Son
deepened the virgin mother's love for you,
and increased her holiness.
May the humanity of Christ
give us courage in our weakness;
may it free us from our sins,
and make our offering acceptable.
We ask this through Christ our Lord.
℟. **Amen.**　　→ No. 21, p. 626 (Pref. P 56-57)

COMMUNION ANT.　　　　See Lk 11, 27
Blessed is the womb of the Virgin Mary; she carried the Son of the eternal Father. ℣

PRAYER AFTER COMMUNION

Lord,
we rejoice in your sacraments and ask your mercy
as we honor the memory of the Virgin Mary.
May her faith and love
inspire us to serve you more faithfully
in the work of salvation.
Grant this in the name of Jesus the Lord.
℟. **Amen.**　　　　→ No. 32, p. 650

————————

2

ENTRANCE ANT.
Blessed are you, Virgin Mary, who carried the creator of all things in your womb; you gave birth to your maker, and remain for ever a virgin.

→ No. 2, p. 614

OPENING PRAYER

God of mercy,
give us strength.
May we who honor the memory of the Mother of
God

rise above our sins and failings with the help of her
  prayers.
Grant this through our Lord Jesus Christ, your Son,
who lives and reigns with you and the Holy Spirit,
one God, for ever and ever. ℟. **Amen.** ℣

OR

Lord,
may the prayers of the Virgin Mary
bring us protection from danger
and freedom from sin
that we may come to the joy of your peace.
We ask this through our Lord Jesus Christ, your Son,
who lives and reigns with you and the Holy Spirit,
one God, for ever and ever. ℟. **Amen.** ℣

READINGS AND INTERVENIENT CHANTS

See pp. 1118-1137.

PRAYER OVER THE GIFTS

Lord,
we honor the memory of the mother of your Son.
May the sacrifice we share
make of us an everlasting gift to you.
Grant this through Christ our Lord.
℟. **Amen.**   ➤ No. 21, p. 626 (Pref. P 56-57)

COMMUNION ANT.   Lk 1, 49

**The Almighty has done great things for me. Holy
is his name.** ℣

PRAYER AFTER COMMUNION

Lord,
you give us the sacraments of eternal redemption.
May we who honor the memory of the mother of
  your Son
rejoice in the abundance of your grace
and experience your unfailing help.
We ask this through Christ our Lord.
℟. **Amen.**   ➤ No. 32, p. 650

3

ENTRANCE ANT. See Jdt 13, 23. 25

You have been blessed, O Virgin Mary, above all other women on earth by the Lord the most high God; he has so exalted your name that your praises shall never fade from the mouths of men.

➔ No. 2, p. 614

OPENING PRAYER

Lord,
as we honor the glorious memory of the Virgin Mary,
we ask that by the help of her prayers
we too may come to share the fullness of your grace.
Grant this through our Lord Jesus Christ, your Son,
who lives and reigns with you and the Holy Spirit,
one God, for ever and ever. ℟. **Amen.** ↓

OR

Lord Jesus Christ,
you chose the Virgin Mary to be your mother,
a worthy home in which to dwell.
By her prayers keep us from danger
and bring us to the joy of heaven,
where you live and reign with the Father and the Holy Spirit,
one God, for ever and ever. ℟. **Amen.** ↓

READINGS AND INTERVENIENT CHANTS

See pp. 1118-1137.

PRAYER OVER THE GIFTS

Lord,
we bring you our sacrifice of praise
at this celebration in honor of Mary, the mother of your Son.
May this holy exchange of gifts
help us on our way to eternal salvation.
We ask this in the name of Jesus the Lord.
℟. **Amen.** ➔ No. 21, p. 626 (Pref. P 56-57)

COMMUNION ANT.   See Lk 1, 48
**All generations will call me blessed, because God
has looked upon his lowly handmaid.** ℣

PRAYER AFTER COMMUNION

Lord,
we eat the bread of heaven.
May we who honor the memory of the Virgin Mary
come one day to your banquet of eternal life.
Grant this through Christ our Lord.
℟. **Amen.**   ➤ No. 32, p. 650

—————————————

4. ADVENT SEASON

ENTRANCE ANT.   Is 45, 8
**Let the clouds rain down the Just One, and the earth
bring forth a Savior.**

OR   Lk 1, 30-32
**The angel said to Mary: You have won God's favor.
You will conceive and bear a Son, and he will be
called Son of the Most High.**   ➤ No. 2, p. 614

OPENING PRAYER

Father,
in your plan for our salvation
your Word became man,
announced by an angel and born of the Virgin Mary.
May we who believe that she is the Mother of God
receive the help of her prayers.
We ask this through our Lord Jesus Christ, your Son,
who lives and reigns with you and the Holy Spirit,
one God, for ever and ever. ℟. **Amen.** ℣

READINGS AND INTERVENIENT CHANTS
See pp. 1118-1137.

PRAYER OVER THE GIFTS

Lord,
may the power of your Spirit,
which sanctified Mary the mother of your Son,
make holy the gifts we place upon this altar.
We ask this through Christ our Lord.
R︠. **Amen.** ➤ No. 21, p. 626 (Pref. P 56-57 or P 2)

COMMUNION ANT. Is 7, 14

**The Virgin is with child and shall bear a son, and
she will call him Emmanuel.** ↓

PRAYER AFTER COMMUNION

Lord our God,
may the sacraments we receive
show us your forgiveness and love.
May we who honor the mother of your Son
be saved by his coming among us as man,
for he is Lord for ever and ever.
R︠. **Amen.** ➤ No. 32, p. 650

_____

5. CHRISTMAS SEASON

ENTRANCE ANT.

**Giving birth to the King whose reign is unending,
Mary knows the joys of motherhood together with
a virgin's honor; none like her before, and there
shall be none hereafter.**

OR

**O virgin Mother of God, the universe cannot hold
him, and yet, becoming man, he confined himself in
your womb.** ➤ No. 2, p. 614

OPENING PRAYER

Father,
you gave the human race eternal salvation
through the motherhood of the Virgin Mary.

May we experience the help of her prayers in our
   lives,
for through her we received the very source of life,
your Son, our Lord Jesus Christ,
who lives and reigns with you and the Holy Spirit,
one God, for ever and ever. ℟. **Amen.** ▼

READINGS AND INTERVENIENT CHANTS

See pp. 1118-1137.

PRAYER OVER THE GIFTS

Lord,
accept our gifts and prayers
and fill our hearts with the light of your Holy Spirit.
Help us to follow the example of the Virgin Mary:
to seek you in all things
and to do your will with gladness.
We ask this in the name of Jesus the Lord.
℟. **Amen.**   ➙ No. 21, p. 626 (Pref. P 56-57)

COMMUNION ANT.   Jn 1, 14

**The Word of God became man, and lived among us,
full of grace and truth.** ▼

PRAYER AFTER COMMUNION

Lord,
as we celebrate this feast of the Blessed Virgin Mary,
you renew us with the body and blood of Christ your
   Son.
May this sacrament give us a share in his life,
for he is Lord for ever and ever.
℟. **Amen.**   ➙ No. 32, p. 650

6. EASTER SEASON

ENTRANCE ANT.   See Acts 1, 14

**The disciples were constantly at prayer together,
with Mary the mother of Jesus, alleluia.**
                                    ➙ No. 2, p. 614

OPENING PRAYER

God our Father,
you give joy to the world
by your resurrection of your Son, our Lord Jesus
   Christ.
Through the prayers of his mother, the Virgin Mary,
bring us to the happiness of eternal life.
We ask this through our Lord Jesus Christ, your Son,
who lives and reigns with you and the Holy Spirit,
one God, for ever and ever. ℟. **Amen.** ✓

OR

God our Father,
you gave the Holy Spirit to your apostles
as they joined in prayer with Mary, the mother of
   Jesus.
By the help of her prayers
keep us faithful in your service
and let our words and actions be so inspired
as to bring glory to your name.
Grant this through our Lord Jesus Christ, your Son,
who lives and reigns with you and the Holy Spirit,
one God, for ever and ever. ℟. **Amen.** ✓

READINGS AND INTERVENIENT CHANTS

See pp. 1118-1137.

PRAYER OVER THE GIFTS

Father,
as we celebrate the memory of the Virgin Mary,
we offer you our gifts and prayers.
Sustain us by the love of Christ,
who offered himself as a perfect sacrifice on the
   cross,
and is Lord for ever and ever.

℟. **Amen.**   ➤ No. 21, p. 626 (Pref. P 56-57)

COMMUNION ANT.

Rejoice, virgin mother, for Christ has arisen from his grave, alleluia. ℣

PRAYER AFTER COMMUNION

Lord,
may this sacrament strengthen the faith in our
    hearts.
May Mary's Son, Jesus Christ,
whom we proclaim to be God and man,
bring us to eternal life
by the saving power of his resurrection,
for he is Lord for ever and ever.
℟. **Amen.** ➔ No. 32, p. 650

OTHER PRAYERS FOR MASSES OF THE BLESSED VIRGIN MARY

OPENING PRAYER

All-powerful God,
we rejoice in the protection of the holy Virgin Mary.
May her prayers help to free us from all evils here
    on earth
and lead us to eternal joy in heaven.
Grant this through our Lord Jesus Christ, your Son,
who lives and reigns with you and the Holy Spirit,
one God, for ever and ever. ℟. **Amen.** ℣

READINGS AND INTERVENIENT CHANTS

See pp. 1118-1137.

PRAYER OVER THE GIFTS

Lord,
accept the prayers and gifts we present today
as we honor Mary, the Mother of God.
May they please you
and bring us your forgiveness and help.
We ask this in the name of Jesus the Lord.
℟. **Amen.** ➔ No. 21, p. 626

PRAYER AFTER COMMUNION

Lord,
we are renewed with the sacraments of salvation.
May we who celebrate the memory of the Mother
  of God
come to realize the eternal redemption you promise.
We ask this through . . . ℟. **Amen.**   ➜ No. 32, p. 650

COMMON OF MARTYRS

The Common of Martyrs comprises ten Mass formularies and three Prayer formularies. Since the Martyrs
were associated in a very special way with the mystery
of Christ's death and resurrection, their worship takes
on special significance when it is celebrated during the
Easter Season. That is why the formularies are separated into those for Martyrs "outside the Easter Season"
and "in the Easter Season."

1. FOR SEVERAL MARTYRS, OUTSIDE THE EASTER SEASON

ENTRANCE ANT.

**The saints are happy in heaven because they followed
Christ. They rejoice with him for ever because they
shed their blood for love of him.**   ➜ No. 2, p. 614

OPENING PRAYER

Father,
we celebrate the memory of Saints N. and N.
who died for their faithful witnessing to Christ.
Give us the strength to follow their example,
loyal and faithful to the end.
We ask this through our Lord Jesus Christ, your Son,
who lives and reigns with you and the Holy Spirit,
one God, for ever and ever. ℟. **Amen.** ℣

READINGS AND INTERVENIENT CHANTS

See pp. 1138-1154.

PRAYER OVER THE GIFTS

Father,
receive the gifts we bring

in memory of your holy martyrs.
Keep us strong in our faith
and in our witness to you.
Grant this through Christ our Lord.
℟. **Amen.**   ➤ No. 21, p. 626

COMMUNION ANT.   Lk 22, 28-30

**You are the men who have stood by me faithfully
in my trials, and now I confer a kingdom on you,
says the Lord. You will eat and drink at my table
in my kingdom.** ✟

PRAYER AFTER COMMUNION

God our Father,
in your holy martyrs you show us the glory of the
     cross.
Through this sacrifice, strengthen our resolution
to follow Christ faithfully
and to work in your Church for the salvation of all.
We ask this through Christ our Lord.
℟. **Amen.**   ➤ No. 32, p. 650

---

2. FOR SEVERAL MARTYRS, OUTSIDE THE EASTER SEASON

ENTRANCE ANT.   Ps 34, 20-21

**Many are the sufferings of the just, and from them
all the Lord has delivered them; the Lord preserves
all their bones, not one of them shall be broken.**

➤ No. 2, p. 614

OPENING PRAYER

All-powerful, ever-living God,
turn our weakness into strength.
As you gave your martyrs N. and N.
the courage to suffer death for Christ,
give us the courage to live in faithful witness to you.
Grant this through our Lord Jesus Christ, your Son,

who lives and reigns with you and the Holy Spirit,
one God, for ever and ever. ℟. **Amen.** ℣

READINGS AND INTERVENIENT CHANTS

See pp. 1138-1154.

PRAYER OVER THE GIFTS

Lord,
accept the gifts we bring
to celebrate the feast of your martyrs.
May this sacrifice free us from sin
and make our service pleasing to you.
We ask this through Christ our Lord.
℟. **Amen.**   ➤ No. 21, p. 626

COMMUNION ANT.   Jn 15, 13

**No one has greater love, says the Lord, than the man
who lays down his life for his friends.** ℣

PRAYER AFTER COMMUNION

Lord,
we eat the bread from heaven
and become one body in Christ.
Never let us be separated from his love
and help us to follow your martyrs N. and N.
by having the courage to overcome all things through
    Christ,
who loved us all,
and lives and reigns with you for ever and ever.
℟. **Amen.**   ➤ No. 32, p. 650

———————————

3. FOR SEVERAL MARTYRS, OUTSIDE THE EASTER SEASON

ENTRANCE ANT.   Ps 40, 39

**The salvation of the just comes from the Lord. He
is their strength in time of need.**   ➤ No. 2, p. 614

OPENING PRAYER

Lord,
may the victory of your martyrs give us joy.
May their example strengthen our faith,
and their prayers give us renewed courage.
We ask this through our Lord Jesus Christ, your Son,
who lives and reigns with you and the Holy Spirit,
one God, for ever and ever. ℟. **Amen.** ⍒

OR

Lord,
hear the prayers of the martyrs N. and N.
and give us courage to bear witness to your truth.
Grant this through our Lord Jesus Christ, your Son,
who lives and reigns with you and the Holy Spirit,
one God, for ever and ever. ℟. **Amen.** ⍒

READINGS AND INTERVENIENT CHANTS

See pp. 1138-1154.

PRAYER OVER THE GIFTS

Lord,
accept the gifts of your people
as we honor the suffering and death
of your martyrs N. and N.
As the eucharist gave them strength in persecution
may it keep us faithful in every difficulty.
We ask this through Christ our Lord.
℟. **Amen.**   ➤ No. 21, p. 626

COMMUNION ANT.   Mk 8, 35

**Whoever loses his life for my sake and the gospel,
says the Lord, will save it.** ⍒

PRAYER AFTER COMMUNION

Lord,
keep this eucharist effective within us.
May the gift we receive
on this feast of the martyrs N. and N.

bring us salvation and peace.
Grant this in the name of Jesus the Lord.
℟. **Amen.** ➤ No. 32, p. 650

4. FOR SEVERAL MARTYRS, OUTSIDE THE EASTER SEASON

ENTRANCE ANT. Ps 34, 18
The Lord will hear the just when they cry out, from all their afflictions he will deliver them.
➤ No. 2, p. 614

OPENING PRAYER
God our Father,
every year you give us the joy
of celebrating this feast of Saints N. and N.
May we who recall their birth to eternal life
imitate their courage in suffering for you.
Grant this through our Lord Jesus Christ, your Son,
who lives and reigns with you and the Holy Spirit,
one God, for ever and ever. ℟. **Amen.** ✟

OR

God our Father,
your generous gift of love
brought Saints N. and N. to unending glory.
Through the prayers of your martyrs
forgive our sins and free us from every danger.
We ask this through our Lord Jesus Christ, your Son,
who lives and reigns with you and the Holy Spirit,
one God, for ever and ever. ℟. **Amen.** ✟

READINGS AND INTERVENIENT CHANTS
See pp. 1138-1154.

PRAYER OVER THE GIFTS
Lord,
you gave Saints N. and N. the fulfillment of their
faith

in the vision of your glory.
May the gifts we bring to honor their memory
gain us your pardon and peace.
We ask this in the name of Jesus the Lord.
℟. **Amen.**   ➤ No. 21, p. 626

COMMUNION ANT.   2 Cor 4, 11
**We are given over to death for Jesus, that the life
of Jesus may be revealed in our dying flesh.** ⅴ

PRAYER AFTER COMMUNION
Lord,
may this food of heaven
bring us a share in the grace you gave the martyrs
    N. and N.
From their bitter sufferings may we learn to become
    strong
and by patient endurance earn the victory of re-
    joicing in your holiness.
Grant this through Christ our Lord.
℟. **Amen.**   ➤ No. 32, p. 650

──────────────────

5. FOR SEVERAL MARTYRS, OUTSIDE THE EASTER SEASON

ENTRANCE ANT.
**The holy martyrs shed their blood on earth for
Christ; therefore they have received an everlasting
reward.**   ➤ No. 2, p. 614

OPENING PRAYER
Lord,
we honor your martyrs N. and N.
who were faithful to Christ
even to the point of shedding their blood for him.
Increase our own faith and free us from our sins,
and help us to follow their example of love.
We ask this through our Lord Jesus Christ, your Son,

who lives and reigns with you and the Holy Spirit,
one God, for ever and ever. ℞. **Amen.** ✟

READINGS AND INTERVENIENT CHANTS

See pp. 1138-1154.

PRAYER OVER THE GIFTS

Lord,
be pleased with the gifts we bring.
May we who celebrate the mystery of the passion
   of your Son
make this mystery part of our lives
by the inspiration of the martyrs N. and N.
Grant this through Christ our Lord. ℞. **Amen.**

OR

Lord,
may these gifts which we bring you in sacrifice
to celebrate the victory of Saints N. and N.
fill our hearts with your love
and prepare us for the reward you promise
to those who are faithful.
We ask this in the name of Jesus the Lord. ℞. **Amen.**

➤ No. 21, p. 626

COMMUNION ANT.   See Rom 8, 38-39

**Neither death nor life nor anything in all creation
can come between us and Christ's love for us.** ✟

PRAYER AFTER COMMUNION

Lord,
you give us the body and blood of Christ your only
   Son
on this feast of your martyrs N. and N.
By being faithful to your love
may we live in you,
receive life from you,
and always be true to your inspiration.
We ask this in the name of Jesus the Lord.
℞. **Amen.**   ➤ No. 32, p. 650

6. FOR ONE MARTYR, OUTSIDE THE EASTER SEASON

ENTRANCE ANT.

This holy man fought to the death for the law of his God, never cowed by the threats of the wicked; his house was built on solid rock.   → No. 2, p. 614

OPENING PRAYER

God of power and mercy,
you gave N., your martyr, victory over pain and suffering.
Strengthen us who celebrate this day of his triumph
and help us to be victorious over the evils that threaten us.
Grant this through our Lord Jesus Christ, your Son,
who lives and reigns with you and the Holy Spirit,
one God, for ever and ever. ℟. **Amen.** ℣

READINGS AND INTERVENIENT CHANTS

See pp. 1138-1154.

PRAYER OVER THE GIFTS

Lord,
bless our offerings and make them holy.
May these gifts fill our hearts
with the love which gave St. N. victory
over all his suffering.
We ask this through Christ our Lord. ℟. **Amen.**

OR

Lord,
accept the gifts we offer in memory of the martyr N.
May they be pleasing to you
as was the shedding of his blood for the faith.
Grant this through Christ our Lord. ℟. **Amen.**

→ No. 21, p. 626

COMMUNION ANT.   Mt 16, 24

If anyone wishes to come after me, he must renounce
himself, take up his cross, and follow me, says the
Lord. ℣

PRAYER AFTER COMMUNION

Lord,
may the mysteries we receive
give us the spiritual courage which made your mar-
    tyr N.
faithful in your service and victorious in his suf-
    fering.
Grant this in the name of Jesus the Lord.
℟. **Amen.**   → No. 32, p. 650

7. FOR ONE MARTYR, OUTSIDE THE EASTER SEASON

ENTRANCE ANT.

Here is a true martyr who shed his blood for Christ;
his judges could not shake him by their menaces,
and so he won through to the kingdom of heaven.
→ No. 2, p. 614

OPENING PRAYER

All-powerful, ever-living God,
you gave St. N. the courage to witness to the gospel
    of Christ
even to the point of giving his life for it.
By his prayers help us to endure all suffering for love
    of you
and to seek you with all our hearts,
for you alone are the source of life.
Grant this through our Lord Jesus Christ, your Son,
who lives and reigns with you and the Holy Spirit,
one God, for ever and ever. ℟. **Amen.** ℣

READINGS AND INTERVENIENT CHANTS
See pp. 1138-1154.

PRAYER OVER THE GIFTS
God of love,
pour out your blessing on our gifts
and make our faith strong,
the faith which St. N. professed by shedding his
    blood.
We ask this through Christ our Lord. ℟. **Amen.**

OR

Lord,
accept these gifts we present in memory of St. N.,
for no temptation could turn him away from you.
We ask this through Christ our Lord. ℟. **Amen.**

➤ No. 21, p. 626

COMMUNION ANT.   Jn 15, 5
**I am the vine and you are the branches, says the
Lord; he who lives in me, and I in him, will bear
much fruit. ↓**

PRAYER AFTER COMMUNION
Lord,
we are renewed by the mystery of the eucharist.
By imitating the fidelity of St. N. and by your
    patience
may we come to share the eternal life you have
    promised.
We ask this in the name of Jesus the Lord.
℟. **Amen.**   ➤ No. 32, p. 650

8. FOR SEVERAL MARTYRS, IN THE EASTER SEASON

ENTRANCE ANT.   Mt 25, 34

Come, you whom my Father has blessed; inherit the kingdom prepared for you since the foundation of the world, alleluia. → No. 2, p. 614

OPENING PRAYER

Father,
you gave your martyrs N. and N.
the courage to die in witness to Christ and the gospel.
By the power of your Holy Spirit,
give us the humility to believe
and the courage to profess
the faith for which they gave their lives.
We ask this through our Lord Jesus Christ, your Son,
who lives and reigns with you and the Holy Spirit,
one God, for ever and ever. ℟. **Amen.** ⍒

OR

God our all-powerful Father,
you strengthen our faith
and take away our weakness.
Let the prayers and example of your martyrs N. and
   N. help us
to share in the passion and resurrection of Christ
and bring us to eternal joy with all your saints.
We ask this through our Lord Jesus Christ, your Son,
who lives and reigns with you and the Holy Spirit,
one God, for ever and ever. ℟. **Amen.** ⍒

READINGS AND INTERVENIENT CHANTS

See pp. 1138-1154.

PRAYER OVER THE GIFTS

Lord,
we celebrate the death of your holy martyrs.

May we offer the sacrifice which gives all martyr-
     dom its meaning.
Grant this through Christ our Lord.
℟. **Amen.**   ➤ No. 21, p. 626

COMMUNION ANT.   Rv 2, 7
**Those who are victorious I will feed from the tree
of life, which grows in the paradise of my God, alleluia.** ⍒

PRAYER AFTER COMMUNION
Lord,
at this holy meal
we celebrate the heavenly victory of your martyrs
     N. and N.
May this bread of life
give us the courage to conquer evil,
so that we may come to share the fruit of the tree
     of life in paradise.
We ask this through Christ our Lord.
℟. **Amen.**   ➤ No. 32, p. 650

————————————

9. FOR SEVERAL MARTYRS, IN THE
EASTER SEASON

ENTRANCE ANT.   Rv 12, 11
**These are the saints who were victorious in the blood
of the Lamb, and in the face of death they did not
cling to life; therefore they are reigning with Christ
for ever, alleluia.**   ➤ No. 2, p. 614

OPENING PRAYER
Lord,
you gave your martyrs N. and N.
the privilege of shedding their blood
for boldly proclaiming the death and resurrection
     of your Son.

May this celebration of their victory give them
  honor among your people.
We ask this through our Lord Jesus Christ, your Son,
who lives and reigns with you and the Holy Spirit,
one God, for ever and ever. ℟. **Amen.** ↯

READINGS AND INTERVENIENT CHANTS
See pp. 1138-1154.

PRAYER OVER THE GIFTS
Lord,
fill these gifts with the blessing of your Holy Spirit
and fill our hearts with the love
which gave victory to Saints N. and N.
in dying for the faith.
We ask this through Christ our Lord.
℟. **Amen.**   ➤ No. 21, p. 626

COMMUNION ANT.   2 Tm 2, 11-12
**If we die with Christ, we shall live with him, and if
we are faithful to the end, we shall reign with him,
alleluia.** ↯

PRAYER AFTER COMMUNION
Lord,
we are renewed by the breaking of one bread
in honor of the martyrs N. and N.
Keep us in your love
and help us to live the new life Christ won for us.
Grant this in the name of Jesus the Lord.
℟. **Amen.**   ➤ No. 32, p. 650

_____

10. FOR ONE MARTYR, IN THE EASTER SEASON

ENTRANCE ANT.   See 4 Ezr 2, 35
**Light for ever will shine on your saints, O Lord, al-
leluia.**   ➤ No. 2, p. 614

OPENING PRAYER

God our Father,
you have honored the Church with the victorious
    witness of St. N.,
who died for his faith.
As he imitated the sufferings and death of the Lord,
may we follow in his footsteps and come to eternal
    joy.
We ask this through our Lord Jesus Christ, your Son,
who lives and reigns with you and the Holy Spirit,
one God, for ever and ever. ℟. **Amen.** ↓

READINGS AND INTERVENIENT CHANTS

See pp. 1138-1154.

PRAYER OVER THE GIFTS

Lord,
accept this offering of praise and peace
in memory of your martyr N.
May it bring us your forgiveness
and inspire us to give you thanks now and for ever.
Grant this in the name of Jesus the Lord.
℟. **Amen.**   ➤ No. 21, p. 626

COMMUNION ANT.   Jn 12, 24-25

**I tell you solemnly: Unless a grain of wheat falls on
the ground and dies, it remains a single grain; but
if it dies, it yields a rich harvest, alleluia.** ↓

PRAYER AFTER COMMUNION

Lord,
we receive your gifts from heaven
at this joyful feast.
May we who proclaim at this holy table
the death and resurrection of your Son
come to share his glory with all your holy martyrs.
Grant this through Christ our Lord.
℟. **Amen.**   ➤ No. 32, p. 650

OTHER PRAYERS FOR MARTYRS

FOR MISSIONARY MARTYRS

OPENING PRAYER

God of mercy and love,
through the preaching of your martyrs N. and N.
you brought the good news of Christ
to people who had not known him.
May the prayers of Saints N. and N.
make our own faith grow stronger.
We ask this through our Lord Jesus Christ, your Son,
who lives and reigns with you and the Holy Spirit,
one God, for ever and ever. ℟. **Amen.** ↓

READINGS AND INTERVENIENT CHANTS

See pp. 1138-1154.

PRAYER OVER THE GIFTS

Lord,
at this celebration of the eucharist
we honor the suffering and death of your martyrs N. and N.
In offering this sacrifice
may we proclaim the death of your Son
who gave these martyrs courage not only by his words
but also by the example of his own passion,
for he is Lord for ever and ever.
℟. **Amen.** ➔ No. 21, p. 626

PRAYER AFTER COMMUNION

Lord,
may we who eat at your holy table
be inspired by the example of Saints N. and N.
May we keep before us the loving sacrifice of your Son,
and come to the unending peace of your kingdom.
We ask this in the name of Jesus the Lord.
℟. **Amen.** ➔ No. 32, p. 650

FOR A VIRGIN MARTYR

OPENING PRAYER

God our Father,
you give us joy each year
in honoring the memory of St. N.
May her prayers be a source of help for us,
and may her example of courage and chastity be
    our inspiration.
Grant this through our Lord Jesus Christ, your Son,
who lives and reigns with you and the Holy Spirit,
one God, for ever and ever. ℟. **Amen.** ↓

READINGS AND INTERVENIENT CHANTS

See pp. 1138-1154.

PRAYER OVER THE GIFTS

Lord,
receive our gifts
as you accepted the suffering and death of St. N.
in whose honor we celebrate this eucharist.
We ask this through Christ our Lord.
℟. **Amen.**   ➤ No. 21, p. 626

PRAYER AFTER COMMUNION

Lord God,
you gave St. N. the crown of eternal joy
because she gave her life
rather than renounce the virginity she had promised
in witness to Christ.
With the courage this eucharist brings
help us to rise out of the bondage of our earthly
    desires
and attain to the glory of your kingdom.
Grant this through Christ our Lord.
℟. **Amen.**   ➤ No. 32, p. 650

FOR A HOLY WOMAN MARTYR

OPENING PRAYER
Father,
in our weakness your power reaches perfection.
You gave St. N. the strength
to defeat the power of sin and evil.
May we who celebrate her glory share in her
    triumph.
We ask this through our Lord Jesus Christ, your Son,
who lives and reigns with you and the Holy Spirit,
one God, for ever and ever. R̶̷. **Amen.** ∀

READINGS AND INTERVENIENT CHANTS
See pp. 1138-1154.

PRAYER OVER THE GIFTS
Lord,
today we offer this sacrifice in joy
as we recall the victory of St. N.
May we proclaim to others the great things
you have done for us
and rejoice in the constant help of your martyr's
    prayers.
Grant this through Christ our Lord.
R̶̷. **Amen.**   ➜ No. 21, p. 626

PRAYER AFTER COMMUNION
Lord,
by this sacrament you give us eternal joys
as we recall the memory of St. N.
May we always embrace the gift of life
we celebrate at this eucharist.
We ask this in the name of Jesus the Lord.
R̶̷. **Amen.**   ➜ No. 32, p. 650

The Common of Pastors comprises twelve Mass formularies: two for a Pope or Bishop (nos. 1-2); two for a Bishop (nos. 3-4); one for a Pastor (no. 5); two for several Pastors (nos. 6-7); one for a Founder of Churches (no. 8); one for several Founders of Churches (no. 9); and three for a Missionary Pastor (nos. 10-12).

1. FOR POPES OR BISHOPS

ENTRANCE ANT.

The Lord chose him to be his high priest; he opened his treasures and made him rich in all goodness.

➜ No. 2, p. 614

OPENING PRAYER
(for popes)

All-powerful and ever-living God,
you called St. N. to guide your people
by his word and example.
With him we pray to you:
watch over the pastors of your Church
with the people entrusted to their care,
and lead them to salvation.
We ask this through our Lord Jesus Christ, your Son,
who lives and reigns with you and the Holy Spirit,
one God, for ever and ever. ℟. **Amen.** ▼

OR (for bishops)
Father,
you gave St. N. to your Church
as an example of a good shepherd.
May his prayers help us on our way to eternal life.
Grant this through our Lord Jesus Christ, your Son,
who lives and reigns with you and the Holy Spirit,
one God, for ever and ever. ℟. **Amen.** ▼

READINGS AND INTERVENIENT CHANTS
See pp. 1154-1176.

PRAYER OVER THE GIFTS
Lord,
we offer you this sacrifice of praise
in memory of your saints.

May their prayers keep us from evil
now and in the future.
Grant this through Christ our Lord.
℞. **Amen.** ➝ No. 21, p. 626

COMMUNION ANT. See Jn 10, 11
The good shepherd gives his life for his sheep. ⩔

PRAYER AFTER COMMUNION
Lord God,
St. N. loved you
and gave himself completely in the service of your
    Church.
May the eucharist awaken in us that same love.
We ask this in the name of Jesus the Lord.
℞. **Amen.** ➝ No. 32, p. 650

---

2. FOR POPES OR BISHOPS

ENTRANCE ANT. See Sir 45, 30
**The Lord sealed a covenant of peace with him, and
made him a prince, bestowing the priestly dignity
upon him for ever.** ➝ No. 2, p. 614

OPENING PRAYER
(for popes)
Father,
you made St. N. shepherd of the whole Church
and gave to us the witness of his virtue and teaching.
Today as we honor this outstanding bishop,
we ask that our light may shine before men
and that our love for you may be sincere.
Grant this through our Lord Jesus Christ, your Son,
who lives and reigns with you and the Holy Spirit,
one God, for ever and ever. ℞. **Amen.** ⩔

OR (for bishops)

All-powerful God,
you made St. N. a bishop and leader of the Church
to inspire your people with his teaching and example.
May we give fitting honor to his memory
and always have the assistance of his prayers.
We ask this through our Lord Jesus Christ, your Son,
who lives and reigns with you and the Holy Spirit,
one God, for ever and ever. ℟. **Amen.** ↓

READINGS AND INTERVENIENT CHANTS
See pp. 1154-1176.

PRAYER OVER THE GIFTS
Lord,
may the sacrifice which wipes away the sins of all
    the world
bring us your forgiveness.
Help us as we offer it
on this yearly feast in honor of St. N.
Grant this through Christ our Lord.
℟. **Amen.**   ➔ No. 21, p. 626

COMMUNION ANT.   Jn 21, 17
**Lord, you know all things: you know that I love
you.** ↓

PRAYER AFTER COMMUNION
Lord God,
let the power of the gifts we receive
on this feast of St. N.
take full effect within us.
May this eucharist bring us your help in this life
and lead us to happiness in the unending life to
    come.
We ask this through Christ our Lord.
℟. **Amen.**   ➔ No. 32, p. 650

----

3. FOR BISHOPS

ENTRANCE ANT.   Ez 34, 11. 23-24
I will look after my sheep, says the Lord, and I will
raise up one shepherd who will pasture them. I, the
Lord, will be their God.   ➤ No. 2, p. 614

OPENING PRAYER
All-powerful, ever-living God,
you made St. N. bishop and leader of your people.
May his prayers help to bring us your forgiveness
    and love.
We ask this through our Lord Jesus Christ, your Son,
who lives and reigns with you and the Holy Spirit,
one God, for ever and ever. R̶. **Amen.** ⅴ

READINGS AND INTERVENIENT CHANTS
See pp. 1154-1176.

PRAYER OVER THE GIFTS
Lord,
accept the gifts we bring to your holy altar
on this feast of St. N.
May our offering bring honor to your name
and pardon to your people.
We ask this through Christ our Lord.
R̶. **Amen.**   ➤ No. 21, p. 626

COMMUNION ANT.   Jn 15, 16
You have not chosen me; I have chosen you. Go and
bear fruit that will last. ⅴ

PRAYER AFTER COMMUNION
Lord,
may we who receive this sacrament
be inspired by the example of St. N.
May we learn to proclaim what he believed
and put his teaching into action.
We ask this in the name of Jesus the Lord.
R̶. **Amen.**   ➤ No. 32, p. 650

4. FOR BISHOPS

ENTRANCE ANT.   1 Sm 2, 35
**I will raise up for myself a faithful priest; he will do
what is in my heart and in my mind, says the Lord.**

OPENING PRAYER
Lord God,
you counted St. N. among your holy pastors,
renowned for faith and love which conquered evil
   in this world.
By the help of his prayers
keep us strong in faith and love
and let us come to share his glory.
Grant this through our Lord Jesus Christ, your Son,
who lives and reigns with you and the Holy Spirit,
one God, for ever and ever. R̸. **Amen.** ⍒

READINGS AND INTERVENIENT CHANTS
See pp. 1154-1176.

PRAYER OVER THE GIFTS
Lord,
accept the gifts your people offer you
on this feast of St. N.
May these gifts bring us
your help for which we long.
We ask this through Christ our Lord.
R̸. **Amen.**   ➤ No. 21, p. 626

COMMUNION ANT.   Jn 10, 10
**I came that men may have life, and have it to the full,
says the Lord.**

PRAYER AFTER COMMUNION
Lord our God,
you give us the holy body and blood
of your Son.

May the salvation we celebrate
be our undying hope.
Grant this through Christ our Lord.
℟. **Amen.** → No. 32, p. 650

---

5. FOR PASTORS

ENTRANCE ANT. Lk 4, 18

**The Spirit of God is upon me; he has anointed me.
He sent me to bring good news to the poor, and to
heal the broken-hearted.** → No. 2, p. 614

OPENING PRAYER

God our Father,
in St. (bishop) N. you gave
a light to your faithful people.
You made him a pastor of the Church
to feed your sheep with his word
and to teach them by his example.
Help us by his prayers to keep the faith he taught
and follow the way of life he showed us.
Grant this through our Lord Jesus Christ, your Son,
who lives and reigns with you and the Holy Spirit,
one God, for ever and ever. ℟. **Amen.** ⌄

READINGS AND INTERVENIENT CHANTS
See pp. 1154-1176.

PRAYER OVER THE GIFTS

Father of mercy,
we have these gifts to offer in honor of your saints
who bore witness to your mighty power.
May the power of the eucharist
bring us your salvation.
Grant this through Christ our Lord.
℟. **Amen.** → No. 21, p. 626

COMMUNION ANT. Mt 28, 20

**I, the Lord, am with you always, until the end of the
world.** ⌄

PRAYER AFTER COMMUNION

Lord,
may the mysteries we receive
prepare us for the eternal joys
St. N. won by his faithful ministry.
We ask this in the name of Jesus the Lord.
℟. **Amen.** ↓

OR

All-powerful God,
by our love and worship
may we who share this holy meal
always follow the example of St. N.
Grant this in the name of Jesus the Lord. ℟. **Amen.**

➤ No. 32, p. 650

---

6.   FOR PASTORS

ENTRANCE ANT.   Jer 3, 15

**I will give you shepherds after my own heart, and
they shall feed you on knowledge and sound teaching.**

OR   Dan 3, 84. 87

**Priests of God, bless the Lord; praise God, all you
that are holy and humble of heart.**

➤ No. 2, p. 614

OPENING PRAYER

Lord God,
you gave your Saints (bishops) N. and N.
the spirit of truth and love
to shepherd your people.
May we who honor them on this feast
learn from their example
and be helped by their prayers.
We ask this through our Lord Jesus Christ, your Son,

who lives and reigns with you and the Holy Spirit,
one God, for ever and ever. ℟. **Amen.** ↓

READINGS AND INTERVENIENT CHANTS
See pp. 1154-1176.

PRAYER OVER THE GIFTS
Lord,
accept these gifts from your people.
May the eucharist we offer to your glory
in honor of Saints N. and N.
help us on our way to salvation.
Grant this in the name of Jesus the Lord.
℟. **Amen.**   ➤ No. 21, p. 626

COMMUNION ANT.   Mt 20, 28
**The Son of Man did not come to be served, but to
serve, and to give his life as a ransom for many.** ↓

PRAYER AFTER COMMUNION
Lord,
we receive the bread of heaven
as we honor the memory of your Saints N. and N.
May the eucharist we now celebrate
lead us to eternal joys.
Grant this in the name of Jesus the Lord.
℟. **Amen.**   ➤ No. 32, p. 650

_____

7. FOR PASTORS

ENTRANCE ANT.   Ps 131, 9
**Lord, may your priests be clothed in justice, and
your holy ones leap for joy.**   ➤ No. 2, p. 614

OPENING PRAYER
All-powerful God,
hear the prayers of Saints N. and N.
Increase your gifts within us
and give us peace in our days.

We ask this through our Lord Jesus Christ, your Son,
who lives and reigns with you and the Holy Spirit,
one God, for ever and ever. ℟. **Amen.** ▼

READINGS AND INTERVENIENT CHANTS
See pp. 1154-1176.

PRAYER OVER THE GIFTS
Lord,
accept the gifts we bring to your altar
in memory of your Saints N. and N.
As you led them to glory through these mysteries,
grant us also your pardon and love.
We ask this in the name of Jesus the Lord.
℟. **Amen.**   ➜ No. 21, p. 626

COMMUNION ANT.   Mt 24, 46-47
**Blessed is the servant whom the Lord finds watching
when he comes; truly I tell you, he will set him over
all his possessions.** ▼

OR   Lk 12, 42
**The Lord has put his faithful servant in charge of his
household, to give them their share of bread at the
proper time.** ▼

PRAYER AFTER COMMUNION
All-powerful God,
by the eucharist we share at your holy table
on this feast of Saints N. and N.
increase our strength of character and love for you.
May we guard from every danger the faith you have
    given us
and walk always in the way that leads to salvation.
Grant this in the name of Jesus the Lord.
℟. **Amen.**   ➜ No. 32, p. 650

8. FOR FOUNDERS OF CHURCHES

ENTRANCE ANT. Is 59, 21; 56, 7

My words that I have put in your mouth, says the Lord, will never be absent from your lips, and your gifts will be accepted on my altar. → No. 2, p. 614

OPENING PRAYER

God of mercy,
you gave our fathers the light of faith
through the preaching of St. N.
May we who glory in the Christian name
show in our lives the faith we profess.
We ask this through our Lord Jesus Christ, your Son,
who lives and reigns with you and the Holy Spirit,
one God, for ever and ever. ℟. **Amen.** ↓

OR

Lord,
look upon the family whom your St. (bishop) N.
  brought to life
with the word of truth
and nourished with the sacrament of life.
By his ministry you gave us the faith;
by his prayers help us grow in love.
Grant this through our Lord Jesus Christ, your Son,
who lives and reigns with you and the Holy Spirit,
one God, for ever and ever. ℟. **Amen.** ↓

READINGS AND INTERVENIENT CHANTS
See pp. 1154-1176.

PRAYER OVER THE GIFTS

Lord,
may the gifts your people bring
in memory of St. N.
bring us your gifts from heaven.
We ask this in the name of Jesus the Lord.
℟. **Amen.** → No. 21, p. 626

COMMUNION ANT.   Mk 10, 45

The Son of Man came to give his life as a ransom for many. ⍒

PRAYER AFTER COMMUNION

Lord,
may this pledge of our eternal salvation
which we receive on this feast of St. N.
be our help now and always.
Grant this through Christ our Lord.
℞. **Amen.**   ➔ No. 32, p. 650

---

9. FOR FOUNDERS OF CHURCHES

ENTRANCE ANT.

The Lord chose these holy men for their unfeigned love, and gave them eternal glory. The Church has light by their teaching.   ➔ No. 2, p. 614

OPENING PRAYER

Lord,
look with love on the church of N.
Through the apostolic zeal of Saints N. and N.
you gave us the beginnings of our faith:
through their prayers keep alive our Christian love.
We ask this through our Lord Jesus Christ, your Son,
who lives and reigns with you and the Holy Spirit,
one God, for ever and ever. ℞. **Amen.** ⍒

OR

God,
you called our fathers to the light of the gospel
by the preaching of your bishop N.
By his prayers help us to grow in the love and
    knowledge
of your Son, our Lord Jesus Christ,
who lives and reigns with you and the Holy Spirit,
one God, for ever and ever. ℞. **Amen.** ⍒

READINGS AND INTERVENIENT CHANTS
See pp. 1154-1176.

PRAYER OVER THE GIFTS
Lord,
accept the gifts your people bring
on this feast of Saints N. and N.
Give us purity of heart
and make us pleasing to you.
We ask this through Christ our Lord.
℟. **Amen.**   ➔ No. 21, p. 626

COMMUNION ANT.   Jn 15, 15
**No longer shall I call you servants, for a servant
knows not what his master does. Now I shall call
you friends, for I have revealed to you all that I have
heard from my Father.** ↓

PRAYER AFTER COMMUNION
Lord,
as we share in your gifts,
we celebrate this feast of Saints N. and N.
We honor the beginnings of our faith
and proclaim your glory in the saints.
May the salvation we receive from your altar
be our unending joy.
Grant this through Christ our Lord.
℟. **Amen.**   ➔ No. 32, p. 650

----

10. FOR MISSIONARIES

ENTRANCE ANT.
**These are holy men who became God's friends and
glorious heralds of his truth.**   ➔ No. 2, p. 614

OPENING PRAYER
Father,
through your St. (bishop) N.
you brought those who had no faith

out of darkness into the light of truth.
By the help of his prayers,
keep us strong in our faith
and firm in the hope of the gospel he preached.
Grant this through our Lord Jesus Christ, your Son,
who lives and reigns with you and the Holy Spirit,
one God, for ever and ever. ℟. **Amen.** ▼

OR

All-powerful and ever-living God,
you made this day holy
by welcoming St. N. into the the glory of your king-
    dom.
Keep us true to the faith he professed with untiring
    zeal,
and help us to bring it to perfection by acting in love.
We ask this through our Lord Jesus Christ, your Son,
who lives and reigns with you and the Holy Spirit,
one God, for ever and ever. ℟. **Amen.** ▼

READINGS AND INTERVENIENT CHANTS
See pp. 1154-1176.

PRAYER OVER THE GIFTS

All-powerful God,
look upon the gifts we bring on this feast
in honor of St. N.
May we who celebrate the mystery of the death of
    the Lord
imitate the love we celebrate.
We ask this through Christ our Lord.
℟. **Amen.**   ➜ No. 21, p. 626

COMMUNION ANT.   Ez 34, 15
**I will feed my sheep, says the Lord, and give them
repose.** ▼

PRAYER AFTER COMMUNION

Lord,
St. N. worked tirelessly for the faith,

spending his life in its service.
With the power this eucharist gives
make your people strong in the same true faith
and help us to proclaim it everywhere
by all we say and do.
℟. **Amen.**   ➤ No. 32, p. 650

_____

11. FOR MISSIONARIES

ENTRANCE ANT.   Is 52, 7
**How beautiful on the mountains are the feet of the
man who brings tidings of peace, joy and salvation.**
➤ No. 2, p. 614

OPENING PRAYER
Father,
you made your Church grow
through the Christian zeal and apostolic work of
    St. N.
By the help of his prayers
give your Church continued growth in holiness and
    faith.
Grant this through our Lord Jesus Christ, your Son,
who lives and reigns with you and the Holy Spirit,
one God, for ever and ever. ℟. **Amen.** ▼

READINGS AND INTERVENIENT CHANTS
See pp. 1154-1176.

PRAYER OVER THE GIFTS
Lord,
be pleased with our prayers
and free us from all guilt.
In your love, wash away our sins
that we may celebrate the mysteries which set us
    free.
Grant this in the name of Jesus the Lord.
℟. **Amen.**   ➤ No. 21, p. 626

COMMUNION ANT.   Mk 16, 15; Mt 28, 20

Go out to all the world, and tell the good news: I am with you always, says the Lord. ℣

OR   Jn 15, 4-5

Live in me and let me live in you, says the Lord; he who lives in me, and I in him, will bear much fruit. ℣

PRAYER AFTER COMMUNION

Lord our God,
by these mysteries help our faith grow to maturity
in the faith the apostles preached and taught,
and the faith which St. N. watched over with such
    care.
We ask this through Christ our Lord.
℞. **Amen.**   ➤ No. 32, p. 650

---

12. FOR MISSIONARIES

ENTRANCE ANT.   Ps 95, 3-4

Proclaim his glory among the nations, his marvelous deeds to all the peoples; great is the Lord and worthy of all praise.   ➤ No. 2, p. 614

OPENING PRAYER

God of mercy,
you gave us St. N. to proclaim the riches of Christ.
By the help of his prayers
may we grow in knowledge of you,
be eager to do good,
and learn to walk before you
by living the truth of the gospel.
Grant this through our Lord Jesus Christ, your Son,
who lives and reigns with you and the Holy Spirit,
one God, for ever and ever. ℞. **Amen. ℣**

OR (for martyrs)

All-powerful God,
help us to imitate with steadfast love
the faith of Saints N. and N.
who won the crown of martyrdom
by giving their lives in the service of the gospel.
We ask this through our Lord Jesus Christ, your Son,
who lives and reigns with you and the Holy Spirit,
one God, for ever and ever. ℟. **Amen.** ▼

READINGS AND INTERVENIENT CHANTS
See pp. 1154-1176.

PRAYER OVER THE GIFTS

Lord,
we who honor the memory of St. N.
ask you to send your blessing on these gifts.
By receiving them may we be freed from all guilt
and share in the food from the heavenly table.
We ask this through Christ our Lord.
℟. **Amen.**   ➔ No. 21, p. 626

COMMUNION ANT.   See Lk 10, 1. 9

**The Lord sent disciples to proclaim to all the towns:
the kingdom of God is very near to you.** ▼

PRAYER AFTER COMMUNION

Lord,
let the holy gifts we receive fill us with life
so that we who rejoice in honoring the memory of
     St. N.
may also benefit from his example of apostolic zeal.
Grant this through Christ our Lord.
℟. **Amen.**   ➔ No. 32, p. 650

COMMON OF DOCTORS OF
THE CHURCH

The Common of Doctors of the Church comprises only
two Mass formularies. One of the reasons for this is
that the relatively few saints who fit into this category
also fall into another—for example, pastors or religious.
Thus a combination of the texts of these categories
offers ample opportunity for the desired variety.

1

ENTRANCE ANT.   Sir 15, 5

**The Lord opened his mouth in the assembly, and
filled him with the spirit of wisdom and understanding, and clothed him in a robe of glory.**

OR   Ps 37, 30-31

**The mouth of the just man utters wisdom, and his
tongue speaks what is right; the law of his God is in
his heart.**   No. 2, p. 614

OPENING PRAYER

God our Father,
you made your St. (bishop) N. a teacher in your
  Church.
By the power of the Holy Spirit
establish his teaching in our hearts.
As you give him to us as a patron,
may we have the protection of his prayers.
Grant this through our Lord Jesus Christ, your Son,
who lives and reigns with you and the Holy Spirit,
one God, for ever and ever. R̹. **Amen.** ♦

READINGS AND INTERVENIENT CHANTS
See pp. 1177-1187.

PRAYER OVER THE GIFTS
Lord,
accept our sacrifice on this feast of St. N.,
and following his example
may we give you our praise
and offer you all we have.
Grant this in the name of Jesus the Lord.
R̹. **Amen.**   → No. 21, p. 626

COMMUNION ANT. Lk 12, 42

The Lord has put his faithful servant in charge of his household, to give them their share of bread at the proper time. ℣

PRAYER AFTER COMMUNION

God our Father,
Christ the living bread renews us.
Let Christ our teacher instruct us
that on this feast of St. N.
we may learn your truth
and practice it in love.
We ask this through Christ our Lord.
℟. **Amen.** ➔ No. 32, p. 650

2

ENTRANCE ANT. Dn 12, 3

The learned will shine like the brilliance of the firmament, and those who train many in the ways of justice will sparkle like the stars for all eternity.

OR See Sir 44, 15. 14

Let the peoples declare the wisdom of the saints and the Church proclaim their praises; their names shall live for ever. ➔ No. 2, p. 614

OPENING PRAYER

Lord God,
you filled St. N. with heavenly wisdom.
By his help may we remain true to his teaching
and put it into practice.
We ask this through our Lord Jesus Christ, your Son,
who lives and reigns with you and the Holy Spirit,
one God, for ever and ever. ℟. **Amen.** ℣

READINGS AND INTERVENIENT CHANTS
See pp. 1177-1187.

PRAYER OVER THE GIFTS

Lord,
by this celebration,
may your Spirit fill us with the same light of faith
that shines in the teaching of St. N.
We ask this through Christ our Lord.
℞. **Amen.**   ➤ No. 21, p. 626

COMMUNION ANT.   1 Cor 1, 23-24

We preach a Christ who was crucified; he is the power and the wisdom of God. ℣

PRAYER AFTER COMMUNION

Lord,
you renew us with the food of heaven.
May St. N. remain our teacher and example
and keep us thankful for all we have received.
Grant this in the name of Jesus the Lord.
℞. **Amen.**   ➤ No. 32, p. 650

COMMON OF VIRGINS

The Common of Virgins comprises four Mass formularies, three for one Virgin and the last for several Virgins. The saint who is a Virgin in many cases also fits into another category. One may thus use both categories in choosing the texts for each celebration.

1

ENTRANCE ANT.

Here is a wise and faithful virgin who went with lighted lamp to meet her Lord. → No. 2, p. 614

OPENING PRAYER

God our Savior,
as we celebrate with joy the memory of the virgin N.,
may we learn from her example of faithfulness and love.
We ask this through our Lord Jesus Christ, your Son,
who lives and reigns with you and the Holy Spirit,
one God, for ever and ever. ℞. **Amen.** ℣

READINGS AND INTERVENIENT CHANTS
See pp. 1188-1194.

PRAYER OVER THE GIFTS

Lord,
we see the wonder of your love
in the life of the virgin N.
and her witness to Christ.
Accept our gifts of praise
and make our offering pleasing to you.
Grant this through Christ our Lord.
℞. **Amen.** → No. 21, p. 626

COMMUNION ANT. Mt 25, 5

The bridegroom is here; let us go out to meet Christ the Lord. ℣

PRAYER AFTER COMMUNION

Lord God,
may this eucharist renew our courage and strength.
May we remain close to you, like St. N.,

by accepting in our lives
a share in the suffering of Jesus Christ,
who lives and reigns with you for ever and ever.
℟. **Amen.**   ➤ No. 32, p. 650

———————

2

ENTRANCE ANT.

**Let us rejoice and shout for joy, because the Lord
of all things has favored this holy and glorious virgin
with his love.**   ➤ No. 2, p. 614

OPENING PRAYER

Lord God,
you endowed the virgin N. with gifts from heaven.
By imitating her goodness here on earth
may we come to share her joy in eternal life.
We ask this through our Lord Jesus Christ, your Son,
who lives and reigns with you and the Holy Spirit,
one God, for ever and ever. ℟. **Amen.** ⍌

OR (for a virgin foundress)

Lord our God,
may the witness of your faithful bride the virgin N.
awaken the fire of divine love in our hearts.
May it inspire other young women to give their lives
to the service of Christ and his Church.
Grant this through our Lord Jesus Christ, your Son,
who lives and reigns with you and the Holy Spirit,
one God, for ever and ever. ℟. **Amen.** ⍌

READINGS AND INTERVENIENT CHANTS
See pp. 1188-1194.

PRAYER OVER THE GIFTS

Lord,
may the gifts we bring you
help us follow the example of St. N.
Cleanse us from our earthly way of life,
and teach us to live the new life of your kingdom.
We ask this through Christ our Lord.
℟. **Amen.**   ➤ No. 21, p. 626

COMMUNION ANT. Mt 25, 4. 6
The five sensible virgins took flasks of oil as well as their lamps. At midnight a cry was heard: the bridegroom is here; let us go out to meet Christ the Lord. ℣

PRAYER AFTER COMMUNION
Lord,
may our reception of the body and blood of your
    Son
keep us from harmful things.
Help us by the example of St. N.
to grow in your love on earth
that we may rejoice for ever in heaven.
We ask this in the name of Jesus the Lord.
℟. **Amen.**
➤ No. 32, p. 650

3

ENTRANCE ANT.
Come, bride of Christ, and receive the crown, which the Lord has prepared for you for ever.
➤ No. 2, p. 614

OPENING PRAYER
Lord,
you have told us that you live for ever
in the hearts of the chaste.
By the prayers of the virgin N.,
help us to live by your grace
and to become a temple of your Spirit.
Grant this through our Lord Jesus Christ, your Son,
who lives and reigns with you and the Holy Spirit,
one God, for ever and ever. ℟. **Amen.** ℣

OR
Lord,
hear the prayers of those who recall the devoted
    life of the virgin N.

Guide us on our way and help us to grow
in love and devotion as long as we live.
We ask this through our Lord Jesus Christ, your Son,
who lives and reigns with you and the Holy Spirit,
one God, for ever and ever. ℟. **Amen.** ♥

READINGS AND INTERVENIENT CHANTS
See pp. 1188-1194.

PRAYER OVER THE GIFTS
Lord,
receive our worship in memory of N. the virgin.
By this perfect sacrifice
make us grow in unselfish love for you
and for our brothers.
We ask this through Christ our Lord.
℟. **Amen.** ➤ No. 21, p. 626

COMMUNION ANT. See Lk 10, 42
**The wise virgin chose the better part for herself,
and it shall not be taken away from her.** ♥

PRAYER AFTER COMMUNION
God of mercy,
we rejoice that on this feast of St. N.
you give us the bread of heaven.
May it bring us pardon for our sins,
health of body,
your grace in this life,
and glory in heaven.
Grant this through Christ our Lord.
℟. **Amen.** ➤ No. 32, p. 650

4

ENTRANCE ANT. Ps 148, 12-14
**Let virgins praise the name of the Lord, for his name
alone is supreme; its majesty outshines both earth
and heaven.** ➤ No. 2, p. 614

OPENING PRAYER

Lord,
increase in us your gifts of mercy and forgiveness.
May we who rejoice at this celebration
in honor of the virgins N. and N.
receive the joy of sharing eternal life with them.
We ask this through our Lord Jesus Christ, your Son,
who lives and reigns with you and the Holy Spirit,
one God, for ever and ever. ℟. **Amen.** ⱱ

READINGS AND INTERVENIENT CHANTS
See pp. 1188-1194.

PRAYER OVER THE GIFTS

Lord,
we bring you our gifts and prayers.
We praise your glory on this feast of the virgins
    N. and N.,
whose witness to Christ was pleasing to you.
Be pleased also with the eucharist we now offer.
Grant this through Christ our Lord.
℟. **Amen.**   ➔ No. 21, p. 626

COMMUNION ANT.   Mt 25, 10
**The bridegroom has come, and the virgins who were
ready have gone in with him to the wedding.** ⱱ

OR   Jn 14, 21. 23
**Whoever loves me will be loved by my Father.
We shall come to him and make our home with him.** ⱱ

PRAYER AFTER COMMUNION

Lord,
may the mysteries we receive
on this feast of the virgins N. and N.
keep us alert and ready to welcome your Son at his
    return,
that he may welcome us to the feast of eternal life.
Grant this through Christ our Lord.
℟. **Amen.**   ➔ No. 32, p. 650

COMMON OF HOLY MEN AND WOMEN

The Common of Holy Men and Women comprises twelve Mass formularies. The first six refer to the saints in general: the first to one (no. 1) and the others to several (nos. 2-6). The other six refer to some specific state and field of endeavor: religious (nos. 7-8), those who worked for the underprivileged (no. 9), teachers (no. 10), and those who were especially noteworthy for holiness (nos. 11-12).

The following Masses, if indicated for a particular rank of saints, are used for saints of that rank. If no indication is given, the Masses may be used for saints of any rank.

1

ENTRANCE ANT.   Ps 145, 10-11

May all your works praise you, Lord, and your saints bless you; they will tell of the glory of your kingdom and proclaim your power.   ➔ No. 2, p. 614

OPENING PRAYER

Ever-living God,
the signs of your love are manifest
in the honor you give your saints.
May their prayers and their example encourage us
to follow your Son more faithfully.
We ask this through our Lord Jesus Christ, your Son,
who lives and reigns with you and the Holy Spirit,
one God, for ever and ever. ℟. **Amen.** ▼

READINGS AND INTERVENIENT CHANTS
See pp. 1195-1233.

PRAYER OVER THE GIFTS

Lord, in your kindness hear our prayers
and the prayers which the saints offer on our behalf.
Watch over us that we may offer fitting service
     at your altar.
Grant this in the name of Jesus the Lord.
℟. **Amen.**   ➔ No. 21, p. 626

COMMUNION ANT.   Ps 68, 4

May the just rejoice as they feast in God's presence, and delight in gladness of heart. ▼

OR Lk 12, 37

Blessed are those servants whom the Lord finds watching when he comes; truly I tell you, he will seat them at his table and wait on them. ℣

PRAYER AFTER COMMUNION
Father, our comfort and peace,
we have gathered as your family
to praise your name and honor your saints.
Let the sacrament we have received
be the sign and pledge of our salvation.
We ask this through Christ our Lord.
℟. **Amen.** ➤ No. 32, p. 650

2

ENTRANCE ANT. Ps 64, 11
The just man will rejoice in the Lord and hope in him, and all the upright of heart will be praised.
➤ No. 2, p. 614

OPENING PRAYER
God our Father,
you alone are holy;
without you nothing is good.
Trusting in the prayers of St. N.
we ask you to help us
to become the holy people you call us to be.
Never let us be found undeserving
of the glory you have prepared for us.
We ask this through our Lord Jesus Christ, your Son,
who lives and reigns with you and the Holy Spirit,
one God, for ever and ever. ℟. **Amen.** ℣

READINGS AND INTERVENIENT CHANTS
See pp. 1195-1233.

PRAYER OVER THE GIFTS

All-powerful God,
may the gifts we present
bring honor to your saints,
and free us from sin in mind and body.
We ask this in the name of Jesus the Lord.
℞. **Amen.**   ➤ No. 21, p. 626

COMMUNION ANT.   Jn 12, 26

**He who serves me, follows me, says the Lord; and
where I am, my servant will also be.** ⱴ

PRAYER AFTER COMMUNION

Lord,
your sacramental gifts renew us
at this celebration of the birth of your saints to
    glory.
May the good things you give us
lead us to the joy of your kingdom.
We ask this through Christ our Lord.
℞. **Amen.**   ➤ No. 32, p. 650

3

ENTRANCE ANT.   Ps 21, 2-3

**Lord, your strength gives joy to the just; they greatly
delight in your saving help. You have granted them
their heart's desire.**   ➤ No. 2, p. 614

OPENING PRAYER

Father,
your saints guide us when in our weakness we tend
    to stray.
Help us who celebrate the birth of St. N. to glory
grow closer to you by following his (her) example.
We ask this through our Lord Jesus Christ, your Son,
who lives and reigns with you and the Holy Spirit,
one God, for ever and ever. ℞. **Amen.** ⱴ

READINGS AND INTERVENIENT CHANTS
See pp. 1195-1233.

PRAYER OVER THE GIFTS
Lord,
let the sacrifice we offer
in memory of St. N.
bring to your people the gifts of unity and peace.
Grant this in the name of Jesus the Lord.
℟. **Amen.**   ➔ No. 21, p. 626

COMMUNION ANT.   Mt 16, 24
**If anyone wishes to come after me, he must re-
nounce himself, take up his cross, and follow me,
says the Lord.** ℣

PRAYER AFTER COMMUNION
Lord,
may the sacraments we receive
on this feast in honor of N.
give us holiness of mind and body
and bring us into your divine life.
We ask this through Christ our Lord.
℟. **Amen.**   ➔ No. 32, p. 650

4

ENTRANCE ANT.   Mal 2, 6
**The teaching of truth was in his mouth, and no
wrong was found on his lips; he walked with me
in peace and justice, and turned many away from
wickedness.**   ➔ No. 2, p. 614

OPENING PRAYER
Merciful Father,
we fail because of our weakness.
Restore us to your love
through the example of your saints.

We ask this through our Lord Jesus Christ, your Son,
who lives and reigns with you and the Holy Spirit,
one God, for ever and ever. ℟. **Amen.** ↓

READINGS AND INTERVENIENT CHANTS
See pp. 1195-1233.

PRAYER OVER THE GIFTS
Lord,
may this sacrifice we share
on the feast of your St. N.
give you praise
and help us on our way to salvation.
Grant this in the name of Jesus the Lord.
℟. **Amen.**   ➜ No. 21, p. 626

COMMUNION ANT.   Mt 5, 8-9
**Happy are the pure of heart for they shall see God.
Happy the peacemakers; they shall be called the
sons of God. Happy are they who suffer persecution
for justice' sake; the kingdom of heaven is theirs.** ↓

PRAYER AFTER COMMUNION
Lord,
our hunger is satisfied by your holy gift.
May we who have celebrated this eucharist
experience in our lives the salvation which it brings.
We ask this in the name of Jesus the Lord.
℟. **Amen.**   ➜ No. 32, p. 650

_____

5

ENTRANCE ANT.   Ps 92, 13-14
**The just man will flourish like the palm tree. Planted
in the courts of God's house, he will grow great like
the cedars of Lebanon.**   ➜ No. 2, p. 614

OPENING PRAYER

Lord,
may the prayers of the saints
bring help to your people.
Give to us who celebrate the memory of your saints
a share in their eternal joy.
Grant this through our Lord Jesus Christ, your Son,
who lives and reigns with you and the Holy Spirit,
one God, for ever and ever. ℟. **Amen.** ↓

READINGS AND INTERVENIENT CHANTS

See pp. 1195-1233.

PRAYER OVER THE GIFTS

Lord,
give to us who offer these gifts at your altar
the same spirit of love that filled St. N.
By celebrating this sacred eucharist with pure minds and loving hearts
may we offer a sacrifice that pleases you,
and brings salvation to us.
Grant this through Christ our Lord.
℟. **Amen.** ➔ No. 21, p. 626

COMMUNION ANT. Mt 11, 28

Come to me, all you that labor and are burdened, and I will give you rest, says the Lord. ↓

PRAYER AFTER COMMUNION

Lord,
may the sacrament of holy communion which we receive
bring us health and strengthen us
in the light of your truth.
We ask this in the name of Jesus the Lord.
℟. **Amen.** ➔ No. 32, p. 650

6

ENTRANCE ANT.   Jer 17, 7-8

**Blessed is the man who puts his trust in the Lord;
he will be like a tree planted by the waters, sinking
its roots into the moist earth; he will have nothing
to fear in time of drought.**   ➤ No. 2, p. 614

OPENING PRAYER

All-powerful God,
help us who celebrate the memory of St. N.
to imitate his (her) way of life.
May the example of your saints
be our challenge to live holier lives.
Grant this through our Lord Jesus Christ, your Son,
who lives and reigns with you and the Holy Spirit,
one God, for ever and ever. ℞. **Amen.** ▾

READINGS AND INTERVENIENT CHANTS

See pp. 1195-1233.

PRAYER OVER THE GFTS

Lord,
we bring our gifts to your holy altar
on this feast of your saints.
In your mercy let this eucharist
give you glory
and bring us to the fullness of your love.
Grant this through Christ our Lord.
℞. **Amen.**   ➤ No. 21, p. 626

COMMUNION ANT.   Jn 15, 9

**As the Father has loved me, so have I loved you;
remain in my love.** ▾

PRAYER AFTER COMMUNION

Lord our God,
may the divine mysteries we celebrate
in memory of your saint

fill us with eternal peace and salvation.
We ask this in the name of Jesus the Lord.
℟. **Amen.**   ➜ No. 32, p. 650

_____

7. FOR RELIGIOUS

ENTRANCE ANT.   Ps 16, 5-6
**The Lord is my inheritance and my cup; he alone
will give me my reward. The measuring line has
marked a lovely place for me; my inheritance is my
great delight.**   ➜ No. 2, p. 614

OPENING PRAYER
Lord God,
you kept St. N. faithful to Christ's pattern of poverty
  and humility.
May his (her) prayers help us to live in fidelity to
  our calling
and bring us to the perfection you have shown us
  in your Son,
who lives and reigns with you and the Holy Spirit,
one God, for ever and ever. ℟. **Amen.** ↓

OR (for an abbot)
Lord,
in your abbot N.
you give an example of the gospel lived to perfection.
Help us to follow him
by keeping before us the things of heaven
amid all the changes of this world.
Grant this through our Lord Jesus Christ, your Son,
who lives and reigns with you and the Holy Spirit,
one God, for ever and ever. ℟. **Amen.** ↓

READINGS AND INTERVENIENT CHANTS
See pp. 1195-1233.

PRAYER OVER THE GIFTS

God of all mercy,
you transformed St. N.
and made him (her) a new creature in your image.
Renew us in the same way
by making our gifts of peace acceptable to you.
We ask this in the name of Jesus the Lord.
℟. **Amen.**   ➔ No. 21, p. 626

COMMUNION ANT.   See Mt 19, 27-29
**I solemnly tell you: those who have left everything
and followed me will be repaid a hundredfold and
will gain eternal life.** ✣

PRAYER AFTER COMMUNION

All-powerful God,
may we who are strengthened by the power of this
    sacrament
learn from the example of St. N.
to seek you above all things
and to live in this world as your new creation.
We ask this through Christ our Lord.
℟. **Amen.**   ➔ No. 32, p. 650

----

8. FOR RELIGIOUS

ENTRANCE ANT.   See Ps 24, 5-6
**These are the saints who received blessings from
the Lord, a prize from God their Savior. They are
the people that long to see his face.** ➔ No. 2, p. 614

OPENING PRAYER

God our Father,
you called St. N. to seek your kingdom in this world
by striving to live in perfect charity.
With his (her) prayers to give us courage,
help us to move forward with joyful hearts in the
    way of love.

We ask this through our Lord Jesus Christ, your Son,
who lives and reigns with you and the Holy Spirit,
one God, for ever and ever. ℟. **Amen.** ↓

READINGS AND INTERVENIENT CHANTS
See pp. 1195-1233.

PRAYER OVER THE GFTS
Lord,
may the gifts we bring to your altar
in memory of St. N.
be acceptable to you.
Free us from the things that keep us from you
and teach us to seek you as our only good.
We ask this through Christ our Lord.
℟. **Amen.**   ➔ No. 21, p. 626

COMMUNION ANT.   Ps 33, 9
**Taste and see the goodness of the Lord; blessed is
he who hopes in God.** ↓

PRAYER AFTER COMMUNION
Lord,
by the power of this sacrament and the example of
  St. N.
guide us always in your love.
May the good work you have begun in us
reach perfection in the day of Christ Jesus
who is Lord for ever and ever.
℟. **Amen.**   ➔ No. 32, p. 650

---

9. FOR THOSE WHO WORK FOR THE UNDERPRIVILEGED

ENTRANCE ANT.   Mt 25, 34. 36. 40
**Come, you whom my Father has blessed, says the
Lord: I was ill and you comforted me. I tell you,
anything you did for one of my brothers, you did
for me.**   ➔ No. 2, p. 614

OPENING PRAYER

Lord God,
you teach us that the commandments of heaven
are summarized in love of you and love of our
   neighbor.
By following the example of St. N.
in practicing works of charity
may we be counted among the blessed in your kingdom.
Grant this through our Lord Jesus Christ, your Son,
who lives and reigns with you and the Holy Spirit,
one God, for ever and ever. ℟. **Amen.** ⩗

READINGS AND INTERVENIENT CHANTS
See pp. 1195-1233.

PRAYER OVER THE GIFTS

Lord,
accept the gifts of your people.
May we who celebrate the love of your Son
also follow the example of your saints
and grow in love for you and for one another.
We ask this through Christ our Lord.
℟. **Amen.**   ➜ No. 21, p. 626

COMMUNION ANT.   Jn 15, 13

**No one has greater love, says the Lord, than the man
who lays down his life for his friends.** ⩗

OR   Jn 13, 35

**By the love you have for one another, says the Lord,
everyone will know that you are my disciples.** ⩗

PRAYER AFTER COMMUNION

Lord,
may we who are renewed by these mysteries
follow the example of St. N.
who worshiped you with love
and served your people with generosity.
We ask this through Christ our Lord. ℟. **Amen.**

OR

Lord,

we who receive the sacrament of salvation ask your
  mercy.

Help us to imitate the love of St. N.

and give to us a share in his (her) glory.

Grant this through Christ our Lord. ℞. **Amen.**

➜ No. 32, p. 650

---

10. FOR TEACHERS

ENTRANCE ANT.   Mk 10, 14

**Let the children come to me, and do not stop them,
says the Lord; to such belongs the kingdom of God.**

OR   Mt 5, 19

**The man that keeps these commandments and teach-
es them, he is the one who will be called great in
the kingdom of heaven, says the Lord.**

➜ No. 2, p. 614

OPENING PRAYER

Lord God,

you called St. N. to serve you in the Church

by teaching his (her) fellow man the way of salvation.

Inspire us by his (her) example:

help us to follow Christ our teacher,

and lead us to our brothers and sisters in heaven.

We ask this through our Lord Jesus Christ, your Son,

who lives and reigns with you and the Holy Spirit,

one God, for ever and ever. ℞. **Amen.** ▼

READINGS AND INTERVENIENT CHANTS
See pp. 1195-1233.

PRAYER OVER THE GIFTS

Lord,

accept the gifts your people bring

in memory of your saints.

May our sharing in this mystery
help us to live the example of love you give us.
Grant this in the name of Jesus the Lord.
Ry. **Amen.** ➤ No. 21, p. 626

COMMUNION ANT. Mt 18, 3

Unless you change, and become like little children, says the Lord, you shall not enter the kingdom of heaven. ℣

OR Jn 8, 12

I am the light of the world, says the Lord; the man who follows me will have the light of life. ℣

PRAYER AFTER COMMUNION

All-powerful God,
may this holy meal help us
to follow the example of your saints
by showing in our lives
the light of truth and love for our brothers.
We ask this in the name of Jesus the Lord.
Ry. **Amen.** ➤ No. 32, p. 650

---

11. FOR HOLY WOMEN

ENTRANCE ANT. See Prv 31, 30. 28

Honor the woman who fears the Lord. Her sons will bless her, and her husband praise her.

➤ No. 2, p. 614

OPENING PRAYER

God our Father,
every year you give us joy on this feast of St. N.
As we honor her memory by this celebration,
may we follow the example of her holy life.
We ask this through our Lord Jesus Christ, your Son,
who lives and reigns with you and the Holy Spirit,
one God for ever and ever. Ry. **Amen.** ℣

OR (for several)

All-powerful God,
may the prayers of Saints N. and N. bring us help
   from heaven
as their lives have already given us
an example of holiness.
We ask this through our Lord Jesus Christ, your Son,
who lives and reigns with you and the Holy Spirit,
one God for ever and ever. ℞. **Amen.** ▼

READINGS AND INTERVENIENT CHANTS
See pp. 1195-1233.

PRAYER OVER THE GIFTS
Lord,
may the gifts we present in memory of St. N.
bring us your forgiveness and salvation.
We ask this in the name of Jesus the Lord.
℞. **Amen.**   ➤ No. 21, p. 626

COMMUNION ANT.   Mt 13, 45-46
**The kingdom of heaven is like a merchant in search
of fine pearls; on finding one rare pearl he sells
everything he has and buys it.** ▼

PRAYER AFTER COMMUNION
All-powerful God,
fill us with your light and love
by the sacrament we receive on the feast of St. N.
May we burn with love for your kingdom
and let our light shine before men.
We ask this through Christ our Lord.
℞. **Amen.**   ➤ No. 32, p. 650

---

12. FOR HOLY WOMEN
ENTRANCE ANT.   See Prv 14, 1-2
**Praise to the holy woman whose home is built on
faithful love and whose pathway leads to God.**

➤ No. 2, p. 614

OPENING PRAYER

Father,
rewarder of the humble,
you blessed St. N. with charity and patience.
May her prayers help us, and her example inspire us
to carry our cross and to love you always.
We ask this through our Lord Jesus Christ, your Son,
who lives and reigns with you and the Holy Spirit,
one God for ever and ever. ℞. **Amen.** ↓

OR

Lord,
pour upon us the spirit of wisdom and love
with which you filled your servant St. N.
By serving you as she did,
may we please you with our faith and our actions.
Grant this through our Lord Jesus Christ, your Son,
who lives and reigns with you and the Holy Spirit,
one God for ever and ever. ℞. **Amen.** ↓

READINGS AND INTERVENIENT CHANTS
See pp. 1195-1233.

PRAYER OVER THE GIFTS

Lord,
receive the gifts your people bring to you
in honor of your saints.
By the eucharist we celebrate
may we progress toward salvation.
Grant this in the name of Jesus the Lord.
℞. **Amen.**   ➔ No. 21, p. 626

COMMUNION ANT.   Mt 12, 50
**Whoever does the will of my Father in heaven is my
brother and sister and mother, says the Lord.** ↓

PRAYER AFTER COMMUNION

Lord,
we receive your gifts

at this celebration in honor of St. N.
May they free us from sin
and strengthen us by your grace.
We ask this in the name of Jesus the Lord.
℟. **Amen.** ➤ No. 32, p. 650

OPTIONAL ANTIPHONS FOR SOLEMNITIES AND FEASTS

1. Let us rejoice in the Lord, and keep a festival in honor of the holy (martyr, pastor) N. Let us join with the angels in joyful praise to the Son of God.

2. Let us all rejoice in the Lord as we honor St. N., our protector. On this day this faithful friend of God entered heaven to reign with Christ for ever.

3. Let us rejoice in celebrating the victory of our patron saint. On earth he proclaimed Christ's love for us. Now Christ leads him to a place of honor before his Father in heaven.

4. Let us rejoice in celebrating the feast of the blessed martyr N. He fought for the law of God on earth; now Christ has granted him an everlasting crown of glory.

5. All his saints and all who fear the Lord, sing your praises to our God; for the Lord our almighty God is King of all creation. Let us rejoice and give him glory.

6. We celebrate the day when blessed N. received his reward; with all the saints he is seated at the heavenly banquet in glory.

COMMON OF SAINTS

READINGS AND INTERVENIENT CHANTS

DEDICATION OF A CHURCH

READING I

OUTSIDE THE EASTER SEASON

1   Gn 28, 11-18

A reading from the book of Genesis

When Jacob came upon a certain shrine, as the sun had already set, he stopped there for the night. Taking one of the stones at the shrine, he put it under his head and lay down to sleep at that spot. Then he had a dream: a stairway rested on the ground, with its top reaching to the heavens; and God's messengers were going up and down on it. And there was the Lord standing beside him and saying:

"I, the Lord, am the God of your forefather Abraham and the God of Isaac; the land on which you are lying I will give to you and your descendants. These shall be as plentiful as the dust of the earth, and through them you shall spread out east and west, north and south. In you and your descendants all the nations of the earth shall find blessing. Know that I am with you; I will protect you wherever you go, and bring you back to this land. I will never leave you until I have done what I promised you."

When Jacob awoke from his sleep, he exclaimed, "Truly, the Lord is in this spot, although I did not know it!" In solemn wonder he cried out: "How awesome is this shrine! This is nothing else but an abode of God, and that is the gateway to heaven!" Early the next morning Jacob took the stone that he had put under his head, set it up as a memorial stone, and poured oil on top of it.

2

1 Kgs 8, 22-23. 27-30

A reading from the first book of Kings

Solomon stood before the altar of the Lord in the presence of the whole community of Israel, and stretching forth his hands toward heaven, he said, "Lord, God of Israel, there is no God like you in heaven above or on earth below; you keep your covenant of kindness with your servants who are faithful to you with their whole heart.

"Can it indeed be that God dwells among men on earth? If the heavens and the highest heavens cannot contain you, how much less this temple which I have built! Look kindly on the prayer and petition of your servant, O Lord, my God, and listen to the cry of supplication which I, your servant, utter before you this day. May your eyes watch night and day over this temple, the place where you have decreed you shall be honored; may you heed the prayer which I, your servant, offer in this place. Listen to the petitions of your servant and of your people Israel which they offer in this place. Listen from your heavenly dwelling and grant pardon."

3

2 Chr 5, 6-10. 13—6, 2

A reading from the second book of Chronicles

King Solomon and the entire community of Israel gathered about him before the ark were sacrificing sheep and oxen so numerous that they could not be counted or numbered. The priests brought the ark of the covenant of the Lord to its place beneath the wings of the cherubim in the sanctuary, the holy of holies of the temple. The cherubim had their wings spread out over the place of the ark, sheltering the ark and its poles from above. The poles were long enough so that their ends could be seen from that part of the holy place nearest the sanctuary; however, they could not be seen beyond. The ark has remained there to this day. There was nothing in it but the two tablets which Moses put there on Horeb, the tablets of the covenant which the Lord made with the Israelites at their departure from Egypt.

When the trumpeters and singers were heard as a single voice praising and giving thanks to the Lord, and when they raised the sound of the trumpets, cymbals and other musical instruments to "give thanks to the Lord, for he is good, for his mercy endures forever," the building of the Lord's temple was filled with a cloud. The priests could not continue to minister because of the cloud, since the Lord's glory filled the house of God.

Then Solomon said: "The Lord intends to dwell in the dark cloud. I have truly built you a princely house and dwelling, where you may abide forever."

---

4   1 Mc 4, 52-59

[For the consecration of an altar]

A reading from the first book of Maccabees

Early in the morning on the twenty-fifth day of the ninth month, that is, the month of Chislev, in the year one hundred and forty-eight, they arose and offered sacrifice according to the law on the new altar of holocausts that they had made. On the anniversary of the day on which the Gentiles had defiled it, on that very day it was reconsecrated with songs, harps, flutes, and cymbals. All the people prostrated themselves and adored and praised Heaven, who had given them success.

For eight days they celebrated the dedication of the altar and joyfully offered holocausts and sacrifices of deliverance and praise. They ornamented the façade of the temple with gold crowns and shields; they repaired the gates and the priests' chambers and furnished them with doors. There was great joy among the people now that the disgrace of the Gentiles was removed. Then Judas and his brothers and the entire congregation of Israel decreed that the days of the dedication of the altar should be observed with joy and gladness on the anniversary every year for eight days from the twenty-fifth day of the month Chislev.

---

5   Is 56, 1. 6-7

A reading from the book of the prophet Isaiah

Thus says the Lord:
Observe what is right, do what is just;
    'for my salvation is about to come,
    my justice, about to be revealed.

And the foreigners who join themselves to the Lord,
   ministering to him,
Loving the name of the Lord,
   and becoming his servants—
All who keep the sabbath free from profanation
   and hold to my covenant,
Them I will bring to my holy mountain
   and make joyful in my house of prayer;
Their holocausts and sacrifices
   will be acceptable on my altar,
For my house shall be called
   a house of prayer for all peoples.

---

6   Ez 43, 1-2. 4-7

A reading from the book of the prophet Ezekiel

The angel led me to the gate which faces the east, and
there I saw the glory of the God of Israel coming from the
east. I heard a sound like the roaring of many waters, and
the earth shone with his glory. I fell prone as the glory of
the Lord entered the temple by way of the gate which
faces the east, but spirit lifted me up and brought me to
the inner court. And I saw that the temple was filled with
the glory of the Lord. Then I heard someone speaking to
me from the temple, while the man stood beside me. The
voice said to me: Son of man, this is where my throne shall
be, this is where I will set the soles of my feet; here I will
dwell among the Israelites forever.

READING I

IN THE EASTER SEASON

1   Acts 7, 44-50

A reading from the Acts of the Apostles

[Stephen spoke to the people, the elders and the scribes:]
"Our fathers in the desert had the meeting tent as God
prescribed it when he spoke to Moses, ordering him to
make it according to the pattern he had seen. The next
generation of our fathers inherited it. Under Joshua, they

brought it into the land during the conquest of those peoples whom God drove out to make room for our fathers. So it was until the time of David, who found favor with God and begged that he might 'find a dwelling place for' the house of 'Jacob.' It was Solomon who ultimately constructed the building for that house. Yet the Most High does not dwell in buildings made by human hands, for as the prophet says:

'The heavens are my throne,
     the earth is my footstool;
What kind of house can you build me?
     asks the Lord.
     What is my resting-place to be like?
Did not my hand make all these things?' "

---

2   Rv 8, 3-4

[For the consecration of an altar]

A reading from the book of Revelation

I, John saw another angel come in holding a censer of gold. He took his place at the altar of incense and was given large amounts of incense to deposit on the altar of gold in front of the throne, together with the prayers of all God's holy ones. From the angel's hand the smoke of the incense went up before God, and with it the prayers of God's people.

---

3   Rv 21, 1-5

A reading from the book of Revelation

I, John, saw new heavens and a new earth. The former heavens and the former earth had passed away, and the sea was no longer. I also saw a new Jerusalem, the holy city, coming down out of heaven from God, beautiful as a bride prepared to meet her husband. I heard a loud voice from the throne cry out: "This is God's dwelling among men. He shall dwell with them and they shall be his people, and he shall be their God who is always with them. He shall wipe every tear from their eyes, and there shall be no more death or mourning, crying out or pain, for the former world has passed away."

The One who sat on the throne said to me, "See, I make all things new!"

---

4   Rv 21, 9-14

A reading from the book of Revelation

The angel said to me, "Come, I will show you the woman who is the bride of the Lamb." He carried me away in spirit to the top of a very high mountain and showed me the holy city Jerusalem coming down out of heaven from God. It gleamed with the splendor of God. The city had the radiance of a precious jewel that sparkled like a diamond. Its wall, massive and high, had twelve gates at which twelve angels were stationed. Twelve names were written on the gates, the names of the twelve tribes of Israel. There were three gates facing east, three north, three south, and three west. The wall of the city had twelve courses of stones as its foundation, on which were written the names of the twelve apostles of the Lamb.

RESPONSORIAL PSALM

1   1 Chr 29, 10. 11. 11-12. 12

℟. (13) **We praise your glorious name, O mighty God.**
Blessed may you be, O Lord,
  God of Israel our father,
  from eternity to eternity.
℟. **We praise your glorious name, O mighty God.**
Yours, O Lord, are grandeur and power,
  majesty, splendor, and glory.
  For all in heaven and on earth is yours.
℟. **We praise your glorious name, O mighty God.**
Yours, O Lord, is the sovereignty;
  you are exalted as head over all.
  Riches and honor are from you.
℟. **We praise your glorious name, O mighty God.**
You have dominion over all.
  In your hand are power and might;
  it is yours to give grandeur and strength to all.
℟. **We praise your glorious name, O mighty God.**

---

2   Ps 84, 3. 4. 5-6. 8. 11

℟. (2) **How lovely is your dwelling-place,**
   Lord, mighty God!
My soul yearns and pines
   for the courts of the Lord.
My heart and my flesh
   cry out for the living God.
℟. **How lovely is your dwelling-place, Lord, mighty God!**
Even the sparrow finds a home,
   and the swallow a nest
   in which she puts her young—
Your altars, O Lord of hosts,
   my king and my God!
℟. **How lovely is your dwelling-place, Lord, mighty God!**
Happy they who dwell in your house!
   continually they praise you.
Happy the men whose strength you are!
   They go from strength to strength.
℟. **How lovely is your dwelling-place, Lord, mighty God!**
I had rather one day in your courts
   than a thousand elsewhere;
I had rather lie at the threshold of the house of my God
   than dwell in the tents of the wicked.
℟. **How lovely is your dwelling-place, Lord, mighty God!**
℟. Or: (Rv 21, 3) **Here God lives among his people.**

————————

3   Ps 95, 1-2. 3-5. 6-7

℟. (2) **Let us come before the Lord and praise him.**
Come, let us sing joyfully to the Lord;
   let us acclaim the Rock of our salvation.
Let us greet him with thanksgiving;
   let us joyfully sing psalms to him.
℟. **Let us come before the Lord and praise him.**
For the Lord is a great God,
   and a great king above all gods;
In his hands are the depths of the earth,
   and the tops of the mountains are his.
His is the sea, for he has made it,
   and the dry land, which his hands have formed.
℟. **Let us come before the Lord and praise him.**

Come, let us bow down in worship;
  let us kneel before the Lord who made us.
For he is our God,
  and we are the people he shepherds, the flock he guides.
℟. **Let us come before the Lord and praise him.**

---

4   Ps 122, 1-2. 3-4. 4-5. 8-9

℟. **(1) I rejoiced when I heard them say:**
  let us go to the house of the Lord.
I rejoiced because they said to me,
  "We will go up to the house of the Lord."
And now we have set foot
  within your gates, O Jerusalem—
℟. **I rejoiced when I heard them say:**
  let us go to the house of the Lord.
Jerusalem, built as a city
  with compact unity.
To it the tribes go up,
  the tribes of the Lord.
℟. **I rejoiced when I heard them say:**
  let us go to the house of the Lord.
According to the decree for Israel,
  to give thanks to the name of the Lord.
In it are set up judgment seats,
  seats for the house of David.
℟. **I rejoiced when I heard them say:**
  let us go to the house of the Lord.
Because of my relatives and friends
  I will say, "Peace be within you!"
Because of the house of the Lord, our God,
  I will pray for your good.
℟. **I rejoiced when I heard them say:**
  let us go to the house of the Lord.
℟. Or: **Let us go rejoicing to the house of the Lord.**

READING II

1   1 Cor 3, 9-13. 16-17

A reading from the first letter of Paul to the Corinthians
You are God's building. Thanks to the favor God showed
me I laid a foundation as a wise master-builder might do,

and now someone else is building upon it. Everyone, how-ever, must be careful how he builds. No one can lay a foundation other than the one that has been laid, namely Jesus Christ. If different ones build on this foundation with gold, silver, precious stones, wood, hay or straw, the work of each will be made clear. The Day will disclose it. That day will make its appearance with fire, and fire will test the quality of each man's work.

Are you not aware that you are the temple of God, and that the Spirit of God dwells in you? If anyone destroys God's temple, God will destroy him. For the temple of God is holy, and you are that temple.

---

2   Eph 2, 19-22

A reading from the letter of Paul to the Ephesians

You are strangers and aliens no longer. No, you are fellow citizens of the saints and members of the household of God. You form a building which rises on the foundation of the apostles and prophets, with Christ Jesus himself as the capstone. Through him the whole structure is fitted to-gether and takes shape as a holy temple in the Lord; in him you are being built into this temple, to become a dwelling place for God in the Spirit.

---

3   Heb 12, 18-19. 22-24

A reading from the letter to the Hebrews

You have not drawn near to an untouchable mountain and a blazing fire, and gloomy darkness and storm and trum-pet blast, and a voice speaking words such that those who heard begged that they be not addressed to them. No, you have drawn near to Mount Zion and the city of the living God, the heavenly Jerusalem, to myriads of angels in festal gathering, to the assembly of the first-born enrolled in heaven, to God the judge of all, to the spirits of just men made perfect, to Jesus, the mediator of a new covenant, and to the sprinkled blood which speaks more eloquently than that of Abel.

4   1 Pt 2, 4-9

A reading from the first letter of Peter

Come to the Lord, a living stone, rejected by men but approved, nonetheless, and precious in God's eyes. You too are living stones, built as an edifice of spirit, into a holy priesthood, offering spiritual sacrifices acceptable to God through Jesus Christ. For Scripture has it:

"See, I am laying a cornerstone in Zion,
an approved stone, and precious.
He who puts his faith in it shall not be shaken."

The stone is of value for you who have faith. For those without faith, it is rather

"A stone which the builders rejected,
that became a cornerstone."

It is likewise "an obstacle and a stumbling stone." Those who stumble and fall are the disbelievers in God's word; it belongs to their destiny to do so.

You, however, are "a chosen race, a royal priesthood, a consecrated nation, a people he claims for his own to proclaim the glorious works" of the One who called you from darkness into his marvelous light.

ALLELUIA VERSE AND
VERSE BEFORE THE GOSPEL

1   2 Chr 7, 16

I have chosen and sanctified this house, says the Lord,
that my name may remain in it for all time.

2   Is 66, 1

Heaven is my throne and earth is my footstool, says the
Lord;
what is the house that you would build for me?

3   Ez 37, 27

My dwelling-place shall be with them, says the Lord,
and I will be their God and they will be my people.

4   See Mt 7, 8

In my house, says the Lord, everyone who asks will
   receive;
whoever seeks shall find; and to him who knocks it shall
   be opened.

GOSPEL

1   Mt 5, 23-24

✠ A reading from the holy gospel according to Matthew

Jesus said to his disciples: "If you bring your gift to the
altar and there recall that your brother has anything
against you, leave your gift at the altar, go first to be reconciled with your brother, and then come and offer your
gift."

---

2   Lk 19, 1-10

✠ A reading from the holy gospel according to Luke

Entering Jericho, Jesus passed through the city. There
was a man there named Zacchaeus, the chief tax collector
and a wealthy man. He was trying to see what Jesus was
like, but being small of stature, was unable to do so because of the crowd. He first ran on in front, then climbed
a sycamore tree which was along Jesus' route, in order to
see him. When Jesus came to the spot he looked up and
said, "Zacchaeus, hurry down. I mean to stay at your
house today." He quickly descended, and welcomed him
with delight. When this was observed, everyone began
to murmur, "He has gone to a sinner's house as a guest."
Zacchaeus stood his ground and said to the Lord: "I
give half my belongings, Lord, to the poor. If I have
defrauded anyone in the least, I pay him back fourfold."
Jesus said to him: "Today salvation has come to this house,
for this is what it means to be a son of Abraham. The Son
of Man has come to search out and save what was lost."

---

3   Jn 2, 13-22

✠ A reading from the holy gospel according to John

As the Jewish Passover was near, Jesus went up to Jerusalem. In the temple precincts he came upon people engaged in selling oxen, sheep and doves, and others seated changing coins. He made a [kind of] whip of cords and drove them all out of the temple area, sheep and oxen alike, and knocked over the moneychangers' tables, spilling their coins. He told those who were selling doves: "Get them out of here! Stop turning my Father's house into a marketplace!" His disciples recalled the words of Scripture: "Zeal for your house consumes me."

At this the Jews responded, "What sign can you show us authorizing you to do these things?" "Destroy this temple," was Jesus' answer, "and in three days I will raise it up." They retorted, "This temple took forty-six years to build, and you are going to 'raise it up in three days'!" Actually he was talking about the temple of his body. Only after Jesus had been raised from the dead did his disciples recall that he had said this, and come to believe the Scripture and the word he had spoken.

---

4   Jn 4, 19-24

✠ A reading from the holy gospel according to John

The [Samaritan] woman said to Jesus: "Sir, I can see you are a prophet. Our ancestors worshiped on this mountain, but you people claim that Jerusalem is the place where men ought to worship God." Jesus told her:

"Believe me, woman,
an hour is coming
when you will worship the Father
neither on this mountain
nor in Jerusalem.
You people worship what you do not understand,
while we understand what we worship;
after all, salvation is from the Jews.
Yet an hour is coming, and is already here,
when authentic worshipers
will worship the Father in Spirit and truth.

Indeed, it is just such worshipers
the Father seeks.
God is Spirit,
and those who worship him
must worship in Spirit and truth."

COMMON OF THE
BLESSED VIRGIN MARY

READING I

OUTSIDE THE EASTER SEASON

1   Gn 3, 9-15. 20

A reading from the book of Genesis

[After Adam had eaten of the fruit of the tree,] the Lord
God then called to the man and asked him, "Where are
you?" He answered, "I heard you in the garden; but I was
afraid, because I was naked, so I hid myself." Then he
asked, "Who told you that you were naked? You have
eaten, then, from the tree of which I had forbidden you to
eat!" The man replied, "The woman whom you put here
with me—she gave me fruit from the tree, and so I ate it."
The Lord God then asked the woman, "Why did you do
such a thing?" The woman answered,

"The serpent tricked me into it, so I ate it."

Then the Lord God said to the serpent:

"Because you have done this, you shall be banned
    from all the animals
    and from all the wild creatures;
On your belly shall you crawl,
    and dirt shall you eat
    all the days of your life.
I will put enmity between you and the woman,
    and between your offspring and hers;
He will strike at your head,
    while you strike at his heel."

The man called his wife Eve, because she became the
mother of all the living.

2

Gn 12, 1-7

A reading from the book of Genesis

The Lord said to Abram: "Go forth from the land of your kinsfolk and from your father's house to a land that I will show you.

"I will make of you a great nation,
  and I will bless you;
I will make your name great,
  so that you will be a blessing.

"I will bless those who bless you
  and curse those who curse you.
All the communities of the earth
  shall find blessing in you."

Abram went as the Lord directed him, and Lot went with him. Abram was seventy-five years old when he left Haran. Abram took his wife Sarai, his brother's son Lot, all the possessions that they had accumulated, and the persons they had acquired in Haran, and they set out for the land of Canaan. When they came to the land of Canaan, Abram passed through the land as far as the sacred place at Shechem, by the terebinth of Moreh. (The Canaanites were then in the land.)

The Lord appeared to Abram and said, "To your descendants I will give this land." So Abram built an altar there to the Lord who had appeared to him.

3

2 Sm 7, 1-5. 8-11. 16

A reading from the second book of Samuel

When King David was settled in his palace, and the Lord had given him rest from his enemies on every side, he said to Nathan the prophet, "Here I am living in a house of cedar, while the ark of God dwells in a tent!" Nathan answered the king, "Go, do whatever you have in mind, for the Lord is with you." But that night the Lord spoke to Nathan and said: "Go, tell my servant David, 'Thus says the Lord: Should you build me a house to dwell in? It was I who took you from the pasture and from the care of the flock to be commander of my people Israel. I have been with you wherever you went, and I have destroyed all your enemies before you. And I will make you famous like the great ones of the earth. I will fix a place for my people Israel; I will plant them so that they may dwell in their place without further disturbance. Neither shall the wicked continue to afflict them as they did of old, since the time I first appointed judges over my people Israel. I will give you rest from all your enemies. The Lord also reveals to you that he will establish a house for you. Your house and your kingdom shall endure forever before me; your throne shall stand firm forever.'"

---

4 1 Chr 15, 3-4. 15-16; 16, 1-2

A reading from the first book of Chronicles

David assembled all Israel in Jerusalem to bring the ark of the Lord to the place which he had prepared for it. David also called together the sons of Aaron and the Levites. The Levites bore the ark of God on their shoulders with poles, as Moses had ordained according to the word of the Lord.

David commanded the chiefs of the Levites to appoint their brethren as chanters, to play on musical instruments, harps, lyres, and cymbals to make a loud sound of rejoicing.

They brought in the ark of God and set it within the tent which David had pitched for it. Then they offered up holocausts and peace offerings to God. When David had finished offering up the holocausts and peace offerings, he blessed the people in the name of the Lord.

5 ——— Prv 8, 22-31

A reading from the book of Proverbs

[Thus speaks the Wisdom of God:]
"The Lord begot me, the firstborn of his ways,
  the forerunner of his prodigies of long ago;
From of old I was poured forth,
  at the first, before the earth.
When there were no depths I was brought forth,
  when there were no fountains or springs of water;
Before the mountains were settled into place,
  before the hills, I was brought forth;

While as yet the earth and the fields were not made,
  nor the first clods of the world.
"When he established the heavens I was there,
  when he marked out the vault over the face of the deep;
When he made firm the skies above,
  when he fixed fast the foundations of the earth;
When he set for the sea its limit,
  so that the waters should not transgress his command;
Then was I beside him as his craftsman,
  and I was his delight day by day,
Playing before him all the while,
  playing on the surface of his earth;
  [and I found delight in the sons of men.]"

---

6   Sir 24, 1. 3-4. 8-12. 19-21
A reading from the book of Sirach

Wisdom sings her own praises,
  before her own people she proclaims her glory.
"From the mouth of the Most High I came forth,
  and mistlike covered the earth.
In the highest heavens did I dwell,
  my throne on a pillar of cloud.

"Then the Creator of all gave me his command,
  and he who formed me chose the spot for my tent,
Saying, 'In Jacob make your dwelling,
  in Israel your inheritance.'
Before all ages, in the beginning, he created me,
  and through all ages I shall not cease to be.
In the holy tent I ministered before him,
  and in Zion I fixed my abode.
Thus in the chosen city he has given me rest,
  in Jerusalem is my domain.
I have struck root among the glorious people,
  in the portion of the Lord, his heritage.

"You will remember me as sweeter than honey,
  better to have than the honey comb.
He who eats of me will hunger still,
  he who drinks of me will thirst for more;
He who obeys me will not be put to shame,
  he who serves me will never fail."

7   Is 7, 10-14

A reading from the book of the prophet Isaiah

The Lord spoke to Ahaz: Ask for a sign from the Lord, your
God; let it be deep as the nether world, or high as the sky!
But Ahaz answered, "I will not ask! I will not tempt the
Lord!" Then he said: Listen, O house of David! Is it not
enough for you to weary men, must you also weary my
God? Therefore the Lord himself will give you this sign:
the virgin shall be with child, and bear a son, and shall
name him Immanuel.

---

8   Is 9, 1-6

A reading from the book of the prophet Isaiah

The people who walked in darkness
   have seen a great light;
Upon those who dwelt in the land of gloom
   a light has shone.
You have brought them abundant joy
   and great rejoicing,
As they rejoice before you as at the harvest,
   as men make merry when dividing spoils.
For the yoke that burdened them,
   the pole on their shoulder,
And the rod of their taskmaster
   you have smashed, as on the day of Midian.
For every boot that tramped in battle,
   every cloak rolled in blood,
   will be burned as fuel for flames.
For a child is born to us, a son is given us;
   upon his shoulder dominion rests.
They name him Wonder-Counselor, God-Hero,
   Father-Forever, Prince of Peace.
His dominion is vast
   and forever peaceful,
From David's throne, and over his kingdom,
   which he confirms and sustains
By judgment and justice,
   both now and forever.
The zeal of the Lord of hosts will do this!

9   Is 61, 9-11

A reading from the book of the prophet Isaiah

The descendants of my people shall be renowned among
the nations,
and their offspring among the peoples;
All who see them shall acknowledge them
as a race the Lord has blessed.

I rejoice heartily in the Lord,
in my God is the joy of my soul;
For he has clothed me with a robe of salvation,
and wrapped me in a mantle of justice,
Like a bridegroom adorned with a diadem,
like a bride bedecked with her jewels.

As the earth brings forth its plants,
and a garden makes its growth spring up,
So will the Lord God make justice and praise
spring up before all the nations.

———————

10   Mi 5, 1-4

A reading from the book of the prophet Micah

You, Bethlehem-Ephrathah,
too small to be among the clans of Judah,
From you shall come forth for me
one who is to be ruler in Israel;
Whose origin is from of old,
from ancient times.
(Therefore the Lord will give them up, until the time
when she who is to give birth has borne,
And the rest of his brethren shall return
to the children of Israel.)
He shall stand firm and shepherd his flock
by the strength of the Lord,
in the majestic name of the Lord, his God;
And they shall remain, for now his greatness
shall reach to the ends of the earth;
he shall be peace.

———————

11   Zec 2, 14-17

A reading from the book of the prophet Zechariah

Sing and rejoice, O daughter Zion! See, I am coming to
dwell among you, says the Lord. Many nations shall join
themselves to the Lord on that day, and they shall be his
people, and he will dwell among you, and you shall know
that the Lord of hosts has sent me to you. The Lord will
possess Judah as his portion in the holy land, and he will
again choose Jerusalem. Silence, all mankind, in the presence of the Lord! for he stirs forth from his holy dwelling.

READING I

IN THE EASTER SEASON

1   Acts 1, 12-14

A reading from the Acts of the Apostles

[After Jesus had ascended to heaven,] the apostles returned to Jerusalem from the mount called Olivet near
Jerusalem—a mere sabbath's journey away. Entering the
city, they went to the upstairs room where they were
staying: Peter and John and James and Andrew; Philip
and Thomas, Bartholomew and Matthew; James son of Al-
pheus; Simon, the Zealot party member, and Judas son of
James. Together they devoted themselves to constant
prayer. There were some women in their company, and
Mary the mother of Jesus, and his brothers.

---

2   Rv 11, 19; 12, 1-6. 10

A reading from the book of Revelation

God's temple in heaven opened and in the temple could
be seen the ark of his covenant.

A great sign appeared in the sky, a woman clothed with
the sun, with the moon under her feet, and on her head
a crown of twelve stars. Because she was with child, she
wailed aloud in pain as she labored to give birth. Then
another sign appeared in the sky: it was a huge dragon,

flaming red, with seven heads and ten horns; on his heads were seven diadems. His tail swept a third of the stars from the sky and hurled them down to the earth. Then the dragon stood before the woman about to give birth, ready to devour her child when it should be born. She gave birth to a son—a boy destined to shepherd all the nations with an iron rod. Her child was snatched up to God and to his throne. The woman herself fled into the desert, where a special place had been prepared for her by God.

Then I heard a loud voice in heaven say:

"Now have salvation and power come,
   the reign of our God and the authority of his Anointed
   One."

---

3   Rv 21, 1-5

A reading from the book of Revelation

I, John, saw new heavens and a new earth. The former heavens and the former earth had passed away, and the sea was no longer. I also saw a new Jerusalem, the holy city, coming down out of heaven from God, beautiful as a bride prepared to meet her husband. I heard a loud voice from the throne cry out: "This is God's dwelling among men. He shall dwell with them and they shall be his people, and he shall be their God who is always with them. He shall wipe every tear from their eyes, and there shall be no more death or mourning, crying out or pain, for the former world has passed away."

The One who sat on the throne said to me, "See, I make all things new!"

RESPONSORIAL PSALM

1   1 Sm 2, 1. 4-5. 6-7. 8

℞. (1) **My heart rejoices in the Lord, my Savior.**
As Hannah worshiped the Lord, she said:
"My heart exults in the Lord,
   my horn is exalted in my God.
I have swallowed up my enemies;
   I rejoice in my victory.

℟. **My heart rejoices in the Lord, my Savior.**
The bows of the mighty are broken,
    while the tottering gird on strength.
The well-fed hire themselves out for bread,
    while the hungry fatten on spoil.
The barren wife bears seven sons,
    while the mother of many languishes.
℟. **My heart rejoices in the Lord, my Savior.**
The Lord puts to death and gives life;
    he casts down to the nether world;
    he raises up again.
The Lord makes poor and makes rich,
    he humbles, he also exalts.
℟. **My heart rejoices in the Lord, my Savior.**
He raises the needy from the dust;
    from the ash heap he lifts up the poor,
To seat them with nobles
    and make a glorious throne their heritage."
℟. **My heart rejoices in the Lord, my Savior.**

---

2   Jdt 13, 18. 19. 20

℟. (9) **You are the highest honor of our race.**
Blessed are you, daughter, by the Most High God, above
all the women on earth; and blessed be the Lord God, the
creator of heaven and earth.
℟. **You are the highest honor of our race.**
Your deed of hope will never be forgotten by those who
tell of the might of God.
℟. **You are the highest honor of our race.**
May God make this redound to your everlasting honor,
rewarding you with blessings, because you risked your
life when your people were being oppressed, and you
averted our disaster, walking uprightly before our God.
And all the people answered, "Amen! Amen!"
℟. **You are the highest honor of our race.**

---

3   Ps 45, 11-12. 14-15. 16-17

℟. (11) **Listen to me, daughter;**
    see and bend your ear.

Hear, O daughter, and see; turn your ear,
  forget your people and your father's house.
So shall the king desire your beauty;
  for he is your lord, and you must worship him.
℟. **Listen to me, daughter;**
  see and bend your ear.
All glorious is the king's daughter as she enters;
  her raiment is threaded with spun gold.
In embroidered apparel she is borne in to the king;
  behind her the virgins of her train are brought to you.
℟. **Listen to me, daughter;**
  see and bend your ear.
They are borne in with gladness and joy;
  they enter the palace of the king.
The place of your fathers your sons shall have;
  you shall make them princes through all the land.
℟. **Listen to me, daughter;**
  see and bend your ear.

---

4   Ps 113, 1-2. 3-4. 5-6. 7-8

℟. (2) **Blessed be the name of the Lord for ever.**
Praise, you servants of the Lord,
  praise the name of the Lord.
Blessed be the name of the Lord
  both now and forever.
℟. **Blessed be the name of the Lord for ever.**
From the rising to the setting of the sun
  is the name of the Lord to be praised.
High above all nations is the Lord;
  above the heavens is his glory.
℟. **Blessed be the name of the Lord for ever.**
Who is like the Lord, our God, who is enthroned on high
  and looks upon the heavens and the earth below?
℟. **Blessed be the name of the Lord for ever.**
He raises up the lowly from the dust;
  from the dunghill he lifts up the poor
To seat them with princes,
  with the princes of his own people.
℟. **Blessed be the name of the Lord for ever.**
℟. Or: **Alleluia.**

---

5   Lk 1, 46-47. 48-49. 50-51. 52-53. 54-55

℟. (49) **The Almighty has done great things for me and holy is his name.**

Mary said:

"My being proclaims the greatness of the Lord,
  my spirit finds joy in God my savior.

℟. **The Almighty has done great things for me and holy is his name.**

For he has looked upon his servant in her lowliness;
  all ages to come shall call me blessed.
God who is mighty has done great things for me,
  holy is his name.

℟. **The Almighty has done great things for me and holy is his name.**

His mercy is from age to age
  on those who fear him.
He has shown might with his arm;
  he has confused the proud in their inmost thoughts.

℟. **The Almighty has done great things for me and holy is his name.**

He has deposed the mighty from their thrones
  and raised the lowly to high places.
The hungry he has given every good thing,
  while the rich he has sent empty away.

℟. **The Almighty has done great things for me and holy is his name.**

He has upheld Israel his servant,
  ever mindful of his mercy;
Even as he promised our fathers,
  promised Abraham and his descendants forever."

℟. **The Almighty has done great things for me and holy is his name.**

℟. Or: **O Blessed Virgin Mary, you carried the Son of the eternal Father.**

READING II

1

Rom 5, 12. 17-19

A reading from the letter of Paul to the Romans

Just as through one man sin entered the world and with sin death, so death came to all men inasmuch as all sinned. If death began its reign through one man because of his offense, much more shall those who receive the overflowing grace and gift of justice live and reign through the one man, Jesus Christ.

To sum up, then: just as a single offense brought condemnation to all men, a single righteous act brought all men acquittal and life. Just as through one man's disobedience all became sinners, so through one man's obedience all shall become just.

2

Rom 8, 28-30

A reading from the letter of Paul to the Romans

We know that God makes all things work together for the good of those who have been called according to his decree. Those whom he foreknew he predestined to share the image of his Son, that the Son might be the first-born of many brothers. Those he predestined he likewise called; those he called he also justified; and those he justified he in turn glorified.

3

Gal 4, 4-7

A reading from the letter of Paul to the Galatians

When the designated time had come, God sent forth his Son born of a woman, born under the law, to deliver from the law those who were subjected to it, so that we might receive our status as adopted sons. The proof that you are sons is the fact that God has sent forth into our hearts the spirit of his Son which cries out "Abba!" ("Father!") You are no longer a slave but a son! And the fact that you are a son makes you an heir, by God's design.

---

4   Eph 1, 3-6. 11-12

A reading from the letter of Paul to the Ephesians

Praised be the God and Father of our Lord Jesus Christ, who has bestowed on us in Christ every spiritual blessing in the heavens! God chose us in him before the world began, to be holy and blameless in his sight, to be full of love; he likewise predestined us through Christ Jesus to be his adopted sons—such was his will and pleasure—that all might praise the divine favor he has bestowed on us in his beloved.

In him we were chosen; for in the decree of God, who administers everything according to his will and counsel, we were predestined to praise his glory by being the first to hope in Christ.

ALLELUIA VERSE AND
VERSE BEFORE THE GOSPEL

1   Lk 1, 28

Hail, Mary, full of grace, the Lord is with you;
blessed are you among women.

2   Lk 1, 45

Blessed are you, O Virgin Mary, for your firm believing,
that the promises of the Lord would be fulfilled.

3   See Lk 2, 19

Blessed is the Virgin Mary who kept the word of God,
and pondered it in her heart.

4

Happy are you, holy Virgin Mary, deserving of all praise;
from you rose the sun of justice, Christ the Lord.

GOSPEL

1   Mt 1, 1-16. 18-23 or 1, 18-23

[If the "Short Form" is used, the indented text in brackets is omitted.]

✠ The beginning (or: A reading) of the holy gospel
            according to Matthew

[A family record of Jesus Christ, son of David, son
of Abraham. Abraham was the father of Isaac,
Isaac the father of Jacob, Jacob the father of Ju-
dah and his brothers.
Judah was the father of Perez and Zerah, whose
mother was Tamar.
Perez was the father of Hezron,
Hezron the father of Ram.
Ram was the father of Amminadab,
Amminadab the father of Nahshon,
Nahshon the father of Salmon.
Salmon was the father of Boaz, whose mother was
Rahab,
Boaz was the father of Obed, whose mother was
Ruth.
Obed was the father of Jesse,
Jesse the father of King David.
David was the father of Solomon, whose mother had
been the wife of Uriah.
Solomon was the father of Rehoboam,
Rehoboam the father of Abijah,
Abijah the father of Asa.
Asa was the father of Jehoshaphat,
Jehoshaphat the father of Joram,
Joram the father of Uzziah.
Uzziah was the father of Jotham,
Jotham the father of Ahaz,
Ahaz the father of Hezekiah.
Hezekiah was the father of Manasseh,
Manasseh the father of Amos,
Amos the father of Josiah.

Josiah became the father of Jechoniah and his broth-
ers at the time of the Babylonian exile.
After the Babylonian exile
Jechoniah was the father of Shealtiel,
Shealtiel the father of Zerubbabel.
Zerubbabel was the father of Abiud,
Abiud the father of Eliakim,
Eliakim the father of Azor.
Azor was the father of Zadok,
Zadok the father of Achim,
Achim the father of Eliud.
Eliud was the father of Eleazar,
Eleazar the father of Matthan,
Matthan the father of Jacob.
Jacob was the father of Joseph the husband of Mary.
It was of her that Jesus who is called the Messiah
was born.]

Now this is how the birth of Jesus Christ came about.
When his mother Mary was engaged to Joseph, but before
they lived together, she was found with child through the
power of the Holy Spirit. Joseph her husband, an upright
man unwilling to expose her to the law, decided to divorce
her quietly. Such was his intention when suddenly the
angel of the Lord appeared in a dream and said to him:
"Joseph, son of David, have no fear about taking Mary
as your wife. It is by the Holy Spirit that she has conceived
this child. She is to have a son and you are to name him
Jesus because he will save his people from their sins." All
this happened to fulfill what the Lord had said through
the prophet:

"The virgin shall be with child
and give birth to a son,
and they shall call him Emmanuel,"
a name which means "God is with us."

---

2   Mt 2, 13-15. 19-23

✠ A reading from the holy gospel according to Matthew
After the astrologers had departed from Bethlehem, the
angel of the Lord suddenly appeared in a dream to Joseph
with the command: "Get up, take the child and his mother,
and flee to Egypt. Stay there until I tell you otherwise.

Herod is searching for the child to destroy him." Joseph got up and took the child and his mother and left that night for Egypt. He stayed there until the death of Herod, to fulfill what the Lord had said through the prophet:

"Our of Egypt I have called my son."

But after Herod's death, the angel of the Lord appeared in a dream to Joseph in Egypt with the command: "Get up, take the child and his mother, and set out for the land of Israel. Those who had designs on the life of the child are dead." He got up, took the child and his mother, and returned to the land of Israel. He heard, however, that Archelaus had succeeded his father Herod as king of Judea, and he was afraid to go back there. Instead, because of a warning received in a dream, Joseph went to the region of Galilee. There he settled in a town called Nazareth. In this way what was said through the prophets was fulfilled:

"He shall be called a Nazorean."

---

3   Lk 1, 26-38

✠ A reading from the holy gospel according to Luke

The angel Gabriel was sent from God to a town of Galilee named Nazareth, to a virgin betrothed to a man named Joseph, of the house of David. The virgin's name was Mary. Upon arriving, the angel said to her: "Rejoice, O highly favored daughter! The Lord is with you. Blessed are you among women." She was deeply troubled by his words, and wondered what his greeting meant. The angel went on to say to her: "Do not fear, Mary. You have found favor with God. You shall conceive and bear a son and give him the name Jesus. Great will be his dignity and he will rule over the house of Jacob forever and his reign will be without end."

Mary said to the angel, "How can this be since I do not know man?" The angel answered her: "The Holy Spirit will come upon you and the power of the Most High will overshadow you; hence, the holy offspring to be born will be called Son of God. Know that Elizabeth your kinswoman has conceived a son in her old age; she who was thought to be sterile is now in her sixth month, for nothing is impossible with God."

Mary said: "I am the maidservant of the Lord. Let it be done to me as you say." With that the angel left her.

4

Lk 1, 39-47

✠ A reading from the holy gospel according to Luke

Mary set out, proceeding in haste into the hill country to a town of Judah, where she entered Zechariah's house and greeted Elizabeth. When Elizabeth heard Mary's greeting, the baby stirred in her womb. Elizabeth was filled with the Holy Spirit and cried out in a loud voice: "Blessed are you among women and blessed is the fruit of your womb. But who am I that the mother of my Lord should come to me? The moment your greeting sounded in my ears, the baby stirred in my womb for joy. Blessed is she who trusted that the Lord's words to her would be fulfilled."

Then Mary said:
"My being proclaims the greatness of the Lord,
    my spirit finds joy in God my savior."

5

Lk 2, 1-14

✠ A reading from the holy gospel according to Luke

In those days Caesar Augustus published a decree ordering a census of the whole world. This first census took place while Quirinius was governor of Syria. Everyone went to register, each to his own town. And so Joseph went from the town of Nazareth in Galilee to Judea, to David's town of Bethlehem—because he was of the house and lineage of David—to register with Mary, his espoused wife, who was with child.

While they were there the days of her confinement were completed. She gave birth to her first-born son and wrapped him in swaddling clothes and laid him in a manger, because there was no room for them in the place where travelers lodged.

There were shepherds in the locality, living in the fields and keeping night watch by turns over their flocks. The angel of the Lord appeared to them as the glory of the Lord shone around them, and they were very much afraid. The angel said to them: "You have nothing to fear! I come to proclaim good news to you— tidings of great joy to be shared by the whole people. This day in David's city a savior has been born to you, the Messiah and Lord. Let this be a sign to you: in a manger you will find an infant wrapped in swaddling clothes." Suddenly, there was with the angel a multitude of the heavenly host, praising God and saying,

"Glory to God in high heaven,
peace on earth to those on whom his favor rests."

---

6   Lk, 2, 15-19

✠ A reading from the holy gospel according to Luke

The shepherds said to one another: "Let us go over to Bethlehem and see this event which the Lord has made known to us." They went in haste and found Mary and Joseph, and the baby lying in the manger; once they saw, they understood what had been told them concerning this child. All who heard of it were astonished at the report given them by the shepherds.

Mary treasured all these things and reflected on them in her heart.

---

7   Lk 2, 27-35

✠ A reading from the holy gospel according to Luke

Simeon came to the temple, inspired by the Spirit; and when the parents brought in the child Jesus to perform for him the customary ritual of the law, he took him in his arms and blessed God in these words:

"Now, Master, you can dismiss your servant in peace;
you have fulfilled your word.
For my eyes have witnessed your saving deed
displayed for all the peoples to see:
A revealing light to the Gentiles,
the glory of your people Israel."

The child's father and mother were marveling at what was being said about him. Simeon blessed them and said to Mary his mother: "This child is destined to be the downfall and the rise of many in Israel, a sign that will be opposed— and you yourself shall be pierced with a sword—so that the thoughts of many hearts may be laid bare."

---

8   Lk 2, 41-52

✠ A reading from the holy gospel according to Luke

The parents of Jesus used to go every year to Jerusalem for the feast of the Passover, and when he was twelve they went up for the celebration as was their custom. As they were returning at the end of the feast, the child Jesus remained behind unknown to his parents. Thinking he was in the party, they continued their journey for a day, looking for him among their relatives and acquaintances.

Not finding him, they returned to Jerusalem in search of him. On the third day they came upon him in the temple sitting in the midst of the teachers, listening to them and asking them questions. All who heard him were amazed at his intelligence and his answers.

When his parents saw him they were astonished, and his mother said to him: "Son, why have you done this to us? You see that your father and I have been searching for you in sorrow." He said to them: "Why did you search for me? Did you not know I had to be in my Father's house?" But they did not grasp what he said to them.

He went down with them then, and came to Nazareth, and was obedient to them. His mother meanwhile kept all these things in memory. Jesus, for his part, progressed steadily in wisdom and age and grace before God and men.

---

9   Lk 11, 27-28

✠ A reading from the holy gospel according to Luke

While Jesus was speaking to the crowd a woman called out, "Blest is the womb that bore you and the breasts that nursed you!" "Rather," he replied, "blest are they who hear the word of God and keep it."

---

10   Jn 2, 1-11

✠ A reading from the holy gospel according to John

There was a wedding at Cana in Galilee, and the mother of Jesus was there. Jesus and his disciples had likewise been invited to the celebration. At a certain point the wine ran out, and Jesus' mother told him, "They have no more wine."

Jesus replied, "Woman, how does this concern of yours involve me? My hour has not yet come." His mother instructed those waiting on table, "Do whatever he tells you." As prescribed for Jewish ceremonial washings, there were at hand six stone water jars, each one holding fifteen to twenty-five gallons. "Fill those jars with water," Jesus ordered, at which they filled them to the brim. "Now," he said, "draw some out and take it to the waiter in charge." They did as he instructed them. The waiter in charge tasted the water made wine, without knowing where it had come from; only the waiters knew, since they had drawn the water. Then the waiter in charge called the groom over and remarked to him: "People usually serve the choice wine first; then when the guests have been drinking a while, a lesser vintage. What you have done is keep the choice wine until now." Jesus performed this first of his signs at Cana in Galilee. Thus did he reveal his glory, and his disciples believed in him.

---

11 Jn 19, 25-27

✠ A reading from the holy gospel according to John

Near the cross of Jesus there stood his mother, his mother's sister, Mary the wife of Clopas, and Mary Magdalene. Seeing his mother there with the disciple whom he loved, Jesus said to his mother, "Woman, there is your son." In turn he said to the disciple, "There is your mother." From that hour onward, the disciple took her into his care.

COMMON OF MARTYRS

READING I

OUTSIDE THE EASTER SEASON

1   2 Chr 24, 18-22

A reading from the second book of Chronicles

The princes of Judah forsook the temple of the Lord, the God of their fathers, and began to serve the sacred poles and the idols; and because of this crime of theirs, wrath came upon Judah and Jerusalem. Although prophets were sent to them to convert them to the Lord, the people would not listen to their warnings. Then the spirit of God possessed Zechariah, son of Jehoiada the priest. He took his stand above the people and said to them: "God says, 'Why are you transgressing the Lord's commands, so that you cannot prosper? Because you have abandoned the Lord, he has abandoned you.'" But they conspired against him, and at the king's order they stoned him to death in the court of the Lord's temple. Thus King Joash was unmindful of the devotion shown him by Jehoiada, Zechariah's father, and slew his son. And as he was dying, he said, "May the Lord see and avenge."

---

2   2 Mc 6, 18. 21. 24-31

A reading from the second book of Maccabees

Eleazar, one of the foremost scribes, a man of advanced age and noble appearance, was being forced to open his mouth to eat pork. Those in charge of that unlawful ritual meal took the man aside privately because of their long acquaintance with him and urged him to bring meat of his own providing such as he could legitimately eat, and to pretend to be eating some of the meat of the sacrifice prescribed by the king. He told them: "At our age it would be unbecoming to make such a pretense; many young men would think the ninety-year-old Eleazar had gone over to an alien religion. Should I thus dissimulate for the sake of a brief moment of life, they would be led astray by me, while I would bring shame and dishonor on my old age.

Even if, for the time being, I avoid the punishment of men, I shall never, whether alive or dead, escape the hands of the Almighty. Therefore, by manfully giving up my life now, I will prove myself worthy of my old age, and I will leave to the young a noble example of how to die willingly and generously for the revered and holy laws."

He spoke thus, and went immediately to the instrument of torture. Those who shortly before had been kindly disposed, now became hostile toward him because what he had said seemed to them utter madness. When he was about to die under the blows, he groaned and said: "The Lord in his holy knowledge knows full well that, although I could have escaped death, I am not only enduring terrible pain in my body from this scourging, but also suffering it with joy in my soul because of my devotion to him." This is how he died, leaving in his death a model of courage and an unforgettable example of virtue not only for the young but for the whole nation.

---

3   2 Mc 7, 1-2. 9-14

A reading from the second book of Maccabees

It happened that seven brothers with their mother were arrested and tortured with whips and scourges by the king, to force them to eat pork in violation of God's law. One of the brothers, speaking for the others, said: "What do you expect to achieve by questioning us? We are ready to die rather than transgress the laws of our ancestors."

[The second brother] at the point of death said: "You accursed fiend, you are depriving us of this present life, but the King of the world will raise us up to live again forever. It is for his laws that we are dying."

After him the third suffered their cruel sport. He put out his tongue at once when told to do so, and bravely held out his hands, as he spoke these noble words: "It was from Heaven that I received these; for the sake of his laws I disdain them; from him I hope to receive them again." Even the king and his attendants marveled at the young man's courage, because he regarded his sufferings as nothing.

After he had died, they tortured and maltreated the fourth brother in the same way. When he was near death, he said, "It is my choice to die at the hands of men with the God-given hope of being restored to life by him; but for you, there will be no resurrection to life."

---

4   2 Mc 7, 1. 20-23. 27-29

A reading from the second book of Maccabees

It happened that seven brothers with their mother were arrested and tortured with whips and scourges by the king, to force them to eat pork in violation of God's law.

Most admirable and worthy of everlasting remembrance was the mother, who saw her seven sons perish in a single day, yet bore it courageously because of her hope in the Lord. Filled with a noble spirit that stirred her womanly heart with manly courage, she exhorted each of them in the language of their forefathers with these words: "I do not know how you came into existence in my womb; it was not I who gave you the breath of life, nor was it I who set in order the elements of which each of you is composed. Therefore, since it is the Creator of the universe who shapes each man's beginning, as he brings about the origin of everything, he, in his mercy, will give you back both breath and life, because you now disregard yourselves for the sake of his law.

"Son, have pity on me, who carried you in my womb for nine months, nursed you for three years, brought you up, educated and supported you to your present age. I beg you, child, to look at the heavens and the earth and see all that is in them; then you will know that God did not make them out of existing things; and in the same way the human race came into existence. Do not be afraid of this executioner, but be worthy of your brothers and accept death, so that in the time of mercy I may receive you again with them."

---

5   Wis 3, 1-9

A reading from the book of Wisdom

The souls of the just are in the hand of God,
    and no torment shall touch them.
They seemed, in the view of the foolish, to be dead;
    and their passing away was thought an affliction
    and their going forth from us, utter destruction.

But they are in peace.
For if before men, indeed, they be punished,
    yet is their hope full of immortality;
Chastised a little, they shall be greatly blessed,
    because God tried them
    and found them worthy of himself.
As gold in the furnace, he proved them,
    and as sacrificial offerings he took them to himself.
In the time of their visitation they shall shine,
    and shall dart about as sparks through stubble;
They shall judge nations and rule over people,
    and the Lord shall be their King forever.
Those who trust in him shall understand truth,
    and the faithful shall abide with him in love:
Because grace and mercy are with his holy ones,
    and his care is with his elect.

———————————

6   Sir 51, 1-8
        A reading from the book of Sirach
I give you thanks, O God of my father;
    I praise you, O God my savior!
I will make known your name, refuge of my life;
    you have been my helper against my adversaries.
You have saved me from death,
    and kept back my body from the pit.
From the clutches of the nether world you have snatched
        my feet;
    you have delivered me, in your great mercy
From the scourge of a slanderous tongue,
    and from lips that went over to falsehood;
From the snare of those who watched for my downfall,
    and from the power of those who sought my life;
From many a danger you have saved me,
    from flames that hemmed me in on every side;
From the midst of unremitting fire,
    from the deep belly of the nether world;
From deceiving lips and painters of lies,
    from the arrows of dishonest tongues.
I was at the point of death,
    my soul was nearing the depths of the nether world;
I turned every way, but there was no one to help me,
    I looked for one to sustain me, but could find no one.

But then I remembered the mercies of the Lord,
   his kindness through ages past;
For he saves those who take refuge in him,
   and rescues them from every evil.

READING I

IN THE EASTER SEASON

1   Acts 7, 55-60

A reading from the Acts of the Apostles

Stephen, filled with the Holy Spirit, looked to the sky
above and saw the glory of God, and Jesus standing at
God's right hand. "Look!" he exclaimed, "I see an opening
in the sky, and the Son of Man standing at God's right
hand." The onlookers were shouting aloud, holding their
hands over their ears as they did so. Then they rushed at
him as one man, dragged him out of the city, and began
to stone him. The witnesses meanwhile were piling their
cloaks at the feet of a young man named Saul. As Stephen
was being stoned he could be heard praying, "Lord Jesus,
receive my spirit." He fell to his knees and cried out in a
loud voice, "Lord, do not hold this sin against them." And
with that he died.

---

2   Rv 7, 9-17

A reading from the book of Revelation

I, John, saw before me a huge crowd which no one could
count from every nation and race, people and tongue.
They stood before the throne and the Lamb, dressed in
long white robes and holding palm branches in their hands.
They cried out in a loud voice, "Salvation is from our God,
who is seated on the throne, and from the Lamb!" All
the angels who were standing around the throne and the
elders and the four living creatures fell down before the
throne to worship God. They said: "Amen! Praise and
glory, wisdom, thanksgiving, and honor, power and might
to our God forever and ever. Amen!"

Then one of the elders asked me, "Who are these, all dressed in white? And where have they come from?" I said to him, "Sir, you should know better than I." He then told me, "These are the ones who have survived the great period of trial; they have washed their robes and made them white in the blood of the Lamb.

"It was this that brought them before God's throne:
   day and night they minister to him in his temple;
   he who sits on the throne will give them shelter.
Never again shall they know hunger or thirst,
   nor shall the sun or its heat beat down on them,
   for the Lamb on the throne will shepherd them.
He will lead them to springs of life-giving water,
   and God will wipe every tear from their eyes."

---

3   Rv 12, 10-12

A reading from the book of Revelation

I, John, heard a loud voice in heaven say:
"Now have salvation and power come,
   the reign of our God and the authority of his Anointed
      One.
For the accuser of our brothers is cast out,
   who night and day accused them before our God.
They defeated him by the blood of the Lamb
   and by the word of their testimony;
   love for life did not deter them from death.
So rejoice, you heavens,
   and you that dwell therein!"

---

4   Rv 21, 5-7

A reading from the book of Revelation

The One who sat on the throne said to me, "See, I make all things new!" Then he said, "Write these matters down, for the words are trustworthy and true!" He went on to say: "These words are already fulfilled! I am the Alpha and the Omega, the Beginning and the End. To anyone who thirsts I will give to drink without cost from the spring of life-giving water. He who wins the victory shall inherit these gifts; I will be his God and he shall be my son."

RESPONSORIAL PSALM

1   Ps 31, 3-4. 6. 7. 8. 17. 21

℟. (6) **Into your hands, O Lord,**
  I entrust my spirit.
Be my rock of refuge,
  a stronghold to give me safety.
You are my rock and my fortress;
  for your name's sake you will lead and guide me.
℟. **Into your hands, O Lord,**
  I entrust my spirit.
into your hands I commend my spirit;
  you will redeem me, O Lord, O faithful God.
My trust is in the Lord.
  I will rejoice and be glad of your kindness.
℟. **Into your hands, O Lord,**
  I entrust my spirit.
Let your face shine upon your servant;
  save me in your kindness.
You hide them in the shelter of your presence
  from the plottings of men.
℟. **Into your hands, O Lord,**
  I entrust my spirit.

---

2   Ps 34, 2-3. 4-5. 6-7. 8-9

℟. (5) **The Lord set me free from all my fears.**
I will bless the Lord at all times;
  his praise shall be ever in my mouth.
Let my soul glory in the Lord;
  the lowly will hear me and be glad.
℟. **The Lord set me free from all my fears.**
Glorify the Lord with me,
  let us together extol his name.
I sought the Lord, and he answered me
  and delivered me from all my fears.
℟. **The Lord set me free from all my fears.**
Look to him that you may be radiant with joy,
  and your faces may not blush with shame.
When the afflicted man called out, the Lord heard,
  and from all his distress he saved him.

R̸. **The Lord set me free from all my fears.**
The angel of the Lord encamps
   around those who fear him, and delivers them.
Taste and see how good the Lord is;
   happy the man who takes refuge in him.
R̸. **The Lord set me free from all my fears.**

---

3   Ps 124, 2-3. 4-5. 7-8

R̸. (3) **Our soul has escaped like a bird from the hunter's net.**
Had not the Lord been with us—
   when men rose up against us,
Then would they have swallowed us alive,
   when their fury was inflamed against us.
R̸. **Our soul has escaped like a bird from the hunter's net.**
Then would the waters have overwhelmed us;
   the torrent would have swept over us;
Over us then would have swept
   the raging waters.
R̸. **Our soul has escaped like a bird from the hunter's net.**
Broken was the snare,
   and we were freed.
Our help is in the name of the Lord,
   Who made heaven and earth.
R̸. **Our soul has escaped like a bird from the hunter's net.**

---

4   Ps 126, 1-2. 2-3 4-5. 6.

R̸. (5) **Those who sow in tears, shall reap with shouts
   of joy.**
When the Lord brought back the captives of Zion,
   we were like men dreaming.
Then our mouth was filled with laughter,
   and our tongue with rejoicing.
R̸. **Those who sow in tears, shall reap with shouts of joy.**
Then they said among the nations,
   "The Lord has done great things for them."
The Lord has done great things for us;
   we are glad indeed.
R̸. **Those who sow in tears, shall reap with shouts of joy.**

Restore our fortunes, O, Lord,
  like the torrents in the southern desert.
Those that sow in tears
  shall reap rejoicing.
℟. **Those who sow in tears, shall reap with shouts of joy.**
Although they go forth weeping,
  carrying the seed to be sown,
They shall come back rejoicing,
  carrying their sheaves.
℟. **Those who sow in tears, shall reap with shouts of joy.**

READING II

1   Rom 5, 1-5

A reading from the letter of Paul to the Romans

Now that we have been justified by faith, we are at peace
with God through our Lord Jesus Christ. Through him we
have gained access by faith to the grace in which we
now stand, and we boast of our hope for the glory of God.
But not only that—we even boast of our afflictions! We
know that affliction makes for endurance, and endurance
for tested virtue, and tested virtue for hope. And this hope
will not leave us disappointed, because the love of God
has been poured out in our hearts through the Holy Spirit
who has been given to us.

2   Rom 8, 31-39

A reading from the letter of Paul to the Romans

If God is for us, who can be against us? Is it possible that
he who did not spare his own Son but handed him over
for the sake of us all will not grant us all things besides?
Who shall bring a charge against God's chosen ones? God,
who justifies? Who shall condemn them? Christ Jesus, who
died or rather was raised up, who is at the right hand of
God and who intercedes for us?

Who will separate us from the love of Christ? Trial, or
distress, or persecution, or hunger, or nakedness, or danger, or the sword? As Scripture says; "For your sake we

are being slain all the day long; we are looked upon as sheep to be slaughtered." Yet in all this we are more than conquerors because of him who has loved us. For I am certain that neither death nor life, neither angels nor principalities, neither the present nor the future, nor powers, neither height nor depth nor any other creature, will be able to separate us from the love of God that comes to us in Christ Jesus, our Lord.

---

3   2 Cor 4, 7-15

A reading from the second letter of Paul to the Corinthians

We possess our treasure in earthen vessels to make it clear that its surpassing power comes from God and not from us. We are afflicted in every way possible, but we are not crushed; full of doubts, we never despair. We are persecuted but never abandoned; we are struck down but never destroyed. Continually we carry about in our bodies the dying of Jesus, so that in our bodies the life of Jesus may also be revealed. While we live we are constantly being delivered to death for Jesus' sake, so that the life of Jesus may be revealed in our mortal flesh. Death is at work in us, but life in you. We have that spirit of faith of which Scripture says, "Because I believed, I spoke out." We believed and so we speak, knowing that he who raised up the Lord Jesus will raise us up along with Jesus and place both us and you in his presence. Indeed, everything is ordered to your benefit, so that the grace bestowed in abundance may bring greater glory to God because they who give thanks are many.

---

4   2 Cor 6, 4-10

A reading from the second letter of Paul to the Corinthians

In all that we do we strive to present ourselves as ministers of God, acting with patient endurance amid trials, difficulties, distresses, beatings, imprisonments and riots; as men familiar with hard work, sleepless nights, and fastings; conducting themselves with innocence, knowledge, and patience, in the Holy Spirit, in sincere love; as men with the message of truth and the power of God; wielding the weapons of righteousness with right hand and left, whether honored or dishonored, spoken of well or ill. We are called imposters, yet we are truthful; nobodies who in fact are well known; dead, yet here we are, alive; punished, but not put to death; sorrowful, though we are always rejoicing; poor, yet we enrich many. We seem to have nothing, yet everything is ours!

---

5   2 Tm 2, 8-13; 3, 10-12

A reading from the second letter of Paul to Timothy

Remember that the Lord Jesus Christ, a descendant of David, was raised from the dead. This is the gospel I preach; in preaching it I suffer as a criminal, even to the point of being thrown into chains—but there is no chaining the word of God! Therefore I bear with all of this for the sake of those whom God has chosen, in order that they may obtain the salvation to be found in Christ Jesus and with it eternal glory.

You can depend on this:
If we have died with him
we shall also live with him;
If we hold out to the end
we shall reign with him.
But if we deny him he will deny us. If we are unfaithful he will still remain faithful for he cannot deny himself.

You have followed closely my teaching and my conduct. You have observed my resolution, fidelity, patience, love, and endurance, through persecutions and sufferings in Antioch, Iconium, and Lystra. You know what persecutions I had to bear, and you know how the Lord saved me from them all. Anyone who wants to live a godly life in Christ Jesus can expect to be persecuted.

---

6   Heb 10, 32-36

A reading from the letter to the Hebrews

Recall the days gone by when, after you had been enlightened, you endured a great contest of suffering. At times you were publicly exposed to insult and trial; at other times you associated yourselves with those who were being so dealt with. You even joined in the sufferings of those who were in prison and joyfully assented to the confisca-

tion of your goods, knowing that you had better and more
permanent possessions. Do not, then, surrender your confidence; it will have great reward. You need patience to
do God's will and receive what he has promised.

------

7   Jas 1, 2-4. 12
A reading from the letter of James

My brothers, count it pure joy when you are involved in
every sort of trial. Realize that when your faith is tested
this makes for endurance. Let endurance come to its perfection so that you may be fully mature and lacking in
nothing.

Happy the man who holds out to the end through trial!
Once he has been proved, he will receive the crown of life
the Lord has promised to those who love him.

------

8   1 Pt 3, 14-17
A reading from the first letter of Peter

Even if you should have to suffer for justice' sake, happy
will you be. "Fear not and do not stand in awe of what
this people fears. Venerate the Lord," that is, Christ, in
your hearts. Should anyone ask you the reason for this
hope of yours, be ever ready to reply, but speak gently
and respectfully. Keep your conscience clear so that, whenever you are defamed, those who libel your way of life in
Christ may be disappointed. If it should be God's will that
you suffer, it is better to do so for good deeds than for evil
ones.

------

9   1 Pt 4, 12-19
A reading from the first letter of Peter

Do not be surprised, beloved, that a trial by fire is occurring in your midst. It is a test for you, but it should not
catch you off guard. Rejoice, instead, insofar as you share
Christ's sufferings. When his glory is revealed, you will
rejoice exultantly. Happy are you when you are insulted
for the sake of Christ, for then God's Spirit in its glory has
come to rest on you. See to it that none of you suffers for
being a murderer, a thief, a malefactor, or a destroyer of
another's rights. If anyone suffers for being a Christian,

however, he ought not to be ashamed. He should rather glorify God in virtue of that name. The season of judgment has begun, and begun with God's own household. If it begins this way with us, what must be the end for those who refuse obedience to the gospel of God? And if "the just man is saved only with difficulty, what is to become of the godless and the sinner?" Accordingly, let those who suffer as God's will requires continue in good deeds and entrust their lives to a faithful Creator.

---

10   1 Jn 5, 1-5

A reading from the first letter of John

Everyone who believes that Jesus is the Christ
has been begotten by God.
Now, everyone who loves the father
loves the child he has begotten.
We can be sure that we love God's children
when we love God
and do what he has commanded.
The love of God consists in this:
that we keep his commandments —
and his commandments are not burdensome.
Everyone begotten of God conquers the world,
and the power that has conquered the world
is this faith of ours.
Who, then, is conqueror of the world?
The one who believes that Jesus is the Son of God.

ALLELUIA VERSE AND

VERSE BEFORE THE GOSPEL

1   Mt 5, 10

Happy are they who suffer persecution for justice' sake;
the kingdom of heaven is theirs.

2   2 Cor 1, 3-4

Blessed be the Father of mercies and the God of all comfort,
who consoles us in all our afflictions.

3   Jas 1, 12

Happy the man who stands firm when trials come;
he has proved himself, and will win the crown of life.

4   1 Pt 4, 14

If you are insulted for the name of Christ, blessed are you,
for the Spirit of God rests upon you.

5

We praise you, God; we acknowledge you as Lord;
the radiant army of martyrs acclaims you.

GOSPEL

1   Mt 10, 17-22

✠ A reading from the holy gospel according to Matthew

Jesus said to his apostles: "Be on your guard with respect
to others. They will hale you into court, they will flog you
in their synagogues. You will be brought to trial before
rulers and kings, to give witness before them and before
the Gentiles on my account. When they hand you over, do
not worry about what you will say or how you will say it.
When the hour comes, you will be given what you are to
say. You yourselves will not be the speakers; the Spirit of
your Father will be speaking in you.

"Brother will hand over brother to death, and the father
his child; children will turn against parents and have them
put to death. You will be hated by all on account of me.
But whoever holds out till the end will escape death."

---

2   Mt 10, 28-33

✠ A reading from the holy gospel according to Matthew

Jesus said to his disciples: "Do not fear those who deprive
the body of life but cannot destroy the soul. Rather, fear
him who can destroy both body and soul in Gehenna. Are
not two sparrows sold for next to nothing? Yet not a single
sparrow falls to the ground without your Father's consent.
As for you, every hair of your head has been counted; so
do not be afraid of anything. You are worth more than an

entire flock of sparrows. Whoever acknowledges me before men I will acknowledge before my Father in heaven. Whoever disowns me before men I will disown before my Father in heaven."

---

3   Mt 10, 34-39

✠ A reading from the holy gospel according to Matthew

Jesus said to his disciples: "Do not suppose that my mission on earth is to spread peace. My mission is to spread, not peace, but division. I have come to set a man at odds with his father, a daughter with her mother, a daughter-in-law with her mother-in-law: in short, to make a man's enemies those of his own household. Whoever loves father or mother, son or daughter more than me is not worthy of me. He who will not take up his cross and come after me is not worthy of me. He who seeks only himself brings himself to ruin, whereas he who brings himself to nought for me discovers who he is."

---

4   Lk 9, 23-26

✠ A reading from the holy gospel according to Luke

Jesus said to all: "Whoever wishes to be my follower must deny his very self, take up his cross each day, and follow in my steps. Whoever would save his life will lose it, and whoever loses his life for my sake will save it. What profit does he show who gains the whole world and destroys himself in the process? If a man is ashamed of me and my doctrine, the Son of Man will be ashamed of him when he comes in his glory and that of his Father and his holy angels."

---

5   Jn 12, 24-26

✠ A reading from the holy gospel according to John

Jesus said to his disciples:
    "I solemnly assure you,
    unless the grain of wheat falls to the earth and dies,
    it remains just a grain of wheat.
    But if it dies,
    it produces much fruit.

The man who loves his life
loses it,
while the man who hates his life in this world
preserves it to life eternal.
If anyone would serve me,
let him follow me;
where I am,
there will my servant be.
Anyone who serves me,
the Father will honor."

6

Jn 15, 18-21

✠ A reading from the holy gospel according to John

Jesus said to his disciples:
"If you find that the world hates you,
know it has hated me before you.
If you belonged to the world,
it would love you as its own;
the reason it hates you
is that you do not belong to the world.
But I chose you out of the world.
Remember what I told you:
no slave is greater than his master.
They will harry you
as they harried me.
They will respect your words
as much as they respected mine.
All this they will do to you because of my name,
for they know nothing of him who sent me."

7

Jn 17, 11-19

✠ A reading from the holy gospel according to John

Jesus looked up to heaven and prayed:
"O Father most holy,
protect them with your name which you have given
me,
[that they may be one, even as we are one.]
As long as I was with them,
I guarded them with your name which you gave me.
I kept careful watch,

and not one of them was lost,
none but him who was destined to be lost—
in fulfillment of Scripture.
Now, however, I come to you;
I say all this while I am still in the world
that they may share my joy completely.
I gave them your word,
and the world has hated them for it;
they do not belong to the world,
[any more than I belong to the world].
I do not ask you to take them out of the world,
but to guard them from the evil one.
They are not of the world,
any more than I am of the world.
Consecrate them by means of truth—
'Your word is truth,'
As you have sent me into the world,
so I have sent them into the world;
I consecrate myself for their sakes now,
that they may be consecrated in truth."

COMMON OF PASTORS

READING I

OUTSIDE THE EASTER SEASON

1   Ex 32, 7-14

A reading from the book of Exodus

The Lord said to Moses, "Go down at once to your people,
whom you brought out of the land of Egypt, for they have
become depraved. They have soon turned aside from the
way I pointed out to them, making for themselves a molten
calf and worshiping it, sacrificing to it and crying out,
'This is your God, O Israel, who brought you out of the
land of Egypt!' I see how stiff-necked this people is," continued the Lord to Moses. "Let me alone, then, that my
wrath may blaze up against them to consume them. Then
I will make of you a great nation."

But Moses implored the Lord, his God, saying, "Why, O Lord, should your wrath blaze up against your own people, whom you brought out of the land of Egypt with such great power and with so strong a hand? Why should the Egyptians say, 'With evil intent he brought them out, that he might kill them in the mountains and exterminate them from the face of the earth'? Let your blazing wrath die down; relent in punishing your people. Remember your servants Abraham, Isaac and Israel, and how you swore to them by your own self, saying, 'I will make your descendants as numerous as the stars in the sky; and all this land that I promised, I will give your descendants as their perpetual heritage.' " So the Lord relented in the punishment he had threatened to inflict on his people.

---

2   Dt 10, 8-9

A reading from the book of Deuteronomy

Moses said to the people: "At that time the Lord set apart the tribe of Levi to carry the ark of the covenant of the Lord, to be in attendance before the Lord and minister to him, and to give blessings in his name, as they have done to this day. For this reason, Levi has no share in the heritage with his brothers; the Lord himself is his heritage, as the Lord, your God, has told him."

---

3   1 Sm 16, 1. 6-13

A reading from the first book of Samuel

The Lord said to Samuel: "Fill your horn with oil, and be on your way. I am sending you to Jesse of Bethlehem, for I have chosen my king from among his sons." As Jesse and his sons came, he looked at Eliab and thought, "Surely the Lord's anointed is here before him." But the Lord said to Samuel: "Do not judge from his appearance or from his lofty stature, because I have rejected him. Not as man sees does God see, because man sees the appearance but the Lord looks into the heart." Then Jesse called Abinadab and presented him before Samuel, who said, "The Lord has not chosen him." Next Jesse presented Shammah, but Samuel said, "The Lord has not chosen this one either." In the same way Jesse presented seven sons before Samuel, but Samuel said to Jesse, "The Lord has not chosen any one of these." Then Samuel asked Jesse, "Are these all the sons you have?" Jesse replied, "There is still the youngest, who is tending the sheep." Samuel said to Jesse, "Send for him; we will not begin the sacrificial banquet until he arrives here." Jesse sent and had the young man brought to them. He was ruddy, a youth handsome to behold and making a splendid appearance. The Lord said, "There— anoint him, for this is he!" Then Samuel, with the horn of oil in hand, anointed him in the midst of his brothers; and from that day on, the spirit of the Lord rushed upon David.

---

4   Is 6, 1-8

A reading from the book of the prophet Isaiah

In the year King Uzziah died, I saw the Lord seated on a high and lofty throne, with the train of his garment filling the temple. Seraphim were stationed above; each of them had six wings: with two they veiled their faces, with two they veiled their feet, and with two they hovered aloft.

"Holy, holy, holy is the Lord of hosts!" they cried one to the other. "All the earth is filled with his glory!" At the sound of that cry, the frame of the door shook and the house was filled with smoke.

Then I said, "Woe is me, I am doomed! For I am a man of unclean lips, living among a people of unclean lips; yet my eyes have seen the King, the Lord of hosts!" Then one of the seraphim flew to me, holding an ember which he had taken with tongs from the altar.

He touched my mouth with it. "See," he said, "now that this has touched your lips, your wickedness is removed, your sin purged."

Then I heard the voice of the Lord saying, 'Whom shall I send? Who will go for us?" "Here I am," I said; "send me!"

---

5   Is 52, 7-10

[For missionaries]

A reading from the book of the prophet Isaiah

How beautiful upon the mountains
are the feet of him who brings glad tidings,

Announcing peace, bearing good news,
  announcing salvation, and saying to Zion,
  "Your God is King!'"
Hark! Your watchmen raise a cry,
  together they shout for joy,
For they see directly, before their eyes,
  the Lord restoring Zion.
Break out together in song,
  O ruins of Jerusalem!
For the Lord comforts his people,
  he redeems Jerusalem.
The Lord has bared his holy arm
  in the sight of all the nations;
All the ends of the earth will behold
  the salvation of our God.

---

6   Is 61, 1-3

A reading from the book of the prophet Isaiah

The spirit of the Lord is upon me,
  because the Lord has anointed me;
He has sent me to bring glad tidings to the lowly,
  to heal the brokenhearted,
To proclaim liberty to the captives
  and release to the prisoners,
To announce a year of favor from the Lord
  and a day of vindication by our God,
  to comfort all who mourn;
To place on those who mourn in Zion
  a diadem instead of ashes,
To give them oil of gladness in place of mourning,
  a glorious mantle instead of a listless spirit.

---

7   Jer 1, 4-9

A reading from the book of the prophet Jeremiah

The word of the Lord came to me thus:
Before I formed you in the womb I knew you,
  before you were born I dedicated you,
  a prophet to the nations I appointed you.
    "Ah, Lord God!" I said,
    "I know not how to speak; I am too young."

But the Lord answered me,
Say not, "I am too young."
To whomever I send you, you shall go;
whatever I command you, you shall speak.
Have no fear before them,
because I am with you to deliver you, says the Lord.
Then the Lord extended his hand and touched my mouth,
saying,
See, I place my words in your mouth!

---

8   Ez 3, 17-21

A reading from the book of the prophet Ezekiel

The word of the Lord came to me: Son of man, I have appointed you a watchman for the house of Israel. When you hear a word from my mouth, you shall warn them for me.

If I say to the wicked man, You shall surely die; and you do not warn him or speak out to dissuade him from his wicked conduct so that he may live: that wicked man shall die for his sin, but I will hold you responsible for his death. If, on the other hand, you have warned the wicked man, yet he has not turned away from his evil nor from his wicked conduct, then he shall die for his sin, but you shall save your life.

If a virtuous man turns away from virtue and does wrong when I place a stumbling block before him, he shall die. He shall die for his sin, and his virtuous deeds shall not be remembered; but I will hold you responsible for his death if you did not warn him. When, on the other hand, you have warned a virtuous man not to sin, and he has in fact not sinned, he shall surely live because of the warning, and you shall save your own life.

---

9   Ez 34, 11-16

A reading from the book of the prophet Ezekiel

Thus says the Lord God: I myself will look after and tend my sheep. As a shepherd tends his flock when he finds himself among his scattered sheep, so will I tend my sheep. I will rescue them from every place where they were scattered when it was cloudy and dark. I will lead them out from among the peoples and gather them from the foreign lands; I will bring them back to their own country and pasture them upon the mountains of Israel [in the land's ravines and all its inhabited places]. In good pastures will I pasture them, and on the mountain heights of Israel shall be their grazing ground. There they shall lie down on good grazing ground, and in rich pastures shall they be pastured on the mountains of Israel. I myself will pasture my sheep; I myself will give them rest, says the Lord God. The lost I will seek out, the strayed I will bring back, the injured I will bind up, the sick I will heal [but the sleek and the strong I will destroy], shepherding them rightly.

READING I

IN THE EASTER SEASON

1   Acts 13, 46-49

[For missionaries]

A reading from the Acts of the Apostles

Paul and Barnabas said to the Jews: "The word of God has to be declared to you first of all; but since you reject it and thus convict yourselves as unworthy of everlasting life, we now turn to the Gentiles. For thus were we instructed by the Lord: 'I have made you a light to the nations, a means of salvation to the ends of the earth.' " The Gentiles were delighted when they heard this and responded to the word of the Lord with praise. All who were destined for life everlasting believed in it. Thus the word of the Lord was carried throughout that area.

---

2   Acts 20, 17-18. 28-32. 36

A reading from the Acts of the Apostles

Paul sent word from Miletus to Ephesus, summoning the elders of that church. When they came to him he delivered this address: "Keep watch over yourselves, and over the whole flock the Holy Spirit has given you to guard. Shepherd the church of God, which he has acquired at the price of his own blood. I know that when I am gone, savage wolves will come among you who will not spare the flock. From your own number, men will present themselves distorting the truth and leading astray any who follow them.

Be on guard, therefore. Do not forget that for three years, night and day, I never ceased warning you individually even to the point of tears. I commend you now to the Lord, and to that gracious word of his which can enlarge you, and give you a share among all who are consecrated to him."

After this discourse, Paul knelt down with them all and prayed.

---

3   Acts 26, 19-23

[For missionaries]

A reading from the Acts of the Apostles

Paul said: "King Agrippa, I could not disobey that heavenly vision. I preached a message of reform and of conversion to God, first to the people of Damascus, then to the people of Jerusalem and all the country of Judea; yes, even to the Gentiles. I urged them to act in conformity with their change of heart. That is why the Jews seized me in the temple court and tried to murder me. But I have had God's help to this very day, and so I stand here to testify to great and small alike. Nothing that I say differs from what the prophets and Moses foretold: namely, that the Messiah must suffer, and that, as the first to rise from the dead, he will proclaim light to our people and to the Gentiles."

RESPONSORIAL PSALM

1   Ps 16, 1-2. 5. 7-8. 11

℟. (5) **You are my inheritance, O Lord.**
Keep me, O God, for in you I take refuge;
   I say to the Lord, "My Lord are you."
O Lord, my allotted portion and my cup,
   you it is who hold fast my lot.
℟. **You are my inheritance, O Lord.**
I bless the Lord who counsels me;
   even in the night my heart exhorts me.
I set the Lord ever before me;
   with him at my right hand I shall not be disturbed.
℟. **You are my inheritance, O Lord.**

You will show me the path to life,
fullness of joys in your presence,
the delights at your right hand forever.
℟. **You are my inheritance, O Lord.**

---

2   Ps 23, 1-3. 3-4. 5. 6

℟. (1) **The Lord is my shepherd;**
   there is nothing I shall want.
The Lord is my shepherd; I shall not want.
   In verdant pastures he gives me repose;
Beside restful waters he leads me;
   he refreshes my soul.
℟. **The Lord is my shepherd;**
   there is nothing I shall want.
He guides me in right paths
   for his name's sake.
Even though I walk in the dark valley
   I fear no evil; for you are at my side
With your rod and your staff
   that give me courage.
℟. **The Lord is my shepherd;**
   there is nothing I shall want.
You spread the table before me
   in the sight of my foes;
You anoint my head with oil;
   my cup overflows.
℟. **The Lord is my shepherd;**
   there is nothing I shall want.
Only goodness and kindness follow me
   all the days of my life;
And I shall dwell in the house of the Lord
   for years to come.
℟. **The Lord is my shepherd;**
   there is nothing I shall want.

---

3   Ps 89, 2-3. 4-5. 21-22. 25. 27

℟. (2) **For ever I will sing the goodness of the Lord.**
The favors of the Lord I will sing forever;
   through all generations my mouth shall proclaim your
      faithfulness.

For you have said, "My kindness is established forever";
  in heaven you have confirmed your faithfulness.
℟. **For ever I will sing the goodness of the Lord.**
"I have made a covenant with my chosen one,
  I have sworn to David my servant:
Forever will I confirm your posterity
  and establish your throne for all generations."
℟. **For ever I will sing the goodness of the Lord.**
I have found David, my servant;
  with my holy oil I have anointed him,
That my hand may be always with him,
  and that my arm may make him strong.
℟. **For ever I will sing the goodness of the Lord.**
My faithfulness and my kindness shall be with him,
  and through my name shall his horn be exalted.
He shall say of me, "You are my father,
  my God, the Rock, my savior."
℟. **For ever I will sing the goodness of the Lord.**

---

4   Ps 96, 1-2. 2-3. 7-8. 10

℟. (3) **Proclaim his marvelous deeds to all the nations.**
Sing to the Lord a new song;
  sing to the Lord, all you lands.
Sing to the Lord; bless his name.
℟. **Proclaim his marvelous deeds to all the nations.**
Announce his salvation, day after day.
  Tell his glory among the nations;
Among all peoples, his wondrous deeds.
℟. **Proclaim his marvelous deeds to all the nations.**
Give to the Lord, you families of nations,
  give to the Lord glory and praise;
  give to the Lord the glory due his name!
℟. **Proclaim his marvelous deeds to all the nations.**
Say among the nations: The Lord is king.
  He has made the world firm, not to be moved;
He governs the people with equity.
℟. **Proclaim his marvelous deeds to all the nations.**

---

5 Ps 110, 1. 2. 3. 4

℞. (4) **You are a priest for ever,**
  in the line of Melchizedek.
The Lord said to my Lord: "Sit at my right hand
  till I make your enemies your footstool."
℞. **You are a priest for ever,**
  in the line of Melchizedek.
The scepter of your power the Lord will stretch forth
    from Zion:
"Rule in the midst of your enemies.
℞. **You are a priest for ever,**
  in the line of Melchizedek.
Yours is princely power in the day of your birth, in holy
    splendor;
before the daystar, like the dew, I have begotten you."
℞. **You are a priest for ever,**
  in the line of Melchizedek.
The Lord has sworn, and he will not repent:
  "You are a priest forever, according to the order of
    Melchizedek."
℞. **You are a priest for ever,**
  in the line of Melchizedek.

———————————

6 Ps 117, 1. 2

℞. (Mk 16, 15) **Go out to all the world,**
  and tell the Good News.
Praise the Lord, all you nations;
  glorify him, all you peoples!
℞. **Go out to all the world,**
  and tell the Good News.
For steadfast is his kindness toward us,
  and the fidelity of the Lord endures forever.
℞. **Go out to all the world,**
  and tell the Good News.
℞. Or: **Alleluia.**

———————————

READING II

1   Rom 12, 3-13

A reading from the letter of Paul to the Romans

In virtue of the favor given to me, I warn each of you not to think more highly of himself than he ought. Let him estimate himself soberly, in keeping with the measure of faith that God has apportioned him. Just as each of us has one body with many members, and not all the members have the same function, so too we, though many, are one body in Christ and individually members one of another. We have gifts that differ according to the favor bestowed on each of us. One's gift may be prophecy; its use should be in proportion to his faith. It may be the gift of ministry; it should be used for service. One who is a teacher should use his gift for teaching; one with the power of exhortation should exhort. He who gives alms should do so generously; he who rules should exercise his authority with care; he who performs works of mercy should do so cheerfully.

Your love must be sincere. Detest what is evil, cling to what is good. Love one another with the affection of brothers. Anticipate each other in showing respect. Do not grow slack but be fervent in spirit; he whom you serve is the Lord. Rejoice in hope, be patient under trial, persevere in prayer. Look on the needs of the saints as your own; be generous in offering hospitality.

---

2   [For missionaries]   1 Cor 1, 18-25

A reading from the first letter of Paul to the Corinthians

The message of the cross is complete absurdity to those who are headed for ruin, but to us who are experiencing salvation it is the power of God. Scripture says,

"I will destroy the wisdom of the wise,
and thwart the cleverness of the clever."

Where is the wise man to be found? Where the scribe? Where the master of worldly argument? Has not God turned the wisdom of this world into folly? Since in God's wisdom the world did not come to know him through its wisdom, it pleased God to save those who believe through the absurdity of the preaching of the gospel. Yes, Jews demand "signs" and Greeks look for "wisdom," but we preach Christ crucified, a stumbling block to Jews and an absurdity to Gentiles, but to those who are called, Jews and Greeks alike, Christ the power of God and the wisdom of God. For God's folly is wiser than men, and his weakness more powerful than men.

---

3   1 Cor 4, 1-5

A reading from the first letter of Paul to the Corinthians

Men should regard us as servants of Christ and administrators of the mysteries of God. The first requirement of an administrator is that he prove trustworthy. It matters little to me whether you or any human court pass judgment on me. I do not even pass judgment on myself. Mind you, I have nothing on my conscience. But that does not mean that I am declaring myself innocent. The Lord is the one to judge me, so stop passing judgment before the time of his return. He will bring to light what is hidden in darkness and manifest the intentions of hearts. At that time, everyone will receive his praise from God.

---

4   1 Cor 9, 16-19. 22-23

A reading from the first letter of Paul to the Corinthians

Preaching the gospel is not the subject of a boast; I am under compulsion and have no choice. I am ruined if I do not preach it! If I do it willingly, I have my recompense; if unwillingly, I am nonetheless entrusted with a charge. And this recompense of mine? It is simply this, that when preaching I offer the gospel free of charge and do not make full use of the authority the gospel gives me.

Although I am not bound to anyone, I made myself the slave of all so as to win over as many as possible. To the weak I became a weak person with a view to winning the weak. I have made myself all things to all men in order to save at least some of them. In fact, I do all that I do for the sake of the gospel in the hope of having a share in its blessings.

---

5   2 Cor 3, 1-6

A reading from the second letter of Paul to the Corinthians

Am I beginning to speak well of myself again? Or do I
need letters of recommendation to you or from you as
others might? You are my letter, known and read by all
men, written on your hearts. Clearly you are a letter of
Christ which I have delivered, a letter written not with
ink but by the Spirit of the living God, not on tablets of
stone but on tablets of flesh in the heart.

This great confidence in God is ours, through Christ. It
is not that we are entitled of ourselves to take credit for
anything. Our sole credit is from God, who has made us
qualified ministers of a new covenant, a covenant not of
a written law but of spirit.

———————

6   2 Cor 4, 1-2. 5-7

A reading from the second letter of Paul to the Corinthians

Because we possess the ministry through God's mercy,
we do not give in to discouragement. Rather, we repudiate
shameful, underhanded practices. We do not resort to
trickery or falsify the word of God. We proclaim the
truth openly and commend ourselves to every man's
conscience before God. It is not ourselves we preach but
Christ Jesus as Lord, and ourselves as your servants for
Jesus' sake. For God, who said, "Let light shine out of
darkness," has shone in our hearts, that we in turn might
make known the glory of God shining on the face of
Christ. This treasure we possess in earthen vessels to make
it clear that its surpassing power comes from God and
not from us.

———————

7   2 Cor 5, 14-20

A reading from the second letter of Paul to the Corinthians

The love of Christ impels us who have reached the conviction that since one died for all, all died. He died for all so
that those who live might live no longer for themselves,
but for him who for their sakes died and was raised up.

Because of this we no longer look on anyone in terms of mere human judgment. If at one time we so regarded Christ, we no longer know him by this standard. This means that if anyone is in Christ, he is a new creation. The old order has passed away; now all is new! All this has been done by God, who has reconciled us to himself through Christ and has given us the ministry of reconciliation. I mean that God, in Christ, was reconciling the world to himself, not counting men's transgressions against them, and that he has entrusted the message of reconciliation to us. This makes us ambassadors for Christ, God as it were appealing through us. We implore you, in Christ's name: be reconciled to God!

---

8   Eph 4, 1-7. 11-13

A reading from the letter of Paul to the Ephesians

I plead with you as a prisoner for the Lord, to live a life worthy of the calling you have received, with perfect humility, meekness, and patience, bearing with one another lovingly. Make every effort to preserve the unity which has the Spirit as its origin and peace as its binding force. There is but one body and one Spirit, just as there is but one hope given all of you by your call. There is one Lord, one faith, one baptism; one God and Father of all, who is over all, and works through all, and is in all.

Each of us has received God's favor in the measure in which Christ bestows it.

It is he who gave apostles, prophets, evangelists, pastors and teachers in roles of service for the faithful to build up the body of Christ, till we become one in faith and in the knowledge of God's Son, and form that perfect man who is Christ come to full stature.

---

9   Col 1, 24-29

A reading from the letter of Paul to the Colossians

Even now I find my joy in the suffering I endure for you. In my own flesh I fill up what is lacking in the sufferings of Christ for the sake of his body, the church. I became a minister of this church through the commission God gave me to preach among you his word in its fullness, that mystery hidden from ages and generations past but now revealed to his holy ones. God has willed to make known to them the glory beyond price which this mystery brings to the Gentiles — the mystery of Christ in you, your hope of glory. This is the Christ we proclaim while we admonish all men and teach them in the full measure of wisdom, hoping to make every man complete in Christ. For this I work and struggle, impelled by that energy of his which is so powerful a force within me.

---

10 1 Thes 2, 2-8

A reading from the first letter of Paul to the Thessalonians

We drew courage from our God to preach his good tidings to you in the face of great opposition. The exhortation we deliver does not spring from deceit or impure motives or any sort of trickery; rather, having met the test imposed on us by God, as men entrusted with the good tidings, we speak like those who strive to please God, "the tester of our hearts," rather than men.

We were not guilty, as you well know, of flattering words or greed under any pretext, as God is our witness! Neither did we seek glory from men, you or any others, even though we could have insisted on our own importance as apostles of Christ.

On the contrary, while we were among you we were as gentle as any nursing mother fondling her little ones. So well disposed were we to you, in fact, that we wanted to share with you not only God's tidings but our very lives so dear had you become to us.

---

11 2 Tm 1, 13-14; 2, 1-3

A reading from the second letter of Paul to Timothy

Take as a model of sound teaching what you have heard me say, in faith and love in Christ Jesus. Guard the rich deposit of faith with the help of the Holy Spirit who dwells within us.

So you, my son, must be strong in the grace which is

ours in Christ Jesus. The things which you have heard from me through many witnesses you must hand on to trustworthy men who will be able to teach others. Bear hardship along with me as a good soldier of Christ Jesus.

---

12   2 Tm 4, 1-5

A reading from the second letter of Paul to Timothy

In the presence of God and of Christ Jesus, who is coming to judge the living and the dead, and by his appearing and his kingly power, I charge you to preach the word, to stay with this task, whether convenient or inconvenient —correcting, reproving, appealing—constantly teaching and never losing patience. For the time will come when people will not tolerate sound doctrine, but, following their own desires, will surround themselves with teachers who tickle their ears. They will stop listening to the truth and will wander off to fables. As for you, be steady and self-possessed; put up with hardship, perform your work as an evangelist, fulfill your ministry.

---

13   1 Pt 5, 1-4

A reading from the first letter of Peter

To the elders among you I, a fellow elder, a witness of Christ's sufferings and sharer in the glory that is to be revealed, make this appeal. God's flock is in your midst; give it a shepherd's care. Watch over it willingly as God would have you do, not under coercion; and not for shameful profit either, but generously. Be examples to the flock, not lording it over those assigned to you, so that when the chief Shepherd appears you will win for yourselves the unfading crown of glory.

ALLELUIA VERSE AND
VERSE BEFORE THE GOSPEL

1   Mt 28, 19-20

Go and teach all people my gospel.
I am with you always, until the end of the world.

2   Mk 1, 17

Come, follow me, says the Lord,
and I will make you fishers of men.

3   Lk 4, 18-19

The Lord sent me to bring Good News to the poor,
and freedom to prisoners.

4   Jn 10, 14

I am the good shepherd, says the Lord;
I know my sheep, and mine know me.

5   Jn 15, 15

I call you my friends, says the Lord,
for I have made known to you all that the Father has told
    me.

6   2 Cor 5, 19

God was in Christ, to reconcile the world to himself;
and the Good News of reconciliation he has entrusted to us.

GOSPEL

1   Mt 16, 13-19

[For a pope]

✠ A reading from the holy gospel according to Matthew

When Jesus came to the neighborhood of Caesarea Philippi, he asked his disciples this question: "Who do people say that the Son of Man is?" They replied, "Some say John the Baptizer, others Elijah, still others Jeremiah or one of the prophets." "And you," he said to them, "who do you say that I am?" "You are the Messiah," Simon Peter answered, "the Son of the living God!" Jesus replied, "Blest are you, Simon son of John! No mere man has revealed this to you, but my heavenly Father. I for my part declare to you, you are 'Rock,' and on this rock I will build my church, and the jaws of death shall not prevail against it. I will entrust to you the keys of the kingdom of heaven. Whatever you declare bound on earth shall be bound in heaven; whatever you declare loosed on earth shall be loosed in heaven."

---

2   Mt 23, 8-12

✠ A reading from the holy gospel according to Matthew

Jesus said to his disciples: "Avoid the title 'Rabbi.' One among you is your teacher, the rest are learners. Do not call anyone on earth your father. Only one is your father, the One in heaven. Avoid being called teachers. Only one is your teacher, the Messiah. The greatest among you will be the one who serves the rest. Whoever exalts himself shall be humbled, but whoever humbles himself shall be exalted."

---

3   Mt 28, 16-20

[For missionaries]

✠ A reading from the holy gospel according to Matthew

The eleven disciples made their way to Galilee, to the mountain to which Jesus had summoned them. At the sight of him, those who had entertained doubts fell down in homage. Jesus came forward and addressed them in these words:

"Full authority has been given to me
both in heaven and on earth;
go, therefore, and make disciples of all the nations.
Baptize them in the name
  'of the Father,
  and of the Son,
  and of the Holy Spirit.'
Teach them to carry out everything I have commanded
  you.
And know that I am with you always, until the end of
  the world!"

---

4   Mk 1, 14-20

✠ A reading from the holy gospel according to Mark

After John's arrest, Jesus appeared in Galilee proclaiming God's good news: "This is the time of fulfillment. The reign of God is at hand! Reform your lives and believe in the good news!"

As he made his way along the Sea of Galilee, he observed Simon and his brother Andrew casting their nets into the sea; they were fishermen. Jesus said to them, "Come after me; I will make you fishers of men." They immediately abandoned their nets and became his followers. Proceeding a little farther along, he caught sight of James, Zebedee's son, and his brother John. They too were in their boat putting their nets in order. He summoned them on the spot. They abandoned their father Zebedee, who was in the boat with the hired men, and went off in his company.

---

5   Mk 16, 15-20

[For missionaries]

✠ A reading from the holy gospel according to Mark

Jesus appeared to the Eleven and said to them: "Go into the whole world and proclaim the good news to all creation. The man who believes in it and accepts baptism will be saved; the man who refuses to believe in it will be condemned. Signs like these will accompany those who have professed their faith: they will use my name to expel demons, they will speak entirely new languages, they will be able to handle serpents, they will be able to drink deadly poison without harm, and the sick upon whom they lay their hands will recover." Then, after speaking to them, the Lord Jesus was taken up into heaven and took his seat at God's right hand. The Eleven went forth and preached everywhere. The Lord continued to work with them throughout and confirm the message through the signs which accompanied them.

---

6   Lk 5, 1-11

[For missionaries]

✠ A reading from the holy gospel according to Luke

As Jesus stood by the Lake of Gennesaret, and the crowd pressed in on him to hear the word of God, he saw two boats moored by the side of the lake; the fishermen had disembarked and were washing their nets. He got into one of the boats, the one belonging to Simon, and asked him to pull out a short distance from the shore; then, remaining seated, he continued to teach the crowds from the boat. When he had finished speaking he said to Simon, "Put out into deep water and lower your nets for a catch." Simon answered, "Master, we have been hard at it all night long and have caught nothing; but if you say so, I will lower the nets." Upon doing this they caught such a great number of fish that their nets were at the breaking point. They signaled to their mates in the other boat to come and help them. These came, and together they filled the two boats until they nearly sank.

At the sight of this, Simon Peter fell at the knees of Jesus saying, "Leave me, Lord. I am a sinful man." For indeed, amazement at the catch they had made seized him and all his shipmates, as well as James and John, Zebedee's sons, who were partners with Simon. Jesus said to Simon, "Do not be afraid. From now on you will be catching men." With that they brought their boats to land, left everything, and became his followers.

---

7 Lk 10-1-9

✠ A reading from the holy gospel according to Luke

The Lord appointed a further seventy-two and sent them in pairs before him to every town and place he intended to visit. He said to them: "The harvest is rich but the workers are few; therefore ask the harvest-master to send workers to his harvest. Be on your way, and remember: I am sending you as lambs in the midst of wolves. Do not carry a walking staff or traveling bag; wear no sandals and greet no one along the way. On entering any house, first say, 'Peace to this house.' If there is a peaceable man there, your peace will rest on him; if not, it will come back to you. Stay in the one house eating and drinking what they have, for the laborer is worth his wage. Do not move from house to house.

"Into whatever city you go, after they welcome you, eat what they set before you, and cure the sick there. Say to them, 'The reign of God is at hand.' "

---

8 Lk 22, 24-30

✠ A reading from the holy gospel according to Luke

A dispute arose among the apostles about who should be regarded as the greatest. Jesus said: "Earthly kings lord it over their people. Those who exercise authority over them are called their benefactors. Yet it cannot be that way with you. Let the greater among you be as the junior, the leader as the servant. Who, in fact, is the greater—he who reclines at table or he who serves the meal? Is it not the one who reclines at table? Yet I am in your midst at the one who serves you. You are the ones who have stood loyally by me in my temptations. I for my part assign to you the dominion my Father has assigned to me. In my kingdom you will eat and drink at my table, and you will sit on thrones judging the twelve tribes of Israel."

9 Jn 10, 11-16

✠ A reading from the holy gospel according to John

Jesus said:

"I am the good shepherd;
the good shepherd lays down his life for the sheep.
The hired hand—who is no shepherd,
nor owner of the sheep—
catches sight of the wolf coming
and runs away, leaving the sheep
to be snatched and scattered by the wolf.
That is because he works for pay;
he has no concern for the sheep.

"I am the good shepherd.
I know my sheep
and my sheep know me
in the same way that the Father knows me
and I know the Father;
for these sheep I will give my life.
I have other sheep
that do not belong to this fold.
I must lead them, too,
and they shall hear my voice.
There shall be one flock then, one shepherd."

---

10 Jn 15, 9-17

✠ A reading from the holy gospel according to John

Jesus said to his disciples:

"As the Father has loved me,
so I have loved you.
Live on in my love.
You will live in my love
if you keep my commandments,
even as I have kept my Father's commandments,
and live in his love.
All this I tell you
that my joy may be yours
and your joy may be complete.

This is my commandment:
love one another
as I have loved you.
There is no greater love than this:
to lay down one's life for one's friends.
You are my friends
if you do what I command you.
I no longer speak of you as slaves,
for a slave does not know what his master is about.
Instead, I call you friends,
since I have made known to you all that I heard from my
    Father.
It was not you who chose me,
it was I who chose you
to go forth and bear fruit.
Your fruit must endure,
so that all you ask the Father in my name
he will give you.
The command I give you is this:
that you love one another."

___

11   Jn 21, 15-17

[For a pope]

✠ A reading from the holy gospel according to John

Jesus appeared to his disciples again and when they had
eaten their meal, he said to Simon Peter, "Simon, son of
John, do you love me more than these?" "Yes, Lord," Peter
said, "you know that I love you." At which Jesus said,
"Feed my lambs."

A second time he put his question, "Simon, son of John,
do you love me?" "Yes, Lord," Peter said, "you know that I
love you." Jesus replied, "Tend my sheep."

A third time Jesus asked him, "Simon, son of John, do
you love me?" Peter was hurt because he had asked a third
time, "Do you love me?" So he said to him: "Lord, you
know everything. You know well that I love you." Jesus
told him, "Feed my sheep."

___

COMMON OF DOCTORS
OF THE CHURCH

READING I

OUTSIDE THE EASTER SEASON

1   1 Kgs 3, 11-14

A reading from the first book of Kings

The Lord said to Solomon: "Because you have asked—not for a long life for yourself, nor for riches, nor for the life of your enemies, but for understanding so that you may know what is right—I do as you requested. I give you a heart so wise and understanding that there has never been anyone like you up to now, and after you there will come no one to equal you. In addition, I give you what you have not asked for, such riches and glory that among kings there is not your like. And if you follow me by keeping my statutes and commandments, as your father David did, I will give you a long life."

---

2   Wis 7, 7-10. 15-16

A reading from the book of Wisdom

I prayed, and prudence was given me;
   I pleaded, and the spirit of Wisdom came to me.
I preferred her to scepter and throne,
And deemed riches nothing in comparison with her,
   nor did I liken any priceless gem to her;
Because all gold, in view of her, is a little sand,
   and before her silver is to be accounted mire.
Beyond health and comeliness I loved her,
And I chose to have her rather than the light,
   because the splendor of her never yields to sleep.

Now God grant I speak suitably
   and value these endowments at their worth:
For he is the guide of Wisdom
   and the director of the wise.

For both we and our words are in his hand,
  as well as all prudence and knowledge of crafts.

---

3   Sir 15, 1-6

A reading from the book of Sirach

He who fears the Lord will do this;
  he who is practiced in the law will come to wisdom.
Motherlike she will meet him,
  like a young bride she will embrace him,
Nourish him with the bread of understanding,
  and give him the water of learning to drink.
He will lean upon her and not fall,
  he will trust in her and not be put to shame.
She will exalt him above his fellows;
  in the assembly she will make him eloquent.
Joy and gladness he will find,
  an everlasting name inherit.

---

4   Sir 39, 6-11

A reading from the book of Sirach

If it pleases the Lord Almighty,
  he will be filled with the spirit of understanding;
He will pour forth his words of wisdom
  and in prayer give thanks to the Lord,
Who will direct his knowledge and his counsel,
  as he meditates upon his mysteries.
He will show the wisdom of what he has learned
  and glory in the law of the Lord's covenant.
Many will praise his understanding;
  his fame can never be effaced;
Unfading will be his memory,
  through all generations his name will live;
Peoples will speak of his wisdom,
  and in assembly sing his praises.
While he lives he is one out of a thousand,
  and when he dies his renown will not cease.

READING I

IN THE EASTER SEASON

1   Acts, 2, 14. 22-24. 32-36

A reading from the Acts of the Apostles

[On the day of Pentecost] Peter stood up with the Eleven, raised his voice, and addressed them: "Men of Israel, listen to me! Jesus the Nazorean was a man whom God sent to you with miracles, wonders and signs as his credentials. These God worked through him in your midst, as you well know. He was delivered up by the set purpose and plan of God; you even made use of pagans to crucify and kill him. God freed him from death's bitter pangs, however, and raised him up again, for it was impossible that death should keep its hold on him.

"This is the Jesus God has raised up, and we are his witnesses. Exalted at God's right hand, he first received the promised Holy Spirit from the Father, then poured this Spirit out on us. This is what you now see and hear. David did not go up to heaven, yet David says,

'The Lord said to my Lord,
Sit at my right hand
until I make your enemies your footstool.'

Therefore let the whole house of Israel know beyond any doubt that God has made both Lord and Messiah this Jesus whom you crucified."

---

2   Acts 13, 26-33

A reading from the Acts of the Apostles

When Paul came to Antioch in Pisidia, he spoke in the synagogue and said: "My brothers, children of the family of Abraham and you others who reverence our God, it was to us that this message of salvation was sent forth. The inhabitants of Jerusalem and their rulers failed to recognize him, and in condemning him they fulfilled the words of the prophets which we read sabbath after sabbath. Even though they found no charge against him which deserved death, they begged Pilate to have him executed. Once they had thus brought about all that had been written of him, they took him down from the tree and laid him in a tomb. Yet God raised him from the dead, and for many days thereafter Jesus appeared to those who had come up with him from Galilee to Jerusalem. These are his witnesses now before the people.

"We ourselves announce to you the good news that what God promised our fathers he has fulfilled for us, their children, in raising up Jesus, according to what is written in the second psalm, 'You are my son; this day I have begotten you.' "

RESPONSORIAL PSALM

1   Ps 19, 8. 9. 10. 11

℟. (10) **The judgments of the Lord are true,**
   and all of them are just.
The law of the Lord is perfect,
   refreshing the soul;
The decree of the Lord is trustworthy,
   giving wisdom to the simple.
℟. **The judgments of the Lord are true,**
   and all of them are just.
The precepts of the Lord are right,
   rejoicing the heart;
The command of the Lord is clear,
   enlightening the eye.
℟. **The judgments of the Lord are true,**
   and all of them are just.
The fear of the Lord is pure,
   enduring forever;
The ordinances of the Lord are true,
   all of them just.
℟. **The judgments of the Lord are true,**
   and all of them are just.
They are more precious than gold,
   than a heap of purest gold;
Sweeter also than syrup
   or honey from the comb.

℟. **The judgments of the Lord are true,**
and all of them are just.
℟. Or: **Your words, Lord are spirit and life.**

---

2   Ps 37, 3-4. 5-6. 30-31

℟. (30) **The mouth of the just man murmurs wisdom.**
Trust in the Lord and do good,
that you may dwell in the land and enjoy security.
Take delight in the Lord,
and he will grant you your heart's requests.
℟. **The mouth of the just man murmurs wisdom.**
Commit to the Lord your way;
trust in him, and he will act.
He will make justice dawn for you like the light;
bright as the noonday shall be your vindication.
℟. **The mouth of the just man murmurs wisdom.**
The mouth of the just man tells of wisdom
and his tongue utters what is right.
The law of his God is in his heart,
and his steps do not falter.
℟. **The mouth of the just man murmurs wisdom.**

---

3   Ps 119, 9. 10. 11. 12. 13. 14

℟. (12) **Lord, teach me your decrees.**
How shall a young man be faultless in his way?
By keeping to your words.
℟. **Lord, teach me your decrees.**
With all my heart I seek you;
let me not stray from your commands.
℟. **Lord, teach me your decrees.**
Within my heart I treasure your promise,
that I may not sin against you.
℟. **Lord, teach me your decrees.**
Blessed are you, O Lord;
teach me your statutes.
℟. **Lord, teach me your decrees.**
With my lips I declare
all the ordinances of your mouth.
℟. **Lord, teach me your decrees.**

In the way of your decrees I rejoice,
  as much as in all riches.
℟. **Lord, teach me your decrees.**

READING II

1   1 Cor 1, 18-25

A reading from the first letter of Paul to the Corinthians

The message of the cross is complete absurdity to those
who are headed for ruin, but to us who are experiencing
salvation it is the power of God. Scripture says,

  "I will destroy the wisdom of the wise,
    and thwart the cleverness of the clever."

Where is the wise man to be found? Where the scribe?
Where is the master of worldly argument? Has not God
turned the wisdom of this world into folly. Since in God's
wisdom the world did not come to know him through
wisdom, it pleased God to save those who believe through
the absurdity of the preaching of the gospel. Yes, Jews demand "signs" and Greeks look for "wisdom," but we preach
Christ crucified, a stumbling block to Jews and an absurdity to Gentiles, but to those who are called, Jews and
Greeks alike, Christ the power of God and the wisdom of
God. For God's folly is wiser than men, and his weakness
more powerful than men.

---

2   1 Cor 2, 1-10

A reading from the first letter of Paul to the Corinthians

Brothers, when I came to you I did not come proclaiming
God's testimony with any particular eloquence or "wisdom." No, I determined that while I was with you I would
speak of nothing but Jesus Christ and him crucified. When
I came among you it was in weakness and fear, and with
much trepidation. My message and my preaching had none
of the persuasive force of "wise" argumentation, but the
convincing power of the Spirit. As a consequence, your

faith rests not on the wisdom of men but on the power of God.

There is, to be sure, a certain wisdom which we express among the spiritually mature. It is not a wisdom of this age, however, nor of the rulers of this age, who are men headed for destruction. No, what we utter is God's wisdom: a mysterious, a hidden wisdom. God planned it before all ages for our glory. None of the rulers of this age knew the mystery; if they had known it, they would never have crucified the Lord of glory. Of this wisdom it is written:

"Eye has not seen, ear has not heard,
   nor has it so much as dawned on man
   what God has prepared for those who love him."

Yet God has revealed this wisdom to us through the Spirit.

---

3   1 Cor 2, 10-16

A reading from the first letter of Paul to the Corinthians

The spirit scrutinizes all matters, even the deep things of God. Who, for example, knows a man's innermost self but the man's own spirit within him? Similarly, no one knows what lies at the depths of God but the Spirit of God. The Spirit we have received is not the world's spirit but God's Spirit, helping us to recognize the gifts he has given us. We speak of these, not in words of human wisdom but in words taught by the Spirit, thus interpreting spiritual things in spiritual terms. The natural man does not accept what is taught by the Spirit of God. For him, that is absurdity. He cannot come to know such teaching because it must be appraised in a spiritual way. The spiritual man, on the other hand, can appraise everything, though he himself can be appraised by no one. For, "Who has known the mind of the Lord so as to instruct him?" But we have the mind of Christ.

---

4   Eph 3, 8-12

A reading from the letter of Paul to the Ephesians

To me, the least of all believers, was given the grace to preach to the Gentiles the unfathomable riches of Christ

'
and to enlighten all men on the mysterious design which
for ages was hidden in God, the Creator of all. Now, therefore, through the church, God's manifold wisdom is made
known to the principalities and powers of heaven, in accord with his age-old purpose, carried out in Christ Jesus
our Lord. In Christ and through faith in him we can speak
freely to God, drawing near him with confidence.

---

5   Eph 4, 1-7. 11-13

A reading from the letter of Paul to the Ephesians

I plead with you, as a prisoner for the Lord, to live a life
worthy of the calling you have received, with perfect humility, meekness, and patience, bearing with one another
lovingly. Make every effort to preserve the unity which
has the Spirit as its origin and peace as its binding force.
There is but one body and one Spirit, just as there is but
one hope given all of you by your call. There is one Lord,
one faith, one baptism; one God and Father of all, who is
over all, and works through all, and is in all.

Each of us has received God's favor in the measure in
which Christ bestows it. It is he who gave apostles, prophets, evangelists, pastors, and teachers in roles of service
for the faithful to build up the body of Christ, till we become one in faith and in the knowledge of God's Son, and
form that perfect man who is Christ come to full stature.

---

6   2 Tm 1, 13-14; 2, 1-3

A reading from the second letter of Paul to Timothy

Take as a model of sound teaching what you have heard
me say, in faith and love in Christ Jesus. Guard the rich
deposit of faith with the help of the Holy Spirit who dwells
within us.

So you, my son, must be strong in the grace which is
ours in Christ Jesus. The things which you have heard
from me through many witnesses you must hand on to
trustworthy men who will be able to teach others. Bear
hardship along with me as a good soldier of Christ Jesus.

---

7   2 Tm 4, 1-5

A reading from the second letter of Paul to Timothy

In the presence of God and of Christ Jesus, who is coming to judge the living and the dead, and by his appearing and his kingly power, I charge you to preach the word, to stay with this task whether convenient or inconvenient—correcting, reproving, appealing—constantly teaching and never losing patience. For the time will come when people will not tolerate sound doctrine, but, following their own desires, will surround themselves with teachers who tickle their ears. They will stop listening to the truth and will wander off to fables. As for you, be steady and self-possessed; put up with hardship, perform your work as an evangelist, fulfill your ministry.

ALLELUIA VERSE AND
VERSE BEFORE THE GOSPEL

1   Mt 5, 16

Let your light shine before men,
that they may see your good works and glorify your
    Father.

2   1Cor 1, 18

The message of the cross is folly to those who turn away,
but to those who are saved it is the power of God.

3   1 Cor 2, 7

We teach a secret and hidden wisdom of God,
which he decreed for our glory before time began.

4

The seed is the word of God, Christ is the sower;
all who come to him will live for ever.

GOSPEL

1   Mt 5, 13-16

✠ A reading from the holy gospel according to Matthew

Jesus said to his disciples: "You are the salt of the earth. But what if salt goes flat? How can you restore its flavor? Then it is good for nothing but to be thrown out and trampled underfoot.

"You are the light of the world. A city set on a hill cannot be hidden. Men do not light a lamp and then put it under a bushel basket. They set it on a stand where it gives light to all in the house. In the same way, your light must shine before men so that they may see goodness in your acts and give praise to your heavenly Father"

---

2   Mt 23, 8-12

✠ A reading from the holy gospel according to Matthew

Jesus said to his disciples: "Avoid the title 'Rabbi.' One among you is your teacher, the rest are learners. Do not call anyone on earth your father. Only one is your father, the One in heaven. Avoid being called teachers. Only one is your teacher, the Messiah. The greatest among you will be the one who serves the rest. Whoever exalts himself shall be humbled, but whoever humbles himself shall be exalted."

---

3   Mk 4, 1-10. 13-20 or 4, 1-9

[If the "Short Form" is used, the indented text in brackets is omitted.]

✠ A reading from the holy gospel according to Mark

[Jesus began to teach beside the lake. Such a huge crowd gathered around him that he went and sat in a boat on the water, while the crowd remained on the shore nearby. He began to instruct them at great length, by the use of parables, and in the course of his teaching said: "Listen carefully to this. A farmer went out sowing. Some of what he sowed landed on the footpath, where the birds came along and ate it. Some of the seed landed on rocky ground where it had little soil; it sprouted immediately because the soil had no depth. Then, when the sun rose and scorched it, it began to wither for lack of roots. Again, some landed among thorns, which grew up and choked it off, and there was no yield of grain. Some seed, finally, landed on good soil and yielded grain that sprang up to produce at a rate of thirty- and sixty- and a hundredfold." Having spoken this parable, he added: "Let him who has ears to hear me, hear!"]

Now when he was away from the crowd, those present with the Twelve questioned him about the parables. He said to them: "You do not understand this parable? How then are you going to understand other figures like it? What the sower is sowing is the word. Those on the path are the ones to whom, as soon as they hear the word, Satan comes to carry off what was sown in them. Similarly, those sown on rocky ground are people who on listening to the word accept it joyfully at the outset. Being rootless, they last only a while. When some pressure or persecution overtakes them, because of the word, they falter. Those sown among thorns are another class. They have listened to the word, but anxieties over life's demands, and the desire for wealth and cravings of other sorts come to choke it off; it bears no yield. But those sown on good soil are the ones who listen to the word, take it to heart, and yield at thirty- and sixty- and a hundred-fold."

———

COMMONS OF VIRGINS

READING I
OUTSIDE THE EASTER SEASON

1   Sg 8, 6-7

A reading from the Song of Solomon

Set me as a seal on your heart,
  as a seal on your arm;
For stern as death is love,
  relentless as the nether world is devotion;
  its flames are a blazing fire.
Deep waters cannot quench love,
  nor floods sweep it away.
Were one to offer all he owns to purchase love,
  he would be roundly mocked.

------

2   Hos 2, 16. 17. 21-22

A reading from the book of the prophet Hosea

I will lead her into the desert
  and speak to her heart.
She shall respond there as in the days of her youth,
  when she came up from the land of Egypt.

I will espouse you to me forever:
  I will espouse you in right and in justice,
  in love and in mercy;
I will espouse you in fidelity,
  and you shall know the Lord.

READING I

DURING THE EASTER SEASON

1   Rv 19, 1. 5-9

A reading from the book of Revelation

I, John, heard what sounded like the loud song of a great assembly in heaven. They were singing:

"Alleluia!
Salvation, glory, and might belong to our God."
A voice coming from the throne cried out:
"Praise our God, all you his servants,
the small and the great, who revere him!"

Then I heard what sounded like the shouts of a great crowd, or the roaring of the deep, or mighty peals of thunder, as they cried:

"Alleluia!
The Lord is king,
our God, the Almighty!
Let us rejoice and be glad,
and give him glory!
For this is the wedding day of the Lamb;
his bride has prepared herself for the wedding.
She has been given a dress to wear
made of finest linen, brilliant white."

(The linen dress is the virtuous deeds of God's saints.)

The angel then said to me: "Write this down: Happy are they who have been invited to the wedding feast of the Lamb."

---

2   Rv 21, 1-5

A reading from the book of Revelation

I, John, saw new heavens and a new earth. The former heavens and the former earth had passed away, and the sea was no longer. I also saw a new Jeruslem, the holy city, coming down out of heaven from God, beautiful as a bride prepared to meet her husband. I heard a loud voice from the throne cry out: "This is God's dwelling among men. He shall dwell with them and they shall be his people, and he shall be their God who is always with them. He shall wipe every tear from their eyes, and there shall be no more death or mourning, crying out or pain, for the former world has passed away."

The One who sat on the throne said to me, "See, I make all things new!"

RESPONSORIAL PSALM

1   Ps 45, 11-12. 14-15. 16-17

℟. (11) **Listen to me, daughter;**
    see and bend your ear.
Hear, O daughter, and see; turn your ear,
    forget your people and your father's house.
So shall the king desire your beauty;
    for he is your lord, and you must worship him.
℟. **Listen to me, daughter;**
    see and bend your ear.
All glorious is the king's daughter as she enters;
    her raiment is threaded with spun gold.
In embroidered apparel she is borne in to the king;
    behind her the virgins of her train are brought to you.
℟. **Listen to me, daughter;**
    see and bend your ear.
They are borne in with gladness and joy;
    they enter the palace of the king.
The place of your fathers your sons shall have;
    you shall make them princes through all the land.
℟. **Listen to me, daughter;**
    see and bend your ear.
℟. Or: (Mt 25, 6) **The bridegroom is here;**
    let us go out to meet Christ the Lord.

2 Ps 148, 1-2. 11-12. 13-14. 14

℞. **Alleluia.**
Praise the Lord from the heavens,
   praise him in the heights;
Praise him, all you his angels,
   praise him, all you his hosts.
℞. **Alleluia.**
Let the kings of the earth and all peoples,
   the princes and all the judges of the earth,
Young men too, and maidens,
   old men and boys.
℞. **Alleluia.**
Praise the name of the Lord,
   for his name alone is exalted;
His majesty is above earth and heaven.
℞. **Alleluia.**
He has lifted up the horn of his people.
   Be this his praise from all his faithful ones;
From the children of Israel, the people close to him.
   Alleluia.
℞. **Alleluia.**

READING II

1 1 Cor 7, 25-35

A reading from the first letter of Paul to the Corinthians
With respect to virgins, I have not received any commandment from the Lord, but I give my opinion as one who is
trustworthy, thanks to the Lord's mercy. It is this: In the
present time of stress it seems good to me for a person to
continue as he is. Are you bound to a wife? Then do not
seek your freedom. Are you free of a wife? If so, do not go
in search of one. Should you marry, however, you will not
be committing sin. Neither does a virgin commit a sin if
she marries. Such people, however, will have trials in this
life, and these I should like to spare you.

   I tell you, brothers, the time is short. From now on those
with wives should live as though they had none; those who
weep should live as though they were not weeping, and

those who rejoice as though they were not rejoicing; buyers should conduct themselves as though they owned nothing, and those who make use of the world as though they were not using it, for the world as we know it is passing away.

I should like you to be free of all worries. The unmarried man is busy with the Lord's affairs, concerned with pleasing the Lord; but the married man is busy with this world's demands and occupied with pleasing his wife. This means he is divided. The virgin—indeed, any unmarried woman—is concerned with things of the Lord, in pursuit of holiness in body and spirit. The married woman, on the other hand, has the cares of this world to absorb her and is concerned with pleasing her husband. I am going into this with you for your own good. I have no desire to place restrictions on you, but I do want to promote what is good, what will help you to devote yourselves entirely to the Lord.

---

2   2 Cor 10, 17—11, 2

A reading from the second letter of Paul to the Corinthians

"Let him who would boast, boast in the Lord." It is not the man who recommends himself who is approved but the man whom the Lord recommends.

You must endure a little of my folly. Put up with me, I beg you! I am jealous of you with the jealously of God himself, since I have given you in marriage to one husband, presenting you as a chaste virgin to Christ.

ALLELUIA VERSE AND

VERSE BEFORE THE GOSPEL

1

This is the wise bridesmaid, whom the Lord found waiting; at his coming, she went in with him to the wedding feast.

2

Come, bride of Christ, and receive the crown, which the Lord has prepared for you for ever.

GOSPEL

1   Mt 19, 3-12

✠ A reading from the holy gospel according to Matthew

Some of the Pharisees came up to Jesus and said, to test him, "May a man divorce his wife for any reason whatever?" He replied, "Have you not read that at the beginning the Creator made them male and female and declared, 'For this reason a man shall leave his father and mother and cling to his wife, and the two shall become as one'? Thus they are no longer two but one flesh. Therefore, let no man separate what God has joined." They said to him, "Then why did Moses command divorce and the promulgation of a divorce decree?" "Because of your stubbornness Moses let you divorce your wives," he replied: "but at the beginning it was not that way. I now say to you, whoever divorces his wife (lewd conduct is a separate case) and marries another commits adultery, and the man who marries a divorced woman commits adultery."

His disciples said to him, "If that is the case between man and wife, it is better not to marry." He said, "Not everyone can accept this teaching, only those to whom it is given to do so. Some men are incapable of sexual activity from birth; some have been deliberately made so; and some there are who have freely renounced sex for the sake of God's reign. Let him accept this teaching who can."

---

2   Mt 25, 1-13

✠ A reading of the holy gospel according to Matthew

Jesus told this parable to his disciples; "The reign of God can be likened to ten bridesmaids who took their torches and went out to welcome the groom. Five of them were foolish, while the other five were sensible. The foolish ones, in taking their torches, brought no oil along, but the sensible ones took flasks of oil as well as their torches. The groom delayed his coming, so they all began to nod, then to fall asleep. At midnight someone shouted, 'The groom is here! Come out and greet him!' At the outcry all the virgins woke up and got their torches ready. The foolish ones said to the sensible, 'Give us some of your oil. Our torches are going out.' But the sensible ones replied, 'No, there may not be enough for you and us. You had better go to the dealers and buy yourselves some.' While they went off to buy it the groom arrived, and the ones who were ready went in to the wedding with him. Then the door was barred. Later the other bridesmaids came back. 'Master, master!' they cried. 'Open the door for us.' But he answered, 'I tell you, I do not know you.' The moral is: keep your eyes open, for you know not the day or the hour."

---

3   Lk 10, 38-42

✠ A reading of the holy gospel according to Luke

Jesus entered a village where a woman named Martha welcomed him to her home. She had a sister named Mary, who seated herself at the Lord's feet and listened to his words. Martha, who was busy with all the details of hospitality, came to him and said, "Lord, are you not concerned that my sister has left me all alone to do the household tasks? Tell her to help me."

The Lord in reply said to her: "Martha, Martha, you are anxious and upset about many things; one thing only is required. Mary has chosen the better portion and she shall not be deprived of it."

COMMON OF HOLY MEN AND WOMEN

READING I

OUTSIDE THE EASTER SEASON

1   Gn 12, 1-4

A reading from the book of Genesis

The Lord said to Abram: "Go forth from the land of your
kinsfolk and from your father's house to a land that I will
show you.

"I will make of you a great nation,
    and I will bless you;
I will make your name great,
    so that you will be a blessing.
I will bless those who bless you
    and curse those who curse you.
All the communities of the earth
    shall find blessing in you."

Abram went as the Lord directed him.

---

2   Lv 19, 1-2. 17-18

A reading from the book of Leviticus

The Lord said to Moses, "Speak to the whole Israelite community and tell them: Be holy, for I, the Lord, your God, am
holy.

"You shall not bear hatred for your brother in your
heart. Though you may have to reprove your fellow man,
do not incur sin because of him. Take no revenge and cherish no grudge against your fellow countrymen. You shall
love your neighbor as yourself. I am the Lord."

---

3   Dt 6, 3-9

A reading from the book of Deuteronomy

Moses said to the people: "Hear, Israel, and be careful to
observe the commandments, that you may grow and pros-

1195

per the more, in keeping with the promise of the Lord, the
God of your fathers, to give you a land flowing with milk
and honey.

"Hear, O Israel! The Lord is our God, the Lord alone!
Therefore, you shall love the Lord, your God, with all your
heart, and with all your soul, and with all your strength.
Take to heart these words which I enjoin on you today.
Drill them into your children. Speak of them at home and
abroad, whether you are busy or at rest. Bind them at
your wrist as a sign and let them be as a pendant on your
forehead. Write them on the doorposts of your houses and
on your gates."

---

4   Dt 10, 8-9

[For religious]

A reading from the book of Deuteronomy

Moses said to the people: "At that time the Lord set apart
the tribe of Levi to carry the ark of the covenant of the
Lord, to be in attendance before the Lord and minister to
him, and to give blessings in his name, as they have done
to this day. For this reason, Levi has no share in the heritage with his brothers; the Lord himself is his heritage,
as the Lord, your God, has told him."

---

5   1 Kgs 19, 4-9. 11-15

[For religious]

A reading from the first book of Kings

Elijah went a day's journey into the desert, until he came
to a broom tree and sat beneath it. He prayed for death:
"This is enough, O Lord! Take my life, for I am no better
than my fathers." He lay down and fell asleep under the
broom tree, but then an angel touched him and ordered
him to get up and eat. He looked and there at his head was

a hearth cake and a jug of water. After he ate and drank, he lay down again, but the angel of the Lord came back a second time, touched him, and ordered, "Get up and eat, else the journey will be too long for you!" He got up, ate and drank; then, strengthened by that food, he walked forty nights to the mountain of God, Horeb.

There he came to a cave, where he took shelter. Then the Lord said, "Go outside and stand on the mountain before the Lord; the Lord will be passing by." A strong and heavy wind was rending the mountains and crushing rocks before the Lord—but the Lord was not in the wind. After the wind there was an earthquake—but the Lord was not in the earthquake. After the earthquake there was fire— but the Lord was not in the fire. After the fire there was a tiny whispering sound. When he heard this, Elijah hid his face in his cloak and went and stood at the entrance of the cave. A voice said to him, "Elijah, why are you here?" He replied, "I have been most zealous for the Lord, the God of hosts. But the Israelites have forsaken your covenant, torn down your altars, and put your prophets to the sword. I alone am left, and they seek to take my life." "Go, take the road back to the desert near Damascus," the Lord said to him.

---

6   1 Kgs 19, 16. 19-21

[For religious]

A reading from the first book of Kings

The Lord said to Elijah: "You shall anoint Elisha, son of Shaphat of Abel-meholah, as prophet to succeed you.

Elijah set out, and came upon Elisha, son of Shaphat, as he was plowing with twelve yoke of oxen; he was following the twelfth. Elijah went over to him and threw his cloak over him. Elisha left the oxen, ran after Elijah, and said, "Please, let me kiss my father and mother goodbye, and I will follow you." "Go back!" Elijah answered. "Have I done anything to you?" Elisha left him and, taking the yoke of oxen, slaughtered them; he used the plowing equipment for fuel to boil their flesh, and gave it to his people to eat. Then he left and followed Elijah as his attendant.

---

7   Tb 8, 5-7

A reading from the book of Tobit

On their wedding night Sarah got up, and she and Tobiah
started to pray and beg that deliverance might be theirs.
He began with these words:

"Blessed are you, O God of our fathers;
   praised be your name forever and ever.
Let the heavens and all your creation
   praise you forever.
You made Adam and you gave him his wife Eve
   to be his help and support;
   and from these two the human race descended.
You said, 'It is not good for the man to be alone;
   let us make him a partner like himself.'
Now, Lord, you know that I take this wife of mine
   not because of lust
   but for a noble purpose.
Call down your mercy on me and on her,
   and allow us to live together to a happy old age."

---

8   Tb 12, 6-13

[For those who work for the underprivileged]

A reading from the book of Tobit

The angel said to Tobit and his son: "Thank God! Give him
the praise and the glory. Before all the living, acknowledge
the many good things he has done for you, by blessing and
extolling his name in song. Before all men, honor and proclaim God's deeds, and do not be slack in praising him. A
king's secret it is prudent to keep, but the works of God
are to be declared and made known. Praise them with due
honor. Do good, and evil will not find its way to you. Prayer
and fasting are good, but better than either is almsgiving
accompanied by righteousness. A little with righteousness
is better than abundance with wickedness. It is better to
give alms than store up gold; for almsgiving saves one
from death and expiates every sin. Those who regularly
give alms shall enjoy a full life; but those habitually guilty
of sin are their own worst enemies.

"I will now tell you the whole truth; I will conceal nothing at all from you. I have already said to you, 'A king's secret it is prudent to keep, but the works of God are to be made known with due honor.' I can now tell you that when you, Tobit, and Sarah prayed, it was I who presented and read the record of your prayer before the Glory of the Lord; and I did the same thing when you used to bury the dead. When you did not hesitate to get up and leave your dinner in order to go and bury the dead, I was sent to put you to the test."

---

9   Jdt 8, 2-8

[For widows]

A reading from the book of Judith

Judith's husband, Manasseh, of her own tribe and clan, had died at the time of the barley harvest. While he was in the field supervising those who bound the sheaves, he suffered sunstroke; and he died of this illness in Bethulia, his native city. He was buried with his forefathers in the field between Dothan and Balamon. The widowed Judith remained three years and four months at home, where she set up a tent for herself on the roof of her house. She put sackcloth about her loins and wore widow's weeds. She fasted all the days of her widowhood, except sabbath eves and sabbaths, new moon eves and new moons, feastdays and holidays of the house of Israel. She was beautifully formed and lovely to behold. Her husband, Manasseh, had left her gold and silver, servants and maids, livestock and fields, which she was maintaining. No one had a bad word to say about her, for she was a very God-fearing woman.

---

10   Est C, 1-7. 10

A reading from the book of Esther

Mordecai recalled all that the Lord had done and he prayed to him and said: "O Lord God, almighty King, all things are in your power, and there is no one to oppose you in your will to save Israel. You made heaven and earth and every wonderful thing under the heavens. You are Lord of all,

and there is no one who can resist you, Lord. You know
all things. You know, O Lord, that it was not out of inso-
lence or pride or desire for fame that I acted thus in not
bowing down to the proud Haman. Gladly would I have
kissed the soles of his feet for the salvation of Israel. But
I acted as I did so as not to place the honor of man above
that of God. I will not bow down to anyone but you. my
Lord. It is not out of pride that I am acting thus. Hear my
prayer; have pity on your inheritance and turn our sorrow
into joy: thus we shall live to sing praise to your name, O
Lord. Do not silence those who praise you."

---

11   Prv 31, 10-13. 19-20. 30-31

A reading from the book of Proverbs

When one finds a worthy wife,
    her value is far beyond pearls.
Her husband, entrusting his heart to her,
    has an unfailing prize.
She brings him good, and not evil,
    all the days of her life.
She obtains wool and flax
    and makes cloth with skillful hands.
She puts her hands to the distaff,
    and her fingers ply the spindle.
She reaches out her hands to the poor,
    and extends her arms to the needy.
Charm is deceptive and beauty fleeting;
    the woman who fears the Lord is to be praised.
Give her a reward of her labors,
    and let her works praise her at the city gates.

---

12   Sir 2, 7-11

A reading from the book of Sirach

You who fear the Lord, wait for his mercy,
    turn not away lest you fall.
You who fear the Lord, trust him,
    and your reward will not be lost.

You who fear the Lord, hope for good things,
   for lasting joy and mercy.
Study the generations long past and understand;
   has anyone hoped in the Lord and been disappointed?
Has anyone persevered in his fear and been forsaken?
   has anyone called upon him and been rebuffed?
Compassionate and merciful is the Lord;
   he forgives sins, he saves in time of trouble.

---

13   Sir 3, 17-24

A reading from the book of Sirach

My son, conduct your affairs with humility,
   and you will be loved more than a giver of gifts.
Humble yourself the more, the greater you are,
   and you will find favor with God.
For great is the power of God;
   by the humble he is glorified.
What is too sublime for you, seek not,
   into things beyond your strength search not.
What is committed to you, attend to;
   for what is hidden is not your concern.
With what is too much for you meddle not,
   when shown things beyond human understanding.
Their own opinion has misled many,
   and false reasoning unbalanced their judgment.
Where the pupil of the eye is missing, there is no light,
   and where there is no knowledge, there is no wisdom.

---

14   Sir 26, 1-4. 13-16

A reading from the book of Sirach

Happy the husband of a good wife,
   twice-lengthened are his days;
A worthy wife brings joy to her husband,
   peaceful and full is his life.
A good wife is a generous gift
   bestowed upon him who fears the Lord;
Be he rich or poor, his heart is content,
   and a smile is ever on his face.

A gracious wife delights her husband,
   her thoughtfulness puts flesh on his bones;
A gift from the Lord is her governed speech,
   and her firm virtue is of surpassing worth.
Choicest of blessings is a modest wife,
   priceless her chaste person.
Like the sun rising in the Lord's heavens,
   the beauty of a virtuous wife is the radiance of her home.

---

15   Is 58, 6-11

[For those who work for the underprivileged]

A reading from the book of the prophet Isaiah

Thus says the Lord:
This is the fasting that I wish:
   releasing those bound unjustly,
   untying the thongs of the yoke;
Setting free the oppressed,
   breaking every yoke;
Sharing your bread with the hungry,
   sheltering the oppressed and the homeless;
Clothing the naked when you see them,
   and not turning your back on your own.

Then your light shall break forth like the dawn,
   and your wound shall quickly be healed;
Your vindication shall go before you,
   and the glory of the Lord shall be your rear guard.
Then you shall call, and the Lord will answer,
   you shall cry for help, and he will say: Here I am!
If you remove from your midst oppression,
   false accusation and malicious speech;
If you bestow your bread on the hungry
   and satisfy the afflicted;
Then light shall rise for you in darkness,
   and the gloom shall become for you like midday;
Then the Lord will guide you always
   and give you plenty even on the parched land.
He will renew your strength,
   and you shall be like a watered garden,
   like a spring whose water never fails.

16

Jer 20, 7-9

A reading from the book of the prophet Jeremiah

You duped me, O Lord, and I let myself be duped;
  you were too strong for me, and you triumphed.
All the day I am an object of laughter;
  everyone mocks me.
Whenever I speak, I must cry out,
  violence and outrage is my message;
The word of the Lord has brought me
  derision and reproach all the day.
I say to myself, I will not mention him,
  I will speak in his name no more.
But then it becomes like fire burning in my heart,
  imprisoned in my bones;
I grow weary holding it in,
  I cannot endure it.

17

Mi 6, 6-8

A reading from the book of the prophet Micah

With what shall I come before the Lord,
  and bow before God most high?
Shall I come before him with holocausts,
  with calves a year old?
Will the Lord be pleased with thousands of rams,
  with myriad streams of oil?

Shall I give my first-born for my crime,
  the fruit of my body for the sin of my soul?
You have been told, O man, what is good,
  and what the Lord requires of you:
Only to do the right and to love goodness,
  and to walk humbly with your God.

18

Zep 2, 3; 3, 12-13

A reading from the book of the prophet Zephaniah

Seek the Lord, all you humble of the earth,
  who have observed his law;

Seek justice, seek humility;
  perhaps you may be sheltered
    on the day of the Lord's anger.
But I will leave as a remnant in your midst
  a people humble and lowly,
Who shall take refuge in the name of the Lord:
  the remnant of Israel.
They shall do no wrong
  and speak no lies;
Nor shall there be found in their mouths
  a deceitful tongue;
They shall pasture and couch their flocks
  with none to disturb them.

READING I

IN THE EASTER SEASON

1   Acts 4, 32-35

[For religious]

A reading from the Acts of the Apostles

The community of believers were of one heart and one mind. None of them ever claimed anything as his own; rather, everything was held in common. With power the apostles bore witness to the resurrection of the Lord Jesus, and great respect was paid to them all; nor was there anyone needy among them, for all who owned property or houses sold them and donated the proceeds. They used to lay them at the feet of the apostles to be distributed to everyone according to his need.

---

2   Rv 3, 14. 20-22

A reading from the book of Revelation

The Amen, the faithful Witness and true, the Source of God's creation, has this to say: "Here I stand, knocking at the door. If anyone hears me calling and opens the door,

I will enter his house and have supper with him, and he with me. I will give the victor the right to sit with me on my throne, as I myself won the victory and took my seat beside my Father on his throne.

"Let him who has ears to hear heed the Spirit's word to the churches."

---

3   Rv 19, 1. 5-9

A reading from the book of Revelation

I, John, heard what sounded like the loud song of a great assembly in heaven. They were singing:
   "Alleluia!
   Salvation, glory, and might belong to our God."
A voice coming from the throne cried out:
   "Praise our God, all you his servants,
   the small and the great, who revere him!"
Then I heard what sounded like the shouts of a great crowd, or the roaring of the deep, or mighty peals of thunder, as they cried:
   "Alleluia!
   The Lord is king,
   our God, the Almighty!
   Let us rejoice and be glad,
   and give him glory!
   For this is the wedding day of the Lamb,
   his bride has prepared herself for the wedding.
   She has been given a dress to wear
   made of finest linen, brilliant white."
(The linen dress is the virtuous deeds of God's saints.)
   The angel then said to me: "Write this down: Happy are they who have been invited to the wedding feast of the Lamb."

---

4   Rv 21, 5-7

A reading from the book of Revelation

The One who sat on the throne said to me, "See, I make all things new!" Then he said, "Write these matters down, for the words are trustworthy and true!" He went on to say: "These words are already fulfilled! I am the Alpha and the Omega, the Beginning and the End. To anyone who thirsts I will give drink without cost from the spring of life-giving water. He who wins the victory shall inherit these gifts; I will be his God and he shall be my son."

RESPONSORIAL PSALM

1   Ps 1, 1-2. 3. 4. 6

R̶. (Ps 40, 5) **Happy are they who hope in the Lord.**
Happy the man who follows not
   the counsel of the wicked
Nor walks in the way of sinners,
   nor sits in the company of the insolent,
But delights in the law of the Lord.
   and meditates on his law day and night.
R̶. **Happy are they who hope in the Lord.**
He is like a tree
   planted near running water,
That yields its fruit in due season,
   and whose leaves never fade.
   [Whatever he does, prospers.]
R̶. **Happy are they who hope in the Lord.**
Not so the wicked, not so;
   they are like chaff which the wind drives away.
For the Lord watches over the way of the just,
   but the way of the wicked vanishes.
R̶. **Happy are they who hope in the Lord.**
R̶. Or: (Ps 92, 13-14) **The just man will flourish like a palm tree**
  in the garden of the Lord.

---

2   Ps 15, 2-3. 3-4. 5

R̶. (1) **He who does justice shall live on the Lord's holy mountain.**
He who walks blamelessly and does justice;
   who thinks the truth in his heart
   and slanders not with his tongue;
R̶. **He who does justice shall live on the Lord's holy mountain.**

Who harms not his fellow man,
   nor takes up a reproach against his neighbor,
By whom the reprobate is despised,
   while he honors those who fear the Lord.
℟. **He who does justice shall live on the Lord's holy
    mountain.**
Who lends not his money at usury
   and accepts no bribe against the innocent.
He who does these things
   shall never be disturbed.
℟. **He who does justice shall live on the Lord's holy
    mountain.**

---

3   Ps 16, 1-2. 5. 7-8. 11

℟. (5) **You are my inheritance, O Lord.**
Keep me, O God, for in you I take refuge;
   I say to the Lord, "My Lord are you."
O Lord, my allotted portion and my cup,
   you it is who hold fast my lot.
℟. **You are my inheritance, O Lord.**
I bless the Lord who counsels me;
   even in the night my heart exhorts me.
I set the Lord ever before me;
   with him at my right hand I shall not be disturbed.
℟. **You are my inheritance, O Lord.**
You will show me the path to life,
   fullness of joys in your presence,
   the delights at your right hand forever.
℟. **You are my inheritance, O Lord.**

---

4   Ps 34, 2-3. 4-5. 6-7. 8-9. 10-11

℟. (2) **I will bless the Lord at all times.**
I will bless the Lord at all times;
   his praise shall be ever in my mouth.
Let my soul glory in the Lord;
   the lowly will hear me and be glad.
℟. **I will bless the Lord at all times.**
Glorify the Lord with me,
   let us together extol his name.

I sought the Lord, and he answered me
  and delivered me from all my fears.
℟. **I will bless the Lord at all times.**
Look to him that you may be radiant with joy,
  and your faces may not blush with shame.
When the afflicted man called out, the Lord heard,
  and from all his distress he saved him.
℟. **I will bless the Lord at all times.**
The angel of the Lord encamps
  around those who fear him, and delivers them.
Taste and see how good the Lord is;
  happy the man who takes refuge in him.
℟. **I will bless the Lord at all times.**
Fear the Lord, you his holy ones,
  for nought is lacking to those who fear him.
The great grow poor and hungry;
  but those who seek the Lord want for no good thing.
℟. **I will bless the Lord at all times.**
℟. Or: (9) **Taste and see the goodness of the Lord.**

---

5   Ps 103, 1-2. 3-4. 8-9. 13-14. 17-18

℟. (1) **Oh, bless the Lord, my soul.**
Bless the Lord, O my soul;
  and all my being, bless his holy name.
Bless the Lord, O my soul;
  and forget not all his benefits.
℟. **Oh, bless the Lord, my soul.**
He pardons all your iniquities,
  he heals all your ills.
He redeems your life from destruction,
  he crowns you with kindness and compassion.
℟. **Oh, bless the Lord, my soul.**
Merciful and gracious is the Lord,
  slow to anger and abounding in kindness.
He will not always chide,
  nor does he keep his wrath forever.
℟. **Oh, bless the Lord, my soul.**
As a father has compassion on his children,
  so the Lord has compassion on those who fear him,
For he knows how we are formed;
  he remembers that we are dust.

℞. **Oh, bless the Lord, my soul.**
But the kindness of the Lord is from eternity
  to eternity toward those who fear him,
And his justice toward children's children
  among those who keep his covenant.
℞. **Oh, bless the Lord, my soul.**

——————

6   Ps 112, 1-2. 3-4. 5-6. 7-8. 9

℞. (1) **Happy the man who fears the Lord.**
Happy the man who fears the Lord,
  who greatly delights in his commands.
His posterity shall be mighty upon the earth;
  the upright generation shall be blessed.
℞. **Happy the man who fears the Lord.**
Wealth and riches shall be in his house;
  his generosity shall endure forever.
He dawns through the darkness, a light for the upright;
  he is gracious and merciful and just.
℞. **Happy the man who fears the Lord.**
Well for the man who is gracious and lends,
  who conducts his affairs with justice;
He shall never be moved;
  the just man shall be in everlasting remembrance.
℞. **Happy the man who fears the Lord.**
An evil report he shall not fear;
  his heart is firm, trusting in the Lord.
His heart is steadfast; he shall not fear
  Till he looks down upon his foes.
℞. **Happy the man who fears the Lord.**
Lavishly he gives to the poor;
  his generosity shall endure forever;
  his horn shall be exalted in glory.
℞. **Happy the man who fears the Lord.**
℞. Or: **Alleluia.**   ——————

7   Ps 128, 1-2. 3. 4-5

℞. (1) **Happy are those who fear the Lord.**
Happy are you who fear the Lord,
  who walk in his ways!
For you shall eat the fruit of your handiwork;
  happy shall you be, and favored.

℞. **Happy are those who fear the Lord.**
Your wife shall be like a fruitful vine
 in the recesses of your home;
Your children like olive plants
 around your table.
℞. **Happy are those who fear the Lord.**
Behold, thus is the man blessed
 who fears the Lord.
The Lord bless you from Zion:
 may you see the prosperity of Jerusalem
 all the days of your life.
℞. **Happy are those who fear the Lord.**

───────────

8   Ps 131, 1. 2. 3

℞. **In you, Lord, I have found my peace.**
O Lord, my heart is not proud,
 nor are my eyes haughty;
I busy not myself with great things,
 nor with things too sublime for me.
℞. **In you, Lord, I have found my peace.**
Nay rather, I have stilled and quieted
 my soul like a weaned child.
Like a weaned child on its mother's lap,
 [so is my soul within me.]
℞. **In you, Lord, I have found my peace.**
O Israel, hope in the Lord,
 both now and forever.
℞. **In you, Lord, I have found my peace.**

───────────

READING II

1   Rom 8, 26-30

A reading from the letter of Paul to the Romans
The Spirit too helps us in our weakness, for we do not
know how to pray as we ought; but the Spirit himself
makes intercession for us with groanings which cannot
be expressed in speech. He who searches hearts knows
what the Spirit means, for the Spirit intercedes for the
saints as God himself wills.

We know that God makes all things work together for the good of those who have been called according to his decree. Those whom he foreknew he predestined to share the image of his Son, that the Son might be the first-born of many brothers. Those he predestined he likewise called; those he called he also justified; and those he justified he in turn glorified.

---

2   1 Cor 1, 26-31

A reading from the first letter of Paul to the Corinthians

Brothers, you are among those called. Consider your own situation. Not many of you are wise, as men account wisdom; not many are influential; and surely not many are well-born. God chose these whom the world considers absurd to shame the wise; he singled out the weak of this world to shame the strong. He chose the world's low-born and despised, those who count for nothing, to reduce to nothing those who were something; so that mankind can do no boasting before God. God it is who has given you life in Christ Jesus. He has made him our wisdom and also our justice, our sanctification, and our redemption. This is just as you find it written, "Let him who would boast, boast in the Lord."

---

3   1 Cor 12, 31— 13, 13 or 13, 4-13

[If the "Short Form" is used, the indented text in brackets is omitted.]

A reading from the first letter of Paul to the Corinthians

[Set your hearts on the greater gifts.

Now I will show you the way which surpasses all the others. If I speak with human tongues and angelic as well, but not have love, I am a noisy gong, a clanging cymbal. If I have the gift of prophecy and, with full knowledge, comprehend all mysteries, if I have faith great enough to move mountains, but have not love, I am nothing. If I give everything I have to feed the poor and hand over my body to be burned, but have not love, I gain nothing.]

Love is patient; love is kind. Love is not jealous, it does not put on airs, it is not snobbish. Love is never rude, it is not self-seeking, it is not prone to anger; neither does it brood over injuries. Love does not rejoice in what is wrong but rejoices with the truth. There is no limit to love's forbearance, to its trust, its hope, its power to endure.

Love never fails. Prophecies will cease, tongues will be silent, knowledge will pass away. Our knowledge is imperfect and our prophesying is imperfect. When the perfect comes, the imperfect will pass away. When I was a child I used to talk like a child, think like a child, reason like a child. When I became a man I put childish ways aside. Now we see indistinctly, as in a miror; then we shall see face to face. My knowledge is imperfect now; then I shall know even as I am known. These are in the end three things that last: faith, hope, and love, and the greatest of these is love.

---

4   2 Cor 10, 17—11, 2

A reading from the second letter of Paul to the Corinthians
"Let him who would boast, boast in the Lord." It is not the man who recommends himself who is approved but the man whom the Lord recommends.

You must endure a little of my folly. Put up with me, I beg you! I am jealous of you with the jealousy of God himself, since I have given you in marriage to one husband, presenting you as a chaste virgin to Christ.

---

5   Gal 2, 19-20

A reading from the letter of Paul to the Galatians
It was through the law that I died to the law, to live for God. I have been crucified with Christ, and the life I live now is not my own; Christ is living in me. I still live my human life, but it is a life of faith in the Son of God, who loved me and gave himself for me.

6

Gal 6, 14-16

A reading from the letter of Paul to the Galatians

May I never boast of anything but the cross of our Lord Jesus Christ! Through it, the world has been crucified to me and I to the world. It means nothing whether one is circumcised or not. All that matters is that one is created anew. Peace and mercy on all who follow this rule of life, and on the Israel of God.

7

Eph 3, 14-19

A reading from the letter of Paul to the Ephesians

I kneel before the Father from whom every family in heaven and on earth takes its name; and I pray that he will bestow on you gifts in keeping with the riches of his glory. May he strengthen you inwardly through the working of his Spirit. May Christ dwell in your hearts through faith, and may charity be the root and foundation of your life. Thus you will be able to grasp fully, with all the holy ones, the breadth and length and height and depth of Christ's love, and experience this love which surpasses all knowledge, so that you may attain to the fullness of God himself.

8

Eph 6, 10-13. 18

A reading from the letter of Paul to the Ephesians

Draw your strength from the Lord and his mighty power. Put on the armor of God so that you may be able to stand firm against the tactics of the devil. Our battle ultimately is not against human forces but against the principalities and powers, the rulers of this world of darkness, the evil spirits in regions above. You must put on the armor of God if you are to resist on the evil day; do all that your duty requires, and hold your ground.

At every opportunity pray in the Spirit, using prayers and petitions of every sort. Pray constantly and attentively for all in the holy company.

---

9   Phil 3, 8-14

A reading from the letter of Paul to the Philippians

I have come to rate all as loss in the light of the surpassing knowledge of my Lord Jesus Christ. For his sake
I have forfeited everything; I have accounted all else
rubbish so that Christ may be my wealth and I may be
in him, not having any justice of my own based on observance of the law. The justice I possess is that which
comes through faith in Christ. It has its origin in God
and is based on faith. I wish to know Christ and the power
flowing from his resurrection; likewise to know how to
share in his sufferings by being formed into the pattern
of his death. Thus do I hope that I may arrive at resurrection from the dead.

It is not that I have reached it yet, or have already
finished my course; but I am racing to grasp the prize if
possible, since I have been grasped by Christ [Jesus].
Brothers, I do not think of myself as having reached the
finish line. I give no thought to what lies behind but push
on to what is ahead. My entire attention is on the finish
line as I run toward the prize to which God calls me —
life on high in Christ Jesus.

———

10   Phil 4, 4-9

A reading from the letter of Paul to the Philippians

Rejoice in the Lord always! I say it again. Rejoice! Everyone should see how unselfish you are. The Lord himself
is near. Dismiss all anxiety from your minds. Present your
needs to God in every form of prayer and in petitions full
of gratitude. Then God's own peace, which is beyond all
understanding, will stand guard over your hearts and
minds, in Christ Jesus.

Finally, my brothers, your thoughts should be wholly
directed to all that is true, all that deserves respect, all
that is honest, pure, admirable, decent, virtuous, or worthy
of praise. Live according to what you have learned and
accepted, what you have heard me say and seen me do.
Then will the God of peace be with you.

———

11   1 Tm 5, 3-10

[For widows]

A reading from the first letter of Paul to Timothy

Honor the claims of widows who are real widows — that is, who are alone and bereft. If a widow has any children or grandchildren, let these learn that piety begins at home and that they should fittingly support their parents and grandparents; this is the way God wants it to be. The real widow, left destitute, is one who has set her hope on God and continues night and day in supplications and prayers. A widow who gives herself up to selfish indulgence, however, leads a life of living death.

Make the following rules about widows, so that no one may incur blame. If anyone does not provide for his own relatives and especially for members of his immediate family, he has denied the faith; he is worse than an unbeliever. To be on the church's roll of widows, a widow should be not less than sixty years of age. She must have been married only once. Her good character will be attested to by her good deeds. Has she brought up children? Has she been hospitable to strangers? Has she washed the feet of Christian visitors? Has she given help to those in distress? In a word, has she been eager to do every possible good work?

---

12   Jas 2, 14-17

A reading from the letter of James

My brothers, what good is it to profess faith without practicing it? Such faith has no power to save one, has it? If a brother or sister has nothing to wear and no food for the day, and you say to them, "Good-bye and good luck! Keep warm and well fed," but do not meet their bodily needs, what good is that? So it is with the faith that does nothing in practice. It is thoroughly lifeless.

---

13   1 Pt 3, 1-9

A reading from the first letter of Peter

You married women must obey your husbands, so that any of them who do not believe in the word of the gospel may be won over apart from preaching, through their wives' conduct. They have only to observe the reverent purity of your way of life. The affectation of an elaborate hairdress, the wearing of golden jewelry, or the donning of rich robes is not for you. Your adornment is rather the hidden character of the heart, expressed in the unfading beauty of a calm and gentle disposition. This is precious in God's eyes. The holy women of past ages used to adorn themselves in this way, reliant on God and obedient to their husbands — for example, Sarah, who was subject to Abraham and called him her master. You are her children when you do what is right and let no fears alarm you.

You husbands, too, must show consideration for those who share your lives. Treat women with respect as the weaker sex, heirs just as much as you to the gracious gift of life. If you do so, nothing will keep your prayers from being answered.

In summary, then, all of you should be like-minded, sympathetic, loving toward one another, kindly disposed, and humble. Do not return evil for evil or insult for insult. Return a blessing instead. This you have been called to do, that you may receive a blessing as your inheritance.

---

14   1 Pt 4, 7-11

A reading from the first letter of Peter

Remain calm so that you will be able to pray. Above all, let your love for one another be constant, for love covers a multitude of sins. Be mutually hospitable without complaining. As generous distributors of God's manifold grace, put your gifts at the service of one another, each in the measure he has received. The one who speaks is to deliver God's message. The one who serves is to do it with the strength provided by God. Thus, in all of you God is to

be glorified through Jesus Christ: to him be glory and
dominion throughout the ages. Amen.

---

15   1 Jn 3, 14-28

[For those who work for the underprivileged]

A reading from the first letter of John

That we have passed from death to life we know
because we love the brothers.
The man who does not love is among the living dead.
Anyone who hates his brother is a murderer,
and you know that eternal life
abides in no murderer's heart.
The way we came to understand love
was that he laid down his life for us;
we too must lay down our lives for our brothers.
I ask you, how can God's love survive in a man
who has enough of this world's goods
yet closes his heart to his brother
when he sees him in need?
Little children,
let us love in deed
and not merely talk about it.

---

16   1 Jn 4, 7-16

A reading from the first letter of John

Beloved,
let us love one another
because love is of God;
everyone who loves is begotten of God
and has knowledge of God.
The man without love has known nothing of God,
for God is love.
God's love was revealed in our midst in this way:
he sent his only Son to the world
that we might have life through him.
Love, then, consists in this:

not that we have loved God
but that he has loved us
and has sent his Son as an offering for our sins.
Beloved,
if God has loved us so,
we must have the same love for one another.
No one has ever seen God.
Yet if we love one another
God dwells in us,
and his love is brought to perfection in us.
The way we know we remain in him
and he in us
is that he has given us of his Spirit.
We have seen for ourselves, and can testify,
that the Father has sent the Son as savior of the
world.
When anyone acknowledges that Jesus is the Son
of God,
God dwells in him
and he in God
We have come to know and to believe in
the love God has for us.
God is love,
and he who abides in love
abides in God,
and God in him.

---

17   **1 Jn 5, 1-5**

A reading from the first letter of John
Everyone who believes that Jesus is the Christ
has been begotten of God.
Now, everyone who loves the father
loves the child he has begotten.
We can be sure that we love God's children
when we love God
and do what he has commanded.
The love of God consists in this:
that we keep his commandments—
and his commandments are not burdensome.
Everyone begotten of God conquers the world,

and the power that has conquered the world
is this faith of ours.
Who, then, is conqueror of the world?
The one who believes that Jesus is the Son of God.

ALLELUIA VERSE AND

VERSE BEFORE THE GOSPEL

1   Mt 5, 3

Happy the poor in spirit;
the kingdom of heaven is theirs!

2   Mt 5, 6

Happy those who hunger and thirst for what is right;
they shall be satisfied.

3   Mt 5, 8

Happy are the pure of heart, for they shall see God.

4   Mt 11, 25

Blessed are you, Father, Lord of heaven and earth;
you have revealed to little ones the mysteries of the
   kingdom.

5   Mt 11, 28

Come to me, all you that labor and are burdened,
and I will give you rest, says the Lord.

6   Jn 8, 12

I am the light of the world, says the Lord;
the man who follows me will have the light of life.

7   Jn 8, 31-32

If you stay in my word, you will indeed be my disciples,
and you will know the truth, says the Lord.

8   Jn 13, 34

I give you a new commandment:
love one another as I have loved you.

9   Jn 14, 23

If anyone loves me, he will hold to my words,
and my Father will love him, and we will come to him.

10   Jn 15, 4-5

Live in me and let me live in you, says the Lord;
my branches bear much fruit.

GOSPEL

1   Mt 5, 1-12

✠ A reading from the holy gospel according to Matthew

When Jesus saw the crowds he went up on the mountainside. After he had sat down his disciples gathered around him, and he began to teach them:

"How blest are the poor in spirit: the reign of God is theirs.
Blest too are the sorrowing; they shall be consoled.
[Blest are the lowly; they shall inherit the land.]
Blest are they who hunger and thirst for holiness; they shall have their fill.
Blest are they who show mercy; mercy shall be theirs.
Blest are the single-hearted for they shall see God.
Blest too the peacemakers; they shall be called sons of God.
Blest are those persecuted for holiness' sake; the reign of God is theirs.
Blest are you when they insult you and persecute you and utter every kind of slander against you because of me.
Be glad and rejoice, for your reward in heaven is great."

---

2   Mt 5, 13-16

✠ A reading from the holy gospel according to Matthew

Jesus said to his disciples: "You are the salt of the earth. But what if salt goes flat? How can you restore its flavor?

Then it is good for nothing but to be thrown out and trampled underfoot.

"You are the light of the world. A city set on a hill cannot be hidden. Men do not light a lamp and then put it under a bushel basket. They set it on a stand where it gives light to all in the house. In the same way, your light must shine before men so that they may see goodness in your acts and give praise to your heavenly Father."

---

3 Mt 11, 25-30

✠ A reading from the holy gospel according to Matthew

On one occasion Jesus said: "Father, Lord of heaven and earth, to you I offer praise; for what you have hidden from the learned and the clever you have revealed to the merest children. Father, it is true. You have graciously willed it so. Everything has been given over to me by my Father. No one knows the Son but the Father, and no one knows the Father but the Son—and anyone to whom the Son wishes to reveal him.

"Come to me, all you who are weary and find life burdensome, and I will refresh you. Take my yoke upon your shoulders and learn from me, for I am gentle and humble of heart. Your souls will find rest, for my yoke is easy and my burden light."

---

4 Mt 13, 44-46

✠ A reading from the holy gospel according to Matthew

Jesus said to the crowds: "The reign of God is like buried treasure which a man found in a field. He hid it again, and rejoicing at his find went and sold all he had and bought that field. Or again, the kingdom of heaven is like a merchant's search for fine pearls. When he found one really valuable pearl, he went back and put up for sale all that he had and bought it."

5
                                                    Mt 16, 24-27

✠ A reading from the holy gospel according to Matthew
Jesus said to his disciples: "If a man wishes to come after
me, he must deny his very self, take up his cross, and begin
to follow in my footsteps. Whoever would save his life
will lose it, but whoever loses his life for my sake will
find it. What profit would a man show if he were to gain
the whole world and ruin himself in the process? What
can a man offer in exchange for his very self? The Son
of Man will come with his Father's glory accompanied
by his angels. When he does, he will repay each man
according to his conduct."

———————————

6
                                                    Mt 18, 1-4

✠ A reading from the holy gospel according to Matthew
The disciples came up to Jesus with the question, "Who
is of greatest importance in the kingdom of God?" He
called a little child over and stood him in their midst and
said: "I assure you, unless you change and become like
little children, you will not enter the kingdom of God.
Whoever makes himself lowly, becoming like this child,
is of greatest importance in that heavenly reign."

———————————

7
                                                    Mt 19, 3-12

[For religious]

✠ A reading from the holy gospel according to Matthew
Some Pharisees came up to Jesus and said, to test him,
"May a man divorce his wife for any reason whatever?"
He replied, "Have you not read that at the beginning the
Creator made them male and female and declared, 'For
this reason a man shall leave his father and mother and
cling to his wife, and the two shall become as one'? Thus
they are no longer two but one flesh. Therefore, let no
man separate what God has joined." They said to him,
"Then why did Moses command divorce and the promulgation of a divorce decree?" "Because of your stubbornness

Moses let you divorce your wives," he replied; "but at the beginning it was not that way. I now say to you, whoever divorces his wife (lewd conduct is a separate case) and marries another commits adultery, and the man who marries a divorced woman commits adultery."

His disciples said to him, "If that is the case between man and wife, it is better not to marry." He said, "Not everyone can accept this teaching, only those to whom it is given to do so. Some men are incapable of sexual activity from birth; some have been deliberately made so; and some there are who have freely renounced sex for the sake of God's reign. Let him accept this teaching who can."

------

8 Mt 25, 1-13

✠ A reading from the holy gospel according to Matthew
Jesus told this parable to his disciples: "The reign of God can be likened to ten bridesmaids who took their torches and went out to welcome the groom. Five of them were foolish, while the other five were sensible. The foolish ones, in taking their torches, brought no oil along, but the sensible ones took flasks of oil as well as their torches. The groom delayed his coming, so they all began to nod, then to fall asleep. At midnight someone shouted, 'The groom is here! Come out and greet him!' At the outcry all the virgins woke up and got their torches ready. The foolish ones said to the sensible, 'Give us some of your oil. Our torches are going out.' But the sensible ones replied, 'No, there may not be enough for you and us. You had better go to the dealers and buy yourselves some.' While they went off to buy it the groom arrived, and the ones who were ready went in to the wedding with him. Then the door was barred. Later the other bridesmaids came back. 'Master, master!' they cried. 'Open the door for us.' But he answered, 'I tell you, I do not know you.' The moral is: keep your eyes open, for you know not the day or the hour."

------

9   Mt 25, 14-30 or 25, 14-23

[If the "Short Form" is used, the indented text in brackets is omitted.]

✠ A reading from the holy gospel according to Matthew

Jesus told his disciples this parable: "It is the case of a man who was going on a journey. He called in his servants and handed his funds over to them according to each man's abilities. To one he disbursed five thousand silver pieces, to a second two thousand, and to a third a thousand. Then he went away. Immediately the man who received the five thousand went to invest it and made another five. In the same way, the man who received the two thousand doubled his figure. The man who received the thousand went off instead and dug a hole in the ground, where he buried his master's money. After a long absence, the master of those servants came home and settled accounts with them. The man who had received the five thousand came forward bringing the additional five. 'My lord,' he said, 'you let me have five thousand. See, I have made five thousand more.' His master said to him, 'Well done! You are an industrious and reliable servant. Since you were dependable in a small matter I will put you in charge of larger affairs. Come, share your master's joy!' The man who had received the two thousand then stepped forward. 'My lord,' he said, 'you entrusted me with two thousand and I have made two thousand more.' His master said to him, 'Cleverly done! You too are an industrious and reliable servant. Since you were dependable in a small matter I will put you in charge of larger affairs. Come, share your master's joy!'

["Finally the man who had received the thousand stepped forward. 'My lord,' he said, 'I knew you were a hard man. You reap where you did not sow and gather where you did not scatter, so out of fear I went off and buried your thousand silver pieces in the ground. Here is your money back.' His master exclaimed: 'You worthless, lazy lout! You know I reap where I did not sow and gather where I did not scatter. All the more reason to deposit my money with the bankers, so that on my return I could have had it back with interest. You, there! Take the thousand away from him and give it to the man with the ten thousand. Those who have, will get more until they grow rich, while those who have not, will lose even the little they have. Throw this worthless servant into the darkness outside, where he can wail and grind his teeth.' "]

---

10   Mt 25, 31-46 or 25, 31-40

[**For those who work for the underprivileged**]

[If the "Short Form" is used, the indented text in brackets is omitted.]

✠ A reading from the holy gospel according to Matthew
Jesus said to his disciples: "When the Son of Man comes in his glory, escorted by all the angels of heaven, he will sit upon his royal throne, and all the nations will be assembled before him. Then he will separate them into two groups, as a shepherd separates sheep from goats. The sheep he will place on his right hand, the goats on his left. The king will say to those on his right: 'Come. You have my Father's blessing! Inherit the kingdom prepared for you from the creation of the world. For I was hungry and you gave me food, I was thirsty and you gave me drink. I was a stranger and you welcomed me, naked and you clothed me. I was ill and you comforted me, in prison and you came to visit me.' Then the just will ask him: 'Lord, when did we see you hungry and feed you or see you thirsty and give you drink? When did we welcome you away from home or clothe you in your nakedness? When did we visit you when you were ill or in prison?' The king will answer them: 'I assure you, as often as you did it for one of my least brothers, you did it for me.'

["Then he will say to those on his left: 'Out of
my sight, you condemned, into that everlasting fire
prepared for the devil and his angels! I was hungry
and you gave me no food, I was thirsty and you

gave me no drink. I was away from home and you gave me no welcome, naked and you gave me no clothing. I was ill and in prison and you did not come to comfort me.' Then they in turn will ask: 'Lord, when did we see you hungry or thirsty or away from home or naked or ill or in prison and not attend you in your needs?' He will answer them: 'I assure you, as often as you neglected to do it to one of these least ones, you neglected to do it to me.' These will go off to eternal punishment and the just to eternal life."]

---

11 Mk 3, 31-35

✠ A reading from the holy gospel according to Mark

The mother of Jesus and his brothers arrived, and as they stood outside [the house] they sent word to Jesus to come out. The crowd seated around him told him, "Your mother and your brothers and sisters are outside asking for you." He said in reply, "Who are my mother and my brothers?" And gazing around him at those seated in the circle he continued, "These are my mother and my brothers. Whoever does the will of God is brother and sister and mother to me."

---

12 Mk 9, 34-37

[For teachers]

✠ A reading from the holy gospel according to Mark

The disciples of Jesus had been arguing along the way about who was the most important. So he sat down and called the Twelve around him and said, "If anyone wishes to rank first, he must remain the last one of all and the servant of all." Then he took a little child, stood him in their midst, and putting his arms around him, said to them, "Whoever welcomes a child such as this for my sake welcomes me. And whoever welcomes me welcomes, not me, but him who sent me."

---

13 Mk 10, 13-16

[For teachers]

✠ A reading from the holy gospel according to Mark

People were bringing their little children to Jesus to have him touch them, but the disciples were scolding them for this. Jesus became indignant when he noticed it and said to them: "Let the children come to me and do not hinder them. It is to just such as these that the kingdom of God belongs. I assure you that whoever does not accept the kingdom of God like a little child shall not enter into it." Then he embraced them and blessed them, placing his hands on them.

---

14 Mk 10, 17-30 or 10, 17-27

[If the "Short Form" is used, the indented text in brackets is omitted.]

[For religious]

✠ A reading from the holy gospel according to Mark

As Jesus was setting out on a journey a man came running up, knelt down before him and asked, "Good Teacher, what must I do to share in everlasting life?" Jesus answered, "Why do you call me good? No one is good but God alone. You know the commandments:

'You shall not kill;
You shall not commit adultery;
You shall not steal;
You shall not bear false witness;
You shall not defraud;
Honor your father and your mother.' "

He replied, "Teacher, I have kept all these since my child-hood." Then Jesus looked at him with love and told him, "There is one thing more you must do. Go and sell what you have and give to the poor; you will then have treasure in heaven. After that come and follow me." At these words the man's face fell. He went away sad, for he had many possessions. Jesus looked around and said to his disciples, "How hard it is for the rich to enter the kingdom of God!" The disciples could only marvel at his words. So Jesus re-peated what he had said: "My sons, how hard it is to enter the kingdom of God! It is easier for a camel to pass through a needle's eye than for a rich man to enter the kingdom of God."

They were completely overwhelmed at this, and ex-claimed to one another, "Then who can be saved?" Jesus fixed his gaze on them and said, "For man it is impossible but not for God. With God all things are possible."

[Peter was moved to say to him: "We have put aside everything to follow you!" Jesus answered: "I give you my word, there is no one who has given up home, brothers or sisters, mother or father, children or property, for me and for the gospel who will not receive in this present age a hundred times as many homes, brothers and sisters, mothers, children and property—and persecution besides—and in the age to come, everlasting life."]

———

15 Lk 9, 57-62

[For religious]

✠ A reading from the holy gospel according to Luke

As Jesus and his disciples were making their way along, someone said to him, "I will be your follower wherever you go." Jesus said to him, "The foxes have lairs, the birds of the sky have nests, but the Son of Man has nowhere to lay his head." To another he said, "Come after me." The man replied, "Let me bury my father first." Jesus said to him, "Let the dead bury their dead; come away and proclaim the kingdom of God." Yet another said to him, "I will be your follower, Lord, but first let me take leave of my people at home." Jesus answered him, "Whoever puts his hand to the plow but keeps looking back is unfit for the reign of God."

---

16   Lk 10, 38-42

✠ A reading from the holy gospel according to Mark

Jesus entered a village where a woman named Martha welcomed him to her home. She had a sister named Mary, who seated herself at the Lord's feet and listened to his words. Martha, who was busy with all the details of hospitality, came to him and said, "Lord, are you not concerned that my sister has left me all alone to do the household tasks? Tell her to help me."

The Lord in reply said to her: "Martha, Martha, you are anxious and upset about many things; one thing only is required. Mary has chosen the better portion and she shall not be deprived of it."

---

17   Lk 12, 32-34

[For religious]

✠ A reading from the holy gospel according to Luke

Jesus said to his disciples: "Do not live in fear, little flock. It has pleased your Father to give you the kingdom. Sell what you have and give alms. Get purses for yourselves that do not wear out, a never-failing treasure with the Lord which no thief comes near nor any moth destroys. Wherever your treasure lies, there your heart will be."

---

18 Lk 12, 35-40

✠ A reading from the holy gospel according to Luke

Jesus said to his disciples: "Let your belts be fastened around your waists and your lamps be burning ready. Be like men awaiting their master's return from a wedding, so that when he arrives and knocks, you will open for him without delay. It will go well with those servants whom the master finds wide-awake on his return. I tell you, he will put on an apron, seat them at table, and proceed to wait on them. Should he happen to come at midnight or before sunrise and find them prepared, it will go well with them. You know as well as I that if the head of the house knew when the thief was coming he would not let him break into his house. Be on guard, therefore. The Son of Man will come when you least expect him."

---

19 Lk 14, 25-33

[For religious]

✠ A reading from the holy gospel according to Luke

On one occasion when a great crowd was with Jesus, he turned to them and said, "If anyone comes to me without turning his back on his father and mother, his wife and his children, his brothers and sisters, indeed his very self, he cannot be my follower. Anyone who does not take up his cross and follow me cannot be my disciple. If one of you decides to build a tower, will he not first sit down and calculate the outlay to see if he has enough money to complete the project? He will do that for fear of laying the foundation and then not being able to complete the work; at which all who saw it would then jeer at him, saying, 'That man began to build what he could not finish.'

"Or if a king is about to march on another king to do battle with him, will he not sit down first and consider whether, with ten thousand men, he can withstand an enemy coming against him with twenty thousand? If he cannot, he will send a delegation while the enemy is still at a distance, asking for terms of peace. In the same way, none of you can be my disciple if he does not renounce all his possessions."

---

20   Jn 15, 1-8

✠ A reading from the holy gospel according to John

Jesus said to his disciples:

"I am the true vine
and my Father is the vinegrower.
He prunes away
every barren branch,
but the fruitful ones
he trims clean
to increase their yield.
You are clean already,
thanks to the word I have spoken to you.
Live on in me, as I do in you.
No more than a branch can bear fruit of itself
apart from the vine
can you bear fruit
apart from me.
I am the vine, you are the branches.
He who lives in me and I in him,
will produce abundantly,
for apart from me you can do nothing.

A man who does not live in me
is like a withered, rejected branch,
picked up to be thrown in the fire and burnt.
If you live in me,
and my words stay a part of you,
you may ask what you will—
it will be done for you.
My Father has been glorified
in your bearing much fruit
and becoming my disciples."

---

21   Jn 15, 9-17

✠ A reading from the holy gospel according to John
Jesus said to his disciples:
"As the Father has loved me,
so I have loved you.
Live on in my love.
You will live in my love
if you keep my commandments,
even as I have kept my Father's commandments,
and live in his love.
All this I tell you
that my joy may be yours
and your joy may be complete.
This is my commandment:
love one another
as I have loved you.
There is no greater love than this:
to lay down one's life for one's friends.
You are my friends
if you do what I command you.
I no longer speak of you as slaves,
for a slave does not know what his master is about.
Instead, I call you friends,
since I have made known to you all that I heard from
    my Father.
It was not you who chose me,
it was I who chose you
to go forth and to bear fruit.
Your fruit must endure
so that all you ask the Father in my name
he will give you.
The command I give you is this,
that you love one another."

———————

✠ A reading from the holy gospel according to John

Jesus looked up to heaven and prayed:

"Holy Father,

I do not pray for my disciples alone.

I pray also for those who will believe in me through
their word,

that all may be one

as you, Father, are in me, and I in you;

I pray that they may be [one] in us,

that the world may believe that you sent me.

I have given them the glory you gave me

that they may be one as we are one—

I living in them, you living in me—

that their unity may be complete.

So shall the world know that you sent me,

and that you loved them as you loved me.

"Father,

all those you gave me

I would have in my company

where I am,

to see this glory of mine

which is your gift to me,

because of the love you bore me before the world
began.

Just Father,

the world has not known you,

but I have known you;

and these men have known that you sent me.

To them I have revealed your name,

and I will continue to reveal it

so that your love for me may live in them,

and I may live in them."

———————

APPENDIX I
SELECTED MASSES AND PRAYERS

This section contains excerpts of selected Masses and Prayers that the celebrant may use on certain days of low rank. (See Tables of Choices of Masses and Texts, pp. [18]-[19].) For convenient reference the numbers attached to these Masses and Prayers in the Sacramentary have been retained. The complete series of Masses and Prayers (including the Readings) for Various Needs and Occasions, Votive Masses, and Masses for the Dead will be found in the last volume of this Weekday Missal. It is always preferable to use *weekday* Readings, as indicated herein.

MASSES AND PRAYERS FOR VARIOUS NEEDS AND OCCASIONS

On Weekdays of Ordinary Time and certain other occasions, the complete Mass formulary found in the Sacramentary (processional chants and presidential prayers) or only the Opening Prayer may be taken from the following Masses and Prayers for Various Needs and Occasions. (See Introduction to Proper of Saints, pp. 917ff and the Tables of Choices of Masses and Texts, pp. [18]-[19].)

1. FOR THE UNIVERSAL CHURCH

OPENING PRAYER

God our Father,
in your care and wisdom
you extend the kingdom of Christ to embrace the
　　world
to give all men redemption.
May the Catholic Church be the sign of our salvation,
may it reveal for us the mystery of your love,
and may that love become effective in our lives.
Grant this . . . for ever and ever. ℟. **Amen.**

PRAYER OVER THE GIFTS

God of mercy,
look on our offering,

and by the power of this sacrament
help all who believe in you
to become the holy people you have called to be
   your own.
We ask this in the name of Jesus the Lord. ℟. **Amen.**

PRAYER AFTER COMMUNION

God our Father,
we are sustained by your sacraments;
we are renewed by this pledge of love at your altar.
May we live by the promises of your love which we
   receive,
and become a leaven in the world
to bring salvation to mankind.
Grant this through Christ our Lord. ℟. **Amen.**

---

2. FOR THE POPE

OPENING PRAYER

Father of providence,
look with love on N. our Pope,
your appointed successor to St. Peter
on whom you built your Church.
May he be the visible center and foundation
of our unity in faith and love.
Grant this . . . for ever and ever. ℟. **Amen.**

PRAYER OVER THE GIFTS

Lord,
be pleased with our gifts
and give guidance to your holy Church
together with N. our Pope,
to whom you have entrusted the care of your flock.
We ask this in the name of Jesus the Lord. ℟. **Amen.**

PRAYER AFTER COMMUNION

God our Father,
we have eaten at your holy table.
By the power of this sacrament,

make your Church firm in unity and love,
and grant strength and salvation
to your servant N.,
together with the flock you have entrusted to his
care.
Grant this through Christ our Lord. ℟. **Amen.**

---

3. FOR THE BISHOP

OPENING PRAYER

God, eternal shepherd,
you tend your Church in many ways,
and rule us with love.
Help your chosen servant N.
as pastor for Christ,
to watch over your flock.
Help him to be a faithful teacher,
a wise administrator, and a holy priest.
We ask this . . . for ever and ever. ℟. **Amen.**

PRAYER OVER THE GIFTS

Lord,
accept these gifts which we offer for your servant
N., your chosen priest.
Enrich him with the gifts and virtues of a true apostle
for the good of your people.
We ask this through Christ our Lord. ℟. **Amen.**

PRAYER AFTER COMMUNION

Lord,
by the power of these holy mysteries
increase in our bishop N. your gifts of wisdom and
love.
May he fulfill his pastoral ministry
and receive the eternal rewards
you promise to your faithful servants.
Grant this through Christ our Lord. ℟. **Amen.**

---

4. ON THE ANNIVERSARY OF ORDINATION

OPENING PRAYER
Father,
unworthy as I am, you have chosen me
to share in the eternal priesthood of Christ
and the ministry of your Church.
May I be an ardent but gentle servant
of your gospel and your sacraments.
Grant this . . . for ever and ever. Ry. **Amen.**

PRAYER OVER THE GIFTS
Lord,
in your mercy, accept our offering
and help me to fulfill the ministry you have given me
in spite of my unworthiness.
Grant this through Christ our Lord. Ry. **Amen.**

PRAYER AFTER COMMUNION
Lord,
on this anniversary of my ordination
I have celebrated the mystery of faith
to the glory of your name.
May I always live in truth
the mysteries I handle at your altar.
Grant this in the name of Jesus the Lord. Ry. **Amen.**

---

9. FOR PRIESTLY VOCATIONS

ENTRANCE ANT. Mt 9, 38
Jesus says to his disciples: ask the Lord to send workers into his harvest. → No. 2, p. 614

OPENING PRAYER
Father,
in your plan for our salvation you provide shepherds
   for your people.
Fill your Church with the spirit of courage and love.
Raise up worthy ministers for your altars

and ardent but gentle servants of the gospel.
Grant this . . . for ever and ever. ℟. **Amen.**

READINGS AND INTERVENIENT CHANTS
The current weekday *readings and intervenient chants
are used.*

PRAYER OVER THE GIFTS
Lord,
accept our prayers and gifts.
Give the Church more priests
and keep them faithful in their love and service.
Grant this in the name of Jesus the Lord.
℟. **Amen.**   ➔ No. 21, p. 626

COMMUNION ANT.   1 Jn 3, 16
**This is how we know what love is: Christ gave up his
life for us; and we too must give up our lives for our
brothers.** ✛

PRAYER AFTER COMMUNION
Lord,
hear the prayers of those who are renewed
with the bread of life at your holy table.
By this sacrament of love
bring to maturity
the seeds you have sown
in the field of your Church;
may many of your people choose to serve you
by devoting themselves to the service of their bro-
    thers and sisters.
We ask this through Christ our Lord.
℟. **Amen.**   ➔ No. 32, p. 650

---

11. FOR RELIGIOUS VOCATIONS

ENTRANCE ANT.   Mt 19, 21
**If you want to be perfect, go, sell what you own,
give it all to the poor, then come, follow me.**
                                                ➔ No. 2, p. 614

OPENING PRAYER

Father,
you call all who believe in you to grow perfect in love
by following in the footsteps of Christ your Son.
May those whom you have chosen to serve you as
     religious
provide by their way of life
a convincing sign of your kingdom
for the Church and the whole world.
We ask this . . . for ever and ever. R̸. **Amen.** ♦

READINGS AND INTERVENIENT CHANTS

The current weekday *readings and intervenient chants
are used.*

PRAYER OVER THE GIFTS

Father,
in your love accept the gifts we offer you,
and watch over those who wish to follow your Son
     more closely,
and to serve you joyfully in religious life.
Give them spiritual freedom
and love for their brothers and sisters.
We ask this through Christ our Lord.
R̸. **Amen.** ➤ No. 21, p. 626

COMMUNION ANT. See Mt 19, 27-29

**I solemnly tell you: those who have left everything
and followed me will be repaid a hundredfold and
will gain eternal life.** ♦

PRAYER AFTER COMMUNION

Father, make your people grow strong
by sharing this spiritual food and drink.
Keep them faithful to the call of the gospel
that the world may see in them
the living image of your Son, Jesus Christ,
who is Lord for ever and ever.
R̸. **Amen.** ➤ No. 32, p. 650

12. FOR THE LAITY

OPENING PRAYER

God our Father,
you send the power of the gospel into the world
as a life-giving leaven.
Fill with the Spirit of Christ
those whom you call to live in the midst of the
    world
and its concerns;
help them by their work on earth
to build up your eternal kingdom.
We ask this . . . for ever and ever. ℟. **Amen.**

PRAYER OVER THE GIFTS

Father, you gave given your Son
to save the whole world by his sacrifice.
By the power of this offering,
help all your people
to fill the world with the Spirit of Christ.
Grant this through Christ our Lord. ℟. **Amen.**

PRAYER AFTER COMMUNION

Lord,
you share with us the fullness of your love,
and give us new courage at this eucharistic feast.
May the people you call to work in the world
be effective witnesses to the truth of the gospel
and make your Church a living presence
in the midst of that world.
We ask this through Christ our Lord. ℟. **Amen.**

---

13. FOR UNITY OF CHRISTIANS

ENTRANCE ANT.   Jn 10, 14-15

**I am the Good Shepherd. I know my sheep, and mine
know me, says the Lord, just as the Father knows
me and I know the Father. I give my life for my
sheep.**
➤ No. 2, p. 614

OPENING PRAYER

Almighty and eternal God,
keep together those you have united.
Look kindly on all who follow Jesus your Son.
We are all consecrated to you by our common baptism;
make us one in the fullness of faith
and keep us one in the fellowship of love.
We ask this . . . for ever and ever. ℟. **Amen.** ↓

READINGS AND INTERVENIENT CHANTS

The current weekday readings and intervenient chants are used.

PRAYER OVER THE GIFTS

Lord,
by one perfect sacrifice
you gained us as your people.
Bless us and all your Church
with gifts of unity and peace.
We ask this in the name of Jesus the Lord.
℟. **Amen.**   ➔ No. 21, p. 626 (P 76)

COMMUNION ANT.   See 1 Cor 10, 17

Because there is one bread, we, though many, are one body, for we all share in the one loaf and in the one cup. ↓

PRAYER AFTER COMMUNION

Lord,
may this holy communion,
the sign and promise of our unity in you,
make that unity a reality in your Church.
We ask this through Christ our Lord.
℟. **Amen.**   ➔ No. 32, p. 650

14. FOR THE SPREAD OF THE GOSPEL

OPENING PRAYER

God our Father,
you will all men to be saved
and come to the knowledge of your truth.
Send workers into your great harvest
that the gospel may be preached to every creature
and your people, gathered together by the word of
  life
and srengthened by the power of the sacraments,
may advance in the way of salvation and love.
We ask this . . . for ever and ever. ℟. **Amen.**

PRAYER OVER THE GIFTS

Lord,
look upon the face of Christ your Son
who gave up his life to set all men free.
Through him may your name be praised
among all peoples from East to West,
and everywhere may one sacrifice be offered to give
  you glory.
We ask this through Christ our Lord. ℟. **Amen.**

PRAYER AFTER COMMUNION

Lord,
you renew our life with this gift of redemption.
Through this help to eternal salvation
may the true faith continue to grow throughout the
  world.
We ask this in the name of Jesus the Lord. ℟. **Amen.**

---

16. FOR PASTORAL OR SPIRITUAL MEETINGS

ENTRANCE ANT.   Mt 18, 20
**Where two or three are gathered together in my
name, says the Lord, I am there among them.**

➤ No. 2, p. 614

OPENING PRAYER

Lord,
pour out on us the spirit of understanding, truth,
   and peace.
Help us to strive with all our hearts
to know what is pleasing to you,
and when we know your will
make us determined to do it.
We ask this . . . for ever and ever. ℟. **Amen.** ❦

READINGS AND INTERVENIENT CHANTS

*The current weekday readings and intervenient chants
are used.*

PRAYER OVER THE GIFTS

God our Father,
look with love on the gifts of your people.
Help us to understand what is right and good in
   your sight
and to proclaim it faithfully to our brothers and
   sisters.
We ask this through Christ our Lord.
℟. **Amen.**   ➜ No. 21, p. 626

COMMUNION ANT.

**Where charity and love are found, God is there.
The love of Christ has gathered us together.** ❦

PRAYER AFTER COMMUNION

God of mercy,
may the holy gifts we receive
give us strength in doing your will,
and make us effective witnesses of your truth
to all whose lives we touch.
We ask this in the name of Jesus the Lord.
℟. **Amen.**   ➜ No. 32, p. 650

17. FOR THE NATION, (STATE,) OR CITY

OPENING PRAYER

God our Father,
you guide everything in wisdom and love.
Accept the prayers we offer for our nation;
by the wisdom of our leaders and integrity of our
    citizens,
may harmony and justice be secured
and may there be lasting prosperity and peace.
We ask this . . . for ever and ever. ℟. **Amen.**

---

18. FOR THOSE WHO SERVE IN PUBLIC OFFICE

OPENING PRAYER

Almighty and eternal God,
you know the longings of men's hearts
and you protect their rights.
In your goodness,
watch over those in authority,
so that people everywhere may enjoy
freedom, security, and peace.
We ask this . . . for ever and ever. ℟. **Amen.** ▼

---

19. FOR THE ASSEMBLY OF NATIONAL LEADERS

OPENING PRAYER

Father,
you guide and govern everything with order and love.
Look upon the assembly of our national leaders
and fill them with the spirit of your wisdom.
May they always act in accordance with your will
and their decisions be for the peace and well-being
    of all.
We ask this . . . for ever and ever. ℟. **Amen.**

---

22. FOR PEACE AND JUSTICE

ENTRANCE ANT.   See Sir 36, 18-19

Give peace, Lord, to those who wait for you; listen to the prayers of your servants, and guide us in the way of justice.   ➤ No. 2, p. 614

OPENING PRAYER

God our Father,
you revealed that those who work for peace
will be called your sons.
Help us to work without ceasing
for that justice
which brings true and lasting peace.
We ask this . . . for ever and ever. ℞. **Amen.**

READINGS AND INTERVENIENT CHANTS

The current weekday *readings and intervenient chants are used.*

PRAYER OVER THE GIFTS

Lord,
may the saving sacrifice of your Son, our King and
    peacemaker,
which we offer through these sacramental signs of
    unity and peace,
bring harmony and concord to all your children.
We ask this through Christ our Lord.
℞. **Amen.**   ➤ No. 21, p. 626

COMMUNION ANT.   Jn 14, 27

Peace I leave with you, my own peace I give you, says the Lord. ℣

PRAYER AFTER COMMUNION

Lord, you give us the body and blood of your Son
and renew our strength.
Fill us with the spirit of love
that we may work effectively to establish among
    men

Christ's farewell gift of peace.
We ask this through Christ our Lord.
℟. **Amen.**   ➔ No. 32, p. 650

---

25. FOR THE BLESSING OF MAN'S LABOR

OPENING PRAYER

God our Creator,
it is your will that man accept the duty of work.
In your kindness may the work we begin
bring us growth in this life
and help to extend the kingdom of Christ.
We ask this . . . for ever and ever. ℟. **Amen.**

PRAYER OVER THE GIFTS

God our Father,
you provide the human race with food for strength
and with the eucharist for its renewal;
may these gifts which we offer
always bring us health of mind and body.
Grant this through Christ our Lord. ℟. **Amen.**

PRAYER AFTER COMMUNION

Lord,
hear the prayers
of those who gather at your table of unity and love.
By doing the work you have entrusted to us
may we sustain our life on earth
and build up your kingdom in faith.
Grant this through Christ our Lord. ℟. **Amen.**

28A. FOR THOSE WHO SUFFER FROM FAMINE

OPENING PRAYER

All-powerful Father,
God of goodness,
you provide for all your creation.

Give us an effective love for our brothers and sisters
who suffer from lack of food.
Help us do all we can to relieve their hunger,
that they may serve you with carefree hearts.
We ask this . . . for ever and ever. ℞. **Amen.**

PRAYER OVER THE GIFTS

Lord,
look upon this offering which we make to you
from the many good things you have given us.
This eucharist is the sign of your abundant life
and the unity of all men in your love.
May it keep us aware of our Christian duty
We ask this through Christ our Lord. ℞. **Amen.**

PRAYER AFTER COMMUNION

God, all-powerful Father,
may the living bread from heaven
give us the courage and strength
to go to the aid of our hungry brothers and sisters.
We ask this through Christ our Lord. ℞. **Amen.**

---

32. FOR THE SICK

ENTRANCE ANT.   Ps 6, 3
**Have mercy on me, God, for I am sick; heal me, Lord,
my bones are racked with pain.**

OR   See Is 53, 4
**The Lord has truly borne our sufferings; he has
carried all our sorrows.**   ➤ No. 2, p. 614

OPENING PRAYER

Father,
to teach us the virtue of patience in human illness.
your Son accepted our sufferings
Hear the prayers we offer for our sick brothers and
    sisters.
May all who suffer pain, illness or disease

realize that they are chosen to be saints,
and know that they are joined to Christ
in his suffering for the salvation of the world,
who lives and reigns with you and the Holy Spirit,
one God, for ever and ever. ℞. **Amen.** ▼

OR

All-powerful and ever-living God,
the lasting health of all who believe in you,
hear us as we ask your loving help for the sick;
restore their health,
that they may again offer joyful thanks in your
    Church.
Grant this . . . for ever and ever. ℞. **Amen.** ▼

READINGS AND INTERVENIENT CHANTS

The current weekday *readings and intervenient chants
are used.*

PRAYER OVER THE GIFTS

God our Father,
your love guides every moment of our lives.
Accept the prayers and gifts we offer
for our sick brothers and sisters;
restore them to health
and turn our anxiety for them into joy.
We ask this in the name of Jesus the Lord.
℞. **Amen.**   ➔ No. 21, p. 626

COMMUNION ANT.   Col 1, 24
**I will make up in my own body what is lacking in
the suffering of Christ, for the sake of his body, the
Church.** ▼

PRAYER AFTER COMMUNION

God our Father,
our help in human weakness,
show our sick brothers and sisters
the power of your loving care.
In your kindness make them well

and restore them to your Church.
We ask this through Christ our Lord.
℟. **Amen.**   ➔ No. 32, p. 650

_____

33. FOR THE DYING

Mass for the Sick, p. 1247, with the following prayers:

OPENING PRAYER

God of power and mercy,
you have made death itself
the gateway to eternal life.
Look with love on our dying brother (sister),
and make him (her) one with your Son in his suffering and death,
that, sealed with the blood of Christ,
he (she) may come before you free from sin.
We ask this . . . for ever and ever. ℟. **Amen.**

PRAYER OVER THE GIFTS

Father, accept this sacrifice we offer
for our dying brother (sister),
and by it free him (her) from all his (her) sins.
As he (she) accepted the sufferings you asked him (her) to bear in this life,
may he (she) enjoy happiness and peace for ever in the life to come.
We ask this through Christ our Lord.
℟. **Amen.**   ➔ No. 21, p. 626

PRAYER AFTER COMMUNION

Lord, by the power of this sacrament,
keep your servant safe in your love.
Do not let evil conquer him (her) at the hour of death,
but let him (her) go in the company of your angels
to the joy of eternal life.
We ask this through Christ our Lord.
℟. **Amen.**   ➔ No. 32, p. 650

_____

34. IN TIME OF EARTHQUAKE

OPENING PRAYER

God our Father,
you set the earth on its foundation.
Keep us safe from the danger of earthquakes
and let us always feel the presence of your love.
May we be secure in your protection
and serve you with grateful hearts.
We ask this . . . for ever and ever. ℞. **Amen.**

---

35. FOR RAIN

OPENING PRAYER

Lord God,
in you we live and move and have our being.
Help us in our present time of trouble,
send us the rain we need,
and teach us to seek your lasting help
on the way to eternal life.
We ask this . . . for ever and ever. ℞. **Amen.**

---

36. FOR FINE WEATHER

OPENING PRAYER

All-powerful and ever-living God,
we find security in your forgiveness.
Give us the fine weather we pray for
and use them always for your glory and our good.
We ask this . . . for ever and ever. ℞. **Amen.**

---

38. FOR ANY NEED

ENTRANCE ANT.

I am the Savior of all people, says the Lord. Whatever their troubles, I will answer their cry, and I will always be their Lord.   ➤ No. 2, p. 614

OPENING PRAYER

God our Father,
our strength in adversity,
our health in weakness,
our comfort in sorrow,
be merciful to your people.
As you have given us the punishment we deserve,
give us also new life and hope as we rest in your
    kindness.
We ask this . . . for ever and ever. ℟. **Amen.**

READINGS AND INTERVENIENT CHANTS

The current weekday *readings and intervenient chants
are used.*

PRAYER OVER THE GIFTS

Lord,
receive the prayers and gifts we offer:
may your merciful love set us free from the punish-
    ment we receive for our sins.
We ask this in the name of Jesus the Lord.
℟. **Amen.**   ➤ No. 21, p. 626

COMMUNION ANT.   Mt 11, 28

**Come to me, all you that labor and are burdened,
and I will give you rest, says the Lord.** ℣

PRAYER AFTER COMMUNION

Lord, look kindly on us in our sufferings,
and by the death your Son endured for us
turn away from us your anger
and the punishment our sins deserve.
We ask this through Christ our Lord.
℟. **Amen.**   ➤ No. 32, p. 650

---

39. IN THANKSGIVING

ENTRANCE ANT.   Eph 5, 19-20
Sing and play music in your hearts to the Lord,

always giving thanks for everything to God the
Father in the name of our Lord Jesus Christ.
➤ No. 2, p. 614

OPENING PRAYER

Father of mercy,
you always answer your people in their sufferings.
We thank you for your kindness
and ask you to free us from all evil,
that we may serve you in happiness all our days.
We ask this . . . for ever and ever. R̸. **Amen.** ↓

READINGS AND INTERVENIENT CHANTS

The current weekday *readings and intervenient chants
are used.*

PRAYER OVER THE GIFTS

Lord,
you gave us your only Son
to free us from death and from every evil.
Mercifully accept this sacrifice
in gratitude for saving us from our distress.
We ask this through Christ our Lord.
R̸. **Amen.**
➤ No. 21, p. 626 (P 40)

COMMUNION ANT.   Ps 138, 1

I will give thanks to you with all my heart, O Lord,
for you have answered me. ↓

OR   Ps 116, 12-13

What return can I make to the Lord for all that he
gives to me? I will take the cup of salvation, and call
on the name of the Lord. ↓

PRAYER AFTER COMMUNION

All-powerful God,
by this bread of life
you free your people from the power of sin
and in your love renew their strength.

Help us grow constantly in the hope of eternal glory.
Grant this through Christ our Lord.
℟. **Amen.**

➔ No. 32, p. 650

44. FOR RELATIVES AND FRIENDS

OPENING PRAYER

Father,
by the power of your Spirit
you have filled the hearts of your faithful people
with gifts of love for one another.
Hear the prayers we offer for our relatives and
    friends.
Give them health of mind and body
that they may do your will with perfect love.
We ask this . . . for ever and ever. ℟. **Amen.**

PRAYER OVER THE GIFTS

Lord,
have mercy on our relatives and friends
for whom we offer this sacrifice of praise.
May these holy gifts gain them the help of your
    blessing
and bring them to the joy of eternal glory.
We ask this through Christ our Lord. ℟. **Amen.**

PRAYER AFTER COMMUNION

Lord,
we who receive these holy mysteries
pray for the relatives and friends you have given us
    in love.
Pardon their sins.
Give them your constant encouragement
and guide them throughout their lives,
until the day when we, with all who have served you,
will rejoice in your presence for ever.
Grant this through Christ our Lord. ℟. **Amen.**

VOTIVE MASSES

(For rules governing these Masses, see p. 1234)

2. HOLY CROSS

ENTRANCE ANT.   See Gal 6, 14

We should glory in the cross of our Lord Jesus Christ, for he is our salvation, our life and our resurrection; through him we are saved and made free.

➤ No. 2, p. 614

OPENING PRAYER

God our Father,
in obedience to you
your only Son accepted death on the cross
for the salvation of mankind.
We acknowledge the mystery of the cross on earth.
May we receive the gift of redemption in heaven.
We ask this . . . for ever and ever. ℞. **Amen.** ℣

READINGS AND INTERVENIENT CHANTS

The current weekday *readings and intervenient chants are used.*

PRAYER OVER THE GIFTS

Lord,
may this sacrifice once offered on the cross
to take away the sins of the world
now free us from our sins.
We ask this through Christ our Lord.
℞. **Amen.**   ➤ No. 21, p. 626 (Pref. P 17)

COMMUNION ANT.   Jn 12, 32

When I am lifted up from the earth, I will draw all men to myself, says the Lord. ℣

PRAYER AFTER COMMUNION

Lord Jesus Christ,
you are the holy bread of life.
Bring to the glory of the resurrection

the people you have redeemed by the wood of the cross.
We ask this through Christ our Lord.
℟. **Amen.**   ➤ No. 32, p. 650

3B. HOLY EUCHARIST

JESUS THE HIGH PRIEST

ENTRANCE ANT.   Ps 109, 4

The Lord has sworn an oath and he will not retract: you are a priest for ever, in the line of Melchisedech.
                                    ➤ No. 2, p. 614

OPENING PRAYER
Father,
for your glory and our salvation
you appointed Jesus Christ eternal High Priest.
May the people he gained for you by his blood
come to share in the power of his cross and resurrection
by celebrating his memorial in this eucharist,
for he lives and reigns with you and the Holy Spirit,
one God, for ever and ever. ℟. **Amen.** ↓

READINGS AND INTERVENIENT CHANTS
The current weekday *readings and intervenient chants are used.*

PRAYER OVER THE GIFTS
Lord,
may we offer these mysteries worthily and often,
for whenever this memorial sacrifice is celebrated
the work of our redemption is renewed.
We ask this through Christ our Lord.
℟. **Amen.**   ➤ No. 21, p. 626 (Pref. P 47-48)

COMMUNION ANT.   1 Cor 11, 24-25
This body will be given for you. This is the cup of

the new covenant in my blood; whenever you receive them, do so in remembrance of me. ℣

PRAYER AFTER COMMUNION

Lord,
by sharing in this sacrifice
which your Son commanded us to offer as his me-
　morial,
may we become, with him, an everlasting gift to you.
We ask this through Christ our Lord.
℞. **Amen.**   → No. 32, p. 650

---

5. PRECIOUS BLOOD

ENTRANCE ANT.   Rv 5, 9-10
By your blood, O Lord, you have redeemed us from
every tribe and tongue, from every nation and people: you have made us into the kingdom of God.
→ No. 2, p. 614

OPENING PRAYER

Father,
by the blood of your own Son
you have set all men free and saved us from death.
Continue your work of love within us,
that by constantly celebrating the mystery of our
　salvation
we may reach the eternal life it promises.
We ask this . . . for ever and ever. ℞. **Amen.** ℣

READINGS AND INTERVENIENT CHANTS

The current weekday *readings and intervenient chants
are used.*

PRAYER OVER THE GIFTS

Lord,
by offering these gifts in this eucharist
may we come to Jesus, the mediator of the new cove-
　nant,

find salvation in the sprinkling of his blood
and draw closer to the kingdom
where he is Lord for ever and ever.
℟. **Amen.**   ➤ No. 21, p. 626 (Pref. P 17)

COMMUNION ANT.   See 1 Cor 10, 10
**The cup that we bless is a communion with the blood
of Christ; and the bread that we break is a communion with the body of the Lord.** ⍖

PRAYER AFTER COMMUNION
Lord,
you renew us with the food and drink of salvation.
May the blood of our Savior
be for us a fountain of water
springing up to eternal life.
We ask this through Christ our Lord.
℟. **Amen.**   ➤ No. 32, p. 650

_____

6. THE SACRED HEART OF JESUS

ENTRANCE ANT.   Ps 33, 11. 19
**The thoughts of his heart last through every genera-
tion, that he will rescue them from death and feed
them in time of famine.**   ➤ No. 2, p. 614

OPENING PRAYER
Lord God,
give us the strength and love of the heart of your
    Son
that, by becoming one with him,
we may have eternal salvation.
We ask this . . . for ever and ever. ℟. **Amen.** ⍖

READINGS AND INTERVENIENT CHANTS
The current weekday _readings and intervenient chants
are used._

PRAYER OVER THE GIFTS

Father of mercy,
in your great love for us
you have given us your only Son.
May he take us up into his own perfect sacrifice,
that we may offer you fitting worship.
We ask this through Christ our Lord. ℟. **Amen.** ↓

PREFACE (P 45)

Father, all-powerful and ever-living God,
we do well always and everywhere to give you thanks
through Jesus Christ our Lord.

Lifted high on the cross,
Christ gave his life for us,
so much did he love us.

From his wounded side flowed blood and water,
the fountain of sacramental life in the Church.
To his open heart the Savior invites all men,
to draw water in joy from the springs of salvation.

Now, with all the saints and angels,
we praise you for ever: ➤ No. 23, p. 627

COMMUNION ANT.   Jn 7, 37-38

The Lord says: If anyone is thirsty, let him come to me; whoever believes in me, let him drink. Streams of living water shall flow out from within him. ↓

OR   Jn 19, 34

One of the soldiers pierced Jesus' side with a lance, and at once there flowed out blood and water. ↓

PRAYER AFTER COMMUNION

Lord,
we have received your sacrament of love.
By becoming more like Christ on earth
may we share his glory in heaven,
where he lives and reigns for ever and ever.
℟. **Amen.**   ➤ No. 32, p. 650

7B. HOLY SPIRIT

ENTRANCE ANT. Jn 16, 13

When the Spirit of truth comes, says the Lord, he will lead you to the whole truth. ➤ No. 2, p. 614

OPENING PRAYER

Lord,
may the Helper, the Spirit who comes from you,
fill our hearts with light
and lead us to all truth
as your Son promised,
for he lives and reigns with you and the Holy Spirit,
one God, for ever and ever. ℟. **Amen.** ℣

READINGS AND INTERVENIENT CHANTS

The current weekday readings and intervenient chants are used.

PRAYER OVER THE GIFTS

Father, look with kindness
on the gifts we bring to your altar.
May we worship you in spirit and truth:
give us the humility and faith
to make our offering pleasing to you.
We ask this through Christ our Lord.
℟. **Amen.** ➤ No. 21, p. 626 (Pref. P 55)

COMMUNION ANT. Jn 15, 26; 16, 14

The Lord says, the Spirit who comes from the Father will glorify me. ℣

PRAYER AFTER COMMUNION

Lord our God,
you renew us with food from heaven;
fill our hearts with the gentle love of your Spirit.
May the gifts we have received in this life
lead us to the gift of eternal joy.
We ask this through Christ our Lord.
℟. **Amen.** ➤ No. 32, p. 650

8. BLESSED VIRGIN MARY
MASS OF THE IMMACULATE HEART OF MARY

See p. 1023.

DAILY MASSES FOR THE DEAD

These Masses may be celebrated according to the rules given on p. 1234.

C. FOR MORE THAN ONE PERSON OR FOR ALL THE DEAD

ENTRANCE ANT.

Give them eternal rest, O Lord, and let them share your glory.   ➤ No. 2, p. 614

OPENING PRAYER

God, our creator and redeemer,
by your power Christ conquered death
and returned to you in glory.
May all your people who have gone before us in faith
share his victory
and enjoy the vision of your glory for ever,
where Christ lives and reigns with you and the Holy
   Spirit,
one God, for ever and ever. ℟. **Amen.** ⍗

READINGS AND INTERVENIENT CHANTS

The current weekday *readings and intervenient chants are used.*

PRAYER OVER THE GIFTS

Lord,
receive this sacrifice
for our brothers and sisters.
On earth you gave them the privilege of believing in
   Christ:
grant them the eternal life promised by that faith.
We ask this through Christ our Lord.
℟. **Amen.**   ➤ No. 21, p. 626 (Pref. P 77-81)

COMMUNION ANT.   1 Jn 4, 9

God sent his only Son into the world so that we could have life through him. ℣

PRAYER AFTER COMMUNION

Lord,
may our sacrifice bring peace and forgiveness
to our brothers and sisters who have died.
Bring the new life given to them in baptism
to the fullness of eternal joy.
We ask this through Christ our Lord.
℟. **Amen.**   → No. 32, p. 650

OTHER POSSIBLE READINGS

Reading I:
        Is 25, 6. 7-9—p. 11 (omit last line).
        Rom 6, 3-9—p. 751 (omit last two sentences).
        2 Tm 2, 8-13—p. 411 (omit last paragraph).
        1 Jn 3, 14-16—p. 1217 (omit last seven lines)
Responsorial Psalm:
        Ps 23—p. 1161.
        Ps 122—p. 5.
Gospel:
        Mt 11, 25-30—p. 1221.
        Mt 25, 1-13—p. 1193.
        Mt 25, 31-46—p. 1225
        Lk 12, 35-40—p. 1230.
        Lk 24, 13-35—p. 777.
        Jn 14, 1-6—p. 849.

VARIOUS PRAYERS FOR THE DEAD

1A. FOR A POPE

OPENING PRAYER

God our Father,
you reward all who believe in you.
May your servant, N. our Pope, vicar of Peter, and
   shepherd of your Church,
who faithfully administered the mysteries of your
   forgiveness and love on earth,

rejoice with you for ever in heaven.
We ask this . . . for ever and ever. ℟. **Amen.**

PRAYER OVER THE GIFTS

Lord,
by this sacrifice which brings us peace,
give your servant, N. our Pope,
the reward of eternal happiness
and let your mercy win for us
the gift of your life and love.
We ask this through Christ our Lord. ℟. **Amen.**

PRAYER AFTER COMMUNION

Lord,
you renew us with the sacraments of your divine
   life.
Hear our prayers for your servant, N. our Pope.
You made him the center of the unity of your Church
   on earth,
count him now among the flock of the blessed in your
   kingdom.
Grant this through Christ our Lord. ℟. **Amen.**

2A. FOR THE DIOCESAN BISHOP

OPENING PRAYER

All-powerful God,
you made N. your servant
the guide of your family.
May he enjoy the reward of all his work
and share the eternal joy of his Lord.
We ask this . . . for ever and ever. ℟. **Amen.**

PRAYER OVER THE GIFTS

Merciful God,
may this sacrifice,
which N. your servant offered during his life
for the salvation of the faithful,
help him now to find pardon and peace.
We ask this through Christ our Lord. ℟. **Amen.**

PRAYER AFTER COMMUNION

Lord,
give your mercy and love to N. your servant.
He hoped in Christ and preached Christ.
By this sacrifice may he share with Christ
the joy of eternal life.
We ask this through Christ our Lord. ℟. **Amen.**

3A. FOR A PRIEST

OPENING PRAYER

Lord,
you gave N. your servant and priest
the privilege of a holy ministry in this world.
May he rejoice for ever in the glory of your kingdom.
We ask this . . . for ever and ever. ℟. **Amen.**

PRAYER OVER THE GIFTS

All-powerful God,
by this eucharist may N. your servant and priest
rejoice for ever in the vision of the mysteries
which he faithfully ministered here on earth.
We ask this through Christ our Lord. ℟. **Amen.**

PRAYER AFTER COMMUNION

God of mercy,
we who receive the sacraments of salvation
pray for N. your servant and priest.
You made him a minister of your mysteries on earth.
May he rejoice in the full knowledge of your truth
   in heaven.
We ask this through Christ our Lord. ℟. **Amen.**

6A. FOR ONE PERSON

OPENING PRAYER

Lord,
those who die still live in your presence
and your saints rejoice in complete happiness.

Listen to our prayers for N. your son (daughter)
who has passed from the light of this world,
and bring him (her) to the joy of eternal radiance.
We ask this . . . for ever and ever. ℟. **Amen.**

PRAYER OVER THE GIFTS

Lord,
be pleased with this sacrifice we offer for N. your
    servant.
May he (she) find in your presence
the forgiveness he (she) always longed for
and come to praise your glory for ever
in the joyful fellowship of your saints.
We ask this through Christ our Lord. ℟. **Amen.**

PRAYER AFTER COMMUNION

Lord,
we thank you for the holy gifts we receive
and pray for N. our brother (sister).
By the suffering and death of your Son
free him (her) from the bonds of his (her) sins
and bring him (her) to endless joy in your presence.
We ask this through Christ our Lord. ℟. **Amen.**

11A. FOR SEVERAL PERSONS

OPENING PRAYER

Lord,
be merciful to your servants N. and N.
You cleansed them from sin in the fountain of new
    birth.
Bring them now to the happiness of life in your king-
    dom.
We ask this . . . for ever and ever. ℟. **Amen.**

PRAYER OVER THE GIFTS

Lord,
we offer you this sacrifice.
Hear our prayers for N. and N.,

and through this offering
grant our brothers (sisters) your everlasting forgiveness.
We ask this through Christ our Lord. ℟. **Amen.**

PRAYER AFTER COMMUNION

Lord,
we who receive your sacraments
ask your mercy and love.
By sharing in the power of this eucharist
may our brothers (sisters) win forgiveness of their
sins,
enter your kingdom,
and praise your for all eternity.
We ask this through Christ our Lord. ℟. **Amen.**

---

13. FOR PARENTS

OPENING PRAYER

Almighty God,
you command us to honor father and mother.
In your mercy forgive the sins of my (our) parents
and let me (us) one day see them again
in the radiance of eternal joy.
We ask this . . . for ever and ever. ℟. **Amen.**

PRAYER OVER THE GIFTS

Lord,
receive the sacrifice we offer for my (our) parents.
Give them eternal joy in the land of the living,
and let me (us) join them one day in the happiness of
the saints.
We ask this through Christ our Lord. ℟. **Amen.**

PRAYER AFTER COMMUNION

Lord,
may this sharing in the sacrament of heaven
win eternal rest and light for my (our) parents

and prepare me (us) to share eternal glory with
  them.
We ask this through Christ our Lord. ℟. **Amen.**

---

14. FOR RELATIVES, FRIENDS, AND BENEFACTORS

OPENING PRAYER

Father,
source of forgiveness and salvation for all mankind,
hear our prayer.
By the prayers of the ever-virgin Mary,
may our friends, relatives, and benefactors
who have gone from this world
come to share eternal happiness with all your saints.
We ask this . . . for ever and ever. ℟. **Amen.**

PRAYER OVER THE GIFTS

God of infinite mercy,
hear our prayers
and by this sacrament of our salvation
forgive all the sins of our relatives, friends, and
  benefactors.
We ask this through Christ our Lord. ℟. **Amen.**

PRAYER AFTER COMMUNION

Father all-powerful, God of mercy,
we have offered you this sacrifice of praise
for our relatives, friends, and benefactors.
By the power of this sacrament
free them from all their sins
and give them the joy of eternal light.
We ask this through Christ our Lord. ℟. **Amen.**

APPENDIX II

ALLELUIA VERSE
FOR WEEKDAYS OF THE YEAR

DECEMBER 1 TO DECEMBER 16

1   See Ps 79, 4
R̸. **Alleluia.** Come and save us, Lord our God;
let us see your face, and we shall be saved. R̸. **Alleluia.**

2   Ps 85, 8
R̸. **Alleluia.** Lord, let us see your kindness,
and grant us your salvation. R̸. **Alleluia.**

3   Is 33, 22
R̸. **Alleluia.** The Lord will judge us by his law;
he is our King and Savior. R̸. **Alleluia.**

4   Is 40, 9. 10
R̸. **Alleluia.** Raise your voice and tell the Good News:
the Lord our God comes in strength. R̸. **Alleluia.**

5   Is 45, 8
R̸. **Alleluia.** Let the clouds rain down the Just One,
and the earth bring forth a Savior. R̸. **Alleluia.**

6   Is 55, 6
R̸. **Alleluia.** Seek the Lord while he can be found.
Call on him while he is near. R̸. **Alleluia.**

7   Lk 3, 4. 6
R̸. **Alleluia.** Prepare the way for the Lord, make straight his paths:
all mankind shall see the salvation of God. R̸. **Alleluia.**

8
R̸. **Alleluia.** Come, O Lord, do not delay:
forgive the sins of your people. R̸. **Alleluia.**

9
R̸. **Alleluia.** Behold, our Lord shall come with power,
he will enlighten the eyes of his servants. R̸. **Alleluia.**

10
R̸. **Alleluia.** Come, Lord, bring to us your peace;
let us rejoice before you with a perfect heart. R̸. **Alleluia.**

11
R̸. **Alleluia.** Behold, the king will come, the Lord of earth:
and he will set us free. R̸. **Alleluia.**

12
R̸. **Alleluia.** The day of the Lord is near:
he comes to save us. R̸. **Alleluia.**

13
℟. **Alleluia.** The Lord will come; go out to meet him!
He is the prince of peace. ℟. **Alleluia.**

14
℟. **Alleluia.** The Lord is coming to save his people;
happy are those prepared to meet him. ℟. **Alleluia.**

DECEMBER 17 TO DECEMBER 24

1
℟. **Alleluia.** Come,
Wisdom of our God Most High,
guiding creation with power and love:
teach us to walk in the paths of knowledge: ℟. **Alleluia.**

2
℟. **Alleluia.** Come,
Leader of ancient Israel,
giver of the Law to Moses on Sinai:
rescue us with your mighty power. ℟. **Alleluia.**

3
℟. **Alleluia.** Come,
Flower of Jesse's stem,
sign of God's love for all his people:
save us without delay. ℟. **Alleluia.**

4
℟. **Alleluia.** Come,
Key of David,
opening the gates of God's eternal Kingdom:
free the prisoners of darkness! ℟. **Alleluia.**

5
℟. **Alleluia.** Come,
Radiant Dawn,
splendor of eternal light, sun of justice:
shine on those lost in the darkness of death! ℟. **Alleluia.**

6
℟. **Alleluia.** Come,
King of all nations,
source of your Church's unity and faith:
save all mankind, your own creation! ℟. **Alleluia.**

7
℟. **Alleluia.** Come,
Emmanuel,
God's presence among us, our King, our Judge:
save us, Lord our God! ℟. **Alleluia.**

BEFORE EPIPHANY

1   Jn 1, 14. 12
℟. **Alleluia.** The Word of God became a man and lived among us.
He enabled those who accepted him
to become the children of God. ℟. **Alleluia.**

2   Heb 1, 1-2
℟. **Alleluia.** In the past God spoke to our fathers through the prophets; now he speaks to us through his Son. ℟. **Alleluia.**

3
℟. **Alleluia.** A holy day has dawned upon us.
Today a great light has come upon the earth.
Come you nations and adore the Lord. ℟. **Alleluia.**

AFTER EPIPHANY

1   Mt 4, 16
℟. **Alleluia.** A people in darkness have seen a great light;
a radiant dawn shines on those lost in death. ℟. **Alleluia.**

2   Mt 4, 23
℟. **Alleluia.** Jesus preached the Good News of the Kingdom
and healed all who were sick. ℟. **Alleluia.**

3   Lk 4, 18-19
℟. **Alleluia.** The Lord sent me to bring Good News to the poor,
and freedom to prisoners. ℟. **Alleluia.**

4   Lk 7, 16
℟. **Alleluia.** A great prophet has risen among us;
God has visited his people. ℟. **Alleluia.**

5   See 1 Tm 3, 16
℟. **Alleluia.** Glory to Christ who is proclaimed to the world;
glory from all who believe in him! ℟. **Alleluia.**

VERSES BEFORE THE GOSPEL FOR THE WEEKDAYS OF LENT

See p. 620 for the various responses before and after each verse.

See p. 620 for the various responses before and after each verse.

1   Ps 51, 12. 14
Create a clean heart in me, O God;
give back to me the joy of your salvation.

2   Ps 95, 8
If today you hear his voice, harden not your hearts.

3   Ps 130, 5. 7
I hope in the Lord, I trust in his word;
with him there is mercy and fullness of redemption.

4   Ex 18, 31
Rid yourselves of all your sins;

and make a new heart and
a new spirit.

5   Ez 33, 11
I do not wish the sinner to
die, says the Lord,
but to turn to me and live.

6   Jl 2, 12-13
With all your heart turn
to me
for I am tender and com-
passionate.

7   Am 5, 14
Seek good and not evil
so that you may live,
and the Lord will be with
you.

8   Mt 4, 4
Man does not live on bread
alone,
but on every word that
comes from the mouth of
God.

9   Mt 4, 17
Repent, says the Lord,
the kingdom of heaven is at
hand.

10   See Lk 8, 15
Happy are they who have
kept the word with a
generous heart,
and yield a harvest through
perseverance.

11   Lk 15, 18
I will rise and go to my
Father and tell him:
Father, I have sinned
against heaven and
against you.

12   Jn 3, 16
God loved the world so
much, he gave us his only
Son,
that all who believe in him
might have eternal life.

13   Jn 6, 64. 69
Your words, Lord, are spir-
it and life;
you have the message of
eternal life.

14   Jn 8, 12
I am the light of the world,
says the Lord:
he who follows me will have
the light of life.

15   Jn 11, 26. 26
I am the resurrection and
the life, said the Lord:
he who believes in me will
not die for ever.

16   2 Cor 6, 2
This is the favorable time,
this is the day of salvation.

17
The seed is the word of God,
Christ is the sower;
all who come to him will
live for ever.

EASTER SEASON UP TO THE ASCENSION

1   Lk 24, 46
℟. **Alleluia.** Christ had to
suffer and to rise from
the dead,
and so enter into his glory.
℟. **Alleluia.**

2   Jn 10, 14
℟. **Alleluia.** I am the good

shepherd, says the Lord;
I know my sheep and mine know me. ℟. **Alleluia.**

3 Jn 10, 27
℟. **Alleluia.** My sheep listen to my voice, says the Lord;
I know them and they follow me. ℟. **Alleluia.**

4 Jn 20, 29
℟. **Alleluia.** You believe in me, Thomas, because you have seen me;
happy those who have not seen me, but still believe! ℟. **Alleluia.**

5 Rom 6, 9
℟. **Alleluia.** Christ now raised from the dead will never die again;
death no longer has power over him. ℟. **Alleluia.**

6 Col 3, 1
℟. **Alleluia.** If then you have been raised with Christ, seek the things that are above,
where Christ is seated at the right hand of God. ℟. **Alleluia.**

7 Rv 1, 5
℟. **Alleluia.** Jesus Christ, you are the faithful witness, first-born from the death;
you have loved us and washed away our sins in your blood. ℟. **Alleluia.**

8
℟. **Alleluia.** Christ has risen and shines upon us,
whom he has redeemed by his blood. ℟. **Alleluia.**

9
℟. **Alleluia.** Nailed to the cross for our sake,
the Lord is now risen from the grave. ℟. **Alleluia.**

10
℟. **Alleluia.** Christ is risen, and makes all things new;
he has shown pity to all mankind. ℟. **Alleluia.**

11
℟. **Alleluia.** We know that Christ is truly risen from the dead;
victorious king, deal kindly with us. ℟. **Alleluia.**

EASTER SEASON AFTER THE ASCENSION

1 Mt 28, 19. 20
℟. **Alleluia.** Go and teach all people my gospel;
I am with you always, until the end of the world. ℟. **Alleluia.**

2 Jn 14, 16
℟. **Alleluia.** The Father will send you the Holy Spirit, says the Lord,
to be with you for ever. ℟. **Alleluia.**

3   Jn 14, 18
℟. **Alleluia.** The Lord said:
   I will not leave you or-
   phans.
I will come back to you, and
   your hearts will rejoice.
   ℟. **Alleluia.**

4   Jr. 14, 26
℟. **Alleluia.** The Holy Spirit
   will teach you all things,
and remind you of all I have
   said to you. ℟. **Alleluia.**

5   Jn 16, 7. 13
℟. **Alleluia.** I will send you
   the Spirit of truth, says
   the Lord;

he will lead you to the
   whole truth. ℟. **Alleluia.**

6   Jn 16, 28
℟. **Alleluia.** I went from the
   Father and came into the
   world;
and now I leave the world
   to return to the Father.
   ℟. **Alleluia.**

7   Col 3, 1
℟. **Alleluia.** If then you
   have been raised with
   Christ, seek the things
   that are above,
where Christ is seated at
   the right hand of God.
   ℟. **Alleluia.**

ORDINARY TIME

1   1 Sm 3, 9; Jn 6, 69
℟. **Alleluia.** Speak, O Lord,
   your servant is listening;
you have the words of everlasting life. ℟. **Alleulia.**

2   Ps 19, 9
℟. **Alleluia.** Your words,
   O Lord, give joy to my
   heart,
your teaching is light to
   my eyes. ℟. **Alleluia.**

3   Ps 25, 4. 5
℟. **Alleluia.** Teach me your
   paths, my God,
and lead me in your truth.
   ℟. **Alleluia.**

4   Ps 27, 11
℟. **Alleluia.** Teach me your
   way, O Lord,
and lead me on a straight
   road. ℟. **Alleluia.**

5   Ps 95, 8
℟. **Alleluia.** If today you
   hear his voice,
harden not your hearts. ℟.
   Alleluia.

6   Ps 111, 8
℟. **Alleluia.** Your laws are
   all made firm, O Lord,
established for ever more.
   ℟. **Alleluia.**

7   Ps 119, 18
℟. **Alleluia.** Unveil my eyes,
   O Lord,
and I will see the marvels
   of your law. ℟. **Alleluia.**

8   Ps 119, 27
℟. **Alleluia.** Instruct me in
   the way of your rules,
and I will reflect on all your
   wonders. ℟. **Alleluia.**

9   Ps 119, 34

℟. **Alleluia.** Teach me the meaning of your law, O Lord,
and I will guard it with all my heart. ℟. **Alleluia.**

10   Ps 119, 35. 29

℟. **Alleluia.** Turn my heart to do your will;
teach me your law, O God. ℟. **Alleluia.**

11   Ps 119, 88

℟. **Alleluia.** Give me life, O Lord,
and I will do your commands. ℟. **Alleluia.**

12   Ps 119, 105

℟. **Alleluia.** Your word is a lamp for my feet,
and a light on my path. ℟. **Alleluia.**

13   Ps 119, 135

℟. **Alleluia.** Let your face shine on your servant,
and teach me your laws. ℟. **Alleluia.**

14   Ps 130, 5

℟. **Alleluia.** I hope in the Lord,
I trust in his word. ℟. **Alleluia.**

15   Ps 145, 13

℟. **Alleluia.** The Lord is faithful in all his words
and holy in his deeds. ℟. **Alleluia.**

16   Ps 147, 2. 15

℟. **Alleluia.** O praise the Lord, Jerusalem;
he sends out his word to the earth. ℟. **Alleluia.**

17   Mt 4, 4

℟. **Alleluia.** Man does not live on bread alone,
but on every word that comes from the mouth of God. ℟. **Alleluia.**

18   Mt 11, 25

℟. **Alleluia.** Blessed are you, Father, Lord of heaven and earth;
you have revealed to little ones the mysteries of the kingdom. ℟. **Alleluia.**

19   See Lk 8, 15

℟. **Alleluia.** Happy are they who have kept the word with a generous heart,
and yield a harvest through perseverance. ℟. **Alleluia.**

20   Jn 6, 64. 69

℟. **Alleluia.** Your words, Lord, are spirit and life,
you have the words of everlasting life. ℟. **Alleluia.**

21   Jn 10, 27

℟. **Alleluia.** My sheep listen to my voice, says the Lord;
I know them, and they follow me. ℟. **Alleluia.**

23   Jn 14, 5

℟. **Alleluia.** I am the way, the truth, and the life, says the Lord;
no one comes to the Father, except through me. ℟. **Alleluia.**

24   Jn 14, 23

℟. **Alleluia.** If anyone loves

me, he will hold to my words,
and my Father will love him, and we will come to him. ℟. **Alleluia.**

25   Jn 15, 15
℟. **Alleluia.** I call you my friends, says the Lord, for I have made known to you all that Father has told me. ℟. **Alleluia.**

26   Jn 17, 17
℟. **Alleluia.** Your word, O Lord, is truth;
make us holy in the truth. ℟. **Alleluia.**

27   See Acts 16, 14
℟. **Alleluia.** Open our hearts, O Lord, to listen to the words of your Son. ℟. **Alleluia.**

28   2 Cor 5, 19
℟. **Alleluia.** God was in Christ, to reconcile the world to himself;
and the Good News of reconciliation he has entrusted to us. ℟. **Alleluia.**

29   See Eph 1, 17-18
℟. **Alleluia.** May the Father of our Lord Jesus Christ enlighten the eyes of our heart
that we might see how great is the hope
to which we are called. ℟. **Alleluia.**

30   Phil 2, 15-16
℟. **Alleluia.** Shine on the world like bright stars;
you are offering it the word of life. ℟. **Alleluia.**

31   Col 3, 16. 17
℟. **Alleluia.** Give thanks to God our Father through Jesus Christ our Lord,
and may the fullness of his message live within you. ℟. **Alleluia.**

32   1 Thes 2, 13
℟. **Alleluia.** Receive this message not as the words of man,
but as truly the word of God. ℟. **Alleluia.**

33   2 Thes 2, 14
℟. **Alleluia.** God has called us with the gospel;
the people won for him by Jesus Christ our Lord. ℟. **Alleluia.**

34.   2 Tm 1, 10
℟. **Alleluia.** Our Savior Jesus Christ has done away with death,
and brought us life through his gospel. ℟. **Alleluia.**

35   Heb 4, 12
℟. **Alleluia.** The word of God is living and active;
it probes the thoughts and motives of our heart. ℟. **Alleluia.**

36   Jas 1, 18
℟. **Alleluia.** The Father gave us birth by his message of truth,
that we might be as the first fruits of his creation. ℟. **Alleluia.**

37   Jas 1, 21
℟. **Alleluia.** Receive and
submit to the word plant-
ed in you;
it can save your souls. ℟.
Alleluia.

38   1 Pt 1, 25
℟. **Alleluia.** The word of
the Lord stands for ever;

it is the word given to you,
the Good News. ℟. **Alle-
luia.**

39   1 Jn 2, 5
℟. **Alleluia.** He who keeps
the word of Christ,
grows perfect in the love of
God. ℟. **Alleluia.**

For the Last Week

1   Mt 24, 42. 44
℟. **Alleluia.** Be watchful
and ready;
you know not when the Son
of Man is coming. ℟. **Alleluia.**

2   Lk 21, 28
℟. **Alleluia.** Lift up your
heads and see;
your redemption is near at
hand. ℟. **Alleluia.**

3   Lk 21, 36
℟. **Alleluia.** Be watchful,
pray constantly,
that you may be worthy to
stand before the Son of
Man. ℟. **Alleluia.**

4   Rv 2, 10
℟. **Alleluia.** Be faithful
until death, says the Lord,
and I will give you the
crown of life. ℟. **Alle-
luia.**

APPENDIX III

Dec. 30 — HOLY FAMILY

(Only for years 1977, 1983, 1988, 1994)

When Christmas falls on a Sunday, the Mass of the Holy Family is celebrated on Dec. 30.

ENTRANCE ANT.   Lk 2, 16

The shepherds hastened to Bethlehem, where they found Mary and Joseph, and the baby lying in a manger.

➜ No. 2, p. 614

OPENING PRAYER

Father,
help us to live as the holy family,
united in respect and love.
Bring us to the joy and peace of your eternal home.
Grant this through our Lord Jesus Christ, your Son,
who lives and reigns with you and the Holy Spirit,
one God, for ever and ever. ℟. **Amen.** ▼

ALTERNATIVE OPENING PRAYER

Father in heaven, creator of all,
you ordered the earth to bring forth life
and crowned its goodness by creating the family of man.
In history's moment when all was ready,
you sent your Son to dwell in time,
obedient to the laws of life in our world.
Teach us the sanctity of human love,
show us the value of family life,
and help us to live in peace with all men
that we may share in your life for ever.
We ask this through Christ our Lord. ℟. **Amen.** ▼

READING I   Sir 3, 2-6. 12-14

Respect, reverence, and love for our parents brings upon us God's blessing and mercy.

A reading from the book of Sirach

The Lord sets a father in honor over his children;
   a mother's authority he confirms over her sons.
He who honors his father atones for sins;

1276

he stores up riches who reveres his mother.
He who honors his father is gladdened by children,
  and when he prays he is heard.
He who reveres his father will live a long life;
  he obeys the Lord who brings comfort to his mother.
My son, take care of your father when he is old;
  grieve him not as long as he lives.
Even if his mind fail, be considerate with him;
  revile him not in the fullness of your strength.
For kindness to a father will not be forgotten,
  it will serve as a sin offering—it will take lasting root.
This is the Word of the Lord. ℟. **Thanks be to God.** ⍦

Responsorial Psalm   Ps 128, 1-2. 3. 4-5
℟. (1) **Happy are those who fear the Lord and walk in his
  ways.**

Happy are you who fear the Lord,
  who walk in his ways!
For you shall eat the fruit of your handiwork;
  happy shall you be, and favored. — ℟

Your wife shall be like a fruitful vine
  in the recesses of your home;
Your children like olive plants
  around your table. — ℟

Behold, thus is the man blessed
  who fears the Lord.
The Lord bless you from Zion:
  may you see the prosperity of Jerusalem
  all the days of your life. — ℟ ⍦

READING II   Col 3, 12-21

Mutual respect and love for one another will bring Christ's peace to
our hearts. Strive to practice all the virtues.

A reading from the letter of Paul to the Colossians

Because you are God's chosen ones, holy and beloved,
clothe yourselves with heartfelt mercy, with kindness,
humility, meekness, and patience. Bear with one another.
Forgive as the Lord has forgiven you. Over all these virtues put on love, which binds the rest together and makes
them perfect. Christ's peace must reign in your hearts,
since as members of the one body you have been called to
that peace. Dedicate yourselves to thankfulness. Let the

word of Christ, rich as it is, dwell in you. In wisdom made
perfect, instruct and admonish one another. Sing grateful-
ly to God from your hearts in psalms, hymns, and inspired
songs. Whatever you do, whether in speech or in action,
do it in the name of the Lord Jesus. Give thanks to God
the Father through him.

   You who are wives, be submissive to your husbands.
This is your duty in the Lord. Husbands, love your wives.
Avoid any bitterness toward them. You children, obey
your parents in everything as the acceptable way in the
Lord. And fathers, do not nag your children lest they lose
heart. — This is the Word of the Lord. ℟. **Thanks be to
God.** ℣

GOSPEL   Mt 2, 13-15. 19-23 (A); Lk 2, 22-40 (B);
Alleluia   Lk 2, 41-52 (C)

℟. **Alleluia.** May the peace of Christ rule in your hearts;
and the fullness of his message live within you. ℟. **Alleluia.**

See p. 1132 (A), 957 (B), 1126 (C).   3

PRAYER OVER THE GIFTS
Lord,
accept this sacrifice
and through the prayers of Mary, the virgin Mother of
   God,
and of her husband, Joseph,
unite our families in peace and love.
℟. **Amen.**   ➤ No. 21, p. 626 (Pref. P 3-5)

COMMUNION ANT.   Bar 3, 38
Our God has appeared on earth, and lived among men.

PRAYER AFTER COMMUNION
Eternal Father,
we want to live as Jesus, Mary, and Joseph,
in peace with you and one another.
May this communion strengthen us
to face the troubles of life.
Grant this through Christ our Lord.
℟. **Amen.**   ➤ No. 32, p. 650

Optional Solemn Blessings, p. 682, and Prayers over the People, p. 689

TREASURY OF PRAYERS

MORNING PRAYERS

Most holy and adorable Trinity, one God in three Persons, I praise you and give you thanks for all the favors you have bestowed upon me. Your goodness has preserved me until now. I offer you my whole being and in particular all my thoughts, words and deeds, together with all the trials I may undergo this day. Give them your blessing. May your Divine Love animate them and may they serve your greater glory.

I make this morning offering in union with the Divine intentions of Jesus Christ who offers himself daily in the holy Sacrifice of the Mass, and in union with Mary, his Virgin Mother and our Mother, who was always the faithful handmaid of the Lord.

Glory be to the Father, and to the Son, and to the Holy Spirit. Amen.

Prayer for Divine Guidance through the Day

Partial indulgence (No. 21) *

Lord, God Almighty, you have brought us safely to the beginning of this day. Defend us today by your mighty power, that we may not fall into any sin, but that all our words may so proceed and all our thoughts and actions be so directed, as to be always just in your sight. Through Christ our Lord. Amen.

---

* The indulgences quoted in this Missal are taken from the 1968 Vatican edition of the "Enchiridion Indulgentiarum" (published by Catholic Book Publishing Co.).

Partial indulgence (No. 1)

Direct, we beg you, O Lord, our actions by your holy inspirations, and carry them on by your gracious assistance, that every prayer and work of ours may begin always with you, and through you be happily ended. Amen.

NIGHT PRAYERS

I adore you, my God, and thank you for having created me, for having made me a Christian and preserved me this day. I love you with all my heart and I am sorry for having sinned against you, because you are infinite Love and infinite Goodness. Protect me during my rest and may your love be always with me. Amen.

Eternal Father, I offer you the Precious Blood of Jesus Christ in atonement for my sins and for all the intentions of our Holy Church.

Holy Spirit, Love of the Father and the Son, purify my heart and fill it with the fire of your Love, so that I may be a chaste Temple of the Holy Trinity and be always pleasing to you in all things. Amen.

Plea for Divine Help

Partial indulgence (No. 24)

Hear us, Lord, holy Father, almighty and eternal God; and graciously send your holy angel from heaven to watch over, to cherish, to protect, to abide with, and to defend all who dwell in this house. Through Christ our Lord. Amen.

CONFESSION PRAYERS

Prayer before Confession

O Holy Spirit, enlighten my mind that I may know my sins, and inspire true sorrow for them. Make me firmly resolve not to commit them again.

Most loving Savior, Lamb of God, you freely gave your life for sinners. Help me to make an act of contrition that is animated by perfect love of God.

Immaculate Virgin Mary, refuge of sinners, help me to fulfill my resolution of henceforth accepting and fulfilling God's Holy Will, as you have done. Amen.

Helpful Suggestions for Confession

1. It is well to personalize our confession by identifying ourselves, e.g., "I am a married woman and have three children," or "I am a widower," or "I am a teacher," etc. This reveals us to the Celebrant as a real person, living in a real situation and serving God in a particular vocation. It helps the Celebrant to judge our service to Christ and to direct us in conforming ourselves to Him.

2. The Sacrament of Penance is a means of Christian perfection. We should use it in a manner that will help us to grow more like Christ. We could refer to the progress, or lack of it, that we think we have made since our last visit to this Sacrament, e.g., "In my last confession I resolved to love Christ more in the people with whom I work; since then, I have improved, but still I have failed many times." Again, this personalizes our confession and avoids automatic listing of sins.

3. Our sorrow and purpose of amendment should be expressed before we receive the Sacrament, and is evidenced by our "Amen" in response to the principal prayer of absolution. It can also be expressed in the very confession of our sins. For example, we could say "In the past month I was irritable many times with my wife and family, hurting the spirit of our home. This month I really want to correct this."

4. How often should I meet the Lord in this Sacrament?
If we have consciously chosen against the Lord in our life, in some serious matter, we should promptly seek his mercy in this Sacrament, as long as we are truly repentant. If there is no question of a turning away from God in this way, Confession is not necessary for us, regardless of how long it may be since our last Confession. However, received with the proper dispositions, it will help us to grow in the Christian life. If we receive the Sacrament often, but without necessity, the burden is on us to receive it fruitfully. The Christian's life is one of constant conversion, of a continually renewed commitment. If our regular confession is made in that light, and with that purpose, the Lord's grace will effect things in our spiritual life.

Examination of Conscience

How long has it been since my last confession?

Did I conceal any sin?

Did I say my penance?

Have I neglected my home and my family duties?

Have I been lazy, neglectful, or willfully distracted during my prayers or at Mass?

Have I used God's name irreverently, or taken false or needless oaths?

Have I missed Mass through my own fault on Sundays or holydays, or worked unnecessarily on Sunday?

Have I disobeyed, angered, or been disrespectful toward my parents, teachers, employers, or other superiors?

Have I been unjust and unkind to those over whom I have authority?

Have I quarreled with or willfully hurt anyone?

Have I refused to forgive?

Have I been guilty of cruelty, mental or physical, toward anyone?

Have I caused another to commit sin?

Have I offended in any way by thought, word, or deed against the holy virtue of purity?

Have I led others into sin?

Have I stolen or destroyed property belonging to any other person, or company?

Have I neglected my home and my family duties?

Have I given a bad example to the members of my family
or others?

Have I knowingly accepted stolen goods?

Have I paid all my just debts?

Have I told lies, repeated gossip, or injured another person's character?

Have I been angry, greedy, proud, envious, jealous, lazy,
immodest; or intemperate in eating or drinking?

Have I willfully broken any of the Church laws concerning fast or abstinence?

Have I failed to support my Church?

Have I received Communion during Easter Time?

For married people.

Have I failed to show love, respect, and good example
towards my partner?

Have I neglected my duty to my children in regard to their
religious instruction, to their training in good habits,
and to their schooling?

Have I sinned against the duties of married life?

We must confess the number of our grave sins.

The Penitent's Formula for the Sacrament of Penance

Penitent: Bless me Father, for I have sinned.

Celebrant: The Lord be on your lips and in your heart that
you may properly confess all your sins, in the Name of the
Father, ✠ and of the Son, and of the Holy Spirit.

Penitent: It is . . . . . . since my last confession . . . . . .

(The penitent confesses)

Penitent: For these and all my sins I am truly sorry.

(The Celebrant instructs and gives the penance)

Celebrant: Now absolves the Penitent, who does not say
the Act of Contrition but reverently listens, and answers
"Amen" to the principal prayer of absolution. Our "Amen"
is a sign of our acceptance of God's mercy, and an evidence
of our sorrow.

"May Our Lord Jesus Christ absolve you, and by his authority I absolve you, [from every bond of excommunica-
tion and interdict to the extent of my power and your need.
And finally, I absolve you] from your sins, in the Name of
the Father, ✠ and of the Son, and of the Holy Spirit."

Penitent: Amen

After Confession

My dearest Jesus, I have told all my sins as well as I could. I have tried hard to make a good confession. I feel sure that you have forgiven me. I thank you. It is only because of all your sufferings that I can go to confession and free myself from my sins. Your Heart is full of love and mercy for poor sinners. I love you because you are so good to me.

My loving Savior, I shall try to keep from sin and to love you more each day. My dear Mother Mary, pray for me and help me to keep my promises. Protect me and do not let me fall back into sin.

COMMUNION PRAYERS

See p. 606.

BENEDICTION OF THE MOST BLESSED SACRAMENT

At the opening of Benediction any Eucharistic Hymn may be sung.

Hymn: Down in adoration falling,
   Lo! The sacred Host we hail;
Lo! O'er ancient forms departing
   Newer rites of grace prevail;
Faith for all defects supplying
   Where the feeble senses fail.

To the everlasting Father
   And the Son who reigns on high,
With the Spirit blest proceeding,
   Forth from each eternally,
Be salvation, honor, blessing,
   Might, and endless majesty. Amen.

℣. You have given them bread from heaven. (P.T. Alleluia.)

℟. Having all sweetness with it. (P.T. Alleluia.)

Celebrant: Let us pray: O God, who in this wonderful sacrament left us a memorial of your passion, grant, we implore you, that we may so venerate the sacred mysteries of your Body and Blood as always to be conscious of the fruit of your redemption. You who live and reign, forever and ever. ℟. Amen.

Partial indulgence (No. 59)

The Divine Praises

Blessed be God. * Blessed be his holy name. * Blessed be Jesus Christ, true God and true man. * Blessed be the name of Jesus. * Blessed be his most Sacred Heart. * Blessed be his most Precious Blood. * Blessed be Jesus in the most Holy Sacrament of the Altar. * Blessed be the Holy Spirit, the Paraclete. * Blessed be the great Mother of God, Mary most holy. * Blessed be her holy and Immaculate Conception. * Blessed be her glorious Assumption. * Blessed be the name of Mary, Virgin and Mother. * Blessed be St. Joseph, her most chaste spouse. * Blessed be God in his angels and in his saints.

THE STATIONS OF THE CROSS

THE Stations of the Cross is a devotion in which we accompany, in spirit, our Blessed Lord in His sorrowful journey to Calvary, and devoutly meditate on His sufferings and death.

1. Jesus Is Condemned to Death
Dear Jesus, help me to sin no more and to be very obedient.

4. Jesus Meets His Mother
Dear Jesus, may Your Mother console me and all who are sad.

2. Jesus Bears His Cross
Dear Jesus, let me suffer for sinners in union with You.

5. Jesus Is Helped by Simon
Dear Jesus, may I do all things to please You all day long.

3. Jesus Falls the First Time
Dear Jesus, help those who sin to rise and to be truly sorry

6. Veronica Wipes His Face
Dear Jesus, give me courage and generosity to help others.

7. Jesus Falls a Second Time
Dear Jesus, teach us to be sorry for all our many sins.

11. Jesus Is Nailed to the Cross
Dear Jesus, keep me close to You from this moment until I die.

8. Jesus Speaks to the Women
Dear Jesus, comfort those who have no one to comfort them.

12. Jesus Dies on the Cross
Dear Jesus, be with me when I die and take me to heaven.

9. Jesus Falls a Third Time
Dear Jesus, show me how to be obedient and to be very kind.

13. He Is Taken from the Cross
Dear Jesus, teach me to place all my trust in Your holy Love.

10. Stripped of His Garments
Dear Jesus, teach me to be pure in thought, word and deed.

14. He Is Laid in the Tomb
Dear Jesus, help me to keep the commandments You have given.

THE HOLY ROSARY OF THE
BLESSED VIRGIN MARY

THE Rosary calls to mind the five Joyful, the five Sorrowful, and the five Glorious Mysteries in the life of Christ and His Blessed Mother. It is composed of fifteen decades, each decade consisting of one "Our Father," ten "Hail Marys," and one "Glory be to the Father."

How to Say the Rosary

The Apostles' Creed is said on the Crucifix; the Our Father is said on each of the Large Beads; the Hail Mary on each of the Small Beads; the Glory Be to the Father after the three Hail Marys at the beginning of the Rosary, and after each group of Small Beads.

When the hands are occupied (driving a car, etc.) the indulgences for saying the Rosary may be gained as long as the beads are on one's person.

The Five

Joyful

Mysteries

1. The Annunciation
For love of humility.

2. The Visitation
For charity.

3. The Nativity
For poverty.

4. The Presentation
For obedience.

5. Finding in Temple
For piety.

1. Agony in Garden
For true contrition

2. Scourging at Pillar
For purity.

The Five
Sorrowful
Mysteries

3. Crowned with Thorns
For moral courage.

4. Carrying of Cross
For patience.

5. The Crucifixion
For final perseverance.

1. The Resurrection
For faith.

2. The Ascension
For hope.

The Five
Glorious
Mysteries

3. Descent of Holy Spirit
For love of God.

4. Assumption of B.V.M.
For devotion to Mary.

5. Crowning of B.V.M.
For eternal happiness.

1289

INDICES
GENERAL INDEX

PROPER OF SAINTS

COMMON OF SAINTS
(Antiphons and Prayers)

COMMON OF SAINTS
(Readings and Intervenient Chants)

APPENDICES

TREASURY OF PRAYERS

INDICES

INDEX OF SAINTS

INDEX OF BIBLICAL
READINGS

INDEX OF PSALMS

INDEX OF PREFACES

See pp. 626-627.